THE OXFORD GUIDE TO TREATIES

The Oxford Guide to Treaties

Edited by
DUNCAN B. HOLLIS

OXFORD
UNIVERSITY PRESS

OXFORD
UNIVERSITY PRESS

Great Clarendon Street, Oxford, OX2 6DP,
United Kingdom

Oxford University Press is a department of the University of Oxford.
It furthers the University's objective of excellence in research, scholarship,
and education by publishing worldwide. Oxford is a registered trade mark of
Oxford University Press in the UK and in certain other countries

First published in 2012
First published in paperback 2014

Impression: 1

Published in the United States of America by Oxford University Press
198 Madison Avenue, New York, NY 10016, United States of America

British Library Cataloguing in Publication Data
Data available

Library of Congress Cataloging in Publication Data
Data available

ISBN   978–0–19–960181–3 (hbk.)
ISBN   978–0–19–871296–1 (pbk.)

Printed and bound by
Lightning Source UK Ltd

For Emily

Acknowledgments

This is a big book. It required a lot of helping hands to come to fruition. I must first and foremost thank my wife Emily, not just for putting up with my long hours toiling away editing chapters, looking at treaty clauses and drafting my own contributions, but for how much good advice she offered along the way. Similar suffering was endured by my three children, Bram, Maggie, and Arlo, who may have offered less in the way of advice, but inspired me nonetheless with their boundless energy and enthusiasm.

I am deeply indebted to John Louth, who has guided this project from the start. This book would quite literally not exist without his support and assistance. Similar gratitude goes to the other OUP editors, Merel Alstein, Anthony Hinton, and Briony Ryles for dealing with my sundry questions, delays, and many of the important details that made this idea into a reality.

Here at Temple, the *Oxford Guide to Treaties* had its own research team of student assistants and graduate fellows. In the last few months, Sarah Happy, Ed Shirreffs, Melissa Mazur, Emma Tuohy, Mary Topper, and Jessica Winchell all put in long hours of research and editorial assistance for which I am eternally grateful. They were aided in that effort by earlier contributions from Heather Bourne, Kashish Chopra, John Holovrat, Will Hummel, and last, but certainly not least, Dan Tyman. I must also thank my colleague, office-mate, and friend, Jeff Dunoff, who provided a nearly constant stream of advice and generous counsel on the framework for the book as well as my chapter and other contributions to it.

Finally, I must extend my sincere thanks to those others who have contributed to this volume. I am so honored to have so many of the world's leading treaty lawyers accept my invitation and contribute their extensive expertise. The *Oxford Guide to Treaties* would not exist without their willingness to take the time to craft works of such relevance, interest, and insight. Of course, I should emphasize, as some of the authors themselves do, that they were invited to write in their individual capacities. None of the chapters should be read to represent the views of any government, international organization or tribunal with which a contributor may currently or previously have an association.

Contents

III. TREATY APPLICATION

IV. TREATY INTERPRETATION

V. AVOIDING OR EXITING TREATY COMMITMENTS

Table of Cases

European Court of Justice (ECJ)/Court of Justice of the European Union (CJEU)

International Criminal Tribunal for former Yugoslavia (ICTY)

Table of Instruments

MATERIALS ON RESPONSIBILITY OF STATES AND INTERNATIONAL ORGANIZATIONS

MULTILATERAL TREATIES AND INTERNATIONAL AGREEMENTS

INSTRUMENTS AND ACTS OF
LEGISLATION OR REGULATION

Australia

Austria

Belgium

Bosnia

Canada

Chile

China

Czech Republic

European Union

List of Abbreviations

AJIL	American Journal of International Law
ARIEL	Austrian Review of International and European Law
ASR	Articles of State Responsibility
ATS	Australian Treaty Series
BYBIL	British Yearbook of International Law
CETS	Council of Europe Treaty Series
CJEU	Court of Justice of the European Union
CTS	Consolidated Treaty Series
DR	Decisions and Reports (European Commission of Human Rights)
EC	European Community
ECHR	European Convention on Human Rights and Fundamental Freedoms
ECR	European Court Reports
ECtHR	European Court of Human Rights
EHRR	European Human Rights Reports
EJIL	European Journal of International Law
EPIL	Encyclopedia of Public International Law
EU	European Union
HILJ	Harvard International Law Journal
HRC	Human Rights Committee
HRQ	Human Rights Quarterly
ICJ	International Court of Justice
ICLQ	International and Comparative Law Quarterly
ICSID	International Centre for the Settlement of Investment Disputes
IHRR	International Human Rights Reports
IJIL	Indian Journal of International Law
ILC	International Law Commission
ILIB	International Law in Brief
ILM	International Legal Materials
ILR	International Law Reports
IO	International Organizations
LJIL	Leiden Journal of International Law
LNTS	League of Nations Treaty Series
MPEPIL	Max Planck Encyclopedia of Public International Law
MTDSG	Multilateral Treaties Deposited with the Secretary General
MTLP	*Modern Treaty Law and Practice* (CUP, 2nd edn, 2007)
NTLP	*National Treaty Law and Practice* (Martinus Nijhoff, 2005)
OJ	Official Journal (EU)
PCIJ	Permanent Court of International Justice
RBDI	Revue Belge de Droit International
RcD	Recueil des cours de l'Académie de droit international
RGDIP	Revue Générale de Droit International Public
RIAA	Reports of International Arbitral Awards
Trb	Tractatenblad (Dutch Treaty Series)

UKTS	United Kingdom Treaty Series
UN	United Nations
UNCLOS	United Nations Convention on the Law of the Sea
UNCTAD	United Nations Conference on Trade and Development
UNGA	United Nations General Assembly
UNJY	United Nations Juridical Yearbook
UNTS	United Nations Treaty Series
USC	United States Code
UST	United States Treaties and International Agreements
VCLT	1969 Vienna Convention on the Law of Treaties
VJIL	Virginia Journal of International Law
YBILC	Yearbook of the International Law Commission
YJIL	Yale Journal of International Law

List of Contributors

Anthony Aust is a former Deputy Legal Adviser of the Foreign and Commonwealth Office, London, and now a consultant to law firms, governments and international organizations. He is the author of *Modern Treaty Law and Practice* (2nd edn CUP 2007, 3rd edn in 2013) and the *Handbook of International Law* (2nd edn CUP 2010).

David J Bederman (1961–2011) was the KH Gyr Professor in Private International Law at Emory University. He was the author of a dozen books, including *Globalization and International Law* (Palgrave Macmillan 2008), *The Spirit of International Law* (University of Georgia Press 2002) and *International Law Frameworks* (Foundation Press 2001), as well as many articles on treaty-law topics.

Christopher J Borgen is Associate Dean for International Studies and Professor of Law at St John's University School of Law in New York and is a co-founder of *Opinio Juris*, an international law blog. He was previously the Director of Research and Outreach at the American Society of International Law.

Curtis A Bradley is the Richard A Horvitz Professor of Law and Professor of Public Policy Studies at Duke Law School and co-director of its Center for International and Comparative Law. He is the author of numerous articles on international law and US foreign relations law. In 2004, he served as Counselor on International Law in the Legal Adviser's Office of the US Department of State.

Catherine Brölmann is an Associate Professor of International Law at the University of Amsterdam's Faculty of Law. She is the author of *The Institutional Veil in Public International Law: International Organisations and the Law of Treaties* (Hart 2007).

Jutta Brunnée is a Professor at the University of Toronto Faculty of Law where she holds the Metcalf Chair in Environmental Law. She has authored numerous books and articles on international law, including, with Stephen Toope, *Legitimacy and Legality in International Law: An Interactional Account* (CUP 2010). From 1998–99, she served as Scholar-in-Residence at the Canadian Department of Foreign Affairs and International Trade, where she advised on matters such as the Biodiversity and Climate Change Conventions.

Başak Çalı is Senior Lecturer in Human Rights at University College London's Department of Political Science, a fellow of the University of Essex Human Rights Centre, and a Council of Europe Expert on the European Convention on Human Rights. She is also the editor of *International Law for International Relations* (OUP 2009) and co-editor of *The Legalisation of Human Rights: Multidisciplinary Perspectives on Human Rights and Human Rights Law* (Routledge 2006).

Marise Cremona is a Professor of European Law and the Head of the Law Department at the European University Institute in Florence. She is the editor of *Developments in EU External Relations Law* (OUP 2008) and co-editor of *EU Foreign Relations Law: Constitutional Fundamentals* (Kluwer Law International 2008) and the author of numerous articles on EU law and EU external relations.

Robert E Dalton is Senior Adviser on Treaty Practice at the US Department of State, where he previously served as the Assistant Legal Adviser for Treaty Affairs and the Counselor on International Law. He is an adjunct faculty member, Georgetown University Law Center. He was also a member of the US delegation to the UN Conference on the Law of Treaties that adopted the Vienna Convention in 1969. He has authored numerous articles and chapters on the law of treaties and US treaty law and practice.

Olufemi Elias is the Executive Secretary of the World Bank Administrative Tribunal and previously served as Legal Adviser at the UN Compensation Commission and as Senior Legal Officer to the Organisation for the Prohibition of Chemical Weapons. He is a Visiting Professor at Queen Mary, University of London, and co-author with Malgosia Fitzmaurice of *Contemporary Issues in the Law of Treaties* (Eleven International Publishing 2005).

Malgosia Fitzmaurice holds a Chair of Public International Law at the Department of Law, Queen Mary, University of London. She specializes in the law of treaties and international environmental law and has published widely on both subjects, including co-authoring with Olufemi Elias *Contemporary Issues in the Law of Treaties* (Eleven International Publishing 2005) and co-editing *Issues of State Responsibility before International Judicial Institutions* (Hart 2004).

Richard Gardiner practiced as a barrister and was then a legal adviser at the Foreign and Commonwealth Office for some twelve years. For the next two decades he was a member of the Faculty of Laws at University College London where he is now a Visiting Professor. He is the author of *Treaty Interpretation* (OUP 2008) and *International Law* (Pearson/Longman 2003).

Tom Grant is a fellow of Wolfson College and senior associate of the Lauterpacht Center for International Law at the University of Cambridge. His books include *Admission to the United Nations: Charter 4 and the Rise of Universal Organization* (Martinus Nijhoff 2009) and *The Recognition of States: Law and Practice in Debate and Evolution* (Praeger 1999). He has served on the legal teams in a number of ICJ cases and international arbitrations and is a co-founder and Associate Editor of the *Journal of International Dispute Settlement*.

Gerhard Hafner is a Professor of International Law at the University of Vienna, a member of the *Institut du Droit International,* a *Chevalier of the Ordre des Palmes Académiques* (France), and a past member of the International Law Commission. The author of over a hundred works, Professor Hafner's research interests include *inter alia* the codification of public international law and the succession of States.

Laurence R Helfer is the Harry R Chadwick, Sr Professor of Law at Duke Law School and co-director of its Center for International and Comparative Law. He has authored more than sixty publications relating to his diverse research interests, which include interdisciplinary analysis of international law and institutions, treaty design, international adjudication, and human rights.

Arancha Hinojal-Oyarbide joined the United Nations in 1993. She oversees the legal areas of the registration of treaties under Article 102 of the UN Charter and the depositary functions of the UN Secretary-General within the UN Office of Legal Affairs. Before taking up her position at the UN Office of Legal Affairs, she served at the UN Department of Administration and Management where she dealt with administration of peace-keeping operations. She has also served in legal and judicial affairs positions with the Office of the

High Commissioner for Refugees and the United Nations Interim Administration Mission in Kosovo (UNMIK).

Duncan B Hollis is James E. Beasley Professor of Law and Associate Dean for Academic Affairs at Temple University's James E Beasley School of Law. He is the co-editor of *National Treaty Law and Practice* (Martinus Nijhoff 2005) and the author of numerous articles on treaties and other forms of international commitment. He is a member of the American Law Institute, a regular contributor to *Opinio Juris*, and from 1998–2004 served in the US State Department Legal Adviser's Office, including several years as the Attorney-Adviser for Treaty Affairs.

Syméon Karagiannis is ordinary professor for public law at the University of Strasbourg, France. He is occasionally legal expert for the Parliamentary Assembly of the Council of Europe (eg report on 'Some Recent Security Council Attitudes Concerning Human Rights. On Sanctions Committee's "Black Lists"' (2007), in French) and has been counsel for a State at the International Tribunal for the Law of the Sea. His main fields of teaching and academic research cover general international law, the law of the sea, European law and human rights law in which he has written numerous articles, mostly in French, and co-edited *Environnement et renouveau des droits de l'homme* (Environmental Law and New Human Rights) (Documentation française 2006) and *Le médiateur européen. Bilan et perspectives* (The European Ombudsman. An assessment and the Prospects) (Bruylant 2007).

Jan Klabbers is Professor of International Law at the University of Helsinki, Faculty of Law. He has written extensively on the law of treaties, including *The Concept of Treaty in International Law* (Kluwer Law International 1996) along with numerous works on international subjects, including *Treaty Conflict and the European Union* (CUP 2008), *An Introduction to International Institutional Law* (2nd edn CUP 2009), and with Anne Peters and Geir Ulfstein, *The Constitutionalization of International Law* (OUP 2009).

George Korontzis has been working in the Office of Legal Affairs of the United Nations since 1988. He has participated in various international conferences including the UN Conference on the Law of the Sea and the Vienna Conference on the Law of Treaties between States and International Organizations or between International Organizations. He is currently the Deputy Director of the Codification Division of the UN Office of Legal Affairs and Deputy Secretary of the International Law Commission.

Gregor Novak holds a Masters of Law and is a Doctoral candidate in law at the University of Vienna. He is also an Associate Editor of the *Oxford Reports on International Law in Domestic Courts*.

Kal Raustiala holds a joint appointment between the University of California Los Angeles (UCLA) Law School and the UCLA International Institute, and is the Director of the UCLA Ronald W Burkle Center for International Relations. His most recent book is *Does the Constitution Follow the Flag? The Evolution of Territoriality in American Law* (OUP 2009).

Annebeth Rosenboom is Senior Legal Officer, Division for Ocean Affairs and the Law of the Sea, UN Office of Legal Affairs. She was Chief of the Treaty Section of the UN Office of Legal Affairs from 2007–10, where she also worked from 1985–87. For twenty years, she worked with Martinus Nijhoff Publishers as a publisher, responsible for the programmes of public international law, international institutional law, and law of the sea.

Bruno Simma served as a Judge on the International Court of Justice from 2003–12. From 1987–96 he was a member of the UN Committee on Economic, Social and Cultural Rights; from 1997–2003 he served on the International Law Commission. He has held faculty positions at the University of Munich Faculty of Law and the University of Michigan Law School, to which he has returned as a Professor of Law in 2012. He has written extensively on a great variety of subjects of international law and taught the 2009 Hague Academy of International Law General Course on 'The Impact of Human Rights on International Law'. More recently, he has also served as an arbitrator both in inter-State cases and in investment arbitrations.

David Sloss is a Professor of Law at Santa Clara University School of Law, where he serves as the Director of the Center for Global Law and Policy. He is the editor of *The Role of Domestic Courts in Treaty Enforcement: A Comparative Study* (CUP 2009), and co-editor of *International Law in the U.S. Supreme Court: Continuity and Change* (CUP 2011). He has published numerous articles on the history of US foreign affairs law and the judicial enforcement of treaties in US courts.

Edward T Swaine is Professor of Law at the George Washington University Law School. He is the author of numerous articles on international law and US foreign relations law, and co-author of *Foreign Relations and National Security Law: Cases, Materials* (4th edn West 2011). In 2005–06, he served as the Counselor on International Law at the US Department of State.

Christian J Tams is Professor of International Law at the University of Glasgow. His publications include *Enforcing Obligations Erga Omnes in International Law* (revised edn CUP 2010) and, with Ranier Hofmann, he is co-editor of *International Investment Law and General International Law* (Nomos 2011). He has authored numerous articles on the law of state responsibility, treaty law, and dispute resolution. In addition to his academic work, he has advised States in proceedings before the International Court of Justice and the International Tribunal for the Law of the Sea.

Geir Ulfstein is Professor of Law at the University of Oslo and from 2004–07 he served as the Director of the Norwegian Centre for Human Rights. He is the author with Anne Peters and Jan Klabbers of *The Constitutionalization of International Law* (OUP 2009), and was the principal editor of *Making Treaties Work: Human Rights, Environment and Arms Control* (CUP 2007).

Introduction

Duncan B Hollis

The treaty is an august instrument. Since antiquity, treaty-makers have recognized the sacrosanct nature of commitments embedded in treaty form. The Bible, for example, records the obligatory character of a treaty forged by Joshua and the Gibeonites. The Hebrew God had directed Israelites to destroy all neighbours living in the promised land of Canaan—'save nothing alive that breathes'[1]—but permitted them to spare foreigners from distant lands. The inhabitants of Gibeon lived in Canaan and knew they faced extinction. They sent a mission to the Israelite leader, Joshua, using worn sandals, cracked wineskins, and mouldy bread to disguise themselves as a delegation from afar. Joshua fell for their deception and made a treaty of peace with Gibeon that Israelite leaders ratified by oath. When the Israelites learned the Gibeonites' true identity days later, they proposed to ignore that covenant and annihilate the city. But their leaders refused to breach the treaty with Gibeon: 'We have sworn to them by the Lord, the God of Israel, and now we may not touch them ... let them live lest wrath be upon us, because of the oath which we swore to them.'[2]

The Gibeon story reveals both the treaty's power and its sacred origins. Despite clear fraud in its formation, Israel considered the treaty binding. It did so by viewing the treaty to include not one, but two, promises: first, a secular promise between Israel and Gibeon to behave in certain ways, and, second, a divine promise by the Israelites to their God to perform the first promise. Whatever irregularities characterized that first promise, the second (divine) promise remained. As a result, the treaty's original binding authority depended not so much on promises amongst parties, but on the divine pledges accompanying them to guarantee performance.[3]

Today, of course, we no longer associate treaties with divine promises. Starting (loosely) with the Peace of Westphalia, international relations secularized. In the process, the existence and force of divine pledges and oaths in treaty-making eroded

---

[1] Deuteronomy 20:10–18 (English Standard Version).

[2] Joshua 9:3–21 (English Standard Version).

[3] In one of the earliest surviving treaty texts—a 1259 BCE treaty between Egypt and the Hittite Empire—the two rulers call upon the Gods of Egypt and Hitii to bear witness to their promises. See G Beckman, *Hittite Diplomatic Texts* (Scholars Press, Atlanta 1996) 92 (Treaty between Hattusili IIII of Hatti and Ramses II of Egypt). A few centuries later in China, Sun Tzu advised that 'peace proposals unaccompanied by a sworn covenant indicate a plot'. Sun Tzu, *The Art of War* (L Giles trans) (El Paso Norte Press, El Paso 2009) 30. The Romans, however, did not rely on promises, but demanded hostages to ensure the performance of their agreements. See D Bederman, *International Law in Antiquity* (CUP, Cambridge 2001) 190.

and has now largely disappeared. So what gives modern treaties their binding authority? The standard response is *pacta sunt servanda*. Article 26 of the 1969 Vienna Convention on the Law of Treaties (VCLT) defines this principle as follows: '[e]very treaty in force is binding upon the parties to it and must be performed by them in good faith'.[4] But *pacta sunt servanda* does not make treaties binding simply because a treaty says so, even one as venerable as the VCLT. Basing the binding character of treaties on consent to a treaty has obvious tautological problems (as do explanations based on State consent through customary practice).[5] Rather, *pacta sunt servanda* exists as a general principle of 'natural law', independent of party promises or State practice.[6] As such, it is a secular cousin to the divine law family of pledges that gave earlier treaties force. Unlike those oaths, however, *pacta sunt servanda* requires no secondary promises (to the divine or otherwise); it flows directly from the primary promise(s) among treaty parties.

Pacta sunt servanda thus serves as the necessary starting point for any study of treaties; it identifies an important function—to obligate performance—that treaties serve. But it is just a starting point. To say treaties are binding, says nothing about *what* qualifies as a treaty in the first place, *who* can make one, or *how* a treaty should be applied, interpreted, avoided, or ended.

Those questions *are* addressed in the law of treaties' seminal document—the VCLT. For more than four decades, this instrument, its *travaux preparatoires* and the critical earlier work of the International Law Commission (ILC) and its four Special Rapporteurs, have served as *the* lens through which States and their lawyers address treaty questions.[7] Today, the VCLT has 111 States parties, but that

---

[4] Vienna Convention on the Law of Treaties (opened for signature 23 May 1969, entered into force 27 January 1980) 1155 UNTS 331, Art 26; ibid preamble (noting *pacta sunt servanda* 'rule' is 'universally recognized').

[5] See eg TM Franck, *The Power of Legitimacy Among Nations* (OUP, Oxford 1990) 187 ('"Why are treaties binding?" is a question usually answered by the superficial assertion that "treaties are binding because states have agreed to be bound"... But the binding force... cannot emanate solely from the agreement of the parties. It must come from some ultimate unwritten rule of recognition, the existence of which may be inferred from the conduct and belief of states.'); A Rubin, *Ethics and Authority in International Law* (CUP, Cambridge 1997) 15 (consent must be 'a natural law rule or a rule that rests on prior consent, thus introducing an infinite regress').

[6] GG Fitzmaurice, 'Some Problems Regarding the Formal Sources of International Law' in *Symbolae Verzijl* (Martinus Nijhoff, The Hague 1958) 153, 164 ('the rule *pacta sunt servanda*... does not require to be accounted for in terms of any other rule. It could neither not be, nor be other than what it is. It is not dependent on consent, for it would exist without it.'). 'Natural law' generally refers to international law sources that exist independent of State consent whether based on divine dictates or secular moral argument. See eg A Verdross and HF Koeck, 'Natural Law: The Tradition of Universal Reason and Authority' in RJ Macdonald and D Johnston (eds), *The Structure and Process of International Law: Essays in Legal Philosophy, Doctrine and Theory* (Martinus Nijhoff, Dordrecht 1983) 31 (discussing religious-based approaches to natural law); FR Tesón, *A Philosophy of International Law* (Westview Press, Boulder 1998) 2 (articulating a Kantian conception of international law based on certain 'morally legitimate' principles).

[7] The ILC first took up the law of treaties in 1949. Four renowned British international lawyers served as Special Rapporteurs—JL Brierly, Sir Hersch Lauterpacht, Sir Gerald Fitzmaurice, and Sir Humphrey Waldock. Together, they authored sixteen reports on the law of treaties between 1950 and 1966. The ILC reported on its progress to the UN General Assembly in 1959, and in 1966 forwarded draft articles on the law of treaties and accompanying commentary, which formed the

number understates its true reach. Much of the VCLT codified or has since come to constitute customary international law.[8]

But even the VCLT affords an incomplete image of the treaty. Its provisions do not deal with all types of treaties or the questions they raise. Some further illumination may be gleaned from the far less widely invoked, but often still useful 1978 and 1986 Vienna Conventions,[9] or more recent ILC work.[10] But even considered collectively, those sources still leave important issues unaddressed (eg treaty-making by other subjects of international law, the role of NGOs, or the application of treaties in domestic law). Moreover, even where the VCLT or its companions do deal with a topic, it is often without great detail, and may even, in some cases, leave a false impression of actual practice. Such outcomes are a necessary byproduct of the VCLT's celebrated flexibility—the fact that its 'rules' are frequently drafted so that States may contract around them or choose from among a list of available options.[11] With a few notable exceptions (the prohibition on treaties that violate pre-emptory norms or *jus cogens*), the law of treaties that the VCLT presents is a default one.

The present *Oxford Guide to Treaties* endeavours to tackle all of the major treaty-related topics in a single volume. It provides a comprehensive and current guide to treaty law and practice, including (but not limited to) issues raised in the VCLT and later codification efforts. There is a strong need for such a treatment. Many earlier, important works on treaty law are now dated (although still quite useful).[12] More recent work has tended to focus on the Vienna Convention(s) exclusively,[13] a

---

basis for the VCLT negotiations. Online access to all of the ILC's work is available at <http://untreaty.un.org/ilc/guide/1_1.htm>.

[8] Indeed the VCLT's pull is so strong that it is often applied without regard to the fact that VCLT Art 4 purports to limit its application to treaties concluded after the VCLT's 1980 entry into force. See eg *Kasikili/Sedudu Island (Botswana v Namibia)* [1999] ICJ Rep 1059 [18] (applying the VCLT's interpretive provisions to an 1890 treaty).

[9] Vienna Convention on the Law of Treaties between States and International Organizations or between International Organizations (adopted 21 March 1986, not yet in force) [1986] 25 ILM 543 ('1986 VCLT'); Vienna Convention on Succession of States in Respect of Treaties (adopted 23 August 1978, entered into force 6 November 1996) 1946 UNTS 3.

[10] Eg ILC, Draft Articles on the Responsibility of States for Internationally Wrongful Acts, Report of the International Law Commission on the Work of its Fifty-first Session (3 May–23 July, 1999), UN Doc A/56/10 55 [3]; ILC, 'Guide to Practice on Reservations to Treaties' at <http://untreaty.un.org/ilc/texts/instruments/english/draft%20articles/1_8_2011.pdf> (forthcoming in [2011] YBILC, vol II(2)).

[11] Thus, the VCLT frequently frames its rules or some of their elements as endorsing the application of whatever the treaty provides (eg Arts 10, 12–17, 19–20, 22, 24–25, 28–31, 33, 40–41, 44, 54–58, 72, 76–78). It also regularly authorizes parties to 'otherwise agree' (eg Arts 11, 22, 25, 37, 44, 70, 72, 77, 79) or to allow the establishment of a different intention to vary the rule's application (eg Arts 7, 12–15, 28–29, 37, 39, 44, 59).

[12] Eg P Reuter, *Introduction au droit des traités* (2nd edn Presses universitaires de France, Paris 1985); H Blix and J Emerson, *The Treaty Maker's Handbook* (Oceana, Dobbs Ferry 1973); A McNair, *Law of Treaties* (2nd edn OUP, Oxford 1961).

[13] O Corten and P Klein, *The Vienna Conventions on the Law of Treaties: A Commentary* (OUP, Oxford 2011); ME Villiger, *Commentary on the 1969 Vienna Convention on the Law of Treaties* (Martinus Nijhoff, Leiden 2009); I Sinclair, *The Vienna Convention on the Law of Treaties* (2nd edn MUP, Manchester 1984).

subset of treaty topics,[14] or a single topic in particular.[15] The most current comprehensive treatment, Anthony Aust's *Modern Treaty Law and Practice* is superb, but reflects the views of one author and does not 'presume to be an academic work'.[16]

This *Guide* seeks to explore treaty questions from theoretical, doctrinal, and practical perspectives. Thus, in addition to reviewing the relevant rules and case law, it offers some theoretical grounding for that doctrine and, where necessary, explores the actual practice, particularly if it differs from the VCLT's terms. In terms of structure, the *Guide to Treaties* is divided into six Sections. The first five sections contain twenty-five chapters on treaty issues by leading international lawyers and political scientists from the academy, diplomatic service, the International Court of Justice, the United Nations, and the World Bank. As the leading experts on their respective topics, these contributors were tasked with describing a particular treaty-related concept, rule, or practice and, where applicable, existing challenges and areas of disagreement. Contributors were also invited, where appropriate, to offer normative claims and discuss the need for some evolution or change in their respective areas. Thus, each chapter constitutes a stand-alone essay. Read together, however, the chapters presents an overarching introduction to the current state of treaty law and practice as well as the tensions and pressure points that arise in modern treaty-making.

Section I addresses foundational issues for treaty-making. Chapter 1 explores the definitional question of what is a treaty, while Chapter 2 contrasts the treaty with its current chief competition, the political commitment. Chapters 3 to 5 then tackle a separate question—who can make treaties? Treaty-making (and thus treaty law) is most often associated with States. But a host of non-State actors also now purport to make treaties, raising questions about their authority, the circumstances in which they do so, and complicated issues of procedure and responsibility. Chapter 3 explores these questions with respect to International Organizations (IOs), and the import of the 1986 VCLT in the process. Chapter 4 looks at the EU's robust and complex treaty-making. Chapter 5 takes on a rarely addressed topic—treaty-making by 'other subjects of international law' including overseas dependencies, sub-federal territorial units, and insurgencies. In contrast to those actors, non-governmental organizations (NGOs) generally lack the formal capacity to make treaties. Nonetheless, as Chapter 6 explains, NGOs are highly visible and occasionally influential actors in the multilateral treaty context.

Section II moves beyond initial questions of definition and capacity to examine issues surrounding treaty formation. Chapter 7 surveys the often complicated

---

[14] G Ulfstein and others, *Making Treaties Work; Human Rights, Environment and Arms Control* (CUP, Cambridge 2007); DB Hollis, MR Blakeslee, and LB Ederington (eds), *National Treaty Law & Practice* (Martinus Nijhoff, Leiden 2005); M Fitzmaurice and O Elias, *Contemporary Issues in the Law of Treaties* (Eleven Publishing, Utrecht 2005).

[15] Eg R Gardiner, *Treaty Interpretation* (OUP, Oxford 2008); J Klabbers, *The Concept of Treaty in International Law* (Kluwer, The Hague 1996); S Rosenne, *Breach of Treaty* (CUP, Cambridge 1985).

[16] A Aust, *Modern Treaty Law and Practice* (2nd edn CUP, Cambridge 2007) 3. Despite this caveat, Aust's volume is fairly well earmarked in academic circles.

process of treaty-making—from negotiations, to conclusion, to expressions of consent to be bound, to entry into force—exploring not just the law but the actual practice at each stage. Chapter 8 explores one area where a treaty may have legal effects prior to its entry into force: the practice of 'simple signature', signing a treaty as a prelude to potential ratification. Beyond signature, treaty-makers occasionally desire to apply their treaties sooner than the text's entry-into-force provisions (or more pertinently their domestic legal requirements) allow. Chapter 9 explains the concept of provisional application as a response to such scenarios. Chapter 10 surveys the role of the depositary and the legal requirements of registering and publishing treaties once they are in force, with particular attention to *the* predominant actor: the United Nations. Section II concludes with the issue most likely to complicate a treaty's formation—unilateral statements, particularly reservations. Chapter 11 surveys the history of reservations and examines how to evaluate their permissibility and legal effects, particularly in cases of objections by other States.

Section III addresses issues such as where, to whom, how and when treaties apply once they are in force. Chapter 12 assesses the rules as to *where* a treaty applies, examining the general rule of integral territorial application and the important questions associated with when and how a treaty may bind a State extraterritorially. Chapter 13 turns to the question of *to whom* a treaty applies by exploring two exceptions to *pacta tertii* (the notion that a treaty binds its parties and *only* its parties): (a) third party rights and duties and (b) the resurgent idea of objective regimes, which apply certain types of treaties to non-parties irrespective of consent. Chapter 14 explores treaty amendments, an area where the practice regularly departs from the VCLT's default rules, including procedural mechanisms that affect amendments without requiring each party's explicit consent.

Of course, treaties are not just applied internationally; in terms of a treaty's efficacy, its application under one or more domestic laws may be as (if not more) important than international law. Chapter 15 surveys how domestic legal systems approach treaty application and the varied treatment that results from different treaty types and domestic actor preferences. Chapter 16 returns to the international frame, asking how treaties apply in cases of disruption to the international legal order—State succession—a topic addressed (albeit not entirely successfully) by the 1978 Vienna Convention.

The final two chapters of Section III examine treaty application beyond the confines of the treaty text itself. Chapter 17 takes up the recent phenomenon by which treaties create so-called 'treaty bodies'. It considers why and how States establish them, and what authority they have to flesh out the treaty's commitments via substantive decision-making, compliance efforts, or coordination with other international actors. Chapter 18 examines treaty conflicts and the normative fragmentation of international law more generally. It explains why and how treaties may conflict and surveys techniques for resolving conflicts, whether by drafting or interpreting around them, relying on the VCLT's default rules, or employing classic canons of treaty construction: *lex posterior, lex prior,* and *lex specialis.*

Section IV focuses on a critical treaty issue—its interpretation. Chapter 19 offers a nuanced account of one of the VCLT's seminal contributions to international law—a single set of interpretative 'principles' if not actual rules. The uniformity of VCLT Articles 31–33, however, operates in some tension with claims that the nature of certain treaties warrants exceptional, or at least specialized, interpretative frameworks. This *Guide* offers two case studies of such claims. First, Chapter 20 examines the extent to which the VCLT interpretative rules apply to treaties that constitute an IO and the boundaries between IO law and the law of treaties. Second, Chapter 21 asks whether VCLT Article 31 is sufficiently flexible to apply to normative treaties, including those involving human rights. It concludes that the VCLT can accommodate interpretative rules specialized for human rights treaties and that the principle of effectiveness in particular is a necessary application of these treaty provisions, rather than some extra-legal choice to elevate human rights treaties above other treaties.

Section V concludes the substantive chapters with an examination of the rules and practices associated with avoiding or exiting treaty commitments. Chapter 22 discusses the importance of validity rules to the law of treaties, while reviewing the relative dearth of practical examples implementing the VCLT rules for invalidating treaties because of constitutional concerns, error, fraud, corruption, coercion, or *jus cogens*. Chapter 23 catalogues the various remedies available when a party breaches a treaty commitment. It explains how reliance on the law of State responsibility or treaty-specific provisions are better options than VCLT provisions on termination or suspension in cases of material breach. Chapter 24 examines various claims of exceptional circumstances, including supervening impossibility of performance, fundamental change of circumstances and necessity, which a State may invoke to try and exit a treaty commitment or excuse its non-performance. Finally, Chapter 25 brings the experts' contributions to a close with an overview of the various ways to denounce, withdraw from, or terminate a treaty alongside a discussion of how and why international law governs treaty exit, including the VCLT's key provisions.

The *Guide to Treaties* sixth and final section adopts a different approach. In 1973, Hans Blix and Jirina Emerson edited the *Treaty Maker's Handbook* to help newly emerging States appreciate the intricacies of treaty-making as a matter of both domestic and international law post-decolonization.[17] One of the work's lasting legacies was the inclusion of sample provisions drawn from existing treaties on various treaty topics such as participation, duration, and amendment. The volume remains a staple among treaty negotiators even as it has become increasingly dated.[18]

---

[17] Blix and Emerson (n 12) Foreword.

[18] The UN and the Council of Europe have each issued their own highly useful explanations of treaty-making, including some similar sampling of treaty clauses, all of which are available online. UN Office of Legal Affairs, *Treaty Handbook* (2006) <http://treaties.un.org>; UN Office of Legal Affairs, *Final Clauses of Multilateral Treaties Handbook* (2003) <http://treaties.un.org/doc/source/publications/FC/English.pdf>; COE, 'Model Final Clauses for Conventions and Agreements Concluded within the Council of Europe' (February 1980) <http://conventions.coe.int/Treaty/EN/Treaties/Html/ClausesFinales.htm>.

Section 6 offers a new set of approximately 350 sample clauses, building off the *Treaty Maker's Handbook* framework with several modifications. First, based on current practice, Section 6 includes samples of clauses not found in Blix and Emerson's earlier work (eg participation clauses for regional integration organizations, NGO participation clauses, clauses signalling an intent to conclude a political commitment). Second, this new treatment reorganizes the treatment of other topics Blix and Emerson did consider; for example, in lieu of simply reproducing Preambles, clauses that implicate a treaty's object and purpose are presented instead. This change reflects a third key difference in the current sampling. The *Treaty Maker's Handbook* was compiled at a time when newly emerging States needed a how-to manual to build their own treaty law and practice, often from scratch. Thus, that volume included samples of constitutional provisions on treaty-making and examples of the instruments States used to do so (eg full powers, instruments expressing consent to be bound, succession instruments). In contrast, today, most States and other treaty-makers have developed and standardized their own specific rules, practices, and instruments for treaties and treaty-making. As a result, there is less need for a compilation of such rules or instruments, and they are not included in the current *Guide*.[19] Instead, the current set of sample clauses focuses on illustrating variations and precedents in treaties themselves. Doing so, it is hoped, may better inform those who actually work with treaties when they encounter future issues of treaty formation, application, interpretation, and exit.

So, who should read this book? Certainly, Section VI and many of the earlier chapters are drafted for international lawyers and policy-makers who attend treaty conferences and negotiations. But, it would be a mistake to characterize this book as some sort of practitioner's manual; the chapter treatments were also designed with academics in mind. Indeed, there is a largely unspoken expectation in international law, that written work will adopt either an academic or practical approach, but never both. The current *Oxford Guide to Treaties* rejects this dichotomy as a false one. Theories about treaties and explanations of actual treaty practice are neither mutually exclusive nor adversarial in nature. Practitioners who operate without understanding the scope and rationale for a particular treaty rule are short-handing themselves when it comes to working with that rule in the novel situations that inevitably arise. Similarly, those who focus only on theoretical explanations for treaty-making without understanding how States and other subjects of international law actually use them risk making disabling assumptions. In other words, a true *guide* to treaties requires an appreciation of the theories that generated a particular treaty law, the content of that law, *and* the ways that law is (or is not) applied in practice. It is such a holistic approach that lies at the root of the current compilation. Thus, the *Oxford Guide to Treaties* is designed to serve as a first reference point

---

[19] Modern compilations of such rules and instruments are, in any case, available elsewhere. See eg Aust (n 16) Appendices B–J, L–O (modelling various treaty and MOU forms and providing examples of various treaty-related instruments); Hollis and others (n 14) (including national treaty-related legislation and documentary samples from nineteen representative States); see also *Treaty Handbook* (n 18); *Final Clauses Handbook* (n 18).

for everyone who works with treaties, whether international lawyers, diplomats, IO officials, NGO representatives, academics, or students.

***

Today, treaties are an essential vehicle for organizing international cooperation and coordination. In both quantitative and qualitative terms, they are the primary source for international legal commitments and, indeed, international law generally. States, IOs and other subjects of international law have concluded tens of thousands of treaties; some 64,000 treaties have been registered with the UN alone.[20] From a qualitative perspective, treaties dictate the content (and contours) of every field of international law, from trade to the environment, from human rights to aviation. They now occupy, in whole or in part, most areas of international relations and quite a few areas of domestic regulation as well. As the 2006 ILC Study Group argued, moreover, the law of treaties may prove key to addressing international law's fragmentation as its fields deepen, mature, and increasingly interact.[21]

Simply put, a facility with treaties has become an indispensable part of the job description for all those who work in the fields of international law or international relations. Chances are that when a lawyer or policy-maker confronts a question of international law today, it is likely (if not inevitable) that one or more treaty provisions will prove relevant to the inquiry. The *Oxford Guide to Treaties* seeks to broaden and deepen how we approach and answer such questions and to assist all those who study treaties in appreciating the potential (and limits) of this august form of international agreement.

---

[20] See Chapter 10 (Part II).

[21] ILC Study Group, 'Fragmentation of International Law: Difficulties Arising from the Diversification and Expansion of International Law' (13 April 2006) UN Doc A/CN.4/L.682, 15 (finalized by M Koskenniemi).

SECTION I
FOUNDATIONAL ISSUES

1

Defining Treaties

Duncan B Hollis

Introduction

What is a treaty? Simply put, it is an international legal agreement. But unpacking the treaty concept further—whether in terms of the nature of that agreement, its legality, or its 'international' character—depends on the *context* in which it is used. Different contexts can produce different meanings for the same term. For example, international law has a specific meaning for the 'high seas' that may differ from the one given by a State's domestic law,[1] let alone in more colloquial settings.

Moreover, even within the same context, the treaty concept may be defined using different formulations. Many (if not most) definitions are *constitutive*; they explain what a concept 'is' by listing its essential elements or the processes for its creation. Thus, for purposes of international law, three essential elements comprise the 'high seas': (a) an area of open ocean; (b) shared by all States; (c) in which no State may exercise territorial sovereignty.[2] Alternatively, definitions may be *differential*, looking outward to explain a concept by its relationship to—and differences from—other concepts. Under this approach, international law defines the 'high seas' as 'all parts of the sea that are *not* included in the exclusive economic zone, in the territorial sea or in internal waters of a State, or in the archipelagic waters of an archipelagic State'.[3] Other definitions are *functional*—they give meaning by explaining what a concept does or how it works. From this perspective, the 'high seas' delineates an area subject to specific international legal rights (or 'freedoms') in the absence of sovereign authority.[4] Unlike different contexts, these definitional approaches—*constitutive, differential,* and *functional*—do not generate alternative meanings. Rather, they express the same meaning in different ways depending on whether the definition needs to explain how to (a) identify; (b) differentiate; or (c) evaluate a concept.

---

[1] Eg 16 USC §1802 (defining 'high seas' for US fisheries law as 'all waters beyond the territorial sea of the United States and beyond any foreign nation's territorial sea').

[2] See UN Convention on the Law of the Sea (10 December 1982, entered into force 16 November 1994) 1833 UNTS 3, Arts 87, 89 (UNCLOS).

[3] Ibid Art 86 (emphasis added).

[4] Cf ibid Art 87 (describing six freedoms of the 'high seas').

When it comes to the 'treaty', a conventional (in both senses of that word) definition already exists. Article 2(1)(a) of the 1969 Vienna Convention on the Law of Treaties (VCLT) provides that:

For the purposes of the present Convention: (a) 'treaty' means an international agreement concluded between States in written form and governed by international law, whether embodied in a single instrument or in two or more related instruments and whatever its particular designation.

This definition is widely accepted. The International Court of Justice (ICJ) has suggested it reflects customary international law.[5] Most States endorse it,[6] and scholars frequently cite it when defining the treaty concept.[7]

For all its popularity, however, the VCLT treaty definition is incomplete and underdeveloped.[8] Its reach is (expressly) limited to the VCLT; it does not address other contexts where the term 'treaty' requires definition. Moreover, Article 2(1)(a) adopts an almost exclusively *constitutive* approach. It identifies elements necessary to constitute a treaty—namely (a) an international agreement; (b) concluded between States; (c) in writing; (d) governed by international law—while dismissing other elements—the title(s) and number of instruments—as non-essential. In doing so, the VCLT does not explicitly differentiate the treaty from other concepts of commitment or agreement. And the VCLT definition says little, if anything, about how treaties function.

This chapter aims to produce a more comprehensive and robust overview of the treaty than the VCLT's now-standard treatment. Part I elaborates three contexts beyond the VCLT where the 'treaty' acquires a different definition, and what purposes that definition serves in each setting. Part II then unpacks the treaty's meaning in a specific context—international law—along *constitutive, differential,* and *functional* lines. It explains how to *constitute* a treaty using Article 2(1)(a) as a baseline, but clarifying and supplementing its list of ingredients. It *differentiates* the treaty from other concepts of commitment (unilateral statements) and agreement (contracts and political commitments) while acknowledging questions about the mutual exclusivity of these concepts. Finally, this chapter adopts a *functional* perspective to explain the evolution in what treaties do across several distinct

---

[5] Cf *Land and Maritime Boundary between Cameroon and Nigeria (Cameroon v Nigeria; Equitorial Guinea Intervening)* [2002] ICJ Rep 249 [263]. Other international tribunals take the same position, eg *Texaco v Libyan Arab Republic* (1977) 53 ILR 389, 474.

[6] DB Hollis, 'A Comparative Approach to Treaty Law and Practice' in DB Hollis, MR Blakeslee, and LB Ederington (eds), *National Treaty Law and Practice* (Martinus Nijhoff, Leiden 2005) 9 (*NTLP*) (among nineteen representative States, 'virtually every state surveyed' accepts the VCLT treaty definition).

[7] Eg J Klabbers, *The Concept of Treaty in International Law* (Kluwer Law International, The Hague 1996) 40 (VCLT definition is 'the obvious starting point' for investigating the nature of treaties); see also A Aust, *Modern Treaty Law and Practice* (2nd edn CUP, Cambridge 2007) 14; M Fitzmaurice and O Elias, *Contemporary Issues in the Law of Treaties* (Eleven International Publishing, Utrecht 2005) 6–25.

[8] Klabbers questions if a definition of 'treaty' is even possible, preferring to focus instead on explaining the 'concept of treaty'. Klabbers (n 7) 8.

dimensions. It concludes by asking if the treaty concept might benefit from further clarification or disaggregation as these treaty functions continue to evolve.

I. Defining Treaties in Context

The VCLT cabins its definition of a 'treaty' to a specific context. Article 1 limits its application 'to treaties between States', while Article 2 says it does so just 'for the purposes of the present Convention'.[9] Thus, the VCLT definition serves a specific purpose—to identify inter-State agreements subject to the VCLT's other eighty-four articles, which deal with the conclusion, application, interpretation, amendment, invalidation, and termination of such treaties. Of these, undoubtedly the most important is *pacta sunt servanda*: 'Every treaty in force is binding upon the parties to it and must be performed by them in good faith.'[10]

As noted, the VCLT definition's influence now expands well beyond its original confines. But it would be a mistake to suggest that it represents a universal definition. On the contrary, definitions of a 'treaty' and the consequences that flow from that label can—and will—vary by context. To say what a treaty 'is' thus requires knowing whether the question is posed for purposes of (a) international law, (b) domestic law, or (c) those pursuing international coordination or cooperation.

A. The 'treaty' for purposes of international law

Today, most States accept the VCLT definition of 'treaty' as customary international law.[11] But, as the VCLT itself acknowledges, this definition is not comprehensive. Article 3 emphasizes that the VCLT's exclusion of (i) agreements concluded between States and other subjects of international law; (ii) between such other subjects of international law; and (iii) unwritten international agreements, does not affect 'the legal force of such agreements'.[12] Such agreements may also qualify as 'treaties' for purposes of international law.

The international law context provides distinct consequences for calling an agreement a treaty as well. First, like the VCLT, the international law 'treaty' triggers an associated set of rules and procedures—the so-called 'law of treaties'— including *pacta sunt servanda*. The VCLT and the two 'other' Vienna Conventions[13] now codify many, but not all, of these rules and procedures. Thus, the law

---

[9] The International Law Commission (ILC) had advocated for such qualifications. See [1966] YBILC, vol II, 188 [1]; H Waldock, 'Fourth Report on the Law of Treaties' [1965] YBILC, vol II, 11 [1] ('Waldock, Fourth Report').

[10] VCLT Art 26.

[11] See n 6; Aust (n 7) 16 (VCLT treaty 'elements now represent customary international law'); ME Villiger, *Commentary on the 1969 Vienna Convention on the Law of Treaties* (Martinus Nijhoff, Leiden 2009) 83 (same).

[12] The ILC originally proposed these exclusions. [1966] YBILC, vol II, 188–9 [5], [7].

[13] Vienna Convention on the Law of Treaties between States and International Organizations or between International Organizations (adopted 21 March 1986, not yet in force) [1986] 25 ILM 543

of treaties exists independently of these conventions and with a wider ambit than the VCLT alone.[14]

Second, the binding quality of *pacta sunt servanda* means that, once in force, treaties constitute a source of international obligations for parties. International obligations implicate a separate area of international law—the law of responsibility. The breach of an 'international obligation' attributable to a State constitutes an internationally wrongful act, which is subject to an increasingly well-developed set of customary international law rules and remedies.[15] Thus, when international law defines a State's agreement as a treaty, its operation (including questions of breach and termination) may become subject to *both* the law of treaties and the law of State responsibility.[16] And, although the rules and remedies are less well developed (and more complicated) for breaches of international obligations attributable to International Organizations (IOs), similar consequences may flow from their 'treaties' as well.[17]

Third, beyond the law of treaties and the law of State responsibility, applying the 'treaty' label may have an even more important role—identifying a source of international law itself. The ICJ Statute lists treaties, or 'conventions', as one of three primary sources—along with custom and recognized general principles—for the Court to apply to a dispute before it.[18] Most international lawyers view this list as a roster for the sources of international legal rules generally. There are some theoretical difficulties with assigning treaties such status; Sir Gerald Fitzmaurice questioned whether treaties can operate as a source of law if they only bind parties.[19] And, aside from a few 'objective regimes', treaties generally do bind only parties.[20] Nonetheless, conventional wisdom has largely overlooked such finer points and treaties are now widely regarded as one of the primary sources of international law.[21]

('1986 VCLT'); Vienna Convention on Succession of States in Respect of Treaties (adopted 23 August 1978, entered into force 6 November 1996) 1946 UNTS 3.

[14] For example, none of the Vienna Conventions deal with oral treaties or how armed conflicts affect treaties. See eg VCLT Arts 3, 73.

[15] ILC, Draft Articles on the Responsibility of States for Internationally Wrongful Acts, Report on the Work of its Fifty-first Session (3 May–23 July, 1999) UN Doc A/56/10, 55 [3] (ASR).

[16] For a discussion of how this affects remedies for breach or exceptional circumstances as grounds for treaty exit, see Chapters 23 and 24, respectively.

[17] On IO responsibility, see Chapter 3, Part III, 84 *et seq.*; on EU responsibility, see Chapter 4, Part II.C, 118 *et seq*; see also ILC, Draft Articles on the Responsibility of International Organizations, UNGA, Report of the International Law Commission, UN GAOR 63rd Session Supp No 10 (2011) UN Doc A/66/10.

[18] Statute of the International Court of Justice (26 June 1945) 33 UNTS 993, Art 38(1).

[19] GG Fitzmaurice, 'Some Problems Regarding the Formal Sources of International Law' in *Symbolae Verzijl* (Martinus Nijhoff, The Hague 1958) 153, 157.

[20] See Chapter 13, Part III, 341 *et seq*. If a treaty codifies or comes to express customary international law, it may bind non-parties, but in such instances, it is the customary international law rule that does so, not its placement within a treaty.

[21] Martti Koskenniemi opined that we do this 'by default' because of continuing controversy over other potential sources and differing theories about the international legal order's structure. M Koskenniemi, 'Introduction' in M Koskenniemi (ed), *Sources of International Law* (Ashgate, Dartmouth 2000) xii; see also DB Hollis, 'Why State Consent Still Matters—Non-State Actors, Treaties, and the Changing Sources of International Law' (2005) 23 Berkeley J Intl L 137, 142.

B. Defining treaties for purposes of domestic law

Most existing studies of the treaty focus on differences in meaning under the VCLT and international law.[22] But this overlooks an equally, if not more important, context in which the treaty exists and requires definition—the domestic level. Although domestic law (occasionally supplemented by practice) differs from State to State, invariably treaties are defined within this context in at least two distinct ways. First, domestic law defines the treaty for purposes of elaborating the conditions for its formation. Second, domestic law also defines treaties to specify whether and how they operate within the national legal order.[23]

To be clear, domestic laws do not have to define treaties differently than international law. Some States (eg Japan, Russia) simply mimic the VCLT definition for domestic purposes.[24] But other States *do* depart from the VCLT formula, defining treaties by their requisite domestic procedures. Thus, France limits its domestic definition of treaties (*traités*) to agreements receiving Presidential ratification; other international agreements (*accords internationaux*) are subject to parliamentary approval. Despite differing domestic law terminology, France regards both concepts as identical for purposes of international law.[25] In the United States, a 'Treaty' is an international agreement approved by two-thirds of the US Senate followed by Presidential ratification.[26] Other 'international agreements' arise through different procedures—congressional approval, reliance on Presidential powers, or authorization by a prior Treaty.[27] Like France, the United States views both 'Treaties' and 'international agreements' as treaties in the international law sense of that term.[28] Chile and the Netherlands make similar domestic distinctions.[29]

For purposes of domestic law, therefore, treaty definitions implicate the State's allocation of international treaty-making capacity among domestic political actors.

---

[22] Eg Aust (n 7) 6; Klabbers (n 7) 8; K Widdows, 'What is an Agreement in International Law?' (1979) 50 BYBIL 117.

[23] Some States also use domestic law to impose procedures on a State's exit from its treaty commitments.

[24] Eg T Kawakami, 'Japan' in *NTLP* (n 6) 415, 416 (Art 4 of Japan's Law for the Establishment of the Ministry of Foreign Affairs tracks the VCLT definition); WE Butler, 'Russia' in *NTLP* (n 6) 537, 540 (1995 Russian Federal Law on International Treaties incorporates the VCLT definition verbatim).

[25] PM Eisemann and R Rivier, 'France' in *NTLP* (n 6) 253–4; ibid 276–7 (1958 French Constitution, Art 52).

[26] US Constitution, Art II, §2, cl 2.

[27] See eg R Dalton, 'United States' in *NTLP* (n 6) 770–1, 780–5. Unfortunately, it is not always clear *which* agreements go through *which* processes. See eg O Hathaway, 'Treaties' End: The Past, Present and Future of International Lawmaking in the United States' (2008) 117 Yale L J 1236.

[28] US federal regulations suggest that even considered together, 'Treaties' and 'international agreements' do not include all international law treaties; US 'international agreements' must meet additional requirements of significance—'minor or trivial undertakings, even if couched in legal language and form are not considered international agreements'—and specificity, including objective criteria for determining enforceability. 22 CFR 181.2 (2011).

[29] FO Vicuña and FO Bauzá, 'Chile' in *NTLP* (n 6) 123, 142 (Chile Constitution, Art 50(1)); ibid 123–4; JG Brower, 'The Netherlands' in *NTLP* (n 6) 485–6 (distinguishing 'treaties' requiring parliamentary approval from other 'administrative agreements').

Every State empowers its executive to represent the State in negotiating and concluding treaties.[30] Frequently, however, States counterbalance this authority by allowing other domestic actors (most often the legislature, but sometimes courts, sub-national units, or even the general populace) to exercise their interests by having a say in what treaties the State makes.[31] As noted, some States, like France and the United States, explicitly use the 'treaty' definition to do this by requiring additional democratic approval (via legislative participation) for certain international law 'treaties'. But even States that do not limit their domestic treaty definition this way, still define the 'treaty' (or different categories of 'treaties') with an eye to the domestic procedures involved in their formation and implementation.[32] And where those procedures are not followed, domestic law may not regard the resulting agreement as a 'treaty'.[33]

Beyond procedures, States also define treaties domestically to situate them within the national legal order. All States may endorse *pacta sunt servanda* as a matter of international law, but States have not interpreted that principle to require any particular priority for treaties as a matter of domestic law. In the national context, the State's constitutional framework, not international law, dictates the legal status of treaties. Some States do not regard treaties as part of their domestic legal order at all, relying on new or existing legislation to implement treaty obligations domestically. Other States give some treaties (but never all of them) direct effect as domestic law, whether upon the treaty's entry into force internationally or the completion of some domestic procedures (eg publication).[34] Moreover, States that grant treaties direct legal effect adopt differing approaches to their positions in the domestic law hierarchy. Some prioritize treaties over all national laws, including the Constitution; some subordinate them below all national laws; and some States afford treaties an intermediate status, equating them, for example, to statutes enacted by the national legislature.[35]

---

[30] Not every State empowers the same officials that VCLT Art 7 (and customary international law) empowers with treaty-making authority. Israel, Japan, and Switzerland deny their Head of State such authority; the Netherlands denies it to the Head of Government; while Colombia does so for its Foreign Minister. Hollis (n 6) 20–1.

[31] Colombia, for example, conditions treaty ratification on Constitutional Court approval; France and Switzerland put certain treaties to a popular referendum. Ibid 30. Germany involves its Länder in federal treaty-making. H Beemelmans and HD Treviranus, 'Germany' in *NTLP* (n 6) 329.

[32] Colombia requires parliamentary approval of all treaties while Commonwealth countries such as the United Kingdom require no parliamentary involvement in treaty formation (as distinct from treaty implementation). Intermediate positions include States such as Chile, Switzerland, the Netherlands, and South Africa who specify exceptions to a general requirement of legislative approval. Austria, China, Egypt, Germany, Israel, Russia, and Thailand have specific lists of treaties that do (or do not) require legislative approval. Whatever approach a State uses, legislative involvement appears more likely if the treaty requires changes to domestic law or has political, social, or economic significance. See Hollis (n 6) 19–38.

[33] For purposes of international law, a failure to follow domestic procedures will not invalidate the treaty absent a manifest violation of a rule of fundamental importance. VCLT Art 46; see also Chapter 22, Part III.A, 561 *et seq*.

[34] On the role of treaties in domestic law, see Chapter 15; Aust (n 7) ch 10; Hollis (n 6) 39–49.

[35] Hollis (n 6) 47–9.

C. Defining treaties for purposes of international cooperation and coordination

Defining the 'treaty' has clear legal consequences with respect to both international and national law. But lawyers are not the only actors interested in treaties; they also matter to those working on transnational issues. Negotiators (and the policy-makers they represent) are more interested in a treaty's capacity to achieve desired goals than the specific legal criteria by which they are defined. Those goals vary but most often involve (a) international *cooperation* that would otherwise not occur due to a collective action problem, or (b) international *coordination* of future behaviour that might otherwise be dissonant.[36] Cooperation and coordination may arise through a coincidence of interests, coercion, or pursuant to a commitment. In this context, the treaty is one of several forms of commitment (others include unilateral declarations and political commitments). For political scientists, a treaty may be defined by its ability to enhance the credibility of the commitments it contains.[37]

What makes a treaty commitment credible? It appears to come from the seriousness and stability such instruments provide.[38] Treaties are serious because their legal form communicates to States, their respective domestic constituencies, and third parties an expectation of performance that may not accompany the same commitment in a non-legal form.[39] Their stability derives from the treaty's existence under *both* international and national laws. In international law, the law of treaties provides default rules that create shared expectations for how treaty commitments will be formed, applied, and interpreted. The law of treaties also explicitly prefers treaty continuity; it has relatively few options for (and significant restrictions on) unilateral exit. Moreover, violations of treaty commitments may trigger reputational consequences that treaty parties likely wish to avoid.[40]

Meanwhile, at the national level, procedural conditions on State consent help to ensure that information about the treaty is distributed internally within the State. Participation by domestic actors other than the executive in a treaty's formation can

---

[36] Why individual actors agree to pursue (or continue) cooperation and coordination is a hard question, the answers to which have generated entire schools of thought in international relations. *Realism* explains cooperation and coordination as a product of self-interested State action and a function of the distribution of power among States; *liberal theory* emphasizes domestic political actors as the driving influence of State behaviour; *institutionalism* describes the need to reduce uncertainty and transaction costs to correct for 'market failures'; while *constructivism* highlights the impact of a social context from which a shared identity, subjective understandings and norms emerge. See generally J Dunoff and M Pollack (eds), *International Law and International Relations: Insights from Interdisciplinary Scholarship* (CUP, Cambridge 2012).

[37] K Raustiala, 'Form and Substance in International Agreements' (2005) 99 AJIL 581, 592.

[38] See eg J Goldsmith and E Posner, *The Limits of International Law* (OUP, Oxford 2005) 91–9; C Lipson, 'Why are Some International Agreements Informal?' (1991) 45 IO 495, 508.

[39] Goldsmith and Posner (n 38) 98–9.

[40] R Brewster, 'Unpacking the State's Reputation' (2009) 50 HILJ 231, 235; see also A Guzman, *How International Law Works: A Rational Choice Theory* (OUP, New York 2008). Treaties may also provide compliance mechanisms or dispute settlement procedures that enhance the treaty's seriousness and stability.

also increase expectations of performance. For States giving treaties direct domestic legal effect, additional mechanisms—judicial interpretation and enforcement— may further ensure continued treaty performance.

Thus, for those concerned with international cooperation and coordination, the treaty cannot be defined solely in international *or* national law terms, but requires a separate, more hybrid, definition. At the same time, questions have arisen about using treaties as a discrete category of international commitment. In recent years, international relations scholars began to think of international commitments in terms of *legalization*, a concept that can be disaggregated along three independent dimensions: (i) obligation, which asks the extent to which a commitment is legally binding; (ii) precision, which involves the clarity of the commitment and expected means of performance; and (iii) delegation, which entails the extent to which third parties (eg courts and administrative organs) are designated to implement the commitment.[41] Although the legalization perspective does not redefine the treaty, this approach to international coordination and cooperation impacts the treaty concept in two key ways.[42]

First, evaluating the extent of a commitment's 'obligation' suggests that its 'bindingness' exists along a continuum of possibilities. Thus, unlike the traditional binary approach to defining treaties (ie a commitment is either a legally binding treaty or it is not), this view highlights the possibility that negotiators may vary how strongly (or weakly) a commitment legally binds its participants. The existence of a legal obligation thus shifts from a black-or-white issue to one encompassing various shades of grey. Second, by emphasizing variables other than obligation—precision and delegation—the essentiality of legal obligations is called into question. A commitment may be fully binding but of little practical use if its content is imprecise or there are no external checks on implementation. Conversely, a non- binding or 'soft' obligation might actually achieve cooperation or coordination if it is stated in highly precise terms and/or delegates responsibility for implementation to third parties.[43] Taken together, a graduated view of bindingness and an emphasis on precision and delegation suggest that the treaty may not be an optimal (let alone essential) vehicle for achieving international cooperation and coordination.

On the other hand, whatever explanatory value legalization may have for analysing cooperation and coordination, it remains contested in certain respects. Some scholars deny any 'spectrum of legality', insisting that the legal quality of a commitment cannot be differentiated, rejecting any concept of 'soft law' in the process.[44] For them, the treaty remains a highly relevant category. States, moreover, appear to agree: they regularly and consciously employ the treaty concept in a

---

[41] KW Abbott and others, 'The Concept of Legalization' (2000) 54 IO 401, 401; CM Chinkin, 'The Challenge of Soft Law: Development and Change in International Law' (1989) 38 ICLQ 850, 865–6.

[42] See Abbott and others (n 41) 403 (declaiming any intent to define (or redefine) law).

[43] Hence the rise in attention to 'soft law'. K Abbott and D Snidal, 'Hard and Soft Law in International Governance' (2000) 54 IO 421; Chinkin (n 41) 850.

[44] Raustiala (n 37) 588; P Weil, 'Towards Relative Normativity in International Law' (1983) 77 AJIL 413. *Jus cogens* is the one widely recognized exception.

binary fashion, choosing it as the label for those commitments they intend to create legal obligations and using other labels (eg political commitment) for other forms of agreement. Nor are these labels merely international rhetoric. At the domestic level especially, the treaty concept implicates domestic law in ways distinct from the impact (if any) of other international commitments. Those impacts, moreover, may be precisely what give the treaty commitment its credibility and hence its utility in facilitating international cooperation and coordination.

The foregoing highlights a range of contexts in which the treaty concept appears: international law, national law, and international relations. In each, the treaty's meaning varies, even as the core concept of an international legal agreement remains. Moreover, each context defines the treaty for very different purposes. Sketching out these differences does not, of course, tell us exactly what the treaty 'is' in any particular context. The remainder of this chapter endeavours to do so for a specific context: international law. It examines how to identify a treaty; how to distinguish it from other commitments and agreements; and what functions it may perform.

II. Defining the 'Treaty' in International Law

A. The *constitutive* definition: identifying treaties by their ingredients

For those concerned with identifying what constitutes a treaty for purposes of international law, the VCLT provides a natural starting point. As noted, it lists four basic ingredients, namely (a) an international agreement; (b) concluded among States; (c) in writing; (d) governed by international law. It also takes two potential ingredients—the agreement's designation and its number of instruments—off the table. As the context shifts from the VCLT to customary international law, this basic recipe requires some variations and substitutions. The resulting formula provides some clarity in deciding whether to apply the 'treaty' label to an international agreement. But, like other recipes, debates continue on how to procure specific ingredients and their relative importance to the treaty concept itself.

1. An international agreement

In international law—as in all contexts—a treaty requires an international agreement. The universality of this criterion, however, belies its ambiguity. International law offers little guidance on what qualifies as an 'agreement' let alone an 'international' one.[45] Nonetheless, this criterion adds value to the treaty concept in three distinct ways.

---

[45] Klabbers (n 7) 51; Fitzmaurice and Elias (n 7) 10. In practice, States often explicitly state their intention to make an agreement. Samples of such statements are excerpted in No 6 of Section VI of this *Guide*. For more on intent, see Part II.A.4 of this chapter.

First, by requiring an *'international* agreement', the VCLT definition clarifies that treaties are a specific category of agreement. All treaties qualify as agreements, but not all agreements qualify as treaties.[46] It is not clear, however, what else the 'international' qualification does. It has not, for example, been interpreted to constrain treaties to specific 'international' subjects. During the Vienna Conference, Spain proposed deleting the adjective as 'unnecessary and liable to cause confusion',[47] but the Drafting Committee declined, without explanation, to do so. Today, the 'international' qualification is best understood as bounding the scope of agreement, whether in terms of the international actors who make it or its basis of obligation in international law, which the rest of the definition then proceeds to clarify.[48]

Second, although the International Law Commission (ILC) gave the idea of 'agreement' little attention,[49] this requirement does significantly impact our understanding of the treaty. It has (at least) two elements. Agreements do not arise from a single actor *sua sponte*; they involve *mutuality*—an interchange or communication among multiple participants.[50] Furthermore, that interchange must generate a normative *commitment*—a shared expectation of future behaviour whether in terms of a change from the status quo or a continuation of existing behaviour.[51] Communications limited to explaining a particular position, or even articulating an 'agreed view', are generally not agreements. The depth of a commitment may vary widely. It may also be one-sided; agreements do not require an exchange of commitments (or what the common law calls 'consideration'); a single commitment by one party to another party or parties will suffice.

Third, by simply requiring an agreement, the definition leaves open the question of where agreement lies. On the one hand, an agreement (and consequently a treaty) could be defined as the actual shared expectation of commitment—the parties' subjective 'meeting of the minds'. Alternatively, an agreement might refer

---

[46] Villiger (n 11) 77. This point was repeated throughout the ILC's preparatory work. See JL Brierly, 'First Report on the Law of Treaties' (1950) YBILC, vol II, 227 [19] ('Brierly, First Report'); Waldock, Fourth Report (n 9) 11 [1]; [1965] YBILC, vol I, 10 [10] (Briggs).

[47] UN Conference on the Law of Treaties, Summary Records of First Session, A/CONF.39/11, 23 [20] ('Vienna Conference, First Session'); UN Conference on the Law of Treaties, Official Records: Documents of the Conference, A/CONF.39/11/Add.2, 111 ('Vienna Conference, Official Records'); see also Klabbers (n 7) 54. Several States supported Spain's proposal. Eg Vienna Conference, First Session, 21 [2] (Chile); ibid 25 [7] (Syria). The United States favoured retaining the 'international' qualifier. Ibid 31 [115].

[48] This follows from Waldock's earlier understanding. H Waldock, 'First Report on the Law of Treaties' [1962] YBILC, vol II, 32 Art 1(a) (defining an 'international agreement' as 'an agreement intended to be governed by international law and concluded between two or more States or other subjects of international law') ('Waldock, First Report'); see also Villiger (n 11) 78.

[49] None of the four ILC Special Rapporteurs explained what they meant by 'agreement'. Brierly (n 46) 227 [19]–[20]; H Lauterpacht, 'First Report on the Law of Treaties' [1953] YBILC, vol II, 90, 93–4 (Art 1) ('Lauterpacht, First Report'); GG Fitzmaurice, 'First Report on the Law of Treaties' [1956] YBILC, vol II, 117 ('Fitzmaurice, First Report'); Waldock, First Report (n 48) 31 (Art 1(a)).

[50] DB Hollis and JJ Newcomer, ' "Political" Commitments and the Constitution' (2009) 49 VJIL 507, 522; Klabbers (n 7) 51–3.

[51] Hollis and Newcomer (n 50) 522; Klabbers (n 7) 51–3; Raustiala (n 37) 584–5 (discussing 'depth' by reference to the departure an agreement requires from what States would do in the absence of agreement).

to the instrument(s) recording the parties' expectations. In other words, do we define treaties as obligations or instruments?[52] That choice has important interpretative consequences, particularly where one side claims the instrument purporting to be the treaty does not fully capture the parties' actual commitment(s).

VCLT Article 2(1)(a)'s 'agreement' reference might appear to conceptualize the treaty in terms of the commitment, rather than the instrument that conveys it.[53] But, the remainder of the VCLT undercuts this view; almost all of its provisions on the formation, application, interpretation, and termination of treaties turn on the text of the treaty instrument. Of course, the VCLT's instrument-centered approach need not govern the treaty concept in the wider ambit of international law. But, the other Vienna Conventions and State practice suggest that it presently does so. Thus, a treaty requires an international agreement evincing a sense of mutuality and commitment manifested through one or more specific instruments.

2. 'Concluded among States' or *other subjects of international law*

Assuming an international agreement, the VCLT requires that a treaty be 'concluded among States'. This criterion implicates the timing of the treaty's creation and the identity of its creators.

As a temporal matter, a treaty must be 'concluded' to exist. What constitutes conclusion? Loosely, it refers to the entire process from the negotiations' end to a 'definitive engagement that the parties are bound by the instrument under international law'.[54] Pinpointing the exact moment of conclusion is a bit more difficult. For some, that moment does not occur until after the parties express their consent to be bound by the treaty and no 'further formalities' are required.[55] In practice, however, a treaty is usually considered concluded at an earlier point: when the parties adopt the treaty text or it is opened for their signature.[56] The VCLT's structure favours this later formulation.[57] In either case, it is clear that a treaty can be 'concluded' even if it has not yet entered into force (or it never does so[58]); conclusion and entry into force are not synonymous.[59] *Pacta sunt servanda* only applies to a subset of treaties, namely those 'in force'. Thus, it is important to

---

[52] See eg S Rosenne, *Breach of Treaty* (CUP, Cambridge 1993) 3–5; Widdows (n 22) 118.

[53] See Villiger (n 11) 77.

[54] Ibid 78–9. This was Waldock's view. Waldock, First Report (n 48) 30 [9]. Fitzmaurice noted conclusion could refer to either a process or a specific point in time. Fitzmaurice, First Report (n 49) 121 [48]–[52]. Brierly supported linking treaty conclusion to the establishment of the agreed text in final form. JL Brierly, 'Second Report on the Law of Treaties' [1951] YBILC, vol II, 70–1.

[54] Villiger (n 11) 79.

[55] Ibid 79; see also R Gardiner, *Treaty Interpretation* (OUP, Oxford 2009) 209–11.

[56] Gardiner (n 55) 209; Aust (n 7) 92.

[57] VCLT Arts 7–10 discuss the 'text of the treaty' when referring to full powers, adoption and authentication of a treaty text, but then refer to the 'treaty' in Arts 11–18, which elaborate various means of expressing consent to be bound. See Gardiner (n 55) 209–11. The 1986 VCLT adopts the same approach.

[58] Unperfected treaties—those that do not enter into force—are thus still considered treaties.

[59] Aust (n 7) 93; Villiger (n 11) 79.

differentiate the legal effects that arise when a treaty merely exists from those imposed upon its entry into force.[60]

In terms of party identity, a VCLT 'treaty' only involves States. But States may still conclude treaties at different levels. Some treaties will be done on behalf of (and in the name of) the State itself; others may be done by the State's government or one of its agencies, ministries, or departments. Austria, China, Germany, India, and Russia all conclude treaties at State-to-State, government-to-government, and agency-to-agency levels.[61] Some States, however, prohibit their agencies from engaging in treaty-making.[62] Regardless of the level at which the agreement is concluded, international law generally treats the 'State' as the responsible party. A few States (notably France and Mexico) have domestic laws suggesting that their agency-level agreements only bind their agencies,[63] but it is not clear if international law respects such attempts to limit State responsibility.

More importantly, although treaty-making was historically the province of States, that limitation no longer holds.[64] The ILC clearly limited its attention to inter-State agreements as a matter of expediency rather than any sense of legal requirement.[65] As Article 3 of the VCLT notes, it was understood at the time that 'other subjects of international law' could conclude treaties as well.[66]

Who are these 'other subjects'? For starters, international organizations (IOs) may have a treaty-making capacity. To the extent it reflects customary international

[60] See eg VCLT Art 24(4) (noting various provisions of 'a treaty' that 'apply from the time of the adoption of its text' rather than on entry into force).

[61] G Hafner, 'Austria' in NTLP (n 6) 59, 64; X Hanqin and others, 'China' in NTLP (n 6) 155, 159; Beemelmans and Treviranus (n 31) 317, 319–20 (Germany); K Thakore, 'India' in NTLP (n 6) 352, 352; Butler (n 24) 540 (Russia).

[62] NJ Botha, 'South Africa' in NTLP (n 6) 581, 584 (South Africa generally does not authorize its agencies to conclude treaties); Kawakami (n 24) 417 (with few exceptions, ministries other than Japan's Ministry of Foreign Affairs have no authority to conclude international agreements).

[63] Eisemann and Rivier (n 25) 254–5 (discussing French practice of *arrangements administratifs* that 'do not bind the State, only the signatory agency'); L Díaz, 'Mexico' in NTLP (n 6) 450 (discussing Mexican Treaty Law authorization of inter-institutional agreements that 'are only binding upon those agencies, which have entered into them').

[64] A McNair, *The Law of Treaties* (OUP, Oxford 1961) 755 ('Fifty years ago it might have been possible to say that only States could conclude treaties, but today any such statement would be out of date.').

[65] All four ILC Special Rapporteurs proposed including non-State actors (whether IOs or 'other subjects of international law') within their treaty definition, and thus within the codification project itself. See Brierly, First Report (n 46) 223; Lauterpacht, First Report (n 49) 90, 94; Fitzmaurice, First Report (n 49) 117; Waldock, First Report (n 48) 32, 35. By 1965, after debate and government input, the ILC decided to focus solely on 'treaties of States'. Waldock, Fourth Report (n 9) 11 (citing ILC decision at its 14th session).

[66] See eg P Gautier, 'Article 1 Convention of 1969' in O Corten and P Klein (eds), *The Vienna Conventions on the Law of Treaties: A Commentary* (OUP, Oxford 2011) vol I, 22–4; Villiger (n 11) 57–8; Fitzmaurice and Elias (n 7) 16–18; Klabbers (n 7) 47–9; S Rosenne, *Developments in the Law of Treaties 1945–1986* (CUP, Cambridge 1989) 10–23. At the Vienna Conference, US and Vietnamese efforts to expand the VCLT treaty definition to include 'other subjects' fell short. See Vienna Conference, First Session (n 47) 20 [64]; Vienna Conference, Official Records (n 47) 110. The Vienna Conference instead adopted a resolution recommending the ILC study IO treaty-making. Vienna Conference, Official Records (n 47) 285.

law, the 1986 VCLT now defines the treaty in terms of IO agreements.[67] Much less attention has been paid to the possibility of treaties involving actors other than States or IOs like the UN or EU. In practice, however, various 'other subjects of international law' may conclude treaties, including (i) federal territorial units, (ii) external territories, (iii) insurgent groups, and maybe (iv) even (very rarely) private actors.[68]

The fact that IOs and other subjects of international law can make *some* treaties does not mean these actors can make *all* treaties. International law imposes two qualifications on their treaty-making: internal authorization and external consent. IOs can only make a treaty where (a) member States have authorized it in the constituent treaty or acquiesced to it in practice; *and* (b) other States, IOs, or subjects of international law are willing to conclude such a treaty with that IO.[69] Similarly, sub-State actors require '(1) the consent of the State responsible for the sub-state actor; and (2) the willingness of the sub-State actor's treaty partners to regard it as capable of entering into treaties' on the subject-matter.[70] Where authorization is absent or potential treaty-partners unavailable, IOs and other subjects of international law cannot make treaties.

3. 'In written form' or otherwise recorded

The VCLT requires a treaty to be in writing. The form of that writing is not terribly relevant. Signature, for example, is not required.[71] Nor is publication.[72] What is required is some permanent and readable evidence of agreement.[73] Thus, the ILC's first Special Rapporteur, JL Brierly, noted a treaty may exist via 'typewriting and printing and, indeed, any other permanent method of recording'.[74] Aust adds more modern forms, including 'telegram, telex, fax message or even an e-mail'.[75] As the Information Age evolves, this list could expand to newer forms of electronic communication, such as text messages or use of social media.

Are oral agreements treaties? The VCLT excluded them for practical reasons and without prejudice to their legal force.[76] Today, many States accept that, in

---

[67] 1986 VCLT (n 13) Art 1(a). IO treaty-making is the subject of Chapters 3 and 21; Chapter 4 deals specifically with EU treaty-making.

[68] Chapter 5, Part I.A.1–4, 127 *et seq*, discusses treaties and each of these 'other subjects'. See also Hollis (n 21) 146–55.

[69] See Chapter 3, Part IV, 87 *et seq*.

[70] Hollis (n 21) 163.

[71] Gautier (n 66) 38; Aust (n 7) 24–5; *Pulp Mills on the River Uruguay (Argentina v Uruguay)* (Judgment, 20 April 2010) [132]–[150] (ICJ treats unsigned joint press communiqué as an 'agreement').

[72] Fitzmaurice and Elias (n 7) 23–4; Klabbers (n 7) 85–6.

[73] Aust (n 7) 19.

[74] Brierly, First Report (n 46) 227. Fitzmaurice implied Brierly's formulation required clarification, asking if it would include an 'oral agreement, recorded . . . on a disc or tape recorder . . .'? Fitzmaurice, First Report (n 49) 117 n4. The topic was not, however, discussed at the Vienna Conference. Klabbers (n 7) 50.

[75] Aust (n 7) 19.

[76] VCLT Art 3. The ILC emphasized it focused exclusively on written agreements 'in the interests of clarity and simplicity' and had 'not intended to deny the legal force of oral agreements under

principle, customary international law may recognize oral agreements as treaties.[77] US domestic law goes so far as to require the commitment of oral international agreements, once made, to writing.[78] Other States, however, oppose concluding oral treaties raising questions about their current status in international law.[79] Moreover, actual practice is quite sparse. There are just a handful of recorded 'oral treaties', the most notable being the so-called Ihlen Declaration.[80] A more recently cited example is Finland and Denmark's oral settlement of their Great Belt bridge dispute.[81]

Assuming oral agreements can constitute treaties, serious questions remain as to the applicable rules. It is not clear what evidence demonstrates the existence of an oral treaty; must it be recorded in some permanent and observable form (eg an audio or video recording, written transcription) akin to an original writing, or can later testimony alone establish the existence of a prior oral treaty? Lauterpacht's charge that 'what matters is the existence of a record of an agreement'[82] cautions against finding oral treaties absent *some* record of the treaty's existence and its content. What other requirements surround oral treaties is also murky. To the extent it codifies customary international law, some VCLT rules may govern oral treaties,[83] but others (ie those on signature or ratification) are obviously inapplicable. To date, there have been few efforts to identify the relevant rules, presumably because of the rarity with which such agreements arise.

international law or to imply that some of the principles contained in later parts of the Commission's draft articles on the law of treaties may not have relevance in regard to oral agreements'. [1966] YBILC, vol II, 189 [7].

[77] See eg Hollis (n 6) 12–13 (surveying treaty law and practice of States, including Canada, Germany, Japan, Switzerland, and the UK, which accept the possibility of oral treaties even if they do not make them).

[78] See 1 USC §112b.

[79] Eg Brower (n 29) 486 (Dutch Government has opposed practice of oral agreements since 1983); G Cavelier, 'Colombia' in *NTLP* (n 6) 196 (Colombia not bound by verbal agreements because of domestic promulgation requirements); Thakore (n 61) 352 (oral agreements 'are not resorted to in Indian practice'); Botha (n 62) 583 (neither South African law or practice makes any provision for oral agreements and they lack official sanction).

[80] See *Legal Status of Eastern Greenland (Denmark v Norway)* [1933] PCIJ Rep Ser A/B No 53, 22–3, 69–73 (viewing Norwegian Foreign Minister Ihlen's oral promise not to interfere with Danish claims to sovereignty in Eastern Greenland (after Denmark agreed not to interfere with Norwegian claims to Spitzbergen) as an internationally legally binding obligation); ibid 91 (dissent of Judge Anzilotti). Its status as an oral treaty remains, however, contested. See n 143 and accompanying text

[81] Aust (n 7) 9; Klabbers (n 7) 50 n71; (1992) 3 Finnish Ybk Intl L 610; but see Hollis and Newcomer (n 50) 527 n78 (suggesting Great Belt settlement might be a political commitment instead). See also Gautier (n 66) 39 n38 (citing oral declaration by Canada on signing a treaty on deep seabed mining accepted by other delegations on hand); McNair (n 64) 8–9 (characterizing Silesian loan affair as an oral treaty).

[82] [1953] YBILC, vol II, 160.

[83] VCLT Art 3 ('The fact that the present Convention does not apply . . . to agreements not in written form, shall not affect: . . . (b) the application to them of any of the rules set forth in the present Convention to which they would be subject under international law independently of the Convention').

4. 'Governed by international law'

Undoubtedly, the most important (and most controversial) part of a treaty's ingredients is the final one—the requirement that it be 'governed by international law'. When questions arise as to whether a particular instrument *is* a treaty, debate almost always centres on this criterion. This may be due to the tautology inherent in saying that, for purposes of international law, a treaty is an 'agreement... governed by international law'. This allows the phrase to operate as a sort of empty vessel, which can be deployed for multiple purposes.

For starters, 'governed by international law' need not be read as an ingredient for making a treaty at all; rather, it can be read as the consequence of doing so. In other words, it describes the effect that follows from a recorded international agreement among States, IOs, and other qualified subjects of international law. That perspective was clearly at work in the ILC's origination of the phrase.[84] At the Vienna Conference, however, efforts to elaborate on a treaty's functions were unavailing. Chile proposed defining the treaty as an agreement 'governed by international law, which produces legal effects' but its amendment was not adopted.[85]

The Chilean proposal, however, highlighted another motivation for the 'governed by international law' qualification—to distinguish treaties from other forms of agreement. The ILC clearly viewed treaties as distinct from agreements governed by 'national' law[86] and agreements not governed by law at all.[87] At the Vienna Conference, clarifications were proposed first by Mexico and Malaysia,[88] and later by Switzerland,[89] to make such distinctions more explicit. But the Drafting Committee considered such proposals 'superfluous' and the original formula remained unaltered.[90]

---

[84] Eg [1959] YBILC, vol II, 95 [3] ('the Commission felt that the element of subjection to international law was so essential an aspect of a treaty... that this should be expressly mentioned in any definition or description').

[85] Vienna Conference, Official Records (n 47) 111. Thus, it becomes difficult to define treaties, if not international law more generally, based on their normative effects. See J Pauwelyn, 'Is it International Law or Not and Does it Even Matter?' in J Pauwelyn and others (eds), *Informal International Lawmaking* (OUP, Oxford 2012).

[86] [1966] YBILC, vol II, 189 [6]; [1959] YBILC, vol II, 95 [3]; At the Vienna Conference, Waldock emphasized that: 'The phrase "governed by international law" serves to distinguish between international agreements regulated by public international law and those, which although concluded between States, are regulated by the national law of one of the parties (or by some other national law system chosen by the parties)'. Vienna Conference, Official Records (n 47) 9 [6].

[87] Eg [1959] YBILC, vol II, 96–7 [8] ('instruments which, although they might look like treaties, merely contained declarations of principle or statements of policy, or expressions of opinion, or *voeux*, would not be treaties').

[88] Vienna Conference, Official Records (n 47) 111–12; Vienna Conference, First Session (n 47) 23 [26] (Mexican delegate distinguishes treaties from 'declarations of principle or political instruments'); ibid 28 [65].

[89] The Swiss Government proposed to exclude 'agreements concluded between States at the international level but not constituting treaties, such as declarations of intent, political declarations and "gentleman's agreements"'. UN Conference on the Law of Treaties, Summary Records of Second Session, A/CONF.39/11/Add.1, 225 [13] ('Vienna Conference, Second Session').

[90] Ibid 346 [21]–[22]; RD Kearney and R Dalton, 'The Treaty on Treaties' (1970) 64 AJIL 495, 504–5.

The real controversy over 'governed by international law', however, comes in its employment in claiming (or denying) treaty status for an agreement. The ILC's Special Rapporteurs had proposed identifying treaties based on their legal content and/or the authors' intentions. For Brierly, a treaty had to establish 'a relationship under international law'.[91] His successor, Lauterpacht, took a different tack, defining treaties as agreements 'intended to create legal rights and obligations'.[92] Fitzmaurice originally combined these approaches, defining the treaty as 'an international agreement . . . intended to create legal rights and obligations, to establish relationships, governed by international law'.[93] Ultimately though, Fitzmaurice fell back on the simpler 'governed by international law' criterion, which the ILC (and later the VCLT) adopted.[94]

Given this history, the intent to create a treaty emphasized by Lauterpacht and Fitzmaurice is widely thought to be subsumed in the 'governed by international law' element. That was certainly the ILC's understanding.[95] The Vienna Conference delegates agreed.[96] Thus, any question as to whether the parties intended to create a treaty (not to mention what relevance to attach to their intentions) ends up being discussed under the 'governed by international law' heading.

Today, a majority of States and scholars regard intent as *the* essential criterion for identifying an agreement as a treaty.[97] Simply put, if qualified parties intend their agreement to be a treaty, it is a treaty; if they lack this intent, the agreement will be denied treaty status. Despite such widespread emphasis, however, the intent element is not without difficulties. During the ILC debates, Ago and others resisted the idea 'that states could always pick and choose from among various legal systems' since international law might regard agreements on certain subjects (eg boundaries, territorial seas) as treaties regardless of what States parties intended.[98] And some scholars continue to suggest that the role of intent in defining treaties should be

---

[91] Brierly, First Report (n 46) 223.

[92] Lauterpacht, First Report (n 49) 93.

[93] [1959] YBILC, vol II, 96. Fitzmaurice reintroduced Brierly's 'legal relations' component to include agreements that might only create legal rights and obligations by implication, such as where a peace treaty just establishes a particular relationship among the parties. Fitzmaurice, First Report (n 49) 117 [6].

[94] See [1966] YBILC, vol II, 187 (draft Art 1(a)).

[95] [1966] YBILC, vol II, 189 [6] ('The Commission concluded that, in so far as it may be relevant, the element of intention is embraced in the phrase "governed by international law", and it decided not to make any mention of the element of intention in the definition').

[96] Vienna Conference, Second Session (n 89) 346 [22] (Drafting Committee 'considered the expression "agreement . . . governed by international law" . . . covered the element of intention to create obligations and rights in international law').

[97] Pauwelyn (n 85) (intent is 'generally accepted under international law for purposes of distinguishing what is international law from what is not'); Aust (n 7) 20–1 ('It is the negotiating states which decide whether they will conclude a treaty, or something else'); Klabbers (n 7) ('Notwithstanding its awkwardness, there is virtual unanimity among international lawyers that, at the very least, intent is one of the main determinants of international legal rights and obligations'); see also Hollis and Newcomer (n 50) 517–18; Widdows (n 22) 120–39. On intent in the interpretative process, see Chapter 19, Part II.B, 487 *et seq*.

[98] [1962] YBILC, vol I, 52 [19].

limited, or supplanted by more substantive criteria.[99] As a result, there has been what Martti Koskenniemi called an 'oscillation between subjective and objective approaches' in defining treaties.[100]

Whether the parties' intent is a definitive or merely important criterion, there is a separate question of *how* to determine what the parties intended. Identifying subjective intent is notoriously difficult among individuals, let alone institutional entities such as States or IOs. Thus, it is generally accepted that the *manifest* intent of the parties is what matters. As Oscar Schachter noted, 'inferences as to such intent have to be drawn from the language of the instrument and the attendant circumstances of its conclusion and adoption'.[101] In this vein, parties may try to short-circuit the intent inquiry by indicating within the instrument itself whether or not they regard it as a treaty. They may label it a treaty, for example, or expressly declaim any intent to create one.[102] In other cases, indications of intent may exist in the specific choice of words used—eg 'shall' usually signifies an intent to create legal rights or obligations—or the adoption of compulsory dispute settlement.[103] But these are mere indications of intent—there are no magic words to create a treaty or deny an agreement that status. Such determinations require consideration of the agreement itself, the text used, and the surrounding circumstances.

More difficult are cases where the text remains silent or is ambiguous as to the parties' intentions. Indeed, it is not hard to imagine treaty texts artfully papering over parties' differences on whether to create a treaty. In such cases, the ICJ has focused on the commitment's content and objective manifestations of intent rather than post-hoc rationalizations. In the *Aegean Sea Continental Shelf Case*, the Court found there was no intent to submit a dispute to the Court under the commitment in question.[104] Scholars disagree whether this was because the commitment was not intended to be legally binding or because its scope did not trigger ICJ jurisdiction on the facts presented.[105]

More recently, in *Qatar v Bahrain*, the ICJ found the parties *had* concluded a legally binding agreement accepting ICJ jurisdiction, notwithstanding protestations

---

[99] See eg Klabbers (n 7) 249 ('The role of intent in the concept of treaty is a limited role' which 'can only refer to the intent to become bound, which inevitably means legally bound. Moreover, intent, rather than having to be proven, will normally be presumed'); Pauwelyn (n 85) (surveying possible substantive criteria for establishing the existence of international law).

[100] M Koskenniemi, 'Theory: Implications for the Practitioner' in P Allott and others (eds), *Theory and International Law: an Introduction* (BICIL, London 1991) 19–20.

[101] O Schachter, 'The Twilight Existence of Nonbinding International Agreements' (1977) 71 AJIL 296, 297.

[102] For examples see Chapter 2, Part I.D, 50–1.

[103] Page 49 of Chapter 2 contains a chart of terminology commonly associated with treaties or political commitments. Although not all treaties contain compulsory dispute settlement, the existence of such a provision may provide evidence of an intent to make a treaty. See Klabbers (n 7) 78.

[104] *Aegean Sea Continental Shelf (Greece v Turkey)* [1978] ICJ Rep 3, 43. For a review of international tribunal analyses of the treaty concept, see Klabbers (n 7) Chs VI–VII.

[105] Compare Aust (n 7) 20 ('The Court found that there had been no intention to conclude an international agreement to submit to the jurisdiction of the Court'); with C Chinkin, 'A Mirage in the Sand? Distinguishing Binding and Non-Binding Relations Between States' (1997) 10 LJIL 223, 234 ('The Court did not dismiss the [joint communiqué] as being without any legal effect but only as insufficient to support a unilateral application of the dispute to the Court').

by Bahrain's Foreign Minister that he had not intended to do so.[106] The Court based the agreement's existence on the 'terms of the instrument itself and the circumstances of its conclusion, not from what the parties say afterwards was their intention'.[107] Aust suggests this approach is consistent with using intent to determine a treaty's existence.[108] Others disagree. Chinkin and Klabbers both read the Court to adopt a more objective approach to delineating a treaty's existence, diminishing the importance of intent in the process.[109] In contrast, Fitzmaurice and Elias question how broadly to read the *Qatar* opinion, suggesting that the ICJ's approach might be limited to agreements to accept ICJ jurisdiction, rather than for use in identifying treaties more generally.[110]

Ultimately, the question of intent may be resolved by imposing a presumption. Where States or IOs enter into an agreement without explicitly manifesting an intention as to its status, treaty status might simply be presumed.[111] This would not mean such agreements would always be treaties; presumptions may be rebutted by countervailing evidence. But it would provide a default rule on which States and other actors could rely in making choices about whether and how to satisfy the 'governed by international law' prong of the treaty definition. To date, there is strong (but not universal) support for imposing such a presumption.[112]

5. Non-essential ingredients: designation, number of instruments, and registration

International law defines the treaty as 'an international agreement ... governed by international law', but does so largely without regard to the form that agreement takes or the formalities that accompany its conclusion. The oaths that used to accompany treaty-making are long gone. Now the VCLT provides that a treaty will exist 'whatever its particular designation'. Thus, the VCLT (and by extension

---

[106] *Maritime Delimitation and Territorial Questions (Qatar v Bahrain)* (Jurisdiction and Admissibility) [1994] ICJ Rep 112 [27].

[107] Ibid ('The two Ministers signed a text recording commitments accepted by their Governments, some of which were to be given immediate application. Having signed such a text, the Foreign Minister is not in a position to say that he intended to subscribe only to a "statement recording a political understanding", and not to an international agreement'); see also *Maritime Delimitation and Territorial Questions (Qatar v Bahrain)* (Judgment) [1995] ICJ Rep 6.

[108] Aust (n 7) 51–2.

[109] Chinkin (n 105) 236–7; Klabbers (n 7) 212–16.

[110] See Fitzmaurice and Elias (n 7) 26–7.

[111] The opposite presumption might apply to 'other subjects of international law' since their treaty-making capacity is usually so limited.

[112] Klabbers devoted an entire book to establishing this presumption. For others favouring it, see A Aust, 'The Theory and Practice of Informal International Instruments' (1986) 35 ICLQ 787, 798; Widdows (n 22) 142; H Lauterpacht, 'Second Report on the Law of Treaties' [1954] YBILC, vol II, 125. In contrast, some have suggested a presumption against treaty-making absent a clearly manifested intent to do so. See Schachter (n 101) 297; JES Fawcett, 'The Legal Character of International Agreements' (1953) 30 BYBIL 381, 400.

international law more generally) do not require a treaty to be titled as such, or indeed, to bear any particular appellation.[113]

In practice, international agreements bear an impressive array of titles, including act, agreed minute, charter, convention, covenant, declaration, memorandum of agreement, memorandum of understanding (MOU), note verbale, protocol, statute, and, of course, treaty. There is little rhyme or reason to the selection of a particular title.[114] But the term 'treaty' is widely accepted as a generic label for 'all kinds of international agreements in written form'.[115]

Thus, the name an international agreement bears should not determine its treaty status. It may, however, have relevance in other respects. For example, a document concluded by States bearing the title 'treaty' likely evidences an intent that international law govern the agreement, which may, in turn, make it a treaty. Caution should be exercised in making such inferences, particularly as so many of the titles used for treaties (eg declaration, charter, MOU) are often also used in documents *not* intended to be governed by international law, namely political commitments.[116]

Like its title, the number of instruments used will not prevent an agreement from having treaty status; treaties may be 'embodied in a single instrument or in two or more related instruments'.[117] Traditionally, the treaty was a single, formal instrument in contrast to less formal agreements such as an exchange of notes or letters.[118] The ILC debated whether to maintain that distinction, but by a close vote (6 to 5) opted to group all of these international agreements under the treaty concept.[119] Thereafter, any controversy over the question died away.

Today, a treaty may still arise via a single, formal instrument. But a treaty may also arise through multiple texts. In the traditional exchange of notes (or letters), one party proposes an agreement in a first note, which the other party's reply note accepts; the agreement consists of both notes considered collectively.[120] More complex combinations are also possible; the North American Free Trade Agreement (NAFTA), for example, consists of an original agreement along with a series of subsequent notes, signed on 8, 11, 14, and 17 December 1992.[121] The Algiers Accords embodied commitments of the US and Iran to settle claims reproduced in

---

[113] See eg *Qatar v Bahrain* (n 106) [21]–[30] (analysing 1990 'Minutes' as a treaty); see also *South West Africa (Ethiopia/Liberia v South Africa)* (Preliminary Objections) [1962] ICJ Rep 331 ('terminology is not a determinant factor as to the character of an international agreement').

[114] See [1966] YBILC, vol II, 188 [3]; Waldock, First Report (n 48) 31. The one exception is the concordat, which is reserved for agreements involving the Holy See. Klabbers (n 7) 43 n33.

[115] [1966] YBILC, vol II, 188 [3].

[116] See Chapter 2, Part I.B, 48–50.

[117] VCLT Art 2(1)(a).

[118] The 1935 *Harvard Draft Convention on the Law of Treaties* originally excluded exchanges of notes from its treaty definition. (1935) 29 AJIL (Supp) 653, 698.

[119] [1950] YBILC, vol I, 78; ibid 68–78. It took the ILC until 1966 to decide a related issue, including treaties done in 'simplified form' (ie without ratification) within its treaty definition. [1966] YBILC, vol II, 188 [3].

[120] In practice, moreover, the reply note will often reproduce the text of the first note verbatim.

[121] NAFTA (Canada–Mexico–US) (signed 8, 11, 14, and 17 December 1992, entered into force 1 January 1994) [1993] 32 ILM 296 and [1993] 32 ILM 605.

two declarations by Algeria, accompanied by a US–Iranian undertaking and an Escrow Agreement.[122] Even instruments that appear as unilateral declarations might actually constitute acceptance of an earlier offer of agreement, thus creating a treaty. That seems to be the case with the Ihlen Declaration and similar claims are made for unilateral declarations accepting the ICJ's compulsory jurisdiction.[123]

Finally, there is an issue left unaddressed by the VCLT—whether the fact than an agreement is registered with the UN is determinative of its status as a treaty. In short, the answer is no.[124] Like its title, registration may indicate an intent (albeit of only the registering party) that the agreement constitutes a treaty. But since States do not regularly monitor treaty registrations, registration says little, if anything, about the other State(s)' intentions. Moreover, although the UN Charter[125] and the VCLT[126] both require treaty registration, neither requirement denies unregistered agreements the status of a treaty.[127] For its part, the UN is careful to regularly indicate that the Secretariat's acceptance of an instrument for registration 'does not confer on the instrument the status of a treaty or an international agreement if it does not already have that status'.[128]

Similarly, the fact that an agreement goes unregistered does not imply denial of treaty status. Some States appear to continue to endorse the making of 'secret' treaties.[129] But even for other treaties, the obligation to register is often 'honoured in the breaking' whether as a result of inattention or a conscious choice to avoid publicity. As a result, the ICJ has noted that '[n]on-registration or late

---

[122] All four documents of the Algiers Accords are reprinted in [1981] 20 ILM 224 *et seq.*

[123] Lauterpacht initially endorsed this idea. Lauterpacht, First Report (n 49) 101. The ICJ has indicated that 'unilateral acts' accepting ICJ jurisdiction establish a 'series of bilateral engagements with other States accepting the same obligation': *Military and Paramilitary Activities in and against Nicaragua (Nicaragua v United States of America)* (Jurisdiction and Admissibility) [1984] ICJ Rep 418 [59].

[124] Accord Aust (n 7) 344–6; Fitzmaurice and Elias (n 7) 23; Klabbers (n 7) 84; D Hutchinson, 'The Significance of the Registration or Non-Registration of an International Agreement in Determining Whether or Not it is a Treaty' (1993) *Current Legal Problems* 257, 265–76.

[125] UN Charter Art 102(1) ('Every treaty and every international agreement entered into by any Member of the United Nations after the present Charter comes into force shall as soon as possible be registered with the Secretariat and published by it'). In contrast, Art 18 of the League of Nations' Covenant indicated that 'a treaty or international engagement' was not binding until registered.

[126] VCLT Art 80(1) ('Treaties shall, after their entry into force, be transmitted to the Secretariat of the United Nations for registration or filing and recording, as the case may be, and publication').

[127] Parties are not allowed to invoke an unregistered 'treaty' before any UN organ, suggesting that unregistered agreements are still treaties. See UN Charter Art 102(2). The ICJ has largely overlooked this proscription in any case. See *Qatar v Bahrain* (n 106) 123 [31]–[33] (analysing unregistered 1987 exchange of letters).

[128] Secretary-General, 'Note by the Secretariat' 2486 UNTS XXXV. In cases of doubt, the UN favours registration, but it has occasionally refused to register a text that it did not consider a treaty. See Chapter 10, Part II.B.2, 270 *et seq.*

[129] Several States' domestic laws acknowledge the possibility of secret treaties. See eg 1 USC 112b (a) (congressional reporting requirements for international agreements whose public disclosure would be 'prejudicial to the national security'); Kingdom Act on the Approval and Publication of Treaties (20 August 1994) (The Netherlands) Art 7(d) reprinted in Brower (n 29) 512–14 (noting 'in exceptional circumstances of a compelling nature' that a 'treaty should remain secret or confidential').

registration . . . does not have any consequence for the actual validity of the agreement, which remains no less binding upon the parties'.[130]

B. A *differential* definition: distinguishing the treaty from its alternatives

The foregoing suggests that, for international law purposes, a treaty is an (a) international agreement (b) among States (or other subjects of international law with the necessary internal authority and external consent to engage in treaty-making) that is (c) recorded in a way that evidences (d) a shared and manifest intent that the agreement be governed by international law (e) without regard as to its form. Most questions of treaty identification can be resolved using these criteria. But questions remain, particularly on the margins. Some of this may be due to the need to further elaborate specific elements, particularly how to identify when an agreement exists or the intent that it be a treaty.

Part of the problem, however, lies in the limitations of a constitutive definition. A constitutive approach seeks to explain the treaty concept from the inside-out, unpacking its individual components. But it is also possible to understand a concept from the outside-in; to explore what a treaty is by elaborating its boundaries with surrounding concepts. For example, international law acknowledges that commitments may arise not only via treaty, but also through unilateral declarations. Similarly, not all international agreements are treaties; other possibilities include political commitments, which are not governed by law, and contracts, which are governed by domestic, as opposed to international, law.

1. Unilateral declarations

In the *Nuclear Tests* case, the ICJ found that France was bound under international law by public statements of its President and Foreign and Defence Ministers to cease nuclear tests in the South Pacific, obviating the need for the Court to rule on the case at hand.[131] Based on this ruling, in 2006, the ILC articulated a basic *Guiding Principle*: 'Declarations publicly made and manifesting the will to be bound may have the effect of creating legal obligations.'[132] What obligations

---

[130] *Qatar v Bahrain* (n 106) 122 [29]. The failure to register or publish a 1983 US–UK MOU was, however, a factor in the Heathrow Arbitration's decision to regard it as non-legally binding. Award on the First Question, US/UK Arbitration concerning Heathrow Airport User Charges (1992) ch 5, 155 [6.5]; see Chapter 2, Part I.F, 52–3.

[131] *Nuclear Tests (Australia/New Zealand v France)* [1974] ICJ Rep 267–8 [43]–[50]. Although the underlying principle is now widely accepted, its application in this case was controversial. Klabbers (n 7) 196–9; A Rubin, 'The International Legal Effect of Unilateral Declarations' (1977) 71 AJIL 1–30.

[132] ILC, Guiding Principles applicable to unilateral declarations of States capable of creating legal obligations, with commentaries thereto (2006) 58th Session, UN Doc A/61/10, Guiding Principle 1 ('ILC, Unilateral Acts'). VR Cedeño served as Special Rapporteur and issued eight reports on the topic. See generally ILC, Analytical Guide: Unilateral Acts of States, <http://untreaty.un.org/ilc/guide/9_9. htm>. Several States, including Austria, Finland, Germany, Italy, Sweden, and the UK, questioned the utility of the ILC project given the wide range of unilateral acts. See ILC, 'Unilateral Acts of States, Replies of Governments to the Questionnaire' (6 July 2000) UN Doc A/CN.4/51, 2–5.

such declarations create is a function of 'their content, of all the factual circumstances in which they were made, and of the reactions to which they gave rise'.[133]
Examples of unilateral declarations include Egypt's 1957 Declaration on the Suez
Canal, Jordan's 1988 waiver of claims to the West Bank, US representations before
the WTO Dispute Settlement Body in the *1974 Trade Act* case, and (at least
potentially) Cuba's 2002 declarations about the supply of vaccines to Uruguay.[134]

International law thus treats unilateral declarations as a form of international
legal commitment.[135] What distinguishes them from treaty commitments? There
are, in fact, many similarities. In each case, intention rather than formality dictates
their creation.[136] Like treaties, unilateral declarations may be formulated orally or
in writing, by 'heads of State, heads of Government, and ministers for foreign
affairs'.[137] Pre-emptory norms (*jus cogens*) limit both categories of commitment.[138]
And unilateral declarations do not bind other States unless they 'clearly accepted
such a declaration'.[139]

On the other hand, unilateral declarations may operate under a different interpretative framework than treaties. The ILC's *Guiding Principles* propose a cautious
approach: in 'cases of doubt as to the scope of obligations resulting from such a
declaration, such obligations must be interpreted in a restrictive manner'.[140]
Unilateral declarations must be stated in clear and specific terms to bind the
declaring State.[141]

More fundamentally, treaties differ from unilateral declarations by virtue of their
mutuality. Unilateral declarations are just that—unilateral commitments by a
single State. Their legal effect derives from the general principle of 'good faith'
since other States may rely on such statements in their own actions or inactions.[142]
In contrast, the treaty rests on an *agreement* where there is a shared expectation
among two or more parties as to the existence of an international legal

---

[133] ILC, Unilateral Acts (n 132) Guiding Principle 3.

[134] Other than the WTO example, these are all discussed in VR Cedeño, 'Eighth Report on
Unilateral Acts of States' (26 May 2005) UN Doc A/CN.4/557. For the WTO's views, see *United
States—Sections 301–310 of the Trade Act of 1974* (Report of the Panel) (1999) WT/DS152/R
[7.118]–[7.123].

[135] ILC, Unilateral Acts (n 132) Guiding Principle 2. Neither the ICJ nor the ILC has opined on
whether this principle extends to IOs or other subjects of international law.

[136] See *Case concerning the Frontier Dispute (Burkina Faso v Republic of Mali)* (Judgment) [1986]
ICJ Rep 573–4 [39]–[40] (existence and content of unilateral declarations 'all depends on the
intention of the State in question').

[137] ILC, Unilateral Acts (n 132) Guiding Principles 4 and 5. Other State representatives may make
unilateral declarations within areas of their competence. Ibid Principle 4.

[138] See VCLT Art 53; ILC, Unilateral Acts (n 132) Guiding Principle 8.

[139] Ibid Guiding Principle 9 and commentary [1] (analogizing to VCLT Art 34).

[140] Ibid Guiding Principle 7. The ILC's Commentary suggest this principle is analogous to one of
the VCLT rules of interpretation—Art 31. But that article is not overtly restrictive and operates in
concert with other rules (eg VCLT Art 32).

[141] Ibid. Accord *Armed Activities in the Territory of the Congo (New Application: 2002) (Democratic
Republic of the Congo v Rwanda)* (Jurisdiction and Admissibility) [50]–[52]; *Nuclear Tests* (n 131)
267 [44].

[142] ILC, Unilateral Acts (n 132) Guiding Principle 1. Actual reliance, however, is not required; a
unilateral declaration arises based on the public setting and specific intentions of its maker.

commitment. And although good faith certainly plays a role, the legal effect of treaty commitments depends not on reliance, but *pacta sunt servanda*.

Since treaties and unilateral declarations both decry formalities, however, it can be difficult at times to distinguish instances of mutual agreement from unilateral action. Debates persist, for example, as to whether the Ihlen Declaration constituted an oral treaty or a unilateral declaration.[143] Similar problems arise in categorizing declarations accepting the ICJ's compulsory jurisdiction; the ICJ has suggested they are *sui generis*[144] while the ILC declined to address them in its *Guiding Principles*. In practice, therefore, it may be difficult to differentiate the acceptance of an earlier offer to make a treaty from a unilateral commitment absent clear evidence of the State's intentions.

2. Political commitments

Intention remains just as important in cases where there is clearly an agreement, and the question is what type of agreement was made. Political commitments are agreements made by States intending to establish non-legal commitments of an exclusively political or moral nature.[145] Like treaties, they involve mutuality and a shared expectation of commitment. The key distinguishing criterion is intent.[146] States can constitute political commitments without legal force if that is their intention; just as they may choose to create treaties governed by international law.[147] The concepts exist largely in contraposition; political commitments do not have *any* legal force, while treaty commitments are, by definition, binding under international law (*pacta sunt servanda*).[148]

State practice in making political commitments is now quite robust and overlaps the subjects of treaty-making in many respects.[149] Exploring the rationales for— and boundaries between—political commitments and treaties is thus critical to refining the treaty concept. Chapter 2 of this *Guide* takes up that task specifically, with particular attention to MOUs.

---

[143] Klabbers (n 7) 178. Cedeño sees it as a unilateral declaration and implies the PCIJ did so too. See Cedeño (n 134) 21–2 [116]–[126]. McNair viewed it as an 'international agreement'. McNair (n 64) 10.

[144] *Fisheries Jurisdiction (Spain v Canada)* (Jurisdiction) [1998] ICJ Rep 453 [46].

[145] See Hollis and Newcomer (n 50) 517. Although the topic is understudied, it seems there is no bar to non-State actors making political commitments. Ibid 521.

[146] Ibid 522.

[147] Ibid 522–3; Schachter (n 101) 296–7; Aust (n 7) 20.

[148] Hollis and Newcomer (n 50) 518–20. Confusion may arise if behaviour based on a political commitment has legal effects because of the good faith reliance by other States. In such cases, however, the legal effects flow from the underlying behaviour rather than by ascribing any legal force to the political commitment itself. I Sinclair, 'Book Review: The Concept of Treaty in International Law' (1997) 91 AJIL 748, 750.

[149] See Hollis and Newcomer (n 50) 528–35 (offering a typology of political commitments). Although States widely accept the political commitment practice, Klabbers has critiqued it at an ontological level. See generally Klabbers (n 7); J Klabbers, 'Not Re-visiting the Concept of Treaty' in A Orakhelashvili and S Williams (eds), *40 Years of the Vienna Convention on the Law of Treaties* (BIICL, London 2010) 29–40.

For present purposes, it is sufficient to note that political commitments complicate our understanding of the treaty in two respects. First, if intent is the dominant criterion in identifying both treaties and political commitments, that doubles the evidentiary possibilities for how parties express their intentions. Just as there may be positive evidence that States meant to constitute a treaty or negative evidence that they did not, there may also be positive evidence that States meant to create a political commitment or (more rarely perhaps) negative evidence that they lacked such intent.

Second, even if political commitments are not treaties in the sense that they do not contain *any* commitments intended to have legal force, the inverse may not follow. Treaties can contain provisions that the parties did not intend to have legal force alongside those that do. The Algiers Accords, for example, contain legal commitments on the functioning of the US–Iran Claims Tribunal alongside a US 'pledge' to maintain a policy of non-interference with Iran's internal affairs.[150] The possibility that political commitments may be contained within a treaty revives the problem of defining the treaty in terms of an instrument versus an agreement embodied in an instrument.[151] It also complicates the intent inquiry, requiring evaluation of intent on a provision-by-provision basis rather than simply assigning one label or another to the instrument as a whole. In the end, such questions are best resolved through an interpretative exercise, examining whether the parties intended to conclude a treaty first, and then more specifically inquiring as to the nature and number of legal commitments assumed therein.

3. Contracts and other agreements governed by domestic law

The existence of an international agreement intended to have legal force may exclude unilateral declarations and political commitments, but it does not necessarily constitute a treaty. As the ILC emphasized, States (and presumably IOs and other subjects of international law) may choose to use laws other than international law to govern their agreements.[152] Thus, contracts concluded under the domestic law of one or more States serve as another alternative to treaty-making. In such cases, it is domestic, rather than international, law that provides the relevant rules for the agreements' formation, application, and interpretation.[153] Austria,

---

[150] Declaration of the Government of the Democratic and Popular Republic of Algeria (20 January 1981) [1981] 20 ILM 224, 224–5. The US has insisted, over Iranian objections, that the pledge constitutes a political commitment. US Statement of Defense, *Islamic Republic of Iran v United States, Claim A-30* (Iran–US Claims Tribunal) 40–5, available at <http://www.state.gov/documents/organization/65779.pdf>; see also *South West Africa* (n 113) 139–40 (ICJ characterizes UN Charter Arts 75 and 77 as imposing 'political or moral duties' rather than legal obligations on mandatory States).

[151] See n 52 and accompanying text.

[152] [1966] YBILC, vol II, 189 [6].

[153] To say a contract is governed by domestic law does not mean it can never have international legal effect. Depending on the circumstances, international legal responsibility may follow a State's breach of contract. But, as the ILC noted, 'this did not entail the consequence that the undertaking itself, or rather the instrument embodying it, was...a treaty or international agreement. While the obligation to carry out the undertaking might be an international law obligation, the incidents of its execution would not be governed by international law': [1959] YBILC, vol II, 95 [3].

Colombia, the Netherlands, Russia, and Thailand, for example, recognize the ability of States to conclude contracts regulated by domestic law.[154]

In creating a contract, intent once again plays a large role. States (and other subjects of international law) may choose to conclude a contract by indicating their intention to apply a particular State's domestic law to their agreement.[155] The same complications in discerning intent apply in such a case. Likewise, where there is doubt, State and IO agreements will likely be presumed to be treaties.[156] The same presumption may not hold, however, for 'other subjects', particularly sub-State actors, for whom the majority of agreements are, in fact, contracts.

But even where there is no question of the parties' intent to conclude a contract, its status as such is not assured. The domestic legal system selected could deny the agreement contract status under its own rules.[157] In such cases, there is a question whether international law would step in to govern such agreements.[158] There is even the possibility of a 'mixed' agreement. Paul Reuter, for example, proposed redefining the treaty to be '*principally* governed by international law' since he noted it 'often happens that a legal situation is covered as a whole by international law but some of its aspects are subject to the rules and concepts of national law'.[159] The ILC did not adopt Reuter's proposal. Nevertheless, the prospect of contractual provisions within a treaty complicates the treaty concept in much the same way as the notion of treaties including political commitment provisions.

Overall, the treaty may be better understood by differentiating it from other forms of international commitment: unilateral declarations, political commitments, and contracts. By existing in contradistinction to the treaty, each of these concepts helps illuminate the treaty within broader categories of commitment and agreement. Each re-emphasizes the importance of intent in the process of identification. At the same time, however, the boundaries among these concepts are not as clear in practice as the theory might suggest. There is room for (reasonable) debate over how to qualify a commitment. Further complications arise from the prospect that treaty instruments may contain commitments that are not only legal, but also political or contractual in nature.

---

[154] See Hollis (n 6) 14 (surveying State practice).

[155] Ibid (noting how Canada, Germany, India, Switzerland, and the UK support the ability of States to decide if an inter-State agreement should be governed by international or domestic law).

[156] See nn 111–12 and accompanying text.

[157] In addition, there may be questions about whether the selected domestic law is limited to its substantive provisions, or includes its choice of law rules.

[158] Lauterpacht was of this view, as was the ILC, at least initially. Lauterpacht, First Report (n 49) 100; [1959] YBILC, vol II, 95.

[159] P Reuter, 'Third Report on the Question of Treaties Concluded between States and International Organizations or Between Two or More International Organizations' [1974] YBILC, vol II(1), 139 (emphasis added); see also Widdows (n 22) 145–6 (noting there might be 'an agreement constituting a "treaty" in international law and a "contract" under a private law system at the same time').

C. A *functional* definition: understanding treaties by what they do

More than eighty years ago, Lord McNair described the treaty as the 'only and sadly overworked instrument with which international society is equipped for the purposes of carrying out its multifarious transactions'.[160] In many respects, that characterization remains true today. Certainly, there have been attempts to disaggregate the treaty concept along various lines, whether by party identity (eg distinguishing bilateral and multilateral treaties) or subject matter.[161] McNair himself proposed four categories based on whether the treaty's functions were akin to: (a) conveyances; (b) contracts; (c) law-making (whether constitutional or ordinary); or (d) charters of incorporation.[162]

Neither the VCLT definition nor its international law analogue, however, differentiate treaties by their functions.[163] At most, these definitions establish that treaties are 'governed by international law'. This is not to suggest that the law of treaties ignores *all* functional distinctions. Several rules do focus only on multilateral treaties and one exists just for bilateral treaties.[164] There are two special rules for treaties relating to IOs.[165] And there are a few cases where what the treaty regulates matters; for example, the standard grounds for termination/suspension in case of material breach are not available for 'provisions relating to the protection of the human person contained in treaties of a humanitarian character'.[166] Likewise, claims of fundamental change of circumstances are unavailable for boundary treaties.[167] But such distinctions are exceptional. The conventional approach is to conceive of the treaty as a single, uniform concept.

The treaty thus serves as a sort of Swiss army knife for international law. By design, it incorporates several tools within a single instrument capable of performing multiple functions. The standard constitutive treaty definition describes only the unopened knife; it does not differentiate what treaties do or to what ends.

A *functional* treaty definition opens up the concept by examining different ways treaties work. This examination might be done multiple ways. For present purposes,

---

[160] A McNair, 'The Functions and Differing Legal Character of Treaties' (1930) 11 BYBIL 100, 101. For similar sentiments see Kearney and Dalton (n 90) 495.

[161] See M Fitzmaurice, 'Treaties' in R Wolfrum (ed), *Max Planck Encyclopedia of Public International Law* (OUP, Oxford 2010) online at <www.mpepil.com>.

[162] McNair envisioned different rules for each category: eg treaties involving conveyances would survive war; *travaux préparatoires* would be more relevant to contractual treaties than law-making ones. McNair (n 160) 101–18.

[163] Brölmann suggests this was because Waldock and the ILC focused their work more on treaty form than functions. See C Brölmann, 'Law-making Treaties: Form and Function in International Law' (2005) 74 Nordic J Intl L 383, 390.

[164] VCLT Arts 40, 41, 58, and 60 have provisions on multilateral treaties; Art 60(1) addresses material breach of a bilateral treaty.

[165] VCLT Art 5 (VCLT applies to IO treaties and treaties adopted within an IO 'without prejudice to any relevant rules of the organization'); VCLT Art 20(3) (reservations to IO's constituent treaty require 'the acceptance of the competent organ of that organization').

[166] Ibid Art 60(5).

[167] Ibid Art 62(2)(a); see also ibid Arts 53, 64 (voiding treaties in conflict with *jus cogens*).

the goal is simply to outline the contours of such an approach. Doing so will reveal how greatly treaty functions have evolved along (at least) three distinct spectrums, *how* treaties regulate, *what* they regulate, and *who* enforces their regulations. Describing such variation is more than a merely taxonomic exercise. It helps explain why there are ongoing efforts to devise specialized (or even exceptional) rules for certain types of treaties. Indeed, a functional approach may actually provide support for such differentiation. More importantly, focusing on treaty functions creates space to evaluate the treaty's utility more generally. In the end, the treaty, like the Swiss army knife, may be a merely serviceable, as opposed to optimal, tool for some of the functions that international law asks it to perform.

1. How treaties regulate

Customarily, treaties regulate by mandating what 'must be *performed*'.[168] Treaty 'obligations' impose a duty of performance (whether in terms of action or inaction) with which the party bound must comply. Much (if not most) attention on how treaties work has focused on the various ways treaties obligate future behaviour and the remedies available in cases of breach. Indeed, regulation by obligation is an extraordinarily flexible tool that varies widely in terms of its (a) normativity; (b) precision; and (c) duties established.

Normativity refers to the extent of expectation accompanying a treaty obligation. Expectations may relate to efforts or results. Some treaties require parties to guarantee a specific result (eg promises to abolish the death penalty).[169] Others may obligate effort irrespective of whether it leads to a particular result, such as where parties promise to negotiate, notify, or consult.[170] Expectations may equally vary in terms of whether the anticipated behaviour involves a dispositive act(s) that constitutes performance or an ongoing obligation to act so long as the treaty is in force. For example, a treaty of cession involves a single, dispositive act in which a sovereign transfers a territory, while a treaty requiring national treatment of goods requires that the expected behaviour be repeated over time.[171]

---

[168] Ibid Art 26 (emphasis added).

[169] Eg Protocol No 6 to the Convention for the Protection of Human Rights and Fundamental Freedoms Concerning the Abolition of the Death Penalty (28 April 1983) [1983] 22 ILM 539, Art 1; see also Montreal Protocol on Substances that Deplete the Ozone Layer, as adjusted and amended (adopted 16 September 1987, entered into force 1 January 1989) 1522 UNTS 3, Art 2a (requiring certain parties to reduce consumption and production of chlorofluorocarbons to zero by specific dates).

[170] See eg Treaty on the Non-Proliferation of Nuclear Weapons (opened for signature 1 July 1968, entered into force 5 March 1970) 729 UNTS 161, Art VI (duty to negotiate in good faith towards cessation of the nuclear arms race); Convention on Early Notification of a Nuclear Accident (adopted 26 September 1986, entered into force 26 October 1986) 1439 UNTS 275, Arts 2, 6 (duties to notify and consult in case of nuclear accident).

[171] For an example of a dispositive obligation see eg Treaty for the Cession of Louisiana (US–France) (signed 30 April 1803, entered into force 21 October 1803) Art 1. Boundary treaties and treaties settling/waiving claims may also involve dispositive obligations. NAFTA's national treatment obligation, in contrast, serves as an example of a continuing obligation. See NAFTA (n 121) Art 301.

By contrast, *precision* relates not to the extent of expectation in the obligation, but to its content. Participating States may convey the same level of normativity in two treaties, stating in each that parties 'shall do X'. But 'X' can vary greatly in generality or specificity. For example, obligations may take the form of rules, standards, or principles.[172] Rules bind parties to respond in specific, determinate ways when certain facts exist; once the facts are clear, under a rule, so too is the expected behaviour.[173] Standards afford decision-makers more discretion to decide (often *ex post*) on what behaviour satisfies an obligation by either widening the range of relevant facts (often a totality of the circumstances) or authorizing direct application of some background policy or principle.[174] Principles, in contrast, set forth broad considerations for evaluating future behaviour without providing any particular norm for the behaviour itself.[175]

Obligations may also differ in the scope of the *duties* they impose. The classic treaty obligation was contractual—*traités contrat*—involving rights and duties paired reciprocally in a synallagmatic manner.[176] Bilateral treaties often take this form, but certain multilateral treaty obligations do so too.[177] However, as Fitzmaurice noted,[178] other multilateral obligations may be 'interdependent', where one party's duty to perform depends on performance by all other parties, as, for example, in a disarmament treaty.[179] Finally, there are what Fitzmaurice called

---

[172] See eg R Dworkin, *Taking Rights Seriously* (Harvard University Press, Cambridge 1977) 22–8; D Bodansky, 'Rules vs Standards in International Environmental Law' (2004) 98 Proc Am Socy Intl L 275; KM Sullivan, 'The Justices of Rules and Standards' (1992) 106 Harvard L Rev 22, 57–9.

[173] Sullivan (n 172) 58. For examples of rules, see eg Convention Against Torture and Other Cruel, Inhuman or Degrading Treatment or Punishment (opened for signature 10 December 1984, entered into force 26 June 1987) 1465 UNTS 85, Art 4 (rule requiring parties to criminalize all acts of torture); Treaty Between the United States and Great Britain Relating to Boundary Waters Between the United States and Canada (signed 11 January 1909) 36 Stat 2448, Art 4 (rule prohibiting pollution of certain waters 'on either side to the injury of health or property on the other').

[174] Sullivan (n 172) 59. For examples of standards, see Convention on the Rights of the Child (opened for signature 20 November 1989, entered into force 2 September 1990) 1577 UNTS 3, Art 2 (1) (imposing non-discrimination standard on performance); General Agreement on Tariffs and Trade (opened for signature 30 October 1947, provisional application from 1 January 1948) 55 UNTS 187, Art III(2) (providing a national treatment standard for internal taxes); Treaty concerning the Encouragement and Reciprocal Protection of Investments (Germany–Afghanistan) (done 19–20 April 2005, entered into force 12 October 2007) <http://www.unctadxi.org/templates/docsearch.aspx?id=779> (establishing a 'fair and equitable' treatment standard for covered investments).

[175] For examples of principles, see Treaty on Principles Governing the Activities of States in the Exploration and Use of Outer Space, including the Moon and Other Celestial Bodies (opened for signature 18 December 1979, entered into force 11 July 1984) 610 UNTS 205, Art 1 (subjecting Outer Space to the common heritage of mankind principle) ('Outer Space Treaty'); International Covenant on Civil and Political Rights (opened for signature 19 December 1966, entered into force 23 March 1976) 999 UNTS 171, Art 1 (affirming principle of self-determination) (ICCPR).

[176] Rosenne (n 66) 182–3.

[177] Eg Agreement on Reciprocal Encouragement and Protection of Investments (People's Republic of China–Spain) (adopted 6 February 1992, entered into force 1 May 1993) 1746 UNTS 185; Vienna Convention on Diplomatic Relations (adopted 14 April 1961, entered into force 24 April 1964) 500 UNTS 95. For an analysis of whether WTO obligations are bilateral or multilateral in nature, see J Pauwelyn, 'A Typology of Multilateral Treaty Obligations' (2003) 14 EJIL 907.

[178] GG Fitzmaurice, 'Second Report on the Law of Treaties' [1957] YBILC, vol II, 31.

[179] See generally South Pacific Nuclear Free Zone Treaty (signed 6 August 1985, entered into force 11 December 1986) 1445 UNTS 171.

'inherent' treaty obligations, where one party's duty to perform is not linked to any other party's performance (eg treaties prohibiting genocide or child labour).[180] Treaties in this third category are often described as 'law-making' or *traités loi* because the duties they impose are akin to domestic law rules of general application. That analogy, however, would also support including treaty 'regimes' such as those for the maritime or aviation environments within the inherent duty category.[181]

Even as treaty obligations vary greatly in terms of their normativity, precision, and duties, it would be a mistake to characterize treaty regulations solely in obligatory terms. As complicated as the available options are for crafting performance obligations, not to mention the emphasis *pacta sunt servanda* gives them, treaties do not always require action (or inaction) from the parties. Treaty provisions may employ at least three other regulatory options.

First, treaties may empower or facilitate behaviour that parties may elect—but are not obligated—to undertake. Thus, UNCLOS allows a right of innocent passage without requiring States to exercise it.[182] In addition to requiring and prohibiting certain conduct, the Geneva Conventions actually facilitate specific conduct—such as killing—that would otherwise be legally impermissible.[183] Second, treaties can create new subjects of international law, including IOs or treaty bodies. Such provisions express agreement on, and in fact 'constitute' the new entity, detail the purpose(s) it will serve, and the specific authorities delegated to it.[184] Finally, not all treaty regulations involve so-called 'primary rules' regulating conduct by international actors; treaties may also devise secondary rules—ie rules on the formation, modification, or termination of primary rules.[185] The VCLT may be the paradigmatic example of this phenomenon as the 'treaty on treaties'.

A single treaty instrument may contain multiple provisions that mix and match these regulatory functions. The UN Charter, for example, simultaneously (a) constitutes the UN as an IO with specific objectives and distinct powers;[186] (b) imposes varying levels of obligation on member States, ranging from the prohibition on the threat or use of force[187] to the requirement that member States promote human rights;[188] (c) empowers and facilitates State behaviour such as the

---

[180] See generally ILO Convention (No 182) Concerning the Prohibition and Immediate Action for the Elimination of the Worst Forms of Child Labour (adopted 17 June 1999, entered into force 19 November 2000) 2133 UNTS 161; Convention on the Prevention and Punishment of the Crime of Genocide (adopted 9 December 1948, entered into force 12 January 1951) 78 UNTS 277.

[181] See eg International Convention for the Safety of Life at Sea, as updated and amended (adopted 1 November 1974, entered into force 25 May 1980); Convention on International Civil Aviation, as amended (adopted 7 December 1944, entered into force 4 April 1947) 15 UNTS 295.

[182] UNCLOS (n 2) Art 17.

[183] Geneva Convention for the Amelioration of the Condition of the Wounded and Sick in Armed Forces in the Field (adopted 12 August 1949, entered into force 21 October 1950) 75 UNTS 31, Arts 3–18.

[184] See eg Treaty of the Economic Community of West African States (adopted 28 May 1975, entered into force 1 August 1995) 1010 UNTS 17, Art 1.

[185] See generally HLA Hart, *The Concept of Law* (OUP, Oxford 1961) 94–9.

[186] UN Charter Arts 1, 11, 12, 13.

[187] Ibid Art 2(4).

[188] Ibid Arts 1(2), 2.

right of self-defence;[189] and (d) includes secondary rules for the maintenance of international peace and security, namely Chapter VII.

The extensive variation in how treaties regulate—by obligation, empowerment, constitution, or secondary rules—raises questions about the existing uniformity of the treaty concept and its associated rules. A treaty obligating an immediate result via a precise rule in a reciprocal relationship is a very different creature than one laying out secondary rules or constituting an IO. Such differences help to explain why the VCLT gave IO treaties specialized treatment; it also explains calls to adopt more specialized methods of treaty interpretation for provisions on IO authorities and those establishing inherent obligations (eg human rights treaties).[190] The lack of differentiation in the current treaty concept, however, gives such efforts an ad hoc quality. A more concerted effort to disaggregate the treaty along functional lines might illuminate additional areas where 'how' a treaty regulates warrants distinct treatment under the law of treaties itself. That has yet to happen, but as the diversity in how treaties regulate continues to evolve, such efforts may gain traction.

2. What treaties regulate

Just as treaties customarily mandated performance, this was traditionally required of a single set of actors—States. Treaties regulated inter-State conduct. Today, many treaties retain that function. But they now frequently regulate in other ways as well. Modern treaties may regulate how States interact with a geographic space (eg the oceans, outer space, Antarctica) as well as how States interact with each other in that space.[191] Similarly, treaties regulate States' use of shared or public goods, whether migratory birds, fisheries, or atmospheric conditions such as the ozone layer or greenhouse gas emissions.[192]

Undoubtedly the most significant shift in what treaties regulate relates to their regulation of persons (whether corporate or individual). As long ago as the Peace of Westphalia, treaties regulated States' behaviour toward individuals with respect to religious freedom.[193] Modern human rights treaties can be seen as a continuation of this phenomenon albeit in broader and more robust terms. These treaties are also

---

[189] Ibid Art 51. Admittedly, self-defence is described as an 'inherent' right which exists outside the Charter. Still, Art 51 frames State authority to engage in self-defence and thus helps empower or facilitate it.

[190] See Chapters 20–21 for discussion of specialized interpretative rules for IO and human rights treaties.

[191] See eg UNCLOS (n 2) Part XII; The Antarctic Treaty (adopted 1 December 1959, entered into force 23 June 1961) 402 UNTS 71, Arts I, III; Outer Space Treaty (n 175) Arts 1, 4.

[192] See eg Convention for the Protection of Migratory Birds in the United States and Canada (US–UK) (adopted 16 August 1916, entered into force 7 December 1916) 2478 UNTS 33; Convention for the Conservation and Management of Highly Migratory Fish Stocks in the Western and Central Pacific Ocean (adopted 5 September 2000, entered into force 19 June 2004) [2001] 40 ILM 278; Montreal Protocol (n 169); Kyoto Protocol to the UN Framework Convention on Climate Change (opened for signature 11 December 1997, entered into force 16 February 2005) 2303 UNTS 148.

[193] L Gross, 'The Peace of Westphalia 1648–1948' (1948) 42 AJIL 20, 33–4.

novel in that they give individuals avenues to hold States accountable for compliance. Certain human rights treaties allow individuals to petition a human rights treaty body about alleged violations of their treaty rights.[194] Bilateral investment treaties (BITs) also grant private investors a right to binding dispute settlement against host States.[195] Most notably, treaties have begun to regulate individual behaviour itself. The Rome Statute holds individuals responsible for certain heinous acts.[196] The various Hague conventions on private law also regulate how individuals conduct themselves vis-à-vis other individuals.[197]

Except with respect to its rules on boundary and humanitarian treaties, international law does not presently differentiate among treaties according to the objects they regulate. Indeed, in the human rights context, the ILC has specifically declined to do so.[198] Nonetheless, certain interpretative principles—eg the principle of effectiveness for human rights treaties—may be explained as an implicit recognition of such distinctions. If such recognition was more explicit, the functional approach might support new rules; for example extending the VCLT's support for the stability of boundary treaties to other treaties involving public goods and shared spaces.

3. Who enforces treaty regulations

The existing international legal order is notable for its essentially horizontal organization, where the makers of international law, States, are also most often its subjects. Similarly, in the absence of global or universal enforcement mechanisms, international law leaves treaty enforcement to States. As a matter of 'good faith', States making treaty commitments are primarily responsible for their own compliance.[199]

Where self-enforcement fails, however, other peaceful mechanisms such as reprisal (now dubbed 'counter-measures'), retorsion, or a claim for reparations may be brought to bear.[200] These mechanisms may be structured bilaterally, in

---

[194] Eg First Optional Protocol to the International Covenant on Civil and Political Rights (opened for signature 16 December 1966, entered into force 23 March 1976) 999 UNTS 171.

[195] Eg *Sempra Energy Int'l v Argentine Republic* ICSID Case No ARB/02/16 (2005) (re California company arbitration claim under US–Argentine BIT).

[196] Rome Statute of the International Criminal Court (adopted 17 July 1998, entered into force 1 July 2002) 2187 UNTS 3, Art 25.

[197] Eg Convention on the Taking of Evidence Abroad in Civil and Commercial Matters (opened for signature 18 March 1970, entered into force 7 October 1972) 847 UNTS 231.

[198] See Chapter 11, Part IV, 291 *et seq.* (discussing ILC decision not to craft separate reservation rules for human rights treaties).

[199] Thus, Louis Henkins's oft-cited, albeit anecdotal, formulation that 'almost all nations observe almost all principles of international law and almost all of their obligations almost all of the time'. L Henkin, *How Nations Behave* (Columbia University Press, New York 1979) 47. IOs would appear to have a similar role. 1986 VCLT (n 13) Art 26. Treaty compliance by other subjects of international law may vary since the responsible State could take the lead in ensuring the 'other subject' performs the obligation assumed.

[200] UN Charter Art 33. Reprisal involves States responding to unlawful activity with behaviour that itself would be unlawful but for the fact that it comes in response to a prior breach; retorsion is the use of otherwise lawful measures to induce a breaching party to return to a state of compliance.

which a single party—usually limited to the party 'injured' by the breach—exercises a right of response. On occasion, these mechanisms have been extended to multilateral settings.[201] For its part, the VCLT allows for the possibility of termination or suspension (although technically these focus on the treaty relationship itself, rather than inducing wayward parties to return to compliance).[202] Today, many treaties rely exclusively on these State-centered approaches to compliance and enforcement.

But, the relative weakness of this system of individualized and collective enforcement has generated treaties that transfer compliance or enforcement functions to third parties.[203] The most obvious example is the ICJ; numerous treaties empower the World Court to judicially resolve treaty questions or disputes and impose appropriate remedies.[204] Other treaties create their own court to perform this function, such as the International Tribunal on the Law of the Sea or the European Court of Human Rights.[205] The WTO's Dispute Settlement Understanding provides a multi-level approach to consideration of WTO compliance questions.[206] Treaty provisions calling for arbitration (whether through a permanent or ad hoc forum) perform a similar function.[207]

Aside from judicial and quasi-judicial actors, treaties may also designate a 'treaty body' to serve in one or more compliance or enforcement roles. In the human rights context, treaty bodies provide general comments about the treaty; specific comments on a single party's performance; and responses to individual petitions.[208] Certain arms control treaties empower the Secretariat or the IO's plenary body to supervise party compliance.[209] In the environmental context, treaty bodies have adopted an explicitly non-adversarial approach through the adoption of

---

[201] The threshold for such action is frequently high—for example, collective action requires unanimity for suspension or termination under the VCLT. VCLT Art 60(2)(a).

[202] VCLT Art 60 restricts the availability of both options, limiting suspension or termination to cases of 'material' breach and then only for cases of unanimity or 'specially affected' parties or if it 'radically changes the position of every other party with respect to the further performance of its obligations'. For details on these rules, see Chapter 23, Parts II–III, 582 *et seq*.

[203] The weakness of the existing system reflects the reality that, as Leo Gross noted, 'each state has a right to interpret the law, the right of autointerpretation, as it might be called'. L Gross, 'States as Organs of International Law and the Problem of Autointerpretation' in GA Lipsky (ed), *Law and Politics in the World Community* (University of California Press, Berkeley 1953) 59. A State's view, however, remains just that—one interpretation, not a final decision on the law's content or applicability. Ibid. Hence the move by States to agree on more definitive vehicles for discerning compliance and enforcing treaty commitments.

[204] See eg UN Convention against Illicit Traffic in Narcotic Drugs and Psychotropic Substances (adopted 20 December 1988, entered into force 11 November 1990) 1582 UNTS 95, Art 32.

[205] Eg UNCLOS (n 2) Annex VI.

[206] See Understanding on Rules and Procedures Governing the Settlement of Disputes, Marrakesh Agreement establishing the WTO (adopted 15 April 1994, entered into force 1 January 1995) 1869 UNTS 299.

[207] Eg Afghanistan–Germany BIT (n 174) Arts 10–11.

[208] See eg Rights of the Child Convention (n 174) Arts 43–45; ICCPR (n 175) Part IV; ICCPR First Optional Protocol (n 194).

[209] See eg Convention on the Prohibition of the Development, Production, Stockpiling and Use of Chemical Weapons and on their Destruction (opened for signature 3 September 1992, entered into force 29 April 1997) 1974 UNTS 45, Art VIII, Verification Annex.

non-compliance procedures. Here treaty bodies provide technological or financial assistance to 'assist' parties in returning to compliance or 'naming and shaming' them into doing so.[210] Thus, they tend to adopt a 'managerial' approach to compliance questions in lieu of the more traditional 'enforcement' model.[211]

As with the issues of how and what treaties regulate, the singularity of the treaty concept does not acknowledge the growing diversity in how treaties task third parties with compliance and enforcement functions. The VCLT (and its 1986 companion) largely ignore questions of compliance and enforcement, viewing them as subjects for the law of State responsibility. But States often prefer to draft their own treaty-specific approaches rather than relying on State responsibility generally.[212] Nothing in the treaty concept (or the law of treaties generally) precludes this. At the same time, however, the treaty concept has not adapted to incorporate these new actors and mechanisms. The law of treaties remains largely geared toward a world of bilateral engagements (even within the multilateral setting) that may be ill-suited to dealing with multi-stakeholder issues.

A functional definition of the treaty concept, therefore, aids our understanding of the treaty concept, not by refining it so much as suggesting the possibility (and perhaps even some need) for its further disaggregation. Differentiating treaties by the types of obligations, objects, or compliance functions they employ helps to explain areas of on-going contestation and potential areas for specialization.

Conclusion

Today, the treaty is *the* dominant instrument through which international law operates. The aim of this chapter has been to illuminate its defining characteristics on two levels. First, it demonstrates that what a treaty 'is' and the consequences for its use vary by context. The treaty may be born of international law, but it is equally at home within domestic legal systems, and remains a key form of commitment for those seeking international coordination and cooperation.

Second, in the context of international law, this chapter sought to explain and expand upon the VCLT's definition of the treaty. It shows how the existing list of treaty ingredients is both incomplete (excluding oral treaties and treaties involving IOs and other subjects of international law) and underdeveloped (in terms of what constitutes an 'international agreement' and what 'governed by international law' means, especially in terms of the parties' intentions). It is difficult, however, to

---

[210] See eg Montreal Protocol (n 169) Art 8 (directing parties to adopt non-compliance procedures); Convention on Biological Diversity (opened for signature 5 June 1992, entered into force 29 December 1993) 1760 UNTS 79, Arts 20–1 (providing financial resources and a mechanism to assist developing parties in meeting the treaty's obligations).

[211] A Chayes and AH Chayes, *The New Sovereignty: Compliance with International Regulatory Agreements* (Harvard University Press, Cambridge 1995) 230.

[212] On this phenomenon, see Chapter 23, Part I.B, 578 *et seq.*

understand treaties solely by dissection. Thus, this chapter also explored how differentiating the treaty from other forms of commitment (unilateral declarations) and agreements (political commitments and contracts) informs our understanding of treaties themselves.

Finally, this chapter has surveyed the widely divergent functions the treaty concept serves. Its flexibility and the law of treaties' openness to contracting around default rules has generated a spectrum of approaches in how treaties operate, what they regulate, and who acts as a regulator. The range of the modern treaty suggests that the single, generic approach to defining 'the' treaty and its associated rules ought to be revisited. This need not mean dispensing with international law's existing definition, but perhaps augmenting the definition to situate various species of treaties within a larger treaty genus.

In the end, the project of defining treaties reveals the strength of McNair's 'sadly overworked' label for the treaty concept and raises a key question: should treaty-making remain the primary method for regulating *all* international problems? If international law owes much of its success to the treaty concept, might that concept also be responsible for some of its failures? The current chapter does not seek to answer these questions. But it lays the necessary foundation for such analysis by offering a deeper and more comprehensive approach to the treaty concept. In doing so, it may also aid treaty practitioners in identifying what 'is' a treaty, distinguishing it from other instruments, and appreciating the treaty's limits. Defining treaties may not be a simple task, but given the present state of international law, it is a critical one.

Recommended Reading

A Aust, *Modern Treaty Law and Practice* (2nd edn CUP, Cambridge 2007) Chs 2–4

C Brölmann, 'Law-Making Treaties: Form and Function in International Law' (2005) 74 Nordic J Intl L 383

C Chinkin, 'A Mirage in the Sand? Distinguishing Binding and Non-Binding Relations between States' (1997) 10 LJIL 223

O Corten and P Klein (eds), *The Vienna Conventions on the Law of Treaties: A Commentary* (OUP, Oxford 2011)

JES Fawcett, 'The Legal Character of International Agreements' (1953) 30 BYBIL 381

M Fitzmaurice, 'Treaties' in R Wolfrum (ed), *Max Planck Encyclopedia of Public International Law* (OUP, Oxford 2010) online at <http://www.mpepil.com>

M Fitzmaurice and O Elias, *Contemporary Issues in the Law of Treaties* (Eleven International Publishing, Utrecht 2005) Ch 1

DB Hollis, MR Blakeslee and LB Ederington (eds), *National Treaty Law and Practice* (Martinus Nijhoff, Leiden 2005)

DB Hollis and JJ Newcomer, ' "Political" Commitments and the Constitution' (2009) 49 VJIL 507

J Klabbers, *The Concept of Treaty in International Law* (Kluwer Law International, The Hague 1996)

A McNair, 'The Functions and Differing Legal Character of Treaties' (1930) 11 BYBIL 100

J Pauwelyn, 'Is it International Law or Not and Does it Even Matter?' in J Pauwelyn and others (eds), *Informal International Lawmaking* (OUP, Oxford 2012)

ME Villiger, *Commentary on the 1969 Vienna Convention on the Law of Treaties* (Martinus Nijhoff, Leiden 2009)

K Widdows, 'What is an Agreement in International Law?' (1979) 50 BYBIL 117

2

Alternatives to Treaty-Making: MOUs as Political Commitments

*Anthony Aust**

Open covenants of peace, openly arrived at, after which there shall be no private international understandings of any kind, but diplomacy shall proceed always frankly and in the public view.[1]

Introduction

Since 1919, when US President Woodrow Wilson issued this sincere, but hopelessly unworldly, appeal, diplomacy has continued to develop many new ways of doing business. Even when the subject matter is proper and lawful, diplomats know that it is not possible for all international deals to be embodied in treaties, whether or not they are on important matters. Yet, the deal needs to be formalized on paper in some way. Hence, the relentless rise of political commitments; instruments concluded between States that are not legally binding.

Such non-legally binding instruments have also been variously described as 'political agreements', 'gentlemen's agreements', 'non-legally binding agreements', 'non-binding agreements', '*de facto* agreements', 'non-legal agreements', etc. Diplomats—who are well aware of such instruments—generally refer to them, and not only in English, as 'Memorandums of Understanding' or 'MOUs'. Calling an instrument a Memorandum of Understanding does not, in itself, determine its status, since—and most confusingly—some treaties are also called Memorandums of Understanding.[2] MOUs (properly so-called) operate as political commitments, however, and may be distinguished from treaties according to the International Law Commission (ILC) because they are not agreements

---

* This chapter mostly draws upon Chapters 2 and 3 of the author's *Modern Treaty Law and Practice* (2nd edn CUP, Cambridge 2007) (MTLP), Chapter 3 being based on the author's article 'The Theory and Practice of Informal International Instruments' (1986) 35 ICLQ 787–812. The author retains the copyright to those two chapters of MTLP. A reference to the present book will of course be made in the next edition of MTLP.

[1] GA Finch, 'The Peace Conference of Paris, 1919' (1919) 13 AJIL 161 (quoting Woodrow Wilson).
[2] See A Aust, *Modern Treaty Law and Practice* (2nd edn CUP, Cambridge 2007) 26–7 (MTLP).

governed by international law.[3] An MOU may still loosely be referred to as an 'agreement', however, since it represents a deal between States, even if there is no intention that it should be binding in international law.

The existence of MOUs, and the extent to which they are a significant vehicle for the conduct of business between States, has until relatively recent years *not* been well known outside government circles.[4] In fact, a large number of such instruments, bilateral and multilateral, are concluded every year covering a wide range of subjects.[5] But, most are never published. A (published) example of an MOU is the Memorandum of Understanding on Port State Control in the Caribbean Region 1996.[6] The UK–Jordan Memorandum of Understanding on Deportations 2005,[7] and similar ones with Libya (18 October 2005) and Lebanon (23 December 2005), are more widely publicized examples, and have been rightly described as no more than 'diplomatic assurances'.

This chapter will discuss ways to distinguish more easily between a treaty and an MOU. It does so based on the evidence of negotiating States' intent, whether through express provisions as to the instrument's status, the circumstances in which it was concluded, or registration (but, not, as discussed, based on the instrument's content). This chapter also reviews the existing practice of States in concluding MOUs, how and why MOUs are used, and their possible legal consequences.

But first, a word of warning—because the use of MOUs is now so widespread, some officials may see the MOU as the norm, a treaty being used only when it cannot be avoided. The very word 'treaty' may conjure up some of the apparent fearsome formalities of diplomacy. One of the tasks of international lawyers is to explain the legal differences between a treaty and an MOU. This includes, most importantly, the advantages and disadvantages of a treaty and an MOU, and why, in the particular circumstances, an MOU might be preferable to a treaty. But, in general, unless there is a particular advantage in having an MOU—such as confidentiality—there should be no reason to avoid having a treaty. On the other hand, in principle, there is no reason to prefer a treaty to an MOU unless there is a need to create *legally* binding rights and obligations in international law, or there are *real* constitutional or other domestic legal requirements for a treaty.

---

[3] See M Leir, 'Canadian Practice in International Law' (1999) 37 Canadian Ybk Intl L 317, 342 (note on treaties and Memorandums of Understanding); S Rosenne, *Developments in the Law of Treaties 1945–1986* (CUP, Cambridge 1989) 104, 107.

[4] See H Hillgenberg, 'A Fresh Look at Soft Law' (1999) 10 EJIL 499–515.

[5] For Canadian practice, see H Kindred and others (eds), *International Law Chiefly as Interpreted and Applied in Canada* (4th edn Emond Montgomery Publ Ltd, Toronto 1987) 119–20; Lier (n 3) 342. For evidence of US practice, see DB Hollis and JJ Newcomer, ' "Political Commitments" and the Constitution' (2009) 49 VJIL 507, 516–38.

[6] [1997] 36 ILM 237. See also the list of MOUs at MTLP (n 2) xlviii–xlix.

[7] [2005] 44 ILM 1511; see the UK special Immigration Appeals Commission judgments in 2007 in *Abu Qatada* and *DD and AS* <http://www.bailii.org/uk/cases/SIAC/2007/15_2005.html>.

I. Distinguishing Between an MOU and a Treaty

A. Evidence of an intention to conclude (or not conclude) a treaty

Negotiating States can determine if they will conclude an agreement as a treaty, an MOU, or a contract governed by domestic law. According to the ILC Commentary[8] on its draft which became the Vienna Convention on the Law of Treaties 1969 (VCLT), in the definition of 'treaty' the phrase 'governed by international law' embraced the element of an _intention to create obligations under international law_.[9] So, an instrument concluded between States which they do _not intend to be governed by international law_ is therefore not binding in international law, and will therefore not be a treaty.[10] Discerning the intent of the parties can involve an intensive analysis. In the _Aegean Sea Continental Shelf_ case in 1978, the International Court of Justice (ICJ), in order to determine its nature, considered the terms of a joint communiqué issued by the Greek and Turkish Prime Ministers, and the particular circumstances in which it was drawn up. The Court found that there had been no intention to conclude an international agreement (ie a treaty) to submit to the jurisdiction of the Court.[11] Intention, thus, must be gathered from the terms of the instrument itself and the circumstances of its conclusion, not from what the parties say _afterwards_ was their intention.[12] The intention to create obligations under international law also distinguishes treaties from agreements between States governed by domestic law.[13]

B. Terminology and form

How do negotiating States indicate their intentions? Although the law of treaties does not require a treaty to be in any particular form or to use special wording,[14] lawyers practising in foreign or other ministries usually use instruments that employ carefully chosen terminology. Most States now follow a practice of manifesting their intention to conclude a treaty by consciously employing a fairly standard form, and mandatory terminology such as 'shall', 'agree', 'undertake', 'rights',

---

[8] See A Watts, _The International Law Commission 1949–1998_ (OUP, Oxford 2004) vol II, 621–4.

[9] VCLT Art 2(1)(a) provides that a '"treaty" means an international agreement concluded between States in written form and _governed by international law_, whether embodied in a single instrument or in two or more related instruments and _whatever its particular designation_' (emphasis added). For further discussion of the definition of a 'treaty', see Chapter 1.

[10] See the exhaustive analysis of 'non-legal agreements' in C Ahlström, _The Status of Multilateral Export Control Regimes: An Examination of Legal and Non-Legal Agreements in International Cooperation_ (Acta Universitatis Upsaliensis, Uppsala 1999) 49–51, 102–298.

[11] _Aegean Sea Continental Shelf Case (Greece v Turkey)_ [1978] ICJ Rep 40, 39–44; H Thirlway, 'The Law and Procedure of the International Court of Justice 1960–1989' (1991) 62 BYBIL 13–15 (interpreting the intention of the parties in the Brussels Communiqué of 31 May 1975).

[12] _Qatar v Bahrain (Jurisdiction and Admissibility)_ [1994] ICJ Rep 40, 112 [26]–[27]; see also MTLP (n 2) 51–2.

[13] See MTLP (n 2) 30.

[14] _Temple of Preah Vihear (Preliminary Objections)_ [1961] ICJ Rep 17, 27, 31–2.

'obligations', and 'enter into force'. In contrast, when they do *not* intend to conclude a treaty, but rather an MOU, instead of 'shall' they use a less mandatory term, such as 'will'; such terms as 'agree' or 'undertake' are avoided; the instrument is expressed to 'come into operation' or 'come into effect'; and most of the final clauses usually found in treaties, and the testimonium, are omitted or simplified. The following table illustrates some of the words most commonly used in a treaty and MOU, respectively:[15]

Treaty	MOU
article	paragraph
agree	decide, accept, approve
agreement	arrangement, understanding
authentic	equally valid
continue in force	continue to have effect
done	signed
enter into force	come into effect, come into operation
obligations	commitments
parties	participants, governments
rights	benefits
shall	will
undertake	carry out
undertakings	understandings

But, it should be stressed that the terminology used for MOUs is analogous to the practice (at least in common law countries) with domestic law contracts, where the use of 'will', as opposed to 'shall' should not necessarily be read to deny the intent to create a legally binding obligation.

Although an MOU will normally be designated 'Memorandum of Understanding' ('*mémorandum d'entente*' or '*memorándum de entendimiento*') or 'Arrangement', such terminology is not dispositive. Taken on its own the designation of an instrument can actually be most misleading; a 'Memorandum of Understanding' or an 'Exchange of Notes' may be a treaty or an MOU, depending on how it is worded.[16] It should also not be assumed that just because a document contains treaty terminology it is a treaty. A joint governmental statement will often use such language even though it is conveying only a political message, such statements being sometimes more impressive if couched in more forceful terms.[17]

---

[15] For specific examples see Section VI of this volume, 635 *et seq*. A larger table comparing treaty and MOU terminology is at Appendix G of this author's book MTLP. The treaty (Appendix B) and the MOUs (Appendices C and D) illustrate the main differences. Guidance on treaty and MOU drafting is given in Chapter 23 of that book.

[16] MTLP (n 2) 23–7.

[17] See the Joint Statement on Terrorism by the Iranian and Russian Foreign Ministers (26 September 1998), UN Doc A/C.6/53/6; 'The Atlantic Charter 1941' (1941) AJIL, Supp 191; and A McNair, *Law of Treaties* (2nd edn OUP, Oxford 1961) 6.

Lest it be thought that the MOU only exists in an Anglo-American context, this thought will be quickly dispelled by an examination of similar 'agreements' concluded between other parties.[18]

C. Content

Unlike form and terminology, the subject of an instrument is not a guide to its status, since the same subject can be found in both treaties and MOUs. And, a treaty can be pretty insubstantial (see the UK–Albania Agreement on Cooperation in the Field of Tourism 1994),[19] and an MOU can be extremely important *politically* (see the Helsinki Final Act 1975).[20] Though, when an instrument contains an article providing for the settlement of disputes by compulsory international judicial process, such a provision is hardly consistent with an intention not to enter into a legally binding instrument.[21]

D. Express provisions as to non-legally binding status

In many cases, negotiating States will clearly evince an intention to conclude an MOU through language in the text itself. In such cases, determining the instrument's legal status is a more simple affair. The States which adopted the Helsinki Final Act 1975 made clear their intention not to enter into a treaty by stating at the end of the instrument that it was 'not eligible for registration [ie as a treaty] under Article 102 of the Charter'.[22] When the Organization for Security and Co-operation in Europe (OSCE)[23] adopts important instruments which are not treaties, it continues to make this clear. The OSCE Document of the Stockholm Conference on Confidence- and Security-Building Measures and Disarmament in Europe 1987 provides that: '[t]he measures adopted in this document are politically binding'.[24] The OSCE Charter of Paris 1990 provides that it is not eligible for registration.[25] In the OSCE Code of Conduct on Politico-Military Aspects of Security, 1994,

---

[18] See eg Joint Communiqué of the Government of Japan and the Government of the People's Republic of China, 29 September 1972, translated and appended to T Kuriyama, 'Some Legal Aspects of the Japan-China Joint Communiqué' (1973) 16 Jap An Intl L 42, 80.

[19] Agreement on Cooperation in the Field of Tourism between the Government of the United Kingdom of Great Britain and Northern Ireland and the Government of the Republic of Albania, in MTLP (n 2) App B.

[20] Conference on Security and Co-operation in Europe (CSCE), 'Final Act' (Helsinki 1975) [1975] 14 ILM 1292; The Global Fund to Fight AIDS, Tuberculosis and Malaria, 'The Framework Document of the Global Fund to Fight AIDS, Tuberculosis and Malaria' <http://www.theglobalfund.org/en/library/documents>; UNEP Guidelines for the Exchange of Information on Chemicals in International Trade, pt II, § 6 [1989] 28 ILM 220.

[21] See Thirlway (n 11) 7–8.

[22] [1975] 14 ILM 1293, 1325. Only treaties can be registered under UN Charter Art 102 ('[E]very treaty and every international agreement entered into by any member of the United Nations . . . shall as soon as possible be registered with the Secretariat'). For more on Art 102, see MTLP (n 2) 339–40.

[23] The OSCE used to be the CSCE; see the author's *Handbook of International Law* (2nd edn CUP, Cambridge 2010) 178 ('*Handbook*').

[24] [1987] 26 ILM 190, 195 [101].

[25] [1991] 30 ILM 193, 208.

paragraph 39 provides that it is 'politically binding', and, accordingly, 'this Code is not eligible for registration under Article 102'.[26]

An MOU adopted by the UN Conference on Environment and Development (UNCED) is 'engagingly' entitled *Non-legally Binding* Authoritative Statement of Principles for a Global Consensus on the Management, Conservation and Sustainable Development of all Types of Forests 1992.[27] The NATO–Russia Founding Act 1997 refers in its preamble to 'political' commitments.[28] When transmitting a copy of it to the UN Secretary-General, the NATO Secretary-General stated that it was not eligible for registration under Article 102 of the UN Charter.

Sometimes a bilateral instrument includes a statement that it represents a political commitment and does not constitute a legally binding agreement. Any doubt as to the status of the Israel–United States Declaration on Trade in Services 1985 is dispelled by the preamble which declares that 'the principles set forth below shall not be legally binding'.[29] Such express statements seem to be a growing trend, particularly in MOUs with the United States.[30] They, and other categorical statements, are conclusive as to the intended status of the instrument. But, the use of such formulas is not yet common, and omitting them certainly does *not* indicate that the instrument was intended to be a treaty. Therefore, one should *not* equate use of such formulas with a formula such as 'subject to contract', used by lawyers in many (common law) countries to prevent a document containing proposals from being held to be legally binding.

E. Circumstances in which the instrument was concluded

If the form, terminology, or express terms of the instrument do not contain enough evidence of the intention of the authors as to its status, it is necessary to consider any evidence of the practice of the States, the circumstances in which the instrument was drawn up, and the subsequent acts of the States, such as registration or non-registration. During the Copenhagen meeting of the parties to the UN Framework Convention on Climate Change, efforts to devise a treaty to redress climate change failed, but interested parties did 'associate' themselves with a

[26] Organization for Security and Co-operation in Europe, Code of Conduct on Politico-Military Aspects of Security, DOC.FSC/1/95 (3 December 1994); see also Section 1.3 of the Charter of the International Energy Convention 2011 (ASIL, ILIB, 27 April 2011).

[27] [1992] 31 ILM 882 (emphasis added).

[28] [1997] 36 ILM 1007, 1008.

[29] [1985] 24 ILM 679.

[30] See Memorandum of Understanding between Environment Canada and the US Department of the Interior for the Conservation and Management of Shared Polar Bear Populations (8 May 2008) <http://www.asil.org/ilib/2008/05/ilib080516.htm#t1>. At the end is the unequivocal statement that 'This [MOU] is not legally-binding and creates no legally-binding obligations on the Participants'. Similarly, the 2009 Russia–US MOU on Antitrust Cooperation is drawn in MOU style and at the end states that 'nothing in it is intended to change existing law, agreements, or treaties, or create enforceable rights'. Memorandum of Understanding on Antitrust Cooperation Between the US Department of Justice and the US Federal Trade Commission, on the One Hand, and the Russian Federal Anti-Monopoly Service, on the Other Hand, 10 November 2009 <http://www.justice.gov/atr/public/international/251836.pdf> ('US–Russia Antitrust MOU').

political commitment known as the Copenhagen Accord.[31] Further, the Terms of Reference of the International Nickel Study Group 1986[32] speak of the 'parties to this arrangement' having reached 'an understanding' about establishing the Group. But it then uses 'shall' throughout. There is provision for it to 'come into effect' rather than enter into force. It is not subject to signature, though that is not essential.[33] It was registered with the UN. Although the drafting is poor, and includes some MOU phraseology, there seems no doubt that the Member States intended to conclude a treaty.[34] Ultimately, an international court or tribunal may decide such questions.

F. Registration and non-registration

Registration of an instrument with the UN pursuant to Article 102 of the UN Charter is generally good evidence that the States concerned regard the instrument as a treaty, although registration cannot, in itself, confer treaty status if the instrument is not a treaty.[35] Usually, only one party registers an instrument (usually a bilateral one), although non-registration—rather than registration—is less of an indication of the status of an instrument. Nor is the lack of any protest at the registration necessarily evidence that the other party or parties accept that the instrument is a treaty, since States do not routinely monitor registrations. In the US–UK Heathrow User Charges Arbitration 1988–92 the Tribunal held that a UK–US MOU of 1988 was not legally binding, citing, among other factors, that it had neither been published nor registered with the UN or the International Civil Aviation Organization (ICAO).[36] But, equally, failure to register a treaty does not

---

[31] 'Report of the Conference of the Parties on its Fifteenth Session, held in Copenhagen from 7 to 19 December 2009, Addendum Part Two: Action taken by the Conference of the Parties at its Fifteenth Session' UN Doc FCCC/CP/2009/11/Add.1, Decision 4/CP.15 (Copenhagen Accord).

[32] (Adopted 2 May 1986) 1566 UNTS 29.

[33] See MTLP (n 2) 24–5.

[34] There is some disagreement among scholars as to whether in the face of silence as to legal intention, an instrument concluded among States should carry a presumption of treaty status. Sir Hersh Lauterpacht was the most notable proponent of a presumption of legal intent. See H Lauterpacht, 'Second Report on the Law of Treaties' [1954] YBILC, vol II, 123; see also K Widdows, 'What is an Agreement in International Law?' (1979) 50 BYBIL 117, 144–9. Others such as Fawcett and Schachter, took the opposite position. See eg JES Fawcett, 'The Legal Character of International Agreements' (1953) 30 BYBIL 381, 400; O Schachter, 'The Twilight Existence of Nonbinding International Agreements' (1977) AJIL 296, 303.

[35] See Chapter 10 for a detailed discussion of UN registration practice; see also MTLP (n 2) 344–6; *Reparatory of Practice of United Nations Organs*, Ch XVI, Art 102, at <http://www.un.org/law/repertory>. An examination of every tenth volume of the *United Nations Treaty Series* from 1980 to 1989 (inclusive) produced only four instruments that are clearly MOUs. All were registered (presumably in error) by the US, three at the same time. See US–Japan Joint Determination for Reprocessing of Special Nuclear Material of US Origin (1981) 1550 UNTS 3; US–Canada Memorandum of Understanding on Co-operation in a 1979 High Plains Co-operative Experiment in Weather Modification (1979) 1180 UNTS 83; US–Japan Exchange of Notes Constituting an Arrangement Relating to Trade in Textiles (1979) 1180 UNTS 163; US–Japan Record of Discussion Constituting an Agreement Relating to Trade in Textiles (1979) 1180 UNTS 179.

[36] On ICAO registration, see MTLP (n 2) 43.

deprive it of treaty status, even if, in theory at least, the treaty cannot be invoked before an organ of the UN.[37]

G. Disagreement as to status

A potentially tricky, and indeed embarrassing, problem can arise when differing views are held by the States concerned as to the status of an instrument, though this appears to happen chiefly with bilateral instruments. The author is aware of at least two instances of this coming to light when a bilateral instrument was on the point of being signed, and four after it had become effective. In two of the latter cases, the disagreement only became apparent once a dispute had arisen, and this may well have been a factor. In both cases, the instrument was supplementary to a treaty.[38]

For example, in 1997, a (self-contained) bilateral *MOU* concluded by a UK home ministry was submitted to the Parliament of the other (European) State for approval as a *treaty*. The misunderstanding about its status was discovered only when the other State asked if the UK's treaty procedures had been completed. The error was mainly due to the home ministry and the British Embassy concerned not reporting to the Foreign and Commonwealth Office (FCO) that an MOU was being negotiated. One solution to the problem is for the State which intended to conclude no more than an MOU to send—and well in advance—a diplomatic note to the other State on the following lines: all the necessary legal requirements having been completed, the instrument will now come into operation on the understanding that it does not constitute a treaty and neither side will publish it as a treaty or seek to register it as a treaty with the UN. Hopefully, the other side will either reply agreeing with this, or not reply. Either should be enough. A reference to the point should of course be made at the outset of the negotiation of the instrument.

Difficult problems can arise when an MOU, which is subsidiary to a treaty, contains provisions purporting to amend, or which are otherwise inconsistent with, the treaty. This raises the question whether the inconsistent provisions have any legal effect. In certain cases, the MOU might be regarded as evidence of a mutual waiver of rights under the treaty. But the deliberate or mistaken use of MOUs to

---

[37] See further MTLP (n 2) 344–6; D Hutchinson, 'The Significance of the Registration or Non-Registration of an International Agreement in Determining Whether or Not it is a Treaty' (1993) *Current Legal Problems* 257–90. For its part, the ICJ has not applied the prohibition on invoking unregistered treaties strictly, or perhaps at all. See *Qatar v Bahrain (Jurisdiction and Admissibility)* [1994] ICJ Rep 112 [17]–[19], [22] and [29].

[38] MOUs are rarely referred to expressly in treaties, but a 1998 UK–US treaty says expressly that it *replaces* a *bi*lateral MOU and *preserves* a *tri*lateral MOU. See the preamble to, and Arts 23 and 24 of, the Maritime and Aerial Operations to Suppress Illicit Trafficking by Sea in the Waters of the Caribbean and Bermuda Agreement (UK–US) (13 July 1998) 2169 UNTS 251; UKTS (2001) 2. Whereas the UKTS gives the references for previous treaties mentioned in the Agreement, it gives none for the '1990 MOU' or the '1990 TRIPART MOU'. See also the text of a UK–US MOU in (1997) 67 BYBIL 500.

modify treaty provisions can be dangerous and can lead to uncertainty as to the precise effect on the treaty. They should therefore be avoided.

It is not usually necessary to determine the precise status of a subsidiary instrument which is in the nature of a statement of interpretation of a treaty. The rules in Article 31 of the Convention deal with most cases adequately.[39]

II. The Practice of States

States have long used political commitments. In their early form, they were conceived as personal commitments among officials, but later came to accommodate national commitments. In 1907, for example, Japan and the US promised to constrain emigration to the United States via a commitment described as a non-binding agreement by its drafter Secretary of State Robert Lansing.[40] In recent decades, State practice has resulted in widespread use of MOUs. As the practice emerged, foreign government negotiators may have been rather bemused by requests, usually from Commonwealth States, to change the title of a draft from 'Agreement' to 'Memorandum of Understanding' or 'Arrangement', and every 'shall' to 'will'. But, what some may have previously seen as a slightly tiresome—even quaint—obsession is now a firmly established practice in international relations.

A. Commonwealth States

The over fifty States which are members of the Commonwealth tend to use MOUs, bilateral or multilateral, among themselves even in those cases where other States might employ a treaty, though there are exceptions.[41] The Commonwealth Secretariat itself was established in 1965 by an MOU entitled 'Agreed Memorandum'.[42]

B. European Union States

In 1996, the Secretariat of the (then EC) Council of Ministers circulated a questionnaire to all (then fifteen) Member States concerning: '[t]he internal procedures of Member States for the conclusion of international agreements approved under a simplified procedure or agreements *without legally-binding force*'.[43] For almost all the Member States, the key factor in distinguishing a non-legally binding instrument from a treaty was the *intention* of the States. Ireland, which, like the

---

[39] See MTLP (n 2) 234 *et seq.*

[40] 'Memorandum by the Division of Far Eastern Affairs' (11 January 1924), *US Dept of State, Papers Relating to the Foreign Relations of the United States 1924* (1939) vol 2, 339–74.

[41] See the India–UK Extradition Agreement (September 1992) 1824 UNTS 190.

[42] [1965] 4 ILM 1108. For more on the Commonwealth and law making, see MTLP (n 2) 412–13.

[43] (Emphasis added.) The replies are summarized in Commission (EC) Doc PESC/SEC 899 (9 August 1996).

other Member States (except the UK) has a written constitution, replied that if an instrument was not intended to be binding it would be worded to reflect that intention; and that the Irish courts had distinguished between MOUs and treaties on the basis of the intentions of the governments as reflected in the language of the text and the formalities, or lack of them, associated with the instrument. The replies of other Member States echoed these points and added further factors which for them distinguished MOUs from treaties: (a) the title of the instrument; (b) the avoidance of mandatory language; (c) the omission of treaty-type final clauses; and, (d) generally, the absence of a parliamentary procedure.[44] One expects that the twelve new Member States which joined between 2004 and 2007, so making twenty-seven in total, either already follow established MOU practice, or are eager to do so.

C. The United States

Examining the practice of the US is valuable because it is well-documented. The purpose of the US Federal Regulations dealing with international agreements is to implement the federal law known as the 'Case Act' by giving guidance to departments and agencies of the US Government as to the types of instruments which the Act requires to be notified to Congress.[45] The Regulations thus cover those instruments which fall within the definition of treaty (as that term is understood by international law),[46] and lay down criteria by which to judge whether a particular instrument is a *treaty*.[47] The following extracts are particularly relevant:

(1) *Identity and intention of the parties*... The parties must intend their undertakings to be legally binding, *and not merely of political or personal effect. Documents intended to have political or moral weight, but not intended to be legally binding, are not international agreements*... [emphasis added]

...

(5) *Form.* Form as such is not normally an important factor, but it does deserve consideration. Documents which do not follow the customary form for international agreements [ie treaties], as to matters such as style, final clauses, signatures, or entry into force dates, may or may not be international agreements. Failure to use the customary form may constitute evidence of a lack of intent to be legally bound by the arrangement. If, however, the general content and context reveal an intention to enter into a legally binding relationship, a departure from customary form will not preclude the arrangement from being an international agreement. Moreover, the title of the agreement will not be determinative. Decisions will be made on the basis of the substance of the arrangement, rather than on its denomination as an international agreement, a memorandum of understanding,

---

[44] See also the Opinion of the Advocate-General of the European Court of Justice in *France v Commission* [1994] ECR I-3641.

[45] 'United States International Agreements' 1 USC §112b; [1979] 18 ILM 82.

[46] See MTLP (n 2) 196 and the following sections for an *attempt* to explain the place of treaties in the US Constitution.

[47] 22 CFR §181.1–2.

exchange of notes, exchange of letters, technical arrangement, protocol, note verbale, aide-memoire, agreed minute, or any other name.

These extracts adopt a not dissimilar approach to that of other States: there must be an intention to enter into legally binding obligations. Use of non-customary treaty form may indicate that the parties did not intend to enter into a legally binding relationship. But, it is also clear that in US practice use of non-treaty language does not necessarily preclude the instrument from being an international agreement if 'the general content and context reveal an intention to enter into a legally binding relationship'. Since less weight is given to terminology, it is more difficult to predict whether a particular instrument will be regarded by the US as a treaty or an MOU.

It must be remembered that the purpose of the Regulations is to help people with the 'Case Act'.[48] Under the Act, every 'international agreement' has to be published annually and the text submitted to Congress within sixty days of entry into force. The term 'international agreement' is defined in the Act so as to exclude 'Treaties', that is those treaties which under the US Constitution have to be submitted to the Senate for approval.[49] Furthermore, the Act requires oral agreements (which are not covered by the VCLT)[50] to be reduced to writing and notified to Congress. Also, the Act excludes any 'agreement' if its public disclosure would be prejudicial to national security. This would seem contrary to the UN Charter obligation to register all treaties,[51] unless of course the exclusion covers only classified *MOUs*.

In practice, the US appears to regard as treaties some instruments which other States would see as no more than MOUs. This may, in part, be due to the tendency of the US to name as a Memorandum of Understanding what is without doubt a treaty.[52] This has led to some instruments which are clearly MOUs, or perhaps only contracts under federal law, being erroneously regarded as treaties. A 1981 Memorandum of Understanding between the 15th Air Base Wing, Hickham Air Force Base, Hawaii and the Royal Air Force Detachment is drawn in the form of an agreement. But it is not expressed to have been made on behalf of the UK and US Governments or even departments of them, and the parties are described as 'Host' and 'Tenant'. The 'final clauses' are not in normal treaty form. The US Base Commander and a British non-commissioned sergeant were the only signatories. The subject is the supply to the RAF detachment at the Base of various goods and services, including fuel and coffins. The preamble cites certain US federal legislation. The inescapable conclusion is that it was no more than a contract drawn up under US federal law, but the US still registered it as a treaty.[53]

---

[48] 1 USC §112b.

[49] See MTLP (n 2) 196. Most US treaties do not have to be submitted to the US Senate for its approval, and are known as 'congressional-executive agreements' or 'sole executive agreements'.

[50] 1 USC §112b(a).

[51] MTLP (n 2) 339–40. See also ibid 185 about Dutch legislation.

[52] See the Austria–US Memorandum of Understanding on Double Taxation (signed 31 May 1996, entered into force 1 February 1998) 2009 UNTS 328.

[53] (Signed 21 April 1981) 1285 UNTS 97.

Whereas the practice of other States seems to be fairly consistent as to the use of particular terminology to distinguish MOUs from treaties, US practice is less consistent. This results in some instruments having uncertain status in international law. The China–US Memorandum of Understanding on Protection of Intellectual Property 1992 states that the two governments 'reached a mutual understanding' but includes some treaty language.[54] The Memorandum of Understanding between the same two States on Prohibitions on Import and Export Trade of Prison Labour Products 1992 says in the preamble that they 'have reached the following understanding', but then says that 'The Parties agree'.[55] The operative provisions use MOU terminology, but the final clauses and testimonium[56] are in treaty form.

Most collaborative defence projects with the US are effected by means of MOUs because of the, often and readily understandable, need for confidentiality, and the ease with which MOUs can be amended.[57] But, perhaps because of perceived requirements of US federal law, the US Government has sometimes regarded them as treaties. By 1993, the US had some twenty-two defence Memorandums of Understanding with the UK.[58] Some were clearly treaties, but the rest, although only MOUs, had been registered by the US as treaties.[59] This was unacceptable to the UK. Australia and Canada had the same problem with the US. As a result, the US concluded a so-called 'Chapeau Agreement' with each of the three States. This is a treaty containing ready-made provisions on matters such as the legal status of armed service personnel and liability.[60] When an MOU for a collaborative defence project with the US needs to provide for such matters, it will state that the relevant terms of the Chapeau Agreement will apply; and the US should not register the MOU as a treaty. In a similar way, an MOU provision that specified persons will be accorded certain immunities may well make reference to provisions of the 1961 Vienna Convention on Diplomatic Relations.[61]

It seems that from at least 1993 even unclassified US defence MOUs have not been registered as treaties with the UN, but references to them still appear in the US *Treaties and Other International Acts Series* (TIAS), which includes all those instruments that have to be notified to Congress under the Case Act. These

---

[54] (Signed 17 January 1992) 2249 UNTS 314.

[55] [1992] 31 ILM 1071, 1072.

[56] For an explanation of these two terms, see MTLP (n 2) 434–44.

[57] For a recent example, see the MOU Regarding Prevention of the Supply of Arms and Related Material to Terrorist Groups (Israel–US) (2009) *International Law In Brief* (ILIB). Paragraph 7 refers to the Memorandum as containing 'ongoing political commitments' and is drawn up in strict MOU form.

[58] See Office of the Legal Adviser, *Treaties in Force* (US State Dept Pub 9433 1997) 290–3.

[59] See eg MOU concerning the Transfer of Technical Data relating to the JT-1OD Jet Engine Collaboration Agreement to Third Countries (signed 30 December 1976) 1068 UNTS 437.

[60] See Defence Co-operation Arrangements Exchange of Notes (UK–US) (1993) 1967 UNTS 86. See also J McNeill, 'International Agreements: Recent US–UK Practice Concerning the Memorandum of Understanding' (1994) 88 AJIL 821–6, though his views on the status of MOUs must be treated with caution since they were based on an unfortunate misunderstanding of the approach taken by the ILC to MOUs.

[61] (Opened for signature 18 April 1961, entered into force 24 April 1964) 500 UNTS 95.

instruments do not seem to figure in the US *Treaties in Force*.[62] Generally, the US continues to conclude instruments it regards as non-legally binding without any legislative involvement, although there are recent questions about the practice's constitutionality.[63]

III. How and Why States Use MOUs Rather Than Treaties

Today MOUs are employed in most areas of international relations—defence, trade, aid, transport, diplomacy, etc. In fact, they may be found in any area. In many cases, all things being equal, a treaty could be used. Frequently MOUs supplement treaties, like the MOUs accompanying many bilateral air services agreements, and which are treated as commercially confidential. The UK had over one hundred air services agreements, and most were supplemented by confidential MOUs.[64] But the UK is by no means exceptional in this; it has been normal practice in international civil aviation for decades.

MOUs like the Helsinki Final Act 1975[65] and the NATO–Russia Founding Act 1997[66] were of course disseminated widely because of their high *political* importance. Although such instruments are most often cited as examples of MOUs, they are not typical of the numerous MOUs concluded each year, which are usually concerned with more mundane matters, and are of little interest outside the narrow circle of those who have to negotiate and implement them. But all who wish to know more about treaties should be aware of the thousands of such MOUs and the important role they play.[67]

Even when the subject matter is not particularly sensitive, it may still be convenient to conclude a quite short 'umbrella' *treaty*, with the detailed provisions being put into one or more *MOUs*. All ministers prefer to be photographed signing treaties rather than MOUs and so their press officers may describe a *classified* MOU as an 'agreement', especially when copies cannot be made available to the media.

The main reasons for using MOUs in preference to treaties are confidentiality and convenience, of which there are various aspects.[68]

---

[62] See US–Russia Antitrust MOU (n 30). *Treaties in Force* may now be a defunct publication, having fallen decades behind TIAS as a publication source for US treaties. The best source of current US treaty-making now appears to be on the US Department of State website at <http://www.state.gov/s/l/treaty>.

[63] See generally Hollis and Newcomer (n 5).

[64] See A Aust, 'Air Services Agreements: Current UK Procedures and Policies' [1985] *Air Law* 189, 200–1. Many air services agreements between the US and EU States have wholly or partially been overtaken by so-called 'open skies' agreements.

[65] [1975] 14 ILM 1293.

[66] [1997] 36 ILM 1007.

[67] See MTLP (n 2) App C (it may be the first time an MOU on such an ordinary subject has been published, a *Memorandum of Understanding on Defence Contacts and Cooperation Between the Government of the Republic of Austria and the Government of the United Kingdom of Great Britain and Northern Ireland*).

[68] Other scholars have used different labels—such as flexibility, credibility, confidentiality, and domestic law—to identify the same criteria discussed here. See C Lipson, 'Why are Some International Agreements Informal?' (1991) 45 IO 495; K Raustiala, 'Form and Substance in International Agreements' (2005) 99 AJIL 581, 613.

A. Confidentiality

An obvious reason for preferring an MOU to a treaty is confidentiality. Since an MOU is not a treaty, there is generally no national or international requirement, or indeed need, to publish it. In the UK, even an unclassified MOU is not published unless there is a special reason, such as the political importance of the subject, or because it is closely associated with a treaty. Being neither a 'treaty' nor an 'international agreement', an MOU is not required by Article 102 of the UN Charter to be registered with the UN.[69] Of the many thousands of MOUs which have been concluded since 1945, only a handful appear in the *United Nations Treaty Series*, and then probably in error.[70] In any case, the mere act of registration does *not* make them treaties.[71]

Unlike Article 102 of the UN Charter, Article 83 of the Chicago Convention on International Civil Aviation 1944 provides that:

[A]ny contracting State may make *arrangements* not inconsistent with the provisions of this Convention. Any such arrangement shall be forthwith registered with the [ICAO] Council, which shall make it public as soon as possible.[72]

One might think this requirement is more extensive than Article 102. But whatever the original intention, the practice of the parties to the Chicago Convention shows that the vast majority do not consider the requirement extends to MOUs. Not surprisingly, very few of the MOUs which accompany air services agreements have been registered with ICAO. The registration rules adopted by ICAO define 'arrangements' to include arrangements between States and *airlines*, and a few of these have been registered with ICAO.

Many arrangements, especially in the defence field and other sensitive areas, are naturally kept confidential for reasons of national security, and are therefore found only in classified MOUs.[73] All States do this, and no one would suggest that they should be publicly available, although it is sometimes necessary for national parliaments to be informed of their contents on a selective or confidential basis.[74] Often, a defence treaty will have numerous MOUs supplementing it. Given the importance of the subject matter, the UK–US Polaris Sales Agreement 1963 might seem surprisingly short, just fifteen articles.[75] But a careful reading will show that it is an

---

[69] See MTLP (n 2) 339–40.

[70] About US practice, see nn 45–63 above and MTLP (n 2) 39–42.

[71] See MTLP (n 2) 344–6.

[72] Convention on International Civil Aviation (signed 7 December 1944, entered into force 4 April 1947) 15 UNTS 295 (emphasis added).

[73] For example, US Secretary of State Henry Kissinger gave confidential security assurances to Israel in the context of negotiating the Sinai Peace Accords. Some of these he clearly regarded as non-legally binding (although at least one of the MOUs *was* a treaty). See Early Warning System Agreement (US–Israel) (1975) 26 UST 2271; Memorandum of Understanding (Israel–US) (1975) 32 UST 2150; M Medzini (ed), *Israeli Ministry of Foreign Affairs, 3 Israel's Foreign Relations: Selected Documents 1974–77* (Ministry of Foreign Affairs, Jerusalem 1982) 281–90 (reproducing texts of Sinai Peace Accords).

[74] See n 45 *et seq* about the Case Act.

[75] (Signed 6 April 1963) 479 UNTS 49. Polaris was a submarine-launched ballistic missile with a nuclear warhead. It has now been replaced by Trident.

'umbrella' treaty. Article II(2) provides that each party's representatives are author-ized 'to enter into such *technical arrangements*, consistent with this Agreement, as may be necessary' (emphasis added). This is a reference to the immensely detailed (and very highly classified) technical and financial MOUs which were necessary during the life of the Agreement. The UK–US Agreement on the use of Ascension Island 1985 is even more explicit on the question of the instrument to be used for recording the detailed arrangements. The treaty has only one substantive para-graph, which provides that the arrangements:

shall be established in a *memorandum of understanding* to be concluded between the Ministry of Defence representing the Government of the United Kingdom and the Department for Defense [*sic*] representing the Government of the United States.[76]

Another reason for the use of MOUs is to protect sensitive commercial information or other security concerns.[77] This is particularly so when governments are involved in obtaining concessions or contracts for their companies, or where governments act as proxies for companies. The confidential MOU associated with an air services agreement, under which traffic rights and capacity entitlements are laid down, is the prime example.[78]

Although most implementing MOUs are made under bilateral treaties, they are also done for certain multilateral treaties, especially in the defence field.

B. Convenience

1. Lack of formality

With an MOU, there is no need for elaborate final clauses or the formalities (international or national) which surround treaty-making. More often than in the case of a treaty, an MOU will become effective on signature without the need for *any* further procedure. Thus, an MOU can generally be negotiated, signed and come into effect more quickly than a treaty. Even when a treaty enters into force on signature, the internal procedures required before it can be adopted may be lengthy. In some cases, these problems may be such that the only practicable way of proceeding is by way of an MOU. Not being a treaty, an MOU is generally not subject to any constitutional procedures, such as presentation to Parliament, though that will depend on the constitution, laws, and practice of each State. The liberalized arrangements regarding air services which the UK negotiated in the 1980s with several European States were each embodied in an MOU called 'Agreed Record of Discussions'. This enabled the arrangements, which were experimental,

---

[76] (Signed 25 March 1985) 1443 UNTS 25 (emphasis added). See also Art 7 (reference to 'implementing arrangements') of the Co-operation in Research and Development of Weapons Detec-tion and Protection-Related Technologies Agreement 2002 (UK–US) (2004) UKTS 23.

[77] Channel Tunnel Act 1987 Ch 53 §11(1)(a), 49 (provides for secondary legislation to implement 'international arrangements'). In 1993, France and the UK concluded an MOU, the Special Arrange-ment on Security Measures. See also *R (Channel Tunnel Group Limited) v Secretary of State* [2000] EWHC Admin 425.

[78] See text accompanying n 72.

to come into effect quickly; and the MOU form made it much easier to modify them in the light of experience.

Like treaties, MOUs are signed by ministers or senior officials, though probably more often by senior officials than is the case for treaties.[79] This is, however, more a reflection of the generally lower importance of the subject matter. There are significant exceptions when the MOU is a statement of high political intent, such as the Helsinki Final Act 1975[80] and the NATO–Russia Founding Act 1997,[81] both of which were signed by Heads of State and Government.

2. Amendment

A distinct advantage of the MOU is the ease with which it can be amended. Since it is not a treaty, any amendment can be effected with the same ease and speed as the MOU itself was concluded. Even when a treaty has a built-in simplified procedure for amendment, that will still involve certain formalities.[82] In the case of arrangements, such as on collaborative defence projects or development aid, that involve complicated technical or financial provisions, there is often a need to make frequent (and sometimes major) modifications. When the arrangements are multilateral, the need for a method of amendment with the least possible formality and delay is often essential for their effectiveness.[83] This is where the MOU form comes in very useful.

3. Termination

The termination provisions of many MOUs can be quite similar to those found in treaties. A period of notice is usually provided for, although this may be less than the six to twelve months commonly found in treaties. Sometimes there is no provision for termination, especially when the MOU is supplementary to a treaty. Difficult questions can then arise. A free-standing MOU can probably be terminated by giving reasonable notice, although, since it is not a legally binding instrument, failure to give due notice may, at least as a matter of law, have no consequences. On the other hand, if the MOU is supplementary to a treaty, and the MOU has no termination clause, can it be terminated before the treaty itself is

---

[79] Signature, however, may not always be required to create an MOU. Neither the Rio Declaration nor the Shanghai Communiqué were signed by the participants. See Rio Declaration on Environment and Development (1992) UN Doc A/CONF.151/26 vol I; US–China Joint Communiqué (1972) Dept State Bull 435 ('Shanghai Communiqué').

[80] [1975] 14 ILM 1293.

[81] [1997] 36 ILM 1007.

[82] For further discussion of traditional and tacit forms of treaty amendment, see Chapter 14.

[83] The MOUs accompanying the Basel Banking Accords and the work of the Financial Action Task Force are two examples of this phenomenon. Basel Committee on Banking Supervision, 'Basel II Accords: International Convergence of Capital Measurement and Capital Standards: A Revised Framework 2006' available at <http://www.bis.org/publ/bcbs128.pdf>; 'Recommendations of the Financial Action Task Force 2003' available at <http://www.fatf-gafi.org/dataoecd/7/40/34849567. PDF>.

terminated? Much may depend upon its purpose. If it is essential for the implementation of the treaty, the arguments against termination of the MOU only are stronger. But again, since it is not legally binding, there should be no *legal* obstacle to giving immediate notice, although *politically* it could be damaging.

4. Dispute settlement

An MOU will usually have some provision regarding the settlement of disputes about its interpretation or application, and typically will provide that they will be settled by negotiation and *not* referred to any third party, court or tribunal. This provision is sometimes inserted as a further indication that the instrument is not intended to be legally binding.

Although Article 102(2) of the UN Charter provides that unregistered treaties cannot be invoked before organs of the UN, including the ICJ, in practice they can be invoked before that Court.[84] It therefore follows that an MOU could also be invoked, though whether this would help the legal argument may depend on whether, in the particular circumstances, the MOU has any legal consequences.[85]

5. Interpretation

For the interpretation and application of MOUs, it is convenient and reasonable to apply by analogy the rules for the interpretation of treaties in so far as they are not at variance with the non-legally binding nature of MOUs. The *travaux* of an MOU may be as important as those of a treaty, though they may be even more difficult to find. In certain cases, an MOU might well constitute a subsidiary or subsequent agreement for the purposes of Article 31(2)(a) or (3)(a).[86]

6. Agreements With non-States

When a State wishes to enter into an agreement with a non-State, or part of a federal State which has not been given delegated treaty-making power, it can often best be done by using an MOU.[87] To the extent that MOUs rest on political and moral bases, rather than international law, there is no reason to limit their creation to the actors who can make treaties.

C. Dangers in using MOUs

A too easy recourse to MOUs can carry dangers. We have already seen the problem of disagreement as to status, but there are other problems.

---

[84] See MTLP (n 2) 346 (discussing *Qatar v Bahrain* (*Jurisdiction and Admissibility*) [1994] ICJ Rep 112 [26]–[27]).
[85] See the discussion accompanying nn 113–17.
[86] See MTLP (n 2) 234 *et seq*; see also Chapter 19, Part II.A.2, 482 *et seq*.
[87] See MTLP (n 2) 61–5.

1. Respect for MOUs may be seen as less important than for treaties

Because an MOU is not legally binding, sometimes there may be a temptation not to take the commitments in it as seriously as those in a treaty. This would be to ignore the fact that *political* commitments engage the good faith of States. Even though failure to carry out an MOU does not usually have *legal* consequences, that certainly does not mean that a State is free, politically or morally, to disregard it. In transmitting an arms control treaty to the US Senate for example, the United States Department of State advised:

An undertaking or commitment that is understood to be legally binding carries with it both the obligation of each Party to comply with the undertaking and the right of each Party to enforce the obligation under international law. A 'political' undertaking is not governed by international law . . . Until and unless a party extricates itself from its 'political undertaking', which it may do without legal penalty, it has given a promise to honor that commitment, and the other Party has every reason to be concerned about compliance with such undertakings. If a Party contravenes a political commitment, it will be subject to an appropriate political response.[88]

Thus, not only would it be dishonourable to disregard an MOU, but it could also provoke a damaging political response.[89] For example, when North Korea failed to follow through on a political commitment to suspend uranium enrichment, the US suspended aid it had promised to provide and sought international sanctions.[90]

2. Possible lack of care in drafting

There may still be a slight tendency among some government officials to regard the drafting of an MOU as not requiring quite the same close attention as the drafting of a treaty. If so, this is most regrettable. In many cases, the content of an MOU could equally well be put into a treaty, and an error in the drafting of an MOU could give rise to the same friction in relations as an error in a treaty. Even though the commitments in an MOU are only political, that is no reason for them to be expressed with less precision than they would be in a treaty.

Depending on the constitution and internal procedures of each State, it will not usually be essential for the foreign ministry to draft all MOUs. However, when another ministry drafts an MOU it should consult the foreign ministry before sending the draft to another government, and at all key stages thereafter. It is the task of the foreign ministry to explain the differences between a treaty and an MOU; why one rather than the other may be advantageous (or not) in the particular case; and to ensure that the form and wording is appropriate for

---

[88] 'Transmittal of the Treaty with the USSR on the Reduction and Limitation of Strategic Offensive Arms' (1991) S Treaty Doc 102–20, 1086.

[89] See also P Kooijmans, 'The International Court of Justice and the Law of the Sea—Some Reflections' in J Makarczyk (ed), *The Theory of International Law at the Threshold of the 21st Century* (Brill Academic Publishers, Dordrecht 1995) 425–30.

[90] See S Harrison, 'Time to Leave Korea' (2001) 80(2) *Foreign Affairs* 62, 67.

whichever instrument is chosen. Unfortunately, too often another ministry may produce a draft which is a mixture of treaty and MOU language, or a draft which uses mostly treaty language but is headed 'Memorandum of Understanding' in the mistaken belief that this is the magic phrase which makes it not legally binding. The foreign ministry must then try to put matters right.

3. Lack of implementing legislation

Although an MOU is not legally binding, that does not mean that it may not need to be implemented in domestic law. The US, for example, implemented the multilateral Kimberley Process MOU on eliminating trade in 'blood diamonds' via statute.[91] MOUs are also often on the status of armed forces sent to another State. Sometimes the law needed to implement such an MOU will already be in place, but if not, care must be taken to ensure that the MOU will not come into effect until any necessary primary or secondary implementing legislation has been made. This possible complication may be more important for those States with so-called 'monist' constitutions under which treaties (but not MOUs) have to be approved by the legislature, whereupon they may automatically become part of the law of that State.[92] Some 'dualist' constitutions, including that of the UK, make use of 'umbrella' primary legislation which authorizes the government to make secondary legislation to give effect to 'arrangements' entered into with another State, the term 'arrangements' being chosen because it is broad enough to embrace both treaties and MOUs.[93]

4. Difficulty in finding MOUs

One important practical advantage of a treaty is that, being published (usually in a special series) and, hopefully, also registered with the UN, it is much easier to find, not only by members of the public, but also by officials. MOUs are very easily 'mislaid'. Those officials responsible for implementing an MOU should keep a copy of it (the signed text, *not* even what seems to be the final draft) somewhere easily accessible and, perhaps even more important, where their successors will be able to find it (ie not only in the archives). As a fail-safe measure, since January 1997 the Treaty Section of the UK MFA (Foreign and Commonwealth Office (FCO)), in principle, keeps a copy of each MOU concluded either by the FCO or by other ministries. If this practice is kept up, it should have the added advantage of providing a set of useful precedents.

---

[91] Clean Diamond Trade Act, 19 USC §§3901–13 (2003); Interlaken Declaration on Kimberley Process Certification Scheme for Rough Diamonds (5 November 2002) available at <http://www.kimberleyprocess.com/download/getfile/5>.

[92] About monism and dualism, see MTLP (n 2) 181–2.

[93] See the (UK) Visiting Forces Act 1952, s 1(2).

IV. The Legal Status of MOUs

A. Are MOUs really treaties?

This question is still being asked, and so needs a reply. MOUs do not fit neatly into international law simply because they are a means of *avoiding* international legal obligations. But, Professor Klabbers has expressed doubts whether the distinction between MOUs and treaties is valid in international law. He has argued that every 'agreement' concluded between States which is of a normative nature (in that it attempts to influence future behaviour), and is not made subject to another system of law (eg domestic law), is a treaty.[94] He sees no distinction between a treaty (as defined in the VCLT) and an MOU, since each embodies an agreement, though this argument does not take into account the clear views of the ILC.[95]

Professor Klabbers' sweeping assertion also runs up against the fact that when States do not intend to enter into a legally binding instrument they generally make this clear by a deliberate and careful choice of words. He argues that intention is not decisive. But to argue so ignores, *first*, the history behind the definition of 'treaty' in the VCLT. We have already seen that the ILC saw the definition in its draft articles as including the intention to create legal obligations. The records of the Conference which adopted the VCLT confirm this vital element. A Swiss amendment to exclude expressly 'political declarations and gentlemen's agreements' was rejected, apparently because it was believed to be unnecessary since such documents were not 'governed by international law' and were therefore already excluded.[96] *Second*, Professor Klabbers' theory is incompatible with the basic principle that a State is free to exercise (or not to exercise) its treaty-making power. States can make agreements between themselves which are binding only in domestic law.[97] Moreover, there is no principle or rule in the law of treaties or general international law that requires that every transaction between States has to be legally binding, or, more particularly, to be embodied in a treaty. *Third*, the hypothesis is just not supported by the *extensive practice* of States.

To take a recent prominent example, the NATO Member States and Russia were from the start of their negotiations at pains to ensure that there would be no misunderstanding about the status of their Founding Act 1997.[98] Since it was eventually agreed that it should be only politically binding, it was most carefully

---

[94] J Klabbers, *The Concept of Treaty in International Law* (Kluwer Law International, The Hague 1996). See the critical reviews by practitioners and academics: I Sinclair (1997) 91 AJIL 748–50; P Keller (1998) 47 ICLQ 240–1; C Hopkins (1997) 67 BYBIL 278–80, and especially Ahlström (n 10) 60–5. For Professor Klabbers most recent views on the subject, see 'Not Revisiting the Concept of Treaty' in A Orakhelashvili and S Williams (eds), *Forty Years of the Vienna Convention on the Law of Treaties* (BIICL, London 2010).

[95] See n 8 and accompanying text.

[96] See UN Conference on the Law of Treaties, Official Records: Documents of the Conference, A/CONF. 39/11/Add 2, 234; Schachter (n 34) n19.

[97] See MTLP (n 2) 30–1.

[98] [1997] 36 ILM 1007.

drafted to avoid all the normal treaty language, thus demonstrating their mutual intention not to conclude a treaty.[99]

Although not decisive, registration with the UN naturally raises a presumption that the instrument is a treaty. The act of registration is rarely challenged at the time, yet, due to the failure by States to register, the process of registration is far from perfect.[100] Moreover, non-registration is not necessarily evidence of lack of an intention to conclude a treaty.[101] Yet, if MOUs are really treaties one would expect this to be reflected in the registration practice of States under Article 102 of the Charter. MOUs are numerous, and many—possibly the majority—are not confidential. But, as we have seen, the assertion that there is no real distinction between a treaty and an MOU is not supported by the registration practice of States. Few MOUs are registered. At the same time, of the 1,000 instruments called 'Memorandum of Understanding' so far submitted for registration, roughly 10 per cent have been rejected. This may indicate that when an instrument is clearly not a treaty, it will be refused registration. In borderline cases, the United Nations seems to err on the side of caution by registering the instrument, registration not being conclusive as to whether it is a treaty.[102]

The theory of Professor Klabbers, although thought provoking, relies heavily on academic writings, interpretations of judicial decisions and philosophical arguments. He finds strong support in the 1994 decision of the ICJ in *Qatar v Bahrain (Jurisdiction and Admissibility)*,[103] which held that an instrument not in customary treaty form was nevertheless a treaty. The Court had to consider the legal effect of two instruments. The first was the treaty constituted by a double exchange of letters between Bahrain and Saudi Arabia and between Qatar and Saudi Arabia.[104] The second were the minutes of a meeting in 1990 between representatives of the three States, the minutes being signed by their foreign ministers. The minutes listed the matters which had been 'agreed' (the term, in Arabic, used in the minutes). The minutes were not registered with the UN by Qatar until six months later, and only ten days before it made its Application to the Court. Bahrain protested the registration, and asserted before the Court that the minutes were not legally binding. But the Court found that they constituted a treaty. Professor Klabbers sees the judgment as 'monumental' in that, in his view, it demonstrates that any document containing commitments by States is a treaty, regardless of form or other considerations, in particular whether or not the States intended it to be binding.[105]

---

[99] R Mullerson, 'NATO Enlargement and the NATO-Russia Founding Act: The Interplay of Law and Politics' (1998) 47 ICLQ 192–204.

[100] See MTLP (n 2) ch 19.

[101] See text accompanying nn 35–6, 69–72; MTLP (n 2) 344–6.

[102] See Chapter 10, Part I, 250 *et seq.* for a discussion of depositary practices, particularly at the UN.

[103] [1994] ICJ Rep 112.

[104] See MTLP (n 2) 22.

[105] See J Klabbers, 'Qatar v. Bahrain: The Concept of "Treaty" in International Law' (1995) 33 Archiv des Völkerrechts 361–76, and summarized in his doctoral thesis. See also E Vierdag, 'The International Court of Justice and the Law of Treaties', and E Lauterpacht, '"Partial" Judgments and the Inherent Jurisdiction of the International Court of Justice', in V Lowe and M Fitzmaurice (eds), *Fifty Years of the International Court of Justice* (CUP, Cambridge 1996) 145–66 and 465–86

Although the decision was almost certainly a compromise to paper over a difference of opinion between the judges, given the particular facts of the case the Court's decision is not so remarkable. The commitments were written down, the text recording what the parties had 'agreed'. The three foreign ministers signed the minutes. The form of minutes of a meeting may have been unusual, but the form—as opposed to the wording—does not determine whether an instrument is a treaty. The minutes may well be at the other end of a spectrum which begins with treaties drawn up in the most formal manner, such as the UN Charter. Although it is not for the Court to speculate as to the intention of the parties, it did what any court has to do, it *inferred* their intention from the text of the minutes and the surrounding circumstances, not from what the parties asserted later. The Court had previously approached the matter in various ways, and it would be wrong to conclude that the judgment is a significant departure from basic treaty principles or practice.[106] The judgment will certainly be valuable if it means that States will be more careful in future in the way they express themselves, particularly when drafting minutes of meetings and diplomatic communiqués. Also, it should not be forgotten that the circumstances which led to the judgment in *Qatar v Bahrain* were exceptional and the case was decided on its own particular facts. In the vast majority of cases, the status of an instrument may not be in dispute.

Professor Klabbers seems to have assumed that State practice in the use of MOUs is neither widespread nor unambiguous. But he did not test his theory by finding out what is the actual practice. States usually choose, consciously and deliberately, to express their intentions by using either the well-established forms and terminology of the treaty, or that of the MOU. All too often, he cites untypical international instruments, instead of the vast quantity of MOUs on ordinary—yet admittedly often mind-numbing—subjects. And, he does not deal at all with the need to keep certain arrangements confidential. Although MOUs are generally not published, and therefore not easy to find, Professor Klabbers, though still holding his theory, has acknowledged that he did not give much weight to State practice, finding it advisable to distance himself somewhat from it, being not necessarily convinced of its normative effect.[107]

B. Are MOUs 'soft law'?

It is not easy to answer this question since there is no agreement on what is 'soft law', or indeed if it exists at all as a distinct source of law.[108] However, 'soft law' is generally used to describe international instruments which their makers recognize

respectively; S Rosenne, 'The Qatar/Bahrain Case: What is a Treaty? A Framework Agreement and the Seising of the Court' (1995) 8 LJIL 161, 165.

[106] See Ahlström (n 10) 165–70; C Chinkin, 'A Mirage in the Sand? Distinguishing Binding and Non-Binding Relations Between States' (1997) 10 LJIL 223–47.

[107] Letter to the author, 28 August 1996.

[108] *Handbook* (n 23) 11; see also A Boyle, 'Some Reflections on the Relationship of Treaties and Soft Law' (1999) 48 ICLQ 901–13; H Hillgenberg, 'A Fresh Look at Soft Law' (1999) 10 EJIL 499; P Birnie and others, *International Law and the Environment* (3rd edn OUP, Oxford 2009) 34–7.

are not treaties, even if they employ mandatory language such as 'shall', but have as their purpose the promulgation of principles or rules (albeit not legally binding) which the authors of the text hope will become of general or universal application. (It can also be a description of provisions in a treaty which are of such generality that they cannot form the basis of legal rights and obligations.) Such non-treaty instruments are typically given names such as Guidelines, Principles, Declarations, Codes of Practice, Recommendations, and Programmes. They are frequently found in the economic, social, and environmental fields. The Rio Declaration on Environment and Development 1992 is just one example.[109] The subject matter is usually not yet well enough developed, or there is no consensus on the content of the principles or rules for them to be embodied in a treaty. Raustiala perceptively points out that since a soft law instrument is not intended to be legally binding, it cannot be law; and that the choice between what he calls, 'contracts' (treaties) and 'pledges' (non-treaties) is made consciously by the negotiating States.[110]

Soft law instruments can therefore represent an intermediate stage in treaty-making,[111] and sometimes never get beyond that stage. But some norms do, such as those in the Universal Declaration of Human Rights 1948, which have been the inspiration for many universal and regional human rights treaties. All such soft law instruments are MOUs in the sense that there is no intention that they should themselves be legally binding. The main difference between them and most other MOUs is that soft law MOUs are usually multilateral, seek to lay down universal norms, and are published and disseminated widely. In contrast, the majority of MOUs are bilateral. Even when they are multilateral, they do not generally lay down universal norms, and (whether multilateral or bilateral) are seldom published even when unclassified.

C. The possible international legal consequences of MOUs: estoppel

But can a non-legally binding instrument, like an MOU, nevertheless give rise to some legal consequences? The question is perplexing. At first sight, it would seem that an MOU has effect only in the realm of politics. If a State does not carry out its commitments the sanction is political, which may be why MOUs are often said to be 'politically binding'. Another State cannot take the matter to an international court or tribunal or impose the countermeasures it might be entitled to take in the case of breach of a treaty,[112] though the State can, of course, show its displeasure by resorting to the (undervalued) right of retorsion (retaliation by a State by means

---

[109] [1992] 31 ILM 876. Other examples include the Non-Legally Binding Authoritative Statement of Principles for a Global Consensus on the Management, Conservation and Sustainable Development of all Types of Forests (n 27); UN Conference on the Human Environment, Final Declaration (5–16 June 1972) (1973) UN Doc A/CONF.48/14, [1972] 11 ILM 1416; American Declaration of the Rights and Duties of Man (1948) OAS Res XXX, OAS Official Rec OEA/Ser.L./V./II.23, doc 21 rev 6; Universal Declaration of Human Rights (10 December 1948) GA Res 217A (III), UN Doc A/810 71.

[110] Raustiala (n 68) 588–91.

[111] See A Boyle and C Chinkin, *The Making of International Law* (OUP, Oxford 2007) esp ch 5.

[112] See MTLP (n 2) 362 *et seq*; *Handbook* (n 23) 391–4.

which are not illegal, such as breaking off diplomatic relations) in response to an act done by another State.[113] But might there nevertheless be some means of legal redress?

The question can be posed thus: can one State conclude bilateral arrangements (to use a neutral term) about, say, status of forces, with two other States, using in one case a treaty and in the other an MOU (there are many examples where the difference is only in the form and terminology, the substance being very similar). Can the State then treat the MOU as no more than an expression of political will? In choosing an MOU rather than a treaty, does a State have to give up all the advantages of a legally binding instrument, in particular enforceability, in return for confidentiality, speed, flexibility, etc?

Take the case of an MOU between State A and State B under which State A expresses its 'intention' to pay State B four billion euros over a period of ten years to pay half the cost of building a dam. State B then starts building the dam. After five years, the dam is half-built and State A has paid out two billion euros. It then has a change of government, and the new one decides to stop the funding. Although much may depend on the circumstances and the precise terms of the MOU, the intention of State A as expressed in the MOU *may* have legal consequences. Depending on the intention of the State making it and the circumstances, a unilateral declaration can be binding in international law. Underlying this is the fundamental international law principle of good faith.[114] *Good faith* also underpins the legal doctrine of estoppel (preclusion), which in international law is a substantive rule and broader and less technical than estoppel in the common law, being founded on the principle that *good faith* must prevail throughout international relations. The exact scope of the international law doctrine is far from settled, but in general it may be said that where a clear statement or representation is made by State A to State B, which then in good faith State B *relies upon it to its detriment*, State A is estopped from going back on its statement or representation.[115] Similarly, if two States choose to record the settlement of a dispute between them in an MOU rather than in a treaty—perhaps for reasons of confidentiality—each is clearly estopped from denying that the terms of the settlement are binding, though it is rather the agreement to settle (as expressed in the MOU) that is binding in international law, not the MOU itself—a fine distinction perhaps, but nevertheless critical.[116]

But if there are certain cases where the conclusion and operation of an MOU could give rise to legal consequences, does it make sense not to regard it as a treaty?

---

[113] See *Handbook* (n 23) 311.

[114] Ibid 8; A Watts, 'The Legal Position in International Law of Heads of States, Heads of Government and Foreign Ministers' (1994-III) 247 RcD 114–28.

[115] See *Land, Island and Maritime Frontier (El Salvador/Honduras/Nicaragua)* [1990] ICJ Rep 92 [63]; R Jennings and A Watts, *Oppenheim's International Law* (9th edn OUP, Oxford 2008) 527 n6; Thirlway (n 11) 36. See also Ahlström (n 10) 188–224.

[116] See the award in the *UK–US Heathrow User Charges Arbitration* (1994) 102 ILR 215, 261–564; B Cheng, *General Principles of Law: As Applied by International Courts and Tribunals* (CUP, Cambridge 1987) 137 *et seq*, in particular the discussion of the *Portendic* case.

The distinction between a treaty (which creates legal rights and obligations) and an MOU (which does not, but which may in certain, special circumstances have legal consequences) may seem rather subtle, but in diplomacy, subtlety is often essential. No State is obliged to conclude a treaty.[117] In the exercise of its sovereignty, each State is free to deny itself the benefits—such as they are—of a treaty in exchange for the different advantages offered by an MOU. The MOU has shown itself to be essential for the efficient conduct of much business between States. Used properly the MOU poses no threat; rather, it has been proved to be an indispensable complement to the process of treaty-making.

D. MOUs in domestic courts[118]

A final question is: to what extent will domestic courts apply an MOU? Domestic judges are probably right to be suspicious at first of anything that is not a treaty, and yet is not made under domestic or foreign law. Fortunately common law courts (I cannot write with any authority about other national legal systems) are now more open to arguments that draw on less traditional sources. For example, judges are right to consider scholarly writings.[119] A modern judge will try to look at material that is not either legislation or treaties and ask whether it might be relevant to an issue in the case. If so, does it come from an authoritative source? Might it help to do justice in the case? Is there a legal 'hook' (ie basis) on which the material can be hung?

Although in dualist systems international customary law is part of domestic law, if legislation is ambiguous it must be interpreted so as to avoid any conflict with obligations of international customary law. But if the legislation is clear, it will prevail even if it conflicts with those obligations.[120] Even when a treaty is in force for the dualist forum State it is only part of the domestic law to the extent that legislation has made it part of domestic law (ie incorporated).[121]

But, common law judges are now much more familiar with international law. If a judge is referred to an *un*incorporated treaty, or an MOU, which might be relevant to an issue before him, he would usually agree to read it and hear argument about its relevance to the dispute before the judge. Whether he will refer to the instrument in his judgment will depend on how relevant it is and whether he can find a legal 'hook'. In the celebrated case of *Kuwait Airways v Iraqi Airways (No 2)*[122] the House of Lords (sitting as the highest court of appeal of the UK on 1 October 2009; now replaced by the Supreme Court of the UK) decided that it would be

---

[117] See MTLP (n 2) 31 about *pactum de contrahendo*.

[118] See A Aust, 'Domestic Consequences of Non-Treaty (Non-Conventional) Treaty-Making' in R Wolfrum and V Röben (eds), *Developments of International Law in Treaty Making* (Springer, Berlin 2005) 487–96.

[119] That is to say writings which are based on careful analysis of the materials.

[120] See MTLP (n 2) 193 *et seq*.

[121] Ibid 187–8.

[122] [2002] UKHL 19; 125 ILR 677, 680–7.

contrary to public policy[123] to recognize the legal effectiveness of foreign legislation that was in breach of the UN Charter, and various resolutions of the Security Council, even though neither the Charter nor the resolutions had been incorporated into English law. Similarly, if a British airline seeks judicial review of the decision of the UK civil aviation authorities refusing it a licence to fly to a foreign country,[124] in deciding whether the decision had been properly arrived at the court will consider all relevant material, which includes the (unincorporated) air services agreement between the UK and the other State *and*, if helpful, any accompanying MOU. Most air services agreements are accompanied by such MOUs, which may also be regarded as subsidiary or subsequent agreements or instruments for the purposes of Article 31(2) or (3) of the Convention.[125]

The fact that an MOU is not legally binding means that to a common law court it may have a status similar to a treaty to which the State is *not* bound—even lower than an unincorporated treaty. But, if, for example, the case concerns legislation conferring discretionary powers on the government or other public bodies, the court should consider the lawfulness of the exercise of that discretion in the light of all relevant factors. So, if a court is considering whether a port authority has lawfully detained a foreign vessel, for example, it might well examine MOUs, such as the Paris Memorandum of Understanding on Port State Control 1982,[126] equivalent ones for the Caribbean (1996)[127] and other parts of the world, especially since they are now considered as reflecting customary international law.[128]

Conclusion

This chapter has reviewed the availability of States to create non-legally binding agreements, known generally as MOUs because of the title 'Memorandum of Understanding' that so many of these instruments bear. As non-legally binding agreements, MOUs are in a distinct category from treaties, although to confuse things sometimes treaties also have the title 'Memorandum of Understanding'. Thus, attention must be given to the parties' intentions in identifying which type of commitment was undertaken: legal or political.

MOUs offer several distinct advantages over treaty-making. Because an MOU is *not legally binding* like a treaty, it does not have to be published (though a few are). As a result, MOUs offer a greater chance at preserving confidentiality. Similarly, MOUs are generally more convenient to make than treaties; they are frequently less

---

[123] 'Public policy' is a common law principle developed through case law. It concerns legal acts that are seen by the courts as injurious to the public good, and this can change over time. It is not the policy of any British Government. See *Halsbury's Laws of England* (4th edn reissue, 1998) vol 9(1), [841]–[2].

[124] Given the 'open skies' type of regime for air services within the EU, the scope for relying on restrictive provisions in air services agreements between EU States must now be considerably less.

[125] See MTLP (n 2) 234 *et seq.*

[126] [1982] 21 ILM 1. It has been amended several times.

[127] [1997] 36 ILM 237.

[128] R Churchill and V Lowe, *The Law of the Sea* (3rd edn MUP, Manchester 1999) 274–6.

formal, and often can be quickly amended or terminated. On the other hand, MOUs do not supplant the treaty entirely; treaty commitments will frequently have greater credibility, and there is less risk in treaty-making of sloppy drafting or a lack of domestic implementation. All told, MOUs now reflect a significant component of States' practice, and that will likely continue to grow in the years to come.

Recommended Reading

C Ahlström, *The Status of Multilateral Export Control Regimes—An Examination of Legal and Non-Legal Agreements in International Cooperation* (Acta Universitatis Upsaliensis, Uppsala 1999)

A Aust, 'Domestic Consequences of Non-Treaty (Non-Conventional) Treaty-Making' in R Wolfrum and V Röben (eds), *Developments of International Law in Treaty Making* (Springer, Berlin 2005) 487

A Aust, *Modern Treaty Law and Practice* (2nd edn CUP, Cambridge 2007)

A Aust, 'The Theory & Practice of Informal International Instruments' (1986) 35 ICLQ 787

M Bothe, 'Legal and Non-Legal Norms—A Meaningful Distinction in International Relations?' (1980) 11 Netherlands Ybk Intl L 65

C Chinkin, 'A Mirage in the Sand? Distinguishing Binding and Non-Binding Relations Between States' (1997) 10 LJIL 223

PM Eisemann, '*Le* Gentleman's agreement *comme source du droit international*' (1979) 106 Journal du Droit International 326 (Fr)

W Fidler, 'Gentleman's Agreements' (1981) 7 EPIL 106

DB Hollis and JJ Newcomer, '"Political Commitments" and the Constitution' (2009) 49 VJIL 507

J Klabbers, *The Concept of Treaty in International Law* (Kluwer Law International, The Hague 1996)

C Lipson, 'Why are Some International Agreements Informal?' (1991) 45 IO 495

A McNair, *Law of Treaties* (Clarendon Press, Oxford 1961)

F Münch, 'Comments on the 1968 Draft Convention on the Law of Treaties: Non-binding Agreements' (1969) 29 Zeitschrift für Ausländisches Öffentliches Recht und Völkerrecht 1 (Gr)

K Raustiala, 'Form and Substance in International Agreements' (2005) 99 AJIL 581

O Schachter, 'The Twilight Existence of Nonbinding International Agreements' (1977) 71 AJIL 296

I Sinclair, *The Vienna Convention on the Law of Treaties* (2nd edn MUP, Manchester 1984)

M Virally, 'La distinction entre textes internationaux de portée juridique et textes internationaux déprouvus de portée juridique' (1983) 60 Annuaire de l'Institut de Droit International (Fr)

3

Who Can Make Treaties?
International Organizations

Olufemi Elias

Introduction

International organizations (IOs) are subjects of international law typically created by agreement between States, usually through treaties, for the achievement or furtherance of a common objective of the IO's creators. Modern international organizations play a variety of direct and indirect roles in the treaty process.[1] Indirectly, IOs provide a permanent forum where technical and legal experts may gather to facilitate treaty-making. Bodies such as the International Law Commission (ILC) or the UN Commission on International Trade Law regularly identify and research issues worthy of treaty-making, drafting texts that may form the basis for agreement among nation States. IOs also frequently set the agenda for treaty-making, initiating and hosting treaty negotiations that, depending on the IO and the subject, may produce treaties involving a limited number of States (for example, the Council of Europe's Convention on Cybercrime) or those having universal aspirations (for example, the UN-initiated Rome Statute on the International Criminal Court). Once a treaty exists, moreover, IOs can have extensive involvement in supervising the legal regime or directing its evolution.[2] Modern treaties:

often embrace a 'managerial' framework that ... provide[s] for continuing interpretation/modification or for supervision/monitoring through an existing IO, an IO created by the treaty itself, or 'treaty organs' that may or may not constitute an 'international organization' with distinct legal personality or a secretariat of its own.[3]

---

[1] On the roles of IOs in the treaty-making process, see Chapters 7, 10, 14, 16, and 17; see also P Sands and P Klein, *Bowett's Law of International Institutions* (5th edn Sweet & Maxwell, London 2001) (distinguishing between 'real law making by international organizations' and 'the preparation of inter-state law-making within an international organization'); JE Alvarez, *International Organizations as Law-makers* (OUP, Oxford 2005) 269–400; C Brölmann, *The Institutional Veil in Public International Law: International Organisations and the Law of Treaties* (Hart Publishing, Oxford 2007), Chapters 5–7; J Klabbers, *An Introduction to International Institutional Law* (2nd edn CUP, Cambridge 2009) 198–200, Chapters 5–6.

[2] See Chapter 17, Part III.C, 439 *et seq.* on how 'treaty bodies' play this role.

[3] Alvarez (n 1) 317.

Through all of these indirect mechanisms, IOs have undoubtedly and substantially changed how nation States form, apply, and interpret treaties.[4]

But IOs also play a direct role in treaty-making. They have the capacity to—and regularly do—become parties to treaties in their own right, within the scope of their competencies and where other parties are willing to enter into treaty relations with them.[5] This direct role is the focus of this chapter. In the 1948 *Reparations for Injuries* case, the International Court of Justice (ICJ) concluded that the UN exercised and enjoyed functions and rights that could only be explained on the basis of its possession of a large measure of international legal personality.[6] One of the considerations on which the Court based this conclusion was that 'practice—in particular the conclusion of conventions to which the Organization is a party—has confirmed the character of the Organization, which occupies a position in certain aspects in detachment from its Members'.[7] Today, more than sixty years on, the treaty-making capacity of IOs is certainly beyond doubt, as is clearly evident from the extensive literature on the subject[8] and the ILC's work leading to the Vienna Convention on the Law of Treaties between States and International Organizations or between International Organizations (1986 VCLT).[9]

---

[4] Whether these changes have improved treaty-making is a separate question. On the one hand, IO permanence improves the availability of information and technical expertise. It may also facilitate greater transparency particularly by expanding the diversity of actors involved in treaty-making, namely less powerful governments, non-governmental organizations, and the growing ranks of the international civil service. On the other hand, IOs may be perceived to favour one group of States over others, leading to forum shopping by interested States. IOs themselves, meanwhile, may seek to expand their authority or work to justify their continued existence in ways that may not be efficient for the international system as a whole. See the excellent treatment of this question by Alvarez (n 1) Chapter 6.

[5] Cf DB Hollis, 'Why State Consent Still Matters: Non-State Actors, Treaties, and the Changing Sources of International Law' (2005) 23 Berkeley J Intl Law 137, 161–5.

[6] *Reparations for Injuries Suffered in the Service of the United Nations* (Advisory Opinion) [1949] ICJ Rep 174, 178–9.

[7] Ibid 179.

[8] See eg R Higgins, *The Development of International Law through the Political Organs of the United Nations* (OUP, Oxford 1963); H Chiu, *The Capacity of International Organizations to Conclude Treaties and the Special Legal Aspects of Treaties so Concluded* (Martinus Nijhoff, Leiden 1966); K Zemanek (ed), *Agreements of International Organizations and the Vienna Convention on the Law of Treaties* (Springer Verlag, Vienna 1971) (38 Österreichisches Zeitschrift für öffentliches Recht und Völkerrecht, Supplementum 1); P Reuter, 'First Report on the Question of Treaties Concluded Between States and International Organizations or Between Two or More International Organizations' [1972] YBILC, vol II, 171; P Reuter, 'Second Report on the Question of Treaties Concluded Between States and International Organizations or Between Two or More International Organizations' [1973] YBILC, vol II, 75; P Reuter, 'Third Report on the Question of Treaties Concluded Between States and International Organizations or Between Two or More International Organizations' [1974] YBILC, vol II(1), 135; P Reuter, 'Fourth Report on the Question of Treaties Concluded Between States and International Organizations or Between Two or More International Organizations' [1975] YBILC, vol II, 25; P Reuter, 'Fifth Report on the Question of Treaties Concluded Between States and International Organizations or Between Two or More International Organizations' [1976] YBILC, vol II(1), 137; P Reuter, 'Sixth Report on the Question of Treaties Concluded Between States and International Organizations or Between Two or More International Organizations' [1977] YBILC, vol II(1), 119; J Dobbert, 'Evolution of Treaty-making Capacity of International Organizations' in *The Law and the Sea: Essays in Memory of Jean Carroz* (FAO, Rome 1987) 21–102; H Schermers and N Blokker, *International Institutional Law: Unity Within Diversity* (4th edn Martinus Nijhoff, Leiden 2004) esp §§ 1743–99; C Brölmann (n 1); J. Klabbers (n 1) Chapter 5.

[9] (Adopted 21 March 1986, not yet in force) [1986] 25 ILM 543.

This chapter begins with an overview of the early practice regarding IOs as parties to treaties. Part II reviews the main issues in the 1986 VCLT, including the ways in which it differs from the 1969 VCLT. Part III considers who is bound when an IO is a party to a treaty and Part IV reviews the types of treaties to which IOs are parties.

I. Recognizing the Capacity of IOs to Become Parties to Treaties

The traditional view was that only States had the capacity to make treaties.[10] Examples of treaty-making by IOs existed in the period before the Second World War but were uncommon.[11] In their 1962 Joint Dissenting Opinion in the *South-West Africa* cases, Judges Spender and Fitzmaurice expressed doubts as to whether international legal opinion in the 1920s would have accepted the conclusion that the League of Nations 'could have a legal personality separate and distinct from their Members and rank as entities "subjects of international law"'.[12] After the Second World War, however, doubts as to the distinct treaty-making capacity of IOs all but disappeared. The ability to enter into agreements was deemed necessary for IOs, in particular the nascent UN, to function.[13] Article 43 of the UN Charter provided for the Security Council to conclude agreements with Member States on the provision of armed forces, assistance, and facilities for the maintenance of international peace and security.[14] The regulations adopted by the General Assembly to give effect to Article 102 of the Charter expressly contemplated that the UN, specialized agencies, and intergovernmental organizations could be parties to a treaty.[15] The ICJ opinion in the *Reparations* case further confirmed these developments.[16] Seyersted famously wrote in 1964 that the treaty-making capacity of IOs derived from customary law to the effect that all intergovernmental organizations have inherent general treaty-making capacity: 'it has never been claimed in a concrete case that any of these treaties are invalid because the organization did

---

[10] See Chiu (n 8) 4.

[11] See eg ibid 8–15 (noting examples of agreements the League of Nations entered into in the 1920s, including the Treaty between the Principal and Allied and Associated Powers and the Serb-Croat-Slovene State (adopted 10 September 1919) UKTS 1919 17 [Cmd 461]. Such treaties were concluded and placed under the guarantee of the League of Nations and Chiu argues that the acceptance of this function by the Council of the League of Nations was equivalent to its concluding treaties).

[12] *South West Africa Cases (Ethiopia v South Africa; Liberia v South Africa)* (Preliminary Objections) [1962] ICJ Rep 465, 475 n1 (Joint Dissenting Opinion of Sir Percy Spender and Sir Gerald Fitzmaurice).

[13] See Higgins (n 8) 241–9.

[14] UN Charter Art 43(3) ('the agreement or agreements shall be negotiated as soon as possible on the initiative of the Security Council. They shall be concluded between the Security Council and Members or between the Security Council and groups of Members and shall be subject to ratification by the signatory States in accordance with their respective constitutional processes').

[15] See UNGA Res 97(1) (14 December 1946) (Arts 4(1)(a) and 10(a) of the 'Regulations to give effect to Article 102 of the Charter of the UN').

[16] *Reparations* case (n 6).

not have the power under any provision of its constitution to conclude them, provided that no constitutional provision precluded it from so doing'.[17]

This view is supported by the ILC's draft articles that were to become the 1969 Vienna Convention on the Law of Treaties (VCLT). There, the ILC asked not whether IOs had treaty-making capacity, but rather whether it was desirable to include treaties concluded by IOs alongside those concluded between States.[18] All four Special Rapporteurs in the first, second, third, and fourth ILC sessions[19] favoured the inclusion of IOs within the scope of the VCLT, but this was ultimately rejected by the Commission.[20]

The ILC acknowledged the possibility that IOs may enter into treaties, but left the rules to govern their treaty-making capacity to be determined elsewhere, thereby paving the way for a dual legal regime: both the VCLT and a new Convention that would be adopted later. The ILC decided not to include IOs in the final draft because 'it would both unduly complicate and delay the drafting of the present [1969] articles if it were to attempt to include in them satisfactory provisions concerning treaties of international organizations'.[21] Hence the VCLT applies only to States.[22] However, Article 3 of the VCLT provides:

The fact that the present Convention does not apply to international agreements concluded between States and other subjects of international law or between such other subjects of international law, or to international agreements not in written form, shall not affect:

(a) the legal force of such agreements;

(b) the application to them of any of the rules set forth in the present Convention to which they would be subject under international law independently of the Convention;

(c) the application of the Convention to the relations of States as between themselves under international agreements to which other subjects of international law are also parties.

Moreover, in reviewing the ILC report on the work of its 21st session, regarding the VCLT, the General Assembly adopted a resolution 'recommending that the International Law Commission should study . . . the question of treaties concluded between States and international organizations or between two or more international organizations, as an important question'.[23] The ILC was furthermore mandated to consult with principal IOs as appropriate.[24]

---

[17] See F Seyersted, 'International Personality of Intergovernmental Organizations: Do Their Capacities Really Depend Upon Their Constitutions?' (1964) 4 Indian J Intl L 1, 9–10 ('Seyersted 1964'); see also F Seyersted, *Common Law of International Organizations* (Martinus Nijhoff, Leiden 2008) 401–5 ('Seyersted 2008'); Chiu (n 8) 34.

[18] See Dobbert (n 8) 5–10.

[19] JL Brierly, Sir Hersch Lauterpacht, Sir Gerald Fitzmaurice, and Sir Humphrey Waldock served as Special Rapporteurs from the ILC's first session in 1949 and in 1952, 1955, and 1961 respectively. For an excellent account of discussions in the ILC, the Sixth Committee of the UN General Assembly, and at the 1968–69 Vienna Conference, see Brölmann (n 1) Chapter 8.

[20] [1982] YBILC, vol II(2), 9 [12]. The *travaux préparatoires* of the VCLT reveal that some participants, eg, the UN Food and Agriculture Organization (FAO), cautioned against creating a dual system.

[21] [1966] YBILC, vol II, 187. See Dobbert (n 8) 25–6.

[22] There are, however, references to IOs in VCLT Arts 2, 3, 5, and 20.

[23] UNGA Res 2501 (XXIV) (12 November 1969).

[24] Ibid.

In 1982, the ILC, with Paul Reuter as Special Rapporteur, submitted draft articles for a new Convention on treaties concluded between States and IOs or between IOs to the UN General Assembly. A conference was convened in 1986 which ended with the adoption of the 1986 VCLT. It is noteworthy that many IOs were reluctant to participate in the 1986 conference, perhaps out of fear that this Convention would impede the liberties they already enjoyed in the field of treaty-making.[25] Relatively few organizations were invited to participate, and even fewer actually participated.[26]

II. The 1986 Convention

Though the 1986 VCLT has yet to enter into force, its provisions are generally accepted as the applicable international law.[27] In its work on the draft articles that led to the 1986 VCLT, the ILC's approach was to take the 'the text of each provision in the 1969 VCLT in turn and consider what changes of drafting or substance were needed to adapt it to treaties concluded between States and international organizations or between international organizations'.[28] As a result, the 1986 VCLT bears a striking resemblance to its 1969 counterpart.[29] In this sense, the 1986 VCLT was anticlimactic, especially given the background assumption that IOs had a special nature warranting special treatment in the treaty context.[30]

---

[25] Klabbers (n 1) 253.

[26] Brölmann (n 1) 185–90 (also noting that IOs did not have the right to vote, and that proposals put forward by organizations could not be put to a vote unless formally supported by a State). IOs of the UN system were in favour of a non-binding declaration that would serve as the basis for the development of customary law, rather than a binding treaty, on the basis, *inter alia*, that the 1969 VCLT provided an adequate legal framework. See Administrative Committee on Co-ordination Decision 1982/17 (December 1982) UN Doc A/C.6/37/L.12.

[27] 1986 VCLT Art 85 requires ratification by thirty-five States—not IOs—for its entry into force. IOs may deposit an instrument of formal confirmation or accession to the Convention, but this does not serve to bring the Convention into force. Thus, while the Convention has been ratified by forty-one parties as of July 2011, only twenty-nine of these are States. The twenty-nine States are: Argentina, Australia, Austria, Belarus, Belgium, Bulgaria, Colombia, Croatia, Cyprus, Czech Republic, Denmark, Estonia, Gabon, Germany, Greece, Hungary, Italy, Liberia, Liechtenstein, Mexico, the Netherlands, Moldova, Senegal, Slovakia, Spain, Sweden, Switzerland, United Kingdom, and Uruguay. IOs that have formally confirmed or acceded to the 1986 Convention are: the International Atomic Energy Agency (IAEA), the International Civil Aviation Organization (ICAO), the International Criminal Police Organization, the International Labour Organization, the International Maritime Organization (IMO), the Organization for the Prohibition of Chemical Weapons (OPCW), the Preparatory Commission for the Comprehensive Nuclear Test-Ban Treaty Organization, the UN, the United Nations Industrial Development Organization, the Universal Postal Union, the World Health Organization (WHO), and the World Intellectual Property Organization (WIPO).

[28] Dobbert (n 8) 8; see also Brölmann (n 1) Chapter 10.

[29] A Aust, *Modern Treaty Law and Practice* (2nd edn CUP, Cambridge 2007) 401. Aust notes that while the 1969 VCLT did not apply to IOs, its rules were already applicable to IOs as a matter of customary international law.

[30] See Brölmann (n 1) 197.

The 1986 VCLT does, however, differ from the 1969 VCLT in a number of respects.[31] In most cases, as may be expected, references were added to IOs in provisions where the 1969 VCLT only referred to States. In fewer cases, provisions dealing specifically with IOs were inserted into the 1986 Convention.[32] Key differences contained in the 1986 Convention include the following:

- the use of the term 'act of formal confirmation' in place of 'ratification' in some of the provisions on entry into force of treaties (eg Articles 2(b)(*bis*), 14, 16, and 83);[33]

- the insertion of references to the governing role of 'the (relevant) rules of the organization' (eg Article 5 on the applicability of the Convention to constituent instruments of IOs and to treaties adopted within IOs; Article 6 on the capacity of IOs to conclude treaties; Articles 27(2) and 46 on the inability of an IO to avoid treaty obligations by referring to its own rules or violations thereof; Articles 35–37 on rights and obligations of third States or organizations; Article 39 on the consent of an organization to the amendment of treaties; and Article 65 on the procedure for invoking defects in consent);

- the insertion of a reference to Article 96 of the UN Charter (on the ICJ's advisory jurisdiction, which is open only to IOs) in Article 66(b) on dispute settlement;

- a clarification that where there is overlap with the 1969 VCLT—for example where two State parties to the 1969 VCLT enter into a multilateral treaty with an IO—the 1969 VCLT will prevail as between the States (Article 73); and

- provisions indicating that the 1986 VCLT shall not prejudge questions regarding (i) the international responsibility of an IO; (ii) the termination of the existence of an IO; (iii) the termination of a State's membership in an IO; and (iv) the establishment of obligations and rights for States members of an IO under a treaty to which that organization is a party (Article 74).[34]

In spite of the otherwise striking likeness between the two Conventions, the doctrinal division of opinion regarding the international legal personality of IOs, of which their capacity to conclude treaties is an important indicator, remains.[35]

---

[31] In a few cases, these differences are not related to differences between States and IOs. Article 9(2) of the 1986 Convention, for example, states that the procedure for adopting the text of a treaty at an international conference is to be determined by the participants, and if this fails to produce agreement, the procedure adopted by two-thirds of the participants present and voting would apply. Its 1969 VCLT counterpart contains only the two-thirds rule. Another example is the Annex to the 1986 Convention, setting out rules relating to the arbitration and conciliation procedures under Art 66, which are more detailed and elaborate than those set out in the 1969 VCLT.

[32] See Brölmann (n 1) Chapter 10 (analysing the ILC debates and the drafting Conference); ibid 273–81 (describing actual differences between the two VCLTs).

[33] The procedures by which an IO consents to be bound by a treaty are discussed in Chapter 7, Part III.E, 200.

[34] See Schermers and Blokker (n 8) §§1783–99 for a discussion of the legal character, validity, binding force, conclusion, entry into force and termination of agreements to which IOs are a party. See also Klabbers (n 1) Chapter 5.

[35] For recent discussion of this long-standing issue, see eg Alvarez (n 1) 129–45; Klabbers (n 1) generally. Brölmann provides a sustained examination of the conceptualization of IOs as legal subjects,

A. The capacity of IOs to conclude treaties

Article 6 of the 1969 VCLT states clearly that 'every State possesses capacity to conclude treaties', but the formulation of a general provision on the capacity of IOs was more difficult; indeed, it had been one of the reasons why IOs were excluded from the scope of the 1969 VCLT. ILC discussions revealed divergent views. Some held the view that international legal capacity could only be conferred by the States parties to the constituent documents and that 'an organization's capacity to conclude treaties depends only on the organization's rules'.[36] Others held the view that IOs, in and of themselves, had the capacity to conclude treaties that were necessary for them to function.[37] Article 6 of the 1986 Convention provides that 'the capacity of an international organization to conclude treaties is governed by the relevant rules of that organization'. The ILC's commentary to its draft articles explained that this provision reflects the absence of a general capacity for all IOs to conclude treaties. Any treaty-making capacity must, instead, be derived from the individual circumstances of each IO: 'It reflects the fact that every organization has its own distinctive legal image which is recognizable, in particular, in the individualized capacity of that organization to conclude treaties.'[38] However, that is not to say that international law does not recognize the general capacity of IOs to conclude treaties; the 1986 VCLT's preamble states that 'IOs possess the capacity to conclude treaties, which is necessary for the exercise of their functions and the fulfilment of their purposes'.[39] Thus, the effect of Article 6 is to contextualize the general treaty-making capacity of IOs—international law empowers IOs to con-clude treaties as long as 'the rules of the organization' are observed.

The phrase 'the rules of the organization', according to Article 2(1)(j) of the 1986 Convention refers to a number of sources, 'in particular, the constituent instruments, decisions and resolutions ... and established practice of the organiza-tion'. The constituent instruments are typically the primary source for identifying the rules of the organization, and usually contain provisions that accord specific treaty-making capacity to the organizations they establish.[40] IOs may also be

and argues that their 'dual image' as both vehicles for their member States and as independent legal actors 'cannot fully be accommodated in the current one-dimensional system of international law'. Brölmann (n 1) 1.

[36] [1974] YBILC, vol II(1), 299.

[37] See ibid 298–9.

[38] [1982] YBILC, vol II(2), 24. See also Brölmann (n 1) 83–90, 203–5 (referring to the criticism levelled at Art 6 for not resolving this debate). On the related distinction between IO 'capacity' and 'competence' to conclude treaties, see G Hartmann, 'The Capacity of IOs to Conclude Treaties' in Zemanek (n 8) 127–63, especially 149–51. This is, however, a distinction that is largely unavailing in practice. See Klabbers (n 1) 251–2; Brölmann (n 1) 90–4.

[39] See F Seyersted, 'Treaty-making Capacity of Intergovernmental Organizations: Article 6 of the International Law Commission's Draft Articles on the Law of Treaties between States and Interna-tional Organizations or between International Organizations' (1983) 34 Österreichisches Zeitschrift für öffentliches Recht und Völkerrecht 261, for a forceful defence of this view that the capacity of IOs must derive from international law.

[40] The treaty establishing the Economic Community of West African States, for example, empow-ers the Community to enter into cooperation agreements with other regional communities, non-

competent to conclude treaties on the basis of the necessary intendment of the provisions of their constituent instrument or other treaties; ie they may be empowered to conclude treaties even where their constituent instruments do not expressly empower the organization to do so.[41] Decisions of the competent organs of the organization, or the development of the law of IOs, may subsequently vest the organization with this capacity.[42] Consistent with the ICJ's ruling in the *Certain Expenses* case, an IO's treaty-making power may also be implied when 'appropriate for the fulfilment of one of the stated purposes of the [organization]'.[43] Thus, even in the absence of express provisions in its constituent documents, the right to conclude treaties that relate to its headquarters and to the privileges and immunities of its staff is regarded as inherent to an IO.[44]

Article 2(1)(j) of the 1986 Convention also identified practice as a source of the 'rules of the organization'. The ILC cautioned, however, against the temptation to regard the reference to practice as establishing a general capacity for all IOs to conclude treaties, noting that 'the reference in question is in no way intended to suggest that practice has the same standing in all organizations; on the contrary, each organization has its own characteristics in that respect'.[45] Article 6 thus sought to specify that treaty-making capacity may be governed by the practice of a particular organization. There is some circularity in the reasoning here; the ILC explained in its commentaries to Article 6:

member States and other organizations. See Revised Treaty of the Economic Community of West African States (adopted 24 July 1993, entered into force 23 August 1995) 2373 UNTS 233, Arts 79–85; see also Convention Establishing the European Free Trade Association (EFTA) Art 43 (empowering the EFTA Council to enter into agreements with other States or IOs).

[41] See eg Treaty on the Non-Proliferation of Nuclear Weapons (adopted 1 July 1968, entered into force 5 March 1970) 729 UNTS 61, Art 3. Article 3 provides that non-nuclear weapons States shall enter into agreements on acceptable safeguards with the IAEA in accordance with the IAEA Statute and its safeguards system, even though the IAEA Statute preceded the Non-Proliferation Treaty in time. By decision of the competent organ pursuant to Art XVI of the IAEA Statute, the IAEA may thus accept rights and obligations assigned to it by a treaty other than its own Statute.

[42] Schermers and Blokker (n 8) §1750. See eg Decision VI/3 of the sixth meeting of the Conference of the Parties of the Basel Convention on the Transboundary Movements of Hazardous Wastes and their Disposal, in which the Conference of the Parties adopted a 'core set of elements for inclusion in the Framework Agreement to be signed between the secretariat of the Basel Convention (on behalf of the Conference of the Parties) and the representative of the host countries' Governments' for the purposes of establishing Regional Centres for the organization. UNEP, 'Report of the Conference of the Parties to the Basel Convention on the Transboundary Movements of Hazardous Wastes and their Disposal' (10 February 2003) UN Doc UNEP/CHW.6/40, 36. Also, in its *WHO Advisory Opinion*, the ICJ noted that 'in the World Health Assembly and in some of the written and oral statements before the Court there seems to have been a disposition to regard international organizations as possessing some form of absolute power to determine and, if need be, change the location of the sites of their headquarters and regional offices'. *Interpretation of the Agreement of 25 March 1951 between the WHO and Egypt* (Advisory Opinion) [1980] ICJ Rep 89 [37]. Regarding headquarters agreements, it is noteworthy that, while the UN Charter expressly authorizes the conclusion of agreements only with specialized agencies, the UN has signed agreements with the IAEA—UNGA Res 1145 (XII) (14 November 1957)—and the OPCW—UNGA Res 55/283 (24 September 2001)—which are not specialized agencies. See, further, Seyersted 2008 (n 17) 357–71.

[43] *Certain Expenses of the United Nations (Article 17, paragraph 2, of the Charter)* (Advisory Opinion) [1962] ICJ Rep 151, 168.

[44] Schermers and Blokker (n 8) §1751.

[45] [1982] YBILC, vol II(2), 21.

that the question how far practice can play a creative part, particularly in the matter of international organization's capacity to conclude treaties, cannot be answered uniformly for all international organizations. This question, too, depends on the 'rules of the organization'; indeed, it depends on the highest category of those rules[46]

The intention, however, was to underscore the importance of giving due consideration to the IO's specific circumstances when determining the extent of its treaty-making capacity.[47]

B. Excess of competence

As the ICJ stated in the *Legality of the Use by a State of Nuclear Weapons in Armed Conflict* case:

international organizations are subjects of international law which do not, unlike States, possess a general competence. International organizations are governed by the 'principle of speciality', that is to say, they are invested by the States which create them with powers, the limits of which are a function of the common interest whose promotion those States entrust to them.[48]

Thus, even if an IO may clearly have the capacity to conclude *some* treaties, it does not follow that it has the capacity to conclude *any* treaty.

Article 46 of the 1986 Convention is the principal rule dealing with issues of competence arising from the rules of the organization. It provides that an IO:

may not invoke the fact that its consent to be bound by a treaty has been expressed in violation of the rules of the organization regarding competence to conclude treaties as invalidating its consent unless that violation was manifest and concerned a rule of fundamental importance.

This provision replicates Article 46 of the 1969 VCLT, and accords priority to the preservation of legal relations at the international level, rather than allowing the rules of an organization to govern the validity of the agreement.[49] Thus, an IO, save for exceptional circumstances, is bound by the obligations under a treaty concluded by an organ that had not been appropriately vested with the competence to do so.

---

[46] Ibid 24.

[47] The ILC further noted in its commentaries:

It is theoretically conceivable that, by adopting a rigid legal framework, an organization might exclude practice as a source of its rules. Even without going as far as that, it must be admitted that international organizations differ greatly from one another as regards the part played by practice and the form which it takes, *inter alia* in the matter of their capacity to conclude international agreements. There is nothing surprising in this; the part which practice has played in this matter in an organization like the United Nations, faced in every field with problems fundamental to the future of all mankind, cannot be likened to the part played by practice in a technical organization engaged in humble operational activities in a circumscribed sector.

Ibid.

[48] (Advisory Opinion) [1996] ICJ Rep 66 [25]. The Court further explained that 'in order to delineate the field of activity or the area of competence of an international organization, one must refer to the relevant rules of the organization and, in the first place, to its constitution'. Ibid [19].

[49] For further discussion of 1969 VCLT Art 46 see Chapter 23, Part III.A, 561 *et seq*.

The condition of a 'manifest' violation of a rule was the subject of considerable ILC discussion. The Commission apparently intended that, in determining whether a violation is 'manifest', the knowledge of the other parties to the treaty was to be considered to ascertain whether they could in good faith rely on the treaty's validity. Accordingly, if the other party was aware, or ought to have been aware of the violation, the IO may be able to invoke this against that party so as to invalidate the IO's consent.[50] This puts the onus on the other party to ensure that the IO is competent to conclude the treaty. This seems reasonable where an IO concludes a treaty with its own members—as its members would have knowledge and, indeed, an interest in ensuring that the organization acts in accordance with the competence accorded to it—but less so where IOs conclude treaties with non-parties or other IOs. It seems doubtful that an IO's governing body would be able to successfully argue that a treaty to which it was a party was invalid on the grounds that its consent to be bound was expressed in 'manifest violation' of a rule of that organization 'of fundamental importance'. This is not much different, however, from the situation facing States; difficulties were acknowledged in relation to the equivalent provision in the 1969 VCLT, since 'practical cases in which they could be invoked will be rather rare'.[51] In the case of IOs, it is similarly difficult to imagine a situation in which an IO acts in accordance with the will of its member States but in so doing manifestly violates a rule of that IO that is of fundamental importance.[52]

The way Article 46 operates in the context of the compromise reflected in the 1986 VCLT also warrants some reflection. As we have seen, the 1986 VCLT reflects a compromise between the view that 'an organization's capacity to conclude treaties depends only on the organization's rules' and the view that 'international law lays down the principle of such capacity'.[53] Article 46, however, clearly assumes the latter view, ie that IOs have the capacity to enter into treaties as a matter of international law. Indeed, Article 46 necessarily implies that an IO can be bound by treaty obligations even when its member-

---

[50] [1982] YBILC, vol II(2), 52.

[51] I Sinclair, *The Vienna Convention on the Law of Treaties* (2nd edn MUP, Manchester 1984) 172.

[52] Klabbers makes the point most eloquently:

If supported by all members (or even by only a majority) three possible arguments may be used in support of the conclusion of the agreement in question. First, the members were of the apparent conviction that the agreement was *intra vires*... Second, if the power to conclude an agreement is not expressly provided for in the organization's constituent document, it may nonetheless be implied in it. Third... the conclusion itself qualifies as subsequent practice of the organization and, if meeting with support, can be deemed to be acquiesced in... Hence, even where the outside observer may have doubts about the legality (and therewith validity) of an agreement in terms of the powers of the organization concerned, as long as the members do not agree with the outside observer, any finding of invalidity is bound to fall upon deaf ears, and this in turn renders the doctrine of *ultra vires* a paper tiger.

Klabbers (n 1) 254. Recall, furthermore, that Art 8 of both the 1969 and 1986 VCLT allows for subsequent confirmation of acts relating to the conclusion of a treaty by persons without the required authority.

[53] [1982] YBILC, vol II(2), 24.

ship may have not expressly permitted it to do so under its internal rules. This reflects the pervasive tension between the view that strictly ties IO treaty-making capacity to the will of its members and the view imposing a much less strict connection that underlies the 1986 VCLT—a tension masked by the similarity between the 1969 and 1986 VCLT.

Specific questions may also arise with respect to the IO's internal distribution of any treaty-making power it possesses. Such powers are usually entrusted to the supreme governing body of the organization composed of its full membership.[54] Some organizations provide for other subsidiary organs to bear the exclusive competence to conclude agreements in their field of activity.[55] The competence to conclude treaties on certain matters may thus be delegated from the plenary governing body to a subsidiary organ or to the Secretariat.[56] Ultimately, however, the governing body retains supervision over the exercise of this competence.

What happens when the governing body determines that the subsidiary organ or the Secretariat has exceeded its delegated competence to conclude a treaty is, however, less clear. Article 7 of the 1986 Convention provides that a person is considered as representing an IO for the purpose of:

expressing the consent of that organization to be bound by a treaty, if: (*a*) that person produces appropriate full powers; or (*b*) it appears from the circumstances that it was the intention of the States and international organizations concerned to consider that person as representing the organization for such purposes, in accordance with the rules of the organization, without having to produce full powers.

In drafting this provision, the ILC felt that, similar to States, representatives of IOs should be subject to the requirement for full powers. But it appears that the ILC's primary purpose in requiring full powers was only to identify the individual who could represent the organization and sign the treaty, rather than to determine the extent of that individual's competence (in terms of the matters on which that representative could commit the organization). In the rare circumstances in which this problem presents itself in practice, however, Article 46 will almost certainly provide the solution, in favour of upholding the validity of a treaty concluded as a result of any excess of competence.

[54] JL Brierly, the ILC's first Special Rapporteur for the law of treaties, took the view that 'in the absence of provision in its constitution to the contrary, the capacity of an international organization to make treaties is deemed to reside in its plenary organ'. JL Brierly, 'Report on the Law of Treaties' [1950] YBILC, vol II, 231. Most organizations do not have detailed rules regarding the form and procedure for concluding treaties; the FAO's Guidelines are a notable exception. See Schermers and Blokker (n 8) §§1789–90.

[55] See Schermers and Blokker (n 8) §1765, citing as examples the UN Security Council on matters of peace and security, UNICEF and UNDP in their fields, and the boards of the IMO, ICAO, and IAEA on several matters specifically attributed to them.

[56] See H Neuhold, 'Organs Competent to Conclude Treaties for International Organizations and the Internal Procedure Leading to the Decision to be Bound by a Treaty and Negotiation and Conclusion of Treaties by International Organizations' in Zemanek (n 8) 195.

III. Who is Bound when the IO is a Party to a Treaty?

Under the principle of *pacta sunt servanda* set out in Article 26 of the 1986 VCLT, the organization itself is bound by the treaty it concludes, and accordingly it bears the incumbent responsibilities and duties. This is also true where an organ of the organization[57] or the secretariat has concluded the agreement on the basis of delegated powers. When the organization is bound by the treaty, all its organs are bound to act in accordance with these obligations. In its Advisory Opinion on the *Effect of Awards Case*, the ICJ confirmed this in the context of the binding force of judgments of the UN Administrative Tribunal regarding employment contracts concluded by the Secretary-General with UN employees.[58]

The effect of treaties concluded by IOs on its member States or its member IOs[59] is, however, less straightforward. Are States bound by the obligations of the organization of which they are members? Article 216(2) of the Treaty on the Functioning of the European Union (formerly Article 300 of the EC Treaty) makes it clear that they are in providing that 'Agreements concluded by the Union are binding upon the institutions of the Union and on its Member States'. Where the position is not stated so clearly, competing views have been expressed. One early view saw IO treaty-making as essentially an act of its member States, suggesting that IOs do not have legal personality but for the collective legal personality of its member States.[60] The ILC, however, adopted a different view. Its draft Article 36*bis* sought to clarify the obligations incumbent upon IO members where an IO entered into a treaty:

Obligations and rights arise for States members of an international organization from the provisions of a treaty to which that organization is a party when the parties to the treaty intend those provisions to be the means of establishing such obligations and according such rights and have defined their conditions and effects in the treaty or have otherwise agreed thereon, and if:

(*a*) the States members of the organization, by virtue of the constituent instrument of that organization or otherwise, have unanimously agreed to be bound by the said provisions of the treaty; and

---

[57] See Case C-327/91 *France v Commission* [1994] ECR I-3641, where the European Court of Justice confirmed that an agreement entered into by the Commission binds the European Community in its entirety. For more discussion of the allocation of responsibility in treaties to which the EU is a party, see Chapter 4, Part II.C, 118, *et seq*.

[58] *Effect of Awards of Compensation made by the UN Administrative Tribunal* (Advisory Opinion) [1954] ICJ Rep 47, 53.

[59] Cf Art 18 of the Draft Articles on the Responsibility of International Organizations (DARIO), in UNGA 'Report of the International Law Commission' UN GAOR 63rd Session Supp No 10 (2011) UN Doc A/66/10, 55.

[60] See eg H Lauterpacht, 'Report on the Law of Treaties' [1953] YBILC, vol II, 100 ('the treaty-making power of international organizations is one of the significant instruments for their proper functioning and it seems desirable that that instrument should receive adequate recognition and elaboration. In fact, there would appear to be no reason why, in the sphere of the treaty-making power, States acting collectively should not be in the position to do what they can do individually').

(*b*) the assent of the States members of the organization to be bound by the relevant provisions of the treaty has been duly brought to the knowledge of the negotiating States and negotiating organizations.[61]

In proposing this draft article, the ILC had in mind instances where an IO treaty specifically contemplates the creation of rights and obligations for its member States;[62] and even then, member States could become third parties to the treaty only when such a result was explicitly specified and accepted by those same member States.[63] Ultimately, the proposal was not adopted,[64] but draft Article 36*bis* demonstrates that there was significant consensus within the ILC that an IO, and not its member States, bears the legal consequences of its treaty relations. Still, there are real difficulties with this position:

if it is true that decision making (including decisions to conclude treaties) usually takes place by the unanimous consent of member States, then it follows that the will of the organization is identical to the will of all its members. Therefore, whatever the will of the organization may be, it can usually be considered to be the aggregate will of the member States, rather than the distinct will of the international organization. With that in mind, organizations could simply be regarded as exercising a delegated power: there would be no need for specific acts of consent, because it would be clear that all the organization's acts would be based on consent anyway . . . Such a conception, however, would mean getting rid of the element of the distinct will, and therefore getting rid of an important justification for the existence of organizations. For if an organization does not have a distinct will, then why establish one to begin with?[65]

In some cases, the IO may not itself be a party to the treaty, but States may enter into agreements on its behalf. This concept is illustrated by some agreements on the privileges and immunities of IOs. The 1949 Agreement on the Privileges and Immunities of the Council of Europe, for example, is a treaty between the member

---

[61] [1982] YBILC, vol II(2), 43.

[62] In Professor Paul Reuter's 10th report to the ILC on the 'Questions of Treaties Concluded between States and International Organizations or Between Two or More International Organizations', he observed: 'what is beyond dispute is that the functions of international organizations lead them to conclude treaties which by their very nature will establish rights and obligations for their member States. This is the case with headquarters agreements between an organization and a host State; this is the case when an international organization is empowered to conclude certain agreements on economic matters, for the implementation of which States members are at least partially responsible'. [1981] YBILC, vol II(1), 67.

[63] The ILC referred to the need for the initial consent not only of the States parties to the treaty concluded by the IO, but also the consent of the States members of that organization. The ILC included an additional condition that the consent of those member States must have been brought to the knowledge of the States and organizations that participated in the negotiation of the treaty. [1982] YBILC, vol II(2), 46.

[64] The debates in the ILC revealed divergent views on the part of members of the ILC and IOs, as well as a range of objections to the idea of considering member States as bearing rights and obligations on the basis of treaties concluded by IOs. For a full discussion, see Brölmann (n 1) 212–25. The remnants of draft Art 36*bis* are set out in Art 74(3) of the 1986 VCLT: 'The provisions of the present Convention shall not prejudge any question that may arise in regard to the establishment of obligations and rights for States members of an international organization under a treaty to which that organization is a party.'

[65] Klabbers (n 1) 262.

States only.[66] An IO may thus become a party to a treaty which has been concluded by its members, rather than by an organ of the organization itself.

Special questions with regard to identifying the entity that is bound by agreements of IOs are raised by so-called 'mixed agreements'.[67] Both member States and the organization are parties to mixed agreements, each in respect of its own area of competence as determined by the rules of the organization, usually where the subject matter of the agreement falls partly within the competence of each. Where the IO's entire membership subscribes to the treaty together with the IO itself, such mixed agreements provide a degree of reassurance to the other contracting party that the treaty will be deemed valid and the obligations performed. In such cases, questions as to whether the IO exceeded its competence to enter into an agreement would become an internal matter to be resolved between the organization and its member States; it appears that such excess will not serve to invalidate the treaty with respect to the other contracting parties.[68] Incomplete mixed agreements—where an IO enters into a treaty but not all its member States follow suit—pose more difficulties. Situations could arise in which some of the treaty's obligations apply in the territory of the member States by virtue of their IO membership, while other parts of the treaty falling within the competence of member States (eg rules on implementation and enforcement of the treaty by national authorities) would not be applied by those States that are not parties to the treaty as such.[69] Such a situation is not necessarily problematic; it should be remembered that the

---

[66] The Agreement on the Privileges and Immunities of the International Criminal Court (adopted 9 September 2002, entered into force 22 July 2004) 2271 UNTS 3, is another treaty concluded by States Parties. It was adopted by the Assembly of States Parties, an organ of the Court, in 2002, but was opened for ratification, acceptance or approval by signatory States and entered into force when the requisite number of States became parties. The Convention on the Privileges and Immunities of the United Nations (adopted 13 February 1946, entered into force 22 July 1946) 1 UNTS 15, was concluded by the member States and adopted by the General Assembly in 1946. See also Chiu (n 8) 71; Schermers and Blokker (n 8) §§1763–4.

[67] Schermers and Blokker (n 8) §§1756–62. The EU is the greatest contributor to the practice regarding the conclusion of mixed agreements and is the subject of Chapter 4.

[68] See *France v Commission* [1994] (n 57). Where a State becomes a new member of an IO, it will, generally speaking, be bound by the agreements already entered into by that organization. Schermers and Blokker argue that these new members should be required to adhere to the mixed agreements as a condition for their membership. Schermers and Blokker (n 8) §1761.

[69] See eg 1982 UN Convention of the Law of the Sea (adopted 10 December 1982, entered into force 16 November 1994) 1833 UNTS 3 (UNCLOS) (Annex IX, Art 2 authorizes an IO to sign the Convention if the majority of its members are signatories while Art 3 provides for an IO to confirm or accede to the Convention if the majority of its members have done so. Article 4(3) of Annex IX provides that 'an international organization shall exercise the rights and perform the obligations which its member States which are Parties would otherwise have under this Convention, on matters relating to which competence has been transferred to it by those member States'. Article 5 sets out the requirement that the other parties to the treaty be notified, upon formal confirmation or accession, of the allocations of competences between an organization that becomes a party to a treaty and its member States). See also Convention on International Liability for Damage caused by Space Objects (adopted 29 March 1972, entered into force 3 October 1973) 961 UNTS 187, Art 22 (references to States shall be deemed to apply to organizations which have declared their acceptance of the rights and obligations of the Convention if a majority of the members of the organization are parties to the Convention).

decision whether to accept selective participation depends on the preferences of the drafters, who may have agreed to tolerate such partial adherence.[70]

Another facet of the question of which entities are bound by the IO's treaty obligations lies in identifying where responsibility and liability ultimately lie in case of a breach of the agreement. The matter goes beyond the law of treaties, and is the subject of debate. For those who view the separate legal personality of IOs as paramount, it is the IO that is responsible and liable for breach of the treaty. On the other hand, those who view IOs as mere vehicles for their members find it easier to assume the responsibility and liability of the members: injured parties ought to be protected through 'indirect' or 'secondary' responsibility of the members of the IO.[71] The view taken by the ILC in the recently adopted Draft Articles on the Responsibility of International Organizations (DARIO) is that membership in an IO alone does not imply or create a presumption of responsibility for the acts of that IO.[72] In cases of mixed agreements, the allocation of liability for a breach may prove much more difficult, depending on a determination of the allocation of competences between the IO and its member States. Treaties rarely address this issue, although Annex IX of the 1982 UN Convention on the Law of the Sea (UNCLOS) provides for joint and several liability between an IO and its member States should they fail to inform other contracting parties of how they divide responsibility for specific matters covered by that treaty.[73]

IV. Types of Treaties Concluded by IOs

IOs have concluded treaties on a wide range of issues with their own member States, with non-member States, and with other IOs.[74] The types of treaties IOs

---

[70] See eg Schermers and Blokker (n 8) §§1759–61 (describing the Memorandum of Understanding of 19 September 1974 between the United States on the one hand and Euratom and some of its member States on the other concerning nuclear science and technology information, in which the United States agreed that it would receive information on the research carried out by Euratom and some of its member States, and would for its part provide information 'which would be beneficial' to all members of Euratom, including those that were not party to the Memorandum).

[71] For further discussion of the question of responsibility and liability beyond the confines of the law of treaties, see ibid §§1582–90; Klabbers (n 1) Chapter 14, esp 285–7; R Higgins, 'Report of the Institut de droit international on the Legal Consequences for Member States of the Non-Fulfilment by International Organisations of Their Obligations toward Third Parties' (1995) 66 Ybk Institute Intl L 251; CF Amerasinghe, 'Liability to Third Parties of Member States of International Organisations: Practice, Principle and Judicial Precedent' (1995) 85 AJIL 259; M Hirsch, *The Responsibility of International Organisations towards Third Parties: Some Basic Principles* (Martinus Nijhoff, Leiden 1995); I Brownlie, 'The Responsibility of States for the Acts of International Organizations' in M Ragazzi (ed), *International Responsibility Today: Essays in Memory of Oscar Schachter* (Martinus Nijhoff, Leiden 2005); Seyersted 2008 (n 17) Chapter 10.

[72] See DARIO (n 59) 80–1, 157–68 (draft Art 3 and Part 5, and the commentary thereto, which include the comments of States and IOs).

[73] UNCLOS (n 69) Annex IX, Art 6.

[74] See Schermers and Blokker (n 8) §§1749–50,1769–82 for a discussion of the varied subject matter of agreements concluded by IOs. In terms of numbers, by 1983, the *UN Treaty Series* had published more than 2,000 treaties to which IOs were parties. Ibid §1749 n244. See also Brölmann (n 1) Chapter 7. Treaties concluded by IOs must be distinguished from 'internal' agreements

actually conclude are a function of their competence to act *and* the acceptance of that competence by the other contracting parties.[75] IOs most often enter into bilateral agreements such as headquarters agreements delineating their status within host States and relationship agreements in which they coordinate activities with another IO or a State. An IO may have the competence to enter into law-making treaties (such as the 1986 Convention) but there is little evidence of IO adherence to such treaties, especially human rights treaties.[76] This paucity of practice may be attributed to the limited powers of the organization to effectively and fully meet the obligations incumbent in such treaties. In considering the question of UN accession to the 1949 Geneva Conventions for the Protection of War Victims,[77] the UN Office of Legal Affairs issued a memorandum stating:

the United Nations is not substantively in a position to become a party to the 1949 Conventions, which contain many obligations that can only be discharged by the exercise of juridical and administrative powers which the Organization does not possess, such as the authority to exercise criminal jurisdiction over members of the Forces, or administrative competence relating to territorial sovereignty. Thus the United Nations is unable to fulfil obligations which for their execution require the exercise of powers not granted to the Organization, and therefore cannot accede to the Conventions.[78]

The Office of Legal Affairs explained that it takes steps to ensure compliance with the Geneva Conventions, through 'exchanges of letters' and 'regulations issued by the organization',[79] but was reluctant to enter into the treaty knowing that it was unable to perform the obligations therein.

Even if an IO has the competence to perform the treaty's obligations, its ability to join will also depend on its acceptance by the other contracting parties. Many treaties limit participation exclusively to States. Thus, even if an organization such as the North Atlantic Treaty Organization (NATO) is competent (whether by itself or in concert with its member States) to comply with the obligations of certain international humanitarian law treaties, often these treaties lack provisions for IO

concluded between different organs of the same IO, or other agreements relating to the functioning of the organization, as these agreements are governed by the internal law of the IO. See Schermers and Blokker (n 8) §1746. For the same reason, other agreements are not to be considered as treaties. Ibid § 1783. For example, because members of NATO did not wish to create legal relations with the Russian Federation, the 1997 Founding Act on Mutual Relations, Cooperation and Security between NATO and the Russian Federation was concluded as a political instrument and is not a treaty; the test being whether the agreement in question is governed by international law. [1997] 36 ILM 1006; see also Chapter 2 on political commitments.

[75] See Hollis (n 5) 163.
[76] See Schermers and Blokker (n 8) §§1773–5.
[77] Eg Geneva Convention Relative to the Protection of Civilian Persons in Time of War (adopted 12 August 1949, entered into force 21 October 1950) 75 UNTS 287, Art 3.
[78] UN Office of Legal Affairs 'Memorandum on the Question of the Possible Accession of Intergovernmental Organizations to the Geneva Conventions for the Protection of War Victims' (1972) UNJY 153 [3].
[79] Ibid [4].

membership.[80] In such cases, as with new treaty negotiations, the participants must consent to the IO becoming a contracting party.[81]

IOs may also enter into agreements for the establishment of a new IO, although they cannot do so independently. In creating a new IO by treaty, negotiating States may agree to participation in that IO by other IOs. But, the UN Office of Legal Affairs has expressed the view that IOs, as entities with a will distinct from its members, may not establish other IOs:

The capacity to establish international intergovernmental organizations having separate legal personality is, under international law, conferred upon States through the conclusion of agreements. International intergovernmental organizations which are the creation of States cannot in and of themselves create new international organizations, endowed with the same international legal personality, unless they are specifically mandated to do so by States.[82]

Thus if an IO wishes to enter into an agreement for the establishment of a new organization, it must carry with it the will of its member States. This was achieved by the UN and the FAO through the passing of parallel resolutions in the governing body of their respective organizations in order to establish the World Food Programme.[83]

IOs often enter into agreements with other IOs on a multitude of issues, such as cooperation on technical activities or the sharing of facilities. Where there is an overlap between the membership of the IOs that are party to the treaty, this creates an anomalous situation when one organization seeks to enforce an obligation under the treaty. Those member States seeking enforcement would be calling upon themselves to comply with the obligations set forth in the treaty, or to compel the organization to which they are members to do so.[84] IOs may also enter into agreements so that they can become members, alongside their member States, of other IOs. In such cases, specific rules must be adopted to determine that IO's role in decision-making. This often entails an arrangement between the member IO

---

[80] For example, the 1980 Convention on Prohibitions or Restrictions on the Use of Certain Conventional Weapons which may be deemed to be Excessively Injurious or to have Indiscriminate Effects (adopted 10 October 1980, entered into force 2 December 1982) 1342 UNTS 137, Art 3, limits membership to States, but several of its Protocols restrict or prohibit contracting parties from using certain weapons in conflict, obligations with which NATO could comply. See eg Protocol on Blinding Laser Weapons (Protocol IV) (adopted 13 October 1995, entered into force 30 July 1998) 1380 UNTS 370.

[81] See eg the 1999 Protocol to Amend the 1949 Convention on the Establishment of an Inter-American Tropical Tuna Commission [2000] 40 ILM 1494, pursuant to which the parties to the Convention amended it to permit EC (now EU) participation and to prohibit the participation of EU member States unless those States represented territory outside the EU.

[82] UN Office of Legal Affairs, 'Legal Capacity of International Intergovernmental Organizations to Establish Other International Organizations—Legal Capacity of the United Nations Development Programme to Participate in the Establishment of Other International Organizations or to Establish its own Subsidiary Organs' (1991) UNJY 296 [4].

[83] UNGA Res 1496 (XV) (27 October 1960); UNGA Res 1714 (XVI) (19 December 1961); UNGA Res 2095 (XX) (20 December 1964); and FAO Resolution 1/61 (FAO, 'Report of the Conference of FAO 11th Session' (1961) [54]) and FAO Resolution 4/65 (FAO, 'Report of the Conference of FAO 13th Session' (1965) [119]).

[84] See Klabbers (n 1) 267.

and the States that are members to both organizations to determine, for example, where the member IO may speak (and vote) on behalf of the States, and where it cannot,[85] and, where applicable, how the member IO will be represented in the organs of the other organization, and the respective liabilities of the organization and its member States for financial contributions.[86]

Concluding Remarks

The purposes for which an IO was established plays an essential role in delimiting the scope of its powers, including its treaty-making powers.[87] It is no surprise then that the 1986 Convention, including especially Article 6, leaves decisions regarding particular issues arising from the exercise of treaty-making power to be decided on a case-by-case basis depending on the particular rules of the organization in question. Nevertheless, the deliberations surrounding the conclusion of the 1986 Convention and academic research have identified a number of outstanding issues. Most notably, there is a continuing tension between the status of IOs as independent subjects of international law distinct from member States, on the one hand, and the fact that these organizations—like international law—are the creation of sovereign States who retain that status in several important respects, even as they operate behind the institutional veil. As a result of this 'constant oscillation between the position of the organization as a party in its own right, and the position of the organization as a vehicle for its own member States',[88] issues remain over who is bound and the division of competences, responsibility, and liability. These ambiguities are often masked by the similarities between the provisions of the 1969 and 1986 VCLT. Despite this tension, with the notable exception of the rich jurisprudence developed by the European Court of Justice (now the Court of Justice of the European Union), in practice major problems have not arisen with any significant frequency.[89] And any problems relating to treaty-making capacity are but a subset of broader issues relating to the (independent) personality of IOs. Since IOs are corporate entities that must be, to a greater or lesser extent, vehicles for their member States, who retain important roles in decision-making, it may be expected

---

[85] Klabbers gives the example of the practice of the European Community in FAO meetings where the European Community declares the distribution of powers between itself and its members on various issues on the agenda. Ibid 268. Klabbers also argues that if the member States of the member organization contribute to the budget of the target IO, it is unlikely that the member organization would be required to do the same, 'save perhaps to cover any additional costs arising out of its separate membership'. Ibid 269. See also UNCLOS (n 69) Art 4(4) of Annex IX ('Participation of such an international organization shall in no case entail an increase of the representation to which its member States which are States Parties would otherwise be entitled, including rights in decision-making').

[86] See Schermers and Blokker (n 8) §1762.

[87] But see Klabbers (n 1) Chapter 4, for a recent account of the challenges faced by the implied powers doctrine.

[88] Ibid 269.

[89] As noted above, the phenomenon of mixed agreements has generated a considerable amount of jurisprudence to a very large extent in the context of European law. See Chapter 4, Part II.A.2, 113 *et seq.*

that most of the conceivable problems will be addressed internally within the organization.

The fact that the 1986 VCLT is not in force over twenty-five years after its adoption should be of limited concern. As noted above, most of the rules set out in the Convention are considered to reflect customary law, and would therefore be applicable regardless of the status of the Convention. It has been written that '[w]hile the equal and independent status of organisations is the most likely cause for the reluctance of States to bind themselves to the 1986 Convention, for organisations this would rather be the apprehension that the Convention will curtail IGO treaty-making practice'.[90] Whatever the reason, contemporary international relations require IOs to conclude treaties as a matter of course on a wide range of matters, and organizations routinely do, and indeed must, conclude such agreements. Thus, the fact that the Convention has not entered into force does not detract from the competence of IOs to enter into treaties. In the conclusion and operation of such treaties, reference to the provisions of customary law and the 1986 VCLT—and ironically, the 1969 VCLT[91]—will continue to be instructive.

Recommended Reading

JE Alvarez, *International Organizations as Law-makers* (OUP, Oxford 2005)

C Brölmann, *The Institutional Veil in Public International Law: International Organisations and the Law of Treaties* (Hart Publishing, Oxford 2007)

H Chiu, *The Capacity of International Organizations to Conclude Treaties and the Special Legal Aspects of Treaties so Concluded* (Martinus Nijhoff, Leiden 1966)

G do Nascimento e Silva, 'The 1986 Vienna Convention and the Treaty-making Power of International Organizations' (1986) 29 German Ybk Intl L 68

J Dobbert, 'Evolution of Treaty-making Capacity of International Organizations' in *The Law and the Sea: Essays in Memory of Jean Carroz* (FAO, Rome 1987)

M Footer, 'International Organizations and Treaties: Ratification and (Non)-implementation of the *Other* Vienna Convention on the Law of Treaties' in A Orakhelashvili and S Williams (eds), *40 Years of the Vienna Convention on the Law of Treaties* (BIICL, London 2010)

G Gaja, 'A "New" Vienna Convention on the Law of Treaties between States and International Organizations or between International Organizations: A Critical Commentary' (1987) 58 BYBIL 253

R Higgins, *The Development of International Law through the Political Organs of the United Nations* (OUP, Oxford 1963)

DB Hollis, 'Why State Consent Still Matters: Non-State Actors, Treaties, and the Changing Sources of International Law' (2005) 23 Berkeley J Intl L 137

H Isak and G Loibl, 'The United Nations Conference on the Law of Treaties between States and International Organizations or Between International Organizations' (1987) 38 Österreichische Zeitschrift für öffentliches Recht und Völkerrecht 49

---

[90] Brölmann (n 1) 192–3.

[91] Ibid (noting, for example, that 'the European Court of Justice, when relying on the international law of treaties, always refers to the 1969 Convention and not to the 1986 Convention').

J Klabbers, *An Introduction to International Institutional Law* (2nd edn CUP, Cambridge 2009)

P Reuter, 'La conférence de Vienne sur les traités des organisations internationals et la securité des engagement conventionnels' in F Capotorti and others (eds), *Du droit international de l'intégration: Liber Amicorum Pierre Pescatore* (Nomos, Baden Baden 1987)

H Schermers and N Blokker, *International Institutional Law: Unity Within Diversity* (4th edn Martinus Nijhoff, Leiden 2003) especially §§1743–99

F Seyersted, *Common Law of International Organizations* (Martinus Nijhoff, Leiden 2008)

F Seyersted, 'International Personality of Intergovernmental Organizations: Do Their Capacities Really Depend Upon Their Constitutions?' (1964) 4 Indian J Intl L 1

K Zemanek (ed), *Agreements of International Organizations and the Vienna Convention on the Law of Treaties* (Springer Verlag, Vienna 1971) (38 Österreichische Zeitschrift für öffentliches Recht und Völkerrecht, Supplementum 1)

4

Who Can Make Treaties? The European Union

Marise Cremona

Introduction

The European Union is unique as a treaty-making actor. It is one of the most prolific makers of treaties, and although it is certainly true that treaties in general have gained in importance as a source of law over the last century, the EU's use of the treaty as a key component of its foreign policy is striking. The EU uses treaties to structure and define its relations with third countries, to devise different models of agreement for groups of partners, to promote its vision of 'an international system based on stronger multilateral cooperation and good global governance',[1] and engages actively in the construction of new multilateral conventions and campaigns for their ratification. At the time of writing, according to the EU's treaty office, the EU is party to 778 bilateral and 240 multilateral treaties.[2] Despite an initially relatively narrow scope of activity, the EU now engages in treaty-making over a very wide field beyond its core competence for trade agreements, ranging from private international law to air services, from climate change to organized crime. As such the EU's treaty-making activity has profoundly affected the Member States, not so much because they have been replaced as treaty parties, but in that they now operate alongside the EU and the other Member States in negotiating treaties and implementing their treaty obligations. The Member States may, with some exceptions, continue to conclude treaties but in so doing they are constrained by both substantive and procedural EU law obligations.

All international organizations (IOs) that possess treaty-making power exhibit the tension that flows from being both a creation and a creator of international law. In the case of the EU this tension is particularly pronounced as a result of the

---

[1] Treaty on European Union (TEU) Art 21(2). Treaty references: the abbreviation 'TEU' refers to the Treaty on European Union [2010] OJ C83/13 (the version in force after 1 December 2009), while 'TFEU' refers to the Treaty on the Functioning of the European Union [2010] OJ C83/47. 'EC' refers to a provision of the Treaty Establishing the European Community [2002] OJ C325/33 (the version in force until 30 November 2009); similarly, 'EU' refers to the Treaty on European Union [2002] OJ C325/5 (the version in force until 30 November 2009).

[2] See European Commission, 'Treaties Office Database' <http://ec.europa.eu/world/agreements/default.home.do>.

evolution of its founding Treaty (now Treaties) into a 'constitutional charter'.[3] The relationship between the EU and its Member States represents a level of mutual trust and interdependence greater than is normally implied by IO membership,[4] and this affects the way that the EU and its Member States engage in treaty-making. While the form of integration represented by the EU may be described as supranational,[5] or as containing elements of federalism,[6] the EU is nonetheless an (advanced form of) IO. It is perhaps in its external relations and in its treaty-making that this is most clearly felt; in defining its external treaty-making powers the Court of Justice of the European Union (CJEU) has developed key doctrines including implied powers, exclusivity, and the autonomy of the Union legal order. At the same time the CJEU has regularly affirmed the key principle of conferred powers: the EU only has those powers which have been granted to it, expressly or impliedly, by its Member States in the EU Treaties.[7] Thus, the EU legal order may possess autonomy (by which the CJEU means the power to determine its relations with other legal orders) with respect both to the domestic law of its Member States and international law, but the EU does not possess sovereignty, nor in the last resort the ability to determine its own powers.

A further special feature of the EU has been the evolution of its architecture. In its initial phase, the European Economic Community was one of three separate Communities (alongside the European Coal and Steel Community—ECSC, and the European Atomic Energy Community—EAEC or Euratom) each with its own separate legal personality and external treaty-making powers, although soon sharing institutions. The single institutional framework was maintained on the creation of the European Union by the Treaty of Maastricht in 1992, and the relation between the European Union and the European Communities (as the renamed European Community—EC, ECSC and EAEC—were termed) was legally intricate.[8] The three European Communities retained their separate legal personalities, and since the Treaty of Maastricht made no express grant of legal personality to the EU, the international legal capacity of the Union was subject to debate.[9] The Treaty of Amsterdam of 1997 still did not mention an express legal personality for the Union

---

[3] Opinion 1/91 [1991] ECR I-6079 [21].

[4] Cf the 'principle of sincere cooperation' established by TEU Art 4(3).

[5] For a discussion of the spectrum between intergovernmental and supranational politics and the way in which different EU policies may be placed and move along the spectrum, see A Stone Sweet and W Sandholtz, 'European Integration and Supranational Governance' (1997) 4 JEPP 297.

[6] R Schütze, *From Dual to Cooperative Federalism: The Changing Structure of European Law* (OUP, Oxford 2009).

[7] The term 'EU Treaties' is used in this chapter to denote the founding treaties of the EU and in particular the current TEU and TFEU. The latter simply use the term 'the Treaties' to refer to these two treaties together (TEU Art 1 and TFEU Art 1), EU Treaties being used here to avoid confusion. Similarly it will be noticed that the CJEU will normally refer simply to 'the Treaty' or 'Treaties' by which it means the EC Treaty or TEU and TFEU Treaties respectively. EU instruments generally refer to treaties in the generic sense as 'international agreements': see eg TFEU Arts 216–19.

[8] DM Curtin and IF Dekker, 'The European Union from Maastricht to Lisbon: Institutional and Legal Unity out of the Shadows' in P Craig and G de Búrca (eds), *The Evolution of EU Law* (2nd edn OUP, Oxford 2011).

[9] J Klabbers, 'Presumptive Personality: The European Union in International Law' in M Koskenniemi (ed), *International Law Aspects of the European Union* (Kluwer Law International,

but this was presumed since it gave the EU treaty-making capacity in the fields of foreign and security policy and criminal justice cooperation.[10] In the following decade, therefore, what was known collectively as the 'European Union' actually encompassed four treaty-making organizations: the EU itself, the EC, the EAEC, and until 2002 the ECSC.[11] Although the three European Communities frequently concluded treaties jointly, only once, in the context of the Schengen *acquis* agreement with Switzerland, did the EU and EC conclude a treaty together. The Member States preferred to keep to the traditional formula of the 'mixed agreement' (an agreement concluded by both the EC and Member States) where an agreement contained foreign policy-related provisions. The Treaty of Lisbon, which came into force in December 2009, made major structural changes to this system. The European Union 'replaced and succeeded' the European Community (Article 1 TEU) and was granted an explicit legal personality (Article 47 TEU). The EU's former rather limited treaty-making powers therefore now encompass the more extensive treaty-making powers of the former European Community.[12]

The EU institutions often rightly stress the special nature of the EU as an international actor and seek specific solutions for EU participation in treaties.[13] And the EU's treaty partners certainly do need to appreciate its specificities. However, the EU works within the same international legal framework as its treaty partners and is constrained not only by its own constitutional requirements but by what its partners will accept and expect. Although the focus of this chapter is therefore on the perspective of EU law, it does address the ways in which international treaty law and practice has—or has not—accommodated the EU.

The first section of the chapter deals with the EU's treaty-making capacity, from the perspective first of EU law, and then of international treaty practice. In determining the rules which govern EU treaty-making, we need to consider first the principle of conferral, express and implied powers, and the importance of identifying a legal basis in the EU Treaties, then treaty-making procedures within EU law, and the role of the CJEU in reviewing the EU's powers. We next examine the ways in which international treaty-making practice has accommodated EU participation in bilateral and, especially, in multilateral agreements. The chapter's second section discusses the legal effects of treaties concluded by the EU, first as regards the EU legal order, including their enforcement and interpretation by the CJEU and the legal effects of mixed agreements. A discussion of the impact of EU treaty-making on the powers of the Member States follows: through the doctrines

---

The Hague 1998); RA Wessel, 'Revisiting the International Legal Status of the EU' (2000) 5 EFA Rev 507; R Gosalbo Bono, 'Some Reflections on the CFSP Legal Order' (2006) 43 CML Rev 337, 354–7.

[10] Formally, these were commonly referred to as the second and third pillars; the European Communities representing the 'first pillar'. The treaty-making powers for the EU were at that time based on EU Arts 24 and 38, introduced by the Treaty of Amsterdam in 1997.

[11] The ECSC Treaty was concluded for only fifty years and since its powers could be exercised by the EC this Community was allowed to die in 2002.

[12] It should be noted that the EAEC (Euratom) was not replaced and succeeded by the European Union and still retains its separate constitutive Treaty, its legal personality, and its treaty-making power.

[13] M Licková, 'European Exceptionalism in International Law' (2008) 19 EJIL 463.

of exclusivity and pre-emption, the impact of EU law on treaties concluded by the Member States, and finally EU treaty-making from the perspective of international responsibility.

I. The European Union's Capacity to Make Treaties

The EU's treaty-making capacity depends on two factors: the treaty-making power granted by its Member States, and external acceptance of such power. First, the Member States must by the EU Treaties have conferred on the EU competence over the subject matter of the proposed agreement, and the authority to enter into international agreements on such matters. As discussed below, under the EU Treaties that authority may be expressed or implied and its exercise is subject to specific procedural requirements and judicial review. Second, even if the EU has authority to conclude a treaty, its ability to do so depends on the acceptance of that authority by any potential treaty partners. The EU may participate in lieu of its Member States or alongside them in what is known as a mixed agreement, depending on the nature of the EU's powers in relation to the treaty's subject matter. In the case of multilateral mixed agreements, increasingly States have agreed to EU treaty participation through the use of a particular formula allowing Regional Economic Integration Organizations (REIOs) to join the treaty alongside its Member States. In the case of certain older treaties such as the UN Charter and treaties concluded under the auspices of some of the UN agencies, participation by IOs is not envisaged and the EU still cannot consent to the treaty notwithstanding any internal competence to do so.

A. The treaty-making powers of the European Union

1. *The conferral of EU treaty-making powers*

(i) Establishing express and implied treaty-making powers
The extent to which the EU may exercise its capacity to act externally is defined, first and foremost, by the scope of the competences granted to it by its Member States in the EU Treaties. The EU has limited, albeit extensive, powers and operates under the principle of conferral.[14] The CJEU, with its formulation of implied powers and its willingness to take an open approach to uses of express treaty-making power, was instrumental in shaping the treaty-making capacity of the EC, and although the EU is now the relevant international actor, we still need to be aware of the evolution of the European Community's external powers to understand how these are reflected in the existing EU Treaties. Indeed, a number of the

---

[14] TEU Art 5(1); TEU Art 5(2) specifies that under the principle of conferral 'the Union shall act only within the limits of the competence conferred on it by the Member States in the Treaties to attain the objectives set out therein'.

provisions relating to competences in the current EU Treaties are in effect a codification of earlier CJEU case law.

The original Treaty of Rome granted to the then European Economic Community (EEC) two express treaty-making powers, one in the field of trade (the common commercial policy, now considerably amended as Article 207 TFEU), the other establishing the power to conclude association agreements with third States or groups of States (now Article 217 TFEU).[15] Since then, the treaty-making powers of first the EEC, then the European Community (EC), and now the European Union (EU) have expanded in three different ways. First, new express competences have been added, including development cooperation, environment, humanitarian aid, and the common foreign and security policy. Second, the scope of the original trade competence has expanded to include trade in services, commercial aspects of intellectual property, and foreign direct investment. And, third, through the CJEU's willingness to imply an external treaty-making power from the existence of internal powers, implied external competence has been recognized in fields as varied as transport and civil justice.

In the 1964 *Costa v ENEL* judgment, the CJEU first recognized the Community's international legal personality, explicitly linking its international legal capacity to the transfer of powers from the Member States to the Community.[16] The autonomy of the Community legal order represented by this transfer of powers thus formed the legal basis for its effective international action. In its 1971 *ERTA* judgment, the Court built on the statement of legal personality in the then EEC Treaty to conclude that the Community's external capacity extended over the 'whole extent of the field of the objectives defined in Part I' of the Treaty and— crucially—that its competence to enter into international agreements was not limited to those cases where there was express provision for external action.[17]

Since this seminal judgment, the existence of an implied external competence to conclude treaties has become well-established in the CJEU's case law,[18] although its extent and the precise nature of the EU's implied competences are still the subject of academic discussion, institutional debate, and new case law. In *Opinion 1/03*,[19] which confirmed the existence (and exclusivity) of Community competence to conclude the revised Lugano Convention, an agreement within a relatively new field of action for the Community (judicial cooperation in civil matters), the Court summarized its earlier case law on the existence of implied powers:

---

[15] Association Agreements provide 'reciprocal rights and obligations, common action and special procedures' (TFEU Art 217). They were initially concluded with the former colonies of Member States and with the EEC's close neighbours, but developed into a political vehicle for establishing substantial long-term ties with the EU, irrespective of geographic or historical linkages.

[16] Case 6/64 *Costa v ENEL* [1964] ECR 585, 593.

[17] Case 22/70 *Commission v Council* [1971] ECR 263 [14] (*ERTA* case).

[18] Opinion 2/91 [1993] ECR I-1061; Opinion 1/94 [1994] ECR I-5267; Opinion 1/03 [2006] ECR I-1145; A Dashwood and J Heliskoski, 'The Classic Authorities Revisited' in A Dashwood and C Hillion (eds), *The General Law of EC External Relations* (Sweet and Maxwell, London 2000).

[19] Opinion 1/03 (n 18).

The competence of the Community to conclude international agreements may arise not only from an express conferment by the Treaty but may equally flow implicitly from other provisions of the Treaty and from measures adopted, within the framework of those provisions, by the Community institutions (see *ERTA*, paragraph 16). The Court has also held that whenever Community law created for those institutions powers within its internal system for the purpose of attaining a specific objective, the Community had authority to undertake international commitments necessary for the attainment of that objective even in the absence of an express provision to that effect (Opinion 1/76, paragraph 3, and Opinion 2/91, paragraph 7). That competence of the Community may be exclusive or shared with the Member States.[20]

The Court here mentions the two traditional bases for implied powers: first, the existence of Community legislation, ie 'Community rules' whether or not adopted within the framework of a common policy;[21] and second, the existence of a Community objective for the attainment of which internal powers under the EC Treaty may be complemented by external treaty-making powers. The first basis is founded on pre-emption, the occupation of the field by existing Community law (hence the equation in the *ERTA* case between the existence of the competence and its exclusive nature[22]). The second basis derives from the principle of *effet utile*, the implication of powers necessary to achieve an expressly defined objective. In *Opinion 1/03* itself the Court spends little time on establishing the existence of implied competence, but appears to rely on the first basis—existence of (internal) Community legislation, specifically the EC Regulation on jurisdiction and the recognition and enforcement of judgments in civil and commercial matters.[23]

In contrast, the second basis for implied powers requires attention to the nature and content of the EU's internal rules, and in particular the EU Treaties, to identify the 'specific objective' for which internal powers have been granted and for which implied external powers may be necessary. The importance of that objective was underlined in *Opinion 1/94* in the context of the EC's conclusion of the WTO agreements.[24] There, the Court defined the EC Treaty provisions on services as being essentially concerned with its internal market objective, namely the liberalization of services within the Community, rather than services liberalization *tout court*. This explains why an additional *express* provision for concluding agreements on international trade in services was subsequently included within what is now Article 207 TFEU.

In some cases where implied treaty-making powers are still required (eg taxation or competition policy), a similar link to the completion or functioning of the internal market will be necessary. In other cases (eg capital movements), the EU Treaties themselves include external as well as internal objectives thereby clearly suggesting an implied treaty-making power. Sometimes the extent of the objective

---

[20] Ibid [114]–[115].
[21] Case 22/70 *Commission v Council* (n 17); Opinion 2/91 (n 18).
[22] Where it exists, EU competence can vary in its nature: exclusive, shared with the Member States, supporting or supplementary (TFEU Art 2).
[23] Opinion 1/03 (n 18) [134].
[24] Opinion 1/94 (n 18) [82]–[86].

in the EU Treaties is not so clear (eg social policy), or the link between pursuing an external policy and its impact on the internal Union regime is so close that it is difficult to disentangle the two (eg energy policy). These variations point to the need to examine the internal objectives and powers carefully when determining the potential scope of implied external powers.

The emphasis on EU Treaty objectives is certainly a logical consequence of applying an *effet utile* principle. *Opinion 1/03* suggests that this principle does not play a central role where the basis for external competence is simply the existence of internal rules. The two alternative bases for implied powers thus may attach very different significance to the objectives of the relevant EU Treaty provisions, something which is implicit in the case law and now reflected in Article 216 TFEU (discussed below), but not explicitly explained or justified. A justification may be found in the fact that where the external power is based on internal legislation, that legislation itself will reflect the objectives of its legal basis in the EU Treaties. The result, in either case, is that implied external powers are inherently (and properly) limited and cannot provide the basis for developing an external policy independent of the needs and functioning of the internal regime. For that, under the current Treaty system, explicit powers are needed (such as are granted in fields such as trade, development cooperation, environmental policy, and the common foreign and security policy). This is coherent in terms of the balance between the necessary flexibility of an implied powers doctrine and the need to ensure compliance with the principle of conferred powers.

(ii) Extending the scope of EU powers

The development of implied treaty-making powers under EU law has been complemented by two other mechanisms that effectively extended the scope of the EU's external action. First, there was the extensive interpretation of the scope of the two original express bases for international agreements. The Court held that Association Agreements could cover all fields of Community (and now Union) policy, even those where no common action had yet been adopted by the Union.[25] The Court was also prepared to see the Union's express trade powers used for purposes beyond traditional trade policy, including development,[26] the protection of the environment,[27] and the adoption of politically motivated economic sanctions against third countries.[28]

Second, Article 352 TFEU has been used for treaty-making; it provides a legal basis for action by the Union (including external action) if such 'should prove necessary, within the framework of the policies defined in the Treaties, to attain one of the objectives set out in the Treaties, and the Treaties have not provided the

[25] Case 12/86 *Demirel v Stadt Schwäbisch Gmünd* [1987] ECR 3719.
[26] Opinion 1/78 [1979] ECR 2871; Case 45/86 *Commission v Council* [1987] ECR 1493.
[27] Case C-281/01 *Commission v Council* [2002] ECR I-12049.
[28] Case C-124/95 *R v HM Treasury and Bank of England Ex p Centro-Com* [1997] ECR I-81; Case C-84/95 *Bosphorus Hava Yollari Turizm ve Ticaret AS v Ministry of Transport, Energy and Communications* [1996] ECR I-3953. Powers in each of these fields are now expressly granted to the EU.

necessary powers'. This provision proved particularly useful in the early years of the European Community. It was used alongside trade powers to conclude international agreements that envisaged cooperation over a number of fields but which the Union did not wish to conclude as Association Agreements. However, the limits of Article 352 TFEU were illustrated in both *Opinion 1/94* and *Opinion 2/94*.[29] In the latter ruling in particular, the Court held that it should not be used in such a way as to undermine the principle of conferral. It held that Article 235 EC (now Article 352 TFEU):

being an integral part of an institutional system based on the principle of conferred powers, cannot serve as a basis for widening the scope of Community powers beyond the general framework created by the provisions of the Treaty as a whole and, in particular, by those that define the tasks and the activities of the Community. On any view, Article 235 [now Article 352 TFEU] cannot be used as a basis for the adoption of provisions whose effect would, in substance, be to amend the Treaty without following the procedure which it provides for that purpose.[30]

Successive amendments, including most recently the Treaty of Lisbon, have indeed added new express legal bases to those in the original Treaty of Rome. To some extent this has lessened the need to use implied powers. Express external powers now include specific fields of external policy: common commercial policy (Article 207 TFEU); Association Agreements (Article 217 TFEU); development cooperation (Article 209(2) TFEU); economic, financial, and technical cooperation (Article 212(3) TFEU); humanitarian aid (Article 214(4) TFEU); neighbourhood agreements (Article 8 TEU); and the common foreign and security policy (Article 37 TEU). There are also express references to international agreements in general policy provisions, such as environmental policy (Articles 191(4) and 192 TFEU), asylum (Article 78(2)(g) TFEU) and immigration (Article 79(3) TFEU on readmission agreements). However, it remains the case that important areas of policy, including transport policy, energy and cooperation on serious transnational crime and terrorism, are still subject to implied powers as far as EU treaty-making is concerned.

The Treaty of Lisbon attempts to synthesize all the different possibilities for deriving EU treaty-making powers in a single article:

The Union may conclude an agreement with one or more third countries or international organisations where the Treaties so provide or where the conclusion of an agreement is necessary in order to achieve, within the framework of the Union's policies, one of the objectives referred to in the Treaties, or is provided for in a legally binding Union act or is likely to affect common rules or alter their scope.[31]

The aim of this provision is to increase certainty in establishing clearly the principle of implied treaty-making powers in the Union legal order, and to achieve a clearer definition of EU competence. Difficulties emerge, however, in the article's attempt

---

[29] Opinion 1/94 (n 18); Opinion 2/94 [1996] ECR I-1759.
[30] Opinion 2/94 (n 29) [30]. See Declarations 41 and 42 annexed to the Treaty of Lisbon.
[31] TFEU Art 216(1).

to reflect the case law on this issue—case law that is complex and sometimes obscure.

Three alternative conditions for implied EU treaty-making power are included in Article 216(1) TFEU. According to the first of these, external powers exist 'where the conclusion of an agreement is necessary in order to achieve, within the framework of the Union's policies, one of the objectives referred to in the Treaties'. Although clearly intended to reflect the case law, this text seems on its face to establish a potentially wider basis for implied powers. No longer is there a need for the agreement to be necessary to achieve an objective for which internal powers have been provided (and which is therefore likely, though not inevitably, to be internal in orientation). Rather, all that is needed is for the objective to be referred to in the EU Treaties (which include the very widely drawn general external objectives of Articles 3(5) and 21(2) TEU), and for the action to take place 'within the framework of the Union's policies'. This last phrase is ambiguous. It could mean that the objective must be a stated objective of an internal EU policy field, but this is not required by a simple reading of the text. Despite, therefore, the ostensible aim of the Treaty of Lisbon's drafters to delimit the Union's powers more closely, and despite the strengthening of the conferred powers principle by an express provision that 'competences not conferred upon the Union in the Treaties remain with the Member States',[32] the Treaty of Lisbon has potentially extended the scope of implied powers by loosening the requisite link between 'internal' objectives and external action.

Turning to the second condition of competence, it clearly makes sense for the Article on general treaty-making powers to provide that 'a legally binding Union act' may provide for the conclusion of an international agreement. This provision is intended to reflect CJEU case law.[33] Although it does not give any guidance as to the limits of the powers potentially conferred by a legally binding act, this provision should not be seen as granting the legislature carte blanche to authorize external competence for EU treaty-making. The principle of conferred powers would require that the authorized agreement facilitates an EU objective as well as the existence of a link between the legal basis for the competence-conferring act of secondary EU law and the scope of the envisaged agreement.[34] The existence of a valid internal act will thus ensure that the international agreement has an appropriate legal basis in the EU Treaties.[35]

The third possible basis for action specified in Article 216(1) TFEU is more problematic. The EU, according to this provision, has the power to conclude an

---

[32] TEU Art 5(2); note also the reiterations of the conferred powers principle in TEU Art 4(1), TFEU Art 7, and Declaration 18.

[33] Opinion 1/94 (n 18) [95].

[34] Although the provision is phrased in terms of EU treaty-making, it is also possible for a legislative act to establish an agency with its own treaty-making powers such as Europol or Eurojust, albeit under EU institutional control. See eg Council Decision of 6 April 2009 establishing the European Police Office [2009] OJ L121/37.

[35] And as a corollary that the annulment of the authorizing internal act would imply the illegality of the act concluding the agreement.

international agreement where its conclusion 'is likely to affect common rules or alter their scope'. The purpose of this provision is not clear. It is presumably intended to reflect CJEU case law which has based implied external competence on the existence of a body of (internal) Union legislation in the field, but without any reference to 'effects'.[36] In fact, this basis for competence to conclude an agreement is arguably unnecessary. It is difficult to conceive of a situation where an agreement should be concluded by the Union because it is 'likely to affect common rules or alter their scope', but which, on the other hand, does not fulfil the first condition for action (that it would be 'necessary in order to achieve, within the framework of the Union's policies, one of the objectives referred to in the Treaties'). Worse, the phrase introduces confusion between the existence of competence and its exclusivity, that is, between the capacity of the EU to conclude a treaty and the nature (exclusive or shared) of Union competence over its contents, although elsewhere in the EU Treaties this distinction is carefully drawn.

(iii) The importance of legal basis
To sum up: EU treaty-making powers may be derived from express provisions in the EU Treaties, as well as implied from the large number of those Treaty provisions granting internal powers and establishing objectives that require external action. In these circumstances it is not surprising that the choice of legal basis may become an issue, whether for the adoption of internal measures or the conclusion of international agreements. The legal basis for Union acts and international agreements has been said by the Court to be a matter 'of constitutional significance'.[37] The choice of legal basis is relevant in determining the type of act that may be adopted and the procedures to be followed (eg the role of the European Parliament and voting procedure in the Council) as well as the relative scope of different policies and how they interrelate. To what extent, for example, may a trade measure pursue environmental objectives and when might an additional (or alternative) environmental legal basis be needed? Choice of legal basis may also have implications for the relative powers of the Union and its Member States, with a few, including trade, carrying exclusive competence, and others being a matter of shared competence.

---

[36] Exemplified by Opinion 1/03 (n 18), which summarized earlier case law; note, however, that this particular Opinion of the Court was delivered after the drafting of the draft Constitutional Treaty, from which the wording of TFEU Art 216 is taken.

[37] 'The choice of the appropriate legal basis has constitutional significance. Since the Community has conferred powers only, it must tie the Protocol to a Treaty provision which empowers it to approve such a measure. To proceed on an incorrect legal basis is therefore liable to invalidate the act concluding the agreement and so vitiate the Community's consent to be bound by the agreement it has signed'. Opinion 2/00 [2001] ECR I-9713 [5]. Note, however, that although the internal concluding act may be invalidated, this does not in itself vitiate the Union's consent to be bound by the agreement as a matter of international law. Case C-327/91 *France v Commission* [1994] ECR I-3641 [24]–[25]. See also Joined Cases C-317/04 and C-318/04 *European Parliament v Council* [2006] ECR I-4721 [73] (*PNR* case).

The Court of Justice has consistently held that 'the choice of the legal basis for a Community measure, including one adopted with a view to conclusion of an international agreement, must be based on objective factors which are amenable to judicial review and include in particular the aim and content of the measure'.[38] Further the Court has developed what has become known as the 'predominant purpose' or 'centre of gravity' test: if it appears that a measure 'pursues a twofold purpose or that it has a twofold component and if one is identifiable as the main or predominant purpose or component, whereas the other is merely incidental, the measure must be founded on a single legal basis, namely that required by the main or predominant purpose or component'.[39] A joint legal basis is only to be used where it is impossible to conclude that one or the other predominates in aim or content.[40] The Court has been consistent in applying the same criteria for determining the legal basis of an international agreement as for an internal measure, based on its aim and content, the predominant purpose test, and with a bias against a dual legal basis.[41]

It is worth asking whether this approach needs adjustment in the context of international agreements. Is the bias against multiple legal bases appropriate given that the EU's international agreements often contain a wide range of subject matters and the need to integrate different objectives? Cross-sectoral agreements still regularly give rise to legal basis disputes, fuelled both by different decision-making procedures and by differences in the nature of Union competence. In resolving these disputes the Court's application of the predominant purpose test has not enhanced predictability.

In practical terms, and from the perspective of third countries, these arguments may appear esoteric; the position is made easier for the Union's negotiating partners by the practice of determining a negotiating mandate without prejudice to a final determination of legal basis (thus allowing negotiations to proceed while internal discussions continue over the proper legal basis). However, from time to time a CJEU Opinion has been necessary to determine the proper legal basis before an agreement could be formally concluded, thus considerably delaying its conclusion.[42] Where an agreement is concluded on a legal basis which the Court subsequently holds to be incorrect, the decision concluding the agreement must be re-adopted on the correct legal basis; this does not, however, affect the binding nature of the agreement in international law as far as the Union is concerned.

---

[38] Case C-94/03 *Commission v Council* [2006] ECR I-1 [34].

[39] Ibid [35].

[40] Case C-411/06 *Commission v European Parliament and Council* [2009] ECR I-7585 [47].

[41] See eg Case C-94/03 *Commission v Council* (n 38) and Case C-178/03 *Commission v European Parliament and Council* [2006] ECR I-107, where the Court used exactly the same approach in establishing the legal basis for the decision concluding the Rotterdam Convention and for the internal Regulation.

[42] See eg Opinion 1/94 (n 18); Opinion 2/00 (n 37); Opinion 1/08 [2009] ECR I-11129. An Opinion from the Court will typically take around eighteen months and may take longer.

2. Treaty-making procedures

Alongside the substantive power-conferring provisions, Article 218 TFEU provides a set of procedural rules for the conclusion of treaties by the EU.[43] Importantly, it applies to all EU international treaty-making, including the common foreign and security policy (CFSP), albeit that its rules do differentiate between this and other policy fields.[44] This means that where a treaty is concluded under implied powers, Article 218 TFEU procedures apply, not the internal decision-making procedures established in the provision from which the power is implied. Thus, the Commission's implementation powers in the field of competition policy do not entitle it to conclude on its own international agreements on competition; such agreements must be negotiated and concluded according to Article 218.[45]

The procedure begins with a recommendation from the European Commission to the Council of Ministers that negotiations should be opened. The Council then adopts a decision authorizing the negotiation. It will normally also adopt 'negotiating directives' outlining the envisaged agreement or the Union's negotiating goals. The content of this negotiating mandate is not made public. Council decisions are also necessary to approve the agreement's signature, its provisional application (if necessary), and conclusion. Such decisions are formal legal acts, requiring a Commission proposal and a specific legal basis, which will be stated in its Preamble. In general, the Council will act by qualified majority vote (a system of weighted voting), but will need to act unanimously (i) where the agreement concerns a field for which unanimity is required (this is increasingly rare, but includes the CFSP and direct taxation), (ii) in the case of Association Agreements and certain agreements with candidate states, and (iii) in the special case of the agreement (under negotiation at time of writing) for the EU's accession to the European Convention for the Protection of Human Rights and Fundamental Freedoms. Under Article 218(9) TFEU, a Council decision is also required to suspend the application of an agreement.[46]

The European Parliament plays an increasing role in the adoption of the decision to approve an international agreement. Parliamentary consent is required in a number of cases, which are significantly increased by the Treaty of Lisbon:

(i) Association agreements based on Article 217 TFEU.

(ii) Union accession to the European Convention for the Protection of Human Rights and Fundamental Freedoms envisaged by Article 6 TEU.

(iii) Agreements 'establishing a specific institutional framework by organizing cooperation procedures'; these might include neighbourhood agreements

---

[43] The current provision amends, amplifies, and simplifies the pre-existing provision in EC Art 300.
[44] TFEU Art 219 establishes specific rules for agreements concerning monetary and foreign exchange regime matters.
[45] Case C-327/91 *France v Commission* (n 37).
[46] See eg Council Decision (EC) 91/586 suspending the application of the Agreement between the European Community, its Member States and the Socialist Federal Republic of Yugoslavia [1991] OJ L315/47; see further Case C-162/96 *Racke GmbH & Co v Hauptzollamt Mainz* [1998] ECR I-3655.

(Article 8 TEU), cooperation agreements (Article 212 TFEU) and development cooperation agreements (Article 209(2) TFEU). Agreements establishing institutions capable of taking binding decisions clearly fall under this head but 'cooperation procedures' has a potentially wider scope.

(iv) Agreements with important budgetary implications for the Union; what amounts to 'important' depends of course on the context in which the expenditure is assessed.[47]

(v) Agreements covering fields to which either the ordinary legislative procedure applies or the special legislative procedure with consent of the European Parliament. Here, the Treaty of Lisbon has made a significant difference. Previously in cases where internal decisions were taken by co-decision of Council and Parliament only parliamentary consultation was required; now Parliament must consent. A number of significant sectors, including trade agreements, are governed by the ordinary legislative procedure and consequently, the number of international agreements requiring parliamentary consent has increased.

Article 218 thus foresees Parliament's involvement at the end of the process, prior to formal conclusion of the agreement. Article 218(10) also requires that the Parliament is to be kept 'immediately and fully informed' at all stages of the procedure, and—at least in cases where the Parliament's consent will ultimately be required—this may entail a substantial involvement and even observer status in the negotiations.[48] In contrast to this increased role generally, Article 218 provides for no formal parliamentary involvement where international agreements relate *exclusively* to the common foreign and security policy; there is only a general obligation on the part of the High Representative to consult the European Parliament on the 'main aspects and basic choices' of the CFSP.[49]

3. Judicial control of EU international agreements

The EU's international agreements may be subject to judicial control both *ex ante* and *ex post*. *Ex ante* control takes the form of an 'opinion' of the CJEU, requested under Article 218(11) TFEU 'as to whether an agreement envisaged is compatible with the Treaties'. Although called an opinion, this is a binding ruling in the sense that, should the Court determine that there is an incompatibility between the agreement and the EU Treaties, 'the agreement envisaged may not enter into

---

[47] See eg Case C-189/97 *European Parliament v Council* [1999] ECR I-4741.

[48] For example, see the Parliament's detailed involvement through its International Trade (INTA) Committee with the agreement with South Korea negotiated in 2009–10. Committee on International Trade, 'Recommendation on the draft Council decision on the conclusion of the Free Trade Agreement between the European Union and its Member States, of the one part, and the Republic of Korea, of the other part' (9 February 2011, PE441.233v02-00/A7-0034/2011). On the possibility of observer status in negotiations, see European Parliament, 'Rules of Procedure' (2010) Annex XIV [25].

[49] TEU Art 36.

force unless it is amended or the Treaties are revised'.[50] The opinion may be requested by the Council, Commission, European Parliament, or a Member State (but not an individual). In *Opinion 1/75* (the first such opinion) the Court explained the purpose of the procedure: it is designed to avoid the complications that would arise both within the Union system and in international law were the Court to find that an international agreement to which the Union has already consented is incompatible with the Treaty.[51]

The fact that an agreement has already been negotiated does not prevent it from being 'envisaged.' However once an agreement has been formally concluded it is no longer envisaged and this *ex ante* procedure can no longer be used.[52] On the other hand, the fact that certain aspects of the agreement have not yet been definitely agreed does not prevent the Court from giving a ruling.[53] It has even been possible to request an opinion on a prospective agreement where there is not yet a draft agreement and before negotiations have started, although in such a case, the Court may be limited to addressing issues of Union competence since questions of substantive compatibility may not be determinable in the absence of a text.[54] Although the CJEU has found a substantive incompatibility in a proposed agreement in only a few cases,[55] the Court has interpreted the concept of compatibility widely, to cover the functions and powers of the EU institutions including the CJEU itself,[56] the role and duties of the domestic courts of the Member States in interpreting Union law,[57] legal basis,[58] the existence of Union competence,[59] and the division of competence between the Union and the Member States.[60] As a consequence the fifteen opinions handed down by the CJEU have been important for the development of EU external relations law. Where such issues are not resolved beforehand, there is the possibility of *ex post* control, through judicial review of the decision concluding the agreement. This may be a question of substantive compatibility,[61] lack of competence,[62] or (more commonly) a dispute as to the choice of the legal basis for the agreement.[63] The relationship between the *ex ante* and *ex post* forms of control is worth a brief note. The opinion procedure can

---

[50] TFEU Art 218(11).   [51] Opinion 1/75 [1975] ECR 1355.

[52] Opinion 3/94 [1995] ECR I-4577.   [53] Opinion 1/78 (n 26).

[54] Opinion 2/94 (n 29) [1]–[22] on the possibility of EU accession to the ECHR. The Court's conclusion was that 'as Community law now stands, the Community has no competence to accede to the Convention'. Ibid [36]. The Treaty of Lisbon has inserted an explicit competence for the Union to accede to the ECHR in TEU Art 6(2), and a specific procedure in TFEU Art 218(8) TFEU.

[55] Eg Opinion 1/91 (n 3) on the European Economic Area agreement, and most recently Opinion 1/09 [2011] OJ C211/28 on the draft agreement establishing a European Patent Court.

[56] Eg Opinion 1/76 [1977] ECR 741; Opinion 1/91 (n 3); Opinion 1/92 [1992] ECR I-2821; Opinion 1/00 [2002] ECR I-3493; Opinion 1/09 (n 55).

[57] Opinion 1/09 (n 55).

[58] Opinion 2/00 (n 37); Opinion 1/08 (n 42).

[59] Opinion 2/94 (n 30).

[60] Opinion 2/91 (n 18); Opinion 1/94 (n 18); Opinion 1/03 (n 18).

[61] Case C-122/95 *Germany v Council* [1998] ECR I-973.

[62] Case C-327/91 *France v Commission* (n 37); Joined Cases C-317/04 and C-318/04 *European Parliament v Council* (n 37).

[63] Case C-268/94 *Portugal v Council* [1996] ECR I-6177; Case 45/86 *Commission v Council* (n 26); Case C-281/01 *Commission v Council* (n 27).

only be used before an agreement has been concluded, but the request for an opinion does not have a suspensive effect;[64] there is thus nothing to prevent the Council from concluding the agreement before the CJEU has given its ruling. In such a case, Article 218(11) TFEU ceases to be applicable and the Member State or institution affected will have to bring an action *ex post* for the annulment of the Council's concluding decision under Article 263 TFEU.[65]

B. Exercising the EU's treaty-making powers

Despite the Member States' grant of treaty-making powers to the EU, its ability to do so depends on the acceptance of that authority by its potential treaty partners. The treaty-making authority of the EEC, as well as of its sister organizations the ECSC and the Euratom were relatively quickly accepted by the international community, with the exception of members of the Council for Mutual Economic Assistance (CMEA or Comecon).[66] Once the European Union was granted treaty-making powers by the Treaty of Amsterdam in 1997, third countries started concluding treaties with the EU despite the absence of a clear attribution of legal personality.[67] Following the Treaty of Lisbon, the international community seems to have accepted the succession of the European Community by the European Union—which now has an explicit legal personality—without demur.

However there are still limitations; the UN and most of its agencies are open only to States and as a result the EU is not able to participate in international agreements negotiated within the framework of such bodies. The Food and Agriculture Organization changed its founding constitution to allow for EC (and now therefore EU) membership, as has the Hague Conference on Private International Law. But despite efforts to secure change, organizations including the IMO, ILO, and IMF are still closed to the EU. The same may apply to older multilateral conventions open only to State parties, such as the Convention on International Trade in Endangered Species (CITES).[68] In such cases, especially but not only where EU competence is exclusive, Member States may participate in treaties on behalf of the EU. Thus (according to the CJEU) the Union is not prevented from

---

[64] Opinion 3/94 (n 52).

[65] This happened in the so-called *PNR* case, concerning the conclusion of an agreement with the United States on the transfer by airline companies of passenger name records in Joined Cases C-317/04 and C-318/04 *European Parliament v Council* (n 37). The Court held that the legal basis of the agreement was invalid, the Council decision approving it was annulled, the agreement having to be renegotiated and concluded under a different legal basis. Council Decision (EU) 2006/729 on the signing, on behalf of the European Union, of an Agreement between the European Union and the United States of America on the processing and transfer of passenger name record (PNR) data by air carriers to the United States Department of Homeland Security [2006] OJ L298/27.

[66] The CMEA officially 'recognized' the EEC in 1988; even before that date individual members of the CMEA had concluded treaties with the EEC.

[67] See eg Council Decision (EU) 2006/313 concerning the conclusion of the Agreement between the International Criminal Court and the European Union on cooperation and assistance [2006] OJ L115/49.

[68] The amendment (the Gabarone amendment) which would allow the accession of REIOs to the Convention was agreed in 1983 but has not yet entered into force.

exercising its competence, since it does so through the Member States acting jointly in the Union's interest.[69]

Given acceptance of the EU as a treaty partner, how then is EU participation dealt with? In the case of bilateral treaties concluded by the EU alone, no special provision is normally made, although in a few cases it has been thought necessary to specify how an agreement with the EU affects the Member States.[70] As will be discussed below, a treaty concluded by the EU alone will, as a matter of EU law, bind the Member States; however, they are not bound as a matter of international law. Third countries do not in general see this as a problem, although it has been suggested that it may account in part for the willingness of third countries to accept the phenomenon of mixed agreements, even when mixity may not be strictly necessary in terms of EU competence.[71]

In the case of bilateral mixed agreements,[72] again special provision for EU participation is not normally made, but an indication may be given as to the different meanings attributed to the term 'Contracting Party'.[73] Where the EU is accepted as a party to a multilateral mixed agreement, this may be dealt with in a number of ways. In some cases, participation by the EU is expressly provided for in the treaty.[74] In others, a more elaborate Regional Economic Integration Organization (REIO) clause is used, which apart from allowing for accession to the specific treaty, will sometimes require a declaration of competence, and will specify the voting arrangements so as to avoid concurrent voting by the EU and any of its Member States.[75]

---

[69] Case C-45/07 *Commission v Greece* [2009] ECR I-701 [31]; see also Opinion 2/91 (n 18) [5].

[70] For example, the Agreement between the EU and the ICC (n 67), defines 'EU' so as to exclude 'the Member States in their own right', Art 2(1), and provides that requests for information originating from an individual Member State must be addressed directly to the relevant Member State, Art 3, thereby maintaining a clear separation between the EU and its Member States.

[71] PJ Kuijper, 'International Responsibility for EU Mixed Agreements' in C Hillion and P Koutrakos (eds), *Mixed Agreements Revisited—The EU and its Member States in the World* (Hart Publishing, Oxford 2010) 223–4, referring to the history of Art 36*bis* of the 1986 VCLT.

[72] Where a mixed agreement is concluded by the EU and its Member States 'of the one part' and a third country or group of countries 'of the other part', it has an 'essentially bilateral character'. Case C-316/91 *European Parliament v Council* [1994] ECR I-625 [33].

[73] For example, the European Economic Area Agreement [1994] OJ L1/3, Art 2(c) provides that 'the term "Contracting Parties" means, concerning the Community and the EC Member States, the Community and the EC Member States, or the Community, or the EC Member States. The meaning to be attributed to this expression in each case is to be deduced from the relevant provisions of this Agreement and from the respective competences of the Community and the EC Member States as they follow from the Treaty establishing the European Economic Community and the Treaty establishing the European Coal and Steel Community'.

[74] Eg Marrakesh Agreement Establishing the World Trade Organization (adopted 15 April 1994, entered into force 1 January 1995) 1867 UNTS 4, Art XI.

[75] See eg Stockholm Convention on Persistent Organic Pollutants (adopted 22 May 2001, entered into force 17 May 2004) 2256 UNTS 119, Art 2 (defining 'Party' to include a REIO and defining a REIO as 'an organization constituted by sovereign States of a given region to which its member States have transferred competence in respect of matters governed by this Convention and which has been duly authorized, in accordance with its internal procedures, to sign, ratify, accept, approve or accede to this Convention'); ibid Art 23(2) (dealing with the right to vote); ibid Art 25(2) (providing that a REIO that accedes without any of its member States being a Party will be bound by all the obligations under the Convention. Where one or more of its member States is a party, the REIO and its member States 'shall decide on their respective responsibilities for the performance of their obligations under the

While facilitating EU participation, these REIO clauses do not resolve all issues relating to the joint participation of the EU and its Member States, especially those concerning international responsibility for performance of the agreement.

One further aspect of practice in EU treaty-making deserves a brief mention here. Where the EU Member States, with or without the EU, enter into a multilateral treaty which overlaps to some extent with EU internal legislation, the parties may agree to include a so-called 'disconnection clause'. These clauses are designed to ensure that as between the EU and its Member States, it is EU law which is applied rather than the multilateral treaty. They thus emphasize that the EU and its Member States, if not one party, are at least in a special relationship to each other in their performance of the agreement. Disconnection clauses have been accepted in particular in Conventions concluded within the framework of the Council of Europe.[76] They differ from other 'without prejudice' and 'non-affect' clauses in that they operate automatically and are peremptory: they do not merely allow the Member States to apply EU law instead of the Convention's rules, but require them to do so. They are thus less a conflict rule than a choice of law rule. From the EU point of view, the disconnection clause facilitates mixed agreements by stipulating, at the level of international law and in the agreement itself, the obligation to apply Union law which the doctrine of primacy of Union law imposes on the Member States. This increases transparency, but there is no doubt that the clause can be controversial, notwithstanding EU assurances that the rights of other parties are not affected, and it will not be appropriate in all cases.[77]

II. The Legal Effects of EU Treaty-Making

A. International agreements and the EU legal order

1. Enforcement and interpretation

Once a treaty has been concluded by the EU it is, according to Article 216(2) TFEU, binding on the institutions of the Union and on the Member States. The

---

Convention' and shall not be entitled to exercise their rights concurrently); ibid Art 25(3) (providing for a declaration of competence by the REIO at the time of ratification or accession).

[76] For an example of a standard disconnection clause see Council of Europe Convention on Laundering, Search, Seizure and Confiscation of the Proceeds from Crime and on the Financing of Terrorism (adopted 16 May 2005, entered into force 1 May 2008) CETS No 198, Art 52(4): 'Parties which are members of the European Union shall, in their mutual relations, apply Community and European Union rules in so far as there are Community or European Union rules governing the particular subject concerned and applicable to the specific case, without prejudice to the object and purpose of the present Convention and without prejudice to its full application with other Parties.' The clause is accompanied by a Declaration which affirms that the clause does not affect the application of the Convention as between the EU and its Member States on the one hand and the other Parties to the Convention on the other.

[77] For example, since the disconnection clause leads to differentiation, it may raise issues where the Convention's aim is to establish a regime of common rules applicable to all parties. M Cremona, 'Disconnection Clauses in EU Law and Practice' in C Hillion and P Koutrakos (eds), *Mixed Agreements Revisited—The EU and its Member States in the World* (Hart Publishing, Oxford 2010).

agreement becomes, in the words of the Court of Justice, an integral part of the EU legal system,[78] and has primacy over legal acts adopted by the EU institutions (EU secondary legislation).[79] Consequently, such internal legal acts should be interpreted, so far as is possible, in a manner that is consistent with Union agreements.[80] Where that is not possible there is at least the possibility (although it is unusual in practice) of challenging the legality of such acts on grounds of incompatibility with an international agreement concluded by the EU.[81] Such an action requires not only that the agreement is binding on the EU, but also that 'the nature and the broad logic of the [agreement] do not preclude this'.[82] In addition, at least where the argument is raised before a national court and referred to the Court of Justice under Article 267 TFEU, it is necessary for the provisions of the agreement to 'appear, as regards their content, to be unconditional and sufficiently precise'.[83] The Court has consistently refused to accept that the WTO agreements satisfy these conditions,[84] and has come to the same conclusion with respect to the UN Convention on the Law of the Sea,[85] with the consequence that it will not impugn the legality of internal Union acts on grounds of incompatibility with these treaties.

Although international agreements in principle take precedence over secondary legislation, they do not prevail over EU primary law, and this includes not only the EU Treaties but also the EU's general principles of law, including fundamental human rights.[86] This follows logically from Article 218(11) TFEU, to the effect that agreements incompatible with the EU Treaties cannot enter into force unless either they or the Treaties are amended.

Article 216(2) TFEU applies to all treaties concluded by the Union, including in the field of the common foreign and security policy (CFSP). However, the jurisdiction of the Court of Justice with regard to the CFSP is limited. Under Article 275 TFEU, the Court does not have jurisdiction with respect to the Treaty provisions relating to the CFSP nor over acts adopted on the basis of those provisions. However, this exclusion is subject to exceptions: in the case of actions for annulment brought by natural or legal persons under Article 263(4) TFEU, the Court may review the legality of CFSP decisions providing for restrictive measures

---

[78] Case 181/73 *Haegeman v Belgium* [1974] ECR 449.

[79] Case C-61/94 *Commission v Germany* [1996] ECR I-3989 [52]; Case C-308/06 *R v Secretary of State for Transport* [2008] ECR I-4057 [42]–[45]; Joined Cases C-402/05 P and C-415/05 P *Yassin Abdullah Kadi v Council* [2008] ECR I-06351 [307].

[80] Case C-61/94 *Commission v Germany* (n 79) [52].

[81] Case C-377/98 *Netherlands v Council* [2001] ECR I-7079.

[82] Case C-344/04 *R v Department for Transport* [2006] ECR I-403 [39].

[83] Case C-308/06 *R v Secretary of State for Transport* (n 79) [45]; compare Case C-377/98 *Netherlands v Council* (n 81) [54]. For a clear exposition of the current position, see AG Kokott's opinion in Case C-366/10 *Air Transport Association of America and Others*, 6 October 2011.

[84] Case C-149/96 *Portugal v Council* [1999] ECR I-8395 [47]. Among the voluminous literature, see F Snyder, 'The Gatekeepers: The European Courts and the WTO' (2003) 40 CML Rev 313; PJ Kuijper and M Bronckers, 'WTO Law in the European Court of Justice' (2005) 42 CML Rev 1313.

[85] Case C-308/06 *R v Secretary of State for Transport* (n 79) [53]–[65]. See further M Mendez, 'The Legal Effect of Community Agreements: Maximalist Treaty Enforcement and Judicial Avoidance Techniques' (2010) 21 EJIL 83.

[86] Joined Cases C-402/05 P and C-415/05 P *Yassin Abdullah Kadi* (n 79) [306]–[309].

against natural or legal persons.[87] There is no reason in principle why a Council decision concluding a treaty should not be subject to review under this provision, although it is probably more likely that a measure implementing the agreement would satisfy these conditions. In addition, under Article 275 TFEU the Court may 'monitor compliance' with Article 40 TEU. This provides that CFSP action shall not 'affect' other policy fields, and also that non-CFSP action shall not 'affect' the CFSP. No doubt it will be possible for an opinion to be requested under Article 218(11) TFEU on the ground that an envisaged agreement does not comply with Article 40 TEU—for example, by use of an incorrect legal basis.

As we have already seen, according to Article 216(2) TFEU treaties concluded by the EU are binding on the Member States as a matter of Union law.[88] Thus in the *Kupferberg* case the Court was able to say:

In ensuring respect for commitments arising from an agreement concluded by the Community institutions the Member States fulfil an obligation not only in relation to the non-member country concerned but also and above all in relation to the Community which has assumed responsibility for the due performance of the Agreement.[89]

A corollary of this is that the Commission, in its role as 'guardian of the Treaties', may bring an enforcement action under Article 258 TFEU against a Member State on grounds of failure to comply with an international agreement concluded by the EU.[90] Such an action may be brought in relation to a mixed agreement where the provision breached is within the scope of Union law. Thus, in *Commission v France (Étang de Berre)*, the Court held that it was enough that the field was 'covered in large measure' by Community legislation; in such a case 'there is a Community interest in compliance by both the Community and its Member States with the commitments entered into under those instruments'.[91]

This 'Union interest' in compliance carries further implications for the Member States. Under Article 344 TFEU the Member States are under an obligation 'not to submit a dispute concerning the interpretation or application of the Treaties to any method of settlement other than those provided for therein'. Applying the concept of the autonomy of the Union legal system, the Court has interpreted this to mean that it has exclusive jurisdiction to resolve disputes between Member States concerning a breach of a mixed agreement provision within the scope of EU law. It is thus a breach of Article 344 TFEU for a Member State to use the agreement's

---

[87] TFEU Art 275(2).
[88] This applies to agreements concluded by the Union before the accession of a Member State as well as after its accession; these agreements form part of the Union 'acquis' accepted by each acceding Member State. Eg Act concerning the conditions of accession of the Czech Republic, the Republic of Estonia, the Republic of Cyprus, the Republic of Latvia, the Republic of Lithuania, the Republic of Hungary, the Republic of Malta, the Republic of Poland, the Republic of Slovenia and the Slovak Republic and the adjustments to the Treaties on which the European Union is founded, OJ 23.09.2003, 33, Art 6(1).
[89] Case 104/81 *Hauptzollampt Mainz v Kupferberg* [1982] ECR 3641 [13].
[90] Case C-61/94 *Commission v Germany* (n 79).
[91] Case C-239/03 *Commission v France* [2004] ECR I-9325 [29]; see also Case C-13/00 *Commission v Ireland* [2002] ECR I-2943.

dispute settlement procedure in a dispute with another EU Member State which raises issues of EU law.[92]

EU enforcement actions before the CJEU are not the only way to enforce international agreements against Member States. As an integral part of Union law, these treaties may be capable of creating individual rights enforceable directly in Member States' national courts ('direct effect'), subject to meeting a two-fold test based on the nature of the agreement as a whole and the nature of the specific obligation to be enforced:

> A provision in an agreement concluded by the Community with non-member countries must be regarded as being directly applicable when, regard being had to its wording and the purpose and nature of the agreement itself, the provision contains a clear and precise obligation which is not subject, in its implementation or effects, to the adoption of any subsequent measure.[93]

With the notable exception of the WTO, the Court has been relatively willing to grant direct effect to provisions of international agreements binding the EU, and this direct effect may extend to the binding decisions of institutions set up under those agreements, such as decisions of an Association Council.[94] Four points should be noted in this regard. First, the Court is clear that the determination of whether or not an EU agreement creates directly effective rights enforceable in national courts is not a matter to be decided by those national courts, but only by the CJEU itself.[95] The status granted to the treaty by EU law thus prevails over the determination of the status of international treaties in the Member States' national constitutional law. Second, as regards individual rights, the Court will defer to the parties' intentions as expressed in the agreement itself, or implied from its 'nature and structure';[96] it is this which has ultimately deterred the Court from granting direct effect to the WTO agreements. Third, where there is no expressed intention in the agreement, the Court will not be deterred from interpreting an agreement as capable of direct effect simply because other parties to the agreement may not grant it such effect.[97] Fourth, even where the provision of an EU agreement does not have direct effect, the courts of the Member States are required to interpret the

---

[92] See Case C-459/03 *Commission v Ireland* [2006] ECR I-4635 which concerned the 1982 UN Convention on the Law of the Sea (UNCLOS); the Court held that Ireland was in breach of its EU Treaty obligations for bringing dispute settlement proceedings against the UK before an Arbitral Tribunal established under Annex VII of the UNCLOS and the International Tribunal for the Law of the Sea with respect to an alleged breach of the UNCLOS that was within the scope of EU law.

[93] Case 12/86 *Demirel* (n 25) [14].

[94] See eg Case 104/81 *Kupferberg* (n 89); Case C-192/89 *S Z Sevince v Staatssecretaris van Justitie* [1990] ECR I-3461; Case C-18/90 *Office national de l'emploi v Kziber* [1991] ECR I-199; Case C-257/99 *R v Secretary of State for the Home Dept, ex p Barkoci and Malik* [2001] ECR I-6557; Case C-162/00 *Land Nordrhein-Westfalen v Pokrzeptowicz-Meyer* [2002] ECR I-1049; Case C-213/03 *Syndicat professionnel coordination des pêcheurs de l'étang de Berre v Électricité de France* [2004] ECR I-07357; Case C-265/03 *Simutenkov v Ministerio de Educación y Cultura* [2005] ECR I-2579; Case C-228/06 *Soysal v Germany* [2009] ECR I-01031.

[95] Case 104/81 *Kupferberg* (n 89) [14].

[96] Ibid [17].

[97] Ibid [18]. Having said this, the CJEU does give the practice of other parties to the WTO some weight: Case C-149/96 *Portugal v Council* (n 84) [43]–[45].

relevant national law in such a way as, to the fullest extent possible, to give effect to the objectives of the agreement.[98]

As this might suggest, the Court has jurisdiction to interpret the provisions of EU agreements, including by way of preliminary reference from national courts under Article 267 TFEU. In doing so, it regularly makes reference to Article 31 of the Vienna Convention on the Law of Treaties, to the effect that a treaty is to be interpreted in good faith in accordance with the ordinary meaning to be given to its terms in their context and in the light of its object and purpose.[99] Although it often makes the point that as a result, provisions of agreements binding the Union will not necessarily be interpreted in the same way as provisions of the EU Treaties which they closely resemble,[100] in practice the Court will often refer to its case law on the EU Treaties to assist in interpreting a similar provision of a Union agreement.[101]

2. Mixed agreements

Some of the most difficult issues in relation to the enforcement and interpretation of EU agreements arise in the context of mixed agreements. To what extent is a Member State under a Union law obligation (as opposed to an international law obligation) to implement a mixed agreement? To what extent does the CJEU have jurisdiction to interpret a mixed agreement? What follows is a summary of the case law as it stands at present, but this is an area subject to continuing litigation and the approach of the Court has evolved over time.[102]

First, the Court has jurisdiction to interpret the agreement as a whole in order to determine the relative competence of the Union and the Member States and responsibility for performance of the agreement.[103] Second, the provisions of a mixed agreement fall within the scope of Union law in so far as they relate to a field in which the EU has exercised its powers and adopted legislation. As such, the Member States are under an EU law obligation to implement those provisions and there is a Union interest to ensure compliance;[104] and the Court of Justice has jurisdiction to interpret those provisions and to determine their legal effects

---

[98] Joined Cases C-300/98 and C-392/98 *Parfums Christian Dior SA v TUK Consultancy BV* [2000] ECR I-11307 [47]; Case C-240/09 *Lesoochranárske zoskupenie VLK v Ministerstvo životného prostredia Slovenskej republiky* [2011] OJ C130/4 [50]–[51].

[99] Case C-416/96 *El-Yassini v Secretary of State for Home Department* [1999] ECR I-1209 [47]; Case C-268/99 *Jany v Staatssecretaris van Justitie* [2001] ECR I-8615 [35]; Case C-386/08 *Brita Gmbh v Hauptzollamt Hamburg-Hafen* [2010] OJ C100/4 [42]–[43].

[100] See eg Case 270/80 *Polydor Ltd v Harlequin Records Shops Ltd* [1982] ECR 329; Opinion 1/91 (n 3); Case 104/81 *Kupferberg* (n 89) [29]–[31].

[101] See eg Case C-438/00 *Deutscher Handballbund eV v Kolpak* [2003] ECR I-4135; Case C-265/03 *Simutenkov* (n 94).

[102] For a clear exposition of the current position, see AG Sharpston's opinion in Case C-240/09 *Lesoochranárske zoskupenie VLK* (n 98).

[103] Case C-431/05 *Merck Genéricos-Produtos Farmacêuticos Lda v Merck & Co Inc* [2007] ECR I-7001 [33]. See also Case C-459/03 *Commission v Ireland* (n 92).

[104] Case C-239/03 *Commission v France* (n 91).

(whether they are capable of creating directly effective rights).[105] Even where there is no EU legislation covering the specific issue, the above principle may apply where the field is 'in large measure' covered by EU law.[106] It will not always be easy to determine in a specific case whether these conditions are satisfied (and it is for the CJEU itself to decide the question).[107]

Third, if a provision of a mixed agreement lies in a field in which the Union has not legislated, then it will be left to the national courts to determine the legal effect of that provision. However, even in such cases the CJEU may interpret the provision, if it may apply both to situations governed by EU law and to situations governed by national law, and there is an interest in ensuring a uniform interpretation.[108] It will be seen from this that, just as the division of competences within a mixed agreement is subject to evolution, so too is the scope of jurisdiction of the Court to interpret such an agreement.

Mixed agreements impose obligations of cooperation on both the Member States and the Union institutions.[109] The duty includes the obligation to inform and consult, to contribute to the formation of a common Union position to be upheld in institutional structures established under a mixed agreement, as well as the duty not to pursue an autonomous position where a Union strategy exists.[110] As parties to mixed agreements, the Member States are not only parties in their own right, they are parties as Member States of the EU and as such do not have complete autonomy of action.

B. The impact of the EU on the Member States' treaty-making powers

1. Exclusivity, shared competence, and pre-emption

Prior to the Treaty of Lisbon, the EU Treaties contained no general statement categorizing competences as exclusive or shared, and the characteristics of exclusive Community (now Union) competence were developed by the Court of Justice. Within the field of external relations, the conditions under which exclusive competence arises, especially within implied powers, and the implications of exercising shared competence, are the subject of ongoing debate and continuing litigation. Recent case law has emphasized a rationale for exclusivity based on the need 'to ensure a uniform and consistent application of the [Union] rules and the proper functioning of the system which they establish in order to preserve the full

---

[105] Case C-431/05 *Merck Genéricos-Produtos Farmacêuticos* (n 103) [35]; Case C-240/09 *Lesoochranárske zoskupenie VLK* (n 98) [33].

[106] Case C-239/03 *Commission v France* (n 91) [29]–[31].

[107] For an example, see Case C-240/09 *Lesoochranárske zoskupenie VLK* (n 98) in which AG Sharpston and the Court of Justice came to different conclusions.

[108] Case C-130/95 *Giloy v Hauptzollamt Frankfurt am Main-Ost* [1997] ECR I-4291 [28]; Case C-53/96 *Hermès International v FHT Marketing Choice BV* [1998] ECR I-3603 [32].

[109] C Hillion, 'Mixity and Coherence in EU External Relations: the Significance of the Duty of Cooperation' in C Hillion and P Koutrakos (eds), *Mixed Agreements Revisited—The EU and its Member States in the World* (Hart Publishing, Oxford 2010).

[110] Case C-246/07 *Commission v Sweden* [2010] ECR I-3317.

effectiveness of [Union] law'.[111] This rationale, founded on the unity of the Union legal order and the uniform application of EU law, forms the basis of implied exclusive competence; it was also behind the Court-determined exclusivity of common commercial policy powers.[112] In the context of implied powers the need for exclusivity is expressed in terms of the possibility that an external agreement, if concluded by the Member State(s), would 'affect' Union rules. An actual conflict between rules is not necessary for this to occur.[113] Rather, it must be shown that the agreement covers a field which is within the scope of common Union rules, or within an area which is already largely covered by such rules. Its effect must then be judged by examining the nature and content of both the terms of the EU agreement and the Union measures.

The Treaty of Lisbon attempted to codify these principles; it may be read as a restatement of what was perceived by the drafters to be the current state of the law. First, it establishes different categories of competence: exclusive, shared, and complementary or supporting.[114] Certain competences are allocated to the exclusive and to the complementary categories and all others are declared to be shared. The list of complementary competences does not include any specifically external relations fields of activity, but, of course, the external dimensions of some of these areas (health, culture, tourism, and education) may well be important. Exclusive competences include the customs union and the common commercial policy as well as other fields which have an external dimension, such as conservation of marine biological resources and competition policy.

This a priori or constitutional exclusivity, where the Member States are as such precluded from acting, is different from pre-emption which applies in the case of shared competence where, as expressed in Article 2(2) TFEU, 'Member States shall exercise their competence to the extent that the Union has not exercised its competence'. The distinction is a useful one: pre-emption (unlike exclusivity) depends on Union action, and although the exercise of shared competence by the EU may pre-empt Member States' action, the right to exercise their competence may also be 'returned' to the Member States, at least in theory.[115] However, the Lisbon Treaty then unfortunately muddies this distinction. Article 3(2) TFEU provides:

The Union shall also have exclusive competence for the conclusion of an international agreement when its conclusion is provided for in a legislative act of the Union or is necessary to enable the Union to exercise its internal competence, or insofar as its conclusion may affect common rules or alter their scope.

---

[111] Opinion 1/03 (n 18) [128].

[112] Opinion 1/75 (n 51). See M Cremona, 'The External Dimension of the Single Market: Building (on) the Foundations' in C Barnard and J Scott (eds), *The Law of the Single European Market: Unpacking the Premises* (Hart Publishing, Oxford 2002).

[113] Case C-476/98 *Commission v Germany* [2002] ECR I-9855 [108]; Opinion 1/03 (n 18) [129].

[114] TFEU Art 2.

[115] TFEU Art 2(2) and Declaration 18.

Not only does this provision fail to distinguish between a priori exclusivity and pre-emption, it also appears to confuse the two separate questions of the existence of implied external competence and the exclusivity of that competence. It does not make any reference to Article 216(1) TFEU (discussed above) and yet they are clearly connected—in fact the almost identical wording of the phrases in the two provisions might suggest that implied *shared* competence would in effect disappear, that all 'implied' competence, as defined in Article 216(1), would be exclusive, as defined in Article 3(2). Such a reading is hard to defend in terms of outcome and is—it is to be hoped—unlikely in practice. It would entail a potentially large expansion of exclusive competence to insist that except where the Treaty expressly provides for treaty-making powers, the Union must have either exclusive competence or no external competence at all. Although exclusive competence is necessary in some external policy situations, it does not need to become the norm.

In cases where the EU's powers are exclusive, or Member States' powers have been pre-empted by Union action, the Member States may act—as a matter of EU law—only by way of authority from the EU. This authority may be granted, for example, where the EU is not itself able to conclude a particular agreement even though it possesses exclusive competence to do so; examples include agreements concluded within the framework of UN agencies such as the IMO or ILO and open only to State parties.

2. Impact of EU law on treaties concluded by Member States

As we have seen, EU treaty-making competence, and the exercise of that competence, has the effect of restricting the Member States' own treaty-making powers. However, the impact of EU law can be felt even in those domains which are still clearly within Member State competence, or where the EU has not yet exercised its powers so as to pre-empt Member State action. The obligations on the Member States stem from the so-called loyalty clause, or principle of sincere cooperation, now found in Article 4(3) TEU. Two aspects of this loyalty obligation are noteworthy.

First, even where Member States conclude an international agreement within their own sphere of competence, they must comply with their general Union law obligations. For example, Member State bilateral agreements with third countries on double taxation must observe the EU law principles of non-discrimination and rights of establishment. Although direct taxation is a matter for the Member States, they must nevertheless exercise their taxation powers consistently with Union law. So, any advantage granted by a Member State under a bilateral agreement with a third country must, on the basis of the equal treatment requirement in Article 49 TFEU, be extended to all EU companies established in that Member State.[116] A Member State will need to justify differential treatment, even where it flows from the existence of a bilateral agreement; the agreement does not in itself remove the

---

[116] Case C-307/97 *Saint-Gobain v Finanzamt Aachen-Innenstadt* [1999] ECR I-6161.

application of EU law rules.[117] In the *Open Skies* cases[118] the principle of equality of treatment was taken further. There, the Court found bilateral Air Services Agreements concluded by several Member States to contain ownership and control clauses in contravention of Article 43 EC (now Article 49 TFEU) on rights of establishment, since, under the bilateral agreements, rights of access to the US market were granted to companies under the ownership and control of nationals of the Member State party, but not to other EU companies established in that Member State.[119] Thus, the bilateral agreement itself conflicted with EU law, since it effectively allowed the third country to discriminate between EU companies, and renegotiation of the agreements was required.[120]

Second, the EU Treaties make special provision for international agreements concluded by Member States before the entry into force of the Treaty of Rome, or the date of the State's accession to the EU. Under Article 351 TFEU the rights of third countries under such 'prior agreements' are protected from a Member State's potentially conflicting EU Treaty obligation.[121] However, this protection is limited. It is designed to protect the rights of third States under the agreement and it does not permit the Member States to exercise rights under the prior agreement if to do so would conflict with an EU Treaty obligation.[122] Nor does it create any obligations of the Union towards the third State. Although it does extend to obligations of the Member States under the EU Treaties, it cannot absolve the Member States from complying with 'the principles that form part of the very foundations of the [Union] legal order, one of which is the protection of fundamental rights'.[123] In addition, the Member States are put under an obligation to eliminate any incompatibilities, by renegotiation and if necessary by denunciation of the prior agreement.

In a series of cases concerning Member States' bilateral investment treaties (BITs), the Court took a broad view of what might amount to an incompatibility. The Commission was concerned that a number of BITs contain commitments to ensure the transfer of payments relating to investments without including any safeguard clause or proviso which would allow the Member State to implement swiftly restrictions on capital movements which might in the future be required as a result of restrictive measures adopted by the Union. Since such restrictive measures had not in fact been adopted in relation to the third countries in question, this was

---

[117] Case C-55/00 *Gottardo v Istituto nazionale della previdenza sociale* [2002] ECR I-413.

[118] Case C-466/98 *Commission v UK* [2002] ECR I-9427; Case C-467/98 *Commission v Denmark* [2002] ECR I-9515; Case C-468/98 *Commission v Sweden* [2002] ECR I-9575; Case C-469/98 *Commission v Finland* [2002] ECR I-9627; Case C-471/98 *Commission v Belgium* [2002] ECR I-9681; Case C-472/98 *Commission v Luxembourg* [2002] ECR I-9741; Case C-475/98 *Commission v Austria* [2002] ECR I-9797; Case C-476/98 *Commission v Germany* (n 113).

[119] Case C-476/98 *Commission v Germany* (n 113) [153]–[154].

[120] This was done both by renegotiating the Member States' bilateral agreements, and by replacing them with EU agreements: Regulation 847/2004 on the negotiation and implementation of air service agreements between Member States and third countries [2004] OJ L157/7.

[121] Case C-124/95 *R v HM Treasury and Bank of England Ex p Centro-Com* (n 28); Case C-62/98 *Commission v Portugal* [2000] ECR I-5171.

[122] Case 812/79 *Attorney General v Burgoa* [1980] ECR 2787.

[123] Joined Cases C-402/05 P and C-415/05 P *Yassin Abdullah Kadi* (n 79) [304].

not a direct breach of any such act; rather, the Commission alleged a breach of Article 351 TFEU.[124] The Court agreed with the Commission; in its view this was not merely a hypothetical future incompatibility, but a situation in which the *effet utile* of the power-conferring Treaty provisions on restrictions of capital movements was put in question. There is obviously a question as to whether it is really possible to establish an incompatibility between a substantive treaty commitment (movement of capital in the BIT) and a power-conferring provision of the EU Treaties. If defensible at all, it must be on the grounds that the power in this special case (restrictive measures against capital flows) is effectively negated if it cannot be used with immediate effect.[125] Nevertheless, the cases serve to illustrate the extent to which EU obligations—including the obligation to facilitate possible future EU action—constrain the Member States in the exercise of their treaty-making powers.

C. International responsibility and EU treaty-making

The effects of a treaty concluded by the EU in EU law are of course complemented by its effects in international law. On a number of occasions, the Court of Justice has recognized that the EU is bound in international law by the agreements it has concluded.[126] As such, the EU will be responsible for breach of its treaty obligations in the same way as other treaty parties. The European Commission has participated in the debate over the ILC's Draft Articles on the International Responsibility of International Organizations (DARIO),[127] and has continued in this context to defend an argument it has used with some success before WTO Panels, to the effect that the specific relationship between Member States and the EU, when the former implement EU law, renders it difficult to accommodate a standard approach to attribution.[128]

Three scenarios may be briefly considered here. First, where the EU alone is a party to the international agreement, it alone will be responsible under international law for the performance of the agreement. This does not necessarily mean that the Member States have no part to play in fulfilling the commitments made by the Union; who actually implements the agreement will depend on 'the state of [Union] law for the time being in the areas affected by the provisions of the agreement'.[129] It only means that the EU's responsibility is not affected by the internal question of how the competence to implement the agreement is distributed. The EU may, in this way, take responsibility for measures taken, or omissions, by its Member States (including Member States acceding to the Union

---

[124] Cases C-205/06 *Commission v Austria* [2009] ECR I-01301; C-249/06 *Commission v Sweden* [2009] ECR I-01335; C-118/07 *Commission v Finland* [2009] ECR I-10889.

[125] See P Koutrakos, 'Annotation on Case C-205/06, *Commission v Austria* and Case C-249/06, *Commission v Sweden*' (2009) 46 CML Rev 2059.

[126] Eg Joined Cases C-317/04 and C-318/04 *European Parliament v Council* (n 37) [73].

[127] ILC, Report on the International Law Commission on the Work of its Sixty-first Session (15 January 2010) UN Doc A/64/10.

[128] See eg E Paasivirta and PJ Kuijper, 'Does One Size Fit All? The European Community and the Responsibility of International Organisations' (2005) 36 Netherlands Ybk Intl L 169.

[129] Case 104/81 *Kupferberg* (n 89) [12].

after the conclusion of the treaty).[130] This scenario is by no means uncommon: EU agreements on subjects ranging from air services to visa facilitation and customs will in practice be implemented by Member State authorities.[131] Nevertheless, there may be cases where the third State concerned in concluding a treaty with the EU alone feels the need for greater certainty that the Member States themselves are fully committed to the new treaty.[132]

Second, and conversely, the EU is not responsible in international law for a failure to perform a treaty to which it is not a party, despite the Member States being parties, merely because it would have had the competence to conclude the agreement and does have the competence to implement it. In situations where the EU is exclusively competent over (part of) the subject matter of an international treaty, but cannot conclude the treaty because it is open only to State parties, the Member States may be authorized by the EU to conclude the treaty on behalf of, and in the interests of, the Union.[133] In such a case the Member States, as parties, are responsible in international law for its performance, but in terms of EU law they may not have the competence to (for example) enact the necessary domestic legislation, relying on the Union institutions to do so. From the perspective of the EU the position is also problematic, since it is expected by its Member States to implement the provisions of a treaty by which it is not legally bound and over the content of whose provisions it has no direct control.[134] For third parties the concern has been that the Member States may somehow seek to escape from their treaty obligations by way of their EU membership and—in some instances—their consequent inability to implement a treaty obligation themselves.[135]

In these scenarios, the specificity of the EU's position derives from the fact that the (external) capacity to conclude an international treaty does not necessarily coincide with the (internal) allocation of powers in its implementation. Neverthe-

---

[130] Ibid [13].

[131] Cf PJ Kuijper, 'Introduction to the Symposium on Responsibility of International Organizations and of (Member) States: Attributed or Direct Responsibility or Both?' (2010) 7 IOLR 9, 14.

[132] Especially where there are existing bilateral agreements between the Member State and the third State on the matter in question. For example, the two agreements on mutual legal assistance and on extradition between the EU and the US contain detailed references to existing bilateral US–Member State agreements, and both required the Union to 'ensure that each Member State acknowledges, in a written instrument' between that Member State and the US, the implications of the EU agreement for its bilateral treaty with the US. Agreement on extradition between the European Union and the United States of America [2003] OJ L181/27, Art 3(2); Agreement on mutual legal assistance between the European Union and the United States of America [2003] OJ L181/34, Art 3(2).

[133] Eg Council Decision (EC) 2008/431 of 5 June 2008 authorising Member States to ratify or accede to the 1996 Hague Convention on Jurisdiction, Applicable Law, Recognition, Enforcement and Cooperation in respect of Parental Responsibility and Measures for the Protection of Children and authorising certain Member States to make a declaration on the application of the relevant internal rules of Community law [2008] OJ L151/36.

[134] An example would be the international rules adopted within the IMO framework, such as the International Convention for the Prevention of Pollution from Ships (MARPOL Convention). For this reason, where EU competence is exclusive it is important for EU law purposes that the Member States act only via commonly agreed positions: Case C-45/07 *Commission v Greece* (n 69).

[135] E Paasivirta, 'Responsibility of a Member State of an International Organization: Where Will It End? Comments on Article 60 of the ILC Draft on the Responsibility of International Organizations' (2010) 7 IOLR 49.

less, in terms of international responsibility the position of the EU is clear in both cases. The third scenario, the case of the mixed agreement, is more complex. Here the international treaty is concluded by both the EU and its Member States, and this fact, combined with the complex division of competence and (internal) responsibility for implementation, has given rise to differences of opinion and largely ineffective attempts to provide some certainty over questions of international responsibility. Three points of view can be identified. First, those who seek to define the EU's responsibility under a mixed agreement in terms of its exercise of competence, including those who hold that the Union is only engaged to the extent of its exclusive competence, everything else being reserved to the Member States on the grounds that their participation is an indication that the EU has chosen not to exercise its shared competence.[136] A second approach holds that since the EU and its Member States have both concluded the treaty, both are contractually liable for its performance as a whole and may be jointly and severally responsible for its breach.[137] On this view, the division of competence between the EU and its Member States is an internal matter.[138] A third approach seeks to base responsibility not solely on the exercise of competence in concluding the treaty, nor simply on the consent to be bound expressed in the formal act of conclusion, but on the exercise of legislative or regulatory authority by the EU.

A competence-based approach to responsibility has been the basis of the practice in multilateral conventions since the United Nations Convention on the Law of the Sea (UNCLOS), which required a declaration of competence as a condition for REIO participation.[139] The EU is a party to approximately forty treaties which include a declaration of competence by the EU, all of them multilateral.[140] The declarations vary. Some merely assert a general EU competence over the field of the treaty,[141] some distinguish between exclusive and shared competence,[142] some list relevant items of EU legislation (often out of date),[143] and most recent ones include a statement to the effect that the scope of EU competence 'is, by its nature, subject to continuous change'.[144] UNCLOS Annex IX, which contains rules for the

---

[136] Eg J Heliskoski, *Mixed Agreements as a Technique for Organizing the International Relations of the European Community and its Member States* (Kluwer Law International, The Hague 2001) 46–7.

[137] A Rosas, 'The European Union and International Dispute Settlement' in L Boisson de Chazournes, C Romano, and R Mackenzie (eds), *International Organisations and International Dispute Settlement: Trends and Prospects* (Transnational Publishers, Ardsley 2002).

[138] Case C-53/96 *Hermès International* (n 108) [14].

[139] UNCLOS (adopted 10 December 1982, entered into force 16 November 1994) 1833 UNTS 3, Annex IX, Art 5(1).

[140] See European Commission, 'Treaties Office Database' (n 2).

[141] Eg Convention on the Protection and Use of Transboundary Watercourses and International Lakes (adopted 17 March 1992, entered into force 6 October 1996) 1936 UNTS 269, declaration by the Union pursuant to Art 25(4).

[142] Eg International Tropical Timber Agreement (adopted 26 January 1994, entered into force 1 January 1997) 1163 UNTS 81, declaration by the Union pursuant to Art 36(3).

[143] Eg Statute of the International Renewable Energy Agency (IRENA) (adopted 26 January 2009, entered into force 8 July 2010) [2010] OJ L178/18.

[144] Eg United Nations Convention against Corruption (adopted 31 October 2003, entered into force 14 December 2005) 2349 UNTS 145, declaration of competence by the Union pursuant to Art 67(3).

participation in the Convention of IOs, clearly links responsibility to the distribution of competence as evidenced by the declaration of competence; it also provides that an IO or its Member States may be asked by any other party to provide information as to who has responsibility in respect of any specific matter and that 'failure to provide this information within a reasonable time or the provision of contradictory information shall result in joint and several liability'.[145] Despite this practice, it is not possible to point to a single case in which the EU declaration of competence has been determinative in allocating responsibility in dispute settlement under an EU agreement.[146]

In contrast, practice under the WTO, where there is no declaration of competence, appears to be based rather on the second approach: shared responsibility.[147] The fact that the EU operates under a system of executive federalism means that even in areas of exclusive Union competence, EU law will be applied and administered by Member State authorities. WTO panels have accepted that the EU should be held responsible in such cases.[148] In other cases, complaints have been brought against the EU and several Member States together,[149] or against the EU alone in respect of measures taken by Member States.[150] This pragmatic approach perhaps works best in the context of a highly institutionalized dispute settlement process, and where the Union and its Member States closely cooperate in management of the treaty regime.

It is not easy to find, in the case law of the Court of Justice, a clear preference for one of these approaches to responsibility for mixed agreements. In the *Mox Plant* case,[151] elements of all three approaches were evident. First, the Court stressed that the UNCLOS as a whole had been concluded by the Community and its provisions therefore 'now form an integral part of the Community legal order'.[152] It then referred to the assumption of responsibility by the Union for the due performance of the UNCLOS as a whole.[153] Despite this starting point, which seems to coincide with the second approach, the Court still examined to what extent the Union had chosen to exercise its (shared) competence in concluding the UNCLOS—an

---

[145] UNCLOS Annex IX, Art 6.

[146] A Delgado Casteleiro, 'International Responsibility of the European Union: From Competence to Normative Control' (PhD thesis, European University Institute 2011).

[147] Kuijper (n 131).

[148] WTO, *European Communities: Customs Classification of Certain Computer Equipment—Report of the Appellate Body* (the LAN case) (15 June 1998) WT/DS62/AB/R, WT/DS67/AB/R, and WT/DS68/AB/R; WTO, *European Community: Protection of Trademarks and Geographical Indications for Agricultural Products and Foodstuffs—Complaint by the United States—Report of the Panel* (15 March 2005) WT/DS174/R.

[149] Eg WTO, *European Communities and Certain Member States: Measures Affecting Trade in Large Civil Aircraft—Report of the Appellate Body* (18 May 2011) WT/DS316/AB/R.

[150] Eg WTO, *European Communities: Measures Affecting Asbestos and Asbestos-Containing Products—Report of the Appellate Body* (12 March 2001) WT/DS135/AB/R; WTO, *European Communities: Measures Affecting the Approval and Marketing of Biotech Products—Reports of the Panel* (26 September 2006) WT/DS291/R, WT/DS292/R, and WT/DS293/R.

[151] Case C-459/03 *Commission v Ireland* (n 92) (*Mox Plant* case).

[152] Ibid [82].

[153] Ibid [85]; cf Case 104/81 *Kupferberg* (n 89) [13]; see also Case C-316/91 *European Parliament v Council* (n 72) [33].

enquiry which, especially in referencing the declaration of competence, reflects the first, competence-based approach. However, the parties to the case drew very different conclusions from the declaration of competence as to the extent to which the EU had in fact exercised its shared competence in concluding the Convention. The Court's conclusion was that it had done so over all parts of the Convention where Union rules (internal Union legislation) existed; for those parts of the Convention in which there are no Union rules, 'competence rests with the Member States'.[154] This final result is most consistent with the third approach identified above. Of course, the *Mox Plant* case was not directly concerned with Union or Member State responsibility to third countries: it concerned a dispute between Ireland and the UK which, in the CJEU's view, should have been dealt with via EU and not UNCLOS enforcement mechanisms. Therefore, the Court was concerned essentially with defining the scope of Union law. But to the extent that the EU regards compliance with a mixed agreement by a Member State party as a matter of EU law to be enforced internally, then it should assume international responsibility for its performance vis-à-vis third parties.[155]

While it seems unlikely that the EU will be the subject of a special provision in the DARIO, the provision in the draft articles for a *lex specialis* recognizing the 'rules of the organisation' should make it possible in principle to take the EU's specificity, and its own approach, into account.[156] From this perspective it would no doubt be helpful were the EU itself to establish a set of guiding principles to apply to responsibility for mixed agreements.[157] As things stand, the model of Article 6 of Annex IX to UNCLOS, which puts the onus on the EU to inform its treaty partners whether responsibility for a specific matter lies with the EU or its Member States, offers a procedural and perhaps sufficiently secure solution to third countries.

Conclusion

This chapter has highlighted the distinctive features of the EU as an international, treaty-making actor. Structurally, the Treaty of Lisbon has simplified the position by merging the EU and EC together into a single organization with a single,

---

[154] Case C-459/03 *Commission v Ireland* (n 92) [107]–[08].

[155] See also Case C-239/03 *Commission v France* (n 91) [25]–[30], in which the Court uses the potential international responsibility of the Union as a basis for its argument that France's breach of the treaty was also a failure to fulfil an internal EU law obligation.

[156] DARIO (n 127) Art 63 ('("lex specialis"): These articles do not apply where and to the extent that the conditions for the existence of an internationally wrongful act or the content or implementation of the international responsibility of an international organization, or a State for an internationally wrongful act of an international organization, are governed by special rules of international law, including rules of the organization applicable to the relations between the international organization and its members.'); C Ahlborn, 'The Rules of International Organizations and the Law of International Responsibility' (Amsterdam Centre for International Law Research Paper 2011–03, 2011) <http://ssrn.com/abstract=1825182> 2.

[157] Kuijper (n 131) 225–7. Kuijper suggests adding a clause to the Council's approval decision for mixed agreements which would either clearly allocate responsibility or establish a rule of allocation.

explicit, legal personality. It also sought to codify (with mixed success) the case law developed by the CJEU on the EU's treaty-making powers. The Court of Justice's early espousal of a doctrine of implied powers enabled the EU from the beginning to use international agreements as well as internal legislation to achieve its objectives, and since then amendments of the EU Treaties have steadily added to its external and internal competence.

The distinctiveness of EU treaty-making is in the volume and extent of its activity, its use of both bilateral and multilateral treaties as a key instrument of its foreign policy, and its complex institutional and constitutional structure. The latter, in particular, entails a rich system of rules encompassing the EU and its Member States, their respective powers and responsibilities, and the legal effects of international agreements in the EU legal order. When considering the EU as a treaty-maker, therefore, both the EU's own internal structures and rules and international practice must be considered. The CJEU has almost never denied the EU external competence,[158] and it is very rare for the Court to question substantive foreign policy choices made by the EU institutions.[159] But nor has it denied its own jurisdiction over international agreements concluded by the EU. As a constitutional court it has been able to define the internal allocation of competence within the Union and in so doing to establish the constitutional framework for international action.

Although EU external competence may exclude that of the Member States, either through a priori exclusivity or through pre-emption, in very many cases, especially complex modern multilateral treaties, the EU and its Member States will participate together and it is these agreements which pose the most difficult challenges, both for EU law and for its treaty partners. Mechanisms such as the REIO clause and declarations of competence have been developed to enable the joint participation of the EU and its Member States, but questions still remain over the extent to which the interpretation and enforcement of these agreements are subject to the jurisdiction of the CJEU and over the allocation of international responsibility. Efforts to resolve these debates take place in the context of internal constitutional (and power) struggles among EU institutions and between the EU and Member States. EU treaty-making, and the conduct of policy within international treaty regimes, can be intensely political and within the EU's institutional structures politics often transforms itself into legal disputes. The nature of the EU as a treaty-making power—and the distinctiveness and complexity with which third countries are faced—is the result of this incremental and reiterative political and legal process. At the same time, in engaging with and posing these questions, the EU is making a contribution to the development of international law.

---

[158] The two existing examples are accession to the ECHR, Opinion 2/94 (n 29), now provided for explicitly in the EU Treaties, and the Passenger Name Records Agreement with the US, which having been wrongly concluded under EC powers was then renegotiated and approved under EU powers (n 65).

[159] Cf Joined Cases C-402/05 P and C-415/05 P *Yassin Abdullah Kadi* (n 79), in which the Court draws a distinction (albeit not convincing to all) between the internal constitutional issues it was addressing and their external policy implications.

Recommended Reading

E Cannizzaro (ed), *The European Union as an Actor in International Relations* (Kluwer Law International, The Hague 2002)

M Cremona (ed), *Developments in EU External Relations Law* (OUP, Oxford 2008)

M Cremona, 'External Relations and External Competence of the European Union: The Emergence of an Integrated Policy' in P Craig and G de Búrca (eds), *The Evolution of EU Law* (2nd edn OUP, Oxford 2011)

M Cremona and B de Witte (eds), *EU Foreign Relations Law: Constitutional Fundamentals* (Hart Publishing, Oxford 2008)

M Cremona, J Monar, and S Poli (eds), *The External Dimension of the Area of Freedom, Security and Justice* (Peter Lang, Brussels 2011)

A Dashwood and C Hillion (eds), *The General Law of EC External Relations* (Sweet & Maxwell, London 2000)

A Dashwood and M Maresceau (eds), *Law and Practice of EU External Relations* (CUP, Cambridge 2008)

G De Baere, *Constitutional Principles of EU External Relations* (OUP, Oxford 2008)

P Eeckhout, *External Relations of the European Union* (2nd edn OUP, Oxford 2011)

J Heliskoski, *Mixed Agreements as a Technique for Organizing the International Relations of the European Community and its Member States* (Kluwer Law International, The Hague 2001)

C Hillion and P Koutrakos (eds), *Mixed Agreements Revisited—The EU and its Member States in the World* (Hart Publishing, Oxford 2010)

J Klabbers, *Treaty Conflict and the European Union* (CUP, Cambridge 2009)

M Koskenniemi (ed), *International Law Aspects of the European Union* (Kluwer Law International, The Hague 2000)

P Koutrakos, *EU International Relations Law* (Hart Publishing, Oxford 2006)

P Koutrakos (ed), *European Foreign Policy: Legal and Political Perspectives* (Edward Elgar, Cheltenham 2011)

V Kronenberger (ed), *The EU and the International Legal Order: Discord or Harmony?* (TMC Asser Press, The Hague 2001)

M Maresceau, 'Bilateral Agreements Concluded by the European Community' (2006) 309 RcD 125

D Thym, 'Foreign Affairs' in A von Bogdandy and J Bast (eds), *Principles of European Constitutional Law* (2nd edn Hart Publishing, Oxford 2011)

JHH Weiler, 'The External Legal Relations of Non-unitary Actors: Mixity and the Federal Principle' in JHH Weiler (ed), *The Constitution of Europe: Do the New Clothes Have an Emperor?* (CUP, Cambridge 1999)

5

Who Can Make Treaties? Other Subjects of International Law

Tom Grant

Introduction

'[T]he right of entering international engagements is an attribute of State sovereignty.'[1] That an entity has entered into a treaty, however, does not necessarily mean that it is a State. The ILC, when considering the law of treaties, did not dispute that other subjects besides States and international organizations could conclude agreements whose 'obligatory force is . . . derived from international law'.[2] The decision of the ILC to limit the 1969 Vienna Convention on the Law of Treaties (VCLT) to treaties concluded between States[3] implicitly acknowledged the broader principle: Article 3 of the VCLT excludes international agreements involving 'other subjects of international law', which is to say, though the Convention does not apply to such agreements, they certainly exist.

Earlier chapters of the present volume examined the treaty-making powers of international organizations and of the European Union. The present chapter concerns other non-State actors. Though this would suggest a residual category, the other subjects considered here need not be defined in the negative—ie, by reference to what they are not. True, they are not international legal persons in the sense of actors holding 'the totality of international rights and duties recognized by international law'[4]—but nor are international organizations, the member States of

---

[1] *The Wimbledon (Great Britain, France, Italy & Japan v Germany; Poland intervening)* (Judgment of 17 August 1923) PCIJ Rep Ser A No 1 25.

[2] This was Brierly's view as the ILC's first Special Rapporteur. JL Brierly, 'Report on the Law of Treaties' [1950] YBILC, vol II, 222, 229 [34]. In 1962, the fourth Special Rapporteur, Sir Humphrey Waldock even proposed to define a 'treaty' to mean 'any international agreement in any written form . . . which is intended to be governed by international law and is concluded between two or more states *or other subjects of international law having capacity to enter into treaties*' [1962] YBILC, vol I, 51 [3] (emphasis added).

[3] ILC, 'Draft Articles on the Law of Treaties' [1966] YBILC, vol II, 187 (comment (2) on Art 1).

[4] *Reparation for Injuries Suffered in the Service of the United Nations* (Advisory Opinion) [1949] ICJ Rep 174, 180.

which, while investing legal personality in them, limit their competences under each organization's constitution.[5] Some of these other subjects are entities like Kosovo before independence and Taiwan since 1949, which are called (perhaps in default of a better analytic category) *sui generis*[6]—but the EU has been described that way as well.[7]

Instead, it might be said that this category of 'other subjects' is comprised of entities over which a State holds authority—or perhaps in the case of a territory administered under condominium, trusteeship, or analogous arrangement, where authority lies in a combination of States or in an international organization—and which do not themselves normally hold international legal responsibility. Such subjects may engage in social, political, and economic transactions at the international level, but they are not presumed competent to negotiate or conclude treaties. This chapter examines exceptions to the usual practice. It concerns non-State actors that have exercised the competence to assume obligations under formal agreements with others—or, at least, to conclude such agreements, if not in their own name. These other subjects of international law may be divided into four categories. First, there are territories integral to a State—especially the units which constitute a federal State. Second, there are external territories, the foreign relations of which normally are the responsibility of a State albeit under a variety of relationships. Third, insurgent groups—entities which seek to displace an existing State in all or part of its territory and themselves to assume the functions of the State—have been said to enter into international agreements as well. Finally, as is now widely acknowledged, private actors—including corporations, non-governmental organizations and individuals—may be international law subjects for some purposes; the extent to which this is the case remains in flux. In at least one field—international investment protection—engagements between States and private actors have become sufficiently routine and display such characteristics to merit attention here.

The present chapter considers treaty-making under each category of these other subjects in turn. It also takes up two more general topics: first, the relationship of treaty-making by such other subjects to the VCLT and to the general international law of treaties; and, second, international responsibility in connection with the obligations arising when such subjects make treaties.

---

[5] Ibid; *Conditions of Admission of a State to Membership in the United Nations (Article 4 of the Charter)* (Advisory Opinion) [1948] ICJ Rep 57, 64.

[6] See eg *Accordance with International Law of the Unilateral Declaration of Independence in Respect of Kosovo* (Advisory Proceedings), Written Statement of the United Kingdom (17 April 2009) 9–15 [0.17]–[0.23]; DB Hollis 'Unpacking the Compact Clause' (2010) 88 Texas L Rev 741, 753 n55; I Brownlie *Principles of Public International Law* (7th edn OUP, Oxford 2008) 65.

[7] As the Bundesverfassungsgericht called it in *Internationale Handelgesellschaft mbH v Einfuhrund Vorratsstelle für Getreide und Futtermittel* (1974) 37 BverfGE 271, trans in [1974] 2 Common Mkt L Rev 540, 549 [19].

I. Treaty-Making by 'Other Subjects of International Law'

A. Federal units and other integral territories

1. The assignment of treaty-making competence

Treaty-making is one of the classic functions of the central government of the State.[8] Although international law is agnostic generally as to the manner in which a State assigns its foreign policy functions, Article 7 of the VCLT lists who, in the absence of full powers, may represent the State in treaty-making. Representatives of a federal territory are not among the officers 'considered as representing their State' unless they are granted full powers or happen to hold one of the State offices that are agreed to include treaty-making powers.[9]

In any case, Article 7 only governs treaty-making by the State; treaty-making by the federal territorial unit presents a distinct situation. Here the question arises whether the federal territorial unit has the capacity to enter into a treaty, not as agent of the State, but on its own account. General international law does not grant federal units this capacity, although it does not withhold it either.[10] Rather, treaty-making by federal territorial units is a function of two elements: on the one hand, the particular rules and practices of the State of which it is a constituent, and on the other, the willingness of another party to enter into international agreements with the unit.

First, to enter into treaties, a federal territorial unit must have explicit treaty-making authority from the State of which it is a component part. Agreement-making by constituents of the federal State is typically constrained to narrow limits or not allowed at all. The restrictive position in Australia was summarized by Justice Murphy in *Koowarta v Bjelke-Petersen* (1982):

> Any purported treaty or agreement between any or all the Australian states and a foreign country is a nullity. States have entered into arrangements with other countries either in the belief they could do so or because of the neglect of the Commonwealth to make arrangements which were thought to be practically necessary ... All such arrangements are within the exclusive authority of the Commonwealth.[11]

To say that the resultant 'arrangements' are a 'nullity' is a legal judgment; it does not preclude political statements. Accordingly, territorial units of federal States may enter into arrangements with foreign States or sub-national counterparts that

---

[8] To the extent a federal State's constitution limits its ability to legislate in respect of matters within the competence of its component territorial units, treaty practice has developed a number of accommodations, most notably, the 'federal-state clause'. For examples and a discussion of its various forms, see Chapter 12, Part II.B, 313 *et seq.*

[9] See Chapter 7, Part II.A, 184 *et seq.* for a detailed discussion of VCLT Art 7.

[10] Cf [1965] YBILC, vol 1, 25 [39] (Tunkin).

[11] High Court (Australia) *Koowarta v Bjelke-Peterson & Others; State of Queensland v Commonwealth of Australia* (1982) 68 ILR 238. India has adopted a similar position although the State will conclude agreements on behalf of its sub-national entities. See K Thakore, 'India' in DB Hollis and others (eds), *National Treaty Law and Practice* (Martinus Nijhoff, Leiden 2005) 369 ('*NTLP*').

appear to contain political, rather than, legal commitments; the intention is to avoid national constitutional objection; a further result is that questions of treaty law are also avoided.[12]

Inversely, if a territorial unit purports to adopt a legal commitment but lacks authorization, a treaty law problem arises. As Hersch Lauterpacht noted while serving as ILC Special Rapporteur on the law of treaties:

[I]n the absence of such authority conferred by federal law, member States of a Federation cannot be regarded as endowed with the power to conclude treaties. For according to international law it is the Federation which, in the absence of provisions of constitutional law to the contrary, is the subject of international law and international intercourse. It follows that a treaty concluded by a member state in disregard of the constitution of the Federation must also be considered as having been concluded in disregard of the limitations imposed by international law upon its treaty-making power. As such it is not a treaty in the contemplation of international law. As a treaty, it is void.[13]

In short, it is not that international law prevents a federation from conferring treaty-making powers on its constituent units. Rather, absent an express decision of the central government, it is assumed that this power is exclusive to the federation. Any treaty-making capacity of constituent units of a federation depends on the particular arrangements under the relevant federal system.[14]

2. Federal rules on treaty-making

So the presumption against treaty-making is subject to the willingness of particular States to make exceptions. Several federal systems allocate or reserve treaty-making competence to their territorial units. No one example is representative. As the ILC observed, 'the practice differed too widely for the Commission to be able to lay down a general rule'.[15] Nevertheless, at least four general types of treaty-making authorization have been discerned: (i) authority to conclude treaties on matters falling within the powers possessed by sub-federal units; (ii) authority to conclude treaties on matters that do not interfere with federal interests or supremacy;

---

[12] Hollis (n 6) 747–8, 769.

[13] 'Report on the Law of Treaties' [1953] YBILC, vol II, 139 ('Lauterpacht, First Report'). Waldock (and the ILC generally) originally favoured making the treaty-making capacity of territorial units of federal States dependent on the municipal constitutional system. [1962] YBILC, vol I, 65 [7]–[9] (Waldock, Special Rapporteur); ILC, 'Report of the Commission, Law of Treaties' [1962] YBILC, vol II, 164 (draft Art 3). Waldock later echoed Lauterpacht's views, objecting to a draft text suggesting a presumption that federal territorial units had a treaty-making capacity. [1965] YBILC, vol I, 250 [10]. There were additional concerns that a provision authorizing sub-federal treaty-making might give States room to plead constitutional limitations to avoid treaty obligations. Eg [1962] YBILC, vol I, 65 [13] (Jiménez de Aréchaga). Ultimately, the ILC did adopt a federal States provision, but it was rejected at the Vienna Conference. [1970] YBILC, vol II, 196 n108.

[14] See eg [1962] YBILC, vol I, 61–2 [58] (Ago).

[15] [1965] YBILC, vol I, 29 [83] (Bartoš, as Chairman). At the time, there was also a division of opinion on whether the capacity of the constituent unit to make treaties flowed from the constitutional law of the federation or from international law. See eg ibid 251 [27]–[30] (Yasseen); ibid [32] (Ago).

(iii) authority to conclude treaties on local matters; and (iv) ad hoc authorization. A few examples suggest the range of possibilities.

The Constitution of the Swiss Confederation confers a (limited) treaty-making power on constituent units. It does so by reference to the powers those units possess. Article 56 provides that a 'Canton may conclude treaties with foreign states on matters that lie within the scope of its powers' so long as those treaties do 'not conflict with the law or the interests of the Confederation, or with the law of any other Cantons'.[16] Article 56 requires the Canton to give the Confederation advance notice before concluding a treaty, in order to facilitate federal supervision, detailed in Article 172, which authorizes the Federal Assembly to 'decide whether to approve intercantonal agreements and treaties between Cantons and foreign countries where the Federal Council or a Canton raises an objection to any such treaty'. The Cantons have concluded some 140 international agreements, which deal mostly with bilateral and administrative matters.[17]

Germany has adopted a similar approach for its territorial units. Article 32(3) of the Basic Law provides that '[i]nsofar as the *Länder* have power to legislate, they may conclude treaties with foreign states with the consent of the Federal Government'.[18] Based on this authority, the *Länder* have concluded dozens of international agreements with neighbouring European regional and national governments.[19] Belgium's Constitution also grants Community and Regional Governments authority to conclude 'treaties regarding matters that fall within the competence of their Parliament', subject to that Parliament's approval.[20] Under this authority, Belgium's three regional governments—Flanders, Wallonia, and Brussels-Capital—entered into two multilateral agreements with France and the Netherlands, one for the protection of the River Scheldt and the other for that of the River Meuse.[21] For Germany and Belgium, however, EU law exercises a limiting effect: the European Court of Justice (now the Court of Justice of the European Union (CJEU)) denies the competence of sub-national territorial units to appear before the Court, which thus restricts their ability to effectuate agreements they might make.[22]

---

[16] Federal Constitution of the Swiss Confederation (18 April 1999) HeinOnline World Constitutions (unofficial trans).

[17] L Wildhaber and others, 'Switzerland' in *NTLP* (n 11) 667.

[18] Basic Law for the Federal Republic of Germany (23 May 1949) HeinOnline World Constitutions (unofficial trans). Austria amended its constitution in 1988 allow its *Länder* to do the same. Austria Constitution, HeinOnline World Constitutions (unofficial trans), Art 16.

[19] HD Treviranus and H Beemelmans, 'Federal Republic of Germany' in *NTLP* (n 11) 328–9.

[20] Constitution of Belgium (17 February 1994 as amended), HeinOnline World Constitutions, Art 167(3).

[21] Agreements on the Protection of the Rivers Meuse and Scheldt (Belgium (Brussels-Capital, Flanders, Wallonia Regional Governments)-France-Netherlands) (26 April 1994) [1995] 34 ILM 851.

[22] Case C-180/97 *Regione Toscana v Commission* [1997] ECR I-5245 [6]; see also Case C-95/97 *Région Wallonne v Commission* [1997] ECR I-1787 [6]. Outside Europe, Mexico's Treaty Law authorizes sub-federal entities to make 'international agreements', evidently to provide a legal foundation for an existing practice. L Diaz, 'Mexico' in *NTLP* (n 11) 450 (citing *Ley de tratados* (Mexico: SRE, 1992)). It has also been suggested that the Russian Constitution leaves room for constituent territories of the Federation to enter into international agreements, 'at least for matters over which they have exclusive jurisdiction'. GM Danilenko, 'The New Russian Constitution and International Law'

In other national systems, the central government may authorize international agreements that do not interfere with federal interests. Under the US Constitution, US States are prohibited from entering into treaties.[23] Article 1, Section 10, Clause 3 also prohibits US States from entering 'into any Agreement or Compact . . . with a foreign Power' without the consent of the US Congress.[24] The 'Agreement or Compact' Clause does not distinguish clearly, however, between a treaty, which US States cannot make, and an agreement or compact, which they can make subject to Congress' consent.[25] The situation in the US is complicated further by the introduction of a third category of commitments that US States can conclude without congressional involvement: these are the agreements identified by the US Supreme Court as not 'directed to the formation of any combination tending to the increase of political power in the states, which may encroach upon or interfere with the just supremacy of the United States'.[26] It is an open question whether this last category is a matter of *ex ante* affirmative grant or *ex post* review.[27] In practice, US States evidently do not interpret federal powers as requiring express permission from Congress in advance of every State engagement with a foreign entity, and US States have concluded hundreds of them in recent years.[28]

The Constitution of Bosnia and Herzegovina appears to permit agreements by its constituent 'Entities' so long as they are consistent with federal interests. Article III(2) grants Entities 'the right to establish special parallel relationships with neighboring states consistent with the sovereignty and territorial integrity of Bosnia and Herzegovina'.[29]

In some States, sub-federal treaty-making is expressly limited to local matters. The Constitution of the United Arab Emirates allocates treaty-making power to the constituent Emirates for 'agreements of a local and administrative nature with the neighbouring states or regions'.[30] The competence is constrained further

---

(1994) 88 AJIL 451, 453. Any such power, however, has been closely circumscribed by Russian federal law. See text (annotated) of Constitution of the Russian Federation at <http://www.wipo.int/clea/docs_new/pdf/en/ru/ru003en.pdf>.

[23] US Const, Art I §10 cl 1.

[24] US Const, Art I §10 cl 3.

[25] Hollis (n 6) 769–83 (reviewing the Constitution's drafting history and subsequent practice).

[26] *State of Virginia v State of Tennessee* 148 US 503, 519 (1893). Although this case involved an agreement between US States, its holding is widely assumed to apply to agreements between US States and foreign States. Hollis (n 6) 766–9.

[27] Whether US States can negotiate with a foreign State remains unresolved. *Clark v Allen* 331 US 503, 517 (1947).

[28] M Schaefer, 'Constraints on State Level Foreign Policy: (Re)Justifying, Refining and Distinguishing the Dormant Foreign Affairs Doctrine' (2011) 41 Seton Hall L Rev 201; Hollis (n 6) 750 (noting US States have concluded at least 340 international agreements and political commitments with foreign powers); see also DB Hollis 'The Elusive Foreign Compact' (2008) 73 Missouri L Rev 1071.

[29] Constitution of Bosnia in General Framework Agreement for Peace in Bosnia and Herzegovina (14 December 1995) Annex 4, Art III(2)(a), reprinted in [1996] 35 ILM 75, 120.

[30] Constitution of the United Arab Emirates (2 December 1971) HeinOnline World Constitutions (unofficial trans), Art 123.

by requirements (i) that such agreements not be 'inconsistent with the interests of the Union or with Union laws', and (ii) that 'the Supreme Council of the Union is informed in advance'. The Supreme Council has the authority, on objection, to block conclusion and operation of such agreements.[31]

Finally, certain States authorize sub-federal treaty-making only on a case-by-case basis. In 1981, Canada concluded a social security agreement with the United States authorizing Quebec, in light of that province's distinct pension system, to conclude its own agreement with the United States.[32] The US–Quebec agreement was concluded in 1983.[33] States may differ as to the legal effect, if any, to accord provincial agreements made without consent. For example, while Canada denies the treaty character of some 230 *ententes* adopted by Quebec without consent, France views them as binding under international law.[34]

The importance of domestic legal authorization should not obscure the important second point, already noted above (and considered further below): it takes more than one party to make a treaty. As Briggs noted early in the ILC's work on treaties:

The international capacity of an entity which is not fully independent to become a party to treaties depends upon: (1) the recognition of that capacity by the state or union of states of which it forms a part, or by the state which conducts its international relations; and (2) *the acceptance by the other contracting parties of its possession of that international capacity.*[35]

In practice, many States will accept a treaty with a sub-federal territorial unit only if they can confirm that the unit has domestic legal authority to engage in the particular treaty envisioned.[36] The situation could also arise in which municipal law says that a territorial unit may act as treaty-maker at the international level, but no potential partner accepts the proposition. As a result, there would be no international agreement.[37]

---

[31] Ibid.

[32] Agreement With Respect to Social Security (US–Canada) (11 March 1981) 35 UST 3403, 3417, Art XX.

[33] Understanding and Administrative Arrangement with the Government of Quebec (US–Quebec) (30 March 1983) TIAS No 10,863.

[34] DB Hollis, 'Why State Consent Still Matters: Non-State Actors, Treaties and the Changing Sources of International Law' (2005) 23 Berkeley J Intl L 151; B Nikravesh, 'Quebec and Tatarstan in International Law' (1999) 23 Fletcher Forum World Affairs 227, 239.

[35] [1962] YBILC, vol I, 59 [20] (Briggs) (emphasis added).

[36] Hollis (n 34) 152.

[37] What of territorial units belonging to the same municipal system and electing, in proper exercise of their rights, to make international law the law of an agreement of their own? Are these treaties? Lauterpacht thought so. Lauterpacht, First Report (n 13) 95 (Art 1, comment (1)); see also *State of Georgia v State of South Carolina* 497 US 376, 407 (1990). The ILC, while acknowledging the analogy, concluded that it was 'impossible to regard the ... agreements [between constituent territories within a federation] as examples of the exercise of *international* treaty-making capacity without risking confusion between the spheres of operation of international and domestic law'. H Waldock, 'First Report on the Law of Treaties' [1962] YBILC, vol II, 37 (draft Art 3, comment (4)).

3. Special administrative regions

In addition to sub-federal treaty-making, States from time to time have established special administrative regions (SARs). Some of these are separate treaty territories.[38] The main modern examples are the SARs of China: Hong Kong and Macao. Like federal States, a SAR's treaty-making capacity depends on both internal authorization and external acceptance of its competence. Both Hong Kong and Macau came under Chinese sovereignty by means of treaties in which China agreed that these regions would have a continuing capacity to make treaties in certain areas (eg, investment, tourism, cultural matters).[39] But China's constitutional provisions do not permit a SAR treaty implying its independence.[40] Other States have accepted the capacity of the SARs in designated fields.[41] Article XII of the Agreement establishing the World Trade Organization (WTO) authorizes any 'customs territory possessing full autonomy in the conduct of its external commercial relations and of the other matters provided for in this Agreement and the Multilateral Trade Agreements' to accede on terms agreed to between it and the WTO.[42] Hong Kong and Macao joined the WTO as original members as they had each acceded to the preceding 1947 General Agreement on Tariffs and Trade under a similar provision (Article XXXIII); they retained their individual membership after China joined the WTO in 2001.

The question arises as to how Taiwan—the other part of China—is to be categorized. Its own government has not made any unequivocal declaration of independence from China; and for much of the time since the de facto truce in the civil war, Taiwanese authorities were clear that the effective control they exercised was over a province of China. However it is to be categorized, Taiwan is certainly a treaty-making entity. Like Hong Kong and Macao, Taiwan has joined the WTO in its own right. In addition, a number of bilateral investment treaties are in force between Taiwan and States still recognizing it as the 'Republic of China'— and also between Taiwan and States which have ceased to recognize it as such.[43]

---

[38] Other special regions, such as duty free zones and the like, generally have no international treaty-making capacity, but, again, this is subject, *inter alia*, to each State's particular rules. By contrast, the interests of the inhabitants of such zones, under an international rule, may merit special consideration in the treaty practice of the responsible States. See *Case of the Free Zones of Upper Savoy and the District of Gex (Switzerland v France)* [1932] PCIJ Rep Series A/B No 46 95, 169.

[39] Eg Joint Declaration on the Question of Hong Kong (China–United Kingdom) (done 19 December 1984, entered into force 27 May 1985) 1399 UNTS 33, Annex I, §XI.

[40] See J Crawford, *The Creation of States in International Law* (2nd edn OUP, Oxford 2006) 244–52.

[41] Hong Kong, between 2000 and 2005, concluded sixty-three bilateral treaties on topics within its competence such as investment protection, mutual legal assistance, and air services, in addition to joining several multilateral treaty organizations. A Aust, *Modern Treaty Law & Practice* (2nd edn CUP, Cambridge 2007) 67–71.

[42] Marrakesh Agreement Establishing the World Trade Organization adopted 15 April 1994, entered into force 1 January 1995, 1867 UNTS 3, 162, Art XII.

[43] UNCTAD lists fifteen States as having entered into BITs with Taiwan: Costa Rica, Dominican Republic, El Salvador, Guatemala, India, former Yugoslav Republic of Macedonia, Malaysia, Nicaragua, Nigeria, Panama, Paraguay, Philippines, Singapore, Thailand, and Vietnam. UNCTAD, 'Country-Specific List of BITs' <http://www.unctad.org/sections/dite_pcbb/docs/bits_taiwan.pdf>.

The willingness of other parties to enter into treaties with Taiwan is nevertheless a limiting factor in respect of Taiwan's treaty practice.[44]

4. Indigenous peoples

Another category of integral territory presenting special considerations is territory inhabited by an indigenous people.[45] Colonizing powers entered into agreements with these peoples especially in Africa, Australasia and the Americas. The 1840 Treaty of Waitangi is perhaps the best-known treaty between a colonizing power and an indigenous people.[46] Eventually, many if not most treaties with indigenous peoples were largely submerged in national constitutional systems—a process which has been called (critically) 'domestication'.[47] The process was by no means direct; constitutional considerations led national courts to struggle with the fate of such agreements.[48] The result, however, was typically the dismantling (judicially and by legislation) of the capacity of the indigenous entity to make treaties.

The United States, for example, concluded some 367 treaties with Native American tribes prior to 1868.[49] The federal government at first accepted these as equivalent to treaties with foreign powers, subject to special interpretative accommodations to avoid prejudice to the Native American parties.[50] By act of Congress in 1871, the treaty-making of these 'domestic dependent sovereigns' was ended.[51] Elsewhere, other processes led to similar results.

Judge Dillard famously said that it 'is for the people to determine the destiny of the territory and not the territory the destiny of the people'.[52] The *Western Sahara* question concerned the people of a Non-Self-Governing Territory and therefore

For its part, the United States concludes agreements, which are legally binding under US law with Taiwan through two non-profit corporations (the American Institute in Taiwan and the Taipei Economic and Cultural Representative Office). See 22 USC §3301 *et seq.*

[44] For example, Taiwan was not allowed to join the Convention on the Conservation and Management of Highly Migratory Fish Stocks in the Western and Central Pacific Ocean as a party, although negotiating States allowed it to make analogous commitments (as Chinese Taipei) through an accompanying Memorandum of Understanding. Aust (n 41) 61.

[45] On treaties with indigenous peoples, see G Alfredsson 'Indigenous Peoples, Treaties with' in R Wolfrum (ed), *Max Planck Encyclopedia of Public International Law* (OUP, Oxford 2007).

[46] Treaty of Cession between Great Britain and New Zealand, Waitangi (5/6 February 1840) 89 CTS 473. See I Brownlie *Treaties and Indigenous Peoples: The Robb Lectures 1990* (FM Brookfield (ed) Clarendon Press, Oxford 1992) 8.

[47] UNCHR (Sub-Commission), 'Third progress report submitted by Miguel Alfonso Martínez, Special Rapporteur, Treaties, Agreements and Other Constructive Arrangements between States and Indigenous Populations' (15 August 1996) UN Doc E/CN.4/Sub.2/1996/23, 3-4 [8] ('Martínez Third Report'); and more extensively UNCHR (Sub-Commission), 'Final report submitted by Miguel Alfonso Martínez, Special Rapporteur, Treaties, Agreements and Other Constructive Arrangements between States and Indigenous Populations' (22 June 1999) UN Doc E/CN.4/Sub.2/1999/20, 26–38 [168]–[244].

[48] See eg *Worcester v State of Georgia*, 31 US 515, 575–7 (1832).

[49] FP Prucha, *American Indian Treaties* (University of California Press, Berkeley 1995) 1.

[50] *Worcester* (n 48) 575–7.

[51] Act of 3 March 1871, 16 Stat 566; P Thornberry, *Indigenous Peoples and Human Rights* (MUP, Manchester 2002) 80–1 and n117 (citing cases).

[52] *Western Sahara* (Advisory Opinion) [1975] ICJ Rep 12, 122 (Separate Opinion, Judge Dillard).

presented special considerations not relevant to an indigenous people. Nevertheless, it is striking that State parties to treaties with indigenous peoples very largely took the reverse approach. More often than not, they sought to secure control of territory, under legal title, regardless of the interests of the prior inhabitants. Modern constitutional measures, including agreements with indigenous groups, have been inspired, to some extent, as a reparative measure for this past practice.

In the Constitution Act, 1982, for example, Canada 'recognized and affirmed' the treaty rights of the aboriginal peoples of Canada.[53] The Canadian Charter of Rights and Freedoms provides that it 'shall not be construed so as to abrogate or derogate from any aboriginal treaty'.[54] Canadian Courts have since recognized the government's obligation to implement these earlier treaties.[55]

There have also been attempts at international legislation. In the 1990s, the UN Commission on Human Rights undertook a number of studies concerning indigenous treaty rights and treaty-making in particular.[56] In 2007, on the recommendation of the new Human Rights Council, the UN General Assembly adopted a UN Declaration on the Rights of Indigenous Peoples.[57] Two operative provisions of the Declaration concern the treaty-making of indigenous peoples—one potentially looking backward, the other forward. Article 37 provides that '[i]ndigenous peoples have the right to the recognition, observance and enforcement of treaties, agreements and other constructive arrangements concluded with States or their successors and to have States honour and respect such treaties, agreements and other constructive arrangements.'[58] The Declaration thus recognizes the existence of earlier treaties with indigenous peoples, although it does not say which ones continue to apply or what rights and obligations they continue to confer. Article 36(1) is in a prospective vein, providing that:

1. Indigenous peoples, in particular those divided by international borders, have the right to maintain and develop contacts, relations and cooperation, including activities for spiritual, cultural, political, economic and social purposes, with their own members as well as other peoples across borders.[59]

Consistent with the approach in a number of federal systems, Article 36(1) seems to restrict treaty-making capacity to agreements with entities at like level ('with ... other peoples') and in designated substantive fields ('activities for spiritual, cultural, political, economic and social purposes'). It does not contemplate a general treaty-making power for indigenous groups.

---

[53] Constitution Act, 1982, Part II §35(1) ('Rights of the Aboriginal Peoples of Canada').
[54] Canadian Charter of Rights and Freedoms §25.
[55] *Haida Nation v British Columbia (Minister of Forests)* [2004] 3 SCR 511, 2004 SCC 73 [17], [25]. In Australia, the *Mabo* case rejected the 'enlarged notion of *terra nullius*' that had allowed Australia's government to deny indigenous peoples' legal capacity. *Mabo v Queensland* (No 2) [1992] HCA 23, (1992) 175 CLR 1 (High Court of Australia) [36]–[39], [63].
[56] Eg Martínez Third Report (n 47); Martínez Final Report (n 47).
[57] UNGA Res 61/295 (13 September 2007) Annex.
[58] Ibid Art 35(1).
[59] Ibid Art 36.

The UN Declaration was adopted 143 votes to 4, with 11 abstentions.[60] The negative votes and abstentions, however, comprised the principal States containing indigenous groups.[61] The four objecting States—Australia, Canada, New Zealand, and the United States—all drew attention to their domestic processes for dealing with indigenous rights and agreements; Canada and Australia specifically rejected that the 2007 Declaration either reflected customary international law or provided a new basis of indigenous rights.[62]

In summary, early agreements with colonizing powers constituted international law acts at the time, and their abrogation is sometimes referred to as conduct for which reparation is due. Though a question of such reparation is likely to be decided as a matter of national law, claimants well may describe the State's conduct with reference to prior international engagements. As reflected in statements such as the 2007 Declaration, some support exists in favour of recognizing a greater international competence in indigenous groups, but given the significant objections to date this hardly has crystallized into a new rule. Finally, as with territorial units of federal States, newly formed indigenous territorial entities within a State may be accorded certain competences at the international level, including treaty-making. The scope and content of any such competence will depend in the first instance on each particular national law arrangement.

B. Treaty-making and external territories

1. The range of juridical relations

External territories differ from integral territory in that international law appears to grant them a distinct international status. Based on the Charter's provisions, the United Nations found that overseas colonies constitute external territories for which administering powers bore special obligations.[63] With decolonization, this category may seem on the verge of disappearing. But sixteen Non-Self-Governing Territories remain,[64] and since the late 1990s, international administration of territory has presented new situations where questions of treaty-making may arise. There are also the Associated States, such as the Cook Islands and Niue, which under Article 305(1)(c) and (d) of UNCLOS, may become parties to that instrument.[65] These would appear to be a special type of State, not another

---

[60] UN Declaration on the Rights of Indigenous Peoples (12 September 2007) UN Doc A/61/L.67.

[61] UN GAOR, 61st Sess, 107th Plenary Meeting, UN Doc A/61/PV.107, 19. The United States, Canada, Australia, and New Zealand voted against the draft. Azerbaijan, Bangladesh, Bhutan, Burundi, Colombia, Georgia, Kenya, Nigeria, the Russian Federation, Samoa, and Ukraine abstained.

[62] Ibid 12 (Australia); ibid 12–13 (Canada); ibid 13–14 (New Zealand); ibid 15 (United States). For a review of the Declaration, see S Allen and A Xanthaki (eds), *Reflections on the UN Declaration on the Rights of Indigenous Peoples* (Hart Publishing, Oxford 2011).

[63] UNGA Res 1542 (XV) (15 December 1960).

[64] Crawford (n 40) 634, Table 5 ('Remaining non-self-governing territories').

[65] UN Convention on the Law of the Sea (adopted 10 December 1982, entered into force 16 November 1994) 1833 UNTS 396, 517 (UNCLOS).

non-State actor, but that questions remain reflects the lack of a clear dividing line between issues of status and the capacity to make treaties.

It is said that international legal personality is the prerequisite for an entity to enter into a treaty; Ago, for example, said that 'all subjects of international law had, as a rule, the capacity to become parties to a treaty'.[66] If one determines that an entity is a State—or, for that matter according to Ago some other 'subject of international law'—then treaty-making capacity follows. However, it has also been said that the practice of treaty-making indicates international status—ie, that status is 'not a precondition for holding international obligations or authorizations, but is the consequence of possessing them'.[67] This is consistent with Kelsen's view.[68] The matter tends to become more complicated as the juridical relations between a State and the external territories for which it is responsible vary from territory to territory and, for a given relation, vary over time as well.[69] If there is a single concept of legal personality, then it would appear to have a considerable range of manifestations.

To what extent then can external territories make treaties in their own right? The answer varies, because as with federal States, States generally differ in how they characterize the territories for which they are responsible. Indeed, what might be an external territory to one State, another might characterize as integral. And like federal States, where a treaty-making capacity is contemplated, its scope will depend on the authorization of the responsible State *and* acceptance of that competence by potential treaty-partners. With respect to external territories, there may also be a third criterion—the responsible States' international commitments to third States vis-à-vis its external territories.

2. Non-Self-Governing Territories

Non-Self-Governing Territories today are the principal remaining form of dependent overseas territory. They 'enjoy a separate legal status, and with it a measure of legal personality'.[70] The ILC early on suggested a general presumption that a 'dependent State' relinquished treaty-making to the State responsible for its international relations. But the ILC's Special Rapporteur, Sir Humphrey Waldock, proposed an exception:

(b) A dependent State may, however, possess international capacity to enter into treaties if and in so far as:
  (i) The agreements or arrangements between it and the State responsible for the conduct of its foreign relations may reserve to it the power to enter into treaties in its own name; and

---

[66] [1962] YBILC, vol I, 61 [57] (Ago).
[67] R Portmann, *Legal Personality in International Law* (CUP, Cambridge 2010) 174.
[68] H Kelsen, *General Theory of Law and State* (Harvard University Press, Cambridge 1945) 96.
[69] For a discussion of the complications external territories pose to the territorial application of treaties, see Chapter 12.
[70] Crawford (n 40) 618.

(ii) The other contracting parties accept its participation in the treaty in its own name separately from the State which is responsible for the conduct of its international relations.[71]

In most instances, therefore, Non-Self-Governing Territories do not make their own treaties; the responsible State will instead conclude treaties in the form of an agreement by the administering power acting on behalf of the dependencies. For a Non-Self-Governing Territory to make a treaty, it will usually require some authorization from the State responsible for its international relations. The United Kingdom, for example, uses an 'Instrument of Entrustment' to authorize certain overseas territories such as Bermuda, the British Virgin Islands, and Jersey to enter into specific treaties in their own name. In 2002, for example, the United Kingdom entrusted the Authorities of Guernsey, Jersey, and the Government of the Isle of Man to negotiate and conclude Tax Information Exchange Agreements with the United States on the understanding that the United Kingdom remained responsible for the international relations of these territories.[72]

In some cases, the responsible State may combine approaches. For example, the parties to the 1960 Agreement establishing the Caribbean Organization were France, the Netherlands, the United Kingdom, and the United States of America.[73] The accompanying Statute of the Caribbean Organization was open, however, to dependent territories specifically named, including the Netherlands Antilles, the Bahamas, and Puerto Rico. France, however, did not agree to give its dependencies of French Guiana, Guadeloupe, and Martinique this right, French constitutional law considering them integral territories. Instead, France joined the Organization on their behalf and exercised their voting rights.[74] Both agreements contained a savings clause, denying that either agreement should be interpreted to affect the present or future constitutional status of the dependencies involved.[75]

In contrast, after a 1999 constitutional amendment afforded New Caledonia a separate treaty-making capacity, France sought agreement that it and New Caledonia could each join the Convention on the Conservation and Management of Highly Migratory Fish Stocks in the Central and Western Pacific Ocean.[76] Other States objected to separate French and New Caledonian membership where the Convention contemplated decision-making by a supermajority vote, and the final treaty text was not open to direct participation by external territories.[77]

---

[71] Waldock, First Report (n 37) 36 (draft Art 3, comment 3).

[72] US Treasury Dept, Press Release, 'United States and Jersey Sign Agreement to Exchange Tax Information' (4 November 2002) <http://www.treas.gov/press/releases/po3595.htm>. See also Pre-clearance Agreement (US–Bermuda) (15 January 1974) 928 UNTS 95.

[73] Agreement for the Establishment of the Caribbean Organization and Annexed Statute of the Caribbean Organization (21 June 1960, entered into force 29 December 1961) 418 UNTS 110.

[74] Ibid 124–6 (Statute Art III).

[75] Ibid 112 (Agreement Art II); ibid 136.

[76] Law No 99–209 (19 March 1999) JO 21 March 1999 4197-99, Arts 21, 22 (giving New Caledonia authority to conclude international conventions in respect, *inter alia*, of exploration, exploitation and conservation of marine resources in the Exclusive Economic Zone).

[77] Though they did not object to the membership of Niue and the Cook Islands as Associated States. See FAO, 'UN Fish Stocks Agreement' <http://www.fao.org/fishery/topic/13701/en> n4.

Indeed, although external territories were original members of international organizations like the Universal Postal Union, it is relatively rare for a multilateral treaty
to allow their participation; most current practice involves bilateral agreements,
though the special treatment which Article 305 of UNCLOS accords to Associated
States applies as well to at least some Non-Self-Governing Territories.[78]

The New Caledonia example also illustrates how potential treaty partners have a
significant say in treaty-making by external territories. States typically exercise
caution before concluding such treaties. Israel, for example, has a practice of consult-
ing with the responsible State to confirm that the territory is authorized to conclude
the treaty; if it is not, then Israel will redraft the instrument in the form of a political
commitment.[79] When the United Kingdom informed the United States that
the Cayman Islands lacked the necessary entrustment to sign a Tax Information
Exchange Agreement in its own name, the United States concluded the agreement
with the United Kingdom, which acted on behalf of the Cayman Islands.[80]

So parallels exist between integral constituent units and external territories. The
agreement-making of both will depend on the readiness of other parties to enter
into agreements; and on the extent to which the responsible State permits such
agreements. A salient difference is that the administering State in respect of its
external territory may have additional international obligations. A mandate, trusteeship agreement, or the UN Charter (especially Chapter XI) may govern the
relationship between the external territory and its responsible State. Depending
on the content of those commitments, they may affect the treaty-making capacities
of the external territory.

3. Territories under international administration

The establishment of international administrations in East Timor and in Kosovo
in the late 1990s led to renewed interest in such arrangements, including in
their provisions for treaty-making.[81] In *Petition for Transfer of Luan Goci and
Bashkim Berisha*, the authority of the UN Interim Administration in Kosovo
(UNMIK) to enter into agreements on criminal matters with the United Kingdom
and Switzerland was challenged; the Supreme Court of Kosovo determined that the
transactions did not constitute international agreements for purposes of Kosovar
criminal procedure.[82] On the other hand, UNMIK adopted treaties on certain
functional matters in respect of Kosovo, and these evidently have not been
invalidated.[83] Concern that an agreement might prejudice the final status of the

---

[78] Cf UNCLOS (n 65) Art 305(1)(e).

[79] R Lapidoth, 'Israel' in *NTLP* (n 11) 400.

[80] Agreement for the Exchange of Information Relating to Taxes, for the Cayman Islands (US–UK)
(signed 27 November 2001, entered into force 10 March 2006) TIAS 13175.

[81] See generally C Stahn, *The Law and Practice of International Territorial Administration. Versailles
to Iraq and Beyond* (CUP, Cambridge 2008) 570–5.

[82] *Decision on Petition for Transfer of Luan Goci and Bashkim Berisha*, Pn-Kr 333/005 (30 January
2006) (Supreme Court of Kosovo), about which see Stahn (n 81) 574–5.

[83] For examples see Stahn (n 81) 573 nn187–188.

territory seems to have restricted the subject matters on which the administering institutions believed they held treaty-making competence.[84]

The Kosovo Government observed in the advisory proceedings on the *Declaration of Independence* that its Constitution provides that 'the Republic concludes international agreements'.[85] Kosovo further observed that it had begun to exercise that treaty-making by (i) 'establishing with its treaty partners the status of treaties to which Kosovo was bound as a former constituent part of the SFRY';[86] and (ii) entering into new bilateral treaties.[87] An example of the latter is an Agreement on the Mutual Abolition of Visas between Kosovo and Turkey.[88]

4. Pre-independence agreements and the competence of pre-independence governments

A separate issue for certain external territories is presented when, prior to independence, they enter into agreements with the administering power. To the extent a Non-Self-Governing Territory holds international legal personality distinct from the administering power, it may also hold a treaty-making competence. The main question will be to *what* extent it holds that competence. If it is competent to enter into agreements with other States, it stands to reason that it is competent to enter into agreements with the administering power. But there is a question—if a dependent territory purports to bind the future State by agreeing with the administering power to fundamental changes in its territorial constitution, will it in truth have acted freely? The question arises especially where negotiations are underway over the territory's final exercise of self-determination at the time of the agreement.

The United Kingdom, shortly before Mauritius and the Seychelles became independent, enacted a municipal law separating certain territory from each to create a new territory—which it titled the British Indian Ocean Territory (BIOT). The transaction was made with the consent of the (pre-independence) governments of both territories.[89] Under the UN Charter, the United Kingdom had an obligation for both territories 'to develop self-government, to take due account of the political aspirations of the peoples, and to assist . . . in the progressive development of their free political institutions'.[90] They both were also territories the 'partial or total disruption of the national unity and the territorial integrity' of which had been

---

[84] Ibid 573–4.

[85] 'Written Contribution of the Republic of Kosovo' in *Declaration of Independence* Proceedings (n 6) (17 April 2009) 22 [2.36].

[86] Ibid 23 [2.39].

[87] Ibid 23 [2.40].

[88] Adopted 13 January 2009 and discussed in 'Written Contribution of the Republic of Kosovo' (n 85) 23 [2.40].

[89] Working Paper prepared by the Secretariat, 'Report of the Special Committee on the Situation with regard to the implementation of the Declaration on the Granting of Independence to Colonial Countries and Peoples' (16 March 1972) UN Doc A/8723/Rev.1 Supp No 23, vol IV.

[90] UN Charter Art 73(b).

declared 'incompatible with the purposes and principles of the Charter'.[91] Despite the local governments' agreement, there were doubts as to whether they (particularly the Mauritius Government) adequately represented the interests of the inhabitants of the territories.[92] Mauritius has since contested the validity of BIOT's creation as a violation of the UK's UN Charter obligations.[93]

Another example is the separation of the Strategic Trust Territory of the Pacific Islands into three eventual Associated States[94] and one territory in political union with the United States.[95] Before the territories attained final status, there were objections that the separation was a breach of the territorial integrity of the Trust Territory.[96] But the UN Trusteeship Council, '[h]aving heard the statements of the elected representatives of the Trust Territory Governments requesting early termination of the Trusteeship Agreement, and believing this to reflect the freely expressed wishes of the people of the Trust Territory', considered that the United States had 'satisfactorily discharged its obligations under the terms of the Trusteeship Agreement'.[97] Unlike the BIOT, moreover, no serious subsequent objection appears to have been made.

The International Court of Justice in its *Kosovo* Advisory Opinion found no general international law rule to restrict political acts within a State having the intention of separating one part of the State territory.[98] A pre-independence agreement between a Non-Self-Governing Territory and its administering power therefore might be characterized as a decision belonging to one legal order and having no special significance under international law. The agreement, taken in that light, would be a municipal constitutional settlement, not a treaty. But whether the territory is subject exclusively to one national order is the central question in contention. Charter Articles 73 and 74, as developed by UN General

[91] Declaration on the Granting of Independence to Colonial Countries and Peoples, UNGA Res 1514 (XV) (14 December 1960) [6].

[92] UNGA, 'Report of the Special Committee on the Situation with regard to the Implementation of the Declaration on the Granting of Independence to Colonial Countries and Peoples, 31 December 1964–12 January 1965' UN Doc A/5800/Rev.1 and A/6000/Rev.1, Conclusions [154], endorsed in UNGA Res 2066 (XX) (16 December 1965) [1].

[93] UNHCR, 'Comments by the Government of Mauritius to the concluding observations of the Human Rights Committee on the United Kingdom of Great Britain and Northern Ireland and Overseas Territories: International Covenant on Civil and Political Rights' (28 May 2002) CCPR/CO/73/UK-CCPR/CO/73/UKOT/Add.1, 1 [4].

[94] Palau, the Marshall Islands, and the Federated States of Micronesia. See *People of Bikini, ex rel Kili/Bikini/Ejit Local Gov Council v United States* 77 Fed Cl 744, 749, 755–60 (US Ct of Fed Claims, 2007).

[95] The Commonwealth of the Northern Mariana Islands. See Covenant to Form a Commonwealth of the Northern Mariana Islands in Political Union with the United States of America (10 March 1975) T/1759; 121 Cong Rec No 43 4083–91. For a summary of transactions leading to the Covenant, see *Temengil & Others v Trust Territory of the Pacific Island & Others* 881 F2d 647, 639–51 (9th Cir 1989) (concurring opinion of Judge Beezer and Chief Judge Kozinski).

[96] Eg Letter dated 12 November 1986 from the Permanent Representative of the USSR to the United Nations addressed to the Secretary-General, UN Doc A/41/822, S/18455.

[97] TC Res 2183 (LIII) (28 May 1986) preambular [7] and operative [3]. Eventually Russia accepted the outcome as satisfactory. See Mr Sidorov (Russian Federation), Trusteeship Council, 1703rd mtg (18 January 1994) UN Doc T/PV.1703, 12.

[98] *Declaration of Independence* Opinion (n 6) [79]–[84].

Assembly resolutions, subject Non-Self-Governing Territories as a category to international rules. As the *Kosovo* proceedings illustrated, outside the relatively clear situation of Chapter XI, the resultant questions may be even more difficult to resolve.

C. Insurgent groups

The UN Secretary-General made clear in 2001 that armed groups that are party to a conflict are subject to international humanitarian law rules found in multilateral treaties as much as States and their governments.[99] The correlation between the capacity of an actor to be subject to rights and obligations under an international instrument and the capacity to conclude such an instrument is imprecise. How a national liberation movement is treated for purposes of humanitarian law does not necessarily determine how it is treated as treaty-maker.[100] Nevertheless, the modern development of international law suggests that the two bear some relation.

As non-State actors, insurgent groups are not parties to the Geneva Conventions of 1949. Some unilaterally have asserted the applicability of the Conventions but have been rebuffed.[101] However, Common Article 3, in addition to its stipulation of *de minimis* rules for parties engaged in a non-international armed conflict, provides that: 'The Parties to the conflict should further endeavour to bring into force, by means of special agreements, all or part of the other provisions of the present Convention.'[102] This evidently invites the State party (or parties) and the insurgent group(s) to enter into 'special agreements' for the purpose of further regulating the conflict.

One such agreement was that adopted by the Government of El Salvador and the Frente Farabundo Martí para la Liberación (FMLN).[103] The text's preambular and substantive provisions are unclear on whether it constitutes a treaty. The preamble refers to 'obligations of this nature under the many international conventions to which [El Salvador] is a party' but refers, rather elliptically, to the FMLN's 'capacity and . . . will . . . to respect the inherent attributes of the human person'.[104] Human rights are defined in terms of UN and OAS declarations and principles as well as those 'rights recognized by the Salvadorian legal system, including treaties to which El Salvador is a party'. Based on these provisions, it

---

[99] UNSC, 'Report of the Secretary-General' (30 March 2001) UN Doc S/2001/331 [48] (finding prohibition on targeting civilians in Common Art 3 to the Geneva Conventions and Additional Protocol II on non-international armed conflicts 'enshrined in customary international law' and applicable to armed groups). For discussion, see C Schaller, 'Guerrilla Forces' in R Wolfrum and others (eds), *Max Planck Encyclopedia of Public International Law* (OUP, Oxford 2009) [3]–[6].

[100] See generally A Cassesse, *International Law* (2nd edn OUP, New York 2005) 140–2.

[101] For examples, see L Zegveld, *Accountability of Armed Opposition Groups in International Law* (CUP, Cambridge 2002) 14 n18.

[102] See Geneva Convention for the Amelioration of the Wounded and Sick in Armed Forces in the Field (adopted 12 August 1949, entered into force 21 October 1950) 75 UNTS 30, Art 3.

[103] Zegveld (n 101) 16–17, 25–6, 49–51, 186–7, 212.

[104] Agreement on Human Rights, San Jose (26 July 1990) UN Doc A/44/971, S/21541, Annex 2 (2nd and 3rd preambular paragraphs).

might be said that the agreement is governed by national, rather than international, law. But the Agreement conferred a mandate on the UN Human Rights Verification Mission to observe its implementation,[105] and the report of the Inter-American Commission on Human Rights later suggested that the Agreement established international obligations on both parties.[106] An international character was also suggested by the Verification Mission in its reports on the situation.[107] Writers take the view, generally, that such agreements establish international law obligations binding on the insurgent group.[108]

D. Private actors

Corporations created under national law and individuals generally do not possess international legal personality. Nevertheless, States at times have empowered such private actors with personality, including (infrequently) the capacity to make treaties.[109] For example, at the end of the First World War, Article 304 of the Treaty of Trianon provided that 'the administrative and technical reorganization of [certain railway concessions in the former Austro-Hungarian empire] . . . shall be regulated in each instance by an agreement between the owning company and the States territorially concerned', subject to arbitration at the election of the States, the Board of Management of the Company operating the line (the Südbahn Company), or a Committee representing the bondholders who financed it.[110] The Yugoslav State, Hungary, Italy, and the Südbahn Company concluded a further Agreement at Rome on 29 March 1923, with a view to implementing Article 304.[111] There is little question that the Rome Agreement constituted a

[105] Inter-American Commission on Human Rights, 'Report on the Situation of Human Rights in El Salvador' (11 February 1994) OEA/Ser.L/V/II.85 Doc 28 rev 2.1.b, 2.4.

[106] Ibid 7.

[107] UNGA, 'First Report of the United Nations Observer Mission in El Salvador' (16 September 1991) UN Doc A/45/1055, S/23037 12–13 [17]–[25], esp [19] (indicating that the 'normative framework' of the Mission is contained in international law instruments).

[108] See eg P Kooijmans, 'The Security Council and Non-State Entities as Parties to Conflicts' in K Wellens (ed), *International Law: Theory and Practice. Essays in Honour of Eric Suy* (Martinus Nijhoff, The Hague 1998) 333, 338.

[109] *Restatement (Third) of Foreign Relations Law of the United States* (1987) Pt II, 'Persons in International Law', Introductory Note.

[110] *Award of the Arbitrators Appointed by Resolution of the Council of the League of Nations of January 17, 1934* (1935) 29 AJIL 523, 524–5 ('1934 Arbitration'). And see identical language in Treaty of Peace between Allied and Associated Powers and Austria (Treaty of St Germain-en-Laye) (10 September 1919) in FL Israel (ed), *Major Peace Treaties of Modern History* (Chelsea House Publishers, New York 1967) Art 320.

[111] Agreement with a View to the Administrative and Technical Re-organization of the Southern Railway Company's System (Austria-Hungary-Italy-Serbs, Croats and Slovenes-Southern Railway Company (Südbhan)) (29 March 1923) 23 LNTS 336 (title indicates that agreement was 'drawn up with the concurrence of the holders of bonds issued by the above Company') ('Rome Agreement'). Disputes over Yugoslavia's performance led to an arbitration at the election of the Committee representing the bondholders, which had also apparently signed the Rome Agreement. See 1934 Arbitration (n 110) 527–8. Although the Committee was mentioned in the title as having concurred in the Agreement and listed as having signed it, questions later arose as to whether the Committee that invoked arbitration was the same as the one mentioned in Art 304 of the Treaty of Trianon. Cf Rome Agreement 368.

treaty granting private rights directly in lieu of the more traditional method of diplomatic protection.[112] This thus was an early example of how States may use a treaty to authorize private parties to participate in the formation and application of a separate international agreement.[113] It is also an early reflection of how the willingness of other parties to conclude an international agreement is at least as consequential as general rules announcing who can (or cannot) do so.

Under modern bilateral investment treaties (BITs) too, private parties may participate in the creation of international agreements—namely, agreements to arbitrate. As the English Court of Appeal indicated in *Ecuador v Occidental Petroleum*, investors obtain rights under international law through BITs directly, rather than derivatively.[114] The arbitration clause of the BIT was once typically described as consent by a State to arbitration. In more recent years, however, it has come to be accepted that the arbitration clause, instead, is an offer by the host State to arbitrate, with the investor's acceptance constituting a necessary step to completing an agreement to arbitrate.[115] Modern ICSID tribunals have understood that their jurisdiction is created in this way.[116]

Once the investor has accepted the offer—whether the offer is contained in a BIT, multilateral treaty, a statute, or a contract—what is contemplated is an agreement to arbitrate, adopted by a State and an investor and—at least potentially—governed by international law. The *travaux préparatoires* to the ICSID Convention suggest that the drafters saw no particular problem in describing a host State's consent to arbitrate as an international agreement between State and investor to which the law of treaties (eg *pacta sunt servanda*) would apply.[117] Indeed, it would

[112] A French court concluded as such with respect to the Committee representing the bondholders. *Vigoureux v Comité des Obligataires Danube-Save-Adriatique* (Tribunal Civil de la Seine) (12 December 1951) 18 ILR 1, 2. On diplomatic protection see V Lowe, 'Injuries to Corporations' in J Crawford and others (eds), *Law of International Responsibility* (OUP, Oxford 2010) 1005, 1006–7 ('*Law of International Responsibility*').

[113] To the extent doubts existed as to whether the Committee that signed the Rome Agreement (n 111) was the one contemplated in Art 304, an alternative theory would be that States do not need to use a treaty to authorize private party treaty-making, but may do so contemporaneously; the Committee's participation in the Rome Agreement alone may have been sufficient to establish its capacity—whoever it was—to make a treaty (or at least that treaty).

[114] *Republic of Ecuador v Occidental Petroleum & Production Co* [2005] EWHC Comm 774 [61]; *Republic of Ecuador v Occidental Petroleum & Production Co* [2006] EWHC Comm 345 [8]. See also C Tomuschat, 'Individuals' in *Law of International Responsibility* (n 112) 985, 990.

[115] International Bank for Reconstruction and Development, 'Report of the Executive Directors on the Convention on the Settlement of Investment Disputes between States and Nationals of Other States (18 March 1965)' reprinted in *History of the ICSID Convention: documents concerning the origin and the formulation of the Convention* (ICSID, Washington 1968) vol II(2), 1077 [24] ('*ICSID History*'); ibid, vol II(1), 275 (Consultative Meeting of Legal Experts, Summary Record of Proceedings (30 April 1964) Fifth Sess, 18 November 1963).

[116] *Tradex Hellas SA v Republic of Albania* ICSID Case No ARB/94/2 (24 December 1996) 5 ICSID Rep 43, 63; *Zhinvali v Georgia* ICSID Case No ARB/00/1 (24 January 2003) 10 ICSID Rep 3, 81 [342]; CH Schreuer and others, *The ICSID Convention. A Commentary* (2nd edn CUP, Cambridge 2009) 202–5 [416]–[426], 211–14 [447]–[455].

[117] Memorandum of the meeting of the Committee of the Whole, 27 December 1962, SID/62-2 (7 January 1963) *ICSID History* (n 115), vol II(1), 68 [48]; Paper prepared by the General Counsel and transmitted to the members of the Committee of the Whole, SID/63-3 (18 February 1963) *ICSID History* (n 115), vol II(1), 74 [8], 79–80 [18].

appear that one of the rationales behind the ICSID Convention was to make this point clear.[118]

Thus, private party capacity to make an agreement binding under international law is found at the heart of modern investment arbitration. This remains a limited capacity; it only applies to one potential agreement—an agreement to arbitrate. For private parties to make other international agreements would require additional authorization by States or other subjects of international law, whether in advance or contemporaneously with the agreement's creation. A contract between a State and a private party is still not normally an international instrument.[119]

II. Other Subjects of International Law and the Law of Treaties

The foregoing demonstrates that various actors—federal territorial units, external territories, insurgent groups, and even private actors—can make treaties. The VCLT does not, however, apply to such other subjects of international law.[120] The question then may arise what are the relevant rules for the agreements they make? The VCLT itself recognizes that a general law of treaties subsists outside its text. As noted at the outset, Article 3 of the VCLT accepts the possibility that instruments concluded by 'other subjects of international law' may be binding under international law.[121] Article 3, moreover, distinguishes between 'the rules set forth in the . . . Convention' and those to which other actors 'would be subject under international law independently of the Convention'. Thus, where the VCLT codifies general international law rules, its provisions may apply independently to other subjects of international law. It remains open, moreover, for other subjects of international law to stipulate that the VCLT rules apply in their entirety when they enter into an international agreement.

At least in respect of the VCLT's central propositions—eg *pacta sunt servanda*, and, probably, the general rule of interpretation (Article 31)—the applicability of treaty law to other subjects of international law can be seen. For example, in a dispute involving the Hamburg customs authorities, the European Court of Justice (ECJ) considered the EC–PLO and EC–Israel Association Agreements.[122] The

---

[118] Consultative Meeting of Legal Experts, Santiago, Chile, 3–7 February 1964, Summary Record of Proceedings, 12 June 1964, First Sess (3 February 1964) *ICSID History* (n 115), vol II(1), 303.

[119] See eg *SGS Société Générale de Surveillance SA v Republic of the Philippines* ICSID Case No ARB/02/6 (29 January 2004) 8 ICSID Rep 515, 553 [126]–[128] (citing *SGS v Pakistan* (5 May 2004) 8 ICSID Rep 451, 456 [172], for the principle that a BIT's umbrella clause—by which the State agrees to observe other obligations (eg contracts) which the State has assumed in respect of an investor—does not convert those obligations into treaty commitments).

[120] The VCLT may, however, apply to such treaties to the extent they involve more than one State; VCLT Art 3(c) extends the Convention rules to States *inter se* even when the agreement involves other subjects of international law.

[121] See Brierly's earlier point on this. Brierly (n 2) 229 ('it is not implied that agreements to which such entities, in addition to States or international organizations, are parties, lack binding force, or that their obligatory force is not derived from international law').

[122] Council Decision (2 June 1997) [1997] OJ L187, 3; Decision of the Council and Commission (19 April 2000) [2000] OJ L147, 3.

Court referred to Article 3(b) of the VCLT and applied certain substantive rules of the VCLT; their status as general international law apparently was self-evident.[123]

No general rule limits the subject matter which non-State actors may regulate through international agreement. There likewise is no general requirement of form. Nevertheless, agreements of other subjects of international law are less likely to be effective if the party seeking to assert them can argue their existence and content only by inference. The Regione Siciliana, for example, sought to establish, by referring to practice but not to text, that the European Commission had assumed a legal obligation to consult on and continue to finance an infrastructure project.[124] The Court did not accept that practice had created a legal commitment of the Commission to the Region.[125] The absence of a text thus proved fatal to this non-State actor's reliance on a putative international agreement.

This suggests a more general problem for parties seeking to rely on the agreements of non-State actors. Article 102 of the UN Charter and Article 80 of the VCLT oblige States to register their treaties which thus assures publication (or at least assures acknowledgment of the existence of the instrument, if not publication of its full text); but the obligation does not extend to the international instruments of other non-State actors.[126] This may present a problem of evidence, though probably not of opposability.[127] Practice on the point remains sparse.

III. Responsibility for Breach of the Non-State Treaty

As Lord Atkin wrote: '[It is] essential to keep in mind the distinction between (1) the formation, and (2) the performance, of the obligations constituted by a treaty'.[128] This chapter has been concerned chiefly with the powers of non-State

---

[123] Case C-386/08 *Brita GmbH v Hauptzollamt Hamburg-Hafen* [2010] ECR I-10289 [40]–[42]. The ECJ did not, however, refer to VCLT Art 3(b) when it reached a similar result in Case C-268/99 *Jany & Others* [2001] ECR I-8615 [35].

[124] Opinion of Advocate General Ruiz-Jarabo Colomer, Case C-417/04P *Regione Siciliana v Commission of the European Communities* [2006] ECR I-03881 [12]–[15].

[125] Case C-417/04P *Regione Siciliana v Commission of the European Communities* (Judgment of 2 May 2006 (Grand Chamber)) [30]; see also Colomer (n 124) [98].

[126] Cf Vienna Convention on the Law of Treaties between States and International Organizations or between International Organizations (adopted 21 March 1986, not yet in force) [1986] 25 ILM 543, Art 81.

[127] UN Charter Art 102(2) provides that '[n]o party to any such treaty or international agreement which has not been registered in accordance with the provisions of paragraph 1 of this Article may invoke that treaty or agreement before any organ of the United Nations'. This, however, would seem to apply only to treaties of States; and failure to register 'does not have any consequence for the actual validity of the agreement, which remains no less binding upon the parties'. *Maritime Delimitation and Territorial Questions between Qatar and Bahrain (Qatar v Bahrain)* (Judgment, Jurisdiction and Admissibility) [1994] ICJ Rep 112, 122 [129].

[128] *Attorney-General for Canada v Attorney-General for Ontario and Others* [1937] AC 326, 347 (Labour Conventions Case). The second category raises issues of international responsibility for breaches by such units, including breaches of obligations under a treaty, which the ILC addressed in its 2001 Draft Articles. See Draft Articles on the Responsibility of States for Internationally Wrongful Acts with Commentaries [2001] YBILC, vol II(2), Art 4(1) and comments (8), (9) and (10) (UN Doc A/56/10, as corrected) (ASR).

actors to enter into international agreements—ie the formation of treaties by a category of actors which ordinarily have no treaty practice of their own. Once it is seen that such actors have entered into treaties, the question follows what the consequences are to be, in the event a failure occurs in the performance of the resultant obligations.

It is axiomatic that, where a State has committed an internationally wrongful act, the international responsibility of the State is entailed.[129] But for the act to be a wrongful act of the State, it must (a) be attributable to the State under international law; and (b) constitute a breach of an international obligation of the State.[130] The question arises whether other subjects of international law entering into international agreements in their own names attract responsibility to themselves, or are mere agents to a State or other entity superior in a legal hierarchy.

It is the State in the usual situation which is treated as the party. After a federal or other constituent unit has entered into an international agreement, for example, a breach will usually entail the responsibility of the State.[131] In Germany, though the *Länder* may enter into international agreements on certain subjects, a breach, it has been said, 'clearly involved' the responsibility of the State.[132] Exceptions might be possible, but experts at the ILC and elsewhere have doubted whether exceptions in truth exist, let alone whether they would be desirable.[133] Fitzmaurice, for example, thought that there was no possibility for separate responsibility.[134]

Yet the view has not been unanimous that only the State may hold responsibility. Lauterpacht accepted that, under certain circumstances, the constituent unit could act separately and thus it would be to that unit, not the State, that responsibility would attach.[135] Elias and Yasseen both thought it possible that federated states could bear responsibility for international agreements concluded within their areas of competence.[136] Moreover, according to a 1974 ILC report:

In the cases—comparatively rare nowadays—in which component states retain an international personality of their own with a relatively restricted legal capacity, it seems evident that the conduct of their organs is likewise attributable to the federal State where such conduct amounts to a breach of the federal State's international obligations. On the other hand, where the conduct of organs of a component state amounts to a breach of an international obligation incumbent upon the component state, such conduct is to be attributed to the component state and not to the federal State.[137]

---

[129] ASR (n 128) Art 1.
[130] Ibid Art 2.
[131] See R Ago, 'Third Report on State Responsibility' [1971] YBILC, vol II(1), 259 [179] ('Ago, Third Report').
[132] [1998] YBILC, vol I, 240 [59] (Simma).
[133] Eg [1973] YBILC, vol I, 30 [45] (Sette Câmara); ibid 29 [31] (Ago); [1965] YBILC, vol I, 249 [7] (Verdross); [1998] YBILC, vol I, 240 [178] (Simma).
[134] GG Fitzmaurice, 'First Report on the Law of Treaties' [1956] YBILC, vol II, 118 [11].
[135] Lauterpacht, First Report (n 13) (comments to Arts 1 and 10).
[136] [1973] YBILC, vol I, 30 [53] (Elias); [1973] YBILC, vol I, 11 [23] (Yasseen).
[137] ILC, 'Report of the Commission' [1974] YBILC, vol II(1), 280 (draft Art 7, comment (10)).

The commentaries on State responsibility, as adopted, acknowledge the possibility of an exceptional situation: by express agreement, a treaty party might limit itself to recourse against the constituent unit.[138] Some national legislation also seems to envisage that result.[139] Ago, as Special Rapporteur, shifted from a sceptical view to entertaining the possibility of responsibility resting with the constituent unit rather than the State.[140]

These debates over responsibility are largely confined to component units of a federal State. But as this chapter has shown, those are not the only 'other subjects of international law' capable of treaty-making. Insurgent groups, for example, raise different issues. Assuming that an insurgent group entered into an international agreement, the question may arise whether the agreement continues in force as part of the international obligations of the State, in the event that the group becomes the government of the State. Insurgent group agreements like the El Salvador example already noted tend to be limited to matters concerning the internal armed conflict. It is unclear whether there is much point in talking about the primary obligation— ie the obligation created under the treaty—continuing in effect for the State if the insurgent group party to the agreement overthrows the government. The agreement was particular to an internal armed conflict which, by definition, no longer exists at the time one side has prevailed.[141] Moreover, where there had been two parties, now there is only one. Nevertheless, the Articles on State Responsibility are clear that 'the conduct of an insurrectional movement which becomes the new Government of a State shall be considered an act of that State under international law'.[142] There is also the prior case: responsibility for a breach before the end of hostilities of an obligation created under an agreement. Presumably, the group bears that responsibility, when the breach is by its own act. If that were not the case, then it would make little sense to refer to the agreement as an agreement *of* the insurgent group.

It is important in any case to distinguish attribution for purposes of international legal responsibility of 'other subjects of international law' from attribution for purposes of the law of treaties.[143] The ILC cautioned that attribution of State responsibility is not the same as the 'international law processes by which particular organs are authorized to enter into commitments on behalf of the State'.[144] Whether or not a convention is in force depends on the law of treaties, not the law of responsibility.[145] The law of State responsibility does not say what the

---

[138] See ASR (n 128) Art 4, comment (10).

[139] Eg Diaz (n 22) 450 (re Mexico's law authorizing inter-institutional agreements 'governed by public international law').

[140] Compare Ago, Third Report (n 131) 259 [179] with R Ago, 'Eighth Report on State Responsibility' [1979] YBILC, vol II, 5 n7 [3].

[141] See generally P Dumberry, 'New State Responsibility for Internationally Wrongful Acts by an Insurrectional Movement' (2006) 17 EJIL 605.

[142] ASR (n 128) Art 10(1).

[143] J Crawford, 'First Report on State Responsibility' [1998] YBILC, vol II(1), 33 [147].

[144] ASR (n 128) Ch II ('Attribution of Conduct to a State'), comment (5).

[145] *Gabčíkovo-Nagymoros Project (Hungary/Slovakia)* (Judgment) [1997] ICJ Rep 7, 38 [47]. And see J Verhoeven, 'The Law of Responsibility and the Law of Treaties' in *Law of International Responsibility* (n 112) 105–13.

primary obligations of States or other subjects of international law are; nor does it say how exactly States or other subjects might assume obligations.[146] Their treaty-making to this extent is a distinct domain.[147]

Conclusion

Other subjects of international law have exhibited a range of treaty-making capacities. Their treaty-making practice is modest in comparison to that of States, but it is by no means negligible. Under some federal systems (eg the United States and Canada), sub-federal units have entered into many hundreds of international agreements.

When considering such agreements, certain issues can arise. It may be asked whether they are legally binding commitments or, instead, political undertakings. Relevant here will be the scope of authorization, if any, which the central government has granted. With respect to external territories, it may further be asked whether some multilateral or general legal requirement restricts the permissible scope of agreements entered into by a pre-independence entity. Moreover, as it is not the sub-State unit which presumptively concludes treaties (either on its own behalf or on that of the State to which it belongs), any other party which contemplates a treaty relationship with such a unit cannot be sure of the legal effects of the intended transaction if it does not consider with care the constitutional or other special arrangements between the unit and its central government.

At least the basic rules of the law of treaties would seem to apply to these agreements. As suggested in Part III above, however, treaty-making and international responsibility operate on different terms: that an entity may conclude a treaty is not in itself an answer to the questions which may arise as to attribution of responsibility in the event of a failure to satisfy the primary obligations that result.

To say that an entity has international legal personality suggests that it can enter into international agreements. The inverse is also true: if there is treaty-making, then, at least to that extent, international personality is to be deduced. A hallmark of modern international law is the recognition of international rights in more and more actors, including those like individuals and business organizations traditionally considered subjects strictly of national law. The scope of obligations also has grown, even if not in complete symmetry with the scope of rights. The breadth and frequency of international agreement making by other subjects of international law bears a relation, albeit imprecise, to these developments; the treaty practice of such other subjects thus seems likely to increase and the questions to which it gives rise to acquire greater urgency.

---

[146] ASR (n 128) Art 12.

[147] But see Judge Simma's Separate Opinion in *Application of the Interim Accord of 13 September 1995 (the former Yugoslav Republic of Macedonia v Greece)* (Judgment of 5 December 2011) [29], which seems to suggest that VCLT Art 60 occupies the field entirely in respect of the consequences of breach, a position not easily reconcilable with the distinction between primary and secondary obligations.

Recommended Readings

G Alfredsson, 'Indigenous Peoples, Treaties with' in R Wolfrum and others (eds), *Max Planck Encyclopedia of Public International Law* (OUP, Oxford 2007) online at <http://www.mpepil.com>

A Aust, *Modern Treaty Law & Practice* (2nd edn CUP, Cambridge 2007) 67

GM Danilenko, 'The New Russian Constitution and International Law' (1994) 88 AJIL 451

L Diaz, 'Mexico' in DB Hollis and others (eds), *National Treaty Law and Practice* (Martinus Nijhoff, Leiden 2005) 450

P Dumberry, 'New State Responsibility for Internationally Wrongful Acts by an Insurrectional Movement' (2006) 17 EJIL 605

DB Hollis, 'The Elusive Foreign Compact' (2008) 73 Missouri L Rev 1071

DB Hollis, 'Unpacking the Compact Clause' (2010) 88 Texas L Rev 741

DB Hollis, 'Why State Consent Still Matters: Non-State Actors, Treaties and the Changing Sources of International Law' (2005) 23 Berkeley J Intl L 151

P Kooijmans, 'The Security Council and Non-State Entities as Parties to Conflicts' in K Wellens (ed), *International Law: Theory and Practice. Essays in Honour of Eric Suy* (Martinus Nijhoff, The Hague 1998) 333

R Lapidoth, 'Israel' in DB Hollis and others (eds), *National Treaty Law and Practice* (Martinus Nijhoff, Leiden 2005) 400

OJ Lissitzyn, 'Territorial Entities in the Law of Treaties' (1968/III) 125 RcD 64

B Nikravesh, 'Quebec and Tatarstan in International Law' (1999) 23 Fletcher Forum World Affairs 227

M Schaefer, 'Constraints on State Level Foreign Policy: (Re)Justifying, Refining and Distinguishing the Dormant Foreign Affairs Doctrine' (2011) 41 Seton Hall L Rev 201

K Thakore, 'India' in DB Hollis and others (eds), *National Treaty Law and Practice* (Martinus Nijhoff, Leiden 2005) 369

HD Treviranus and H Beemelmans, 'Federal Republic of Germany' in DB Hollis and others (eds), *National Treaty Law and Practice* (Martinus Nijhoff, Leiden 2005) 328

A Wildhaber and others, 'Switzerland' in DB Hollis and others (eds), *National Treaty Law and Practice* (Martinus Nijhoff, Leiden 2005) 667

L Zegveld, *Accountability of Armed Opposition Groups in International Law* (CUP, Cambridge 2002)

6

NGOs in International Treaty-Making

*Kal Raustiala**

Introduction

Non-governmental organizations (NGOs) are a fixture of many contemporary treaty negotiations. Consider the effort to negotiate a successor agreement to the 1997 Kyoto Protocol on climate change. Meeting in Copenhagen in December 2009 to hammer out a deal were 192 State delegations and 120 heads of State and government.[1] Yet alongside these delegations, some of which comprised hundreds of diplomats and advisers, were nearly 1,000 private organizations and over 20,000 individuals seeking to influence the terms of agreement and shape broader public opinion about climate change.[2] This phenomenon is not unique to environmental treaty-making. In a surprisingly wide range of contemporary contexts, NGOs are very active participants in treaty-making. That is to say, they address negotiators formally, lobby them informally, put forward proposals and procedures, and generally act as cheerleaders and roadblocks on the way to final signature or failure. Later on, NGOs may monitor implementation, chastise the non-compliant, and encourage reform and renegotiation.

This was not always the case. Indeed, treaty negotiations were long marked—as they sometimes still are—by substantial secrecy, and took place, if not secretly, at least behind several sets of closed doors. The relevant actors were few, both because fewer earlier treaties were multilateral and because the number of States recognized as capable of entering into treaties was much more limited. Even as famous and significant a negotiation as the Paris peace talks of 1919 vividly illustrates the differences between the traditional approach to treaty-making and the contemporary one. Woodrow Wilson famously campaigned against secret agreements and

* I thank Andrew Guzman, Duncan Hollis, Peter Spiro, and Lara Stemple for helpful comments on earlier drafts, Gabriele Goettsche-Wanli, Chief of the Treaty Section at the UN Office of Legal Affairs, for her insights, and Phil Rucker and Nell Moley of UCLA for research assistance.

[1] S Roberts, 'GHG Finding Could be Fuel for Lawsuits' 15 Waste & Recycling News (4 January 2010) 7; UN Framework Convention on Climate Change, 'The United Nations Climate Change Conference in Copenhagen' (COP 15 and CMP 5 Reports, 7–19 December 2009) <http://unfccc. int/meetings/cop_15/items/5257.php>.

[2] P Wilson, 'Security Moving in for the Cull—Copenhagen Summit' *The Australian* (17 December 2009) Local 2.

sought to ensure that after the Great War covenants would be openly arrived at; indeed, he made this Point 1 of his Fourteen Points.[3] Yet there was much secrecy in Paris, and while newspapers covered the event avidly, and several NGOs of the time sent delegations, their level of participation was minimal and all working sessions were closed to the public.[4] Still, the Paris peace talks were a high point compared to the practices of the past, and in their own way they augured a new form of global governance in which NGOs and governments would work together far more closely.

As this suggests, NGOs were hardly unknown in 1919. The nineteenth century saw the formation of many NGOs, some of which—such as the British and Foreign Anti-Slavery Society, formed in 1839—focused expressly on reforming or influencing international law.[5] As early as 1911, Elihu Root, the former US Secretary of State (and Zelig of progressive-era American foreign policy and international law)[6] noted that such 'international societies' were growing in number and often actively propelling forward the negotiation of new treaties.[7]

But in the early twentieth century, NGOs remained limited in number and in scope compared to what we see today. There were few established norms or practices about how they ought to participate in the treaty process. That changed with the creation of the United Nations, which increasingly became an important, if not central, forum for treaty-making and, in roughly the same period, began accrediting large numbers of NGOs for participation in UN activities. This process has accelerated ever since. While not all contemporary treaty negotiations resemble the complex (one might say chaotic) mix of actors present in Copenhagen in 2009, the climate talks there were not unusual. For many treaties today, in particular major multilateral treaties, NGOs play a very visible role in both negotiation and implementation.

This chapter surveys the role of NGOs[8] in treaty-making. It focuses primarily on multilateral treaty-making, where NGOs are most prominent and active. Bilateral

---

[3] For the full list see 'President Woodrow Wilson's Fourteen Points' (8 January 1918) <http://avalon.law.yale.edu/20th_century/wilson14.asp>.

[4] S Charnovitz, 'The Emergence of Democratic Participation in Global Governance (Paris, 1919)' (2003) 10 Ind J Global L Stud 45, 62. Nonetheless, the Treaty of Versailles created the International Labour Organization discussed at n 29 and accompanying text.

[5] Other anti-slavery groups date back longer. A Hochschild, *Bury the Chains: Prophets and Rebels in a Fight to Free an Empire's Slaves* (Houghton Mifflin, New York 2005).

[6] For a discussion of Root's pervasive influence (and original use of the 'Zelig' metaphor), see J Zasloff, 'Law and the Shaping of American Foreign Policy: From the Gilded Age to the New Era' (2003) 78 NYU L Rev 239.

[7] S Charnovitz, 'Nongovernmental Organizations and International Law' (2006) 100 AJIL 348, 349.

[8] For the purposes of this chapter I define NGOs broadly, as non-state organizations that seek to influence international law and politics. This definition includes firms and also their associations, the latter of which are generally non-profit but lobby on behalf of profit-making enterprises (eg the International Chamber of Commerce). In this sense NGOs are a species of non-state actor, but that latter category includes, *inter alia*, international organizations (IOs) such as the UN itself. Unlike IOs, NGOs are generally constituted under the domestic law of some State, which may or may not be where they do most of their work or have the largest number of members. For more on the definition of NGOs see eg S Ripinsky and P van den Bossche, *NGO Involvement in International Organizations* (BIICL, London 2007) Ch 1.

treaties tend to be negotiated in processes and forums which do not lend themselves as readily to active NGO participation. Some of the key areas of bilateral treaty-making, such as arms control, investment, and trade, are guided by rules of confidentiality that limit NGO access, at least formally.[9] And bilateral treaty negotiations are less likely to take place under the aegis of international organizations (IOs), which tend—especially, as I will describe, in the case of the UN—to have entrenched norms of openness that facilitate NGO participation. Consequently, the line between NGO participation in treaty-making and participation in the general work of an IO is often blurry, since treaties are often updated and extended via rules and decisions taken within the framework of an IO.

This chapter asks four key questions about the relationship between NGOs and treaties. First, what roles do NGOs play today in treaty processes, and how have these roles changed? Second, what explains the increased prominence of NGOs? Third, are NGOs a salutary addition to treaty-making or illegitimate special interests? And finally, fourth, what is the broader significance of NGO activity for international law and international order? NGOs are clearly important players in treaty-making today. But their roles remain, to a large degree, circumscribed and controlled by States. Indeed, NGO participation is frequently useful to governments, and the rules and practices regulating their participation in treaties reflect this often symbiotic relationship. At the most fundamental level, the presence of NGOs in contemporary treaty-making and implementation—which for brevity I will refer to as *treaty processes*—is a sign of the expansion of the domain of treaty-making. As international law has expanded its substantive ambit, it has come to govern more and more of what has traditionally been thought to fall within the sphere of national law. In turn, the process of *international* law-making has come to resemble the process of *national* law-making. Like lobbyists in national capitals, NGOs tell us where governing power is; increasingly, that power rests at the international level.

I. NGOs and International Treaty-Making: An Overview

The oldest NGO active in international law is probably the Catholic Church,[10] but for most purposes, NGOs, as we conventionally understand them today, first became internationally active in the nineteenth century. The aforementioned anti-slavery societies, the Red Cross/Red Crescent movement (born shortly after Swiss businessman Henry Dunant witnessed the brutal aftermath of the Battle of Solferino in 1859), the International Peace Union, and many others first became

---

[9] Why this is true is less clear, but perhaps it is that bilateral negotiations are more nearly zero-sum in nature, and therefore each side has an incentive to resist the participation of NGOs the other side wants to involve. I thank Andrew Guzman for this idea.

[10] The Catholic Church is of course a complicated actor in international law, one that has an arguably unique status as a sovereign in certain contexts. See J Crawford, *The Creation of States in International Law* (2nd edn Clarendon Press, Oxford 2006) 221–33.

operational in this period.[11] By the early twentieth century, NGOs expressly focused on the then-nascent global governance movement began to emerge, such as the International Federation of the League of Nations Societies.[12] (Today, the analogous World Federation of United Nations Associations operates out of offices in New York and Geneva.) International legal scholars of the time noted this growing phenomenon and its significance for international law-making. Writing in the inaugural 1907 issue of the *American Journal of International Law*, Simeon Baldwin argued that 'it has often been found that the public congress of moment to the world has been the immediate consequence of a private congress'.[13]

Nonetheless, NGOs were hardly welcomed into the international negotiations of the time. The 1899 Hague Peace Conference, for instance, kept interested NGOs away from the proceedings. The desire for confidentiality was widespread, and NGOs were seen as interlopers in a fundamentally State-driven process. Still, NGOs were increasingly drawn to and sought greater roles in the treaty-making process. It was largely after the Second World War that NGOs grew more prominent in world politics, aided by at least five broad but important changes.

At a very basic level, technological change made travel and communication ever easier and cheaper; the proverbial 'three people with a fax machine' became a reality once phones and faxes (now internet connections) made it feasible for even a small NGO to lobby governments for a new international agreement or provision. Jet travel had a similar, and maybe even more profound, effect, enabling frequent and large multilateral negotiations that in turn opened up the door to greater NGO participation. In short, technology enhanced access. Today, many NGOs active in international law-making crisscross the globe en route to whatever negotiation is pressing.

A second, perhaps less obvious factor, was the move to codification in international law. The League of Nations adopted a project on codification in 1924; the result was the Conference for the Codification of International Law in 1930, and, fifteen years later, the United Nations Charter imposed on the General Assembly the duty to 'initiate studies and make recommendations... encouraging the progressive development of international law and its codification'.[14] The resulting International Law Commission spurred the creation of many new treaties in the post-war era. These treaty-making efforts often blended codification and progressive development, but the key here is that NGOs now had many more opportunities to weigh in on issues, like the law of the sea, that had previously only been governed by customary law.

---

[11] Like the Catholic Church, the International Committee for the Red Cross is a highly unusual organization with a designated role in the area of international humanitarian law that is perhaps *sui generis*.

[12] B Seary, 'The Early History: From the Congress of Vienna to the San Francisco Conference' in P Willetts (ed), *The Conscience of the World: The Influence of Non-Governmental Organizations in the UN System* (Hurst, London 1996) 17.

[13] SE Baldwin, 'The International Congresses and Conferences of the Last Century as Forces Working Toward the Solidarity of the World' (1907) 1 AJIL 565, 576.

[14] UN Charter Art 13.

Closely related to the codification movement was the creation of the United Nations itself, which provided a focal point and a formalized means of access—accreditation—that spurred significant NGO involvement in UN-related negotiations (I say more on this factor below). The UN is of course only the most important of a myriad of contemporary IOs. In a broad sense, the twentieth century move to IOs was NGO-friendly. As Jose Alvarez writes:

Matters of interstate diplomacy were, at least in the 19th century, regarded as confidential interstate matters. Modern treaty-making under IO auspices, by contrast, is characterized by a much greater openness to the accumulated wisdom, shared experiences, and institutional biases and blind spots, of a variety of actors beyond the government representatives set to negotiate... Certain structural aspects of IOs, including provision for access to documents and for 'observer' or other forms of non-voting status, have provided entry points for NGOs' growing participation in various forms of inter-state diplomacy, including treaty-making.[15]

A fourth factor promoting NGO participation was the post-war growth in democratic States, which, thanks to their more vibrant and open domestic civil societies, often birth NGOs that in turn may address or expressly focus on international issues.[16] These States also unsurprisingly tend to be more comfortable with the active involvement of NGOs at international negotiations than are more autocratic regimes.

A fifth factor was the increasing propensity for treaties in areas that were traditionally the province of domestic law. Many issues, such as tobacco regulation, banking, and transboundary air pollution, were long thought of as subjects for national law, not international law. Over the course of the last several decades, however, international law embraced a much wider concept of regulation and blurred the lines between intrinsically 'domestic' and 'international' topics.[17] Consequently, many NGOs have moved from a purely domestic orientation to an embrace of international law, as international law itself has expanded its ambit. The US-based National Rifle Association, for example, is increasingly involved in global gun regulation, and gained accreditation at the UN in 1997. Many multinational firms and trade associations that traditionally lobby parliaments and executives are also now more active in trade, labour, and environmental treaty negotiations, which often result in multilateral agreements that shape or

---

[15] JE Alvarez, *International Organizations as Law-Makers* (OUP, New York 2005) 277, 284. This may be because NGOs help provide an alternative power and legitimacy base to IOs. On this point see K Anderson, 'What NGO Accountability Means—And Does Not Mean' (2009) 103 AJIL 170, 170 (reviewing L Jordan and P van Tuijl (eds), *NGO Accountability: Politics, Principles & Innovations* (Earthscan, London 2006)).

[16] This growth is of course uneven. See LJ Diamond, *The Spirit of Democracy: The Struggle to Build Free Societies Throughout the World* (Times Books, New York 2008). On the relationship between NGOs, democracy, and treaties, see HK Jacobson and E Brown Weiss, 'Assessing the Record and Designing Strategies to Engage Countries' in HK Jacobson and E Brown Weiss (eds), *Engaging Countries: Strengthening Compliance with International Environmental Accords* (MIT Press, Cambridge 1998) 533–4.

[17] A Chayes and A Handler Chayes, *The New Sovereignty: Compliance with International Regulatory Agreements* (Harvard University Press, Cambridge 1995) 123–4.

determine national regulatory policies. One result, among others, is more extensive NGO demands for inclusion in international institutions and processes, and arguably a change in the style of treaty negotiations, as these organizations bring expectations and lobbying approaches forged in national capitals into the diplomatic arena.

The result of all these factors, and others, was a very large increase in the post-war era in the number of NGOs interested in treaty matters. This has been particularly true since the 1990s wave of treaty-making and UN conferencing; as one observer noted a decade ago, NGOs 'have enjoyed a phenomenally rapid rise on the world scene'.[18] Today, many of the large NGOs active in treaty processes have a global presence befitting their global interests. For example, Greenpeace International is legally incorporated in the Netherlands, but has dozens of affiliate offices around the world. These are independent actors in many respects, though in others (such as the use of the Greenpeace trademark) control is kept in Amsterdam. The rise to prominence of large and well-financed groups with international reach, like Greenpeace, is particularly noteworthy from the 1970s onwards. Several well-known transnational NGOs, such as Human Rights Watch, Oxfam, *Medecins Sans Frontieres*, and Greenpeace itself, were established in the 1970s. At the same time, more active multinational firms and higher levels of foreign direct investment and world trade led many firms to be more interested in international rules.[19]

This newly expanded and active cohort of NGOs sought to influence a very wide range of treaties negotiated over the last several decades and continues to do so today. (NGOs are likewise active in negotiations over instruments and documents other than treaties—such as non-binding declarations and conference action plans.) To be sure, much NGO influence is exercised at the domestic level, by shaping the demands and negotiating positions of governments as they enter into treaty processes. How effective particular NGOs are at this is a function of both skill and knowledge and the domestic politics and institutions of their home nation. But a meaningful look at how NGOs shape domestic positions vis-à-vis treaties is not possible in a brief survey such as this. However, it is possible to discuss in general terms the direct access and participation of NGOs in international negotiations and the broad variations that exist across different areas of international law. It is to that inquiry that I now turn.

[18] P Spiro, 'Accounting for NGOs' (2002) 3 Chi J Intl L 161. See also M Edwards, *NGO Rights and Responsibilities: A New Deal for Global Governance* (Foreign Policy Centre 2000) 9 ('the 176 "international" NGOs of 1909 . . . blossomed into 28,900 by 1993, and over 20,000 transnational NGO networks are already active on the world stage, 90 per cent of which were formed during the last thirty years').

[19] This increased attention to NGO activity, is dramatically reflected in a Google Ngram search on 'NGO' or 'nongovernmental organization', both of which (but in particular 'NGO') exhibit an extremely sharp leap in usage after 1980. Google Ngram allows searches of particular words or phrases in books catalogued in Google Books. A search in French of 'ONG' yields a very similar pattern, though at lower levels of usage. According to Steve Charnovitz, the term NGO (in English) was first used in 1919. Charnovitz (n 7) 351.

II. NGO Participation: Provisions and Practice

A. IO provisions for NGO participation

Much of contemporary treaty-making flows through the UN system, and thus UN rules and practices play an outsize role in shaping what NGOs can do with regard to treaties. Indeed, legal rules governing NGO participation are almost always the product of IOs; the Vienna Convention on the Law of Treaties, though central to many treaty issues, is silent on NGOs' role. Although the initial proposals for a UN that emerged in Dumbarton Oaks during the Second World War made no mention of NGOs, the United States pushed for their express recognition in the emerging UN Charter. (And about 1,200 NGOs attended the San Francisco conference in June of 1945 establishing the UN.[20]) Ultimately, Article 71 of the Charter formalized the role of NGOs within the organization. It states that the Economic and Social Council (ECOSOC):

may make suitable arrangements for consultation with nongovernmental organizations which are concerned with matters within its competence. Such arrangements may be made with international organizations and, where appropriate, with national organizations after consultation with the Member of the United Nations concerned.[21]

Forty-one NGOs were granted consultative status with ECOSOC in 1946. By 1992, the dawn of the age of UN mega-conferences, some 700 NGOs held that status. Today, the number is over 3,000, and many more have been granted access to specific treaty negotiations and meetings.[22] Any contemporary UN-sponsored treaty negotiation or conference routinely includes a sizeable, sometimes enormous, NGO component. Indeed, the NGO side of a major UN negotiating process is often far larger, and certainly more colourful, than the actual State-based negotiation. Still, ECOSOC accreditation remains an important filter for NGOs, and one that States control carefully. If NGOs are perceived to threaten the interests of important States, they can be denied accreditation, as was the case recently with a gay rights NGO, the International Gay and Lesbian Human Rights Commission.[23]

ECOSOC rules lay out several requirements for accreditation.[24] Among the most important are that the NGO must be concerned 'with matters falling within

---

[20] P Willetts, 'Pressure Groups as Transnational Actors' in Willetts (n 12) 1, 11.

[21] UN Charter Art 71.

[22] UN Department of Economic and Social Affairs, 'Introduction to ECOSOC Consultative Status' <http://esango.un.org/paperless/Web?page=static&content=intro>.

[23] L Charbonneau, 'U.N. Committee moves to keep out gay-lesbian NGO' *Reuters* (3 June 2010) <http://www.reuters.com/article/2010/06/03/us-un-gays-idUSTRE6526BQ20100603>. Ultimately, on 19 July 2010, the group was accredited, a move applauded by President Obama. See 'Statement by President Obama on UN Accreditation of IGLHRC' (19 July 2010) <http://www.iglhrc.org/cgi-bin/low/article/pressroom/iglhrcinthenews/1171.html>.

[24] See ECOSOC Res 1996/31 (25 July 1996) <http://www.un.org/documents/ecosoc/res/1996/eres1996-31.htm>. There are in turn three categories of status: General, Special, and Roster. As ECOSOC's website explains: *General* consultative status is reserved for international NGOs whose area of work covers most of the issues on the agenda of ECOSOC and its subsidiary bodies. These tend

the competence of the Economic and Social Council and its subsidiary bodies', and that the 'aims and purposes of the organization' must conform with the 'spirit, purposes and principles of the Charter of the United Nations'. In addition, the NGO 'shall be of recognized standing within the particular field of its competence or of a representative character', and must have an established headquarters, a democratically adopted constitution (a copy of which shall be deposited with the UN), and the authority to speak for its members through its authorized representatives. Finally, 'organizations established by governments or intergovernmental agreements are not considered NGOs'.[25]

NGOs have also been granted access within the many departments and affiliated bodies of the UN. As a 1998 report by then-Secretary-General Kofi Annan noted:

the United Nations Secretariat's relationship with NGOs is manifold...the majority of funds, agencies, and programmes of the United Nations system have also received a clear mandate from their governing bodies to work with NGOs, and have developed a wide range of mechanisms to do so.[26]

For example, the World Health Organization (WHO) accredits NGOs (what it terms 'official relations with WHO') who may participate, though not vote, in WHO meetings, conferences, and treaty negotiations. A similar approach is taken by the World Intellectual Property Organization (WIPO). WIPO is empowered by its constitutive convention to consult and cooperate with NGOs. NGOs can be granted observer status, and today nearly 300 NGOs are permanent observers at WIPO.[27] Observer status permits these NGOs to participate in all WIPO assemblies, diplomatic conferences, committees, and working groups. Moreover, NGO observers can participate in WIPO debates when allowed by the session chairman.[28] These NGO arrangements and practices are fairly typical within the UN family.

to be fairly large, established international NGOs with a broad geographical reach. *Special* consultative status is granted to NGOs which have a special competence in, and are concerned specifically with, only a few of the ECOSOC fields of activity. These NGOs tend to be smaller and more recently established. Organizations that apply for consultative status but do not fit in any of the other categories are usually included in the *Roster*. These NGOs tend to have a rather narrow and/or technical focus. NGOs that have formal status with other UN bodies or specialized agencies (FAO, ILO, UNCTAD, UNESCO, UNIDO, WHO, and others) can be included on the ECOSOC Roster. The roster lists NGOs that ECOSOC or the UN Secretary-General considers can make 'occasional and useful contributions to the work of the Council or its subsidiary bodies'. 'Introduction to ECOSOC Consultative Status' (n 22).

[25] Ibid. There are today many government-organized or friendly NGOs, typically from autocratic societies, that are derisively referred to as 'GONGOs', or government-sponsored NGOs. This phenomenon speaks to the power of NGOs and their relatively secure place in treaty processes; governments that rarely tolerate opposition from private associations at home seek to tap into the influence of NGOs by creating or tolerating NGOs that largely hew to their preferred line. See M Naim, 'What is a GONGO?' (18 April 2007) Foreign Policy 96.

[26] Report of the Secretary-General, 'Arrangements and Practices for the Interactions of Non-Governmental Organizations in All Aspects of the United Nations System' (1998) UN Doc A/53/170 [11], [15].

[27] WIPO, 'How WIPO Works' <http://www.wipo.int/about-wipo/en/how_wipo_works.html>.

[28] WIPO, 'WIPO General Rules of Procedure' (4th edn 2 October 1979) 10 <http://www.wipo.int/freepublications/en/index.jsp?cat=general%20information>.

Somewhat less typical, though noteworthy as a result, is the approach of the International Labour Organization (ILO). The ILO was founded in 1919 and thus preceded the UN model. The ILO has a highly unusual structure in which labour unions and businesses are formal participants in the ILO's work and deliberative processes—what the ILO calls 'tripartism'. Moreover, the ILO Governing Body consists of twenty-eight government members and twenty-eight non-government members, divided equally among employers and workers. In addition, the ILO Constitution states that the ILO may 'make suitable arrangements for such consultation as it may think desirable with recognized [NGOs], including international organizations of employers, workers, agriculturalists and co-operators'.[29] The ILO has its own multifaceted accreditation process for these NGOs, which includes NGOs that fall outside these enumerated and now somewhat dated categories, such as those concerned with human rights or child labour issues.

B. NGO participation in treaty formation and implementation

NGOs have also been active in treaty processes that occur outside a pre-existing international organization such as the UN or the ILO. A well-known example is the Ottawa Mine Ban Treaty,[30] which was spearheaded by a group of NGOs operating under the banner of the International Campaign to Ban Landmines (ICBL). In the 1970s, the International Committee of the Red Cross (ICRC) convened a conference on indiscriminate weapons that ultimately influenced Protocol II of the 1980 Convention on Certain Conventional Weapons. Amid continuing concern over the horrific and indiscriminate effects of landmines, the ICBL formed in the early 1990s and convened an NGO Conference on Landmines. By the 1995 Review Conference of the Convention on Certain Conventional Weapons, more than seventy NGOs were participating. The ICRC was invited by the UN Secretariat to attend as an expert observer, and was allowed to speak and submit proposals, as well as asked to prepare two working papers for the delegates. Members of other NGOs served on the delegations of certain key States, including Canada and Australia.[31]

When no ban on mines emerged from the review conference, the ICBL grew in scope and scale; by May of 1996 it comprised some 600 NGOs in forty States.[32] After a coordinated and sophisticated media campaign, and substantial lobbying by NGOs in many national capitals, the Mine Ban Treaty was signed in 1997. That same year the ICBL and its leader, Jody Williams, jointly received the Nobel Peace

---

[29] ILO Constitution (established 9 October 1919) 15 UNTS 40, Art 12(3).

[30] Formally, The Convention on the Prohibition of the Use, Stockpiling, Production and Transfer of Anti-Personnel Mines and on their Destruction (adopted 18 September 1997, entered into force 1 March 1999) 2056 UNTS 241. For an account focused on NGOs' role see K Anderson, 'The Ottawa Convention Banning Landmines, the Role of International Non-Governmental Organizations and the Idea of International Civil Society' (2000) 11 EJIL 91.

[31] R Price, 'Reversing the Gun Sights: Transnational Civil Society Targets Land Mines' (1998) 52 Intl Org 613, 620–1.

[32] Ibid.

Prize for their efforts. Highlighting the importance of NGOs to the treaty's promulgation, then-Minister of Foreign Affairs for Canada, Lloyd Axworthy, declared that:

[n]o other issue in recent times has mobilized such a broad and diverse coalition of countries, governments, and nongovernmental organizations. Much of this momentum has been the result of the tremendous efforts made by NGOs to advance the cause to ban mines.[33]

A similar, if less dramatic, recent example of NGO involvement in a treaty negotiation was the WHO's 2003 Framework Convention on Tobacco Control. The WHO generally tracks the UN in terms of NGO access. Early on in the negotiating process, WHO held public hearings. One hundred and forty-four health-related NGOs provided testimony during the hearings, with a total of 500 written submissions received.[34] As in the landmines case, many NGOs banded together (here, into the 'Framework Convention Alliance') to maximize their impact on the treaty process. The Framework Convention Alliance was an important lobbying force in producing the tobacco treaty. Nonetheless, as I will discuss further below, the Alliance NGOs' access was greater in the early stages of the negotiation than in the later stages.

NGOs have also influenced the development of a host of major human rights treaties, as well as the landmark (though formally nonbinding) Universal Declaration on Human Rights (UDHR).[35] Their participation has been expanding in recent years. For example, in 2001 the UN General Assembly established an Ad Hoc Committee to negotiate a new convention on disability rights, which ultimately resulted in the 2006 UN Convention on the Rights of Persons with Disabilities. Delegates to the Ad Hoc Committee 'represented NGOs, governments, national human rights institutes, and international organizations'.[36] Indeed, the Ad Hoc Committee went beyond standard contemporary practice and invited NGOs to 'to participate in all public (and later also all informal and closed) meetings of the Ad Hoc Committee, with extensive formal representation in the Working Group, permitting them to make substantive statements on the UN floor following discussion of each draft article'.[37] Moreover, this extends to post-negotiation issues: the Convention dictates that 'civil society, in particular persons

---

[33] K Rutherford, 'Implications of the Role of NGOs in Banning Antipersonnel Landmines' (2000) 53 Wld Pol 74, 74.

[34] WHO, 'Public Hearings on the WHO Framework Convention on Tobacco Control' (2000) <http://www.who.int/fctc/about/public_hearings/en/index.html>.

[35] A Cassese, *Human Rights in a Changing World* (Polity, Cambridge 1990) 173; W Korey, *NGOs and the Universal Declaration of Human Rights* (Palgrave MacMillan, New York 2001). The UDHR is legally non-binding but widely seen as highly influential and perhaps now reflective, or constitutive, of customary international law.

[36] United Nations Enable (Frequently Asked Questions) <http://www.un.org/esa/socdev/enable/convinfofaq.htm#q3>.

[37] G de Burca, 'The EU in the Negotiation of the UN Disability Convention' (2010) 35 EL Rev 174, 184.

with disabilities and their representative organizations, shall be involved and participate fully in the [treaty] monitoring process'.[38]

As this last point indicates, NGOs have been active not only in negotiating human rights treaties but also in their implementation. Many human rights NGOs, for example, produce 'shadow reports' on the implementation of impor-tant treaties, which 'shadow' the official reports produced by States parties and are intended to critique and influence treaty implementation in various States parties. These reports are distributed among the parties, the media, and other interested actors. In 1993, in advance of the Fourth World Conference on Women in Beijing, the International Women's Rights Action Watch even created a guide to producing shadow reports on the Convention to Eliminate All Forms of Discrimination Against Women, so as to aid other women's rights groups around the world interested in weighing in on matters of implementation. Some regional human rights treaties go further in incorporating NGOs; the European and Inter-American human rights systems both permit NGOs to bring forward claims about abuses, and some others, such as the African Charter on Human and People's Rights, have regularly considered communications filed by NGOs.[39]

NGOs have been similarly active in the related and rapidly growing field of international criminal law. For example, the successful creation of the International Criminal Court in the 1990s was due in part to an active and highly organized NGO effort. The Coalition for an International Criminal Court, a group encom-passing over 1,000 NGO members, was a key player in the often-contentious negotiation of the Rome Statute. As one observer notes:

[NGOs] lobbied intensively. Their influence was felt on a variety of issues, particularly the protection of children, sexual violence, forced pregnancy, enforced sterilization, and an independent role for the prosecutor. Throughout [the negotiations] they provided briefings and legal memoranda for sympathetic delegations . . . and even assigned legal interns to small delegations.[40]

Then-UN Secretary-General Kofi Annan, who generally supported much wider NGO access and engagement with UN activities, later stated that the NGO presence at the Rome Conference represented 'an unprecedented level of participa-tion by civil society in a law-making conference'.[41]

There are many similar examples of NGOs' participation in treaty-making; NGOs are an important and even central component of most treaty processes today. In broad terms, the trend over the last century has been toward markedly greater access and participation for NGOs in these processes. The history of environmental treaties illustrates this pattern of steadily increasing NGO

---

[38] Convention on the Rights of Persons with Disabilities (adopted 13 December 2006, opened for signature 30 March 2007) UN Doc A/AC.265/2006/L.6, Art 33.

[39] RG Steinhardt and others, *International Human Rights Lawyering* (West, New York 2009) 855.

[40] MH Arsanjani, 'The Rome Statute of the International Criminal Court' (1999) 93 AJIL 22, 23.

[41] K Annan, 'Preface' to C Bassiouni, *The Statute of the International Criminal Court: A Documentary History* (Transnational, Ardsley 1999) ix.

incorporation. Early environmental treaties, such as the 1933 Convention Relative to the Preservation of Flora and Fauna in Their Natural State, typically said nothing about NGOs. The 1946 Whaling Convention was similarly silent, though from 1977 onwards NGOs were permitted to participate as observers at whaling negotiations, and in the years since have become so active that they have arguably transformed the regime's purpose entirely—from one of conservation of whales to one of their preservation.

The first major multilateral environmental treaty to include explicit language on the role of NGOs was the 1973 Convention on International Trade in Endangered Species, which stated that the treaty secretariat may seek assistance from 'suitable ... non-governmental international or national agencies and bodies technically qualified in protection, conservation, and management of wild fauna and flora', unless one-third of the parties object.[42] Nearly identical language appears in subsequent treaties, such as the 1987 Montreal Protocol on Ozone Depletion. The 1992 UN Framework Convention on Climate Change (UNFCCC) likewise declares that:

[a]ny body or agency, whether national or international, governmental or non-governmental, which is qualified in matters covered by the Convention, and which has informed the secretariat of its wish to be represented at a session of the Conference of the Parties as an observer, may be so admitted unless at least one third of the Parties present object.[43]

Moreover, the Conference of the Parties must '[s]eek and utilize, where appropriate, the services and cooperation of, and information provided by, competent international organizations and intergovernmental and non-governmental bodies'.[44]

Actual practice generally reflects these formal changes in NGO participation, and at times even outpaces it. In contemporary environmental treaty processes, NGOs are quite active attending meetings, contributing materials, speaking to plenary negotiating sessions, working the corridors, and generally aiming to influence the details of treaty terms and principles. In some environmental treaty regimes, NGOs have even greater formal powers, such as in the North American Agreement on Environmental Cooperation, where, in a process analogous to that in some human rights regimes, NGOs can directly bring complaints alleging that governments have failed to adequately enforce their own domestic environmental laws.[45] In short, contemporary environmental treaty-making is unimaginable today without NGOs, even if they are simply outside the negotiating room shaping the terms of debate and channeling political pressure (or creating media circuses, depending on one's view).

---

[42] Convention on International Trade in Endangered Species of Wild Fauna and Flora (concluded 3 March 1973, entered into force 1 July 1975) 27 UST 1087, Art 12.

[43] UNFCCC (concluded 9 May 1992, entered into force 21 March 1994) 1771 UNTS 107, Art 7.

[44] Ibid.

[45] K Raustiala, 'Citizen Submissions and Treaty Review in the NAAEC' in J Knox and D Markell (eds), *The North American Commission on Environmental Cooperation: An Evaluation* (Stanford University Press, Stanford 2003).

NGOs play a less noticeable role in some areas of treaty-making, however. While NGOs were instrumental in shaping the progress and content of the Land Mines Convention, as described above, they generally have played a minor role in major arms control treaties. Arms treaties in recent decades typically have been bilateral and in many cases negotiated in significant secrecy. In some cases, such as the 1972 Treaty on the Limitation of Anti-Ballistic Missile Systems, the negotiating records of the agreements themselves were classified.[46] While today an active arms control NGO community exists, it tends to focus more on broad policy matters and proliferation concerns, and works primarily to seek change via informal lobbying and public opinion formation rather than direct participation in treaty negotiations. Still, this role should not be underestimated; in the late 2010 debate over the US–Russian New START treaty in the US Senate, arms control NGOs played important roles in shaping media coverage and persuading various senators of the merits and demerits of the accord.

Trade agreements also tend to feature a comparatively low level of NGO activity, even in multilateral contexts. The 1994 Agreement Establishing the World Trade Organization (WTO) states that the WTO General Council 'may make appropriate arrangements for consultations and cooperation with [NGOs] concerned with matters related to those of the WTO'.[47] This marks a change from the GATT (General Agreement on Tariffs and Trade) years, when there were no formal provisions governing NGO participation. NGOs at that time were also not permitted to participate directly in meetings and conferences. Even at the Marrakesh Conference, where the WTO Agreement was signed, there were no accredited NGOs; those NGOs present were registered as members of the press.[48]

In 1996, the WTO General Council promulgated guidelines on NGO participation. These took a decidedly cautious approach compared to those of other IOs. As the guidelines note:

[t]here is currently a broadly held view that it would not be possible for NGOs to be directly involved in the work of the WTO or its meetings. Closer consultation and cooperation with NGOs can also be met constructively through appropriate processes at the national level where lies primary responsibility for taking into account the different elements of public interest which are brought to bear on trade policy-making.[49]

In 2003, however, the WTO created an 'Informal NGO Advisory Body' (and a parallel body for businesses) as a way to reach out to non-State actors in a manner consistent with the limitations present in the 1996 guidelines. NGOs also now attend the WTO Ministerial Conferences, held every two years, and the number of NGOs accredited to these has grown dramatically: from 159 in 1996 to over 1,000 in 2005. In the context of global trade cooperation these changes are marked, but

---

[46] See 'Statement by State Department Legal Adviser Abraham Sofaer' in JL Dunoff, SR Ratner, and D Wippman, *International Law* (3rd edn Aspen Publishers, New York 2010) 291.
[47] Marrakesh Agreement Establishing the World Trade Organization (adopted 15 April 1994, entered into force 1 January 1995) 1867 UNTS 154, Art 5.
[48] Ripinsky and van den Bossche (n 8) 190.
[49] Ibid.

NGOs still remain outside the room in many negotiating sessions and meetings. Likewise, NGO participation in the all-important WTO dispute settlement process has been highly controversial, with most member States opposed to even amicus briefs submitted by interested NGOs.[50] While NGOs (in particular, firms and their trade associations) may greatly influence the decision to bring a case before the dispute settlement body, 'once the proceeding is initiated, direct participation by business and NGOs in the WTO's judicial process is much more limited'.[51]

The preceding brief survey illustrates a fundamental point. Over the last few decades NGOs have become a regular part of the treaty process in a wide range of issue-areas in international law. NGOs are active at many treaty negotiations, where they receive negotiating documents, informally present proposals, and are consulted by and lobby State delegations. NGOs participate actively as well in the corridor diplomacy and media outreach that is so central to many complex multilateral negotiations. States nonetheless maintain meaningful control over NGO access through various accreditation processes, as the experience of the International Gay and Lesbian Human Rights Commission in ECOSOC shows. Once accredited, NGOs tend to stay accredited and involved—though here too States remain the gatekeepers of these processes and can, when they desire, convene in private and informal sessions apart from NGOs. (And outside of unusual structures such as that of the ILO, only governments may vote.) Still, the wide array of NGO activities described above are either relatively new or much more pervasive than in the past, and have, in many important ways, transformed the process of treaty-making. The picture of what NGOs *do* varies somewhat from issue to issue, but the major themes are reasonably clear. Less clear is the *significance* of this activity for international cooperation.

III. States and NGOs in Treaty-making

Why have NGOs become such a common feature of treaty-making, and what does it signify? Some observers in the past have suggested that the active role of NGOs may be just 'window-dressing', intended to satisfy vocal NGOs and public opinion but of no real or lasting importance.[52] But most observers perceive more significance to the move to incorporate a wide range of NGOs into treaty processes. For some, NGOs are important guardians of the public interest, who protect values

---

[50] For the official description of the issue, see WTO, 'Participation in Dispute Settlement Proceedings' <http://www.wto.org/english/tratop_e/dispu_e/disp_settlement_cbt_e/c9s3p1_e.htm>. On opposition see eg CL Lim, 'The Amicus Brief Issue at the WTO' (2005) 4 Chinese JIL 1.

[51] J Barton and others, *The Evolution of the Trade Regime: Politics, Law, and Economics of the GATT and the WTO* (Princeton University Press, Princeton 2006) 199.

[52] B Hagerhall, 'The Evolving Role of NGOs' in G Sjostedt (ed), *International Environmental Negotiation* (Sage Publications, Newbury Park 1993) 75. For an extensive discussion of NGOs and their impact see B Arts, M Noortmann, and B Reinalda (eds), *Non-State Actors in International Relations* (Ashgate, Aldershot 2000).

that States will not guard reliably.[53] In this view, NGO participation will shift the terms of debate on many issues and result in better international law-making. Indeed, one observer of NGOs suggests that 'had NGOs never existed, international law would have a less vital role in human progress'.[54]

Indeed, to some observers, NGOs may even increasingly be the driving force behind much global law-making, usurping some of the power of sovereign States.[55] Anyone who has participated in or closely observed a major multilateral negotiation, in particular a UN-sponsored one, will concede that NGOs can and sometimes do effectively shape debate. But this must be put into perspective. Indeed, one of the core propositions of this chapter is that the access to and participation in treaty processes that NGOs now enjoy is not a hijacking of the law-making process. Rather, NGO participation is shaped by governments and is often beneficial to governments. That NGOs often serve the interests of governments is one reason— and I would argue the most important one—that NGOs have become so pervasive in contemporary treaty processes.[56]

In short, the NGO–State relationship is in many respects symbiotic. The sovereign State remains the leading actor in the international system, and NGOs need the coercive power of States to realize the social and legal changes they seek. But conversely, the political incentives modern governments face frequently compel them to work with NGOs, especially those that possess specialized and useful resources and political power. Nonetheless, States still largely control the terms of the relationship, because international law is built and predicated on a system of sovereign States.

Why then do States permit NGOs to participate so closely and vigorously in treaty-making? There are several distinct benefits for States in doing so. Although not all States enjoy or value these benefits, and some oppose NGO participation in particular cases or even more widely, in the aggregate States benefit often enough that broad, general rules and practices permitting NGO participation make sense. The structure of NGO participation in most treaty processes supports this argument.

Perhaps the central benefit for States of NGO inclusion is the provision of information. NGOs can provide important information about policy options, especially in issue-areas with high levels of uncertainty and technical or scientific complexity. Consider climate change, the issue that opened this chapter. There are many large, expertly staffed NGOs that devote considerable resources to policy

[53] PK Wapner, *Environmental Activism and World Civic Politics* (State University of New York Press, Albany 1996) 5–7, 11; PJ Sands, 'Environment, Community and International Law' (1989) 30 HILJ 393, 394. See also M Keck and K Sikkink, *Activists Beyond Borders: Advocacy Networks in International Politics* (Cornell University Press, Ithaca 1998).

[54] Charnovitz (n 7) 348.

[55] JR Bolton, 'Should We Take Global Governance Seriously?' (2000) 1 Chi J Intl L 205, 215–17; DB Hollis, 'Private Actors in Public International Law: Amicus Curiae and the Case for the Retention of State Sovereignty' (2002) 25 BC Intl & Comp L Rev 235.

[56] For earlier elaborations of this argument see K Raustiala, 'States, NGOs, and International Environmental Institutions' (1997) 41 ISQ 719; K Raustiala, '"The Participatory Revolution" in International Environmental Law' (1997) 21 Harv Envtl L Rev 537.

research and development—research that can help the negotiating parties develop and evaluate often-complex policy options. NGOs commonly provide such information to government policy-makers freely, and indeed compete to do so. Many such groups exist, and the plurality of sources provides a check on exaggeration, obfuscation, and poor logic and data. The result is that governments can gain useful and creative policy advice from many independent sources—and typically at no cost. To be sure, much of the world's policy expertise on climate change rests within governments or is directly accessible by them. (States have also created the Intergovernmental Panel on Climate Change (IPCC) as a way to gather and channel the best scientific advice.) But NGO policy research provides perspectives and ideas that may not have emerged from a bureaucratic review process, whether within a given State or the IPCC. Moreover, many State delegates, especially from smaller States, are generalists and unlikely to be expert in the particular area under negotiation, and this is particularly so in highly technical areas like climate change. Like lobbyists in a domestic setting, NGOs act as conduits for ideas and political pressures to these negotiators.

The formal record from many treaty negotiations reveals a very active information-providing role for NGOs. Consider a report, chosen at random, of the WIPO Standing Committee on the Law of Patents from the 3rd Session in September 1999. The various government delegations debated the then-draft Patent Law Treaty, which was adopted the following year. Yet at WIPO, NGOs such as the American Bar Association, Federation of German Industry, the Korean Patent Attorneys Association, and the World Association for Small and Medium Enterprises were also introducing proposals and raising objections to the draft Patent Treaty text.[57] These groups contained much expertise on patent law and conveyed that expertise (and opinion) to the assembled negotiators. It is not always necessary to admit NGOs into negotiating sessions to convey this kind of information. But in practice that is a helpful way to do it, since expertise transcends official position papers, and NGO members can and do speak informally with many delegates at negotiations to flesh out details and provide commentary on other ideas. All of this activity can greatly improve the suite of options negotiators can draw upon in drafting and revising treaty texts.

NGOs also may provide useful information on treaty implementation. Groups like Human Rights Watch have a global reach, and they expend significant resources documenting problems around the world. Much of this effort uses a legal frame and often identifies specific treaty commitments that are being violated or improperly implemented. These reports can be influential and may garner significant media attention. (And given that many treaties lack meaningful review of implementation, or rely merely on self-reporting by parties about their implementation of treaty commitments, NGO monitoring can be an important addition to what little occurs via more official channels.) The role of NGOs in monitoring is

---

[57] WIPO Standing Committee on the Law of Patents, 'Third Session—Report Adopted by the Standing Committee' (6–14 September 1999) <http://www.wipo.int/edocs/mdocs/scp/en/scp_3/scp_3_11.pdf>.

clearly contentious, and States differ on how much NGOs should participate. But it also reflects some political realities that make it attractive to many governments. Principles of sovereignty and general political disinterest in monitoring in some States make it relatively costly to create direct, formal evaluation of treaty compliance by other States parties or IOs. Due to their informal, decentralized nature, NGO efforts are less readily blocked; NGOs would have to be kept out of negotiations altogether, for even formal bans on compliance discussions or papers can be circumvented 'in the corridors'. In short, in many instances NGOs 'supply the personnel and resources for managing compliance that States have been increasingly reluctant to provide'.[58] Again, not all States welcome this role, but others do. And once NGOs are present within treaty frameworks, even if they are welcomed for other reasons, such as technical expertise, they may gravitate toward monitoring and enforcement efforts.[59]

NGOs may also provide another important form of information: information about the actions of State delegations to treaty negotiations. Governments—in particular, legislatures—want to control the decisions of their national delegations. Treaty negotiations often create tensions between branches of government, especially in presidential systems, where important aspects of foreign affairs may not be directly controlled or overseen by legislatures. But the desire to control negotiators is not limited to legislators, since other executive branch officials may also fear that treaty negotiators will exceed their mandates or create political headaches through their positions. NGO participation in treaty negotiations is one means by which legislatures, as well as executive branch officials, can enable outside parties to alert them to undesired delegation actions. In other words, NGOs can help minimize an important principal–agent problem. As interested parties, NGOs have an incentive to both monitor delegates' actions and inform governmental principals of their findings. Because NGOs of many persuasions exist, movement in many directions can be covered. This decentralized process is both effective and low-cost. Delegates that move too far away from the preferences of their principals are thus more likely to be identified and checked.[60]

Yet another way NGOs provide practical information to governments is via reporting on treaty negotiations themselves. This may seem trivial, but in practice it is often very useful. During the course of large-scale multilateral talks there is often a numbing array of detail to be followed. Delegates cannot keep track of everything that is going on, particularly if the negotiations occur through multiple working groups. In several arenas, NGOs have alleviated this information overload

---

[58] Chayes and Chayes (n 17) 250–1.

[59] NGOs remain imperfect monitoring agents, however. NGO monitoring is often less concerned with compliance in the narrow sense—adherence to the letter of an agreement—than it is with NGO approval or disapproval of particular actions, even if those actions are not violations of the relevant accord. A classic case is whaling; NGOs have criticized and monitored nations engaged in scientific research whaling or that took reservations to the Whaling Convention, despite the legality of their actions under that treaty.

[60] Unless the NGOs present agree more with the delegates than their principals. But from the principal's point of view, creating a fire alarm of this kind that is only occasionally pulled in the presence of a fire is still superior to having no alarm at all. On this analogy see Raustiala (n 45) 256–73.

by supplying regular bulletins. The Canada-based International Institute for Sustainable Development, for example, runs a widely read reporting service called Linkages that covers a wide array of treaty processes, including water, oceans, and wetlands; chemicals management; trade and investment; and sustainable development.[61] Similarly, the International Centre for Trade and Sustainable Development in Geneva provides a daily information service during all ministerial conferences of the World Trade Organization.[62] The Coalition for the International Criminal Court similarly supplied an 'Informal Daily Summary' at the 2010 Kampala Review Conference for the ICC.[63] 'Ongoing negotiations reporting' is something governments and even IOs cannot do easily—or effectively—on their own. If any one government were to attempt to provide such reporting, the reports would likely be derided as biased and unrepresentative. If the UN itself or a formal secretariat published daily reports, they would have the status of official documents, and member governments would find it difficult or impossible to agree on content, style, tone, and so forth.

Bringing NGOs into the treaty-making process also has political benefits for many States. NGOs allowed to participate in State-to-State deliberations get a closer look at the positions of relevant parties. Specific areas of controversy are more apparent, as are the areas where compromise is possible. Negotiating positions have sometimes been described by scholars in spatial terms, with various positions corresponding to points in a multidimensional 'policy space'. The set of points acceptable to all parties is the bargaining zone. By taking part as observers and as participants, NGOs become more aware of the shape and location of the bargaining zone. Revealing the structure of the international bargaining process in this way may help to diffuse NGO criticism and placate at least some unsatisfied interests, as NGOs become more knowledgeable about obstacles—and perhaps more invested in the negotiating process. It may also lead to new ideas about how to reach that bargaining space, since NGOs have many incentives to provide practical proposals that overcome apparent deadlocks in negotiations.

Relatedly, NGO participation in treaty processes may facilitate the approval of treaties at the domestic level. While States vary in the processes by which they approve treaties, many have some legally mandated process of domestic review and consent that is required prior to ratification.[64] In broadly democratic States this nearly always involves the legislature. Legislatures (and other domestic actors) may well reject a treaty that has been painstakingly negotiated—think of the famous rejection by the US Senate of the Treaty of Versailles settlement in 1919, or the more recent rejection by French voters of the Treaty Establishing a Constitution for Europe. One way to reduce the odds of such an event is to bring some of the

---

[61] International Institute for Sustainable Development—Reporting Services Division, 'Linkages' <http://www.iisd.ca>.

[62] International Centre for Trade and Sustainable Development, 'Latest News' <http://ictsd.org>.

[63] Coalition for the International Criminal Court, 'Delivering on the promise of a fair, effective and independent Court: Review Conference of the Rome Statute' (Daily Summaries Provided) <http://www.iccnow.org/?mod=review>.

[64] See Chapter 1, Part I.B, 15 *et seq.*

important domestic players directly to the international table, thereby 'bridging' the two levels of the negotiating game, in political scientist Robert Putnam's famous terms.[65] Problems with accords can be rectified early, during the negotiation process, rather than late, when renegotiation may be extremely difficult. As I noted earlier, NGOs are not only active at the international level; they are powerful domestic actors in many States. Treaty regimes must have domestic support to succeed, and NGOs, as interest groups, can provide this support or withhold it. Bridging thus is an attractive strategy for minimizing ratification risk. By bringing these important societal actors into the negotiations process directly, information flow is enhanced, and more importantly, potential opponents may be turned into supporters or at least abstainers.

If NGO skills, resources, and political power are useful to States, demand for these resources should increase when the scope, complexity, and obligations of a treaty regime grow. And indeed, the major treaties of the 1980s, 1990s, and 2000s—such as climate change, chemical weapons control, tobacco use, disability rights—are generally more complex and more demanding than earlier treaties. And as described above, the rules and practices governing NGO participation in treaty-making have generally become more inclusive and given NGOs greater access and participation over time. Moreover, the ways in which NGOs are included in treaty processes are broadly consistent with a symbiotic understanding of NGO-State relations in treaty-making. NGOs possess many resources, but those resources and skills are not uniformly useful over time. Policy expertise is most useful at the early stages of negotiations, monitoring most useful in the implementation phase. When governments desire secrecy to air possible compromises, or are at the stage of log-rolling once positions have solidified, they may find NGO participation undesirable or not useful. Hence, States face incentives to keep NGOs out at some times, and bring them in at others. By this logic, they ought to attempt to meter or calibrate NGO participation.

In practice, States have achieved this calibration through the proliferation of working groups and informal meetings in treaty negotiations. Consider the pattern in the 1992 UN Conference on Environment and Development (UNCED). The early preparatory meetings ('prep-coms') preceding UNCED, where basic positions were hashed out and the scope and shape of the negotiating space determined, were most open to NGO participation. However:

by the penultimate meeting, as the bargaining became heated . . . all governments agreed to close the doors, and the NGOs frequently suffered the humiliation of being turned out . . . the governments introduced a new type of forum: 'informal informals'—too informal for NGOs to participate, but indeed where the decisions were made.[66]

---

[65] RD Putnam, 'Diplomacy and Domestic Politics: The Logic of Two-Level Games' (1988) 42 Intl Org 427.

[66] E Enge and R Malkenes, 'Non-Governmental Organizations at UNCED: Another Successful Failure?' in HO Bergesen and G Parmann (eds), *Green Glove Yearbook of International Co-operation on Environment and Development* (OUP, Oxford 1993) 25, 27.

The same pattern can be observed in the negotiations of the 2003 Framework Convention on Tobacco Control. There, the Framework Convention Alliance, as one observer notes:

encompassed more than 180 NGOs from over 70 countries and had established itself as an important lobbying alliance. Its impact in the final negotiations was, however, hampered by the imposition of restrictions on NGO access to the negotiating sessions. Most sessions of the final INB [the negotiating body] were designated as informal, thus providing a pretext for the exclusion of NGO participants.[67]

As at UNCED, the overall pattern in the Tobacco Convention negotiation was one of greater NGO access and participation early on—as the basic structure of the negotiation is being defined and policy prescriptions debated—and less NGO access later, when the details of essentially fixed positions were being hammered out. This pattern is what we would expect to observe if NGOs are admitted to treaty processes not as an act of grace, or under pressure, but instead mainly for the ideas and resources they bring to the table.

Thus, when looked at in light of the many informational and political benefits to States of NGO participation, the generally high level of NGO participation in most treaty processes is not surprising. NGOs are often—though not always—helpful to governments, even when they appear opposed to a particular policy or provision. And this symbiosis is not limited to governments; as noted above, IOs, in particular the UN, have been major sites and proponents of NGO inclusion. Indeed, officials at these organizations may embrace NGOs for an additional reason: 'as a source of legitimacy through "representativeness" that bypass[es] the increasingly problematic legitimacy of international organizations through nation-States'.[68]

IV. The Legitimacy of NGO Participation

Whatever the putative benefits to governments, the increase in NGO participation in treaty processes over the last several decades has not been without critics. While many observers (and participants) approve of NGOs' newfound prominence, and see NGOs as an essential part of a global 'civil society',[69] others see NGOs as vectors for unattractive ideas and policies. Indeed, there is a:

growing chorus of complaint that sees NGOs as unrepresentative, unaccountable, and often plain uninformed—distorting the democratic process, eroding the authority of elected officials, and excluding the voices of those directly affected by global change in favour of an urban, middle-class minority of armchair radicals, based largely in the industrial world.[70]

As this suggests, this debate often takes on a North-South dimension, with NGOs characterized as fellow travellers of Northern, or Western, governments. In trade,

---

[67] J Collin, 'Tobacco Politics' (2004) 47 Dev 91, 93.
[68] Anderson (n 15) 174.
[69] J Keane, *Global Civil Society?* (CUP, New York 2003) 2.
[70] Edwards (n 18) 2.

for example, 'developing country negotiators have ... tended to argue against more direct NGO participation in part because their countries lack active, indigenous NGOs and in part because they perceive active NGOs as representing interests rooted in Western, advanced, industrialized countries'.[71] To be sure, NGOs do not always line up neatly with the views of their 'home' States; indeed, they sometimes oppose them straightforwardly. But they may share some world views and general principles, and this can make those NGOs seem like stalking horses for government interests. (Some NGOs, moreover, are nearly arms of the government, organized by them for the purpose of providing other modes of support to government positions).[72] NGOs also need resources to survive, and many are funded by wealthy, often Western, donors, in whole or in part. This too is a source of unease over NGO participation in treaty-making. In short, opposition to NGOs is sometimes driven by straightforward differences over interests, and the belief that increased NGO participation will tend to favour the interests of some parties over those of others.

Yet debate over NGOs also has centred on questions of legitimacy. Do NGOs warp the essentially State-to-State nature of international law? Is their presence in treaty processes fundamentally undemocratic? And is it appropriate that NGOs can—and often do—attempt to influence negotiating positions domestically, but then go on to do the same at the international level, giving them 'two bites at the apple'?

These questions are not amenable to easy answers, and have spawned a wide range of reactions. Whether international law is inherently a State-to-State endeavour that NGOs should remain distant from is a large question that transcends the treaty context. In the ICJ's 1996 *Nuclear Weapons* decision, for instance, some judges expressed concern about the role of NGOs in pushing the UN General Assembly to seek an opinion from the ICJ.[73] As Judge Oda wrote:

The idea behind the resolution whereby the General Assembly ... requested advisory opinions, had previously been advanced by a handful of [NGOs] which initiated a campaign for the total prohibition of nuclear weapons but failed to persuade the States' delegations in the forum of the General Assembly ... Some NGOs seem to have tried to compensate for the vainness of their efforts by attempting to get the principal judicial organ of the United Nations to determine the absolute illegality of nuclear weapons[74]

Judge Oda's tenor suggests that this effort was inappropriate, and that NGOs' catalysing role casts doubt on the legitimacy of the whole advisory exercise. While these particular concerns addressed the process of a General Assembly resolution, and not a treaty, they starkly reflect a more general view: NGOs increasingly are intruding in matters beyond their competence or appropriate role.

Proponents of active NGO involvement, by contrast, see NGOs as representative of important public interests that need to be heard. Many NGOs 'present

[71] Barton and others (n 51) 201–2.
[72] See n 25 (discussing these GONGOs).
[73] *Legality of the Threat or Use of Nuclear Weapons, Advisory Opinion* [1996] ICJ Rep 287, 300 (Separate Opinion of Judge Guillaume and Dissenting Opinion of Judge Oda).
[74] Ibid 330, 335 [8].

themselves as custodians of the observance of elementary principles of international law, such as human rights'.[75] NGOs are representative in a different—but, proponents believe, equally if not more significant way—than are governments, especially undemocratic governments. If true representativeness requires that society and not just the State have a place at the table, then organized groups of individuals have a reasonable claim to that place.[76] And it is undeniable that NGOs often bring views to the negotiating table that simply would not be heard otherwise. They can think big and be creative in ways that States simply cannot—and can provide a voice to those who are otherwise voiceless.

Still, NGO participation can be and often is criticized on the grounds that NGOs are just lobbyists with a particular interest to push. Moreover, NGOs not only favour particular interests; they may favour *particularistic* interests—their special interests—at the expense of larger balances that often must be struck in policy-making. Governments must make tradeoffs and accommodate differing views; NGOs do not have that burden and they can, and do, lobby hard for their view to triumph. As a result, their more prominent role in treaty-making may undermine the often essential process of accommodation, unless there are enough varied NGOs involved to represent a truly wide array of interests.

What then gives NGOs, few of which formulate their positions via elections of their membership, any greater claim to representativeness than autocratic governments or monarchs? The answer is not clear. As two writers bluntly put it: 'NGOs claim to represent global civil society. But nobody elects them.'[77] Many, perhaps most, NGOs are not even internally democratic. Yet even these NGOs do in a sense represent their supporters, who 'vote' with their dollars and support. As one NGO leader argued, 'we have a certain democratic legitimacy . . . by having millions of supporters. And while they do not give us a specific mandate, they decide by the membership fee whether they agree with us or not'.[78] As Steve Charnovitz argues, unlike the State, NGOs enjoy a relationship with individuals that is voluntary: 'Individuals join and support an NGO out of commitment to its purpose. That purpose, plus organization, gives NGOs whatever "authority" they have, and it will be moral authority rather than legal authority'.[79] Comparing NGOs to governments, in sum, is a category mistake; they have a different role. Perhaps, as

---

[75] A Vedder, 'Questioning the Legitimacy of Non-Governmental Organizations' in A Vedder (ed), *NGO Involvement in International Governance and Policy: Sources of Legitimacy* (Martinus Nijhoff, Boston 2007) 11.

[76] For example, Robert Keohane and Joseph Nye argue that NGO participation in institutions of global governance can improve legitimacy and help arrest concerns about democratic deficits. R Keohane and J Nye, 'The Club Model of Multilateral Cooperation and Problems of Democratic Legitimacy' in R Porter and others (eds), *Efficiency, Equity, and Legitimacy: The Multilateral Trading System at the Millennium* (Brookings Institution Press, Washington 2001).

[77] J Micklethwait and A Wooldridge, 'The Globalization Backlash' (September/October 2001) Foreign Pol 16, 24. See also D Rieff, 'The False Dawn of Civil Society' (22 February 1999) The Nation 11.

[78] Anonymous representative of an NGO, quoted in V Collingwood and L Logister, 'Perceptions of the Legitimacy of international NGOs' in A Vedder (n 75) 35.

[79] Charnovitz (n 7) 348. On these general issues see also the work of D Held, in particular *Democracy and Global Order: From the Modern State to Cosmopolitan Governance* (Stanford University

another close observer of NGO politics put it, they are 'the conscience of the world'.[80]

Of course, conscience is in the eye of the beholder. Much of the supportive commentary on NGOs reflects or assumes a largely Western, liberal orientation on the part of most NGOs. Even within the West, however, there are sizeable political differences among NGOs, and the NGO community active on treaty matters increasingly evidences that diversity, from gun rights advocates to anti-abortion activists. None of this vitiates the idea that NGOs wield moral, not legal authority, but it does underscore how context- and viewpoint-specific that authority may be.

Whether NGOs (mis)use the international treaty-making process as a way to influence domestic law or policy—which is a central aspect of the 'two bites at the apple' concern—is really a concern about the integrity or fairness of domestic law-making, not of international law-making. But since so many areas of law that were traditionally seen as domestic are now the purview of international law, this issue is bound to arise. In many ways this parallels Judge Oda's concern in *Nuclear Weapons*—that there is something untoward about NGOs using international processes to achieve ends that could not be achieved politically and domestically.[81] Another aspect of the two-bites critique is that lobbying at the domestic level is simply different from lobbying at the international level, and the latter is much more troublesome. NGO lobbying at the domestic level, at least within democratic States, 'must contend with an electorate, a ballot box, and the checks upon the legitimacy claims of the NGO' that a well-functioning democratic system provides.[82] At the international level, these checks, or countervailing pressures, are thought to be less present and effective—perhaps giving NGOs excessive power.

These concerns and critiques have some merit. As a practical matter, however, the international community has largely—at least in multilateral settings, and certainly in UN-led settings—ceded significant roles to NGOs in treaty-making. Whatever concerns may exist about legitimacy have not stopped the steady accretion of greater power and participation on the part of NGOs over the last hundred years.

Conclusion

NGOs are ubiquitous in treaty processes today. While they have been active in one form or another in international lawmaking for well over a century, the quantity

---

Press, Stanford 1995) and R Keohane, eg, 'Accountability in World Politics' (2006) Scandinavian Political Studies 29, 75.

[80] P Willetts (n 12). Some defenders of NGOs also note that since many domestic governments in the world are non-democratic, NGOs are not necessarily any less democratic than States. See eg P Wapner, 'Defending Accountability in NGOs' (2002) 3 Chi J Intl L 197, 198 ('States and NGOs possess various mechanisms of accountability, each of which works imperfectly. When compared to each other, it is not the case that states come out shining while NGOs are tarnished . . . the argument is that NGOs are not *more* accountable than states but *differently* accountable').
[81] See also Bolton (n 55) 215–21. Bolton (later) was US Ambassador to the UN.
[82] Anderson (n 15) 177.

and quality of participation today is unprecedented. International law 'has been forever changed by the empowerment of NGOs'.[83] In this brief chapter, I have sketched how NGO participation in treaty processes has developed and how it is structured. While there is no uniform pattern, in a wide array of issue-areas—from global health to environment to labour—NGOs have become important and even central players who actively and vigorously participate in the negotiation of new treaties and the implementation and adjustment of existing ones.

The move to a greater participatory role for NGOs has many causes. But it should not be viewed as necessarily antagonistic to State interests. Nor does it undermine the centrality of States in international law-making. The roles played by NGOs remain formally subject to State control. This control ranges from the accreditation process, which keeps out the overly radical or insufficiently organized (or just deeply disliked), to the use of informal negotiating venues and forums, which keeps out everyone. Yet this control is used sparingly and, I have argued, often strategically. The reality is that NGOs remain active in a wide range of treaty settings.

In the aggregate, States have benefited from the new-found prominence of NGOs in treaty-making. This complementarity broadly tracks the relationship between national governments and domestic interest groups in many democracies. In the United States, for instance, the rise of the modern regulatory State in the twentieth century led to and benefited from the participation of a wide array of interest groups. The vastly increased scope of governmental regulation in the post-New Deal era encouraged the courts—and Congress—to facilitate and guarantee the participation of many stakeholders and interested parties in the regulatory process.[84] Citizen groups, firms, and associations became fixtures in regulatory governance, wielding seemingly great power. Yet one could hardly argue that the federal government in the United States began to wither away as a result. The power of the central government to regulate was never stronger; the very presence and participation of these groups indicated just where the power lay. In a similar fashion, the participation of NGOs in treaty processes demonstrates not the growing weakness of States, but the increasing importance of international law.

Of course, none of this means that all NGOs are legitimate actors that should be welcomed without qualification onto the global stage. Many governments and observers continue to oppose greater participation by NGOs in treaty processes because they believe many (or all) NGOs are simply special interests who will warp the process of treaty-making. This view is more persuasive in the abstract than in practice, however. In a world of well-functioning governments that are responsive and open to varied interests, a prominent role for NGOs at the international level might well be unnecessary. But in the real world, where many important views and perspectives are often left out of State-to-State processes, NGOs fill an important

---

[83] Alvarez (n 15) 611.

[84] See generally RB Stewart, 'The Reformation of American Administrative Law' (1975) 88 Harv L Rev 1669; RB Stewart and CR Sunstein, 'Public Programs and Private Rights' (1982) 95 Harv L Rev 1193.

void in treaty-making. For this reason, they will, for the foreseeable future, continue to be a significant presence in many treaty processes.

Recommended Reading

K Anderson, 'What NGO Accountability Means—And Does Not Mean' (2009) 103 AJIL 170 (reviewing L Jordan and P van Tuijl (eds), *NGO Accountability: Politics, Principles & Innovations* (Earthscan, London 2006))

S Charnovitz, 'Nongovernmental Organizations and International Law' (2006) 100 AJIL 348

PM Dupuy and L Vierucci (eds), *NGOs in International Law* (Edward Elgar, Northampton MA 2008)

M Keck and K Sikkink, *Activists Beyond Borders: Advocacy Networks in International Politics* (Cornell University Press, Ithaca 1998)

R Price, 'Reversing the Gun Sights: Transnational Civil Society Targets Land Mines' (1998) 52 Intl Org 613

S Ripinsky and P van den Bossche, *NGO Involvement in International Organizations* (BIICL, London 2007)

A Vedder (ed), *NGO Involvement in International Governance and Policy: Sources of Legitimacy* (Martinus Nijhoff, Boston 2007)

P Willetts (ed), *The Conscience of the World: The Influence of Non-Governmental Organizations in the UN System* (Hurst, London 1996)

SECTION II
TREATY FORMATION

7

Making the Treaty

George Korontzis [*]

Introduction

From time immemorial, States have concluded treaties on all possible matters under the sun.[1] Today, treaty-making has become an almost indispensable aspect of sovereignty—the 'outward-looking' facet of a State and one of the cornerstones of its relations with other States. Questions of treaty formation play a similarly central role in the formation of international law, witnessed most recently during the Copenhagen discussions on 'formalizing' an international environmental strategy and ongoing consultations on finalizing a comprehensive convention against terrorism.[2]

As a process, the term 'treaty-making' used herein actually encompasses four different stages: (a) treaty negotiations; (b) the conclusion of the treaty text; (c) expressions of consent to be bound; and (d) entry into force.[3] Various legal acts take place at each stage that operate in two parallel and cross-cutting legal orders, namely international law and the domestic law systems of the States involved. This chapter focuses on treaty-making solely under international law. But, it should be understood at the outset that domestic legal orders also regulate these acts, whether in delineating which organ of a State can conclude treaties, how to issue full powers, what domestic steps are necessary for treaty ratification, or whether and how incorporation of the treaty's provisions into the domestic legal order occurs.[4]

---

[*] The views expressed in this chapter are solely those of the author and do not necessarily reflect the views of the United Nations. The author would also like to thank Mr G Buzzini for his valuable comments.

[1] Paul Guggenheim refers to a treaty concluded in 1280 BC between Ramses II of Egypt and Khatisir, King of the Hittites. P Guggenheim, 'Contribution à l'histoire des sources du droit des gens' (1954) 85 RcD 54, 55.

[2] See UN Doc FCCC/CP/2009/11/Add.1 (containing the Copenhagen Accord and a proposed Amendment to the UN Framework Convention on Climate Change); UN Doc A/C.6/65/L.10 (containing the latest proposals concerning a comprehensive anti-terrorism convention).

[3] Treaty-making is often thought to only involve the process of negotiations, conclusion and expressions of consent to be bound, but this chapter expands the term to include entry into force as well.

[4] For a discussion of the role of treaties in domestic law, see Chapter 15.

At the international level, a certain formalism has always characterized treaty-making. As instruments that by design, signal permanence and stability, treaties require a record. Today, that record is almost universally required to be a written one. Through a series of treaties and practice, States have agreed on specific rules and processes for how they will record treaty commitments.[5] The 1969 Vienna Convention on the Law of Treaties (VCLT) in particular, has achieved an almost 'sacrosanct' status; what started out as codification of certain customary rules and the progressive development of others, has now all mostly taken on the character of customary norms.[6]

On the other hand, for all its formality and customary character, treaty-making remains a remarkably flexible process. The field of treaty law is vast and very complex, leaving room for indefinite variations. Tens of thousands of treaties now exist that can be classified along any number of criteria, including the treaty's content, the presumed or proven intent of the negotiating parties, or the identity of participating parties. For our purposes, the distinction between multilateral (involving three or more parties) and bilateral (involving two parties) treaties reveals the most significant differences in practice (although additional gradations within these categories can, and do, occur).[7]

Within such a vast and varied terrain, the rules found in the relevant Vienna Conventions are mostly residual in character. They generally only apply in the absence of any other specific agreement between the parties (the absolute prohibition of agreements contrary to *jus cogens* being a notable exception).[8] Otherwise, parties are 'free to agree on anything'. In recent years, the process has become even more complex. Changes in domestic regimes, particularly the rise of democratic institutions, have led States to different practices and processes of treaty-making. The presence of possible or potential additional treaty-makers—first of all international organizations (IOs), but also entities like liberation movements, and possibly non-governmental organizations—have further complicated the landscape.[9] In such a labyrinth, the fundamental rules embodied in the three Vienna Conventions provide useful signposts to those engaged in the often messy work of constructing a treaty.

Taken together, this chapter focuses on all aspects of treaty-making, in the light, inevitably, of the Vienna Conventions, while cognizant of the actual variations from its terms in practice. Given the difficulty of presenting in detail the minutiae of all the procedural and legal aspects, this chapter seeks to provide an overview of

---

[5] Eg VCLT; Vienna Convention on Succession of States in Respect of Treaties (adopted 23 August 1978, entered into force 6 November 1996) 1946 UNTS 3; Vienna Convention on the Law of Treaties Between States and International Organizations or Between International Organizations (opened for signature 21 March 1986, not yet in force) UN Doc A/CONF.129/15 ('1986 VCLT').

[6] *Gabcikovo-Nagymaros Project* [1997] ICJ Rep 7 [46]; S Bastid, *Les Traités Dans la Vie Internationale: Conclusion et Effets* (Economica, Paris 1985).

[7] H Waldock, 'First Report on the Law of Treaties' [1962] YBILC, vol II, 34.

[8] For a discussion of *jus cogens*, see Chapter 22, Part III.D, 570 *et seq.*

[9] See eg Wye River Memorandum of 23 October 1998 between Israel and PLO [1988] 37 ILM 1251; Agreements concluded in the context of the conflict in Yugoslavia with local authorities or communities (including Croatia and Local Serbian Community) [1996] 35 ILM 1.

the four essential stages of the treaty-making process: first, the negotiation of the treaty; second, the conclusion of the treaty; third, the expression of consent to be bound by the treaty; and, fourth and finally, the entry into force of the treaty.

I. Negotiation of the Treaty

Treaty negotiations have not really been made the object of any international regulation *stricto sensu*.[10] In 1962, Waldock, as the International Law Commission's (ILC's) fourth Special Rapporteur on the law of treaties, proposed a provision—Article 5—on negotiation.[11] As adopted by the ILC in 1962, Article 5 read:

A treaty is drawn up by a process of negotiation which may take place either through the diplomatic channel or some other agreed channel, or at meetings of representatives or at an international conference. In the case of treaties negotiated under the auspices of an international organization, the treaty may be drawn up either at an international conference or in some organ of the organization itself.[12]

The Commission indicated that the process of drawing up the treaty text is an essential preliminary to the legal act of its adoption. At the same time, it recognized that the article's content, as drafted, was more descriptive than normative. This attracted much adverse comment from governments. Although Waldock attempted to revise it to meet those criticisms, the ILC ultimately decided to drop the article since it lacked normative content.[13]

To say that international law does not dictate particular rules for treaty negotiations, however, does not mean that negotiations are immune from legal questions. Particularly at their commencement, two issues may dominate a negotiation. First, does the negotiation seek to produce a treaty, or some other commitment? To negotiate a treaty, the participants should intend that their result will constitute a legally binding agreement governed by international law. Only from that viewpoint will negotiations constitute a first, and necessary, step towards the conclusion of a treaty in whatever field (political, economic, military, cultural, etc) they address. As Shabtai Rosenne noted:

On the other hand, if the participants in that negotiation, for whatever reason, do not intend the arrangement which comes out of the negotiation, however formal that arrangement might look, to be an agreement governed by international law, it will not be a 'treaty' for the purposes of international law, whatever else it might be, and however much of a 'commitment' it might express.[14]

---

[10] In a substantively legal normative sense. The practice of conferences and diplomatic meetings has been addressed, as far as the technical aspect is concerned, in handbooks, manuals, etc, such as *Satow's Diplomatic Practice* or even the still invaluable V Pastuhov, *A Guide to the Practice of International Conferences* (Carnegie Endowment for International Peace, Washington 1945).

[11] The issue was first introduced by the ILC's third Special Rapporteur, Sir Gerald Fitzmaurice. [1957] YBILC, vol II, 104–28.

[12] [1962] YBILC, vol II, 166.

[13] [1965] YBILC, vol I, 255.

[14] S Rosenne, *Developments in the Law of Treaties 1945–1986* (CUP, Cambridge 1989) 87.

Thus, treaty negotiations should be distinguished from those designed to produce a political commitment such as an MOU or a contract governed by the domestic law of one or more of the participating States.[15]

Second, treaty negotiations must address questions of participation. As detailed in earlier chapters, international law *does* dictate who can make treaties. States and IOs are without doubt the main subjects of international law having the treaty-making capacity, while there are fewer examples of treaty-making by entities such as occupied States or semi-autonomous territories. Most notably, negotiating States allowed certain territories that did not possess full independence to participate in the Third UN Conference on the Law of the Sea; they had similar roles in the 1974 Geneva Conference entrusted with the preparation of two Protocols to the 1949 Geneva Conventions relating to international humanitarian law.[16]

In terms of treaty-making by States, they have broad authority, although occasionally there are questions about whether an entity qualifies as a State, a topic that has given rise to long and difficult debates, inevitably affected by political or other considerations.[17] Assuming a State exists, international law leaves the State with great discretion on whether and when to make treaties. Moreover, that discretion extends to include who may negotiate a treaty on behalf of the State, although, suffice it here to say that at the national level, it is mainly the Executive Branch that in most national systems has the competence to negotiate.[18]

The authority of IOs[19] to make treaties is more circumspect. It remains an open question whether all IOs have the capacity to conclude treaties and on what basis they could do so.[20] If an organization has treaty-making authority, the Executive Head of the organization (Secretary-General, Director General, etc) usually has the capacity to represent the organization in the negotiation and conclusion of treaties. That said, it is not clear if this assignment is considered to be part of the 'inherent powers' of the Executive or if some previous authorization by the deliberative/parliamentary body is required. Certainly such authorization is necessary for the expression by the organization of its consent to be bound by the treaty.[21] In the UN, however, the Secretary-General (or his representatives) may on certain occasions conclude treaties *on behalf of the organization*, either on his own initiative or to give effect to resolutions of UN organs even if they did not specifically request him to enter into such an agreement.[22]

---

[15] For more on this distinction, see Chapter 1, Part II.B, 31 *et seq.*

[16] Final Act, 1125 UNTS 438 [3]; on treaty-making by other subjects of international law, see also Chapter 5.

[17] For example, participation of entities such as the Palestine Liberation Organization (PLO) in the 1974 Geneva Conference and the revolutionary government of South Vietnam gave rise to many difficulties.

[18] DB Hollis, 'A Comparative Approach to Treaty Law and Practice' in DB Hollis and others (eds), *National Treaty Law and Practice* (Martinus Nijhoff, Leiden 2005) 19–23.

[19] IOs usually include inter-governmental organizations following in this respect the definition in Art 2(1)(i) of the 1986 VCLT.

[20] For a detailed discussion of the treaty-making capacity of IOs, see Chapter 3.

[21] See eg UNGA Res 53/100 (8 December 1998) (authorizing the UN to deposit an act of formal confirmation of the 1986 VCLT).

[22] *Repertory of Practice of UN Organs*, Supp 7, vol VI, Art 98 [610].

Conditions for participating in treaties are not set solely by international law; in practice, many negotiations are limited by the negotiating participants themselves. The 1986 Vienna Convention anticipates IOs negotiating an array of treaties. In practice, however, they are mainly involved in concluding *bilateral* treaties with States or other organizations. The multilateral treaty process is still dominated by States.[23] Similarly, a negotiating State may choose to limit the number of other States, IOs, or other entities with which it wishes to negotiate a treaty. Thus, many multilateral treaties themselves contain clauses determining which States may become parties or even giving the possibility to the parties to invite other States to become parties. Examples of various participation clauses are included in Section VI(3)–(4) of this volume.

In deciding with whom to partner in a treaty, the threshold for States is whether to conclude a bilateral or a multilateral treaty. Bilateral treaties are negotiated between the representatives of each State mostly in a formal setting. These negotiations usually begin after representatives of each party receive, exchange, and examine their respective full powers.[24] In other cases, negotiations are more informal or take place at various levels, starting with the involvement of mid-level diplomatic agents and going up to that of high level officials or even Cabinet Ministers, Prime Ministers, or Heads of State. Negotiations may also take place in successive 'rounds', whether in a formal setting, or in more informal contexts, on the occasion of a meeting or summit.

Bilateral agreements also commonly include agreements between a State and an IO. A 2009 UN–US Agreement concerning the establishment of security for the UN presence in Iraq is a recent example.[25] For the UN, such negotiations usually take place between a specific department or office of the Secretariat and representatives of the interested State (usually part of the personnel of its Permanent Mission to the UN). IOs, including the UN, may also negotiate bilateral agreements with other IOs, usually on matters of mutual cooperation.[26]

Despite the moniker, some bilateral treaty negotiations may involve more than two parties. Especially in the case of treaties between former opponents that purport to end a conflict, third parties may act as intermediaries and play a crucial role in the course of the negotiations. The most well-known example of this phenomenon involved Algeria's role in negotiating an agreement between the United States and Iran.[27]

---

[23] Increasing participation of IOs or other entities may occur in the future given their enhanced roles in international relations.

[24] See nn 38–45 and accompanying text.

[25] Agreement between the United Nations Organization and the Government of the United States of America concerning the establishment of security for the United Nations presence in Iraq (31 December 2008) (2009) UNJY 5.

[26] See eg Memorandum of Understanding between the United Nations Industrial Development Organization and the Latin American Energy Organization (16 and 25 February 2009) (2009) UNJY 56; Memorandum of Understanding on Cooperation between the Commission of the African Union and the Technical Secretariat of the Organization for the Prohibition of Chemical Weapons (24 January 2006) (2009) UNJY 78.

[27] P Guilland, 'Le rôle de l'Algérie dans la conclusion de l'accord entre les Etats-Unis et l'Iran' (1981) AFDI 29. The fourth agreement on a peaceful resolution of the situation in Afghanistan

In the case of multilateral treaties, treaty negotiations usually take place within an *international conference*, whether convened under the auspices of a standing IO, or in specific ad hoc bodies established to that effect. Elaboration of treaties was among the first functions of early unions created in the nineteenth century, which prepared their own constituent acts.[28] The League of Nations prepared the Statute of the Permanent Court of International Justice and other multilateral conventions.[29] Article 62(3) of the UN Charter expressly includes the negotiation of treaties among the UN's functions.

Over the years, the UN General Assembly has elaborated many treaties either through its main Committees or through ad hoc organs. Other organizations like the Council of Europe (COE) or the International Maritime Organization (IMO) are essentially permanent treaty-making mechanisms. Thus, large multilateral conventions will almost always be negotiated within pre-established institutional frameworks. These entities facilitate the process and offer expertise to the increasingly specialized and fragmented field of treaty-making.

Beyond the role of IOs in multilateral treaty-making, the negotiation process itself has evolved. The 1960s witnessed a period of intensive treaty-making on the codification and progressive development of international law driven by the ILC. At that time, the usual pattern started with a set of draft articles prepared by the Commission, which it submitted to the UN General Assembly. A codification conference was then convened in which 'all States' were invited to participate.[30]

But scarcely any large codification conferences have taken place during the last twenty-five years. The one notable exception (although not strictly a codification conference) was the 1998 Rome Conference convened after several years of preparation to conclude the final statute of the International Criminal Court (ICC).[31] Otherwise, the last conference of such calibre was the negotiations leading to the conclusion of the 1986 VCLT.

In place of codification conferences, States adopted other processes of negotiation. The UN Conference on the Law of the Sea, convened over a period of several years, was notable both for the variety of techniques used and for ingenious solutions to a wide-range of problems.[32] A more recent trend has been the UN General Assembly's establishment of ad hoc committees or working groups of the

---

concluded on 14 April 1988, constitutes another variation; it was concluded apparently between two different sets of parties (United States–USSR/Afghanistan–Pakistan). [1988] 27 ILM 577.

[28] J Siotis, *Essai sur le Secrétariat international* (Droz, Geneva 1963).

[29] Eg General Act for the Pacific Settlement of Disputes (adopted 26 September 1928, entered into force 16 August 1929) 93 LNTS 344.

[30] For a discussion of the meaning of the 'all States' formula see nn 72–4 and accompanying text.

[31] The Rome Conference was preceded by an initial ILC draft as well as involvement by an Ad Hoc Committee and a Preparatory Committee established by the UNGA.

[32] See the lectures by T Koh, 'The Negotiating Process of UNCLOS III' and 'The Art and Science of Chairing Major Inter-governmental Conferences' <http://untreaty.un.org/cod/avl/ls/Koh_T_LS. html>. (noting the conference's innovative use of the principle 'No agreement until final agreement'; the Gentleman's Agreement on consensus; the emergence of new interest groups of States based on geographical factors, and parallel formal and informal negotiating processes).

Sixth Committee to negotiate sensitive treaties.[33] The UN Commission on International Trade Law (UNCITRAL) and the UN Environment Programme (UNEP) have similarly negotiated treaties as part of their mandates.[34] While diplomatic conferences have a more formal organization—including discussion in sub-committees and a drafting committee—UN ad hoc commissions or committees follow a more informal pattern. They may establish working groups open to all members of the commission or committee and which focus on specific thematic areas to be covered by the treaty. The final outcome is submitted to the plenary of the committee (or commission), which endorses or adopts the text, and then submits it to its parent body, whether the UN General Assembly or the Assembly of the specialized agency or other organization.

Negotiations themselves may be conducted in myriad ways. In the UN, sometimes the Secretariat may prepare a first draft of the convention. At other times, negotiations may be conducted informally on the basis of 'non-papers',[35] working papers, or more formal modalities. In the latter case, each delegation may present (simultaneously or successively) a complete text of the proposed outcome (agreement). Counter proposals are then submitted (formally or informally, orally or in writing) by other delegations. The question of the status of each proposal or counter proposal may be an extremely thorny one that can become politically charged. Procedural rules together with clarifications on the exact status of each proposal at every stage of the negotiating process may acquire great importance.

In terms of procedural rules, diplomatic conferences convened for the purpose of concluding a multilateral treaty mainly follow parliamentary practices. Several attempts to codify such procedures have not, however, produced any conclusive result. States prefer instead to keep open the possibilities of elaborating specifically tailored rules of procedure for any conference based on its specific subject and presumed goal.[36] The fact remains, however, that the Rules of Procedure of the UN General Assembly still provide an acceptable model. Tacitly or expressly, treaty-making conferences and related bodies (such as ad hoc committees) have referred to them whenever a procedural problem arises.

The really important aspect of the negotiation process is, of course, the decision-making rules; for example, whether the negotiating participants will require unanimity, consensus, or required majorities to reach a collective decision. Generally,

---

[33] See UNGA Res 56/93 (28 January 2002) (establishing the Ad Hoc Committee for the purpose of considering the elaboration of an international convention against the reproductive cloning of human beings).

[34] See eg UNCITRAL, Convention on the Use of Electronic Communications in International Contracts (adopted 23 November 2005, opened for signature 16 January 2006) UN Doc A/Res/60/21; Convention on Biological Diversity (adopted 5 June 1992, entered into force 29 December 1993) 1760 UNTS 79.

[35] 'Non-papers' are texts distributed on an informal basis and designed to facilitate the process of negotiating an agreement. It is not a proposal (although it may foreshadow one) and does not engage its author. UNITAR, *Glossary of Terms* 116.

[36] See eg documents establishing the Rules of Procedure for the UN Diplomatic Conference of Plenipotentiaries on the Establishment of an International Criminal Court. UN Doc A/CONF.183/2/Add.2; UN Doc A/CONF.183/3.

the recent trend—both in the UN and diplomatic conferences—is to seek the widest possible agreement at every step of the treaty-making process and on any draft provision of the treaty under negotiation. Resort to voting is viewed as divisive or counter-productive on the logical assumption (not always proved in practice) that treaty-making resulting from a consensual process will eventually produce a more widely accepted treaty. At the same time, another recent phenomenon for multilateral treaty negotiations is the 'package deal', according to which 'nothing is agreed until everything is agreed'. Under this approach, any delegation has the right to reserve its position on certain points until it obtains satisfaction on others.[37]

II. Conclusion of the Treaty

The conclusion of the treaty has various stages, beginning with the establishment of the text and usually ending with its signature. A treaty text is established by its adoption and/or authentication by duly authorized representatives of the negotiating parties, who are usually identified in IOs through the presentation of credentials or, when an adoption entails signature, through full powers. Adoption is the act by which the negotiating parties express their *agreement* with the final text of the treaty. Adoption thus formally acknowledges substantive agreement on a text by the negotiating parties. Authentication, in contrast, is more in the nature of a 'notarial' certification or witnessing that the very text as finally established and adopted constitutes the 'authentic' (genuine, real) text of the treaty. Multiple linguistic versions of a single, multilateral treaty can frequently complicate the authentication process. An adopted or authenticated text may be signed by representatives of the negotiating participants. In addition, participants may adopt a 'Final Act', recording the history of the negotiation process in ways that can provide valuable information for the treaty's later interpretation or application.

A. Full powers

The question of who can represent a State (or an IO) is central to the whole process of adopting and authenticating a treaty.[38] According to Article 7(1) of the VCLT:

a person is considered as representing a State for the purpose of adopting or authenticating the text of a treaty or for the purpose of expressing the consent of the State to be bound by a treaty if:

a. he produces appropriate full powers; or

b. it appears from the practice of the States concerned or from other circumstances that their intention was to consider that person as representing the State for such purposes and to dispense with full powers.

---

[37] RY Jennings, 'Law Making and the Package Deal', in *Mélanges Offerts à Paul Reuter* (Pedone, Paris 1981) 347–55; G de Lothaire, 'Aspects juridiques de la négociation sur un Package deal à la Conférence des Nations Unies sur le droit de la mer' in *Essays in Honor of Erik Castren* (Finnish Branch of the International Law Association, Helsinki 1979) 30–45.

[38] In some cases, it will also be a necessary prerequisite to any treaty negotiations whatsoever.

Article 2(c) of the VCLT defines the full powers as 'a document emanating from the competent authority of a State designating a person or persons to represent the State for negotiating, adopting or authenticating the text of a treaty, for expressing the consent of the State to be bound by a treaty, or for accomplishing any other act with respect to a treaty'.[39] Full powers must be distinguished from credentials, which are documents authorizing a person merely to participate in a conference.[40]

Full powers clarify what authority a representative has in relation to formation of the treaty under negotiation. The content of full powers can range from authorization simply to negotiate the treaty, to authorization to negotiate and sign the final text; it may also include signature alone or some other variation. They must usually name the person authorized (authorizing a particular office holder is insufficient), be signed by someone authorized to issue full powers, and mention the date and place of signature, often accompanied by the official seal.

Who can issue full powers? Practice varies from State to State, but it is widely admitted that Heads of State, Heads of Government, and Ministers for Foreign Affairs may sign the full powers document. It is also customary that those officials by their very function do not require full powers, a principle confirmed in Article 7(2) of the VCLT. All other Ministers, as well as Deputy or Vice-Ministers (including Vice-Ministers for Foreign Affairs) do require full powers.[41] The VCLT's only exceptions are for the principle of 'limited automatic representativeness' where (a) heads of diplomatic missions (usually having the rank of Ambassadors) can adopt a treaty between the accrediting State and the State to which they are accredited,[42] and (b) representatives accredited by States to an IO or to an international conference (or one of its organs) may adopt the text of a treaty in that conference, organization, or organ.[43] This function of a diplomatic mission is reinforced in Article 3(1)(c) of the Vienna Convention on Diplomatic Relations (VCDR).[44] In UN practice, accredited representatives of States (and only those representatives) are considered as having full powers to adopt the text of treaties concluded within the UN (but not to sign or to express the consent of the State to be bound by the treaty).

---

[39] '[A]ny other act with respect to the treaty' can include authority to terminate or suspend the treaty for a State, to provisionally apply it, or to extend its territorial reach. See UN Office of Legal Affairs, *Treaty Handbook* (2006) Sales No. E.02.V.2 <http://treaties.un.org>.

[40] Credentials are mainly used in multilateral settings but may also arise in bilateral negotiations, especially those involving a more formal framework. In UN practice, credentials to participate in a conference are also considered sufficient for the signature of the Final Act.

[41] Officials serving as 'acting' Foreign Ministers or running those Ministries *ad interim* may issue full powers.

[42] It is remarkable that this is the only instance in which a *lettre de créance* (accreditation) may also have the function of 'full powers'.

[43] As the ILC noted, however, the principle of limited automatic representativeness 'is not considered in practice to extend, without production of full powers, to expressing the consent of the State to be bound by the treaty': [1966] YBILC, vol II, 193. Thus, the principle's coverage extends to initialling of a treaty, but not to expressing the State's consent to be bound by it.

[44] Vienna Convention on Diplomatic Relations (adopted 18 April 1961, entered into force 24 April 1964) 500 UNTS 95 (VCDR).

It often happens that full powers to sign are given to other representatives coming from the capital for a particular conference. Despite the overlap in authority, all full powers emanating from the competent authority of a State have equal validity. Indeed, it is not unusual that more than one representative of the same State sign a treaty at the same time, provided, of course, that each has a duly signed full powers.

In terms of procedures, full powers are transmitted to the Secretariat of the Conference or the IO hosting the negotiations through means of a notification or *note verbale*.[45] The Secretariat checks them and reports any problem to the State concerned. In bilateral treaties or treaties negotiated among a small number of States, full powers are produced either at the beginning of the meeting set out for the treaty's signature, at the beginning of the negotiations, or even earlier through mutual notifications/*notes verbales* from the foreign ministries concerned.

Finally, it should be noted that in certain contexts in practice, the negotiating participants may agree to dispense with full powers. This frequently occurs in bilateral contexts, and may also particularly characterize certain early and informal stages of multilateral negotiations. Ultimately, negotiating participants need to decide in each case whether or not full powers will be needed.

B. Adoption of a treaty text

At the end of the negotiations, there should be agreement on a treaty text. Treaty texts are generally comprised of certain, standard parts:

(a) a Preamble containing the names of the parties, a summary description of its object and purpose, the names and official designations of the representatives of the parties (plenipotentiaries) and, often, a paragraph stating that the plenipotentiaries have produced their full powers which were found to be in good and due form and then they have agreed upon the following articles;

(b) the various substantive articles of the treaty;

(c) a set of what are known as 'final clauses', dealing with matters such as territorial application of the treaty, signature, ratification (acceptance or approval), accession, entry into force, amendments, denunciation (withdrawal) and duration, or (in the case of a multilateral treaty) reservations;

(d) a clause (testimonium) stating: 'In witness thereof (en foi de quoi) the respective plenipotentiaries have signed the treaty'; and

(e) the location and date.

For bilateral treaties, there is rarely a specific or distinct process of adoption. The parties' very signature of the final text (which may be 'simple' signature acting as a precursor to ratification, or a signature that actually expresses the State's consent to

---

[45] Notifications of full powers have, in the past, been acceptable by telegram or facsimile, followed by delivery of the actual full powers. Today, electronic copies (eg a .pdf) may also precede actual delivery.

be bound)[46] constitutes the act adopting the text. Depending on the form chosen, 'adopting' the treaty in the bilateral context may also take the form of an exchange of letters, which have identical contents. The letters (with the required changes in names, etc) are duly signed by the representatives of each party. They may be exchanged either through diplomatic channels or during a solemn meeting between the representatives of the two parties.

In the case of multilateral treaties, in contrast, adoption constitutes a specific and distinct process for the formal establishment of the text. In practice, adoption actually often comprises two distinct stages. First, the negotiating body (ad hoc committee, commission, etc) will 'finalize' the text that represents the negotiations' result. This 'finalization' takes place in accordance with the relevant rules of procedure of that negotiating body, but, in practice, is mostly achieved through consensus.[47] What constitutes 'consensus' or 'general agreement' has occasionally been the subject of some dispute, but generally 'consensus' is distinguished from unanimity, and involves the absence of formal objection, including from States that would not vote affirmatively in favour of adoption.[48]

Second, once the negotiating body has 'adopted' the text, it transmits it with a recommendation (included in a draft resolution) to the parent body such as the UN General Assembly. In theory, the General Assembly may still bring changes or modify substantially the prepared text. In the UN, the General Assembly adopts treaties through a resolution to which the treaty is annexed. For example, on 2 December 2004 the UN General Assembly adopted the UN Convention on Jurisdictional Immunities of States and their Property by Resolution 59/38.[49] In UN practice, the treaty is very often adopted by consensus, although UN General Assembly rules of procedure do allow for voting if necessary.[50]

Outside the UN General Assembly, diplomatic conferences that elaborate a treaty may use another method of adoption. The 'final text' (usually prepared within the Conference's Drafting Committee) is adopted by the Conference Plenary. But in the Plenary context, voting may often occur if consensus is unattainable. Thus, the Rome Conference adopted the ICC Statute by a vote of

---

[46] See nn 88–113, and accompanying text.

[47] Where the negotiating body is constituted ad hoc, rules of procedure, including the voting rules, are usually among the first items agreed by the negotiating participants. As a general matter, VCLT Art 9 suggests a preference for unanimity in adoption, but allows for it to occur by a two-thirds vote of States present and voting (unless those two-thirds decide to apply a different rule).

[48] A Aust, *Modern Treaty Law & Practice* (2nd edn CUP, Cambridge 2007) 86–9.

[49] UNGA Res 59/38 (2 December 2004).

[50] See UNGA, *Rules of Procedure of the General Assembly* (2007) UN Doc A/520/Rev 17, Rules 82–93. For examples of treaties adopted by the UN General Assembly without a vote, see Convention Against Torture and Other Cruel, Inhuman or Degrading Treatment or Punishment (adopted 10 December 1984, entered into force 26 June 1987) 1465 UNTS 85; International Convention for the Suppression of Acts of Nuclear Terrorism (adopted 13 April 2005, entered into force 7 July 2007) 2445 UNTS 89. For examples of treaties adopted by a vote of the General Assembly, see International Covenant on Civil and Political Rights (adopted 16 December 1966, entered into force 23 March 1976) 999 UNTS 171 (ICCPR); Comprehensive Nuclear Test-Ban Treaty (opened for signature 24 September 1996, not yet in force) [1996] 35 ILM 1439 (CTBT).

120 in favour, 7 against, and 21 States abstaining.[51] According to Article 9 of the VCLT, adoption of a treaty text occurs with the consent of all States participating in the negotiations, or by the vote of two-thirds of the States present and voting (unless those two-thirds decide to apply a different rule). In practice, however, different international fora and conferences have established different majorities, or established that the principle of adoption of the text must be mainly by consensus.[52]

The adoption of a treaty marks the end of the negotiation; it does not mean that the treaty is already legally binding in all respects.[53] Adoption instead signals the moment from which certain of the treaty's provisions apply, namely those on authentication, consent to be bound, reservations, depositary functions, and 'other matters arising necessarily before the entry into force of the treaty'.[54] In certain cases, the adoption of a large, multilateral treaty may also constitute an important element in the formation of a customary rule.[55] Depending on the number of adopting States, the treaty may also take on independent political significance.

C. Authentication

The next step in establishing the final text of the treaty is authentication. There are various standard methods of authentication, such as initialling, signature ad referendum, signature, or adoption of the Final Act. Article 10 of the VCLT, however, allows negotiating participants to agree on their own procedures for authentication as well.[56]

Initialling involves participants placing their initials at the bottom of each page of the treaty text. It signals that after having been read, this initialled text is found to correspond to the one agreed upon and, therefore, constitutes the 'authentic' or definitive text of the treaty. Initialling is mostly used in bilateral or very restricted multilateral treaties. It is not a method used in UN processes involving a large number of participants.

---

[51] Rome Statute of the International Criminal Court (adopted 17 July 1998, entered into force 1 July 2002) 2187 UNTS 90 (Rome Statute).

[52] During the Third Conference on the Law of the Sea, a declaration incorporating the 'Gentlemen's Agreement' approved by the General Assembly made by the President and endorsed by the Conference was appended to the rules of procedure and provided that: 'The Conference should make every effort to reach agreement on substantive matters by way of consensus and there should be no voting on such matters until all efforts at consensus have been exhausted.': '167th Plenary Meeting' Third United Nations Conference on the Law of the Sea (7 April 1982) UN Doc A/CONF.62/SR.167 [2].

[53] A notable exception, discussed in the text accompanying n 135, is the 1994 Agreement relating to the implementation of Part XI of the United Nations Convention on the Law of the Sea of 10 December 1982 (adopted 28 July 1994, entered into force 28 July 1996) 2167 UNTS 3, which was subject to provisional application.

[54] VCLT Art 24(4).

[55] N Quoc Dinh, A Pellet, and P Dailler, *Droit international public* (6th edn LGDJ, Paris 1999) 135; R Baxter, 'Treaties and Custom' (1970) 129 RcD 25–106.

[56] VCLT Art 10.

In multilateral treaties, the authentication process is sometimes more complicated. The adoption of the treaty by the Plenary of the Conference or the
General Assembly constitutes at the same time also the 'authentication of its
text'. Alternatively, the signature of a Final Act (discussed below) may constitute
a means of authentication of the treaty text to which the Final Act is usually
attached. In the UN, the final text of a treaty is also reproduced in the form of a
brochure duly certified (at its last page) by the Legal Counsel as containing the
authentic text of the treaty in all languages. Normally, once adopted on the basis of
a working document, an 'authentic' final text of the treaty is processed on 'official'
illustrative paper, in all languages in which it has been finalized and which all
together constitute the original text of the treaty. At the end of all the linguistic
versions, signature pages contain the name of each State having the capacity to
become party, again in all official languages. The pages are then bound into a
volume, which is the one signed when the treaty is open for signature. If this process
is followed, then there is no other stage of 'authentication'.

D. Multiple linguistic versions of treaties

Treaty texts will often come in multiple languages. Article 35(3) of the VCLT
provides that the terms of a treaty are presumed to have the same meaning in each
authentic text. Paragraph 4 of that Article provides that comparison of the authentic texts is a part of the process of interpretation.[57]

In the case of bilateral treaties, the treaty is usually concluded in the languages of
the negotiating Parties, which are each equally authentic. In some cases, however,
one of the languages may be given priority over the other. Or, these languages may
(but need not) be accompanied by a text in a commonly agreed language (most
frequently English or French), which often prevails in the event of any divergence
of interpretation. Sometimes, a treaty may even be drawn up in a language which is
not that of the contracting parties. For example, the 1905 Treaty of Peace between
Japan and Russia was drawn up in English and French.[58] In multilateral treaties,
the text is established in two or more languages. In the UN, most treaties are
established in the six official languages (Arabic, Chinese, English, French, Russian,
and Spanish) which all constitute the authentic text of the treaty.

Simultaneous drafting of all the authentic texts is today technically possible and
even expert bodies such as the ILC or UNCITRAL conduct their work and prepare
their texts in all official languages. Usually the text of treaties concluded under UN

---

[57] The ILC commentary on draft Art 29 (subsequently Art 35) provided that: 'The plurality of the
authentic texts of a treaty is always a material factor in its interpretation, since both or all the texts
authoritatively state the terms of the agreement between the parties. But it needs to be stressed that in
law there is only one treaty—one set of terms accepted by the parties and one common intention with
respect to those terms—even when two authentic texts appear to diverge': [1966] YBILC, vol II, 225.
For a discussion of the interpretative issues associated with plurilingual treaties, see Chapter 19,
Part II.C, 490 *et seq*.

[58] The Conclusion of the Russo-Japanese War (Russia-Japan) (5 September 1905), Art XV ('The
present treaty shall be signed in duplicate in both the English and French languages. The texts are in
absolute conformity, but in case of a discrepancy in the interpretation the French text shall prevail.').

.

auspices is authentic in all its official languages. The number of authentic texts may vary depending on the body adopting them. Signature pages of treaties deposited with the UN Secretary-General are always, however, in *all* official languages irrespective of the authentic languages of the treaty text itself. This avoids, in particular, any terminological or diplomatic difficulties that might arise from establishing signature pages in non-official languages.

In some cases, participants may request the depository to prepare an authentic text of a treaty subsequent to its adoption on the basis of other existing authentic texts.[59] In other cases, the agreement may contain no provisions on the subject. In the latter case, the Secretary-General's practice has been to consider as authentic the texts in all official languages and to prepare the original accordingly.[60] Even then, exceptions sometimes occur. For example, the Convention on the Privileges and Immunities of the UN exists in English and French only; the working languages of the Secretariat.[61] Section VI(9) of this Volume contains examples of various clauses dealing with the conclusion of multiple linguistic versions of a treaty text.

The most complex and sometimes thorny question surrounding treaty languages lies in the correction of errors or lack of concordance in the original of a multilateral treaty.[62] The VCLT devotes a whole, detailed article (Article 79) to the correction of errors in multilateral treaties by the parties themselves, or, where there is one, through the depository.[63] Since 1964, the Secretary-General has adopted a consistent practice as depositary of communicating proposed corrections not only to signatory States but to all States that participated in the treaty's elaboration. Objections to the correction of the original must be notified to the depositary within a certain period of time; Article 79(2) of the VCLT provides that the depositary 'shall specify an appropriate time-limit within which objection to the proposed correction may be raised'. For the UN, that time limit is normally ninety days from the date of the notification of proposed corrections. Any objections

---

[59] Such was the case for example with the Chinese text of the International Tropical Timber Agreement (2006) [2007] OJ L262/8, the testimonium of which read: 'Done at Geneva on the eighteenth day of November, one thousand nine hundred and eighty-three, the texts of this Agreement in the Arabic, English, French, Russian and Spanish languages being equally authentic. The authentic Chinese text of this Agreement shall be established by the depositary and submitted for adoption to all signatories and States and intergovernmental organizations which have acceded to this Agreement.'

[60] See eg UNGA Resolution 317 (IV) (21 March 1950) by which the General Assembly adopted the Convention for the Suppression of the Traffic in Persons and of the Exploitation of the Prostitution of Others; *Summary of Practice of the Secretary-General as Depositary of Multilateral Treaties*, ST/LEG/7/Rev 1, 11–12.

[61] Convention on the Privileges and Immunities of the United Nations (adopted 13 February 1946, entered into force 17 September 1946) 1 UNTS 15 (Official Texts in English and in French).

[62] The origin of this practice of correction of errors goes back to the Genocide Convention and the request from the Government of China for revision of the Chinese text of the Convention. The Secretary-General submitted a comprehensive memorandum (UN Doc A/2221) on that matter. The question of lack of concordance in the original of a multilateral treaty may even arise during the conference in which the text of the treaty is elaborated. Such was the case during the Rome Conference with regard to the Spanish text.

[63] Where there is no depositary, the parties may allow duly authorized representatives to initial a correction; execute and exchange instruments making the correction; execute a corrected text by the same procedure used in the case of the original text; or decide upon some other means of correction. VCLT Art 79(1).

received are also notified to the parties concerned.[64] Where a State is neither a signatory nor a contracting party, the Secretary-General communicates the objection to all interested States only for their *information*; that objection is not considered valid for the purpose of rejecting the correction.

What legal effects flow from objections to proposed corrections by a signatory or contracting party? The topic was not addressed in the VCLT or by the ILC.[65] In practice, the Secretary-General has consistently tried to consult with the objecting State so that any corrections are firstly accepted unanimously. This practice, however, should not be construed to mean that the existence of an isolated objection may, by itself, ultimately prevent the corrections from taking effect. At the same time, it is also clear that, while many corrections are technical in nature and relate only to the authentic text of the treaty, some go beyond that and, in effect, constitute a proposal of amendment. In those cases, the Secretary-General should not treat the proposal as a correction, but insist it proceed under the completely different procedures for amendment, which vary depending on the relevant treaty provisions. The line of distinction between a correction and an amendment is sometimes very thin; in such cases the depositary may have a role to play informally. Otherwise, the communication of such a 'disguised' amendment to all States could always trigger objections from other States through the usual mechanism of amendments to treaties.

Where, however, there are no objections to the proposed corrections within ninety days, the corrections are deemed adopted. The Secretary-General circulates a procès-verbal of rectification containing the already deemed 'as accepted' correction.[66] Sometimes and under exceptional circumstances a more simplified procedure has been followed by the Secretary-General: the text of the corrections may simply be communicated to all parties with a request that they make them in any appropriate documentation or regulation.

E. Signature or signature ad referendum

In bilateral treaties, a treaty will normally be signed by each party following the completion of negotiations and the 'conclusion' of the treaty (ie adoption and/or authentication). Signature may take place in a more or less formal setting, whether a ceremony vested with political significance or more discreetly. It may occur at the highest possible level (by Heads of State) or at the level of ministers or ambassadors.

Signature takes place on the authentic text of the treaty (which in this case is a duplicate). The parties then 'exchange' their signed texts, which differ only to the extent that in the text kept by each party its own name comes first in the title and preambular paragraphs of the treaty that contain the names of the parties (a practice known as the principle of the *alternat*).

---

[64] Summary of Practice (n 60) 15.
[65] [1962] YBILC, vol I, [8].
[66] Summary of Practice (n 60) 16.

Most multilateral treaties are usually open for signature (either on the day of their adoption or, for practical reasons associated with the preparation of the text in all its authentic languages, a little later). For both bilateral and multilateral treaties, signature does more than serve as a means of concluding the treaty; it is also the first (but not necessarily the last) step of the expression of a State's consent to be bound to a treaty.

The treaty itself will usually delineate which States or other entities can sign it.[67] Most multilateral treaties are normally open to signature by all States having participated in its adoption.[68] For many years, this was accomplished by the treaty containing the following clause:

The present Convention shall be open for signature by all States Members of the United Nations or of any of the specialized agencies, parties to the Statute of the International Court of Justice, and by any other State invited by the General Assembly of the United Nations to become a Party to the Convention, as follows: until 31 October 1961 at the Federal Ministry for Foreign Affairs of Austria and subsequently, until 31 March 1962, at the United Nations Headquarters in New York.[69]

This type of clause is called the 'Vienna' formula, since it was consistently used by all the Vienna Conventions, starting with the VCDR.[70] It allows those States that, for political or other reasons, are not members of the UN to participate in the treaty because they can be members of specialized agencies (where the veto[71] does not exist concerning admission of new members).

In addition to the Vienna formula, today, most multilateral treaties are simply open to participation by 'all States' (which is accordingly referred to as the

---

[67] Article 305 of the 1982 United Nations Convention on the Law of the Sea (adopted 10 December 1982, entered into force 16 November 1994) 1833 UNTS 396 (UNCLOS) provides a good example of the various participants that can sign a treaty:
This Convention shall be opened for signature by:

    (a) all States;
    (b) Namibia, represented by the United Nations Council for Namibia;
    (c) all self-governing associated States which have chosen that status in an act of self-determination supervised and approved by the United Nations in accordance with General Assembly resolution 1514(XV) and which have competence over the matters governed by this Convention, including the competence to enter into treaties in respect of those matters;
    (d) all self-governing associated States which, in accordance with their respective instruments of association, have competence over the matters governed by this Convention, including the competence to enter into treaties in respect of those matters;
    (e) all territories which enjoy full internal self-government, recognized as such by the United Nations, but have not attained full independence in accordance with General Assembly resolution 1514(XV) and which have competence over the matters governed by this Convention, including the competence to enter into treaties in respect of those matters;
    (f) international organizations, in accordance with annex IX.
[68] Eg UNGA Res 1450 (XIV) (7 December 1959) [3] (convening the International Conference of Plenipotentiaries on Diplomatic Intercourse and Immunities).
[69] VCDR (n 44) Art 48.
[70] Ibid.
[71] This is the 'veto' accorded to the five permanent members of the Security Council by virtue of UN Charter Art 27(3).

'all States' formula).[72] In these cases, the Secretary-General has a practice, set out in the understanding adopted by the General Assembly at its 2202nd plenary meeting on 14 December 1973, whereby:

the Secretary-General, in discharging his functions as a depositary of a convention with an 'all States' clause, will follow the practice of the Assembly in implementing such a clause and, whenever advisable, will request the opinion of the Assembly before receiving a signature or an instrument of ratification or accession.[73]

The Secretary-General's *Summary of Practice* explains that the 'practice of the General Assembly', referred to in this understanding concerns situations where there are unequivocal indications from the Assembly that it considers a particular entity to be a State even if it does not fall within the 'Vienna formula'.[74]

Aside from the Vienna and 'all States' formulas, there are many other ways in which participation in the treaty via signature can be limited. A treaty may be open for signature only for the States engaged in the negotiation, only for those State members of a particular organization (such as the COE), or only for other States specifically invited to sign the treaty.[75] Limitations on signature do not, however, always preclude excluded States from joining the treaty; they may just be limited to using accession as the means to do so.[76] Examples of various types of signature clauses are included in Section VI of this Volume.

The legal effects of signature vary widely. In most multilateral treaties, signature does not have any real legal effect except triggering the rather general obligation of the signatory not to act in a way contrary or detrimental to the provisions of the treaty.[77] As discussed below, however, in some cases signature may be simultaneously an expression of the consent to be bound if the treaty so provides.

The representative may also sign *ad referendum*, a signature that needs to be 'confirmed' at a later stage. The representative thus signs the treaty in a purely ceremonial or symbolic manner declaring that (for constitutional or other reasons) this signature (for which full powers are still required) will be duly confirmed. Signature *ad referendum* occurs in both bilateral and multilateral treaties.

---

[72] See eg Convention on Cluster Munitions (adopted 3 December 2008, entered into force 1 August 2010) [2009] 48 ILM 354, art 15 ('This Convention...shall be open for signature at Oslo by all States').

[73] [1973] UNJY 79.

[74] Summary of Practice (n 60) 23.

[75] See eg Customs Convention on Containers (adopted 18 May 1956, entered into force 4 August 1959) 338 UNTS 103, Art 12 ('Countries members of the Economic Commission for Europe and countries admitted to the Commission in a consultative capacity... may become contracting parties to this Convention... (a) by signing it'); see also Charter of the Asian and Pacific Development Centre (adopted 1 April 1982, entered into force 1 July 1983) 1321 UNTS 203, Arts III and XVI; European Anti-Doping Convention (opened for signature 16 November 1989, entered into force 1 March 1990) CETS No 135, Art 14.

[76] See Agreement Concerning the Adoption of Uniform Conditions of Approval and Reciprocal Recognition of Approval for Motor Vehicle Equipment and Parts (adopted 20 March 1958, entered into force 20 June 1959) 335 UNTS 218, Art 6.

[77] See VCLT Art 18 (signatory state 'is obliged to refrain from acts which would defeat the object and purpose of a treaty... until it shall have made its intention clear not to become a party to the treaty'). For a more detailed discussion, see Chapter 8 ('Treaty Signature').

In general, multilateral treaties have separate provisions concerning signature, on the one hand, and ratification, accession, approval, etc, on the other. These provisions will often specify when signature can occur. Some signature clauses leave the treaty open for signature indefinitely as, for example, the one in the International Covenant on Civil and Political Rights.[78] In other cases, a signature clause may leave the treaty open for signature for a specified period of time (from a few months to a number of years).[79]

There is little practice concerning treaty signature by IOs. The head of the organization (Secretary-General or Director-General) has the authority to sign on behalf of the organization after he has been duly authorized by the competent body of the organization (General Assembly, Council, Executive Board, etc). But it is an open question as to what other officials may sign on behalf of the IO. In the UN, the practice has not always been consistent. Generally speaking, any other official who signs a multilateral treaty on behalf of the organization needs full powers signed by the Secretary-General. In the case of bilateral agreements between the UN and a State or another organization, this practice might be more flexible depending on the nature of the agreement. Agreements of limited duration or of technical or specific content have been signed by the head of the relevant department of the Secretariat under whose competence the agreement falls without full powers from the Secretary-General[80] and that signature will also express the UN's consent to be bound.

Finally, a very different type of signature can occur when a treaty text is 'witnessed' by the signature of one or more representatives of third States or IOs. Witnessing has no legal effect for the participants or for those engaged in the witnessing; it is done more for its political effect in promoting the agreement or its effects.[81] Thus, the Dayton Agreement was witnessed by various heads of State and government, who added their signatures after the parties.[82]

F. The Final Act

The Final Act consists of a document (usually attached to the main text of the treaty) containing a summary of the proceedings of a conference (dates and place, participants, organization, etc) as well as of the organization of its work. Final Acts

---

[78] ICCPR (n 50) Art 48.

[79] Convention on Consent to Marriage (adopted 10 December 1962, entered into force 9 December 1964) 521 UNTS 231, Art 4 ('The present Convention shall, until 31 December 1963, be open for signature'); UN Convention Against Corruption (adopted 31 October 2003, entered into force 14 December 2005) 2349 UNTS 41, Art 67 ('This Convention shall be open to all States for signature from 9 to 11 December 2003 in Merida, Mexico, and thereafter at United Nations Headquarters in New York until 9 December 2005').

[80] An example of this bilateral practice is the Memorandum of Agreement between the United Nations and France for the Provision of Personnel to the United Nations Assistance Mission in Afghanistan of 4 March 2003, signed for the United Nations by the then Under-Secretary-General, Head of the Department of Peacekeeping Operations (2003) UNJY 12.

[81] Aust (n 48) 101–2.

[82] Ibid.

accompany the conclusion of almost any international conference, not just those associated with the adoption of a treaty. But where a treaty is involved, the Final Act serves as the 'certificate of birth'. It is often signed separately from the treaty text, but doing so has no effect on whether or not a State signs or joins the treaty itself.

An accurate and concise definition can be found in *Satow*'s classic guide to diplomatic practice:

The term 'Final Act' (*Acte Final*) is normally used to designate a document which constitutes a formal statement or summary of the proceedings of an international conference recording the result of its deliberations, including, as the case may be, enumerating the treaties or related treaty instruments drawn up together with any resolutions or vœux adopted by the Conference. The signature of an instrument of this nature does not in itself entail any expression of consent to be bound by the treaties or related treaty instruments so enumerated.[83]

The Final Act is not normally part of the treaty and does not usually contain substantive provisions. They may, however, contain vœux, recommendations, or even resolutions with 'semi-binding' force, in the sense that they constitute strong policy orientations or indications.

In some cases, however, the Final Act may constitute what Shabtai Rosenne dubbed 'informal treaty making'. Resolutions can be annexed to the Final Act that are intended to produce legal consequences.[84] Or, they may incorporate resolutions or decisions intended to complement a treaty.[85] Accordingly, and in the absence of any specific clause of the treaty to that effect, a case-by-case examination of Final Acts is appropriate to determine whether a Final Act includes precise legal commitments (deriving from or pertaining to the treaty).[86] Indeed, such scrutiny is also warranted given that a Final Act may be part of the *context* associated with the treaty for interpretative purposes.[87]

III. Expression of the Consent to be Bound by the Treaty

For historical and other reasons, the adoption of a treaty or even its signature does not necessarily mean that a State has consented to be bound by the treaty (unless, of course, the contracting parties have agreed that signature has this effect). Instead, States, IOs, and other treaty-making entities must consent to a concluded treaty before they can be legally bound to comport with its substantive contents (and

---

[83] I Roberts (ed), *Satow's Diplomatic Practice* (6th edn OUP, Oxford 2009) 569 [37.5].

[84] Rosenne (n 14) 118. For a famous example, see Resolutions I and II contained in Annex I of the Final Act of the 3rd UN Conference on the Law of the Sea.

[85] The Final Act of the Rome Conference included in its Annex I resolutions of more than recommendatory nature, establishing, for example, the ICC Preparatory Commission. UN Doc A/CONF.183/13, vol 1, Resolution F.

[86] Shabtai Rosenne wrote at length about the origin of the modern forms of Final Acts ('as a deliberately non-binding instrument') going back to the Hague Peace Conference of 1899. Rosenne (n 14) 107.

[87] For a more detailed discussion of treaty interpretation, see Chapter 19, Part II.A.2, 482 *et seq.*

then, as discussed below, only when the treaty has entered into force). There are various distinct procedures for the expression of such consent:

(a) signature (as a form of expression of the consent to be bound by the treaty);
(b) exchange of instruments constituting a treaty;
(c) ratification;
(d) acceptance/approval;
(e) formal confirmation; or
(f) accession.[88]

As with other aspects of treaty formation, to perform any of these acts, the representative must normally have sufficient authority (whether as a matter of the office held or full powers) to express the State's consent to be bound to a treaty.

A. Agreements in simplified form: signature as a form of expression of the consent to be bound by the treaty

Article 12(1)(a) of the 1969 and 1986 VCLT states that consent to be bound by a treaty can be expressed by signature when the treaty provides that signature shall have this effect. This is known as a *definitive* signature. Treaties containing such a provision are generally referred to as 'simplified agreements' or agreements in simplified form (*Accords en forme simplifiée*). The main reason for this simplified procedure is to have the treaty operative as soon as possible in lieu of the cumbersome and lengthy process of ratification.[89] Beside this procedural difference, there is not any substantial difference between simplified agreements and other treaties. Suffice it to say that some very important international treaties were in simplified form.[90] Today, the practice of simplified agreements is widespread and represents a large proportion of international agreements.

In addition to recognizing the consent to be bound by signature where the treaty so provides, the Vienna Conventions provide that signature may constitute consent where it is otherwise established that the negotiating States agreed on that effect for signature (Article 12(1)(b)), or that intention appears from the full powers, or was expressed during the negotiation (Article 12(1)(c)). In practice, however, these circumstances rarely, if ever, arise; indeed, it seems difficult to contemplate these conditions occurring in the absence of specific provisions of the treaty to such

[88] This is not an exclusive list. VCLT Art 11 authorizes these methods 'or by any other means if so agreed'. As Aust notes, the 'other means' language has given treaty-makers room to utilize a variety of alternative procedures. Aust (n 48) 113.

[89] In American practice, simplified agreements are often called 'executive agreements' and are concluded under the authority of the President without a role for the Senate; consent to be bound usually occurs via signature or an exchange of instruments. See R Dalton, 'United States' in DB Hollis and others (eds), *National Treaty Law and Practice* (Martinus Nijhoff, Leiden 2005) 780–3.

[90] Eg the 1938 Munich Agreement which is silent on the date of its entry into force and is presumed to have entered into force upon signature. Munich Pact (signed and entered into force 29 September 1938) 204 LNTS 378.

effect.[91] In the absence of any clause, the assumption is that signature also expresses the consent to be bound by the treaty and consequently triggers its entry into force.

B. Exchange of instruments

For many bilateral treaties, consent to be bound comes through an exchange of diplomatic notes or letters. Usually, one side proposes the terms of an agreement to the other side, accompanied by notice that a positive reply will constitute consent to an international agreement. The reply note (or letter) will usually reproduce *verbatim* the substantive language of the first note and then indicate the replying State's agreement to those terms. Thus, the reply note functions to signal the replying State's consent to be bound, the proposing State's consent having come in the initial offer to make a treaty. The treaty's terms will often indicate that completion of this exchange also serves to bring the treaty into force. In some cases, however, the treaty may condition entry into force on a further exchange (usually involving notifications of each side's completion of any necessary domestic procedures). An exchange of instruments may, on occasion, involve more than two parties, although as Aust notes, doing so may generate technical difficulties.[92]

C. Ratification

Ratification is among the most time-honoured means for a State to consent to be bound by a treaty; it is 'definitive confirmation of a willingness to be bound'.[93] It is a method, however, usually available only to those States that have signed a treaty. Basically, ratification involves a two-faceted process: (a) the introduction of the treaty into the internal legal order of the State through the completion of an 'instrument of ratification'; and (b) the notification of this act of ratification at the international level through an exchange of such instruments or providing them to a depositary.

Ratification thus has both an internal and an international component. The modalities of the internal process leading to the establishment of an instrument of ratification can vary depending on the State's internal legislation (including its constitution). It may involve approval by legislative bodies, the Executive, or both. In some States, ratification of certain treaties may also require approval of the people.[94] The historic development of ratification and its modern iteration reflect

---

[91] Nor does the ILC's commentary illuminate the meaning of these cases. See [1966] YBILC, vol II, 196. With regard to Art 12(1)(b), the ILC simply noted that 'it is simply a question of demonstrating the intention from the evidence'. But which evidence? Certainly the treaty itself provides the most decisive evidence. Article 12(1)(c) might be more conceivable; however, it would take place only if Art 12(1)(a) also allows it—that is to say, that the treaty provides for this effect of the signature.

[92] Aust (n 48) 103 (citing double exchange of letters involving Bahrain, Saudi Arabia, and Qatar).

[93] [1982] YBILC, vol II, 19.

[94] For instance, Art 140 of the Federal Constitution of the Swiss Confederation (18 April 1999) provides for a mandatory referendum in the case of 'accession to organizations for collective security or to supranational communities' and Art 141 provides for an optional referendum concerning particularly significant treaties.

its utility 'in the majority of cases as the means of submitting the treaty-making power of the executive to parliamentary control'.[95] Thus, in most contemporary democracies, involvement of legislative or parliamentary bodies in the decision to ratify is usually required.[96]

Once the internal processes necessary for a State to establish an instrument of ratification are complete, ratification requires an international act; either the formal deposit of the instrument of ratification with the depositary, or in the case of bilateral treaties an exchange of the instruments of ratification between the two sides. To satisfy the international process of ratification, an instrument of ratification must usually state solemnly that the State has ratified the treaty; it may also contain any reservations, understandings, or declarations the State wishes to make with respect to the treaty. An instrument of ratification should be precise and state in full the title of the ratified treaty, contain an unambiguous expression of the will to be bound of the government acting on behalf of the State, and undertake to implement its provisions. It has to be signed by the Head of State, the Head of Government or the Minister for Foreign Affairs or, as the case may be, by another organ which has received the full powers. Usually, however, instruments of ratification are signed by the Head of State or the Minister for Foreign Affairs.

In the case of an exchange of instruments of ratification, each party transmits to the other its own instrument duly signed.[97] The transmission may take place through diplomatic channels. Or, it may occur in a solemn meeting between the representatives of each party, which may include signature of an additional document—a certificate of exchange or *procès-verbal*.[98] Deposits are made in the capital of the depositary State or the headquarters of an IO serving in that role.

Where a treaty is deposited with the UN, in contrast, a *procès-verbal* no longer accompanies the deposit of the instrument of ratification. The Secretary-General, in his capacity as depository, announces immediately (usually the next day) the deposit in the *Official Journal* of the UN and subsequently issues a depositary notification (addressed to all States).[99] Consent itself takes effect from the date of exchange or deposit, but is 'activated' when the treaty enters into force.

According to the VCLT, ratification is an available option when the treaty expressly so provides or the representative signs the treaty subject to ratification.[100]

---

[95] [1966] YBILC, vol II, 197.

[96] Hollis (n 18) 33.

[97] Earlier practice allowing for notification of the instrument of ratification to other contracting parties is 'hardly, if ever, done now.' Aust (n 48) 106.

[98] VCLT Art 13 refers to this method.

[99] Because in most cases they potentially may become parties to the multilateral treaty. But in cases of closed or restricted treaties, the notification is addressed only to those having the capacity to become parties.

[100] VCLT Art 14. An exceptional procedure was included in Art 36(5) of the International Agreement on Olive Oil, 1956, as amended by the Protocol of 3 April 1958, providing that for purposes of entry into force a simple undertaking by a government to endeavour to obtain as speedily as possible in accordance with its constitutional procedure, either ratification or accession would be considered equivalent to ratification or accession. Such an undertaking was to emanate from one of the government authorities competent to sign an instrument of ratification or accession. See Summary of Practice (n 60) 39.

Like definitive signature, moreover, the VCLT also contemplates ratification where it can be an inferred option if it can be otherwise established that the negotiating States so agreed, or that intention is evidenced in the full powers or was expressed during the negotiations. If, however, a treaty is silent on the question of ratification, there is a presumption that ratification is not required.[101]

What purpose does ratification serve? As McNair explained, 'the interval between the signature and the ratification of a treaty gives the appropriate departments of Government that have negotiated the treaty an opportunity of studying the advantages and disadvantages involved in the proposed treaty as a whole'.[102] It affords to governments a time of reflection and the space to obtain any parliamentary or other approvals. This does not mean that the negotiation may be reopened (although this should not be excluded in bilateral treaties). But logically this 'reflection' leads to the possibility of formulating reservations or declarations at the time of the deposit of the instrument of ratification. Moreover, States can use the interval to enact any necessary domestic legislation.

Generally, it should be stressed that there is not any general obligation to ratify an already signed treaty or to apply its provisions.[103] At one time, the Permanent Court of International Justice suggested there might be, in exceptional cases, an abuse of right in case of a refusal to ratify.[104] But there has been no subsequent practice or jurisprudence to that effect.

D. Acceptance or approval

The terms 'acceptance' or 'approval', although they may not be quite identical, are usually used alternatively to designate a form of expression of consent to be bound by a State which does not want to use the 'ratification' process. Usually this occurs due to a desire to avoid the internal, domestic legal processes required for ratification. One case where the acceptance of a treaty (instead of its ratification) was politically expedient occurred in 1934 when the US Congress authorized the US President to accept, for the US Government, membership in the International Labour Organization (ILO); at the time, ratification was excluded since the ILO Constitution formed part of the Treaty of Versailles, to which the US Senate had declined to give its advice and consent to ratification.[105]

At the international level, acceptance and approval are usually treated as equivalent either to ratification or accession.[106] Some treaties adopted within the UN system, however, mention only the term 'acceptance' in the context of discussing

---

[101] Aust (n 48) 104.

[102] A McNair, *Law of Treaties* (Clarendon Press, Oxford 1961) 133–4.

[103] *North Sea Continental Shelf* (Advisory Opinion) [1969] ICJ Rep 25.

[104] *Case of the German Interests in Polish Upper Silesia (Germany v Poland)* PCIJ Rep Series A No 7, 30.

[105] S Bastid (n 6) 69.

[106] Ibid. As Bastid notes, the use of the word 'acceptance' intends to avoid, as in the United States, the obligation to submit the treaty to the Senate.

consent to be bound, without referring to ratification or even accession.[107] In that context, 'acceptance' is used as a generic term that may be fulfilled by any form of expression of consent to be bound (ie ratification or accession). As the ILC has confirmed: 'on the international plane "acceptance" is an innovation which is more one of terminology than of method'.[108]

E. Act of formal confirmation

Signature, ratification, acceptance, and approval were all methods of consent designed with the State in mind. For IOs, however, the 1986 VCLT mentions an act of formal confirmation as the technical mechanism amounting to the confirmation of the will to be bound. As the ILC's commentary noted:

> in the absence of an accepted term, the Commission has confined itself to describing this mechanism [of consent] by the words 'act of formal confirmation'...When necessary, international organizations, using a different terminology, can thus establish on an international plane their consent to be bound by a treaty by means of a procedure which is symmetrical with that which applies to States.[109]

At present, however, there is no generally accepted international designation of such a mechanism. In practice, the process followed for depositing an act of formal confirmation is the same as for an IO's signature of a treaty, namely, prior authorization by the deliberative body of the IO concerned (General Assembly, Executive Council, etc).[110] The UN, the World Health Organization, and the International Maritime Organization, among others, have all deposited just such an instrument to indicate their consent to the 1986 VCLT.

F. Accession

States which have not participated in the negotiation and signature of the treaty may become parties subsequently through accession. At the internal level, the procedure remains the same (it is that of ratification, albeit by another name). At the international level, an instrument of accession differs from one of ratification because the State concerned did not previously *sign* the treaty. As noted above, treaties usually provide for a certain period during which they can be signed; thereafter they are open only to accession. But even in cases when treaties are permanently open for signature such as the ICCPR, an instrument of accession may

---

[107] This has occurred especially in the case of amendments to treaties—eg Amendments to the Agreement Establishing the African Development Bank (adopted 17 May 1979, entered into force 7 May 1982) 1276 UNTS 501—or treaties constituent of IOs—eg Convention on the International Maritime Organization, as amended (adopted 6 March 1948, entered into force 17 March 1958) 289 UNTS 3. Sometimes, the terms ratification or acceptance are used in an interchangeable manner, such as in the Constitution of the Asia-Pacific Telecommunity (adopted 27 March 1976, entered into force 25 February 1979) 1129 UNTS 3, Art 17.

[108] [1966] YBILC, vol II, 198.

[109] [1982] YBILC, vol II(2), 19 [9].

[110] Ibid.

still constitute a method of consenting to a treaty without signing it. In a few cases, such as the 1928 General Act for the Pacific Settlement of Disputes or the Convention on the Privileges and Immunities of the UN, treaties may only authorize consent by accession.[111]

There is, however, no guaranteed right for States to consent by accession; accession is only available where the treaty so provides or the parties agree to a State's accession. Thus, accession may be restricted to specific categories of States or subject to specified conditions (eg requiring an acceding State to be party to another treaty).[112] Practically speaking, most multilateral treaties include an accession clause. The opinion that accession is possible only after the entry into force of the treaty, moreover, is no longer valid.[113] Finally, the international procedures for depositing instruments of accession follow those for instruments of ratification.

For each of the methods of expressing consent to be bound discussed above, Section VI(6) of this Volume contains a set of sample clauses illustrating the precise form and terminology used.

IV. Entry into Force of a Treaty

A State, IO, or other treaty-making entity is not necessarily legally bound to a treaty by its consent; the treaty must also have entered into force for it. Where a State consents *and* the treaty is in force for that State, it is considered a 'party' to the treaty. Moreover, the fact that a treaty is in force for some States does not mean that it is in force for all States in general; only those States that have expressed their consent are so bound.

According to Article 24 of the VCLT, a treaty enters into force 'in such manner and upon such date as it may provide or as the negotiating States may agree'.[114] As a general rule, bilateral treaties enter into force upon the completion of the formalities required for their ratification and the exchange of diplomatic notes or notifications informing the other party about such a completion. In the case of simplified agreements, bilateral treaties may enter into force on signature, the date of the last signature if not done simultaneously, or—in case of an exchange of notes—on the replying States' affirmative acceptance of the proposed treaty. Sometimes the procedure of a *procès-verbal* of entry into force is followed. Usually, bilateral treaties stipulate that they enter into force on the date (or after a certain period of time following this date) of receipt of the last of any notifications. In case of silence, there

---

[111] General Act (n 29) Art 43; Convention on the Privileges and Immunities of the United Nations (n 61).

[112] See the International Convention to Facilitate the Importation of Commercial Samples and Advertising Material (adopted 7 November 1952, entered into force 20 November 1955) 221 UNTS 225, Art X, whereby the Convention is open to accession (as well as for signature) by the GATT contracting parties.

[113] [1966] YBILC, vol II, 199. Usually treaties provide in their final clauses the details of the entry into force for each State depositing an instrument of accession.

[114] If the treaty is silent on entry into force—a rarity in the modern era—it may be presumed that it will enter into force when all the negotiating States have consented to be bound (or upon its signature).

is a presumption that the entry into force takes place on the date of exchange of the notifications.[115]

In the case of a multilateral treaty, the conditions for entry into force are stated in the treaty itself, usually in its final clauses. As indicated in Article 24(4) of the VCLT, those provisions, whether regulating the number of ratifications or accessions needed for its entry into force or the date of such entry into force, *apply from the time of the adoption of its text.*[116] The treaty may provide that it shall enter into force on a specific date or on the date when certain conditions are met.[117] The determination of such conditions is relatively simple in the case of bilateral treaties, but may be more complicated when multilateral treaties are involved. Usually, in such a case, the date and the fulfilment of the conditions of entry into force are determined by the depositary.

There are many variations with regard to the conditions for entry into force of a treaty. The treaty may require ratification, acceptance, or accession by a minimum number of negotiating States (eg two) or any number all the way up to unanimity by all signatories.[118] UNCLOS required sixty ratifications, while the VCLT itself required thirty-five.[119] Other treaties may add additional conditions, stipulating, for example, that a number of parties should belong to a particular geographic area or region or that certain percentages are reached or exceeded.[120] Or, treaties may link entry into force to consent by specific States—the 1996 Comprehensive Test

---

[115] *Arbitral Award made by the King of Spain on 23 December 1906 (Honduras v Nicaragua)* [1960] ICJ Rep 208.

[116] VLCT Art 24(4).

[117] For example, the Agreement providing for the Provisional Application of the Draft International Customs Conventions on Touring, on Commercial Road Vehicles and on the International Transport of Goods by Road (adopted 16 June 1949) 45 UNTS 149, stipulated in its Art III that it was to enter into force on 1 January 1950. In the absence of other provisions, this Agreement entered into force on that date for those States that, at that date, had accepted to be bound by the Agreement. However, such a clause is unusual in multilateral treaties.

[118] The 1949 Geneva Conventions came into force with two ratifications, while the Treaty of Rome required unanimity. Eg Geneva Convention Relative to the Treatment of Prisoners of War (adopted 12 August 1949, entered into force 21 October 1950) 75 UNTS 135, Art 138 ('The present Convention shall come into force six months after not less than two instruments of ratification have been deposited'); Treaty Establishing the European Economic Community (Treaty of Rome) (adopted 25 March 1957, entered into 1 January 1958) 298 UNTS 3, Art 247 ('The Treaty shall enter into force on the first day of the month following the deposit of the instrument of ratification by the last signatory State to comply with this formality').

[119] UNCLOS (n 67) Art 316(1) ('Amendments to this Convention . . . shall enter into force for the States Parties . . . on the thirtieth day following the deposit of instruments of ratification or accession by two thirds of the States Parties or by 60 States Parties, whichever is greater'); VCLT Art 84(1) ('The present Convention shall enter into force on the thirtieth day following the date of deposit of the thirty-fifth instrument of ratification or accession').

[120] Protocol of 28 September 1984 to the 1979 Convention on Long Range Transboundary Air Pollution on Long Term Financing of the Cooperative Programme for Monitoring and Forwarding of the Long Range Transmission of Air Pollutants in Europe (EMEP) (adopted 28 September 1984, entered into force 28 January 1988) 1491 UNTS 167, Art 10 ('The present Protocol shall enter into force on the ninetieth day following the date on which: a) Instruments of ratification, acceptance, approval or accession have been deposited by at least nineteen States and Organizations referred to in article 8(1) which are within the geographical scope of EMEP'). A second condition was provided for by subpara (b) of Art 10(1): 'The aggregate of the United Nations assessment rates for such States and organizations exceeds forty per cent.' Ibid.

Ban Treaty requires consent by forty-four named States.[121] Commodities agreements such as the 2001 International Cocoa Agreement may stipulate even more complex conditions for entry into force relating, for example, to ratification by certain governments representing a number of exporting and importing members and holding various percentages of votes.[122] In some cases, especially agreements that are constituent treaties of IOs, a supplementary condition may be an additional agreement (after the required number of ratifications has been reached) of the contracting parties.[123] Examples of entry into force clauses may be found in Section VI(11) of this Volume.

Despite substantial variation in entry into force clauses, the issue of reservations tends to constitute a general complication to their application. What is the fate of an expression of consent to be bound accompanied by reservations? In 1951, at the request of the General Assembly, the ICJ issued an advisory opinion on this question. It indicated that a:

State which has made and maintained a reservation which has been objected to by one or more of the parties to the Convention but not by others, *can be regarded as being a party to the Convention* if the reservation is compatible with the object and purpose of the Convention, otherwise that State cannot be regarded as being a party to the Convention.[124]

The opinion, however, did not address what happens if one contracting party considers the reservation of another contrary to the object and purpose of the treaty. Should the reserving State not be counted for the determination of the date of entry into force? Technically, that seems the correct result, but only if the objecting State is correct in its belief that the reservation is inadmissible. Divergent views on the admissibility of reservations thus create the possibility for much confusion on questions of entry into force.

Since 1952, the practice of the UN Secretary-General has been to avoid such confusion by accepting the deposit of all instruments containing reservations or objections.[125] Consequently, the Secretary-General simply counts these instruments to determine whether the required number of ratifications for the entry into force of the treaty has been attained.[126]

The ILC has also opted for a more 'nuanced' orientation in its *Guide to Practice* finalized in 2011; Guideline 4.2.2 provides that, when 'a treaty *has not* yet entered into force, the author of a reservation shall be included in the number of contracting States and contracting organizations required for the treaty to enter into force

---

[121] CTBT (n 50) Art XIV.

[122] International Cocoa Agreement (adopted 2 March 2001, entered into force 2 November 2005) 2229 UNTS 2.

[123] See Constitution of the United Nations Industrial Development Organization (adopted 8 April 1979, entered into force 21 June 1985) 1401 UNTS 3, Art 25.

[124] *Reservations to the Convention on the Prevention and Punishment of the Crime of Genocide* (Advisory Opinion) [1951] ICJ Rep 15, 18 (emphasis added).

[125] This practice is also followed by several others depositaries such as the IMO, UNESCO, etc.

[126] It was the General Assembly, in Resolution 598 (VI) (12 January 1952), which advised the Secretary-General as depositary of multilateral treaties, to follow this practice.

once the reservation is established'.[127] But, concomitantly even the author of an invalid reservation is considered to be a party to the treaty 'without the benefit of the reservation', 'unless [it] has expressed a contrary intention or such an intention is otherwise established'.[128] This position differs from the 1951 Advisory opinion, which had seemed to leave the admissibility of reservations to the subjective views of the contracting States; the *Guide to Practice* seems to opt for a more objective system where the incompatibility of the reservation with the object and purpose of the treaty may exist as such irrespective of the 'subjective' views of States parties. On the other hand, the *Guide* does allow for counting a reserving State within the number of contracting States if no contracting State is opposed to it in a particular case.[129]

Beyond such theoretical debates, in practice, most final clauses use wording to the effect that the treaty will enter into force [X] days following the deposit of the (Xth) instrument of ratification. It could be argued that this formulation further reflects a formalistic approach, stressing the act of depositing an instrument rather than the effectiveness of the ratification itself. Indeed, this approach is also an indication of a 'limitation' in the system of entry into force of treaties, which seems to repose on a tacit 'fictional' belief that all instruments are prima facie valid; otherwise this system would crash like a house of cards.

Assuming a depositary will count all deposited instruments, there are still other potential complications that may arise in determining when the treaty enters into force. A depositary may not recognize an instrument of ratification for purposes of entry into force for a variety of reasons such as where the contracting State has disappeared. It is also possible, according to State practice, for a State to withdraw its instrument of ratification *before* the treaty enters into force.[130] These sorts of adjustments may be decisive for the calculation of the number of instruments required for the treaty's entry into force.

In terms of timing, the calculation of the effective date of initial entry into force is based on the provision of the relevant final clauses of the treaty. If the treaty provides for entry into force 'on the thirtieth day following [or after] the deposit of the [Xth] instrument of ratification', the practice of the UN Secretary-General is to have the time run from the day *following* the deposit of the last required instrument. Thus, in the above example, if the deposit of the last instrument is affected on

---

[127] ILC, 'Guide to Practice on Reservations to Treaties' 63rd session (2011) UN Doc A/66/10, forthcoming in [2011] YBILC, vol II(2) ('Guide to Practice') (emphasis added). For the meaning of the term 'established reservation', see Guideline 4.1 which states that 'a reservation formulated by a State or an IO is established with regard to a contracting State or a contracting organization if it is permissible and was formulated in accordance with the required form and procedures, and if that contracting State or contracting organization has accepted it'.

[128] Ibid, Guideline 4.5.3.

[129] Ibid, Guideline 4.2.2 [2].

[130] An interesting question would be if such a withdrawal is possible if the treaty itself does not provide for withdrawal. It is here submitted that, even in such a case, the inferred withdrawal before the entry into force should be allowed because the treaty itself is not yet applicable and, secondly, this would constitute a convenient solution in case such a drastic measure is required—usually for serious reasons—without jeopardizing any legal principles or legal security.

15 March, the period of thirty days will begin on 16 March, and the Convention will enter into force on 14 April. In contrast, for entry into force 'three months after the deposit', the time runs from the day of the deposit of the last required instrument. Thus, in this last example, if the deposit was affected on 31 March, since there is no corresponding 31 June, the Convention would then enter into force on the last day of June, ie 30 June. Similarly, upon the relevant deposit on 30 November the Convention would enter into force on 28 February (or on 29 February for leap years). But whenever there is a 'same' day [X] months later, that day is the day of entry into force.[131] Nowadays there is no *procès-verbal* for entry into force unless the treaty so requires.[132]

Finally, it is possible for the treaty to stipulate provisional application or even a provisional entry into force.[133] For example, the General Agreement on Tariffs and Trade (GATT) included a Protocol of Provisional Application, which provided for provisional application on and after 1 January 1948 ('provided this Protocol shall have been signed on behalf of all the foregoing Governments not later than 15 November 1947, to apply provisionally on and after 1 January 1948').[134] Usually a date of provisional application or provisional entry into force is stipulated in the treaty itself. The Agreement on Implementation of Part XI of the UNCLOS, however, incorporated implicit consent to the provisional application of that Agreement, merely upon the adoption of the Agreement or its signature.[135]

Conclusion

This chapter has attempted to summarize in a comprehensive and not too cumbersome manner the very complex question of treaty-making. From an overview of the treaty-law rules as well as practice, three major points seem to emerge.

First, treaty-making is a manifestation of the sovereignty and free will of States and other subjects of international law. Entities such as States participate willingly and freely in this exercise and, consequently, there is a presumption that States can sacrifice a portion of sovereignty that the participation in the treaty implies to the extent that they undertake obligations (as also they may acquire rights) in an eminently (although not perfectly) symmetrical exercise.

Second, treaty-making is characterized by a combination of formality and flexibility. The formalism of some rules (full powers, expressions of consent to be bound) is complemented by the flexibility of others (required majorities for the adoption of texts). In many ways, everything is dependent on the will of the parties; even the strictest rules may be set aside if the parties so *wish*. Ultimately, however,

---

[131] See Summary of Practice (n 60) 70.

[132] For an earlier example, see Agreement for Facilitating the International Circulation of Visual and Auditory Materials of an Educational, Scientific and Cultural Character (adopted 15 July 1949, entered into force 12 August 1954) 197 UNTS 3.

[133] For a discussion of the provisional application of treaties, see Chapter 9.

[134] Protocol of Provisional Application (30 October 1947) 55 UNTS 308.

[135] (28 July 1994) 1836 UNTS 3, Art 7. See also Summary of Practice (n 60) 71.

there are limits to such flexibility since extreme informality might defeat the security towards which all treaty relations aspire.

Third and finally, treaty-making is and will continue to be an important aspect of international law and international relations. As long as States, IOs, and other entities are willing to enter into *contractual* relations and mutual undertakings, treaty-making will remain an essential factor in the establishment of such relations and an indispensable mechanism.

What does the future hold? If in the field of bilateral treaties the techniques have not much changed, the same does not seem to be exactly true in the case of multilateral treaties. The era of great codification conferences now appears finished, although some resurgence might not be excluded in the future. IOs now provide more and more frequently for multilateral treaty-making. We might expect future treaty-making to take place in even smaller and less institutionalized settings (eg, the G20, various diplomatic 'summits'). Treaties themselves may take a more 'inchoate', hybrid form (under titles such as declarations, findings, principles, etc), creating thus a sort of legal limbo, a cross between treaties and instruments whose binding force is not clear. Technological development (especially the use of the Internet) may affect the rules of treaty-making as well. None of this should detract, however, from the fundamental premise: the combined will of States or other entities can make treaties. It will be for the lawyer and historian of the future to shed light on any new practices and emerging patterns, to clarify them and, if necessary, to revise and restate the codified rules.

Recommended Reading

A Aust, *Modern Treaty Law and Practice* (2nd edn CUP, Cambridge 2007)

S Bastid, *Les Traités dans la vie internationale: Conclusion et Effets* (Economica, Paris 1985)

C Brölmann, *The Institutional Veil in Public International Law: International Organisations and the Law of Treaties* (Hart Publishing, Oxford 2007)

O Corten and P Klein, *Les conventions de Vienne sur le droit des traités: commentaires article par article* (Bruylant, Brussels 2006)

O Corten and P Klein, *The Vienna Conventions on the Law of Treaties: A Commentary* (OUP, New York 2011)

M Craven, *The Decolonization of International Law: State Succession and the Law of Treaties* (OUP, Oxford 2007)

Y Dinstein, 'The Interaction between Customary International Law and Treaties' (2006) 322 RcD 243

M Fitzmaurice and O Elias, *Contemporary Issues in the Law of Treaties* (Eleven International Publishers, Utrecht 2005)

RK Gardiner, *Treaty Interpretation* (OUP, Oxford 2008)

DB Hollis, MR Blakeslee, and LB Ederington (eds), *National Treaty Law and Practice* (Martinus Nijhoff, Leiden 2005)

M Lang, J Schuch, and C Staringer (eds), *Tax Treaty Law and EC Law* (Kluwer Law International, Alphen aan den Rijn 2007)

U Linderfalk, *On the Interpretation of Treaties: The Modern International Law as Expressed in the 1969 Vienna Convention on the Law of Treaties* (Springer, Dordrecht 2007)

VD Pastuhov, *A Guide to the Practice of International Conferences* (Carnegie Endowment for International Peace, Washington 1945)

N Quoc Dinh, P Daillier, and A Pellet, *Droit international public* (6th edn LGDJ, Paris 1999)

I Roberts (ed), *Satow's Diplomatic Practice* (6th edn OUP, Oxford 2009)

S Rosenne, *Developments in the Law of Treaties 1945–1986* (CUP, Cambridge 1989)

J Siotis, *Essai sur le Secrétariat international* (Droz, Geneva 1963)

UN Legislative Series, *Review of the Multilateral Treaty-Making Process*, ST/LEG/SGR.13/21

ME Villiger, *Commentary on the 1969 Vienna Convention on the Law of Treaties* (Martinus Nijhoff, Leiden 2009)

R Wolfrum and R Volker (eds), *Developments of International Law in Treaty Making* (Springer, Berlin 2005)

8

Treaty Signature

Curtis A Bradley

Introduction

To become a party to a treaty, a State must express its consent to be bound by the treaty. Such consent can be expressed in a variety of ways, including through signature of the treaty by a proper representative of the State.[1] Under modern treaty practice, however, States often express their consent to be bound by a separate act of ratification that is carried out after signature. For bilateral treaties, this ratification is typically manifested by the exchange of instruments of ratification. For multilateral treaties, it is typically manifested by the deposit of an instrument of ratification or accession with a central depository, such as the UN. When a treaty is subject to discretionary ratification after signature, the signature is referred to as a 'simple signature', whereas a signature that indicates consent to be bound is referred to as a 'definitive signature'.[2]

A simple signature does not commit a State to ratify a treaty, let alone comply with its terms. In the popular press, parties to a treaty are often referred to as 'signatories', but this reference confusingly blurs the distinction between definitive and simple signature. Although a simple signature does not make a State a party to a treaty, it can create benefits and obligations for the signatory State. This chapter considers those benefits and obligations and examines in particular why States often prefer simple signature subject to ratification in lieu of other methods of joining a treaty, the legal consequences of a simple signature, and the process by which a State can terminate its signatory obligations.

I. Why Do States Utilize Simple Signature?

When the Western world was composed primarily of monarchies rather than representative democracies, signature was more commonly viewed as consent to

---

[1] International organizations can also consent to treaties in a variety of ways, including through signature. VCLT Arts 11–17; for more details see Chapter 7, Part III.E, 200.

[2] UN Office of Legal Affairs, *Treaty Handbook* (2006) Sales No E.02.V.2 <http://treaties.un.org/pages/Publications.aspx?pathpub=Publication/TH/Page1_en.xml> 2–3. For a detailed discussion of the methods for expressing consent to be bound and for bringing a treaty into force, see Chapter 7, Parts III and IV, 195 *et seq*.

be bound, since monarchs (and thus their agents, or 'plenipotentiaries') had the authority to unilaterally bind their States to treaties.[3] The central legal issue under that regime was one of agency—that is, whether the monarch's purported representative actually had the authority to make the commitment. The conferral of 'full powers' on an agent would define the scope of the agent's authority to bind the State in treaty negotiations. 'Ratification', under that regime, was a confirmation by the monarch that the agent had acted with authority.

This treaty practice became more complicated after the American and French revolutions of the late eighteenth century. Both the United States and post-revolutionary France included a clause in the full powers of their agents reserving the right of the State to decide whether to ratify the treaty after signature.[4] The US repeatedly had to remind other countries during the nineteenth century that its signature did not constitute a promise of ratification.[5] Eventually, 'European governments ceased to protest against the American practice; and unratified treaties became a common feature of international relations'.[6] Similarly, in countries following the approach of the French Constitution, 'only the Legislative Power... could approve a treaty', and thus 'the plenipotentiary, receiving his powers from the Executive, could not bind the State with his signature'.[7]

This history suggests one of the primary reasons that modern States frequently prefer simple over definitive signature: it better accommodates domestic treaty-making requirements. Many countries today divide their treaty power between the executive and legislative departments, at least for certain types of agreements.[8] In these countries, the executive department will typically have the authority to engage in a simple signature on behalf of the State but may lack the authority to commit the State more fully to the treaty, whether through definitive signature or some other mechanism. In the US, for example, the President often is required to obtain either the consent of a supermajority of the Senate or the agreement of a majority of both houses of Congress before concluding a treaty.[9] In the UK, by contrast, the

---

[3] JS Camara, *The Ratification of International Treaties* (Ontario Publishing, Toronto 1949) 22–5; FO Wilcox, *The Ratification of International Conventions* (Allen & Unwin, London 1935) 21–2. Even in the eighteenth century, however, not all rulers had 'the power to make public treaties on their own authority; some are forced to take counsel of a senate or of the representative body of the Nation'. E de Vattel, *The Law of Nations or the Principles of Natural Law Applied to Conduct and to the Affairs of Nations and of Sovereigns* (CG Fenwick (trs), Carnegie Institute, Washington 1916) (1758) 160.

[4] SB Crandall, *Treaties: Their Making and Enforcement* (2nd edn John Byrne & Co, Washington 1916) 94.

[5] JM Jones, *Full Powers and Ratification* (CUP, Cambridge 1946) 76–7. See also JB Moore, *A Digest of International Law* (Government Printing Office, Washington 1906) vol 5, 189 (describing a treaty negotiation with Spain in 1819 in which Secretary of State John Quincy Adams explained to the Spanish minister that 'by the nature of our Constitution, the full powers of our ministers never are or can be unlimited').

[6] Jones (n 5) 77.

[7] Camara (n 3) 28–9.

[8] DB Hollis, 'A Comparative Approach to Treaty Law and Practice' in DB Hollis, MR Blakeslee, and LB Ederington (eds), *National Treaty Law and Practice* (Martinus Nijhoff, Leiden 2005) 25–6, 32–7 (*NTLP*).

[9] The US Constitution states that the president has the power to make treaties 'by and with the Advice and Consent of the Senate... provided two thirds of the Senators present concur'. US Const

executive has essentially plenary treaty-making authority, although the treaties that are concluded by the executive do not become part of the domestic law of the UK until they are implemented by the Parliament.[10] In some countries, such as France and Germany, parliamentary approval is not required as a general matter but is required for certain categories of treaties.[11] As a result, domestic law will in some instances prevent a country from expressing its consent to be bound to a treaty through signature. When this is the case, the executive will typically have the authority to sign the treaty but will be required to wait to ratify it until the completion of required domestic procedures.

Even when domestic law allows the executive to commit the State to a treaty without legislative approval, the executive may have other reasons for not wanting to utilize a definitive signature. For example, the executive may want time to consider more fully the implications of the treaty, to gauge domestic reactions to the treaty, or to obtain necessary implementing legislation before the treaty becomes binding. As a result, most modern multilateral treaties (and many bilateral ones) allow for ratification after signature as an available means for States to consent.[12] This does not mean, of course, that States no longer use definitive signature to consent to a treaty. Indeed, this method of expressing consent is still common, especially for bilateral treaties.[13]

Commentators have debated whether, when a treaty is silent about how consent to be bound is to be expressed, there is a presumption in favour of either definitive signature or ratification.[14] The 1969 Vienna Convention on the Law of Treaties (VCLT) does not take a position on this issue, instead simply referring to the intention of the States parties as expressed in negotiations and in the full powers of the representatives.[15] In any event, the issue has little practical significance today since most modern treaties specify how consent to be bound is to be expressed.[16]

Multilateral treaties are often open for signature for only a limited period of time.[17] Even after the period for signing has expired, however, a State may have the

---

Art II, §2. Despite this language, the US often concludes international agreements through a 'congressional-executive agreement' process that involves a majority of both houses of Congress rather than a supermajority of the Senate. In some instances, such as when settling international claims, presidents have the authority to conclude 'sole executive agreements' without any participation by Congress.

[10] I Sinclair and others, 'United Kingdom' in *NTLP* (n 8) 733–5.

[11] M Eisemann and R Rivier, 'France' in *NTLP* (n 8) 258–60; H Beemelmans and HD Treviranus, 'Federal Republic of Germany' in *NTLP* (n 8) 323–4.

[12] *Restatement (Third) of the Foreign Relations Law of the United States* §312, cmt d (American Law Institute, Philadelphia 1987) ('A state can be bound upon signature, but that has now become unusual as regards important formal agreements'); MA Rogoff, 'The International Legal Obligations of Signatories to an Unratified Treaty' (1980) 32 Maine L Rev 263, 266–7 ('While at one time signature played a more important role in the process whereby a state assumed treaty obligations, today the crucial event is ratification').

[13] A Aust, *Modern Treaty Law and Practice* (2nd edn CUP, Cambridge 2007) 96.

[14] I Sinclair, *The Vienna Convention on the Law of Treaties* (2nd edn MUP, Manchester 1984) 39–40.

[15] VCLT Arts 12(1)(c) and 14(1)(d).

[16] Aust (n 13) 96–7; Sinclair (n 14) 40.

[17] Aust (n 13) 98.

ability to join the treaty by submitting an instrument of accession with the treaty depository, if the treaty so permits.[18] Accession, like ratification, avoids the domestic legal issues that can be associated with definitive signature, since the executive department can wait to accede until after it has obtained legislative agreement.

Simple signature nevertheless carries potential benefits for States over accession. For States that have participated in treaty negotiations, a simple signature can be a useful means of marking the conclusion of those negotiations. A simple signature might also indicate to other States that 'the results of the negotiations are apparently approved by the executive department of government'.[19] Depending on the treaty, a simple signature can also confer certain entitlements, such as (i) the ability to participate in preparatory commissions or meetings of the treaty body,[20] (ii) the right to formulate objections to reservations,[21] and (iii) the right to participate in the correction of errors.[22]

II. Legal Obligations Triggered by Simple Signature

In the nineteenth century, some countries, such as the US, maintained that, when a treaty was ratified, it would operate retroactively to the time of signature, at least with respect to inter-state obligations, as opposed to private rights.[23] This view was abandoned in the twentieth century, and the modern presumption under international law is that treaties do not operate retroactively.[24] Article 28 of the VCLT now provides that '[u]nless a different intention appears from the treaty or is otherwise established, its provisions do not bind a party in relation to any act or

[18] *UN* Treaty Handbook (n 2) 2. For more information on accession as a method of consent to be bound, see Chapter 7, Part III.F, 200 *et seq.*

[19] Wilcox (n 3) 27.

[20] For example, under the Rome Statute of the International Criminal Court, signatories are entitled to observer status in the Assembly of States Parties. Rome Statute of the International Criminal Court (opened for signature 17 July 1998, entered into force 1 July 2002) 2176 UNTS 90, Art 112. In addition, signatories were entitled to participate in the Preparatory Commission for the Court. L Boisson de Chazournes, A La Rosa, and MM Mbengue, 'Article 18' in O Corten and P Klein (eds), *The Vienna Convention on the Law of Treaties: A Commentary* (OUP, Oxford 2011) vol 1, 369, 391–2.

[21] *Reservations to the Convention on the Prevention and Punishment of the Crime of Genocide* (Advisory Opinion) [1951] ICJ Rep 15, 28; see also Rogoff (n 12) 275 ('The *Reservations* case thus recognizes signature as conferring certain legal rights on a signatory').

[22] VCLT Art 79(1).

[23] Wilcox (n 3) 39–40; CC Hyde, *International Law Chiefly as Interpreted and Applied by the United States* (Little, Brown, Boston 1922) 49–50 ('It is laid down as a rule of the law of nations, that in the absence of special agreement, a treaty upon the exchange of ratifications operates retroactively, as from the date of signature'); *Haver v Yaker* (1869) 76 US 32, 34 ('[A]s respects the rights of either government under it, a treaty is considered as concluded and binding from the date of its signature... But a different rule prevails where the treaty operates on individual rights').

[24] Camara (n 3) 121–4; JM Jones, 'The Retroactive Effect of the Ratification of Treaties' (1935) 29 AJIL 51. However, as provided in Art 24(4) of the VCLT, '[t]he provisions of a treaty regulating the authentication of its text, the establishment of the consent of States to be bound by the treaty, the manner or date of its entry into force, reservations, the functions of the depositary and other matters arising necessarily before the entry into force of the treaty apply from the time of the adoption of its text'.

fact which took place or any situation which ceased to exist before the date of the entry into force of the treaty with respect to that party'.[25] Since this rule is only a presumption, however, it can be overridden by the parties to the treaty.[26]

There was also some debate in the nineteenth and early twentieth centuries over whether a State that had signed a treaty subject to ratification was obligated to proceed with the ratification. Surveying the literature on the topic, one commentator noted in the early twentieth century that '[a]n examination of the opinions of writers and authorities shows that upon the subject of ratification three fairly distinguishable views prevail: 1, that no obligation to ratify exists, ratification being purely a matter of discretion; 2, that a moral obligation exists; 3, that where the negotiator has remained within his instructions, a perfect or legal obligation exists'.[27] The modern view is that a simple signature does not carry with it any legal obligation of ratification.[28]

A simple signature may nevertheless trigger some legal obligations, stemming either from the VCLT or customary international law.[29] Article 18 of the VCLT provides that, after a State has signed a treaty, it 'is obliged to refrain from acts which would defeat the object and purpose' of the treaty 'until it shall have made its intention clear not to become a party to the treaty'.[30] It is not clear to what extent this provision reflects customary international law. Some commentators contend that, at least at the time it was included in the VCLT, it reflected progressive development rather than established State practice.[31] In any event, the VCLT has now been in force for many years and has been ratified by over 110 States, and even some countries that are not parties to it (such as the US) appear to accept that the obligation recited in Article 18 is now a matter of customary international law.[32]

---

[25] VCLT Art 28.

[26] Camara (n 3) 121.

[27] JE Harley, 'The Obligation to Ratify Treaties' (1919) 13 AJIL 389, 404.

[28] Aust (n 13) 106; AD McNair, *Law of Treaties* (Clarendon, Oxford 1961) 133–5. See also *Research in International Law*, 'Law of Treaties' (1935) 29 AJIL 657, 770 ('[M]odern writers are practically unanimous in holding that there is no *legal* obligation to ratify a treaty which has been signed on its behalf') ('Research in Internationl Law').

[29] Sometimes treaties will specify obligations that apply in the interim between signature and ratification. JS Charme, 'The Interim Obligation of Article 18 of the Vienna Convention on the Law of Treaties: Making Sense of an Enigma' (1991) 25 Geo Wash J Intl L and Econ 71, 78–9; Rogoff (n 12) 280–1.

[30] VCLT Art 18(a). Under Art 18(b), a State that has expressed its consent to be bound by a treaty is 'obliged to refrain from acts which would defeat the object and purpose . . . pending the entry into force of the treaty and provided that such entry into force is not unduly delayed'. For discussion of the meaning of 'undue delay' see ME Villiger, *Commentary on the 1969 Vienna Convention on the Law of Treaties* (Martinus Nijhoff, Leiden 2009) 252.

[31] S Rosenne, *Developments in the Law of Treaties, 1945–1986* (CUP, Cambridge 1989) 149 (noting that 'article 18 . . . is in many circles regarded as highly controversial, at least with regard to the question of whether it is declaratory of customary international law or innovative'); Sinclair (n 14) 43 (noting that Art 18 'in all probability constitutes at least a measure of progressive development').

[32] For statements by US officials suggesting at various times that Art 18 reflects customary international law, see CA Bradley, 'Unratified Treaties, Domestic Politics, and the U.S. Constitution' (2007) 48 HILJ 307, 315 n36.

That is also the view of a number of commentators.[33] To the extent that Article 18 does reflect customary international law, the signing obligation would apply even to States that have not ratified the VCLT.

The VCLT does not define the circumstances under which actions by a State will 'defeat the object and purpose' of a treaty. The phrase 'object and purpose' appears in a number of places in the VCLT, but each time the context has potentially different connotations.[34] For example, under Article 19, States are precluded from attaching a reservation to their ratification of a treaty if the reservation is 'incompatible with the object and purpose of the treaty'.[35] The word 'incompatible' in that limitation may not signify the same limitation as the word 'defeat' in Article 18.

There is almost no State practice that would help clarify the content of the signing obligation.[36] There is also relatively little judicial precedent, and most of what there is long predates the VCLT. In its commentary on the draft article that became Article 18, the International Law Commission (ILC) cited a 1926 decision by the Permanent Court of International Justice (PCIJ), *Case Concerning Certain German Interests in Polish Upper Silesia*.[37] In that case, Poland challenged the right of Germany to alienate property located in territory that Germany was ceding to Poland in the Treaty of Versailles between the time of Germany's signing of the treaty and the treaty's entry into force. The court concluded that Germany's action would not have violated the treaty even after ratification, and the court therefore observed that it 'need not consider the question whether, and if so how far, the signatories of a treaty are under an obligation to abstain from any action likely to interfere with its execution when ratification has taken place'.[38] As a result, the court did not actually address the existence or scope of an interim signing obligation.

Another decision that is often cited in support of the Article 18 signing obligation is a 1928 decision by an arbitral tribunal, *Megalidis v Turkey*.[39] In that case, the tribunal held invalid a Turkish seizure of a Greek national's property that had occurred between the time that Turkey had signed a peace treaty with Greece and the time when the treaty entered into force. The tribunal reasoned that 'from the time of the signature of the Treaty and before its entry into force the contracting parties were under the duty to do nothing which might impair the operation of its

---

[33] Boisson de Chazournes and others (n 20) 382–3; P Palchetti, 'Article 18 of the 1969 Vienna Convention: A Vague and Ineffective Obligation or a Useful Means of Strengthening Legal Cooperation?' in E Cannizzaro (ed), *The Law of Treaties Beyond the Vienna Convention* (OUP, Oxford 2011) 25, 26; Villiger (n 30) 252.

[34] DS Jonas and TN Saunders, 'The Object and Purpose of a Treaty: Three Interpretive Methods' (2010) 43 Vanderbilt J Transnat'l L 565.

[35] VCLT Art 19(c). On reservations and the object-and-purpose test for their permissibility, see Chapter 11, Part III, 285 *et seq*.

[36] Aust (n 13) 94; ET Swaine, 'Unsigning' (2003) 55 Stanford L Rev 2061, 2078.

[37] *Draft Articles on the Law of Treaties with Commentaries* [1966] YBILC, vol II, 169, 202; see also *Certain German Interests in Polish Upper Silesia* (*Germany v Poland*) [1926] PCIJ Rep Series A No 7.

[38] *Upper Silesia Case* (n 37) 40.

[39] *Megalidis v Turkey* (Turkish-Greek Mixed Arb Trib 1928) 4 Ann Dig Pub Intl L 395.

clauses'.[40] Although this decision is more directly supportive of a signing obligation than the *Upper Silesia* decision, it involved the behaviour of a State that had become a party to the treaty by the time of the decision and thus does not necessarily speak to the obligations of a signatory that has not ratified a treaty.[41]

The intellectual history of the Article 18 signing obligation can be traced to a 1935 Harvard research project that attempted to codify international law, the treaty portions of which were an early precursor to the VCLT. The Harvard project stated that a signatory State was 'under no duty to perform the obligations stipulated' in the treaty until the State ratified the treaty, but that 'under some circumstances' the State would be obligated as a matter of 'good faith' to 'refrain from taking action which would render performance by any party of the obligations stipulated impossible or more difficult'.[42] Subsequently, the ILC, led by a series of four prominent Rapporteurs, spent two decades drafting the Vienna Convention, building on the work of the Harvard project.

The first Rapporteur, JL Brierly, concluded that even the modest obligation referred to in the Harvard research project was moral rather than legal in nature. He subsequently explained that, while '[a] certain amount of material exists concerning an alleged obligation on the part of States not to do anything, between the signature of a treaty on their behalf, and its ratification, that would render ratification by other States superfluous or useless', the material supporting even this narrow obligation was 'of too fragmentary and inconclusive a nature to form the basis of codification'.[43] Perhaps not surprisingly, in light of the position of the Rapporteur, the possibility of including such an obligation in the proposed treaty was initially rejected.

A subsequent Rapporteur, Hersch Lauterpacht, believed that the interim signing obligation did have legal status, but described the obligation narrowly as 'prohibit[ing] action in bad faith deliberately aimed at depriving the other party of the benefits which it legitimately hoped to achieve from the treaty and for which it gave adequate consideration'.[44] The subsequent Rapporteurs, Gerald Fitzmaurice and Humphrey Waldock, continued to focus on actions that would impair the ability of the parties to comply with or obtain the benefits of the treaty. Waldock, for example, referred to an obligation to 'refrain during at least some period from acts calculated to frustrate the objects of the treaty'.[45]

This drafting history makes clear that the signing obligation was not intended as a general obligation to comply with the terms of the treaty, or even an obligation to comply with the most important provisions in the treaty. Instead, the signing

---

[40] Ibid 396.
[41] Swaine (n 36) 2070 n44. See also Palchetti (n 33) 32 ('[T]he few cases which are generally regarded as the most notable precedents in relation to the obligation now laid down in Article 18 mainly concern claims addressed to a state which ultimately became party to the treaty'). In addition, Turkey's actions in the case may have independently violated a restriction in international law on the expropriation of alien property. Charme (n 29) 81 n39.
[42] Research in International Law (n 28) 781.
[43] [1952] YBILC, vol II, 54.
[44] [1953] YBILC, vol II, 110.
[45] [1962] YBILC, vol II, 110.

obligation appears to have been designed to ensure that one of the signatory parties, typically in a bilateral arrangement, does not change the status quo in a way that substantially reduces either its ability to comply with its treaty obligations after ratification or the ability of the other treaty parties to obtain the benefit of the treaty.[46] Considered in these terms, the signing obligation may have little relevance to some treaties, such as human rights treaties, where pre-ratification conduct inconsistent with the treaty is not likely to undo the bargain reflected in the treaty.[47]

The examples of prohibited signatory conduct provided by the Harvard research project are illustrative:

(1) A treaty contains an undertaking on the part of a signatory that it will not fortify a particular place on its frontier or that it will demilitarize a designated zone in that region. Shortly thereafter, while ratification is still pending, it proceeds to erect the forbidden fortifications or to increase its armaments within the zone referred to.

(2) A treaty binds one signatory to cede a portion of its public domain to another; during the interval between signature and ratification the former cedes a part of the territory promised to another State.

(3) A treaty binds one signatory to make restitution of certain property to the other signatory from which it has been wrongfully taken, but, while ratification is still pending, it destroys or otherwise disposes of the property, so that in case the treaty is ratified restitution would be impossible.

(4) A treaty concedes the right of the nationals of one signatory to navigate a river within the territory of the other, but the latter soon after the signature of the treaty takes some action which would render navigation of the river difficult or impossible.

(5) By the terms of a treaty both or all signatories agree to lower their existing tariff rates, but while ratification of the treaty is pending one of them proceeds to raise its tariff duties.

---

[46] Bradley (n 32) 308. For descriptions of the signing obligation in similarly narrow terms, see Aust (n 13) 119 ('The state must therefore not do anything which would prevent it being able fully to comply with the treaty once it has entered into force'); Villiger (n 30) 249 ('A State's act will defeat the treaty's object and purpose if it renders meaningless subsequent performance of the treaty, and its rules'); Rogoff (n 12) 298–9 ('The most likely conclusion to be drawn . . . is that the purpose of the rule is to prevent a signatory from claiming the benefits to which it is entitled under the treaty while at the same time engaging in acts that would materially reduce the benefits to which the other signatory or signatories are entitled'); UNGA, *Report of the International Law Commission*, UN GAOR 62nd Session Supp No 10 (2007) (A/62/10) 67 ('It is unanimously accepted that article 18, paragraph (a), of the Convention does not oblige a signatory State to respect the treaty, but merely to refrain from rendering the treaty inoperative prior to its expression of consent to be bound').

[47] Bradley (n 32) 308. See also J Klabbers, 'How to Defeat a Treaty's Object and Purpose Pending Entry into Force: Toward Manifest Intent' (2001) 34 Vanderbilt J Transnat'l L 283, 330 ('[P]articularly with non-contractual, normative, multilateral arrangements, the interim obligation laid down in Article 18 of the Vienna Convention does not provide much relief').

(6) A treaty provides that one of the signatories shall undertake to deliver to the other a certain quantity of the products of a forest or a mine, but while ratification is pending the signatory undertaking the engagement destroys the forest or the mine, or takes some action which results in such diminution of their output that performance of the obligation is no longer possible.[48]

The records of the ILC's deliberations on the VCLT suggest additional possible examples. The Italian jurist Roberto Ago stated that if a treaty 'provided for the cession by a State of installations owned by it in the territory of another State' or 'relat[ed] to the return by a State of works of art formerly taken from the territory of another State', there would be a violation of the signing obligation if the State destroyed the installations or works of art prior to ratification.[49] The Polish jurist Manfred Lachs expressed the view that if a group of countries signed a treaty calling for a reduction of their armed forces and one of them increased their armed forces between the time of signature and ratification, there would be a violation of an obligation 'not to invalidate the basic presumption of the agreement'.[50] Again, these examples suggest a narrow obligation not to negate the reasons for having the treaty in the first place.

III. Terminating the Legal Effects of Simple Signature

Whatever the extent of the signing obligation, Article 18 of the VCLT makes clear that it lasts only until the signatory State 'shall have made its intention clear not to become a party to the treaty'.[51] There is little State practice involving this provision. Although it is not uncommon for signatory States to delay their ratification of a treaty, these States generally do not make express statements indicating that they do not intend to ratify the treaty.

A much-discussed example of a signatory making such an intention clear is the US announcement in 2002 that it did not intend to ratify the Rome Statute of the International Criminal Court (ICC). The US signed the treaty in December 2000, shortly before President William J Clinton left office. At that time, President Clinton expressed concern about what he referred to as 'significant flaws' in the treaty and noted that he did 'not recommend that [his] successor submit the Treaty to the Senate for advice and consent until our fundamental concerns are satisfied'.[52] He also observed, however, that by signing the treaty the US was 'reaffirm[ing] [its] strong support for international accountability and for bringing to justice

---

[48] Research in International Law (n 28) 781–2.
[49] [1965] YBILC, vol I, 87, 92 (remarks of R Ago).
[50] Ibid 97 (remarks of M Lachs).
[51] VCLT Art 18. See also Rogoff (n 12) 296 ('Any obligations imposed on a signatory should terminate when that state indicates that it will not ratify the treaty, since a signatory is under no obligation to ratify a signed agreement, and may refuse ratification for any reason').
[52] President William J Clinton, 'Statement on Signature of the International Criminal Court Treaty' (31 December 2000) <http://clinton4.nara.gov/textonly/library/hot_releases/December_31_2000.html>.

perpetrators of genocide, war crimes, and crimes against humanity', and that, as a signatory, the US would 'be in a position to influence the evolution of the Court'.[53]

Two years later, under the administration of President George W Bush, the US sent a letter to the Secretary-General of the UN stating that 'the United States does not intend to become a party to the treaty', and that '[a]ccordingly, the United States has no legal obligations arising from its signature [of the treaty]'.[54] In deciding to send this letter, the Bush administration may have been concerned that its plan to conclude 'non-surrender' agreements with individual States, whereby these States would agree not to extradite US personnel to the ICC, would be viewed as an effort to defeat the object and purpose of the treaty.[55]

The US announcement was referred to by a number of commentators as an 'unsigning' of the ICC treaty, although there was no attempt to physically remove the earlier signature. Nor does the VCLT or State practice provide any support for the possibility of such a physical 'unsigning'. In fact, the UN Treaty Collection still lists the US as a signatory to the Rome Statute, albeit with a footnote referencing the letter from 2002.[56] Despite criticism of the US announcement on policy grounds, it appears to have been consistent with the terms of Article 18.[57]

A more recent example of such an announcement concerns Russia's relationship to the Energy Charter Treaty, which provides protections to foreign investors in the energy sector and sets forth rules designed to promote trade in energy materials.[58] Along with a number of other countries, Russia signed the treaty in 1994, and it also accepted provisional application of the treaty pending ratification. In 2009, however, Russia sent a notice to Portugal, the depository for the treaty, stating that Russia did not intend to become a party to the treaty.[59]

---

[53] Ibid.

[54] Letter from JR Bolton, Under Sec'y for Arms Control and Intl Security, US Dept of State, to Kofi Annan, Sec'y General, United Nations (6 May 2002) <http://usinfo.org/wf-archive/2002/020506/epf110.htm>. For discussion of the US action, see Bradley (n 32) 311–12, 317.

[55] These non-surrender agreements are also referred to as 'Article 98 agreements', because the US was seeking to obtain the benefit of Art 98(2) of the Rome Statute, which provides that:

> The Court may not proceed with a request for surrender which would require the requested State to act inconsistently with its obligations under international agreements pursuant to which the consent of a sending State is required to surrender a person of that State to the Court, unless the Court can first obtain the cooperation of the sending State for the giving of consent for the surrender.

Rome Statute (n 20) Art 98(2).

[56] Rome Statute of the International Criminal Court, *Multilateral Treaties Deposited with the Secretary General*, Ch XVIII.10 <http://treaties.un.org/pages/ViewDetails.aspx?src=TREATY&mtdsg_no=XVIII-10&chapter=18& lang=en#10>.

[57] Aust (n 13) 117–18. More generally, see Villiger (n 30) 250 (noting that a State that has signed but not ratified a treaty 'is free at any time to make its intention clear not to become a party to the treaty, *ie*, either by means of an express statement or through implied conduct, in which case Article 18 can no longer be invoked'); H Blix, 'Developing International Law and Inducing Compliance' (2002) 41 Columbia J Transnat'l L 1, 5 ('Clearly, in the cases where signature does not signal the state's consent to be bound, a simple but formal announcement by a government clarifying that it will not proceed with ratification or any other form of confirmation will be enough to terminate the limited legal effect that flowed from the signature').

[58] Energy Charter Treaty (17 December 1994) [1995] 34 ILM 360.

[59] For more on this incident, see the discussion in Chapter 9, Part III.B, 241 *et seq*.

Absent an express statement such as the one that the US made with respect to the Rome Statute, or that Russia made with respect to the Energy Charter Treaty, it will often be unclear whether a State that has signed a treaty continues to have an intent to ratify the treaty. Although a long passage of time might suggest a lack of such an intent,[60] this is not entirely clear, since States sometimes ratify treaties many years after signature.[61]

The ability of States to decide not to ratify a treaty after signature can create strategic issues in the treaty process, especially for multilateral treaties that are the product of extensive negotiation.[62] In particular, there is a danger that a signatory could influence the text and implementation of a treaty without ever intending to become a party to it and thereby compromise the interests of those States that do become parties. The 'object and purpose' obligation probably does not significantly alleviate this danger, since it operates only until such time as a State makes clear its intent not to ratify the treaty, and its scope is sufficiently modest that it may not deter signatures that do not reflect a good faith intent of ratification.

Presumably, States will face reputational incentives not to sign treaties in bad faith, and one can imagine that a pattern of signatures that do not lead to ratification will reduce a State's negotiating leverage over time. In addition, there may be ways to design treaties to address the problem of disingenuous signatures— for example, by specifying that the treaty does not take effect unless and until particular States ratify it.[63] As an example, the Nuclear Non-Proliferation Treaty required ratification by Great Britain, the Soviet Union, and the US, along with forty other States, before it would take effect.[64] It might also make sense to impose some sort of statute of limitations on the legal effect of a signature, so that other States will stop relying on it after a certain period of time has elapsed.[65] In any event, at least to date it does not appear that there have been substantial abuses by States of the ability to decide not to ratify a treaty after signature.

Conclusion

In sum, there are a variety of reasons why it is common today for States to sign treaties subject to ratification, including perhaps most notably domestic constitutional considerations. Such simple signature can confer legal and other benefits on States and also potentially create an obligation, as set forth in Article 18 of the

---

[60] *Restatement (Third)* (n 12) §312, cmt i ('The obligation [not to take actions that would defeat the object and purpose of the treaty] ... continues until the state has made clear its intention not to become a party *or if it appears that entry into force will be unduly delayed*' (emphasis added)).

[61] For a particularly dramatic example of a long delay between signature and ratification, the US signed the Convention on the Prevention and Punishment of the Crime of Genocide in 1948 but did not ratify it until forty years later, in 1988.

[62] Swaine (n 36) 2071–7.

[63] Bradley (n 32) 331 n111.

[64] Treaty on the Non-Proliferation of Nuclear Weapons (opened for signature 1 July 1968, entered into force 5 March 1970) 729 UNTS 161, Art IX.

[65] Bradley (n 32) 336.

VCLT, not to take actions that would defeat the object and purpose of the treaty. The precise scope of this obligation is uncertain, although the drafting history of Article 18 suggests that the obligation was intended to apply only to acts that would substantially reduce either the signatory State's ability to comply with its treaty obligations after ratification or the ability of the other treaty parties to obtain the benefit of the treaty. A State can terminate the legal effect of a simple signature by making clear its intent not to ratify the treaty, although this ability to terminate can present some strategic concerns for the treaty process itself.

Recommended Reading

A Aust, *Modern Treaty Law and Practice* (2nd edn CUP, Cambridge 2007)

L Boisson de Chazournes, A La Rosa, and MM Mbengue, 'Article 18' in O Corten and P Klein (eds), *The Vienna Convention on the Law of Treaties: A Commentary* (OUP, Oxford 2011) vol I

CA Bradley, 'Unratified Treaties, Domestic Politics, and the U.S. Constitution' (2007) 48 HILJ 307

JS Camara, *The Ratification of International Treaties* (Ontario Publishing, Toronto 1949)

JS Charme, 'The Interim Obligation of Article 18 of the Vienna Convention on the Law of Treaties: Making Sense of an Enigma' (1991) 25 Geo Wash J Intl L and Econ 71

DS Jonas and TN Saunders, 'The Object and Purpose of a Treaty: Three Interpretive Methods' (2010) 43 Vanderbilt J Transnat'l L 565

JM Jones, *Full Powers and Ratification* (CUP, Cambridge 1946)

J Klabbers, 'How to Defeat a Treaty's Object and Purpose Pending Entry into Force: Toward Manifest Intent' (2001) 34 Vanderbilt J Transnat'l L 283

A McNair, *Law of Treaties* (Clarendon, Oxford 1961)

P Palchetti, 'Article 18 of the 1969 Vienna Convention: A Vague and Ineffective Obligation or a Useful Means of Strengthening Legal Cooperation?' in E Cannizzaro (ed), *The Law of Treaties Beyond the Vienna Convention* (OUP, Oxford 2011)

MA Rogoff, 'The International Legal Obligations of Signatories to an Unratified Treaty' (1980) 32 Maine L Rev 263

I Sinclair, *The Vienna Convention on the Law of Treaties* (2nd edn MUP, Manchester 1984)

ET Swaine, 'Unsigning' (2003) 55 Stanford L Rev 2061

ME Villiger, *Commentary on the 1969 Vienna Convention on the Law of Treaties* (Martinus Nijhoff, Leiden 2009)

FO Wilcox, *The Ratification of International Conventions* (Allen & Unwin, London 1935)

9

Provisional Application of Treaties

*Robert E Dalton**

Introduction

Article 24(1) of the 1969 Vienna Convention on the Law of Treaties (VCLT) dictates that a treaty enters into force as its text 'may provide or as the negotiating States may agree'.[1] Some bilateral agreements are concluded in simplified form, entering into force on signature alone. But agreements that require approval of a parliamentary body, including most multilateral agreements dealing with important subjects, typically provide for entry into force following ratification, acceptance, or approval. In the latter cases, a substantial period of time may elapse before a treaty enters into force, particularly if the treaty further conditions the number or percentage of consenting parties required for initial entry into force.[2] Indeed, it is not unusual for ten years to pass between the adoption of the text of a major multilateral treaty and its entry into force. In certain instances, however, States or international organizations (IOs) may wish to apply certain treaty provisions prior to the treaty's entry into force. This desire may arise for a variety of reasons, including the treaty addressing a matter of some urgency or the need for legal continuity or consistency with other treaty regimes.[3] The doctrine of provisional application has developed to respond to such circumstances.

* The views expressed are the author's personal views and are not to be attributed to the US Department of State. The author thanks Francis J Holleran for his technical assistance in preparing this chapter.

[1] The corresponding article of the 1986 Vienna Convention on the Law of Treaties between States and International Organizations or between International Organizations (adopted 21 March 1986, not yet in force) [1986] 25 ILM 543, is substantively identical but for a few modifications taking account of the differences in the nature of international organizations. [1981] YBILC, vol II, 141; [1982] YBILC, vol II, 38.

[2] For general discussions of consent to be bound and entry into force, see Chapter 7, Parts III and IV, 195 *et seq*.

[3] Although scholars often cite urgency as the primary rationale for applying treaty provisions before entry into force, Michie identifies seven distinct rationales for doing so: (i) *urgency*; (ii) *certainty of ratification*, which may encourage negotiators to propose such action; (iii) *legal continuity* to avoid gaps in a treaty regime; (iv) *legal consistency* so amendments can be applied as early as possible among parties able to provisionally apply them; (v) *circumvention of obstacles to entry into force*; (vi) *confidence-building*, particularly with respect to arms limitation treaties; and (vii) *playing a special role in the process of establishing new international institutions*, in particular interim special arrangements for IOs. A Michie,

Provisional application is the application of an international agreement or one or more of its substantive provisions prior to its entry into force.[4] It generally takes place after the signatories have agreed—in a treaty, by an exchange of notes, or in some other manner—to apply such provisions prior to completing the steps that must be taken under their internal law before the treaty can be brought into force.[5] Thus, agreements concluded in simplified form (ie that enter into force on signature) are not normally susceptible of provisional application. Most cases of provisional application occur with treaties that have been signed but cannot enter into force until the signatories or a specified number of them have completed their domestic processes and brought the treaty into force.

The practice of provisionally applying treaties dates back to the 1648 Peace of Westphalia, but did not attract much attention until the International Law Commission (ILC) took up the project of codifying the law of treaties.[6] The ILC's commentary on its 1966 draft article explained the practice as follows: 'Owing to the urgency of the matters dealt with in the treaty or for other reasons the States concerned may specify in a treaty, which it is necessary for them to bring before their constitutional authorities for ratification or approval, that it shall come into force provisionally.'[7] The ILC emphasized, moreover, that provisional application produces international legal effects, arising:

with some frequency to-day and requir[ing] notice in the draft articles . . . Whether in these cases the treaty is to be considered as entering into force in virtue of the treaty or of a subsidiary agreement concluded between the States concerned in adopting the text may be a question. But there can be no doubt that such clauses have legal effect and bring the treaty into force on a provisional basis.[8]

In recent years, the incidence of provisional application between States has continued to increase. The practice, moreover, is the subject of Article 25 of the VCLT:

'The Provisional Application of Treaties in South African Law and Practice' (2005) 30 S Africa Ybk Intl L 8–10.

[4] VCLT Art 24(4) provides that certain non-substantive clauses of a treaty (eg those on authentication, entry into force, reservations, depositary functions) necessarily arise from the time of the text's adoption. Sinclair (n 38) 46 explains that the rule also applies to provisional application clauses.

[5] In more recent practice, participants adopting a treaty text may establish preparatory commissions to prepare for an IO's future operation. P Daillier, M Forteau, and A Pellet, *Droit international public* (8th edn LGDJ, Paris 2009) 180; A Aust, *Modern Treaty Law and Practice* (2nd edn CUP, Cambridge 2007) 175, 176. Often, preparatory commissions disappear once the treaty establishing the IO enters into force.

[6] Provisional application was not proposed when American States sought to devise a multilateral convention on treaties. Multilateral Convention on Treaties (adopted 28 February 1928) in M Hudson (ed), *International Legislation* (Oceana, New York 1950) vol IV, 2378. The 1935 *Harvard Draft Convention on the Law of Treaties* examined the issue, but did not include it among 'the more common problems . . . arising with respect to treaties'. (1935) 29 AJIL (Supp) 653, 671 (commentary on Art 7(b)) ('Harvard Draft Convention').

[7] [1966] YBILC, vol II, 210; see also Michie (n 3) for a compilation of rationales for provisional application.

[8] [1966] YBILC, vol II, 210.

1. A treaty or a part of a treaty is applied provisionally pending its entry into force if:
   (*a*) the treaty itself so provides; or
   (*b*) the negotiating States have in some other manner so agreed.

2. Unless the treaty otherwise provides or the negotiating States have otherwise agreed, the provisional application of a treaty or a part of a treaty with respect to a State shall be terminated if that State notifies the other States between which the treaty is being applied provisionally of its intention not to become a party to the treaty.

As early as 1984, Article 25 was invoked as reflecting customary international law in the *Kuwait v AMINOIL Arbitration*, a position echoed in recent scholarship.[9]

This chapter examines the provisional application of treaties in three parts. The first part traces an 'already ancient' practice that has become 'more and more frequent'.[10] The second examines the ILC's work and subsequent negotiating history, resulting in Article 25. The third part discusses how necessary provisional application has become to modern practice, including the important precedents of the extended provisional application of the General Agreement on Tariffs and Trade and the Agreement relating to Part XI of the Convention on the Law of the Sea. In addition, it assesses the legal consequences of agreeing to, and withdrawing from, a treaty's provisional application, in light of recent decisions of arbitral tribunals in a series of cases concerning the provisional application of the Energy Charter Treaty.

I. Practice Relating to 'Provisional Application' of Treaties Through the 1930s

The term 'provisional application' was rarely used prior to the adoption of Article 25 of the VCLT. But the practice itself was evident as early as the two treaties comprising the 1648 Peace of Westphalia, which brought an end to the Thirty Years' War. The final clauses of the Treaties of Peace signed at Münster and Osnabrück both provided that, notwithstanding the normal rule that treaties entered into force only after ratification, the substantive provisions were to be executed as quickly as possible after signature and to the extent practicable before ratification.[11]

Dr JHW Verzijl's work identified a series of eighteenth century examples of provisional application. These treaties generally provided for entry into force of certain provisions immediately upon signature even though the treaties called for

---

[9] *The Government of the State of Kuwait v The American Independent Oil Company (AMINOIL)* (1984) 66 ILR 568 (arbitral panel comprised of P Reuter, A Sultan, and GG Fitzmaurice, finding parties did not reach agreement on provisional application of their contract).

[10] Dallier and others (n 5) 179–80.

[11] Treaty of Peace between France and the Holy Roman Empire (signed at Münster 24 October 1648) Arts CIV, CV, CVI, C Parry (ed), 1 *Consolidated Treaty Series* (CTS) 319 (English trans), 349–50; Treaty of Peace between Sweden and the Holy Roman Empire (signed at Osnabrück, 24 October 1648) Art XVI, 1 CTS 119, 198 (English trans), 256.

later ratification.[12] Article 22 of the 1760 Peace Treaty between Great Britain and Morocco, for example, provides: 'It is moreover agreed, that the peace shall commence from the signing of this treaty'. However, that language is immediately followed by the parenthetical 'ratification within six months or sooner, if possible'.[13]

The earliest example of a separate agreement permitting partial application of a treaty prior to its entry into force appears to be the 1840 'Quadruple Alliance' Treaty for the Pacification of the Levant.[14] The parties wanted to act immediately to assist the Sublime Porte in its struggle to regain control over Syria from Egypt, but they avoided saying so in the treaty, which was to be ratified. Instead, they signed a separate *Protocole réservé*, stating that the naval measures mentioned in Article II 'shall be carried into execution at once, without waiting for exchange of ratifications'.[15]

Before the American and French revolutions, treaty ratifications generally occurred relatively quickly. The 1648 Münster and Osnabrück treaties, for example, were each ratified in approximately three months. Over the course of the nineteenth century, however, many countries' domestic laws began to require parliamentary consultation or approval prior to treaty ratification.[16] These domestic law requirements led to significant delays in ratification—delays compounded by the rise in the number of important multilateral treaties requiring the deposit of a large number of ratifications prior to entry into force. Where these delays were unacceptable to negotiating States, they agreed to apply the treaty (or, more commonly, certain provisions of the treaty) prior to its entry into force. Thus, the concept of provisional application emerged as a limited escape valve from the delay in entry into force of multilateral treaties occasioned by these new requirements at both the national and international level to the entry into force process.

This long-standing practice of applying treaties prior to ratification seldom received scrutiny in the nineteenth century. One exception occurred in 1880, when representatives of thirteen governments signed a Convention for the Settlement of the Right of Protection in Morocco. That treaty supplemented a standard ratification paragraph with a second paragraph, providing: 'By exceptional consent of the high contracting parties the stipulations of this convention shall take effect on the day on which it is signed at Madrid.'[17] On receipt of the Convention, US Secretary of State William Evarts noted the apparent provisional application clause and stated: '[t]his government could not accord validity to such an international

---

[12] JHW Verzijl, *International Law in Historical Perspective, Part VI* (HW Sijthoff, Leiden 1973) 261–8.

[13] 1760 Peace Treaty between Great Britain and Morocco (28 July 1760) 42 CTS 1, 3 (English trans) 11.

[14] Convention between Great Britain, Austria, Prussia, Russia and Turkey for the pacification of the Levant (signed 15 July 1840) 90 CTS 285, 291.

[15] W Cargill, *The Foreign Affairs of Great Britain Administered by The Right Honourable Henry John Viscount Palmerston* (John Reid and Co, London 1841) 232–3.

[16] For more on these developments, see Chapter 8, Part I, 208 *et seq.*

[17] 156 CTS 487, 488 (in French).

compact in advance of the consent of the Senate'. However, Secretary Evarts continued:

[I]n view of the exceptional circumstances under which the convention had been framed and of its limited operation within the territory of Morocco involving apparently no domestic legislation of this country, I deem it entirely unlikely that any issue would arise, pending formal ratification, which would call for diplomatic intervention on the part of the Executive in a sense opposed to the convention.[18]

The US Senate gave advice and consent to US ratification of the treaty on 5 May 1881, without raising the provisional application issue; the US deposited its instrument of ratification at Tangier on 9 March 1882. Moreover, there is no information to suggest that any other country objected to the treaty's provisional application.

By the 1920s, with parliamentary participation in the ratification process firmly established, States began to formally recognize and accept exceptions to that rule. Some countries enacted domestic legislation authorizing the conclusion of certain agreements without subsequent parliamentary approval to permit their prompt application and avoid the delay inherent in the two-step ratification process.[19] At the same time, State practice in using the provisional application concept continued to evolve.

One of the first treaties to use the term 'provisional application' was the 1929 Convention of Commerce, Navigation, and Establishment between France and Greece; Article 38 provided: 'It shall be brought into *provisional application* as soon as possible and on a date to be agreed upon by the two Governments.'[20] The duration of the treaty was two years. The part dealing with wine tariffs was renewed in 1931, but the parties chose an expression other than 'provisional application' to allow for the application of the tariff provisions prior to the 1931 treaty's ratification. Many similar treaties concluded during the League of Nations period used the phrase 'provisional entry into force' to describe the process by which parties agreed to give effect to a treaty provision prior to its entry into force.

The 1935 *Harvard Draft Articles on the Law of Treaties* had no article on provisional application, but did discuss the anomalous situation where a provision of a treaty was to have effect before the exchange of instruments of ratification:

A treaty which is subject to ratification by a State may nevertheless provide that it, or a certain part of it, shall come into force so as to bind the State prior to such ratification. The agreement signed at Rapallo on April 16, 1922, by Germany and the Soviet Union, for example, provided (Article 6):

---

[18] Letter from WM Evarts, US Secretary of State, to L Fairchild, 11 August 1889, reprinted in [1880] Foreign Relations of the United States 922.

[19] A number of older examples may be found in A McNair, *The Law of Treaties* (Clarendon, Oxford 1961) 192–3. McNair uses the rubric *entry into force pending ratification* instead of *provisional application*, a practice widely followed through the 1960s.

[20] Convention of Commerce, Navigation, and Establishment between France and Greece (adopted 11 March 1929, entered into force 19 October 1929) 95 LNTS 403, 423 (emphasis added).

Articles 1(b) and 4 of this Agreement shall come into force on the day of ratification, and the remaining provisions shall come into force immediately. (19 *League of Nations Treaty Series*, p. 247.)

In such cases it is evident that ratification by a State is not intended to be, and in practice it is not, a condition precedent to the treaty's coming into force so as to bind the States concerned. It does not seem, however, that such cases are the same as those in which ratification is dispensed with entirely; in fact the right of ratification is specifically provided for. Perhaps it can be said that in such cases the treaty comes into force at the time prescribed subject to the conditions subsequent that ratification is forthcoming.[21]

At about the same time, a German scholar, Dr Herbert Kraus, provided one of the first full analyses of the provisional application concept in discussing bilateral treaties concluded with third States by France and Germany. In his 1934 course at The Hague Academy of International Law, Dr Kraus explained:

A new type of treaty, particularly interesting from the point of view of time, is the *provisionally applicable treaty*. It always appears in a bilateral commercial agreement, which is signed as a solemn treaty but which is placed in force provisionally by particular agreements, on the basis of authority under the national law of the contracting Parties, and declared applicable by the executive organs of the competent Parties, as a rule the ministry of foreign affairs.

This kind of treaty has actually become so frequent that one can justly speak of a regime of treaties provisionally applied in the domain of international economic life today. Germany has thus far concluded more than one hundred treaties of this kind.

To give a recent example, I would cite Article 35 of the Convention on Commerce, Establishment and Navigation concluded between Germany and France July 28, 1934 ... It says:

'The present convention will be ratified and the exchange of ratifications will take place at Paris'.

'It will enter into force fifteen days after the exchange of instruments of ratification. However, the High Contracting Parties are agreed to provisionally apply it as of August 1, 1934'.

The authority of the Government of Germany to insert in solemn treaties such clauses and then to apply them under internal law is based on a governmental law dated April 4, 1933 ... which reads as follows:

'The Ministry of Foreign Affairs is authorized, in cases of urgent economic necessity, to provide for provisional application of economic bilateral agreements with foreign states'.[22]

---

[21] Harvard Draft Convention (n 6) 760 (comment on Art 7). Article 7(b) itself provided that ratification of a State is necessary 'when the treaty provides for ratification by that State and does not provide for its coming into force prior to such ratification'. Ibid 759.

[22] H Kraus, 'System and Functions of International Treaties' (1934–1935-IV) 50 RcD 358 (author's translation) (emphasis in original).

Dr Kraus continued:

Without a doubt we have here a species of administrative accord concerning the obligations under international law that encompasses the period between the signature and the exchange of ratifications of the treaty. From the constructivist point of view one must recognize that we are faced here with *two* treaties relating to the same subject, one of which is designed to continue the other and assumes—this is what is essential for us—a provisional character (that is to say) operates for an indeterminate time while the other will not become obligatory.[23]

The provisional application practice was not, however, confined to commercial treaties nor to bilateral ones. The 1936 Protocol to the Montreux Straits Convention, for example, provided that, notwithstanding Article 26's requirement of ratification by six signatories, including Turkey, prior to entry into force, that '[a]t the moment of signing the Convention . . . the plenipotentiaries declare for their respective Governments that they accept' Turkey's ability to remilitarize the Straits and that '[a]s from 15 August 1936, Turkey shall provisionally apply the regime specified in the Convention'.[24]

II. The Development of Article 25 of the VCLT

A. The ILC's preparatory work

The desire to establish institutions and arrangements quickly following the Second World War led to a resurgence of the practice providing for provisional application of bilateral treaties and to a marked increase in the number of multilateral treaties that provided for provisional application.[25] All four of the ILC's Special Rapporteurs on the Law of Treaties favoured including an article on provisional application. But only Sir Gerald Fitzmaurice and his successor, Sir Humphrey Waldock, proposed texts, and the ILC itself only addressed Waldock's proposal (which built on Fitzmaurice's earlier work). Waldock's decision to include parts of his proposal in different articles made it difficult to understand. Draft Article 20(6) provided that a treaty might 'prescribe that it shall come into force provisionally on signature or on a specified date or event, pending its full entry into force in accordance with the rules laid down in this article'. The second part of his proposal in the article that followed contains a provision permitting any party to terminate its rights and obligations six months after giving notice of termination if 'the entry into full

---

[23] Ibid 359 (author's translation) (emphasis in original).

[24] Montreux Convention Regarding the Regime of the Turkish Straits (adopted 20 July 1936, entered into force 9 November 1936) 173 LNTS 213, 215 (noting in margin, 'The present Convention, the provisions of which were provisionally applied as from 15 August 1936, came finally into force on 9 November 1936'); see also ibid 241 (Protocol text).

[25] See, in this regard, the impressive marshalling and analysis of bilateral treaties in P Picone, *L'applicazione in via provisoria degli accordi internazionale* (Eugenio Jovenc, Naples 1973) passim.

force of the treaty is unreasonably delayed and, unless the parties have concluded a further agreement to continue the treaty in force on a provisional basis'.[26] Waldock conceded his termination provision was *de lege ferenda*, but argued that it was evident termination must occur in instances where entry into force was unreasonably delayed and that it seemed 'desirable for the Commission to try and give a little more definition to the rule, and perhaps to make withdrawal from the provisional application and (sic) orderly process'.[27]

The ILC did not, however, accept Waldock's termination proposal, with several ILC members emphasizing in particular its destabilizing potential for treaty relations.[28] As a result, Waldock agreed to drop the provision on termination of provisional application, with the ILC accepting the idea that States could decide the issue for themselves or turn to the rules on treaty termination for guidance.[29]

The ILC developed the text of its draft provisional application article (Article 22) between 1962 and 1966.[30] It accepted that provisional application could occur with respect to a treaty 'in whole or in part' and Waldock's proposal that States could agree outside the treaty (eg through an exchange of notes) that a treaty may enter into force provisionally.[31] During that period Paul Reuter argued that the term 'entry into force provisionally' was, despite its use in practice, 'quite incorrect', and proposed that the Commission substitute the term 'provisional application'.[32] The ILC debate ended with the Commission deciding to retain the term 'entry into force provisionally'.[33]

B. The Vienna Conference's adoption of Article 25

The Diplomatic Conference on the Law of Treaties in 1968 and 1969 made significant changes in the ILC's proposed text as a result of its consideration of nine proposed amendments. While not all were adopted, Article 25 differs in several key respects from the ILC's proposed final draft. For ease of reference, the texts are set out side by side.[34]

---

[26] H Waldock, 'First Report on the Law of Treaties' [1962] YBILC, vol II, 71.

[27] Ibid.

[28] See [1962] YBILC, vol I, 179–80 [14] (Jimínez de Aréchaga); Ibid 180 [15] (Tunkin).

[29] Ibid 180 [18]; see also [1965] YBILC, vol II, 58.

[30] The most complete presentation of the ILC's versions of the provisional application article is R Wetzel and D Rauschning, *The Vienna Convention on the Law of Treaties: Travaux Preparatoires* (Alfred Metzner Verlag GmbH, Frankfurt am Main 1978) 206–8.

[31] [1965] YBILC, vol I, 107 [90].

[32] Ibid 106 [75]; see also [1962] YBILC, vol I, 259.

[33] As a member of the ILC, TO Elias questioned both the inclusion of a provisional application article and the ILC's ability to agree on it. [1965] YBILC, vol I, 111. While he remained reluctant to endorse the concept, Elias subsequently acknowledged that 'the laws of most States often provide for any contingency that may arise out of the provisional application of a treaty'. TO Elias, *The Modern Law of Treaties* (Oceana, New York 1974) 38–9.

[34] S Rosenne, *The Law of Treaties: A Guide to the Legislative History of the Vienna Convention* (Oceana Publications, Dobbs Ferry 1970) 192.

| ILC Proposed Text | Text Adopted by Diplomatic Conference |
Article 22	Article 25
Entry into force provisionally	Provisional application
1. A treaty may enter into force provisionally if:	1. A treaty or a part of a treaty is applied provisionally pending its entry into force if:
(a) The treaty itself prescribes that it shall enter into force provisionally pending ratification, acceptance, approval or accession by the contracting States; or	(a) the treaty itself so provides; or
(b) The negotiating States have in some other manner so agreed.	(b) the negotiating States have in some other manner so agreed.
2. The same rule applies to the entry into force provisionally of part of a treaty.	2. Unless the treaty otherwise provides or the negotiating States have otherwise agreed, the provisional application of a treaty or a part of a treaty with respect to a State shall be terminated if that State notifies the other States between which the treaty is being applied provisionally of its intention not to become a party to the treaty.

Three changes warrant particular attention as they illuminate the current contours of provisional application: (a) the substitution of provisional application for provisional entry into force; (b) the replacement of 'may' by 'is' to avoid ambiguity in the chapeau of paragraph 1; and (c) the change to paragraph 2 to permit States to terminate provisional application unilaterally unless the treaty otherwise provides or the States otherwise agree.

First, the Conference substituted the title 'Provisional Application' for the ILC's title of 'Entry into force provisionally'. As noted earlier, treaties had employed both terms. However, the absence of any discussion in contemporary treatises such as those of McNair and Charles Rousseau[35] suggests that there was no agreed vocabulary at the time; indeed, it is almost certain that many of the Vienna Conference delegates were unfamiliar with the issue. Nonetheless, the Vienna Conference preferred 'provisional application' because of a disinclination to have two kinds of entry into force—provisional and definitive—as a residual rule. In this regard, the Conference followed Professor Reuter's earlier critique during the ILC discussions.[36] At the Conference in 1968, Mr Maresca (Italy) urged

---

[35] C Rousseau, *Droit international public* (Sirey, Paris 1971) vol I.

[36] See nn 32–3 and accompanying text. Although the ILC had declined to change its terminology, the United States, after proposing the article's deletion at the Conference, stated that if it were retained, the expression 'entry into force provisionally' should be replaced by 'provisional application'. UN Conference on the Law of Treaties, Summary Records of First Session, A/CONF.39/11, 140 [23]–[24] ('Vienna Conference, First Session'). The US oral amendment was followed by a supporting written amendment by Czechoslovakia and Yugoslavia and was approved without a vote of the

that 'confusion should be avoided between mere application, which was a question of practice, and entry into force, which was a formal legal notion. Mere . . . application did not involve entry into force'.[37]

In his treatise on the Convention, Sir Ian Sinclair noted:

In terms of theory and doctrine, this change would appear to be justified, since the better view is that provisional application results from an accessory or secondary informal agreement among the parties to a treaty that the substantive provisions of the treaty, or certain selected substantive provisions, should be applied pending the formal entry into force of the treaty.[38]

Second, the Drafting Committee replaced the expression 'a treaty may . . . be applied provisionally' with the words 'a treaty . . . is applied provisionally'. The Drafting Committee considered that the former expression might be interpreted to mean that the parties were left free not to apply the treaty provisionally, even when such application was prescribed by the treaty.[39] Later, during the Conference's final deliberations on the Article, the UK's delegation emphasized that it understood the *pacta sunt servanda* rule applied to the provisional application of treaties. With the exception of India, which stated that principle only governed treaties in force, there was no objection to this statement.[40]

Third, the Drafting Committee included a second paragraph to Article 25, permitting a party to terminate provisional application as a result of the Committee of the Whole's acceptance of amendments to that effect. This change was important in several respects. It eased concerns that provisional application might thwart compliance with a State's constitutional law since the executive could terminate a treaty's provisional application should a parliamentary body indicate that it would not consent to the treaty or to its provisional application. It also permitted the delegations from a number of Latin American States whose Constitutions prohibited provisional application to abstain on the Article 25 vote rather than voting against it as a matter of principle (which they would have done had the original text been maintained).[41]

The plenary session of the Conference approved the final text of Article 25 by a vote of 87 to 1 (Tanzania), with 13 abstentions.[42] Normally, this vote would have completed the Conference's discussion of Article 25. However, the Polish delegate

Committee of the Whole, and by the Conference itself the following year. UN Conference on the Law of Treaties, Summary Records of Second Session, A/CONF.39/11/Add.1, 43 [101] ('Vienna Conference, Second Session').

[37] Vienna Conference, First Session (n 36) 142 [43].

[38] I Sinclair, *The Vienna Convention on the Law of Treaties* (2nd edn MUP, Manchester 1984) 247. For a discussion of how the practice of provisional entry into force has continued see n 58 and accompanying text.

[39] Vienna Conference, First Session (n 36) 426–27 [24]–[27]. The Committee of the Whole approved this change without discussion. Ibid [28].

[40] Vienna Conference, Second Session (n 36) 39–40 [55]–[58] (UK statement); Ibid 41 [68]–[70] (India's response).

[41] Nevertheless, four Latin American States reserved as to Art 25 when they ratified the Convention.

[42] Vienna Conference, Second Session (n 36) 43 [101].

proposed an amendment to Article 25(2), requiring the passage of six months before a notification to terminate provisional application would become effective. In order to allow the text's adoption, the delegate agreed not to press for a vote on his amendment, provided that the Drafting Committee would review it and report on it to the Conference.[43]

That report turned out to be perhaps the Conference's most significant document on the binding nature of provisional application. Ambassador Yasseen, the Drafting Committee chairman, stated that the Committee was not persuaded that the oral proposals (by Poland) would improve Article 25 and thus did not propose any changes to it.[44] In the interim, however, the Committee had received a Yugoslavian proposal to insert the following new article: 'Every treaty applied provisionally in whole or in part is binding on the contracting States and must be performed in good faith'. Yasseen stated that the Drafting Committee considered the proposed article 'was self-evident and that provisional application also fell within the scope of Article 23 [eventually Article 26 of the VCLT] on the *pacta sunt servanda* rule' and that there was no need to emphasize its specific application to this particular case; the ILC thus 'did not recommend the adoption of the proposed new article'.[45] Taken as a whole, this record of consideration of Article 25 provides strong evidence that the negotiating States understood that obligations under treaty provisions being provisionally applied were governed by the *pacta sunt servanda* rule and thus legally binding.

Article 25 does not, however, provide a complete explication of the rules on provisional application. Article 2 of the VCLT does not define 'provisional application' and Article 25 does not make clear the relationship between provisional application and the underlying treaty. However, over the years acceptance has grown for the view that provisional application is the product of a separate, ancillary, or collateral agreement. This view—following Dr Kraus' earlier position—was favoured by Professor Briggs during the ILC's discussions and later adopted by Professor Nascimento e Silva, Brazil's Representative to the Vienna Conference.[46] Briggs emphasized:

> If the provisional application was prescribed by the treaty itself, the States concerned could be said to be parties to an informal understanding on such application. The legal nature of the operation could also be described by saying that one and the same instrument contained two transactions: the treaty itself and the agreement on provisional application pending its formal entry into force.[47]

Some scholars, including Mark Villiger and Esperanza Orihuela Calatayud, have observed a tension between Article 25 on provisional application and Article 28 on

---

[43] Ibid 42–3 [87]–[100].

[44] Ibid 157 [45]–[47].

[45] Ibid [47]. The only subsequent comment on Yasseen's report was by the Polish delegate who had sent the article to the Drafting Committee, agreeing with the Committee's views on the binding quality of provisionally applied treaties. Ibid 158 [3].

[46] GE Nascimento e Silva, 'Le Facteur Temps et Les Traités' (1977-I) 154 RcD 229, 231.

[47] [1965] YBILC, vol I, 109.

non-retroactivity of treaties.[48] But as Frédéric Dopagne argued in his commentary on Article 28 of the VCLT, 'when a treaty is applied provisionally pending its entry into force, it seems that the critical date to appraise the retroactivity is the date of the provisional application, and no longer that of the entry into force'.[49]

Other outstanding questions are whether a State can exit provisional application without indicating an intent not to ratify a treaty that is being provisionally applied, or if having done so, it is precluded from again provisionally applying (or joining the treaty itself) if their intention changes. These issues were raised, but not resolved, at the Vienna Conference.[50] In his recent commentary, Villiger stated that Article 25 appears misleading in linking termination of provisional application with a State's 'intention not to become a party to the treaty' because notification under paragraph 2 'cannot exclude subsequent entry into force of the treaty for that State'.[51]

In the end, Article 25 leaves provisional application very much in the hands of the negotiating States, a point Waldock emphasized just before its adoption by the Plenary at the Vienna Conference:

89. Sir Humphrey Waldock (Expert Consultant) said that he had been surprised at the degree of anxiety to which paragraph 2 had given rise during the discussion, since to him that paragraph seemed to offer a protection to the constitutional position of certain States rather than the contrary. The practice of provisional application was now well established among a large number of States and took account of a number of different requirements. One was where, because of a certain urgency in the matter at issue, particularly in connexion with economic treaties, it was highly desirable that certain steps should be taken by agreement in the very near future. If the treaty was one which had to come before a parliament, for example, there might be a certain delay in securing its ratification which would deprive it of some of its value. States might also resort to the process of provisional application when it was not so much a question of urgency, as that the matter was regarded as manifestly highly desirable and almost certain to obtain parliamentary approval.

90. As drafted, article 25 did not seem to involve any real risks to States which might have very strict constitutional requirements because, as had already been pointed out, there was

---

[48] ME Villiger, *Commentary on the 1969 Vienna Convention on the Law of Treaties* (Martinus Nijhoff, Leiden 2009) 385; E Orihuela Calatayud, *Los tratados internacionales su aplicación en el tiempo* (Dykinson, Madrid 2004) 53–62, 245–65.

[49] FF Dopagne, 'Commentary on Article 28, Non-retroactivity of Treaties' in O Corten and P Klein (eds), *The Vienna Convention on the Law of Treaties: A Commentary* (OUP, Oxford 2011) vol I, 720 (stating that acts on or after the date of the Energy Charter Treaty's provisional application 'come within the scope of the treaty even though it has not yet entered into force, without this entailing any retroactive application of the treaty').

[50] See Vienna Conference, Second Session (n 36) 41 [73] (Professor Eustathiades on behalf of Greece). The Eustathiades question was being examined at the end of 2011 in connection with an announcement by the EU of its intention to terminate certain benefits under trade agreements with a number of African, Caribbean, and Pacific countries that have not fully implemented economic partnership agreements with the EU by 1 January 2014. However, a claim has been made on behalf of those countries that in order to take such action the EU would have to state its own intention not to become a party to such economic partnership agreements. Thus, there may be further developments relating to this question prior to 2014.

[51] Villiger (n 48) 356.

no need for the State concerned to resort to the procedure of provisional application at all. On the other hand, there were many States which did have important constitutional requirements but which also had a very general practice of entering into treaties in simplified form. In those cases, the practice of provisional application had been found highly convenient. Paragraph 2 offered a perfect safeguard, since if a treaty was brought before parliament and it became apparent that parliamentary approval was not likely to be forthcoming, the government could change its decision and terminate the treaty.[52]

For multilateral treaties, provisional application ends among parties for which the treaty enters into force. However, it continues to apply among States that have not become parties unless they choose to terminate such application.

C. The customary international law status of Article 25 of the VCLT

The ILC's commentary on Article 25 says nothing about it being a rule of customary international law.[53] But State practice has largely comported with Article 25(1) in agreements to apply a treaty provisionally. As a result, two recent commentators on provisional application have found paragraph 1 to be custom.[54] Article 25(2)'s status was initially less clear; it had not been proposed by the ILC and only emerged to ensure States did not oppose the Article's inclusion in the VCLT. But, the author is not aware of any case in which a party wishing to terminate provisional application in accordance with paragraph 2 has encountered any difficulty. Moreover, as discussed below, the International Atomic Energy Agency (IAEA) has established a mechanism for dealing with withdrawals from provisional application that suggests that they are automatic.[55] These and other developments lead Villiger to conclude that Article 25(2) 'indubitably reflects an established customary rule of international law'.[56]

D. The residual character of Article 25 of the VCLT

Even as a rule of custom, Article 25 only provides a default rule. Thus, Article 25(2) provides for termination of provisional application on notice '[u]nless the treaty

---

[52] Vienna Conference, Second Session (n 36) 43 [89]–[90]. A current example of the application of Art 25, para 2 is the recent termination by the EU of the provisional application of the EU–Morocco Protocol relating to the Fisheries Partnership Agreement between the European Community and the Kingdom of Morocco after the European Parliament refused to approve the Protocol. The EU communication notifies Morocco of the immediate termination of provisional application and relies on the corresponding article in the Vienna Convention on the Law of Treaties between States and International Organizations or between International Organizations (n 1). A draft of the EU communication appears in a document of the Council of the European Union, No 18678/11 (14 December 2011).

[53] A point noted in *Kardassopoulos v Georgia*, Decision on Jurisdiction (6 July 2007) ICSID Case No ARB/05/18 [217].

[54] D Mathy, 'Article 25 Provisional Application' in Corten and Klein (n 49), vol 2, 639, 641; Villiger (n 48) 357.

[55] See nn 82–84 and accompanying text.

[56] Villiger (n 48) 357.

otherwise provides or the negotiating States have otherwise agreed'. States have taken advantage of this caveat to craft their own termination provisions. For example, the Arrangement on Provisional Application of the Agreement on the Establishment of the ITER (International Thermonuclear Experimental Reactor) International Fusion Energy Organization for the Joint Implementation of the ITER Project provides for withdrawal on 120 days written notice.[57]

In some cases, moreover, States have agreed to avoid Article 25 altogether and instead employ the older practice of having a treaty enter into force provisionally and/or definitively. Although such two-tiered provisions are rare today, multilateral commodity agreements continue to use them since those treaties have shorter durations and require measures that avoid gaps between regimes. The 2010 International Cocoa Agreement provides an example of this approach:

Article 57
Entry into force

1. This Agreement shall enter into force definitively on 1 October 2012, or anytime thereafter, if by such date Governments representing at least five exporting countries accounting for at least 80 per cent of the total exports of countries listed in annex A and Governments representing importing countries having at least 60 per cent of total imports as set out in annex B have deposited their instruments of ratification, acceptance, approval or accession with the Depositary. It shall also enter into force definitively once it has entered into force provisionally and these percentage requirements are satisfied by the deposit of instruments of ratification, acceptance, approval or accession.

2. This Agreement shall enter into force provisionally on 1 January 2011 if by such date Governments representing at least five exporting countries accounting for at least 80 per cent of the total exports of countries listed in annex A and Governments representing importing countries having at least 60 per cent of total imports as set out in annex B have deposited their instruments of ratification, acceptance, approval or accession, or have notified the Depositary that they will apply this Agreement provisionally when it enters into force. Such Governments shall be provisional Members.

3. If the requirements for entry into force under paragraph 1 or paragraph 2 of this article have not been met by 1 September 2011, the Secretary-General of the United Nations Conference on Trade and Development shall, at the earliest time practicable, convene a meeting of those Governments which have deposited instruments of ratification, acceptance, approval or accession, or have notified the Depositary that they will apply this Agreement provisionally. These Governments may decide whether to put this Agreement into force definitively or provisionally among themselves, in whole or in part, on such date as they may determine or to adopt any other arrangement as they may deem necessary.[58]

---

[57] (16 December 2006) OJ L0081, 358, Arts 4–5.
[58] [2011] 50 ILM 673, Art 57 (not yet in force).

III. Provisional Application in Modern Practice

Recent practice illustrates that States now provide for provisional application for a wide range of treaties. In her study on provisional application of treaties, Albane Geslin states that approximately 3 per cent of the (mostly bilateral) treaties that she examined in the UN database contained provisional application provisions.[59] This figure appears consistent with those for post-Second World War multilateral treaties contained in Christian L Wiktor's magisterial *Multilateral Treaty Calendar/Repertoire des Traités Multilateraux*.[60] That said, certain subjects appear more susceptible to provisional application, with the UN Secretary-General's records identifying commodity conventions and the law of the sea as areas generating the largest number of actions for provisional application of treaties. The EU also appears to be particularly willing to engage in provisional application where there is a need to gain member States' consent to mixed agreements concluded by the EU.

States today pursue provisional application to serve several functions. Most often, provisional application provides a way for States to fill an urgent need to apply a signed but unratified treaty. It may also allow States for whom domestic ratification requirements are no bar to apply a treaty that they favour in advance of its entry into force. It may, as in arms limitation treaties, provide a timeline for taking measures following signature to pave the way for application of the treaty once it enters into force. Further, in some cases, provisional application gives States room to prepare rules and regulations for an IO that the treaty will bring into existence, and even, if necessary, to modify the terms by which that IO will function. Finally, provisional application may serve as a second-best alternative to applying all or parts of a treaty where circumstances preclude a treaty temporarily (or even permanently) from entering into force.

In terms of urgency, for example, there seems to be a substantial practice of initiating arbitrations on the basis of provisional application agreements to ensure that the issuance of an award and the ability to implement it are not delayed. Belgium and the Netherlands' 2003 Arbitration Agreement concerning the reactivation of the Iron Rhine railway line provided for the Agreement's provisional application pending the completion of the constitutional formalities in both countries.[61] As a result of provisional application, the arbitration proceeded to an award on 24 May 2005, notwithstanding that parties did not bring the Arbitration Agreement itself into force until 1 July 2005.[62]

---

[59] A Geslin, *La Mise en Application Provisoire des Traités* (Pedone, Paris 2005) 347.

[60] CL Wiktor, *Multilateral Treaty Calendar/Repertoire des Traités Multilateraux* (Martinus Nijhoff, The Hague 1998) passim.

[61] (22 July 2003) 2332 UNTS 486–7 (parties agreed 'to execute the Arbitral Tribunal's decision as soon as possible by taking a decision on the definitive route, and on the temporarily and restricted re-use of the historical route').

[62] Ibid; *Arbitration regarding the Iron Rhine ('Ijzeren Rijn') Railway (Belgium/Netherlands)* (2005) XXVII RIAA 35.

In other instances, provisional application provides space for the necessary groundwork to enable the treaty's operation once it enters into force. The most recent example of this may be the Protocol on Provisional Application that is part of the New START Treaty.[63] It has also become relatively common for a treaty to establish a preparatory commission that operates in advance of the entry into force of a treaty establishing a new organization. One of the earliest and best known examples of this is the UN Convention on the Law of the Sea (UNCLOS), Article 308(4) of which provides:

4. The rules, regulations and procedures drafted by the Preparatory Commission shall apply provisionally pending their formal adoption by the Authority in accordance with Part XI.[64]

Without Article 308(4), it would have been impossible for the seabed regime to have functioned until UNCLOS entered into force. The actual establishment of the Preparatory Commission and the entrustment to it of important functions is found in the Final Act of the Conference (Annex I, resolution II).[65] Article 308(4)'s purpose was to give legal effect to the stated materials to allow the Preparatory Commission to take action having binding effect prior to the 1982 Convention's entry into force.

An even more fundamental and significant provisional application precedent was Article 7 of the 1994 Agreement relating to the Implementation of Part XI of the United Nations Convention on the Law of the Sea, 10 December 1982.[66] Although Article 7 of the implementing Agreement is entitled provisional application, it is atypical in addressing partial implementation of a separate treaty—Part XI of UNCLOS—that had not entered into force. The implementing agreement provided that if on 16 November 1994 it had not entered into force—and it had not—it would be applied provisionally by those States that had consented to its adoption in the UN General Assembly or had signed it, except for those States that notified the depositary otherwise. Professor Aust characterized the arrangement as amounting to '*implied* consent to provisional application, but with an opt-out'.[67] According to the Secretary-General's status list for the 1994 Agreement, sixteen States opted out of provisional application although they later approved the agreement itself.

---

[63] New START Treaty (13 May 2010) US Senate Treaty Doc 111–5, 111th Congress 2nd Session, 358.

[64] UN Convention on the Law of the Sea (adopted 10 December 1982, entered into force 16 November 1994) 1833 UNTS 3, 518 (UNCLOS).

[65] Final Act of the Third UN Conference on the Law of the Sea (10 December 1982) <http://www.un.org/depts/los/convention_agreements/texts/final_act_eng> 21–6. However, a Final Act is not the only vehicle for establishing Preparatory Commissions; for others, see Aust (n 5) 175–6; Michie (n 3) 8–10.

[66] Agreement relating to the Implementation of Part XI of the United Nations Convention on the Law of the Sea of 10 December 1982 (provisional application on 16 November 1994, definitive entry into force 28 July 1996) 1836 UNTS 42.

[67] Aust (n 5) 194.

Another function served by provisional application is to deal with problems where the body that normally ratifies treaties is not functioning and thus is unable to do so. In 2010, for example, Iraq wanted to ratify an Additional Protocol it had signed with the IAEA but, owing to the absence of a parliament, it could not do so in accordance with its internal law. Iraq did, however, agree with the IAEA to apply the Additional Protocol provisionally,[68] with the understanding that it would revisit the ratification issue after it had a parliament.

In May 2004, the Committee of Ministers of the Council of Europe (COE) adopted Protocol 14 to the European Convention on Human Rights to streamline the Court's procedures in light of the large increase in its caseload.[69] Protocol 14 required ratification by all parties for entry into force; as of 2006, all parties except Russia had ratified Protocol 14, because Russia's Duma had failed to approve it. In response, the Council of Ministers opened a new protocol—14*bis*—for signature in 2009 that allowed the Court to implement its revised procedures for its parties in cases involving nationals of States that have ratified that agreement. In addition, Protocol 14*bis* required consent from only three parties to enter into force, with termination tied to Protocol 14's entry into force. After the Russian Federation ratified Protocol 14 bringing it into force for all COE member States, Protocol 14*bis* terminated on 1 June 2010.

Clearly, the treaty most extensively applied provisionally in the second half of the twentieth century was the Protocol of Provisional Application of the General Agreement on Tariffs and Trade of 30 October 1947. That instrument not only survived but grew, until it was replaced by the General Agreement on Tariffs and Trade 1994 in concert with the Marrakesh Agreement establishing the WTO, which entered into force on 1 January 1995.[70]

The 1947 General Agreement on Tariffs and Trade (GATT) never entered into force because it was linked to the Charter of the International Trade Organization, a treaty not yet drafted in 1947.[71] Article XXIX(4) of GATT provided that if the Charter did not enter into force before January 1949, or once it became clear it would not enter into force, the GATT contracting parties should meet 'to agree whether this Agreement shall be supplemented, amended, or maintained'.[72] As it turned out, the Havana Charter for an International Trade Organization was adopted at Havana on 24 March 1948, but it never entered into force. The United States failed to obtain congressional approval, and by 1950 gave up even seeking

---

[68] Additional Protocol to Nuclear Safeguards Agreement between Iraq and the International Atomic Energy Agency (signed 9 October 2008; provisionally applied 17 February 2010), IAEA Status list (20 February 2011).

[69] See L Caflisch, 'The Reform of the European Court of Human Rights: Protocol No. 14 and Beyond' (2006) 6 Human Rts L Rev, vol 2, 403–15.

[70] Texts of the WTO Agreements can be found on the WTO website at <http://www.wto.org/english/docs_e/legal_e/legal_e.htm#GATT94>.

[71] Protocol of Provisional Application of the General Agreement on Tariffs and Trade (1947) 55 UNTS 308, Arts XXVI(5)(b) and XXIX(2)(a).

[72] Ibid.

it.[73] Other States followed the US lead and declined to deposit instruments accepting the Charter.[74]

However, as Professor Jackson has shown, there was domestic legal authority for the US to apply the GATT provisionally.[75] Other States found a way as well; 128 States did so before the Protocol on Provisional Application came to an end in 1994.[76] One reason for this may have been that, in contrast to the GATT itself, the Protocol on Provisional Application required provisional application of Parts I and III of GATT, but allowed governments to apply Part II 'to the fullest extent not inconsistent with existing legislation'.[77]

Thus, according to Professor Jackson:

GATT became, by default, the general regulatory institution for world trade, filling the gap left by the demise of the ITO. This misdirected beginning . . . and the shifting of power over foreign economic affairs from the legislative to the executive . . . caused GATT to be established in a halting 'provisional' manner that continues to make it an anomaly among major international institutions.[78]

By 1968 there were more than a hundred international agreements that could officially be called 'GATT agreements' being provisionally applied by the United States.[79] As Professor Jackson explained:

The general practice within GATT has been to assume that protocols amending Pt. II are subject to the Protocol of Provisional Application by which GATT was originally applied. One could argue that the subsequent protocols and amendments stand upon their own feet and thus circumvent the Protocol of Provisional Application. A more appropriate analysis seems to be that technically the subsequent protocols or amendments are amendments to the Protocol of Provisional Application, which in turn incorporates by reference the General Agreement on Tariffs and Trade including the amending article, which article provides the authority for amending the Protocol of Provisional Application.[80]

In short, modern State practice reveals provisional application of a wide array of treaties for a variety of reasons, most notably urgency and in response to domestic and other barriers to a treaty's entry into force.[81] The various IOs that serve as

---

[73] (1950) 23 Dept State Bulletin 977.

[74] For a comprehensive discussion of the Charter's failure, see MM Whiteman (ed), *Digest of International Law* (Government Printing Office, Washington 1970) vol 14, 618–21.

[75] JH Jackson, 'The General Agreement on Tariffs and Trade in United States Domestic Law' (1967–68) 66 Mich L Rev 249, 253.

[76] Based on information from the WTO website <http://www.wto.org/english/thewto_e/gattmem_e.htm>.

[77] Protocol of Provisional Application (n 71) Art 1(b). Such provisions appear with some frequency in multilateral treaties. Broader formulations appear in the IAEA nuclear accident conventions, the Energy Charter Treaty, and in most of the commodity agreements, all of which are discussed in this chapter.

[78] Jackson (n 75) 252.

[79] Ibid 276.

[80] Ibid n147.

[81] There may be limits, however, on the capacity to apply a treaty provisionally; the Cook Islands and Niue's attempts to provisionally apply the 1972 Customs Convention on Containers were unperfected, presumably because those entities were not eligible to become parties to the conventions.

treaty depositaries provide additional records of State practice. The IAEA offers two instructive examples with respect to the Convention on Early Notification of a Nuclear Accident[82] and the Convention on Assistance in the Case of a Nuclear Accident or Radiological Emergency.[83] Ten States provisionally applied both with variously worded declarations.[84]

A. The legal effect of provisional application

Since the adoption of Article 25 of the VCLT, it has generally been accepted that provisional application provisions in treaties are legally binding. Rogoff and Gauditz noted, however, that the term 'applied provisionally' is ambiguous, leaving provisional application to create either 'definitive' obligations subject to *pacta sunt servanda* or obligations analogous to those in Article 18 of the VCLT not to defeat a treaty's object and purpose prior to its entry into force.[85] Rogoff and Gauditz seemed to view the alternatives as in equipoise. Other authors have gone further, suggesting *pacta sunt servanda* does not apply to provisionally applied treaties.[86] And in its section on provisional application, the 2003 edition of the UN Treaty Handbook takes an unexampled view in its discussion[87] of the 1993 International Cocoa Agreement.[88]

Most scholars, however, reject the analogy to Article 18, and as discussed in Section B below, so have cases under the Energy Charter Treaty which adopt the

---

See 988 UNTS 43 and the UN Treaty Section's Status Page on the Convention <http://treaties.un. org/pages/ViewDetails.aspx?src=TREATY&mtdsg_no=XI-A-15&chapter=11&lang=en>.

[82] Convention on Early Notification of a Nuclear Accident (adopted 26 September 1986, entered into force 27 October 1986) 1439 UNTS 275, Art 13.

[83] Convention on Assistance in the Case of a Nuclear Accident or Radiological Emergency (adopted 26 September 1986, entered into force 26 February 1987) 1457 UNTS 133, Art 15.

[84] See 'Declarations/reservations made upon signature' on the depositary status lists for the Early Notification and Assistance Conventions, at <http://www.iaea.org/Publications/Documents/Conventions/ cenna_reserv.pdf> and <http://www.iaea.org/Publications/Documents/Conventions/cacnare_reserv. pdf> respectively.

[85] MA Rogoff and BE Gauditz, 'The Provisional Application of International Agreements' (1987) 39 Maine L Rev 29, 50. For a discussion of Art 18, see Chapter 8.

[86] See eg D Vignes, 'Une notion ambiguë: l'application à titre provisoire des traités' (1972) 18 Annuaire français de droit international 181, 192; Geslin (n 59) 330; H Hillgenberg, 'A Fresh Look at Soft Law' (1999) 10 EJIL 499, 508.

[87] UN Office of Legal Affairs, *Final Clauses of Multilateral Treaties Handbook* (UN Sales No E04V3 2003) 44. Citing the 1993 Cocoa Agreement as an example, the *Handbook* states that provisional application is an 'option . . . open to a State that may wish to give effect to the treaty without incurring the legal commitments under it'. Ibid. Whatever the case under the 1993 Cocoa Agreement, the relevant text of that agreement does not represent a general rule. Still, a State reading the *Handbook* might understand the text as establishing such a rule and provisionally apply another multilateral agreement at its peril. Rather than relying on the *Handbook*, therefore, a State wishing to avoid legal obligations should examine the agreement provisions to identify any possible legal obligations before agreeing to provisionally apply an agreement. For example, the text of the 2010 International Cocoa Agreement does appear to legally bind 'provisional members' (ie those who apply it provisionally) including the EU and several other States, who are responsible for *inter alia* financial contributions. 2010 Cocoa Agreement (n 58) Art 57.

[88] International Cocoa Agreement (adopted 16 July 1993, provisional entry into force 22 February 1994) 1766 UNTS 80.

pacta sunt servanda view.[89] The majority of authorities take the view that a provisionally applied treaty constitutes a binding legal instrument, which is consistent with Article 25's own *travaux préparatoires*.[90] These views, moreover, match what the author believes may be the only ruling by a depositary for a treaty having a provisional application article. As depositary to the 1971 Food Aid Convention, the United States rejected the claim that the treaty's provisional application provision was only morally and not legally binding, explaining that:

It is very difficult, if not impossible, to perceive any valid basis for considering the effect of the deposit of a declaration of provisional application as being limited to 'moral implications'. There does not appear to be any basis for such an interpretation either in the provisions of the Convention itself or in generally recognized treaty law and practice...

The expression 'provisional application' is the subject of Article 25 of the Vienna Convention on the Law of Treaties which, although not yet in force, is the most recent consensus of the world community on the law of treaties.[91]

Under the Convention, the United States noted, specific States and the European Economic Community (EEC) could deposit a declaration of provisional application, after which Article IX provided they 'shall provisionally apply this Convention and be provisionally regarded as parties thereto'. Furthermore, the United States assumed Article 25 of the VCLT applied to the Convention, noting how it:

makes no distinction between the effect of a treaty being provisionally applied and a treaty deemed to be fully in force other than to recognize the right, unless the treaty otherwise provides, of a state to notify the other states between which the treaty is being applied provisionally of its intention not to become a party to the treaty.

The expression 'intention not to become a party to the treaty' in the last sentence of Article 25 of the Vienna Convention does not derogate from the effect of the provisions of the last sentence of Article IX of the Food Aid Convention, 1971, particularly because that sentence also contains the phrase 'and be provisionally regarded as parties thereto'.

In Article 2, paragraph 1(g) of the Vienna Convention on the Law of Treaties the word 'party' is defined as meaning 'a State which has consented to be bound by the treaty and for which the treaty is in force'.

It appears that under the provisions of the Food Aid Convention, 1971 both the European Economic Community and governments which deposited declarations of provisional application are on the same level as to rights and obligations as Governments which deposit instruments of ratification or accession except for two minor exceptions.[92]

---

[89] These authorities include G Hafner, 'The "Provisional Application" of the Energy Charter Treaty' in L Binder and others (eds), *International Investment Law for the 21st Century, Essays in Honour of Christoph Schreurer* (OUP, Oxford 2009) 593, 599–606; R Jennings and A Watts, *Oppenheim's International Law* (9th edn Longman, London 1996) vol 1, 584 n1; R Lefeber, 'The Provisional Application of Treaties' in J Klabbers and R Lefeber (eds), *Essays on the Law of Treaties. A Collection of Essays in Honour of Bert Vierdag* (Martinus Nijhoff, Leiden 1998) 90; Mathy (n 54) 652; Michie (n 3) 5–7; Villiger (n 48) 354–6; Aust (n 5) 172; and Professors James Crawford and Michael Reisman in presenting evidence to the *Yukos* arbitral tribunal; see nn 116–118 and accompanying text.

[90] See nn 39–40, 45 and accompanying text.

[91] A Rovine (ed), *Digest of United States Practice in International Law 1974* (Government Printing Office, Washington 1975) 235–6.

[92] Ibid. The exceptions being (i) the ability to give notification of an intent not to ratify, which would provide relief from any subsequent obligation pursuant to VCLT Art 25(2); and (ii) under Art X

Article 18 of the Land Mines Convention provides an alternative, and perhaps unique, set of legal effects from provisional application, applicable between a party's consent to be bound (rather than, as usual, on signature) and the Convention's entry into force for that State:

Any State may at the time of its ratification, acceptance, approval or accession, declare that it will apply provisionally paragraph 1 of Article 1 of this Convention pending its entry into force.[93]

Article 1(1) has a large scope, including commitments 'never under any circumstances' to use, develop, produce, stockpile, retain, transfer anti-personnel mines, or to assist anyone in engaging in activity prohibited by the Convention.[94] However, the period of provisional application is necessarily shorter than it would have been if, as in most cases, the obligation began on signature rather than a period of approximately six months after a State that has made a declaration under Article 18 has expressed its consent to be bound by the Convention. Five States, Austria, Mauritius, South Africa, Sweden, and Switzerland, made declarations under Article 18.

An area where provisional application's legal effects remains problematic is the accelerated application of amendments to constituent instruments of IOs, particularly absent relevant rules of the organization on the subject or agreement of all the parties.[95] The International Telecommunication Union (ITU), for example, adopted a resolution urging provisional application of amendments to certain of its basic legal instruments. It sought to avoid conflicting structures and working methods among States that have ratified amendments to the ITU Constitution and Convention and those that have not by appealing to the latter group to provisionally apply those amendments pending ratification.[96]

The application of Article 25 to the 2006 and 2008 amendments to the International Mobile Satellite Organization (IMSO) Convention proved more problematic.[97] The IMSO Assembly decided by a two-thirds majority vote to

(2) of the Convention, governments that consented by 18 June 1971 to be bound by the treaty or deposited declarations of provisional application could decide by 'mutual consent' to bring the treaty into force (provided the 1971 Wheat Convention is in force), but that such entry into force would only extend to governments that had previously consented to be bound by the Convention. Ibid.

[93] Convention on the Prohibition of the Use, Stockpiling, Production, and Transfer of Anti-Personnel Mines and on their Destruction (adopted 18 September 1997, entered into force 1 March 1999) 2056 UNTS 211, Art 18 ('Land Mines Convention'). For the evolution of the text of Art 18, see S Maslen, *Commentaries on Arms Control Treaties* (2nd edn OUP, Oxford 2005) vol I, 311–13.

[94] Land Mines Convention (n 93) Art 1(1).

[95] As Villiger points out, '(p)artial provisional application of a multilateral treaty, ie, among some States *inter se* is possible where the treaty lends itself to a fragmentation of treaty relations and other future parties will not be affected. Conversely, provisional application appears difficult in the case of so-called integral treaties (e.g., on human rights) which are to be applied collectively by all treaty parties'. Villiger (n 48) 355.

[96] ITU Resolution 69 (Kyoto, 1994) at <http://www.itu.int/aboutitu/basic-texts/resolutions/res69.html>.

[97] International Mobile Satellite Organization Convention (adopted 3 September 1976, entered into force 16 July 1979) 1143 UNTS 105 (originally the 'International Maritime Satellite Organization Convention').

apply both amendments provisionally even though its constituent instruments did not give it that authority. Switzerland objected, indicating it was unwilling to accept provisional application of the amendments (which it had voted against), and that in the absence of a provision within the organizational and constitutional documents on consensus of the members on the subject, it was not possible for the IMSO to provisionally apply the amendments to States that opposed their adoption.[98] Consistent with Article 25(1), Switzerland accepted that States favouring the amendments could provisionally apply them among themselves. It called for the depositary to notify the parties of its opposition, which was joined by ten other States.[99] These incidents suggest that IO collective action on provisional application of amendments will remain controversial (if not prohibited) unless their constituent instruments grant them such authority.[100]

On one final question of legal effect Article 25 has not proven as troublesome as initially feared. Some commentators originally expressed concern that the provisional application concept in international law would be used to evade parliamentary review and, where required, approval of ratification.[101] In practice, that does not appear to have happened. Perhaps that is attributable to the good judgment of States, who refrain from provisional application of treaties where it would likely cause domestic difficulties.

B. The Energy Charter cases on provisional application

On 17 December 1994 the European Energy Charter Conference adopted the Energy Charter Treaty (ECT) at Lisbon.[102] Part III (Articles 10–17) of the ECT provides significant protection for foreign energy sector investments in the territory of the parties. Article 26 of the ECT provides for investor-state arbitration of investment disputes under Part III arising while the Treaty was in effect. Under paragraph 3, parties give unconditional consent to nationals of a party submitting disputes concerning alleged breaches of investment-related obligations to an arbitral tribunal established 'to decide the issues in dispute in accordance with the Treaty and applicable rules and principles of international law'.[103] Finally, Article 45 of the ECT contains a particularly robust and highly complex article on provisional application:

---

[98] Cf IMO, 'Status of Multilateral Conventions and Instruments in respect of which the International Maritime Organization or its Secretary-General performs Depositary or other Functions' (29 February 2012) <http://www.imo.org/About/Conventions/StatusOfConventions/Documents/Status%20-%202012.pdf> 334.

[99] Ibid; L Caflisch, 'La pratique suisse en matière de droit international public 2008' (2009) 19 Swiss Rev Intl and Europ L 537–607 (2009).

[100] Aust's work supports this view as well. Aust (n 5) 172.

[101] See eg Lefeber (n 89) 81.

[102] Energy Charter Treaty (opened for signature 17 December 1994, entered into force 16 April 1998) [1995] 34 ILM 360, Art 45 (ECT). The ECT established a structural framework to implement the principles of a political commitment, the European Energy Charter of 17 December 1991. For an early, comprehensive treatment see TW Wälde (ed), *The Energy Charter Treaty: An East-West Gateway for Investment and Trade* (Kluwer Law International, The Hague 1996).

[103] ECT (n 102) Art 26.

Article 45—Provisional Application

(1) Each signatory agrees to apply this Treaty provisionally pending its entry into force for such signatory in accordance with Article 44, to the extent that such provisional application is not inconsistent with its constitution, laws or regulations.

(2)(a) Notwithstanding paragraph (1) any signatory may, when signing, deliver to the Depository a declaration that it is not able to accept provisional application. The obligation contained in paragraph (1) shall not apply to a signatory making such a declaration. Any such signatory may at any time withdraw that declaration by written notification to the Depository.

(b) Neither a signatory which makes a declaration in accordance with subparagraph (a) nor Investors of that signatory may claim the benefits of provisional application under paragraph (1).

(c) Notwithstanding subparagraph (a), any signatory making a declaration referred to in subparagraph (a) shall apply Part VII provisionally pending the entry into force of the Treaty for such signatory in accordance with Article 44, to the extent that such provisional application is not inconsistent with its laws or regulations.

(3)(a) Any signatory may terminate its provisional application of this Treaty by written notification to the Depository of its intention not to become a Contracting Party to the Treaty. Termination of provisional application for any signatory shall take effect upon the expiration of 60 days from the date on which such signatory's written notification is received by the Depository.

(b) In the event that a signatory terminates provisional application under subparagraph (a), the obligation of the signatory under paragraph (1) to apply Parts III and V with respect to any Investments made in its Area during such provisional application by Investors of other signatories shall nevertheless remain in effect with respect to those Investments for twenty years following the effective date of termination, except as otherwise provided in subparagraph (c).

(c) Subparagraph (b) shall not apply to any signatory listed in Annex PA. A signatory shall be removed from the list in Annex PA effective upon delivery to the Depository of its request therefor.[104]

The ECT is the first multilateral treaty to provide jurisdiction for binding dispute settlement between foreign investors and the State in which they invested to parties provisionally applying a treaty, albeit with specific caveats for domestic legal requirements and signatories that do not wish to be so bound. Under Article 45(3)(b), moreover, parties terminating provisional application cannot escape jurisdiction over disputes arising during the period of provisional application for twenty years. The ECT has been ratified by forty-five States and the EC, with five additional 'signatory' States who applied it provisionally pursuant to Article 45. One of those signatories, the Russian Federation, terminated its provisional application by notifying the depositary on 20 August 2009 that it did not intend to become a party to the ECT.[105] Under Article 45(3)(a) of the ECT, this terminated Russia's provisional application as of 19 October 2009.

---

[104] Ibid Art 45.
[105] Government Ordinance 1055-r issued by Prime Minister Putin on 30 July 2009. The notice addressed to the depositary, the Government of Portugal, is attached to the Ordinance.

By 2010, 23 cases had been brought by investors to international arbitration under the Treaty.[106] Four of these cases addressed issues of provisional application, with two of principal interest: (i) *Ioannis Kardassopoulos v Georgia (Decision on Jurisdiction)*[107] and (ii) *Yukos Universal Limited (Isle of Man) v The Russian Federation*.[108] These cases further support the binding nature of provisional application, categorically rejecting the argument that such provisions are only 'aspirational in character'.[109]

In the *Kardassopoulos* case, a Greek investor charged that the Republic of Georgia had expropriated a pipeline construction concession and failed to reimburse him for the loss of his investment. Both Greece and Georgia signed the ECT in December 1994. The alleged expropriations took place between 1995 and 1997, when both parties were provisionally applying the treaty.

Kardassopoulos argued that under Article 45(1) of the ECT Georgia was bound by the Treaty's obligations between the date of its signature and ECT entry into force. Georgia argued that provisional application was 'only aspirational in nature' and thus it had no legal obligation to refrain from expropriation during the provisional application period.[110] After categorically rejecting Georgia's argument that provisional application was only aspirational, the Tribunal reasoned that 'properly interpreted in accordance with international law' Article 45(1) obliged both States to apply the whole Treaty as if it had entered into force on 17 December 1994, the date on which they both had signed it:

> 209. Applying the ECT provisionally is used in contradistinction to its entry into force: '[...] agrees to apply this Treaty provisionally pending its entry into force [...]'. Provisional application is therefore <u>not the same as</u> entry into force. But the ECT's provisional application is a course to which each signatory 'agrees' in Article 45(1): it is (subject to other provisions of the paragraph) thus a matter of legal obligation. The Tribunal cannot therefore accept Respondent's argument that provisional application is only aspirational in character.

> 210. It is 'this Treaty' which is to be provisionally applied, *i.e.,* the Treaty as a whole and in its entirety and not just a part of it; and use of the word 'application' requires that the

---

[106] K Hobér, 'Investment Arbitration and the Energy Charter Treaty' (2010) 1 J Intl Disp Settlement 153–90.

[107] *Kardassopoulos v Georgia* (n 53).

[108] *Yukos Universal Ltd v Russian Federation, Interim Award on Jurisdiction and Admissibility* (2009) PCA Case No AA 227 <http://ita.law.uvic.ca/documents/YULvRussianFederation-InterimAward-30Nov2009.pdf>. *Yukos'* two companion cases are not discussed here because the tribunal handed down substantially identical decisions affirming jurisdiction and admissibility, although the three cases will proceed separately on the merits. *Hulley Enterprises Ltd v Russian Federation, Interim Award on Jurisdiction and Admissibility* (2009) PCA Case No AA 226; *Veteran Petroleum Trust v Russian Federation, Interim Award on Jurisdiction and Admissibility* (2009) PCA Case No AA 228.

[109] In addition to the cases discussed in the text, two others have addressed provisional application. See Arbitration Institute of Stockholm Chamber of Commerce, *Petrobart Ltd v The Kyrgyz Republic, Final Award* (2005) Arbitration Case No 126/2003 (adopting a formal approach and finding the UK's failure to include Gibraltar in its ECT instrument of ratification did not mean the UK intended to revoke its earlier ECT declaration of provisional application to Gibraltar); *Plama Consortium Ltd v Bulgaria, Decision on Jurisdiction* (2005) ICSID Case No ARB/03/24 [140] ('ECT Article 26 provisionally applied from the date of a state's signature unless that state declared itself exempt from provisional application under Article 45(2)(a)' which Bulgaria had not done).

[110] *Kardassopoulos v Georgia* (n 53) [84].

ECT be 'applied'. Since that application is to be provisional 'pending its entry into force' the implication is that it would be applied on the same basis as would in due course result from the ECT's (definitive) entry into force, and as if it had already done so.

211. It follows that the language used in Article 45(1) is to be interpreted as meaning that each signatory State is obliged, even before the ECT has formally entered into force, to apply the whole ECT as if it had already done so.[111]

Noting that if, as Georgia had argued, investments made before the date of definitive entry into force were not protected during the provisional application period, the tribunal stated that 'such a result would strike at the heart of the clearly intended provisional application regime'.[112]

The most recent ECT arbitral tribunal award dealing with provisional application is *Yukos Universal Limited (Isle of Man) v the Russian Federation*.[113] Like the award in the *Kardassopoulos* case, it is an interim award on jurisdiction and admissibility, focused on issues arising before Russia's provisional application terminated on 19 October 2009.[114] The *Yukos* award specifically adopted some of the findings of the *Kardassopoulos* case on the scope of provisional application under Article 45(1) quoted above.[115] The opinion made the additional point that what it called the Limitation Clause in Article 45(1) (providing for provisional application only to 'to the extent that such provisional application is not inconsistent with its constitution, laws, or regulations') comprises an 'all-or-nothing' proposition: either the entire Treaty is applied provisionally, or it is not applied provisionally at all.[116]

The *Yukos* Tribunal then considered the applicability of the *pacta sunt servanda* rule and Article 27 of the VCLT to the Russian Federation's argument for limiting ECT provisional application as contrary to its internal law.[117] The tribunal— relying on evidence and testimony it received—identified 'a strong presumption of the separation of international from national law'.[118] It found that the negotiating parties had consented to a strong system of immediate provisional application and placed the burden of proof on the defendant State—Russia—to show whether or not its law triggered Article 45(1)'s Limitation Clause.[119]

---

[111] Ibid [209]–[210] (emphasis in original), [223].

[112] Ibid [222].

[113] *Yukos v Russian Federation* (n 108).

[114] As noted, Russia indicated it did not intend to ratify the ECT on 20 August 2009. Russia's notice to the depositary, however, focused on bringing its VCLT Art 18 obligations to an end.

[115] The similarities between the cases may not be surprising given that L Yves Fortier was the Chairman of both tribunals.

[116] *Yukos v Russian Federation* (n 108) [311]. Although the Tribunal relied primarily on VCLT Arts 31 and 32 in interpreting the ECT provisional application articles, at times the Tribunal referred to the opinions of witnesses who appeared before it, with particular emphasis on those of Mr Fremantle, a British lawyer who played a leading role in the ECT negotiations, and Professors James Crawford and W Michael Reisman on the issue of whether ECT provisional application was consistent with Russian law. See eg ibid 46–86, esp [268] n44, [285] n50.

[117] Ibid [313]; see also VCLT Art 27 ('A party may not invoke the provisions of its internal law as justification for its failure to perform a treaty').

[118] *Yukos v Russian Federation* (n 108) [316].

[119] Ibid [317]–[319].

The tribunal noted that Russia specifically allowed provisional application both under its treaty law and in its treaty practice. Here, like earlier cases, the tribunal relied on earlier official statements by the government regarding their internal laws on provisional application made in response to a 1999 COE questionnaire. In response to the question 'Is the provisional application of a treaty before its entry into force possible in your legal system and under what conditions?', Russia's succinct reply was: 'Yes, if a treaty itself so provides or signatory States so agreed'.[120] And, as the tribunal noted, Russian law adopted the same position.[121] In the end, the *Yukos* tribunal indicated that Russia was bound by its provisional application of the ECT, denying that it could invoke 'internal legislation as a justification for failure to perform a treaty'.[122]

Some commentators disagreed with certain positions taken by the *Yukos* and *Kardassopoulos* tribunals.[123] But most appear to accept the overall approach, which confirms the legally binding effect of provisional application and the customary international law status of Article 25. Moreover, the ECT is expected to produce more cases.[124] As Kaj Hobér and Sophie Nappert conclude '[p]rovisional application as it appears at Art. 45 is a deceptively simple concept, like the Russian *matryoshka* dolls, one issue leads to another'.[125] To this author, it seems inevitable that additional provisional application issues will be addressed in subsequent ECT cases.

Conclusion

The adoption of Article 25 of the VCLT clarified the law and facilitated provisional application of treaties. Today, the prevailing view is that Article 25 establishes that provisionally applied treaties are legally binding. The most authoritative decisions

---

[120] COE and BIICL (eds), *Treaty Making: Expression of Consent by States to be Bound by a Treaty* (Kluwer Law International, The Hague 2001) 245. These and similar statements by Bulgaria and Greece have made it difficult for those States to invoke ECT Art 45(1)'s Limitation Clause. See ibid 132 (Bulgaria), 183 (Greece).

[121] *Yukos v Russian Federation* (n 108) [332] (examining Art 23(1) of Russia's 1995 Federal Law on International Treaties).

[122] Ibid [313].

[123] See eg T Roe and M Happold, *Settlement of Investment Disputes under the Energy Charter Treaty* (CUP, Cambridge 2011) 77 (questioning whether tribunal's views and reliance on Professor Crawford's expert evidence 'are sufficient to outweigh what' (in their view) 'Article 45(1) clearly provides'); MH Arsanjani and WM Reisman, 'Provisional Application of Treaties in International Law: The Energy Charter Treaty Awards' in E Cannizzaro (ed), *The Law of Treaties beyond the Vienna Convention* (OUP, Oxford 2011) (finding certain aspects of the *Kardassopoulos* tribunal's interpretation of Art 45 (2)(a) unpersuasive and indicating other aspects of its interpretation of the ECT provisional application regime are 'not without problems').

[124] Professor James Crawford has noted how the ECT 'remains a hot topic' even after the *Yukos* award, and that even with Russia's cessation of provisional application, 'Russia remains bound to apply the Treaty provisionally until 2029 with respect to investments made between 17 December 1994 and 19 October 2009. Article 45 has a long arm—it remains to be seen whether it is an equally strong one': J Crawford, 'Introductory Remarks' in G Coop (ed), *Energy Dispute Resolution: Investment Protection, Transit and the Energy Charter Treaty* (Juris, Huntington 2011) 189.

[125] 'Provisional Application and the Energy Charter Treaty, The Russian Doll Provision' (2007) 10 Intl Arb L Rev 53, 57.

on the matter are those of the ECT arbitral tribunals since the ECT is the only multilateral treaty that contains a jurisdictional basis for resolution of disputes concerning provisional application of those matters. Thus, the ECT arbitral tribunal decisions, along with other State practice, confirm the position taken in Article 25.

Exactly how provisional application of treaties works, however, remains the subject of some ambiguity, which will require clarification in the ECT context and elsewhere. For example, Article 46 of the ECT prohibits reservations but does not clarify if that prohibition limits State discretion to opt out of provisional application under Article 45(2)(a) to circumstances where the Limitation Clause applies. If States must be legally unable (as opposed to politically unwilling) to provisionally apply the ECT, questions then arise about the legal effect of declarations States such as Australia and Norway made when they opted out of ECT provisional application.[126]

Regardless of whether these or different issues are resolved, it seems inevitable that in the coming years governments (and in some cases tribunals and subsidiary bodies of international organizations) will have abundant opportunities to enhance our understanding of provisional application and its potential. Thus, the ILC's August 2011 decision to add the topic of provisional application to its long-term programme of work is a welcome development. In light of the changes made to Article 25 at the Vienna Conference and the absence of either a definition of 'provisional application' or an authoritative commentary on the revised text, such additional work should add clarity to the article and reflect relevant State practice over the four decades since its adoption.

In the end, the pressures of globalization and the dynamic nature of modern international problems put States under increasing pressure to apply treaty provisions as early as possible. The provisional application of treaties gives States a vehicle for doing this. It allows them to respond to such urgency (and other interests) in quickly binding themselves to agreed courses of action.

Recommended Reading

D Anderson, 'Legal Implications of the Entry into Force of the UN Convention on the Law of the Sea' (1995) 44 ICLQ 313

M Brown, 'Report on the Law of the Sea Treaty—Alternative approach to provisional application' (4 March 1974) 93rd Cong, 2nd Sess, Committee Print of the House Committee of Foreign Affairs

COE and BIICL, *Treaty Making: Expression of Consent by States to be Bound by a Treaty* (Kluwer Law International, The Hague 2001)

P Daillier, M Forteau, and A Pellet, *Droit international public* (8th edn LGDJ, Paris 2009) 179–80

N Galus, *The Temporal Scope of Investment Protection Treaties* (BIICL, London 2008)

---

[126] For more on this question see M Polkinghorn and L Gouiffés, 'Provisional Application of the Energy Charter Treaty: The Conundrum' in Coop (n 124) 249, 261–4.

A Geslin, *La Mise en Application Provisoire des Traités* (Pedone, Paris 2005)

G Hafner, 'The "Provisional Application" of the Energy Charter Treaty' in L Binder and others (eds), *International Investment Law for the 21st Century, Essays in Honour of Christoph Schreuer* (OUP, Oxford 2009)

H Krieger, 'Article 25 Provisional Application' in O Dörr and K Schmalenbach (eds), *Vienna Convention on the Law of Treaties: A Commentary* (Springer-Verlag, Berlin 2012)

R Lefeber, 'The Provisional Application of Treaties' in J Klabbers and R Lefeber (eds), *Essays on the Law of Treaties. A Collection of Essays in Honour of Bert Vierdag* (Martinus Nijhoff, The Hague 1998) 81

D Mathy, 'Article 25–1969 Convention' in O Corten and P Klein (eds), *The Vienna Conventions on the Law of Treaties: A Commentary* (OUP, Oxford 2011) 1047

A Michie, 'The Provisional Application of Arms Control Treaties' (2005) 10 J of Conflict and Security L 345

A Michie, 'The provisional application of treaties with special reference to arms control, disarmament and non-proliferation instruments' (University of South Africa LLM thesis, 2004) <http://etd.unisa.ac.za/ETD-db/theses/available/etd-07292005-085331.unrestricted/02dissertation.pdf>

F Montag, *Völkerrechtliche Verträge mit vorläufigen Wirkungen* (Duncker & Humblot, Berlin, 1985)

P Picone, *L'applicazione in via provisoria degli accordi internazionale* (Eugenio Jovenc, Naples 1973)

MA Rogoff and BE Gauditz, 'The Provisional Application of International Agreements' (1987) 39 Maine L Rev 9

Senate Executive Report (1980) No 49, 98th Cong, 2d Sess

I Sinclair, *The Vienna Convention on the Law of Treaties* (2nd edn MUP, Manchester 1984)

L Sohn, 'The 1994 [LOS] Agreement and the Convention' (1994) 88 AJIL 687, 704–05

JHW Verzijl, *International Law in Historical Perspective, Part VI* (HW Sijthoff, Leiden 1973)

ME Villiger, *Commentary on the 1969 Vienna Convention on the Law of Treaties* (Martinus Nijhoff, Leiden 2009)

TW Wälde (ed), *The Energy Charter Treaty: An East-West Gateway for Investment and Trade* (Kluwer Law International, The Hague 1996)

10

Managing the Process of Treaty Formation

Depositaries and Registration

*Arancha Hinojal-Oyarbide and Annebeth Rosenboom**

Introduction

This chapter describes two very distinct functions. On the one hand, the function of the depositary of a multilateral treaty, which includes the performance of many tasks, some even before the adoption of a treaty and many before its entry into force; on the other hand, the registration of treaties, which is a process that only occurs once a treaty has entered into force.[1] Practice shows that these two functions often get confused.

When two States conclude a treaty, they commonly prepare and sign two originals.[2] Each State then keeps one. If the treaty is subject, for example, to notification of the completion of internal procedures as a condition for its entry into force, the two States will notify each other that such procedures have been fulfilled. If the treaty is amended, denounced, or subject to any other action affecting its substance or life, the parties will simply communicate with each other and solve the issues between themselves.

When more than two parties conclude a treaty, procedural complexities begin. In the past, when a multilateral treaty provided for subsequent ratification, the instruments of ratification were exchanged among all States to which the treaty was open, as in the case of bilateral treaties. The practice of designating a 'depositary' originated from the increasing number of parties to multilateral treaties and the growing complexity of the procedural issues this created. A multilateral treaty would then be prepared and signed in one copy only, which would be entrusted to one of the parties that acted as depositary, usually the State that hosted the conference at which the treaty was adopted. The depositary would subsequently

---

* The views expressed herein are those of the authors and do not necessarily reflect the views of the United Nations.

[1] In this chapter the term 'treaty' means any international agreement binding under international law.

[2] In this chapter, unless otherwise noted, the term 'State' may also mean an international organization entitled to negotiate and become party to a treaty.

prepare certified copies of the treaty; verify the acceptability of signatures, instruments of ratification, and related reservations, declarations, etc; and inform all States concerned of such actions and also of the entry into force of the treaty. Later, international organizations (IOs) started to perform depositary functions. Today, the complexities involving treaties are even greater, not only due to the increasing number of States and IOs, but also due to the increasing volume and widening scope of the treaties that they conclude.

The registration of treaties has its origin in the vision of US President Woodrow Wilson to eliminate secret diplomacy, which he believed was the main cause of war, to advance the cause of peace.[3] The registration of treaties (and subsequent publication) is of critical importance for States, IOs, law practitioners, and scholars, as the recording and dissemination of treaties keeps them abreast of the developments in substantive international law and procedural treaty matters, which contributes, in turn, to the development of legal principles and the rule of law. Today, around 64,000 treaties are registered with the United Nations. The number of treaties registered is however smaller than the number of treaties UN members have actually entered into since the UN Charter's entry into force.[4]

The Treaty Section of the Office of Legal Affairs of the Secretariat in New York ('Treaty Section') discharges the functions of the UN Secretary-General as depositary of multilateral treaties and performs the registration functions of treaties submitted by UN member States in the fulfilment of their obligation under Article 102 of the Charter.

The first part of this chapter elaborates on the role of the depositary, tracking chronologically the depositary's functions following treaty conclusion. The problems, solutions, and current practices relevant to each phase are discussed in turn. Given the fact that the UN Secretary-General, depositary of more than 550 multilateral treaties, performs depositary functions for the largest collection of treaties of universal scope, this chapter focuses on the role of the Secretary-General and States' practices relating to the multilateral treaties deposited with him. The publication *Summary of Practice of the Secretary-General as Depositary of Multilateral Treaties* (*Summary of Practice*),[5] prepared by the Treaty Section, describes the main features of the practice followed by the Secretary-General in the exercise of his depositary functions through 1994, when the *Summary of Practice* was last published.[6] Since that time, the Secretary-General, as depositary, has sought to solve problems arising out of new situations involving the application and interpretation of international law with respect to treaties, including changes in the structure of States and the emergence of new States and IOs. The Secretary-General's practice

---

[3] RB Lillich, 'The Obligation to Register Treaties and International Agreements with the United Nations' (1971) 65 AJIL 771.

[4] An estimated 25 per cent of treaties are not registered. See also A Aust, *Modern Treaty Law and Practice* (2nd edn CUP, Cambridge 2007) 342.

[5] Treaty Section, *Summary of Practice of the Secretary-General as Depositary of Multilateral Treaties* (UN, New York 1994) UN Doc ST/LEG/7/Rev 1 ('Summary of Practice').

[6] It was reissued in 1999.

has evolved over time in response to experience, actions by UN organs, and government feedback, much of which will be highlighted in this chapter.

Other depositaries often look to the Secretary-General's practice for guidance. States and IOs perform depositary functions for a number of important multilateral treaties. An example of a State acting as depositary is the Netherlands. In addition to a number of other treaties, all Hague conventions on private international law, negotiated within the framework of the Hague Conference on Private International Law, are deposited with the Kingdom of the Netherlands.[7] The US, which is depositary for the UN Charter and Switzerland, depositary of the four 1949 Geneva Conventions and the three Additional Protocols of 1977 and 2005,[8] are other examples. IOs such as the International Labour Organization (ILO), the United Nations Educational, Scientific and Cultural Organization (UNESCO), the Food and Agriculture Organization of the United Nations (FAO), the International Atomic Energy Agency (IAEA), and the Council of Europe (COE) are, to mention a few, likewise important depositaries of multilateral treaties.[9]

The second part of this chapter explains the functions of the UN Secretariat in relation to the registration of treaties, both bilateral and multilateral, and the Secretariat's obligation to publish treaties registered with it. It discusses the scope and consequences of the registration with the Secretariat of treaties submitted by a party or the depositary and the Secretariat's publication of these treaties.

I. The Role of the Depositary

Professor Shabtai Rosenne observed that:

At the Vienna Conference on the Law of Treaties, the British delegation submitted an amendment, adopted as article 24(4) VCLT, on the entry into force of a treaty. That new paragraph established that the provisions of a treaty regarding the authentication of its text, the establishment of the consent of States to be bound by the treaty, the manner or date of its entry into force, reservations, *the functions of the depositary* and other matters arising necessarily before the entry into force of the treaty (all of these being final clauses) apply from the time of the adoption of its text. This clarified the question of the binding force of clauses relating to bringing the treaty into force. That binding force commences with the adoption of the treaty text, regardless of whether or not or when the treaty as a whole comes into force.[10]

---

[7] Ministry of Foreign Affairs, 'Depositary Duties of the Kingdom of the Netherlands' <http://www.minbuza.nl/en/key-topics/treaties/depositary-duties-of-the-kingdom-of-the-netherlands>.

[8] Eg Federal Department of Foreign Affairs, 'Switzerland as Depositary State of the Geneva Conventions' <http://www.eda.admin.ch/eda/en/home/topics/intla/humlaw/gecons/gechde.html>.

[9] In the 1960s, a practice of multiple depositaries for multilateral treaties developed to accommodate participation by entities not universally recognized. That practice has not been seen in recent years, and although it may be satisfying from a political point of view, the use of multiple depositaries causes practical problems, such as uncertainty about the effective date of an action.

[10] S Rosenne, 'Final Clauses' in R Wolfrum (ed), *The Max Planck Encyclopedia of Public International Law* (OUP, Oxford 2008) online edition at <http://www.mpepil.com> (emphasis added).

Thus, the binding force of clauses relating to the exercise of depositary functions commences with the adoption of the treaty's text. Usually, if the negotiating States wish to designate a State or IO (normally its chief administrative officer) to act as depositary, this will be mentioned in the treaty's final clauses. Most modern treaties include such a provision. The depositary's role may even begin prior to the adoption of the treaty text; it can provide advice on final clauses during the negotiation phase.

The 1969 Vienna Convention on the Law of Treaties (VCLT), which codified and to some extent developed the law and practice of States in relation to treaties between States, entered into force on 27 January 1980. Articles 76 and 77 of the VCLT were dedicated to the depositary. However, well before this time the UN Secretary-General, as well as his predecessor, the Secretary-General of the League of Nations, carried out the functions of depositary of multilateral treaties. The general mandate for the Secretary-General to perform depositary functions emanates from Article 98 of the UN Charter, which provides that the Secretary-General, besides acting in all meetings of the UN General Assembly, the Security Council, the Economic and Social Council, and the Trusteeship Council,[11] and making his annual report to the General Assembly on the work of the Organization, shall perform such other functions as are entrusted to him by these organs. Depositary functions relating to multilateral treaties deposited with the Secretary-General are discharged by the Treaty Section.[12]

At the same time, the Secretary-General, in his capacity as chief administrative officer (and not as depositary), may be requested to carry out administrative functions in relation to multilateral treaties deposited with him, such as the convening of a conference of States parties. These administrative functions are not considered depositary but rather secretariat functions and are, accordingly, normally carried out by one of the substantive offices of the Secretariat of the United Nations. Thus, for example, the Convention on Cluster Munitions provides that 'the first Meeting of States Parties shall be convened by the Secretary-General of the United Nations'.[13] After its entry into force on 1 August 2010, the first such conference was convened by the UN Office for Disarmament Affairs, which also provided the necessary secretariat assistance to the conference. Similarly, the Office of the High Commissioner for Human Rights is the substantive UN office that provides secretariat support for most human rights treaties deposited with the UN Secretary-General. Such support is often solicited in the treaties themselves. Thus, most human rights treaties establish that proposals of amendments must be transmitted to the Secretary-General of the United Nations and circulated by him to all States parties. Again, these functions are performed by the

---

[11] The Trusteeship Council suspended operation on 1 November 1994.

[12] One exception is the depositary functions in relation to mandatory deposit of charts and lists of geographical coordinates under the UN Convention on the Law of the Sea (adopted 10 December 1982, entered into force 16 November 1994) 1833 UNTS 3 (UNCLOS), which is discharged by the Division for Ocean Affairs and the Law of the Sea of the UN Office of Legal Affairs.

[13] Convention on Cluster Munitions (adopted 30 May 2008, entered into force 1 August 2010) (I-47713) [2009] 38 ILM 354, Art 11(2).

substantive office (eg the Office of the High Commissioner for Human Rights), and not by the depositary (the Treaty Section). Other multilateral treaties deposited with the Secretary-General, like the Convention on Biological Diversity,[14] set up their own secretariat to perform such administrative tasks regarding those treaties.[15]

In carrying out his depositary functions, the Secretary-General is guided by the provisions found in the treaty deposited with him and in resolutions of the General Assembly and other organs of the UN. He is also guided by international law, including customary international law, and by his own practice.

The acceptance of depositary functions by the Secretary-General is not automatic. It is the Secretary-General's practice to restrict the assumption of depositary functions to treaties of global scope, usually those adopted by the General Assembly or concluded by plenipotentiary conferences convened by UN organs and to regional treaties drawn-up within the framework of the UN regional commissions and open to participation by their entire membership. However, it remains within the Secretary-General's discretion to make exceptions to this policy and to accept the depositary role for any multilateral treaty he deems appropriate. Treaties that are intended to be deposited with the Secretary-General must confer the depositary functions on the Secretary-General and not on any other official. The Secretary-General does not accept the role of co-depositary.[16]

Where a treaty is adopted within the UN framework, the Secretary-General has to be consulted in advance, particularly so that he, as depositary, may comment on the final clauses. In 2001, the sheer volume of treaties deposited with the Secretary-General (and some difficulties regarding the interpretation and application of final clauses) led the Secretary-General to issue a bulletin establishing procedures to be followed by UN departments, offices, and officials with regard to treaties concluded by or under the UN's auspices.[17] The bulletin describes, *inter alia*, the procedure to be followed when a multilateral treaty is intended to be deposited with the Secretary-General, including a requirement that draft final clauses must be submitted by the relevant department, office, or regional commission to the Treaty Section for review and comment prior to finalization.

Even though this bulletin is addressed to the departments, offices, and other entities of the UN, the same procedures apply to treaties drawn up outside the UN framework where it is intended that the Secretary-General be the depositary. In these cases he also must receive and accept a request to perform depositary functions. For example, requests for the Secretary-General to act as the depositary were made in the case of the Convention on the Prohibition of the Use, Stockpiling, Production and Transfer of Anti-Personnel Mines and on their Destruction

---

[14] Convention on Biological Diversity (adopted 5 June 1992, entered into force 29 December 1993) 1760 UNTS 79.

[15] See also Summary of Practice (n 5) [31]–[33].

[16] Ibid [15]–[19].

[17] See UN Secretariat, 'Procedures to be followed by the departments, offices and regional commissions of the United Nations with regard to treaties and international agreements' (28 August 2001) UN Doc ST/SGB/2001/7.

(Anti-Personnel Landmines Convention)[18] and the Convention on Cluster Munitions.[19] Both conventions were negotiated outside of the UN framework.

As stipulated in Article 76 of the VCLT, the functions of the depositary of a treaty are international in character and the depositary is obliged to act impartially in performing those functions. Such impartiality is of utmost importance. Article 76 reads:

1. The designation of the depositary of a treaty may be made by the negotiating States, either in the treaty itself or in some other manner. The depositary may be one or more States, an international organization or the chief administrative officer of the organization.

2. The functions of the depositary of a treaty are international in character and the depositary is under an obligation to act impartially in their performance. In particular, the fact that a treaty has not entered into force between certain of the parties or that a difference has appeared between a State and a depositary with regard to the performance of the latter's functions shall not affect that obligation.

The specific functions of the depositary are established and codified in Article 77 of the VCLT:

1. The functions of a depositary, unless otherwise provided in the treaty or agreed by the contracting States, comprise in particular:
(*a*) keeping custody of the original text of the treaty and of any full powers delivered to the depositary;
(*b*) preparing certified copies of the original text and preparing any further text of the treaty in such additional languages as may be required by the treaty and transmitting them to the parties and to the States entitled to become parties to the treaty;
(*c*) receiving any signatures to the treaty and receiving and keeping custody of any instruments, notifications and communications relating to it;
(*d*) examining whether the signature or any instrument, notification or communication relating to the treaty is in due and proper form and, if need be, bringing the matter to the attention of the State in question;
(*e*) informing the parties and the States entitled to become parties to the treaty of acts, notifications and communications relating to the treaty;
(*f*) informing the States entitled to become parties to the treaty when the number of signatures or of instruments of ratification, acceptance, approval or accession required for the entry into force of the treaty has been received or deposited;
(*g*) registering the treaty with the Secretariat of the United Nations;
(*h*) performing the functions specified in other provisions of the present Convention.

2. In the event of any difference appearing between a State and the depositary as to the performance of the latter's functions, the depositary shall bring the question to the attention of the signatory States and the contracting States or, where appropriate, of the competent organ of the international organization concerned.[20]

---

[18] Anti-Personnel Landmines Convention (adopted 18 September 1997, entered into force 1 March 1999) 2056 UNTS 211, Art 21.
[19] Cluster Munitions Convention (n 13) Art 22.
[20] For the negotiating history of VCLT Arts 76 and 77, see ME Villiger, *Commentary on the 1969 Vienna Convention on the Law of Treaties* (Martinus Nijhoff, Leiden 2009) 921–46.

Because these articles establish the depositary's basic role and functions, there is no need for negotiating States to specify these in the treaty. Unless a new function is to be set up, simply designating a depositary will suffice. The depositary will be guided by the treaty's procedural provisions, normally contained in its final clauses, in carrying out its functions. The final clauses, however, also describe the actions that States must undertake vis-à-vis the treaty. Accordingly, the final clauses need to be clear to avoid difficulties of interpretation and application for both States and the depositary. This is precisely why the depositary should be consulted in the drafting of the final clauses well before the adoption of the treaty. The depositary does not, however, involve itself with the application of other, substantive parts of the treaty.[21]

A. Preparation of the original treaty and the certified true copies

Following adoption of a treaty's text, the depositary prepares the original treaty. As the original treaty will include the treaty text in all authentic languages, the text in all authentic languages must be submitted to the Treaty Section. Today most texts are submitted only electronically. The Treaty Section will then ensure that the various authentic texts are complete before formatting the original treaty. The original treaty consists of a title page including the title of the treaty in all authentic languages listed in English alphabetical order. This is followed by the texts in all authentic languages, also listed in English alphabetical order.[22] Multilateral treaties deposited with the Secretary-General are, in most cases, authentic in the six official languages of the UN: Chinese, English, French, Russian, Spanish, and Arabic. Following the text and right after the testimonium, is a signature page for each State that could sign the particular treaty, again listed in English alphabetical order. The name of the State in all authentic languages of the treaty also appears on this page. The treaty is then bound as a loose-leaf so that the names of potential, new State signatories can be inserted. Those treaties still open for signature are kept in vaults in the Treaty Section for easy access. Contrary to most bilateral treaties whereby each party has its own original, only one original is prepared for a multilateral treaty.

Certified true copies based on the original treaty that contain the title page and text in all authentic languages in the sequence described above are then printed. The Under-Secretary-General for Legal Affairs, the Legal Counsel, certifies that the text is a true copy of the treaty and this certification is included as the last page of the certified true copy. The depositary then sends copies to all that can participate in the treaty. The depositary also announces the opening for signature of the treaty.[23] All communications from the depositary to States are sent through

---

[21] See eg S Rosenne, 'The Depositary of International Treaties' (1967) 61 AJIL 923–45.

[22] Arabic appears at the end to respect the reading from right to left.

[23] See eg UN Secretary-General, 'Convention on the Rights of Persons with Disabilities: Opening for Signature' (22 December 2006) C.N.1236.2006 and UN Secretary-General, 'Convention on the Rights of Persons with Disabilities: Issuance of Certified True Copies' (18 January 2007) C.N.37.2007

Circular Notifications (CNs). CNs are always issued in English and French. Since 1 April 2010, CNs are only issued electronically and are sent to subscribers by e-mail. They are also posted on the website of the Treaty Section, the United Nations Treaty Collection (UNTC).[24] Anyone can subscribe to an automatic service provided by the Treaty Section to receive these CNs.[25]

The Secretary-General adds the new treaty to the publication *Multilateral Treaties Deposited with the Secretary-General* (MTDSG).[26] The MTDSG contains the status list of each treaty deposited with the Secretary-General, including subsequent protocols, amendments, etc. This publication also contains the text of all reservations, declarations, objections, etc, made by States in relation to treaties deposited with the Secretary-General. The MTDSG is maintained and published in English and French. The electronic version of this invaluable publication is updated daily.

B. Signature

The treaty will open for signature at a stipulated date or as soon as the treaty is prepared and the certified true copies are circulated. Some treaties open for signature in solemn and formal ceremonies officiated by a representative of the Secretary-General, which may attract a high number of signatories.[27] The officiating representative, acting as depositary, both declares the treaty open and receives the signatures at a signing ceremony. A message from the Secretary-General may then be read. For instance, the following message was delivered at the opening for signature for the Convention on Cluster Munitions, held in Oslo on 3 December 2008:

The large number of participants here today attests to the broad support enjoyed by the Convention. I am honoured to assume the duties of depositary, and encourage all governments to sign and ratify the Convention without delay. Sadly, there remains much work to do in mitigating the dreadful humanitarian suffering caused by cluster weapons and the United Nations is firmly committed to continuing those efforts. Congratulations again to all who have made this day possible.[28]

---

both relating to the Convention on the Rights of Persons with Disabilities (adopted 13 December 2006, entered into force 3 May 2008) 2515 UNTS 3 ('Convention on Disabilities').

[24] See UN Secretary General, 'Depositary Notifications (CNs) by the Secretary General' (Database) <http://treaties.un.org/pages/CNs.aspx>.

[25] UN Secretary-General, 'Treaty Section—Documents: General Information' (28 January 2010) C.N.31.2010 (28 January 2010).

[26] UN Secretary-General, 'MTDSG' (Database) <http://treaties.un.org/pages/ParticipationStatus. aspx>.

[27] For example, the ceremony for the opening for signature of the Convention on Disabilities (n 23) and its Optional Protocol attracted 127 signatures and the one for the Convention on Cluster Munitions (n 13) attracted 92.

[28] UN Department of Public Information, 'Signing of Cluster Munitions Convention Marks Major Step Forward in Global Efforts to Control Noxious Spread of Deadly, Inhuman Weapons, Says Secretary-General' (3 December 2008) <http://www.un.org/News/Press/docs/2008/sgsm11981. doc.htm>. Similar messages are issued upon the entry into force of conventions deposited with him.

Some treaties remain open for signature indefinitely; others remain open until the date of entry into force. It is also possible that a treaty remains open for signature for only a limited period of time. The VCLT stipulates in its Article 18 that States that have signed a treaty are obliged to refrain from acts that would defeat the object and purpose of that treaty.[29]

Only Heads of State, Government, and Ministers of Foreign Affairs (or a person acting on behalf of one of these authorities *ad interim*) may sign a treaty without full powers. For all other representatives, full powers must be issued before that person may sign a particular treaty on behalf of his or her government.[30] If full powers are needed, they should be delivered to the depositary prior to the treaty signing.[31] A fax of the signed full powers or a scanned, e-mailed copy is, in accordance with established practice, considered sufficient, provided that the original full powers are received as soon as possible following the signing of the treaty. A telegram sent in the name of the person granting the full powers and containing the same information is not sufficient.

Once a treaty is signed, the depositary will update the status list (published in the MTDSG) for that treaty to include the new signatory to the treaty. The date published in the status list is the date that the representative of the State affixed the signature to the treaty. This date, however, may differ from the date at which the State becomes a party to the treaty. Unless the State has signed the treaty definitively, it will need to express its consent to be bound by ratifying, accepting, or approving the treaty. There is no time limit for these actions. States may become a party to a treaty many years after they have signed it, or may never become a party to it.[32]

One sometimes hears about States that have 'unsigned' a treaty. In practice, however, the signature remains where it was put on paper. The signature is not removed from the MTDSG but a footnote containing the text of the communication regarding the State's intention not to ratify the treaty is added. That communication is then reproduced and distributed in a CN by the Treaty Section. Normally, this and other treaty actions are communicated within one to two days of their receipt by the depositary.

C. Consent to be bound and entry into force

The provisions of the treaty itself set up the modalities by which a State may become a party to it. These provisions can be found in the final clauses and can be

---

[29] For more discussion of treaty signature, see Chapter 8.

[30] Exceptionally, some States such as the United Kingdom issue general full powers for the Permanent Representative to the UN in New York.

[31] See Treaty Section, *Treaty Handbook* (UN, New York 2006) available at <http://treaties.un.org/doc/source/publications/THB/English.pdf>.

[32] For more discussion of full powers and methods of consent to be bound, see Chapter 7, Parts II. A, 184 *et seq.* and III, 195 *et seq.*

in the form of ratification, approval, or acceptance[33] following (simple) signature; accession; or definitive signature.[34] Formal confirmation is equivalent to ratification and is normally provided for in case the treaty is open to IO participation. The depositary will follow the final clauses of the treaty. For example, if the treaty indicates the possibility of approval, then the instrument of approval deposited by the State will be accepted as such. If an instrument of approval is received and the treaty only provides for ratification or accession as modalities of expression of the consent to be bound, depending on whether that State has signed the treaty or not, the depositary will indicate in the CN that an instrument of either ratification or accession has been deposited and the State concerned will be informed accordingly.

Before a treaty enters into force, the ratifications will be disseminated in CNs including the effective date of deposit.[35] This is the date of receipt of the instrument by the Secretary-General. It can be the date of receipt of a faxed or e-mailed copy of the instrument, or the date of receipt of the actual instrument. Generally, a State faxing or e-mailing a copy of the instrument will wish to affect the deposit as soon as possible and will have contacted the Treaty Section in advance to express this desire. In such cases, the date of deposit will be the date the fax or e-mail is received. Only after the depositary resolves that the original instrument or its copy is in proper and due form will the instrument be received for deposit. The State can choose to make an appointment for a ceremony in which the instrument is handed over to the officiating representative, acting as depositary (a photographic opportunity). If the treaty requires a mandatory declaration to effectuate consent to be bound, then the instrument cannot be deposited until receipt of such declaration. All actions (ratifications, accessions, etc) are then immediately published in the MTDSG on the internet.

A treaty will enter into force in accordance with its terms. Normally, this occurs sometime after a certain number of ratifications have been deposited. Once these required conditions have been met, the treaty will enter into force and the depositary will issue a CN specifying the date of entry into force. This CN will also cite the treaty's relevant provisions regarding entry into force. For example, the CN announcing the Convention on the Rights of Persons with Disabilities' entry into force reads:

---

[33] For ease of discussion, 'ratification' as used herein refers also to acceptance and approval in addition to ratification.

[34] Succession is another way that a State may express its consent to be bound by multilateral treaties and, unlike the other methods for consent, it is not regulated by the treaties' final clauses. For more on succession, see Chapter 16.

[35] See eg UN Secretary-General, 'Paraguay: Ratification' (4 August 2010) C.N.485.2010 (relating to the International Convention for the Protection of all Persons from Enforced Disappearance (adopted 20 December 2006, entered into force 23 December 2010) (I-48088) <http://treaties.un. org/doc/Publication/CTC/Ch_IV_16.pdf>). Note that instruments of withdrawal or denunciation, if permitted, will also be distributed in a CN. See eg UN Secretary-General, 'United Kingdom of Great Britain and Northern Ireland: Denunciation' (19 October 2007) C.N.1016.2007 (relating to the Convention on a Code of Conduct for Liner Conferences (adopted 6 April 1974, entered into force 6 October 1983) 1334 UNTS 15).

The Secretary-General of the United Nations, acting in his capacity as depositary, communicates the following:

On 3 April 2008, the conditions for the entry into force of the Convention were met. Accordingly, the Convention will enter into force on 3 May 2008, in accordance with its article 45 which reads as follows:

'1. The present Convention shall enter into force on the thirtieth day after the deposit of the twentieth instrument of ratification or accession.

2. For each State or regional integration organization ratifying, formally confirming or acceding to the present Convention after the deposit of the twentieth such instrument, the Convention shall enter into force on the thirtieth day after the deposit of its own such instrument.'[36]

Once the treaty has entered into force, a CN will also be issued for each individual State that ratifies the convention after its entry into force. The CN will precisely indicate on which date the treaty shall enter into force for that State, in accordance with the relevant provisions of the treaty. The status list of the treaty in the MTDSG will indicate the date of entry into force of the treaty and the date of deposit of the instruments of ratification, accession, etc. It does not indicate the date of the entry into force of the treaty for each individual State. As described above, this date can be found in the corresponding CNs.

D. Authorities competent to issue full powers and instruments of consent to be bound

Before a State representative affixes his or her signature to a multilateral treaty, the depositary has to ascertain whether that representative is competent to do so, that is, whether he or she is duly authorized by his or her government. In accordance with customary international law,[37] only certain qualified authorities, that is, Heads of State, Heads of Government, and Ministers for Foreign Affairs may represent their State for the purpose of signing a treaty without producing full powers. Otherwise, a government must authorize its representative by issuing specific full powers to sign a particular treaty or treaties. Some States issue general full powers for a representative to sign (and make certain notifications) for all treaties deposited with a particular depositary.[38] The depositary must then determine whether the full powers are issued by the proper authority, as full powers can only be produced by one of the three qualified authorities.

It is important to distinguish full powers from credentials to represent a State in conferences convened for the purpose of drafting and adopting treaties. Such credentials are not sufficient for treaty-signing purposes.

---

[36] UN Secretary-General, 'Convention on the Rights of Persons with Disabilities: Entry Into Force' (3 April 2008) C.N.226.2008 (relating to the Convention on Disabilities (n 23)).

[37] See VCLT Art 7(2)(a).

[38] This is the practice of eg the United Kingdom, China, and Germany with respect to multilateral treaties deposited with the UN Secretary-General.

Instruments expressing consent to be bound must also be issued by one of the three qualified authorities. Who, among these authorities, must sign the instrument will depend on the internal laws of each State. Occasionally, the depositary receives full powers or instruments issued by an acting Head of State, Government, or Minister for Foreign Affairs. These instruments are also accepted for deposit if the instrument states that the issuing authority is signing in such capacity.[39]

E. Entities that may become parties

Multilateral treaties specify which States or IOs may become parties thereto. The depositary must ensure that only those entities to which the treaty is open sign or express consent to be bound. Final provisions on participation vary, but today multilateral treaties of universal scope are generally open to all States. They may also be open to some or all IOs depending on the substance of the treaty and the competences of organizations in that particular field. Rarely are they open to other entities.[40]

In the past, the Secretary-General, as depositary, encountered problems concerning the possible participation in treaties open to all States of entities that appeared to be States but could not be admitted to the United Nations due to the veto of a permanent member of the Security Council. Since the veto did not affect membership procedures for the UN's specialized agencies, a number of those States joined these organizations and thus gained recognition in the international community. For this reason, multilateral treaties often contained a clause specifying that they were open for participation by States members of the UN, any of its specialized agencies, or the IAEA. Parties to the Statute of the International Court of Justice (ICJ) and States invited by the General Assembly were also permitted to participate. This clause was known as the 'Vienna formula'.

Treaties open to all States have also given rise to the question of whether certain entities, whose status as sovereign States is unclear, could be permitted to participate in a treaty under the 'any State' or 'all States' formula. The Secretary-General, as depositary, has always been of the view that determining whether those entities fall within this formula is beyond his competence and he has sought directives from the General Assembly and other UN organs in this respect. On 14 December 1973, the General Assembly issued an understanding, in which it stated that:

The Secretary-General, in discharging his functions as a depositary of a convention with an 'all States' clause, will follow the practice of the Assembly in implementing such a clause and, whenever advisable, will request the opinion of the Assembly before receiving a signature or an instrument of ratification or accession.[41]

[39] See Summary of Practice (n 5) [104]–[138]; Treaty Handbook (n 31) 6–11.

[40] UNCLOS (n 12) Art 305, for example, sets out a detailed list of entities that can participate in the Convention. In a UN treaty first, Art 42 of the Convention on Disabilities (n 23) provides for the participation of 'regional integration organizations' without using the term 'economic'; this reflects the evolution of the EU's competences in social and other non-economic matters.

[41] See World Health Organization (WHO), 'Resolution of the Twenty-Sixth World Health Assembly Amending the Constitution of the WHO' (1973) UNJY 79 n9.

The practice of the General Assembly this understanding refers to is primarily found in unequivocal indications from the Assembly that it considers a particular entity to be a State. The Secretary-General has implemented this practice in cases such as Guinea-Bissau and the Democratic Republic of Vietnam,[42] which the General Assembly had designated as States. The Secretary-General has also considered decisions of the General Assembly taken during deliberations on the implementation of the Declaration on the Granting of Independence to Colonial Countries and Peoples[43] as allowing the inclusion of newly independent countries in the 'all States' formula. The Secretary-General furthermore followed the indications of the General Assembly and other UN organs in the case of the Cook Islands, Niue, and the Marshall Islands.[44]

In 1992, the General Assembly adopted a resolution, upon the recommendation of the UN Security Council, that held that the Federal Republic of Yugoslavia could not, as it had claimed, automatically continue the former Yugoslavia's UN membership; rather the Federal Republic of Yugoslavia would be required to apply for membership. The UN Legal Counsel took the view, however, that this resolution neither changed the UN membership of the former Yugoslavia nor addressed the status of either the former Yugoslavia or of the Federal Republic of Yugoslavia with regard to multilateral treaties deposited with the Secretary-General. The Legal Counsel decided that the Secretary-General, as depositary, could not either reject or disregard the Federal Republic of Yugoslavia's claim that it continued the legal personality of the former Yugoslavia. Rather, a contrary decision from a relevant body would be required. Such a decision could come from: a competent organ of the UN directing the Secretary-General in the exercise of his depositary functions, a competent treaty organ, the contracting States to a treaty, or a competent organ representing the whole international community of States on the general issue of continuity and discontinuity of statehood. Thus, consistent with the claim of the Federal Republic of Yugoslavia, the Secretary-General did not differentiate between treaty actions performed by the former Yugoslavia and those performed by the Federal Republic of Yugoslavia. Treaty actions of either were listed under the short name 'Yugoslavia'.[45] The General Assembly admitted the Federal Republic of Yugoslavia to membership on 1 November 2000, after the Federal Republic of Yugoslavia renounced its claim to continue the legal personality of the former Yugoslavia. Then, the Secretary-General undertook a review of the multilateral treaties deposited with him in relation to many of which the former Yugoslavia and the Federal Republic of Yugoslavia had undertaken a range of treaty actions.[46]

---

[42] UNGA Res 3061 (XXVIII) (2 November 1973); UNGA Res 3067 (XXVIII) (16 November 1973).

[43] UNGA Res 1514 (XV) (14 December 1960).

[44] See Summary of Practice (n 5) [82]–[87].

[45] UN Secretariat, 'Status of the Federal Republic of Yugoslavia After General Assembly Resolution 47/1, Especially with Regard to the Publication "Multilateral Treaties deposited with the Secretary-General"' (1994) UNJY 460.

[46] See Summary of Practice (n 5) [89]; UN Office of Legal Affairs, *Final Clauses of Multilateral Treaties Handbook* (UN, New York 2003) 17–20; see also MC Wood, 'Participation of Former

Some regional treaties concluded under the auspices of the UN regional commissions are open not only to member States of the commissions that are members of the United Nations, but also to non-UN member States granted consultative status by the Economic and Social Council (ECOSOC). This has given rise to problems of participation of entities, even those recognized by a number of States, that do not meet the 'all States' condition.[47] Also, regional treaties of this kind are sometimes open to associate members that may not be fully recognized States. For example, three of the treaties concluded under the auspices of the UN Economic and Social Commission for Western Asia (ESCWA) are open to its entire membership[48] and Palestine, an associated member,[49] is party to them.

The Secretary-General has also faced difficulties with respect to IO participation in treaties open to IOs.[50] In 2006, a tribunal submitted for deposit an instrument of accession to the Vienna Convention on the Law of Treaties between States and International Organizations or between International Organizations (1986 VCLT).[51] The Secretary-General sought clarification of this tribunal's treaty-making capacity and following various exchanges informed the tribunal that he accepted on face value and good faith its argument that it met the criteria of implicit conferral of treaty-making capacity despite the fact that its constituent instrument, a bilateral agreement, did not explicitly provide for this. However, he reminded the tribunal that the 1986 VCLT explicitly conditioned participation on submission of a declaration of the organization's treaty-making capacity and that, in cases where that capacity was not explicit in the constituent instrument, the depositary's practice had been to request that such a declaration be adopted by the highest decision-making body of the organization in question. The tribunal confirmed that its highest decision-making body, the members of the tribunal, had issued the required declaration, which was submitted for deposit. Not being able to verify these assertions, the depositary informed the parties to the bilateral agreement of his exchanges with the tribunal and suggested that he would accept the instrument of accession for deposit if neither government objected. While one of the parties supported the accession, the other rejected it on the grounds that there was no evidence of intent to grant the tribunal treaty-making capacity and that the tribunal

Yugoslav States in the United Nations and in Multilateral Treaties' (1997) 1 Max Planck Ybk UN L 231 ('Final Clauses Handbook').

47 See Summary of Practice (n 5) [91]–[94].

48 These agreements are: Memorandum of Understanding on Maritime Transport Cooperation in the Arab Mashreq (adopted 9 May 2005, entered into force 4 September 2006) 2385 UNTS 125; Agreement on International Roads in the Arab Mashreq (adopted 10 May 2001, entered into force 19 October 2003) 2228 UNTS 371; and Agreement on International Railways in the Arab Mashreq (adopted 14 April 2003, entered into force 23 May 2005) 2316 UNTS 537.

49 See ECOSOC Res 2089 (LXIII) (22 July 1977), by which the Council amended the terms of reference of ESCWA and the 'Palestinian Liberation Organization' was accepted as a member of ESCWA. UNGA Res 43/177 (15 December 1988) UN Doc A/43/PV.82, changed the name to 'Palestine'.

50 See Summary of Practice (n 5) [98]–[99].

51 1986 VCLT (adopted 21 March 1986, not yet in force) [1986] 25 ILM 543.

was not competent to decide on the matter. Accordingly, the depositary did not accept the instrument for deposit.

F. Amendments to treaties

As with the text of adopted treaties, the circulation of the text of adopted amendments is one of the depositary functions. This function is often indicated in the final clauses regulating the amendment procedure. As with the text of treaties, the text of amendments to treaties deposited with the Secretary-General should be submitted to the Treaty Section for review prior to adoption. Once adopted, the amendment should be sent to the depositary as soon as possible for circulation. The text will then be entered in the MTDSG and a CN will be sent out.[52]

The circulation of proposed amendments (like the convening of conferences of States parties) is, on the contrary, not a depositary function. However, treaties sometimes delegate this duty to the Secretary-General. If so, the depositary will clarify that the Secretary-General as depositary does not perform administrative functions and that usually the relevant treaty secretariat or unit will perform this function. The depositary however has made an exception and circulates proposed amendments to transportation-related treaties concluded under the auspices of the UN Economic Commission for Europe (UNECE). These so-called 'proposals' are usually in fact adopted amendments (proposed by a UNECE technical body but subsequently adopted by the parties prior to circulation by the depositary).[53] In other cases, they are mere proposals for which no adoption procedure is set up and which are directly circulated for acceptance or rejection through a simplified non-objection procedure.[54] Two other exceptions to the practice of non-circulation of proposals of amendment by the depositary relate to the Rome Statute of the International Criminal Court (Rome Statute)[55] and the Single Convention on Narcotic Drugs, 1961, as amended by the Protocol of 25 March 1972 (Amended Single Convention on Narcotic Drugs).[56]

---

[52] See eg UN Secretary-General, 'Adoption of Amendment' (27 September 2005) C.N.992.2005 (announcing adoption of the Amendment to the Convention on Access to Information, Public Participation in Decision-Making and Access to Justice in Environmental Matters (adopted 27 May 2005, not yet in force)).

[53] Eg UN Secretary-General, 'Proposal of Amendments to Articles 14, 15 and 16 of the AGTC Agreement' (3 September 2008) C.N.623.2008 (relating to the European Agreement on Important International Combined Transport Lines and Related Installations (AGTC) (adopted 1 February 1991, entered into force 20 October 1993) 1746 UNTS 3).

[54] Eg UN Secretary-General, 'Proposal of the Kingdom of the Netherlands to the Agreement' (4 October 2006) C.N.806.2006 (relating to the Agreement concerning the Adoption of Uniform Conditions for Periodical Technical Inspections of Wheeled Vehicles and the Reciprocal Recognition of such Inspections (adopted 13 November 1997, entered into force 27 January 2001) 2133 UNTS 117).

[55] UN Secretary-General, 'South Africa: Proposal of Amendment' (30 November 2009) C.N.851.2009 (relating to the Rome Statue (adopted 17 July 1998, entered into force 1 July 2002) 2187 UNTS 3).

[56] UN Secretary-General, 'Bolivia: Proposal of Amendments by Bolivia to Article 49, Paragraphs 1(c) and 2(e)' (6 April 2009) C.N.194.2009 (relating to the Single Convention on Narcotic Drugs, as amended (entered into force 8 August 1975) 976 UNTS 105).

Instruments of expression of consent to be bound by the adopted amendments, which are prepared as separate instruments following amendment of the treaty, will be deposited and reflected in the MTDSG under the amendment itself. Once the amendment enters into force, this information will also be displayed in the status list of the amendment and a CN will be sent out to all States. Where the amendments are subject to a simplified procedure of entry into force, such as a non-objection procedure, and enter into force on the same date for all parties (and thereafter for new parties which become bound by the treaty as amended) the information is also circulated by CN but listed in the MTDSG at the beginning of the status list for the amended treaty under the heading 'text'.

G. Correction of errors

Corrections to the text of a treaty may be needed because of: an error in typing or printing, spelling, numbering, etc; discrepancies with respect to the official records of the adopting diplomatic conference; or incongruence between the different authentic languages of the treaty.[57] The depositary, as custodian of the original of the treaty, initiates the correction procedure *proprio motu* or at the request of one or more of the States that participated in the elaboration and adoption of the treaty. The depositary examines each apparent error, determines whether it does fall in one of those categories, and ensures that a correction will not modify the meaning or substance of the treaty's text. If the corrections are justified, he circulates the proposed corrections and specifies a limited period in which parties may object (usually ninety days). When the depositary is not convinced that the correction is justified, he consults with the State that proposed the correction and tries to persuade it to withdraw its proposal (a practice at which the Secretary-General has always, in practice, been successful). As a last resort, the Secretary-General would refer the matter to all States that may participate in the treaty.[58] If no objections are voiced within the stated period, the corrections are deemed adopted. The corrections are included in a *procès verbal* of rectification, which indicates that the depositary has taken into account the errors in the original of the treaty, has duly circulated the text of the proposed corrections, and that he has caused the said corrections to be effected *ab initio* in the original. These corrections also apply to the certified copies, if already circulated.

An example of this practice of consultation can be seen in the recent case of the extensive corrections that were drawn to the attention of the depositary in relation to the French text of the Nagoya Protocol on Access to Genetic Resources and the Fair and Equitable Sharing of Benefits Arising from their Utilization to the

---

[57] The Rome Statute is an example where extensive errors of all three types occurred. See eg UN Secretary-General, 'Rectification of the Statute and Transmission of the Relevant Procès-Verbal' (30 November 1999) C.N.1075.1999.

[58] The practice of the Secretary-General regarding which States were to be informed of the proposed corrections was apparently not entirely consistent in the past. See Summary of Practice (n 5) [50]–[52]. Today, the practice of the depositary is to inform all States which can participate in the treaty.

Convention on Biological Diversity (Nagoya Protocol).[59] The depositary exhaustively analysed the proposed corrections and, after consultations with those involved, drew up a definitive list of acceptable proposals. The depositary circulated these proposals[60] and received, within the objection period, certain comments that he determined were not in the nature of objections but rather a new set of corrections. Those proposals initially circulated were deemed accepted[61] and the same process of consultation and circulation was followed with respect to the newly suggested corrections.[62]

H. Reservations, objections, and communications

The Secretary-General's depositary practice with respect to reservations is notable for its significant evolution.[63] He has developed his own practice with respect to the deposit of and objections to late reservations. The practice deviates from Article 19 of the VCLT, which stipulates that reservations must be made at the time of signature or when depositing an instrument of ratification, acceptance, approval, or accession. Despite this, the Secretary-General will accept for deposit late reservations that are made after becoming a party to the particular treaty, provided that certain requirements are satisfied. First, the late reservation must be 'lodged'[64] rather than deposited. The text will be circulated and contracting States have a period of twelve months from the date of the notification of the 'lodged' reservation in which they can object to the deposit of the reservation and/or the procedure established for accepting the late reservation.[65] The language in a typical CN announcing a late reservation reads:

In keeping with the depositary practice followed in similar cases, the Secretary-General proposes to receive the reservation in question for deposit in the absence of any objection on the part of one of the Contracting States, either to the deposit itself or to the procedure envisaged, within a period of one year from the date of the present notification. In the absence of any such objection, the said reservation will be accepted for deposit upon the expiration of the above-stipulated period that is on 23 July 2009.[66]

---

[59] Nagoya Protocol (Adopted 29 October 2010) UN Doc UNEP/CBD/COP/DEC/X/1.

[60] UN Secretary-General, 'Proposal of Corrections to the Original Text of the Protocol (French version) and to the Certified True Copies' (18 March 2011) C.N.115.2011.

[61] UN Secretary-General, 'Corrections to the Original Text of the Protocol (French version) and to the Certified True Copies' (17 June 2011) C.N.356.2011.

[62] UN Secretary-General, 'Proposal of Corrections to the Original Text of the Protocol (French version) and to the Certified True Copies' (1 November 2011) C.N.711.2011.

[63] Summary of Practice (n 5) [161]–[203].

[64] UN Secretary-General, 'Bahrain: Reservation' (28 December 2006) C.N.1140.2006 (relating to the International Covenant on Civil and Political Rights (adopted 16 December 1966, entered into force 23 March 1976) 999 UNTS 171).

[65] Prior to 4 April 2000, the objection period was limited to ninety days. It was felt that a ninety-day period was too short in cases of a complex political nature or when a group of States sought to raise a common objection. See 'Statement by Legal Counsel of the UN' (Notes verbales 4 April 2000) UN Doc LA 41 TR/221 (23–1) <http://treaties.un.org/doc/source/publications/nv/2000/4_04_00.pdf>.

[66] UN Secretary-General, 'Kazakhstan: Communication' (23 July 2008) C.N.526.2008 (relating to the International Convention for the Suppression of the Financing of Terrorism (adopted 9

If no objection is received within twelve months, the reservation will be deemed accepted for deposit. If an objection is received within the time limit, the depositary will not accept the reservation for deposit. If an objection is received by the depositary after the period of twelve months, it will be sent around as a 'communication' rather than an objection to the already deposited reservation. The same practice applies to communications from States that seek to modify their existing reservations.

The ILC in its sixty-third session (2011) adopted the *Guide to Practice on Reservations to Treaties* (*Guide to Practice*).[67] The guidelines are accompanied by commentaries.[68] The ILC recommended that the General Assembly take note of the *Guide to Practice* (and it is expected to do so perhaps in 2012) and otherwise ensure its widest possible dissemination (which may include recommending its dissemination to all Member States).

While an analysis of the *Guide to Practice* is beyond the scope of this article, it is worth noting that the ILC discussions on the practice relating to late reservations have evolved to align more with the practice of the Secretary-General.[69] Also, it is worth noting the final outcome of the ILC discussions over the treatment of territorial exclusions. Until recently, the practice of the Secretary-General in relation to the treatment of territorial exclusions differed from the ILC treatment of such statements: while the ILC deemed a statement purporting to exclude the application of a treaty (as a whole) to a territory to which that treaty would be applicable in the absence of such a statement a reservation, the depositary treats it as a mere territorial declaration.[70] However, the *Guide to Practice* finally adopted by the ILC endorses the Secretary-General's approach, as it considers that a declaration by which a State purports to exclude the application of a treaty as a whole to part of its territory is not necessarily a reservation but rather an expression of a 'different intention' in the sense of Article 29 of the VCLT.[71] The comments and observations made by some of the States concerned in 2011 as regards draft guideline 1.1.3 (Reservations having territorial scope) seem to be at the origin of this change.[72]

December 1999, entered into force 10 March 2002) 2178 UNTS 197). The reservation cited here was raised belatedly but accepted in deposit a year after the date of notification. No objections to the reservation or to the procedure envisaged were received. See also, PTB Kohona, 'Some Notable Developments in the Practice of the UN Secretary-General as Depositary of Multilateral Treaties: Reservations and Declarations' (2005) 99 AJIL 433–50.

[67] ILC, 'Guide to Practice' (2011) <http://untreaty.un.org/ilc/texts/instruments/english/draft%20articles/1_8_2011.pdf> (forthcoming [2011] YBILC, vol II(2)). For a more detailed discussion of the ILC's *Guide to Practice*, see Chapter 11.

[68] ILC, 'Report of the International Law Commission on the Work of its 63rd Session' (ILC 63rd Session) (26 April to 3 June and 4 July to 12 August 2011) UN Doc A/66/10 and Add.1 <http://untreaty.un.org/ilc/sessions/62/GuidetoPracticeReservations_commentaries(e).pdf> ('ILC Commentaries on Guide to Reservations Practice').

[69] See ibid 173–185.

[70] See Final Clauses Handbook (n 46) 81–83; Summary of Practice (n 5) 80–85; Kohona (n 66); ILC Guide to Reservations Practice (n 67); ILC Commentaries on Guide to Reservations Practice (n 68).

[71] ILC Commentaries on Guide to Reservations Practice (n 68) 48–51.

[72] ILC, Reservations to Treaties: Comments and observations received from Governments: Addendum (2011) UN Doc A/CN.4/639/Add.1.

I. Conclusions on depositary practice

The practice of the Secretary-General and of States has evolved as the depositary has adapted to new situations. The Secretary-General follows prior practice when similar issues present themselves and when new issues arise he seeks guidance from principles and rules of international law, the final clauses of the relevant treaties, and if required the views of States and of appropriate UN organs.

The Secretary-General's practice also serves as an example for other depositaries, which often seek his guidance. For example, when the Treaty of Lisbon amending the Treaty on European Union and the Treaty establishing the European Community took effect in late 2009, this marked the first time a regional economic integration organization (REIO) succeeded to treaties deposited with the Secretary-General. Other depositaries and IOs were eager to learn how this succession would be dealt with. One sentence of Article 1 of the Lisbon Treaty proved crucial in this respect: 'The Union shall replace and succeed the European Community.' Was this a mere name change or was this a succession? Did the European Union (EU) need to submit information for each treaty to which it wished to succeed or was a change of name in the status of each treaty sufficient? In March 2010, the UN Secretary-General received and communicated the following:

[T]he European Union requests that the depositary notifies the other parties/signatories to the aforementioned Conventions/Agreements that with effect from 1 December 2009, the European Union has *replaced* the European Community and that it has taken over all the rights and obligations of the European Community with respect to the said Conventions/ Agreements.[73]

With a growing number of States and prominent IOs, and their increasing participation in the multilateral treaty framework, the sort of questions the depositary faces as regards the law and practice of treaties that have been discussed above, are likely to arise again, together with new problems and issues. The recently finalized and long awaited *Guide to Practice*, once considered by the General Assembly, may also lead to new developments in the field of reservations.

II. The Registration of Treaties in Accordance with Article 102 of the UN Charter: Scope and Consequences

A. Introduction

Article 102 of the UN Charter imposes on member States the obligation to register all treaties and international agreements that they enter into after the date of entry into force of the Charter.[74] Article 102 reads:

---

[73] UN Secretary-General, 'European Union: Communication' (23 March 2010) C.N.182.2010 (emphasis added).

[74] The UN Charter was adopted 26 June 1945 and entered into force 24 October 1945.

1. Every treaty and every international agreement entered into by any Member of the United Nations after the present Charter comes into force shall as soon as possible be registered with the Secretariat and published by it.

2. No party to any such treaty or international agreement which has not been registered in accordance with the provisions of paragraph 1 of this Article may invoke that treaty or agreement before any organ of the United Nations.

Obligatory registration and publication of treaties has its origin in Article 18 of the Covenant of the League of Nations (Covenant),[75] and is founded in the principle that publicity of treaties would promote public control, awaken public interest, and remove causes for distrust and conflict between States.[76] The Covenant, and later, the UN Charter, sought to ensure publicity by creating a register maintained by its secretariat that would collect and publish the texts of treaties transmitted for registration and relevant information about them.

The VCLT expanded the registration obligation and built on further developments in registration rules and practice. Article 80, 'Registration and publication of treaties', reads:

1. Treaties shall, after their entry into force, be transmitted to the Secretariat of the United Nations for registration or filing and recording, as the case may be, and for publication.

2. The designation of a depositary shall constitute authorization for it to perform the acts specified in the preceding paragraph.

Article 81 of the 1986 VCLT is similarly drafted.[77] These VCLT provisions impose a general obligation of registration, incorporate a 'filing and recording' obligation, and make the depositary's obligatory treaty registration generally applicable. They omit, however, the sanction for non-registration. How Article 80 of the VCLT should be applied, its relation with Article 102 of the UN Charter, and its customary nature have all been debated.[78] Today, though, the general acceptance of the UN registration system by member States, non-member States, and IOs, combined with the UN's quasi-universal membership may have rendered the issue less practically important.

---

[75] The Covenant of the League of Nations was incorporated as Part I of the Treaty of Peace Between the Allied and Associated Powers and Germany (adopted 28 June 1919, entered into force 10 January 1920) UKTS 1919 4 (Treaty of Versailles). Article 18 of the Covenant reads: 'Every treaty or international engagement entered into hereafter by any Member of the League shall be forthwith registered with the Secretariat and shall as soon as possible be published by it. No such treaty or international engagement shall be binding until so registered.'

[76] LON Secretariat, 'The Registration and Publication of Treaties as Prescribed Under Article 18 of the Covenant of the League of Nations' (1920) 1 LNTS 9 (Memorandum approved by the Council of the League of Nations on 19 May 1920).

[77] 1986 VCLT (n 51).

[78] Villiger (n 20) 972–6.

B. Scope of registration and registration practice

1. Obligation to register

Under the UN Charter regime, UN member States must act to register treaties with the Secretariat. The Secretariat is then obliged to publish all registered treaties. The legal obligation to register is thus born by the States, not the Secretariat. The Secretariat publishes registered treaties[79] in the *United Nations Treaty Series* (UNTS), which is one of only two publications mandated by the Charter itself.[80] The Treaty Section is the unit of the Secretariat charged with responsibility for receiving, recording, and publishing treaties. Only treaties concluded by member States after the entry into force of the Charter are to be registered in accordance with the Charter. Even though the Charter's obligation to register can only be imposed on member States, treaties between member States and a non-member State transmitted to the Secretariat by a non-member State may also be registered.[81] A treaty concluded after the entry into force of the Charter that amends a treaty concluded before the entry into force of the Charter is also subject to registration.[82]

The provisions of Article 102 have been further interpreted and developed by the General Assembly, which established detailed Regulations to give effect to Article

[79] An exception exists for treaties submitted to limited publication. By UNGA Res 33/141 (19 December 1978), the General Assembly gave the Secretariat the option not to publish *in extenso* certain categories of bilateral treaties: (i) assistance and cooperation treaties of limited scope concerning financial, commercial, administrative, or technical matters; (ii) treaties relating to the organization of conferences, seminars, or meetings; and (iii) treaties that are to be published elsewhere by the UN Secretariat or by a specialized or related agency. By UNGA Res 52/153 (15 December 1997) UN Doc A/RES/52/153, the General Assembly further extended the opt-out from *in extenso* publication to include multilateral treaties falling within the same categories. Treaties that will not be published *in extenso* are identified by an asterisk in a monthly publication: Treaty Section, *Statement of Treaties and International Agreements: registered or filed and recorded with the Secretariat* (UN, New York) (Monthly Statement), which can be retrieved from the 'Monthly Statements Database' <http://treaties.un.org/pages/MSDatabase.aspx>. A decision not to publish *in extenso* may be reversed at any time.

[80] The other being the annual report of the Secretary-General to the General Assembly on the work of the Organization as mandated in Art 98 of the Charter.

[81] Eg Agreement on the Reciprocal Promotion and Protection of Investments (Switzerland–Uruguay) (adopted 7 October 1988, entered into force 22 April 1991) 1976 UNTS 389, which was registered by Switzerland on 13 May 1997 under Registration number I-33771. Switzerland did not become a UN member State until 2002.

[82] Eg International Labour Organization (ILO) conventions, as modified by the Final Articles Revision Convention, 1946, which were registered on 15 September 1949, under registration numbers 584–640. The Final Articles Revision Convention itself, entitled 'Convention (No. 80) for the partial revision of the conventions adopted by the General Conference of the International Labour Organization at its first twenty-eight sessions for the purpose of making provision for the future discharge of certain chancery functions entrusted by the said conventions to the Secretary-General of the League of Nations and introducing therein certain further amendments consequential upon the dissolution of the League of Nations and the amendment of the Constitution of the International Labour Organization' (agreed 9 October 1946, entered into force 28 May 1947) 38 UNTS 3 was registered on 15 September 1949 under registration number 583; see also Amendments to Arts 23, 27, and 61 of the Charter of the United Nations, adopted by the General Assembly of the United Nations in resolutions 1991 A and B (XVIII) of 17 December 1963 (adopted 17 December 1963, entered into force 31 August 1965) 557 UNTS 143, which were registered on 1 March 1966 under registration number 8132.

102.[83] These Regulations spell out the requirement that the treaty be in force before registration can be effected in Article 1.[84]

Thus, for a member State's treaty to be registered it must have been concluded after the Charter entered into force and be in force. Hence, a treaty in force concluded prior to the Charter's entry into force is not subject to registration in accordance with Article 102. If such a treaty is voluntarily submitted by a UN member State, the Secretariat shall, in accordance with Article 10(b) of the Regulations, 'file and record' it, provided that it was not included in the League of Nations treaty series. Filing and recording is thus an alternative procedure to registration that may be applied to those treaties not subject to registration. While registration and filing and recording are essentially similar procedures, they are kept in separate, parallel registers to reflect their diverse legal character. Member States may submit treaties for filing and recording under Article 10(b) of the Regulations. Treaties between IOs and those submitted by non-member States[85] with other non-member States or IOs, on the other hand, are submitted for filing and recording under Article 10(a)[86] and (c) of the Regulations.

The Regulations also lay down the rules for *ex officio* treaty registration. Article 4 of the Regulations specifies that *ex officio* registration must be undertaken by the UN itself where it is a party to the treaty, is the depositary, or is specifically authorized by the treaty to affect its registration. Registration by the UN exonerates member States from their obligation to register. The Regulations further provide for the registration of subsequent actions (ratifications, accessions, withdrawals, terminations, etc) taken with regards to treaties registered with the Secretariat.

Every year since 1996, the UN Legal Counsel has sent a *note verbale* addressed to the permanent representatives of UN member States and to the heads of IOs recalling the registration obligation, offering assistance, and reminding them of the

---

[83] UNGA Res 97(I) (14 December 1946), as amended by UNGA Res 364B (IV) (1 December 1949); UNGA Res 482(V) (12 December 1950); and UNGA Res 33/141(19 December 1978) (collectively, the Regulations). See Secretariat, 'Note by the Secretariat' (1973) 859 UNTS VIII. See also UNGA Res 52/153 (15 December 1997) UN Doc A/RES/52/153; UN, 'Article 102' in *Repertory of Practice of United Nations Organs (Repertory)* (UN, New York 1955) vol V; UN, 'Article 102' in *Repertory* (UN, New York 1958) supp 1, vol 2; UN, 'Article 102' in *Repertory* (UN, New York 1964) supp 2, vol 3; UN, 'Article 102' in *Repertory* (UN, New York 1972) supp 3, vol 4; UN, 'Article 102' in *Repertory* (UN, New York 1982) supp 4, vol 2; UN, 'Article 102' in *Repertory* (UN, New York 1986) supp 5, vol 5; UN, 'Article 102' in *Repertory* (UN, New York 2001) supp 6, vol 6.

[84] The term 'entry into force' has been broadly interpreted to include treaties provisionally applied by two or more parties.

[85] See UNGA Res 23(I) (10 February 1946).

[86] Article 10(a) of the Regulations provides for the Secretariat to file and record the following categories of treaties where they are not subject to registration under Art 102:

(a) Treaties entered into by the UN or by one or more of the specialized agencies. This covers treaties between:
  (i) The UN and non-member States;
  (ii) The UN and specialized agencies or international organizations;
  (iii) Specialized agencies and non-member States;
  (iv) Two or more specialized agencies; and
  (v) Specialized agencies and international organizations.

registration requirements, including new technical requirements for submission of treaty texts to be published in the UNTS.[87]

All treaties and actions registered or filed and recorded in a month are reflected in the monthly publication *Statement of Treaties and International Agreements registered or filed and recorded with the Secretariat (Monthly Statement).*[88] Additionally, all information and documentation regarding treaties registered or filed and recorded since 1946 are today kept in a complex and comprehensive electronic database. This database is not only an information management system, but also a publication tool. Through this tool, treaties registered or filed and recorded are desktop-published in the UNTS in their original language or languages and in English and French translations where applicable. At present, the database is accessible free of charge not only to States and IOs but also to the general public.[89]

2. The term 'treaty and international agreement'

Article 102 of the Charter does not define the term 'treaty and international agreement'. Article 1 of the Regulations only adds to this term: 'whatever its form and descriptive name'. It can be said, however, that the general position has been not to define treaty and international agreement but to understand it in its broadest sense and leave the question of its scope to development through practice. Hence each UNTS volume starts with a 'Note by the Secretariat', which states:

> The terms 'treaty' and 'international agreement' have not been defined either in the Charter or in the regulations, and the Secretariat follows the principle that it acts in accordance with the position of the Member State submitting an instrument for registration that so far as that party is concerned the instrument is a treaty or an international agreement within the meaning of Article 102. Registration of an instrument submitted by a Member State, therefore, does not imply a judgment by the Secretariat on the nature of the instrument, the status of a party or any similar question. It is the understanding of the Secretariat that its action does not confer on the instrument the status of a treaty or an international agreement if it does not already have that status and does not confer on a party a status which it would not otherwise have.[90]

This statement, however, should not be interpreted as contradictory with the general duty of the Secretariat to determine, when receiving an instrument for registration or for 'filing and recording', whether such an instrument falls within the category of instruments requiring registration or filing and recording. To that end, each *Monthly Statement* also starts with a 'Note by the Secretariat' that adds:

---

[87] Eg UN Legal Counsel (3 February 2010) UN Doc LA 41 TR/230/Registration and Publication Requirements/2010. All of these *notes verbales* can be accessed at <http://treaties.un.org/doc/source/publications/NV/2010/Registration_Publication-2010.pdf>.

[88] Monthly Statement (n 79).

[89] The General Assembly approved the discontinuation of the user-fee mechanism at the end of 2007 in UNGA Res 62/62 (6 December 2007).

[90] Secretary-General, 'Note by the Secretariat' 2486 UNTS XXXV.

when treaties and international agreements are submitted by a party for the purpose of registration or filing and recording, they are first examined by the Secretariat in order to ascertain (i) whether they fall within the category of agreements requiring registration or are subject to filing and recording, and (ii) whether the technical requirements of the Regulations are met. It is noted that an authoritative body of practice relating to registration has been developed in the League of Nations and the United Nations. In some cases, the Secretariat may find it necessary to consult with the registering party concerning the question of registrability.[91]

Where doubts exist as to the nature of an instrument transmitted for registration (or filing and recording), a practice has gradually developed by which the Secretariat ascertains, in accordance with international law and previous registration practice, whether the instrument constitutes a treaty governed by international law and, if necessary, consults with the registering party.[92] States have also raised similar questions when it is unclear whether a particular instrument is subject to registration. The main issues that arise are whether the parties are subjects of international law with treaty-making capacity and whether the parties intended to conclude a treaty binding under international law.

From the very beginning, the Secretariat took a position in relation to the registration of unilateral declarations. It considered declarations pursuant to Article 36(2) of the ICJ Statute recognizing the ICJ's compulsory jurisdiction to be international agreements and registered them *ex officio*.[93] In fact, the first three registrations were such declarations.[94] The Secretariat has subsequently considered the question of whether certain other instruments received could be registered.[95] Thus, questions have commonly arisen regarding: (a) agreements between States and certain organizations, which are not considered to be treaties within the meaning of Article 102, because the organizations concerned are either not inter-governmental or, having been created by inter-governmental agreements, do not appear to have a treaty-making capacity; (b) agreements between States and certain governmental or semi-governmental agencies that, after consultation with the governments concerned, are considered not subject to registration; (c) agreements between States (or IOs) and governments of dependent territories, which are considered treaties for Article 102 purposes only if the agreement formally binds the State responsible for the conduct of the foreign relations of the dependent territory and the State and not the dependent territory is a party to the treaty; and (d) agreements on the establishment of diplomatic relations, such as joint communiqués, which are normally only political declarations and are transmitted for

---

[91] Monthly Statement (n 79) (June 2011) 5.

[92] 'Article 102' in *Repertory* (1955) vol V (n 83) [29]–[31].

[93] Ibid [47].

[94] The first was: Declaration recognizing as compulsory the jurisdiction of the Court, in conformity with Article 36, paragraph 2, of the Statute of the International Court of Justice in all legal disputes concerning the interpretation, application or validity of any treaty relating to the boundaries of British Honduras (adopted and entered into force 13 February 1946) 1 UNTS 3. On the legal nature of the declarations, see S Alexandrov, *Reservations in Unilateral Declarations Accepting the Compulsory Jurisdiction of the International Court of Justice* (Martinus Nijhoff, Dordrecht 1995) 9.

[95] 'Article 102' in *Repertory* (1955) vol V (n 83) 293, 295–6.

informational purposes (and hence will be circulated as a General Assembly document).

In these cases, registrability does not depend on the instrument's particular designation (eg memorandum of understanding, exchange of notes or letters, joint communiqué, decision, minutes, or arrangement). Rather the Secretariat looks to the form, context, and terminology of the instrument and, more importantly, whether the parties regard the instrument as a treaty binding under international law. For example, the UN usually concludes memoranda of understanding with member States for its peacekeeping operations and criminal tribunals or to arrange UN conferences. The UN considers such memoranda of understanding to be binding and registers or files and records them when it is a party to them. Once a treaty is registered, the submitting party receives a certificate of registration and these certificates are made public on the Treaty Section's website.[96] Each certificate bears the stamp of the United Nations and the signature of the Legal Counsel. Yet, this certificate should not be seen as official approval of the UN Secretariat and it is not customary for States to publish this certificate anywhere. The act of registration does not change the status or conditions of a treaty and in that sense the parties can expect no additional benefits from registration.

C. Objection to registration

Once a treaty is registered, the Treaty Section's website will immediately reflect this. The fact of registration will also be announced in the next *Monthly Statement*. This gives other States the opportunity to see whether a particular treaty which they have concluded and which has entered into force has indeed been registered, if they were not the submittor. This also gives States an opportunity to object to treaties that have been registered. One reason an objection might be raised is that the other party did not consider the instrument binding. This is sometimes the case with memorandums of understanding. This circumstance, however, can be avoided by stipulating in the instrument itself that it is not subject to registration. The Secretariat has no formal way to respond to objections to registration.

Unless the other party carefully notes which treaties are registered on a monthly basis to see if it is a party to any one of them, it may not realize that a treaty is registered until the treaty itself is the subject of discussion. In several cases such treaties have not become the subject of discussion until a dispute was submitted to mediation or the ICJ for settlement. For instance, this happened in the case of the 'Agreed Minutes Between the State of Kuwait and the Republic of Iraq Regarding the Restoration of Friendly Relations, Recognition and Related Matters' between

---

[96] See eg the certificate of registration for the Agreement on the Mutual Abolition of Visas on Diplomatic, Consular, Official and Special or Equivalent Passports between the Government of the Federative Republic of Brazil and the Government of the Republic of Panama (adopted 10 April 2000, entered into force 10 May 2000) 2116 UNTS 3, which is found at <http://treaties.un.org/doc/Treaties/2000/07/20000725%2011-46%20PM/Other%20Documents/COR-Reg-36809-Sr-46983.pdf>.

Iraq and Kuwait,[97] which was the basis for Security Council resolution 687 of 3 April 1991,[98] and the so-called 'Minutes of 25 December 1990',[99] which was the basis for the ICJ judgment of 1 July 1994 concerning the jurisdiction and admissibility of a case between Qatar and Bahrain.[100]

In response to the objection to the (late) registration of the 'Minutes of 25 December 1990' and its treaty status by Bahrain, the Court observed:

> that an international agreement or treaty that has not been registered with the Secretariat of the United Nations may not, according to the provisions of Article 102 of the Charter, be invoked by the parties before any organ of the United Nations. Non-registration or late registration, on the other hand, does not have any consequence for the actual validity of the agreement, which remains no less binding upon the parties. The Court therefore cannot infer from the fact that Qatar did not apply for registration of the 1990 Minutes until six months after they were signed that Qatar considered, in December 1990, that those Minutes did not constitute an international agreement … Accordingly Bahrain's argument on these points also cannot be accepted.[101]

D. Reliance on non-registered treaties

Despite the sanction in Article 102(2) that no party to a non-registered treaty may invoke it before any UN organ, in practice parties have invoked non-registered instruments and UN organs have considered them without delving into the issue of whether or not they were registered.[102] Although the Court in *Qatar v Bahrain* made a reference to Article 102 of the Charter, it took the Exchange of Letters of 1987[103] into account in its judgment even though it was not registered. It did so as it considered the Exchange of Letters among the 'treaties and conventions in force' between the parties.[104] Thus, the ICJ will look to a treaty, whether registered or not, if it is in force and invoked before the Court.

In a recent case before the ICJ concerning a territorial and maritime dispute between Nicaragua and Honduras, a regional free-trade treaty was mentioned in the pleadings by one of the parties. During oral argument on 13 March 2007, the counsel for Honduras referred to the 1998 'Tratado de Libre Comercio Centroamerica-Republica Dominicana'.[105] This treaty was signed by the President of Nicaragua, among others, and thereafter ratified by Nicaragua. However, the treaty

---

[97] (Adopted 4 October 1963) 485 UNTS 321.

[98] UN Doc S/RES/687.

[99] Minutes on Settlement of Disputes Regarding Joint Boundaries (Qatar-Bahrain-Saudi Arabia) (adopted 25 December 1990) 1641 UNTS 239.

[100] *Maritime Delimitation and Territorial Questions between Qatar and Bahrain, Jurisdiction and Admissibility (Qatar v Bahrain)* (Judgment) [1994] ICJ Rep 112.

[101] Ibid 122 [28].

[102] See Aust (n 4) 345–6.

[103] *Qatar v Bahrain* (n 100) 116–17 [17].

[104] In this regard, see also ibid 103 (Dissenting opinion of Judge Shigeru Oda).

[105] *Case Concerning Maritime Delimitation between Nicaragua and Honduras in the Caribbean Sea (Nicaragua v Honduras)* (Oral Proceedings of 13 March 2007) <http://www.icj-cij.org/docket/files/120/13737.pdf> [60].

was never registered with the Secretariat. According to the counsel for Honduras, 'the treaty entered into force for Nicaragua on 3 September 2002, shortly after it entered into force for Honduras'.[106] Also, according to the counsel for Honduras, the Annex to Article 2.01, an integral part of the treaty, defined a particular territory as belonging to Honduras.[107] The treaty was published in the Honduran *Gaceta no 226* on 28 November 2000.[108]

On Monday 19 March 2007, the counsel for Nicaragua mentioned the same treaty in an attempt to counter the Honduran assertions: 'A free trade treaty was signed in Santo Domingo on the dates indicated but this treaty had no such description of the Honduran territory.'[109] The counsel for Nicaragua then referred to the publication of the treaty in the Nicaraguan *Gazette* of 7 March 2002, No 46, which included Article 2.01 to which the counsel of Honduras had referred, and denied the existence of annexes tied to this article.[110]

On Thursday 22 March 2007, the counsel for Honduras thanked the Agent of Nicaragua for his assistance in clarifying the situation surrounding the annexes to the disputed treaty.[111] There seemed to have been a subsequent agreement by the parties to make certain amendments, including the removal of the Annex to article 2.01. Apparently, this revised version of the treaty had not been widely posted. According to the counsel for Nicaragua: 'To compound the difficulties the treaty has no depositary and has not been registered at the United Nations. And to make things even more interesting the possibility cannot be excluded that parties have ratified different versions of the treaty.'[112]

In its judgment of 8 October 2007, the Court observed:

The Court has obtained the text of the above-mentioned Annex. It observes that the four islands in dispute are not mentioned by name in the Annex. Moreover, the Court notes that it has not been presented with any convincing evidence that the term 'Media Luna' has the meaning advanced by Honduras. In these circumstances the Court finds that it need not further examine arguments relating to this Treaty nor its status for the purposes of these proceedings.[113]

While Article 102 stipulates that no treaty may be invoked before an organ of the UN (most commonly the ICJ) without its prior registration, in this case an unregistered treaty was invoked and obtained by the Court. After examining the disputed treaty, however, the Court found it not dispositive of the case before it and hence it did not need to determine its status.

---

[106] Ibid [61].
[107] Ibid [60].
[108] Ibid [61].
[109] *Nicaragua v Honduras* (Oral Proceedings of 19 March 2007) <http://www.icj-cij.org/docket/files/120/13751.pdf> [3]; ibid [2]–[6].
[110] Ibid.
[111] *Nicaragua v Honduras* (Oral Proceedings of 22 March 2007) <http://www.icj-cij.org/docket/files/120/13783.pdf> [24].
[112] Ibid [24].
[113] *Case Concerning Maritime Delimitation between Nicaragua and Honduras in the Caribbean Sea (Nicaragua v Honduras)* (Judgment) [2007] ICJ Rep 659 [226].

Would the Court have further considered this treaty for the purposes of these proceedings if the territory in dispute were mentioned by name in the Annex or if convincing evidence was presented to the Court that the territory in dispute was referred to in the treaty, even though the treaty was not registered with the Secretariat? It probably would have, since it had done so in the past. In this particular case, the Court did not look into the status of the treaty because it found no relevant information in the Annex. But the Court did not immediately reject consideration of the treaty on account of its lack of registration.

Would this case have come out differently had the parties stipulated that one of them was obliged to register the treaty in its final clauses, or if one of the parties had registered the treaty at its own initiative? In all likelihood, the party that took it upon itself to register the treaty would have ensured that all annexes were included. If not, the Secretariat would have pointed this out if the treaty itself referred to the annexes as an integral part of the treaty. All subsequent agreements or amendments would have had to be registered and ultimately the text in its authentic language as well as translations into French and English would have been published in the UNTS. In sum, all of the confusion about the treaty could most likely have been avoided if registration had occurred.

E. Conclusions on treaty registration

Publication of the registered treaties facilitates clarity and transparency for all parties involved, including counsel and tribunals. In addition, the publication of treaties offers an excellent source of examples upon which States may draw in drafting similar agreements. The website of the Treaty Section, in particular its UNTS database now offers authentic texts and translations into English and French where needed, for more than 64,000 agreements. In addition, one can find the registration of all treaty actions, amendments, subsequent agreements, termination of the treaty and withdrawal of the parties immediately upon registration.

Recommended Reading

A Aust, *Modern Treaty Law and Practice* (2nd edn CUP, Cambridge 2007) Chapters 18–19

R Caddell, 'Depositary' in R Wolfrum (ed), *The Max Planck Encyclopedia of Public International Law* (OUP, Oxford 2008) online edition at <http://www.mpepil.com>

R Caddell, 'Treaties, Registration and Publication' in R Wolfrum (ed), *The Max Planck Encyclopedia of Public International Law* (OUP, Oxford 2008) online edition at <http://www.mpepil.com>

DN Hutchinson, 'The Significance of the Registration or Non-Registration of an International Agreement in Determining Whether or Not it is a Treaty' (1993) 46 Current Legal Problems 257

Bruno Simma (ed), *The Charter of the United Nations: A Commentary* (2nd edn OUP, Oxford 2002)

Treaty Section, *Final Clauses of Multilateral Treaties: Handbook* (UN, New York 2003) online at <http://treaties.un.org/doc/source/publications/THB/English.pdf>

Treaty Section, *Treaty Handbook* (UN, New York 2006) online edition at <http://treaties.un.org/doc/source/publications/THB/English.pdf>

UN, *Repertory of Practice of United Nations Organs* (UN, New York 1955) online edition at <http://www.un.org/law/repertory>

UN, *United Nations Juridical Yearbook* (UN, New York 1962) online edition at <http://www.un.org/law/UNJuridicalYearbook/index.htm>

ME Villiger, *Commentary on the 1969 Vienna Convention on the Law of Treaties* (Martinus Nijhoff, Leiden 2009)

11

Treaty Reservations

Edward T Swaine

Introduction

Given the common wisdom that the subject of treaty reservations is among the most complicated in treaty law,[1] the relevant law defies easy summary; indeed, a chapter-length treatment can only discuss the most prominent issues and note others of a more incidental character. That said, it is easy enough to provide an orientation in the basic rules of the 1969 Vienna Convention on the Law of Treaties (VCLT). The subject is mostly uncontroversial. While reservations, by definition, seek unilaterally to compromise a State's treaty obligations,[2] States are nonetheless presumptively free to propose them. Generally they do so to adapt the treaty to domestic legal and political circumstances in matters that are usually of keen local (and, happily, minimal international) interest.

The VCLT rules also make clear, however, that the right to make reservations is not unfettered. States are not supposed to propose reservations when doing so is proscribed by a treaty, either because of the way that treaty addresses reservations or because the reservation is incompatible with the treaty's 'object and purpose'. Other States may also object to a proposed reservation. But if a State proposes a reservation, and another State does not object within twelve months, the reservation will modify the treaty as between them. A State that does object may do so on any basis, and if it wishes, may specify that the treaty will not enter into force as between it and the reserving State. Barring such a specification, however, a State's objection establishes relations on the basis of the entire treaty minus the reserved-to provision(s).

At least superficially, the principles set forth in the VCLT rules complicate and diversify treaty relations, but are not themselves hopelessly obscure. Once a State

---

[1] See eg H Lauterpacht, 'Report on the Law of Treaties' [1953] YBILC, vol II, 124 (describing reservations as being 'of unusual—in fact baffling—complexity'); DP O'Connell, *International Law* (2nd edn Stevens & Sons, London 1970) 230 (describing reservations as 'a matter of considerable obscurity in the realm of juristic speculation'); accord A Aust, *Modern Treaty Law and Practice* (2nd edn CUP, Cambridge 2007) 125 (quoting Lauterpacht and O'Connell and indicating such views 'are even truer today').

[2] VCLT Art 1(d) defines a reservation as 'a unilateral statement, however phrased or named, made by a State, when signing, ratifying, accepting, approving or acceding to a treaty, whereby it purports to exclude or to modify the legal effect of certain provisions of the treaty in their application to that State'.

has proposed a reservation to a treaty, three forms of future relations are possible: (i) no relations under that treaty at all, with respect to any State that has objected and made clear that it wishes to deny treaty relations; (ii) treaty relations but for the reserved-to provision(s), with respect to any State that has objected but not declined treaty relations; and (iii) treaty relations as amended by the reservation, with respect to any State that has explicitly (or tacitly) accepted the reservation. Only a fourth type of treaty relationship—application of the entire, original treaty—appears to be squarely foreclosed by a reservation.

Unfortunately, things are not even as straightforward as this suggests. Derived in large part from principles developed by the International Court of Justice (ICJ) in the human rights context, the VCLT establishes rules purportedly germane to all treaties. But they are only one part of the modern landscape, and are also arguably increasingly epiphenomenal. The VCLT's vagueness on some fundamental issues (eg the initial standing of reservations, the effect of objections, and virtually everything having to do with a treaty's 'object and purpose') contributed to its original appeal. Reservations can be initially accepted—and subsequently practised—by States operating on very different premises. However, because these rules are defeasible and expressly invite States to adopt stricter provisions, a number of important multilateral conventions have established different principles. Equally interesting, States parties to treaties that nominally reflect the VCLT default rules have developed practices that seem to diverge from it. The result has been a gradual marginalization of the VCLT regime, including in the original human rights context in which its principles were forged. This retreat from the VCLT generated a sustained effort to reconsider its rules—most prominently, by the International Law Commission (ILC), but also by an increasingly diverse set of other stakeholders.

This Chapter examines current treaty law and practice relating to reservations. It does so in five parts. Part I examines how reservations are made and distinguishes them from other unilateral acts. Part II examines the historical development of the legal rules surrounding reservations. Part III turns to the issues surrounding the initial legal status of reservations, including the continuing tension over whether all reservations must pass an initial threshold of permissibility to trigger the objection system envisaged by the VCLT. Part IV examines that objection system, while Part V examines questions of authority, examining which actors have (or claim) authority to evaluate reservations.

I. Proposing Reservations (and Other Unilateral Statements)

When a State wishes to make a reservation to a multilateral treaty,[3] it can do so fairly simply; the relevant procedures require attention to detail but are not

---

[3] Attempts to make 'reservations' to bilateral treaties are presumptively not reservations but requests for renegotiation, requiring the other party's acceptance before having any legal effect. However, at least one State—the United States—has a lengthy history of labelling such requests 'reservations' given

challenging to master.[4] As Article 19 of the VCLT explains, a 'State may, when signing, ratifying, accepting, approving or acceding to a treaty, formulate a reservation'.[5] Thus, neither informal statements nor formal statements made by a State prior to adopting the treaty constitute reservations. Reservations may accompany signature even if the treaty contemplates ratification, but States doing so must confirm those reservations when expressing their consent to be bound by the treaty.[6] Most multilateral treaties that address reservations, however, anticipate they will be made initially at the time of ratification and State practice (with some exceptions noted below) largely conforms to that understanding.[7]

Reservations must be made in writing and communicated to treaty parties as well as other States (or international organizations) entitled to become parties.[8] Reservations do not, however, need to be labelled as such. Reservations are classified by their attempted effect rather than their billing; in the words of the VCLT, a reservation 'purports to exclude or to modify the legal effect of certain provisions of the treaty in their application to that State'.[9] Reservations are thus distinguishable from two other devices that States frequently deploy in consenting to treaties: (i) interpretative declarations (or 'understandings') and (ii) (other) unilateral statements.

According to the ILC, an interpretative declaration is 'a unilateral statement, however phrased or named, made by a State or an international organization . . . purport[ing] to specify or clarify the meaning or scope of a treaty or of certain of its provisions'.[10] In other words, interpretive declarations do not seek to change or modify a State's treaty obligations, but rather explain to other parties what the State

---

its legislature's role in the treaty-making process. See R Dalton, 'United States' in D Hollis and others (eds), *National Treaty Law and Practice* (Martinus Nijhoff, Leiden 2005) 765, 775. For similar reasons, the United States repeatedly issues interpretative declarations for bilateral treaty provisions. Aust (n 1) 128.

[4] See VCLT Arts 19, 23; Aust (n 1) 153–5, 159. Significant attention is devoted to these and other procedural rules in the ILC's *Guide to Practice*, which should reduce further the possible scope for misunderstanding. ILC, 'Guide to Practice on Reservations to Treaties' (2011) <http://untreaty.un.org/ilc/texts/instruments/english/draft%20articles/1_8_2011.pdf> (forthcoming [2011] YBILC, vol II(2)) ('Guide to Practice').

[5] The rule for treaties involving international organizations is similar with the additional category of allowing reservations when 'formally confirming' a treaty. Vienna Convention on the Law of Treaties between States and International Organizations or between International Organizations (adopted 21 March 1986, not yet in force) [1986] 25 ILM 543, Art 19 ('1986 VCLT'). For more on the 1986 VCLT, see Chapter 3.

[6] VCLT Art 23(2).

[7] Aust (n 1) 154. In contrast, unless the treaty otherwise provides, withdrawal of reservations may occur at any time, provided it is in writing. Withdrawal is operative on notice; the consent of States that accepted the reservation is unnecessary. VCLT Art 22(1), (3). As an example, on 24 September 2009, Spain informed the UN Secretary General of the withdrawal of its reservation to the Genocide Convention's Art IX. See 'End note', *Multilateral Treaties Deposited with the Secretary General* <http://treaties.un.org/Pages/Treaties.aspx?id=4&subid=A&lang=en>, Ch IV.1 n29 (MTDSG).

[8] VCLT Art 23(1); 1986 VCLT (n 5) Art 23(1).

[9] VCLT Art 2(1)(d).

[10] Guide to Practice (n 4) 1.2.

understands its obligations to be. Interpretative declarations are not regulated by the VCLT, although they may play a role in treaty interpretation.[11] Finally, States may make other unilateral statements in consenting to a treaty that are neither reservations nor interpretative declarations. These unilateral statements are most often declarations of political opinion or intention on matters relating to the treaty but not to its specific provisions.[12] As with interpretative declarations, the VCLT says nothing about unilateral declarations. And although depositaries like the UN Secretary General discourage them, they are usually circulated to parties and potential parties along with any reservations or interpretative declarations.[13]

Careful attention must be paid to differentiating among these three categories. The applicability of the VCLT rules and the actual treaty relationships a State assumes can turn on whether a statement is a proposed reservation, an interpretative declaration, or some other form of unilateral statement. And to capitalize on that distinction, States have been known to propose changes to their obligations under the guise of making a 'declaration' or issuing an 'understanding'. States may do this because: (a) the treaty prohibits or restricts reservations; (b) they wish to avoid suggesting to other States the capacity to object; (c) they wish to avoid other negative consequences (such as reputational effects, or inspiring other States to propose reservations); or (d) they genuinely regard their position as within the compass of the treaty's provisions. At bottom, though, they want to limit the treaty's potential effects without overtly altering its terms, often in response to some domestic pressure or interest. States sometimes object to these attempts as reservations-in-fact when they are discovered.[14] Although they cannot be relied upon by the proposing States to alter any determinate obligations, such devices are difficult to formally exclude and run the risk of subtly altering obligations. Experience suggests that it is hard to extinguish reservations while permitting other statements, so long as the enforcement of restrictions is left to States in their individual

---

[11] Aust (n 1) 127. On the (limited) effects of interpretative declarations in the interpretative process, see R Gardiner, *Treaty Interpretation* (OUP, Oxford 2009) 94–9; see also DM McRae, 'The Legal Effect of Interpretative Declarations' (1978) 49 BYBIL 156.

[12] Two of the most common unilateral declarations are statements of non-recognition (where a State indicates its consent to a treaty should not be read as recognition of another State party) and declarations on the modalities by which a State intends to implement the treaty domestically. See Guide to Practice (n 4) 1.5.1–1.5.2.

[13] P Kohona, 'Some Notable Developments in the Practice of the UN Secretary General as Depositary of Multilateral Treaties: Reservations and Declarations' (2005) 99 AJIL 443, 447–8.

[14] In 2003, the United States objected to a Pakistani declaration in acceding to the International Convention for the Suppression of Terrorist Bombings, insisting that it was actually a reservation, and, moreover, one contrary to the Convention's object and purpose. The United States indicated, however, that its objection should not preclude its treaty relations with Pakistan. 'Declaration as reservation contrary to object and purpose' [2003] Digest of United States Practice in International Law 244–5; Aust (n 1) 129–32 (addressing 'disguised reservations', and citing examples of purported interpretations and declarations drawing objection). The ILC's *Guide to Practice* also labels as a reservation something it calls a 'conditional interpretive declaration', the effect of which is to condition a State's consent to be bound to that State's assertion of a particular interpretation of a treaty or its provisions. Guide to Practice (n 4) 1.4.

capacities.[15] And the fact that reservations are determined by their legal effect (and in principal charge other States to object irrespective of their billing) means that those treaties permitting reservations may also be afflicted by statements that have the effect of reservations without calling attention to their status.

II. Background on the Law of Reservations

The modern law of reservations—if not rival kinds of unilateral statements—is highly conventional. It consists of the VCLT rules, as clarified or modified by treaty practice, with only a residual role for customary international law principles governing States that are not constrained by the VCLT. Even in its residual role, customary international law is relevant only to the extent that particular treaties have not themselves restated the VCLT's rules or set out their own deviant principles.

Nonetheless, it is helpful to understand that important features were introduced to the customary law of reservations as it evolved through four, discrete phases.[16] In its first phase, the law reflected propositions that were thought inherent in the very nature of a treaty. The presumption was that when a putative State party to a multilateral convention proposed conditions to its assent, all the other parties would have to agree to these proposed reservations. Such unanimity followed directly from the consensual nature of treaty-making. This same consensualism, however, meant that particular treaties could specify alternative formula for dealing with reservation proposals, whether authorizing approval by some qualified majority of States or removing the issue from subsequent deliberation by banning reservations outright. The predicate, in all events, was that States made collective decisions on any particular State's proposed reservation with the same effect for all

---

[15] The 1982 UN Convention on the Law of the Sea, for example, bars parties from making reservations but permits declarations and comparable statements 'with a view, inter alia, to the harmonization of its laws and regulations with the provisions of this Convention, provided that such declarations or statements do not purport to exclude or to modify the legal effect of the provisions of this Convention in their application to that State'. UN Convention on the Law of the Sea (adopted 10 December 1982, entered into force 16 November 1994) 1833 UNTS 3, Art 310 (UNCLOS). In other instances, reservation-like declarations are tolerated, at least in the short term. For example, Denmark initially ratified the Rome Statute while attaching a territorial declaration excluding its application to the Faroe Islands and Greenland, later withdrawing that declaration following adoption of the necessary domestic decrees. See 'End Note' in MTDSG (n 7) Ch XVIII.10, n2. It is difficult to distinguish between such a declaration and a reservation. A declaration of comparable territorial exclusions relating to the jurisdiction of the European Court of Human Rights was deemed incompatible with the European Convention. See *Loizidou v Turkey* (Preliminary Objections) (1995) 20 EHRR 99 [65]–[89].

[16] This section draws on the description in ET Swaine, 'Reserving' (2006) 31 YJIL 307, 312–3. For other comprehensive accounts, see I Detter, *Essays on the Law of Treaties* (Sweet and Maxwell, London 1967); F Horn, *Reservations and Interpretive Declarations to Multilateral Treaties* (TMC Asser Institute, The Hague 1988); S Rosenne, *Developments in the Law of Treaties 1945–1986* (CUP, Cambridge 1989) 356–7, 424–6; I Sinclair, *The Vienna Convention on the Law of Treaties* (2nd edn MUP, Manchester 1984) Chapter 3; RL Bindschedler, 'Treaties, Reservations' (1984) in (2000) 4 EPIL 965; WW Bishop, 'Reservations to Treaties' (1961-II) 103 RcD 245.

non-reserving States. As a result, the possible effects of a proposed reservation on a State's obligations were reasonably apparent from the outset.

The Pan American system was one important exception to the unanimity approach.[17] It was also consensual in nature: States needed to accept a reservation for it to be effective against them, and if they objected, no relations under that treaty would be established between the reserving and the objecting State. Distinctively, though, diverse bilateral relations could be forged under the same treaty: one between all non-reserving States (the treaty's original terms), one between a reserving State and any States accepting the reservation (the treaty's original terms, as altered by the reservation), and a third kind between a reserving State and any States not accepting the reservation (no treaty relations at all).[18] This necessarily made things more complicated, but put reservations in the hands of non-reserving States, and established a clear rule—the reservation's ineffectiveness—if those States did nothing.

In a second phase, the law of treaty reservations was conceived of as a treaty-specific phenomenon that depended on the nature of the problem at hand. This approach derived from the *Reservations* case.[19] The Court started with the principle that 'in its treaty relations a State cannot be bound without its consent, and that consequently no reservation can be effective against any State without its agreement thereto', but said that this principle required 'a more flexible application' in the Genocide Convention context.[20] It observed, among other things, that in conventions aspiring to a universal character the practice evidenced greater tolerance for tacit acceptance (and for treating reserving States as States parties for all States accepting the reservation), while noting the 'great number of reservations which have been made of recent years to multilateral conventions' (seemingly, not just for conventions of a universal character).[21] The Court rejected the affiliated notion that the 'absolute integrity of the Convention as adopted' invariably required that *all* States parties consent to a reservation, citing again the tolerance of tacit assent, the seeming lack of objections to reservations, and the Pan American practice.[22]

Having dispensed with these absolutes, the Court concluded that States had latitude to forge different reservations rules. This left the issue of the intended rule for the Genocide Convention. The Court drew on the Convention's drafting history to conclude that reservations of some kind and under some conditions were anticipated.[23] For the most part, though, the ICJ emphasized the character-

---

[17] For a description, see MM Whiteman (ed), *Digest of International Law* (US Govt Printing Office, Washington 1970) vol 14, 141–4; 'Report approved by the Council of the Panamerican Union of 4 May 1932', reproduced in [1965] YBILC, vol II, 79.

[18] A Pellet, 'Article 19 of the Convention of 1969' in O Corten and P Klein, *The Vienna Conventions on the Law of Treaties: A Commentary* (OUP, Oxford 2011) vol I, 410–11.

[19] *Reservations to the Convention on the Prevention and Punishment of the Crime of Genocide* (Advisory Opinion) [1951] ICJ Rep 15 ('*Reservations* case').

[20] Ibid 21.

[21] Ibid 21–2.

[22] Ibid 24–6.

[23] It speculated that perhaps the text failed to address reservations in order to avoid encouraging them unduly. Ibid 22–3.

istics of fundamental human rights conventions like the Convention. The Court reasoned that human rights treaties: (i) were back-stopped by binding customary international law obligations (suggesting that reserving States could secure only limited latitude); (ii) tried to attain universality (warranting compromise in order to achieve broader participation); and (iii) put the consensual interests of States confronting reservations at no particular risk (because their true interest was in promoting the Convention's purposes, rather than defending sovereign interests particular to themselves).[24]

These same circumstances, the Court inferred, established a principle that 'limit[ed] both the freedom of making reservations and that of objecting to them':[25] namely, whether a proposed reservation was consistent with the treaty's object and purpose.[26] The Court recognized that States would have varied opinions about the application of this object-and-purpose test, with a resulting prospect for some confusion. (The dissenters were even more concerned, arguing that confusion could be avoided only by a default rule of unanimous consent to reservations, a rule they also felt was required by customary international law.[27]) The Court did not directly confront the question of whether an object-and-purpose test was hard-wired in all treaties (or, at least, in those that permitted reservations with less than unanimous consent). The ICJ clearly found it difficult to imagine otherwise, suggesting that principles of treaty integrity might require it, but it also deferred to the powers of States parties to derogate.[28] Ultimately, the Court's analysis seemed sufficiently context-sensitive to resist easy generalization, and it felt little cause to clarify anything beyond the result for the Genocide Convention itself—or, perhaps, for the greater class of human rights conventions to which it belonged.

The third phase in the development of the law of reservations came with the advent of the VCLT, the rules of which are discussed in the ensuing sections.[29] Although these rules owe a debt to the *Reservations* case and developments under other treaty schemes, the default regime it establishes was plainly constructed: that is, it could not in any sense be characterized as inherent in the nature of treaties generally. Nor, for that matter, can the VCLT's rules be attributed to something imminent in the nature of universal human rights treaties, despite its resemblance to the *Reservations* case approach—not least, because the VCLT establishes a default approach for *all* treaties. That global approach necessarily enhanced the possibility of complaints about the regime's fit.

---

[24] Ibid 23–4.

[25] Ibid 24.

[26] Ibid 26–7.

[27] *Reservations* case (n 19) 31–9 (dissenting opinion of Judges Guerrero, McNair, Read, and Hsu Mo).

[28] Ibid 24.

[29] For more on the ILC and VCLT drafting history, see O Corten and P Klein (eds), *The Vienna Conventions on the Law of Treaties: A Commentary* (OUP, Oxford 2011) vol I, Part II, Section 2 (Reservations); M Villiger, *Commentary on the 1969 Vienna Convention on the Law of Treaties* (Martinus Nijhoff, Leiden 2009) 257–335.

A fourth phase of the law's development, still underway, has involved reconsideration of the VCLT regime by several different constituencies. The most obvious, and most inchoate, review has come from States, which established practices both in negotiating treaties with reservations provisions and in formulating reservations and objections under the VCLT regime. Treaty bodies, particularly in the human rights context, have formed a second constituency, proposing and attempting to effectuate fundamental changes to the rules operating in those quarters.

Both States and treaty bodies are, to varying degrees, anticipated participants in the treaty reservation regime (and their respective roles are discussed further below). But two other participants also deserve note. The first is the ICJ, the body responsible for the pioneering *Reservations* opinion, which has participated in reservations questions surprisingly infrequently. Its most extensive discussion in recent opinions, however, was at pains to limit the *Reservations* case to its original context, suggesting (diplomatically) that the Court had severely underestimated the practical difficulties of relying on States to resist other States' reservations.[30]

The ILC has also returned to the fray. In 1993, the Commission decided to reexamine the VCLT reservations regime it had forged, and embarked on a course of study that took close to twenty years. The objective was ostensibly only to clarify, as opposed to revising, the rules on reservations.[31] But the sheer volume and acuity of the work—including seventeen principal reports from Special Rapporteur, Alain Pellet—has meant the project sometimes strayed, inevitably, from the purely descriptive.[32] In 2011, the ILC adopted a *Guide to Practice on Reservations to Treaties* and commended it to the General Assembly's attention,[33] along with a recommendation on mechanisms of assistance in relation to reservations.[34] Whether the *Guide* will influence the other relevant actors is at this point uncertain, but it will undoubtedly serve as a starting point for further re-examination of the present regime.

---

[30] See *Case Concerning Armed Activities on the Territory of the Congo (New Application: 2002) (Democratic Republic of the Congo v Rwanda)* (Judgment of 3 February 2006) [2006] ICJ Rep 31, 65–71 [4]–[10] (joint separate opinion of Judges Higgins, Kooijmans, Eleraby, Owada, and Simma) ('*Congo* Judgment').

[31] [1995] YBILC, vol II(2), 108 [487] (reporting a 'consensus in the Commission that there should be no change in the relevant provisions of the 1969, 1978, and 1986 Vienna Conventions' regarding reservations).

[32] An extremely succinct timeline may be found in ILC, 'Report of the International Law Commission on the work of its sixty-third session' (2011) UN Doc A/66/10 [51]–[55] ('ILC sixty-third session').

[33] See ibid [72]; Guide to Practice (n 4). The ILC has also provisionally adopted over time accompanying commentaries; these draw in part on more extensive reports prepared by the special rapporteur. ILC, 'Text of the draft guidelines constituting the Guide to Practice on Reservations to Treaties, with commentaries, as provisionally adopted by the International Law Commission' (2011) <http://untreaty.un.org/ilc/sessions/62/GuidetoPracticeReservations_commentaries(e).pdf> ('Guide to Practice Commentaries').

[34] ILC sixty-third session (n 32) [73].

III. The Initial Status of Reservations

The foundational decision made in formulating the VCLT's reservations regime—and certainly the most significant provision relating to the initial status of reservations—was the acceptance in Article 19 of a presumptive right for States to forge reservations.[35] This generalized a practice the ICJ developed in the specific context of the Genocide Convention and explained in terms consistent with other human rights treaties. The ILC and the States ratifying the VCLT apparently regarded it as more universal in nature—subject, significantly, to a contrary collective decision by States forging a treaty.

In consequence, the VCLT generally indulges the making of reservations unless the treaty expressly prohibits reservations or accepts only specific ones.[36] Simultaneously, however, the VCLT also generalized the ICJ's substantive limitation on a reservation's content. According to Article 19(c), States are not supposed to propose reservations that are incompatible with a treaty's object and purpose.[37] This test makes abundant sense as an exhortation. States should, it seems, consider whether a reservation they are considering would, even if accepted by other States, degrade the treaty's essence, and (as discussed below) other States should certainly be vigilant for such reservations when considering whether and when to object.

But putting aside, for the moment, the possibility of objection, the threshold question is whether an object-and-purpose inquiry has independent force in determining a reservation's initial status. This has evolved over time into a debate between the 'permissibility' school (according to which impermissible reservations, usually equated to those violating a treaty's object and purpose, are void *ab initio*) and the 'opposability' school (according to which such reservations are merely opposable by other States through the vehicle of objections).[38]

For permissibility advocates, a reservation's status involves a two-stage inquiry: first, whether the reservation is 'permissible' (or 'admissible') under a treaty and its object and purpose; and second, assuming it is, whether it is 'acceptable' to at least one other State.[39] Under the permissibility approach, the object-and-purpose inquiry *must* have legal significance independent of a State's objection. To a degree, this argument is motivated by a conviction that objections are insufficient to ensure the integrity of multilateral conventions. A more formal argument is that the VCLT's nature requires an objective, threshold inquiry. Article 19(c) says flatly

[35] See n 5 and accompanying text (detailing how a State 'may . . . formulate a reservation').

[36] VCLT Art 19(a)–(b) (States 'may . . . formulate a reservation unless . . . (a) the reservation is prohibited by the treaty; (b) the treaty provides that only specified reservations, which do not include the reservation in question, may be made'). For further discussion of these relatively straightforward provisions, see Aust (n 1) 133–6.

[37] VCLT Art 19(c) (States 'may . . . formulate a reservation unless . . . the reservation is incompatible with a treaty's object and purpose').

[38] See eg DW Bowett, 'Reservations to Non-Restricted Multilateral Treaties' (1976–77) 48 BYBIL 67; JM Ruda, 'Reservations to Treaties' (1975-III) 146 RcD 97, 101.

[39] See M Villiger, *Customary International Law and Treaties* (Kluwer Law International, The Hague 1997) 254–63.

that States may not (even) formulate a reservation if it is incompatible with a treaty's object and purpose—rather than providing, for example, that such reservations are prone to objection. Opposability would, notwithstanding this injunction, put the claim that a reservation is fundamentally treaty-incompatible on the same footing as any other ground for objection (or even no ground at all, since States need no basis whatsoever for an objection under the VCLT).[40] Opposability also seems to wrench the object-and-purpose test out of context: Article 19's other operative parts—on reservations prohibited by a treaty or omitted from the roster of permitted reservations—are enforceable without any State intercession.[41]

The argument for the opposability approach, however, can also draw some support from the VCLT regime. The provisions governing objections do not suggest that they are confined to objections of a less fundamental kind, or that objections relating to a treaty's object and purpose merely serve some kind of expressive function. Rather, the provisions governing acceptance indicate that a reservation is considered to be accepted by a State 'if it shall have raised no objection to the reservation' during a twelve-month period following notice of the reservation or its own consent.[42]

For opposability proponents, the more fundamental problem with permissibility is practical in character. Because the 'object and purpose' of a treaty is not self-evident, a permissibility approach is hardly self-enforcing.[43] Judicial attempts have provided little real guidance.[44] States are free to indicate more clearly when drafting a treaty where its object and purpose(s) lies, but negotiating that kind of point raises an additional obstacle to consensus, not least because it risks marginalizing other

[40] The ILC was initially inclined to follow the ICJ's *Reservations* case in limiting objections to the ground of incompatibility, but removed that limitation in response to the criticism that States might also object on other grounds. See [1966] YBILC, vol II, 279, 287, 346 (comments by Australia, Denmark, and the United States). Accordingly, it is generally accepted that objections to reservations may be made on any ground, and that the effect of an objection is the same regardless of the stated ground.

[41] See eg Treaty Section of the UN Office of Legal Affairs, *Summary of Practice of the Secretary-General as Depositary of Multilateral Treaties* (UN, New York 1994) UN Doc ST/LEG/7/Rev 1 [164], [189]–[193] (noting UN depositary practice to reject proposed reservations that do not conform to treaty provisions on reservations) ('Summary of Depositary Practice').

[42] See VCLT Art 20(5). To be sure, the quoted provision is explicitly '[f]or the purposes of Art 20 (2)–(4), which relate to other aspects of acceptance and objection that apply 'unless the treaty otherwise provides'. So, it may be argued that Art 20(5) does not apply at all to reservations not properly formulated, for which the treaty (implicitly) otherwise provides.

[43] The inscrutability of the object-and-purpose test is widely acknowledged. See eg I Buffard and K Zemanek, 'The "Object and Purpose" of a Treaty: An Enigma?' (1998) 3 AREIL L 311; J Klabbers, 'Some Problems Regarding the Object and Purpose of Treaties' (1997) 8 Finnish Ybk Intl L 138. William Schabas has noted that, in light of the VCLT's approach to treaty interpretation, the object and purpose of a treaty should be determined in light of its object and purpose. WA Schabas, 'Reservations to Human Rights Treaties: Time for Innovation and Reform' (1994) 18 Canadian Ybk Intl L 39, 48. These difficulties were forecast by the dissenters in the *Reservations* case. See (n 19) 44 (dissenting opinion of Judges Guerrero, McNair, Read, and Hsu Mo) ('What is the "object and purpose" of the Genocide Convention? To repress genocide? Of course; but is it more than that? Does it comprise any or all of the enforcement articles of the Convention? That is the heart of the matter').

[44] A Pellet, '10th Report on Reservations to Treaties, First Addendum' (2005) UN Doc A/CN.4/558/Add.1, [81] (describing ICJ case law).

provisions not so designated.[45] Entrusting such inquiries, and their policing, to a treaty-monitoring body is another potential tack, but there have been few (if any) explicit attempts at that.[46]

These limitations mean that, in practice, the permissibility approach requires each reserving State to intuit for itself whether a reservation violates a treaty's object and purpose, potentially at pain of surrendering that reservation if it is wrong.[47] Even States that imitate another State's arguably impermissible reservation may learn little from that State's experience if States failed to object, objected without making clear that they were doing so on object-and-purpose grounds, or conveyed different impressions through their varied action or inaction. Barring something patently obvious (eg a reservation that would enable violation of a *jus cogens* norm), it may be difficult for any State, whether reserving or objecting, to confidently assume common ground as to what violates a treaty's object and purpose.

Notwithstanding these practical concerns, the bulk of academic commentary sides with the permissibility approach, and the ILC's *Guide to Practice* does as well—the guidelines squarely depict reservations that are contrary to object and purpose, among others, as 'null and void, and therefore devoid of any legal effect'.[48] Furthermore, the *Guide* rejects the possibility that a reservation's permissibility or legal effect may be influenced by State acceptances or objections.[49] Nonetheless, it contemplates that 'a State or an international organization which considers that a reservation is invalid should formulate a reasoned objection as soon as possible'.[50] The exhortation, though seemingly without legal effect, is for the edification of the reserving States, other contracting States or organizations, and any treaty bodies or other authorities. Moreover, although the *Guide* suggests that an objection is formally unnecessary—and may only grudgingly be called an objection because the reservation lacks any potential legal effect—the only basis for reckoning treaty

---

[45] An alternative that avoids this problem may be found in the Racial Discrimination Convention, which precludes reservations that would be incompatible with the Convention's object and purpose or inhibit its treaty body's functions, and provides that '[a] reservation shall be considered incompatible or inhibitive if at least two-thirds of the States Parties to the Convention object to it'. International Convention on the Elimination of All Forms of Racial Discrimination (opened for signature 7 March 1966, entered into force 4 January 1969) 660 UNTS 195, Art 20(2). As Anthony Aust observed, it is unclear if this provision is supposed to supplement or supplant the VCLT rules; he also notes that the two-thirds threshold has not been met. Aust (n 1) 151–2; see also ibid 152 (noting other treaties, not framed in object-and-purpose terms, that rely on varying degrees of non-opposition to reservations).

[46] See Part V below, 298 *et seq.*

[47] The precise consequences of being wrong—making an impermissible reservation—are discussed below, but one view, often advanced as a corollary of impermissibility, denies a reservation that violates a treaty's object and purpose the same relatively favourable treatment as other reservations, and would simply disregard it, holding the reserving State bound to the treaty as if it had never proposed the reservation.

[48] Guide to Practice (n 4) 4.5.1.

[49] Ibid 3.3.3 ('Acceptance of an impermissible reservation by a contracting State or by a contracting organization shall not affect the impermissibility of the reservation.'); ibid 4.5.2(1) ('The nullity of an invalid reservation does not depend on the objection or the acceptance by a contracting State or a contracting organization').

[50] Ibid 4.5.2(2).

relations in most instances is, in point of fact, the reactions by States to each other.[51]

Practice has been less decisive than the *Guide* suggests. Several States have articulated the view that reservations that violate a treaty's object and purpose are without any legal effect, and either expressed or implied that objections on that score are not necessary to achieve that end. At the same time, States *do* object to reservations on object-and-purpose grounds, and their usual attention in doing so to the legal niceties attending objection, like the twelve-month deadline, suggests that they regard their objections as more than mere points of information.[52] Judicial bodies seem sometimes to attribute legal significance to objections in describing the validity of reservations,[53] but at the same time may note the object-and-purpose standard as though it describes an additional, independent hurdle.[54] The effect of the prevailing uncertainty is to encourage States to seek legal advantage through the filing of objections, including those claiming a violation of the object-and-purpose test, while at the same time denying to States proposing questionable reservations any confidence in those reservations even after the time for lodging objections has passed.[55]

---

[51] Guide to Practice Commentaries (n 33) 686–92.

[52] See VCLT Art 20(5). For example, the United States recently became party to Protocol III to the Convention on Prohibitions or Restrictions on the Use of Certain Conventional Weapons which may be deemed to be Excessively Injurious or to have Indiscriminate Effects (adopted 10 October 1980, entered into force 2 December 1983) 1342 UNTS 171. As part of its depositary notification, the United States reserved the right to use incendiary weapons against certain military objectives located in concentrations of civilians (Art 2(2)–(3) of Protocol III). See 'Declarations and Reservations' in MTDSG (n 7) Ch XXVI.2. In the final five days before the close of the twelve-month period following the US deposit of its consent to be bound, seventeen States objected to the US reservation, nearly all specifically claiming that it violated the Protocol's object and purpose. See J Abramson, 'US Incendiary-Weapons Policy Rebuffed' (April 2010) Arms Control Today 39. Of course, it is difficult to discern if additional States, convinced that they need not object, refrained from doing so.

[53] See eg *Case Concerning Legality of Use of Force* (Provisional Measures) [1999] ICJ Rep 761, 772 [32] (finding that '[w]hereas the Genocide Convention does not prohibit reservations; whereas Yugoslavia did not object to Spain's reservation to article IX; and whereas the said reservation had the effect of excluding that article from the provisions of the Convention in force between the Parties'). In that instance, however, Yugoslavia does not seem to have put any object-and-purpose issue before the ICJ.

[54] *Congo* Judgment (n 30) 65–71 [15]–[23] (joint separate opinion of Judges Higgins, Kooijmans, Elaraby, Owada, and Simma) (describing practice of judicial and other bodies following *Reservations* case). ICJ discussions of the incompatibility issue tend to be relatively glancing, and in most instances involve a belt-and-suspenders approach to crediting the force of reservations. See eg *Case Concerning Armed Activities on the territory of the Congo (New Application: 2002) (Democratic Republic of the Congo v Rwanda)* (Order of 10 July 2002) [2002] ICJ Rep 219, 245–6 [72] (finding that '[w]hereas the Genocide Convention does not prohibit reservations; whereas the Congo did not object to Rwanda's reservation when it was made; whereas that reservation does not bear on the substance of the law, but only on the Court's jurisdiction; whereas it therefore does not appear contrary to the object and purpose of the Convention'); *Congo* Judgment (n 30) 32 [67] (reservation to dispute settlement provision cannot be regarded as incompatible with the treaty's object and purpose); ibid 33 [68] ('The Court further notes that, as a matter of the law of treaties, when Rwanda acceded to the Genocide Convention and made the reservation in question, the DRC made no objection to it'). For the position of treaty-monitoring bodies on this question see nn 88–91 and accompanying text.

[55] Two related features of practice—the character and effect of the objections made, and the intervention of new participants in the evaluation of reservations—are examined below in Parts IV and V, 291 *et seq*.

Apart from object-and-purpose difficulties, another area of potential ambiguity involves late reservations. The VCLT does not expressly address whether reservations can be made *after* a State has expressed its consent to be bound by a treaty. Even so, the VCLT's listing of when reservations may be formulated implies that, absent State agreement, reservations made at another time are impermissible. Moreover, permitting late reservations would seem to run afoul of the consensual nature of treaty-making, suggesting that States may unilaterally alter their treaty obligations at will. In practice, however, late reservations have been allowed where unanimously accepted (expressly or tacitly) by other parties. For example, as treaty depositary for many (if not most) major multilateral treaties, the UN Secretary General circulates late reservations, provided the treaty text does not prohibit them generally or specifically. It then assumes the reservation to be accepted if no objection is received within twelve months.[56]

In light of these and other ambiguities,[57] it bears emphasis that States may regulate the initial status of reservations more overtly. The VCLT provides that the normal means of determining the status of reservations may be pretermitted if the treaty precludes a given kind of reservation, or omits it from a list of permissible reservations, and a number of treaties have been drawn in that fashion.[58] The conventional view is that such provisions are exceptional, and that too few treaties address the subject of reservations.[59] However, one recent review of a large sample of multilateral conventions deposited with the UN Secretary General suggests that fully 40 per cent of them contained a clause banning reservations.[60] Certainly some

---

[56] UN Office of Legal Affairs, *Treaty Handbook* (Sales No. E.02.V.2 2006) <http://treaties.un.org/doc/source/publications/THB/English.pdf> 3.5.3 and Annex 2 (prior to 2000 UN practice was to only allow ninety days for such objections). Objections received outside the twelve-month period are treated as communications. The UN uses the same twelve-month timeframe for objections to a reserving State withdrawing an earlier reservation and substituting it with a new or modified reservation. Ibid Annex 2.

[57] One other area of ambiguity is whether a State may withdraw from a treaty to which it had no reservations and rejoin with a reservation. Trinidad and Tobago tried this with respect to the First Optional Protocol to the International Covenant on Civil and Political Rights (ICCPR) (adopted 16 December 1966, entered into force 23 March 1976) 999 UNTS 171. Other States objected to this approach, and Trinidad and Tobago ended up withdrawing from the Optional Protocol entirely, suggesting the practice is disfavoured. In 1999, however, Guyana replicated it with more success, and is still a party to the Optional Protocol. Aust (n 1) 159–60.

[58] See eg International Convention on Arrest of Ships (adopted 12 March 1999, entered into force 14 September 2011) UN Doc A/Conf.188/6, Art 10 (identifying provisions as to which reservations are permitted); Patent Cooperation Treaty (adopted 19 June 1970, entered into force 24 January 1978) 1160 UNTS 231, Art 64 (identifying provisions as to which reservations are permitted, but barring other reservations).

[59] See eg Aust (n 1) 151 ('Unfortunately, all too many treaties are simply silent on the matter [of reservations]: sometimes because no agreement could be reached; sometimes because it was not seen as important enough, the matter being dealt with anyway by the VCLT; and sometimes because the problem was just not considered'). What it means to say that the number of treaties addressing reservations is insufficient, however, is unclear—and important. For example, it may rest on a normative preference for fewer reservations or for more focused consideration by States; on the other hand, it may simply test the hypothesis that States are dissatisfied with the way the default rules protect negotiated treaty terms. See eg Swaine (n 16) 325.

[60] See J Galbraith, 'Treaty Options' (draft November 2011) <http://www.asil.org/midyearmeeting/pdfs/papers/November_5_2pm/Treaty%20Options.pdf>, forthcoming (2012) 53 VJIL.

of the most important multilateral conventions in contemporary discourse—the 1982 UN Convention on the Law of the Sea (UNCLOS),[61] the Rome Statute establishing the International Criminal Court,[62] and the Kyoto Protocol,[63] as well as a number of environmental treaties[64]—preclude reservations altogether.

Clauses prohibiting reservations have been explained as a critical safeguard for package deals, because they prevent a State from clawing back by reservation a concession it made at the bargaining table while retaining the benefits of concessions made by other States.[65] (Objections might theoretically be an adequate safeguard, but for reasons explored below, the limited advantages afforded by objecting, and the infrequency of objections—which may result from that limited upside—suggests the need for more dramatic solutions.) Alternatively, such clauses may resolve the practical challenges of administering the permissibility approach, or otherwise validate the VCLT's concern with protecting a treaty's object and purpose. If States cannot agree in advance on the object and purpose[66] (or depend on any process for establishing it afterwards), they may be disposed to preclude all reservations to preclude only the most fundamental ones.

It has proven difficult, however, to maintain any firm bar on reservations and their proxies. A number of treaties appear to prohibit all reservations in the first instance, but enable reservations to affiliated agreements or to technical and dynamic content—which is where the action for agreements on trade, environmental, and arms control matters ultimately may lie.[67] In other instances, States are

---

[61] UNCLOS permits reservations where 'expressly permitted by other articles', but none of its principal clauses permit them. UNCLOS (n 15) Art 309.

[62] Kyoto Protocol to the United Nations Framework Convention on Climate Change (adopted 10 December 1997, entered into force 16 February 2005) [1998] 37 ILM 32, Art 26.

[63] Rome Statute of the International Criminal Court (adopted 17 July 1998, entered into force 1 July 2002) 2187 UNTS 90, Art 120.

[64] UN Office of Legal Affairs, *Final Clauses of Multilateral Treaties Handbook* (UN Sales No E04V3 2003) <http://treaties.un.org/doc/source/publications/FC/English.pdf> 47 n51 (citing examples) ('Final Clauses Handbook'); CL Carr and GL Scott, 'Multilateral Treaties and the Environment: A Case Study in the Formation of Customary International Law' (1999) 27 Denver J Intl L and Poly 313, 322 n29 (indicating ten of forty-one global environmental treaties surveyed contained 'no reservations' provisions).

[65] UNCLOS is the most obvious example. See eg M Nordquist and C Park (eds), *Reports of the United States Delegation to the Third United Nations Conference on the Law of the Sea* (Law of the Sea Institute, Honolulu 1993) 83 ('Since the Convention is an overall "package deal" reflecting different priorities of different States, to permit reservations would inevitably permit one State to eliminate the "quid" of another State's "quo." Thus there was general agreement in the Conference that in principle reservations could not be permitted').

[66] B Oxman, 'The Third United Nations Conference on the Law of the Sea: The Eighth Session (1979)' (1980) 74 AJIL 1, 35 (speculating that 'it is likely that any attempt to achieve a consensus at the conference on the object and purpose of the [Law of the Sea] convention would end, after a long period of time, with the verbatim repetition of almost every provision').

[67] See eg Convention on the Prohibition of the Development, Production, Stockpiling and Use of Chemical Weapons and on their Destruction (opened for signature 13 January 1993, entered into force 29 April 1997) 1974 UNTS 317, Art XXII (barring reservations to the Convention's articles, but permitting reservations to its annexes not incompatible with its object and purpose); Convention on International Trade in Endangered Species of Wild Fauna and Flora (opened for signature 3 March 1973, entered into force 1 July 1975) 993 UNTS 243, Art XXIII (prohibiting 'general reservations' but permitting reservations to specific articles and appendices); see also Marrakesh Agreement establishing the World Trade Organization (adopted 15 April 1994, entered into force January 1995) 1867

permitted to tailor their obligations more indirectly, but in ways that are difficult to distinguish from the effect of a well-tailored reservation. For example, UNCLOS managed to achieve consensus in part by permitting States to opt out of certain dispute settlement provisions.[68] Similarly, States parties to the Rome Statute deferred decisions about the crime of aggression and the elements of crimes, while permitting individual States to defer implementation of war crimes provisions for up to seven years.[69] In addition, as noted, States may try to disguise their reservations through other unilateral forms such as interpretative declarations or unilateral statements.[70]

The most persistent challenge for attempts to limit reservations is simply the problem originally confronted by the *Reservations* case: if reservations to negotiated agreements are not allowed, States may decline to consent at all. Alternatively, if a sufficient number of negotiating States are aware that they will be unable to propose reservations—the number need not be substantial if the text requires consensus for its adoption—they may dilute the original obligations to dispense with the need for reservations in the first place. Or, they may negotiate other release mechanisms to similar effect. The unattractiveness of these options may explain the continued tolerance of reservations, notwithstanding ambiguity around the rules for determining even their initial standing.

IV. Objections to Reservations—and their Effects

The relevance of the object-and-purpose inquiry is not exhausted in determining a reservation's initial status. One of the most vexing reservations questions concerns the remedy for objecting States—or, to the extent it differs, the remedy for reservations determined to be incompatible with the treaty.

The VCLT rules initially appear fairly straightforward. Under Articles 20 and 21, if one State has proposed a reservation, each other State may accept the reservation or object to it—and if an objection is not made within twelve months, the State is deemed to have accepted it.[71] If one State accepts another State's

---

UNTS 154, Art XVI(5) ('No reservations may be made in respect of any provision of this Agreement. Reservations in respect of any of the provisions of the Multilateral Trade Agreements may only be made to the extent provided for in those Agreements. Reservations in respect of a provision of a Plurilateral Trade Agreement shall be governed by the provisions of that Agreement').

[68] UNCLOS (n 15) Art 298. More broadly, provisions permitting amendment and denunciation relieved concerns that States might have about the need to use reservations to secure protection against future changes in circumstances. Ibid Arts 312–14, 317; see TL McDorman, 'Reservations and the Law of the Sea Treaty' (1982) 13 J Maritime L and Comm 481, 496.

[69] See Rome Statute (n 63) Arts 5 (provision relating to crime of aggression), 9 (elements of crimes), 124 (deferral of war crimes provisions).

[70] See nn 10–13 and accompanying text.

[71] The twelve-month period runs from when the non-reserving State is notified of the reservation. VCLT Art 20(5). By operation of VCLT Art 23(2), a reservation is considered as having been made when it is formally confirmed by the reserving State in expressing its consent to be bound, so notice and the twelve-month period do not run from any *earlier* formulation of the reservation (eg from when the reserving State was signing a treaty subject to ratification, acceptance, or approval). The deadline for the

reservation, it modifies the relevant treaty provisions for each in relation to one another.[72] Objections may have one of two effects. If an objecting State so indicates, the objection can preclude the treaty's entry into force as between the two parties. Absent such an indication, objecting means that 'the provisions to which the reservation relates do not apply as between the two States to the extent of the reservation'.[73]

As with reservations, some potentially significant but still secondary procedural questions have arisen relating to objections. For example, tardy objections are sometimes lodged, when on the face of the VCLT these are without legal effect.[74] But a more fundamental issue has to do with the consequences of objections. As the VCLT is written, the results for an accepting State and for any objecting State that does not seek to prevent the treaty from entering into force appear equivalent. The difference between saying that 'to the extent of the reservation' a treaty provision is 'modifie[d]' (in the case of acceptance) or 'does not apply' (in the case of objection) seems a mere formality.[75] Such equivalence would mean that non-reserving States have little cause to object, which in turn means that other States have little reason to refrain from proposing reservations in the first place.

One might rationalize this as at least assuring objecting States that they will not thereby worsen their situations (or as a means of encouraging them to object to any treaty relations at all with the reserving State), but the truth seems to be that the VCLT's text was an imperfect attempt to ensure that objections negate the intended effect of a proposed reservation.[76] One sensible solution, embraced by the ILC's *Guide to Practice*, is to clarify that an objection in all events 'precludes the reservation from having its intended effects' as against the objecting State. The *Guide* differentiates between the consequences of: (i) an objection to an otherwise valid reservation that tries to exclude outright the legal effect of one or more treaty provisions (with the result being that neither relevant State is bound by such provisions) and (ii) an objection that tries instead to modify the provisions' legal effect (with the result being that neither relevant State is bound 'by the provisions . . . as intended to be modified by the reservation').[77] Putting aside the stress this places on differentiating between legal effect-excluding reservations and

non-reserving State is postponed, however, if it expresses its own consent to be bound after the end of the twelve-month period, with the date of its consent marking the last opportunity for it to object—again, at peril of tacit acceptance. VCLT Art 20(5) (tacit acceptance commences from the 'end of a period of twelve months after [the non-reserving State] was notified of the reservation or by the date on which it expressed its consent to be bound by the treaty, whichever is later').

[72] VCLT Arts 20(4)(a), 21(1)(a).

[73] Ibid Arts 20(4)(b), 21(3).

[74] For discussions of the problem of tardy objections, see eg Horn (n 16) 205–9. The *Guide to Practice* does not directly deny them any legal effect, but says their legal effect is not the same as for timely objections. Guide to Practice (n 4) 2.6.13. The UN Secretary General, acting as a depositary, circulates late objections to parties as 'communications'. Treaty Handbook (n 56) 3.5.6. Questions concerning timing are intimately related to the permissibility theory, since concerns with timing diminish if a reservation was never proper. Swaine (n 16) 317–19.

[75] Cf VCLT Art 21(1)(a) and (3).

[76] Guide to Practice Commentaries (n 33) 613–17 (discussing drafting history).

[77] Guide to Practice (n 4) 4.3, 4.3.5.

provision-modifying ones (not to mention the challenge in determining how an objection best counters the latter kind of reservation's intent)[78] it is unclear how this approach respects Article 21(3)'s injunction that the reserved-to provision should be disapplied solely 'to the extent of the reservation'—though it is possible to speculate about ways that text might be redeemed.[79]

These remedies for non-reserving States seem particularly lacklustre for objections claiming that a reservation violates a treaty's object and purpose (or, in the words of the permissibility approach, where a reservation is impermissible regardless of whether any objection is made). Denying a reservation legal effect does not, unfortunately, determine the residual treaty relations between the reserving State and the (other) States parties. As one author summarized, one might imagine three results:

Option 1: The [reserving] state remains bound to the treaty except for the provision(s) to which the reservation related.

Option 2: The invalidity of a reservation nullifies the instrument of ratification as a whole and thus the state is no longer a party to the agreement.

Option 3: An invalid reservation can be severed from the instrument of ratification such that the state remains bound to the treaty including the provision(s) to which the reservation related.[80]

None of these options is free from difficulty. The first, while consistent with the outcome described for objections under Article 21(3), is in obvious tension with the permissibility approach. Article 21 literally applies only to '[a] reservation established with regard to another party in accordance with articles 19, 20 and 23'; arguably a reservation that cannot properly be 'formulate[d]' under Article 19(c) because of an object-and-purpose violation is also not properly 'established' with respect to another party. In more practical terms, the first option permits a reserving State to unilaterally alter its treaty obligations, notwithstanding that they seek to disapply something essential to the negotiated text, since any objection

---

[78] Guide to Practice Commentaries (n 33) 623–7 (suggesting principles).

[79] An objection to a reservation that sought to deny legal effect to a treaty provision would, of course, disapply that provision 'to the extent of the reservation' by disapplying it *en toto*, as Guideline 4.3.5(2) envisions. The function of that limiting proviso would have to be somewhat different with respect to objections to provision-modifying reservations, and different too from the function of that phrase in VCLT Art 21(1)(a) relating to the effect of acceptance, if equivalent effect between an acceptance and an objection is to be avoided. In such cases, 'to the extent of the reservation' might operate to prevent an objection from triggering effects beyond the scope of the original reservation. For example, France formulated a reservation to Art 6 of the 1958 Geneva Convention on the Continental Shelf that sought to prevent the application of the equidistance principle under *certain* circumstances; the United Kingdom objected, and France argued to the Court of Arbitration that the result of the UK objection was that Art 6 as a whole was inapplicable. The Court disagreed, in part by invoking VCLT Art 21(3). Guide to Practice Commentaries (n 33) 620–3. Generalizing this, the 'to the extent of the reservation' condition in VCLT Art 21(3) might not mean that an objection to a provision-modifying reservation would negate the provision only to the extent of the reservation, which would indirectly secure the reservation's intended effect. Rather, that proviso would mean that the objection did not, as an upper bound, negate more of the provision than the reservation touched.

[80] R Goodman, 'Human Rights Treaties, Invalid Reservations, and State Consent' (2002) 96 AJIL 531, 531.

produces essentially the same result as if there were no objection or no incompatibility discerned.[81]

The second option, on the other hand, would essentially assert on behalf of non-reserving States a draconian solution—the preclusion of treaty relations—that they rarely elect for themselves. The third solution would invert consent-based concerns. Rather than compromising the consent-based interests of non-reserving States like the first two options, severing the reservation and creating a binding treaty obligation simply ignores what might have been an indispensable part of the reserving State's expression of its consent to be bound.

Which option is the most consistent with current law? Practice provides no authoritative answer at present. States have sometimes advocated for the first approach, negating the reserved-to provision along with the reservation.[82] Additional supporting evidence exists in the number of circumstances where non-compliance by the reserving State with the reserved-to provision is tolerated. The second option, where the reserving State falls out of treaty relations, has been occasionally suggested by States,[83] and arguably draws some support from the Secretary-General's practice as depositary of multilateral treaties.[84] As to the third, 'severance' option, some States (especially Nordic ones) have indeed asserted a right to objections with 'super-maximum' effect—effectively severing the reservation and asserting a binding relationship between the States under the entire treaty, including any provisions to which the reservations pertain.[85] Such objec-

---

[81] This is a slight exaggeration, since other States remain free in theory to object to any treaty relations with an overreaching State.

[82] See 'Observations by the United States on General Comment 24' (28 March 1995) CCPR A/50/40/Annex VI 126–29, reprinted in (1996) 3 IHRR 265, 269 (taking the view that only this option, and preventing the treaty from coming into force at all between the States, were open to an objecting State) ('US Observations').

[83] Guide to Practice Commentaries (n 33) 670–2. For example, Burundi's reservation to the 1973 Convention on the Prevention and Punishment of Crimes against Internationally Protected Persons, including Diplomatic Agents, drew object-and-purpose objections from Israel, Italy, and the United Kingdom, and those States also objected to considering Burundi a party to the treaty until the reservation was withdrawn; the Federal Republic of Germany and France also objected but did not assert that the treaty was not in force. Both results, however, are fully explicable as options available to objecting States under the VCLT regime. Ibid.

[84] Ibid 671 (citing Summary of Depositary Practice (n 41) [191]–[193]). In fact, the *Summary of Practice* suggests only that the UN Secretary-General will refuse to accept the deposit of instruments with reservations that are prohibited, explicitly or by omission, a test that is much easier to administer than an inquiry into object and purpose. Indeed, the *Summary* indicates that refusal is warranted only if there is no doubt of an unauthorized reservation, which seems to reinforce the distinction between the two operations. Summary of Depositary Practice (n 41) [193].

[85] Guide to Practice Commentaries (n 33) 664–5; A Pellet, 'Ninth Report on Reservations to Treaties' (24 June 2004) UN Doc A/CN.4/544 [8] ('Pellet, Ninth Report'); A Pellet, 'Eighth Report on Reservations to Treaties, First Addendum' (10 July 2003) UN Doc A/CN.4/535/Add.1 [96] (citing examples). For example, Sweden's objection to Qatar's reservation to the Optional Protocol to the Convention on the Rights of the Child on the Sale of Children, Child Prostitution and Child Pornography stated that '[t]he Convention enters into force in its entirety between the two States, without Qatar benefiting from its reservation'. *MTDSG Status as of 1 April 2009* (2009) UN Doc ST/LEG/SER.E/26 <http://treaties.un.org/doc/source/publications/MTDSG/2009/English-I.pdf> 448; see also ibid 309, 312–15, 331–5 (similar objections and communications by Denmark, Finland, Sweden, and Great Britain to reservations to the Convention on the Elimination of all Forms of Discrimination against Women); ibid 219–20, 229 (similar objections by Denmark, Finland, and Sweden to reservations to the ICCPR). This type of

tions have been justified on familiar permissibility grounds, including the claim that 'ordinary' objections and those based on object-and-purpose grounds should not have identical effects.[86] In other cases, States have asserted still different options, claiming a different set of legal effects to object-and-purpose objections that lie between disapplying the reserved-to provision and disapplying the reservation itself. Such objections may, for example, assert the right to disapply not only the reserved-to provisions but also other provisions identified by the objecting State.[87]

The severance approach has been reinforced by the reactions of treaty-monitoring bodies, principally in the human rights context. Most notably, in General Comment 24, the UN Human Rights Committee (HRC) took the position that 'generally' incompatible reservations may be severed, so that the treaty binds the reserving party in its entirety.[88] The HRC comment followed an earlier European Court of Human Rights decision that invalidated reservations and held the reserving State bound to the entire European Convention on Human Rights, albeit in a regional context and without reference to the VCLT.[89] The HRC did not specify conditions under which severability would be eschewed. Unfortunately, too, the linchpin to its approach—the ability to determine a treaty's object and purpose—remained wanting, even in the context of its particular treaty (the ICCPR). The HRC gave examples of provisions to which reservations could not be made, but did

---

objection is not entirely limited to human rights treaties. See eg ibid 131 (objection by Finland to reservations to the Vienna Convention on Consular Relations); ibid 592 (objection by Finland to reservations to the Convention Against Illicit Traffic in Narcotic Drugs and Psychotropic Substances); see also P Kaukoranta, 'Elements of Nordic Practice 1997: Finland' (1998) 67 Nordic J Intl L 321, 327–8.

[86] The Netherlands once reasoned that the authority to object to treaty relations with the reserving State connoted the right to exclude only part of a treaty, providing the provisions were severable. RCR Siekmann, 'Netherlands State Practice for the Parliamentary Year 1982–1983' (1984) 15 Netherlands Ybk Intl L 267, 345–46 (quoting explanatory memorandum from the Dutch Government on VCLT ratification). Subsequent defences have sounded in permissibility terms. See eg L Magnuson, 'Elements of Nordic Practice 1997: The Nordic Countries in Coordination' (1998) 67 Nordic J Intl L 345, 350 (quoting statement by Swedish representative to the UNGA's Sixth Committee); L Mikaelsen, 'Elements of Nordic and International Practice in the Year of 1996 (Denmark)' (1997) 66 Nordic J Intl L 319, 323. States defending innovative objections have, in any event, confined their use to reservations claimed to be inadmissible.

[87] See J Klabbers, 'Accepting the Unacceptable? A New Nordic Approach to Reservations to Multilateral Treaties' (2000) 69 Nordic J Intl L 179. See also F Hampson, 'Final Working Paper on Reservations to Human Rights Treaties' (19 July 2004) UN Doc E/CN.4/Sub.2/2004/43 [16]–[17] (citing other, non-Nordic examples); Pellet, Ninth Report (n 85) [19] (same).

[88] HRC, 'General Comment No 24: General comment on issues relating to reservations made upon ratification or accession to the Covenant or the Optional Protocols thereto, or in relation to declarations under article 41 of the Covenant' (4 November 1994) CCPR/C/21/Rev.1/Add.6 [18] ('General Comment 24'); ibid (stating that '[t]he *normal* consequence of an unacceptable reservation is not that the Covenant will not be in effect at all for a reserving party' (emphasis added)). Other treaty-monitoring bodies have assented in the severability approach. UNGA, 'Report of the Ninth Meeting of Persons Chairing the Human Rights Treaty Bodies' (14 May 1998) UN Doc A/53/125 [18] (reporting chairpersons' 'firm support for the approach reflected in General Comment No. 24'). The authority of such a body to execute this approach—its jurisdiction, as opposed to the merits of such a position—is addressed below.

[89] *Belilos v Switzerland* (App no 10328/83) ECHR 29 April 1988, reprinted in (1998) 10 EHRR 466; see also *Loizidou* (n 15).

not provide much by way of a rationale or explanation;[90] as partial guidance, it suggested that reservations contrary to peremptory norms or customary international law were necessarily incompatible with the ICCPR's object and purpose, but its explanation for this principle was unsatisfying.[91]

The ILC's *Guide to Practice*, drafted in full view of General Comment 24, improves to a degree on the predictability of object-and-purpose determinations. Its attempt to articulate a general test to determine the object and purpose of a treaty was no great improvement on the VCLT, nor was it clear how it was indicated by the VCLT.[92] Nevertheless, the *Guide* indicates that a reservation is not impermissible solely because it relates to a treaty provision reflecting customary international law,[93] follows General Comment 24 in drawing no necessary conclusion from the fact that a treaty provision is non-derogable,[94] and takes a slightly more nuanced view of the relationship between reservations and peremptory norms.[95]

What may be more significant, however, is the *Guide*'s endorsement of a fourth approach to meting out the effects of impermissible objections. The *Guide* suggests severability is a function of the reserving State's intent—specifically, 'whether it intends to be bound by the treaty without the benefit of the reservation or whether it considers that it is not bound by the treaty'—and adopts the presumption that,

---

[90] General Comment 24 (n 88) [7] (explaining that '[i]n an instrument which articulates very many civil and political rights, each of the many articles, and indeed their interplay, secures the objectives of the Covenant', such that '[t]he object and purpose of the Covenant is to create legally binding standards for human rights by defining certain civil and political rights and placing them in a framework of obligations which are legally binding for those States which ratify; and to provide an efficacious supervisory machinery for the obligations undertaken'). Apparently as illustrations of this principle, the HRC cited examples of impermissible reservations: a 'reservation to article 1 denying peoples the right to determine their own political status and to pursue their economic, social and cultural development'; a 'reservation to the obligation to respect and ensure the rights, and to do so on a non-discriminatory basis'; and a reservation of 'an entitlement not to take the necessary steps at the domestic level to give effect to the rights of the Covenant'. Ibid [9].

[91] Ibid [8] (providing examples of reservations perceived to be inadmissible as contrary to *jus cogens* or customary international law). Granting that norms that are established by customary international law (and certainly those that are peremptory in character) are different in kind, proposing a reservation to the treaty-based means of enforcing a norm is not the same as seeking the right to violate the norm itself. See US Observations (n 82) 267. Nor is it necessarily obvious whether a given norm is one established by customary international law.

[92] See Guide to Practice (n 4) 3.1.5 ('A reservation is incompatible with the object and purpose of the treaty if it affects an essential element of the treaty that is necessary to its general tenour, in such a way that the reservation impairs the raison d'être of the treaty').

[93] Ibid 3.1.5.3.

[94] Ibid 3.1.5.4; see also General Comment 24 (n 88) [10].

[95] Whereas General Comment 24 took the view that 'provisions in the Covenant that...have the character of peremptory norms...may not be the subject of reservations', the *Guide to Practice* stated that '[a] reservation cannot exclude or modify the legal effect of a treaty in a manner contrary to a peremptory norm of general international law'; its final version classified that principle among those regulating the effect of reservations on non-treaty rights, seemingly to establish the narrower principle that the treaty could not be modified so as to violate peremptory norms. Guide to Practice (n 4) 4.4.3(2). Other *Guide* provisions addressed the permissibility of reservations concerning internal law, interdependent rights and obligations, and dispute settlement or treaty monitoring provisions. Ibid 3.1.5.5–3.1.5.7.

unless a State has expressed or can otherwise evidence a contrary intent, it is to be considered a full-fledged party to the treaty without the reservation's benefit.[96] A presumption of severability is certainly more moderate than an absolute severability rule or a rule that absolutely precluded party status, and it is an approach that human rights bodies appear to have endorsed.[97] Nonetheless, though the *Guide*'s approach is sensitive in application to the intent of particular States, it is not itself consensualist—being based neither in the VCLT nor in pre-existing State practice—and the inquiry into the counterfactual intentions of a reserving State, in the event its reservation were frustrated, may be as vexed as that into object and purpose.[98]

The *Guide to Practice*'s approach suggests, successfully or otherwise, a persistent tendency in the VCLT regime. As initially noted, the rules' origins in the human rights context evolved into the VCLT's default approach for all treaties. Somewhat ironically, the inadequacy of the VCLT regime has been felt most keenly in its original context. Critics of human rights treaty reservations have contended—with some force—that while the availability of reservations may have increased the number of treaty adherents, the device of objections has proven completely inadequate. The excuse for allowing reservations to compromise the consent-based interests of other States parties to human rights treaties—namely, that reservations were not really defending sovereign interests, and thus States should take less exception to letting others make unilateral changes to their treaty obligations—was also the regime's weakness, precisely because States did in fact object less. The interest and attention of non-reserving States was no match for the interest of reserving States in securing additional latitude, and neither seemed focused on protecting the true subjects of human rights treaties: individuals.[99] In light of these factors, the HRC, among others, felt that severability—which avoided any immediate diminution in the number of adherents to human rights treaties, since it did not entail annulling ratifications—was the only way to preserve treaty integrity and advance the entire object and purpose of these treaties.[100]

---

[96] Guide to Practice (n 4) 4.5.3.

[97] Guide to Practice Commentaries (n 33) 677–82; see UNGA, 'Report of the Sixth Inter-Committee Meeting of Human Rights Treaty Bodies' (2007) UN Doc A/62/224, Annex [48(v)] (endorsing conclusion of a working group).

[98] The *Guide to Practice* also embraces the possibility of 'intermediate' objections, in which an objecting State seeks to disapply a provision other than the one to which the reservation was made, so long as there is some link between the two provisions and the objection does not itself defeat the treaty's object and purpose. Guide to Practice (n 4) 3.4.2. It is unclear how this approach relates to the presumption of severability—whether, that is, the objecting State's intention to achieve a result other than severance should matter.

[99] See eg L Lijnzaad, *Reservations to UN Human Rights Treaties* (TMC Asser Institute, Dordrecht 1994); I Ziemele (ed), *Reservations to Human Rights Treaties and the Vienna Convention Regime* (Martinus Nijhoff, Leiden 2004); R Higgins, 'The United Nations: Still a Force for Peace' (1989) 52 Modern L Rev 1, 11–12.

[100] See General Comment 24 (n 88) [17] (differentiating human rights treaties for purposes of reservations on the ground, *inter alia*, that they 'concern the endowment of individuals with rights', such that '[t]he principle of inter-State reciprocity [ordinarily] has no place'; 'because the operation of the classic rules on reservations is so inadequate for the Covenant, States have often not seen any legal interest in or need to object to reservations', which means that the absence of protest does not inform

The ILC has reacted to this critique in two ways. On the one hand, it consciously rejected the proposal that it differentiate between the reservations scheme for human rights matters and that for other treaties. That is consistent with, and arguably necessitated by, the breadth of the VCLT itself.[101] On the other hand, as part of that undifferentiated approach, the ILC has again generalized from the remedy urged for the particular circumstances of human rights treaties to the adoption of an approach applicable to *all* treaties.[102] Leading advocates of severability, not limited to the HRC, frequently emphasized the peculiar strength of the warrant for severability in the human rights context.[103] The *Guide*'s decision to accept a warrant arising from the human rights context, and to extrapolate it to the world of treaties as a whole, may well influence the practice of States. If it does, however, it is also plausible that States operating outside the human rights context may react by negotiating treaty-specific reservations clauses that purposefully deviate from this practice, even as to the remedy for impermissible reservations. Presumably, they would do so both to account for interests outside the human rights realm and to better inform the State intent that is at the core of the *Guide*'s inquiry.

V. Participants in Evaluating Reservations

By and large, the system laid out in the VCLT reservations regime is limited to States in their individual capacities: individual States propose reservations, individual States accept or object to reservations, and individual States determine what results from these exchanges, subject to the rules they have agreed to in the Convention.[104] The notable exception was a default obligation that proposed reservations to constituent treaties of international organizations (IOs) required

---

the question of whether the object and purpose has been affronted); ibid [18] (extending analysis to severability).

[101] See also Aust (n 1) 149 (rejecting appeals to 'see human rights treaties as a special case').

[102] Interestingly, the *Guide to Practice* transformed one guideline, originally depicted as concerning 'general human rights treaties', into one relating to 'treaties containing numerous interdependent rights and obligations'. While the guideline's substance also changed somewhat, it remains readily applicable to human rights treaties—but is not designed to be dispositive. Guide to Practice (n 4) 3.1.5.6 ('To assess the compatibility of a reservation with the object and purpose of a treaty containing numerous interdependent rights and obligations, account shall be taken of that interdependence as well as the importance that the provision to which the reservation relates has within the general tenor of the treaty, and the extent of the impact that the reservation has on the treaty').

[103] See eg Goodman (n 80) 531 n8 (arguing that severance should be the presumed remedy effectuated by third-party institutions, so long as it is not shown to be an essential condition of ratification, and that this is consistent with the consensual interests of States that wish to be bound by their commitments—but limiting this thesis to human rights treaties); B Simma and GI Hernandez, 'Legal Consequences of an Impermissible Reservation to a Human Rights Treaty: Where Do We Stand?', in E Cannizzaro (ed), *The Law of Treaties Beyond the Vienna Convention* (OUP, Oxford 2011) 60 (supporting severability, but confining argument to multilateral human rights treaties).

[104] Although not addressed in this chapter, States also play a role in evaluating the impact of State succession on treaty reservations. See Chapter 16, Part III, 425–6; Guide to Practice (n 4) Part 5.

that organization's approval.[105] Ultimately, treaties involving IOs as parties became the subject of a different convention, which addressed reservations in parallel terms.[106]

Unsurprisingly, given long-evident trends in international law and international relations, individual States are no longer the only relevant actors. The fact that States often act collectively in proposing and, still more commonly, in evaluating reservations is perhaps the least surprising tendency. Somewhat less predictable, perhaps, has been the tendency of States to develop distinctive approaches to the rules governing reservations, as evident for example in the so-called Nordic approach.[107]

The more dramatic change has been the increased involvement of non-State actors. The most obvious of these are IOs such as the UN, acting as depositaries, who receive reservations that they must occasionally evaluate, particularly where the treaty text addresses reservations explicitly.[108] That international courts and tribunals might also play a role was almost inevitable, at least once the objective character of an object-and-purpose inquiry is granted. The participation by treaty-monitoring bodies, however, has been more controversial. When the HRC asserted its own capacity to evaluate whether reservations to the ICCPR violated that treaty's object and purpose, several prominent States protested. To a degree, those protests hinged on a disputed understanding that the HRC was asserting or seeking definitive or binding authority to sever reservations.[109] As matters have developed, the HRC has been cautious in asserting such authority, and more often engages in attempts to persuade States to consider withdrawing arguably objectionable reservations—a

---

[105] VCLT Art 20(3). Examples of IOs exercising such authority are harder to discern and it is not clear whether the practice tracks the VCLT. The most prominent example involved a pre-VCLT treaty, when Iceland proposed in 2001 to rejoin the International Whaling Convention (adopted 2 December 1946, entered into force 10 November 1948) 1953 UNTS 74, with a reservation to the Convention Schedule's commercial whaling moratorium. The Convention's plenary body, the International Whaling Commission, voted twice in 2001 and 2002 to refuse the reservation (and Iceland's status as a party) before voting 19–18 to accept Iceland and its reservation in October 2002. For its part, the United States treated the issue as one governed by the Convention and subsequent practice rather than any general rule of treaty law. See 'Reservation Practice: Iceland Whaling' [2002] Digest of United States Practice in International Law 206–12. Following the Commission's approval, fifteen States filed objections to Iceland's reservation, three of which claimed to deny treaty relations with Iceland. 'Objection to Reservation' [2003] Digest of United States Practice in International Law 243–4.

[106] 1986 VCLT (n 5) Arts 19–23. It is not clear, however, whether IOs other than the EU have any sustained practice of proposing treaty reservations.

[107] See nn 85–86 and accompanying text.

[108] On the role of depositaries in this respect see Chapter 10, Part I.H, 264 *et seq.*

[109] See General Comment 24 (n 88) [11] (asserting non-contravenable 'competence to interpret the requirements of any provisions of the Covenant'); ibid [18] ('It necessarily falls to the Committee to determine whether a specific reservation is compatible with the object and purpose of the Covenant'). Cf US Observations (n 82) 266 (rejecting the Committee's power to issue 'definitive or binding interpretations of the Covenant'); 'Observations by the United Kingdom on GC No 24' (21 July 1995) CCPR A/50/40/Annex VI 130–34, reprinted in (1996) 3 IHRR 261, 263–4 [9]–[12] (similar criticism); 'Observation by France on GC No 24 on Reservations to the ICCPR' (8 September 1995) CCPR A/51/40/Annex VI 104–6 (same); Aust (n 1) 150–1, with PR Ghandhi, *The Human Rights Committee and the Right of Individual Communication* (Ashgate, Dartmouth 1998) 371.

form of interaction very similar to that of other treaty-monitoring bodies that have more conclusively renounced binding authority for themselves.[110]

The ILC's *Guide to Practice* aims at establishing, somewhat abstractly, the capacity of treaty-monitoring bodies (within their treaty-established competences) to assess the permissibility of reservations, just as that capacity exists for States parties and dispute settlement bodies.[111] The proposal seems unobjectionable on its face, given the deference to the particulars of any particular treaty. But there are potentially serious drawbacks to promoting this kind of authority. Multiplying the number of parties assessing objections increases the likelihood that potentially problematic objections will be caught, but also increases the likelihood of conflicting pronouncements. Treaty-monitoring bodies also accentuate the risks inherent in the permissibility approach. If reservations are not merely opposable by States—a right exhausted within twelve months—there is potentially no real limits on the opportunity to disallow reservations. Although States are presently encouraged to muster their objections—within a year anyway, as that will ensure the objection's resonance regardless of whether the treaty's object and purpose is genuinely involved—a treaty-monitoring body has neither the same incentive nor the capacity unilaterally to control the occasions for its pronouncements. It is unclear, moreover, whether the contribution of treaty-monitoring bodies is so distinctive that it must be added to the entities engaged in reviewing the permissibility of reservations.[112]

Ultimately, the participation by treaty-monitoring bodies must be resolved by the governing treaties, to which the VCLT and the *Guide to Practice* both defer. The ILC's non-binding encouragement of their role—not only in assessing permissibility in their own right, but also to having their views considered by States parties[113]—curiously reinserts the Commission itself as another contributor to the reservations dialogue.

Conclusion

The law of reservations has evolved considerably since the Genocide Convention controversy. While the VCLT rules are quite similar to those indicated by the ICJ—and the reliance on objections and the focus on a treaty's object and purpose continues to bedevil practice—the contemporary landscape provides States with many more options. The assistance of depositaries and treaty-monitoring bodies,

---

[110] Swaine (n 16) 322 n93 (noting Committee's subsequent caution); ibid 321 n87 (noting positions of other treaty-monitoring bodies gainsaying binding authority); see also UNGA, 'Report on Reservations by the Twenty-First Meeting of Chairpersons of the Human Rights Treaty Bodies' (17 June 2008) UN Doc HRI/MC/2009/5.

[111] Guide to Practice (n 4) 3.2–3.2.5.

[112] In terms of other participants, the *Guide to Practice* cites the potential for contributions from domestic courts. See Guide to Practice Commentaries (n 33) 490. The fact that they may independently weigh in on the permissibility of reservations, without heed to the position established by States, remains troublesome.

[113] Guide to Practice (n 4) 3.2.3.

the proliferation of model clauses that deviate from the VCLT, and now the ILC's elaborate *Guide to Practice* all stand ready to help parties avoid any perceived pitfalls in the law of reservations. As practice matures still further, understanding the consequences of any proposed reservation will likely borrow increasingly from other principles of international law. For example, understanding proposed reservations and the reactions thereto, particularly in the context of a diverse array of final clauses governing reservations, will likely depend more and more on questions of treaty interpretation and the customary international law of unilateral acts. It seems unlikely, however, that these developments will ever obviate a default law of reservations or resolve all its puzzles.

Recommended Reading

A Aust, *Modern Treaty Law and Practice* (2nd edn CUP, Cambridge 2007) Chapter 8

RL Bindschedler, 'Treaties, Reservations' (1984), reprinted in (2000) 4 EPIL 965

WW Bishop Jr, 'Reservations to Treaties' (1961-II) 103 RcD 245

DW Bowett, 'Reservations to Non-Restricted Multilateral Treaties' (1976–77) 48 BYBIL 67

RW Edwards Jr, 'Reservations to Treaties' (1989) 10 Mich J Int'l L 363

R Goodman, 'Human Rights Treaties, Invalid Reservations, and State Consent' (2002) 96 AJIL 531

DW Greig, 'Reservations: Equity as a Balancing Factor?' (1995) 16 Australian Ybk Intl L 21

F Horn, *Reservations and Interpretive Declarations to Multilateral Treaties* (TMC Asser Institute, The Hague 1988)

ILC, 'Text of the draft guidelines constituting the Guide to Practice on Reservations to Treaties, with commentaries, as provisionally adopted by the International Law Commission' (2011) <http://untreaty.un.org/ilc/sessions/62/GuidetoPracticeReservations_commentaries(e).pdf>

L Lijnzaad, *Reservations to UN Human Rights Treaties* (TMC Asser Institute, Dordrecht 1994)

DM McRae, 'The Legal Effect of Interpretative Declarations' (1978) 49 BYBIL 156

JM Ruda, 'Reservations to Treaties' (1975-III) 146 RcD 97

ET Swaine, 'Reserving' (2006) 31 YJIL 307

I Ziemele (ed), *Reservations to Human Rights Treaties and the Vienna Convention Regime* (Martinus Nijhoff, Leiden 2004)

SECTION III
TREATY APPLICATION

12

The Territorial Application of Treaties

Syméon Karagiannis

Introduction

Legal texts are traditionally (and conveniently) applied with the aid of some good old Latin expressions: *ratione personae* (personal application), *ratione materiae* (material application), *ratione temporis* (temporal application), and *ratione loci* (spatial application).[1] Although treaties may raise all four issues, the law of treaties does not address them equally. Neither the 1969 Vienna Convention on the Law of Treaties (VCLT) nor its 1986 companion takes an express position on the *ratione materiae* or the *ratione personae* issues. What subjects a treaty covers instead becomes a matter of the interpretation method put down by the Vienna conventions. The *ratione personae* issue is seemingly more ambiguous. Asking which persons or entities within a State party to a treaty are bound by that treaty raises difficult questions about how municipal law incorporates treaties. The Vienna conventions cautiously avoid dictating any answers in light of the different approaches taken by national legal systems. In contrast, the VCLTs contain a large number of articles on a treaty's *ratione temporis* application (entry into force, non-retroactivity, termination, suspension, and so forth). But for the *ratione loci* application of treaties, there is but one article. Article 29 of the VCLT ('Territorial scope of treaties') provides that 'unless a different intention appears from the treaty or is otherwise established, a treaty is binding upon each party in respect of its entire territory'.[2]

Article 29 may not be the VCLT's shortest provision, but it is close. The main principle ('a treaty is binding upon each party in respect of its entire territory') consists of only thirteen words. It is a principle, moreover, rarely encountered in treaty texts, corresponding as it so often does to a text's 'ordinary meaning'. Indeed, a State party that refuses to apply treaty provisions to the whole of its territory would usually not be deemed to act in 'good faith'. The logic of Article 29 thus

---

[1] Thus, *ratione personae* asks to whom the legal text applies; *ratione materiae* asks to what subject matter it applies; *ratione temporis* asks when it applies, and *ratione loci* asks where it applies.

[2] A similar provision is found in Art 29 of the 1986 Vienna Convention on the Law of Treaties between States and International Organizations or between International Organizations (adopted 21 March 1986, not yet in force) [1986] 25 ILM 543 ('1986 VCLT'). See n 92 and accompanying text.

parallels Article 31's rule of interpretation, which relies heavily on both the good faith and 'ordinary meaning' principles.[3]

What saves Article 29 from the most boring banality is its pairing of the main principle favouring integral territorial application with a derogation ('unless a different intention appears from the treaty or is otherwise established'). Combining a legal principle with its opposite cannot but prove thrilling for scholars, puzzling for diplomats, and dramatic for judges. More positively, a provision that permits— almost—everything cannot but attain a high degree of consensus among States. Thus, Article 29 reflects in a certain way customary law in so far as customary law loves above all consensual and flexible solutions. Yet, this approach may also generate confusion. The Greek delegation to the International Law Commission (ILC) characterized it as 'a refutable legal presumption' and queried 'whether the inclusion of such a provision is useful in a formal text'.[4] The ILC, however, took the position that 'a State's territory plays such an essential role in the scope of the application of treaties that it is desirable to formulate a general rule on the matter'.[5]

This chapter examines the legal questions associated with the territorial application of treaties. It begins by reviewing Article 29's *travaux préparatoires* and the sources of exceptions to its main principle of integral territorial application. State practice is then explored in two respects. First, the chapter explores how variations in how States organize themselves—whether through the presence of colonies or a federal form of government—led to particular clauses in treaties delimiting how they would apply to some or all of a State's territory. Second, it examines the question of territorial boundaries as a precursor to a topic left unaddressed by the VCLT, namely the extraterritorial application of treaties, particularly in the human rights context. Finally, this chapter examines the difficulties associated with territorial application in the context of treaties involving international organizations (IOs).

I. Article 29: The Curious Relationship between a Principle and a Derogation

Article 29's actual text differs only slightly from the wording of the earlier 1966 ILC draft.[6] The article was easily approved at the Vienna Conference, with no votes against and no abstentions. Such history might suggest that no particular difficulties

---

[3] Indeed, Paul Reuter, Special Rapporteur for the International Law Commission's (ILC) work on what became the 1986 VCLT observed that 'the authors of [Article 29] had simply wanted to enunciate a rule for the interpretation of treaties': [1977] YBILC, vol I, 117 [24].

[4] [1966] YBILC, vol II, 65.

[5] Ibid 65–6.

[6] The ILC draft stated that 'unless a different intention appears from the treaty or is otherwise established, the application of a treaty extends to the entire territory of each party'. Ibid 213. Article 29's phrasing—'a treaty is binding upon each party in respect of its entire territory'—followed a Ukrainian submission suggesting that the ILC draft did not sufficiently respect dualist legal systems where treaty provisions are not directly applicable as national law.

arise under a *ratione loci* application of treaties. This is unfortunately not the case. Although not related here in detail, Article 29's drafting history was actually lengthy and complicated, undoubtedly due to the political context of decolonization at the end of the 1950s.

The *travaux préparatoires* were further complicated due to the (British) nationality and legal experiences of the ILC Special Rapporteur on the law of treaties, Sir Gerald Fitzmaurice. In 1959, Fitzmaurice drafted a highly sophisticated system for the territorial scope of treaties. Most of his provisions—in four articles— favoured a strict dichotomy between the application of treaties to a State's metropolitan territories and to its so-called 'dependent territories'. Given its colonies, the United Kingdom was, along with some other European powers, most concerned by this discussion. Most of the other States (and non-western European members of the ILC) were less enthused, to the point that no territorial scope draft article was submitted to the UN General Assembly in these years. But even as the issue became blurred by a rather heavy political discussion on the metropolis/colony relationship, Fitzmaurice's early effort hinted at the customary international law on this topic. His draft Article 25 provided that: 'Unless a treaty otherwise provides, it applies automatically to the whole of the metropolitan territory (or to all territories forming part of the metropolitan territory) of each contracting party.'[7]

The next ILC Special Rapporteur, Waldock, simplified Fitzmaurice's approach considerably, paving the way to the ILC's adoption of its first draft article on this point.[8] The ILC's 1964 draft article submitted to the General Assembly stated that 'the scope of application of a treaty extends to the entire territory of each party, unless the contrary appears from the treaty'.[9] That language thus continued Fitzmaurice's idea that territorial application should consist of both a principle and a corresponding exception. As already noted, such duality assured the provision the general consensus among States and its easy adoption at the Vienna Conference. Yet, this very duality (or ambiguity) might also undermine the provision's credibility and effectiveness. For starters, there is the question of what comes first. Is it the principle (applying the treaty to the State's whole territory) or the exception (a partial application of the treaty on the territory)?

Normally, exceptions are interpreted *stricto sensu*, which suggests that the principle of integral application should not be easily defeated. Yet, Article 29's own drafting history reveals a continuing retreat from the principle applying a treaty to the whole of the State's territory. Fitzmaurice's draft had required the treaty itself to express an exception. Waldock's draft extended exceptions to the more vague form of a 'contrary intention' expressed: (i) in the treaty, (ii) 'from the circumstances of its conclusion or the statements of the parties', or (iii) contained in a reservation.[10] The more sources for the exception, the easier it is to establish. The 1964 ILC draft was even more general ('unless the contrary appears from the treaty').[11] The final

---

[7] [1959] YBILC, vol II, 48.   [8] [1964] YBILC, vol II, 12 *et seq.*
[9] Ibid 179.   [10] Ibid 12.
[11] Ibid 179.

1966 ILC draft, as well as the 1969 text, go even further.[12] Not only do they double the material sources for the exception (whether derived from the treaty or 'otherwise established'), they also place (symbolically?) the exception at the head of the sentence.[13]

How do Article 29's exceptions to integral territorial application apply? The first source ('appears from the treaty') simply requires reference to the usual methods of treaty interpretation detailed in Articles 31 and 32 of the VCLT. The alternative source ('otherwise established') poses more difficulties. The term 'otherwise'[14] appears to permit methods for establishing a 'different intention' quite different from those envisaged in Articles 31 and 32. But it is by no means clear what these alternative methods are. There is little doubt that the possibilities for identifying a 'different intention' are numerous. Yet, we should not minimize the importance of the verb 'establish'.[15] Albeit 'otherwise', the 'different intention' still has to be clearly shown. Indeed, if this were not the case, the distinction between the principle and its exception would be thoroughly erased, which hardly seems a correct interpretation of Article 29's phrasing.

Both sources of the exception, moreover, require establishing a 'different intention' from the default rule. Thus, as Waldock recognized in his 1964 commentary: 'The territorial application of a treaty is essentially a question of the intention of the parties.'[16] Admittedly, lawyers may not be particularly fond of the word 'intention'. There is always a question of whose intention matters. It is difficult to prove that a collective 'intention' exists and, assuming this is impossible, there are suggestions that the 'intention' of the State party to the territory of which the treaty would apply should prevail over the 'intention' of other States parties to the same treaty.

Unfortunately, the case law and practice are not coherent. The United Kingdom has a practice of declaring in writing to the depositary to which, if any, of its overseas territories a treaty applies, which it regards as settling any territorial application question.[17] In Application No 8873/80 (*X v United Kingdom*), the former European Commission of Human Rights based its solution on the mere 'intention' of the respondent UK Government not to consider the island of Guernsey as part of UK territory as far as some electoral rights were concerned.[18] The same Commission had previously found, however, in *Wiggins v United*

---

[12] The 'contrary intention', which served as the basis for the exception, was replaced by a 'different intention'. 'Different' is admittedly weaker than 'contrary'; a merely different, but not drastically contrary, intention could thus set aside the main principle favouring integral territorial application.

[13] International law formulae are rarely innocent, although not all the official versions of the VCLT place the exception before the principle. The Chinese, English, French, and Russian versions do, but the Spanish one continues to give grammatical privilege to the principle ('Un tratado será obligatorio para cada una de las partes por lo que respecta a la totalidad de su territorio, salvo que una intención diferente se desprenda de él o conste de otro modo').

[14] The equivalent expression of the Spanish version is quite eloquent ('de otro modo'). The same can be said of the Russian ('иным образом') and the Chinese ones ('另') ['lìng'], whereas the French one is rather vague ('par ailleurs').

[15] Or, 'Etablir', 'constar', 'устанавливать', '确定' ['què dìng'] in the other versions.

[16] [1964] YBILC, vol II, 12.

[17] A Aust, *Modern Treaty Law & Practice* (2nd edn CUP, Cambridge 2007) 206–8.

[18] (1982) 28 DR 99.

Kingdom, that there were not 'any significant social or cultural differences between Guernsey and the United Kingdom' which could have proved relevant for a differentiation between the 'metropolis' and this Channel island, at least as far as housing regulations on this island were concerned,[19] which probably means the mere 'intention' of the UK Government did not prevail on this point. On the other hand, in French case law, the *commissaire du gouvernement* of the *Conseil d'Etat* stated, with respect to the application of a French-Australian extradition treaty to New Caledonia, that the Convention being silent on the point, Australia had the right to think that the Convention applied on the whole of the territory of an indivisible Republic such as France.[20] The UN Secretary-General, as a depositary, has taken to circulating unilateral declarations on exclusions of territorial application, a practice it describes as not 'inconsistent' with Article 29 of the VCLT 'since it may be considered that the constant practice of certain States (which still comprise "non-metropolitan" Territories) in respect of territorial application and the general absence of objections to such practices have "established a different intention" within the meaning of article 29'.[21]

II. Territorial Application in State Practice

How a State organizes its government with respect to the territory under its control may, of course, vary widely. Two practices in particular, however, have had a lasting impact on questions of *ratione loci*—(i) the presence of colonial territory distinct from that of the metropolitan territory; and (ii) the establishment of federal systems of government, which may place constitutional constraints on the federal government's ability to make and apply a treaty on matters within the competence of one or more sub-federal territorial governments. In both contexts, States have devised particular treaty clauses to delineate whether and how a treaty will apply. Although no longer used with as much frequency, these clauses remain relevant both for applying existing treaties and the continuing occasions where States seek a treaty text to overcome the default rule of integral territorial application.

A. Colonial clauses

States endowed with colonies (now referred to as 'overseas territories') have not adopted a uniform internal attitude on whether to apply treaties to such territories. One can generally speak of a British[22] (and similar Dutch) system and a distinct

---

[19] (App no 7456/76) (1978) 13 DR 40 [5]. See also n 32 and accompanying text for the important *Tyrer* judgment.

[20] *Mme Smets*, 14 May 1993, (1993) Rev gén de dr int pub 1056.

[21] Treaty Section of the UN Office of Legal Affairs, *Summary of Practice of the Secretary-General as Depositary of Multilateral Treaties* (United Nations, New York 1999) UN Doc ST/LEG/7/Rev 1 [284]–[285].

[22] Cf JES Fawcett, 'Treaty Relations of British Overseas Territories' (1949) 26 BYBIL 86–107.

French one.[23] The first model clearly distinguishes between the metropolis and colony with connotations that are both negative (the colony may not benefit from an advantageous treaty) and positive (the colony preserves autonomy vis-à-vis its metropolis). The French model, with some exceptions,[24] favours a kind of creeping assimilation between metropolis and colony; the constitutional principle of *égalité* pushing quite naturally to such a solution.

Prior to decolonization, States regularly dealt with colonial territorial application issues. Occasionally, they expressly endorsed the general principle of integral territorial application to all territories for which a State was 'internationally responsible'.[25] Exceptions were allowed via what has come to be known as the 'colonial clause', which took various forms. Some treaties afforded a State with colonial territory the option *to extend* the treaty to those territories by notification at the time it signed or consented to be bound.[26] In others, the treaty provided the colonial State the option *to exclude* colonial territories by similar notification.[27] In a few instances, moreover, a treaty would specify by name covered (or excluded) territories.[28]

With decolonization and the accompanying intense diplomatic and even military fighting against colonial systems, controversy enveloped the idea of allowing the remaining colonial powers the discretion to dictate whether international treaties applied to one or more of their colonies. Trying not to be politically incorrect, the ILC only stated that it preferred to avoid referring to expressions such as 'territories for which the parties are internationally responsible' (previously found in the Fitzmaurice and Waldock drafts) to which treaties could be extended.[29] Although not necessarily warranted, the prevailing sentiment viewed use of colonial clauses as an endorsement of the colonial system itself.[30]

---

[23] P Lampué, 'L'application des traités dans les territoires et départements d'outre-mer' (1960) 6 AFDI 907–24.

[24] See eg Law No 99–209 of 19 March 1999, Arts 21, 22, JO, 21 March 1999, 4197, 4198–99 (giving New Caledonia treaty-making authority in specific areas).

[25] Convention for the Suppression of the Traffic in Persons and of the Exploitation of the Prostitution of Others (adopted 2 December 1949, entered into force 25 July 1951) 96 UNTS 271, Art 23.

[26] Eg Convention on the Prevention and Punishment of the Crime of Genocide (adopted 9 December 1948, entered into force 12 January 1951) 78 UNTS 277, Art XII.

[27] International Convention on the Settlement of Investment Disputes between States and Nationals of Other States (adopted 18 March 1965, entered into force 14 October 1966) 575 UNTS 159, Art 70.

[28] Treaty Establishing the European Economic Community (adopted 25 March 1857, entered into force 1 January 1958) 294 UNTS 17, Art 227. Examples of each of these approaches may be found in Section VI of this volume, 715 *et seq*.

[29] [1966] YBILC, vol II, 213.

[30] See, for example, the reaction of Grigory Tunkin who asked whether it was 'appropriate for the Commission to act as if the world had stood still and give its approval to colonial institutions': [1964] YBILC, vol I, 49 [35]. Others, however, viewed the colonial clause as a potential vehicle for aiding States emerging from colonialism in dealing with the inevitable questions of State succession to treaties. The post-colonial Algerian Government, for example, argued the law of treaties should:

> limit the application of a treaty to the metropolitan territory of the parties, unless the still subject peoples through a valid expression of opinion decide to accept the treaty and its

Of course, just because the VCLT did not address the colonial clause does not mean it is absent from international treaty-making. For starters, many existing treaties (particularly regional European treaties) still contain colonial clauses. Thus, most (if not all) Council of Europe (COE) treaties do so. Article 56(1) of the European Convention on Human Rights (ECHR) is a paradigmatic example, providing that 'any State may at the time of its ratification or at any time thereafter declare by notification addressed to the Secretary General of the Council of Europe that the present Convention shall . . . extend to all or any of the territories for whose international relations it is responsible'.[31] In *Tyrer v United Kingdom*, the European Court of Human Rights (ECtHR) emphasized that Article 56 'was primarily designed to meet the fact that, when the Convention was drafted, there were still certain colonial territories whose state of civilization did not, it was thought, permit the full application of the Convention'.[32] But even after the 1960s collapse of European colonial empires, the clause still garners attention. In the post-colonial era, those territories for which a State party is responsible are more likely to have historical, geographic, and cultural ties to the State, a point emphasized by the Court in its Tyrer judgment which analyses the ECHR's application to the Isle of Man. Nevertheless, efforts to delete Article 56 seem to have met strong resistance from some European States.

Today, the colonial clause remains controversial. For some, it marks an unfortunate mechanism for precluding the universal application of treaty rights (especially human rights). Thus, modern UN human rights treaties do not contain a colonial clause or otherwise allow the protection of fundamental rights to be different depending on the individual's place of residence (whether in a metropolis or overseas territory). On the other hand, some colonial clauses continue to facilitate respect for regional and local differentiation. For example, where a State extends the ECHR to an overseas territory, Article 56(3) provides that 'the provisions of this Convention shall be applied in such territories with due regard, however, to local requirements'. This 'local requirements' ('*necessités locales*') clause allows further discrimination of the Convention's application overseas. To apply, however, the 'local requirements' have to be evidenced beyond doubt. That has proven neither an easy nor frequent occurrence before the ECtHR; the *Tyrer* case, for example, declined to find it applicable to the Isle of Man's governmental use of corporal punishment. In *Py v France*, the Court did make an adjustment to permit a New Caledonian restriction on French citizens who had not resided there for a sufficiently lengthy time to elect the members of the local legislature; a restriction designed to appease strained relations between competing political and ethnic

---

effects. Otherwise the legitimate representatives of those peoples may have no alternative but to denounce treaties in which they have taken no part and which are, in its view, often detrimental to their interests.

[1966] YBILC vol II, 65.

[31] Cf S Karagiannis, 'L'aménagement des droits de l'homme outre-mer: la clause des "nécessités locales" de la Convention européenne' (1995) 28 RBDI 224–305; L Moor and AB Simpson, 'Ghosts of Colonialism in the European Convention on Human Rights' (2006) 76 BYBIL 121–94.

[32] (App no 5856/72) (1978) Series A no 26 [38].

groups.[33] In this sense, 'colonial clauses' do not stand unavoidably against overseas inhabitants and their human rights; they may be seen as vehicles for preserving local traditions and minority cultures for overseas societies, albeit perhaps at the expense of individual human rights.[34]

The sometimes heavy heritage of the colonial clause is also found in the two treaties on the European Union. Article 355 of the Treaty on the Functioning of the European Union (TFEU) divides territories under the sovereignty of the Union's member States into a surprisingly large number of categories. Of course, to most of them, situated in Europe itself, the provisions of the Treaty apply completely. But there are some others to which the Treaty has never applied, for example the Faeroe Islands, under Danish sovereignty.[35] To a large number of overseas territories, globally called 'overseas countries and territories', and listed in Annex II, applies a complex system of special arrangements amounting to a kind of association of these territories to the Union.[36] Article 198 details that the 'association shall serve primarily to further the interests and prosperity of the inhabitants of these countries and territories in order to lead them to the economic, social and cultural development to which they aspire'.[37] Member States, moreover, cannot unilaterally or in groups change the rules and procedures regarding this association; unanimity of the Council of Ministers is required by Article 198. At least officially, therefore, this kind of colonial clause does not purport to discriminate negatively against 'overseas countries and territories'. On the contrary, this status differentiation could be seen as a kind of 'affirmative action'.

A similar approach is taken with respect to French overseas departments in the Caribbean region as well as to the Island of the Réunion in the Indian Ocean. Originally, the treaties of the European Communities as a whole were supposed to eventually apply to these departments. Local authorities, however, resisted. The

---

[33] (App no 66289/01) ECHR 2005-I.

[34] Colonial clauses, of course, are not the only vehicle for doing this. France has used reservations to reserve room for the application of local law in its territories under various Protocols to the ECHR. See eg French reservation to Protocol No 7 (stating that the Protocol 'shall apply to the whole territory of the Republic, due regard being had where the overseas territories and the territorial collectivity of Mayotte are concerned, to the local requirements referred to' in what is now Art 56). Of course, the fact that the French Government thought that the Muslim Sharia in application on Mayotte constitutes a 'local requirement' is not in itself a sufficient proof to establish the existence of such a 'requirement'. Moreover, even if this approach may foster the cohesion of the local communities under the menace of individually coloured Western values, it unavoidably leads to a dwindling of the protection of human rights of individual members of these communities, for example of the women's rights in the case of Mayotte. It is suggested that the ECHR's 'colonial clause' assumes quite boldly such consequences.

[35] Other territories excluded from a complete application of the EU treaties and Union secondary law emerged from accession agreements, and include the Channel Islands, Isle of Man, British Sovereign Base Areas of Akrotiri and Dhekelia in Cyprus, and the Åland Islands. Some other territories are not addressed by Art 355, but only by specific provisions of the respective accession agreement or a simple unilateral declaration, creating doubts as to the applicable legal regime (eg areas traditionally inhabited by the Sami people in Finland or Mount Athos in Greece).

[36] Said territories have special relations with four member States, namely Denmark, France, the Netherlands, and the United Kingdom. Amusingly, French Southern and Antarctic Territories and British Antarctic Territory are listed in Annex II as 'overseas countries and territories', although all the other member States reject any possibility whatsoever to raise territorial claims on the frozen continent.

[37] TFEU Art 198.

Court of Justice of the European Union condemned France for not complying with its Community obligations because of, *inter alia*, the non-abolition of some local taxes on all goods not originating from these departments upon their entry.[38] Eventually, however, rather than implementing EU law, local resistance in the French overseas departments brought about a substantial modification of the application of EU law to these departments. Article 349 TFEU, to which Article 355 refers, enables the EU Council of Ministers to adopt specific measures laying down conditions for the application of the EU Treaties to overseas departments, including common policies, in areas including customs, fishery, and agricultural policy. In doing so, the Council must take into account the overseas departments' 'structural social and economic situation . . . which is compounded by their remoteness, insularity, small size, difficult topography and climate, economic dependence on a few products, the permanence and combination of which severely restrain their development'. At the same time, this adaptation to local situations is not to result in an 'undermining [of] the integrity and [of] the coherence of the Union legal order, including the internal market and common policies'.[39] Today, the four traditional French overseas departments (Réunion, Guadeloupe, Martinique, and Guiana) have been joined in Article 349 by additional territories.[40]

Thus, in these more recent clauses, what one could still call a 'colonial clause' has become a vehicle for adjusting whether and how treaties apply to the people concerned and their elected officials. Although integral territorial application remains the default rule, treaties may still authorize a State to extend (or exclude) the treaty's application to its overseas territories. Today, however, such an extension (or exclusion) is more often done with the involvement of the peoples concerned.[41] Thus, the clause's inclusion is less controversial, although tensions remain with its relationship with treaties that purport to declare universal rights or responsibilities.

B. Federal clauses

Besides States endowed with overseas territories, federal States also present difficulties as far as the territorial application of treaties. The crux of the problem is that international law (with some exceptions discussed in Chapter 5) enables only federal States to enter into international treaties. But many federal States'

---

[38] The Court considers these taxes ('*octroi de mer*') as 'a charge having an effect equivalent to a customs duty on imports, notwithstanding the fact that the charge is also imposed on goods entering that region from another part of the same State'. Case No C-163/90 *Administration des Douanes et Droits Indirects v Léopold Legros* [1992] ECR I-04625 [18].

[39] TFEU Art 349.3.

[40] These are French Saint-Barthélemy and Saint-Martin Islands in the Caribbean, the Portuguese Azores and Madeira Islands, and the Spanish Canary Islands. On 31 March 2011 a fifth French overseas department, Mayotte, in the Indian Ocean, was created. Yet, up to now, Mayotte has not been added to the list of TFEU Art 349. For the time being, this island remains listed in Annex II; which means that the national/unilateral change of the status of a territory does not automatically bind the EU. A formal modification of Art 349 will probably be needed. This is not what one could call a flexible solution for such matters.

[41] Aust (n 17) 207–8 (describing UK practice of consultation with its dependencies and other overseas territories on the extension of treaties).

constitutions entitle their sub-federal governmental units (states, Länder, regions, provinces, or cantons) to implement—either exclusively or concurrently—the measures necessary for the federal State to comply with a treaty. In important areas, such as criminal law, human rights law, environmental law, and civil law, the federal State may simply lack domestic legal authority to apply treaty provisions in the absence of implementation by the sub-federal unit that the federal State may have no authority to require.[42] Federal States thus face difficult choices in deciding whether to consent to treaties in these areas. One alternative would be for the federal State to abstain from entering into the treaty entirely. Such a 'solution' is highly impractical due to the fact that some of the most important States in the world have a federal form of government, while others increasingly favour it nowadays to end internal strife.[43] A second alternative is for the federal State and its sub-federal units to resolve the situation internally through agreed procedures, the most notable example of which is undoubtedly the 1957 Lindau Agreement concluded by the Länder and the German Federal Government, providing that in the case of treaties affecting the Länder, the latter must give their consent (and not merely their opinion) before the Federation can validly enter into such a treaty.

A third option lies in adjusting the treaty obligations for federal States.[44] Expressing a non-federal or even anti-federal view, Fitzmaurice's 1959 report on treaties had suggested that:

the constituent states, provinces or parts of a federal union or federation, notwithstanding such local autonomy as they may possess under the constitution of the union or federation, are considered to be part of its metropolitan territory for treaty and other international purposes.[45]

Unlike the more general question of territorial application, the VCLT never endorsed any provision on federal States. In practice, however, treaty-makers

---

[42] Determining which areas are outside the federal governments' purview can be difficult, particularly in light of inconsistent practice by federal governments in joining treaties on matters that might otherwise seem constitutionally delegated to the sub-federal level. See DB Hollis, 'Executive Federalism: Forging New Federalism Constraints on the Treaty Power' (2006) 79 S Cal L Rev 1327, 1371–2.

[43] Nonetheless, there are several cases where a federal state has declined to join a treaty on federalism grounds, among the most prominent being the US decision not to seek ratification of the International Covenant on Economic, Social and Cultural Rights (adopted 16 November 1966, entered into force 3 January 1976) 993 UNTS 3, or the Convention on the Rights of the Child (adopted 20 November 1989, entered into force 2 September 1990) 1577 UNTS 3. See also Hollis (n 42) 1372–3.

[44] These are not, of course, the only available options. A federal State may also seek to issue reservations or understandings on ratification that address obligations that might otherwise be inconsistent with the State's federal system. The United States has used both approaches, issuing a federalism reservation for its obligations under the UN Transnational Organized Crime Convention (adopted 15 November 2000, entered into force 29 September 2003) 2225 UNTS 209, and an understanding for the International Covenant on Civil and Political Rights (ICCPR) (adopted 16 December 1966, entered into force 23 March 1976) 999 UNTS 171. See also Hollis (n 42) 1361–3, 1379. Alternatively, federal States may seek to adjust the treaty obligations themselves to avoid federalism issues, for example, by limiting implementation requirements to the 'national level'. Ibid 1377.

[45] [1959] YBILC, vol II, 47. Fitzmaurice did, however, anticipate that States might agree to otherwise provide for inclusion of a 'federal clause' adjusting the obligations of Federal States. Ibid 75 [130].

have devised a 'federal clause' to avoid the strains created by the confrontation between international and federal national law.[46]

The principal example of a 'federal clause' remains the Constitution of the International Labour Organization. Article 19(7)(b) provides that the federal State's obligations shall be the same as those of non-federal States for matters appropriate for federal action under the federal State's Constitution. For matters 'appropriate under its constitutional system, in whole or in part, for action by the constituent' units of the federal State, the federal State obligations are limited to referring them to the appropriate sub-federal units 'for the enactment of legislation or other action'.[47] The clause, with slight adaptations, has been repeated in a number of other major multilateral agreements, including the New York Convention on Arbitration and the 1951 Convention Relating to the Status of Refugees.[48] A more recent example of a federal clause appears in the COE's Convention on Cybercrime, authorizing a federal State to avoid the treaty's criminalization obligations 'consistent with its fundamental principles governing the relationship between its central government and constituent States' provided it does not 'exclude or substantially diminish' those criminalization obligations.[49]

A variation of the federal clause—known as a 'territorial clause'—appears in a variety of commercial and so-called private international law treaties. Thus, Article 93(1) of the 1980 UN Convention on Contracts for the International Sale of Goods (CISG) provides that:

If a Contracting State has two or more territorial units in which, according to its constitution, different systems of law are applicable in relation to matters dealt with in this Convention, it may, at the time of signature, ratification, acceptance, approval or accession, declare that this Convention is to extend to all its territorial units or only to one or more of them, and may amend its declaration by submitting another declaration at any time.[50]

---

[46] See generally RL Looper, '"Federal State" Clauses in Multilateral Instruments' (1955–56) 32 BYBIL 162–203.

[47] Constitution of the International Labour Organisation (adopted 9 October 1946, entered into force 20 April 1948) 15 UNTS 35. In addition, the federal State is obligated to consult with its sub-federal units on such matters with a view to promoting coordinated action and reporting back to the ILO on its activities and any implementation done at the sub-federal level. Ibid Art 19(7)(ii)–(v).

[48] Article 34 of the Convention for the Protection of the World Cultural and Natural Heritage is typical, limiting the responsibility of a federal State to provisions 'the implementation of which comes under the legal jurisdiction of the federal or central legislative power' whereas for implementation coming under the jurisdiction of the component units (which have no obligation to legislate), the federal government's only obligation is to inform these units of the provisions and recommend their adoption. (adopted 16 November 1972, entered into force 15 July 1975) 1037 UNTS 151, 161–2; see also Convention on the Recognition and Enforcement of Foreign Arbitral Awards (adopted 10 June 1958, entered into force 7 June 1959) 330 UNTS 38, Art XI (New York Convention on Arbitration); Convention Relating to the Status of Refugees (adopted 28 July 1951, entered into force 22 April 1954) 189 UNTS 150, Art 51.

[49] Council of Europe Convention on Cybercrime (adopted 23 November 2001, entered into force 1 July 2004) CETS No 185, Art 41.

[50] CISG (adopted 11 April 1980, entered into force 1 January 1988) 1489 UNTS 3; see also UN Convention on International Bills of Exchange and International Promissory Notes (adopted 9 December 1988, not yet in force) UN Doc A/Res/43/165, Art 87.

As written, the clause could apply to political sub-divisions of a metropolitan territory, although in practice the clause is most often invoked by federal States such as Canada.[51]

In recent years, there seems to be less enthusiasm for federal clauses, especially regarding treaties on human rights. The objections centre on allowing federal States to assume different (and fewer) obligations than non-federal States, especially where human rights treaties are designed to establish universal minimum standards. Some treaty texts now affirmatively oppose differential treatment for federal States. A typical 'anti-federal clause' is found in Article 50 of the International Covenant on Civil and Political Rights (ICCPR): 'The provisions of the present Covenant shall extend to all parts of federal States without any limitations or exceptions.'[52] Article 28(2) of the American Convention on Human Rights is less brutal, but also more ambiguous:

With respect to the provisions over whose subject matter the constituent units of the federal State have jurisdiction, the national government shall immediately take suitable measures, in accordance with its constitution and its laws, to the end that the competent authorities of the constituent units may adopt appropriate provisions for the fulfillment of this Convention.[53]

In one of the few judgments of the Inter-American Court of Human Rights on this provision, the Court described it as a federal clause, before asserting that, as a matter of estoppel, Argentina had always behaved 'as if the federal State had jurisdiction over human rights matters' although the matter concerned exclusively the attitude of the local police in the Argentinian province of Mendoza.[54] Indeed, quite often, federal tribunals have developed rather a bold (and much discussed) case law in order to bridge the gap between federal and international law.[55]

---

[51] Canada, for example, on joining the Sale of Goods Convention declared that it would extend the treaty to nine of its provinces and territories. Secretary-General, 'Canada: Declaration in Accordance with Article 93' (5 October 1998) C.N. 631.2003.

[52] ICCPR (n 44). In response to this provision, the United States issued the following (controversial) understanding:

The United States shall implement all the provisions of the [Covenant] over whose subject matter the Federal Government exercises legislative and judicial administration; with respect to the provisions over whose subject matter constituent units exercise jurisdiction, the Federal Government shall take appropriate measures, to the end that the competent authorities of the constituent units may take appropriate measures for the fulfillment of this Covenant.

ICCPR, 19 December 1966, S Exec Doc E, 95–2 (1978) xiv. Article 50 does not, moreover, prevent the ICCPR's Human Rights Committee (HRC) from asking States to produce in their reports specific information on how federated state law complies with provisions of the Covenant.

[53] (Adopted 22 November 1969, entered into force 18 June 1978) 1144 UNTS 123.

[54] *Garrido v Argentina* (1998) 4 Inter-American Ybk H Rts 3473.

[55] Cf J Kalb, 'Dynamic Federalism in Human Rights Treaty Implementation' (2010) 84 Tulane L Rev 1025–66.

III. The Concept of 'Territory' in the Territorial Application of Treaties

A. Treaty application to a State's 'territory'

The foregoing analysis focused on territorial application in juridical terms: deciding if a treaty applies to all of a State's territorial units or only to some of them. But even where a treaty clearly applies to a designated territory, two questions still remain. First of all, it is important to differentiate territorial application from the material application of treaty provisions that happen to relate to territory. Waldock, in particular, emphasized this distinction:

[S]ometimes the provisions of a treaty expressly relate to a particular territory or area, e.g. the Antarctic Treaty; and in that event the territory or area in question is undoubtedly the object to which the treaty applies. But this is not what the territorial application of a treaty really signifies, nor in such a case is the application of the treaty confined to the particular territory or area. The 'territorial application' of a treaty signifies the territories which the parties have purported to bind by the treaty and which, therefore, are the territories affected by the rights and obligations set up by the treaty. Thus, although the enjoyment of the rights and the performance of the obligations contained in a treaty may be localized in a particular territory or area, as in the case of Antarctica, it is the territories with respect to which each party contracted in entering into the treaty which determine its territorial scope.[56]

Second, understanding a treaty's territorial application requires understanding what the concept of 'territory' means with respect to a State's consent, regardless of whether the State is consenting to apply the treaty to 'its entire territory' or only to some specific parts of it.

For his part, Waldock simply relied on authorities stating that the territorial scope of a treaty coincides with territory under sovereignty of States parties to the treaty.[57] But the contemporary concept of 'territory' is a more composite one. In its 1966 commentary to what became Article 29, the ILC defined 'the entire territory of each party' to include 'all the land and appurtenant territorial waters and air space which constitute the territory of the State'.[58] This definition, however, does not resolve the issue. Neither the terms 'territorial waters' nor 'appurtenant' were used in previous (or later) treaties on the law of the sea. Moreover, 'appurtenant' seems also likely to instill confusion as it can be interpreted to give States the right to determine which waters belong to them. Looking to the law of the sea, however, it is possible to equate 'appurtenant' to the idea of waters belonging to or coming under a State's sovereignty, namely internal waters, territorial seas, as well as the archipelagic waters of archipelagic States.[59]

---

[56] [1964] YBILC, vol II, 12 [1].

[57] [1964] YBILC, vol II, 13 [3].

[58] [1966] YBILC, vol II, 213 [3]. Given the sensitivities associated with decolonization discussed above, the ILC indicated a preference for this definition in lieu of one that emphasized territories 'for which the parties are internationally responsible'. Ibid.

[59] It is rather curious that the ILC, to which we largely owe the four 1958 Geneva Conventions on the Law of the Sea, did not elaborate on the maritime aspects of a State's 'territory'.

Whether the additional maritime zones beyond the territorial sea are 'appurtenant' to coastal States so as to comprise part of a State's territory is a more difficult question. The exclusive economic zone (EEZ), which post-dated the VCLT, is neither a part of the high seas nor a zone under coastal State sovereignty. Its elusive legal nature is underscored by Article 59 of the 1982 UN Convention on the Law of the Sea (UNCLOS), which suggests conflicts over the EEZ not specifically regulated by the Convention 'should be resolved on the basis of equity and in the light of all the relevant circumstances, taking into account the respective importance of the interests involved to the parties as well as to the international community as a whole'.[60] The most that one can say at present is that, depending on the circumstances, the EEZ may or may not be 'territory' under Article 29 of the VCLT.

In contrast to the EEZ, a coastal State's rights in its contiguous zone (police surveillance powers) and continental shelf (economic rights) are rather devoid of ambiguity. With respect to the continental shelf, the Netherlands proposed that the ILC revise the territorial application provision to include 'the entire territory of each party, and beyond it as far as the jurisdiction of the State extends under international law, unless the contrary appears from the treaty'.[61] Waldock accepted this suggestion by adding a second paragraph to his draft article: 'a treaty may apply also in areas outside the territories of any of the parties in relation to matters which are within their competence with respect to those areas if it appears from the treaty that such application is intended'.[62] Yet, despite additional US support,[63] the Commission rejected this adjunction. The final word on this subject came from Senjin Tsuruoka, who suggested that the clause 'unless the contrary appears from the treaty' contained in the ILC's draft 'should be interpreted fairly broadly, in the positive as well as the negative sense, so that it was understood that the treaty—if its object so required or the intention was clear—was applicable outside the territory of the parties'.[64]

B. Extraterritorial application of treaties

Tsuruoka's observation suggests a certain value in applying some treaties beyond their States parties' territories. Still, formally, Article 29 abstains from addressing the question of extraterritorial application of treaties. Both its history and text focus on choosing between applying the treaty to the entire territory of a State party or to a part of it. As worded, the provision does not easily allow going beyond the 'entire territory' concept; it reads as if one may do less but not more. For its part, the

---

[60] UNCLOS (adopted 10 December 1982, entered into force 16 November 1994) 1833 UNTS 3. See S Karagiannis, 'L'article 59 de la Convention des Nations Unies sur le droit de la mer (ou les mystères de la nature juridique de la zone économique exclusive)' (2004) 37 RBDI 325–418.

[61] [1966] YBILC, vol II, 66.

[62] Ibid.

[63] A similar American proposition was drafted as such: 'a treaty also applies beyond the territory of each party whenever such wider application is clearly intended'. Ibid.

[64] [1966] YBILC, vol I(2), 49 [15].

ILC—without rejecting the idea of extraterritoriality—made clear that its draft article which became Article 29 avoided that topic:

[A]rticle [29] was intended by the Commission to deal only with the limited topic of the application of a treaty to the territory of the respective parties... In its view, the law regarding the extra-territorial application of treaties could not be stated simply in terms of the intention of the parties or of a presumption as to their intention; and it considered that to attempt to deal with all the delicate problems of extra-territorial competence in the present article would be inappropriate and inadvisable.[65]

Quite clearly, this commentary does not exclude applying a treaty in some extra-territorial way. It merely excludes Article 29 from governing such an application, leaving the issue to the law of treaties that lies beyond the VCLT.

But what does it mean for a treaty to apply extraterritorially? Some treaties appear to apply irrespective of territorial boundaries (such as the UN Charter's prohibitions on the unlawful use of force). For our purposes, the concept may actually mean either: (i) that a treaty will apply to territory, 'terrestrial' or not, lying outside the sovereignty of any State or (ii) that it will apply to territory lying under the sovereignty of another State.

The first possibility involves applying treaties to maritime zones outside the limits of the territorial sea.[66] We will not deal again with the contiguous zone, the continental shelf, or the EEZ. The big issue consists in the application of treaties on the high seas. Here, international customary law (and not Article 29 of the VCLT) allows (and more and more often obliges) States to apply treaties on ships flying their flags. As a normative matter, this is an important way to ensure the 'rule of law' on the high seas. But as a descriptive matter, it is no longer acceptable to describe ships as 'floating territory'. By applying treaty provisions to a ship on the high seas, the flag State applies them to its ship and not to the high seas themselves. But is it ever possible to forget that, in this case, the ship is really located on the high seas?[67] We see therefore that a treaty may geographically apply to a territory even if the latter is not under the territorial sovereignty of the State party to it. The case is quite similar to the application of treaties to territories commonly thought not to appertain to any State. The best example for this is Antarctica, even though seven States continue to raise territorial claims to some portions of the frozen continent.

The second understanding of extraterritoriality raises undoubtedly more 'delicate' problems. Applying a treaty to a portion (or even worse, to the whole) of another State's territory runs counter to a fundamental principle of sovereignty and the territorial integrity of States.[68] And States are rarely eager to accept (and

---

[65] [1966] YBILC, vol II, 213–14 [5].

[66] It may, in the future, extend to celestial bodies as well.

[67] The specificity of the high seas allows, however, some adaptations of the treaties concerned. See, for instance, in the case of the ECHR, *Medvedyev and Others v France* (App no 3394/03) ECHR 29 March 2010. See also *Hirsi Jamaa and Others v Italy* (App no 27765/09) ECHR 23 February 2012.

[68] It is possible, of course, for a State to enter into a treaty on behalf not only of itself but also of another State. If the latter agrees, there is not any difficulty. Problems arise when no such agreement can be shown.

even less so to claim openly) that a treaty binding on them applies on territory outside of their own national territory. Ultimately, the issue may be one of treaty interpretation.

In recent years, interpretative disputes have arisen in particular with respect to the extraterritorial application of human rights treaties.[69] The ICCPR, for example, provides that 'each State Party to the present Covenant undertakes to respect and to ensure to all individuals within its territory *and* subject to its jurisdiction the rights recognized in the present Covenant'.[70] In General Comment 31, the ICCPR's Human Rights Committee (HRC) interpreted this provision as a 'disjunctive conjunction', allowing the ICCPR to bind a State party not just for acts within its territory but also in other areas subject to its jurisdiction, which the Committee defined to cover 'anyone within the power or effective control of that State Party'.[71] Others, notably the United States and the Netherlands, however, continue to insist that the text of Article 2 and the accompanying *travaux préparatoires* limit the ICCPR's application to the territory of a State party.[72]

Resolving such interpretative disputes (let alone the issues of State responsibility that they may generate) is difficult absent the consent of the concerned State(s) to judicial review. Several human rights treaties, however, include such consent. The most abundant (and sometimes spectacular) case law on extraterritorial application is that of the ECtHR. The Court (and before it the European Commission of Human Rights) have repeatedly said that a State party to the ECHR is accountable for acts contrary to its conventional commitments even if materially these acts take place outside the territory of that State. The Court bases this interpretation on Article 1 of the ECHR: 'The High Contracting Parties shall secure to everyone within their jurisdiction the rights and freedoms defined in Section I of this

---

[69] M Milanovic, 'From Compromise to Principle: Clarifying the Concept of State Jurisdiction in Human Rights Treaties' (2008) 8 Hum Rts L Rev 411–48 (noting claims by victims of aerial bombardment, inhabitants of territories under military occupation, suspected terrorists detained in Guantánamo, and the family of a former KGB spy assassinated in London that a State has human rights treaty obligation towards individuals located outside its territory).

[70] ICCPR (n 44) Art 2(1) (emphasis added).

[71] HRC, 'General Comment No 31: Nature of the General Legal Obligations Imposed on States Parties to the Covenant' (29 March 2004) UN Doc CCPR/C/21/Rev.1/Add.13. The ICJ endorsed this position in its Advisory Opinion on *Legal Consequences on the Construction of a Wall in the Occupied Palestinian Territory*:

> The Court would observe that, while the jurisdiction of States is primarily territorial, it may sometimes be exercised outside the national territory. Considering the object and purpose of the International Covenant on Civil and Political Rights, it would seem natural that, even when such is the case, States parties to the Covenant should be bound to comply with its provisions.

[2004] ICJ Rep 179 [109] (Wall Opinion).

[72] See KJ Heller, 'Does the ICCPR Apply Extraterritorially ?'[2006] Opinio Juris <http://opinio-juris.org/2006/07/18/does-the-iccpr-apply-extraterritorially> (describing US objections to extraterritorial application); MJ Dennis, 'Application of Human Rights Treaties Extraterritorially in Times of Armed Conflict and Military Occupation' (2005) 99 AJIL 119, 125 (describing the Dutch position). One can also note that the 'dual' expression used in Art 2 of the Covenant is the unfortunate result of the concurrent American ('within its territory') and French ('subject to its jurisdiction') propositions. Unable to choose, the General Assembly preferred to include both of them separated by the conjunction 'and'. Strictly speaking, Art 2 could now become too narrow a provision. This is what the HRC tried to avoid in its case law and in its General Comment (n 71).

Convention.' Unlike the ICCPR, there is no territorial limitation in Article 1, meaning not only that the ECHR might extend to acts committed outside the State's territory but, conversely, acts committed inside the said territory might not trigger the State's ECHR obligations if it has no 'jurisdiction' in a given case.[73]

This rather surprising aspect of the 'jurisdiction' theory is fully admissible in case, for instance, the State has no (more) authority on the territory in which the act contrary to the Convention takes place (provided of course that no agent of the State is involved). This would apply most naturally to instances of military occupation.[74] For example, during the allied occupation of Berlin, it has been argued that West Germany was not responsible for what was happening there.[75] The ECtHR's own case law, however, has not fully endorsed this view. In *Ilaşcu and Others v Moldova and Russia*,[76] the Court held Moldova accountable for acts in Transdniestria during a period in which its government did not control this secessionist territory (and which the Court found was almost occupied by Russia). The Court acknowledged Moldova's lack of de facto authority, but held that the jurisdictional requirement of Article 1 required it to 'endeavour, with all the legal and diplomatic means available to it *vis-à-vis* foreign States and international organisations, to continue to guarantee the enjoyment of the rights and freedoms defined in the Convention'.[77] That finding may explain why States subsequently sought to reserve to any ECHR obligations for territory under foreign occupation or controlled by secessionist forces. Upon ratifying additional Protocol No 7, for example, Azerbaijan declared that 'it is unable to guarantee the application of the provisions of the Protocol in the territories occupied by the Republic of Armenia until these territories are liberated from that occupation'.[78]

---

[73] Several other treaties—the American Convention on Human Rights and the UN Convention on the Rights of the Child—follow the ECHR in imposing obligations on States with respect to 'persons subject to their jurisdiction'. Other treaties—such as the Convention on the Elimination of All Forms of Racial Discrimination (adopted 21 December 1965, entered into force 4 January 1969) 660 UNTS 195, and the Convention Against Torture and Other Cruel, Inhuman or Degrading Treatment or Punishment (adopted 10 December 1984, entered into force 26 June 1987) 1465 UNTS 85—provide specific rights and obligations a State must apply to 'any territories under its jurisdiction'. Milanovic (n 69) 413–14. For a complete review of international bodies' and US practice see SH Cleveland, 'Embedded International Law and the Constitution Abroad' (2010) 110 Columbia L Rev 225–87.

[74] Yet, what qualifies as a military occupation is only apparently clear in law. Cf Adam Roberts, 'What Is A Military Occupation?' (1984) 55 BYBIL 249–345.

[75] *George Vearncombe and Others v United Kingdom and Federal Republic of Germany* (App no 12816/87) (1989) 59 DR 186 (decision of the European Commission on Human Rights that 'acts performed by organs of an occupying State (including members of its army) are generally attributable to this State and not to the occupied State').

[76] *Ilaşcu and Others v Moldova and Russia* (App no 48787/99) ECHR 2004-VII.

[77] Ibid 77 [33].

[78] See 'List of Declarations Made with Respect to Treaty 117' in <http://conventions.coe.int/treaty/Commun/ListeDeclarations.asp?NT=117&CM=8&DF=02/10/2011&CL=ENG&VL=1>. Similarly, Georgia declared upon ratifying Protocol No 12 that it 'declines its responsibility for the violations of the provisions of the Protocol on the territories of Abkhazia and Tskhinvali region until the full jurisdiction of Georgia is restored over these territories'. See 'List of Declarations Made with Respect to Treaty 177' in <http://conventions.coe.int/treaty/Commun/ListeDeclarations.asp?NT=177&CM=8&DF=02/10/2011&CL=ENG&VL=1>.

Still, the genuine extraterritorial effect of the 'jurisdiction' theory arises vis-à-vis the occupying or controlling power.[79] The classic statement of this is found in the ECtHR's *Loizidou v Turkey* judgment (Preliminary Objections): 'although Article 1 sets limits on the reach of the Convention, the concept of "jurisdiction" under this provision is not restricted to the national territory of the High Contracting Parties'.[80] The Court defined this jurisdiction such that 'the responsibility of a Contracting Party may also arise when as a consequence of military action— whether lawful or unlawful—it exercises effective control of an area outside its national territory'.[81] Yet, what has been celebrated (or criticized) as a bold extension of the ECHR's scope created new problems.

In the first place, the 'effective control of an area' test is not always easy to handle. Whereas, for example, some 35,000 Turkish soldiers may be deemed more than enough to secure effective control over Northern Cyprus (with a population of 150,000 to which must be added some 100,000 Turkish settlers), it may be more difficult to ascertain the same as far as Transdniestria is concerned (with just 1,500 Russian soldiers at the time of the *Ilaşcu* case). This being said, a territory 'just' bombed by a State party's war planes is not, according to the famous *Banković* decision, a territory under the effective control of that State.[82] The control of air space apparently does not amount to territorial control proper for purposes of establishing the State's jurisdiction. Obviously (and perhaps due to the heavy political consequences?), *Banković* does not fit with the Court's *Issa* judgment, according to which 'Article 1 of the Convention cannot be interpreted so as to allow a State party to perpetrate violations of the Convention on the territory of another State, which it could not perpetrate on its own territory'.[83] Most recently, the Court attempted to reconcile its earlier case law in *Al-Skeini and Others v UK*. There, the ECtHR interpreted Article 1 to apply to the killing of an Iraqi national in a British military prison in Iraq as well as the killing of five individuals

---

[79] This is especially true where a special legal relationship links the State to the territory even if the State does not exercise sovereignty proper on this territory. Cf 'Decision of 12 March 2002 of the Inter-American Commission on Human Rights in the case of Guantánamo detainees' [2002] 41 ILM 532 (Commission considered that measures requested by petitioners were justified and necessary having regard, *inter alia*, to the fact that the detainees at Guantánamo 'remain wholly within the authority and control of the United States government' despite the fact that the military base at Guantánamo is not strictly speaking US territory but is the subject of a long-term lease from Cuba); Wall Opinion (n 71) 179 [109] (finding Israel in breach of its obligations under the ICCPR and the ICESC with respect to the occupied territories).

[80] *Loizidou v Turkey* (App no 15318/89) (1995) Series A no 310. See also *Cyprus v Turkey* (App no 25781/94) (2001) ECHR 2001-IV.

[81] *Loizidou* (n 80) [62]. In a separate line of cases, the ECtHR has interpreted jurisdiction in personal, rather than territorial terms, to apply where the use of force by a State's agents operating outside its territory may bring the individual thereby under the control of the State's authorities into the State's Art 1 jurisdiction. See *Al-Skeini and Others v UK* (App no 55721/07) ECHR 7 July 2011 [135]–[136].

[82] *Banković and Others v Belgium and Others* (App no 52207/99) ECHR 2001-XII [59]. This said, an absence of jurisdictional link due to a lack of effective control of a territory may be compensated for by judicial actions brought by the tribunals of the respondent State. Cf *Marković and Others v Italy* (App no 1398/03) ECHR 2006-XIV [55].

[83] *Issa and Others v Turkey* (App no 31821/96) ECHR 16 November 2004 [71].

by British troops in the streets of the UK-occupied Basra since the 'United Kingdom (together with the United States) assumed in Iraq the exercise of some of the *public powers normally to be exercised by a sovereign government*'.[84]

The *Loizidou* test and its progeny bear some similarity to the effective/overall control test used to attribute responsibility to a foreign State for the acts of groups of individuals, a test that has proved controversial in cases ranging from the ICJ's *Nicaragua* judgment[85] to the International Criminal Tribunal for former Yugoslavia's (ICTY) *Tadić* judgment.[86] In *Loizidou* (as well as Al-Skeini), the discussion was not about control over a group whose acts might be attributed to a State, but about a foreign State's control over territory. From this point of view, *Loizidou* proves quite restrictive in terms of ascribing to a State jurisdiction.

The Court has emphasized, in any case, it is only 'in exceptional circumstances [that] the acts of Contracting States performed outside their territory or which produce effects there ("extra-territorial act") may amount to exercise by them of their jurisdiction within the meaning of Article 1 of the Convention'.[87] More often, the Court will find it has no competence to examine complaints under Article 1 even where a State's acts have extraterritorial effects. A good example of this was the *Ben El Mahi and Others v Denmark* decision.[88] There, the applicants were Moroccan residents and Moroccan associations operating in Morocco with no jurisdictional link whatsoever with Denmark. As a result, the Court found they could not validly challenge Denmark's decision to allow publication of cartoons on Prophet Muhammad in Denmark. Even if the concept of 'jurisdiction' within the meaning of Article 1 is not necessarily restricted to the national territory, the Court reaffirmed in *Issa*, that:

[F]rom the standpoint of public international law, the words 'within their jurisdiction' in Article 1 of the Convention must be understood to mean that a State's jurisdictional competence is primarily territorial but also that jurisdiction is presumed to be exercised normally throughout the State's territory.[89]

Yet, the control of territory test is not always of paramount importance to the Strasbourg Court's definition of Article 1 jurisdiction. In addition to defining 'jurisdiction' on a territorial/extraterritorial basis, the Court has a separate line of cases that envision it in more personal terms. As *Issa* puts it, 'moreover, a State may also be held accountable for violation of the Convention rights and freedoms of persons who are in the territory of another State but who are found to be under the former State's authority and control through its agents operating—whether

---

[84] *Al-Skeini* (n 81) [149] (emphasis added).
[85] *Case concerning Military and Paramilitary Activities in and against Nicaragua* (Merits) [1986] ICJ Rep 65 [115].
[86] (Judgment) ICTY-1994-1 (15 July 1999) [120].
[87] *Issa* (n 83) [68]; accord *Al-Skeini* (n 81) [149].
[88] (App no 5853/06) ECHR 2006-XV.
[89] *Issa* (n 83) [67].

lawfully or unlawfully—in the latter State'.[90] Policemen, diplomats, secret agents, and so on can then fully engage a State's ECHR commitments through either their acts or even their omissions. A highly sensitive topic, which is not always void of some confusion, the European case law on extraterritoriality will probably need some great clarification in the coming years.[91]

IV. The Territorial Scope of Treaties Concluded between States and International Organizations or between International Organizations

Article 29 of the 1986 VCLT is strikingly similar to Article 29 of the 1969 VCLT. It reads: 'unless a different intention appears from the treaty or is otherwise established, a treaty between one or more States and one or more international organizations is binding upon each State party in respect of its entire territory'.[92] The main principle of integral territorial application for States is thus overtly reaffirmed as well as the bases for derogations. In doing so, the article raises many (if not all) of the same issues discussed above. One might thus ask if this provision was necessary at all. Members of the ILC felt a moral obligation to not introduce any substantial changes from the 1969 VCLT in drafting this treaty. Special Rapporteur Paul Reuter had originally reproduced the 1969 formula literally word by word, although that text had little obvious connection to the conclusion of treaties involving international organizations (IOs).[93] This oddity was corrected by the ILC, when N Ushakov, proposed to add the words 'between one or more States and one or more international organizations' to the draft text.[94] This suggestion was easily accepted and the formula suffered no more changes.

---

[90] Ibid [71]. Similar is the construction of the HRC in cases such as *Burgos v Uruguay* (1981) 1 Selected Decisions of the Human Rights Committee 88, 91 [12.1]–[12.3] and *Casariego v Uruguay* (1981) 1 Selected Decisions of the Human Rights Committee 92, 94 [10.1]–[10.3].

[91] The extraterritorial application of the ECHR has provoked considerable emotion in military and political circles and given rise to much academic writing. See, among many others, F Coomans and M Kamminga (eds), *Extraterritorial Application of Human Rights Treaties* (Intersentia, Antwerp–Oxford 2004); S Karagiannis, 'Le territoire d'application de la Convention européenne des droits de l'homme. Vetera et nova' (2005) 16 Rev trim des droits de l'homme 33–120; M Gondek, 'Extraterritorial Application of the European Convention on Human Rights: Territorial Focus in the Age of Globalization?' (2005) Netherlands Intl L Rev 349–87; V Mantouvalou, 'Extending Judicial Control in International Law: Human Rights Treaties and Extraterritoriality' (2005) 9 Intl J Human Rts 147–63; S Skogly, *Beyond National Borders: States' Human Rights Obligations in International Cooperation* (Intersentia, Antwerp–Oxford 2006); E Lagrange, 'L'application de la Convention de Rome à des actes accomplis par les États parties en dehors du territoire national' (2008) 112 Rev gén de dr int public 521–65; M Gibney and S Skogly (eds), *Universal Human Rights and Extraterritorial Obligations* (U Penn Press, Philadelphia 2010); M Milanovic, *Extraterritorial Application of Human Rights Treaties* (OUP, Oxford 2011).

[92] 1986 VCLT (n 2) Art 29. For a discussion of the status of the 1986 VCLT in customary international law see Chapter 3.

[93] [1977] YBILC, vol I, 117.

[94] Ibid 118 [26].

Despite the satisfactory resolution of a text for Article 29 of the 1986 VCLT, two lacunae still render it somewhat enigmatic. They correspond to the two hypotheses on which the 1986 VLCT is built: (i) the conclusion of a treaty by an IO with a State and (ii) the conclusion of a treaty by an IO with another IO. In the first case, Article 29 allows for unequal treatment between the two contracting parties since the application *ratione loci* concerns only the State and not at all IOs. In the second case, no discrimination whatsoever takes place, but if one sticks to the text itself, the *ratione loci* application issue is irrelevant. Among IOs, territorial scope appears to have nothing to do with their treaty commitments.

A prima facie reaction might logically attribute the wording of Article 29 of the 1986 VCLT to a lack of adequate attention by its authors. Behind this 'clumsiness' explanation, however, lies a more nefarious possibility. Article 29 of the 1986 VCLT suggests that what is actually important when two IOs enter into a treaty is not the IOs themselves but rather their member States, to the whole of the territory of which the treaty will normally apply. Under this reading, IOs become thoroughly transparent, almost non-existent, in so far as, with respect to the territorial application of their treaties, the only thing to behold is their member States' territory. Ultimately, not only the wording (which could have probably been less awkward) but also the global philosophy of Article 29 of the 1986 VCLT are likely to fuel arguments about the very legal existence of IOs. Assuming territorial application of treaties is an important matter (and one can hardly deny this), IOs seem to just be organs of coordination of the international efforts of their respective member States.

In any event, it may be seriously asked why the ILC (and later on the 1986 Conference) took such a stance, especially where it flies in the face of the 1986 Convention's other provisions. Why confirm IO treaty-making powers[95] if one merely wishes to show that IOs are artificial legal constructions (as the Neapolitan school of law around Rolando Quadri or the Soviet one around Grigory Tunkin thought it at a time)? Still, behind this conceptual difficulty lie two additional questions: (1) May an IO ever claim to possess a territory of its own? (2) In the negative, may the territories of IO member States taken together be deemed to constitute the territory of the organization?

The second question is easier to answer. Even IOs that can boast very significant legal powers abstain from considering the territory of their member States as their own. The EU provides a telling example. Article 52 of the Treaty on European Union and Article 355 TFEU only indicate the territories of the Union's member States to which those treaties apply; they by no means indicate that these territories are territories of the EU itself. Speaking of a Union territory (customs territory, for instance) as some scholars do is only a metaphorical extrapolation.

As regards the other question, one may usually think that territory is closely related to the concept of statehood (along with a population and political power). Just as an organization cannot possess a population of its own, in the same way it

---

[95] 1986 VCLT Art 6 ('The capacity of an international organization to conclude treaties is governed by the rules of that Organization').

generally cannot possess a territory. Nevertheless, there are some marginal cases where an IO possesses territory, albeit temporarily and not in an absolute but rather a functional way. This applies where organizations, most of the time the UN, exercise *de jure* (or sometimes both *de jure* and *de facto*) sovereignty on a given territory. A good historical example was the Council of the United Nations for Namibia, created by General Assembly Resolution 2248 (XXII) of 19 May 1967, which represented (until Namibia's independence) something between an IO (it was a subsidiary body of the UN) and a State. Some multilateral conventions in fact dealt with the Council as if it were a State.[96] One may also wonder if the UN or, more exactly, UN subsidiary organs responsible for State-building in a given area (East Timor, Kosovo) play a similar role and might therefore be considered as having a kind of territory during the transition period.[97] Of course, the ephemeral aspect of State-building operations has nothing to do with the permanence of State sovereignty on State territory. We must not forget that IOs are definitely not States and the territory on which they sometimes exercise their jurisdiction cannot generally be equated to a State's territory.

Conclusion

Altogether, the simplicity of the territorial scope of treaties seems to be only apparent. Such sensitive issues as the application of treaties to territories largely autonomous and lying most of the time overseas or the distribution of power (as far as the application of treaties is concerned) between federal States and sub-federal entities have only slightly and somewhat superficially been dealt with by international law. Definitely, it is not easy to say whether Article 29 of the VCLT really deals with them at all, and at the same time diplomatic practice and international or national case law are far from being homogeneous. The mere definition of the components of the State territory to which treaties apply is likely to become of some inextricable complexity (especially at sea). A careful drafting of territorial clauses of treaties could be a kind of remedy. Still, the most sensitive matter concerns not so much the diminution of the State territory to which a treaty applies but the perspective of considerably enlarging the scope of treaties to what

---

[96] Eg UNCLOS (n 60) Art 305(1)(b). A related line of inquiry is whether UNCLOS's International Sea-Bed Authority is an IO exercising power analogous to 'territory', namely the soil and sub-soil of the high seas beyond national continental shelves. At present, such an analogy seems difficult where the sea soil is at a depth of thousands of metres and the Sea-Bed Authority's power is primarily functional and subsequently quite limited; its authority is limited to exploration and exploitation of natural resources and does not extend, for example, to shipwrecks. Ibid Art 149.

[97] Legal writing on this point becomes extensive. See eg B Knoll, *The Legal Status of Territories Subject to Administration by International Organisations* (CUP, New York 2008); C Stahn, *The Law and Practice of International Territorial Administration. Versailles to Iraq and Beyond* (CUP, Cambridge 2008); R Wilde, *International Territorial Administration: How Trusteeship and the Civilizing Mission Never Went Away* (OUP, Oxford 2008); HF Kiderlen, *Von Triest nach Osttimor. Der völkerrechtliche Rahmen für die Verwaltung von Krisengebieten durch die Vereinten Nationen* (Springer Berlin, Heidelberg 2008).

lies outside the national territory, that is, parts of our planet free of any State sovereignty or parts of territories of third States. In particular in the field of modern human rights case law, the perspective of substituting the notion of 'jurisdiction' for one of territorial application leads unavoidably to the accountability of States for acts and omissions of their agents taking place outside the borders of national territory. One still cannot see up to what point exactly this rather strong extraterritoriality movement is likely to lead. Despite some precautions they can take (careful drafting of the treaty, appropriate reservations, declarations, and so on), States seem to be somewhat defenceless. It would be disastrous if they come to consider that the only solution is for them to be less and less committed.

Recommended Reading

SH Cleveland, 'Embedded International Law and the Constitution Abroad' (2010) 110 Columbia L Rev 225

F Coomans and M Kamminga (eds), *Extraterritorial Application of Human Rights Treaties* (Intersentia, Antwerp–Oxford 2004)

MJ Dennis, 'Application of Human Rights Treaties Extraterritorially in Times of Armed Conflict and Military Occupation' (2005) 99 AJIL 119

M Gibney and S Skogly (eds), *Universal Human Rights and Extraterritorial Obligations* (U Penn Press, Philadelphia 2010)

M Gondek, 'Extraterritorial Application of the European Convention on Human Rights: Territorial Focus in the Age of Globalization?' (2005) 52 Netherlands Intl L Rev 349

DB Hollis, 'Executive Federalism; Forging New Federalism Constraints on the Treaty Power' (2006) 79 S Cal L Rev 1327

S Karagiannis, 'L'aménagement des droits de l'homme outre-mer: la clause des "nécessités locales" de la Convention européenne' (1995) 28 RBDI 224

S Karagiannis, 'Le territoire d'application de la Convention européenne des droits de l'homme. Vetera et nova' (2005) 16 Rev trim des droits de l'homme 33

B Knoll, *The Legal Status of Territories Subject to Administration by International Organisations* (CUP, New York 2008)

E Lagrange, 'L'application de la Convention de Rome à des actes accomplis par les Etats parties en dehors du territoire national' (2008) 112 Rev gén de dr int public 521

RL Looper, '"Federal State" Clauses in Multilateral Instruments' (1955–56) 32 BYBIL 162

M Milanovic, *Extraterritorial Application of Human Rights Treaties* (OUP, Oxford 2011)

M Milanovic, 'From Compromise to Principle: Clarifying the Concept of State Jurisdiction in Human Rights Treaties' (2008) 8 Hum Rts L Rev 411

L Moor and AB Simpson, 'Ghosts of Colonialism in the European Convention on Human Rights' (2006) 76 BYBIL 121

13

Third Party Rights and Obligations in Treaties

David J Bederman

Introduction

The law of treaties is full of complexities and nuances. But it has always appeared axiomatic that treaties, in their application, bind only parties. The origins of that maxim are derived from the most basic of 'general principles of law recognized by civilized nations':[1] that the rights and duties contained in contracts adhere to only those that have consented. This 'default' rule for treaty application—that treaty rights and obligations have no effect on third parties (in Latin: *'pacta tertii alieni nec nocere, nec prodissi potest'* or simply *'pacta tertii'*)—seems both intuitive and well-enshrined in the relevant sources of international law, particularly in State practice.

But, as with so many other subjects related to the law of treaties, the *res inter alios acta* principle (things done between others do not create duties for non-parties) has undergone an extraordinary process of reflection and revision over the course of the past half-century. Like the set of rules concerning the scope of permissible reservations to treaties (considered in Chapter 11 of this *Guide*), the default rule for third party treaty application has been dissolved with the solvent of codification, in the form of the 1969 Vienna Convention on the Law of Treaties (VCLT). What impelled this doctrinal modification in third party treaty application will be a major focus of this chapter. This will necessitate a comparison between the case law, State practice, and conclusions of publicists that subsisted prior to the VCLT, and that post-codification. Additionally, a searching analysis of the VCLT's text and *travaux préparatoires* will be undertaken here with respect to the provisions concerning third parties. My aim is to ascertain whether these clauses were truly codification of existing State practice, or, rather, a progressive development in this area of treaty law. Additionally, I hope to assess the success of the current VCLT regime of third party application, in light of the very sparse State practice and decisional law that has transpired on this subject since 1969, including that relevant for agreements concluded with international organizations.

---

[1] Statute of the International Court of Justice (26 June 1945) 33 UNTS 993, Art 38(1)(c). One such general principle is the notion that treaty obligations should be performed in good faith—*pacta sunt servanda*. See VCLT Art 26 ('Every treaty in force is binding upon the parties to it and must be performed by them in good faith').

The biggest puzzle implicated in the topic of treaty application to third parties is a doctrine that was expressly rejected as part of the Vienna Convention project. This was the principle of 'objective regimes', the notion that certain treaties (or provisions therein) were of such significance to the international community that they were to be applied to non-parties, irrespective of consent. The objective regimes doctrine, as part of *pacta tertii*, is a dimmer star in the constellation of principles that includes *erga omnes* obligations and *jus cogens* norms.[2] Although limited in scope to questions concerning third party application of treaties, and as a notional exception to the default rule, objective regimes remain an immensely controversial—but understudied—topic. I intend to remedy that in this chapter.

Third party rights and obligations implicate a variety of correlate issues under treaty law. Among these are a State's obligation not to frustrate the object and purpose of a treaty prior to the entry-into-force of obligations, and the possibility of the provisional application of treaty clauses. These are expressly handled in other sections of the VCLT,[3] and are considered elsewhere in this volume (Chapters 8 and 9). Likewise, a State's duty not to interfere with another State's exercise of treaty rights is beyond the scope of this contribution.[4] Lastly, matters of State succession to treaty obligations—which were the subject of their own International Law Commission (ILC) project and treaty regime[5]—cannot be reviewed in this chapter, despite the obvious connection to what defines a 'party' or 'non-party' to a treaty instrument (for a discussion of treaty succession see Chapter 16).

As a final prefatory matter, for the purposes of this chapter it makes sense to adopt the VCLT's straightforward definition of a 'third party' to a treaty. A 'third State', according to the VCLT, is simply a 'State not a party to the treaty'.[6] A 'party' means a 'State which has consented to be bound by the treaty and for which the treaty is in force'.[7] Taking these definitions together, a 'third party' is a State which has not consented to be bound to a treaty, nor to a particular set of rights or obligations contained in that instrument.

I. Pre-Vienna Convention Doctrine and Practice

It is easy to understand how the general contracts rule, *res inter alios acta* (things done between others do not create duties for non-parties), was elevated as a general

---

[2] *Jus Cogens* norms are those few pre-emptory norms that the international community considers so significant that they will not suffer States to 'contract' out of them by treaty. Obligations *erga omnes* are customary international law obligations that are important enough that the international community permits *any* State to claim for their violation, not just the States that are immediately affected.

[3] VCLT Arts 18 and 25.

[4] But see I Sinclair, *Vienna Convention on the Law of Treaties* (2nd edn MUP, Manchester 1984) 99.

[5] Vienna Convention on Succession of States in Respect of Treaties concluded 23 August 1978, entered into force 6 November 1996, 1946 UNTS 3.

[6] VCLT Art 2(1)(h).

[7] Ibid Art 2(1)(g). These definitions were largely repeated in the 1986 Vienna Convention on the Law of Treaties between States and International Organizations or between International Organizations (adopted 21 March 1986, not yet in force) [1986] 25 ILM 543, Art 2(1)(h) ('1986 VCLT').

principle of law into the maxim of *pacta tertii nec nocent nec prosunt* (treaties do not create rights or duties for third States).[8] In the Anglo-American common law, *res inter alios acta* was well-enshrined, with the exception of the possibility of contractual benefits running to non-parties (either as a matter of trust, assignment, or the law of beneficiaries).[9] In civil law jurisdictions on the Continent, particularly those following the French Code Napoléon,[10] the absolute rule of *res inter alios acta* (derived from Roman law[11]) was followed with the exception of cases where a party made a stipulation of a contractual benefit to be conferred on a non-party (the *stipulation pour autrui*) and that third party expressly accepted the benefit.[12] Likewise, in German and Swiss law, contractual rights could be conferred on non-parties—if that was the intent of the contractors—and the third party need not even expressly accept it.[13] All of these legal systems were unanimous in the conclusion that contractual *obligations* could never be visited on a non-party, but were rather less consistent in expressing the conditions under which contractual *benefits* could (or should) be granted and the manner in which they could be subsequently enforced.

This evidence of 'general principles of law recognized by civilized nations' was cited before international tribunals and bodies in matters concerning treaty application,[14] and came to be relied upon by at least some authorities.[15] Indeed, most of the doctrinal developments for treaty application to third parties can be traced to case law from the inter-War period, particularly in a handful of decisions rendered by the Permanent Court of International Justice (PCIJ), and in some notorious incidents of State practice immediately following the First[16] and Second World

---

[8] R Roxburgh, *International Conventions and Third States* (Longmans, Green and Co, London 1917) 6 (citing to Roman law, as received through Gentili, Grotius, and Pufendorf); DW Arrow, 'Seabed, Sovereignty and Objective Regimes' (1983) 7 Fordham Intl L J 169, 170 n7.

[9] Roxburgh (n 8) 6–12 (absolute rule in English law against third party benefits was modified by exceptions). See also EJ de Aréchaga, 'Treaty Stipulations in Favor of Third States' (1956) 50 AJIL 338, 347–8; Harvard Research on 'International Law, Law of Treaties, Article 18: Treaties and Third States' (1935) 29 AJIL Supp 918, 924 ('Harvard Research').

[10] C Civ Arts 1119, 1121, 1165 (France) (1804). Harvard Research (n 9) 925 (equating the *stipulation pour autrui* to the trust in England).

[11] H Waldock, 'Third Report on the Law of Treaties' [1964] YBILC, vol II, 18.

[12] Roxburgh (n 8) 12–13.

[13] BGB Arts 328–33 (Germany) (1900); CO, Art 112 (Switzerland) (1907). See also Harvard Research (n 9) 919 (discussing municipal law cases from Switzerland, Poland, and Italy); S Williston, 'Contracts for the Benefit of a Third Person in the Civil Law' (1902) 16 Harvard L Rev 43, 50.

[14] Jimenez de Aréchaga (n 9) 346, 348 (discussing the *Free Zones* and *German Interests in Polish Upper Silesia* cases). See also H Lauterpacht, *Private Law Sources and Analogies to International Law* (Longmans, Green and Co, London 1927) 69.

[15] *Case Concerning Certain German Interests in Polish Upper Silesia (Germany v Poland)* [1926] PCIJ Rep Series A No 7, 84 (Finlay J, observations). But see Waldock (n 11) 20 (commentary (1), questioning whether doctrine has been influenced by general principles derived from municipal law); *Case of the Free Zones of Upper Savoy and District of Gex (France v Switzerland)* [1929] PCIJ Rep Series A No 22, 43 (Dreyfus J, dissenting) (noting that diversity of application of third party contractual rights in municipal law precluded its elevation to international law as a general principle) ('*Free Zones 1929*').

[16] See Harvard Research (n 9) 921 (citing examples of Dutch practice). For earlier examples of State practice, see ibid 928–9; Roxburgh (n 8) 42–5 (discussing status of Schleswig based on 1866 treaty between Prussia and Austria, and whether Denmark had any rights thereunder).

Wars. Inasmuch as the codification process which led to the VCLT extensively relied on this decisional law and State practice, it is worth reviewing in detail here.

The vast majority of cases and incidents from the pre-VCLT period concerned the possibility of treaties conferring rights and benefits on non-parties. In the Åland Islands dispute, which arose in 1907 and again just after the conclusion of the First World War, the question was whether Russia's planned fortification of the islands—which was in express violation of its obligations under the Convention of 30 March 1856 (which ended the Crimean War)—was opposable by Sweden, which was not a party to that instrument. Contemporary publicists opined that Sweden had no rights under the 1856 treaty and was not even named as an intended beneficiary by the parties; Sweden's only recourse was to raise its objection through a treaty party, which was under no obligation to take the matter further.[17] A Committee of Jurists, appointed by the League of Nations in 1920, took a different position, finding that even though Sweden was not a party, nor even an intended beneficiary, the 1856 convention nevertheless created an 'objective law whose effects extended beyond the circle of the contracting powers'.[18] This pronouncement, although criticized contemporaneously as being unsupportable as a matter either of State practice or general principles,[19] is still regarded as the *locus classicus* of the 'objective regimes' theory of applying treaty rules to non-parties.[20]

Early PCIJ decisions tended, however, to be unequivocal in upholding the *res inter alios acta* principle. In the 1929 *Territorial Jurisdiction of the International Commission of the River Oder* case, the Court declined to hold that the terms of the 1921 Barcelona Convention on the Regime of Navigable Waterways of International Concern were binding on Poland, inasmuch as Poland was not a party.[21] But, in other decisions, the PCIJ did hold that a non-party to a treaty instrument could nonetheless be bound to an obligation by its acceptance of subsequent instruments.[22]

The Court's jurisprudence was rather more nuanced in relation to the question raised in the Åland Islands dispute: whether rights and benefits (as distinct from obligations) could flow to third States. In the PCIJ's 1926 judgment in *Certain*

---

[17] See Roxburgh (n 8) 41; M Waultrin, 'La Neutralité des Isle d'Aland' (1907) 14 Revue Générale de Droit International Public 517, 529; O Hoijer, *Les Traités Internationaux* (Éditions internationales, Paris 1928) vol 2, 271.

[18] Committee of Jurists, Åland Islands Affair, League of Nations Official Journal, Special Supplement No 3 (October 1920) 18.

[19] See F de Visscher, 'La Question des Iles d'Aland' (1921) 2 Revue de Droit Internationale et de Législation Comparée 262.

[20] GG Fitzmaurice, 'Fifth Report on the Law of Treaties' [1960] YBILC, vol II, 98–9, 106–7; P Cahier, 'Le Problème des Effets des Traités a L'Égard des États Tiers' (1974) 143 RcD 589, 665–8; S Subedi, 'The Doctrine of Objective Regimes in International Law and the Competence of the United Nations to Impose Territorial Settlement on States' (1994) 37 German Ybk Intl L 162, 175, 185–6, 187–8 (discussing PCIJ's 1923 decision in the *Wimbledon* case as implicating an objective regime).

[21] *Case relating to the Territorial Jurisdiction of the International Commission of the River Oder (UK v Poland)* [1929] PCIJ Rep Series A No 23, 20, 22. See also Fitzmaurice (n 20) 85; Waldock (n 11) 18. For related arbitral practice, see *Isle of Palmas Case (Netherlands v US)* (1932) 2 RIAA 831, 842, 850, 870 (Huber, arb); Cahier (n 20) 612; Waldock (n 11) 18.

[22] *Treatment of Polish Nationals in Danzig* [1932] PCIJ Rep Series A/B No 44, 30 (Free City of Danzig had impliedly accepted the constitutive agreement made on its behalf).

German Interests in Polish Upper Silesia, Poland claimed rights under the 1918 Armistice Convention and the Protocol of Spa, even though it was not a party to either of these instruments, or even an intended beneficiary (Poland had not even been revived as a State at the time of these treaties).[23] The Court concluded that '[a] treaty only creates law as between states which are parties to it; in case of doubt no rights can be deduced from it in favor of third states'.[24] The Court's language seems to imply a presumption against the application of treaty benefits in favour of third States; it does not categorically reject the position.[25] Only Judge Finlay would have supported Poland's assertion, and he reached this position through a brief analysis of the intent of the parties to the Armistice and Spa Protocol to extend benefits to Poland as a '*jus quaesitum*, a right acquired for the new State as soon as it should come into existence'.[26] The majority holding itself seems consistent with international arbitral practice from the inter-War period, which tended to preclude third States from invoking the provisions of treaties against another party in a litigation.[27]

The most significant decision on the subject of third State application of treaty rights, at least in the period prior to the VCLT's codification, was undoubtedly the PCIJ's series of rulings in the *Free Zones of Upper Savoy and the District of Gex* case between France and Switzerland.[28] At issue in this dispute was whether Switzerland could continue to enjoy the benefits of a set of free customs zones, established in French territory on the Swiss frontier, by virtue of multilateral agreements entered into by France in 1814 and 1815 (at the end of the Napoleonic Wars) to which the Swiss Confederation was not a party.[29] But Article 435 of the Treaty of Versailles of 1919, to which (again) Switzerland was not a party, declared 'that the stipulations of the Treaties of 1815 and of the other supplementary Acts concerning the free zones of Upper Savoy and the Gex district are no longer

---

[23] See Waldock (n 11) 18–19.

[24] *German Interests in Polish Upper Silesia* (n 15) 29.

[25] See also *Case Concerning the Factory at Chorzów (Germany v Poland)* (Merits) [1928] PCIJ Rep Series A No 17, 45; *Case of Customs Regime Between Germany and Austria* [1931] PCIJ Rep Series A/B No 41, 15 (for language to the same effect).

[26] *German Interests in Polish Upper Silesia* (n 15) 84 (observations of Lord Finlay).

[27] See *Pablo Nájera Claim (France v Mexico)* (1928) 5 RIAA 466 (Verzijl, arb); Cahier (n 20) 612–13; M Hudson, 'Legal Effect of Unregistered Treaties in Practice, Under Article 18 of the Covenant' (1934) 28 AJIL 546, 548. See also *Affair des forêts du Rhodope central (Greece v Bulgaria)* (1931) 3 RIAA 1405, 1417; Waldock (n 11) 19. But see *Steiner and Gross v Polish State* (1927–28) 4 Annual Digest of Public Intl L Cases No 287 (allowing for a claim to be brought by a national of a non-party to the claims settlement instrument) ('Upper Silesian Arbitral Tribunal'); Cahier (n 20) 624–5.

[28] *Free Zones 1929* (n 15); *Case of the Free Zones of Upper Savoy and the District of Gex (Switzerland v France)* (Second Phase) [1930] PCIJ Rep Series A No 24; *Case of the Free Zones of Upper Savoy and the District of Gex (Switzerland v France)* [1932] PCIJ Rep Series A/B No 46 ('*Free Zones 1932*').

[29] A complicating feature of the case was that no less than three zones were at issue, each established by a different set of instruments, and ostensibly Switzerland may have been a party to one or more of these—rendering irrelevant the *pacta tertii* issue. Waldock (n 11) 23 [13]. See also A McNair, *The Law of Treaties* (Clarendon Press, Oxford 1961) 312 (suggesting that the PCIJ's discussion in the *Free Zones* case is *obiter dicta*); Waldock (n 11) 23 [13] (same). It seems evident, though, that Switzerland was definitely not a party to the instrument which created the free zone at Gex. See Cahier (n 20) 625–30.

consistent with present conditions'.[30] Naturally, Switzerland objected to the termination of these long-standing treaty benefits, without its consent.[31]

In its 1929 order in the case, the Permanent Court held that it had been the intent of the Great Powers in 1815 'to create in favour of Switzerland a right, on which she could rely... to the free zone of Gex'.[32] Curiously, though, the Court went on to note that '[i]t need not decide as to the extent to which international law takes cognizance of the principle of stipulations in favour of third Parties [*stipulations pour autrui*]'.[33] In truth, it seems, the Court was (with eight judges concurring) making a qualified endorsement of third State benefits by treaty, at least in view of the dissenting judges to the order. Judge ad hoc Dreyfus (appointed by France) objected to 'the theory of the stipulation "*in favorem tertii*"' and 'giving it such an unlimited field of application'.[34] Judge Negulesco observed that 'even if it be held that several States may, under a Treaty, create rights in favour of a third State... it is difficult to say that this Treaty cannot be abrogated without such third State consent'.[35] Judge Nyholm noted that the stipulation *in favorem tertii* was merely a 'civil obligation', and 'not admissible in inter-states relations' because of its 'unilateral character' which is in tension with 'relations between States which must be placed on a footing defined by reciprocal rights'.[36] Application of the rule, Judge Nyholm observed, 'could not fail to give rise to difficult problems'.[37]

In its 1932 judgment, the PCIJ was obliged to revisit this matter and issue a more definitive opinion. And, again, a majority of the members of the Court agreed that stipulations in favour of third parties were permissible under international law. The Court addressed the subject in these terms:

It cannot be lightly presumed that stipulations favourable to a third State have been adopted with the object of creating an actual right in its favour. There is however nothing to prevent the will of sovereign States from having this object and this effect. The question of the existence of a right acquired under an instrument drawn between other States is therefore one to be decided in each particular case: it must be ascertained whether the States which have stipulated in favour of a third State meant to create for that State an actual right which the latter has accepted as such.[38]

Some elements of the Court's analysis here seem unassailable. Among these is the notion that it certainly lies within the prerogative of parties to a treaty to create rights and benefits for third States. Additionally, it seems reasonable to assume that this will not be the normal or typical approach made by treaty parties, and that, therefore, this will not be their presumed intent. But where treaty parties have

---

[30] *Free Zones 1929* (n 15) 9.
[31] See Cahier (n 20) 625–30; Harvard Research (n 9) 930–1.
[32] *Free Zones 1929* (n 15) 20.
[33] Ibid. See also W Beckett, 'Decisions of the Permanent Court of International Justice on Points of Law and Procedure of General Application' (1930) 11 BYBIL 1, 12–15.
[34] *Free Zones 1929* (n 15) 43 (Dreyfus J, individual opinion).
[35] Ibid 38 (Negulesco J, individual opinion).
[36] Ibid 26 (Nyholm J, individual opinion).
[37] Ibid.
[38] *Free Zones 1932* (n 28) 147–8.

manifested such a volition to create 'an actual right' in favour of a non-party, it will be respected. Lastly, the Court seems clear that the potential beneficiary of the third party right must affirmatively accept it.

The decisive question left open by the Court's 1932 opinion is whether a benefit, once granted to a non-party by treaty, could be later abrogated without the consent of the third party beneficiary. The dissenters to the 1932 judgment clearly believed that was the Court's thrust.[39] And the Court's use of the phrase 'actual right' certainly implies a benefit that cannot be later unilaterally withdrawn without the beneficiary State's agreement.[40] Later commentary—especially the authoritative Harvard Research on the Law of Treaties issued in 1935—sharply questioned whether this was in the orbit of the Court's expectations and whether there was any authority in State practice for the concept of such irrevocable *stipulations pour autrui*.[41]

An ancillary question arising from the PCIJ's *Free Zones* opinions is whether a beneficiary State must expressly accept the benefit. Some contemporaneous commentaries opined that, inasmuch as a treaty benefit may be conferred with conditions, there must be some sort of confirmation that the receiving State acknowledges those limitations.[42] The 1928 Havana Convention on Treaties provided that '[t]he acceptance or non-acceptance of provisions in a treaty, for the benefit of a third State, which was not a contracting party, depends exclusively on the latter's decision'.[43] The *travaux* for the Havana Convention would have gone further and required that the beneficiary State 'express[ly] accept[]' the stipulation.[44]

Thus matters stood, at least until the period in the immediate aftermath of the Second World War. In one well-known incident, the United States was the intended beneficiary of a clause contained in the Peace Treaty with Finland.[45] Because the United States never declared war on Finland, it was not a party to that instrument. After the war, Finnish shipowners brought claims against the United States for requisitioned vessels. The US Comptroller General's office ruled that the 1947 peace treaty conclusively waived the right of Finnish nationals to make their claim and that the US could assert the treaty provision as a vested right. The US State Department, relying on the 1932 *Free Zones* opinion and the 1928 Havana Convention, held that because the United States had not expressly accepted the

---

[39] Ibid 185 (Hurst and Altamira JJ, dissenting) ('mak[ing] every reservation...to a theory' supporting irrevocable *stipulations pour autrui*, as 'such a theory would be fraught with so great peril for the future of conventions of this kind now in force, that it would be most dangerous to rely on it in support of any conclusion whatever').

[40] See ibid 143. See also de Aréchaga (n 9) 342–3.

[41] Harvard Research (n 9) 935–6; Waldock (n 11) 21 [7].

[42] Harvard Research (n 9) 936.

[43] 'Havana Convention on Treaties, 20 February 1928, art 9' (1935) 29 AJIL Supp 1205, 1206.

[44] Intl Commission of American Jurists, Rio de Janeiro, 1929 (1935) 29 AJIL Supp 1222, 1223, Art 9.

[45] (10 February 1947) (1948) 42 AJIL Supp 203, 205, Art 9.

stipulation on its behalf, it had no force and effect.[46] Congress acquiesced in this position and appropriated funds for the payment of the Finnish shipowners' claims.

Two other decisions rendered by the International Court of Justice (ICJ), in the years just after the Second World War, are worth mentioning as having some bearing on treaty application to third parties. In the 1949 *Reparations for Injuries Sustained in the Service of the United Nations* advisory opinion,[47] the Court was obliged to rule on whether the UN had the capacity to bring an international claim, on behalf of the organization, in circumstances arising from the assassination of one of its envoys and the failure of local authorities to protect him.[48] A complicating issue in the case was that the claim was to be addressed to Israel, which, at the time of the incident, was not even recognized as a State much less a member of the United Nations (and thus not a party to the UN Charter).

The Court held that the UN Charter—or at least an obligation to respect the organization's capacity to bring a claim—was binding on Israel even though it was a non-party at the time the dispute arose. The ICJ held that:

> fifty States, representing the vast majority of the members of the international community, had the power, in conformity with international law, to bring into being an entity possessing objective international legal personality, and not merely personality recognized by them alone, together with the capacity to bring international claims.[49]

The Court's use of the phrase, 'objective', was nowhere explained but was certainly resonant with the Committee of Jurists' invocation in the Åland Islands dispute of a treaty creating 'objective law'.[50] Judge Krylov, in his dissent to the *Reparations* opinion, observed that '[i]t is true that the non-member States cannot fail to recognize the existence of the United Nations as an objective fact. But, in order that they may be bound by a legal obligation to the Organization, it is necessary that the latter should conclude a special agreement with these States'.[51] The *Reparations for Injuries* opinion thus extended the basis of a theory of 'objective regimes' as a notional exception to the *res inter alios acta* principle.

More ambiguous in this regard was the ICJ's discussion the following year, in the *International Status of South-West Africa* opinion.[52] A majority of the Court held in that opinion that obligations under the League of Nations' mandate over Southwest Africa (Namibia) survived the death of the organization.[53] Inasmuch as South Africa had concurred with the mandate, issues of third party obligations under

---

[46] See M Whiteman (ed), *Digest of International Law* (Government Printing Office, Washington 1970) vol 14, 337–47. See also de Aréchaga (n 9) 338–9, 354–5; Cahier (n 20) 622–3; Waldock (n 11) 24–5 [19].
[47] [1949] ICJ Rep 179.
[48] See UNGA Res 195 (III) (3 December 1948); [1948] ICJ Rep 121. For background on this dispute, see D Bederman, 'The *Reparations for Injuries* Case: The Law of Nations is Transformed into International Law' in J Noyes, L Dickinson, and M Janis (eds), *International Law Stories* (Foundation Press, New York 2007) 307, 308–17.
[49] *Reparations for Injuries* (n 47) 185.
[50] Committee of Jurists, Åland Islands Affair (n 18) 18.
[51] *Reparations for Injuries* (n 47) 218–19 (Krylov J, dissenting).
[52] *International Status of South-West Africa* (Advisory Opinion) [1950] ICJ Rep 128.
[53] Ibid 132.

treaties did not arise. But Lord McNair, in his separate opinion to the *South-West Africa* opinion, would have premised his decision on the 'objective character' of the mandates system and the analogy to objective regimes as derived from the Åland Islands affair. 'From time to time', McNair wrote:

it happens that a group of great Powers, or a large number of States both great and small, assume a power to create by a multipartite treaty some new international régime or status, which soon acquires a degree of acceptance and durability extending beyond the limits of the actual contracting parties, and giving it an objective existence. This power is used when some public interest is involved, and its exercise often occurs in the course of the peace settlement at the end of a great war.[54]

It appears, however, that no other member of the Court accepted McNair's articulation of objective regimes as a principled basis for imposing obligations as against non-parties to a treaty, especially inasmuch as McNair implied that the 'great Powers' had a unique role to play in imposing settlements on recalcitrant States.[55]

If, prior to the VCLT, judges were muddled about the scope of possible exceptions to the *res inter alios acta* principle in treaty law, publicists were no more consistent.[56] Broad scholarly consensus existed as to the non-applicability of treaty obligations on third States—with the controversial exception of the objective regimes theory. As for the viability of *stipulations pour autrui*, and the modalities of conferring treaty benefits on non-parties, there was little agreement, even in the wake of the *Free Zones* case. The Harvard Research on the Law of Treaties, issued in 1935, had a provision allowing *stipulations pour autrui*, but with the qualification that a beneficiary State could only claim the right for 'so long as the stipulation remains in force between the parties to the treaty'.[57] In other words, stipulations in favour of third States remained revocable by the treaty parties. With all of these cross-currents of views (as expressed in State practice, arbitral and judicial opinions, as well as publicists' writings), the topic was ripe for codification, or, at a minimum, consolidation.

II. The 1969 Vienna Convention on the Law of Treaties

The VCLT's treatment of third party rights and obligations under treaties was handled in five relatively laconic provisions, Articles 34 through 38. The default

---

[54] Ibid 153 (McNair J, separate opinion).

[55] But see *Case relating to the Jurisdiction of the European Commission of the Danube between Galatz and Braila* [1927] PCIJ Rep Series B No 14, 95 (Negulesco J, dissenting) ('decisions of the Great Powers, met together as the Concert of Europe... have never been held to be legally binding upon States not represented in the Concert'). See also F Pollock, 'The Sources of International Law' (1902) LQR 418, 418–29; R Rayfuse, 'The United Nations Agreement on Straddling and Highly Migratory Fish Stocks as an Objective Regime: A Case of Wishful Thinking' (1999) 20 Australian Ybk Intl L 253, 263; Roxburgh (n 8) 99–101.

[56] For collections of publicists' views, see Cahier (n 20) 609–11; Roxburgh (n 8) 20–1; G Scelle, *Précis de droit des gens* (Sirey, Paris 1934) vol 2, 345–6, 367–8.

[57] Harvard Research (n 9) 924 (Art 18(b)).

rule of *res inter alios acta* was established at the outset. Article 34 provides simply that '[a] treaty does not create either obligations or rights for a third State without its consent'.[58] As special rapporteur Gerald Fitzmaurice observed, this principle is 'so fundamental, self-evident and well-known, that [it] does not require the citation of much authority in [its] support'.[59] From early on in the development of the text that would become the VCLT, successive special rapporteurs concluded that the key issue for resolution was whether, and to what extent, the law of treaties would admit of exceptions to the *res inter alios acta* rule.[60] As Christine Chinkin has trenchantly written, the VCLT 'takes a reductivist and formalist approach to treaty law', and particularly to matters of third party application.[61] In so far as the VCLT recognizes exceptions to *res inter alios acta*, they are narrowly circumscribed.

So, for example, Article 35 provides that '[a]n obligation arises for a third State from a provision of a treaty if the parties to the treaty intend the provision to be the means of establishing the obligation and the third State expressly accepts that obligation in writing'.[62] In contrast with pre-VCLT State practice and judicial pronouncements, the requirement that the third State accept an obligation 'expressly... in writing' is assuredly a progressive development. This provision also confirms that such an acceptance takes the form of a recognized international agreement, itself enforceable under the VCLT, or (at a minimum) as a unilateral declaration enforceable on estoppel principles. Article 37(1) makes clear that '[w]hen an obligation has arisen for a third State in conformity with Article 35, the obligation may be revoked or modified only with the consent of the parties to the treaty and of the third State, unless it is established that they had otherwise agreed'.[63] In other words, once a third party has agreed to be bound to an obligation, it requires the concurrence of all States concerned to relieve it of that duty.

The VCLT does not appear to embrace any treaty-based exception to the rule prohibiting assertions of obligations as against non-parties, with the exception of Article 75's provision on aggressor States.[64] As discussed below, the VCLT and its

---

[58] VCLT Art 34. For the *travaux préparatoires* for these VCLT provisions, see S Rosenne, *The Law of Treaties: A Guide to the Legislative History of the Vienna Convention* (Sijthoff, Leiden 1970) 224–37; M Villiger, *Commentary on the 1969 Vienna Convention on the Law of Treaties* (Martinus Nijhoff, Leiden 2009) 465–504.

[59] Fitzmaurice (n 20) 84 [10].

[60] Ibid 73 [3], 86 [19]. See also Arrow (n 8) 208; C Chinkin, *Third Parties in International Law* (Clarendon Press, Oxford 1993) 29–30.

[61] Chinkin (n 60) 35.

[62] VCLT Art 35.

[63] VCLT Art 35(1). Some authorities (see Villiger (n 58) 495) have suggested that this provision does not preclude situations where a treaty right afforded a third party is suspended. I am sceptical of this construction. For the purposes of VCLT Art 35, a suspension would be tantamount to a modification.

[64] See eg VCLT Art 75 ('The provisions of the present Convention are without prejudice to any obligation in relation to a treaty which may arise for an aggressor State in consequence of measures taken in conformity with the Charter of the United Nations with reference to that State's aggression'). For more on this 'aggressor State' exception to the rule of not applying obligations as to non-parties, see Cahier (n 20) 649–52; T Elias, *The Modern Law of Treaties* (Sijthoff, Leiden 1974) 68; Sinclair (n 4) 101–2.

travaux studiously avoids any endorsement of an objective regimes theory as an exception. The VCLT does, however, recognize the international law dynamic by which a State, not a party to a treaty, can become bound by an obligation contained in a parallel rule of customary international law. Article 38 provides that '[n]othing in Articles 34 to 37 precludes a rule set forth in a treaty from becoming binding upon a third State as a customary rule of international law, recognized as such'.[65] This provision builds on a doctrine of an esteemed pedigree; publicists[66] and courts[67] have observed for some time that customary international law obligations can reach States that have not expressly adopted a rule by treaty. Inasmuch as customary norms must be consented to (or, at a minimum, not objected to), this may not constitute a real exception to the *res inter alios acta* principle. Nevertheless, no less than two ILC special rapporteurs felt the necessity of including a provision on parallel obligations arising from customary international law as part of the cluster of articles on third State rights and duties.[68] But at the Vienna Diplomatic Conference, convened to consider the ILC's draft text, substantial controversy arose about this provision and it was modified to include the qualifying notion that the customary rule had to be 'recognized as such'.[69]

The VCLT's approach to the interplay between treaty and customary obligations was essentially confirmed in the ICJ's 1969 judgment in the *North Sea Continental Shelf* cases.[70] Inasmuch as it was relevant to third party application of treaty obligations, the essential question before the ICJ was whether Germany was bound to a customary rule of delimitation by equidistance of its continental shelf, even though it had especially disclaimed any treaty-based obligation by its refusal to sign or ratify the 1958 Geneva Convention on the Continental Shelf. In rejecting Denmark's and the Netherlands' contentions that Germany was bound by the parallel corpus of customary international law, the Court made this observation which certainly resonated with the ILC's work on this subject:

[The Netherlands' and Denmark's] contention is based on the view that Article 6 of the [Geneva] Convention . . . [is] a norm-creating provision which has constituted the foundation of, or has generated a rule which, while only conventional or contractual in origin, has since passed into the general corpus of international law, and is now accepted as such by the

---

[65] VCLT Art 38.

[66] See R Baxter, 'Multilateral Treaties as Evidence of Customary International Law' (1965) 41 BYBIL 275; M Lachs, 'Le Développement et les Fonctions des Traités Multilatéraux' (1957) 92 RcD 229, 317–19; Roxburgh (n 8) 72–95; Sinclair (n 4) 100.

[67] See *Chrichton v Samos Navigation Co*, 2 Annual Digest of Public Intl L No 1 (Mixed Court of Egypt (Port Said) 1927) (rules of 1910 Salvage Convention would be held applicable, even though Egypt was not a party).

[68] Fitzmaurice (n 20) 80, 94–6 [58]–[62]; Waldock (n 11) 27, 34.

[69] See C Rozakis, 'Treaties and Third States in the Reinforcement of the Consensual Standards in International Law' (1975) 35 Zeitschrift für ausländisches öffentliches Recht und Völkerrecht 1, 25–38. This qualification may have been necessary out of a larger concern that the entirety of the VCLT project (and not just the articles on third parties) could have been viewed as exclusively codifying customary international law, perhaps then complicating the position of States (like the United States) that never acceded to the VCLT.

[70] *North Sea Continental Shelf Cases (Federal Republic of Germany v Denmark and Netherlands)* (Judgment) [1969] ICJ Rep 3.

opinio juris, so as to have become binding even for countries which have never, and do not, become parties to the Convention. There is no doubt that this process is a perfectly possible one and does from time to time occur: it constitutes one of the recognized methods by which new rules of customary international law may be formed. At the same time this result is not lightly to have been regarded as having been attained.[71]

As the PCIJ accomplished in the *German Interests in Polish Upper Silesia* and *Free Zones* decisions,[72] the *North Sea Continental Shelf* Court established a presumption *against* the assertion of a treaty-based right or obligation in favour of a third State, even as it recognized the notional possibility that such could occur.

That leaves for consideration the VCLT's provisions concerning treaty benefits running to non-parties. Article 36 provides:

1. A right arises for a third State from a provision of a treaty if the parties to the treaty intend the provision to accord that right either to the third State, or to a group of States to which it belongs, or to all States, and the third State assents thereto. Its assent shall be presumed so long as the contrary is not indicated, unless the treaty otherwise provides.
2. A State exercising a right in accordance with paragraph 1 shall comply with the conditions for its exercise provided for in the treaty or established in conformity with the treaty.

Article 37(2), concerning the revocation or modification of treaty rights granted to third States, provides that '[w]hen a right has arisen for a third State in conformity with Article 36, the right may not be revoked or modified by the parties if it is established that the right was intended not to be revocable or subject to modification without the consent of the third State'.[73] In other words, the States that are granting the right to a third party can determine whether that grant can be revocable.[74]

Article 36 of the VCLT contemplates a potentially broad set of polities that might be the beneficiary of a treaty right: a 'third State, or...a group of States to which it [the third State] belongs, or...all States'.[75] This gives maximum discretion to treaty parties to craft provisions which may be of benefit to the larger international community. The VCLT text did not, however, definitively resolve the earlier controversy as to the precise way that beneficiary States were to accept rights granted under a treaty as a third party. Article 36(1) simply provides that the third State should 'assent[] thereto', and 'assent shall be presumed so long as the contrary is not indicated, unless the treaty otherwise provides'. In other words, the burden is on the beneficiary State to affirmatively disclaim or renounce a treaty benefit, unless the treaty requires a formal and written acceptance.[76]

---

[71] Ibid 41 [71].
[72] See *German Interests in Polish Upper Silesia* (n 15) 29; *Free Zones 1932* (n 28) 148.
[73] VCLT Art 37(2).
[74] See Cahier (n 20) 620–40; R Jennings and A Watts, *Oppenheim's International Law* (9th edn Longman, London 1996) vol 1, 1263; Fitzmaurice (n 20) 102–4 [82]–[90]; Waldock (n 11) 19–26. As discussed later, a treaty beneficiary might also include an international organization or a group of international institutions.
[75] VCLT Art 36(1).
[76] See Chinkin (n 60) 32; Jennings and Watts (n 74) vol 1, 1262–3; Rozakis (n 69) 18–20.

Broadly confirmatory of the VCLT's *pacta tertii* provisions' status as settled law is that they were rendered virtually verbatim in the 1986 Vienna Convention on the Law of Treaties between States and International Organizations or between International Organizations (1986 VCLT).[77] Aside from certain changes rendered necessary by the very character of international institutions,[78] there is no evidence in the *travaux* for the 1986 VCLT of any perceived need to alter the essential premises of the 1969 Convention's provisions on third States.[79] Indeed, it has been suggested[80] that treaties which create referral mechanisms or working relationships between two or more international organizations are an example of the *pacta tertii* principle at work. But one might legitimately wonder whether such mechanisms or relationships are really a 'right', within the meaning of Article 36 of the 1986 VCLT.

In reviewing the entirety of the VCLT's provisions on third States, it is by no means clear the extent to which this project was meant to be a codification of earlier State practice or decisional law. Inasmuch as canonical incidents like the Åland Islands affair and *Free Zones* case were hardly conclusive in their outcomes, it might be too much to expect that the drafters of the 1969 VCLT would slavishly pursue their implications. Rather, the VCLT's approach is formalistic in two respects. The first is in the sharply drawn distinction between the handling of treaty rights and treaty obligations. The entire structure and application of Articles 34 through 38 depends on that differentiation. The means by which an obligation is accepted by a third party are very different than for a treaty right.[81] But is it up to the third State or a contracting State to characterize a provision as a duty? As has been observed,[82] many treaties contain provisions that can be construed as both imposing obligations *and* granting benefits. How, then, to deal with such 'mixed' instruments?

The second formalism of the VCLT's articles on third States is its extolling of the intent of the contracting parties as controlling such issues as (1) how the third State

---

[77] 1986 VCLT Arts 34–8.

[78] See eg ibid Art 35 (adding qualification that 'Acceptance by the third organization of such an obligation shall be governed by the rules of that organization'); ibid Art 37(3) (to same effect).

[79] The only major initiative made in that section of the 1986 VCLT dealing with third States and organizations was one concerning the situation where a supranational organization had the capacity to become a party to the treaty, and did so, even while its member States were not a party. Arguably, this proposal—as reflected in Art 36bis of the 1986 VCLT draft—was intended to deal only with what was then the European Economic Community, and today the EU and Art 216(2) of the Treaty on its Functioning, allow such a result. The ILC special rapporteurs believed that the *pacta tertii* rules of the VCLT did not satisfactorily cover this situation. In any event, the 1986 Vienna Conference ultimately decided that the treaty would not cover this subject, leaving it as a matter not to be 'prejudge[d]'. 1986 VCLT Art 74(2)–(3). See generally C Brölmann, 'The 1986 Vienna Convention on the Law of Treaties: The History of Draft Article 36bis' in J Klabbers and R LeFeber (eds), *Essays on the Law of Treaties* (Kluwer, The Hague 1998) 121–40.

[80] See M Fitzmaurice and O Elias, *Contemporary Issues in the Law of Treaties* (Eleven Intl L Pub, Utrecht 2005) 270–88 (arguing *pacta tertii* is at work in Rome Statute Art 13(b), allowing for the UN Security Council, acting under Chapter VII of the Charter, to refer situations to the ICC Prosecutor).

[81] Cf VCLT Art 35 ('expressly accepts th[e] obligation in writing'), with ibid Art 36(1) ('assent shall be presumed').

[82] See Chinkin (n 60) 40–1.

'expressly accepts'[83] an obligation or 'assents'[84] to a benefit, and (2) whether a right or obligation flowing to a third State will be revocable or subject to modification (under Article 37). Preserving party autonomy and the freedom of States to contract through treaties is a laudable goal, but in some situations it may simply be impossible to divine the intent of the parties concerned. That includes the States parties to the main treaty, as well as the third State that is weighing the acceptance of a benefit or obligation and under what conditions. These formalisms certainly affect the way in which the VCLT's *pacta tertii* provisions were meant to operate.

III. Objective Regimes: The New Flash-Point for *Pacta Tertii*

Nor has State practice in the years following the VCLT's adoption clarified these open issues. Indeed, it is hard to discern any international precedent in the past forty years that has turned on the proper interpretation or application of the VCLT's provisions on third States. We may have well reached a position of doctrinal equipoise on matters related to the granting of benefits to third States—when and how States grant such benefits is simply no longer in dispute. Inasmuch as such issues are left to the treaty parties (and to presumed beneficiary State(s)), the VCLT simply establishes a set of presumptions and default rules which should guide treaty drafters. The key message of the VCLT's third State regime is straightforward enough: treaties must be clear in their intent to grant benefits to non-parties (especially in determining whether such benefits are to be irrevocable), and third States need to take care in their practice of assenting to the stipulation of such rights.

Ironically enough, in recent years the scholarly debate concerning the *res inter alios acta* principle's application to international affairs has returned to where it began: the extent to which obligations can be imposed on recalcitrant States. This has revived the debate, begun in the early years of the twentieth century, over the use of *pacta tertii* rules by Great Powers to their advantage.[85] Under this view,[86] powerful States can, through the selective employment of third State rules, impose political settlements on outside parties. Today, this notion has been subsumed into the principle of objective regimes. And, with a doctrinal pedigree as distinguished as the *Åland Islands* report and the *Reparations for Injuries* opinion,[87] the doctrine has had remarkable staying power despite the fact that it was excluded by the drafters of

---

[83] VCLT Art 35.
[84] Ibid Art 36(1).
[85] See nn 54–5 and accompanying text.
[86] See Chinkin (n 60) 143.
[87] See Lachs (n 66) 316. For early criticism of objective regimes, see Harvard Research (n 9) 922–3; C Rousseau, *Principes généreaux du droit international public* (Pedone, Paris 1944) vol 2, 478; Roxburgh (n 8) 81–2; Q Wright, 'Conflicts between International Law and Treaties' (1917) 11 AJIL 566, 573. For other views, see Waldock (n 11) 32; Cahier (n 20) 660–3; Subedi (n 20) 189–92 (collecting publicists' opinions).

the VCLT as a recognized exception to *res inter alios acta*.[88] Indeed, the reason that objective regimes were not incorporated into the VCLT draft was the perception, based on the work of the ILC's special rapporteurs,[89] that it would be impossible to codify the exception in terms of a 'true' objective regime without leaving it as an immensely broad and sweeping exception to the default rule of not imposing obligations on non-parties. In short, embracing the principle of objective regimes would be tantamount to allowing de facto legislation by select groups of States.

An insuperable problem with objective regimes is determining which kinds of treaties would be eligible and what sorts of obligations would be deemed so significant as to be candidates for application to non-parties.[90] It is not enough to assert, as some publicists have,[91] that any properly qualified *erga omnes* obligation is, by definition, an objective regime. Indeed, this may be quite wrong. The elements, factors, and considerations that make an obligation *erga omnes* (giving standing to any State to make a claim for its violation) cannot be the same as to make it an objective regime for imposition as against third parties. Put another way, the requisites for making a norm binding on non-parties must surely be higher than those for simply granting standing to a polity to raise a claim for that norm's violation. Just as the set of *jus cogens* norms overlaps with (but is a smaller subset of) *erga omnes* obligations, the list of objective regimes may be even shorter.

As originally conceived,[92] objective regimes were regarded as being territorial in scope, creating servitudes, such as the demilitarization of a locale (as with the Åland Islands) or free passage through a strait or canal (as with the Bosporus or Kiel Canal regimes). Additionally, candidates for objective regimes would have included prominent 'international settlements' coming at the end of conflicts or disposing of disputed territories or populations.[93] With the ICJ's 1949 opinion in *Reparations for Injuries*, the ambit of objective regimes was augmented to include the organic or constituent instruments of vitally significant, global international institutions. But the notion of objective regimes has never been extended to cover all multilateral 'law-making' treaties of a general character.[94] To do so would, essentially, subvert the entire *res inter alios acta* principle and allow for 'legislation' by the international community through means other than treaty-making and acceptance. So, there must be some unique ingredient that defines an obligation under an objective regime, apart from the large number of States that have ratified it, the possibility

---

[88] M Ragazzi, *The Concept of International Obligations* Erga Omnes (OUP, Oxford 1997) 41. It might be argued that VCLT Art 36 is at least suggestive of *erga omnes* obligations. VCLT Art 36(1) ('A right arises for a third State from a provision of a treaty if the parties to the treaty intend the provision to accord that right to . . . *all States*' (emphasis added)).

[89] Fitzmaurice (n 20) 80 (Art 18), 97–100; Waldock (n 11) 26–8.

[90] See Rozakis (n 69) 7–8 n19.

[91] See B Simma, 'The Antarctic Treaty as a Treaty Providing for an "Objective Regime"' (1986) 19 Cornell Intl L J 189, 198–200 (discussing E Klein, *Statusverträge im Völkerrecht: Rechtsfragen territorialer Sonderregime* (Springer, Berlin 1980)); A Aust, *Modern Treaty Law and Practice* (2nd edn, CUP, Cambridge 2007) 258.

[92] See Sinclair (n 4) 104.

[93] Cahier (n 20) 671–6 (discussing application of settlements for Cyprus and Danzig); Roxburgh (n 8) 56–61.

[94] Waldock (n 11) 33; Subedi (n 20) 171.

that the UN Security Council adopted it in exercise of its Chapter VII powers,[95] or the fact that few States have (within a specified period of time) objected to the creation of the objective regime.[96] There is, however, no consensus as to what, precisely, makes an objective regime, even though there is some agreement about the few that qualify, irrespective of the standard.

What are the leading candidates for objective regimes? The UN Charter, for reasons expressed in the *Reparations for Injuries* opinion,[97] is certainly one. There is undoubtedly a high degree of scholarly consensus as to the UN's status in this regard,[98] as there was for the earlier League of Nations.[99] Of course, the *Reparations for Injuries* opinion concerned only one aspect of the Charter's *pacta tertii*: the obligation of non-members to respect the organization's legal personality. But the Charter also expressly incorporated provisions directly applicable to non-parties, including Article 2, paragraph 6: 'The Organization shall ensure that states which are not Members of the United Nations act in accordance with these Principles so far as may be necessary for the maintenance of international peace and security'.[100] UN actions have, in the organization's practice,[101] certainly been applied to third States, as has been recognized in the ICJ's *Namibia* opinion[102] and in various sanctions programmes.[103]

Of course, the original conception for objective regimes were those that neutralized or demilitarized territories or placed them under some form of international servitude.[104] While neutralization treaties are rare today, some such regimes still subsist (as, for example, the Panama Canal,[105] Cambodia,[106] and the Iraqi frontier

---

[95] Subedi (n 20) 197–200.

[96] Waldock (n 11) 26–33 (proposing a five-year period for opposing States to object).

[97] See nn 47–51 and accompanying text.

[98] But see H Kelsen, *The Law of the United Nations* (Stevens, London 1950) 791–805; J Verzijl, *International Law in Historical Perspective* (Sijthoff, Leiden 1973) vol 6, 279, for arguments that the Charter's application to non-parties was *ultra vires*.

[99] Cahier (n 20) 707–9; Harvard Research (n 9) 921 (discussing Covenant Art 17).

[100] UN Charter Art 2(6). Under the Charter, non-UN members can be invited to appear before the Security Council, ibid Art 32, and can bring matters to the attention of the organization for peaceful settlement. Ibid Art 35(2). Non-members are even eligible to apply for assistance from the organization if UN measures or sanctions pose 'special economic problems'. Ibid Art 50. See de Aréchaga (n 9) 356; Cahier (n 20) 709–12; Fitzmaurice (n 20) 88.

[101] See Cahier (n 20) 712–16.

[102] *Legal Consequences for States of the Continued Presence of South Africa in Namibia (South-West Africa) notwithstanding Security Council Resolution 276* (Advisory Opinion) [1971] ICJ Rep 16, 44 [126].

[103] See Jennings and Watts (n 74) 1265 and n7 (collecting Security Council resolutions imposing obligations on non-UN members).

[104] See Arrow (n 8) 213–14 (re neutrality of Switzerland, Belgium and Austria); Cahier (n 20) 663–9, 681–95; Roxburgh (n 8) 61–5, 86–8; Subedi (n 20) 175–9 (re neutralization treaties); Waldock (n 11) 27–30 (re Kiel, Suez, and Panama Canal regimes); Fitzmaurice (n 20) 92–3 (re Po river regime), 99 (re Swiss neutrality).

[105] See Protocol Concerning the Permanent Neutrality and Operation of the Panama Canal (7 September 1977, entered into force 1 October 1979) [1977] 16 ILM 1022, Art 2.

[106] Agreement Concerning the Sovereignty, Independence, Territorial Integrity and Inviolability, Neutrality and National Unity of Cambodia (signed and entered into force 23 October 1991) [1992] 31 ILM 180, Art 4.

with Kuwait[107]). One oft-mentioned[108] possibility of an objective regime of this variety is the 1959 Antarctica Treaty.[109] That convention reserves the continent for peaceful purposes and prohibits nuclear testing and disposal of radioactive materials.[110] The treaty grants free access to the continent for all parties.[111] Article X expressly concerns the interests of non-parties: 'Each of the Contracting Parties undertakes to exert appropriate efforts, consistent with the Charter of the United Nations, to the end that no one engages in any activity in Antarctica contrary to the principles or purposes of the present Treaty.'[112] While it has been open to question whether the drafters of the Antarctic Treaty intended to fashion an objective regime thereby,[113] this was certainly the perception of ILC members who were concerned that any provision in what would become the VCLT[114] should not give licence to an abuse of objective regimes as a potential exception to the *pacta tertii* default rule.[115] Indeed, the whole controversy concerning the Antarctic Treaty System's insular character (what with its twenty-eight consultative parties largely representing the developed world) became a proxy contest for the broader issue of applying obligations in objective regimes to non-parties, particularly those activist States that might vehemently oppose a particular regime. Since the 1980s, non-consultative parties have acquiesced in the Antarctic Treaty System's management of the southern continent, and by doing so have at least notionally accepted the Antarctic Treaty's status as an objective regime.

As noted already,[116] objective regimes cannot extend so far as to cover all (or even many) treaties of a general law-making character. Despite proposals to the contrary,[117] to qualify human rights instruments and collective security mechanisms as objective regimes is unlikely to gain much traction. So, for the time being, it would be extravagant to suggest that the objective regimes principle will be employed in such a manner as to impose a substantial set of obligatory norms against States that are non-parties to treaties containing such rules. Any attempt to make a doctrinal congruence of *erga omnes* obligations with objective regimes can (and should) thus be stoutly resisted. There is confusion enough with distinguishing *erga omnes* obligations from *jus cogens* norms. To blend into the mix the

---

[107] UNSC Res 687 (3 April 1991) UN Doc S/RES/687 [5]; UNSC Res 833 (27 May 1993) UN Doc S/RES/833.

[108] See Simma (n 91) 190 (collecting views of publicists). It has also been suggested that treaties which establish rules of visitation for sunken gravesites (as with the MS ESTONIA disaster in 1994) might qualify as objective regimes. See J Klabbers, 'Les cimitières marins sont-ils établis comme des régimes objectifs' (1997) 11 Espaces et Ressources Maritimes 121–33.

[109] (1 December 1959, entered into force 23 June 1961) 402 UNTS 71.

[110] Ibid Arts I, V.

[111] Ibid Art VII.

[112] Ibid Art X.

[113] See Arrow (n 8) 223–5 (reviewing the treaty's *travaux*). See also J Crawford and D Rothwell, 'Legal Issues Confronting Australia's Antarctica' (1992) 13 Australian Ybk Intl L 53, 62–3.

[114] See Fitzmaurice (n 20) 93–4 [54]; Waldock (n 11) 30.

[115] See Chinkin (n 60) 31–2, 140.

[116] See nn 92–6 and accompanying text.

[117] See ILC, 'Report on the Work of its 35th Session' [1983] YBILC, vol II, 41.

completely distinct problem of applying treaty rules to non-parties would be doctrinally irresponsible.

Conclusion

That part of the law of treaties concerned with third party rights and obligations has now reached, through the processes of codification and progressive development, an appropriate level of elaboration and sophistication. The relevant VCLT Articles (Articles 34–38 of both the 1969 and 1986 instruments) provide an acceptable level of guidance to regime designers (who plan the broad objectives and structures of conventional systems) and treaty drafters (who translate these plans into actual treaty language). Armed with the VCLT's default rules and presumptions, States and other interested parties should—with a high degree of confidence—be able to craft treaty provisions which clearly and unambiguously determine whether obligations or rights will flow to non-parties, whether such provisions will be deemed irrevocable, and the modalities by which third States will assent to or accept such benefits or duties. Given that, since 1969, virtually no disputes have arisen on matters of third State application, these VCLT provisions can be judged a success.

If the appropriate metric is, indeed, the absence of subsequent controversy, the VCLT's articles on *pacta tertii*—like those dealing with treaties' territorial application, invalidity, fundamental changes of circumstances (*rebus sic stantibus*), and depositary and registry functions—can also be considered an appropriate exercise of the art of codification. Given that for each of these areas, including third State application (as discussed in Part I), there was a substantial confusion in doctrine and State practice prior to the VCLT, this result is all the more remarkable. But all of this has come at some cost, largely the result of compromises or 'constructive ambiguities' fashioned by the ILC and at the Vienna Diplomatic Conferences. This is especially so with questions arising from the continued invocation of objective regimes. Future gains in our understanding of objective regimes are likely to be produced, not through codification, but by situational rulings or decisions of international institutions and tribunals. So, for the time being, we must be content with what doctrinal certainty we can garner in the law of treaties.

Recommended Reading

E J de Aréchaga, 'Treaty Stipulations in Favor of Third States' (1956) 50 AJIL 338

A Aust, *Modern Treaty Law and Practice* (2nd edn CUP, Cambridge 2007)

P Cahier, 'Le Problème des Effets des Traités a L'Égard des États Tiers' (1974) 143 RcD 589

C Chinkin, *Third Parties in International Law* (Clarendon Press, Oxford 1993)

Harvard Research on International Law, 'Law of Treaties, Article 18: Treaties and Third States' (1935) 29 AJIL Supp 918

'Havana Convention on Treaties, 20 February 1928, art 9' (1935) 29 AJIL Supp 1205

M Lachs, 'Le Développement et les Fonctions des Traités Multilatéraux' (1957) 92 RcD 229

League of Nations, Committee of Jurists, *Åland Islands Affair*, League of Nations Official Journal, Special Supplement No 3 (October 1920)

R Rayfuse, 'The United Nations Agreement on Straddling and Highly Migratory Fish Stocks as an Objective Regime: A Case of Wishful Thinking' (1999) 20 Australian Ybk Intl L 253

R Roxburgh, *International Conventions and Third States* (Longmans, Green & Co, London 1917)

C Rozakis, 'Treaties and Third States in the Reinforcement of the Consensual Standards in International Law' (1975) 35 Zeitschrift für ausländisches öffentliches Recht und Völkerrecht 1

B Simma, 'The Antarctic Treaty as a Treaty Providing for an "Objective Regime"' (1986) 19 Cornell Intl L J 189

I Sinclair, *Vienna Convention on the Law of Treaties* (2nd edn MUP, Manchester 1984) 98

S Subedi, 'The Doctrine of Objective Regimes in International Law and the Competence of the United Nations to Impose Territorial Settlement on States' (1994) 37 German Ybk Intl L 162

M Villiger, *Commentary on the 1969 Vienna Convention on the Law of Treaties* (Martinus Nijhoff, Leiden 2009)

14

Treaty Amendments

Jutta Brunnée

Introduction

Modern treaties, in the majority of cases, are not one-off transactions in which parties exchange commitments or advantages. In particular, multilateral treaties are typically designed to govern relations between States on a given issue for the longer term, often indefinitely. This open-endedness is a feature not only of treaties that establish international institutions, but also those that establish regimes to govern an ever-growing range of issues, such as human rights, international trade, arms control, maritime or air transport, or environmental protection. In all such long-term arrangements, provision must be made for subsequent change. Some issues may have been too difficult to settle in the original negotiations and may become amenable to agreement only once parties have begun to interact under the treaty's auspices. Other issues may be unforeseen by the original negotiators, or may arise due to changes in other areas of international law. In yet other circumstances the underlying issue, or the parties' understanding of the issue (or of appropriate response actions), may change, sometimes rapidly so.

The formal legal device for making changes to the text of a treaty, whether to its core provisions or to annexes or appendices, is an amendment. If the changes apply only among a subset of treaty parties, they are referred to as modifications. In older treaty practice, amendments were also distinguished from revisions, which involved a general review of the entire treaty rather than changes only to particular provisions.[1] While some treaties provide for such a review process,[2] the general view today is that, notwithstanding the terminological distinction, there is no legal difference between amendment and revision processes.[3]

Amendments must be distinguished from other methods for altering or augmenting treaty terms covered elsewhere in this volume. For example, unless

---

[1] ME Villiger, *Commentary on the 1969 Vienna Convention on the Law of Treaties* (Martinus Nijhoff, The Hague 2009) 509–10.

[2] See eg Rome Statute of the International Criminal Court (adopted 17 July 1998, entered into force 1 July 2002) 2187 UNTS 90, Art 123 ('Rome Statute'). On the 2010 Review Conference of the Rome Statute, see also nn 53–8 and accompanying text.

[3] See Rome Statute (n 2) Art 123 (providing that the Statute's amendment provisions apply to any changes considered at a review conference). See also Villiger (n 1) 522.

specifically designed to effect an amendment,[4] subsequent protocols supplement rather than alter the original treaty.[5] Decisions of a treaty's plenary body, in turn, often produce technical, procedural, or even substantive standards applicable to all parties. But unless explicitly provided for in the treaty, such decisions do not constitute amendments and the resultant standards are not legally binding.[6] Finally, substantive change can also be effected through treaty interpretation, notably through subsequent agreement or practice of the parties.[7] In the case of subsequent agreements, the line between interpretation and amendment can be difficult to draw.[8] Still, at least notionally, there is a difference between an authoritative interpretation of treaty terms and changed or new terms.

In earlier treaty-making practice, unanimity tended to be required for amendments. The premium placed on treaty integrity, on the maxim of *pacta sunt servanda*, and on the protection of parties' sovereignty helps explain this default rule, which prevailed through the first half of the twentieth century.[9] Another important factor was the fact that many treaties were bilateral or, if multilateral, involved much smaller numbers of States than they tend to involve today. In the second half of the twentieth century, with the steady increase in the number of sovereign States and growing recourse to long-term multilateral treaty-making, the old customary rule became increasingly impractical and international practice shifted.[10] The new default rule that emerged was that amendments bind only those treaty parties that consent to them. This rule is reflected in the provisions of the 1969 Vienna Convention on the Law of Treaties (VCLT).[11]

The Convention built on draft articles that the International Law Commission (ILC) submitted to the UN General Assembly in 1966, having begun its work on the topic in 1949, the year it was established.[12] With some notable exceptions, the

---

[4] Parties can of course choose to amend a treaty by means of an amending protocol. For example, in 1982, the parties to the Convention on Wetlands of International Importance Especially as Waterfowl Habitat (signed 2 February 1971, entered into force 21 December 1975) 996 UNTS 245, adopted a Protocol to Amend the Convention on Wetlands of International Importance especially as Waterfowl Habitat (Paris Protocol) (signed 3 December 1982, entered into force 1 October 1986) [1983] 22 ILM 698.

[5] For example, the 1997 Kyoto Protocol to the UN Framework Convention on Climate Change (UNFCCC), while drawing in some respects on the UNFCCC, is a separate treaty that creates rights and obligations only for those UNFCCC parties that ratify it. See UNFCCC (adopted 9 May 1992, entered into force 16 November 1994) 1771 UNTS 107; Kyoto Protocol to the UNFCCC (adopted 10 December 1997, entered into force 16 February 2005) [1998] 37 ILM 32. See generally Chapter 17, Part II, 430 *et seq.*

[6] See generally Chapter 17 (on treaty regimes and treaty bodies); R Churchill and G Ulfstein, 'Autonomous Institutional Arrangements in Multilateral Environmental Agreements' (2000) 94 AJIL 623; J Brunnée, 'COPing with Consent: Lawmaking under Multilateral Environmental Agreements' (2002) 15 LJIL 1.

[7] See Chapters 19–21 (on treaty interpretation).

[8] See A Aust, *Modern Treaty Law and Practice* (2nd edn CUP, Cambridge 2007) 239, 263.

[9] E Hoyt, *The Unanimity Rule in the Revision of Treaties: A Re-Examination* (Martinus Nijhoff, The Hague 1959).

[10] I Sinclair, *The Vienna Convention on the Law of Treaties* (2nd edn MUP, Manchester 1984) 106.

[11] See VCLT Art 40(4).

[12] Villiger (n 1) 29, 34.

VCLT codified the existing customary international law on treaties.[13] The topic of treaty amendment came to be included in the ILC's draft articles only relatively late, in 1964.[14] Given the basic principle that a State's rights under a treaty could not be modified without their consent, amendments were widely seen as raising political and diplomatic, rather than legal, issues.[15] At the same time, the rise of international organizations and the proliferation of multilateral treaties increased States' awareness of the need to make advance provision and clarify the procedural requirements for subsequent amendment.[16] Since the considerable diversity in amendment practice made it difficult to identify customary rules,[17] the ILC eventually opted for a broadly framed general principle, along with residual procedural rules intended to guide the amendment of multilateral treaties. In the deliberations leading to the adoption of the VCLT, the provisions relating to amendments did not raise much discussion.[18] Articles 39–41, which make up Part IV of the VCLT (Amendment and Modification of Treaties), read as follows:

Article 39
General rule regarding the amendment of treaties

A treaty may be amended by agreement between the parties. The rules laid down in Part II [on conclusion and entry into force of treaties] apply to such an agreement except insofar as the treaty may otherwise provide.

Article 40
Amendment of multilateral treaties

1. Unless the treaty otherwise provides, the amendment of multilateral treaties shall be governed by the following paragraphs.
2. Any proposal to amend a multilateral treaty as between all the parties must be notified to all the contracting States, each one of which shall have the right to take part in:

(*a*) the decision as to the action to be taken in regard to such proposal;
(*b*) the negotiation and conclusion of any agreement for the amendment of the treaty.

3. Every State entitled to become a party to the treaty shall also be entitled to become a party to the treaty as amended.
4. The amending agreement does not bind any State already a party to the treaty which does not become a party to the amending agreement; article 30, paragraph 4(b), applies in relation to such State.
5. Any State which becomes a party to the treaty after the entry into force of the amending agreement shall, failing an expression of a different intention by that State:

(*a*) be considered as a party to the treaty as amended; and
(*b*) be considered as a party to the unamended treaty in relation to any party to the treaty not bound by the amending agreement.

---

[13] K Zemanek, 'Vienna Convention on the Law of Treaties' (United Nations Audiovisual Library 2009) <http://untreaty.un.org/cod/avl/pdf/ha/vclt/vclt-e.pdf> (referring to reservations, interpretation, and termination of treaties).
[14] See Villiger (n 1) 510–11.   [15] See [1964] YBILC, vol II, 48.   [16] Ibid.
[17] Ibid 49–50.   [18] See Villiger (n 1) 510–11.

Article 41
Agreements to modify multilateral treaties between certain of the parties only

1. Two or more of the parties to a multilateral treaty may conclude an agreement to modify the treaty as between themselves alone if:

  (*a*) the possibility of such a modification is provided for by the treaty; or
  (*b*) the modification in question is not prohibited by the treaty and:

  (i) does not affect the enjoyment by the other parties of their rights under the treaty or the performance of their obligations;
  (ii) does not relate to a provision, derogation from which is incompatible with the effective execution of the object and purpose of the treaty as a whole.

2. Unless in a case falling under paragraph 1 (*a*) the treaty otherwise provides, the parties in question shall notify the other parties of their intention to conclude the agreement and of the modification to the treaty for which it provides.

As these residual rules confirm, amendments require agreement between treaty parties, but not necessarily between all parties.[19] For bilateral treaties, of course, the agreement of both parties is needed to effect any changes. The main question here concerns the form in which the parties' agreement is to be expressed. Some bilateral treaties stipulate that written agreement, for example through exchange of notes, is required.[20] It is worth noting that for plurilateral treaties too the unanimity rule continues to hold sway.[21] For example, the North American Free Trade Agreement (NAFTA) between Canada, Mexico, and the United States stipulates that the 'Parties may agree on any modification of or addition to' NAFTA.[22]

For multilateral treaties, the default rule is that amendments must be proposed and adopted, and that individual parties then decide whether or not they wish to become a party to the amendment.[23] However, parties are free to reach informal agreements on the amendment, and to decide on the details of the amendment process.[24] This open-endedness of the residual rules reflects not only the afore-mentioned variations in State practice, but also the fact that international law does not contain an *acte contraire* principle.[25] In other words, there is no general legal requirement that changes to a treaty be made through the same process or by an act of the same legal nature as the original instrument.[26] When a party joins a treaty for which an amendment is already in force, it normally will be bound by the amendment unless it indicates otherwise.[27] If two or more parties wish to change a treaty as between themselves—as opposed to between all parties—they can do so, subject to certain limitations, by way of a modification.[28]

---

[19] VCLT Art 39.   [20] See Aust (n 8) 264–5 (with examples).
[21] The VCLT does not specifically address amendments of plurilateral treaties. However, the considerations accounting for the unanimity practice is reflected in the VCLT's approach to reservations, according to which the 'limited number of negotiating States' may be a reason why reservations to a treaty requires 'acceptance by all the parties'. See VCLT Art 20(2).
[22] North American Free Trade Agreement (signed 8, 11, 14 and 17 December 1992, entered into force 1 January 1994) [1993] 32 ILM 289, Art 2202 (NAFTA).
[23] VCLT Art 40.   [24] Ibid Arts 39, 40(1).
[25] Aust (n 8) 263–4.   [26] Villiger (n 1) 513.
[27] VCLT Art 40(5).   [28] Ibid Art 41.

A variety of potentially competing considerations must be balanced in devising an amendment process for a multilateral agreement. States' desire to protect their sovereign interests and their attendant preference for formal consent must be balanced against the need for a dynamic, responsive treaty that can facilitate necessary change. Amendment procedures must also balance between the stability of a treaty and its dynamism and, hence, adaptability. In some contexts—for example in the case of treaties that establish international organizations—stability of the organization's institutional and procedural structures will be one of the greatest strengths of the underlying treaty. Stability will also be paramount in some issue areas, such as human rights law.[29] In other settings, for example in the environmental protection context, a treaty's success will be dependent in part upon its dynamism—its ability to adapt and respond to new or evolving challenges, knowledge or political dynamics. The relative importance of stability and change may also differ depending on the type of provision involved. For example, provisions that are central to the integrity of a treaty, such as its main substantive provisions and procedural infrastructure, will be less amenable to change than technical or administrative standards. Finally, the integrity and stability of a treaty may suffer when some parties are bound by an amendment and others are not, or when, as a result of different amendments with different subsets of parties, a treaty ends up proceeding at different speeds. The 1929 Warsaw Convention for the Unification of Certain Rules relating to International Carriage by Air provides an infamous example.[30] It was amended and supplemented multiple times, progressively undercutting the Convention's 'unification' goal because of the divergent memberships of the Convention and the various amendments.[31] The 1999 Montreal Convention for the Unification of Certain Rules relating to International Carriage by Air was intended to remedy the less than satisfactory situation,[32] but so far not all parties to the Warsaw Convention have joined the Montreal Convention.[33] As this chapter will illustrate, how the balance is struck between sovereignty protection, stability, and dynamism is often directly related to the overall effectiveness of the treaty.

Hence, most treaties today contain detailed amendment provisions.[34] Sometimes, however, parties are unable to resolve the underlying policy questions when they negotiate the terms of treaty, leaving the VCLT rules to operate by default. For

---

[29] Indeed, human rights treaties adopted under the auspices of the UN often require approval by the UN General Assembly, in addition to acceptance by a specified majority of parties, for amendments to enter into force. See n 44 and accompanying text.

[30] Convention for the Unification of Certain Rules relating to International Carriage by Air (signed 12 October 1929, entered into force 13 February 1933) 137 LNTS 11 ('Warsaw Convention').

[31] Aust (n 8) 262–3.

[32] Convention for the Unification of Certain Rules for International Carriage by Air (signed 28 May 1999, entered into force 4 November 2003) 2242 UNTS 309.

[33] See EM Giemulla, 'Traffic and Transport, International Regulation' in R Wolfrum (ed), *The Max Planck Encyclopedia of Public International Law* (OUP, Oxford 2008).

[34] The Warsaw Convention (n 30) is an example of an older treaty that did not contain an amendment provision.

example, Article 26(1) of the Convention on Elimination of All Forms of Discrimination against Women (CEDAW) provides only that a request for the revision of the Convention may be made at any time by any party, 'by means of a notification in writing addressed to the Secretary-General of the United Nations'.[35]

This chapter will examine the different options for structuring amendment processes for multilateral treaties, leaving aside the relatively straightforward matter of amendments to bilateral and plurilateral treaties. The focus will be on formal treaty amendments and modifications to multilateral treaties. As the chapter will illustrate, many treaties contain amendment provisions that deviate from the default rules outlined in the VCLT, which require explicit consent for individual parties to be bound by amendments. In order to facilitate change, some treaties employ tacit consent or 'opt-out' processes. In other treaties, amendments ratified by specified majorities will bind all parties, except for States whose party status ends due to non-ratification of the amendment and, in a variation on this approach, for States that choose to withdraw from the treaty. Some treaties even allow, for narrowly defined types of changes, the collapsing of the adoption and consent steps into a vote by the plenary body. Finally, as the following review will illustrate, it is not uncommon for treaties to provide multiple amendment procedures for different parts of the treaty, permitting the treaty to strike a more finely tuned balance between sovereignty protection, stability, and dynamism. The chapter will also briefly touch upon the question whether treaties can be amended prior to their entry into force.

I. The Standard Amendment Process—Explicit Consent

The traditional process for altering existing text or adding new treaty terms is a formal treaty amendment as envisaged in Article 40 of the VCLT. In keeping with the formal model of strictly consent-based treaty-making, the amendment process requires explicit consent for an individual party to be bound by an amendment. Similar to the treaty-making process itself, the amendment process normally proceeds in several steps. The first step is the proposal of an amendment, usually by one or more of the parties (sometimes by a treaty body), and the notification of that proposal to all other parties. If the parties decide to proceed with the amendment they enter into negotiations on the new terms. The amendment must then be adopted by the treaty parties. Once adopted, it enters into force only upon subsequent acceptance by a specified majority of parties, and only for those parties that have ratified it.[36]

The requirements for adoption provide a first opportunity to calibrate the amendment process so as to balance protections for State sovereignty, stability,

---

[35] Convention on Elimination of All Forms of Discrimination against Women (adopted 18 December 1979, entered into force 3 September 1981) 1249 UNTS 13 (CEDAW).
[36] On adoption, ratification, and entry into force of treaties see Chapter 7, Parts III and IV, 195 *et seq.*

and dynamism—with potentially significant implications for the effectiveness of the treaty. For example, if a treaty requires consensus for an amendment to be adopted, individual parties are assured that no amendment can emerge that is unacceptable to them and that all amendments have broad support among parties. Such amendments, one might argue, are more likely to be viable. But the consensus rule can also stifle treaty development, precisely by enabling small numbers of parties or even individual parties to obstruct the adoption of an amendment. Hence, the consensus requirement can also undermine the effectiveness of a treaty by holding up necessary changes. As noted above, what the appropriate balance is between sovereignty, stability, and change will depend in part upon the subject matter of the treaty, and in part upon what type of provision is to be amended.

The entry-into-force threshold presents a further juncture at which sovereignty protection, stability, and treaty development—and so effectiveness considerations—can be factored into the design of the amendment process. If a large number of ratifications are required for entry into force, the amendment may never take effect. At the same time, some amendments will not achieve their intended purpose, or will not be acceptable to parties, unless they bind a significant segment of the treaty membership. For example, if the number of required ratifications for an amendment that is meant to expand the jurisdiction of an international court is too low, the court may not be able to operate effectively. An unduly low entry into force threshold may also deter individual parties from ratifying, for fear of being one of only a few States subject to the expanded jurisdiction. Similar considerations apply in a broad range of issue areas. Consider the example of a global issue like climate change—an amendment to a global climate treaty that contained new emission limits could not deliver meaningful global emission reductions if only a few States were bound by it, nor would individual States be likely to agree to take expensive reduction measures while others 'free-ride'.

It should be noted that, in setting an entry-into-force threshold for amendments, it may not be enough to specify a percentage of parties that must accept it. As the experience with a number of treaties has demonstrated, the question may arise whether the required percentage refers to the number of parties at the time of the adoption of the amendment or the time of its entry into force. When an amendment takes a long time to enter into force, the number of treaty parties required may grow in the intervening time, making it increasingly difficult for the amendment to meet the threshold. For example, the 1960 Convention for the Safety of Life at Sea ('SOLAS Convention') and the 1971 Load Lines Convention were both amended multiple times but none of the amendments entered into force.[37] Since State practice on the percentage question has tended to vary, some treaties do specify that the reference group is parties at the time of adoption of the amend-

---

[37] See M Bowman, 'The Multilateral Treaty Amendment Process—A Case Study' (1995) 44 ICLQ 540, 551 n57.

ment.[38] Others, such as the 1974 successor of the SOLAS Convention,[39] opt for simplified amendment processes to remedy the problem.[40]

In practice, most multilateral treaties permit adoption of amendments by a specified majority of parties, provide for relatively high entry-into-force thresholds, and stipulate individual party consent. For example, amendments to the United Nations Framework Convention on Climate Change (UNFCCC) are adopted by a meeting of the Conference of the Parties (COP), normally by consensus but, as a last resort, by a three-quarters majority of the parties present and voting.[41] However, these amendments will not enter into force unless three-quarters of the 194 parties to the Convention have accepted them.[42] Only parties that accept the amendment are bound by it.[43] Many other multilateral agreements provide for direct recourse to majority voting on the adoption of amendments. For example, amendments to the International Covenant on Civil and Political Rights (ICCPR) can be adopted by a majority of the parties present and voting. However, this relatively lower adoption threshold is counterbalanced by a relatively high bar for entry-into-force of the amendment: approval by the UN General Assembly and acceptance by two-thirds of the ICCPR parties.[44] Another majority-based amendment process can be found in the Constitution of the Food and Agriculture Organization ('FAO Constitution').[45] Amendments that involve new obligations for States can be adopted by a two-thirds majority of the votes cast, so long as this majority represents more than one-half of FAO members. Such amendments enter into force for accepting States once two-thirds of FAO members have accepted them.[46] A variant of this approach is employed by the International Telecommunication Union (ITU).[47] Amendments to its Constitution can be adopted by a two-thirds majority.[48] To enable speedy modification, the ITU Constitution dispenses with an entry-into-force threshold and stipulates that amendments will enter into force between ratifying parties.[49]

---

[38] See eg Convention Establishing the World Intellectual Property Organization (WIPO) (adopted 14 July 1967, entered into force 26 April 1970) 828 UNTS 3, Art 17(3).

[39] International Convention for the Safety of Life at Sea, 1974 (concluded 1 November 1974, entered into force 25 May 1980) 1184 UNTS 2 ('SOLAS Convention').

[40] See nn 80–5 and accompanying text.

[41] UNFCCC (n 5) Art 15(3).

[42] Ibid Art 15(4).

[43] Ibid Art 15(4) and (5).

[44] See International Covenant on Civil and Political Rights (adopted 19 December 1966, entered into force 23 March 1976) 999 UNTS 171, Art 51 (ICCPR). Several other UN human rights treaties similarly require approval of amendments by the UN General Assembly. See eg International Covenant on Economic, Social and Cultural Rights (adopted 19 December 1966, entered into force 3 January 1976) 999 UNTS 3, Art 29; UN Convention on the Rights of the Child (adopted 20 November 1989, entered into force 2 September 1990) [1989] 28 ILM 1448, Art 50.

[45] Constitution of the Food and Agricultural Organization (with Annexes) (adopted 16 October 1945, entered into force 16 October 1945) 145 BSP 910 ('FAO Constitution').

[46] Ibid Arts XX(1), (2).

[47] Constitution and Convention of the International Telecommunication Union (with Annexes and Optional Protocol) (concluded 22 December 1992, entered into force 1 July 1994) 1825 UNTS 143 ('ITU Constitution').

[48] Ibid Art 55(4).   [49] Ibid Art 55(6).

A similar approach is applied to amendments to the 1998 Rome Statute on the International Criminal Court (ICC).[50] All amendments under the Statute are adopted by consensus, or if consensus cannot be reached, by a two-thirds majority of the parties.[51] But amendments to provisions that define the crimes within the jurisdiction of the Court enter into force only for those parties that accept them, one year after the deposit of their instruments of ratification or acceptance.[52] During the 2010 Review Conference of the Rome Statute, parties used this process to adopt, by consensus, an amendment that added a variety of poisonous weapons as well as expanding or flattening bullets to the ICC's jurisdiction over war crimes in non-international armed conflicts.[53] This amendment was relatively uncontroversial, since the Court already had jurisdiction over the relevant weapons in the context of international armed conflicts.[54] Not surprisingly, the adoption of an amendment that defined the crime of aggression and activated the ICC's jurisdiction over it proved rather more difficult.[55] While the parties adopted this amendment too by consensus,[56] the amendment introduced additional barriers to the exercise of jurisdiction by the Court, effectively revising the amendment process for the crime of aggression. In particular, the ICC can exercise jurisdiction only 'with respect to crimes of aggression committed one year after the ratification or acceptance of the amendments by thirty States Parties', and only after a further decision by the parties, 'to be taken after 1 January 2017 by the same majority required for the adoption of an amendment to the Statute'.[57] Except in the case of a Security Council referral of the matter to the ICC, the Court's jurisdiction over the crime of aggression is furthermore excluded when a party has previously declared its non-acceptance.[58]

The examples of the amendments adopted at the Rome Statute Review Conference highlight the crucial importance that amendment procedures may assume, and the difficult political issues that they may raise. They also underscore the earlier observation that treaties frequently provide different amendment procedures for different parts of a treaty, depending on the nature of the provision to be amended and the political sensitivity of the underlying issue. Indeed, the Rome Statute itself provides for two other amendment procedures, one for amendments to provisions of an institutional nature, and one for all other provisions except those outlining the crimes under the Court's jurisdiction.[59]

Before turning to alternatives to the formal amendment process, it is important to note that States' laws and practices with respect to the domestic approval and

---

[50] Rome Statute (n 2) Art 121(5).

[51] Ibid Art 121(3).   [52] Ibid Art 121(5).

[53] See Review Conference of the Rome Statute, 31 May–11 June 2010 (8 June 2010) ICC Doc RC/11/Res 5 (Amendments to Article 8 of the Rome Statute).

[54] See Rome Statute (n 2) Art 8(2)(b)(xvii–xix).

[55] The Rome Statute had left the definition of this crime and the terms of the ICC's jurisdiction over it to be determined by means of an amendment. See ibid Art 5(2).

[56] See Review Conference of the Rome Statute, 31 May–11 June 2010 (11 June 2010) ICC Doc RC/11/Res 6 (the crime of aggression).

[57] Ibid Annex I, Arts 15*bis*(2)–(3), 15*ter*(2)–(3).

[58] Ibid Annex I, Arts 15*bis*(4); Annex III(2).

[59] See Rome Statute (n 2) Arts 122, 124(1)–(4); see also Part IV, 362 *et seq* below.

effects of amendments differ.[60] In some States, the ratification of treaties and amendments to treaties is within the competence of the executive branch, although legislative implementation may be required for the treaty or amendment to have domestic effect. In other States, the approval of the legislature will be required before the executive can consent to a treaty or amendment. In turn, once ratified, the treaty or amendment may then be directly applicable in domestic law. The formal amendment process allows each State to follow its domestic approval process for each change to a treaty to which it is a party. Where treaties provide for simplified consent to amendments, or even dispense with individual party consent, a State's domestic process may be effectively bypassed. Depending on the international amendment process, the vote of a government representative may suffice to bind an individual State. Of course, the State in question would have formally consented to this amendment process as it ratified the original treaty. Still, given the scope and significance of international standard setting through alternative amendment processes, the impact on domestic decision-making has occasioned some concern. Such concern has been voiced notably in the United States, where Senate approval is generally required for treaties and amendments.[61]

II. Amendments With Tacit Consent or 'Opt-Out'

In this variant of an amendment process, the plenary body adopts an amendment, usually by majority decision. The amendment will bind all treaty parties, except those that declare in writing that they do not accept the amendment. Normally, this opt-out must be notified within a specified period of time from the adoption of the amendment. As in the standard process, individual parties retain control over new treaty terms. But rather than requiring their explicit opt-in, this variant presumes parties' consent unless they explicitly opt out. In other words, the opt-out model retains the individual consent requirement but replaces explicit consent with tacit consent.

The first multilateral treaty to employ the opting out procedure was the 1944 Chicago Convention on International Civil Aviation (ICAO).[62] The treaty's plenary body, the ICAO Council, adopts standards on the safety, regularity, and efficiency of air navigation,[63] designating them as annexes to the Convention.[64]

---

[60] See Aust (n 8) 178–99 (providing an overview of major jurisdictions).

[61] See eg RF Blomquist, 'Ratification Resisted: Understanding America's Response to the Convention on Biological Diversity 1989–2002' (2002) 32 Golden Gate Univ L Rev 493, 545–6; *Natural Resources Defense Council v EPA*, 464 F.3d 1 (D.C. Cir. 2006) (concluding that, absent specific ratification or authorization by the US Congress, certain requirements validly agreed upon under the auspices of the Montreal Protocol on Substances that Deplete the Ozone Layer where not 'law' for the purposes of relevant US legislation). For a more detailed discussion of treaties and domestic law, see Chapter 15 (Domestic Application of Treaties).

[62] Convention on International Civil Aviation (signed 7 December 1944, entered into force 4 April 1947) 15 UNTS 295 ('Chicago Convention').

[63] Ibid Art 37.   [64] Ibid Art 54(l).

The Council adopts or amends these annexes by two-thirds majority vote and they become effective within three months unless a majority of the parties register their disapproval with the Council.[65] Individual member States can reject some or all of the standards in the annexes or amendments.[66]

The opting-out process has since come to be commonly employed by international organizations or multilateral agreements to facilitate the adoption or revision of technical standards. For example, world conferences under the auspices of the ITU can revise the international telecommunication regulations,[67] which are binding on members.[68] The revisions enter into force among the ratifying States.[69] They are provisionally applied to member States that have signed but not ratified them, except for States that opposed such provisional application upon signature. If a member State has not communicated its consent to be bound within thirty-six months of its entry into force, it will be deemed to have consented to the revision.[70]

Under the Constitution of the World Health Organization (WHO), the World Health Assembly can adopt regulations on public health matters by majority vote.[71] These regulations become binding on all member States, except those that reject them or formulate reservations to them.[72] In 1951, to replace earlier sanitary conventions, the assembly adopted several international regulations, which in turn have been amended repeatedly to keep up with new health threats and other developments, most recently through International Health Regulations (IHR) adopted in 2005.[73] These regulations introduced the requirement that, if one-third of the WHO member States object to a reservation and the reserving State does not withdraw it, the Assembly must confirm that the reservation is compatible with the IHR's object and purpose.[74] In this case, the relevant regulations will not enter into force for a party that maintains its reservation notwithstanding the Assembly's objection.[75] The 2005 IHR are in force for 194 States. Only two States, India and the United States, lodged reservations. Since there was only one objection, the IHR entered into force for the reserving States, subject to their reservations.[76]

Yet another version of the tacit consent process is used under the auspices of the World Meteorological Organization (WMO) and the International Maritime

---

[65] Ibid Art 90(a).
[66] Ibid Art 38.   [67] ITU Constitution (n 47) Art 25(2).   [68] Ibid Arts 4(3), 54(1).
[69] Ibid Arts 54(2)*bis*, (3)*bis*.   [70] Ibid Art 54(3)*penter*.
[71] Constitution of the World Health Organization (signed 22 July 1946, entered into force 22 July 1946) 14 UNTS 185, Art 21 ('WHO Constitution').
[72] Ibid Art 22.
[73] WHO, International Health Regulations, Resolution WHA 58/3 (adopted 23 May 2005, entered into force 7 June 2007), in WHO, *International Health Regulations* (2nd edn 2008) 1 (IHR).
[74] See ibid Arts 59, 61, 62. According to Art 62(9), the Assembly must object to the reservation by majority vote, on the ground that it is incompatible with the IHR's object and purpose.
[75] Ibid Art 62(9).
[76] See WHO, 'States Parties to the International Health Regulations (2005)' <http://www.who.int/ihr/legal_issues/states_parties/en/index.html>. See also IHR (n 73) Art 62(5). India's reservation concerned responses to Yellow Fever. The US reservation concerned implementation of the IHR in accordance with the fundamental principles of US federalism. Iran objected to the latter reservation.

Organization (IMO), respectively. The WMO's plenary body, the Congress, is empowered to adopt, by two-thirds majority vote, binding regulations on meteorological practices and procedures.[77] However, parties are required only to 'do their utmost to implement the decisions of the Congress' and can advise the WMO that they find it 'impracticable', temporarily or permanently, to implement certain standards.[78] In turn, while the IMO Convention itself does not provide for tacit consent to amendments,[79] many of the conventions and protocols adopted under the IMO umbrella do. The simplified amendment process was introduced because the standard ratification requirement delayed, or even prevented the entry into force of key amendments.[80] For example, the 1960 SOLAS Convention required ratification by two-thirds of the parties for entry into force of an amendment, with the result that several amendments never passed this bar. In response to this state of affairs, parties tasked a working group with an assessment of the tacit amendment procedures used by ICAO, ITU, WHO, and WMO.[81] Since 1972, tacit consent procedures for amendments to technical standards have been incorporated into most IMO Conventions.[82] Under the 1974 SOLAS Convention, a tacit amendment process is available for changes to the technical chapters of the Annex to the Convention.[83] Such amendments are deemed to have been accepted after a stipulated period of time.[84] Unless a specified number of objections are received by a particular date, they enter into force for all parties except those that object.[85] For example, under the Convention on Facilitation of International Maritime Traffic ('Maritime Traffic Convention'), parties can indicate that they find it 'impracticable to comply' with given standards in the annex to the Convention.[86] However, the plenary body can decide by two-thirds majority that these standards are of such nature that a non-accepting State ceases to be a party to the Convention. Revisions or amendments to the Convention itself enter into force for all parties, except those that previously declared that they do not accept the new terms.[87] Although some concerns were initially expressed, notably by developing countries, about the tacit consent process,[88] it has come to be firmly established in IMO

---

[77] Convention of the World Meteorological Organization (done 11 October 1947, entered into force 23 March 1950) 77 UNTS 143, Arts 8(d), 11(b) ('WMO Convention').

[78] Ibid Art 9.

[79] Convention on the Intergovernmental Maritime Consultative Organization (done 6 March 1948, entered into force 17 March 1958) 289 UNTS 3, Art 66 ('IMO Convention').

[80] See n 37 and accompanying text.

[81] D König, 'Tacit Consent/Opting Out Procedures' in R Wolfrum (ed), *The Max Planck Encyclopedia of Public International Law* (OUP, Oxford 2008).

[82] Ibid.

[83] SOLAS Convention (n 39) Art VIII.

[84] Ibid Art VIII(xi)(2).

[85] Ibid Art VIII(xi)(2) and (vii)(2).

[86] Convention on Facilitation of International Maritime Traffic (signed 9 April 1965, entered into force 5 March 1967) 591 UNTS 265, Arts VI–VIII.

[87] Ibid Art IX.

[88] AO Adede, 'Amendment Procedures for Conventions with Technical Annexes: The IMCO Experience' (1976–77) 17 VJIL 201, 206–10 (pointing primarily to sovereignty concerns and capacity limitations).

practice and is generally seen as having been successful in facilitating the expeditious updating of safety and environmental standards.[89]

Some international fisheries commissions also use opt-out procedures. Hence, the North-East Atlantic Fisheries Commission (NEAFC) can adopt 'recommendations' by majority vote. These recommendations will be binding on parties that do not object to them.[90] If three or more parties object, none will be bound, except for individual parties that agree to be bound amongst themselves.[91] An identical process is used by the North Atlantic Fisheries Organization (NAFO) in respect of 'proposals for joint action'.[92]

Finally, under many multilateral environmental agreements (MEAs), the opting-out process is employed in the initial adoption and subsequent amendment of technical or administrative annexes, such as lists of regulated substances or applicable procedures. Relevant examples can be found in the UNFCCC and its Kyoto Protocol,[93] in the Convention on Biological Diversity,[94] and in the Basel Convention on the Control of Transboundary Movements of Hazardous Wastes and Their Disposal.[95]

As these various examples serve to illustrate, the opting-out approach is typically used for technical, scientific, or administrative matters. Such matters are less likely to be politically charged than changes to obligations or other core terms of a treaty. At the same time, to ensure the effectiveness of an organization or treaty, it is particularly important that the relevant standards can be updated easily and in harmonized fashion. The tacit consent process creates a presumption for treaty development. Furthermore, because parties' formal consent is not required, new or updated standards can bypass potentially time-consuming domestic approval processes. The result is a much speedier standard-setting process, albeit at the expense of some of the safeguards that formal consent processes offer.[96] As noted above, at least in domestic systems that require legislative approval of treaties, the opting-out process can shift international standard-setting to the executive. Given the largely technical nature of the relevant standards, this shift may be unproblematic. Still, some treaties permit parties, upon ratification of the treaty, to generally opt-out of tacit amendments or, more specifically, to stipulate that such amendments enter into force for such parties only upon their explicit consent.[97] In addition, it is

---

[89] König (n 81).

[90] North-East Atlantic Fisheries Convention (with Annex) (signed 24 January 1959, entered into force 27 June 1963) 486 UNTS 157, Arts 5–8.

[91] Ibid Art 12.

[92] Convention on Future Multilateral Co-operation in the Northwest Atlantic Fisheries (with Annexes) (done 24 October 1978, entered into force 1 January 1979) 1135 UNTS 369, Arts X–XII.

[93] UNFCCC (n 5) Art 16; Kyoto Protocol (n 5) Art 21.

[94] Convention on Biological Diversity (concluded 5 June 1992, entered into force 29 December 1993) 1760 UNTS 79, Art 30(2).

[95] Basel Convention on the Control of Transboundary Movements of Hazardous Wastes and Their Disposal (done 22 March 1989, entered into force 5 May 1992) 1673 UNTS 57, Art 18(2).

[96] See n 88 and accompanying text (on the concerns of developing countries in the context of IMO's shift to the tacit consent process).

[97] See eg Convention to Combat Desertification in Those Countries Experiencing Serious Drought and/or Desertification, Particularly in Africa (opened for signature 14 October 1994, entered into force

important to note that the boundary between technical and substantive matters cannot always be sharply drawn. For example, when an operative provision in an environmental agreement refers to substances that are listed in an annex to the treaty, the annex directly affects the scope of the binding treaty commitment. For this reason, some environmental agreements use different amendment processes, depending on the annex in question. The Kyoto Protocol provides a good illustration. Its Annex A identifies the greenhouse gases to which the Protocol applies and its Annex B lists each party's assigned amount of emissions, thereby specifying their individual emission reduction commitments. Hence, while the Protocol uses the opt-out procedure for purely technical annexes, it requires the formal amendment process for changes to Annexes A and B.[98] This differentiated approach to amendments provides another illustration of the finely tuned efforts of many treaties to balance between sovereignty protection, stability, and dynamism.[99]

III. Amendments With Majority Ratification

As the example of the Warsaw Convention illustrates,[100] the traditional amendment model can produce increasing differentiation of treaty commitments among parties. When it comes to the amendment of constituent treaties of international organizations or international tribunals, or of other large multilateral treaties, such divergences may be impractical or undesirable from a policy perspective. Some treaties, therefore, provide for amendment procedures that are designed to ensure uniformity of terms and commitments as between all parties. This uniformity is accomplished by a majority ratification requirement, combined with either (i) the stipulation that non-ratifying States cease to be treaty parties or (ii) the stipulation that amendments ratified by a specified majority bind all treaty parties.

An early example of the first approach can be found in a provision of the 1919 Versailles Peace Treaty that dealt with amendments to the Covenant of the League of Nations.[101] Such amendments required ratification by a specified majority of the members of the organization. No member State could be bound without its consent, but non-ratification of an amendment ended that State's membership in the League. The Chicago Convention contains a similar provision with respect to amendments which the ICAO Assembly considers to be 'of such a nature to justify such a course of action'.[102] However, although not all

---

26 December 1996) 1954 UNTS 3, Arts 30, 31, 34(4); Stockholm Convention on Persistent Organic Pollutants (done 22 May 2001, entered into force 17 May 2004) [2001] 40 ILM 532, Arts 20, 21, 25(4).

[98] Kyoto Protocol (n 5) Art 21(7).

[99] See also the Introduction to this chapter, n 59 and accompanying text.

[100] See nn 30–3 and accompanying text.

[101] Treaty of Peace between the Allied and Associated Powers and Germany (Versailles Peace Treaty) (signed 28 June 1919, entered into force 10 January 1920) 225 CTS 188, Art 26.

[102] Chicago Convention (n 62) Art 94(b).

member States have ratified all amendments, none have been expelled.[103] This practice led some commentators to suggest that the amendment in question would have to entail fundamental changes to the Convention to justify expulsion.[104]

A prominent example of the second approach can be found in the UN Charter. A Charter amendment must first be adopted by two-thirds of the members of the UN General Assembly. It enters into force for all member States upon ratification by two-thirds of the membership, including all permanent members of the Security Council.[105] Similar approaches are used for amendments to the constituent treaties of several other UN specialized agencies, including the WHO Constitution,[106] the WMO Convention,[107] and Article XIII(1) of the UNESCO Constitution, which concerns 'fundamental alterations in the aims of the Organization or new obligations for the Member States'.[108] The process can also be found in the Charter of the League of Arab States and in the Statute of the Council of Europe.[109]

In the second variant of the majority consent approach individual States can find themselves bound by the amended treaty without their consent. They can avoid the new terms only by withdrawing from the treaty or organization. In some treaties, this option is provided through, and under the conditions of, the treaty's general withdrawal provisions. In other treaties it is stipulated in the amendment provision itself. For example, under the Rome Statute of the ICC, amendments that pertain neither to the crimes within the jurisdiction of the Court nor to 'exclusively institutional' matters enter into force for all parties one year after ratification by seven-eighths of them.[110] The Rome Statute further provides that a party that does not accept the amendment may withdraw from the Statute with immediate effect.[111] This variant resembles the opting-out process in that the consent to the amendment of all parties that do not withdraw from the treaty is effectively presumed. However, the 'opt-out' itself is significantly different, as the parties' opt-out concerns not merely the amendment but pertains to the treaty as a whole.

Both variants, through the relatively extreme approach of either automatic exclusion or individual withdrawal, underscore the importance that parties attach to uniform application of the underlying treaty terms.

---

[103] See ICAO Council, 'Review of International Governance (Chicago Convention)', Working Paper, 188th Sess (22 June 2009) ICAO Doc C-WP/13416; E Osieke, 'Sanctions in International Law: The Contributions of International Organizations' (1984) 31 Netherlands Intl L Rev 183, 185.

[104] Osieke (n 103) 186.

[105] UN Charter Arts 108, 109.

[106] WHO Constitution (n 71) Art 73.

[107] WMO Convention (n 77) Art 28(c).

[108] UNESCO Constitution (signed 16 November 1945, entered into force 4 November 1946) 4 UNTS 275.

[109] Pact of the League of Arab States (signed 22 March 1945, entered into force 10 May 1945) 70 UNTS 237, Art 19; Statute of the Council of Europe (with Amendments) (signed 5 May 1949, entered into force 3 August 1949) CETS No 1, Art 41.

[110] Rome Statute (n 2) Arts 121(4)–(5), 122.

[111] Ibid Art 121(6).

IV. Amendment By Consensus or Majority Plenary Decision

In the standard amendment process, the opting-out process, and the majority ratification process, individual parties must consent to be bound by an amendment, either explicitly or tacitly. All of these approaches, therefore, require two steps: the adoption of an amendment and its entry into force, triggered by the consent of a specified number of parties. Some amendment processes go further, collapsing the adoption and consent steps into a vote by the treaty's plenary body. The rationale for such a simplified process is not just that it expedites decision-making. It also represents another method for ensuring uniformity of commitments among parties. However, amendments through simple decision-making by treaty plenaries diverge quite significantly from the formal safeguards of treaty law. Like the opt-out process, they also shift powers to executive decision-making in domestic systems that require legislative approval for formal international commitments. For all these reasons, this type of amendment process is rare and tends to be reserved for narrowly defined and relatively uncontroversial matters. Sometimes these changes are referred to as adjustments rather than amendments, to highlight the fact that they involve an updating of a previously agreed regulatory approach, rather than a major substantive change.

Some constituent treaties of international organizations authorize amendments by simple decision of the plenary body. For example, under the FAO Constitution, binding amendments can be adopted by two-thirds majority resolution of the plenary body, so long as they do not involve new obligations for members and associate members and the resolution itself does not require individual acceptances.[112] If new obligations are involved, a formal amendment process is required.[113] Similarly, amendments to the UNESCO Constitution that do not concern fundamental alterations in the aims of the organization or new obligations can be adopted by two-thirds majority resolution of the plenary body with binding effect for all members.[114] In turn, under the Rome Statute of the ICC, amendments that are of an 'exclusively institutional nature' are adopted by consensus or, if consensus cannot be reached, by a two-thirds majority of the parties. Such amendments enter into force for all parties six months after their adoption.[115]

Some MEAs employ a binding majority decision process for a small category of matters. The most frequently cited example is the Montreal Protocol on Substances that Deplete the Ozone Layer.[116] The Protocol contains a provision that allows for certain changes to the control measures for substances that are already regulated under the Protocol, accomplished through so-called 'adjustments' to relevant

---

[112] FAO Constitution (n 45) Art XX(2).
[113] See n 46 and accompanying text.
[114] UNESCO Constitution (n 108) Art XIII(1).
[115] Rome Statute (n 2) Art 122.
[116] Montreal Protocol on Substances that Deplete the Ozone Layer (with Annex) (adopted 16 September 1987, entered into force 1 January 1989) 1522 UNTS 3.

annexes.[117] To date all such adjustments have been adopted by consensus. But if consensus cannot be achieved, the Protocol permits adoption by two-thirds majority decision, including a majority of both industrialized and developing country parties present and voting.[118] Such adjustments are binding upon all Protocol parties.[119]

Comparable procedures exist under other MEAs. For example, the Protocol to the 1979 Convention on Long-Range Transboundary Air-Pollution and Further Reduction of Sulphur Emissions allows for adjustments to standards contained in an annex to the Protocol.[120] Such adjustments must be adopted by consensus decision. While there are numerous other examples of this approach, suffice it here to point to the Convention on the Prior Informed Consent Procedure for Certain Hazardous Chemicals and Pesticides in International Trade ('Rotterdam Convention'), which provides that a consensus decision can amend, with binding effect for all parties, Annex III to the Convention, which lists the chemicals subject to the prior informed consent procedure.[121] Like many other MEAs, the Rotterdam Convention takes a differentiated approach to amendments.[122] Hence, in the case of new annexes, or amendments to annexes other than Annex III, parties can opt out by means of notification.[123] In turn, amendments to the Convention itself must be made through the standard process and require individual parties' consent to bind them.[124]

V. Modifications Between Certain Parties Only

Whereas amendments are intended to alter treaty terms as between all the parties,[125] two or more treaty parties can also agree to modify certain terms of the treaty 'as between themselves alone'.[126] However, given the general interest in the integrity of treaties and preference for harmonized treaty terms, the scope for such modifications is strictly limited. Modifications may be made when the treaty explicitly provides for them.[127] Otherwise, they are possible only when they are not prohibited by the treaty, and when they neither affect other parties' rights or obligations under the treaty nor purport to change a provision 'derogation from which is incompatible with the effective execution of the object and purpose of the treaty as a whole'.[128] In addition, unless modification is permitted by the treaty, the relevant parties must notify the other parties of their intent to conclude a modifi-

---

[117] Ibid Art 2(9).   [118] Ibid Art 2(9)(c).   [119] Ibid Art 2(9)(d).

[120] Protocol to the 1979 Convention on Long-Range Transboundary Air-Pollution and Further Reduction of Sulphur Emissions (concluded 14 June 1994, entered into force 5 August 1998) [1994] 33 ILM 1540, Art 11(6).

[121] Convention on the Prior Informed Consent Procedure for Certain Hazardous Chemicals and Pesticides in International Trade (done 11 September 1998, entered into force 24 February 2004) 2244 UNTS 337, Art 22(5) ('Rotterdam Convention').

[122] See also nn 98–9 and accompanying text.

[123] Rotterdam Convention (n 121) Art 22(3)–(4).

[124] Ibid Art 21(4).   [125] VCLT Art 40(2).

[126] Ibid Art 41(1).   [127] Ibid Art 41(1)(a).   [128] Ibid Art 41(1)(b).

cation agreement and of the modification that they envisage.[129] In practice, States do not appear to avail themselves of this device very often.[130]

VI. Amendment Before Entry Into Force

Technically speaking, a treaty can only be amended once it is in force. However, on occasion, multilateral treaties require changes in order for them to enter into force in the first place.[131] The most commonly cited example is that of the 1994 Agreement relating to the Implementation of Part XI of the UN Convention on the Law of the Sea.[132] The provisions in Part XI of the Law of the Sea Convention, pertaining to deep sea-bed mining, were among the most controversial parts of the Convention.[133] Specifically, leading industrialized countries indicated that, because of the cost-sharing, decision-making, profit-sharing, and other provisions in Part XI, they would not ratify the Convention. As a result, many developing countries too were reluctant to ratify the Convention. Consultations led to the adoption of the Implementation Agreement, which contained agreed interpretations to several provisions of Part XI and several new terms concerning the International Seabed Authority. The Implementation Agreement stipulated that it and the Convention would 'henceforth be interpreted and applied as a single instrument'.[134] It also tied any future consent to the Convention to consent to the Agreement, and vice versa. For States already party to the Convention, a simplified process enabled consent to the Agreement without formal ratification.[135] Since the parties to the Agreement consent to implementing Part XI in accordance with its terms, its effect is similar to that of an amendment. Parties did not avail themselves of the Law of the Sea Convention's amendment provisions, in part because these provisions were available only after entry into force of the Convention and in part because they would not have facilitated the desired speedy alteration of Part XI. The impact of the Implementation Agreement is significant. Although amendments normally have legal effects for those States that accept them, convention parties that did not join the Agreement will find it increasingly difficult to maintain their original interpretation of Part XI.[136]

---

[129] Ibid Art 41(2).

[130] See J Klabbers, 'Treaties, Amendments, and Revision' in R Wolfrum (ed), *The Max Planck Encyclopedia of Public International Law* (OUP, Oxford 2008).

[131] See Aust (n 8) 276 (noting that bilateral treaties are more commonly 'amended' before entry into force).

[132] UN Convention on the Law of the Sea (adopted 10 December 1982, entered into force 16 November 1994) 1833 UNTS 3 (UNCLOS); Agreement relating to the Implementation of Part XI of the UN Convention on the Law of the Sea of 10 December 1982 (adopted 28 July 1994, entered into force provisionally 16 November 1994 and definitively 28 July 1996) 1836 UNTS 3 ('Implementation Agreement').

[133] For an overview, see C Kojima and VS Vereshchetin, 'Implementation Agreements' in R Wolfrum (ed), *The Max Planck Encyclopedia of Public International Law* (OUP, Oxford 2010).

[134] Implementation Agreement (n 132) Art 2(1).

[135] Ibid Arts 4–5.   [136] Villiger (n 1) 524.

Conclusion

At first glance, amendments would appear to be among the more straightforward treaty law topics. They do not raise major theoretical controversies and textbooks on international law tend to give them relatively brief treatment. Yet, especially in the context of large multilateral treaties, amendments often raise intricate design questions. A wide variety of approaches to treaty amendment have gained currency to balance considerations of sovereignty protection, stability, and change. Depending on the circumstances, adoption and entry-into-force thresholds can be higher or lower within the standard amendment process. Alternatively, amendment processes can alter the requirement of individual party consent by relying upon tacit rather than explicit consent (opt-out rather than opt-in); by stipulating that majority ratification creates binding amendments for all parties except for those that, due to their non-acceptance of the amendment, are automatically excluded from the treaty or choose to withdraw from it; or by dispensing altogether with the individual consent step and relying exclusively on the adoption of the amendment by the treaty plenary. As the almost infinite range of variations on the amendment process and the examples provided in this chapter illustrate, there is no one formula for an effective amendment process. The amendment process must be tailored to the treaty in question and the policy context in which the treaty operates. Hence, while amendments may not raise major conceptual issues, the configuration of the amendment process does raise important practical issues in the negotiation of a treaty. An appropriately calibrated amendment process is a crucial ingredient for a successful treaty.

Recommended Reading

D Anderson, 'Further Efforts to Ensure Universal Participation in the United Nations Convention on the Law of the Sea' (1994) 43 ICLQ 886

A Aust, *Modern Treaty Law and Practice* (2nd edn CUP, Cambridge 2007)

M Bowman, 'The Multilateral Treaty Amendment Process—A Case Study' (1995) 44 ICLQ 540

J Brunnée, 'International Legislation' in R Wolfrum (ed), *The Max Planck Encyclopedia of Public International Law* (OUP, Oxford 2008) available online at <http://www.mpepil.com>

J Charney, 'Entry into Force of the 1982 Convention on the Law of the Sea' (1995) 35 VJIL 381

O Corten and P Klein (eds), *Les Conventions de Vienne sur les droits des traités: Commentaire article par article* (Bruylant, Brussels 2006)

O Corten and P Klein (eds), *The Vienna Conventions on the Law of Treaties: A Commentary* (OUP, Oxford 2011)

R Gardiner, 'Revising the Law of Carriage by Air: Mechanisms in Treaties and Contract' (1998) 47 ICLQ 278

E Hoyt, *The Unanimity Rule in the Revision of Treaties: A Re-Examination* (Martinus Nijhoff, The Hague 1959)

W Karl, B Mützelberg, and G Witschel, 'Article 108' in B Simma (ed), *The Charter of the United Nations: A Commentary* (2nd edn OUP, Oxford 2002)

J Klabbers, 'Treaties, Amendments, and Revision' in R Wolfrum (ed), *The Max Planck Encyclopedia of Public International Law* (OUP, Oxford 2008) available online at <http://www.mpepil.com>

C Kojima and VS Vereshchetin, 'Implementation Agreements' in R Wolfrum (ed), *The Max Planck Encyclopedia of Public International Law* (OUP, Oxford 2010) available online at <http://www.mpepil.com>

D König, 'Tacit Consent/Opting Out Procedures' in R Wolfrum (ed), *The Max Planck Encyclopedia of Public International Law* (OUP, Oxford 2008) available online at <http://www.mpepil.com>

G Scelle, *Théorie juridique de la revision des traités* (Librairie du Recueil Sirey, Paris 1936)

J Sommer, 'Environmental Law-Making by International Organizations' (1996) 56 ZaöRV 628

ME Villiger, *Commentary on the 1969 Vienna Convention on the Law of Treaties* (Martinus Nijhoff, The Hague 2009)

15

Domestic Application of Treaties

David Sloss

Introduction

There has been dramatic growth in treaty-making since the Second World War: more than 64,000 treaties have been registered with the United Nations since 1945.[1] Meanwhile, with the rise of globalization, the boundary separating domestic law from international law has become increasingly permeable. Consequently, States are making greater use of treaties to regulate activity that was previously regulated exclusively by domestic law. For example, under the 1993 Hague Convention on Intercountry Adoption,[2] eighty-three States have agreed to regulate child adoption on a transnational scale.[3] Additionally, States are concluding greater numbers of treaties that protect the rights of private parties, including, for example, treaties related to international human rights law,[4] international humanitarian law,[5] and international refugee law.[6] As a consequence of these three trends—growth in the number of treaties, increasing overlap between treaties and domestic law, and a growing emphasis on private rights—domestic courts are playing an increasingly prominent role in treaty application.

Traditional scholarship on the domestic application of treaties has focused on the distinction between monist and dualist legal systems.[7] Part I of this chapter explains that distinction: in brief, the monist-dualist divide hinges on the role of the legislative branch in incorporating and implementing treaties domestically.

---

[1] See United Nations Treaty Series Cumulative Index <http://treaties.un.org/Pages/CumulativeIndexes.aspx>. In contrast, States concluded about 16,000 treaties during the nineteenth century. See JF Witt, 'Internationalism and the Dilemmas of Strategic Patriotism' (2006) 41 Tulsa L Rev 787, 791.

[2] Convention on Protection of Children and Cooperation in Respect of Intercountry Adoption (adopted 29 May 1993, entered into force 1 May 1995) 1870 UNTS 167.

[3] See Status Table, Convention on Protection of Children and Cooperation in Respect of Intercountry Adoption <http://www.hcch.net/index_en.php?act=conventions.status&cid=69>.

[4] See eg International Covenant on Civil and Political Rights (adopted 16 December 1966, entered into force 23 March 1976) 999 UNTS 171 (ICCPR).

[5] See eg Geneva Convention (IV) Relative to the Protection of Civilian Persons in Time of War (adopted 12 August 1949, entered into force 21 October 1959) 75 UNTS 135.

[6] See eg Protocol Relating to the Status of Refugees (adopted 31 January 1967, entered into force 4 October 1967) 606 UNTS 267.

[7] See nn 8–15 and accompanying text.

Although the monist-dualist framework helps illuminate important *formal* differences among States, Part I suggests that scholarly preoccupation with the formal distinction between monism and dualism tends to obscure key *functional* differences among States.

Hence, the remainder of the chapter adopts a functional approach, focusing primarily on the role of domestic courts in promoting compliance with treaty obligations and protecting treaty-based private rights. Part II explains the distinction between horizontal, vertical, and transnational treaty provisions. Part III addresses the functional distinction between nationalist and transnationalist approaches to judicial application of treaties. Part IV discusses the crucial role of domestic courts in promoting compliance with treaty obligations, especially transnational and vertical treaty obligations.

The functional analysis in Parts II to IV shows that domestic courts play a key role in protecting private rights under transnational treaty provisions and promoting compliance with those provisions, but they play virtually no role in promoting compliance with horizontal treaty provisions. This is generally true for both monist and dualist States. The story with respect to vertical treaty provisions is more complicated. When domestic courts adopt a transnationalist approach, they play a key role in protecting private rights under vertical treaty provisions and promoting compliance with those provisions. When domestic courts adopt a nationalist approach, vertical treaty provisions may be under-enforced. There does not appear to be any significant correlation between a State's formal classification as monist or dualist and the tendency of domestic courts in that State to function in a nationalist or transnationalist mode.

I. Monism and Dualism

The terms 'monism' and 'dualism' generate considerable confusion because there is no single, agreed definition of the terms. Some scholars employ the terms to describe contrasting theoretical perspectives on the relationship between international and domestic law.[8] Used in this sense, dualism 'points to the essential difference of international law and municipal law, consisting primarily in the fact that the two systems regulate different subject-matter'.[9] In contrast, monism holds that 'international and municipal law are part of the same system of norms'.[10] Some monist theorists assert 'the supremacy of international law' over domestic law, but this is not an essential feature of monist theory.[11]

Other scholars employ the terms monism and dualism to describe different types of domestic legal systems.[12] Used in this sense, dualist States are States in which

---

[8] See eg I Brownlie, *Principles of Public International Law* (7th edn OUP, Oxford 2008) 31–3.
[9] Ibid 31.
[10] Ibid 32.
[11] See ibid 32–3 (discussing Kelsen's and Lauterpacht's theories).
[12] See eg A Aust, *Modern Treaty Law and Practice* (CUP, Cambridge 2007) 181–95.

'the constitution . . . accords no special status to treaties; the rights and obligations created by them have no effect in domestic law unless legislation is in force to give effect to them'.[13] In contrast, '[t]he essence of the monist approach is that a treaty may, without legislation, become part of domestic law once it has been concluded in accordance with the constitution and has entered into force for the state'.[14] As Professor Aust correctly notes, many national constitutions 'contain both dualist and monist elements'.[15]

This chapter uses the terms monism and dualism in the second sense, to describe different types of domestic legal systems. Dualist States are States in which *no treaties* have the status of law in the domestic legal system; *all* treaties require implementing legislation to have domestic legal force.[16] Monist States are States in which *some* treaties have the status of law in the domestic legal system, even in the absence of implementing legislation.[17] In most monist States, there are some treaties that require implementing legislation and others that do not. There is substantial variation among monist States as to which treaties require implementing legislation. Moreover, monist States differ considerably in terms of the hierarchical rank of treaties within the domestic legal order. Despite these variations, all monist States have one common feature: at least some treaties have the status of law within the domestic legal order.

The question whether a treaty requires legislative implementation after the treaty enters into force internationally must be distinguished from the question whether legislative approval is necessary prior to treaty ratification. In most dualist States, the executive has the constitutional authority to conclude treaties that bind the nation under international law without obtaining prior legislative approval.[18] The executive's power to conclude treaties without prior legislative approval helps explain why, in dualist States, implementing legislation is necessary to grant treaties domestic legal force. In most monist States, though, the constitution requires legislative approval for at least some treaties before the executive can make an internationally binding commitment on behalf of the nation.[19] The fact that the legislature approves (some) treaties before they become binding on the nation helps explain why, in monist States, some treaties have the status of domestic law even in the absence of implementing legislation. In sum, in both monist and dualist States, it is rare for a treaty to have domestic legal force unless the legislature has acted either to approve the treaty before

---

[13] Ibid 187.   [14] Ibid 183.   [15] Ibid 182.

[16] In many dualist States, customary international law has domestic legal force, even in the absence of implementing legislation. See eg N Jayawickrama, 'India' in D Sloss (ed), *The Role of Domestic Courts in Treaty Enforcement: A Comparative Study* (CUP, Cambridge 2009) 244–5 ('Sloss').

[17] These definitions arguably constitute a slight departure from standard terminology. However, these definitions have the advantage of drawing a clear distinction between monism and dualism. Applying these definitions, almost all States can be neatly classified as either monist or dualist without significant overlap between the categories.

[18] See n 25.   [19] See n 72 and accompanying text.

international entry into force, or to implement the treaty after international entry into force.[20]

The following sections summarize key features of monist and dualist systems. The analysis touches upon the domestic legal systems of twenty-one States, relying heavily on two previously published volumes that present a comparative analysis of national treaty law.[21] Those twenty-one States include five dualist States: Australia, Canada, India, Israel, and the United Kingdom. The other sixteen (monist) States are: Austria, Chile, China, Colombia, Egypt, France, Germany, Japan, Mexico, the Netherlands, Poland, Russia, South Africa, Switzerland, Thailand, and the United States.

A. Dualist States

Almost all the British Commonwealth States follow the dualist approach for treaties.[22] Apart from Commonwealth States, Israel, Denmark, and other Nordic States also follow a dualist approach.[23] The key distinguishing feature of dualism is that no treaties have the formal status of law in the domestic legal system unless the legislature enacts a statute to incorporate the treaty into domestic law.[24] Such statutes must be distinguished from legislative acts that authorize the executive to make a binding international commitment, which, as noted above, are unnecessary in these systems.[25] In many dualist States the executive consults with the legislature before concluding 'important' treaties.[26] (There is considerable variation among States concerning which treaties qualify as 'important'.) Moreover, if legislation is needed to ensure that government officials have the requisite authority to implement a treaty, dualist States usually enact the necessary implementing legislation before the treaty enters into force internationally.[27]

For courts in dualist States, there is a crucial distinction between incorporated and unincorporated treaties. As a formal matter, courts in dualist States have no authority to apply treaties directly as law. If the legislature has enacted a statute to incorporate a particular treaty provision into national law, courts apply the statute as law;[28] and they frequently consult the underlying treaty to help construe the

---

[20] See DB Hollis, 'A Comparative Approach to Treaty Law and Practice' in DB Hollis, MR Blakeslee, and LB Ederington (eds), *National Treaty Law and Practice* (Martinus Nijhoff, Leiden 2005) 32–45 ('*NTLP*').

[21] See *NTLP* (n 20); Sloss (n 16).

[22] See Aust (n 12) 194–5.

[23] See ibid.

[24] See DR Rothwell, 'Australia' in Sloss (n 16) 128–30; M Copithorne, 'Canada' in *NTLP* (n 20) 95–101; K Thakore, 'India' in *NTLP* (n 20) 351; R Lapidoth, 'Israel' in *NTLP* (n 20) 396; and I Sinclair, SJ Dickson and G Maciver, 'United Kingdom' in *NTLP* (n 20) 733.

[25] See Copithorne (n 24) 91–4 (Canada); Lapidoth (n 24) 385–90 (Israel); Rothwell (n 24) 128–30 (Australia); Sinclair and others (n 24) 727 (United Kingdom); and Thakore (n 24) 352–5 (India).

[26] See Copithorne (n 24) 96, 98 (Canada); Lapidoth (n 24) 388–9, 393–4 (Israel); Sinclair and others (n 24) 737–9 (United Kingdom); and Thakore (n 24) 365–6 (India).

[27] See Copithorne (n 24) 96 (Canada); Lapidoth (n 24) 396–8 (Israel); Sinclair and others (n 24) 742 (United Kingdom); and Thakore (n 24) 359–60 (India).

[28] See eg A Aust, 'United Kingdom' in Sloss (n 16) 486; Rothwell (n 24) 138–41 (Australia); G van Ert, 'Canada' in Sloss (n 16) 202–4.

meaning of the statute.[29] Thus, in dualist States, courts apply treaties indirectly, not directly. However, one should not overstate the difference between direct and indirect application. Either way, judges who are receptive to the domestic judicial application of treaties can use their judicial power to protect the treaty-based rights of private parties and promote compliance with national treaty obligations.[30]

Dualist States employ a variety of methods for incorporating treaties into national law.[31] In the United Kingdom, for example: the text of a treaty may be attached to a statute stipulating that the attached treaty provisions 'shall have the force of law in the United Kingdom';[32] Parliament may pass an Act granting government officials 'all the powers necessary to carry out obligations under an existing or future treaties';[33] or Parliament may pass an Act authorizing the Crown to enact regulations to implement one or more treaties.[34] Given the wide variety of techniques that dualist States utilize to incorporate treaties,[35] the question whether a particular treaty provision has been incorporated is often ambiguous.[36]

The Australian High Court developed a creative approach to addressing this type of ambiguous situation, which commentators have dubbed 'quasi-incorporation'.[37] The term refers to situations where 'government departments, and administrative decision makers are given [a statutory directive] to take into account the provisions of . . . international instruments to which Australia is a party'.[38] For example, in the *Project Blue Sky* case,[39] an Australian statute specifically directed the Australian Broadcasting Authority (ABA) 'to perform its functions in a manner consistent with "Australia's obligations under any . . . agreement between Australia and a foreign country"'.[40] The petitioners argued that the ABA had violated the statute by enacting regulations inconsistent with a bilateral free-trade agreement between Australia and New Zealand.[41] A three-judge panel of the Federal Court held that 'the ABA was not bound to take into account' the free-trade agreement because that agreement conflicted with a different statutory provision.[42] The High Court

---

[29] See eg Aust (n 28) 482–3 (United Kingdom); Jayawickrama (n 16) 264–6 (India); D Kretzmer, 'Israel' in Sloss (n 16) 290–2 (Israel); Rothwell (n 24) 138–41 (Australia); van Ert (n 28) 175–82 (Canada).

[30] See generally D Sloss, 'Treaty Enforcement in Domestic Courts: A Comparative Analysis' in Sloss (n 16) 8–43 (analysing the practice of national courts in eleven States).

[31] See eg Kretzmer (n 29) 283–5 (Israel); Rothwell (n 24) 159–60 (Australia); van Ert (n 28) 169–71 (Canada).

[32] Aust (n 12) 189.

[33] Ibid 190.

[34] Ibid 190–1.

[35] See eg Aust (n 28) 479–81 (United Kingdom) (discussing, among others, *Cheng v Conn, Inspector of Taxes* [1968] 1 All ER 779); Kretzmer (n 29) 283–5 (Israel); Rothwell (n 24) 158–60 (Australia) (discussing *Project Blue Sky Inc v Australian Broadcasting Auth* (1998) 153 ALR 490); van Ert (n 28) 169–71 (Canada) (discussing, among others, *Pan American World Airways v The Queen* [1981] 2 SCR 565; *Schavernoch v Foreign Claims Commission* [1982] 1 SCR 1092).

[36] See eg van Ert (n 28) 171.

[37] See Rothwell (n 24) 158–64.

[38] Ibid 159.

[39] *Project Blue Sky Inc v Australian Broadcasting Auth* (1998) 153 ALR 490.

[40] Rothwell (n 24) 141 (quoting Broadcasting Services Act 1992).

[41] Ibid 141–2.   [42] Ibid 143.

reversed, holding 'that the ABA was precluded from making a standard inconsistent with the' free-trade agreement, even though that agreement had not been directly incorporated into Australian domestic law.[43] Courts in other dualist States have adopted a similar approach. In the United Kingdom, for example, petitioners in several cases have obtained judicial remedies by invoking statutes that required administrative decision-makers to exercise their authority in conformity with treaty obligations that had not been directly incorporated into domestic law.[44]

More surprisingly, courts in dualist States have developed a variety of strategies for judicial application of unincorporated treaties—even in the absence of any statutory directive for government officials to take account of treaty provisions.[45] In Australia, for example, the High Court held in *Minister of State for Immigration and Ethnic Affairs v Teoh*[46] that administrative decision-makers must exercise their statutory discretion in conformity with the Convention on the Rights of the Child, an unincorporated treaty, because treaty ratification meant that individuals had a 'legitimate expectation' that government officials would act in accordance with the treaty.[47] The Canadian Supreme Court has declined to follow this so-called legitimate expectations doctrine.[48] Even so, the Canadian Supreme Court has held that administrative decision-makers in Canada, like their Australian counterparts, must exercise their statutory discretion in conformity with the Convention on the Rights of the Child, an unincorporated treaty.[49] In Israel, 'it has now become standard practice for the Supreme Court to' apply Geneva Convention IV in cases involving the Occupied Territories, although the Convention has not been incorporated into domestic law.[50] The Court justifies this approach by citing the government's political commitment to 'respect the humanitarian provisions of the Convention'.[51] Similarly, the Indian Supreme Court routinely applies unincorporated treaties to support its interpretation of both statutory and constitutional provisions;[52] the Court has also applied treaties to support its progressive development of common law principles.[53]

---

[43] Ibid 143–5.

[44] See Aust (n 28) 490–1 (noting that 'there have been numerous successful challenges by way of judicial review to [administrative] decisions on claims to refugee status'); ibid 491–2 (discussing *Secretary of State for Foreign and Commonwealth Affairs v Quark Fishing Ltd* [2002] EWCA Civ 1409; [2002] All ER (D) 450 holding that the Director of Fisheries of South Georgia and the South Sandwich Islands 'had not properly carried out his statutory powers' because he failed to take account of relevant treaty provisions).

[45] See MP Van Alstine, 'The Role of Domestic Courts in Treaty Enforcement: Summary and Conclusions' in Sloss (n 16) 608–12.

[46] (1995) 128 ALR 353.

[47] Ibid; See also Rothwell (n 24) 146–8.

[48] See van Ert (n 28) 173 (discussing *Baker v Canada* [1999] 2 SCR 817).

[49] See ibid 194–7.

[50] See Kretzmer (n 29) 305–10 (discussing, among others, HCJ 3278/02, *Hamoked The Center for the Defense of the Individual v IDF Commander* 57 P.D. (1) 385 ('*Hamoked*')).

[51] Ibid 309–10 (discussing *Hamoked* (n 50); HCJ 7862/04, *Abu Dahar v IDF Commander* 59 P.D. (5) 368).

[52] See Jayawickrama (n 16) 247–64 (discussing, among others, *Jolly George Verhese v Bank of Cochin* [1980] 2 SCR 913; *Transmission Corporation of Andhra Pradesh v Ch Prabhakar* Supreme Court of India, Civil Appeal 6131 of 2002, 26 May 2004).

[53] See ibid 255–6 (discussing *MV Elisabeth v Harwan Investment and Trading Pvt Ltd* [1992] 1 SCR 1003).

This increasing judicial reliance on unincorporated treaties by courts in dualist States blurs the traditional distinction between monist and dualist States.[54] Nevertheless, judges in dualist States periodically invoke the dualist dogma that courts are powerless to apply treaties unless the legislature has expressly incorporated the treaty into domestic law.[55] Hence, there remains an uneasy tension between the formalities of strict dualist doctrine and the practical reality that courts in dualist States have developed a variety of strategies to facilitate judicial application of unincorporated and partially incorporated treaties.

B. Monist States

The key distinguishing feature of monist legal systems, as defined herein, is that at least some treaties are incorporated into the domestic legal order without the need for any legislative act, other than the act authorizing the executive to conclude the treaty. Under this definition, Austria,[56] Chile,[57] China,[58] Colombia,[59] Egypt,[60] France,[61] Germany,[62] Japan,[63] Mexico,[64] the Netherlands,[65] Poland,[66] Russia,[67] South Africa,[68] Switzerland,[69] Thailand,[70] and the United States[71] all have monist legal systems. In all sixteen States, some form of legislative approval is required for at least some types of treaties before the executive is authorized to make a binding international commitment on behalf of the nation.[72] Despite these similarities, there are substantial differences among these States concerning the application of treaties within their national legal systems.

---

[54] See MA Waters, 'Creeping Monism: The Judicial Trend Toward Interpretive Incorporation of Human Rights Treaties' (2007) 107 Colum L Rev 628.

[55] See eg B Saul, 'The Kafka-esque Case of Sheikh Manour Leghaei: The Denial of the International Human Right to a Fair Hearing in National Security Assessments and Migration Proceedings in Australia' (2010) 33 UNSW Law J 629.

[56] See F Cede and G Hafner, 'Republic of Austria' in *NTLP* (n 20) 59–60, 67–8.

[57] See F Orrego Vicuna and F Orrego Bauzá, 'Chile' in *NTLP* (n 20) 136–8.

[58] See X Hanqin, H Zhiqiang, and Fan Kun, 'China' in *NTLP* (n 20) 163–4.

[59] See G Cavelier, 'Colombia' in *NTLP* (n 20) 205.

[60] See N Elaraby, M Gomaa, and L Mekhemar, 'Egypt' in *NTLP* (n 20) 238–9.

[61] See PM Eisemann and R Rivier, 'France' in *NTLP* (n 20) 265–7.

[62] See H Beemelmans and HD Treviranus, 'Federal Republic of Germany' in *NTLP* (n 20) 323–6.

[63] See T Kawakami, 'Japan' in *NTLP* (n 20) 424–5.

[64] See LM Díaz, 'Mexico' in *NTLP* (n 20) 451.

[65] See JG Brouwer, 'The Netherlands' in *NTLP* (n 20) 497–9.

[66] See L Garlicki, M Masternak-Kubiak, and K Wójtowicz, 'Poland' in Sloss (n 16) 378.

[67] See WE Butler, 'Russia' in *NTLP* (n 20) 554–6.

[68] See NJ Botha, 'South Africa' in *NTLP* (n 20) 600–2.

[69] See L Wildhaber, A Scheidegger, and MD Schinzel, 'Switzerland' in *NTLP* (n 20) 658–9.

[70] See S Sucharitkul, 'Thailand' in *NTLP* (n 20) 706.

[71] See RE Dalton, 'United States' in *NTLP* (n 20) 788–90.

[72] See Beemelmans and Treviranus (n 62) 323–6 (Germany); Botha (n 68) 590–2 (South Africa); Brouwer (n 65) 489–91 (the Netherlands); Butler (n 67) 544–7 (Russia); Cavelier (n 59) 199 (Colombia); Cede and Hafner (n 56) 64–5 (Austria); Dalton (n 71) 770–4 (United States); Díaz (n 64) 447–8 (Mexico); Eisemann and Rivier (n 61) 258–60 (France); Elaraby and others (n 60) 231 (Egypt); Garlicki and others (n 66) 376–7 (Poland); Hanqin and others (n 58) 161–2 (China); Kawakami (n 63) 419–20 (Japan); Sucharitkul (n 70) 701–3 (Thailand); Vicuna and Bauzá (n 57) 127–30 (Chile); and Wildhaber and others (n 69) 644–8 (Switzerland).

One significant area of variability concerns the types of treaties that require legislative approval before international entry into force of the treaty.[73] In Mexico and Colombia, all treaties require prior legislative approval.[74] Chile, the Netherlands, South Africa, and Switzerland establish a default rule that treaties ordinarily require legislative approval, but they recognize certain exceptions to that rule.[75] In other States, legislative approval is required only for designated categories of treaties.[76]

Another significant area of variability relates to publication requirements. In Egypt, France, Chile, Japan, and Russia, a treaty that has entered into force internationally lacks domestic legal force until the executive branch publishes or promulgates the treaty domestically.[77] In other monist States, though, (at least some) treaties enter into force domestically at the same time they enter into force internationally, without the need for any additional steps.[78]

There is also significant variation among monist States concerning the hierarchical rank of treaties within the domestic legal order. In Austria, Egypt, Germany, and the United States, treaties are equivalent to statutes; they rank lower than the Constitution.[79] In South Africa, treaties rank lower than statutes.[80] In China, France, Japan, Mexico, and Poland, (at least some) treaties rank higher than statutes but lower than the Constitution.[81] In the Netherlands, some treaties rank higher than the Constitution.[82] In Chile, Russia, and Switzerland, the hierarchical rank of treaties is contested, but it is undisputed that at least some treaties rank higher than statutes,[83] and there is some authority for the proposition that some treaties have constitutional rank.[84]

---

[73] For a tabular depiction of the variability in this area, see Hollis, 'Comparative Approach' (n 20) 33.

[74] See Cavelier (n 59) 199 (Colombia); Díaz (n 64) 447–8 (Mexico).

[75] See Botha (n 68) 586–92 (South Africa); Brouwer (n 65) 489–91 (the Netherlands); Vicuna and Bauzá (n 57) 123–4 (Chile); and Wildhaber and others (n 69) 644–51 (Switzerland).

[76] See Hollis, 'Comparative Approach' (n 20) 32–7.

[77] See Butler (n 67) 552–4 (Russia); Eisemann and Rivier (n 61) 265–7 (France); Elaraby and others (n 60) 238–9 (Egypt); Kawakami (n 63) 424–5 (Japan); Vicuna and Bauzá (n 57) 136–8 (Chile).

[78] See Hollis, 'Comparative Approach' (n 20) 41–2.

[79] See Cede and Hafner (n 56) 59–60, 67–8 (Austria); Dalton (n 71) 789–90 (United States); Elaraby and others (n 60) 238–9 (Egypt); A Paulus, 'Germany' in Sloss (n 16) 214–18. In both Austria and Germany, treaties approved by the legislature have the rank of statutes, but treaties concluded without legislative approval have a lower rank. See Cede and Hafner (n 56) 67–8; A Paulus, 'Germany' in Sloss (n 16) 214–18. In the United States, though, there is at least some authority for the proposition that treaties concluded without legislative approval have the same rank as treaties approved by the legislature. See *United States v Pink* 315 US 203 (1942); *United States v Belmont* 301 US 324 (1937).

[80] This follows directly from Art 231(4) of the South African Constitution, which states: 'Any international agreement becomes law in the Republic when it is enacted into law by national legislation; but a self-executing provision of an agreement that has been approved by Parliament is law in the Republic unless it is inconsistent with the Constitution or an Act of Parliament.'

[81] See Díaz (n 64) 451–4 (Mexico); Eisemann and Rivier (n 61) 263–7 (France); Garlicki and others (n 66) 376–9 (Poland); Hanqin and others (n 58) 163–5 (China); and T Webster, 'International Human Rights Law in Japan: The View at Thirty' (2010) 23 Colum J Asian L 241, 245.

[82] See Brouwer (n 65) 498–9.

[83] See Butler (n 67) 554–6 (Russia); Vicuna and Bauzá (n 57) 138–9 (Chile); and Wildhaber and others (n 69) 658–64 (Switzerland).

[84] See Butler (n 67) 556 (contending that '[t]he primacy of international treaties of the Russian Federation extends to Federal laws, including constitutional laws'); Vicuna and Bauzá (n 57) 139 (noting that, in one view, human rights treaties 'now have in Chile a ranking above that of ordinary

In many monist States, even if a treaty has the formal status of law in the absence of implementing legislation, the legislature sometimes enacts legislation to help ensure that courts and executive officers give practical effect to the treaty within the national legal system. Thus, for example, the United States enacted implementing legislation for the New York Convention,[85] and South Africa enacted implementing legislation for the Warsaw Convention.[86] As Professor Nollkaemper observes: '[E]ven if the provisions of a treaty could in principle be applied directly, the Netherlands usually chooses to convert them into national legislation to harmonize Dutch law with the requirements of international law'.[87]

All monist States recognize the possibility, at least theoretically,[88] that domestic courts can apply (at least some) treaties directly as law.[89] Indeed, this is one of the crucial differences between monist and dualist systems: dualist States permit only indirect judicial application of treaties, whereas monist States permit direct judicial application in some cases. Despite this formal distinction, however, there are several reasons why judicial practice exhibits many similarities between monist and dualist States. First, as noted above, courts in dualist States apply various strategies to facilitate judicial application of unincorporated and partially incorporated treaties.[90]

Second, courts in monist States often apply treaties indirectly as an aid to statutory or constitutional interpretation, rather than applying treaties directly as rules of decision to resolve disputed issues.[91] It is difficult to measure the relative frequency of direct versus indirect application, but there is some evidence that courts even in monist States rely more heavily on indirect than direct application.[92] Indeed, courts may prefer indirect application 'in cases where the direct application

---

statutes and at least equal to the Constitution'); and Wildhaber and others (n 69) 662 (Switzerland) ('Treaties in conflict with federal constitutional law have to be applied irrespective of their unconstitutionality').

[85] See Federal Arbitration Act 1970 ss 201–8 (implementing the New York Convention on the Recognition and Enforcement of Foreign Arbitral Awards (adopted 10 June 1958, entered into force 7 June 1959) 330 UNTS 38 ('NY Convention').

[86] See J Dugard, 'South Africa' in Sloss (n 16) 470; Convention for the Unification of Certain Rules Relating to International Carriage by Air (signed 12 October 1929, entered into force 13 February 1933) 137 LNTS 11 ('Warsaw Convention').

[87] A Nollkaemper, 'The Netherlands' in Sloss (n 16) 335.

[88] The South African Constitution expressly contemplates a category of self-executing treaties, but South African courts have not yet held that any particular treaty is self-executing. See Dugard (n 86) 453–5.

[89] See WE Butler, 'Russia' in Sloss (n 16) 410–11; Cede and Hafner (n 56) 69 (Austria); Dalton (n 71) 788–90 (United States); Díaz (n 64) 454 (Mexico); Eisemann and Rivier (n 61) 265–70 (France); Elaraby and others (n 60) 238–9 (Egypt); Garlicki and others (n 66) 400–4 (Poland); Hanqin and others (n 58) 163–5 (China); Nollkaemper (n 87) 341–8 (the Netherlands); Paulus (n 79) 209–12 (Germany); Vicuna and Bauzá (n 57) 136–9 (Chile); Webster (n 81) 244–7 (Japan); and Wildhaber and others (n 69) 644–8 (Switzerland).

[90] See nn 37–53 and accompanying text.

[91] See eg Dugard (n 86) 457–63 (South Africa); Garlicki and others (n 66) 403–4 (Poland); Nollkaemper (n 87) 348–51 (the Netherlands); Paulus (n 79) 209–10 (Germany); and D Sloss, 'United States' in Sloss (n 16) 526–7.

[92] See eg Garlicki and others (n 66) 404 (stating that 'the most typical technique [in Poland] is that of coapplication of an international norm and a domestic norm').

of international law would conflict with national law' because '[c]ourts usually prefer a conciliatory solution over the acknowledgment and resolution of a conflict of law'.[93] Insofar as courts in monist States prefer indirect rather than direct application, this further erodes the practical significance of the traditional distinction between monist and dualist States.

Finally, in certain monist States, courts have articulated a distinction between 'self-executing' and 'non-self-executing' treaties.[94] When domestic courts decide that a treaty is 'non-self-executing', they sometimes behave as if the treaty has not been incorporated into domestic law even though the treaty, as a formal matter, has the status of law within the domestic legal system.[95] Thus, just as judicial practice in some dualist States blurs the monist-dualist divide by applying unincorporated treaties as if they were incorporated, judicial practice in some monist States blurs the monist-dualist divide by handling formally incorporated treaties as if they were unincorporated.

II. Horizontal, Transnational, and Vertical Treaty Provisions

To appreciate the role of domestic courts in treaty application, it is important to understand the nature of modern treaties. There is a widespread misconception that treaties focus exclusively, or almost exclusively, on regulating horizontal relations among States. This was never really true,[96] and it is certainly not true in the twenty-first century. States conclude treaties to regulate three different types of relationships: *horizontal* relations between and among States, *vertical* relations between States and private actors (including natural persons and corporations), and *transnational* relations between private actors who interact across national boundaries.[97] The role of domestic courts in applying treaties varies greatly depending on whether the treaty provision at issue is horizontal, vertical, or transnational.[98]

Domestic courts rarely apply treaties that regulate horizontal relationships among States. If one State believes that another State has violated a horizontal treaty obligation, the complainant might raise the issue in diplomatic negotiations,

---

[93] Nollkaemper (n 87) 349.

[94] See nn 161–77 and accompanying text.

[95] In the United States, for example, courts behave as if non-self-executing treaties are unincorporated, even though the Constitution states expressly that 'all treaties' are 'the supreme Law of the Land'. See Sloss, 'United States' (n 91) 509–14, 527–9, 534–9.

[96] See eg D Sloss, 'When Do Treaties Create Individually Enforceable Rights?' (2006) 45 Colum J Trans'l L 20, 51–91 (analysing US Supreme Court's application of vertical and transnational treaty provisions between 1789 and 1838).

[97] A separate category of treaties involves agreements between States and international organizations. Such treaties involve horizontal provisions (such as a nation's obligation to make financial contributions) and vertical provisions (such as immunities for employees of international organizations). Treaties between States and international organizations do not generally include transnational provisions.

[98] In assessing whether a particular treaty provision is properly characterized as horizontal, vertical, or transnational, it is important to examine the specific provision at issue because a single treaty may contain a combination of horizontal, vertical, and transnational provisions.

or perhaps file suit in an international tribunal, but it would be unusual for the complainant to file suit in a domestic court. Domestic courts typically dismiss cases in which private litigants file suit to resolve disputes that are properly characterized as horizontal disputes between States, because domestic courts generally lack the institutional competence to adjudicate such disputes. For example, a group of Serbian citizens sued the Dutch Government in a domestic court in the Netherlands, alleging that the government violated Article 2(4) of the UN Charter by supporting the NATO bombing of Yugoslavia in 1999. The Supreme Court of the Netherlands held that plaintiffs were not entitled to invoke Article 2(4) in a Dutch court.[99] US Supreme Court Chief Justice Marshall made a similar point two centuries ago. Speaking as a Member of Congress (before he was appointed to the Supreme Court), he asserted that a treaty-related claim falls within the scope of judicial competence where parties 'come into court, who can be reached by its process, and bound by its power...to which they are bound to submit'.[100] However, in a case where '[t]he parties were the two nations...the demand is not a case for judicial cognizance'[101] because sovereign nations are generally not bound to submit to the power of domestic courts.

In contrast to horizontal treaties, domestic courts routinely apply transnational treaty provisions that regulate cross-border relationships between private actors. Such treaties include, for example, the 1958 New York Convention,[102] the 1999 Montreal Convention,[103] and the 1980 Hague Convention on Child Abduction.[104] Although States negotiated and ratified these treaties, they are designed primarily to regulate cross-border relationships among private actors, not horizontal relationships among States. The New York Convention provides rules for recognition and enforcement of arbitral awards arising from transnational commercial activities. The Montreal Convention governs relationships between airlines and their customers: both passengers and shippers. The Hague Convention applies to child custody disputes in which one parent transports a child across national boundaries. For these and other transnational treaties, domestic courts play a vital role in ensuring that private actors behave in accordance with internationally agreed rules regulating cross-border activities. Indeed, domestic courts are arguably the primary enforcers of transnational treaty obligations because most international tribunals lack jurisdiction to adjudicate private disputes involving alleged infractions of transnational treaty provisions.[105] Moreover, such disputes rarely have sufficient political salience to become the subject of interstate diplomacy.

---

[99] See Nollkaemper (n 87) 347.   [100] 10 Annals of Cong 613 (1800).

[101] Ibid.   [102] NY Convention (n 85).

[103] Convention for the Unification of Certain Rules for International Carriage by Air (adopted 28 May 1999, entered into force 4 November 2003) 2242 UNTS 309.

[104] Convention on the Civil Aspects of International Child Abduction (adopted 25 October 1980, entered into force 1 December 1983) 1343 UNTS 89.

[105] Arbitral panels established pursuant to bilateral investment treaties frequently adjudicate disputes between States and private corporations but—in contrast to international commercial arbitration—investment treaty arbitration typically involves vertical treaty provisions, not transnational treaty provisions. The International Court of Justice occasionally adjudicates disputes that originated as transnational, commercial disputes between private parties. See eg *Jurisdiction and Enforcement of*

The preceding comments apply equally to monist and dualist States. Although there are significant formal distinctions between monist and dualist States (as discussed in Part I), there are few, if any, functional distinctions. In both monist and dualist States, domestic courts rarely apply horizontal treaty provisions, but they routinely apply transnational treaty provisions.

The most significant differences among States relate to the judicial application of vertical treaty provisions—provisions that regulate relations between States and private parties. Prominent examples of vertical treaty provisions include the Covenant on Civil and Political Rights (which protects the civil and political rights of citizens in relation to their own governments)[106] and the Refugee Protocol (which protects the rights of individuals who have fled persecution in their home countries to seek asylum in other countries).[107] Domestic courts in both monist and dualist States apply vertical treaty provisions more frequently than they apply horizontal treaty provisions because, in most mature legal systems, domestic courts have an institutional responsibility to protect the rights of private parties, and vertical treaties (unlike horizontal treaties) create rights for private parties.

Whereas both vertical and transnational treaty provisions implicate the rights of private parties—and therefore invite judicial application of treaties—vertical treaty provisions implicate the public functions of government in a way that is not true for transnational treaty provisions. For example, the Refugee Protocol regulates the public functions of government by creating legal (vertical) duties that the government owes to individuals who claim refugee status under the treaty. In contrast, the 1999 Montreal Convention[108] regulates the cross-border commercial activities of airlines, including State-owned airlines, but it does not create significant new duties for governments in the exercise of traditional public functions.

This distinction between vertical and transnational treaty provisions helps explain the distinction between nationalist and transnationalist approaches to the judicial application of treaties. 'Transnationalist' decisions manifest a belief that the judiciary has an independent responsibility to ensure that domestic government officials act in accordance with international treaty obligations. 'Nationalist' decisions manifest a belief that courts should not scrutinize too closely government conduct that is arguably inconsistent with international treaty obligations. In countries where courts adopt a more 'transnationalist' approach—such as South Africa[109] and the Netherlands[110]—domestic courts apply both vertical and transnational treaty provisions with equal vigour. However, in States where courts adopt a more 'nationalist' approach—such as the United States[111] and Israel[112]—domestic

---

Judgments in Civil and Commercial Matters (Belgium v Switzerland) ICJ Press Release 2009/36. However, these types of transnational, private disputes rarely give rise to ICJ jurisdiction.

[106] ICCPR (n 4).
[107] Protocol Relating to the Status of Refugees (n 6).
[108] Convention for the Unification of Certain Rules for International Carriage by Air (n 103).
[109] See Dugard (n 86) 448–75.
[110] See Nollkaemper (n 87) 326–69.
[111] See Sloss, 'United States' (n 91) 504–54.
[112] See Kretzmer (n 29) 273–325.

courts are hesitant to apply vertical treaty provisions, even though they routinely apply transnational provisions.[113]

The contrast between nationalist and transnationalist approaches manifests different judicial attitudes about the relative weight assigned to two competing factors: the judicial responsibility to protect the rights of private parties and the judicial responsibility to refrain from interfering with public governmental functions.[114] Transnationalist judges assign greater weight (implicitly, if not explicitly) to the judicial responsibility to protect the rights of private parties, including rights vis-à-vis government actors, protected by vertical treaty provisions. Nationalist judges assign greater weight (again implicitly, if not explicitly) to the judicial responsibility to defer to the political branches' judgment about how best to interpret and apply vertical treaty provisions. It bears emphasis that the distinction between nationalist and transnationalist approaches is best conceptualized as a spectrum with multiple shades of grey, not a sharp line separating black and white.

One might think that courts in monist States are more transnationalist and courts in dualist States are more nationalist. In fact, though, there is not any significant correlation along these lines. Courts in dualist States sometimes adopt a transnationalist approach and courts in monist States sometimes adopt a nationalist approach.[115] Hence, the monist-dualist dichotomy cannot explain variations among States in judicial decision-making in cases involving vertical treaty provisions. Rather, the extent to which domestic courts apply vertical treaty provisions is best explained by examining whether courts in a particular country are more inclined to adopt a nationalist or transnationalist approach.

III. Nationalist and Transnationalist Approaches

The contrast between nationalist and transnationalist techniques is most visible when litigants ask courts to apply vertical treaty provisions. The tension between nationalist and transnationalist approaches generally does not arise in cases involving horizontal treaty provisions because courts rarely apply horizontal treaty provisions. Similarly, the tension between nationalist and transnationalist approaches rarely arises in cases involving transnational treaty provisions: courts in both monist and dualist States routinely apply transnational treaty provisions without hesitation.

---

[113] For more detailed analysis, see Sloss, 'Treaty Enforcement' (n 30) 1–60; see also Van Alstine (n 45) 555–613.

[114] See PB Stephan, 'Treaties in the Supreme Court, 1946–2000' in DL Sloss, MD Ramsey, and WS Dodge (eds), *International Law in the US Supreme Court: Continuity and Change* (CUP, Cambridge 2011) 338 ('*Intl Law in the US Supreme Court*').

[115] No State is purely nationalist and no State is purely transnationalist. However, courts in some States have more nationalist tendencies and courts in other States have more transnationalist tendencies. See Sloss, 'Treaty Enforcement' (n 30). To obtain more accurate information, a detailed, multi-State empirical study is needed. No such study has been done, but the present author has done an empirical study of nationalist and transnationalist trends in US courts. See Sloss, 'United States' (n 91).

The fact that the tension between nationalist and transnationalist approaches pertains primarily to vertical treaty provisions raises an additional point. Since vertical treaty provisions regulate relations between States and private parties, litigated cases typically pit a private party against a government actor. In some cases, the government invokes a vertical treaty provision to support the exercise of governmental power to regulate private conduct.[116] More commonly, though, a private party invokes a vertical treaty provision as a constraint on government action.[117] Despite the spread of democratization since the end of the Cold War, many States still lack a truly independent judiciary.[118] In such States, transnationalism is not a viable option because judges lack the institutional authority to issue and enforce judgments constraining government conduct. In States that do have an independent judiciary, though, courts must still decide whether to apply treaties—much as they would apply constitutional, statutory, or common law—as a tool to constrain government action. Transnationalist judges apply treaties in precisely this way, whereas nationalist judges employ various rationales to refrain from applying treaties as a constraint on government action. This is the core feature of the distinction between nationalist and transnationalist approaches.

The following analysis of nationalist and transnationalist techniques is divided into four sections: statutory interpretation, treaty interpretation, constitutional interpretation, and self-execution. The first three sections address issues that are common to both monist and dualist States. The final section addresses issues that are unique to monist States.[119]

A. Statutory interpretation

Courts in both monist and dualist States frequently apply an interpretive presumption that statutes should be construed in conformity with the nation's international legal obligations, including obligations derived from both treaties and customary international law. This interpretive presumption is sometimes called a 'presumption of conformity' or a 'presumption of compatibility'.[120] In the United States, the

---

[116] For example, when the Security Council approved the transfer of Charles Taylor to the Netherlands to stand trial before the Special Court for Sierra Leone, the government of the Netherlands relied on the Security Council resolution, and therefore ultimately the UN Charter 'to provide the proper legal basis in domestic law for the arrest and detention of Charles Taylor'. Nollkaemper (n 87) 329–30.

[117] See eg Paulus (n 79) 234–5 (discussing decisions of German courts applying Art 36 of the Vienna Convention on Consular Relations).

[118] The Polity IV Project is the best source of data for estimating the number of countries with independent judiciaries. See Polity IV Project, Political Regime Characteristics and Transitions, 1800–2009: Dataset Users' Manual <http://www.systemicpeace.org/inscr/inscr.htm>. According to the most recent data, there are eighty-one countries whose scores indicate that there are significant constraints on the executive. This is a reasonably good proxy for determining whether a country has an independent judiciary. Thus, approximately half the countries in the world have independent judiciaries.

[119] For a comparable analysis of issues unique to dualist States, see nn 37–55 and accompanying text.

[120] See eg van Ert (n 28) 188–97 (discussing application of the presumption of conformity by Canadian courts in the context of, among others, *R v Hape* [2007] SCC 26); Kretzmer (n 29) 287–92

presumption is referred to as the 'Charming Betsy canon'.[121] Labels aside, the presumption of conformity is probably the most widely used transnationalist tool. Courts in Australia,[122] Canada,[123] Germany,[124] India,[125] Israel,[126] the Netherlands,[127] Poland,[128] South Africa,[129] the United Kingdom,[130] and the United States,[131] among other countries, have applied the presumption in cases involving vertical treaty provisions to help ensure that government conduct conforms to the nation's international treaty obligations.

One recurring issue concerns the threshold conditions necessary to trigger application of the presumption. There is broad agreement that courts may apply the presumption in cases where the statute is facially ambiguous. The Supreme Court of Canada has gone further, holding that 'it is reasonable to make reference to an international agreement at the very outset of the inquiry to determine if there is any ambiguity, even latent, in the domestic legislation'.[132] Justice Kirby advocated a similar approach in Australia, arguing that courts should refer to international treaties 'not only when there exists statutory ambiguity, but also where the construction of a statute would result in an interpretation contrary to international human rights standards'.[133] However, the majority of the Australian High Court has rejected this approach, refusing 'to endorse a wider role for treaties in statutory interpretation other than where the legislature has clearly envisaged such a role or where there exists a clear ambiguity on the face of the statute'.[134]

Judicial application of the presumption is clearly transnationalist, especially in cases where the statute is not facially ambiguous. In contrast, judges with a more

---

(discussing application of the presumption of compatibility by Israeli courts in the context of, among others, Cr. A. 5/51, *Steinberg v Attorney General* 5 P.D. 1061).

[121] The canon takes its name from an 1804 decision by Chief Justice Marshall. See *Murray v Schooner Charming Betsy* 6 US (2 Cranch) 64, 118 (1804).

[122] See Rothwell (n 24) 152–6 (discussing, among others, *Mabo v Queensland (No 2)* (1992) 175 CLR 1).

[123] See van Ert (n 28) 188–97 (discussing, among others, *R v Hape* [2007] SCC 26).

[124] See Paulus (n 79) 209 ('German courts are also bound to interpret domestic law, as far as possible, in a way that avoids the breach of international legal obligations', citing BVerfGE 74, 358, 370).

[125] See Jayawickrama (n 16) 247–51 (discussing, among others, *Jolly George Verghese* [1980] 2 SCR 913).

[126] See Kretzmer (n 29) 287–92 (discussing, among others, HCJ 2599/00, *Yated—Friendly Society of Downs Syndrome Children's Parents v Ministry of Education* 56 P.D. (5) 834).

[127] See Nollkaemper (n 87) 348–51 (discussing, among others, Supreme Court, 27 May 2005, LJN AS7054).

[128] See Garlicki and others (n 66) 404 (noting that 'coapplication of an international norm and a domestic norm' is the most common technique for the judicial application of treaties in Poland).

[129] See Dugard (n 86) 457 (noting that the South African Constitution requires courts, when interpreting legislation, to 'prefer any reasonable interpretation of the legislation that is consistent with international law over any alternative interpretation that is inconsistent with international law', citing *S v Basson* 2005 (1) SALR 171 (CC)).

[130] See Aust (n 28) 482–3 (discussing, among others, *Garland v British Rail Engineering* [1983] 2 AC 751).

[131] See Sloss, 'United States' (n 91) 526–7 (discussing, among others, *Murray* (n 121)).

[132] *National Corn Growers Association v Canada* [1990] 2 SCR 1324, 1372–3.

[133] See Rothwell (n 24) 153–4.

[134] Ibid 156.

nationalist orientation sometimes avoid application of the presumption by declaring that a statute is unambiguous in cases where litigants argue that the statute could reasonably be interpreted in conformity with international treaty obligations.[135] It is likely that courts throughout the world decide numerous statutory interpretation cases where the presumption is not applied, even though it is potentially applicable, because litigants fail to raise a possible treaty argument, or courts decline to address the argument explicitly. It is difficult to perform a systematic analysis of judicial application of the presumption even in a single country because it is hard to identify cases in which courts do not mention potentially applicable treaty arguments.

B. Treaty interpretation

Domestic courts in both monist and dualist States are frequently asked to interpret treaties. In dualist States, this situation commonly arises when the legislature enacts a statute that is expressly intended to implement a treaty.[136] In monist States, courts sometimes interpret treaties when a litigant asks the court to apply a treaty directly, and sometimes when the treaty is applied indirectly. Regardless of the context in which treaty interpretation issues arise, courts have a choice whether to adopt a nationalist or transnationalist approach to treaty interpretation.

Courts applying a transnationalist approach interpret treaties in accordance with the shared understanding of the parties. In accordance with this approach, transnationalist judges cite the Vienna Convention on the Law of Treaties,[137] decisions of foreign courts[138] and international tribunals,[139] and views adopted by non-

---

[135] See eg *Breard v Greene* 523 US 371, 375–6 (1998) (construing a federal statute to be inconsistent with US obligations under the Vienna Convention on Consular Relations).

[136] See eg Aust (n 28) 482–3 (United Kingdom) (discussing, among others, *Sidhu v British Airways* [1997] 1 All ER 193); Jayawickrama (n 16) 264–5 (India) (discussing *Dadu alias Tulsidas v State of Maharashtra* Supreme Court of India, Writ Petition (Criminal) 169 of 1999, 12 October 2000); van Ert (n 28) 177 (Canada) (discussing *Pushpanathan v Canada (Minister of Citizenship and Immigration)* [1998] 1 SCR 982).

[137] See eg Aust (n 28) 483 (United Kingdom) (discussing, among others, *R v Lambert Justices, ex p Yusufu* [1985] Times Law Reports 114); Garlicki and others (n 66) 387–9 (Poland) (discussing, among others, Decision of 9 March 2004, I CK 410/03 (not published Lex 182080)); Nollkaemper (n 87) 360–2 (Netherlands) (discussing, among others, Supreme Court, *State Secretary for Finance v X* 21 February 2003, 36 NYIL 2005, 475); Rothwell (n 24) 151–2 (Australia) (discussing, among others, *Morrison v Peacock* [2002] HCA 44); van Ert (n 28) 175–82 (Canada) (discussing, among others, *Pushpanathan v Canada (Minister of Citizenship and Immigration)* [1998] 1 SCR 982).

[138] See eg Dugard (n 86) 470 (South Africa) (discussing, among others, *Potgieter v British Airways* 2005 (3) SALR 133 (C)); Kretzmer (n 29) 291–2 (Israel) (discussing, among others, F.H. 36/84, *Teichner v Air France* 41 P.D. (1) 589); Nollkaemper (n 87) 364–5 (Netherlands) (discussing, among others, *Administrative Law Division of the Council of State, M.E.D. v State Secretary for Justice* 6 November 1995, 28 NYIL 1997, 353); van Ert (n 28) 185–6 (Canada) (discussing, among others, *Connaught Laboratories Ltd v British Airways* (2002) 61 OR (3d) 2004 (Ont. SCJ)).

[139] See eg Dugard (n 86) 466–70 (South Africa) (discussing, among others, *Ferreria v Levin NO* 1996 (1) SALR 984 (CC)); Garlicki and others (n 66) 389–98 (Poland) (discussing, among others, Judgment of 29 January 2003, V.S.A. 1494/02 (ONSA 2004 nr 2, item 57)); Nollkaemper (n 87) 363–4 (Netherlands) (discussing, among others, *H v Public Prosecutor* Court of Appeal of The Hague, ILDC 636 (NL 2007)); Paulus (n 79) 223–35 (Germany) (discussing, among others, BVerfGE 111,

judicial international bodies[140] to support their interpretations of particular treaty provisions. In contrast, courts applying a nationalist approach emphasize that treaty interpretation is primarily an executive function, not a judicial function. Accordingly, courts applying a nationalist approach tend to defer to the executive branch on treaty interpretation issues.[141] Deference to the executive branch often yields judicial opinions that give greater weight to unilateral national policy interests, and less weight to the shared, multilateral understanding that guides transnationalist interpretations.

Available information, which is admittedly limited, indicates that the nationalist approach to treaty interpretation is a minority approach. The United States may be the only State where courts have adopted an explicit interpretive presumption favouring deference to the executive branch on treaty interpretation issues.[142] In Israel, the Supreme Court has never adopted an express interpretive presumption of this type, but 'in cases relating to the [Occupied Territories], for a long time, the Supreme Court in fact adopted the interpretation of [Geneva Convention IV] favored by the authorities'.[143] In contrast, Polish commentators assert: 'For a court to treat executive branch views [on treaty interpretation issues] as dispositive would be incompatible with the principle of independence of the judicial branch, as understood under the Polish Constitution.'[144] The Polish view appears to be the dominant one. In most countries with independent judiciaries—including both monist and dualist States—domestic courts claim an independent responsibility to construe treaties in accordance with the shared expectations of the parties, without giving undue weight to the unilateral views of their own governments.[145]

---

307 (2004)); van Ert (n 28) 183–4 (Canada) (discussing, among others, *Mugesera v Canada (Minister of Citizenship and Immigration)* [2005] 2 SCR 91).

[140] See eg Dugard (n 86) 466–70 (South Africa) (discussing, among others, *Government of the Republic of South Africa v Grootboom* 2001 (I) SALR 46 (CC); *Minister of Health v Treatment Action Campaign (No 2)* 2002 (5) SALR 721 (CC)); Jayawickrama (n 16) 257 (India) (discussing *Visaka v State of Rajasthan* [1997] 3 LRC 361); Kretzmer (n 29) 298–301 (Israel) (discussing, among others, HCJ 7029/95 *New General Labor Federation v National Labor Court* 51 P.D. (2) 63, 157); van Ert (n 28) 184–5 (Canada) (discussing, among others, *Canadian Foundation for Children, Youth and the Law v Canada (Attorney General)* [2004] 1 SCR 76).

[141] See eg Sloss, 'United States' (n 91) 524–5 (discussing, among others, *El Al Israel Airlines, Ltd v Tsui Yuan Tseng* 525 US 155, 168 (1999)); Kretzmer (n 29) 292–5 (Israel) (discussing, among others, HCJ 785/87, *Afu v IDF Commander* 42(2) P.D. 4 (English tr [1990] 29 ILM 139)).

[142] See eg *Medellin v Texas* 552 US 491, 513 (2008) ('It is, moreover, well settled that the United States' interpretation of a treaty "is entitled to great weight"'). In other States, courts give conclusive weight to executive views on specific treaty-related issues that are constitutionally committed to executive decision-making. See eg Aust (n 28) 484 (United Kingdom); Dugard (n 86) 471–2 (South Africa); van Ert (n 28) 186–8 (Canada). However, to the best of my knowledge, the United States is the only country where the nation's highest court has expressly adopted an interpretive canon favouring deference to the executive branch across the full spectrum of treaty interpretation questions.

[143] Kretzmer (n 29) 292 (discussing, among others, HCJ 785/87 *Afu v IDF Commander* 42(2) P.D. 4).

[144] Garlicki and others (n 66) 399 (discussing, among others, *K Galstyan V. S.A.* 726/99).

[145] See eg Aust (n 28) 482–3 (United Kingdom); Dugard (n 86) 471–2 (South Africa) (discussing, among others, *Kolbarschenko v King* NO 2001 (4) SALR 336 (C)); Jayawickrama (n 16) 267–70 (India); Nollkaemper (n 87) 362–3 (Netherlands) (discussing, among others, Central Appeals Tribunal 21 July 2006, LJN No AY 5560); Paulus (n 79) 221–3 (Germany) (discussing, among others, Görgülü BVerfGE 111, 307, Engl Tr BVerfG, 2 BvR 1481/04 of 14 October 2004); van Ert (n 28)

A distinct interpretive issue concerns treaty-based protection for the rights of private parties. Transnationalist judges recognize that many treaties are designed to protect the rights of private parties. Accordingly, they interpret treaties in a manner that accords significant protection to treaty-based private rights.[146] In contrast, nationalist judges sometimes apply a presumption that treaties ordinarily regulate horizontal relations between States, not vertical relations between States and private parties.[147] Application of this presumption can lead nationalist courts to construe vertical treaty provisions as if they were horizontal provisions, thereby denying protection for treaty-based private rights. This strategy provides nationalist judges a convenient rationale for declining to apply treaty-based (vertical) constraints on governmental conduct.[148]

The United States is the only State whose courts have adopted an explicit interpretive presumption that treaties do not create rights for private parties. Courts in other States approach the matter as a straightforward interpretive question, without adopting a presumption for or against private rights.[149] If the treaty text, on its face, indicates that the parties intended to confer rights on private parties, domestic courts will typically enforce those rights, subject to constraints on judicial enforcement of unincorporated treaties in dualist States.[150]

C. Constitutional interpretation

Courts in both monist and dualist States apply treaties to help elucidate the meaning of constitutional provisions. South Africa and India are two leading

---

186–8 (Canada) (discussing *Pushpanathan v Canada* [1998] 1 SCR 982; *Château-Gai Wines Ltd v Attorney General of Canada* [1970] Ex CR 366).

[146] See eg Aust (n 28) 484–7 (United Kingdom); Dugard (n 86) 472–4 (South Africa); Garlicki and others (n 66) 400–7 (Poland) (discussing, among others, Judgment of 21 November 2003 (I CK 323.02), OSNC 2004 nr 6, item 103); Jayawickrama (n 16) 266–72 (India) (discussing *Basu v State of West Bengal* [1997] 2 LRC 1; *Visaka v State of Rajasthan* [1997] 3 LRC 361); Nollkaemper (n 87) 345–8 (Netherlands) (discussing, among others, *Central Appeals Court for the Public Service and for Social Security Matters X Y and Z v B.O.Z. Regional Compulsory Insurance Fund* 29 May 1996, 30 NYIL 1998, 241); Paulus (n 79) 211 (Germany) ('[W]hen individual citizens claimed rights against the state on the basis of international law, it was quite natural that the state that had given its word to other states could be regarded also bound toward its own citizens'); Rothwell (n 24) 136 (Australia) ('[O]ne clear trend is that the courts have become more open to hearing matters based on the existence not only of a treaty right recognized under Australian law but also of a right that exists entirely under international law by way of a treaty to which Australia is a party'); van Ert (n 28) 202–7 (Canada).

[147] See Sloss, 'United States' (n 91) 525–6 (discussing, among others, *Gandara v Bennett* 528 F.3d 823, 828 (11th Cir 2008)).

[148] See ibid 539–40.

[149] See eg Aust (n 28) at 484 (United Kingdom) ('There is no presumption that a treaty does not create a right for a private party'); Dugard (n 86) 472 (South Africa) (stating that an incorporated treaty 'creates rights and duties for the individual in the same way that an ordinary statute creates rights and duties'); Garlicki and others (n 66) 400 (Poland) ('It is generally recognized that self-executing [treaty] provisions create rights (and obligations) for private parties'); Nollkaemper (n 87) 347 (Netherlands) ('Dutch law recognizes the fact that states may agree by treaty to grant certain rights to individuals, which they are then entitled to enforce before national courts').

[150] See nn 28–30 and accompanying text.

examples of States where courts routinely invoke treaties and other provisions of international law in the context of constitutional interpretation.[151] The South African Constitution states explicitly: 'When interpreting the Bill of Rights, a court, tribunal or forum... must consider international law; and may consider foreign law.'[152] In light of this constitutional mandate, the South African Constitutional Court has adopted the view 'that the spirit, purport and objects of the bill of rights... are inextricably linked to international law and the values and approaches of the international community'.[153] Similarly, the Indian Constitution stipulates: 'The State shall endeavour to... foster respect for international law and treaty obligations in the dealings of organized peoples with one another.'[154] Accordingly, Indian jurisprudence reflects a view 'that any international convention not inconsistent with the fundamental rights provisions in the Constitution and in harmony with its spirit must be read into those provisions to enlarge the meaning and content thereof'.[155]

Courts in Canada, Germany, Israel, and Poland also apply treaties to help interpret domestic constitutional provisions, but they do so less regularly than the Indian Supreme Court or the South African Constitutional Court.[156] The judicial practice of using international law in constitutional interpretation has provoked sharp controversy in both Australia and the United States. In Australia, Justice Kirby was a strong advocate for judicial application of international law in constitutional interpretation, but he never persuaded a majority of the High Court to follow his recommended approach.[157] The United States Supreme Court has occasionally cited treaties to support its interpretation of a contested constitutional provision; in all such cases the majority's reliance on international law provoked a strong critical response from the dissenting Justices.[158]

Recent judicial practice in the United Kingdom merits separate discussion. Since Britain does not have a written, constitutional Bill of Rights, British courts rely on other sources of law to protect the fundamental rights that, in most other countries, are protected by a written Constitution. The Human Rights Act, enacted in 1998,

---

[151] See Dugard (n 86) 457–71 (South Africa) (discussing, among others, *Prince v President Cape Law Society* 2002(2) SALR 794 (CC)); Jayawickrama (n 16) 245–7, 266–72 (India) (discussing, among others, *Visaka v State of Rajasthan* [1997] 3 LRC 361).

[152] S Afr Const s 39(1).

[153] Dugard (n 86) 462 (quoting N Botha, 'The Role of International Law in the Development of South African Common Law' (2001) S Af Ybk Intl L 253, 259).

[154] India Const s 51.

[155] Jayawickrama (n 16) 246 (discussing, among others, *Visaka v State of Rajasthan* [1997] 3 LRC 361).

[156] See Garlicki and others (n 66) 404–5 (Poland) (discussing, among others, Judgment of the Constitutional Court of 20 March 2006 (K 17/05); Judgment of the Constitutional Court of 11 October 2006 (P 3/06)); Kretzmer (n 29) 298–301 (Israel) (discussing, among others, HCJ 112/77 *Foguel v Broadcasting Authority* 31 P.D. (3) 657); Paulus (n 79) 230–3 (Germany) (discussing, among others, BVerfGE 111, 307 (2004)); van Ert (n 28) 197–201 (Canada) (discussing, among others, *R v Hape* [2007] SCC 26).

[157] See Rothwell (n 24) 156–8 (discussing, among others, *Al-Kateb v Godwin* [2004] HCA 37).

[158] See eg *Graham v Florida* 130 S Ct 2011 (2010); *Roper v Simmons* 543 US 551 (2005); *Lawrence v Texas* 539 US 558 (2003).

'effectively incorporated the [European Convention on Human Rights] into English law'.[159] Since passage of the Act, British courts routinely apply the European Convention to protect individual rights that, in many other countries, would be regarded as constitutional rights.[160]

D. Self-execution in monist States

Judicial doctrine in monist States distinguishes between treaties that are directly applicable as law and treaties that are not directly applicable. Many States use the terms 'self-executing' and 'non-self-executing' to distinguish between these two classes of treaty provisions.[161] When a court holds that a treaty is self-executing, it typically acts in a transnationalist mode to facilitate the domestic application of treaty-based international norms. When a court holds that a treaty is not self-executing, it generally acts in a nationalist mode to shield the domestic legal system from the influence of treaty-based legal norms.[162] Judicial doctrine invariably grants judges some discretion to determine which treaties are self-executing. Transnationalist judges exercise their discretion in a manner that pushes more treaties into the self-executing category. Nationalist judges exercise their discretion in a manner that pushes more treaties into the non-self-executing category.

South Africa's Constitution includes an explicit textual distinction between self-executing and non-self-executing treaty provisions.[163] Although the Constitution refers explicitly to 'self-executing' treaties, it does not define the term 'self-executing', nor does it identify criteria for distinguishing between self-executing and non-self-executing treaties. The South African courts have not yet issued a definitive ruling to clarify the meaning of the self-execution clause in the South African Constitution.[164] Accordingly, there is an ongoing scholarly debate as to which treaties, if any, are self-executing in South Africa.[165] Ultimately, the resolution of that question may have little practical significance because the South African Constitutional Court is one of the most transnationalist courts in the world: it regularly applies treaties and customary international law to help construe both statutory and constitutional provisions.[166]

Domestic courts in Germany, Poland, and the Netherlands are also fairly transnationalist, insofar as they take a fairly broad view of which treaties are self-executing. In all three countries, courts generally hold that treaty provisions

---

[159] Aust (n 28) 487.

[160] See ibid 487–91 (discussing, among others, *A(FC) and others v Secretary of State* [2004] UKHL 56).

[161] See eg Dugard (n 86) 453–5 (South Africa); Garlicki and others (n 66) 400–3 (Poland); Wildhaber and others (n 69) 659 (Switzerland).

[162] See Sloss, 'United States' (n 91) 527–9 (discussing, among others, *Intl Café SAL v Hard Rock Café Intl (USA), Inc* 252 F.3d 1274 (11th Cir 2001)).

[163] See S Afr Const s 231(4) (n 80).

[164] See Dugard (n 86) 454.

[165] See ibid 453–5.

[166] See ibid 457–73 (discussing, among others, *S v Makwanyane* 1995 (3) SA 391 (CC); *S v Williams* 1995 (3) SALR 632 (CC)).

designed to benefit private parties are invocable by private parties and directly applicable by the courts, subject to one caveat.[167] To be directly applicable, 'a treaty provision has to be sufficiently clear to function as "objective law" in the domestic legal order'.[168] Courts in all three countries have stated or assumed that most substantive provisions of the European Convention on Human Rights and other human rights treaties are self-executing.[169]

The self-execution jurisprudence in Germany, Poland, and the Netherlands is characteristic of most European Union countries because judicial decision-making in those countries is heavily influenced by the European Court of Justice (ECJ), now known as the Court of Justice of the European Union (CJEU). Earlier ECJ case law 'establishes that European law requires the direct effect of community law in the domestic legal order. Moreover, the ECJ demands supremacy of European over domestic law'.[170] Thus, once a legal instrument 'has been adopted by a competent EU body, it . . . becomes automatically incorporated into the system of law binding on the national level [in Poland] and must be enforced by all national authorities, in particular by the national courts'.[171] For States who are members of the European Union, this is a 'consequence of EU membership', and member States have 'no alternative but to follow the established rules'.[172]

In contrast to European jurisprudence, self-execution doctrine in the United States is analytically incoherent.[173] Courts and commentators agree that non-self-executing treaties are not directly applicable by domestic courts, but they do not agree why this is so. Some sources suggest that non-self-executing treaties are not incorporated into domestic law. A distinct view holds that non-self-executing treaties are part of domestic law, but they are a special type of law that courts are precluded from applying directly.[174] Under the latter approach, there is further

---

[167] See Garlicki and others (n 66) 400–7 (Poland) (discussing, among others, *The Interagra Judgment* Judgment of 14 June 1988 (II CR 367/87), OSP 1990 nr 9, item 705); Nollkaemper (n 87) 341–8 (the Netherlands) (discussing, among others, Central Appeals Tribunal, *Management Board of Employee Insurance Benefits Agency v X* 14 March 2003, 36 NYIL 2006, 466); Paulus (n 79) 209–12 (Germany).

[168] Nollkaemper (n 87) 333 (the Netherlands). See also Garlicki and others (n 66) 400 (courts in Poland recognize a treaty as self-executing if it has been drafted 'in a manner allowing its use as an exclusive legal basis for resolving an individual case or controversy', citing Resolution of the Supreme Court of 5 October 1974, III CZP 71/73, OSN CP 1975, no 5, item 72); Wildhaber and others (n 69) 659 (under Swiss doctrine, 'a treaty is self-executing if it is sufficiently precise and clear to constitute the basis of decision in a concrete case').

[169] See Garlicki and others (n 66) 405 (Poland) (discussing Judgment of 28 November 2001 (V KKN 565/99, Lex nr 51620)); Nollkaemper (n 87) 342 (the Netherlands); Paulus (n 79) 232 (Germany) (discussing BVerfGE 111, 307 (2004); English tr BVerfG, 2 BvR 1481/04 of 14 October 2004).

[170] Paulus (n 79) 210 (citing *Internationale Handelsgesellschaft*, Case 11/70, [1970] ECR 1125).

[171] Garlicki and others (n 66) 385.

[172] Ibid.

[173] For recent commentary, see CA Bradley, 'Self-Execution and Treaty Duality' (2009) Sup Ct Rev 131; CM Vazquez, 'Treaties as Law of the Land: The Supremacy Clause and the Judicial Enforcement of Treaties' (2008) 122 Harv L Rev 599; EA Young, 'Treaties as "Part of Our Law"' (2009) 88 Tex L Rev 91.

[174] See D Sloss, 'Non-Self-Executing Treaties: Exposing a Constitutional Fallacy' (2002) 36 UC Davis L Rev 1, 10–18 (summarizing different theories of non-self-execution).

disagreement as to why courts are precluded from applying non-self-executing treaties.[175] In practice, courts often hold that treaties are non-self-executing when an individual invokes a vertical treaty provision as a constraint on government action, but they almost never hold that transnational treaty provisions are non-self-executing.[176] Thus, the net effect of judicial doctrine is that US courts tend to adopt a transnationalist approach in cases involving transnational treaty provisions, but they tend to adopt a nationalist approach in cases involving vertical treaty provisions.[177] In contrast, courts in Germany, the Netherlands, Poland, and South Africa adopt a fairly consistent transnationalist approach for both vertical and transnational treaty provisions.

IV. Domestic Courts and Treaty Compliance

The final part of this chapter addresses the respective roles of the judicial, executive, and legislative branches in promoting compliance with treaty obligations.[178] My central claim is that these roles vary greatly depending on whether the treaty provision at issue is horizontal, vertical or transnational. In brief, executive officials have primary responsibility for ensuring compliance with horizontal treaty obligations; the judiciary's role is marginal. With respect to transnational treaty provisions, though, the positions are reversed. The judiciary plays a central role in promoting compliance with transnational treaty provisions and the executive is marginalized. The picture for vertical treaty provisions is more complex.

A. Horizontal treaty provisions

As discussed above, domestic courts rarely apply horizontal treaty provisions.[179] Consequently, domestic courts bear little responsibility for promoting compliance with horizontal treaty provisions. This proposition is generally true for both monist and dualist States, regardless of whether courts adopt a nationalist or transnationalist approach.

---

[175] See ibid 12–18. In some cases, courts hold that a treaty provision is not self-executing because it is too vague or ambiguous for judicial enforcement. See CM Vazquez, 'The Four Doctrines of Self-Executing Treaties' (1995) 89 AJIL 695, 713–15. This version of the doctrine is similar to the non-self-execution doctrine applied in many European countries. See nn 167–8 and accompanying text. In other cases, courts hold that a treaty provision is not self-executing—even though it is sufficiently unambiguous to permit judicial enforcement—because the political branches have manifested a desire to preclude or limit judicial enforcement. See Sloss (n 174) 35–44. This version of the doctrine has no apparent analogue in other countries.

[176] See Sloss, 'United States' (n 91) 534–6.

[177] See ibid 529–39.

[178] Given space constraints, the present analysis does not address the role of sub-national governments. However, it is noteworthy that sub-national governments in some States exert significant influence over matters related to treaty compliance. See eg Beemelmans and Treviranus (n 62) 328–9 (Germany); Wildhaber and others (n 69) 635–7 (Switzerland).

[179] See nn 99–101 and accompanying text.

With respect to horizontal treaties, the relationship between the legislative and executive branches depends on the specific treaty provision at issue and the constitutional structure of a given State. For example, the North Atlantic Treaty obligates parties to assist other member States if there is 'an armed attack against one or more of them in Europe or North America'.[180] The duty to provide mutual assistance in the event of an armed attack is a paradigmatic horizontal treaty obligation. If a NATO State was the target of an armed attack, the executive branches in other NATO States would have primary responsibility for providing assistance under the treaty. In some States, depending on constitutional separation of powers considerations, the executive might have to obtain legislative approval before committing troops and weapons to the defense of an ally. Regardless, there is no State in which the judiciary would be responsible for implementing the nation's treaty obligation to help defend against an armed attack.

B. Transnational treaty provisions

Conventional wisdom holds that the executive branch has primary responsibility in most countries for implementing international treaty obligations. This is certainly not true for transnational treaty provisions. Consider, for example, the 1929 Warsaw Convention, which regulates international air carriage.[181] In the United States, Congress never enacted legislation to implement the Convention, but courts routinely apply it as a self-executing treaty.[182] In many dualist States,[183] and even in some monist States,[184] the legislature has enacted legislation to promote effective implementation of the Convention. In all States—whether the treaty is considered self-executing or is implemented by legislation—the judiciary bears primary responsibility for resolving disputes between private parties that are governed by the Convention.[185] In the United States, the executive branch occasionally submits amicus briefs to present its views about the proper interpretation of contested treaty provisions, but that is the extent of executive branch participation in treaty implementation.

Domestic courts play a crucial role in promoting compliance with transnational treaty provisions. A simple example helps illustrate this point. The New York Convention obligates States to recognize and enforce foreign arbitral awards.[186]

---

[180] North Atlantic Treaty (adopted 4 April 1949, entered into force 24 August 1949) 34 UNTS 243, Art 5.

[181] Warsaw Convention (n 86). The Warsaw Convention is the predecessor of the 1999 Montreal Convention (n 103).

[182] See eg *Olympic Airways v Husain* 540 US 644 (2004); *El Al Airlines v Tsui Yuan Tseng* 525 US 155 (1999).

[183] See eg Kretzmer (n 29) 284 (Israel); Rothwell (n 24) 138 (Australia); van Ert (n 28) 186 (Canada).

[184] See Dugard (n 86) 470 (South Africa); Nollkaemper (n 87) 355 (the Netherlands).

[185] See eg Dugard (n 86) 470 (South Africa); Kretzmer (n 29) 290–1 (Israel); Nollkaemper (n 87) 355 (the Netherlands); Rothwell (n 24) 138 (Australia); van Ert (n 28) 186 (Canada).

[186] See New York Convention (n 85) Art III ('Each Contracting State shall recognize arbitral awards as binding and enforce them . . . under the conditions laid down in the following articles').

Assume that a French company and a Japanese company submit a commercial dispute to an arbitral panel in accordance with UNCITRAL arbitration rules.[187] The panel orders the Japanese company to pay damages to the French company, but the Japanese company refuses to pay. That refusal, by itself, does not constitute a violation of Japanese treaty obligations because the company's refusal to pay is not attributable to the Japanese Government.[188] Now assume that the French company files suit in a Japanese court to enforce the arbitral award. If the Japanese court rules against the French company, and that ruling cannot be justified under the New York Convention,[189] the judicial decision would constitute a violation of Japanese treaty obligations because that judicial decision is attributable to the Japanese Government under principles of State responsibility.[190] Conversely, if the Japanese court orders the Japanese company to pay—and especially if the court attaches company assets to secure payment—the court is effectively acting as an agent of the international legal system to ensure Japanese compliance with national treaty obligations. Either way, the domestic court is the primary decision-maker whose decision determines whether the nation complies with its treaty obligations. This is characteristic of transnational treaty provisions: in most cases involving transnational provisions, domestic courts serve as the primary interface between the domestic and international legal systems, and their decisions effectively determine whether the nation complies with its treaty obligations.

The preceding observations about domestic judicial application of transnational treaty provisions apply equally to both monist and dualist States, with one caveat. In dualist States, the legislature typically incorporates a treaty before courts will apply it to resolve private disputes. Once the treaty is incorporated, though, judicial application is quite similar in both monist and dualist States. Moreover, the distinction between nationalist and transnationalist approaches has scant effect on judicial application of transnational treaty provisions. The global record of compliance with transnational treaty provisions is quite good because national courts in most States apply transnational treaty provisions routinely—either directly or indirectly—to help resolve private disputes arising from cross-border activities.

---

[187] UNCITRAL is the UN Commission on International Trade Law. For information, see UNCITRAL <http://www.uncitral.org/uncitral/en/about_us.html>.

[188] See J Crawford, *The International Law Commission's Articles on State Responsibility: Introduction, Text and Commentaries* (CUP, Cambridge 2002) 91–3.

[189] Article V of the New York Convention identifies several circumstances in which '[r]ecognition and enforcement of the [foreign arbitral] award may be refused'. See New York Convention (n 85) Art V. Under the treaty, States are obligated to enforce foreign arbitral awards unless there is a valid reason for non-enforcement as specified in Art V.

[190] See Crawford (n 188) 61 (reprinting Art 4 of the Articles on Responsibility of States for Internationally Wrongful Acts: 'The conduct of any State organ shall be considered an act of that State under international law, whether the organ exercises legislative, executive, judicial or any other functions').

C. Vertical treaty provisions

The relationship among the legislative, executive, and judicial branches in implementing vertical treaty provisions is a complex subject that defies simple generalizations. Patterns vary by nation and by individual treaty.

States sometimes achieve compliance with vertical treaty obligations even if no government official or agency makes a conscious decision to implement that obligation. For example, when the United States ratified the International Covenant on Civil and Political Rights (ICCPR), the executive branch assured the Senate that no implementing legislation was necessary because the United States could fulfil its treaty obligations by applying pre-existing laws.[191] Thus, when a court issues an injunction to enjoin enforcement of a State law that violates federal laws prohibiting race-based discrimination, one could say that the court is promoting compliance with US treaty obligations under Articles 2 and 26 of the ICCPR,[192] even if the court never considers a treaty-based argument. Similarly, commentators have noted that Canadian courts implement Canada's obligations under the ICCPR, at least partially, by applying the Canadian Charter of Rights and Freedoms and other provisions of domestic law.[193]

Leaving aside cases where States achieve compliance almost unwittingly, we turn next to situations where some government actor makes a conscious decision to apply or interpret a particular treaty in a particular way. Here, it is helpful to discuss the 1951 Refugee Convention[194] and the 1967 Refugee Protocol[195] to illustrate the interplay among the legislative, executive, and judicial branches in the domestic application of vertical treaty provisions.

In dualist States, the legislature must first decide whether to enact legislation to incorporate a treaty into domestic law. Professor Aust says: 'It is invariable British practice never to ratify a treaty until any [necessary implementing] legislation has first been made.'[196] Like Britain, other dualist States generally refrain from ratifying treaties with vertical obligations unless or until they have enacted the implementing legislation necessary to ensure compliance with those obligations.[197] Accordingly, Australia, Canada, and the United Kingdom have all adopted

---

[191] See D Sloss, 'The Domestication of International Human Rights: Non-Self-Executing Declarations and Human Rights Treaties' (1999) 24 YJIL 129, 183–8.

[192] See ICCPR (n 4) Art 2(1) (guaranteeing protection of rights 'without distinction of any kind, such as race, colour . . . or other status'); ibid Art 26 (guaranteeing 'all persons equal and effective protection against discrimination on any ground such as race, colour . . . or other status').

[193] See G van Ert, *Using International Law in Canadian Courts* (2nd edn Kluwer Law International, The Hague 2008) 332–51.

[194] Convention Relating to the Status of Refugees (adopted 28 July 1951, entered into force 22 April 1954) 189 UNTS 137.

[195] Refugee Protocol (n 6).

[196] Aust (n 28) 486.

[197] See eg Hollis, 'Comparative Approach' (n 20) 32–4 (concluding that 'the case studies presented support a practice by which States join treaties only after they have established the domestic legal means to comply with the treaty's obligations'); van Ert (n 28) 204 ('The usual Canadian practice is not to allow treaties requiring domestic implementation to enter into force for Canada until the federal government has ensured the treaty's implementation').

legislation to implement the Refugee Convention and Protocol.[198] Even in monist States, legislatures often enact implementing legislation to promote effective domestic implementation of vertical treaty provisions. Although South Africa's Constitution provides expressly for self-executing treaties,[199] the South African legislature enacted legislation in 1998 to implement the nation's treaty obligations under the Refugee Convention and Protocol.[200] Similarly, in the United States, even though the Constitution specifies that ratified treaties are the 'supreme Law of the Land',[201] Congress enacted legislation in 1980 to implement US obligations under the Refugee Protocol.[202] Thus, in both monist and dualist States, legislative decisions about whether and how to implement vertical treaty provisions can have a significant impact on the nation's compliance with its treaty obligations.

Once a vertical treaty provision enters into force domestically, the executive branch assumes primary responsibility for treaty implementation. In most States, if an individual seeks admission to the country as a refugee, an executive officer will make the initial determination whether the individual qualifies for refugee status. That determination might promote or hinder treaty compliance, depending on three factors: first, whether the treaty has been fully or partially incorporated into domestic law (either by legislation or self-execution); second, in so far as the treaty is unincorporated or partially incorporated, whether the executive decision-maker construes relevant domestic laws in conformity with the nation's treaty obligations; and finally, in so far as the decision-maker consults or applies the treaty, whether that decision-maker interprets the treaty in accordance with internationally agreed principles of treaty interpretation.

If a treaty has been fully incorporated into domestic law—either by self-execution or by legislative incorporation—the decision-maker will presumably apply the treaty as a rule of law to reach his/her decision. In the Netherlands, for example, the 2000 Aliens Act authorizes executive officers to grant residence permits for 'Convention refugees', without defining the term. Hence, the statute effectively directs administrative (and judicial) decision-makers to apply the treaty definition of refugees.[203] The statute therefore promotes treaty compliance by directing decision-makers to apply the treaty definition as a rule of domestic law. In contrast, when a treaty remains wholly or partially unincorporated, decision-makers must apply domestic rules in place of or in tandem with the international rule; this raises a greater risk of non-compliance. In Australia, for example, the 1951 Convention has been only partially incorporated into domestic law.[204] Consequently, Australian decision-makers have been hesitant to rely too heavily on the

---

[198] See Aust (n 28) 490–1 (United Kingdom); Rothwell (n 24) 138–40 (Australia); van Ert (n 28) 175 (Canada).

[199] See S Afr Const (n 80).

[200] See Dugard (n 86) 473–4.

[201] US Const Art VI cl 2.

[202] The Refugee Act of 1980, PL No 96-212, 94 Stat 102 (17 March 1980). The United States is not party to the 1951 Refugee Convention, but US ratification of the 1967 Protocol effectively means that the United States is bound by key provisions of the Convention.

[203] See Nollkaemper (n 87) 336–7.

[204] See Rothwell (n 24) 138–40.

Convention in construing domestic statutes,[205] producing a less-than-perfect record of treaty compliance.

If a vertical treaty provision remains wholly or partially unincorporated, executive decision-makers might still construe relevant domestic statutes in harmony with the nation's international treaty obligations. For example, Canada's Immigration and Refugee Protection Act directs executive officers to construe the Act 'in a manner that... complies with international human rights instruments to which Canada is a signatory'.[206] The statutory reference to 'human rights instruments' presumably includes the Refugee Convention and Protocol.[207] Similarly, in other States, executive officers may have a constitutional or statutory duty to perform their governmental functions in a manner that is consistent with the nation's treaty obligations—including, perhaps, obligations contained in unincorporated or partially incorporated treaties.[208] Alternatively, executive officials might simply decide as a policy matter to exercise their statutory responsibilities in a way that promotes compliance with treaty obligations. In any case, if executive officials have a conscious goal of exercising their powers and duties consistently with international treaty obligations, treaty compliance is enhanced. Conversely, if executive officials are heedless of treaty obligations, their actions are less likely to promote treaty compliance.

Executive officials are often required to interpret treaties. An official charged with deciding whether to grant an applicant refugee status would need to interpret the treaty if the treaty itself provides the governing rule of domestic law (via self-execution or full incorporation), or if some law or policy directs the official to take account of the treaty when construing the relevant domestic statute. In construing the treaty, the official might be guided to some extent by unilateral national policy interests. However, he or she might also be guided by internationally agreed principles of treaty interpretation.[209] If executive decision-makers give great weight to internationally agreed principles, their decisions are more likely to promote treaty compliance. Conversely, if decision-makers give more weight to unilateral policy interests, there is a greater risk that their decisions will obstruct treaty compliance.

If the legislative and executive branches both viewed treaty compliance as a paramount objective, the courts would rarely be asked to decide cases involving alleged treaty violations. However, legislatures sometimes fail to implement treaties

---

[205] See ibid 153–6.   [206] van Ert (n 193) 155.

[207] Canada is party to both the 1951 Refugee Convention and the 1967 Refugee Protocol. See United Nations Treaty Collection <http://treaties.un.org/Home.aspx?lang=en>.

[208] In the United States, the President and subordinate executive officers have a constitutional duty to 'take Care that the Laws be faithfully executed'. US Const Art II s 3. Most commentators agree that the Take Care Clause creates a legal duty for executive officers to implement treaties. See ET Swaine, 'Taking Care of Treaties' (2008) 108 Colum L Rev 331. The US Supreme Court decision in *Medellin v Texas*, 552 US 491 (2008), is not to the contrary. *Medellin* stands for the proposition that there are constitutional limits on the President's power to implement treaties, but *Medellin* is consistent with the view that the President has a duty to act within the scope of his constitutional powers to execute treaties.

[209] For more on the VCLT rules on treaty interpretation, see Chapter 19.

that require legislative implementation, and executive officers sometimes fail to honour such treaties. When that happens, courts may be asked to decide whether governmental conduct is consistent with the nation's treaty obligations. Ultimately, the impact of judicial decision-making depends heavily on whether domestic courts pursue a nationalist or transnationalist course. In States where courts tend to adopt a transnationalist approach, domestic courts can play a key role in promoting treaty compliance. India, the Netherlands, and Poland are leading examples of States where domestic courts actively promote compliance with vertical treaty obligations.[210] However, in States where courts tend to apply a nationalist approach, domestic courts effectively cede authority to the legislative and executive branches to make key decisions affecting compliance with vertical treaty provisions. Israel and the United States exemplify this nationalist approach, although judicial decision-making in Israel is moving in a more transnationalist direction.[211]

Finally, it is important to note that legislative action or inaction can nudge courts in a more nationalist or transnationalist direction. In the United Kingdom, for example, Parliament's decision to enact the Human Rights Act 1998 has undoubtedly moved judicial decision-making in British courts in a more transnationalist direction.[212] In the United States, however, the Senate's consistent practice of attaching non-self-executing declarations to human rights treaties has clearly pushed judicial decision-making in a more nationalist direction.[213] These examples illustrate the complexity of the relationship among legislative, executive, and judicial branches in shaping governmental decisions that affect compliance with vertical treaty obligations.

Conclusion

International law and international relations scholars have written extensively about theories of national compliance with international legal obligations, including treaty obligations.[214] However, the scholarly literature has paid scant attention to domestic courts as key institutional actors whose decisions can promote or impede treaty compliance.[215] The preceding discussion suggests that more detailed study of domestic courts is warranted. Granted, domestic judicial decisions have little impact on national compliance with horizontal treaty obligations. However, domestic courts play a central role in ensuring compliance with transnational treaty obligations. Moreover, domestic courts have the potential to play a very significant

---

[210] See Garlicki and others (n 66) (Poland); Jayawickrama (n 16) (India); Nollkaemper (n 87) (the Netherlands).

[211] See Kretzmer (n 29) (Israel); Sloss 'United States' (n 91).

[212] See Aust (n 28) 483–4, 487–90.

[213] See eg MS Flaherty, 'Global Power in an Age of Rights: Historical Commentary, 1946–2000' in *Intl Law in the US Supreme Court* (n 114).

[214] See eg JL Goldsmith and EA Posner, *The Limits of International Law* (OUP, Oxford 2005); AT Guzmán, *How International Law Works* (OUP, Oxford 2008); R Goodman and D Jinks, 'How to Influence States: Socialization and International Human Rights Law' (2004) 54 Duke L J 621.

[215] But see HH Koh, 'Why Do Nations Obey International Law?' (1997) 106 Yale L J 2599.

role in promoting compliance with vertical treaty obligations. Whether that potential is realized depends, to a great extent, on whether domestic courts adopt a nationalist or transnationalist approach to the judicial application of vertical treaty provisions.

Recommended Reading

A Aust, *Modern Treaty Law and Practice* (2nd edn CUP, Cambridge 2007)

E Benvenisti and GW Downs, 'Court Cooperation, Executive Accountability, and Global Governance' (2009) 41 NYU J Intl L and Pol 931

E Benvenisti and GW Downs, 'National Courts, Domestic Democracy, and the Evolution of International Law' (2009) 20 EJIL 59

CA Bradley, 'Self-Execution and Treaty Duality' (2009) Sup Ct Rev 131

X Hanqin and J Qian, 'International Treaties in the Chinese Domestic Legal System' (2009) 8 Chinese J Intl L 299

DB Hollis, MR Blakeslee, and LB Ederington (eds), *National Treaty Law and Practice* (Martinus Nijhoff, Leiden 2005)

D Kretzmer, *The Occupation of Justice: The Supreme Court of Israel and the Occupied Territories* (SUNY Press, Albany 2002)

A Reinisch (ed), *Challenging Acts of International Organizations Before National Courts* (OUP, Oxford 2010)

D Sloss, 'Non-Self-Executing Treaties: Exposing a Constitutional Fallacy' (2002) 36 UC Davis L Rev 1

D Sloss (ed), *The Role of Domestic Courts in Treaty Enforcement: A Comparative Study* (CUP, New York 2009)

DL Sloss, MD Ramsey, and WS Dodge (eds), *International Law in the US Supreme Court: Continuity and Change* (CUP, New York 2011)

ET Swaine, 'Taking Care of Treaties' (2008) 108 Colum L Rev 331

G van Ert, *Using International Law in Canadian Courts* (Irwin Law Inc, Toronto 2008)

CM Vazquez, 'The Four Doctrines of Self-Executing Treaties' (1995) 89 AJIL 695

CM Vazquez, 'Treaties as Law of the Land: The Supremacy Clause and the Judicial Enforcement of Treaties' (2008) 122 Harv L Rev 599

MA Waters, 'Creeping Monism: The Judicial Trend Toward Interpretive Incorporation of Human Rights Treaties' (2007) 107 Colum L Rev 628

T Webster, 'International Human Rights Law in Japan: The View at Thirty' (2010) 23 Colum J Asian L 241

J Wouters, A Nollkaemper, and E de Wet, *The Europeanization of International Law* (TMC Asser Press, The Hague 2008)

EA Young, 'Treaties as "Part of Our Law"' (2009) 88 Tex L Rev 91

16

State Succession in Respect of Treaties

Gerhard Hafner and Gregor Novak

Introduction

In a generally accepted definition that is also enshrined in the 1978 Vienna Convention on Succession of States in Respect of Treaties (VCSST), State succession is conceived as the 'replacement of one State by another in the responsibility for the international relations of territory'.[1] The legal regime governing State succession is significant because no new State or territory can exist outside the legal order of the community of States. In order to avoid jeopardizing predictability and stability—the central objects of international law—it is necessary to regulate the legal status and acceptance of new States as well as other alterations in the responsibility for the international relations of territory within this community. Consequently, the regulation of treaty relations in cases of State succession ('treaty succession') is widely acknowledged to be a critical question for international relations and international law. The law and practice of State succession is highly contextual, with the outcome of each case strongly influenced by the relevant political situation. As a result, there is no single rule for all cases of treaty succession. Nonetheless, for certain cases general rules and practices can be identified that may serve as a guide for future cases related to succession, even if they may not prove truly determinative.

Legal problems associated with State succession have arisen since ancient times.[2] In the modern era of sovereign States, early notable cases included the unifications of Germany[3] and Italy,[4] the transfers of Alsace and Lorraine,[5] the emergence of the United States of America[6] (US), and the independence of colonies in Latin

---

[1] VCSST (concluded 23 August 1978, entered into force 6 November 1996) 1946 UNTS 3, Art 2. This definition does not include cases involving a mere change of government (such as the change from the Soviet Union to the Russian Federation), a constitutional change combined with a name change (such as the change from the Czechoslovak Socialist Republic (CSSR) to the Czechoslovak Federative Republic (CSFR)), or the mere change in the State's designation.

[2] Cf H Grotius, *De jure belli et pacis*, lib II, cap ix, tit xii; see also DP O'Connell, 'State Succession in Relation to New States' (1970-II) 130 RdC 101 *et seq* (quoting Aristotle's *Politics*, noting that when a city lost its identity, its political successor was to bear the burden of paying the city's debts).

[3] A Zimmermann, *Staatennachfolge in völkerrechtliche Verträge* (Springer, Berlin 2000) 136.

[4] DP O'Connell, *The Law of State Succession* (CUP, Cambridge 1956) 17 *et seq* ('O'Connell 1956').

[5] DP O'Connell, 'Reflections on the State Succession Convention' (1979) 39 ZaÖRV 734 *et seq*.

[6] O'Connell 1956 (n 4) 34.

America.[7] The First World War raised a new wave of related problems with the break-up of the Austro-Hungarian Empire,[8] the dissolution of the Ottoman Empire,[9] and the emergence of new States on the territory of Tsarist Russia resulting from its eventual transformation into the Union of Soviet Socialist Republics (USSR).[10]

A further important source for the law and practice of State succession emerged from the period of European colonialism.[11] The process of decolonization in the period after the Second World War was particularly significant, both in quantitative terms and in terms of its impact on international relations.[12] UN membership rose from 50 in 1945 to over 190 today largely due to this process.[13] Decolonization also provided the relevant political context within which the International Law Commission (ILC) formulated draft articles on State succession in respect of treaties, leading up to the 1978 VCSST.[14] The VCSST, however, came relatively late in the decolonization process. The wave of newly emerging States receded soon thereafter, and for a time, the question of State succession seemed to become less significant in international relations and international law.[15]

Prior to 1989, therefore, it was widely assumed that the system of existing States (particularly in Europe) was unlikely to change due to the then existing East-West stalemate.[16] The end of the Cold War and the breakdown of the communist system dramatically changed that situation in Europe and Central Asia. Germany incorporated the former German Democratic Republic (GDR), the Baltic States, liberated from the iron clamp of the Soviet system, gained independence and other former Union Republics of the USSR followed. At about the same time,

---

[7] Cf these and further cases in M Huber, *Die Staatensuccession: völkerrechtliche und staatsrechtliche Praxis im XIX. Jahrhundert* (Duncker & Dumblot, Leipzig 1898); O'Connell 1956 (n 4) 16–74.

[8] O'Connell 1956 (n 4) 4, 35 *et seq*; Zimmermann (n 3) 81 *et seq*.

[9] Zimmermann (n 3) 82.

[10] XJ Eudin and HH Fisher, *Soviet Russia and the West, 1920–1927: A Documentary Survey* (Stanford University Press, Stanford 1957) 6–14.

[11] Cf R Aldrich and J Connell, *The Last Colonies* (CUP, Cambridge 1998); UNGA, 'Report of the Special Committee on the Situation with regard to the Implementation of the Declaration on the Granting of Independence to Colonial Countries and Peoples for 2010' (6 July 2010) 65th Session, UN Doc Supp No 23 (A/65/23).

[12] On the relationship between the decolonization process and treaty succession before 1989, see generally M Craven, *The Decolonization of International Law: State Succession and the Law of Treaties* (OUP, Oxford 2007).

[13] DF Vagts, 'State Succession: The Codifiers' View' (1993) 33 VJIL 275, 277–80.

[14] UN Conference on Succession of States in Respect of Treaties, First Session, Vienna, 4 April–6 May 1977, Official Records, vol I: Summary records of the plenary meetings and of the meetings of the Committee of the Whole (A/CONF.80/16); UN Conference on Succession of States in Respect of Treaties, Resumed Session, Vienna, 31 July–23 August 1978, Official Records, vol II: Summary records of the plenary meetings and of the meetings of the Committee of the Whole, UN Doc A/CONF.80/16/Add.1; UN Conference on Succession of States in Respect of Treaties, 1977 session and resumed session 1978, Vienna, 4 April–6 May 1977 and 31 July–23 August 1978, Official Records, vol III: Documents of the Conference, UN Doc A/CONF.80/16/Add.2.

[15] ST Korman, 'The 1978 Vienna Convention on Succession of States in Respect of Treaties: An Inadequate Response to the Issue of State Succession' (1992) 16 Suffolk Transnat'l L Rev 174, 178.

[16] D Türk, 'The Dangers of Failed States and a Failed Peace in the Post Cold War Era' (1995) 27 NYU J Intl L & Pol 625 *et seq*.

the Socialist Federal Republic of Yugoslavia (SFRY) collapsed in the midst of war and eventually opened the door to the creation of, so far, six or even seven new States.[17] Finally, the Czechoslovak Federative Republic (CSFR) (formerly the Czechoslovak Socialist Republic (CSSR)) peacefully dismembered into two new States: the Czech and the Slovak Republics. Outside the European context, the new State of East Timor seceded from Indonesia after several decades of occupation. This new wave of emerging States imbued the issue of State succession with new significance, especially given the legal problems flowing from the density of pre-existing relations among affected States.[18]

Although this latest and seemingly last major wave of State succession is largely over, legal problems of treaty succession remain relevant. Growing cross-border activities of States and non-State actors have created a need for greater stability and predictability, leading to an even greater density of treaty relations among States and in relation to international organizations (IOs). Future cases of State succession seem likely, if not inevitable, such as the case of the recent independence of South Sudan.[19] These cases will occur under varying circumstances and entail different legal problems and solutions. In the past, different theories of treaty succession, reaching from the continuity doctrine to the clean-slate rule, were developed in conformity with the prevailing political circumstances, although presently the continuity doctrine prevails to a certain extent. Broadly speaking, different treatment can be expected depending on the type of State succession at issue: cession, merger and incorporation, dissolution and separation, as well as (the now largely historical) cases of emerging newly independent States.[20]

---

[17] The relevant number depends on whether Kosovo is counted as a new State.

[18] MA Martins, 'An Alternative Approach to the International Law of State Succession: *Lex Naturae* and the Dissolution of Yugoslavia' (1993) 44 Syracuse L Rev 1019, 1020.

[19] On 14 July 2011, the Republic of South Sudan was admitted to UN membership: UN Doc A/RES/65/308. Prior to South Sudan's independence, a 2009 'handbook' addressed the relevant problems of treaty succession. Cf Office of the President of the Government of Southern Sudan in collaboration with the Public International Law & Policy Group, *South Sudan: A Guide to Critical Post-2011 Issues, Legal Handbook* (December 2009). The handbook noted that the 'Republic of Sudan will be considered the "continuing state" and Southern Sudan will be considered a newly independent or "successor state" '. The handbook also dealt with 'continuing treaty obligations', noting that:

> [a]n examination of international legal principles demonstrates that a successor state . . . has the option of choosing which treaties signed by the predecessor/continuing state (the Republic of Sudan) it would like to uphold. However, based on recent state practice, the international community would likely expect an independent Southern Sudan to continue the Republic of Sudan's treaty obligations. Exceptions to this presumption of continuity occur when: (1) both parties agree otherwise, (2) the treaty is not relevant to the new state's territory, or (3) continuity would frustrate the treaty's object and purpose.

The handbook suggested that South Sudan identify all treaties that fall under the listed exceptions and 'thus would not continue to apply to Southern Sudan after independence'. Likewise, it suggested that South Sudan follow State practice and inform other States of its 'intentions to abide by the terms of the predecessor State's treaty obligations as part of the process of achieving international recognition and establishing diplomatic relations'. The handbook noted that '[i]n some instances, new states must also deposit an instrument of accession with the appropriate treaty depository to affirm a commitment to be bound by a treaty's terms'.

[20] See in more detail Part I.D, 403 *et seq.*

Unlike other areas of the law of treaties, State succession is not governed by the 1969 Vienna Convention on the Law of Treaties (VCLT).[21] The relevant legal regulations must thus generally be found in customary international law. As Brigitte Stern has pointed out,[22] most of this customary international law could be understood as merely the 'translation' of certain general principles of international law into the State succession context, such as the *uti possidetis* principle,[23] the principle of effectiveness of territorial regimes,[24] the fundamental principle of consent as expressed *inter alia* in Article 57 of the VCLT, and the principle relating to a fundamental change of circumstances (Article 62 of the VCLT). As a result of the ILC's codification efforts, some of the relevant customary international law is mirrored in the VCSST. In contrast to the VCLT, however, the VCSST reflects the respective customary rules only to a limited extent. Moreover, as a treaty, the VCSST has not received widespread adherence,[25] although it entered into force due to the limited number of ratifications required.[26]

The present state of affairs relating to treaty succession proves that the VCSST can serve as a reliable guide to the current State of customary international law only regarding some of its provisions (eg Article 11's continuation of all boundary treaties, Article 15's 'moving treaty boundaries' rule), while others constitute progressive development of international law (eg Article 31 in cases of incorporation; Article 34 in cases of separation). In any case, modern treaty succession distinguishes not only among the different cases of State succession, such as merger or dismemberment, but also among specific categories of treaties that are subject to different rules. Thus, it is difficult to identify a generally applicable legal regime of treaty succession. It still depends on the individual case and on the particular political context in which succession occurs.

---

[21] VCLT Art 73 (providing that the VCLT shall not prejudge any question that may arise in regard to a treaty from a succession of States); see also M Villiger, *Commentary on the 1969 Vienna Convention on the Law of Treaties* (Martinus Nijhoff, Leiden 2009) 895–904.

[22] B Stern, 'La Succession d'Etats' (1996) 262 RdC 164–70.

[23] ST Bernárdez, 'The "*Uti Possidetis Juris* Principle" in Historical Perspective' in K Ginther and others (eds), *Völkerrecht zwischen normativem Anspruch und politischer Realität: Festschrift für Karl Zemanek zum 65. Geburtstag* (Duncker & Humblot, Berlin 1994). The ICJ described the *uti possidetis* principle, ie the principle of the intangibility of frontiers inherited from colonization, as a 'general principle, which is logically connected with the phenomenon of the obtaining of independence, wherever it occurs'. *Case concerning the Frontier Dispute (Burkina Faso/Republic of Mali)* [1986] ICJ Rep 554, 565.

[24] Stern (n 22) 167 *et seq.*

[25] As of 2012, twenty-two States are parties to the VCSST; fourteen others are signatories. The latest State to accede was the Republic of Moldova on 9 February 2009.

[26] According to VCSST Art 49(1), the Convention entered into force on the thirtieth day following the date of deposit of the fifteenth instrument of ratification or accession.

I. General Framework: Definitions, Theories, Effects, and Taxonomy of Treaty Succession

A. Definitions

The VCSST's definition of a 'succession of States' as laid out above[27] is widely accepted.[28] Although it only refers to cases of internationally lawful State succession,[29] most cases of interest in this general overview may be subsumed under this definition due to its otherwise broad scope.[30] Similarly, the VCSST provides a definition of 'successor State' as the State 'which has replaced another State on the occurrence of a succession of States'.[31] Accordingly, a successor State need not necessarily be a new State, but could comprise an old one acquiring new territory to which the regime of State succession applies.[32] The law of treaty succession is also structured around a number of other concepts, including those of 'treaty' and 'reservation', which are defined in the VCSST in the same terms as in the VCLT.[33] In contrast, a 'newly independent state' is defined in Article 2(1)(f) of the VCSST as a specific type of successor State, namely one 'the territory of which immediately before the date of the succession of States was a dependent territory for the international relations of which the predecessor State was responsible'.

B. The spectrum of opinions: from *tabula rasa* to universal succession

Over the years, different authors[34] and international institutions, such as the International Law Association (ILA),[35] have tried to come to grips with the legal problems ensuing from State succession. Historically, however, the applicable international law has remained rather vague, primarily because State practice itself has been and remains largely inconsistent. Different theories and approaches to treaty succession have become prominent depending on the respective political context as well as the changing attitude of States regarding the integration of new States into the existing community. As a result, a near permanent fluctuation

---

[27] Cf n 1 and accompanying text.

[28] Cf Opinion No 1 of the Arbitration Commission of the Conference on Yugoslavia (Badinter Commission), 29 November 1991 [1992] 31 ILM 1494–7, 1(e); *Award of the Arbitration Tribunal for the Determination of the Maritime Boundary between Guinea-Bissau and Senegal, 31 July 1989* (1992) RGDIP 265 (English translation available at <http://www.icj-cij.org/docket/files/82/11289.pdf>).

[29] VCSST Art 6 provides: 'The present Convention applies only to the effects of a succession of States occurring in conformity with international law and, in particular, the principles of international law embodied in the Charter of the United Nations.'

[30] Thus, it has been noted that certain revolutionary governments were allowed not to respect entirely the obligations of their predecessors. Whether this was simply a consequence of negotiation or a case of succession is debatable. P Dailler, M Forteau, and A Pellet, *Droit International Public* (8th edn LGDJ, Paris 2009) 601.

[31] VCSST Art 2(1)(c).   [32] Cf VCSST Art 15.

[33] Cf VCSST Art 2(1) on the use of terms.   [34] Cf Craven (n 12) 29–51.

[35] ILA, *The Effect of Independence on Treaties: A Handbook* (Stevens & Sons, London 1965).

between theories has occurred. For instance, Makonnen[36] has distinguished: (i) the theory of universal succession first put forward by Grotius and later adopted by a number of jurists;[37] (ii) the popular continuity theory (a variation of the universal succession theory taking regard of obligations of a 'political character');[38] (iii) the organic substitution theory of continuity (as first advanced by Huber and constituting an adaptation of the universal succession theory);[39] (iv) the clean-slate theory[40] with its socialist aberration (the latter also considering radical changes in government as cases of State succession);[41] (v) a theory of continuity of rights and obligations by virtue of the general principles of law, attributed to O'Connell;[42] and (vi) moderate theories of continuity, which took an intermediate stance between the clean-slate theory and the universal succession theory.[43] It can quite safely be argued that each of these theories was developed subject to a particular political context and ideology. Changes in context and ideology frequently prompted a change of theories.[44]

In general, the spectrum of legal conceptions and attitudes of States to treaty succession has ranged between two poles: the clean-slate rule (*tabula rasa* doctrine or negative theory), on the one hand, and the theory of continuity, on the other. The clean-slate rule holds that upon a change of sovereignty over territory the new sovereign is absolutely free of any of the obligations that bound its predecessor. This doctrine puts emphasis on a theory of complete and automatic discontinuity of all rights and obligations upon State succession.[45] Its adherents emphasize State sovereignty as the reason a new State is not bound by the obligations of its predecessor. They also stress that succession in domestic law, where the successor assumes the rights and obligations of the predecessor, is different from succession in international law, where sovereign States are the main actors.[46] Under the continuity theory, in contrast, all treaties existing at the date of succession continue to bind the successor State, which in some sense inherits all pre-existing treaties whether or not the predecessor State continues to exist.[47]

---

[36] This list is taken from Y Makonnen, *International Law and the New States of Africa: A Study of the International Legal Problems of State Succession in the Newly Independent States of Eastern Africa* (Ethiopian National Agency for UNESCO 1983) 129; cf also A Reinisch and G Hafner, *Staatensukzession und Schuldenübernahme* (Wien, Berlin 1995) 35.

[37] Makonnen (n 36) 129.

[38] Ibid 130. Makonnen associates this theory with Gabba, Appleton, and Gidel.

[39] Ibid 131.

[40] Ibid 132. This theory is also called the *tabula rasa* theory.

[41] NV Zakharova, 'O mezhdunarodnoi pravosub-ektnosti gosudarstv pri socialnoi revolucii' (1960) Soviet Ybk of Intl L 157, 164; Makonnen (n 36) 133.

[42] Makonnen (n 36) 137.

[43] Ibid 142.

[44] EG Bello, 'Reflections on Succession of States in the Light of the Vienna Convention on Succession of States in Respect of Treaties of 1978' (1980) German Ybk Intl L 296–7.

[45] Makonnen (n 36) 133 with reference to a slightly modified theory of Keith according to whom rights would pass to the successor, but not obligations. AB Keith, *The Theory of State Succession: With Special Reference to English and Colonial Law* (Kessinger, London 1907) 5.

[46] R Mullerson, 'New Developments in the Former USSR and Yugoslavia' (1993) 33 VJIL 299, 301.

[47] AM Beato, 'Newly Independent and Separating States' Succession to Treaties: Considerations on the Hybrid Dependency of the Republics of the Former Soviet Union' (1994) 9 Am U J Intl L & Pol'y 525, 536.

As discussed below, under customary international law and the VCSST, more sophisticated and more complex rules have developed than would follow from simply applying either the clean-slate principle or the continuity theory's rule of universal succession. Nevertheless, the dichotomy of universal succession and clean slate sheds light on the varying concepts of international law underlying the respective approaches[48] and serves to frame the variety of available solutions to the highly contextualized problems of State succession.

C. International and domestic legal effects of treaty succession

The international legal effects of treaty succession may be understood as the establishment of new treaty relations different from those that existed between the other State party and the predecessor State. Those effects occur, moreover, irrespective of whether the predecessor State continues to exist or not. Although it may be disputed in some details—in particular with regard to the existence of a norm of general international law and its precise content—the view expressed by Kelsen seems thus still to be adequate: '[D]evolution of obligations and rights of one State on another does not imply identity of these obligations and rights; it means only that general international law imposes upon the successor State certain obligations and confers upon it certain rights which have the same content as certain obligations and rights of the predecessor'.[49]

In contrast to the attention devoted to the international legal effects of treaty succession, with the exception of O'Connell,[50] the doctrine has remained rather silent as to the legal effect of treaty succession in domestic law. That, however, does not diminish the complexity of the issue. If treaty succession is understood as some sort of 'novation'[51] creating new treaty relations, the question remains how the legal effect of these new relations is produced within the domestic legal order. Unlike the conclusion of other new treaties by the relevant State, no parliamentary approval is required in order to establish new treaty relations via treaty succession. This raises several interesting, but as yet, unanswered questions. For example, can a rule of general international law on treaty succession, if it exists, replace the procedure required by the relevant national constitution to make a treaty applicable within that domestic legal system?[52]

---

[48] In this context, Degan discerns, on the one hand, a collectivist (*solidariste*) and, on the other, a voluntarist conception of international law. Cf VD Degan, 'Création et disparition de l'Etat' (1999) 279 RdC 205.

[49] H Kelsen, *Principles of International Law* (Rinehart and Company, New York 1952) 296. Seen as such, the creation of new treaty relations can also be compared to the institution of subrogation relevant, in particular, to the international legal regime of investment protection. Cf O Udokang, *Succession of New States to International Treaties* (Oceana, Dobbs Ferry 1972) 109.

[50] DP O'Connell, *State Succession in Municipal Law and International* Law (CUP, Cambridge 1967) vol II, 335.

[51] Ibid 349 *et seq*.

[52] Thus, it can even be asked whether a treaty subject to implementing legislation because of its non-self-executing nature remains applicable or requires new implementing legislation assuming the continuation of a treaty in relation to a new State. Cf ibid.

D. Taxonomy of State succession

The ILC, when elaborating what became the VCSST, did not consistently differentiate among legal effects according to the various cases of succession. But it is undeniable that certain differences exist, particularly in light of the latest practice.[53] For instance, practice indicates that it is important to distinguish cases of State succession where the predecessor continues to exist from those where it ceases to exist, as in cases of dismemberment. Important cases of State succession broadly include the cession of part of a State forming a new State (eg generally the cases of newly independent States) or becoming part of another already existing State (eg the cases of Hong Kong, Macao, and Walvis Bay), the separation of parts of territory from a continuator State (eg the case of the former USSR), the complete breaking up of a State into different new ones (eg the case of the former SFRY), the uniting of two or more States into a new one (eg the case of Yemen), or the mere disappearance of a State, the territory of which is incorporated into another State (particularly the case of the GDR and the FRG).

Treaty succession operates differently in each of these cases and thus suggests the following taxonomy for devising an overview of the main customary rules: (1) newly independent States, (2) cession, (3) incorporation, (4) merger, (5) dissolution, and (6) separation. Additionally, annexation is discussed as a further category posing special problems due to its unlawful nature. At the same time, treaty succession does not correlate only with a particular category of State succession; it can also turn on the type of treaty at issue. Particular types of treaties, such as those relating to boundaries or those whose continued application would be incompatible with the object and purpose of the treaty concerned, are governed by special rules or are not affected by the legal regime of State succession at all.

1. Newly independent States

The VCSST singles out for special treatment newly independent States, defined as successor States 'the territory of which immediately before the date of the succession of States was a dependent territory for the international relations of which the predecessor State was responsible'.[54] This category of States was based on the wave of new States emerging from the process of decolonization,[55] a process that pushed

---

[53] Cf the collection of recent practice in J Klabbers and others (eds), *State Practice Regarding State Succession and Issues of Recognition: The Pilot Project of the Council of Europe* (Kluwer, London 1999).

[54] VCSST Art 2(1)(f).

[55] The ILC considered the category of 'newly independent states' to include 'any case of emergence to independence of any former dependent territories, whatever its particular type may be', including 'colonies, trusteeships, mandates, protectorates, etc'. Cf [1974] YBILC, vol II(1), 176; Zimmermann (n 3) 228 *et seq*. However, such States raise certain problems regarding the definition of their predecessor; so, for instance, the Vienna Conference on State Succession with Regard to Treaties adopted a resolution that denied South Africa the status as predecessor of Namibia. This resolution, nevertheless, did not decide which other State could qualify as such, whether it was Germany as the former colonial power of Namibia ('Deutsch Südwest Afrika') or whether it was Great Britain whose dominion South Africa was at that time, UN Doc A/CONF.80/32.

the issue of State succession itself onto the ILC's codification agenda.[56] At the time, the ILC could gain very little from precedents outside this process. Many newly created developing countries rejected any idea of a continuity of treaty relations. In their view, the continuity theory was developed by certain industrialized countries under conditions foreign to the situation of these new developing States.[57] These successors to the colonial powers wanted to become free of the treaties concluded by those powers. They invoked principles of State sovereignty, equality, self-determination, and permanent sovereignty over natural wealth and resources to justify this outcome. In terms of treaty succession, they favoured an optional theory where they could choose which treaties to continue; a position they repeatedly voiced during the ILC codification process.

In light of these claims and their historical context, it was no surprise that the ILC felt itself compelled to separate the regime on State succession into two distinct legal regimes, one based on the optional theory and covering 'newly independent States', and the other applying a modified continuity regime to all other cases of State succession. This distinction was then incorporated into the VCSST as well the Vienna Convention on Succession of States in Respect of State Property, Archives, and Debts of 1983.[58] Thus, it was a distinction of great importance for cases of newly independent States, both before and shortly after the adoption of the VCSST. But as the process of decolonization came to an end, the newly independent States classification lost much of its relevance. By 1999, the category was no longer employed when the ILC submitted to the UN General Assembly draft articles on nationality of natural persons in relation to the succession of States.[59]

2. Cession of territory

Cession of territory has resulted from changes of territory without the creation of a new State or the extinction of an old one. Cession was defined by Oppenheim as 'the transfer of sovereignty over state territory by the owner-state to another state'.[60] Cases of cession[61] were seen in the 1867 cession of Alaska,[62] the 1871 cession of Alsace and Lorraine by France to the German Empire, the Treaties of Versailles, St Germain and Trianon following the First World War, the Treaties following the Second World War relating to Germany, Italy, Romania, and Hungary, the 1962

---

[56] At its first session in 1949, the ILC did not give priority to the topic of State succession. [1968] YBILC, vol II, 213 [29]. At its 1962 session, however, prompted by UNGA resolution 1686 (XVI) of 18 December 1961, the ILC included on its priority list the topic of succession of States and governments.

[57] Makonnen (n 36) 201; see also DP O'Connell, 'Independence and Problems of State Succession' in WV O'Brien (ed), *The New Nations in International Law and Diplomacy* (Stevens and Sons, London 1965) 7.

[58] UN Doc A/CONF.117/14 (not yet in force).

[59] But see n 229 and accompanying text with respect to the ILC's current work on reservations.

[60] RY Jennings and AD Watts (eds), *Oppenheim's International Law* (9th edn Longman, London 1992) vol I, 227.

[61] Cf generally in addition to subsequently cited more recent sources O'Connell (n 50).

[62] O'Connell 1956 (n 4) 31 *et seq* and 54 *et seq.*

cession of West New Guinea to Indonesia,[63] the 1994 transfer of Walvis Bay from South Africa to Namibia[64] as well as the retransfers of Hong Kong[65] and Macao[66] from the United Kingdom (UK) and Portugal to China in 1997 and 1999, respectively.

3. Incorporation

The VCSST is silent on a situation of one or more States being incorporated into another and the latter ceasing to exist. However, the incorporation of the GDR, which became part of the FRG in 1990,[67] provides a recent and important example of this situation. Previous cases of incorporation occurred with the United States' 1845 accession of Texas,[68] Italian unification in 1860, the 1866 expansion of Prussia,[69] the 1871 creation of the German Empire,[70] Britain's 1886 incorporation of Burma,[71] France's 1885/96 incorporation of Madagascar,[72] the United States' 1898 incorporation of Hawaii,[73] Belgium's 1908 incorporation of independent Congo,[74] the Kingdom of Yugoslavia's incorporation of Montenegro,[75] Malaysia's 1963 incorporation of Singapore,[76] and arguably, the unification of the two Vietnamese States in 1976.[77]

4. Annexation of territory

Annexation, which may be understood as the 'forcible acquisition of territory' by a State,[78] is to be kept separate from both cession and incorporation. Whereas in former centuries annexation was considered as lawful,[79] presently, it is deemed to contradict basic rules of general international law, such as the principle of the non-use of force. Being wrongful, annexation poses particular problems due to the dependency of the applicability of the respective rules on treaty succession on the lawfulness of State succession.[80]

5. Merger

Important cases of merger, where two or more States decide to form a new State, have been observed in the 1958 merger of Egypt and Syria to form the United Arab

---

[63] Zimmermann (n 3) 176 *et seq.* [64] Ibid 447 *et seq.*
[65] R Mushkat, 'Hong Kong and Succession of Treaties' (1997) 46 ICLQ 181.
[66] Zimmermann (n 3) 444 f. [67] Ibid 245–82.
[68] Ibid 134 *et seq.* [69] Ibid 135 *et seq.* [70] Ibid 136.
[71] Zimmermann (n 3) 137. [72] Ibid. [73] O'Connell 1956 (n 4) 21 *et seq.*
[74] Ibid 22 *et seq.* [75] Zimmermann (n 3) 141 *et seq.*
[76] S Jayakumar, 'Singapore and State Succession: International Relations and Internal Law' (1970) 19 ICLQ 398–423.
[77] Zimmermann (n 3) 123 *et seq.*
[78] See R Hofmann, 'Annexation' in R Wolfrum (ed), *The Max Planck Encyclopedia of Public International Law* (OUP, Oxford 2006) online edition at <www.mpepil.com> [1].
[79] Ibid [5].
[80] Cf notes 29–30 and accompanying text; Zimmermann (n 3) 24–36, who concludes that in the case of an illegal acquisition of territory a modified version of the rules of State succession apply.

Republic (UAR),[81] the 1964 merger of Tanganyika and Zanzibar to form Tanzania as well as the union, based on a 1990 merger, of the Yemen Arab Republic and the State of the People's Democratic Republic of Yemen.[82]

6. Separation

In cases of separation, one of the entities existing on the territory of the predecessor State separates and forms a new State, whereas the other part continues its legal personality and is, as such, identical with that predecessor State, although to a more limited geographical extent. Recent examples of separation include the separation of Eritrea from Ethiopia in 1993,[83] and the USSR. In the latter case, the Russian Federation was generally considered to have continued the legal personality of the USSR as—in the Russian phraseology—a continuator ('prodolžatel'), even if this result was initially controversial in doctrine.[84] Following the dismemberment of former Yugoslavia, Montenegro (and Kosovo if it is recognized as a new State) separated from Serbia, which continued its legal personality.[85]

7. Dissolution

Dissolution occurs when a part (or parts) of the territory of a State separate and form one or more new States with the predecessor State ceasing to exist. The most important recent cases of dissolution are provided by the dissolution of the former Yugoslavia (SFRY) as well as of Czechoslovakia (CSFR). An earlier case arose in the dissolution of the Republic of Great Colombia into Ecuador, New Grenada, and Venezuela.[86]

II. The Substance of the Law of Treaty Succession

As pointed out above, the dichotomy between the clean-slate rule and the continuity theory have framed the debate about the law of treaty succession. At the same time, whatever the default rules of treaty succession may be in particular instances, the ability of successor States and third States to agree on their treaty relations must be kept in mind. Since at least the nineteenth century, the clean-slate (*tabula rasa*) rule[87] was favoured by some and considered complementary to the principle

---

[81] E Cotran, 'Some Legal Aspects of the Formation of the United Arab Republic and the United Arab States' (1959) 8 ICLQ 346–90.

[82] C Dunbar, 'The Unification of Yemen: Process, Politics and Prospects' (1992) Middle East J 456; R Goy, 'La reunification du Yémen' (1990) AFDI 249.

[83] R Goy, 'L'Independence de l'Erythrée' (1993) AFDI 337–56.

[84] Cf also in regard to the case of the former SFRY, Craven (n 12) 67–75.

[85] See nn 153–73 and accompanying text.

[86] E Williamson and J Osborne, 'A U.S. Perspective on Treaty Succession and Related Issues in the Wake of the Breakup of the USSR and Yugoslavia' (1993) 33 VJIL 261.

[87] Makonnen concludes that 'thus the opinions of jurists (were) almost unanimous in holding that the clean-slate rule doctrine is most widely accepted and whatever contrary evidence is available in state

of self-determination.[88] Developing countries especially relied on this doctrine to resist treaties of the former colonial powers that were dictated upon them and in whose elaboration they did not take part. The ILC later accepted it for the category of newly independent States, even if the practice before 1978 was not entirely conclusive in this regard.

On the other hand, the continuity theory is supported by the fact that the rules of general customary international law are likewise binding upon new States, including newly independent States, despite their inability to participate in their formation. As a result, the denial of the continued application of at least certain general multilateral treaties is difficult to justify. Moreover, irrespective of the special case of newly independent States, other political considerations speak against a general application of the clean-slate doctrine and in favour of a presumption of treaty continuity. Modern States are embedded in an intensive set of commonly shared values and interests governing their social life, all of which are the product of very dense treaty relations. The density of these treaty relations rules out any clear-cut clean-slate concept. State social life, which is to a significant extent and increasingly also cross-border, undoubtedly relies on continuity. A breakdown of these relations in the case of a change of Statehood would severely damage the stability of international society. In addition, international society can no longer be—if it ever could have been—conceived as a society merely of States, but also includes non-governmental actors, in particular individuals. This circumstance is visible in nearly all parts of the world, but especially in Europe, where transnational instead of intergovernmental transboundary cooperation is the rule.[89] A termination of treaties carving the legal frame and foundation for those transnational contacts and cooperation would simultaneously and necessarily entail an end to such transnational policy. Only when the new social situation created by a political transformation involving State succession changes radically, would a termination of treaty relations seem an appropriate solution. State practice seems to have sensed this need. Hence, the clean-slate rule has not reflected the state of affairs of existing international relations, particularly in relation to States belonging to the same geographical region or those purporting to share the same basic values.[90]

But despite these considerations in favour of the continuity doctrine, and their applicability to the latest wave of State succession cases, no settled State practice supports the exclusive general validity of this doctrine. The only conclusion which can safely be drawn is that a universally applicable rule of international law for

---

practice (was) governed by treaties and by other political arrangements'. Makonnen (n 36) 129 (referring to authorities like Jenks, Lissitzyn, Bokor-Szegő, and McNair).

[88] Beato (n 47) 525, 537.

[89] According to the universalists who rely on Kant, international relations rest on the transnational bonds between individuals, all of whom share common interests. Cf 'Taking Reichs Seriously: German Unification and the Law of State Succession' (1990) 104 Harv L Rev 588, 602.

[90] Thus, the US departed from the position laid down in the *Restatement (Third) of the Foreign Relations Law of the United States* (1987) in favour of considerations dictated by the need for stability of legal rights and obligations. Cf Williamson and Osborne (n 86) 264.

treaty succession does not yet exist, neither one based on the clean-slate rule nor on that of continuity[91] (although a certain tendency towards the continuity theory cannot be denied). Rather, different rules and practices have emerged for the categories of State succession outlined above and with respect to particular kinds of treaties.

A. Unilateral declarations and devolution agreements

Before assessing the specific categories of State succession and rules for particular types of treaties, a preliminary word is necessary on the practice of unilateral declarations and devolution agreements. As a general matter, the legal effects of treaty succession result from the application of a generally applicable rule of international law, either derived from customary international law or treaty law (eg the VCSST for those States party to it). Moreover, in almost all cases there can be a specific rule agreed upon by the relevant States, ie the new State and the State which is the other party to the relevant treaty.

A new State may also conclude a devolution agreement with the predecessor State or issue a unilateral declaration on treaty succession.[92] Both of these instruments purport to indicate those treaties to which the new State has (or has not) succeeded. As the VCSST confirms, however, neither a unilateral declaration by the successor State (Article 9 of the VCSST) nor a devolution agreement between the predecessor and successor State (Article 8 of the VCSST) can of itself exercise any legal effect on another State party. The other party to the treaty must usually acquiesce or explicitly express its consent thereto pursuant to the notion that a treaty cannot create rights or obligations for a third party without its consent (the *pacta tertiis* rule).[93] A declaration of succession has no legal effect with respect to State succession in treaties, other than as a notification of succession by a newly independent State pursuant to Articles 17 and 18 of the VCSST. In this respect, Article 9(1) of the VCSST undoubtedly reflects customary international law when it provides that a State does not succeed in treaties 'by reason only of the fact that the successor State has made a unilateral declaration providing for the continuance in force of the treaties in respect of its territory'. This understanding is confirmed by the practice of the UN Secretary-General according to which general declarations of succession do not suffice to establish the State's status as a party to a multilateral treaty.[94] Thus, the Secretary-General's practice is to duly comply with a new State's request to circulate its 'general' declaration of succession to all UN members, but not to 'consider such a declaration as a valid instrument of succession to any of the treaties deposited with him' and to inform the new State thereof.[95]

---

[91] Udokang (n 49) 164.

[92] Cf UN Legislative Series, Materials on Succession of States, UN Doc ST/LEG/SER.B/14.

[93] See J Charney, 'Universal International Law' (1993) 87 AJIL 529, 536.

[94] Treaty Section, UN Office of Legal Affairs, *Summary of Practice of the Secretary-General as Depositary of Multilateral Treaties* (UN, New York 1994), UN Doc ST/LEG/7/Rev. 1 ('UN Depositary Practice').

[95] Ibid [303].

Despite the lack of legal effect for third States,[96] devolution agreements remain significant in practice. They can oblige the successor State in relation to the predecessor State in two ways, either by (a) declaring accession or succession in respect of certain treaties covered by the devolution agreement,[97] or, (b) in the case of automatic succession under customary international law, not denying such automatic succession.[98] As to multilateral treaties, it has been the practice of depositaries, particularly the UN Secretary-General, to request a successor State to specially confirm the succession expressed in its respective devolution agreement.[99] In general, devolution agreements enunciate the attitude of the relevant successor State[100] and thus further predictability and stability in the context of an area of law otherwise tending towards uncertainty.

B. Newly independent States

Part III (Articles 16–30) of the VCSST prescribes specific rules for treaty succession involving newly independent States. Article 16 adopts the clean-slate rule as a general rule for these States. Article 17 provides an additional right of optional succession to newly independent States, allowing them to establish their status as parties to any multilateral treaty by a notification of succession, unless it is otherwise established that it would be incompatible with the treaty's object and purpose or would radically change the conditions of the treaty's operation. Article 27 also allows a newly independent State to provisionally apply a multilateral treaty by notification with any other party that expressly agrees to such provisional application or by reason of its conduct can be considered to have so agreed.[101]

The practice was inconsistent at the time of the VCSST's adoption. After 1978, however, newly independent States by and large followed the model prescribed by the VCSST.[102] The VCSST provisions, namely Articles 17 and 27, applied a modified version of the clean-slate doctrine known as Nyerere formula.[103] According to the eponym of this formula, Julius Nyerere, the first president of Tanzania, international agreements dating from colonial times should be renegotiated when a State becomes independent, since the nation should not be bound by a treaty that it was not in a sovereign position to conclude at that time. Accordingly, such a State should be entitled—upon its independence—to review the international treaties of its colonial power and decide which of the agreements it would accept and which repudiate. Such an 'optional' approach to events of State succession was certainly

---

[96] Cf Makonnen (n 36) 281.

[97] K Zemanek, *Gegenwärtige Fragen der Staatensukzession, Berichte der Deutschen Gesellschaft für Völkerrecht* (CF Mueller, Karlshue 1964) 77.

[98] Zimmermann (n 3) 155.

[99] See [1962] YBILC, vol II, 122 [133] (discussed in A Watts, *The International Law Commission, 1949–1998* (Clarendon Press, Oxford 1999) vol II(2), 1019).

[100] See A Aust, *Modern Treaty Law and Practice* (2nd edn CUP, Cambridge 2007) 373.

[101] On provisional application generally, see Chapter 9.

[102] Zimmermann (n 3) 830.

[103] See Y Makonnen, 'State Succession in Africa: Selected Problems' (1986-V) RdC 146–8.

not new; however, it can hardly be stated that it was already recognized by customary international law.

In contrast to the pure *tabula rasa* (clean-slate) doctrine, the Nyerere doctrine differs to the extent that under the former a new State emerges without any of the obligations of the predecessor State whereas, under the latter doctrine, this is only an assumption. The Nyerere doctrine does not rule out or prejudice the possibility or desirability of renewal (after a legal interruption during the succession) of commitments or agreements of mutual interest to the parties concerned. It does, however, reject any categorization of international obligations between those which the successor State would have to accept and those which it could reconsider. Nyerere also created a formula for the practical application of this doctrine, which provides for an interim reflection period during which some of the predecessor's treaties apply provisionally while the successor chooses which treaties it will renew or renegotiate and which it will set aside.[104] Both the doctrine and the formula, with case specific variations, served as a framework for State succession among East African States as well as for many other developing countries. In most instances, predecessor States and third States have accepted—if not indeed supported—the application of the Nyerere doctrine. Thus, while at the time of its elaboration the practice of newly independent States was not entirely consistent, the practice of States after 1978 shows that the provisions of Part III of the VCSST have largely been followed. In particular, States followed the practice of provisional application enshrined in Article 27 of the VCSST in respect of multilateral treaties, in line with the Nyerere formula. With the end of the process of decolonization, however, these rules for newly independent States have ceased to be particularly pertinent in modern practice.

C. Succession of States other than newly independent States

1. Cession of territory

Article 15 of the VCSST prescribes the so-called 'moving treaty boundaries' rule to cases of cession of territory.[105] According to this rule, when part of the territory of

---

[104] See J Nyerere, 'Problems of State Succession in Africa: Statement of the Prime Minister of Tanganyika' (1962) 11 ICLQ 1211 f. ('[W]e are willing on a basis of reciprocity to continue in force for a period of two years from Independence Day all valid bilateral treaties which would otherwise have ended when we became an independent State. During that two-year period we will negotiate with the States concerned with a view, where appropriate, to continuing or changing these treaties in a mutually acceptable manner. We are also willing and anxious that Tanganyika should play her role in the family of nations by participation not only in those multi-lateral treaties which the United Kingdom may have extended or applied to the territory of Tanganyika but also even in those not so applied. However, because of the wide range of subject-matter covered by such treaties and also of the difficulties of applying the interim solution proposed for bilateral treaties, we have considered that the simplest solution is to deal with each of these treaties by specific arrangements as soon as possible. We are, however, prepared on a basis of reciprocity to treat such instruments as being in force vis-a-vis other States who rely upon them in their relations with Tanganyika.')

[105] VCSST Art 15 (Succession in respect of part of territory) provides that:

> When part of the territory of a State, or when any territory for the international relations of which a State is responsible, not being part of the territory of that State, becomes part of the territory of another State: (*a*) treaties of the predecessor State cease to be in force in respect

one State becomes part of the territory of another State, treaties of the former cease to apply to the territory while the treaties of the latter extend to the territory. Both State practice before 1978 as well as thereafter has confirmed the validity of this rule as part of customary international law.[106] For example, the retransfer of Hong Kong by the UK to China was subject to particular agreements,[107] which per se do not have third party effect, but were largely guided by the 'moving treaty boundaries' rule.

2. Incorporation

The VCSST did not anticipate or accommodate the important recent case of the former German Democratic Republic (GDR) that was incorporated into the Federal Republic of Germany (FRG). Neither Article 31 of the VCSST relating to the 'effects of a uniting of States in respect of treaties in force at the date of the succession of States'[108] nor Article 15 relating to the 'succession in respect of part of territory' covered the complete incorporation of one State by another, existing State.

Without embarking on the Berlin question or the FRG and GDR's legal status after the Second World War, it suffices to proceed from the undisputed fact that the GDR enjoyed the status of a State as a separate subject of international law. It was recognized by the community of States irrespective of the particular view of the FRG, and was, like the FRG, a UN member and a State party to numerous bilateral and multilateral treaties. But, by 3 October 1990, the GDR ceased to exist as a separate State and became part of the FRG. This unification did not result in a new State; the FRG remained identical with the FRG before unification, albeit enlarged in terms of territory and population. Still on the eve of this event, both States agreed among themselves on the regulation of questions relating to treaties concluded by them. Article 11 of the Unification Treaty[109] provided for the automatic extension of treaties concluded by the FRG to the entire territory of the State, in application of the principle of 'moving treaty boundaries', except for certain explicitly mentioned treaties deemed of a 'highly political' nature. As to the GDR's treaties, according to Article 12 of the Unification Treaty, these were to become the subject of negotiations between Germany and the relevant other State Party, taking into account various factors, including the need for protection of confidence, the

---

of the territory to which the succession of States relates from the date of the succession of States; and (*b*) treaties of the successor State are in force in respect of the territory to which the succession of States relates from the date of the succession of States, unless it appears from the treaty or is otherwise established that the application of the treaty to that territory would be incompatible with the object and purpose of the treaty or would radically change the conditions for its operation.

[106] Cf eg Stern (n 22) 169; Zimmermann (n 3) 823 *et seq*.

[107] Cf Joint Declaration of the Government of the United Kingdom of Great Britain and Northern Ireland and the Government of the People's Republic of China on the Question of Hong Kong (signed 19 December 1984) 1399 UNTS 61; Joint Declaration of the Government of the People's Republic of China and the Government of the Republic of Portugal on the Question of Macao (signed 13 April 1987) 1498 UNTS 229.

[108] See Part II.C.3, 412 *et seq*.   [109] [1991] 30 ILM 463.

interests of the States concerned, the FRG's treaty obligations, the competence of the EC, as well as the principles of a free, democratic basic order governed by the rule of law.[110] It was further envisaged that Germany would define its final stance concerning those treaties only after consultations with the other parties to the treaty concerned.[111]

For future situations of incorporation, the case of the former GDR[112] indicates that the rule of Article 31 of the VCSST is not a reliable guide to customary law. In contrast, the principle of the 'moving treaty boundaries' rule generally remains applicable, ie the treaties of the incorporated State cease to apply while the remaining State's treaties remain in force and extend to the enlarged territory.[113]

3. Merger

In contrast to incorporation, the case of Yemenite unification and other instances of a union of States with the predecessor States ceasing to exist, point to Article 31 of the VCSST expressing an emerging customary rule for merger.[114] In this context, the VCSST enshrines a territorially limited continuity approach. In particular, Article 31(1) provides that '[w]hen two or more States unite and so form one successor State, any treaty in force at the date of the succession of States in respect of any of them continues in force in respect of the successor State' unless the States otherwise agree or 'it appears from the treaty or is otherwise established that the application of the treaty in respect of the successor State would be incompatible with the object and purpose of the treaty or would radically change the conditions for its operation'. Article 31(2) provides that any treaty continuing in force under Article 31(1) 'shall apply only in respect of the part of the territory of the successor State in respect of which the treaty was in force at the date of the succession of States' unless, in the case of a multilateral treaty not of the category mentioned in Article 17(3),[115] 'the successor State makes a notification that the treaty shall apply in respect of its entire territory' or, in all cases, unless 'the successor State and the other States Parties otherwise agree'.

The unified Republic of Yemen was created pursuant to a 1990 agreement between North and South Yemen.[116] A corresponding joint letter addressed to

---

[110] Ibid 472; JA Frowein, 'The Reunification of Germany' (1992) 86 AJIL 152, 158.

[111] Cf with respect to consultations Klabbers and others (n 53) 88.

[112] Cf certain exceptions in Zimmermann (n 3) 246–82.

[113] See ILA Committee on Aspects of the Law of State Succession, 'Draft Conference Report Rio de Janeiro Conference' (2008) available at <http://www.ila-hq.org/en/committees/index.cfm/cid/11> 8–10; Zimmermann (n 3) 831.

[114] Zimmermann (n 3) 283–5; O'Connell 1956 (n 4) 71 *et seq*; D Cottran, 'Some Legal Aspects of the Formation of the United Arab Republic and the United Arab States' (1959) 8 ICLQ 346; M Shaw, *International Law* (CUP, Cambridge 2008) 973.

[115] VCSST Art 17(3) provides that '[w]hen, under the terms of the treaty or by reason of the limited number of the negotiating States and the object and purpose of the treaty, the participation of any other State in the treaty must be considered as requiring the consent of all the parties, the newly independent State may establish its status as a party to the treaty only with such consent'.

[116] Agreement between the Yemen Arab Republic and the People's Democratic Republic of Yemen on the Establishment of the Republic of Yemen (done 22 April 1990, entered into force 21 May 1990)

the UN Secretary-General accepted Article 31's direction that the treaties of both States should continue, declaring that 'all treaties and agreements concluded between either the Yemen Arab Republic or the People's Democratic Republic of Yemen and other States and international organizations in accordance with international law which are in force on 22 May 1990 will remain in effect'.[117]

4. Separation

Article 34 is one of the core VCSST provisions, adopting a continuity theory for separating States other than newly independent States. It provides that 'any treaty in force at the date of the succession of States in respect of the entire territory of the predecessor State continues in force in respect of each successor State so formed'. Any treaty that applied only to that part of the territory of the predecessor State, which has become a successor State, is likewise to continue in force in respect of the latter only. With regard to a remaining predecessor State, Article 35 of the VCSST provides that existing treaties remain in force after the succession in respect of the remaining territory, likewise subject to special agreement by the States concerned and the nature of the treaty in question. The ILC itself acknowledged in its commentary on draft Articles 32 to 34, which became Articles 33 to 35 of the VCSST, that State practice contained certain inconsistencies.[118] Nevertheless, the ILC found the practice sufficiently consistent to support their formulation of these draft articles.

In reality, however, inconsistencies in the practice before and after the VCSST's adoption cast doubts as to whether the continuity rule expressed in Article 34 of the VCSST applies to all cases of separation.[119] Generally, the most recent practice of successor States in cases of separation has been less uniform than in the recent cases of dissolution.[120] That practice does nevertheless offer support for Article 34's limitations on the continued legal force of treaties insofar as the States concerned (the parties to the relevant treaty) could otherwise agree or continuity as reflected in Article 34(1) of the VCSST would not apply if 'it appears from the treaty or is otherwise established that the application of the treaty in respect of the successor State would be incompatible with the object and purpose of the treaty or would radically change the conditions for its operation'. With regard to bilateral treaties, this limit is usually reflected in the practice of States through an agreement on a list of treaties that are considered to be still applicable. This list is deemed to be declaratory only;[121] it is normally not submitted to parliamentary approval or

---

translation in [1991] 32 ILM 820 ('[T]here shall be established . . . a full and complete union, based on a merger, in which the international personality of each of them shall be integrated in a single international person called "the Republic of Yemen"').

[117] Ibid.

[118] [1974] YBILC, vol II(1), 260–6.

[119] Williamson and Osborne (n 86) 263 *et seq*.

[120] Cf Klabbers and others (n 53) 100, 102.

[121] See eg the list of bilateral treaties drawn up by Austria and the Czech Republic, 'Promulgation of the Federal Chancellor concerning the bilateral treaties in force between the Republic of Austria and

other domestic constitutional procedures generally required for the conclusion of treaties.[122] Practice also shows that, in the case of multilateral treaties, succession has generally been deemed admissible with *ex tunc* effect upon a notification of succession.[123] In the case of bilateral treaties, however, succession was made subject to individual appraisals by the parties, although generally a tendency towards continuity has been maintained.[124]

The most important recent case of separation concerned the former republics of the USSR. Geopolitical changes on the territory of the former USSR commenced with the demand of the Baltic Republics (Lithuania, Latvia, and Estonia) for their independence as sovereign States in 1989, a status which they had already enjoyed prior to the Second World War.[125] Lithuania declared its independence restored as early as 11 March 1990.[126] But it was only on 6 September 1991 after various events[127] and decrees[128] calling on the community of States to recognize their independence[129] that these States obtained recognition as independent States by the Soviet Union still existing at that moment.[130] The Baltic States did not, however, consider themselves to be new States but identical with those existing prior to the Second World War and occupied since then by the USSR. As a result, they declined any succession in treaties entered into by the USSR.[131]

Following the Baltic States, the other Union Republics[132] also called for independence.[133] Ukraine, Belarus, and Russia formally declared the disintegration of the USSR on 8 December 1991. Signatories of the Agreement of Minsk of 8 December 1991 (Belarus, Russian Soviet Federative Socialist Republic (RSFSR),

the Czech Republic' (31 July 1997) Federal Law Gazette III No 123/1997. Similar lists have been annexed to agreements between other States, see ILA Committee Draft Report (n 113) 14.

[122] In contrast, the United States and Ukraine concluded an international agreement detailing the terms of Ukraine's succession to various US–USSR treaties. Agreement Concerning the Succession of Ukraine to Bilateral Treaties between the United States and the Former Union of Soviet Socialist Republics, with Annex (Exchange of notes at Kiev 10 May 1995) reprinted in (1995) 89 AJIL 761–2. See also S Cummins and D Stewart (eds), [2005] *Digest of United States Practice in International Law 1991–1999* 748–50.

[123] Zimmermann (n 3) 831 *et seq.*

[124] ILA Committee Draft Report (n 113) 27; Zimmermann (n 3) 831 *et seq.*

[125] As to the history prior to the Second World War, see Beato (n 47) 548; D Lloyd, 'Succession, Secession, and State Membership in the United Nations' (1994) 26 NYU J Intl L & Pol 761, 757; Mullerson (n 46) 308; R Rich, 'Recognition of States: The Collapse of Yugoslavia and the Soviet Union' (1993) 4 EJIL 37.

[126] Mullerson (n 46) 308.

[127] Ibid 309; Korman (n 15) 174.

[128] Vagts (n 13) 309; P Williams, 'The Treaty Obligations of the Successor States of the Former Soviet Union, Yugoslavia, and Czechoslovakia: Do They Continue in Force?' (1994) 23 Denv J Intl L & Pol 1, 2 (concerning the reluctant recognition by the Soviet Union). As to doubts on Statehood before 1991, see Lloyd (n 125) 776.

[129] Mullerson (n 46) 309.

[130] Lloyd (n 125) 778.

[131] Mullerson (n 46) 310.

[132] Those States were Ukrainskaya SSR, Byelorusskaya SSR, Azerbaijanskaya SSR, Armyanskaya SSR, Gruzinskaya SSR, Kazakhskaya SSR, Turkmenskaya SSR, Uzbekistanskaya SSR, Tajikistanskaya SSR, Kyrgyzstanskaya SSR, and Moldovskaya SSR.

[133] In the Ukraine, 90 per cent of the population voted in favour of independence. Williams (n 128) 2.

and Ukraine) committed themselves 'to discharge the international obligations incumbent on them under treaties and agreements entered into by the former Union of Soviet Socialist Republics'.[134] With the exception of Georgia and the Baltic States, all former Union Republics of the Soviet Union established the Community of Independent States (CIS) with the Declaration of Alma Ata of 21 December 1991. The Alma Ata Declaration also indicated that the USSR had begun the process of ending its existence upon the establishment of this Commonwealth.[135] Through a 21 December 1991 Protocol to the Minsk Agreement, other States forming the CIS joined the commitment under the Minsk Agreement.[136]

As far as their legal status is concerned, the States presently existing on the territory of the former USSR cannot be treated in an equal manner. As to the Baltic States, despite singular views to the contrary,[137] the opinion prevails that they re-established the Statehood they possessed before 1940[138] and, therefore, did not fall under the regime of State succession. Ukraine[139] and Belarus also operated as special cases since they were already members of the UN and parties to several international multilateral and bilateral treaties and had enjoyed a certain restricted international legal personality prior to their full independence and Statehood in 1991.[140]

The Russian Federation raised difficult problems by claiming an identity with the former USSR irrespective of the Declaration of Alma Ata. This posed the question of whether events had produced either a dismemberment of the former USSR or a separation of certain parts of the territory of the USSR combined with a redesignation of the USSR as the Russian Federation. Under the latter view, the Russian Federation would remain party to all treaties that the USSR had entered into.[141] The Russian Federation officially adopted this view,[142] declaring itself as the 'continuator' and not a successor to the USSR. Even though the continuator concept was relatively novel at the time, the Russian Federation's view was generally accepted by other States[143] as well as by the UN where the name 'Union of Soviet Socialist Republics' was only replaced by the new name 'Russian Federation'.

As to the remaining States emerging from the USSR, they undoubtedly became new States subject to the regime of State succession. Although the Baltic States[144]

---

[134] [1992] 31 ILM 145 (Art 12).　　[135] Ibid 149; Rich (n 125) 44.

[136] [1992] 31 ILM 147. However, the Declaration of Alma Ata made the continued legal force of treaties dependent on compatibility with the relevant 'constitutional procedures'.

[137] Cf Klabbers and others (n 53) 96.

[138] Mullerson (n 46) 309; L Love, 'International Agreement Obligations after the Soviet Union's Break-Up: Current United States Practice and its Consistency with International Law' (1993) 26 Vand J Transnat'l L 373, 384.

[139] Cf Rich (n 125) 40.

[140] HJ Uibopuu, *Die Völkerrechtssubjektivität der Unionsrepubliken der UdSSR* (Springer, Vienna 1975) 275 *et seq*; Love (n 138) 389.

[141] This practice accords with VCSST Art 35, which provides that in the case of separation and subject to limited exceptions when 'the predecessor State continues to exist, any treaty which at the date of the succession of States was in force in respect of the predecessor State continues in force in respect of its remaining territory'.

[142] Mullerson (n 46) 305.

[143] Klabbers and others (n 53) 98 *et seq*.

[144] Mullerson (n 46) 311 *et seq*; Beato (n 47) 550. The Baltic States argued in this sense irrespective of the non-applicability of the treaty succession regime to their situation.

and certain other States[145] contended they were newly independent states, they were not entitled to that qualification. Unlike colonies, these entities enjoyed the same legal status as all other Union Republics in the framework of the Soviet Union and were equally represented in the National Council as part of the Supreme Soviet.[146] Thus, irrespective of the concentration of actual political decision-making power in small elite bodies outside the formal government (namely the communist party),[147] these States can hardly be equated with the former colonies[148] according to the UN terminology.[149] As a result, they could not claim the status of newly independent States, and consequently, State practice since then has generally rejected their qualification as such.

5. Dissolution

In contrast to cases of separation where the prior practice was inconsistent, at the time of its adoption, Article 34 of the VCSST did codify the customary international law applicable to cases of dissolution.[150] Moreover, subsequent practice has generally, if not exactly, confirmed this rule, particularly in the cases of the former SFRY and the former CSFR. These two cases of dissolution displayed more consistency in the continued application of multilateral treaties than the USSR's separation. Nevertheless, in the case of multilateral treaties, the practice of the UN Secretary-General additionally requires a declaratory notification of succession by the States concerned.[151] In the case of bilateral treaties, negotiations tend to be the rule, leading to exchanges of notes including non-constitutive lists of treaties to remain in force, similar to cases of separation.[152]

The geopolitical changes relating to the SFRY[153] were connected with much more bloodshed, atrocities, and cruelties than the other cases mentioned here.[154] The dissolution started with the proclamation of independence of Slovenia and Croatia on 29 June 1991. Following the delivery of Opinion No 7 of the EC Arbitration Commission,[155] the EU recognized Slovenia as an independent State

---

[145] Cf U Saxer, 'The Transformation of the Soviet Union: From Commonwealth Socialist Federation to a Commonwealth of Independent States' (1992) 14 Loy LA Intl & Comp L J 581, 674.

[146] Cf USSR Constitution (1977) Art 10.

[147] Even in this respect it must be asked how far the parties of these Union Republics were represented in the inner circles of the CPSU.

[148] Beato (n 47) 554.

[149] Cf [1968] BILC, vol II, 17; cf also on the link between newly independent States and the so-called 'salt-water' colonies, Craven (n 12) 15.

[150] Cf somewhat more restrictively Zimmermann (n 3) 825.

[151] UN Depositary Practice (n 94) [303].

[152] Zimmermann (n 3) 831–2; This understanding was also reflected eg in the opinion of the ECJ's General Advocate Tizzano in *Case C-216/01, Budějovický Budvar, národní podnik v Rudolf Ammersin GmbH* (Opinion of Advocate General Tizzano) ECR 2003 I-13617.

[153] Rich (n 125) 38.

[154] Cf UNSC Res 757 (1992).

[155] Cf (1993) 4 EJIL 80. The 'Badinter' EC Arbitration Commission was an organ of the Conference on Yugoslavia, convened by the European Community in 1991 and tasked with giving advisory opinions, *inter alia*, relating to questions of State succession arising during the process of the SFRY's disintegration. See eg M Craven, 'The European Community Arbitration Commission on Yugoslavia' (1996) BYBIL 333–413.

on 15 January 1992,[156] simultaneously with its recognition of Croatia. Both States became new members of the UN on 22 May 1992 and were accepted, although differently, by the community of States.[157]

Doubts were initially raised as to the ability of Bosnia and Herzegovina to effectively govern its territory.[158] Nevertheless, after it declared independence in November 1991, EU member States and the US recognized it as a State on 7 April 1992, and it was admitted to the UN as a new member on 22 May 1992.[159] As to Macedonia or, in UN terminology, Former Yugoslav Republic of Macedonia (FYROM), the question of its recognition was overshadowed by the dispute over its name. Once it was admitted to the UN on 8 April 1993,[160] it was also accepted by the community of States as an independent State[161] and recognized by a great number of States.

The remaining part of the former SFRY, formerly forming the Republics of Serbia and Montenegro and comprising about 40 per cent of the area and 44 per cent of the population of the SFRY,[162] claimed identity with the SFRY from a legal point of view.[163] However, other States did not accept this claim. The Opinion of the EC Arbitration Commission[164] as well as resolutions of the UN Security Council[165] and the General Assembly required the Federal Republic of Yugoslavia (Serbia and Montenegro) to apply for new membership in the Council of Europe and the UN, respectively.[166] The only conclusion that can be drawn from this is that this State is a new one, succeeding to the former SFRY like all the other new States formed in this region.[167] That view was confirmed by EU member States' recognition of this State in April 1996 and by its admission to the UN as a new State in 2000.[168] Hence, the former SFRY has to be considered as dismembered and that so far, six (and, if Kosovo is regarded as a new State, seven) new States have emerged on its territory.[169]

Notwithstanding the fact that unilateral declarations cannot produce any legal effect for other States,[170] Slovenia included in one of its first constitutional acts a

---

[156] Williams (n 128) 4.   [157] Lloyd (n 125) 780.

[158] In Opinion No 4, the EC Arbitration Commission declared Bosnia Herzegovina as having not yet achieved the status as a 'sovereign and independent State'. (1993) 4 EJIL 74.

[159] UNGA Res 46/237 (22 May 1992).

[160] UNGA Res 47/225 (8 April 1993); Williams (n 128) 4.

[161] In contrast to the findings concerning Bosnia Herzegovina, the EC Arbitration Commission took the view in its Opinion No 6 that Macedonia satisfied the tests of the Guidelines on the Recognition of New States adopted by the Council of the European Communities on 16 December 1991. (1993) 4 EJIL 77 *et seq*.

[162] Lloyd (n 125) 780.

[163] Williams (n 128) 29; cf also the *Case Concerning the Application of the Convention on the Prevention and Punishment of the Crime of Genocide (Bosnia and Herzegovina v Serbia and Montenegro)* ('Bosnian Genocide Case') (Provisional Measures) [1993] ICJ Rep 3, 15.

[164] Cf (1993) 4 EJIL 80.

[165] UNSC Res 777 (1992).

[166] Williams (n 128) 40.

[167] See Opinion No 10 of the EC Arbitration Commission. (1993) 4 EJIL 90.

[168] UNGA Res 55/12 (10 November 2000).

[169] Cf ICJ, *Accordance with International Law of the Unilateral Declaration of Independence in Respect of Kosovo* (Advisory Opinion) 2010 <http://www.icj-cij.org/docket/files/141/15987.pdf>.

[170] See Part II.A, 408 *et seq*.

provision according to which the '[i]nternational agreements concluded by Yugoslavia and relating to the Republic of Slovenia shall be effective in the territory of
the Republic of Slovenia'.[171] In the framework of the Meeting of the Legal Advisers
within the Council of Europe, the representative of Croatia stated that 'his country
would respect all the treaties of former Yugoslavia (unless they conflicted with the
constitution)'.[172] No such acts were produced by the other parts of former
Yugoslavia.[173]

The other, though peaceful, recent case of dismemberment arose with the
emergence of the Czech and Slovak Republics. The first change affecting Czechoslovakia after the Velvet Revolution altered that State's name from CSSR to CSFR,
but this did not affect its legal personality under international law. However, on
25 November 1992, the Federal Assembly of the CSFR adopted legislation
providing that as of midnight, 1 January 1993, the State of Czechoslovakia
would cease to exist and would be succeeded by two independent new States, the
Czech Republic and the Republic of Slovakia (Slovak Republic). By the same date,
both new States were recognized by the member States of the EU and the US.[174]
Thus, these events amounted to a classic case of dismemberment of one State
succeeded by two new States.

Like Slovenia and Croatia, the Parliaments of both component parts of the
CSFR adopted on 2 December 1992[175] and 17 December 1992[176] a Declaration
according to which, as of 1 January 1993, they declared themselves bound by
multilateral and bilateral treaties and agreements to which the CSFR was a party by
that date. The constitutional law of the Czech Republic No 4/1993 stipulates that
the 'Czech Republic takes over rights and obligations... deriving for Czechoslovakia on the date of its extinction from the international law, except those... relating
to the territory which was under (Czechoslovakia's) sovereignty but is not under the
sovereignty of the Czech Republic'.[177] According to Article 153 of the Constitution of the Slovak Republic, this State succeeded to all rights and duties ensuing
from international treaties and agreements binding former Czechoslovakia.[178]

---

[171] Cf Art 3 Republic of Slovenia Assembly Constitutional Law of the Enforcement of the Basic
Constitutional Charter on the Autonomy and Independence of the Republic of Slovenia (25 June
1991) in S Trifunovska (ed), *Yugoslavia Through Documents: From its Creation to its Dissolution*
(Martinus Nijhoff, Dordrecht 1994) 292–8; Williams (n 128) 38 *et seq.*

[172] Doc CAHDI (93)11 of 12 August 1993, 7; see also Williams (n 128) 16 *et seq.*

[173] Williams (n 128) 33.

[174] Ibid 7.

[175] 'Proclamation of the National Council of the Slovak Republic to the Parliaments and Peoples of
the World' (2 December 1992) in UNGA, 'Letter Dated 31 December 1992 from the Permanent
Representative of Czechoslovakia to the United Nations Addressed to the Secretary-General' UN Doc
A/47/848, Annex II.

[176] 'Proclamation of the Czech National Council to all Parliaments and Nations of the World' (17
December 1992) in UNGA, 'Letter Dated 31 December 1992 from the Permanent Representative of
Czechoslovakia to the United Nations Addressed to the Secretary-General' UN Doc A/47/848
Annex I.

[177] Ústavní zákon České národní rady o opatřeních souvisejících se zánikem České a Slovenské
Federativní Republiky (Constitutional Law of the Czech National Council on Measures Connected
with the Dissolution of the CSFR) (done 15 December 1992) č 4/1993 Sb.

[178] Constitution of the Slovak Republic (Slovakia) No 466/1992 Coll.

In sum, with certain modifications, as indicated above, the continuity principle as laid down in Article 34 of the VCSST forms the vantage point for treaty succession in cases of dissolution, frequently accompanied by declaratory notifications of succession in the case of multilateral treaties, and frequently modified by agreement between the parties in accordance with the varying context of each case of succession, especially in the case of bilateral treaties.

D. Legal regimes not affected by State succession

Even where customary legal rules exist for particular categories of treaty succession, those rules will not govern all treaties. Some treaties create legal regimes that are not affected by State succession.

1. Boundary treaties

The law and practice of State succession to boundary treaties is based on the acknowledgment of the particular nature of boundary treaties. As expressed by the ICJ in the *Temple of Preah Vihear* case, the primary object of a boundary treaty is to 'achieve stability and finality'.[179] Article 11(1) of the VCSST provides that a 'succession of States does not as such affect . . . a boundary established by a treaty or . . . obligations and rights established by a treaty and relating to the regime of a boundary'. The ILC's First Report on Succession of States and Governments in Respect of Treaties in 1968 found that:

the weight both of opinion and practice seems clearly to be in favour of the view that boundaries established by treaties remain untouched by the mere fact of a succession. The opinion of jurists seems, indeed, to be unanimous on the point . . . [and] State practice in favour of the continuance in force of boundaries established by treaty appears to be such as to justify the conclusion that a general rule of international law exists to that effect.[180]

Subsequent practice also confirms that this rule may be considered as customary both with regard to land[181] and to maritime boundaries.[182] This rule enhances the stability of boundaries and is in conformity with the principle of the intangibility of frontiers as reflected in the generally applicable principle of *uti possidetis*.[183]

2. Other territorial regimes

Besides the special case of boundary regimes, another traditional distinction was generally made between personal and dispositive treaties. According to one author,

---

[179] *Case Concerning the Temple of Preah Vihear (Cambodia v Thailand)* (Merits) [1962] ICJ Rep 6, 34.
[180] [1968] YBILC, vol II, 92–3.
[181] Cf *Frontier Dispute (Burkina Faso/Republic of Mali)* [1986] ICJ Rep 554, 567; *Territorial Dispute (Libyan Arab Jamahiriya/Chad)* [1994] ICJ Rep 6 ff 38; Opinion No 3 of the Arbitration Commission of the Conference on Yugoslavia (Badinter Commission) [1992] 31 ILM 1499 f; Cf also ILA Committee Draft Report (n 113).
[182] Zimmermann (n 3) 490.   [183] Bernárdez (n 23) 418.

personal treaties are contractual in nature and, therefore, depend on the continued existence of the parties; dispositive treaties, by contrast, create rights in the land and survive all changes in sovereignty.[184] Accordingly, a dispositive treaty has a legal effect similar to a covenant running with land—the territory gains permanent status independent of the personality of the State exercising sovereignty.

According to Article 12 of the VCSST, dispositive treaties, which it terms 'other territorial regimes', are not affected by State succession. Examples include treaties of cession, peace treaties, and treaties that grant 'rights of way over territory'.[185] As the ILC pointed out, the 'weight of the opinion amongst modern writers supports the traditional doctrine that treaties of a territorial character constitute a special category and are not affected by a succession of States'.[186] Although this 'other territorial regimes' category lacks a precise definition, the ILC's first candidates (beside boundary regimes mentioned above) were treaties 'concerning water rights or navigation on rivers'; other candidates included treaties for the neutralization or demilitarization of a particular territory, treaties according freedom of navigation on international waterways or rivers, and treaties for the equitable use of water resources in an international river basin.[187] More generally, according to the ILC, this category is 'limited to cases where a State by a treaty grants a right to use territory, or to restrict its own use of territory, which is intended to attach to territory of a foreign State or, alternatively, to be for the benefit of a group of States or of all States generally'.[188] In the *Gabčíkovo-Nagymaros* case, the ICJ explicitly confirmed the customary nature of Article 12 of the VCSST.[189] That case found that the territorial regime on the Danube established by the 1977 Treaty between Hungary and the CSSR had 'establish[ed] a territorial régime within the meaning of Article 12' of the VCSST since it created rights and obligations 'attaching to the parts of the Danube to which it relates' and therefore the treaty 'itself cannot be affected by a succession of States'.[190]

3. Permanent sovereignty over natural resources

The principle of permanent sovereignty over natural resources, which was derived mostly by developing countries from the principle of self-determination, was a point of contention during the elaboration of the VCSST, particularly due to the principle's connection with the concept of acquired rights.[191] Finally, Article 13 of

---

[184] Love (n 138) 378.   [185] Ibid.

[186] [1974] YBILC, vol II(1), 83.   [187] Ibid 204.

[188] ILC, 'Report on Succession of States' [1974] YBILC, vol II(1), 206; see also ILA, *Effect of Independence on Treaties* (1965) 352.

[189] *Case concerning the Gabčíkovo-Nagymaros Project (Hungary/Slovakia)* (Judgment) [1997] ICJ Rep 7 [123].

[190] Ibid.

[191] See also the respective positions of the US and the UK at the Vienna Conference in Craven (n 12) 196 *et seq.* The doctrine of acquired rights broadly entails that a legal right or status acquired under domestic law must be respected as an international obligation. Cf eg F Francioni, 'Compensation for Nationalisation of Foreign Property: The Borderland between Law and Equity' (1975) ICLQ 255, 258.

the VCSST was elaborated and provided that nothing in the convention 'shall affect the principles of international law affirming the permanent sovereignty of every people and every State over its natural wealth and resources'. The exact extent of the principle of permanent sovereignty over natural resources was—and remains—subject to debate even if it has been generally recognized as a principle of international law,[192] and has been emphasized in Article 1 of both the International Covenant on Economic, Social and Cultural Rights and the International Covenant on Civil and Political Rights, both of 1966.[193] In any case, since the wave of decolonization has passed, this principle has become less relevant in the context of the law of State succession.

4. Other special categories of treaties

The legal effects of State succession may also depend on the nature and content of the relevant treaty in other respects. In particular, issues of succession may arise based on the treaty's subject matter or the nature of the treaty commitment. In some cases, moreover, the rules for these other special categories remain contested or vague, and are thus still emerging.

(i) Human rights and humanitarian law treaties

Times of fundamental change are particularly conducive to occurrences of State succession. In such instances, the guarantees accorded to individuals through various human rights and humanitarian law treaties may be especially relevant—particularly due to the specificity of treaty rules and the existence of compliance mechanisms that are lacking in the case of customary rules. Thus, the breakup of the SFRY was accompanied by numerous violations of international human rights and humanitarian law in the period between the independence of the successor States and their formal notification of succession. In view of such cases, proponents of succession have argued that the nature of human rights and humanitarian treaties should be described as similarly 'attaching' to individuals as territorial treaties attach to land.[194]

The VCSST is silent on the particular fate of human rights or humanitarian treaties in cases of State succession.[195] Today, it remains unclear whether customary international law includes a rule of automatic succession to multilateral humanitarian and human rights treaties.[196] The practice of the Czech and Slovak

---

[192] NJ Schrijver, *Sovereignty over Natural Resources: Balancing Rights and Duties* (CUP, Cambridge 1997, reprinted CUP 2008) 377.

[193] International Covenant on Civil and Political Rights (adopted 19 December 1966, entered into force 23 March 1976) 999 UNTS 171; International Covenant on Economic, Social and Cultural Rights (adopted 16 December 1966, entered into force 3 January 1976) 993 UNTS 3.

[194] A Trindade, 'International Law for Humankind: Towards a New *Jus Gentium*' (2005) 317 RdC 108 *et seq.*

[195] Article 12*bis* of the ILC draft had originally foreseen automatic succession in respect of certain universal multilateral treaties, including particularly human rights treaties. [1974] YBILC, vol II(1), 172.

[196] ILA Committee Draft Report (n 113) 33.

Republics with regard to the ECHR provides some degree of support for such a rule, albeit in a regional context.[197] Moreover, the ICTY[198] and to a certain extent the Eritrea-Ethiopia Claims Tribunal[199] have pronounced themselves in favour of automatic succession in the case of certain universal human rights and humanitarian treaties. But, the ICJ has remained silent on the issue.

Most recently, in its judgment regarding preliminary objections in the *Croatia-Serbian Genocide* case, the ICJ found that the FRY succeeded to the Genocide Convention, without elaborating specifically how this succession occurred.[200] Rather, the ICJ took account of the text of the FRY's declaration and Note of 27 April 1992 on succession, alongside the consistent conduct of the FRY then and thereafter to find 'that from that date onwards the FRY would be bound by the obligations of a party in respect of all the multilateral conventions to which the SFRY had been a party at the time of its dissolution, subject of course to any reservations lawfully made by the SFRY limiting its obligations'. Since the Genocide Convention had been one of these conventions, the ICJ held that the FRY in 1992 had accepted the obligations of that Convention.[201] However, it did not pronounce itself on how this occurred, whether by way of automatic succession or via Article 34's codification of a customary rule of international law.

In contrast, the Appeals Chamber of the ICTY held in the *Čelebići* case that:

irrespective of any findings as to formal succession, Bosnia and Herzegovina would in any event have succeeded to the Geneva Conventions under customary law, as this type of convention entails automatic succession, ie, without the need for any formal confirmation of adherence by the successor State. It may be now considered in international law that there is automatic State succession to multilateral humanitarian treaties in the broad sense, ie, treaties of universal character which express fundamental human rights.[202]

The Appeals Chamber found that:

the Geneva Conventions f[ell] within this category of universal multilateral treaties which reflect rules accepted and recognised by the international community as a whole. The Geneva Conventions enjoy nearly universal participation . . . In light of the object and purpose of the Geneva Conventions, which is to guarantee the protection of certain fundamental values common to mankind in times of armed conflict, and of the customary nature of their provisions, the Appeals Chamber is in no doubt that State

---

[197] See on this issue A Rasulov, 'Revisiting State Succession to Humanitarian Treaties: Is There a Case for Automaticity?' (2003) 14 EJIL 141–70 (concluding that 'in international law, the treaties of humanitarian character are not subject to automatic succession' but favouring transformation of the acquired rights theory so that obligations arising from a human rights treaty are not affected by State succession).

[198] See n 202 and accompanying text.

[199] See nn 204–8 and accompanying text.

[200] *Application of the Convention on the Prevention and Punishment of the Crime of Genocide (Croatia v Serbia)* Judgment (Preliminary Objections) [2008] ICJ Rep 412 [117].

[201] Ibid; see also S Sivakumaran, 'Application of the Convention on the Prevention and Punishment of the Crime of Genocide (Bosnia and Herzegovina v Serbia and Montenegro)' (2007) 56 ICLQ 695–708; Craven (n 12) 7–13.

[202] *Čelebići Case* (Prosecutor v Delacic et al) [2001] ICTY Case No IT-96-21-A [111]–[113].

succession has no impact on obligations arising out from these fundamental humanitarian conventions.[203]

Similarly, in the Partial Award relating to Prisoners of War, the Eritrea Ethiopia Claims Commission found that '[t]reaty succession may happen automatically for certain types of treaties'.[204] However, in the instance at hand, the Commission found that it had 'not been shown evidence that would permit it to find that such automatic succession to the Geneva Conventions occurred in the exceptional circumstances here, desirable though such succession would be as a general matter'[205] since '[f]rom the time of its independence from Ethiopia in 1993, senior Eritrean officials made clear that Eritrea did not consider itself bound by the Geneva Conventions'.[206] Moreover, this evidence was complemented by the fact that '[d]uring the period of the armed conflict and prior to these proceedings, Ethiopia likewise consistently maintained that Eritrea was not a party to the Geneva Conventions'[207] and the 'ICRC, which has a special interest and responsibility for promoting compliance with the Geneva Conventions, likewise did not at that time regard Eritrea as a party to the Conventions'.[208]

These divergent views correspond to a broader analysis of the practice relating to the Genocide Convention[209] undertaken by Gaeta, who concluded that 'it is unclear whether the succession to the Convention is automatic, or voluntary for a new State, though the latter view has more support'.[210] However, it seems clear that for the purposes of international litigation 'the consent of new states is required . . . whether they have as a substantive matter succeeded to the responsibility of their predecessor state or not'.[211]

(ii) 'Political' treaties

Another category of treaties subject to particular rules lacks any clear definition; those treaties the application of which to the successor State would be incompatible with the object and purpose of the treaty or would radically change the conditions for its operation.[212] This characterization—used repeatedly in the VCSST—is borrowed from the VCLT and tends to address those treaties which are also sometimes called 'political treaties'.[213] Some authors try to define this category in a negative manner by arguing that only those treaties should pass on to the successor States from which both Parties to the treaty benefit.[214] But whatever efforts previously undertaken to define these categories of treaties, the definition

---

[203] Ibid [112]–[113].

[204] Eritrea Ethiopia Claims Commission, Partial Award, Prisoners of War, Ethiopia's Claim 4 (The Federal Democratic Republic of Ethiopia v The State of Eritrea), The Hague, 1 July 2003 [24].

[205] Ibid. [206] Ibid. [207] Ibid. [208] Ibid.

[209] Convention on the Prevention and Punishment of the Crime of Genocide (adopted 9 December 1948, entered into force 12 January 1951) 78 UNTS 277.

[210] P Gaeta (ed), *The UN Genocide Convention: A Commentary* (OUP, Oxford 2009) 493.

[211] Ibid.

[212] Cf VCSST Arts 31(3), 32(6), 30(3)(a), 33(5), 34(2)(b), 35(c), 36(3), 37(2).

[213] Jennings and Watts (n 60) 211.

[214] Korman (n 15) 180.

still remains vague. In this respect, these treaties share the lack of a precise definition of the 'object and purpose'.[215] In practice, however, States have overcome the difficulty related to the vagueness of this phrase by drawing up a list of the agreements that were to remain in force.[216]

(iii) Multilateral treaties

As far as multilateral treaties are concerned, the question arises as to whether the clause determining the conditions for becoming a party to the treaty also applies to the successor State or States. Both the VCSST[217] as well as UN practice recognize that the conditions governing the right to become party to a specific treaty define also the category of States which may succeed to this treaty. Thus, the UN Secretary General's *Summary of Practice* states that '[i]n the absence of provisions which set specific conditions for succession or which otherwise restrict succession; the Secretary-General is guided by the participation clauses of the treaties as well as by the general principles governing the participation of States'.[218] This practice even acknowledges the possibility that treaty succession may be excluded.[219]

(iv) Constitutive treaties of international organizations (IOs)

The regulation of the succession to constitutive treaties of IOs is widely subject to the special internal rules of the respective organizations. Generally, these rules do not allow for succession, but rather require accession to the organization's constitutive instrument(s).[220] Both in the practice prior and subsequent to the VCSST's adoption,[221] succession of new States to the constitutive instruments of IOs has generally not been accepted in cases of cession, dissolution, or separation. In cases of merger or incorporation, however, the practice has been for the incorporating State or the unified State to continue, or 'substitute', the IO membership, even if only following a notification of succession.[222] Article 4 of the VCSST also anticipates special internal rules of IOs that would in some cases and under specific

---

[215] See I Buffard and K Zemanek, 'The "Object and Purpose" of a Treaty: an Enigma?' (1998) ARIEL 311–43.

[216] See nn 109–11 and accompanying text.

[217] VCSST Art 17(3) provides: 'When, under the terms of the treaty or by reason of the limited number of the negotiating States and the object and purpose of the treaty, the participation of any other State in the treaty must be considered as requiring the consent of all the parties, the newly independent State may establish its status as a party to the treaty only with such consent.' Moreover, the VCSST frequently refers explicitly to this provision: elsewhere in Art 17 on multilateral treaties and in Arts 29, 30, 31, 32, 33, 36, and 37. The latter articles do not relate to newly independent States, so this restriction must be considered generally applicable.

[218] UN Depositary Practice (n 94) [297].

[219] Ibid [295] ('The provisions of a treaty may even totally rule out succession. Such would be the case if the treaty was open only to the participation of the members of a regional commission which itself would not be open to the new State. In such cases, the situation is clear and the Secretary-General simply abides by the provisions of the treaty').

[220] See generally K Bühler, *State Succession and Membership in International Organizations: Legal Theories versus Political Pragmatism* (Martinus Nijhoff, London 2001).

[221] Cf O'Connell (n 57) 183–211.

[222] Bühler (n 220) 289.

circumstances provide for succession; these are found especially among international and regional financial organizations, such as the World Bank, the International Monetary Fund, and regional development banks.[223]

(v) Disarmament and arms control treaties

Agreements relating to military matters engender particular problems. In this regard, succession issues have been addressed differently in the case of generalized commitments not to possess or use certain weapons, on the one hand, and specific agreements about the number of weapons, on the other.[224] The former could be seen as resembling other treaties codifying customary international law while the latter would lead to further issues concerning the legal status of the respective treaty commitments. Moreover, recent practice suggests that the regulation of both disarmament and arms control treaties largely depends on the intention of the parties. As a result, the specific context of each particular treaty is relevant and no general rule can be discerned, even if the need for stability and predictability supports a general notion of continuity (or at least the obligation to negotiate in good faith towards a regulation of disarmament and arms control).[225]

III. Other Aspects of the Law of Treaty Succession

Article 20 of the VCSST only deals with reservations in the context of newly independent States and is therefore of considerably restricted use today.[226] Recent practice shows that States may only retain reservations of the predecessor State but not formulate new ones with respect to treaties to which they are succeeding.[227] Special problems may arise in the case of merger where reservations of the predecessor States conflict.[228] The ILC, as part of its work on the topic of 'the law and practice relating to reservations to treaties', has dealt with the status of reservations, acceptances of, and objections to reservations, and interpretative declarations in the case of succession of States.[229] In this context, the ILC maintains the specific

---

[223] VCSST Art 4 provides in this regard that the 'Convention applies to the effects of a succession of States in respect of: (a) any treaty which is the constituent instrument of an international organization without prejudice to the rules concerning acquisition of membership and without prejudice to any other relevant rules of the organization; (b) any treaty adopted within an international organization without prejudice to any relevant rules of the organization'.

[224] Vagts (n 13) 292–3.

[225] Zimmermann (n 3) 746 *et seq.*

[226] VCSST Art 20 provides that '[w]hen a newly independent State establishes its status as a party or as a contracting State to a multilateral treaty by a notification of succession under article 17 or 18, it shall be considered as maintaining any reservation to that treaty which was applicable at the date of the succession of States in respect of the territory to which the succession of States relates unless, when making the notification of succession, it expresses a contrary intention or formulates a reservation which relates to the same subject matter as that reservation'.

[227] Zimmermann (n 3) 770.

[228] Ibid 771.

[229] See eg A Pellet (Special Rapporteur), 'Sixteenth report on reservations to treaties: Status of reservations, acceptances of and objections to reservations and interpretative declarations in the case of

category of newly independent States[230] irrespective of the emerging tendency of renouncing such a category of States.

Articles 36 and 37 of the VCSST deal with questions of treaty succession with respect to the status of a predecessor State as contracting and signatory State, respectively. Article 36 of the VCSST provides that in cases of separation or dissolution, a successor State may, 'by making a notification, establish its status as a contracting State to a multilateral treaty which is not in force if, at the date of the succession of States, the predecessor State was a contracting State to the treaty in respect of the territory to which the succession of States relates'. This provision has largely been confirmed by recent State practice.[231] Article 37 of the VCSST provides an analogous provision for cases where, before the date of the succession of States, the predecessor State had signed a multilateral treaty subject to ratification, acceptance, or approval. While this rule did not constitute customary international law before 1978, it has since been largely confirmed by recent State practice.[232]

Another issue relevant for determining the effects of the applicable rules on treaty succession is the determination of the date of succession. Particularly in cases where State succession is the consequence of a protracted process or it is uncertain whether the new entity is a State, it can be difficult to ascertain the exact date when State succession occurs.[233] Thus, one may contrast, for example, the protracted dissolution of the SFRY in the context of conflict or the case of some successor States of the USSR with several cases of decolonization or, more recently, the case of South Sudan's emergence as a new State on a specific date.[234]

Conclusion

With the disappearance of the circumstances of decolonization, States have moved further away from the clean-slate doctrine, which, together with the continuity theory, has traditionally framed the law of treaty succession. Even if the principle of continuity in cases of treaty succession can be said to form a starting point of the law today, negotiations among States often modify this general precept. Likewise, different rules and practices have emerged for various categories of State succession and with respect to particular kinds of treaties. Any generalization thus fails to accord with the contextual nature of the law of treaty succession. At the same time, especially the moving boundaries rule for cases of cession and incorporation enjoys wide support in State practice. Similarly, constitutive treaties of IOs are generally not considered as permitting succession, but rather require accession. There is also

---

succession of States', 19 March 2010, UN Doc A/CN.4/626; in 2011, the ILC's work on the topic has culminated in a Guide to Practice on Reservations to Treaties, UN Doc A/66/10 19-49.

[230] Ibid (Guide to Practice Section 5).

[231] Zimmermann (n 3) 832.

[232] Ibid 833.

[233] Ibid 785 *et seq.*

[234] On South Sudan see n 19; S Salman, 'The New State of South Sudan and the Hydro-Politics of the Nile Basin' (2011) 36 Water Intl 154–66.

legal certainty regarding the rule that certain boundary and territorial regimes are not affected by State succession. At the same time, while oriented towards continuity, particularly in the case of bilateral treaties, negotiation plays an important role in State practice in cases of dissolution and separation, albeit to different extents in each case.

Thus, the law of State succession with regard to treaties illustrates a still existing divergence of views and practice, although certain generally accepted tendencies are already recognizable. These tendencies point in the direction of a continuity of treaties, at least in respect of certain types of treaties such as those on human rights, which is obviously in the interest of the individuals and with the purpose of protecting their rights even if a State succession has occurred.

Recommended Reading

KG Bühler, *State Succession and Membership in International Organizations: Legal Theories versus Political Pragmatism* (Kluwer, London 2001)

M Craven, *The Decolonization of International Law: State Succession and the Law of Treaties* (OUP, Oxford 2007)

PM Eisenmann and M Koskenniemi (eds), *La Succession d'Etats: La Codification à l'Épreuve des Faits/State Succession Tested against the Facts* (Martinus Nijhoff, London 2000)

U Fastenrath, T Schweisfurth, and C Thomas, *Das Recht der Staatensukzession* (Müller, Heidelberg 1996) 49

ILA Committee on Aspects of the Law of State Succession, *Draft Conference Report Rio de Janeiro Conference* (2008)

J Klabbers, M Koskenniemi, O Ribbelink, and A Zimmermann (eds), *State Practice Regarding State Succession and Issues of Recognition: The Pilot Project of the Council of Europe* (Kluwer, London 1999)

Y Makonnen, 'International law and the new states of Africa: a study of the international legal problems of state succession in the newly independent states of Eastern Africa' (Ethiopian National Agency for UNESCO, Addis Ababa 1983)

DP O'Connell, 'State Succession in Relation to New States' (1970-II) 130 RdC 101

P Pazartzis, *La Succession d'États aux Traités Multilateraux á la Lumière des Mutations Territoriales Récentes* (Pedone, Paris 2002)

M Silagi, *Staatsuntergang und Staatennachfolge* (Lang, Frankfurt am Main 1996)

B Stern, 'La Succession d'Etats' (1996) 262 RdC 9

DF Vagts, 'State Succession: The Codifiers' View' (1993) 33 VJIL 275

A Zimmermann, *Staatennachfolge in völkerrechtliche Verträge* (Springer, Berlin 2000)

17

Treaty Bodies and Regimes

Geir Ulfstein

Introduction

Treaties will generally set out the substantive rights and obligations of the treaty parties. But treaties are also used to establish institutions for international cooperation. Such institutions may take many forms such as formal international organizations (IOs) or international courts. But treaties may also set up organs that are neither IOs nor international courts in the traditional sense. Such organs may be labelled 'treaty bodies'.[1]

Today, treaty bodies serve various functions. Some have many characteristics of an IO. In the international environmental context, treaty bodies have a multiplicity of tasks, including developing new substantive commitments, guiding sub-organs and the secretariat, and ensuring implementation of States' obligations. But treaty bodies may also have more specialized competences. For example, the Commission on the Limits of the Continental Shelf, set up by the UN Convention on the Law of the Sea (UNCLOS), has a specific function—to make substantive recommendations on the outer limit of continental shelves. Bodies established by human rights and arms control treaties are essentially limited to controlling implementation of the relevant treaty by States parties, or, in the case of human rights treaty bodies, to resolving disputes between individuals and States.

Treaty bodies have not received much scholarly attention, either in the literature on treaty law, the law of international institutions, or specialized works on international environmental law, human rights, etc. Clearly, treaty law applies to treaty bodies: their powers and procedures must be determined based on the constituting treaty. But treaty law does not have much to say about treaty bodies' competence to establish subsidiary bodies; the legal status of their decisions; or whether treaty bodies have international legal personality (and thus the capacity to possess and act on international legal rights and obligations). Such issues are usually the domain of international institutional law. However, it may be asked whether the tenets of international institutional law as developed for IOs apply wholesale (or even partly)

---

[1] Treaty bodies should be distinguished from forms of cooperation resting on a non-binding foundation, such as the Organization for Security and Co-operation in Europe (OSCE) commitments discussed in Chapter 2.

to treaty bodies. After all, if the parties have carefully determined not to establish an IO, why should the law of IOs—or, as the case may be, the law of international courts—apply?

This chapter examines the current status of treaty bodies in international law and practice. It explores why States have established them, the various structural forms they take, as well as their authority to act both internally and externally, on topics such as substantive decision-making, compliance, and coordination with other treaty bodies, IOs, and States. This analysis reveals how treaty bodies reflect the increasingly public character of international law as international organs exercising functions delegated by States. They may also be seen as aspects of a growing international legalization, judicialization—and even constitutionalization—of international law.

But, in the aggregate, the proliferation of treaty bodies may also be seen as an aspect of de-constitutionalization given the increased institutional fragmentation they have generated. Moreover, as international institutions are increasingly empowered, their exercises of authority are more and more questioned in terms of democratic control, respect for the rule of law, and human rights.[2] Treaty bodies are not immune from such inquiries. Indeed, treaty bodies may be charged with contributing to a deformalization of international law, representing expert bodies and other, more informal organs that may be seen as less accountable than traditional IOs.[3]

I. Why have treaty bodies been established?

The reasons for establishing treaty bodies rather than full-fledged IOs or courts may vary among different subject matters and from case to case. Generally speaking, three rationales stand out. First, States may choose to create treaty bodies to minimize interference in their sovereignty. For example, the minimalist approach to institutional creation was a deliberate choice in Antarctic cooperation. It took forty years before a permanent secretariat was established, in part because of a suspicion that even the establishment of a secretariat could lead to an internationalization of Antarctica, threatening States with sovereignty claims in the territory.[4] Similarly, human rights treaty bodies interfere less with State sovereignty by resolving individual complaints by non-binding decisions rather than the binding judgments produced by international courts.

[2] J Klabbers, 'Setting the Scene' in J Klabbers, A Peters, and G Ulfstein (eds), *The Constitutionalization of International Law* (OUP, Oxford 2009) 37–43.
[3] M Koskenniemi, 'The Fate of Public International Law: Between Technique and Politics' (2007) 70 MLR 1, 9–15.
[4] K Scott, 'Institutional Developments within the Antarctic Treaty System' (2003) 52 ICLQ 473, 476, 479. See also P Vigni, 'The Secretariat of the Antarctic Treaty: Achievements and Weaknesses Three years After its Establishment' in G Triggs and A Riddell (eds), *Antarctica: Legal and Environmental Challenges for the Future* (BIICL, London 2007) 18; F Francioni, 'Establishment of an Antarctic Treaty Secretariat: Pending Legal Issues' in D Vidas (ed), *Implementing the Environmental Protection Regime for the Antarctic* (Kluwer Academic Publishers, Dordrecht 2000) 125–6.

Second, treaty bodies may also be the preferred option due to a reluctance to establish new IOs or a sense that it is inappropriate to use existing IOs for new purposes. In international environmental law, treaty bodies emerged in the 1970s and 1980s in concert with growing dissatisfaction with traditional IOs because of their cost and bureaucracy. Creating treaty bodies thus might seem less costly and more effective. They avoid difficulties in using an existing IO with an already fixed membership. And they make choosing the location of a new IO unnecessary.[5]

Third, the choice of treaty bodies rather than IOs in international human rights and arms control may be due to their limited functions. As noted, supervisory organs usually only supervise States' implementation of treaty obligations while the meeting of the parties' only function is to elect members of such supervisory bodies.

There are, however, cases where it may be difficult to explain why States opted either for an IO or a treaty body. For example, the Convention on Chemical Weapons and the Comprehensive Test Ban Treaty both established IOs. But, despite similarities in subject matter and obligations, the Anti-Personnel Landmine Convention did not, establishing a meeting of the parties instead, whose function is to 'consider any matter with regard to the application or implementation of this Convention'.[6]

II. The Structure of Treaty Bodies

Treaty bodies almost always include a central plenary organ, but depending on their functions and relationship to other treaties, subsidiary bodies and a secretariat may also be established. The plenary organ of treaty bodies may be called the Conference of the Parties (COP) or a different denomination like Meeting of the Parties (MOP). It will meet regularly, often annually. A 'bureau' may be elected to serve on its behalf between regular meetings and to operate as a facilitating organ during plenary body sessions.

Protocols are formally separate treaties from the treaty that spawned them. Nevertheless, substantive overlap between the parent convention and its protocol(s)—and full or partial overlap in membership between the two—sometimes militates in favour of joint institutions. In other cases, a protocol's more specialized functions or different membership may prevent such integration.

The Montreal Protocol on Substances that Deplete the Ozone Layer (Montreal Protocol) is an example of a protocol with a separate treaty body—a MOP—that meets in conjunction with the COP of the foundational Vienna Convention for the Protection of the Ozone Layer. In contrast, the plenary body of the regional Convention on Long-Range Transboundary Air Pollution (LRTAP Convention)

---

[5] R Churchill and G Ulfstein, 'Autonomous Institutional Arrangements in Multilateral Environmental Agreements: A Little-Noticed Phenomenon in International Law' (2000) 94 AJIL 623–60, 629–31.

[6] Convention on the Prohibition of the Use, Stockpiling, Production, and Transfer of Anti-Personnel Mines and on their Destruction (adopted 18 September 1997, entered into force 1 March 1999) 2056 UNTS 211, Art 11.

also serves as the governing body of its relevant protocols. The Kyoto Protocol to the UN Framework Convention on Climate Change (UNFCCC) provides that the Convention's COP shall serve as the Protocol's MOP, but parties to the Convention that are not parties to the Protocol may participate only as observers when the COP acts in this capacity. And while the Antarctic Treaty and the Convention on the Conservation of Antarctic Marine Living Resources (CCAMLR) contain several identical substantive obligations, they generated legally separate institutions.[7] Thus, in so far as cooperation is needed, this must to be undertaken at an inter-institutional level.

Protocols may also increase the competence of existing treaty bodies. In the human rights context, the (First) Optional Protocol to the International Covenant on Civil and Political Rights (ICCPR) establishes the Human Rights Committee's power to deal with individual complaints. On the other hand, the Optional Protocol to the Convention Against Torture establishes a separate Subcommittee to conduct visits to places where persons are deprived of their liberty and to make appropriate recommendations on their protection.[8]

In addition to the plenary organ, subsidiary bodies may be established, whether through express treaty provisions or by plenary body decisions. For example, the meeting of States parties to the Anti-Personnel Landmine Convention established intersessional Standing Committee meetings, contact groups, and an Implementation Support Unit.[9] Subsidiary bodies may have different functions from plenary organs, including providing financial assistance (eg the Montreal Protocol's Executive Body), technology transfer, compliance control (eg the Kyoto Protocol's Compliance Committee), or scientific advice. Membership may replicate the COP or operate with more limited numbers. Subsidiary bodies may even be composed of persons acting in their individual capacity. These organs will generally be under the guidance of the plenary body, but their independent status may prevent such guidance, as is the case for meetings of the parties to human rights supervisory organs vis-à-vis the various committees that oversee State implementation of those treaties or hear individual complaints relating to them.

Aside from a plenary organ and any subsidiary bodies, a treaty body may have a secretariat. The secretariat may be designated in the treaty itself; the treaty may establish an interim secretariat and leave the final decision to the plenary body; or the treaty may not contain any provision on a secretariat. Establishing a secretariat is important to ensure a permanent organ that can act between meetings of the plenary and any subsidiary bodies that otherwise serve these bodies. Typical secretariat functions include conducting studies, preparing draft decisions for the other treaty bodies, providing technical assistance to parties, and receiving and

---

[7] M Jacobsson, 'The Antarctic Treaty System: Future Challenges' in G Triggs and A Riddell (eds), *Antarctica: Legal and Environmental Challenges for the Future* (BIICL, London 2007) 12.

[8] Optional Protocol to the Convention Against Torture and Other Cruel, Inhuman or Degrading Treatment or Punishment (adopted 18 December 2002, entered into force 22 June 2006) 2375 UNTS 237, Art 11.

[9] S Maslen, *The Convention on the Prohibition of the Use, Stockpiling, Production, and Transfer of Anti-Personnel Mines and on their Destruction* (OUP, Oxford 2005) 272.

circulating reports on implementation of commitments. The secretariat may also serve as the conduit for cooperation with relevant IOs and other treaty bodies; a role the Assembly of States Parties to the International Criminal Court (ICC) described as 'necessary for the exercise of the functions of the Assembly and its subsidiary bodies and the fulfilment of the purposes of the Court'.[10]

While plenary and subsidiary bodies are independent organs, many treaties locate their secretariats within existing IOs. Global treaties on human rights and the treaty bodies established by UNCLOS have their secretariats situated as part of the UN. Although some establish more autonomous secretariats, global environmental treaties generally have their secretariat in the UN, UNEP, the UN Economic Commission for Europe (UNECE), or the International Maritime Organization (IMO). For example, the UNFCCC established an interim secretariat and left the final decision to its COP. The COP decided that 'the Convention secretariat shall be institutionally linked to the United Nations, while not being fully integrated in the work programme and management structure of any particular department or programme'.[11] When a treaty body uses an existing IO to perform secretariat functions, the location of that secretariat may be different from that of the host organization. For example, the secretariat of the Convention on Biological Diversity (CBD) is based in Montreal, whereas the 'host', UNEP, is located in Nairobi. In an unusual case, the Ramsar Convention uses a non-governmental organization (NGO)—the International Union for Conservation of Nature (IUCN)—as its secretariat.[12]

III. The Functions and Competences of Treaty Bodies

A treaty body's functions are spelled out in the constitutive treaty, although, as discussed below, it may have 'implied powers' as well. Assigned functions can range widely. Some plenary bodies have fairly limited functions. For example, meetings of the parties in human rights treaties merely elect members of supervisory organs, such as the Human Rights Committee or the Committee against Torture. The UNCLOS Meeting of States Parties (SPLOS) elects members of the International Tribunal for the Law of the Sea and the Commission on the Limits of the Continental Shelf, and deals with budgetary and administrative matters of the Tribunal.[13]

---

[10] Establishment of the Permanent Secretariat of the Assembly of States Parties to the International Criminal Court (12 September 2003) ICC-ASP/2/Res.3.

[11] UNFCC COP Decision 14/CP.1[2], 'Institutional Linkage of the Convention Secretariat to the United Nations' (6 June 1995) FCCC/CP/1995/7/Add.1, 42.

[12] Convention on Wetlands of International Importance Especially as Waterfowl Habitat (Ramsar Convention) (adopted 2 February 1971, entered into force 21 December 1975) 996 UNTS 245 (as amended) Art 8.

[13] UNCLOS (adopted 10 December 1982, entered into force 16 November 1994) 1833 UNTS 397, Art 319(2). There has, however, been disagreement on the mandate of the Meeting of States Parties to discuss 'matters of a substantive nature relating to the implementation of the Convention'. 'Report of the twenty-first Meeting of States Parties' (29 June 2011) SPLOS/231 [119]–[120].

In contrast, plenary bodies such as those associated with multilateral environmental organizations (MEAs) have a wide range of powers. Typical functions include: (i) matters internal to the MEA such as establishing subsidiary bodies, adopting rules of procedure, and giving guidance to subsidiary bodies and the secretariat; (ii) development of the parties' substantive cooperation by adopting new binding or non-binding commitments; (iii) supervision of the MEA's implementation and State party compliance; and (iv) external activity including arrangements with States, IOs, or organs of other MEAs, which raise questions of the treaty body's 'international legal personality'. In each of these areas a treaty body may have delegated competence to act or its powers may evolve over time. For example, the meeting of States parties in the Anti-Personnel Landmine Convention was originally just intended to serve as a permanent forum in the absence of a secretariat and a vehicle for observing the Convention's application and implementation; over time, however, it has developed into a 'major decision-making event'.[14]

A. Treaty bodies at the internal level

A treaty body's internal competence typically includes powers to adopt rules of procedure, financial regulations, the budget, and to establish and give guidance to subsidiary bodies and a secretariat. The Consultative Meeting of the Antarctic Treaty thus distinguishes its 'Decisions' on an 'internal organizational matter' from 'Measures' on substantive matters adopted under Article IX of the Treaty.[15] Powers at the internal level may be explicitly established in the treaty, either by specifying the different treaty body functions, or by setting out more general powers to exercise the functions required for achieving the treaty's objectives.

Sometimes, the treaty may not offer much guidance, and it may be necessary to turn to principles of international institutional law. The ICJ first accepted the doctrine of implied powers for IOs in the 1949 *Reparations* case, which concerned the UN's capacity to bring legal claims externally.[16] In 1954, in the *U.N. Administrative Tribunal* case, the ICJ held that the UN also had competence to establish a subsidiary organ—a tribunal to render binding judgments in disputes with employees.[17]

Should such implied powers also be accepted as a basis for treaty bodies operating at the internal level? At the outset, caution is warranted in applying doctrines applicable to IOs when the treaty parties consciously decided not to establish an IO, but instead established the more modest set-up of a treaty body. On the other hand, it may be difficult to find any determination or intention by the

---

[14] Maslen (n 9) 272.

[15] Decision 1, 'Final Report of the Nineteenth Antarctic Treaty Consultative Meeting' (Seoul 8–19 May 1995); P Gautier, 'Institutional Developments in the Antarctic Treaty System' in T Scovazzi and F Francioni (eds), *International Law for Antarctica* (2nd edn Kluwer, The Hague 1996) 44–6.

[16] *Reparation for Injuries Suffered in the Service of the United Nations* (Advisory Opinion) [1949] ICJ Rep 174.

[17] *Effect of Awards of Compensation Made by the UN Administrative Tribunal* (Advisory Opinion) [1954] ICJ Rep 47, 53.

parties *not* to apply the doctrine of implied powers. The same reasoning used for IOs would seem suitable for treaty bodies: the relevant functions may be considered necessary to achieve the objectives of the cooperation. Furthermore, internal level decisions by the treaty organ will not impose new substantive obligations on member States, and should, as such, be more acceptable than implying substantive decision-making powers. At the same time, the particular—and possibly more limited—functions of a treaty body may militate against accepting as wide a set of internal powers as for IOs.

If we start with the work of the plenary body, there should be no reason not to accept that this organ may adopt its own rules of procedure, to the extent that such rules are not laid down in the treaty itself. For example, meetings of the parties to human rights treaties must have the competence to decide procedures for nomination and election of members of supervisory bodies, and these bodies in turn must be able to decide on procedures for dealing with the examination of State reports, individual complaints, and the adoption of any General Comments interpreting the treaty's obligations.

Treaty bodies will not necessarily have the capacity to dispose of their own financial resources, but if they do, they should also have the power to adopt appropriate financial regulations and the budget. Furthermore, if the treaty body is a political organ, it may have powers concerning the procedural rights and obligations of member States (eg exclusion or suspension of voting and other rights) and representatives of member States (eg approval of credentials). The treaty body should also have the power to implement any rules of procedure in practice (eg adopting meeting agendas, allotting the speaking order, and admitting observers from IOs, NGOs and non-member States).

Treaty bodies will also generally be in a position to establish subsidiary organs. But while plenary political organs may have extensive express or implied powers to establish subsidiary bodies, the competence of more specialized organs may be limited. For example, supervisory human rights bodies consisting of independent experts, due to their function as expert bodies, should not—or only to a limited extent—be allowed to delegate substantive decision-making powers to a secretariat. It is more acceptable that a subgroup—or individual members—of such bodies be allocated special responsibilities in such cases. If subsidiary organs are established, the treaty organ establishing them should have the powers to control such organs—unless they are meant to have an autonomous status, such as scientific bodies or organs for dispute settlement. In this sense, an elaborate hierarchical structure may be developed, which in practice may be comparable to that of an IO.

The establishment of a secretariat itself may also be a controversial issue where the treaty is silent, as evidenced by the Antarctic Treaty experience where it took decades to establish one. If a separate secretariat is designated in the treaty or established by the treaty body, there is no question about the treaty body controlling the secretariat. Furthermore, the treaty body would be the supreme organ when it comes to recruiting and instructing secretariat personnel.

More intricate questions arise if the secretariat functions are undertaken by an existing IO. The treaty body's independent status means that the IO hosting the secretariat may only exercise the powers flowing from this particular function, and has no powers to instruct the treaty body or its subsidiary bodies. As regards the secretariat, however, matters are different. Both the treaty body and the host organization possess powers in relation to the secretariat. The treaty body and its subsidiary bodies must be considered to have the authority to instruct the secretariat in substantive as well as procedural matters. On the other hand, as the host organization employs the secretariat officials, it has the right to appoint, instruct, and terminate staff. If contradictory instructions occur, the relevant officials would be obliged, under the internal law of the IO, to carry out its instructions. These instructions, however, could violate the commitments undertaken by the IO in agreeing to serve as a host organization for the treaty body.

As with IOs, moreover, internal decisions, such as guidance by the treaty body to subsidiary bodies and the secretariat, should be considered to be binding unless the treaty or the relevant decision itself specifically indicates that it was intended to be non-binding.[18]

B. Substantive decision-making

1. Vehicles for treaty body decision-making

Treaty bodies may have important roles in developing the substantive commitments of States parties. In doing so, they contribute to the dynamic character of international law and overcome the cumbersome treaty-making process. On the other hand, treaty bodies may also balance the desire for effective decision-making with the need for State consent, which is sought to ensure democratic legitimacy for international obligations as well as their national implementation. In practice, different treaty bodies have different functions and therefore also different roles and powers when it comes to substantive decision-making, ie establishing new substantive obligations for States parties, either as international 'legislation' or 'executive' decisions in individual cases.

Treaty bodies often have explicit delegated law-making powers comparable to plenary organs of IOs. But only exceptionally will such organs have the competence to adopt binding new obligations for member States by majority voting. One example is Article 2(9) of the Montreal Protocol, which allows the MOP to adopt certain new obligations in the form of 'adjustments'—with binding effect for all parties—by a 'double majority' of developing and developed States. This authority has never been used. However, its mere existence may induce States' willingness to accept such obligations through consensus.

Considerable ingenuity has been demonstrated in making substantive decision-making more effective, short of binding decisions by majority-voting, including amendments and protocols; recommendations; and interpretations of the relevant

---

[18] CF Amerasinghe, *Principles of the Institutional Law of International Organizations* (2nd edn CUP, Cambridge 2005) 163–4; HG Schermers and NM Blokker, *International Institutional Law: Unity within Diversity* (3rd edn Martinus Nijhoff, Leiden 1995) 744.

treaty. First, treaty bodies may have authority to adopt amendments to the relevant treaty text and its annexes or new legal instruments in the form of protocols. Although State consent is required for these new commitments to enter into force, the existence of the treaty body's authority may facilitate recognition of the need for amendments and protocols as well as their eventual negotiation.[19]

A second, more potent, way of decision-making can be found in the Antarctic Treaty. Article IX provides that the Antarctic Treaty Consultative Meeting (ATCM) may adopt recommendations which shall become 'effective'—presumably legally binding—when approved by the States parties.[20] While it is up to each State to decide whether to accept the binding character of the recommendation, such acceptance does not require a ratification procedure.

Third, treaty bodies may also contribute to international 'legislation' by interpreting the relevant treaty or by adopting recommendations in the form of soft law. For example, the Commission on the Limits of the Continental Shelf has a 'quasi-legislative' function. Its recommendations on the outer limit of the continental shelf beyond 200 nautical miles will, if implemented by the coastal State, be 'final and binding'.[21] This represents a unique example of a scientific-administrative international body contributing to a binding determination of the interpretation of a treaty on complex issues, with wide-reaching legal and political implications. Similarly, the ICC Assembly of States Parties has the power to adopt and amend 'elements of crime' which shall 'assist the Court in the interpretation and application of Articles 6, 7, 8 and 8 *bis*' (genocide, crimes against humanity, war crimes and the crime of aggression), subject to the condition that such elements 'shall be consistent' with the Rome Statute.[22]

Interpretative measures adopted by COPs are also important in international environmental law. In some cases, this power of interpretation is expressly conferred by the MEA. Thus, Article 10(1) of the Montreal Protocol authorizes the MOP to interpret the term 'agreed incremental costs' (incurred by developing States parties in complying with the Protocol) by establishing an 'indicative list of... incremental costs'.[23] But, more commonly, a COP will interpret a MEA not because the agreement authorizes it, but because experience in operating the MEA or scientific, technical, or other developments are perceived as requiring it.[24] For example, in 2003, the Montreal Protocol MOP acknowledged 'that the meaning of the term "State not party to this Protocol" may be subject to differing

---

[19] Additional processes, ie tacit consent by States parties, exist to streamline the process by which amendments to annexes of the treaties or protocols enter into force. For further details see Chapter 14, Part II, 356 *et seq*.

[20] Antarctic Treaty (1 December 1959, entered into force 23 June 1961) 402 UNTS 71, Art IX; A Watts, *International Law and the Antarctic Treaty System* (Grotius, Cambridge 1992) 25; Gautier (n 15) 42.

[21] UNCLOS (n 13) Art 76(8).

[22] Rome Statute of the International Criminal Court (adopted 17 July 1998, entered into force 1 July 2002) 2187 UNTS 90, Art 9.

[23] Montreal Protocol (adopted 16 September 1987, entered into force 1 January 1989) 1522 UNTS 3, Art 10(1).

[24] Churchill and Ulfstein (n 5) 636–43.

interpretations with respect to hydrochlorofluorocarbons by Parties to the Beijing Amendment' and made a decision on the definition of this term.[25]

Supervisory bodies of human rights conventions often have authority to issue 'General Comments' on their respective treaties.[26] While such comments are formally not 'legislation', and not issued by a body competent to undertake law-making, they are interpretations of the respective conventions, to be applied in examining State reports and in compliance procedures. Realistically speaking, as they set out in more detail the obligations contained in the conventions, they may be regarded as a form of soft legislation.[27]

2. The sources of treaty body competence over substance

To the extent that treaty bodies have a comparable structure and function as traditional IOs, they should be expected to have comparable law-making powers. But as with powers at the internal level, caution is advised in determining the scope of law-making powers. They may be constrained by both the relevant body's function(s) and the possible intention of the parties to restrict delegated powers by establishing a treaty body rather than an IO.

When assessing more closely whether tenets of IO law should apply, there is no reason to deny the application of the principle of effective interpretation to the relevant treaty.[28] It must be assumed that the parties desired to achieve effects with their cooperation, be it in the field of human rights, arms control, or the environment. But, as with IOs, there is more reason to be sceptical about the doctrine of implied powers when it comes to substantive law-making. Unlike the determination of internal powers, substantive law-making means that new obligations are imposed on States parties. The point of departure should thus be that law-making power must be based on explicit authority in the treaty. Substantive decisions of a non-binding character may, however, be more easily accepted on the basis of implied powers than binding decisions.

Difficult questions may arise when determining substantive powers in concrete cases. For example, the decision by the COP of the Basel Convention on the Control of Transboundary Movements of Hazardous Wastes and their Disposal to ban transboundary movement of covered waste from OECD to non-OECD countries was controversial. Some States argued that the decision was not legally binding because the COP could not alter parties' substantive obligations merely by utilizing its explicit general power to take action to achieve the Convention's

---

[25] Decision XV/3, 'Obligations of Parties to the Beijing Amendment under Article 4 of the Montreal Protocol with respect to hydrochlorofluorocarbons' (Fifteenth Meeting of the Parties to the Montreal Protocol on Substances that Deplete the Ozone Layer 11 November 2003) UNEP/OzL. Pro.15/9, 44–5.

[26] See eg International Covenant on Civil and Political Rights (adopted 19 December 1966, entered into force 23 March 1976) 999 UNTS 171, Art 40(4), (5).

[27] See H Keller and L Grover, 'General Comments of the Human Rights Committee and their Legitimacy' in H Keller and G Ulfstein (eds), *UN Human Rights Treaty Bodies. Law and Legitimacy* (CUP, Cambridge 2012).

[28] For further discussion of interpretation of the constitutive treaties of IOs see Chapter 22.

objectives. The COP sought to resolve the controversy by adopting an amendment to the Convention that incorporated the substance of the decision.[29] As of 20 August 2011 the amendment had received seventy ratifications, but was not yet in force.[30]

In contrast, Article 17 of the Kyoto Protocol enables the MOP to adopt 'rules' relating to the operation of the system for trading in emissions of greenhouse gases. The use of the word 'rules' suggests that such measures are intended to be legally binding. This idea is supported by the fact that Article 17 refers to 'relevant principles, modalities, rules and guidelines', indicating that 'rules' are different from, for example, non-binding 'principles' or 'guidelines'.[31] Such an interpretation is also supported by substantive considerations. For instance, a party that makes use of the 'rules' on emission trading by buying emission quotas cannot, arguably, be accused of non-compliance with the Protocol when it wants to add these quotas to its emission limits in the Protocol.[32] This example demonstrates that there may be a fine distinction between effective interpretation and the use of implied powers: relevant arguments may be found in both the wording and object and purpose of the treaty.

But even if the treaty body is not empowered to make binding interpretations, its decisions are not necessarily without legal significance. Reliance on such practice may, however, raise complex questions regarding the relationship between treaty law and the law of international institutions. Article 31(2)(b) of the Vienna Convention on the Law of Treaties (VCLT) requires that treaty interpretation takes into account 'any subsequent practice in the application of the treaty which establishes the agreement of the parties regarding its interpretation'. Such an agreement might be seen expressed in decisions of treaty organs consisting of representatives of the parties. But it seems more natural to see such practice as the practice of the treaty body, rather than the collective practice of States parties.[33] This view is even clearer when the treaty body does not consist of representatives of States parties, but rather independent experts, as is the case with the supervisory organs of human rights conventions.

Decision-making by treaty bodies has proven more effective than traditional consent-based treaty processes. However, how treaty bodies take these decisions, ie by majority vote or consensus, requires some scrutiny. Since the mid-1960s,

---

[29] Churchill and Ulfstein (n 5) 639.

[30] See Decision IX/26, 'President's statement on the possible way forward on the Ban Amendment' (Report of the Conference of the Parties to the Basel Convention on the Control of Transboundary Movements of Hazardous Wastes and their Disposal on its ninth meeting 27 June 2008) UNEP/CHW.9/39.

[31] Kyoto Protocol to the UN Framework Convention on Climate Change (adopted 16 March 1998, entered into force 16 February 2005) [1998] 37 ILM 22, Art 17.

[32] Churchill and Ulfstein (n 5) 639. More skeptical about the binding character is J Brunnée, 'COPing with Consent: Law-Making Under Multilateral Environmental Agreements' (2002) 15 LJIL 1, 24–6.

[33] See different views on the significance of institutional practice in interpretation of the UN Charter, JE Alvarez, *International Organizations as Law-Makers* (OUP, Oxford 2005) 88–9 and J Klabbers, 'Checks and Balances in the Law of International Organizations' (2008) 1 Ius Gentium 141, 151–2.

treaty bodies have increasingly used a consensus requirement to keep powerful States on board. But a consensus requirement may prevent decisions or make them 'constructively' vague.[34] It may also be contested what is meant by consensus, as evidenced by adoption of the Cancun Agreements by consensus under the UNFCCC in 2010 over the vocal objections of Bolivia.[35] A compromise between consensus and simple majority voting may be to require qualified majorities and/or weighted voting. The Montreal Protocol combines those two techniques by requiring a double majority under the aforementioned Article 2(9); a two-thirds majority must include a majority of developing States parties and a majority of developed States parties. All told, the possibility to object to, and so not be bound by decisions a State does not like, serves also to protect against treaty bodies gaining overly wide-reaching powers on decision-making by majority-voting.[36]

C. Supervisory treaty bodies

International law has traditionally left the enforcement of treaty obligations to individual States parties, whether through: suspension or termination of treaties as a consequence of material breach; invoking State responsibility, including counter-measures; or, by initiating proceedings by international courts. In recent years, States have sought to supplement these essentially bilateral approaches with multi-lateral arrangements to ensure national implementation. Many treaties now establish their own collective and individual mechanisms in the form of supervisory treaty bodies to serve treaty implementation and enforcement. Originally inspired by mechanisms developed in the ILO, so-called 'non-compliance procedures' now exist in several fields, including human rights, international environmental law, and arms control.

Supervisory treaty bodies are well-suited to apply measures of a more facilitative quality in lieu of traditional coercive approaches, consonant with the view that a 'managerial approach' rather than an 'enforcement approach' may better address non-compliance questions.[37] Treaty organs may also be better designed to prevent non-compliance rather than waiting to address reparations for damages post-hoc. Finally, these bodies may also offer a new structure for communication rather than confrontational approaches that might undermine the cooperative spirit in ongoing international cooperation under the same treaties.

These are all plausible reasons why treaties may contain non-compliance procedures. An alternative explanation exists, however; namely that States prefer non-compliance procedures because—instead of leaving decisions to a third party court or an arbitral tribunal—they allow States more control over the process and its

---

[34] Churchill and Ulfstein (n 5) 642–3.
[35] L Rajamani, 'The Cancun Climate Agreements: Reading the Text, Subtext and Tea Leaves' (2011) 60 ICLQ 499, 514–18.
[36] Churchill and Ulfstein (n 5) 643.
[37] G Ulfstein, T Marauhn, and A Zimmermann, 'Introduction' in G Ulfstein, T Marauhn, and A Zimmermann (eds), *Making Treaties Work: Human Rights, Environment and Arms Control* (CUP, Cambridge 2007) 9.

outcome. Furthermore, a decision resulting from a non-compliance procedure is not final in the form of res judicata, and may therefore be seen as less intrusive on State sovereignty.

A fundamental requirement for assessing compliance with international obligations is information about relevant facts, be it the emission of relevant polluting substances, the treatment of human beings, or the manufacturing and storage of weapons. States have traditionally been responsible for providing such data through reporting obligations. Expert Review Teams (ERTs) established under the Kyoto Protocol, however, offer an example of how fact-finding can be done by independent treaty bodies. ERTs provide a 'thorough and comprehensive technical assessment' of 'all aspects of the implementation by a Party of the Kyoto Protocol', and identify 'any problems in, and factors influencing, the fulfilment of commitments' as well as 'questions of implementation' with regard to a party's performance.[38] We find also human rights treaty bodies empowered to conduct fact-finding inquiries on the territory of States parties if they have reason to believe that serious human rights violations are taking place.[39]

Beyond fact-finding, human rights treaty bodies may—to the extent agreed to by the relevant State—consider individual complaints and, as discussed above, issue General Comments on the interpretation of relevant treaty obligations. The Aarhus Convention is special among MEAs in contemplating a right for individuals and NGOs to trigger cases of non-compliance, presumably as an aspect of the Convention's human rights character.[40]

Decisions of supervisory treaty bodies are generally based on express authorization in the respective treaty texts, but 'implied powers' are also occasionally used. For example, it has been disputed whether the adoption of General Comments by human rights treaty bodies can only be based on specific treaty provisions, including subsequent State practice, or may exist by necessary implication.[41] Likewise, the adoption of interim measures lacks an explicit basis in the relevant conventions. Implied powers have also been claimed as the legal basis for follow-up procedures.[42] Human rights treaty bodies have been successful in achieving acceptance for all of these activities. Thus, as noted above, they may be considered to constitute both

[38] UNFCCC, Decision 23/CP.7, 'Guidelines for Review under Article 8 of the Kyoto Protocol' (Report of the Conference of the Parties on its Seventh Sess Marrakesh 29 October–10 November 2001) Annex [4] and [48(b)(iv)].

[39] Convention against Torture and Other Cruel, Inhuman or Degrading Treatment or Punishment (adopted 10 December 1984, entered into force 26 June 1987) 1465 UNTS 85, Art 2; Convention on the Elimination of All Forms of Discrimination Against Women (adopted 18 December 1979, entered into force 3 September 1981) 1249 UNTS 13, Art 8.

[40] Aarhus Convention on Access to Information, Public Participation in Decision-Making and Access to Justice in Environmental Matters (adopted 25 June 1998, entered into force 30 October 2001) [1998] 37 ILM 517, Art 15.

[41] See generally Keller and Grover (n 27).

[42] G Ulfstein, 'Individual Complaints' in H Keller and G Ulfstein (eds), *UN Human Rights Treaty Bodies. Law and Legitimacy* (CUP, Cambridge 2012).

subsequent practice of the treaty bodies (under international institutional law) and the subsequent practice by the States parties (under the law of treaties).[43]

What legal status human rights treaty body findings have is more controversial. Some human rights literature has claimed that views adopted by the Human Rights Committee (HRC) in cases of individual complaints involving the ICCPR are, although formally not binding, to a great extent comparable to judicial decisions.[44] In its General Comment No 33, the HRC accepted that its function is not 'as such, that of a judicial body'.[45] But the HRC stated that its Views exhibit 'some important characteristics of a judicial decision'. The Views are arrived at 'in a judicial spirit', including 'the impartiality and independence of Committee members, the considered interpretation of the language of the Covenant, and the determinative character of the decisions'. Furthermore, the General Comment established that the Views represent 'an authoritative determination'[46] and that States parties 'must use whatever means lie within their power in order to give effect to the views of the Committee'.[47] This gives an impression that, to the HRC at least, its Views are tantamount to legally binding decisions.

Despite opposition from some States, there are arguments for taking the practice of treaty bodies into account because doing so accords with the object and purpose of States parties: they established these organs to ensure the treaty's effective implementation and to obtain authoritative interpretations of treaty obligations. The ICJ endorsed this view in the *Diallo* case, stating that the HRC practice should be accorded 'great weight' since it 'was established specifically to supervise the application of that treaty [the ICCPR]'. The argument was thus based on the parties' intention. But the Court also used a 'systemic' argument for relying on HRC practice, referring to the need 'to achieve the necessary clarity and the essential consistency of international law, as well as legal security'.[48] The same arguments could be made for other treaty bodies to accord their opinions 'great weight', recognizing that there might be more scrutiny by international or national

---

[43] See discussion by the International Law Association, Committee on International Human Rights Law and Practice, *Report of the Seventy-First Conference (Berlin)* (ILA, London 2004) 629.

[44] See R Hanski and M Scheinin, *Leading Cases of the Human Rights Committee* (2nd edn Institute for Human Rights, Åbo Akademi University, Turku 2007) 23; M Nowak, *U.N. Covenant on Civil and Political Rights: CCPR commentary* (2nd edn NP Engel, Kehl 2005) XXVII; HJ Steiner, R Goodman, and P Alston, *International Human Rights in Context: Law, Politics and Morals* (3rd edn OUP, Oxford 2008) 915; M Nowak, K Buchinger, and E McArthur, *The United Nations Convention against Torture* (OUP, Oxford 2008) 777; S Joseph, J Schultz, and M Castan, *The International Covenant on Civil and Political Rights: Cases, Materials, and Commentary* (2nd edn OUP, Oxford 2004) 24; C Tomuschat, *Human Rights: between Idealism and Realism* (2nd edn OUP, Oxford 2008) 220. See also W Kälin and J Künzli, *The Law of International Human Rights Protection* (OUP, Oxford 2009) 225.

[45] HRC, 'General Comment No. 33: The Obligations of States Parties under the Optional Protocol to the International Covenant on Civil and Political Rights' (5 November 2008) CCPR/C/GC/3[11].

[46] Ibid [13].

[47] Ibid [20].

[48] ICJ, *Case Concerning Ahmadou Sadio Diallo (Republic of Guinea v Democratic Republic of Congo)* (2010) [66]. That said, the ICJ only used HRC practice to corroborate its own interpretation, although it did refer to HRC findings in individual Communications (ie Views) as well as its General Comments as 'case law'.

courts since such bodies would have less eminence in judicial decision-making than
the HRC.

Although often contemplated as a facilitative process, a finding of non-compliance may be regarded as a sanction, in the form of 'naming and shaming', creating
political embarrassment for the relevant State. Such finding in itself does not,
however, entail legal consequences—except possibly with respect to internal treaty
cooperation between the parties (eg States that violate their commitments will not
be elected to treaty organs). Therefore, such findings should not require an explicit
treaty basis. Likewise, the introduction of positive measures in the form of incentives, for example of a financial or technological character, should be accepted
without express authorization.

The situation is more complicated when it comes to explicit sanctions. IOs have
imposed different sanctions with or without an explicit basis, such as suspension of
voting rights or representation, or of other rights and privileges of membership.[49]
The reluctance of States to accept imposition of such sanctions in treaty bodies
without an explicit treaty basis is illustrated by Article 18 of the Kyoto Protocol.
It establishes that mechanisms 'entailing binding consequences shall be adopted by
means of an amendment to this Protocol'. It is not obvious what kind of measures
should be regarded as entailing 'binding consequences', but it would be difficult
to accept, eg deduction of emissions quotas at a penalty rate, as adopted by the
MOP as part of its Marrakesh Accords, without a treaty basis in the form of an
amendment.[50]

D. Treaty bodies at the external level

1. Treaty body treaty-making

Treaty bodies may also need to have a 'foreign policy'. For instance, the relationship
to the IO providing a secretariat must be arranged; there may be a need for a
headquarters agreement with the State hosting the secretariat as well as States
hosting meetings of the parties and subsidiary bodies; implementation of commitments by States parties may require financial assistance and capacity-building
and, hence, involvement by treaty bodies may require arrangements with international financial institutions; and, finally, to the extent that relevant international
problems are interconnected, it may be necessary to require cooperation among
different treaty bodies and IOs. These needs raise the question of the 'international
legal personality' of treaty bodies to enter into binding agreements under international law.[51]

---

[49] Schermers and Blokker (n 18) 916–18.

[50] G Ulfstein and J Werksman, 'The Kyoto Compliance System: Towards Hard Enforcement' in
OS Stokke, J Hovi, and G Ulfstein (eds), *Implementing the Climate Regime. International Compliance*
(Earthscan, London 2005) 57–8.

[51] See on international legal personality: JE Nijman, *The Concept of International Legal Personality*
(TMC Asser Press, The Hague 2004) and R Portmann, *Legal Personality in International Law* (CUP,
Cambridge 2010).

Treaties establishing treaty bodies will rarely set out a treaty-making capacity. This absence of explicit provisions is, however, also common to most IOs, without preventing them from enjoying such legal capacity. Thus, although some treaties may be interpreted to include a reference to treaty-making capacity for treaty bodies, the main basis for accepting such powers would, as for IOs, be implied powers. Doing so would accord with the flexible approach used by the ICJ in the *Reparations* case, where it noted that not all subjects of law are identical in their nature or the extent of their rights, which turn instead on 'the requirements of international life' and the 'progressive increase in the collective activities of States'.[52] Furthermore, accepting an external capacity for treaty bodies would allow such bodies to possess rights and obligations under international law, but would not itself provide them with a capacity to create new obligations for States parties or third States.

When it comes to treaty bodies resembling IOs in their structure and functions, such as the organs established by MEAs, there seems little reason not to accord them powers at the external level, to the extent such powers are needed to fulfil their functions. The reason MEAs establish treaty bodies instead of formal IOs comes from a desire to accomplish 'institutional economy', not to prevent their effectiveness. Such capacities may also be based on subsequent practice by treaty bodies.[53] As is demonstrated by the establishment of the Antarctic Treaty Secretariat, the recognition of international legal personality may be highly controversial.[54] But the Headquarters Agreement for the Secretariat of the Antarctic Treaty defines the 2010 Antarctic Treaty Consultative Meeting (ATCM) and the Argentine Republic as its parties, implying that the ATCM possesses a treaty-making capacity.

On the other hand, the constitutive treaty or the functions of a treaty body may restrict its treaty-making capacity. For example, the Rome Statute establishes that the ICC's relationship with the UN shall be regulated 'through an agreement to be approved by the Assembly of States Parties to this Statute and thereafter concluded by the President of the Court on its behalf'.[55] This means that while the consent of the ICC Assembly as a treaty body is necessary, the Court as such, not the Assembly as a treaty body, is party to the agreement with the UN.

The structure and functions of supervisory organs established by treaties on arms control or human rights do not provide the same basis for accepting powers to enter into treaties. There may, however, be a need to coordinate activities, be it between the treaty body and the host IO for the secretariat or between different treaty bodies of the same character, such as harmonizing reporting requirements for States parties to different human rights conventions.[56] While a capacity to enter into binding

---

[52] *Reparations* case (n 16) 174, 178.

[53] Churchill and Ulfstein (n 5) 651. On the international legal personality of MEA secretariats see also B Desai, *Multilateral Environmental Agreements* (CUP, Cambridge 2010) 124–5.

[54] Vigni (n 4) 21–2.

[55] Rome Statute (n 22) Art 2; see also ibid Art 3(2) on a similar procedure for entering into a Headquarters Agreement.

[56] The Secretary-General of the UN called for 'harmonized guidelines on reporting to all treaty bodies' in his report 'In Larger Freedom: Towards Development, Security and Human Rights for All' UNGA (21 March 2005) UN Doc A/59/2005 [147].

international agreements in the form of treaties should not readily be accepted, there should be no reason for denying these bodies' capacity to enter into political understandings or agreements, such as a Memorandum of Understanding (MOU).

Restrictions on treaty body external capacity may also follow from general international law. The ICJ held, for instance, in the *Nuclear Weapons* advisory opinion that the World Health Organization (WHO) could not, under reference to 'the principle of speciality', request an advisory opinion from the ICJ on the legality of the use of nuclear weapons.[57]

2. The fragmentation of treaty regimes

The increasing number of treaty bodies may—in addition to the growth of IOs and courts—contribute to a fragmented international architecture, at the expense of comprehensive policy-making. Inconsistent and contradictory decisions may also occur. On the other hand, the existence of different treaty orders and institutions may have benefits by: providing possibilities for designing the institutional set-up to the specific needs of the problem at hand; giving focus to marginalized interests; and increasing the pool of experience in developing policy-making and jurisprudence.

The coordination problems associated with treaty body proliferation may be met (i) by increased formal or informal cooperation among different treaty regimes and (ii) by taking account of other treaty body decisions as well as those of relevant IOs and international courts. In international environmental law, this challenge has been met by increased cooperation between the COPs of different MEAs[58] and between COPs and IOs.[59] In human rights, the High Commissioner for Human Rights has taken an initiative to streamline and strengthen the human rights treaty body system.[60] As for the ICJ, it takes due account of the practice of human rights treaty bodies, as it did in the *Diallo* case as well as by respecting the complementarity between it and bodies like the Committee on the Elimination of Racial Discrimination (CERD), which it did in the *Georgia v Russian Federation* case.[61] In practice, different treaty regimes interact in different ways and States and other actors may use the existence of different regimes in strategic ways.[62]

---

[57] *Legality of the Use by a State of Nuclear Weapons in Armed Conflict* (Advisory Opinion) [1996] ICJ Rep 226 [25].

[58] See KN Scott, 'International Environmental Governance: Managing Fragmentation through Institutional Connection' (2011) 12 Melbourne J Intl L 1–40.

[59] See eg MA Young, *Trading Fish, Saving Fish: the Interaction between Regimes in International Law* (CUP, Cambridge 2011) 154–84.

[60] See the website titled, 'The Treaty Body Strengthening Process', established by the UN High Commissioner for Human Rights <http://www2.ohchr.org/english/bodies/HRTD/index.htm>.

[61] ICJ, *Case Concerning Application of the International Convention on the Elimination of All Forms of Racial Discrimination (Georgia v Russian Federation)* (2011).

[62] See eg K Raustiala and DG Victor, 'The Regime Complex for Plant Genetic Resources' (2004) 58 Intl Org 277–309; RO Keohane and DG Victor, 'The Regime Complex for Climate Change' Discussion Paper (2010) Harvard Project on International Climate Agreements.

A more ambitious approach to international coordination and comprehensive policy- and decision-making would be to merge different treaty bodies, and possibly replace them by IOs and international courts. Thus, a World Environmental Organization has been proposed to overcome the fragmented institutional framework and strengthen international environmental governance.[63] In international human rights, the UN High Commissioner for Human Rights has proposed a 'unified treaty body',[64] while a more ambitious proposal involves establishing a World Court of Human Rights.[65] Such proposals have, however, been met by considerable reluctance from States. Less ambitious approaches seem more realistic—at least in the short term.

Conclusions

Treaty bodies are established by treaties, but their manifold structures and functions do not easily fit into the traditional scheme of treaty law. To the extent that their legal powers and capacities, their procedures, and the legal status of their decisions must be determined, the law of treaties has to be supplemented by the law of international institutional law, especially the law of IOs.

International institutional law is characterized by its open-ended nature. It may indeed be asked which parts of it are truly general, as opposed to specific rules for each institution.[66] But this also means that this body of law has sufficient flexibility to be adapted to legal issues concerning treaty bodies, taking due account of their explicit foundation in the relevant treaties and their specific functions.

The creation of treaty bodies in various areas of international law raises challenges in ensuring effective and consistent policy- and decision-making. But institutional plurality can also serve important functions in ensuring a design suited to the treaty's particular purposes, and increasing the pool of knowledge-based practice. There are also remedies available to promote coordination—and even to merge these bodies if needed.

Increased power to treaty bodies does raise issues of accountability and legitimacy of their activities, concerns well known from the work of IOs and international courts. It can be argued that treaty bodies present special dilemmas due to their less formal character. There is, however, nothing in the legal technique of using treaty bodies that by itself provides for more or less political or judicial control. Nor do they provide for more or less protection of rule of law guarantees or human rights than IOs and international courts. Control and protection can be instituted,

---

[63] See G Ulfstein, 'International Framework for Environmental Decision-Making' in M Fitzmaurice, DM Ong, and P Merkouris (eds), *Research Handbook on International Environmental Law* (Edward Elgar, Cheltenham 2010) 42–3.

[64] OHCHR, 'Concept Paper on the High Commissioner's Proposal for a Unified Standing Treaty Body' (22 March 2006) HRI/MC/2006/2.

[65] G Ulfstein, 'Do We Need a World Court of Human Rights?' in O Engdahl and P Wrange (eds), *Law at War–The Law as It Was and the Law as It Should Be* (Brill, Leiden 2008).

[66] Amerasinghe (n 18) 16–20.

adjusted for special needs, whether the powers are being exercised by formal IOs, international courts, or treaty bodies.[67]

Today, States may choose cooperation through treaty bodies for several reasons: costs, effectiveness, protection of State sovereignty, or avoiding the need to locate a new IO or court. In the case of single purpose treaty bodies, such as the supervisory bodies of international human rights, establishing an IO seems hardly necessary. But even in more complex institutional settings, States should be allowed flexibility in designing the format of their cooperation, including the use of treaty bodies when considered appropriate. It will then be for the lawyers to adapt the law, including the law of treaties and international institutional law, to suit such institutional innovations.

Recommended Reading

CF Amerasinghe, *Principles of the Institutional Law of International Organizations* (2nd edn CUP, Cambridge 2005)

J Brunnée, 'Coping with Consent: Law-Making under Multilateral Environmental Agreements' (2002) 15 LJIL 1

R Churchill and G Ulfstein, 'Autonomous Institutional Arrangements in Multilateral Environmental Agreements: A Little-Noticed Phenomenon in International Law' (2000) 94 AJIL 623

B Desai, *Multilateral Environmental Agreements* (CUP, Cambridge 2010)

F Francioni, 'Establishment of an Antarctic Treaty Secretariat: Pending Legal Issues' in D Vidas (ed), *Implementing the Environmental Protection Regime for the Antarctic* (Kluwer Academic Publishers, Dordrecht 2000) 125

P Gautier, 'Institutional Developments in the Antarctic Treaty System' in T Scovazzi and F Francioni (eds), *International Law for Antarctica* (2nd edn Kluwer, The Hague 1996) 31

R Hanski and M Scheinin, *Leading Cases of the Human Rights Committee* (2nd edn Institute for Human Rights, Åbo Akademi University, Turku 2007)

M Jacobsson, 'The Antarctic Treaty System: Future Challenges' in G Triggs and A Riddell (eds), *Antarctica: Legal and Environmental Challenges for the Future* (BIICL, London 2007) 1

S Joseph, J Schultz, and M Castan, *The International Covenant on Civil and Political Rights: Cases, Materials, and Commentary* (2nd edn OUP, Oxford 2004)

W Kälin and J Künzli, *The Law of International Human Rights Protection* (OUP, Oxford 2009)

H Keller and G Ulfstein (eds), *UN Human Rights Treaty Bodies. Law and Legitimacy* (CUP, Cambridge, 2012)

RO Keohane and DG Victor, 'The Regime Complex for Climate Change' (2010) Discussion Paper 2010–33, Harvard Project on International Climate Agreements

---

[67] G Ulfstein, 'Institutions and Competences' in J Klabbers, A Peters, and G Ulfstein (eds), *The Constitutionalization of International Law* (OUP, Oxford 2009) 50–1.

J Klabbers, 'Setting the Scene' in J Klabbers and others (eds), *The Constitutionalization of International Law* (OUP, Oxford 2009) 1

M Koskenniemi, 'The Fate of Public International Law: Between Technique and Politics' (2007) 70 MLR 1

S Maslen, *The Convention on the Prohibition of the Use, Stockpiling, Production, and Transfer of Anti-Personnel Mines and on Their Destruction* (OUP, Oxford 2005)

JE Nijman, *The Concept of International Legal Personality* (TMC Asser Press, The Hague 2004)

M Nowak, *UN Covenant on Civil and Political Rights: CCPR Commentary* (2nd edn NP Engel, Kehl 2005)

M Nowak, K Buchinger, and E McArthur, *The United Nations Convention against Torture* (OUP, Oxford 2008)

R Portmann, *Legal Personality in International Law* (CUP, Cambridge 2010)

L Rajamani, 'The Cancun Climate Agreements: Reading the Text, Subtext and Tea Leaves' (2011) 60 ICLQ 499

K Raustiala and DG Victor, 'The Regime Complex for Plant Genetic Resources' (2004) 58 Intl Org 277

HG Schermers and NM Blokker, *International Institutional Law: Unity within Diversity* (5th edn Martinus Nijhoff, Leiden 2011)

K Scott, 'Institutional Developments within the Antarctic Treaty System' (2003) 52 ICLQ 473

K Scott, 'International Environmental Governance: Managing Fragmentation through Institutional Connection' (2011) 12 Melbourne J Intl L 1

HJ Steiner, R Goodman, and P Alston, *International Human Rights in Context: Law, Politics and Morals* (3rd edn OUP, Oxford 2008)

C Tomuschat, *Human Rights: Between Idealism and Realism* (2nd edn OUP, Oxford 2008)

G Ulfstein, 'Do We Need a World Court of Human Rights?' in O Engdahl and P Wrange (eds), *Law at War—the Law as It Was and the Law as It Should Be* (Brill, Leiden 2008) 261

G Ulfstein, 'Institutions and Competences' in J Klabbers and others (eds), *The Constitutionalization of International Law* (OUP, Oxford 2009) 45

G Ulfstein, 'International Framework for Environmental Decision-Making' in M Fitzmaurice and others (eds), *Research Handbook on International Environmental Law* (Edward Elgar, Cheltenham 2010) 26

G Ulfstein, T Marauhn, and A Zimmermann, 'Introduction' in G Ulfstein and others (eds), *Making Treaties Work: Human Rights, Environment and Arms Control* (CUP, Cambridge 2007) 3

G Ulfstein and J Werksman, 'The Kyoto Compliance System: Towards Hard Enforcement' in OS Stokke and others (eds), *Implementing the Climate Regime. International Compliance* (Earthscan, London 2005)

P Vigni, 'The Secretariat of the Antarctic Treaty: Achievements and Weaknesses Three Years after Its Establishment' in G Triggs and A Riddell (eds), *Antarctica: Legal and Environmental Challenges for the Future* (BIICL, London 2007) 17

A Watts, *International Law and the Antarctic Treaty System* (Grotius, Cambridge 1992)

MA Young, *Trading Fish, Saving Fish: The Interaction between Regimes in International Law* (CUP, Cambridge 2011)

18

Treaty Conflicts and Normative Fragmentation

Christopher J Borgen

Introduction

Studies addressing how States can respond to conflicting international legal obligations are nothing new.[1] But warnings of the possible systemic fragmentation of international law are a by-product of the modern conception of international law as an integrated, though primitive, legal system. Fragmentation is thus a more recent 'macroeconomic' or systemic manifestation of the 'microeconomic' or 'firm-level' problem of conflicting legal obligations inherent to international relations.

One recurrent theme in fragmentation discussions is a debate over whether international law has different regional traditions. During the Cold War, 'western' views of international law contrasted with Soviet doctrine. More recently, discussions of regionalization have focused interest in Islamic, East Asian, and Russian (as opposed to Soviet) conceptions of international law and asked if these are compatible with mainstream (essentially Euro–American) views.[2]

Since the end of the Cold War, a second theme has emerged: fragmentation as a result of functional specialization.[3] Trade, international investment, human rights, and environmental protection are all issue areas that have become increasingly legalized, spawning new (and relatively autonomous) treaties, international organizations (IOs), and tribunals. Increasing legalization can have a 'snowball effect', producing even broader and deeper law-making and law-interpreting activity.[4]

---

[1] See eg C Rousseau, 'De la compatibilité des norms juridiques contradictories dans l'ordre international' (1932) 39 RGDIP 33–192; H Lauterpacht, 'The Covenant as the "Higher Law"' (1936) 17 BYBIL 54–65; CW Jenks, 'The Conflict of Law Making Treaties' (1953) 30 BYBIL 403; J Mus, 'Conflicts Between Treaties in International Law' (1998) 45 Netherlands Intl L Rev 208–32.

[2] See CJ Borgen, 'Whose Public, Whose Order?: Imperium, Region, and Normative Friction' (2007) 32 YJIL 331, 338–54.

[3] The ILC Study Group's Fragmentation Report considered functional differentiation of treaty regimes as part of a broader phenomenon of increasing specialization and autonomization, both domestically and internationally. ILC Study Group, Fragmentation of International Law: Difficulties Arising from the Diversification and Expansion of International Law (13 April 2006) UN Doc A/CN.4/L.682, 10–11 ('Fragmentation Report') (defining fragmentation as 'the emergence of specialized and (relatively) autonomous rules or rule-complexes, legal institutions and spheres of legal practice'). See also Jenks (n 1) 403.

[4] Regarding IOs as law-makers, see JE Alvarez, *International Organizations as Law Makers* (OUP, Oxford 2005).

However, increasing legalization also risks two types of potential *normative fragmentation*: (a) one State having conflicting obligations in multiple treaties to which it is a party and (b) fragmentation due to competing interpretations of the same obligation by different international institutions.[5]

The first type is most often discussed in scholarship analyzing (potentially) conflicting obligations between various trade regimes and human rights, environmental, and/or labour regimes.[6] The second type of conflict includes, for example, the overlapping and competing jurisdictions of international tribunals.[7] There is some disagreement over whether fragmentation is or is not occurring at all.[8] And, among commentators who perceive that normative fragmentation exists, there is a second level of debate over whether such fragmentation is necessarily bad or good for international law's development.[9]

This chapter examines treaty conflicts on both the micro and macro levels.[10] This discussion necessarily revolves around three key texts: (i) the 1969 Vienna Convention on the Law of Treaties (VCLT); (ii) the International Law Commission's (ILC's) 2006 Report of the Study Group on Fragmentation of International Law;[11] and (iii) the Conclusions of the work of the Study Group on the Fragmentation of International Law: Difficulties arising from the Diversification and Expansion of International Law.[12]

While numerous canons of construction have been used for centuries to address the clash of obligations under international law, Article 30 of the VCLT codifies

---

[5] For a similar, through tripartite, description of fragmentation types, see Fragmentation Report (n 3) 30–1. Disputes over the environmental effects of the UK 'MOX Plant' nuclear facility exhibited both versions of fragmentation, generating three different proceedings under three different normative regimes: an arbitral tribunal pursuant to the 1982 UN Convention on the Law of the Sea; dispute settlement under the Convention on the Protection of the Marine Environment of the North-East Atlantic; and proceedings before the European Court of Justice pursuant to the European Community and Euratom treaties. Ibid 12–13.

[6] Sometimes this is referred to as 'Trade and . . .' scholarship. For a prominent example, see J Pauwelyn, *Conflict of Norms in International Law: How WTO Law Relates to Other Rules of International Law* (CUP, Cambridge 2003).

[7] See Y Shany, *The Competing Jurisdictions of International Courts and Tribunals* (CUP, Cambridge 2003); CPR Romano, 'The Proliferation of International Judicial Bodies: The Pieces of the Puzzle' (1999) 31 NYU J Intl L & Poly 709; JI Charney, 'Is International Law Threatened by Multiple International Tribunals?' (1998) 271 RdC 101.

[8] Regarding recent scholarship on the diversity of sources of international regulation and fragmentation, see Fragmentation Report (n 3) 11 n11, 12 n14.

[9] Scholarship that exhibits concern about the potential effects of fragmentation includes CJ Borgen, 'Resolving Treaty Conflicts' (2005) 37 GW Intl L Rev 573; Pauwelyn (n 6); G Guillaume, 'The proliferation of international judicial bodies: The outlook for the international legal order', Address by the ICJ President to the UNGA's Sixth Committee (27 October 2000) at <http://www.icj-cij.org/court/index.php?pr=85&pt=3&p1=1&p2=3&p3=1>. Examples of scholarship that does not see fragmentation as a serious problem includes Charney (n 7); M Koskenniemi & P Leino, 'Fragmentation of International Law? Postmodern Anxieties' (2002) 15 LJIL 553.

[10] This chapter does not focus on fragmentation issues that are not a function of treaty conflicts. Thus, it does not deal directly with interpretative fragmentation.

[11] Fragmentation Report (n 3).

[12] ILC Study Group, Conclusions of the work of the Study Group on the Fragmentation of International Law: Difficulties arising from the Diversification and Expansion of International Law (2006) included in ILC, Report on the Work of its 58th Session (1 May to 9 June and 3 July to 1 August 2006) UN Doc A/61/10 [251] ('Study Group Conclusions').

certain techniques concerning conflicts between 'successive treaties relating to the same subject-matter'.[13] As Richard Kearney and Robert Dalton, two US negotiators involved in drafting the VCLT, noted:

> In essence [Article 30 of the VCLT] provides that: (a) if a treaty says it is subject to another treaty, the other treaty governs on any issue of compatibility; (b) as between parties to one treaty who become parties to a second, the second governs on any point where it is incompatible with the first; (c) if some of the parties to the first treaty are not parties to the second treaty, and vice versa, the first governs between a party to both and a party only to the first; the second governs between a party to both and a party only to the second.[14]

Thus, Article 30's normative framework applies only in certain defined instances, making it a necessary, but incomplete, response to treaty conflicts.

Indeed, the VCLT was written before the North American Free Trade Agreement (NAFTA), before the World Trade Organization (WTO) Agreements, before the burgeoning of the European Union (EU), and before the enactment of most of the over 2,700 bilateral investment treaties that now exist among at least 176 States.[15] Consequently, responding to treaty conflicts requires assessing the VCLT's efficacy, and where it fails to provide an answer, considering various older canons of construction and other techniques.

In 2000, the ILC began such a project and, in 2002, organized the Study Group on Fragmentation of International Law (ILC Study Group) to consider fragmentation as a consequence of the expansion and diversification of international law.[16] Preliminary reports served as the basis for a consolidated Study Group report, finalized by Martti Koskenniemi, and issued on 13 April 2006.[17] The ILC Study Group also produced forty-two conclusions regarding fragmentation and possible responses to normative conflicts.[18]

In considering the question of normative fragmentation, the ILC Study Group considered diplomatic and lawyerly tactics for resolving normative conflicts involving treaties, canons of construction, and the VCLT's prescriptions. Though not without some controversy, it is at the time of this writing the most complete

---

[13] VCLT Art 30(1).

[14] RD Kearney and RE Dalton, 'The Treaty on Treaties' (1970) 64 AJIL 495, 517.

[15] Concerning the total number of BITs, see UNCTAD, 'Recent Developments in International Development Agreements (2008–June 2009)' (2009) IIA Monitor no 3, 2. Concerning the number of States parties to BITs, see UNCTAD, 'Investment Instruments Online' at <http://www.unctadxi.org/templates/Page____1007.aspx>.

[16] Fragmentation Report (n 3) 8. The UNGA's Sixth Committee supported the ILC recommendation for a broad study dealing with treaty conflicts oriented on the VCLT as a guide. UNGA, Report of the Study Group on Fragmentation of International Law: Difficulties Arising from the Diversification and Expansion of International Law, UNGA, 55th Session (2003), UN Doc A/CN.4/L.644, 6.

[17] See Fragmentation Report (n 3) 9.

[18] Study Group Conclusions (n 12); but see ILC, Report on the work of its fifty-eighth session (2006): Topical summary of the discussion held in the Sixth Committee of the General Assembly during its sixty-first session, prepared by the Secretariat Addendum (23 January 2007) UN Doc A/CN.4/577/Add.1 [17] ('Sixth Committee Discussion') (noting views of some Sixth Committee representatives that the use of 'vague expressions' in the ILC Study Group Conclusions 'reflected the fact that the general system of international law did not provide clear guidance on how to resolve possible conflicts of norms').

statement on treaty conflicts and the question of fragmentation produced under UN auspices.

This chapter will consider the VCLT, the recent work of the ILC Study Group, and underlying norms and canons of construction. Part I reviews the causes of normative conflict, while Part II examines the various ways a treaty can conflict with another treaty or source of law. Part III surveys different techniques for addressing normative conflict via conflict avoidance clauses, treaty interpretation, the VCLT, and the classic canons of treaty construction (*lex prior, lex posterior*, and *lex specialis*). The chapter concludes with a discussion of the broader theme concerning international law's systemic fragmentation.[19]

I. Drivers of Conflict and Fragmentation

At the micro level, normative conflicts can arise for various reasons. Sometimes they are due to the ignorance of lawyers and policy-makers unaware of the 'legislative and institutional activities in the adjoining fields and the general principles of international law'.[20] Alternatively, the enactment of conflicting treaties can be a deliberate attempt to supersede or pre-empt other obligations. Thus, not all conflicts are mistakes but may 'reflect differing pursuits and preferences that actors in a pluralistic (global) society have'.[21]

At the macro level, the two main sources of normative conflict are regionalization and specialization.

A. Regionalization

Regions are a physical, geographic, space, but also constitute areas of normative similarity. Most generally, regionalism 'refers to particular orientations of legal thought and culture'.[22] Political geographer Harm de Blij has observed that '[t]he world seems to be divided into about a dozen realms within which boundaries are usually, though not always, reasonably "easy," but between which they tend to be tough to cross, surface or otherwise'.[23] De Blij's realms are North America, Middle America (Mexico and Central America), South America, Europe, North Africa/ Southwest Asia, Sub-Saharan Africa, Russia, South Asia, East Asia, Southeast Asia,

---

[19] This chapter will focus on treaty conflicts between States. There is, however, growing scholarship on conflicts involving other subjects of international law, such as IOs. The recent *Behrami* and *Saramati* decisions from the European Court of Human Rights, for instance, considered the possible clash of norms between UN Charter requirements and the European Convention on Human Rights. *Behrami v France* and *Saramati v France* (Joined Application Nos 71412/01 and 78166/01) (2007) 45 EHRR 85.

[20] Fragmentation Report (n 3) 11.

[21] Ibid 15.

[22] Ibid 103.

[23] H de Blij, *Why Geography Matters: Three Challenges Facing America: Climate Change, the Rise of China, and Global Terrorism* (OUP, New York 2005) 121.

the Austral realm (Australia/New Zealand), and the Pacific realm (the Pacific islands).[24] Each area is a geographic space, but each is also a normative realm.[25]

While these ideas have found a receptive audience among political scientists and geographers, '[t]here is a very strong presumption among international lawyers that notwithstanding such influences, the law should be read in a universal fashion'.[26] However, the ILC Study Group Report noted that even Sir Robert Jennings, an advocate of universality, stated that:

Universality does not mean uniformity. It does mean, however, that such regional international law, however variant, is part of the system as a whole, and not a separate system, and it ultimately derives its validity from the system as a whole.[27]

This distinction between universality and uniformity allows for significant regional variation among substantive rules, even if there are common procedural rules. If that is the case, then regionalism (regardless of whether one views it as part of a single international legal system or not) can be quite divergent and robust, leading to significant normative conflicts. The EU is one example of a robust regional system with respect to treaties; the relationship of obligations among EU members to those owed to non-members has spawned numerous studies, including a chapter in this *Guide*.[28]

B. Specialization

The ILC Study Group downplayed the role of geographic regionalism, explaining 'where previously the moving forces behind international law may have been geographical regions, today those forces are often particular interests that are globally diversified: trade interests, globalization lobbies, environmentalist or human rights groups and so on'.[29]

Perceiving States as disaggregated entities, as areas of competition among interest groups, does help in understanding the phenomenon of treaty conflicts. Different interest groups vie for treaties that support their policy preferences. Sometimes one treaty is ratified. Sometimes another. Sometimes both. And so disaggregated domestic interests lead to the aggregated (and possibly conflicting) obligations of the State.

---

[24] Ibid 122–3.

[25] But, particularly in today's Eurasia, many States are themselves the boundaries between two normative systems and have aspects of both. Elsewhere, I have called these countries or regions *systemic borderlands*. See Borgen (n 2) 354–6.

[26] Fragmentation Report (n 3) 105.

[27] Ibid 105 (quoting R Jennings, 'Universal International Law in a Multicultural World' in M Bos and I Brownlie (eds), *Liber Amicorum for the Rt Hon Lord Wilberforce* (OUP, Oxford 1987)). Pierre-Marie Dupuy has argued for the unity of international law as well. See generally PM Dupuy, 'L'unité de l'ordre juridique international' (2002) 297 RcD 9–489; see also Fragmentation Report (n 3) 12.

[28] See Chapter 4, Part II, 109 *et seq*; J Klabbers, *Treaty Conflict and the European Union* (CUP, Cambridge 2009); J Grimes, 'Comment: Conflicts Between EC Law and International Treaty Obligations: A Case Study of the German Telecommunications Dispute' (1994) 35 HILJ 535. See also Borgen (n 9) 608–10.

[29] Fragmentation Report (n 3) 105.

Specialized treaty regimes can further exacerbate fragmentation if each regime also uses its own dispute resolution forum. At times, this simply results in differing substantive regimes having idiosyncratic rules governing the resolution of treaty conflicts.[30] But this can also lead to each dispute resolution forum favouring its own substantive regime over obligations stemming from other specialized regimes or from general rules of international law. Such favouritism may be deliberate or merely a matter of proclivity. For example, in the case of investment regimes:

[I]nvestment tribunals have addressed arguments regarding inconsistencies between the investment agreement and non-investment law in a very cautious (and even suspicious) manner. Thus far, no investment tribunal has absolved a host state from its investment obligations, or significantly reduced its responsibility to compensate the injured investor in such cases.[31]

Results such as this point to the problem that the proliferation of tribunals may lead to a proliferation of parochial—and potentially conflicting—interpretations of the legal obligations of States parties to more than one treaty regime.[32]

II. How a Treaty Can Conflict with Another Source of Law

Having considered the factors that drive normative conflicts, we now turn to describing these conflicts in greater detail. The ILC Study Group noted that conflicts among international legal norms can arise from:

a. relations between special and general law;
b. relations between prior and subsequent law;
c. relations between laws at different hierarchical levels; and
d. relations of law to its 'normative environment' more generally.[33]

The ILC Study Group continued:

Such relations may be conceived in varying ways. At one end of the spectrum is the case where one law (norm, rule, principle, rule-complex) simply invalidates the other law. This takes place only in hierarchical relations involving *jus cogens*. Much more often priority is 'relative'. The 'other law' is set aside only temporarily and may often be allowed to influence 'from the background' the interpretation and application of the prioritized law. Then there is the case where the two norms are held to act concurrently, mutually supporting each

---

[30] M Hirsch, 'Interactions between Investment and Non-investment Obligations' in P Muchlinski and others (eds), *The Oxford Handbook of International Investment Law* (OUP, Oxford 2008) 154, 173 *et seq.*

[31] Ibid 179.

[32] In the discussion held by the Sixth Committee on the report of the ILC for its 58th Session:

It was . . . pointed out that the proliferation of adjudicatory bodies, sometimes with overlapping jurisdiction, had a distinct impact on the integrity of international law. It was therefore necessary that the international community remain alert to the interplay between the substantive and institutional aspects of fragmentation.

Sixth Committee Discussion (n 18) [16]. But see Charney (n 7).

[33] Fragmentation Report (n 3) 16 (cross-references omitted).

other. And at this end of the spectrum is the case where, finally, there appears to be no conflict or divergence at all. The laws are in harmony.[34]

Beyond conflicting relationships, norms may also conflict based on their sources. Thus, a treaty can come into normative conflict with another treaty, with customary international law, or with *jus cogens*.[35] Although each of these areas of conflict will be considered, this chapter focuses on resolving conflicts between treaties, including conflicts that lie along the four dimensions of relations identified by the ILC Study Group.

A. Conflicts between a treaty and *jus cogens*

Conceptually, the simplest conflict is when a treaty conflicts with *jus cogens*. Under the ILC Study Group framework, this is a category 'c' relationship between laws at different hierarchical levels. The hierarchically superior law, the *jus cogens* norm, supersedes the treaty.[36] This is the result regardless as to which of the two was first in time.[37] A recent survey concluded, though, that 'international tribunals have demonstrated a cautious approach and declined to pronounce any treaty void because of conflict with peremptory norms'.[38] Thus, such conflicts are more a matter of theory than actual practice.

B. Conflicts between a treaty and customary international law

The VCLT does not explicitly address the topic of conflicts with customary international law. Article 31(3)(c), however, does require taking account of 'any relevant rules of international law applicable in the relations between the parties' in the good faith interpretation of a treaty.[39] Therefore, inconsistencies between treaty and custom will most likely be resolved through an interpretative exercise, whether by enforcing the parties' manifest intent or, where there is no evidence of an intended relationship between the treaty and custom, as a function of canons of construction such as *lex specialis*, *lex posterior*, or *lex prior*.[40]

---

[34] Ibid 16.

[35] Conflicts with sources of domestic law are not considered in this chapter. Also, inconsistencies between a treaty and a subsidiary source of law, such as tribunal case law, do not normally constitute a conflict; subsidiary sources tend to be interpretations of treaties and customary international law rather than a competing source of law.

[36] *Barcelona Traction, Light and Power Co (Belgium v Spain)* (Merits) [1970] ICJ Rep 32; see also P Daillier, M Forteau, and A Pellet, *Droit International Public* (8th edn LDGJ, Paris 2009) 300.

[37] VCLT Art 53 ('[a] treaty is void if, at the time of its conclusion, it conflicts with a peremptory norm of general international law'); ibid Art 64 ('If a new peremptory norm of general international law emerges, any existing treaty which is in conflict with that norm becomes void and terminates'); see also SA Sadat-Akhavi, *Methods of Resolving Conflicts between Treaties* (Martinus Nijhoff, Leiden 2003) 53.

[38] Hirsch (n 30) 179.

[39] For more discussion of this rule, see Chapter 19, Part II.A.3, 485 *et seq*.

[40] Hirsch (n 30) 160.

C. Conflicts between treaties

So far, this chapter has noted different types of normative conflict without un-packing the idea of how treaties can conflict. Unfortunately, even as '[m]odern developments have led to an unprecedented increase in the number of treaties',[41] there is no generally accepted definition of what constitutes a conflict.[42] A treaty conflict in the strictest sense occurs when a party to two treaties cannot simulta-neously honour its obligations under both. For example, assume State A forms a treaty (Treaty I) with State B promising that B will have access to A's markets at terms no worse than any other State. Some years later, State A becomes part of a regional economic treaty with States C, D, E, and F, and to which B is not a party. This second treaty (Treaty II) requires that member States accord each other, *and only each other*, the best terms of market access. This 'architecture' can be written in shorthand as AB:ACDEF. On these facts there is undoubtedly a conflict as A is required by Treaty I to give B the same terms as C, D, E, and F while Treaty II requires that A deny B those terms of trade.[43]

However, this narrow definition of a conflict between treaties is too restrictive.[44] States are not only concerned when a State cannot abide by two treaties but also where one treaty frustrates the goals of another. Thus, treaty conflicts may be defined more broadly to include cases where a State is party to two or more treaty

---

[41] R Bernhardt, 'Treaties' in R Bernhardt (ed), *Encyclopedia of Public International Law* (North-Holland, New York 1981–1990) vol 4, 926, 930.

[42] Pauwelyn (n 6) 166. In fact, most scholars examining the topic fail to even provide a definition, ignoring the possibility that a mere divergence between treaties does not necessarily constitute a conflict. Ibid 167; Jenks (n 1) 426.

[43] An example of such a conflict architecture was the clash between Germany's obligations to the United States under a Treaty of Friendship, Commerce and Navigation (FCN Treaty) and its obligations under the Treaty of Rome (establishing the European Community) and subsequent European Union (EU) legislation. See FCN Treaty (Germany–United States) (29 October 1954) 7 UST 1839; Treaty Establishing the European Economic Community (25 March 1997) 298 UNTS 11 (Treaty of Rome). The FCN Treaty predated both the Treaty of Rome and subsequent EU regula-tions. It included a section on nondiscrimination in government procurement allowing the United States to receive most favoured nation treatment and entitling US companies to receive the same treatment as the best rate given to the companies of any nationality—German or foreign—in government procurement. In 1993, the EU enacted the EU Utilities Directive (Directive), which provided that when a company from a non-member State bids on a procurement contract solicited by an EU State, the EU State will mark-up the non-member State company's bid by a certain percentage, thus making those companies relatively uncompetitive compared to EU member State bidders. Germany, relying on Art 234 of the Treaty of Rome, concluded that the FCN Treaty governed any utilities-related procurement bids submitted by US companies. Germany's EU partners disagreed with this interpretation, with some concerned about its broader implications, since six other EU members had similar FCN treaty provisions with the United States and there was also a possibility of similar provisions in bilateral treaties with other non-EU countries. The situation was ultimately resolved at the bargaining table, with US companies being able to bid on contracts in certain sectors without a mark-up. See Grimes (n 28) 536–41; Borgen (n 9) 609–10.

[44] Early ILC rapporteurs argued for broader definitions. Sir Hersch Lauterpacht focused on 'inconsistency' of norms and Sir Humphrey Waldock on the idea that conflict occurred when two treaties could not be reconciled. See H Lauterpacht, 'First Report on the Law of Treaties' [1953] YBILC, vol II, 154–5; H Waldock, 'Second Report on the Law of Treaties' [1963] YBILC, vol II, 54–61.

regimes and either the mere existence of (or the actual performance under) one treaty will frustrate the purpose of another treaty. Under either this definition or the stricter construction, policy-makers face the same questions: Which treaty should prevail? And are there any useful, principled methods to resolve the conflict?

Commentators have divided their consideration of such questions into three distinct structural categories of conflicts: (a) where the two treaties have identical parties, (b) where there is partial commonality of parties, and (c) where there is no commonality of parties.

The first category of *complete unity of parties* (AB:AB) has received relatively little interest because the issue of treaty conflict simply turns on whether the later treaty was meant to supersede the earlier treaty. Moreover, as all interested States are parties to both treaties, negotiation and bargaining may be relatively straightforward.

Even if the later treaty is not meant to replace the earlier, a subsequent treaty may provide a binding interpretation of one or more provisions in the earlier agreement. As Richard Gardiner has explained, Article 31(3)(a) of the VCLT addresses situations where 'the parties to a treaty have, subsequent to its conclusion, reached firm agreement on what one of its provisions means'.[45] In *Territorial Dispute (Libyan Arab Jamahiriya/Chad)*, for example, the International Court of Justice (ICJ) considered an 8 September 1919 convention between Great Britain and France, which was 'Supplementary to the Declaration signed at London on 21 March 1899, as an addition to the Convention of 14 June 1898 which regulated the Boundaries between British and French Colonial Possessions'.[46] The Court wrote:

Inasmuch as the two States parties to the Convention are those that concluded the Declaration of 1899, there can be no doubt that the 'interpretation' in question constituted, from 1919 onwards, and as between them, the correct and binding interpretation of the Declaration of 1899.[47]

Where two treaties are not obviously concerned with the same subject, however, a consistent reading may not occur, and one treaty could frustrate the purpose of the other. Thus, while there may be no intent to supersede the earlier treaty, the later treaty may nonetheless render the earlier treaty dysfunctional.

By contrast to instances of complete unity of parties, cases of *no commonality of parties* tend to be the most difficult to resolve. For bilateral treaties, such a conflict occurs when States A and B are parties to Treaty I, States A and C are parties to Treaty II, and A's obligations to C are incompatible with A's obligations to B. This can be diagrammed as AB:AC.[48] As discussed below, neither the VCLT nor the customary canons of treaty construction offer a ready solution to such conflicts.

---

[45] R Gardiner, *Treaty Interpretation* (OUP, Oxford 2008) 217.

[46] Ibid 223. If Treaty II is not meant to be related to Treaty I, then while it may still overlap and conflict with Treaty I, one could argue that it is not consider an *inter se* agreement in the strict sense.

[47] [1994] ICJ Rep 29 [60]; see also Gardiner (n 45) 223.

[48] See W Czaplinski and GM Danilenko, 'Conflict of Norms in International Law' (1990) 21 Netherlands Ybk Intl L 3, 24.

This is a form of conflict that drafters need to attempt to head off in the drafting stage, if at all possible.

Different architectures can occur in the third set of cases involving *partial commonality of parties*. One case involves increasing membership from Treaty I between States A and B to Treaty II involving States A, B, C, and D (diagrammed as AB:ABCD). Conversely, there can be decreasing membership (diagrammed as ABCD:AB), where Treaty II may be an *inter se* agreement.[49] Both increasing and decreasing membership scenarios may produce potential conflicts between States A and B, where there is a unity of parties, or between A and C or D, where there is no commonality between Treaties I and II. Additionally, one can envision a conflict between multilateral treaties where there is a partial unity of parties (diagrammed as ABCD:ABEF), where A and B's obligations to E and F are incompatible with their earlier obligations to C and D.[50]

III. Resolving Normative Conflicts

The foregoing has shown that normative conflicts may be caused by inattention or conscious action by individuals. They may also be driven by regionalization or specialization in international law at the systemic level. Moreover, the sources of norms and the relationships among the parties can also affect how conflicts arise.

With such complexity in the roots and manifestations of conflict, it is not surprising that international law has developed multiple mechanisms for resolving normative conflicts. For treaty conflicts, at least four possible solutions exist involving: (a) careful drafting, (b) interpretative mechanisms, (c) the VCLT, or (d) the application of classic canons of construction.

A. Conflict clauses

Potential treaty conflicts are best addressed in the drafting stage.[51] If the treaties are not actually incompatible, then there is no need to resort to the VCLT or general principles of interpretation.[52] Two types of conflict avoidance clauses are possible: (1) clauses that prioritize the present treaty and (2) clauses that prioritize another treaty.[53]

---

[49] See W Karl, 'Conflicts Between Treaties' in R Wolfrum and others (eds), *Encyclopedia of Public International Law* (Max Planck Institute, Berlin 2000) vol 4, 935, 936.

[50] Ibid.

[51] See eg Karl (n 49) 936.

[52] See ibid (stating that '[i]ncompatibility of contents is an essential condition of conflict').

[53] H Blix and JH Emerson (eds), *The Treaty Maker's Handbook* (Oceana Publications, New York 1973) 210–22 ('Treaty Maker's Handbook'). In a more recent typology, Anthony Aust identifies five types of conflict avoidance clauses that prioritize the present treaty:

1. 'The treaty prevails over all other treaties, past and future'
2. 'The parties shall not enter into later inconsistent treaties'
3. 'An existing treaty shall not be affected'
4. 'For parties to the treaty it prevails over earlier treaties'
5. 'Compatible supplementary treaties are permitted'

1. *Clauses that provide for the priority of the present treaty*

A clause may state that the current treaty will supersede conflicting treaties. Hans Blix and Jirina Emerson catalogued six general types of such clauses, where:

a. the 'present treaty prevails over all other treaties';

b. the 'present treaty prevails over earlier treaties';

c. the 'present treaty prevails over earlier treaties for parties to the present treaty';

d. the parties to the present treaty undertake an '[o]bligation not to enter into later treaties inconsistent with the present one';

e. '[s]upplementary agreements [are] permitted if compatible with the present treaty'; and

f. the parties to the present treaty undertake an obligation to modify existing treaties they may have with third parties.[54]

Conflict avoidance clauses may refer to treaties generally or to specific agreements. For example, the 1999 Food Aid Convention states in Article XXVI that '[t]his Convention shall replace the Food Aid Convention, 1995, as extended, and shall be one of the constituent instruments of the International Grain Agreement, 1995'.[55]

Where clauses prohibit later conflicting treaties, they specifically state that parties shall not enter into later treaties that would conflict with the current agreement. Article 8 of the NATO Treaty provides an example: 'Each Party declares that none of the international engagements now in force between it and any other of the Parties or any third State is in conflict with the provisions of this Treaty, and undertakes not to enter into any international engagement in conflict with this treaty.'[56]

Related to this is the special case of the UN Charter. Article 103 states that the obligations under the Charter will prevail over any conflicting obligation from another international agreement. The ICJ analysed this article in the *Lockerbie* case, finding that a Security Council resolution promulgated under UN auspices, and thus under Article 103, trumped any conflicting treaty including, in that case, the Montreal Convention.[57]

A Aust, *Modern Treaty Law and Practice* (2nd edn CUP, Cambridge 2007) 219–25. See also Daillier and others (n 36) 293–7 for numerous examples of conflict avoidance clauses.

[54] *Treaty Maker's Handbook* (n 53) 210–17.

[55] See UN Office of Legal Affairs, *Treaty Handbook* (UN Sales No E02V2 2006) at <http://treaties.un.org> 86 (citing Food Aid Convention of 1999) ('UN Treaty Handbook').

[56] North Atlantic Treaty (signed 4 April 1949, entered into force 24 August 1949) 34 UNTS 243, Art 8.

[57] Aust (n 53) 219–20 (citations omitted). Article 103 states that 'In the event of a conflict between the obligations of the Members of the United Nations under the present Charter and their obligations under any other international agreement, their obligations under the present Charter shall prevail'.

2. Clauses providing for the priority of another treaty

Alternatively, a clause may state that one or more treaties should be given priority over the current treaty. As Aust puts it, these clauses mean '[a]n existing treaty shall not be affected'.[58] Blix and Emerson list four types of these clauses, where:

a. the 'existing treaties prevail';

b. the 'existing or future treaties giving greater benefits prevail';

c. the 'present treaty [is] to be modified to conform to a future treaty'; or

d. '[s]upplementary agreements, not necessarily consistent with the present treaty, [are] permitted'.[59]

Article 90 of the 1980 UN Convention on Contracts for the International Sale of Goods (CISG) provides the following example: 'This Convention does not prevail over any international agreement which has already been or may be entered into and which contains provisions concerning the matters governed by this Convention, provided that the parties have their places of business in States parties to such agreement.'[60] Other typical phrases declare that the present treaty is 'compatible with, or not to be construed as impairing' an earlier treaty.[61] This is exemplified by Article 4(2) of the 1991 Protocol on Environmental Protection to the Antarctic Treaty: '[n]othing in this Protocol shall derogate from the other instruments in force within the Antarctic Treaty system'.[62]

Conflict avoidance clauses are not mutually exclusive. Clauses providing for the priority of the existing treaty or the priority of another treaty may both exist within a single text. A treaty may thus use a combination of these clauses to provide a comprehensive description of its relations to other treaties.[63]

B. Interpretation to avoid conflict

If there are no express priority provisions within the four corners of the agreements—or if any such clause is ambiguously worded—one must turn to the principles of treaty interpretation and the law of treaty conflicts.[64] In doing so, the first step is to try to find a harmonious interpretation of both treaties.[65] When

---

[58] Aust (n 53) 221.

[59] Treaty Maker's Handbook (n 53) 217–22.

[60] UN Treaty Handbook (n 55) 87 (quoting CISG Art 90).

[61] Karl (n 49) 939.

[62] Protocol on Environmental Protection to the Antarctic Treaty (signed 4 October 1991, entered into force 14 January 1998) [1991] 30 ILM 1461, 1463.

[63] See eg UN Convention on the Law of the Sea (adopted 10 December 1982, entered into force 16 November 1994) 1833 UNTS 3, Art 311; see also UN Treaty Handbook (n 55) 86–7. Additional examples of conflict avoidance clauses may be found in Section VI of this *Guide*.

[64] VCLT Art 31 is of particular importance regarding interpretation to avoid conflicts. For a detailed discussion of the VCLT's interpretative rules (Arts 31–33) see Chapters 19–21.

[65] Or, of the treaty and any potentially conflicting customary rule. See Study Group Conclusions (n 12) [18]–[19]. But see Sixth Committee Discussion (n 18) [25] (noting that some delegations found

there are multiple possible interpretations of a treaty text, one of which would cause a violation of another international norm, lawyers should avoid it in favour of an interpretation that is not violative of other obligations. The ILC Study Group Report quoted the ICJ's opinion in the *Right of Passage* case to support this presumption of compatibility:

It is a rule of interpretation that a text emanating from a Government must, in principle, be interpreted as producing *and intended to produce* effects in accordance with existing law and not in violation of it.[66]

The *Oxford Handbook on International Investment Law* points to two more recent examples of this principle in operation: the NAFTA case *SD Myers v Canada* and the investment arbitration *SPP v Egypt* where tribunals sought harmonious readings of party obligations such that there was no true conflict between the treaties.[67]

One result of this 'generally accepted' presumption against a conflict of norms is that 'the State relying on a conflict of norms will have the burden of proving it'.[68] Thus, in the *EC- Hormones* case, the WTO Dispute Settlement Board indicated that:

WTO members, as sovereign entities, can be *presumed* to act in conformity with their WTO obligations. A party claiming that a Member acted *inconsistently* with WTO rules bears the burden of proving that inconsistency.[69]

This burden may in turn advantage the party that has entered into two supposedly conflicting treaties.

Moreover, given the proliferation of dispute resolution fora, the application of this presumption of compatibility within each forum may (either deliberately or intuitively) ultimately favour the enforcement of the treaty from within that regime. This seems to be the case, for example, in the international investment context.[70] Negotiators who wish to avoid this situation should be cautious and assume that clauses that *may* conflict *will* conflict. Consequently, treaty drafters should clarify *ex ante* the desired relationship between the two norms whether through clauses of abrogation or precedence.

The presumption of compatibility, however, remains only a presumption. Since treaty interpretation is based on the words' 'clear meaning', sometimes interpretation will not make a conflict disappear:

---

that the Conclusions concerning interpretation left open questions as to which principles of international law were generally recognized).

[66] *Case concerning the Right of Passage over Indian Territories (Portugal v India)* (Preliminary Objection) [1952] ICJ Rep 142 (emphasis added).

[67] See Hirsch (n 30) 163–8, 173–4; NAFTA/UNCITRAL Tribunal, *SD Myers Inc v Canada (US-Canada)* (13 November 2000) [2001] 40 ILM 1408; ICSID, *SPP (ME) v Egypt* (Case No ARB/84/3) (1994) 19 Ybk Commercial Arbitration 51.

[68] Pauwelyn (n 6) 240.

[69] WTO, *European Communities—Measures Concerning Meat and Meat Products (Hormones)* (1997) WT/DS28 and WT/DS48 [9].

[70] Hirsch (n 30) 179.

[I]f interpretation leads to the conclusion that one norm in and of itself, or as implemented or relied upon by a state, *does* constitute a breach of another norm, that is where the role of interpretation of treaty terms as a conflict-avoidance technique stops. To put it differently, interpretation of the terms in question may resolve apparent conflicts; it cannot resolve genuine conflicts.[71]

When there is a genuine conflict that was not avoided by drafting and cannot be resolved by interpretation, one may next attempt to apply any relevant rules from the VCLT.

C. The VCLT rules on treaty conflicts

As is often the case in codifications, the VCLT attempts to draw bright line rules. Article 30 contains the main treaty conflict rules, but Articles 26 (*pacta sunt servanda*), 31 (interpretation), and 41 (*inter se* agreements) are also useful in addressing normative conflicts.

Article 30 applies to 'successive treaties relating to the same subject-matter'.[72] Although originally a cause of some disagreement, States now generally agree that determining the timing of the earlier treaty's conclusion is based on date of adoption, not entry into force.[73] According to the ILC's Commentary on an earlier version of Article 30, it 'comes into play only *after it has been determined under [Article 59] that the parties did not intend to abrogate, or wholly to suspend the operation of, the earlier treaty*'.[74] (Article 59, for its part, is of only limited use, applying only when all the parties to Treaty I are also parties to Treaty II.[75])

---

[71] Pauwelyn (n 6) 272.
[72] VCLT Art 30(1). The meaning of 'same subject-matter' is discussed in this chapter's Conclusion. More generally, VCLT Art 30 provides:

1. Subject to Article 103 of the Charter of the United Nations, the rights and obligations of States parties to successive treaties relating to the same subject-matter shall be determined in accordance with the following paragraphs.
2. When a treaty specifies that it is subject to, or that it is not to be considered as incompatible with, an earlier or later treaty, the provisions of that other treaty prevail.
3. When all the parties to the earlier treaty are parties also to the later treaty but the earlier treaty is not terminated or suspended in operation under article 59, the earlier treaty applies only to the extent that its provisions are compatible with those of the latter treaty.
4. When the parties to the later treaty do not include all the parties to the earlier one:
   (a) as between States parties to both treaties, the same rule applies as in paragraph 3;
   (b) as between a State party to both treaties and a State party to only one of the treaties, the treaty to which both States are parties governs their mutual rights and obligations.

5. Paragraph 4 is without prejudice to article 41, or to any question of the termination or suspension of the operation of a treaty under article 60 or to any question of responsibility which may arise for a State from the conclusion or application of a treaty the provisions of which are incompatible with its obligations towards another State under another treaty.

[73] Aust (n 53) 229.
[74] [1966] YBILC, vol II, 253 (emphasis in original); see also EM Vierdag, 'The Time of Conclusion of a Multilateral Treaty' (1988) 59 BYBIL 75, 91 n61; UN Office of Legal Affairs, *Final Clauses of Multilateral Treaties Handbook* (UN Sales No E04V3 2003) 85 ('[U]nless there is evidence of contrary intention, the parties are presumed to have intended to terminate or modify the earlier treaty when they conclude a subsequent treaty that is incompatible with the earlier one.').
[75] See Vierdag (n 74) 91.

Article 30(2) of the VCLT endorses the use of conflict avoidance clauses that give priority to the earlier treaty: '[w]hen a treaty specifies that it is subject to, or that it is not to be considered incompatible with, an earlier or later treaty, the provisions of the other treaty prevail'.[76] Where the treaty lacks such a clause, Article 30(3) provides a rule for cases of complete unity of parties: '[if] the earlier treaty is not terminated or suspended under article 59 [of the VCLT[77]], the earlier treaty applies only to the extent that its provisions are compatible with those of the later treaty'. Article 30(3) thus effectively codifies a default *lex posterior* canon of construction.[78]

Article 30(4) considers the harder case where the later treaty does not include all of the parties to the earlier treaty. It applies the rule set forth in paragraph 3 (the *lex posterior* rule) to States that *are* parties to both treaties. But when one State is party to both treaties and another State is only party to one, then the treaty to which they both belong governs their relationship.[79]

In a conflict where there is no commonality, such as one diagrammed AB:AC, Article 30 of the VCLT allows each treaty to remain effective between each of the parties. The VCLT does, however, acknowledge that this is without prejudice to questions of responsibility that 'may arise for a State from the conclusion or application of a treaty, the provisions of which are incompatible with its obligations towards another State under another treaty'.[80] The issue thus becomes not a question of conflict resolution, but of the law of responsibility.[81] Otherwise, though, the parties are left to negotiate whatever solution they are able.[82]

---

[76] VCLT Art 30(2).

[77] Ibid Art 59 (providing for the termination or suspension of an earlier treaty where it is established that was the parties' intention or if the later treaty's provisions are 'so far incompatible with the earlier one that the two treaties are not capable of being applied at the same time').

[78] See UN Treaty Handbook (n 55) 85 ('[I]n the case of successive treaties relating to the same subject-matter concluded among the same parties, the principle of *lex posterior derogat priori* applies.'); Daillier and others (n 36) 297 ('Cette disposition n'est que l'application du principe lex posterior derogate priori, don't la mise en oeuvre ne fait pas problem puisque les deux traits sont issus des memes États.').

[79] VCLT Art 30(4)(b).

[80] Ibid Art 30(5).

[81] There is increasing focus in scholarship on the relationship between normative conflicts and the law of responsibility. Professor Kristen Boon has written:

As a general proposition . . . the law of responsibility is relevant to all breaches of international obligations, including breaches that originate from conflicting norms.

Thus when one instrument or norm obliges a state to take an action that is incompatible with a second instrument or norm, conflicting international obligations arise. These conflicts can create legal responsibility, because breaches of any international obligations constitute international wrongs. Moreover, conflicting domestic laws are not a valid reason for breaching international obligations. Under the Draft Articles on IO Responsibility, the same principles apply to IOs. IOs may incur responsibility for breaching their international legal commitments, even when this occurs as a result of conflicting obligations.

K Boon, 'Regime Conflicts and the UN Security Council: Applying the Law of Responsibility' (2011) 42 GW Intl L Rev 101, 114 (citations omitted).

[82] The result is like the EU/US/German dispute, where the 'renegotiation' was essentially a trade skirmish. See n 43.

Besides Article 30, other VCLT clauses can play a role in resolving treaty conflict. As described above, interpretation can be used to avoid potential conflicts. Article 31 is particularly important in this respect. Article 26, for its part, codifies *pacta sunt servanda*, stating '[e]very treaty in force is binding upon the parties to it and must be performed by them in good faith'. As discussed below, *pacta sunt servanda* allows for Treaty I to remain in force in the face of a conflicting subsequent norm in Treaty II. Article 41 concerns the status of an *inter se* agreement, a subsequent agreement to modify a multilateral treaty by some, but not all, parties to the original treaty. It provides that the *inter se* agreement cannot adversely affect the object or purpose of the original treaty, nor may it affect a third party's enjoyment of rights or the performance of obligations under the original treaty.

D. Customary canons of construction

No set of black letter rules can fully respond to the multitude of potential treaty conflicts. The variety of conflict architectures, as well as substantive interrelations (general rules, special rules, same subject-matter or different subject-matter), and the temporal element combine and recombine to frustrate any set of bright-line rules. There are too many factors open to interpretation to allow agreement on which rules apply in all but the simplest cases. If the VCLT does not provide applicable rules, one may turn to the customary canons of construction, especially *lex posterior*, *lex prior* (in concert with *pacta sunt servanda*), or *lex specialis*. These canons are generally viewed as techniques, not obligatory rules (except, as discussed below, perhaps in certain circumstances).[83] Although these canons can render opposing results (consider the relationship of *lex posterior* to *lex prior*), there may be a certain consensus on their application under certain circumstances.

1. Lex posterior

Lex posterior derogat legi priori (*lex posterior*) considers the parties' evolving intent and favours the most recent treaty by the same parties.[84] If the same States are

---

[83] As Richard Gardiner explains later in this *Guide*:

> Sir Humphrey Waldock avoided all the principles and maxims of interpretation then in common use. Taking as examples ones frequently referred to in their Latin forms ('*ut res magis valeat quam pereat, contra proferentem, eiusdem generis, expressio unius est exclusio alterius, generalia specialibus non derogant*'), he characterised these as 'for the most part, principles of logic and good sense valuable only as guides to assist in appreciating the meaning', principles whose use was thus discretionary rather than obligatory.

Chapter 19, 477.

[84] Fragmentation Report (n 3) 116 n290. Aufricht's summary of pre-VCLT treaty conflict resolution techniques focused on *lex posterior*. In his view, there were five requirements for *lex posterior* to work: (1) the same subject as the earlier treaty; (2) the later treaty covers the same parties as the earlier treaty; (3) the later treaty is on the same level or a higher level as the earlier treaty; (4) the scope of the later treaty is of the same degree of generality as the earlier treaty; and (5) the legal effect or effects of the later treaty are different from the earlier. H Aufricht, 'Supersession of Treaties in International Law' (1952) 37 Cornell L Q 655, 700.

parties to two treaties, which cannot be interpreted in a compatible manner, then the parties may apply *lex posterior*.[85] It is a technique related to a rule of priority among domestic statues, in which the later in time statute is favoured over the earlier statute.[86]

Lex posterior has sometimes been referred to 'as a general principle of law recognized by civilized nations'.[87] It was applied by the Permanent Court of International Justice (PCIJ) in numerous cases including the *Mavrommatis Concession* cases and the *Electricity Company of Sofia* case.[88] But this does not mean it is universally followed today.[89] *Lex posterior* is most useful when there is a unity of parties (AB:AB) or partial commonality, where the counterparty is the same in both treaties, such as a potential conflict between A and counterparty B in two treaties diagrammed as ABCD:AB. A more serious problem arises when the parties are not identical, which is often the case in conflicting treaties concerning politico-military affairs.[90]

2. *Lex prior* and *pacta sunt servanda*

By contrast, the *lex prior* principle would specifically enforce the earlier treaty. Vattel argued that States were not allowed to enter into conflicting treaties; if there was a conflict, the later treaty would be null and void.[91] *Lex prior* is a technique derived from ideas in domestic law of the illegality of a contract to break a contract.[92] This canon is most often invoked in cases where there is divergent membership between the two treaties.[93]

The ILC Study Group noted that the strongest references to *lex prior* are from the early twentieth century.[94] Both the Central American Court of Justice in *San Juan River (Costa Rica v Nicaragua)* and the PCIJ in *Customs Regime between Austria and Germany*, used *lex prior* where there was a diversity of parties between the first and second treaty.[95] However, both courts also showed a reluctance to void the

---

[85] Borgen (n 9) 583; Fragmentation Report (n 3) 118–19.

[86] Fragmentation Report (n 3) 124.

[87] Ibid 116–17.

[88] Ibid 120–1; see also *Mavrommatis Palestine Concessions (Greece v UK)* [1924] PCIJ Rep Series B No 2, 31; *Jurisdiction of the European Commission of the Danube* (Advisory Opinion) [1927] PCIJ Rep Series B No 14, 23; *Electricity Company of Sofia and Bulgaria (Belgium v Bulgaria)* [1939] PCIJ Rep Series A/B No 77, 92.

[89] Some have questioned whether either *lex prior* or *lex posterior* 'have been generally accepted as default rules of unwritten public international law'. A Schulz, *The Relationship Between the Judgments Project and Other International Instruments* (Hague Conference on Private International Law, December 2003) Preliminary Doc No 24, 14.

[90] Fragmentation Report (n 3) 121.

[91] E de Vattel, *The Law of Nations* (1758) (J Chitty (trans) 1863, reprinted by AMS Press, New York 1982) 196.

[92] Fragmentation Report (n 3) 124.

[93] Karl (n 49) 937.

[94] Fragmentation Report (n 3) 123.

[95] *San Juan River (Costa Rica v Nicaragua)* reprinted in (1917) 11 AJIL 181 (Cent Am Ct of Justice 1917); *Customs Regime between Austria and Germany* (Advisory Opinion) 1931 PCIJ Rep Series A/B No 41, 50.

later treaty, whether based on jurisdictional grounds (*San Juan River*) or by not explicitly recognizing a conflict between the later and earlier treaties (which was the approach used in the PCIJ's *Oscar Chinn* decision[96]). Sir Humphrey Waldock, the ILC's fourth Special Rapporteur on the Law of Treaties, thus emphasized that PCIJ jurisprudence 'had rejected inconsistency as a ground for invalidity'.[97]

In 1951, the ICJ suggested in the *Reservations* case that the Genocide Convention could not be frustrated or impaired by the contracting parties' later agreements.[98] Aside from this somewhat unclear reference, post-World War II examples of international tribunals using *lex prior* have been few and far between.[99] There is some evidence that *lex prior* is re-emerging in a limited way in the investment treaty arbitration context. As one commentator notes: 'Where the host state *voluntarily* undertook the non-investment international obligation after the obligation vis-à-vis the investor had been undertaken, the host state would not be absolved of its investment obligation [by the investment treaty tribunal].'[100] The ILC Study Group noted that although there are few modern examples of the application of *lex prior*, it has survived in the scholarly literature in part due to its relation to contract doctrine, especially as expounded by Lauterpacht.[101]

A similar interpretive rule to *lex prior* is *pacta sunt servanda,* which is codified in the VCLT.[102] While *pacta sunt servanda* is a cornerstone of international law, its effect on conflicting treaties is not clear. Some scholars interpret *pacta sunt servanda* as not *favouring* the earlier treaty but rather simply making each treaty enforceable, even though they may pose potentially incompatible obligations.[103] Others claim that *pacta sunt servanda* favours enforcement of the earlier treaty while preventing enforcement of the later.[104] Under both views, it is clear that Treaty I must be honoured (unless a State makes the policy choice of breaching and incurring responsibility). The disagreement concerns the effect of *pacta sunt servanda* on Treaty II: Is the second treaty abrogated or should it simply be followed to the fullest extent possible without frustrating the first treaty?

Both *lex prior* and *pacta sunt servanda* principles are most likely to be used where there is no commonality between the two treaties (eg AB:AC) or where there may be partial commonality overall (eg ABCD:ABEF) but no commonality among the specific counterparties to the conflict (eg comparing A's obligations to C or D to its obligations to E or F).

---

[96] *Oscar Chinn Case (UK, Ireland v Belgium)* 1934 PCIJ Rep Series A/B No 63 (Hurst, J, dissenting) in (1938) 3 WCR 416, 462.

[97] Kearney & Dalton (n 14) 518.

[98] *Reservations to the Convention on the Prevention and Punishment of the Crime of Genocide* (Advisory Opinion) [1951] ICJ Rep 21; but see Fragmentation Report (n 3) 122–3 (questioning how much the *Reservations* case supports the *lex prior* principle).

[99] Fragmentation Report (n 3) 122–3.

[100] Hirsch (n 30) 174–5.

[101] Fragmentation Report (n 3) 124.

[102] VCLT Art 26.

[103] See eg Schulz (n 89) 14.

[104] See eg Aufricht (n 84) 672–3 (arguing for interdiction of later conflicting treaties even in cases of non-identical parties).

3. *Lex specialis* and self-contained regimes

Instead of deciding which treaty controls based on the timing of the conflicting treaties' conclusion, the interpretive rule *lex specialis* focuses on the treaties' scope and precision by giving effect to the more narrowly gauged treaty.[105] Grotius explained that 'special provisions are ordinarily more effective than those that are general'.[106]

Although the VCLT does not use this interpretive norm, *lex specialis* may still apply in conflicts between multilateral treaties of general application and international regimes for a specific issue area.[107] (*Lex specialis* can also be formulated to focus on the breadth or narrowness of specific clauses or rules that are regional, as opposed to global.) It is used most often when the parties to both the general treaty and the specific treaty are the same,[108] and the treaties deal with the same subject-matter.[109]

Two possible results of *lex specialis* are that the specific rule (a) is interpreted within the context of the general standard, or (b) it replaces the general rule.[110] When applied to treaties as a whole, *lex specialis* is usually understood to mean that the special treaty supersedes the general treaty. But *lex specialis* is not just used for comparing treaties holistically; it is applied at times to find priority between special and general clauses in two instruments. When comparing clauses, there are three possible outcomes: (1) the special clause cancels out the general clause; (2) the special clause is deemed supplementary to the general clause; or (3) the general clause is considered as overriding the special clause.[111]

In Conclusion (10), the ILC Study Group argued that there are certain cases in which the *lex specialis* doctrine could not be invoked and that the general rule, not the special rule, would be enforced.[112] The Sixth Committee discussion noted this

---

[105] For a history of *lex specialis* in Roman law, see Fragmentation Report (n 3) 34 n57.

[106] H Grotius, *De Jure Belli ac Pacis*, Bk II, Ch XVI, Sec XXIX; Fragmentation Report (n 3) 36; but see ibid 37 (noting that Scelle favoured the general rule over the special rule); see also Daillier and others (n 36) 292–3.

[107] Jenks (n 1) 414.

[108] See eg Fragmentation Report (n 3) n141.

[109] The ILC Study Group agreed with Fitzmaurice that *lex specialis* only applies when both treaties are on the same subject-matter. Fragmentation Report (n 3) 62–3; GG Fitzmaurice, 'The Law and procedure of the International Court of Justice 1951–4: Treaty Interpretation and Other Treaty Points' (1957) 33 BYBIL 203, 237.

[110] Fragmentation Report (n 3) 35. The former seems to be the view of both Mus and Fitzmaurice. Ibid n58.

[111] Aufricht (n 84) 697. ILC, Draft Articles on the Responsibility of States for Internationally Wrongful Acts, with Commentaries [2001] YBILC, vol II, Art 55 (ASR) (containing a *lex specialis* rule so that the ASR does not apply 'where and to the extent that the conditions for the existence of an internationally wrongful act or the content of implementation of the international responsibility of a State are governed by special rules of international law'). The commentary accompanying ASR Art 55 notes that *lex specialis* requires more than the same subject matter; there must be an actual inconsistency or one provision intended to exclude the other. Ibid Art 55, Commentary [4]; Fragmentation Report (n 3) 50.

[112] Study Group Conclusions (n 12) [10].

conclusion and expressed concerns that it 'substantially blurred the *lex specialis* principle'.[113]

According to the ILC Commentary to its Draft Articles on State Responsibility, self-contained regimes can be thought of as a strong form of *lex specialis*.[114] The 1923 *SS Wimbledon* and 1980 *Hostages* cases are oft-cited examples of this concept.[115] However, the ILC Study Group argued that the term 'self-contained regime' is a misnomer, as no set of rules operates completely independently of the general rules of public international law and there is no evidence that any rule-regime claims to operate independently of the VCLT.[116] The Sixth Committee, in its discussion of the Study Group's Conclusions, raised the argument that the Study Group's definition of 'self-contained regime' was actually too broad and that regimes, as per the Committee's reading of the *Hostages* case, are self-contained only if they include 'their own system of sanction in case of breach'.[117]

4. *The interrelations of the canons of construction*

It is not uncommon to see more than one of these general principles of interpretation used to resolve a treaty conflict. *Lex specialis* and *lex posterior* are often used in conjunction with one another when the narrower treaty is also the later treaty.[118] Other cases are resolved by techniques that are neither a strict application of *lex posterior* or *lex specialis*, but rather cases where the 'earlier and general instruments remains "in the background", controlling the way the later and more specific rules are being interpreted and implemented'.[119]

Although these general principles may dovetail in certain instances, inasmuch as they are largely adapted from domestic canons of statutory construction, it should be of little surprise that these interpretative principles can conflict. Karl Llewellyn, discussing domestic statutory interpretation, famously argued that 'there are two opposing canons on almost every point'.[120] The same holds true in international law. There is, at the very least, a tension between the notions of *lex posterior* (favouring the later treaty) and *lex prior* and *pacta sunt servanda* (favouring the earlier treaty), if not an outright clash between such principles.

The solution, to the extent there is one, turns on the architecture of the conflict. If the States are parties to both treaties, *lex posterior* or *lex specialis* should most likely

---

[113] Sixth Committee Discussion (n 18) [21].

[114] Fragmentation Report (n 3) 65–6 (citing ILC Commentary on ASR Article 55(5)).

[115] *Case of the SS Wimbledon (Great Britain v Germany)* [1923] PCIJ Rep Ser A No 1; *Case Concerning United States Diplomatic and Consular Staff in Tehran (United States of America v Iran)* [1980] ICJ Rep 3; see also Fragmentation Report (n 3) 66.

[116] Fragmentation Report (n 3) 94. For further critical analysis of the self-contained regime idea, see B Simma, 'Self-contained regimes' (1985) Netherlands Ybk Intl L 111; Sixth Committee Discussion (n 18) [22]–[24].

[117] Sixth Committee Discussion (n 18) [23].

[118] Aufricht (n 84) 698–9.

[119] Fragmentation Report (n 3) 22.

[120] KN Llewellyn, 'Remarks on the Theory of Appellate Decision and the Rules or Canons about How Statutes are to be Construed' (1950) 3 Vand L Rev 395, 401.

apply. If there is no unity of the counterparties, then *lex prior* or *pacta sunt servanda* are more likely responses.[121]

Conclusion: From Treaty Conflicts to Systemic Fragmentation, and Back Again

States undertake conflicting legal obligations. As those obligations aggregate, they may increase the fragmentation of international law. In closing, we return to the central questions of what to do about treaty conflicts at the micro level and fragmentation at the macro level?

For the last fifty years, the micro-level literature on responding to treaty conflicts has mostly examined the VCLT's strengths and weaknesses. Although the VCLT responds to some scenarios, the basic critique is that its description of what is a conflict and thus its prescriptions are too narrow. The two key shortcomings of Article 30 are its emphasis on successive treaties of the 'same subject-matter' and the lack of a clear rule when there is no unity of parties.

The 'same subject-matter' issue has been the source of some debate. Critics contend that although treaties about different policy areas (say, trade and the environment) may actually overlap, they are not about the same subject-matter.[122] Others have responded that this critique is an overly narrow reading of the VCLT.[123] If the obligation of one treaty frustrates or causes a breach of the obligations under another treaty then, the argument goes, they *are* about the same subject-matter. This is a pragmatic work-around, but it should be noted that it is not at all clear that this is what the VCLT's drafters intended.[124]

The second main critique is that most of the clauses in Article 30 of the VCLT assume a unity of parties and that it is on less sure footing even in cases of partial unity,[125] let alone no unity of parties. The VCLT would allow the obligations to each party to survive, thus there is no solution to the conflict in the VCLT, just a recognition that a conflict exists.

Nor do the canons of construction have a clear solution for this dilemma either. Conflicts where there is a unity of parties can often be resolved by *lex posterior*. Where there is no commonality, then *lex prior* (and *pacta sunt servanda*) seems to be used more, rarely superseding the later treaty, but more often giving rise to independent causes of action under both treaties.

---

[121] Daillier and others (n 36) 299.

[122] I argue this in Borgen (n 9) 603–4.

[123] See eg Klabbers (n 28) 93; Sixth Committee Discussion (n 18) [26].

[124] For a third way to interpret the 'same subject-matter' phrase, see Daillier and others (n 36) 291 (defining the phrase in terms of the generality or specificity of each treaty: treaties with the same specificity level may be on the same subject matter, with those that are not falling into the category of *lex specialis*—'Mais il ne faut pas oublier que l'article 30 ne vise que les accords successifs portant "sur la même matière", ce qui a été interprété come significant: "ayant le meme degree de généralité" ').

[125] Such as in the case of ABC:AD, when the issue is whether A's obligations to B and C conflict with its obligations to D. Here, A's obligations to B,C, and D all survive.

For its part, the ILC Study Group proposed a novel approach to treaty conflicts. Rather than focusing on the terminology of 'subject-matter', the Study Group argued that what is important is whether or not treaties are in the same treaty regime:

The distinction between treaties dealing with the 'same subject-matter' and treaties within the same 'regime' may appear slight, but it constitutes an important practical shift of perspective. In the former case, focus is on the object that is being regulated while in the latter case, focus is on the intent of the States parties and the institutions they have established. The former is dependent on an abstract characterization of an issue as a 'human rights issue', an 'environmental problem' or a 'trade question'—and meets with the difficulty that often many characterizations may be applied to a single problem and different actors may have an interest to characterize the problem in different ways so as to ensure that their preferred rule-systems will be applied. By contract, the notion of a 'regime' points to the institutional arrangements that may have been established to link sets of treaties to each other. Treaties may of course enter into conflict both within and across regimes. To make that distinction is merely to point out that the task of settling the conflict—for example, by seeking a 'mutually supportive solution'—may be much easier or more straightforward in the former than in the latter situation where at issue is often a conflict of wider objectives or values underlying the very regimes themselves.[126]

The ILC Study Group noted that VCLT Article 30's techniques are disappointing when applied to conflicts *across* regimes because '[a] straightforward priority of one treaty over another (that is in fact, of one regime over another) cannot be reasonably assumed on a merely chronological basis'.[127]

In considering clashes across regimes, one moves from the micro-level concern of treaty conflicts to the macro-level issue of systemic fragmentation. The ILC Study Group took a decidedly optimistic tone about existing patterns of fragmentation:

the fragmentation of the substance of international law—the object of this study—does not pose any very serious danger to legal practice ... The emergence of new 'branches' of the law, novel types of treaties or clusters of treaties is a feature of the social complexity of a globalizing world. If lawyers feel unable to deal with this complexity, this is not a reflection of problems in their 'tool-box' but of their imagination about how to use it.[128]

While reasonable people may disagree as to whether normative fragmentation is a current or potential future threat, the ILC Study Group made a point worthy of emphasis. International lawyers must expand their repertoire of techniques for resolving conflicts, utilizing the tools already available to them. This is not to say that the current rules—either in the VCLT or in customary cannons of construction—are able to solve all treaty conflicts. They cannot.[129] But lawyers do have other techniques—of interpretation, of drafting, of coordination—that *can* either avoid or draw the sting from potential conflicts.

---

[126] Fragmentation Report (n 3) 131. [127] Ibid 138. [128] Ibid 114–15.
[129] See Daillier and others (n 36) 292 ('Aucune des solutions proposées par les auteurs ne semble d'ailleurs entièrement satisfaisant ... ').

In reviewing the ILC Study Group's Conclusions, the Sixth Committee found that there is further work to be done on the theoretical level, particularly in the relationship of treaty interpretation to conflict resolution.[130] As noted earlier, there is also promising scholarship in the relationship of the law of responsibility to normative conflicts. As a matter of practical lawyering, though, there are already many tools (albeit no 'silver bullet') that one may use to avoid or address treaty conflicts.

Recommended Reading

H Aufricht, 'Supersession of Treaties in International Law' (1952) 37 Cornell L Q 655

A Aust, *Modern Treaty Law and Practice* (2nd edn CUP, Cambridge 2007) 219

G Binder, *Treaty Conflict and Political Contradiction: The Dialectic of Duplicity* (Praeger, New York 1988)

H Blix and JH Emerson (eds), *The Treaty Maker's Handbook* (Oceana Publications, New York 1973) 210

K Boon, 'Regime Conflicts and the UN Security Council: Applying the Law of Responsibility' (2011) 42 GW Intl L Rev 101

CJ Borgen, 'Resolving Treaty Conflicts' (2005) 37 GW Intl L Rev 573

JI Charney, 'Is International Law Threatened by Multiple International Tribunals?' (1998) 271 RdC 101

W Czaplinski and GM Danilenko, 'Conflict of Norms in International Law' (1990) 21 Netherlands Ybk Intl L 3

PM Dupuy, 'L'unité de l'ordre juridique international' (2002) 297 RcD 9

R Gardiner, *Treaty Interpretation* (OUP, Oxford 2008)

ILC, Report on the work of its fifty-eighth session (2006): Topical summary of the discussion held in the Sixth Committee of the General Assembly during its sixty-first session, prepared by the Secretariat, Addendum (23 January 2007) UN Doc A/CN.4/577/Add.1

ILC Study Group, Conclusions of the work of the Study Group on the Fragmentation of International Law: Difficulties arising from the Diversification and Expansion of International Law (2006) included in ILC, Report on the Work of its 58th Session (1 May to 9 June and 3 July to 1 August 2006) UN Doc A/61/10

CW Jenks, 'The Conflict of Law Making Treaties' (1953) 30 BYBIL 403

RD Kearney and RE Dalton, 'The Treaty on Treaties' (1970) 64 AJIL 495

J Klabbers, *Treaty Conflict and the European Union* (CUP, Cambridge 2009)

M Koskenniemi and P Leino, 'Fragmentation of International Law? Postmodern Anxieties' (2002) 15 LJIL 553

J Mus, 'Conflicts between Treaties in International Law' (1998) 45 Netherlands Intl L Rev 208

J Pauwelyn, *Conflict of Norms in International Law: How WTO Law Relates to Other Rules of International Law* (CUP, Cambridge 2003)

---

[130] Sixth Committee Discussion (n 18) [30]–[31].

CPR Romano, 'The Proliferation of International Judicial Bodies: The Pieces of the Puzzle' (1999) 31 NYU J Intl L & Poly 709

C Rousseau, 'De la compatibilité des noms juridiques contradictoires dans l'ordre international' (1932) RGDIP 33

SA Sadat-Akhavi, *Methods of Resolving Conflicts between Treaties* (Martinus Nijhoff, Leiden 2003)

Y Shany, *The Competing Jurisdictions of International Courts and Tribunals* (CUP, Cambridge 2003)

EM Vierdag, 'The Time of Conclusion of a Multilateral Treaty' (1988) 59 BYBIL 75

SECTION IV
TREATY INTERPRETATION

19

The Vienna Convention Rules on Treaty Interpretation

Richard Gardiner

'The Vienna Rules'[1]

SECTION 3. INTERPRETATION OF TREATIES

Article 31
General rule of interpretation

1. A treaty shall be interpreted in good faith in accordance with the ordinary meaning to be given to the terms of the treaty in their context and in the light of its object and purpose.

2. The context for the purpose of the interpretation of a treaty shall comprise, in addition to the text, including its preamble and annexes:

   (*a*) any agreement relating to the treaty which was made between all the parties in connection with the conclusion of the treaty;

   (*b*) any instrument which was made by one or more parties in connection with the conclusion of the treaty and accepted by the other parties as an instrument related to the treaty.

3. There shall be taken into account, together with the context:

   (*a*) any subsequent agreement between the parties regarding the interpretation of the treaty or the application of its provisions;

   (*b*) any subsequent practice in the application of the treaty which establishes the agreement of the parties regarding its interpretation;

   (*c*) any relevant rules of international law applicable in the relations between the parties.

4. A special meaning shall be given to a term if it is established that the parties so intended.

Article 32
Supplementary means of interpretation

---

[1] Rules for treaty interpretation from the 1969 Vienna Convention on the Law of Treaties (VCLT). References in this chapter to 'the Vienna rules' are to the articles reproduced here.

Recourse may be had to supplementary means of interpretation, including the preparatory work of the treaty and the circumstances of its conclusion, in order to confirm the meaning resulting from the application of article 31, or to determine the meaning when the interpretation according to article 31:

> *(a)* leaves the meaning ambiguous or obscure; or
> *(b)* leads to a result which is manifestly absurd or unreasonable.

Article 33
Interpretation of treaties authenticated in two or more languages

1. When a treaty has been authenticated in two or more languages, the text is equally authoritative in each language, unless the treaty provides or the parties agree that, in case of divergence, a particular text shall prevail.

2. A version of the treaty in a language other than one of those in which the text was authenticated shall be considered an authentic text only if the treaty so provides or the parties so agree.

3. The terms of the treaty are presumed to have the same meaning in each authentic text.

4. Except where a particular text prevails in accordance with paragraph 1, when a comparison of the authentic texts discloses a difference of meaning which the application of articles 31 and 32 does not remove, the meaning which best reconciles the texts, having regard to the object and purpose of the treaty, shall be adopted.

Introduction

The idea that there are rules applicable to interpretation of all treaties is one that in past times would have been controversial, or at best uncertain as regards the content of any such rules. Now, however, the rules in the Vienna Convention on the Law of Treaties (VCLT) are accepted as customary international law and not open to challenge.[2] Nevertheless, as a set of principles ancillary to the instruments whose interpretation they assist, and as provisions which are themselves set out in a treaty, these rules require interpretation. Their very brevity leaves considerable scope for this.

The present chapter addresses two questions. The first is in what sense are the Vienna rules on treaty interpretation 'rules'? The second is how are the rules to be used in interpreting treaties? The answer to the first question provides much of the answer to the second one. But the second is worth additional attention, mainly

---

[2] See RK Gardiner, *Treaty Interpretation* (OUP, Oxford 2008 and paperback edition with updating preface, 2010), chapter 1, section 2, and the section on practice below. References to Gardiner below are to the paperback edition.

because the rules' application in practice reveals interpretations that do not stand out from simply reading them.

At the outset, it is important to note that too much should not be claimed for the Vienna rules. In any particular instance, the difficult part of the art of treaty interpretation involves going beyond the rules themselves, that is the evaluation and judgement required in applying the rules to a particular treaty to produce an actual interpretation. The International Law Commission (ILC), which drew up the draft articles, stated in its Commentary on them: '... the Commission confined itself to trying to isolate and codify the comparatively few general principles which appear to constitute general rules for the interpretation of treaties'.[3] This endorsed the analysis by the ILC's Special Rapporteur, Sir Humphrey Waldock, whose proposals avoided all the principles and maxims of interpretation then in common use. Taking as examples ones frequently referred to in their Latin forms ('*ut res magis valeat quam pereat, contra proferentem, eiusdem generis, expressio unius est exclusio alterius, generalia specialibus non derogant*'), he characterized these as 'for the most part, principles of logic and good sense valuable only as guides to assist in appreciating the meaning', principles whose use was thus discretionary rather than obligatory.[4] It is clear that the ILC's approach was not to exclude such principles and maxims, but to concentrate on the minimum necessary to stand as rules.

A more specific indication of the role of the rules describes their structure as having become 'the virtually indispensable scaffolding for the reasoning on questions of treaty interpretation, and this despite the intention of the authors of the Convention that it should not establish anything like a hierarchy of rules'.[5] The image of scaffolding nicely captures the supporting and enabling role of the Vienna rules. The extent to which these rules also sustain the resulting interpretation takes the interpreter beyond this metaphor, reflecting the growing and helpful tendency of courts and tribunals to expose their use of particular elements of the rules while constructing an interpretation.

Preliminary Considerations

A prerequisite to assessment of the VCLT provisions as rules for treaty interpretation is identification of what they aim to achieve. Even if one accepts that they only provide 'scaffolding for the reasoning on questions of treaty interpretation', the ultimate target provides part of the standard for their evaluation. In this respect, the ILC's Special Rapporteur (Waldock) suggested that:

---

[3] [1966] YBILC, vol II, 218–19 [4]–[5]. This chapter is confined to the rules on treaties between States; a discussion of the rules of treaty interpretation involving international organizations is found in Chapter 20 (Specialized Rules of Treaty Interpretation: International Organizations).

[4] H Waldock, 'Third Report on the Law of Treaties' [1964] YBILC, vol II, 54 [5]–[6].

[5] H Thirlway, 'The Law and Procedure of the International Court of Justice 1960–1989, Supplement 2006: Part Three' (2006) 77 BYBIL 1, 19.

The process of interpretation, rightly conceived, cannot be regarded as a mere mechanical one of drawing inevitable meanings from the words in a text, or of searching for and discovering some preexisting specific intention of the parties with respect to every situation arising under a treaty . . . In most instances interpretation involves *giving* a meaning to a text.[6]

This seems unnecessarily cautious. The interpreter is always 'giving' a meaning to the text even where the meaning is perfectly obvious. The same reason gives ground to question the observation of McNair: 'Strictly speaking, when the meaning of the treaty is clear, it is "applied", not "interpreted".'[7] In order to apply a provision of a treaty, it must first be given meaning. Defining interpretation as 'giving meaning' inevitably imports an active role for the interpreter. Noting Waldock's apt observation that the process of interpretation is not to be viewed as a mere mechanical one, the role of the person giving a meaning to the terms of a treaty introduces elements of subjectivity and creativity. Thus, judgement is a necessary component of the process. Rules can assist judgement but cannot replace it.

A widely perceived generalization about the international legal system is that in executing legal rules, judgments are less confined to courts than in national legal systems. The truth of this need not be investigated here because treaty interpretation is not solely the province of international courts and tribunals, nor even of courts more generally. States, their governments, legislative bodies, international organizations and many others also have to give meaning to treaty provisions.[8] National courts increasingly do tackle interpretation of treaties.[9] But so do international organizations, their constitutions being typically in the form of treaties, while their ancillary courts, tribunals, or legal secretariats may have an interpretative role as well.[10] The extent to which the Vienna rules have found a home in the practice of these bodies and within national administrations and legal systems is variable and difficult to assess. However, the trend is towards their use and no evidence exists of their being rejected.

I. The Vienna Rules—Historic Controversy

A full account of the historical development of the rules of treaty interpretation is beyond the scope of this chapter.[11] It is, however, useful to be aware of one of the

---

[6] [1964] YBILC, vol II, 53 [1] (citing Part III of the Harvard draft codification of international law in (1935) 29 AJIL Supp 653, 946 (original emphasis)).

[7] AD McNair, *The Law of Treaties* (Clarendon Press, Oxford 1961) 365 n1. For more on the distinction between interpretation and application, see Gardiner (n 2) 25–9, but cf M Milanovic, 'The ICJ and Evolutionary Treaty Interpretation' <http://www.ejiltalk.org/the-icj-and-evolutionary-treaty-interpretation/>. On the ILC and this distinction, see Part II.A.3, 485 *et seq.*

[8] On the role of national courts see Chapter 15 (Domestic Application of Treaties); Gardiner (n 2), preface and chapter 4, section 4.2.

[9] See eg CH Schreuer, 'The Interpretation of Treaties by Domestic Courts' (1971) 45 BYBIL 255.

[10] See Chapter 20, Part II, 519 *et seq.*

[11] For such an account see Gardiner (n 2), chapter 2. The present chapter covers much that is considered in greater detail in *Treaty Interpretation*, without citing it at every point. For an elaboration

main criticisms originally levelled against the Vienna rules. Professor McDougal, a member of the American delegation at the Vienna Conference where the text of the VCLT was finalized, saw the rules as highly restrictive, with an 'insistent emphasis upon an impossible, conformity-imposing textuality'.[12] McDougal also considered that what he saw as the rigour of the ILC's insistence upon the 'primacy of the text' authorized only 'a minimum recourse to preparatory work'.[13]

That such a restrictive character is *not* the case has been amply demonstrated in practice (as discussed below); but it was equally clearly never the ILC's intention that the rules should be constricting in the way McDougal saw them. That the treaty text was taken by the ILC as the starting point for interpretation, and that wholly extraneous evidence of intention was excluded, is neither open to challenge nor surprising. Using the text as the starting point for interpretation is hardly 'conformity-imposing textuality' and 'the general rule' (which is the *whole* of Article 31) goes well beyond treaty text. At the very least, the inclusion of subsequent practice in the treaty's application and reference to rules of international law applicable in relations between the parties shows that textuality does not reign supreme. Nor was reference to preparatory work relegated to a minimal role or exceptional situations. Article 32 of the VCLT categorizes preparatory work as among the supplementary means of interpretation but, rather contrary to appearances from the text, was neither intended to preclude routine consideration of preparatory work nor has it done so. The ILC's views as reported by the Vienna rules' principal architect, Sir Humphrey Waldock (the fourth Special Rapporteur on this subject), was that:

This formulation [the precursor to Article 32] seemed to the Commission about as near as it is possible to get to reconciling the principle of the primacy of the text . . . with frequent and quite normal recourse to *travaux préparatoires* without any too nice regard for the question whether the text itself is clear. Moreover, the rule . . . is inherently flexible, since the question whether the text can be said to be 'clear' is in some degree subjective.[14]

Somewhat paradoxically, only by adopting an excessively literal approach to interpretation of the Vienna rules—an approach at variance with the text, its preparatory work, and its application in practice—could they be seen, in McDougal's words, as 'highly restrictive principles'.[15] Indeed, acknowledging that these are 'principles' is itself rather at odds with the notion of these rules being 'conformity-imposing' and 'highly restrictive'.

---

of more detailed rules on treaty interpretation see U Linderfalk, *On the Interpretation of Treaties: The Modern International Law as Expressed in the 1969 Vienna Convention on the Law of Treaties* (Springer, Dordrecht 2007). For examples of detailed studies of specialized areas see I Van Damme, *Treaty Interpretation by the WTO Appellate Body* (OUP, Oxford 2009), G Letsas, *A Theory of Interpretation of the European Convention on Human Rights* (OUP, Oxford 2007), and N Shelton, *Interpretation and Application of Tax Treaties* (LexisNexis, London 2004).

[12] MS McDougal, 'The International Law Commission's Draft Articles upon Interpretation: Textuality *Redivivus*' (1967) 61 AJIL 992.

[13] Ibid 995.

[14] Waldock, 'Sixth Report on the Law of Treaties' [1966] YBILC, vol II, 99 [20].

[15] McDougal (n 12) 999.

McDougal's criticisms do, however, appear to have some force in relation to the exact formulation of Article 32 on preparatory work (and other supplementary materials). Quite apart from their general classification as 'supplementary', the differing roles envisaged for preparatory work according to the outcome of applying the general rule seems itself at odds with the ILC's intention as expressed in Waldock's quoted statement. In practice, Article 32 has been applied without too close a regard for its precise terms, being taken more as indicative of a need for caution in using preparatory work and a reflection of its often rather haphazard character.

II. Are the Rules on Treaty Interpretation 'Rules'?

A. The general rule: Article 31

The section of the VCLT covering treaty interpretation opens with Article 31 entitled *General rule of interpretation*. Common usage describes this article, along with the next two, as the 'rules of interpretation'. A starting point for assessing the nature of these provisions as 'rules' is their content and formulation.

The title of Article 31 indicates that the whole of the article is the general rule. The use of the singular 'rule' was deliberate. The ILC's Commentary articulated a 'crucible' approach to interpretation:

The Commission, by heading the article 'General rule of interpretation' in the singular and by underlining the connexion between paragraphs 1 and 2 and again between paragraph 3 and the two previous paragraphs, intended to indicate that the application of the means of interpretation in the article would be a single combined operation. All the various elements, as they were present in any given case, would be thrown into the crucible, and their interaction would give the legally relevant interpretation. Thus, Article 27 [now 31] is entitled 'General *rule* of interpretation' in the singular, not 'General *rules*' in the plural, because the Commission desired to emphasize that the process of interpretation is a unity and that the provisions of the article form a single, closely integrated rule.[16]

The first paragraph of Article 31 is couched in 'mandatory' language: 'A treaty *shall* be interpreted in good faith in accordance with the ordinary meaning to be given to the terms of the treaty in their context and in the light of its object and purpose' (emphasis added). However, while this looks like a rule in the sense of a requirement or regulation, there are a number of reasons to suggest that its meaning is not so firm and inflexible.

First, it has to be accepted that there is commonly no single 'ordinary' meaning of a word and thus there is the need for a direct link to the context and the treaty's object and purpose. That linkage immediately qualifies any impression that the ordinary meaning is simply a literal approach. Context and object and purpose

---

[16] [1966] YBILC, vol II, 219 [8] (emphasis in original).

are not additional or optional elements. They are pointers to the appropriate ordinary meaning and thus must also be put in the crucible.

Second, Article 31's opening paragraph is part of a set of provisions forming the single general rule. Paragraph (3) indicates additional factors to be 'taken into account'. These factors include (a) subsequent agreement between the parties on the meaning, (b) subsequent practice showing the meaning, and (c) applicable rules of international law. The interpreter takes these factors (where present) into account in determining whether they trump any impression given by applying the first paragraph of the general rule. This demonstrates emphatically the error of treating just the first paragraph as the general rule or viewing the later stated elements of the general rule as subsidiary.

Third, paragraph (4) of Article 31 requires a special meaning to be given to a treaty term if it is established that the parties so intended. Hence, the parties to a treaty can deliberately displace the ordinary meaning or themselves guard against an overly literal interpretation.[17]

Fourth, it is apparent from Waldock's statement as the ILC's Special Rapporteur that, though formulated as rules, these provisions have a more liberal character:

The Commission was fully conscious... of the undesirability—if not impossibility—of confining the process of interpretation within rigid rules, and the provisions of [the draft articles] ... do not appear to constitute a code of rules incompatible with the required degree of flexibility... any 'principles' found by the Commission to be 'rules' should, so far as seems advisable, be formulated as such. In a sense all 'rules' of interpretation have the character of 'guidelines' since their application in a particular case depends so much on the appreciation of the context and the circumstances of the point to be interpreted.[18]

Fifth, the ILC's 'crucible' approach described above envisages a fluid interaction of Article 31's elements producing the legally relevant interpretation. The crucial interaction is not to be formulaic in the sense of a purely mechanical process.

1. Context contrasted with circumstances of conclusion

If the effect of these observations indicates that the Vienna rules are as much guidelines as rules, particularly given the great variation in treaties and issues to which they apply, the last part of the ILC's words (quoted at the fourth point above) does reflect a distinction made in the rules between context and circumstances of conclusion. The *context* to which Article 31(1) refers is defined in Article 31(2) to include the whole treaty text, including its preamble and annexes, any agreement relating to the treaty made between all the parties in connection

---

[17] For an example of a special meaning see the terms 'refugee' and '*refouler*' in the Convention Relating to the Status of Refugees (adopted 28 July 1951, entered into force 22 April 1954) 189 UNTS 137, and its 1967 Protocol (adopted 31 January 1967, entered into force 4 October 1967) 606 UNTS 267, considered in *R v Immigration Officer at Prague Airport ex parte European Roma Rights Centre* [2004] UKHL 55, [2005] 2 AC 1, 31 [18], per Lord Bingham and cf *Sale v Haitian Centers Council* 509 US 155 (1993) 179 *et seq*.
[18] H Waldock, 'Sixth Report' (n 14) 94 [1].

with the treaty's conclusion, and any instrument made by one or more parties in connection with the treaty's conclusion and accepted by the other parties as an instrument related to the treaty.

This definition gives 'context' a specific content for purposes of treaty interpretation. McDougal saw it as too prescriptive and narrow. He sought application of a principle of 'contextuality', taking into account anything that could be construed as relevant to the twin tasks of (i) realizing the shared expectation of the parties as to the outcome of the 'continuing process of communication and collaboration between the parties' (which he saw as the true concept of a treaty) and (ii) reflecting the shared values of the community.[19]

It is not, however, because the VCLT is excessively literalist in approach, or that its rules are excessively prescriptive in nature, that context is defined more narrowly than McDougal's posited principle of contextuality. Instead, the Vienna rules distinguish between (a) context as an indispensable adjunct to finding the ordinary meaning of the terms used and (b) 'the circumstances of conclusion' of a treaty which, in the Vienna scheme, are part of the supplementary means of interpretation in Article 32. True, this may place a premium on the texts that provide the element of context in the general rule as against the more general surrounding circumstances. True also that Article 31's interpretative elements are couched in mandatory terms, while the supplementary means in Article 32 are interpretative tools to which 'recourse may be had'. But this difference is more of an attempt to give guidance on priorities or emphasis than an indication that the general rule has the character of a straightjacket. The rather gentle application made in practice of differentiating between the general rule and supplementary means serves to confirm this understanding.

Article 31(2) functions to bring into consideration other material generated in connection with the treaty's conclusion. As with several other elements of the Vienna rules, this is more a description of *what* is to be considered rather than *how* the material should be used to fashion the interpretation. Even so, it still does not provide a rigid rule for demarcation of what is admissible as interpretative material.

2. Agreements and practice: Article 31(2)–(3)

Paragraphs (2)(a) and (2)(b) of Article 31 have a common feature: both refer to acts 'in connection with the conclusion of the treaty'. Beyond that, they are somewhat different. Paragraph (2)(a) defines context by looking to an instrument evidencing the agreement of all parties and hence of direct interpretative significance. An example of such an instrument is a diplomatic conference's 'Final Act', which typically provides a brief account of the proceedings leading up to the treaty's adoption and may include interpretative indications agreed by the negotiators. Paragraph (2)(b) envisages as context an instrument made by one or more parties accepted by the others as related to the treaty, but not necessarily agreed to by those

---

[19] MS McDougal, HD Lasswell, and JC Miller, *The Interpretation of Agreements and World Public Order: Principles of Content and Procedure* (Yale University Press, New Haven 1967) xxiii and 197–9.

others. For example, an interpretative declaration accompanying a State's instrument of ratification is made in connection with a treaty's conclusion and accepted by other parties as related to it, but may not receive those parties' agreement as to whether it is the correct interpretation.

As regards the former category (paragraph 2(a)), the principle of taking into account what amounts to an agreement by the parties relating to the treaty seems clear in a general sense. However, differences in practice as to (i) what constitutes a firm agreement and (ii) the absence of precision as to when a treaty is 'concluded', combine to make the provision less of a clear rule than it may seem. It is easy enough to identify a Protocol of Signature or a specific protocol on interpretation as coming within Article 31(2)(a). An instrument described as a 'Memorandum of Understandings', whether accompanying a treaty or standing alone, may be more difficult to classify.[20] That title provides no conclusive indication as to the legal character of its content. Sometimes this term is used for an instrument containing commitments of the same character as a treaty, while at other times it is used to describe an instrument recording mere understandings or setting out the terms of a 'gentlemen's agreement', which are not viewed as legally binding commitments.

The VCLT's text does not, however, specifically require interpretative agreements to be in a particular form. From the immediate context it seems probable that Article 31(2)(a) requires evidence of the fact of agreement on meaning rather than a formal agreement itself. Article 31(3)(b) requires account to be taken of 'any subsequent practice in the application of the treaty which establishes the agreement of the parties regarding its interpretation'. That clearly attributes interpretative significance to the fact of agreement where there is no formal instrument. Given that approach, there is no particular reason to suppose that Article 32(2)(a) requires an agreement in treaty form. Hence, if a memorandum accompanying a treaty provides sufficiently clear evidence of agreement between the parties as to the treaty's meaning, there is little reason to exclude it.[21]

Article 31(2)(b) separately brings into interpretative play 'any instrument which was made by one or more parties in connection with the conclusion of the treaty and accepted by the other parties as an instrument related to the treaty'. The reference to an 'instrument' does not raise the same potential uncertainty whether the 'agreement' of the parties has to be formal in the sense of a treaty. Nor does the requirement of showing that the parties other than the maker of that instrument accepted it as related to the treaty suggest that they necessarily agree to the instrument's content. The VCLT does not specify what such content may be, but, as in the case of the Article's previous paragraph, Article 31(2)(b) requires that the instrument be connected with the treaty's conclusion. It seems probable that in the context of unilateral instruments, or instruments not reflective of agreement of

---

[20] See Chapter 2, 46 *et seq*; A Aust, *Modern Treaty Law and Practice* (2nd edn CUP, Cambridge 2007) chapter 3; Gardiner (n 2) chapter 3, 'Interpretative Material Generated in Making Treaties'. For an example of a protocol on interpretation, see the Protocol on the Interpretation of Article 69 of the European Patent Convention, Munich, 1973 [1974] 13 ILM 348.

[21] *US–UK Arbitration concerning Heathrow Airport User Charges* (30 November 1992) 102 ILR 215.

all parties, typically the content will involve interpretative declarations. Such declarations are commonly made on signature, ratification, accession, etc, along with reservations.[22]

Moreover, the moment of a treaty's 'conclusion' may be difficult to pinpoint because there is no single procedure for the various stages that follow completion of treaty negotiations and its entry into force. Signature indicates that the process of drawing up the treaty is 'concluded', but it cannot be assumed to be the only key stage when so many treaties are subject to ratification. Even within the VCLT itself, different provisions give different meanings to the term 'conclusion'.[23]

Within the immediate context of the general rule on interpretation, an interpretative agreement connected with a treaty's conclusion (treated as context by Article 31(2)(a)) can be contrasted with 'any subsequent agreement' (to be taken into account pursuant to Article 31(3)(a)). The possibility of 'subsequent' agreement suggests that there must have been an earlier fixed point of agreement appropriate for collective action. The most likely moment for an interpretative agreement among all parties in connection with the treaty's conclusion is at signature because this could affect the basis on which States start the process of committing themselves to the treaty. However, this does not inevitably fix 'conclusion' as the moment of opening for signature. If no States signed, or if very few ratified the treaty, there might follow an agreement among all negotiating States to interpret some offending provision in a particular way, which would overcome the obstacle States had found to participation. Such an agreement seems as likely to be seen as connected with conclusion of the treaty as one made on signature.

Although the instruments to which Article 31(2)(b) refers are in the same immediate context as those in Article 31(2)(a) given their location in the general rule, their situation is somewhat different. There is no contrasting provision in Article 31(3). Nor is there the same sense of collective action involving all parties. The occasion of a deposit of an instrument of ratification may be just the moment for making a unilateral interpretative declaration. Hence 'conclusion' in Article 31 (2)(b) may be more appropriately understood as including the process of successive lodging of instruments of ratification, accession, etc—or what might be viewed as a rolling process of conclusion.

Leaving aside this difficulty over the meaning of 'conclusion', a positive theme unites Articles 31(2)(a), 31(3)(a) and 31(3)(b)—the notion that agreement on interpretation among the treaty parties is the very best indicator of its proper interpretation. They are the entities with the power to amend, terminate, or replace the treaty. Beyond the imposition of a few peremptory rules, international law allows States free reign in treaty-making. Hence the parties can interpret a treaty

---

[22] The ILC has included provisions on interpretative declarations in its work on reservation: see reports of its Special Rapporteur (Pellet) and ILC accounts of its work on reservations in its annual reports: <http://untreaty.un.org/ilc/guide/1_8.htm>. That work culminated in 2011 in a *Guide to Practice*: ILC, 'Guide to Practice on Reservations to Treaties' (2011) <http://untreaty.un.org/ilc/texts/instruments/english/draft%20articles/1_8_2011.pdf> (forthcoming [2011] YBIL, vol II(2)).

[23] See VCLT Part II, Section 1, headed 'Conclusion of Treaties'; Ibid Arts 4, 40; see further Gardiner (n 2) chapter 6, section 2.1.

authoritatively. Those who seek to give the first paragraph of Article 31 a stronger role than agreements of the parties or practice evidencing the parties' agreement on the meaning of a treaty provision perhaps underestimate the difference between a national system of law and international law, the latter reflecting to a major extent the sovereign character of the principal entities that it regulates.

More specifically, in its commentary on the draft articles, the ILC assimilated the effect of subsequent interpretative agreements with those made at a treaty's conclusion, albeit without treating as context such subsequent agreements by virtue of their later adoption:

But it is well settled that when an agreement as to the interpretation of a provision is established as having been reached before or at the time of the conclusion of the treaty it is to be regarded as forming part of the treaty . . . Similarly, an agreement as to the interpretation of a provision reached after the conclusion of the treaty represents an authentic interpretation by the parties which must be read into the treaty for purposes of its interpretation.[24]

The ILC also indicated that the elements in paragraph (3) of Article 31 were no less part of the general rule than paragraph (2)'s provisions: 'But these three elements[25] are all of an obligatory character and by their very nature could not be considered to be norms of interpretation in any way inferior to those which precede them.'[26]

3. Rules of international law: Article 31(3)(c)

Somewhat in contrast to the provisions on subsequent agreement and subsequent practice, Article 31(3)(c) is rather unrevealing of its intentions. It requires account be taken of 'any relevant rules of international law applicable in the relations between the parties'. Such laconic wording rather masks the provision's purpose. It appears to offer a rule requiring attention to other rules. It seems trite to say that an interpretation should take account of applicable law, though in the context of international relations, two particular issues are immediately apparent. The first is whether the law to be taken into account is that as it was at the time the treaty was made or whether evolution in the law affects its interpretation. The second is the extent to which other treaty relations between the parties may have an interpretative role.

First, although it is not clear from the text of Article 31(3)(c), its origins lie in the so-called 'intertemporal' rule. The ILC's initial draft on this topic considered the first limb of the intertemporal rule as requiring that 'a treaty is to be interpreted in the light of the law in force at the time when the treaty was drawn up'.[27] However,

---

[24] [1966] YBILC, vol II, 221 [14].

[25] The comment refers also to relevant rules of international law, which are the subject of Art 31 (3)(c).

[26] [1966] YBILC, vol II, 220 [9].

[27] [1964] YBILC, vol II, 8–9 (including Waldock's commentary). This reflected the classic formulation of the intertemporal rule in the words used by Judge Huber in *Island of Palmas (Netherlands v USA)* Arbitration (1928) 2 RIAA 829, 845: 'a juridical fact must be appreciated in the light of the law contemporary with it, and not the law in force at the time when a dispute in regard to it arises or falls to be settled'.

a second part of the rule required that, subject to the first limb of the rule, 'the application of a treaty shall be governed by the rules of international law in force at the time when the treaty is applied'.[28]

The ILC scrapped this formulation in view of the difficulty of reconciling the principle that terms of a treaty should be interpreted in the light of international law as at the time of the treaty's conclusion with taking appropriate account of developments in the law up to the time when a difference in interpretation is being resolved. It expected intertemporal issues to be resolved by appropriate interpretation of the particular treaty in issue: 'correct application of the temporal element would normally be indicated by interpretation of the term *in good faith*'.[29] Hence, part of the intertemporal rule was ultimately included by reference to good faith in the first part of the general rule. But the main principle, expressed by Waldock (as the ILC's Special Rapporteur) was that: 'The question whether the terms used were intended to have a fixed content or to change in meaning with the evolution of the law could be decided only by interpreting the intention of the parties'.[30] Thus, this outcome leaves scope to the interpreter to decide what the treaty envisages in taking account of developments in international law.

Second, Article 31(3)(c)'s reference to 'rules of international law applicable in the relations between the parties' is somewhat opaque as to whether it includes treaty relations. Once again, reference to the ILC's work is required to clarify the provision. An earlier draft had referred to 'rules of general international law'. The VCLT elsewhere refers to a 'peremptory norm of general international law'. In the latter context the phrase 'general international law' was used in part to avoid confusion with general multilateral treaties.[31] There is no authoritative definition of 'general international law', so it is not possible to say if in other contexts treaties would be excluded from its scope. In Article 31(3)(c), however, the word 'general' was deleted, and a proposal to include the word 'customary' in its place was rejected, suggesting that the distinction required in relation to peremptory norms was not intended here.[32] Further, ILC debate, though sparse, clearly supported the view that treaties are potentially within the scope of Article 31(3)(c). One member of the ILC welcomed the text as amended to delete 'general':

[the] new text should be maintained, because it set out the important principle that a treaty constituted a new legal element which was additional to the other legal relationships between the parties and should be interpreted within the framework of other rules of international law in force between them. But it should not be qualified by the insertion of the word 'general', which would exclude specific or regional rules of international law

---

[28] [1964] YBILC, vol II, 8–9; Judge Huber, *Island of Palmas* (n 27) ('The same principle which subjects the act creative of a right to the law in force at the time the right arises, demands that the existence of the right, in other words its continued manifestation, shall follow the conditions required by the evolution of law').

[29] [1966] YBILC, vol II, 222 [16] (emphasis added).

[30] [1966] YBILC, vol I(2), 199 [9].

[31] See eg debate in [1963] YBILC, vol I(1), 70 [40].

[32] [1966] YBILC, vol I(2), 191 [74].

binding on the parties. That was a particularly important matter where one treaty had to be interpreted in the light of other treaties binding on the parties.[33]

Similarly, another member saw the revised wording as including 'rules of written law', a phrase which must point primarily to treaties:

The omission of the word 'general' before the words 'international law' was justified, because a treaty concluded between several States should be interpreted in the light of the special international rules applying to those States, whether they were customary rules or rules of written law. It must be emphasized, however, that to be taken into consideration in interpreting the treaty, those rules, although not 'general', must be 'common' to the parties to the treaty.[34]

This history and analysis of Article 31(3)(c)'s text only takes one part of the way to understanding its purport. As discussed further below, the provision's role is only gradually being revealed through emerging practice.

B. Supplementary means: Article 32

The contrast between 'means' in the heading of Article 32 and 'rule' in Article 31 combines with the provisions' wording to suggest a clear difference in their interpretative roles. Article 31 ostensibly lays down a prescriptive rule using the mandatory 'shall' in each of its paragraphs. Article 32 offers an option: 'recourse *may* be had to supplementary means'. Yet, any consideration of the general rule's meaning leads almost inevitably to the ILC's preparatory work to achieve a clear interpretation, a process that might be illustrative of the process of treaty interpretation more generally.

It is at this point that McDougal's criticisms of the apparent relegation of preparatory work to supplementary means take on some force. McDougal proposed that supplementary means should have the same engagement in the interpretative process as all the elements in the general rule. As evidence of the important role of supplementary work, he pointed to the need of the Vienna conference delegates to consult Waldock to understand fully the drafts they were discussing:

In parenthesis, it could be added that the mere presence at this Conference of Sir Humphrey Waldock, in the role of former Special Rapporteur, is the best testimony, not always mute, of the impossibility in application of the textuality approach. Time after time during the course of our deliberations, even with the preparatory work of the Commission before us, we have found it necessary to appeal to Sir Humphrey for enlightenment about the 'ordinary' meanings of the simple Convention before us. The tremendous clarity he has brought to our deliberations and the enormous influence he has had with us have been due, I submit, not to his skill in flipping pages of a dictionary or as a logician, but rather his very special knowledge of all the circumstances attending the framing of our draft Convention.[35]

---

[33] Ibid 190 [70] (Jiménez de Arechaga).

[34] Ibid 197 [52] (Yasseen).

[35] 'Statement of Professor McDougal, US Delegation, to Committee of the Whole, Vienna Conference, 19 April 1968', as reproduced in (1968) 62 AJIL 1021, 1025. This differs a little in

This entertaining caricature of the general rule's defects is actually rather destructive of the better points McDougal was advancing. For example, the Vienna Conference was concerned with establishing the final version of treaty provisions, rather than interpreting existing terms. Hence Sir Humphrey's role was not merely as an interpreter of text. Nevertheless, McDougal's reference to use of 'preparatory work' (in context, recorded preparatory work) and surrounding circumstances (in Article 32, 'the circumstances of conclusion') does reflect the direction in which an interpreter's attention is strongly drawn. The question is how far to go down that route?

It seems all too obvious that treaty interpreters cannot generally have the live testimony of all those who had a hand in drawing up a treaty. So the preparatory work must be reasonably limited to permanent records (the *travaux préparatoires*). The ILC sensibly declined to attempt a universal definition of such preparatory work. The ways in which treaties are negotiated and the modes of recording their development are too multifarious. But the ILC followed Waldock's recommended approach:

> Recourse to *travaux préparatoires* as a subsidiary means of interpreting the text, as already indicated, is frequent both in State practice and in cases before international tribunals. Today, it is generally recognized that some caution is needed in the use of *travaux préparatoires* as a means of interpretation. They are not, except in the case mentioned [agreements, instruments, and other documents ultimately covered elsewhere in the Vienna rules], an authentic means of interpretation. They are simply evidence to be weighed against any other relevant evidence of the intentions of the parties, and their cogency depends on the extent to which they furnish proof of the *common* understanding of the parties as to the meaning attached to the terms of the treaty. Statements of individual parties during the negotiations are therefore of small value in the absence of evidence that they were assented to by the other parties.[36]

Noting first that Waldock was not an 'individual party' but, as Special Rapporteur, was the guide, motivator, and mouthpiece of the ILC on this topic, the theme in this extract is integration of the use of preparatory work with the rest of the process of treaty interpretation, albeit with proper caution and appropriate evaluation. The cardinal principle for admissibility and use of preparatory work is that its cogency depends on how far it provides evidence of a 'common understanding of the parties as to the meaning' when weighed against other evidence.

It can be seen, therefore, that there is no clear cut *rule* on preparatory work, but rather a principle requiring interpreters to use judgement. The VCLT's preparatory work reveals acceptance by the Vienna conference of the ILC's draft rules virtually unchanged (the only controversy, which did not result in any change, coming from the admittedly significant issues raised by McDougal). Such acceptance adds justification for importing the ILC's records into the body of preparatory work to

---

tone but not in substance from the summary records of the Statement itself. UN Conference on the Law of Treaties, Summary Records of First Session (26 March–24 May 1968) UN Doc A/Conf.39/11, 167–8 [45].

[36] Waldock, Third Report (n 4) 58 [21] (emphasis in original, footnotes omitted).

be evaluated as evidence of the Vienna rules' meaning.[37] However, acceptance by the conference of texts proposed by the ILC is only one factor in favour of using the records as material for interpreting the rules; others include the strength of agreement within the ILC and at the conference on any particular point and the growing subsequent practice of referring to the ILC's work on the Vienna rules.

Both McDougal and Waldock recognized that preparatory work is very readily considered by treaty interpreters. Where they differed was in the role and content of the principles reflected in Article 32. McDougal saw preparatory work as part of the whole body of interpretative evidence, making the supplementary and circumscribed role ascribed to preparatory work unacceptable. Waldock evidently considered the text to be a fair reflection of the Commission's aim of 'reconciling the principle of the primacy of the text . . . with frequent and quite normal recourse to *travaux préparatoires*'.[38] There is some difficulty in accepting Waldock's view given the wording of the text, but ultimately his view prevails in the liberal interpretation given to that text in practice.

In terms of its content, Article 32 provides two different regimes. The first envisages recourse to supplementary means, including preparatory work, to 'confirm' the meaning established by application of the general rule for treaty interpretation. The second invites recourse to 'determine' the meaning where application of the general rule leaves the meaning ambiguous or obscure, or produces a result which is manifestly absurd or unreasonable. Clearly, this second regime gives preparatory work a potentially crucial role in interpretation. It is therefore hardly surprising, or unreasonable, that the function of preparatory work is defined in Article 32 in more precise terms. Preparatory work is itself notoriously difficult to use in finding proof of the parties' common understanding. Thus, only when the general rule fails, or produces a manifestly questionable result, should primacy be given to preparatory work.

The circumstances in which preparatory work is determinative are rare. However, the opportunity to deploy it to support an interpretation resulting from application of the general rule is more common and is not subject to the qualifying conditions prerequisite to its use to determine meaning. The difficulty centres on the term 'confirm'. In ordinary use, and perhaps misuse, one might be asked to 'confirm' one's name despite not having given it yet; one may confirm an order or reservation only made provisionally or which will lapse if not confirmed; one may confirm a booking that is already firm but for which one has forgotten the details or which one senses may not have registered adequately with the recipient, and so on.

As application of the general rule requires evaluating elements of differing weight and reliability, 'confirming' a meaning may assume a range of roles according to the circumstances. At the lightest end of the scale, it may mean little more than looking at the preparatory work to see whether any help lies there. At the other extreme, the preparatory work may tip the balance. Once again, a distinction made by Waldock at an early stage of deliberations on the role of preparatory work is helpful:

[37] Gardiner (n 2) 102–3.   [38] See text to n 14.

There is, however, a difference between examining and basing a finding upon *travaux préparatoires,* and the [International] Court itself has more than once referred to them as confirming an interpretation otherwise arrived at from a study of the text. Moreover, it is the constant practice of States and tribunals to examine any relevant *travaux préparatoires* for such light as they may throw upon the treaty. It would therefore be unrealistic to suggest, even by implication, that there is any actual bar upon mere reference to *travaux préparatoires* whenever the meaning of the terms is clear.[39]

This support for attributing to preparatory work a role throwing, where possible, light on the treaty's terms was accompanied by an indication of a loose approach on preparatory work being part of the 'supplementary' means of interpretation. Just as the 'crucible' approach does not see the elements of the general rule as hierarchical or sequential (other than as a sequence of thoughts which may be reiterated in a different order), so too the distinction between the general rule and supplementary means was not slotted into any particular sequence. Waldock noted that it was 'unrealistic to imagine that the preparatory work was not really consulted by States, organizations and tribunals whenever they saw fit, before or at any stage of the proceedings, even though they might afterwards pretend that they had not given it much attention'.[40]

Nevertheless, even if the formulation actually used in Article 32 has to be taken with a large pinch of salt, there is something to be said for its clear distinction between the rather loose idea of confirming meaning and the much more clearly circumscribed possibility of relying on preparatory work to determine a treaty's meaning. What is agreed and binding is the treaty, not the preparatory work. The Vienna rules accept the interpretative role of well-defined ancillary material in the general rule and, with due caution, a limited role for the less well-defined preparatory work that can be elevated to a higher role only in controlled situations (ambiguity or obscurity, or manifest absurdity or unreasonableness).

C. Languages: Article 33

The division of the rules of interpretation into a general rule and supplementary means of interpretation engendered the most substantial debate at the Vienna conference; but it did not result in any change from the ILC's scheme. Where there was a change was in how different languages could assist or affect treaty interpretation. To the ILC's draft of what became Article 33 the Vienna conference added a rule of last resort: where a difference of meaning remained after applying all the other Vienna rules, 'the meaning which best reconciles the texts, having regard to the object and purpose of the treaty, shall be adopted' (Article 33(4)).

Though couched in terms of a rule, the idea of 'reconciling' divergent language texts by 'having regard' to the treaty's object and purpose is not a formula of

---

[39] Waldock, Third Report (n 4) 58 [20] (footnotes omitted).
[40] [1964] YBILC, vol I, 314 [65]; the phrase 'verify or confirm' had been used in an early draft of Art 32, but 'verify' was dropped as being included in 'confirm', thus suggesting a broad meaning for the latter term.

scientific precision. The starting point is stated in Article 33(1), namely that parallel language texts are equally authoritative unless it is specifically stated or agreed that a particular text is to prevail. This is accompanied by the presumption in Article 33(3) that terms have the same meaning in each authentic text. The remaining provision, Article 33(2), identifies which translations made after a treaty has been authenticated are to be treated as authentic.

Like many other elements of the Vienna rules, the article on languages is as much about identifying what is admissible material for use in interpretation as how to use that material in the interpretative process. The provision tries to identify relevant concepts and select appropriate terminology. Since the starting point of any interpretation must be a text, identification of the correct text is a prerequisite. However, the Vienna rules recognize that the aim is to interpret the *agreement* of the parties expressed in a text. The ILC therefore attached importance to the idea of there being only a *single* agreement, even if expressed in different languages. Where more than one language is used, describing the expressions of agreement in differing languages as 'texts' could indicate plurality rather than unity. Describing the expressions of agreement in different languages as 'versions' could imply an even greater departure from the concept of the unity of a treaty. Article 33 adopts a pragmatic, if inconsistent, approach. It keeps to the principle of unity by stating that the singular 'text' is equally authoritative in each language unless, where so indicated, 'a particular text' is to prevail. In reality, this acknowledges the customary usage of referring to authentic texts in different languages as 'texts' in the plural. The term 'version' is reserved for describing later translations accepted as authentic.

The article also distinguishes between the descriptions 'authentic' and 'authoritative'. It follows the concept of 'authentication' in Article 10 of the VCLT, the process for establishing a text as definitive at the end of negotiations.[41] Associating the term 'authentic' with the finalized terms in different languages leaves the word 'authoritative' to describe the subsequent status and effect of a text authenticated in different languages.

This approach in itself provides a lesson in treaty interpretation, particularly for the importance attached by the ILC to the link between ordinary meaning and context at the outset of the general rule. The ordinary meaning of 'authentic' in Article 33 is informed by the context, that is by considering use of the term in the Convention's provisions on treaty-making. Elsewhere than in the context of the Convention, 'authentic' may have a different ordinary meaning, as in its use by the ILC in the expression 'authentic interpretation' (meaning one made by the parties).[42] Thus, the ordinary meaning of 'authentic' is not established by a

---

[41] For a more detailed discussion of the process of authentication, see Chapter 7, Part II.C, 188 *et seq.*

[42] See eg the ILC's Commentary on its draft articles noting that an interpretative agreement reached after the treaty's conclusion 'represents an *authentic* interpretation by the parties which must be read into the treaty for purposes of its interpretation', [1966] YBILC, vol II, 221 [14] (emphasis added), cited by the ICJ in *Kasikili/Sedudu Island (Botswana v Namibia)* [1999] ICJ Rep 1045, 1075 [49] and in the NAFTA arbitration *Methanex v USA* (Merits), Award of 3 August 2005, [2005] 44 ILM 1345, 1354 [19].

'conformity-imposing textuality' (in McDougal's terms), but by selecting an ordinary meaning of the term *in its context*.

More generally, the ILC recognized that discrepancies between languages are bound to occur:

Few plurilingual treaties containing more than one or two articles are without some discrepancy between the texts. The different genius of the languages, the absence of a complete *consensus ad idem*, or lack of sufficient time to co-ordinate the texts may result in minor or even major discrepancies in the meaning of the texts.[43]

The result is that the provisions on languages do no more than raise some presumptions, leaving considerable discretion to the interpreter.

III. The Vienna Rules in Practice

The analysis of the Vienna rules thus far has essentially looked at the words of the provisions and the preparatory work recording their development to see how far the provisions have the character of prescriptive rules. It is suggested that though the general rule is couched in mandatory language and identifies in clear terms what must be taken into account, the envisaged interpretative exercise is actually quite flexible. It is dependent on which elements may be present in any given case, and even more so in that any determination made by an interpreter in a particular case depends on the application of judgement in evaluating the relationship between the various elements and their respective values in giving meaning to the treaty's terms by that process.

Just as the Vienna rules give the parties' interpretative agreement (whether express or through practice) a value potentially equal to any treaty term's ordinary meaning in its context and in the light of the treaty's object and purpose, so too do they make it appropriate to consider practice in applying a treaty. There is now very extensive practice in courts and tribunals, both international and national, showing explicit use of the Vienna rules.[44] However, neither this body of case law, nor the much less readily located practice of States in interpreting treaties when applying them, has yet established conclusively the agreement of all the VCLT parties (or of all States when the rules are viewed as customary international law) on many of the issues raised above. Nevertheless, examples from practice are offered here to confirm that the Vienna rules are more in the nature of principles and indications of admissible material. They reveal a quite loose structure for developing interpretations, rather than a straightjacket or formulaic set of requirements.

---

[43] [1966] YBILC, vol II, 225 [6]. For many examples of difficulties and confusions in multilingual treaties see D Shelton, 'Reconcilable Differences? The Interpretation of Multilingual Treaties' (1997) 20 Hastings Intl and Comp L Rev 611.

[44] See Gardiner (n 2) Part II and the preface to the paperback edition.

A. General application of the Vienna rules

There is, however, one preliminary point of practice that does constitute a firm rule: the Vienna rules are now the rules of customary international law applicable to all treaties, even though the VCLT itself is not retroactive. Thus, even though the law of treaties as stated in the VCLT has a more limited scope of application when applied to its parties than do the rules of customary international law, the Convention's provisions on treaty interpretation now reflect the latter and have general application. This is subject to one caveat since the Vienna rules allow parties to attribute special meanings to terms if they deliberately so choose; and it may well follow that they could choose to apply their own specific rules of interpretation as a means of achieving their own special meaning.[45]

How can one be sure that the Vienna rules have the wide applicability just discussed? The American Law Institute stated its test for inclusion of propositions in its *Restatement of Foreign Relations Law* thus: 'this Restatement represents the opinion of The American Law Institute as to the rules that an impartial tribunal would apply if charged with deciding a controversy in accordance with international law'.[46] This test may be extrapolated to apply to the Vienna rules. Thus, in an arbitration in which the President of the ICJ was the presiding arbitrator, the Award stated:

It is now well established that the provisions on interpretation of treaties contained in Articles 31 and 32 of the Convention reflect pre-existing customary international law, and thus may be (unless there are particular indications to the contrary) applied to treaties concluded before the entering into force of the 1969 [VCLT] in 1980. The International Court of Justice has applied customary rules of interpretation, now reflected in Articles 31 and 32 of the 1969 [VCLT], to a treaty concluded in 1955 ... and to a treaty concluded in 1890, bearing on rights of States that even on the day of Judgment were still not parties to the 1969 [VCLT]... *There is no case after the adoption of the* [1969 VCLT] *in which the International Court of Justice or any other leading tribunal has failed so to act.*[47]

That the Vienna rules have been 'acknowledged' by the ICJ, other international courts and tribunals, and national courts as the governing rules does not, however, provide a full indication, still less an assessment, of their actual use by such bodies. In many cases their actual use has only been introduced gradually and

---

[45] cf The American Convention on Human Rights (adopted 22 November 1969, entered into force 18 July 1978) 1144 UNTS 123, Art 19; L Lixinski, 'Treaty Interpretation by the Inter-American Court of Human Rights: Expansionism at the Service of the Unity of International Law' (2010) 21 EJIL 585.

[46] *The Restatement of the Law (Third), The Foreign Relations Law of the United States* (ALI, St Paul 1987) 3.

[47] *Arbitration regarding the Iron Rhine ('Ijzeren Rijn') Railway (Belgium/Netherlands)* (2005) XXVII RIAA 35, 62 [45] (emphasis added). For cases of the ICJ, other international courts and tribunals, and judgments of domestic courts acknowledging the Vienna rules' applicability, see Gardiner (n 2) chapter 1, section 2.

remains limited in scope. Indeed, in practice, the rules are not always fully deployed.[48]

There are, moreover, two reasons why categorical assertions about the extent of use of the Vienna rules are difficult. First, there is no obligation on interpreters to provide a running commentary on how they are applying the rules of interpretation as they develop their argument in a particular instance. Hence, absence of reference to particular elements of the Vienna rules does not necessarily mean that they are not being applied. Second, all the elements of the rules may not be applicable in any particular case. For example, there may be no subsequent agreement on interpretation, no established interpretation through practice, no circumstances warranting determination of meaning by supplementary means, and so on.

Nevertheless, reported instances show a repeated focus on Article 31(1) alone, which does raise the strong suspicion that that paragraph is sometimes viewed by itself as the general rule of interpretation.[49] This suspicion is largely confirmed where a restricted view of Article 31 is stated expressly. Thus, despite longstanding authoritative assertions of the Vienna rules' applicability in UK courts, it has nevertheless been stated that:

article 31 of the 1969 VCLT on the Law of Treaties (1980) (Cmnd 7964) provides that a treaty shall be interpreted 'in accordance with the ordinary meaning to be given to the terms of the treaty in their context and in the light of its object and purpose'. This is the starting point of treaty interpretation to which other rules are supplementary: see articles 31(2), 31(3), 31(4) and 32. The primacy of the treaty language, read in context and purposively, is therefore of critical importance.[50]

This is correct in viewing Article 31(1) of the VCLT as a 'starting point' for interpretation; but the statement that the further paragraphs of Article 31 are 'supplementary' is quite at odds with the indication in that Article's heading that the *whole* of Article 31 is the general rule. The ILC emphatically confirmed and integrated this indication in its 'crucible' approach.[51] Further, Article 32's heading and its preparatory work make it clear that it is those provisions that are the 'supplementary' means of interpretation, not the successive elements of the general rule in Article 31.

The real danger of excessive emphasis on Article 31's first paragraph is that it relegates the further elements of that Article, such as subsequent agreement between the parties on interpretation and subsequent practice amounting to such agreement, to a subordinate role. Yet, such agreements are an 'authentic'

---

[48] See Opinion, Professor WM Reisman, 22 March 2010, on the International Legal Interpretation of the Waiver Provision in CAFTA Chapter 10 in connection with *Pac Rim Cayman LLC v Republic of El Salvador*, ICSID Case No ARB/09/12 (CAFTA) <http://ita.law.uvic.ca> [19].

[49] See the examples, particularly the assessment of the practice of the Inter-American Court of Human Rights, in ME Villiger, *Commentary on the 1969 Vienna Convention on the Law of Treaties* (Martinus Nijhoff, Leiden 2009) 436–7; Gardiner (n 2) lv, 12–19, 120–5.

[50] *In Re Deep Vein Thrombosis and Air Travel Group Litigation* [2006] 1 AC 495, 508, and see further Gardiner (n 2) xxxiv *et seq*. On the approach adopted in certain other States, see Villiger (n 49) 438.

[51] See text to n 16.

interpretation and, where present, could be determinative. The ICJ has observed that 'the subsequent practice of the parties, within the meaning of Article 31(3)(b) of the VCLT, can result in a departure from the original intent on the basis of a tacit agreement between the parties'.[52] Thus, such an interpretative agreement achieved through practice can trump a meaning that might be derived from application of Article 31(1) alone.

B. Ordinary meaning in context

In examining the manner of the rules' application, one finds numerous cases where dictionaries have been used as the starting point for interpreting a treaty. But these neither show that the Vienna rules are based on McDougal's feared 'conformity-imposing textuality', nor do they even typically suggest a single ordinary meaning. Dictionaries tend to produce a range of probable ordinary meanings. The interpretative exercise therefore rapidly moves on to consider further elements of the general rule. In *Kasikili/Sedudu Island (Botswana/Namibia)*,[53] the ICJ stated that it was interpreting words in a treaty of 1890 between Great Britain and Germany to give them their ordinary meaning, and that it was determining the meaning of 'main channel' of the river forming a disputed frontier by 'reference to the most commonly used criteria in international law'. Judge Higgins, concurring but making her own declaration, found this 'somewhat fanciful'. She considered that no 'ordinary meaning' of the term 'main channel' existed either in international law or in hydrology:

The analysis on which the Court has embarked is in reality far from an interpretation of words by reference to their 'ordinary meaning'. The Court is really doing something rather different. It is applying a somewhat general term, decided upon by the Parties in 1890, to a geographic and hydrographic situation much better understood today...

The Court is indeed, for this particular task, entitled to look at all the criteria the Parties have suggested as relevant. This is not to discover a mythical 'ordinary meaning' within the Treaty, but rather because the general terminology chosen long ago falls to be decided today...

At the same time, we must never lose sight of the fact that we are seeking to give flesh to the intention of the Parties, expression [*seemingly*: 'expressed'] in generalized terms in 1890. We must trace a thread back to this point of departure. We should not, as the Court appears at times to be doing, decide what *in abstracto* the term 'the main channel' might today mean, by a mechanistic appreciation of relevant indicia.[54]

This comment follows more closely the ILC's scheme that sought, not simply to avoid a 'mechanistic appreciation' of interpretative elements, but more positively to see that context and a treaty's object and purpose informed the ordinary meaning of treaty terms (at least as a precursor to use of further elements of the rules). Although

---

[52] *Dispute regarding Navigational and Related Rights (Costa Rica v Nicaragua)* ICJ Judgment of 13 July 2009 [64].
[53] *Kasikili/Sedudu Island (Botswana/Namibia)* [1999] ICJ Rep 1045.
[54] Ibid 1113–4 [1]–[4] (Declaration of Judge Higgins).

context is given a broader definition than just immediate context, this does not of course exclude the use of immediate context. The WTO Appellate Body's decision in *Canada—Measures Affecting the Export of Civilian Aircraft* used both elements of context.[55] The case concerned the definition of 'subsidy' in the Agreement on Subsidies and Countervailing Measures (the 'SCM Agreement'). Canada argued that 'subsidy' could mean an amount measured by the cost to the government as much as the benefit to the recipient.

The Appellate Body looked to the immediate context in SCM Article 1's definition of 'benefit', then investigated other relevant elements of that Agreement and the structure of the provision. Finding that a 'benefit does not exist in the abstract, but must be received and enjoyed by a beneficiary or a recipient', logic implied existence of a recipient as did use of the term 'conferred'. The context supported this reading in that a related provision in the same treaty referred to the 'benefit *to the recipient* conferred *pursuant to paragraph 1 of Article 1* [the provision under interpretation]'. The Appellate Body found the structure of the whole provision to have two discrete elements, viz: 'a financial contribution by a government or any public body' and that 'a benefit is thereby conferred', such structure suggesting that a contribution from the government flowed to a beneficiary.[56] Hence, the term referred to what the beneficiary received, not the cost to the government. It can be seen from this reasoning (if not abundantly obvious already) that reference to context cannot be usefully made in a purely mechanistic fashion and pursuing 'conformity-imposing textuality'.

Even less rule orientated is the requirement to make an interpretation 'in the light of' the treaty's object and purpose. This is not a teleological imperative subordinating terms of the treaty to its purpose. Rather, it is an enabling provision allowing the selection of meaning to take this factor into account.[57] It is not therefore a rule in the sense of a prescriptive formula, even though it is an indication of a factor to be considered.

Finding a treaty's object and purpose is a somewhat open-ended operation. The ILC and the ICJ have linked it with the good faith requirement in the opening words of the general rule to produce a 'principle of effectiveness'. This principle has two aspects: (i) it incorporates the Latin maxim preferring a meaning that ascribes some effect to a term rather than no effect (*ut res magis valeat quam pereat*); and (ii) it imports a teleological element into the interpretation. The ILC noted:

When a treaty is open to two interpretations one of which does and the other does not enable the treaty to have appropriate effects, good faith and the objects and purposes of the treaty demand that the former interpretation should be adopted.[58]

---

[55] WTO, *Canada—Measures Affecting the Export of Civilian Aircraft—Decision AB-1999-2* (2 August 1999) WT/DS70/AB/R.

[56] Ibid 39–40 [155]–[157].

[57] See the account in Gardiner (n 2) chapter 2, section 4, of the Harvard draft articles on the law of treaties where the approach to interpretation made pervasive reference to the treaty's purpose as a guide to interpretation.

[58] 'Commentary on draft articles' [1966] YBILC, vol II, 219 [6].

The ICJ applied both aspects of the principle of effectiveness in *Territorial Dispute (Libyan Arab Jamahiriya/Chad)*.[59] Application of the narrower aspect (the Latin maxim) led it to interpret a provision referring to frontiers 'that result from the international instruments' defined in the Annex to the treaty, as meaning *all* the frontiers resulting from those instruments. The Court also applied a more general principle of effectiveness to conclude that the aim of the treaty was to resolve all the issues over these frontiers.[60]

C. Interpretation agreed by the parties

There is relatively little cause for invitations to courts and tribunals to interpret treaties where the parties have themselves reached a clear interpretative agreement. It seems reasonably safe to say that many differences over interpretation will be resolved by the parties' agreement recorded in some form or other. Disputes are most likely to arise where there is uncertainty if there is actually agreement, where agreements are not kept, or where they produce results that one party dislikes and seeks to repudiate. However, the principle seems clear: The parties are the best interpreters of their own agreement.

Adoption of an interpretative agreement may be specifically envisaged in the treaty.[61] Such a situation is really covered by the Vienna provision requiring the context to be taken into account, meaning the full text of the treaty under interpretation. The Vienna provisions on interpretative agreements have an even greater reach than that, including as they do agreement shown by concordant practice. The latter is probably most readily evidenced by practice following an agreement or understanding.[62]

However, the ultimate test of the notion that the parties are the best interpreters of their agreement is whether they can establish by interpretation something others would view as an amendment. If *all* parties agree, it matters little in principle whether they view their agreement as an interpretation or a record of amendment. Unless there is a party who objects to a failure to follow an amending procedure, if such is present, the process of international agreement seems loosely structured in this regard. There may be practical difficulties, particularly if one or more parties has constitutional requirements to follow, but collectively the parties are masters of their own treaty relations subject to the few peremptory rules of international law.

---

[59] *Territorial Dispute (Libyan Arab Jamahiriya/Chad) (Merits)* [1994] ICJ Rep 6.

[60] Ibid 25–6 [51]–[52].

[61] This can, however, raise difficulties where the parties adopt an interpretation of a provision while it is the subject of an arbitration: see Article 1131 of the North American Free Trade Association Agreement (an interpretation by the NAFTA Commission is to be binding on NAFTA tribunals), and *Arbitration under Chapter Eleven of NAFTA, Pope & Talbot v Canada (Award in respect of Damages)* [2002] 41 ILM 1347.

[62] See, for example, Decision XV/3 of the Fifteenth Meeting of the Parties to the Montreal Protocol on Substances that Deplete the Ozone Layer, where the parties indicated their desire 'to decide . . . on a practice in the application of Article 4, paragraph 9 of the Protocol by establishing by consensus a single interpretation of the term "State not party to this Protocol", to be applied by Parties' (11 November 2003) UNEP/OzL.Pro.15/9, 44–5.

That it is difficult to find good examples of this may be explained by the probability that if there is an amending procedure, the parties are likely to follow it if there is a need for a serious change. However, the ICJ has endorsed the possibility of a changed meaning being established by practice of the parties, suggesting this must, a fortiori, be possible by express agreement. The ICJ viewed interpretation by subsequent practice as itself a tacit agreement, noting in *Costa Rica v Nicaragua*:

It is true that the terms used in a treaty must be interpreted in light of what is determined to have been the parties' common intention, which is, by definition, contemporaneous with the treaty's conclusion . . .

This does not however signify that, where a term's meaning is no longer the same as it was at the date of conclusion, no account should ever be taken of its meaning at the time when the treaty is to be interpreted for purposes of applying it.

On the one hand, the subsequent practice of the parties, within the meaning of Article 31(3)(b) of the 1969 VCLT, can result in a departure from the original intent on the basis of a tacit agreement between the parties . . . [63]

More generally, there may be uncertainty over what amounts to an interpretative agreement. The report of the WTO Appellate Body in *EC—Bananas III* provides an example of this.[64] The case concerned a waiver adopted at a Ministerial Conference allowing the EC to apply preferential tariff treatment and a separate tariff quota for certain banana imports. The previous EC Schedule, which included the tariff quota concession for bananas, had an imminent expiry date. Without the waiver, the EC arrangements would have violated the GATT 1994. One issue was whether the waiver constituted a subsequent interpretative agreement or an application of the Schedule of Concessions, extending the Schedule beyond its expiry date. The Appellate Body noted the Panel's view that the waiver in fact modified the original Schedule, rather than simply interpreting or applying it. Hence, the waiver could not be construed as an interpretative agreement, a conclusion supported by the context, which indicated a different regime for adoption of waivers from that for interpretations.[65] This example shows how even though the elements of the general rule reflect various kinds of interpretative agreements (contemporaneous, subsequent, or through practice), leading to strong interpretative evidence in clear cases, nevertheless, that rule's scope allows interpreters to go far beyond 'conformity-imposing textuality'.

D. Rules of international law and evolutionary interpretation

Included among the elements of the general rule of interpretation is the notion that the meaning of treaty provisions may develop or change over time, variously

---

[63] *Dispute regarding Navigational and Related Rights (Costa Rica v Nicaragua)* ICJ Judgment of 13 July 2009 [63]–[64].

[64] WTO, *European Communities—Regime for the Importation, Sale and Distribution of Bananas—Second Recourse to Article 21.5 of the DSU by Ecuador and First Recourse by USA* ('*EC—Bananas III*') (26 November 2008) WT/DS27/AB/RW2/ECU and WT/DS27/AB/RW/USA.

[65] *EC—Bananas III*, Appellate Body Report (n 64) 389–92.

described as 'evolutive' or 'evolutionary' interpretation. The provision requiring account to be taken of any relevant rules of international law applicable in the parties' relations is particularly rooted in this notion. This provision in Article 31(3)(c) has attracted growing attention recently, though recognition of the effect on interpretation of the evolution of rules of international law, as well as of other relevant factors, has long been a feature of case law of the European Court of Human Rights.[66]

The concept of evolutionary or evolutive interpretation has largely overtaken attempts to align principles of interpretation with the difficult formulation of an 'intertemporal rule'. The development of international law and the proliferation of treaties have added complexity to the range of legally relevant material to be taken into account. In this context, the ILC endorsed a study of 'fragmentation' of international law, such fragmentation arising principally through the parallel development of new specialist sets of rules such as those of international environmental law and international economic law. The potential of Article 31(3)(c) for assisting in reconciling divergent regimes was a feature of this study as set out in 'the Koskenniemi Report', which also provides useful accounts of relevant practice.[67]

The ILC's work on Article 31(3)(c) has not produced a comprehensive understanding of the temporal issues in treaty interpretation, but it has offered guidance on the specific issue of using related treaties in interpretative practice:

Application of other treaty rules. Article 31(3)(c) also requires the interpreter to consider other treaty-based rules so as to arrive at a consistent meaning. Such other rules are of particular relevance where parties to the treaty under interpretation are also parties to the other treaty, where the treaty rule has passed into or expresses customary international law or where they provide evidence of the common understanding of the parties as to the object and purpose of the treaty under interpretation or as to the meaning of a particular term.[68]

A more general difficulty over using relevant international law rules in treaty interpretation is shown by the ICJ's approach in the *Oil Platforms* case.[69] The majority judgment invoked the Vienna provision (Article 31(3)(c)) to use the general international law of self-defence as the starting point for interpreting

---

[66] See M Fitzmaurice, 'Dynamic (Evolutive) Interpretation of Treaties: Part I' (2008) 21 Hague Ybk Intl L 101 and 'Part II' (2009) 22 Hague Ybk Intl L 3.

[67] See ILC 58th Session, Report of the Study Group on Fragmentation of International Law: Difficulties arising from the Diversification and Expansion of International Law, finalized by M Koskenniemi (13 April 2006) Un Doc A/CN.4/L.682, 206–44; further, Report (18 July 2006) Un Doc A/CN.4/L.702; and ILC Report on its 58th session (2006), UNGA, 61st Session, Supplement No 10 (Un Doc A/61/10) 400–23 ('ILC Report on its 58th Session'). See also C McLachlan, 'The Principle of Systemic Integration and Article 31(3)(c) of the Vienna Convention' (2005) 54 ICLQ 279; Gardiner (n 2) chapter 7.

[68] ILC Report on its 58th Session (n 67) 'ILC Report on the work of its fifty-eighth session (2006)', UNGA, 61st Session, Supp No 10 (A/61/10) 414–15 [21]. For an example of a resolution of temporal issues in treaty interpretation see *Arbitration regarding the Iron Rhine ('Ijzeren Rijn') Railway* (n 47).

[69] *Oil Platforms (Islamic Republic of Iran v United States of America) (Merits)* Judgment of 6 November 2003; for commentary, see FD Berman, 'Treaty "Interpretation" in a Judicial Context' (2004) 29 YJIL 315; D French, 'Treaty Interpretation and the Incorporation of Extraneous Legal Rules' (2006) 55 ICLQ 281.

whether the United States could justify its destruction of Iranian oil platforms by reference to a provision in a bilateral US–Iranian treaty. The majority found that the United States could not establish self-defence, but held that it had nevertheless not violated any treaty provisions, particularly the provision on freedom of commerce.

Oil Platforms' significance lies in its application of Article 31(3)(c). One of the judges who concurred in the outcome nevertheless considered that the majority had not used the Vienna rules correctly: 'It has rather invoked the concept of treaty interpretation to displace the applicable law.'[70] Similarly, another concurring judge opined that:

the approach taken by the Court is putting the cart before the horse. The Court rightly starts by saying that it is its competence to interpret and apply [the bilateral treaty provision], but it does so by directly applying the criteria of self-defence under Charter law and customary law and continues to do so until it reaches its conclusion . . .

The proper approach in my view would have been to scrutinize the meaning of the words [in the bilateral treaty provision] . . . [71]

What is important to stress about these criticisms is their indication that the majority took an illogical approach by investigating whether a defence under general international law was absent, without deciding first whether there was any breach of the treaty in issue to which a defence needed to be raised. The criticism was thus not that the majority had failed to take a sufficiently literal or textual approach when invoking Article 31(3)(c). Rather, it was that the majority had strayed outside the realm of treaty interpretation using too loose an allusion to the reference to international law in the Vienna rules.

E. Supplementary means

It is harder to find fault with the prevailing loose application of Article 32's provisions, principally as it affects use of preparatory work. As noted above, the provision's use of preparatory work 'to confirm' a meaning built up by application of the general rule does offer a very broad scope for its application. The approach taken in practice by courts and tribunals to use of preparatory work may perhaps be best exemplified by a judgment of the European Court of Human Rights where the typical form is to state the history of the applicable provision of the European Convention as part of an account of the relevant law before applying the law to the particular facts and assertions.

Thus, in *Witold Litwa v Poland*, the Court considered whether the word 'alcoholics' in a provision of the Convention permitting 'the lawful detention . . . of persons of unsound mind, alcoholics or drug addicts or vagrants' applied solely to those having an addiction to alcohol or could justify detention of someone behaving drunkenly.[72] After stating the facts and relevant domestic law, the

---

[70] Judge Higgins, *Oil Platforms* n 69, Separate Opinion [49].
[71] Judge Kooijmans, *Oil Platforms* n 69, Separate Opinion [42]–[43].
[72] ECHR App No 26629/95, Judgment of 4 April 2000.

Court set out the preparatory work, showing that there was an early concern to protect a State's right to take necessary measures to fight vagrancy and alcoholism. As the draft text developed, the right of States to take measures combating 'drunkenness' was translated as *l'alcoolisme* in the French text. That thought was recast consistent with other provisions so that it related to a person rather than a condition. By this route 'drunkenness' became transformed into 'alcoholics'.

Explicitly applying the Vienna rules, the Court accepted that an ordinary meaning of 'alcoholics' was persons who are addicted to alcohol. However, the immediate context of the treaty provision in question included categories of individuals (i) linked by possible deprivation of liberty to be given medical treatment, (ii) because of considerations dictated by social policy, or (iii) on both these grounds.[73] This suggested that the provisions allowed deprivation of liberty not only because such persons were a danger to public safety, but also because their own interests might require their detention.

The Court found that the treaty's object and purpose was not to detain persons in a clinical state of alcoholism, but to give authority for taking into custody those whose conduct and behaviour under the influence of alcohol posed a threat to public order or themselves. Such risk of public disorder or harm to the intoxicated person arose whether or not they were addicted to alcohol.[74] In reaching this interpretation, the Court ostensibly relied on context as well as the treaty's object and purpose to displace an apparently unequivocal ordinary meaning. It then 'confirmed' this view by reference to the provision's preparatory work, noting that the commentary on the preliminary draft acknowledged the right of States to take measures to combat vagrancy and drunkenness.

Although this application of the Vienna rules seems fully in keeping with their proper use, it is difficult not to conclude that consideration of the preparatory work before formal application of the general rule convinced the Court of the correct interpretation. Further, it seems inevitable that courts and tribunals commonly consider preparatory work before formulating their judgment or award. Only in the loosest sense is this process 'confirming' a meaning established by the general rule, even if (as in the example above) care is taken to construct the interpretation giving respect to the structure of the Vienna rules.

Where preparatory work is being used to 'confirm' a meaning, its role is, in effect, cumulative with the application of the general rule. In practice, however, there may be a sliding scale to the effect that the clearer the result from application of the general rule, the less precision is demanded from the preparatory work. Where, for example, a change in terminology in the developing negotiations is not very clearly explained in preparatory work, its significance and reliability may be balanced against the clarity of the text.[75] Likewise, the implications of rejection of a

---

[73] Ibid [60].

[74] Ibid [61]–[62]. A fuller account of the case is given in Gardiner (n 2) chapter 1, section 5.1.

[75] See eg *Maritime Delimitation and Territorial Questions between Qatar and Bahrain (Qatar v Bahrain) (Jurisdiction and Admissibility)* [1994] ICJ Rep 112, where the majority view attached more weight to what those judges saw as a meaning clear in its context as contrasted with unclear preparatory work, while the principal dissenter, Judge Schwebel, saw clear conclusions to be drawn from the

proposed provision or uncontroverted assertions recorded in preparatory work as to an expected meaning can only be assessed in light of the particular circumstances and evaluation of the result of the general rule's application.[76] All too often, preparatory work is confusing and unrevealing. This has led some courts to reject its use unless it very directly and conclusively addresses the point in issue.[77]

However, in the main, from the attention courts and tribunals do give preparatory work, along with consideration of the circumstances of conclusion, it is clear that the separation of these elements into a class of supplementary means of interpretation has neither resulted in undue insistence on the 'primacy of the text' nor been taken as authorizing only the 'minimum recourse to preparatory work' foreseen by McDougal. On the contrary, the classification of preparatory work in a separate and supplementary category of rules appears to have produced little by way of diminution of their interpretative effect.

F. Languages

If anything, the part of the Vienna rules that tends to be viewed as a separate category is the content of Article 33 on interpreting treaties in multiple languages. This may be because the matter only arises in certain cases where there appears to be a potential difference between the languages which could help the interpreter. The language factor is very much individual to each treaty. There is also the considerable difficulty of working with many languages where not only the nuances of the words, but the process of thought and the legal environment behind the words may be quite alien to the interpreter.

It is, therefore, difficult to reveal any trend through the cases as distinct from showing that particular ones tackle particular points. One case from the ICJ shows how even a comparison of two languages from five authentic ones can produce a confusing picture. In the *LaGrand* case, the ICJ indicated by way of provisional measures that the United States should not execute a German national pending the Court's final decision on consular access issues.[78] LaGrand was nevertheless executed before that decision. The Court then had to determine if its indication of provisional measures imposed on the United States an international legal obligation to comply.

---

preparatory work rather than finding a meaning in a term which was ambiguous and not clarified by its context. See Gardiner (n 2) 316–21.

[76] Compare *Hosaka v United Airlines* 305 F.3d 989 (9th Cir 2002), certiorari denied 537 U.S. 1227 with *Pierre-Louis v Newvac* 584 F.3d 1052 (11th Cir 2009); see Gardiner (n 2) preface to paperback edition, xliv–xlix.

[77] See the trend in cases in the UK to require that preparatory work must clearly and indisputably point to a definite legal intention: 'Only a bull's-eye counts. Nothing less will do.' *Effort Shipping Company v Linden Management* [1998] AC 605, 623; see Gardiner (n 2) preface to paperback edition, xxxix–xli.

[78] *LaGrand Case (Germany v USA)* [2001] ICJ Rep 466.

In deciding that its indications of provisional measures did establish legal obligations, the Court only referred in its reasoning to the French and English texts of its Statute (although Germany had included the relevant words in all five authentic languages in its memorial). The Court began by applying Article 31(1) of the VCLT. It noted considerable differences of emphasis, the French terms being of more potential mandatory effect than the English. In the latter language, the use in the Court's statute of 'indicate' instead of 'order', of 'ought' instead of 'must' or 'shall', and of 'suggested' instead of 'ordered' implied that decisions of this kind lacked mandatory effect.

The Court concluded that it was 'faced with two texts which are not in total harmony' and proceeded to apply Article 33(4) of the VCLT, attempting to reconcile the texts by reference to the Statute's object and purpose.[79] The Court considered that the Statute's object and purpose was to enable the Court to fulfil its functions, principally the basic function of judicial settlement of international disputes by binding decisions. Hence, the Court was not to be hampered in the exercise of this function by the respective rights of the parties to a dispute not being preserved. Thus, the Court concluded that indications of provisional measures had to be binding.[80]

Such a brief summary does scant justice to the Court's reasoning and on the language issue it was confronted with only some of the issues that may arise. Others include: how to deploy the presumption of the same meaning in all authentic texts;[81] whether the 'original' language of a treaty has particular significance (that is where one language was used for negotiating and drafting, the others being translations);[82] how to treat texts where translations are of legal concepts in different languages;[83] reconciliation where one or more texts are clear but another is ambiguous;[84] the significance of different punctuation in different languages;[85] and use of preparatory work in reconciling differences between languages.[86]

---

[79] Ibid [101].   [80] Ibid [102].

[81] Cf *Case Concerning Elettronica Sicula SpA (ELSI) (USA v Italy)* [1989] ICJ Rep 15; WTO, *United States—Final Countervailing Duty Determination with Respect to Certain Softwood Lumber from Canada—Appellate Body Report* (2004) WT/DS257/AB/R [59]–[60].

[82] See *LaGrand* (n 78).

[83] See *Ehrlich v Eastern Airlines* 360 F.3d 366 (2nd Cir 2004); *Abbott v Abbott* 130 S.Ct. 1983 (2010).

[84] See *Border and Transborder Armed Actions (Nicaragua v Honduras)* [1988] ICJ Rep 69; *Wemhoff v Germany* Judgment of 27 June 1968, Series A no 7, 23 (European Court of Human Rights); *Busby v State of Alaska* 40 P.3d 807 (Alaska Ct Appeals 2002).

[85] See the discrepancy between a comma and a semi-colon in the Agreement for the Prosecution and Punishment of the Major War Criminals of the European Axis, and Charter of the International Military Tribunal, London, 8 August 1945, in *Trial of Major War Criminals before the International Military Tribunal*, vol 1, Documents (HMSO, London 1947) and E Schwelb, 'Crimes Against Humanity' (1946) 23 BYBIL 178, 188, 193–5; see also *United States—Measures Affecting the Cross-Border Supply of Gambling and Betting Services—WTO Appellate Body Report* (7 April 2005) WT/DS285/AB/R.

[86] See *La Grand* (n 78) and *Case concerning Military and Paramilitary Activities in and against Nicaragua (Nicaragua v USA) (Jurisdiction and Admissibility)* [1984] ICJ Rep 392.

IV. Beyond the VCLT

The Vienna rules only state the general principles of treaty interpretation. There is no indication in these rules what further means are to be used, although the listed supplementary means are not exclusive. As the Vienna rules are mainly concerned with *what* is to be taken into consideration, with only limited indications of *how* evaluation of these elements is to be accomplished, there is scope to look beyond the rules. Thus, use of traditional maxims of construction of legal instruments is not ruled out. As noted above, however, these are really means of analysing the context when applying the first part of the general rule.[87]

Particular approaches are not mandated by the rules such as that of 'restrictive interpretation'. The latter had been taken as applying a presumption that deference to State sovereignty requires a minimalist interpretation of the rights granted by a State in a treaty. However, the ICJ has stated that this is not part of the general rule.[88] In contrast, some general and specific interpretative approaches have developed within individual courts or institutions. For example, the European Court of Human Rights has provided a focus for development of the evolutive approach and, as one of its own doctrines, adopted a 'margin of appreciation' in favour of States' discretion.[89] However, neither of these is at variance with the Vienna rules. If the context in which the provisions of a treaty are located and a full application of the principles of treaty interpretation lead to the conclusion that a particular approach or doctrine is the right one to use, that is quite consistent with the Vienna rules.[90]

Conclusion

The convenient shorthand of describing Articles 31–33 of the VCLT as setting out the 'rules' of interpretation reflects the title given to those provisions, but only in part their content. To the extent that they are a mandatory code, they are rules. However, their content and their proper interpretation show a nature which is more akin to principles than rules. They have not proved to be highly restrictive nor has their application suggested that they import an insistent emphasis on conformity-inducing textuality. Their flexible interpretation and application in practice attest to a character better described by the metaphor imagining them as 'scaffolding'.[91]

---

[87] See text to n 4.
[88] *Dispute regarding Navigational and Related Rights (Costa Rica v Nicaragua)* ICJ Judgment of 13 July 2009 [48]; see also L Crema, 'Disappearance and New Sightings of Restrictive Interpretation(s)' (2010) 21 EJIL 681; Gardiner (n 2) preface to paperback edition, xvii–xviii.
[89] See n 66.
[90] Cf G Letsas, 'Strasbourg's Interpretive Ethic: Lessons for the International Lawyer' (2010) 21 EJIL 509; I Van Damme, 'Treaty Interpretation by the WTO Appellate Body' (2010) 21 EJIL 605.
[91] Thirlway (n 5) 19.

Recommended Reading

DJ Bederman, *Classical Canons: Rhetoric, Classicism and Treaty Interpretation* (Ashgate, Aldershot 2001)

FD Berman, 'Treaty "Interpretation" in a Judicial Context' (2004) 29 YJIL 315

I Buffard and K Zemanek, 'The "Object and Purpose" of a Treaty: An Enigma?' (1999) 3 ARIEL 311

E Criddle, 'The 1969 VCLT on the Law of Treaties in US Treaty Interpretation' (2003–2004) 44 VJIL 431

RA Falk, 'Charybdis Responds: A Note on Treaty Interpretation' (1969) 63 AJIL 510

RA Falk, 'On Treaty Interpretation and the New Haven Approach: Achievements and Prospects' (1967–1968) 8 VJIL 323

GG Fitzmaurice, '*Vae Victis* or Woe to the Negotiators! Your Treaty or Our "Interpretation" of it?' (1971) 65 AJIL 359

M Fitzmaurice, 'Dynamic (Evolutive) Interpretation of Treaties: Part I' (2008) 21 Hague Ybk of Intl L 101 and Part II (2009) 22 Hague Ybk Intl L 3

M Frankowska, 'The 1969 VCLT on the Law of Treaties before United States Courts' (1987–1988) 28 VJIL 281

D French, 'Treaty Interpretation and the Incorporation of Extraneous Legal Rules' (2006) 55 ICLQ 281

DB Hollis, MR Blakeslee, and LB Ederington (eds), *National Treaty Law and Practice* (Martinus Nijhoff, Leiden 2005)

F Horn, *Reservations and Interpretative Declarations to Multilateral Treaties* (North-Holland, Amsterdam 1988)

MS McDougal, 'The International Law Commission's Draft Articles upon Interpretation: Textuality Redivivus' (1967) 61 AJIL 992

MS McDougal, 'Statement of Professor Myres S McDougal, United States Delegation, to Committee of the Whole, April 19, 1968' (1968) 62 AJIL 1021

MS McDougal, HD Lasswell, and JC Miller, *The Interpretation of Agreements and World Public Order: Principles of Content and Procedure* (Yale University Press, New Haven 1967, re-issued as *The Interpretation of International Agreements etc* with a new introduction and appendices, 1994)

C McLachlan, 'The Principle of Systemic Integration and Article 31(3)(c) of the Vienna Convention' (2005) 54 ICLQ 279

DM McRae, 'The Legal Effect of Interpretative Declarations' (1978) 49 BYBIL 155

P Sands, 'Treaty, Custom and the Cross-fertilization of International Law' (1998) 1 Yale Human Rights and Development L J 85

R Sapienza, 'Les Déclarations Interprétatives Unilatérales et l'Interprétation des Traités' (1999) 103 Revue Generale de Droit International Public 601

N Shelton, *Interpretation and Application of Tax Treaties* (LexisNexis, London 2004)

H Thirlway, 'The Law and Procedure of the International Court of Justice 1960–1989, Supplement 2006: Part Three' (2006) 77 BYBIL 1

I Van Damme, *Treaty Interpretation by the WTO Appellate Body* (OUP, Oxford 2009)

C Warbrick, 'Introduction' to B Macmahon (ed), *The Iron Rhine ('Ijzeren Rijn') Railway (Belgium Netherlands) Award of 2005* (TMC Asser Press, The Hague 2007)

ES Yambrusic, *Treaty Interpretation: Theory and Reality* (University Press of America, Lanham 1987)

MK Yasseen, 'L'Interprétation des Traités d'après la Convention de Vienne sur le Droit des Traités' (1976–III) 151 RcD 1

20

Specialized Rules of Treaty Interpretation: International Organizations

Catherine Brölmann

Introduction

International law has generally treated questions of the legal personality and legal powers of international organizations (IOs) as a distinct subject—international institutional law.[1] But IOs, whatever their form or function, will also regularly trigger questions of treaty law and practice.[2] Most (but not all[3]) IOs are created by treaty, and that 'constituent instrument' provides the necessary starting point for delimiting the IO's functions and competences. This chapter addresses treaty interpretation in the IO context, with particular attention to interpreting the founding or constitutive treaties of international organizations.

The choice of topic for this chapter is premised on the idea that not all interpretive rules are the same for all treaties. This is a well-tried proposition. As early as 1930 Arnold McNair recommended that 'we free ourselves from the traditional notion that the instrument known as the treaty is governed by a single set of rules',[4] distinguishing for instance treaties of a category that would now be called 'objective regimes'[5] from 'treaties creating constitutional international law' (comprising the Covenant of the League of Nations and the Statute of the PCIJ) from 'treaties akin to charters of incorporation' (instruments creating the non-political Unions, Institutes and Commissions of the time). More recently, Joseph

---

[1] Cf eg J Klabbers, *An Introduction to International Institutional Law* (2nd edn CUP, Cambridge 2009); H Schermers and NM Blokker, *International Institutional Law* (4th edn Martinus Nijhoff, Dordrecht 2003).

[2] In addition to interpretation issues, IO constituent instruments may also trigger treaty law questions as to who can consent to that instrument; whether and how reservations or amendments can be made to it; and what processes exist for parties to withdraw from the founding treaty or terminate the IO itself.

[3] Klabbers (n 1) 9–10 (noting how the UN Children's Fund (UNICEF) was created by a UN General Assembly resolution, while the IO status of other entities, like the Organization on Security and Cooperation in Europe (OSCE), remains unclear).

[4] A McNair, 'The Function and the Differing Legal Character of Treaties' (1930) 11 BYBIL 100, 118.

[5] Objective regimes are dealt with in detail in Chapter 13 of this *Guide*.

Weiler called for a 're-examination of treaty interpretation' in particular, and proposed identifying and applying different hermeneutics to different treaty regimes.[6]

This recent interest in different canons of treaty interpretation hinges on distinguishing interpretative practices for different areas of substantive law, for example investment treaties or human rights treaties.[7] Constitutive treaties of IOs may be set apart as 'treaties creating organizations' à la Arnold McNair in his early article, or as belonging to the category of 'law-making treaties'.[8] But it must be recalled that they are, beyond these divisions, a special category in their own right. IOs are to some extent separate and 'internal' legal orders, so that interpretation of their founding texts can be said to take place at the cutting edge of treaty law and institutional law.

Is such differentiation accommodated by the interpretative framework set out in Articles 31–33 of the 1969 Vienna Convention on the Law of Treaties (VCLT)? On the one hand, a case can be made that constituent treaties are exceptional, warranting a separate interpretative framework. As discussed below, this position is bolstered by the decisions of the International Court of Justice (ICJ), and of the Court of Justice of the European Union (CJEU), which has developed a 'distinct' teleological approach for interpreting EU Treaties in lieu of the VCLT's more textual orientation.[9] On the other hand, some constituent treaties explicitly disavow a special approach. The World Trade Organization (WTO)'s Dispute Settlement Understanding, for example, anticipates that any clarification of the WTO's constituent agreements will be done 'in accordance with the customary rules of interpretation of public international law'.[10] Moreover, the VCLT framework itself is famously broad, subsidiary and not very hierarchically structured.[11] As a result, it may be best to approach treaty interpretation in this context, not as a separate regime, but rather as a version of the VCLT framework to which additional or

---

[6] J Weiler, 'Prolegomena to a Meso-theory of Treaty Interpretation at the Turn of the Century', *IILJ International Legal Theory Colloquium: Interpretation and Judgment in International Law* (NYU Law School, 14 February 2008) 576; J Weiler, 'The Interpretation of Treaties—A Re-examination' (2010) 21 EJIL 507.

[7] Issues of human rights treaty interpretation are discussed in Chapter 21 of this *Guide*.

[8] 'Law-making treaties' (*traités loi*) involve 'a series of generalized, and not particularly reciprocal, statements of standards, norms, rules, rights, duties and benefits which the contracting parties... postulate' and may be contrasted with 'contractual treaties' (*traités–contrat*), which involve 'a series of reciprocally operating rights, duties and benefits, the treaty being more or less synallagmatic'; law-making treaties generally seem susceptible to a more contextual and functional interpretation than 'contractual treaties'. Cf S Rosenne, *Developments in the Law of Treaties 1945–1986* (CUP, Cambridge 1989) 182–3.

[9] Cf eg R Gardiner, *Treaty Interpretation* (OUP, Oxford 2008) 120.

[10] Understanding on Rules and Procedures Governing the Settlement of Disputes, Marrakesh Agreement Establishing the World Trade Organization, Annex 2, 1869 UNTS 401, Art 3.2. For more on interpretation of WTO Agreements, cf I van Damme, 'Treaty Interpretation by the WTO Appellate Body' (2010) 21 EJIL 605.

[11] Chapter 19 addresses the VCLT's general rules of treaty interpretation. Such interpretation is frequently described as 'an art not an exact science'. Cf eg P Merkouris, 'Interpretation is a Science, is an Art, is a Science' in M Fitzmaurice and others (eds), *Treaty Interpretation and the Vienna Convention on the Law of Treaties: 30 Years on* (Martinus Nijhoff, Leiden 2010) 8–12.

supplementary approaches have emerged in light of the 'special' characteristics that these constitutive instruments possess.

This chapter addresses treaty interpretation in the IO context in two parts. Part I examines the interpretation of constitutive treaties and IO secondary rules. Part II looks at the role of organizations as treaty interpreters. Examples are drawn predominantly from the UN context and to a lesser degree the European Union. These organizations and their constitutive treaties, especially the UN Charter, have received extensive and articulate interpretations. They may also be generally representative of similar treaties, for which concrete examples are less accessible.[12] The ICJ, moreover, has issued several seminal decisions in this field (eg the 1949 *Reparation* and the 1996 *WHO Legality of Nuclear Weapons* cases), which reflect the current state of the law and count as authoritative statements on the nature of IO treaties.

I. Interpretation of Constitutive Treaties

What is a constitutive treaty? Generally, it is a treaty among States[13] that establishes an institution with one or more organs with a will distinct from that of those States creating it. Thus, the constitutive treaty establishes the IO, and in doing so, details its functions and competences. But a constitutive treaty can also create substantive rights or obligations for States parties. Thus, the UN Charter constitutes the UN, but also binds parties to specific conduct (eg Article 2(4)'s prohibition on the unlawful use of force).

The interpretation of constitutive treaties is quite important. It is the primary legal exercise for determining the IO's competences. Thus, it often touches upon— in political terms—the degree to which the IO's member States are 'Masters of the Treaty'.

For a long time after the dawn of IOs in the second half of the nineteenth century, IOs were perceived as open platforms and functional vehicles for State action. They possessed little to no autonomy vis-à-vis their member States, nor did they maintain 'external relations'. The interpretation of a founding treaty for the purpose of establishing the organization's competences was thus not a regular concern. Organizations themselves were very much looked at as a 'contractual agreement' between States, as Otto von Gierke wrote in 1868 about the Administrative Unions of his time.[14]

But the rise of IOs in the UN era led to a dramatic change in outlook on constitutive treaties. As IOs became more independent from their member States, the treaties creating them garnered special attention.

---

[12] Accord Gardiner (n 9) 113.

[13] Although on occasion an IO can be a member of another IO; thus, the EU is a member of the WTO and the Food and Agriculture Organization.

[14] O von Gierke, *Community in Historical Perspective* in M Fisher (trans) of A Black (ed), *Das Deutsche Genossenschaftsrecht* (1868) (CUP, Cambridge 1990).

A. Constitutive treaties as a separate category

Today, Article 5 of the VCLT affirms that constitutive treaties are a distinct class: 'The Present Convention applies to any treaty which is the constituent instrument of an international organization and to any treaty adopted within an international organization *without prejudice to any relevant rules of the organization*' (emphasis added). Thus, the VCLT applies to constitutive treaties by default, reserving to the IO the ability to have its rules govern the treaty creating it. In practice, this reservation clause has been focused on the IO's rules involving consent to be bound, reservations, amendments, etc.[15] But nothing in Article 5 precludes it from applying to interpretation where an IO (as in the aforementioned WTO case) specifies one or more interpretative rules for its founding treaty.

Underlying this distinctive treatment of constitutive treaties is the notion that they have a special nature. They are 'self-contained', albeit not in the traditional sense of a particular area of substantive law or *lex specialis*,[16] but rather as a semi-independent or 'internal' legal order based on specific institutional rules. Constitutive treaties may even be seen as having a 'constitutional'[17] function, binding member States to a set of coherent 'internal' laws on the IO's competences, functions and goals.

Judge Alvarez's dissenting opinion in the ICJ's *Genocide* case emphasized the institutional character of IO constitutive treaties:

... the new international law, so far as concerns multilateral conventions of a special character ... includes ... those which seek to develop world international organization or to establish regional organizations ...

Alvarez went on to argue that such treaties should not be linked to:

The preparatory work which preceded them; they are distinct from that work and have acquired a life of their own ...[18]

Some years later, a majority of the ICJ specifically referred to the 'special' nature of constitutive treaties:

---

[15] Article 5's application to treaties 'adopted within' an IO may be less relevant as a separate category. The practice of big 'open' IOs on matters such as the text's adoption does not differ much from its adoption in an ad hoc diplomatic conference organized by the IO. Cf DH Anderson, 'Article 5 Convention of 1969' in O Corten and P Klein (eds), *The Vienna Conventions on the Law of Treaties: A Commentary* (OUP, Oxford 2011) vol I, 94–5.

[16] Hence IO legal orders arguably do not trigger the criticism of 'self-contained regimes' set forth eg in B Simma and D Pulkovski, 'Of Planets and the Universe: Self-contained Regimes in International Law' (2006) 17 EJIL 483.

[17] Although the 'constitutional' aspect of treaties constituting IOs may explain their distinct treatment, this chapter does not engage with the (rich) debate on possible 'constitutional' features of treaty regimes and constitutional functions for the international community. On that subject cf eg J Dunoff and J Trachtman, *Ruling the World? Constitutionalism, International Law and Global Governance* (CUP, Cambridge 2010); J Klabbers, A Peters, and G Ulfstein, *The Constitutionalization of International Law* (OUP, Oxford 2009).

[18] *Reservations to the Convention on the Prevention and Punishment of the Crime of Genocide* (Advisory Opinion) [1951] ICJ Rep 15, 51 (Dissenting Opinion of Judge Alvarez).

On the previous occasions when the Court has had to interpret the Charter of the United Nations, it has followed the principles and rules applicable in general to the interpretation of treaties, since it has recognised that the Charter is a multilateral treaty, albeit a treaty having certain *special characteristics*.[19]

Nor did the VCLT change the ICJ's views. In a landmark ruling in response to a request of the World Health Organization (WHO) for an Advisory Opinion on the legality of the use of nuclear weapons, the Court emphasized that constitutive treaties are hybrid instruments, combining a multilateral treaty with a self-contained or 'institutional' aspect:

From a formal standpoint, the constitutive instruments of international organizations are multilateral treaties, to which the well-established rules of treaty interpretation apply . . . But the constitutive instruments of international organizations are also treaties of a particular type; their object is to create new subjects of law endowed with a certain autonomy, to which the parties entrust the task of realising common goals. Such treaties can raise specific problems of interpretation owing, inter alia, to *their character which is conventional and at the same time institutional*.[20]

B. Specialized rules of interpretation

Conceptualizing founding treaties as a separate treaty category has, in turn, made room for a specialized interpretive practice. In the same *WHO-Legality* case, the Court pointed out that:

the imperatives associated with the effective performance of its functions, as well as its own practice, are all elements which *may deserve special attention when the time comes to interpret these constitutive treaties*.[21]

What sort of 'special attention' do constitutive treaties receive? Traditionally, treaty interpretation accords considerable weight to the aspect of consent underlying the treaty. Hence, Articles 31 and 32 of the VCLT emphasize a textual approach, whether alone or in concert with an 'intentional' approach; a similar method may be gleaned from the ICJ's practice.[22] Moreover, although part of the VCLT rule, there is generally less concern for 'object and purpose' as a tool to establish the text's

---

[19] *Certain Expenses of the United Nations (Article 17, paragraph 2, of the Charter)* (Advisory Opinion) [1962] ICJ Rep 151, 157 (emphasis added).
[20] *Legality of the Use by a State of Nuclear Weapons in Armed Conflict (Request by WHO)* (Advisory Opinion) [1996] ICJ Rep 66, 74–5 (emphasis added) ('*WHO Legality* case').
[21] Ibid (emphasis added).
[22] Cf eg *Anglo-Iranian Oil Co (United Kingdom v Iran)* (Judgment) [1952] ICJ Rep 104 ('[The Court] must seek the interpretation which is in harmony with a natural and reasonable way of reading the text, having due regard to the intention [of the Parties]'). For analysis of the textual and 'subjective' approach in ICJ jurisprudence, see S Torres Bernárdez, 'Interpretation of Treaties by the International Court of Justice Following the Adoption of the 1969 Vienna Convention on the Law of Treaties' in G Hafner and others (eds), *Liber Amicorum Professor Seidl-Hohenveldern* (Martinus Nijhoff, Leiden 1998) 721–48.

meaning.[23] In contrast, the interpretation of constitutive treaties appears generally inspired by the principle of effectiveness,[24] and by an approach along the lines of Alvarez's dissenting opinion[25] (now *en vogue* for 'objective regimes'), namely, to conceptually separate the treaty from the regime it creates.

Accordingly, we find two trends in the interpretation of constitutive treaties[26] that stand apart from the standard VCLT approaches: (i) a 'teleological approach' to the text, similar to traditions in national law of statutory interpretation in an organic, constitutional context; and (ii) a particular importance attached to the 'practice of the organization' as opposed to the practice of the original treaty parties.

1. The telos of the treaty and the organization's function as an interpretive tool

Some terminological distinctions at this point are helpful. According to Article 31 of the VCLT, the 'object and purpose' is used to elucidate a textual approach for discerning the 'ordinary meaning' to be given to a treaty's terms.[27] This is not quite the same as a 'teleological approach' which in its classic sense is a general interpretive approach, taking the treaty's objective as a guiding principle for interpretation of the text. In addition, there is a third, 'evolutionary' or 'living instrument' interpretative approach, which is different in that it takes into account the social context and may even necessitate reformulation of the original object and purpose.[28] All three approaches play a role in interpreting constitutive treaties, but the teleological approach is most prominent.

In some cases, a constitutive treaty text may be sufficiently clear that a textual approach is employed. The ICJ, for example, did so in the *Conditions of Admission* and *IMCO* cases.[29] But where the text is not sufficiently clear, the interpreter must

---

[23] Cf VCLT Arts 31–33 and identical language found in the 1986 Vienna Convention on the Law of Treaties between States and International Organizations or between International Organizations (adopted 21 March 1986, not yet in force) [1986] 25 ILM 543, Arts 31–33 ('1986 VCLT'). The ICJ applied the 'object and purpose test' in a moderate form, eg, in The Ambatielos Claim (Greece v United Kingdom) [1952] ICJ Rep 28, 45; cf I Sinclair, The Vienna Convention on the Law of Treaties (2nd edn MUP, Manchester 1984) 131 ('there is also the risk that the placing of undue emphasis on the "object and purpose" of a treaty will encourage teleological methods of interpretation').

[24] M Herdegen, 'Interpretation in International Law' in R Wolfrum (ed), Max Planck Encyclopedia of Public International Law (OUP, Oxford 2008) online at <http://www.mpepil.com>.

[25] Alvarez (n 18); see also Territorial Dispute (Libyan Arab Jamahiriya v Chad) [1994] ICJ Rep 6 [72]–[73].

[26] T Sato, Evolving Constitutions of International Organizations (Brill, Dordrecht 1996) esp 41–159 (including all ICJ cases involving constitutive instruments through 1982). Sato's conclusions are more cautious than earlier ones by Denis Simon. Cf D Simon, L'interprétation judiciaire des traités d'organisations internationales: morphologie des conventions et fonction juridictionelle (Pedone, Paris 1981) 194 ('l'interprétation jurisdictionelle des traités constitutifs tend effectivement privilégier le development des finalités institutionelles'); see also CE Amerasinghe, Principles of the International Law of International Organizations (2nd edn CUP, Cambridge 2005) 24–65.

[27] Gardiner (n 9) 190–1.

[28] CM Brölmann, 'Limits to the Treaty Paradigm' in M Craven and M Fitzmaurice (eds), Interrogating the Treaty: Essays in the Contemporary Law of Treaties (Wolf Legal Publishers, Nijmegen 2005) 28–39.

[29] Conditions of Admission of a State to Membership in the United Nations (Advisory Opinion) [1948] ICJ Rep 48, 63. In the IMCO case, the ICJ interpreted 'largest ship-owning nations' to be a function of

decide on a guiding principle for further interpretation. The principle of *in dubio mitius* (favouring interpretations protecting the liberty of the third party or the sovereignty of individual States) is familiar from the context of 'contractual treaties' (*traités–contrat*) and domestic contract law. Indeed, when the legal context suggests the contractual element of the constitutive instrument deserves priority—eg in contentious cases in which acceptance of the Court's compulsory jurisdiction is at issue[30]—the Court has adhered to the traditional rules for treaty interpretation and adopted a fairly conservative approach.[31] But more often when it comes to constitutive treaties, *in dubio mitius* plays little role.[32] In its place, interpreters rely on the principle of *effet utile* or effectiveness (sometimes called 'functionality').[33] And when effectiveness is the guiding principle in the choice of interpretive methods, it generally brings on a teleological approach.

At the ICJ, the *Reparation* case;[34] the *Effects of Awards* case;[35] and the 1971 *Namibia* opinion[36] are all instances where there was little attention to the 'intentions' of the treaty parties, while the degree of teleological reasoning in interpreting the UN Charter exceeded that of traditional interpretive exercises.[37] In all three cases, moreover, the interpretation involved UN competence, suggesting that a teleological approach applies whenever the interpretation of the constitutive instrument is aimed at determining the competences of the IO, and thus moves within an institutional discourse.[38] In such cases, it appears the Court generally departs from the traditional framework, 'proceed[ing] directly to an interpretation of the

registered tonnage based on the treaty text, its drafting history and maritime usage generally. *Constitution of the Maritime Safety Committee of the Inter-Governmental Maritime Consultative Organization* (Advisory Opinion) [1960] ICJ Rep 23. In doing so, the Court endorsed two 'flags of convenience' States falling under the interpreted term, even though from a teleological stance their participation may have been counterproductive to IMCO's purpose of improving safety in shipping.

[30] Rosenne (n 8) 234 (including case law references).

[31] Cf *Case Concerning the Military and Paramilitary Activities in and against Nicaragua (Nicaragua v United States)* (Jurisdiction and Admissibility) [1984] ICJ Rep 392 [24]–[42] (interpreting ICJ Statute Art 36(5)).

[32] J Kokott, 'States, Sovereign Equality' in R Wolfrum (ed), *Max Planck Encyclopedia of Public International Law* (OUP, Oxford 2008) online at <http://www.mpepil.com> [26].

[33] Cf *Interpretation of the Agreement of 25 March 1951 between the WHO and Egypt* (Advisory Opinion) [1980] ICJ Rep 73, 96 (emphasizing 'their [of the host state and the organization] clear obligation to co-operate in good faith to promote the objectives and purposes of the Organization'); cf Sato (n 26) 154.

[34] *Reparation for Injuries Suffered in the Service of the United Nations* (Advisory Opinion) [1949] ICJ Rep 174 ('*Reparation* case').

[35] *Effect of Awards of Compensation made by the United Nations Administrative Tribunal* [1954] ICJ Rep 53 (relying on the teleological approach for the competence of the UNGA to establish the Administrative Tribunal, but on the textual approach for determining the judicial nature of the Tribunal itself).

[36] *Legal Consequences for States of the Continued Presence of South Africa in Namibia (South-West Africa)* (Advisory Opinion) [1971] ICJ Rep 16.

[37] Not everyone endorsed this approach; Rosenne and Sinclair both criticized it. Rosenne (n 8) 237 (seeing teleological approach for constitutive treaties as potentially 'unproductive in the political sense and [...] prejudicial to the authority of the Court'); Sinclair (n 23) 131.

[38] Here, the doctrine of 'implied powers' holds a prominent place. Cf eg *Reparation* case (n 34) 182; *WHO Legality* case (n 20) 79. For examples in which the contractual element of a constitutive treaty is dominant, and the classic interpretive rules are applied, see n 29 and accompanying text.

constitutive instrument as it stands at the time of the interpretation',[39] with a corresponding disinterest for the intention of the parties and the *travaux préparatoires*.[40]

Beyond recognizing an IO's implied powers, the ICJ's *Reparation* case is the canonical example of teleological treaty interpretation, explicitly inspired by the principle of effectiveness. The Court, without precedent of any of the new 'constitutional' perspectives on IO constitutive treaties, attributed legal personality to the organization 'by some unorthodox [viz teleological] reasoning',[41] even though it could have reached the same conclusion along more traditional lines, using the *travaux préparatoires* of the Charter. In fact, part of the San Francisco Conference had considered international legal personality to be *implied* by the Charter as a whole.[42]

The other landmark decision in this respect is the 1996 *WHO Legality* case, where the ICJ seemed to take its interpretive exercise one step beyond a regular (even if teleological) treaty interpretation. After it determined the functions of the organization by reference to the classic law of treaties canon,[43] the Court moved into a teleological discourse, proceeding from the functions of the organization, rather than working towards establishing them. This included not only references to 'the practice followed by the Organization',[44] but also an—unprecedented—constitutional or 'systemic approach' in which it relied on an interpretation of the UN Charter reference to 'specialized agency' as the basis for limiting its reading of the WHO Constitution:

As these provisions [in UN Charter Article 63] demonstrate, the Charter of the United Nations laid the basis of a 'system' designed to organise international co-operation in a coherent fashion...It follows...that the WHO Constitution can only be interpreted, as far as the powers conferred upon that Organization are concerned, by taking due account...also of the *logic of the overall system* contemplated by the Charter...[A]ny other conclusion would render virtually meaningless the notion of a specialised agency.[45]

---

[39] Rosenne (n 8) 234; cf ibid 195 (finding, with regard to ICJ interpretation of the UN Charter, that there is 'little doubt that adherence to "traditional" legal concepts of the law of treaties is not a prominent feature of the interpretation of those provisions by the Court, although it is not displaced entirely').

[40] For in-depth studies of the interpretation of IO constitutions, see Sato (n 26) (re the ICJ); Rosenne (n 8) 234; Simon (n 26). A seminal treatise is the chapter on 'Interpretation of Constitutions' in E Lauterpacht, 'The Development of the Law of International Organization by the Decisions of International Tribunals' (1976/IV) 135 RcD 379, 414–65.

[41] Rosenne (n 8) 238. For the Court's reasoning, see *Reparation* case (n 34) 179.

[42] Rosenne (n 8) 238; 12 UNCIO 703, 710 (Committee no IV/2 of San Francisco Conference of opinion that no explicit reference to UN international personality was needed as '[i]n effect, it will be determined implicitly from the provisions of the Charter taken as a whole').

[43] *WHO Legality* case (n 20) 75–6.

[44] Ibid 76 [21]; see also n 48 and accompanying text.

[45] *WHO Legality* case (n 20) 79–80 [26] (emphasis added). For more on 'functional decentralisation' see Schermers and Blokker (n 1) [1692].

2. Practice of the organization as an interpretive tool

A second feature of constitutive treaty interpretation (especially by the ICJ) involves referencing 'the practice of the organization'.[46] Even in decisions which emphatically rely on traditional methods of interpretation, there seems to be additional recourse to consistent practice by the IO itself.[47] In the *WHO Legality* case, the ICJ reaffirmed that an organization's constitutive treaty was to be:

[i]nterpreted in accordance with their ordinary meaning, in their context and in the light of the object and purpose of the... Constitution, *as well as of the practice followed by the Organization.*[48]

But this practice of the organization is not to be confused with the 'subsequent practice' of the contracting parties from which their anticipatory consent to the treaty's interpretation can be construed. In other words, IO practice cannot be put on the same footing as the interpretive tool envisaged by Article 31(3)(b) of the VCLT.[49] The reason is precisely that the IO's own application of its constitutive treaty should be attributed to the organization itself, independent of the 'will' or intention of the contracting parties.[50] The 'practice of the organization' is thus added to the law of treaties armamentarium, while the 'subsequent practice' of the *parties* mentioned in Article 31 of the VCLT is altogether absent in the ICJ's opinions involving interpretation of IO constitutions.[51]

On occasion, moreover, there have been explicit interpretative references to the practice of a particular IO *organ* rather than to the practice of the organization as such. In such cases, the practice of organs may be considered to have the same legal effect as that of the IO on the principle that organs represent the international legal person in its entirety.[52] Article 2(1) of the VCLT references 'the established practice of the organization' as a form of 'rules of the organization',[53] but leaves the

---

[46] Cf *Certain Expenses* case (n 19) 157; *Namibia* case (n 36) 22 [22]; see also Sato (n 26) 41–159.

[47] *Competence of the General Assembly for the Admission of a State to the United Nations* [1950] ICJ Rep 7, 9.

[48] *WHO Legality* case (n 20) 76 [21] (emphasis added); note that both in the 1986 VCLT (n 23) Art 2(1)(j) and in Art 2(b) of the 2011 ILC Draft Articles on the Responsibility of IOs, UN Doc A/66/10, the 'rules of the organization' are defined as comprising 'the constituent instruments... and... established practice of the organization'.

[49] Article 31(3)(b) of both the 1969 and 1986 VCLT requires interpreters to take account of 'any subsequent practice in the application of the treaty which establishes the agreement of the parties regarding its interpretation'. See discussion of this provision in Chapter 19, Part II.A.2, 482 *et seq*.

[50] But see paragraph 45 of 'Written Statement submitted on behalf of the Secretary-General of the United Nations of 2 October 1998' in relation to *Difference relating to Immunity from Legal Process of a Special Rapporteur of the Commission on Human Rights* [1999] ICJ Rep 62 (implicitly equating 'the established practice of the Organization, as confirmed by the Mazilu opinion' with the 'subsequent practice' of Art 31(3)(b) of the 1969 and 1986 VCLT).

[51] There is a similar dearth of (substantive) references to the intention of the parties. Cf eg Lauterpacht (n 40) 438 *et seq*.

[52] Analogous reasoning justifies extending an IO's treaty-making capacity to its organs—such as the UN's treaty-making capacity extending to the UN High Commissioner for Refugees.

[53] 1986 VCLT Art 2(1)(j) ('"rules of the organization" means, in particular, the constituent instruments, decisions and resolutions adopted in accordance with them, and established practice of the organization').

internal division of IO competences entirely to the institutional discretion of the organization. From the perspective of general international law and the law of treaties such decentralization *within* the organization clearly removes the IO's member States one step further from control of the IO 'practice', which may subsequently shape the interpretation of the treaty to which they originally became a party.

Put differently, relying on the practice of IO organs adds another layer between the general law of treaties and the constitutive treaty to be interpreted. Judge Spender noted this fact in his *Certain Expenses* dissent:

I find difficulty in accepting the proposition that a practice pursued by an *organ* of the United Nations may be equated with the subsequent conduct of parties to a bilateral agreement and thus afford evidence of intention of the parties to the Charter.[54]

Nonetheless, the Court reaffirmed the validity of employing the practice of an IO *organ* (*in casu* the UN's Security Council) as an interpretive tool in the *Namibia* opinion.[55]

The role of the 'practice of the organization' in treaty interpretation may be further complicated if such practice plays dual roles. At times, IO practice might be a tool to establish the correct interpretation of the treaty text; at other times, the IO practice *itself* might be an interpretation of that text. This distinction between interpretation and application is, however, often fuzzy. The premise that 'when the meaning of the treaty is clear, it is "applied", not "interpreted"',[56] has been convincingly questioned with regard to treaties in general and seems especially relevant with respect to organizations.[57] A broad approach appears warranted, where many instances of application can be regarded as implicit acts of interpretation.[58] This is all the more so since interpretation is a key method for IOs to change the rules of the organization when formal amendment of the constitutive treaty is not feasible.[59]

C. Constitutive treaties (in general)

For reasons noted at the outset, the discussion so far has had a UN focus. But interpretation of constitutive treaties other than the UN Charter generally shows the same pattern.[60] Special attention, however, should be given to interpretations of the treaties establishing the EU (including the European Community) by the

---

[54] *Certain Expenses* case (n 19) 189 (italics in the original).

[55] *Namibia* case (n 36) 22 [22].

[56] A McNair, *The Law of Treaties* (2nd edn OUP, Oxford 1961) 365 n1; cf also M Milanovic, 'The ICJ and Evolutionary Treaty Interpretation' (14 July 2009) EJIL Talk! <http://www.ejiltalk.org/the-icj-and-evolutionary-treaty-interpretation> (interpretation is 'the activity of establishing the linguistic or semantic meaning of a text; [application is] the activity of translating that text into workable legal rules to be applied in a given case').

[57] Cf eg Gardiner (n 9) 25–9; Chapter 19, Preliminary Considerations, 477 *et seq*.

[58] See Schermers and Blokker (n 1) [1155]–[1185].

[59] P Kunig, 'Interpretation of United Nations Charter' in R Wolfrum (ed), *Max Planck Encyclopedia of Public International Law* (OUP, Oxford 2008) online at <http://www.mpepil.com>.

[60] See eg Amerasinghe (n 26) 24–65; Schermers and Blokker (n 1) [1346]–[1350].

Court of Justice of the European Union (CJEU).[61] These do not differ substantively from the ICJ's interpretive exercises, even though the CJEU is meant to operate only within the—comparatively 'constitutional'—EU legal order.[62]

Although the CJEU has not rejected the VCLT framework, it has tended to cite only the first paragraph of Article 31.[63] Moreover, in its (sparse) references to the rules of interpretation as part of the general law of treaties, the CJEU can be seen to employ a large degree of teleological reasoning coupled with a reluctance to use the *travaux préparatoires* as a supplementary means of interpretation.[64] In the same vein, the CJEU does not generally recognize subsequent practice of the treaty *parties* as a tool for interpreting the EU Treaties.[65] As a further sign of its self-contained outlook, the European Court has been known to perform, as one commentator put it, a 'Baron von Münchhausen trick' relying on the object and purpose test of Article 31(1) of the VCLT in its interpretation of an EU constitutive treaty[66] to underscore the special character of that treaty, and then using its own case law as 'context' in the sense of Article 31(2) of the VCLT to substantiate the particular character of that EU treaty as opposed to another treaty concluded among EU member States.[67]

Taken together, these patterns show constitutive treaty interpretation moving out of a contractual framework into an institutional one—and thus out of the law of treaties discourse into the institutional law discourse—in which 'treaty parties' become 'member States'. Nor is this move limited to international tribunals. Consider a (lesser known) case before the Netherlands' Council of State by the Dutch Seamen's Welfare Foundation, addressing the interpretation of the constitutive treaty of the International Labour Organization (ILO). The Foundation argued that 'ratification' of an ILO treaty by ILO member States pursuant to Article 19(5) of the ILO Constitution implied that the previous stage of 'adoption' by the ILO Plenary Conference (per ILO Constitution Article 19(1)) equalled 'signature' in terms of the law of treaties. As such, the Netherlands as an ILO member had incurred a legal obligation under Article 18 of the VCLT[68] not to defeat the object and purpose of ILO Treaty No 163 (concerning Seafarers' Welfare) after its 'adoption' in the ILO Plenary Conference—an obligation the Netherlands was claimed to have breached by terminating a subsidy to the Foundation. The Council

---

[61] The CJEU was previously called the European Court of Justice (ECJ).

[62] The CJEU's interpretations address, however, both the founding treaties for the EU as well as treaties between the EU and non-member States. See Gardiner (n 9) 122–4.

[63] Ibid.

[64] Cf eg PJ Kuijper, 'The Court and the Tribunal of the EC and the Vienna Convention on the Law of Treaties 1969' (1999) 25 Legal Issues of European Integration 1–23 ('Kuijper 1999'); PJ Kuijper, 'The European Courts and the Law of Treaties: The Continuing Story' in E Canizzaro (ed), *The Law of Treaties Beyond the Vienna Convention* (OUP, Oxford 2011) 256–78 ('Kuijper 2011').

[65] The Court made this point explicitly in Case C-327/91 *France v Commission* [1994] ECR I-3641 (point 36) and Opinion 1/94 [1994] ECR I-5267 (point 52 and 61). Contrary to the ICJ, however, the CJEU does not seem to accept (as yet) the subsequent practice of Community institutions for purposes of interpretation. See Kuijper 1999 (n 64) esp 9–10.

[66] Cf eg Opinion 1/91 [1991] ECR, I-6079 (point 14); Case 270/80 *Polydor v Harlequin Records* [1982] ECR 329.

[67] Kuijper 1999 (n 64) 2–4.

[68] For a detailed discussion of VCLT Art 18 see Chapter 8, Part II, 211 *et seq*.

of State, however, did not adopt this contractual view of ILO treaty-making. Instead, it considered the adoption of ILO Convention No 163 to be part of an *institutional* legal process, to which Article 18 of the VCLT did not apply.[69]

D. Interpretations of IO secondary law

The grey area between a contractual framework and an institutional framework for IO treaty interpretation is brought out even more by those rules that are the 'secondary law' of IOs. These are the normative acts of IOs, which derive their validity from the primary law of the organization, ie the constitutive treaties.[70] Most IOs have organs which can take decisions binding on the organization (with 'internal' effect) or upon member States. Sometimes this competence is given to non-plenary organs, and sometimes the rules enacted by the organization are binding on a resolutive condition, such as the 'standards' adopted or amended by the Council in the International Civil Aviation Organization by a two-thirds majority.[71] Comparable procedures for the enactment of 'regulatory acts' exist in the WHO (where law-making functions reside in the plenary organ) and in several other UN Specialized Agencies.[72]

There has been some debate as to whether this growing body of rules[73] is either (i) derivative (or 'delegated') treaty obligations for the IO's member States—ie deriving from the constitutive treaty, or (ii) legislative acts by an organization simply binding its member States.[74] Essentially the same question arises in asking if various systems of IO standard-setting are covered by existing categories of sources, or whether they constitute a new source of international law.[75] Both

---

[69] *Dutch Seamen's Welfare Foundation [Stichting Zeemanswelzijn Nederland] v The Minister of Transport, Public Works and Water Management*, 27 July 2005, Administrative Law Division of the Council of State (200410468/1, LJN No. AU0095, AB (2006) No. 177). For an English translation and commentary see *Oxford Reports on International Law in Domestic Courts* (OUP 2009) <http://www.oup.com/online/ildc>.

[70] The scope of normative acts will differ from IO to IO, and will (largely) depend on 'what the constituent treaty says', but as Klabbers notes, a treaty may not be clear on what acts are authorized and unanticipated acts may emerge in practice. Klabbers (n 1) 178. Moreover, distinctions must be made between IO normative acts that are legally binding versus those that are not. Ibid 182.

[71] Convention on International Civil Aviation (opened for signature 7 December 1944, entered into force 4 April 1947) 15 UNTS 295, Arts 37, 54(1), 90.

[72] WHO Constitution (opened for signature 22 July 1946, entered into force 7 April 1948) 14 UNTS 185, Arts 21–22; see also CH Alexandrowicz, *The Law-Making Functions of the Specialised Agencies of the United Nations* (Angus and Robertson, London 1973) 40–69 (on 'quasi-legislative acts' of Specialized Agencies); E Klein, 'United Nations, Specialized Agencies' in R Wolfrum (ed), *Max Planck Encyclopedia of Public International Law* (OUP, Oxford 2008) online at <http://www.mpepil.com>; F Kirgis, 'Specialized Law-Making Processes' in C Joyner (ed), *The United Nations and International Law* (CUP, Cambridge 1997) 65, 70 *et seq*.

[73] M Benzing, 'International Organizations or Institutions, Secondary Law' in R Wolfrum (ed), *Max Planck Encyclopedia of Public International Law* (OUP, Oxford 2008) online at <http://www.mpepil.com>.

[74] Compare M Fitzmaurice, 'Modifications to the Principles of Consent in Relation to Certain Treaty Obligations' (1997) ARIEL 275, 316–17 (adhering to the derivative view) with Alexandrowicz (n 72) 152 (on the regulatory acts of UN Specialised Agencies: 'this is no doubt an extra-treaty process').

[75] Compare GM Danilenko, *Law-Making in the International Community* (Martinus Nijhoff, Boston 1993) 192 ('they hardly qualify as new formal sources of general international law existing

views are defensible: on the one hand, the binding character of regulatory acts can be construed from an *ex ante* expression of consent on the part of States;[76] on the other hand, their binding force can be traced to the competences of the decision-making organ itself.

The latter perspective is increasingly dominant among public international law scholars.[77] The EU serves as an example of an organization, which from the outset expressly had the legislative paradigm prevail for reasons of practical and doctrinal necessity: obligations stemming from EU law (Articles 288 and 289 of the Treaty on the Functioning of the European Union (TFEU)) are clearly set apart from obligations stemming from the EU's founding treaties, or primary European law.

Meanwhile, when it comes to IO secondary law in general, the interpretative practice differs some from the practice relating to constitutive instruments. A principle favouring the 'paramount importance of contextual interpretation' exists, meaning that 'legal acts always have to be construed by reference to and in accordance with the constitutive instrument of the organization' and 'in conformity with general international law binding on the international organization, especially rules of jus cogens'.[78] Moreover, some scholars emphasize that, contrary to primary IO law (ie the constituent treaty), 'interpretation according to the object and purpose, has to be referred to more cautiously . . . This is a result of the delegated character of secondary rules'.[79] In the context of the EU 'law-making' done pursuant to authorities in EU Treaties, the very paradigm of 'treaty interpretation' has retreated into the background.[80]

II. Interpreters of IO Law

A. Organizations as interpreters

The constitutive treaty and the secondary rules of an organization are interpreted first of all by IOs themselves.[81] In the context of the present chapter this excludes

---

independently of a specific treaty arrangement') with V Degan, *Sources of International Law* (Martinus Nijhoff, Boston 1997) 6 (considering 'non-obligatory' rules such as ICAO standards, to which, nevertheless, 'the respective states almost invariably conform themselves', as a possible newly emerging source of international law).

[76] This was the ICJ's approach to dealing with the conflict between the 1971 Montreal Convention and UN Security Council Resolution 748—originating under the UN Charter—as a traditional case of conflicting treaties. Cf *Case concerning Questions of Interpretation and Application of the 1971 Montreal Convention Arising from the Aerial Incident at Lockerbie (Libyan Arab Jamahiriya v United States)* (Provisional Measures) [1992] ICJ Rep 126.

[77] Cf C Tomuschat, 'Obligations Arising for States Without or Against Their Will' (1993) 241 RdC 195, 328 ('An honest assessment of the new legal position created by the establishment of an international organization must find a different justification').

[78] Benzing (n 73) [47].

[79] Ibid [48]; see also A Orakhelashvili, *The Interpretation of Acts and Rules in Public International Law* (OUP, Oxford 2008) 486–93.

[80] Cf Kuijper 2011 (n 64) 268–70 (survey of recent CJEU practice).

[81] O Schachter, 'The UN Legal Order: An Overview' in C Joyner (ed), *The United Nations and International Law* (CUP, Cambridge 1997) 3, 9–13; Rosenne (n 8) 241(with references); Sato (n 26) 161–226 (detailed survey analysing the legal effects of such interpretations); see also 'International

international 'courts and tribunals' (discussed separately below), but includes so-
called treaty bodies,[82] so long as their activity is not limited to (semi-)judicial review
of cases but also entails, *inter alia*, issuing general legal comments. Treaty bodies are
created under a treaty and incorporated within an IO, even if the constitutive treaty
itself did not envision them (eg the Committee on Economic, Social and Cultural
Rights (CESCR) was established by the States parties to the International Covenant
on Economic, Social and Cultural Rights (ICESCR) rather than by the treaty
itself[83]). The CESCR does produce General Comments, as does the Human
Rights Committee under the International Covenant on Civil and Political Rights
(ICCPR).[84] This interpretive role of IOs is an expression of—in institutional rather
than treaty terms—the IO's *compétence de la compétence*.[85]

Traditionally, treaty parties interpreted their treaty, with additional interpretative tools such as 'subsequent practice' easily traced back to the original States
parties' consent. However, in the interpretation of IO functions and competences
laid out in constitutive treaties, the role of the contracting parties seems to have
moved to the background. States are simply less likely to unilaterally interpret
constitutive instruments of treaties, although as the Dutch Seamen's Welfare
Foundation case suggests, States (or their organs) will still do so on occasion. States
undoubtedly continue to auto-interpret substantive provisions of constitutive
treaties (eg UN Charter Article 51 on self-defence; ICCPR Article 7's prohibition
on torture) irrespective of any interpretations of those provisions by the IO or its
organs. But, for IO functions and competence, the IO drives the interpretative
enterprise, as indicated by the fact that essentially all the ICJ's cases involving
interpretations of constitutive treaties came via advisory opinions—requested by
the Organization—not inter-State contentious cases.

Having an organization interpreting the constitutive instrument by which it was
created is, however, a phenomenon that has long served as a point of tension
between treaty and institutional perspectives.[86] From an institutional perspective, it
makes sense that an IO would determine its own competences and test its own
mandate by going back to its constitutive treaty. But, in a contractual framework,
there is less support for the IO doing so in lieu of the contracting parties themselves,

Bureaucracies as Actors in Legal Discourse' in I Venzke, *The Practice of Interpretation and International
Law: On the Semantic Authority of International Institutions in Communicative Law-making* (OUP,
Oxford 2012) Chapter III.A (expounding how international institutions, comprising both international 'bureaucracies' and 'international courts', have a large degree of semantic authority in the attribution
of meaning to treaty texts).

[82] For a discussion of treaty bodies and treaty regimes, see Chapter 17.
[83] (Adopted 16 December 1966, entered into force 3 January 1976) 993 UNTS 3. The CESCR
was established by ECOSOC Res 1985/17 (28 May 1985).
[84] ICCPR (16 December 1966, entered into force 23 March 1976) 999 UNTS 171, Art 28.
[85] Cf DB Hollis, 'Why State Consent Still Matters: Non-State Actors, Treaties, and the Changing
Sources of International Law' (2005) 23 Berkeley J Intl L 137, 165–71; Orakhelashvili (n 79) 511–24.
[86] EP Hexner, 'Interpretation by Public International Organizations of their Basic Instruments'
(1959) 53 AJIL 341, 343 ('the function of authoritative interpretation rests with the ordinary executive
organs of these [Bretton Woods] institutions and not with any tribunal external to them').

and the notion has virtually no place in the VCLT system.[87] It is nonetheless now a generally accepted approach to IO law. Likewise, so-called treaty bodies also regularly engage in interpretation of 'their' treaty. When done teleologically, this can spur a law-making process, as when the CESCR inferred a right to water from Articles 11 and 12 of the ICESCR.[88] In other instances, the body's interpretation may generate controversy, as was the case in 1994 with the Human Rights Committee's self-declared right to judge reservations to the ICCPR.[89]

In a well-known passage in the *Certain Expenses* case, the ICJ examined which IO organs had interpretive authority:

> In the legal systems of States, there is often some procedure for determining the validity of even a legislative or governmental act, but no analogous procedure is to be found in the structure of the United Nations...As anticipated in 1945 therefore, *each organ must, in the first place at least, determine its own jurisdiction.*[90]

Thus, when the question arises which organ(s) are competent to interpret the constituent instrument, it is in the first place the rules of the organization that determine this (as general international law is agnostic on this point).

In the case of the UN, both the Security Council and the General Assembly have claimed (and exercised) such authority.[91] Famous examples include the Security Council's interpretation of UN Charter Article 39's 'threat to the international peace' provision to include situations within existing State borders,[92] and the General Assembly's claim, under the Uniting for Peace Resolution, to a role in furthering international peace and security, including the establishment of peace-keeping missions.[93] If the International Criminal Tribunal for Yugoslavia (ICTY) is viewed not as a distinct IO, but as a subsidiary organ established by the UN Security Council pursuant to UN Charter Article 41, the notorious passage in the 1995 *Tadic* case (where the Tribunal assessed and approved of its own existence based on UNSC competence) is another case in point.[94] Organs of other organizations, such as at the ILO or the Executive Directors of the International Monetary Fund (IMF) and the International Bank for Reconstruction and Development

---

[87] The one notable exception is VCLT Art 20 where, in requiring the competent IO organ to accept reservations to the IO's constituent instrument (unless the treaty otherwise provides), IO organs presumably interpret their constituent instrument.

[88] CESCR General Comment 15, E/C.12/2002/11.

[89] UNCHR, 'General Comment No. 24' (4 November 1994) CCPR/C/21/Rev.1/Add.6; see also 'Observations of the United States and the United Kingdom on General Comment 24' (28 March 1995) UN Doc A/50/40.

[90] *Certain Expenses* case (n 19) 168 (emphasis added).

[91] Cf P Kunig, 'Interpretation of United Nations Charter' in R Wolfrum (ed), *Max Planck Encyclopedia of Public International Law* (OUP, Oxford 2008) online at <http://www.mpepil.com> [16].

[92] Cf UNSC Res 232 (16 December 1966) UN Doc S/RES/232 (1966); UNSC Res 418 (4 November 1977) UN Doc S/RES/418.

[93] UNGA, 'Uniting for Peace Resolution' (3 November 1950) UN Doc A/RES/377 (V).

[94] *Prosecutor v Dusko Tadic a/k/a 'Dule'* (Decision on the Defense Motion for the Interlocutory Appeal on Jurisdiction), International Criminal Tribunal for the former Yugoslavia, 2 October 1995 (Case No IT-94-1-AR72) [26]–[40].

(IBRD), have also produced relevant interpretations, generating subsequent adherence.[95]

B. (Semi-)Judicial interpretation

Although some courts are organs of an IO, it seems better to conceive of them as independent reviewers—and hence interpreters—of the application of legal rules in a constitutive treaty. Hence, in this chapter, international courts and tribunals are not considered 'international organizations', even if they are not domestic courts or stand-alone international tribunals, but rather bodies that institutionally belong to a particular organization (eg the ICJ serves as the UN's principal judicial organ) or functional sphere (eg the European Court of Human Rights operates under the European Convention on Human Rights). Thus, in addition to the IO itself, these bodies exist to interpret constitutive treaties, most often the ones that created them. In performing judicial dispute settlement, these courts can face interpretative questions on a treaty's 'operational' or 'substantive' parts as well as on its 'constituent' parts. This chapter, however, only focuses on the later instances; as indicated above, cases involving disputes over the interpretation of the non-constitutive parts of the treaty are better approached under the VCLT's general interpretative framework.

The act of interpreting an IO's primary or secondary law is singled out and detached from the act of application whenever it is the subject of a declared difference of opinion or dispute. In these cases, the relevant choices of procedure, body, and competence are governed (in principle) by the rules of the organization itself, notably those laid down in the constitutive instrument. Often a (semi-) judicial procedure is at issue.

Some constitutive treaties such as the UN Charter are silent about the competent interpretive authority in case of dispute. At the San Francisco Conference in 1944, the proposal to appoint the ICJ as the authoritative interpreter of the Charter was rejected.[96] However, even without a formal appointment, the Court has subsequently (and logically) assumed a central role in the Charter's interpretation. And that role has been generally accepted (witness the large number of cases). Formally, however, neither the request for an advisory opinion to the Court, nor the outcome is binding, so other (diplomatic) means of resolving an interpretive dispute may always be sought.[97]

Some constitutive treaties do envisage a binding decision, whether by the ICJ (eg ILO Constitution Article 37) or an arbitral tribunal (eg UNESCO Constitution

---

[95] Amerasinghe (n 26) 25–6.

[96] Cf Doc XII UNCIO 709; *Certain Expenses* case (n 19) 168 ('Proposals made during the drafting of the Charter to place the ultimate authority to interpret the Charter in the International Court of Justice were not accepted . . . As anticipated in 1945, therefore, each organ must, in the first place at least, determine its own jurisdiction'); Kunig (n 91) [7].

[97] An assertion by one or more States parties of a right to intervene under ICJ Statute Art 63 when a (binding) interpretation is at issue would greatly complicate the ICJ's interpretation of a constitutive treaty. As yet, however, that situation has not presented itself.

Article XIV). Other founding treaties provide for non-binding opinions by the ICJ or another tribunal, often as a last resort. An alternative mechanism, seen most often with international financial institutions (IFIs), gives final and binding interpretative competence to the IFI's supreme plenary organ.[98]

Concluding Remarks: A Layered Exercise in Interpretation

Interpretive practice *vis-à-vis* constitutive treaties (or the segments in these treaties which regulate the functioning of the organization rather than the behaviour of the States parties) can be said to differ notably from general treaty interpretation because of two features. First, special weight is given to the 'object and purpose' of the treaty by way of a general teleological approach to interpretation, rather than as a means to establish the text's 'ordinary meaning' per Article 31 of the VCLT. Second, special weight is also given to the subsequent practice of the organization. In contrast, classic interpretive methods that safeguard the State party's 'sovereign will'—such as recourse to the *travaux préparatoires,* party intention, and the subsequent practice of treaty parties—seem to have faded into the background.

Arguably, these points of distinction are brought into the interpretive process by the extra layer of the IO legal order over the constituent treaty. Or, from a doctrinal perspective, these distinctions reflect a shift from a contractual (treaty) approach to constitutive treaties to an institutional perspective (or even 'paradigm'). As a result, it is the IO, not the States parties, that ends up taking on any interpretative questions.

Interpretation of the rules of organizations begs a basic question that does not arise with other treaties, that is: whether treaty interpretation is even at issue, or if a different interpretive exercise, viz the institutional law of a particular organization, should apply. In other words, are UN Security Council resolutions a form of treaty law or do they amount to 'international legislation'?[99] Was the 1999 new 'strategic concept' of NATO[100] a (highly 'evolutive') interpretation of the 1949 North Atlantic Treaty or a redefinition of powers and competences by an organization making use of its *compétence de la compétence*? From a formal perspective, the answer to such questions determines the applicability of the law of treaties. And, in accordance with the focus of this book, this chapter has examined these issues from the perspective of *treaty law* rather than that of institutional law.

Some time ago constitutive treaties were stated to be so fundamentally different that 'it is deceptive to see in diplomatic and legal (including judicial) incidents

---

[98] Eg IMF Articles of Agreement (adopted 22 July 1944, entered into force 27 December 1945) 2 UNTS 39, Art XXIX(a). These variations and other provisions are mentioned in an insightful discussion by Amerasinghe (n 26) 26–32.

[99] Cf Gardiner (n 9) 113 (asking whether UNSC resolutions are subject to the Vienna rules or better treated as unilateral acts).

[100] Cf NATO, 'The Alliance's Strategic Concept' (24 April 1999) <http://www.nato.int/cps/en/natolive/official_texts_27433.htm>.

concerning the constitutive instruments "precedents" for the general law of treaties, and *vice versa.*'[101] This perhaps over-emphasizes the special character of constitutive treaties. On a general note, we may conclude that the law of treaties *is* the primary legal tool for their interpretation. But, even so—arguably because of the IO's semi-separated internal legal order—the receptiveness of constitutive treaties to the classic VCLT interpretative framework is somewhat limited. With the multiplication of levels of governance and loci of semantic authority in the world, the mechanism of 'constitutive interpretation' is likely to become more prominent in the future.

Recommended Reading

CE Amerasinghe, *Principles of the International Law of International Organizations* (2nd edn CUP, Cambridge 2005) Chapter 2

M Benzing, 'International Organizations or Institutions, Secondary Law' in R Wolfrum (ed), *Max Planck Encyclopedia of Public International Law* (OUP, Oxford 2008), online at <http://www.mpepil.com>

CM Brölmann, *The Institutional Veil in Public International Law; International Organizations and the Law of Treaties* (Hart, Oxford 2007)

O Corten and P Klein, *The Vienna Conventions on the Law of Treaties: A Commentary* (OUP, Oxford 2011) vol I

RK Gardiner, *Treaty Interpretation* (OUP, Oxford 2008)

M Herdegen, 'Interpretation in International Law' in R Wolfrum (ed), *Max Planck Encyclopedia of Public International Law* (OUP, Oxford 2008), online at <http://www.mpepil.com>

J Klabbers, *An Introduction to International Institutional Law* (2nd edn CUP, Cambridge 2009) 86

P Kunig, 'Interpretation of United Nations Charter' in R Wolfrum (ed), *Max Planck Encyclopedia of Public International Law* (OUP, Oxford 2008), online at <http://www.mpepil.com>

A Orakhelashvili, *The Interpretation of Acts and Rules in Public International Law* (OUP, Oxford 2008) 511

S Rosenne, *Developments in the Law of Treaties 1945–1986* (CUP, Cambridge 1989)

T Sato, *Evolving Constitutions of International Organizations* (Kluwer Law International, The Hague 1996)

H Schermers and NM Blokker, *International Institutional Law: Unity within Diversity* (5th edn Martinus Nijhoff, Dordrecht 2011)

---

[101] Rosenne (n 8) 257–8.

21

Specialized Rules of Treaty Interpretation: Human Rights

Başak Çalı

Introduction

Is the interpretation of treaties regulating international human rights a specialized regime? This question is itself open to interpretation along two dimensions. First, it could be understood to advocate exceptions for human rights treaties from the interpretative regime set out in the Vienna Convention on the Law of the Treaties (VCLT) and the customary international law it codifies. Second, it could instead be understood to ask if there exist specialized interpretive rules due to the demands of the subject matter that these treaties regulate. A discussion of the first dimension is necessary before any analysis of the second dimension (that is, the specific rules of treaty interpretation in the field of human rights law).[1]

Accordingly, this chapter starts by discussing what it means to have specialized rules for treaty interpretation in the field of international human rights. This will focus first on whether human rights treaties call for special interpretive rules that are beyond the VCLT paradigm and then, second, whether the debate on reservations to human rights treaties constitutes a move towards an exceptional regime for human rights. In the third part, attention turns to the interpretive strategies developed for human rights treaties. This section aims to show that human rights treaty interpretation is specialized in the sense that making these treaties and their provisions 'effective' in application animates how human rights interpreters approach treaty interpretation as a whole. In this part of the chapter, I shall also discuss how the interpretation of human rights treaties takes place within the context of general international law and other treaties that may be in force between States parties and why the forum for interpretation matters, be it specialized or generalist international bodies or domestic courts.

---

[1] This chapter will discuss international human rights treaty law and provide examples from human rights treaty interpreting bodies including regional human rights courts and commissions, UN treaty monitoring bodies, and other entities that interpret general international law such as the International Court of Justice (ICJ), International Law Commission (ILC), and domestic Constitutional courts. A comparative analysis of all institutions that interpret international human rights law, however, is beyond the scope of this chapter (and, indeed, this *Guide*).

The central argument of this chapter is two pronged. First, human rights treaty law does not constitute an exceptional regime as some commentators suggest. The principles of interpretation enshrined in Article 31 of the VCLT are flexible enough to incorporate human rights treaties, which are a subset of normative multilateral treaties in international law.[2] Second, international human rights law does have specialized rules of treaty interpretation. As the chapter demonstrates by a close analysis of the structure of human rights treaties, such specialization stems from the necessities of the *application* of the normative and abstract provisions of human rights treaty law in concrete cases and not from an extra-legal choice to elevate human rights treaties to a special status.

I. International Human rights Treaty Interpretation: Exceptional or Specialized?

Does international human rights treaty interpretation have its own interpretive scheme distinct and separate from the general principles of treaty interpretation codified in the VCLT? Or, is it a specialized regime due to the subject matter it regulates, but one nevertheless located within the confines of Article 31 of the VCLT?

There are supporters of both views. On the one hand, scholars argue that the *sui generis* nature of human rights calls for an interpretative practice that disregards traditional principles of general international law.[3] On the other hand, there are those who say that the interpretation of human rights treaties are specialized and that this is an inevitable development in international law.[4] On this latter view, international human rights treaty interpretation may be no more specialized than, for example, international trade law or investment law.[5] In terms of practice, there is no evidence to suggest that UN treaty bodies, regional human rights courts, the ICJ, the ILC, or domestic courts have systematically advocated either of these views. In fact, the evidence shows that these bodies cite the VCLT as a guide to interpretation *and* that regional human rights courts, in particular, are creating their own specialized rules and doctrines in the course of interpreting specific provisions of human rights treaties.[6]

---

[2] The only exception within the VCLT regime as far as human rights treaties and other treaties of a humanitarian character are concerned is Art 60(5). It states that suspension of treaties following material breach does not apply to 'provisions relating to the human person contained in the treaties of a humanitarian character'. For further discussion of this provision, see Chapter 23, Part II.B, 585 *et seq.*

[3] Cf DF Vagts, 'Treaty Interpretation and the New Ways of Law Reading' (1993) 4 EJIL 499. Those who hold this view are famously called '*droit de l'hommistes*' (human rightists) by Alain Pellet. A Pellet, '"Droit de l'hommisme" et droit international' (2001) 1 Revue Droits Fondamenteux 167.

[4] Cf J Tobin, 'Seeking to Persuade: A Constructive Approach to Human Rights Treaty Interpretation' (2010) 23 Harvard Human Rts J 1.

[5] Cf I Van Damme, 'Treaty Interpretation by the WTO Appellate Body' (2010) 21 EJIL 605; A Roberts, 'Power and Persuasion in Investment Treaty Arbitration' (2010) 104 AJIL 179.

[6] See with reference to the Human Rights Committee, R Higgins, 'Human Rights: Some Questions of Integrity' (1989) 52 Modern L Rev 1; with reference to the European Court of Human Rights,

Differences in opinion on this preliminary question are better conceived as disagreements on the rules of treaty interpretation in international law rather than disagreements on the correct interpretations of human rights treaties. What makes up the regime of interpretation set out in the VCLT? What are the rules of interpretation that are in force? What constitutes a diversion from such rules? The way in which one approaches these questions is central to deciding whether the interpretation of human rights treaties is *sui generis* or in line with the VCLT.[7]

The VCLT's rules of interpretation are set out in Articles 31 and 32. Of these two articles, Article 31 sets out the general rule for treaty interpretation. Specifically, Article 31 anchors interpretation in (a) text, (b) context, and (c) the object and purpose of a treaty.[8] The context within the scope of Article 31 has a special meaning; it includes the preamble of a treaty, its annexes, any agreement made between all the parties of that treaty when concluding it, and any instrument made by any of the parties to the treaty in connection with the treaty's conclusion, but accepted by all. Treaty context, according to Article 31, involves respect both for historical context at the time of the conclusion of the treaty together with forward-looking context. Treaties and agreements that are subsequently ratified by member States, and any emerging treaty law or relevant international law, are to be taken into account 'together with the context'. Article 32 further sets out the original intensions of States parties to a treaty as a supplementary means of treaty interpretation.[9] The provision itself is clear in indicating that such *travaux préparatoires* are a secondary means to provide meaning. The method of recovering the intentions of States parties is a means to confirm the outcome of an interpretation that follows Article 31 or to clarify situations where such an interpretation leaves matters 'manifestly absurd or unreasonable'.

Even though the order in which interpretive techniques should be employed is made clear between Articles 31 and 32, it has long been debated how Article 31's tripartite interpretive formula of wording, context, and object and purpose should be understood.[10] Some commentators have understood Article 31 as imposing a literal ordering, where wording, context and object and purpose should be employed as interpretive tools in the order they appear.[11] This formula, associated

---

A Mowbray, *The Development of Positive Obligations Under the European Convention on Human Rights by the European Court of Human Rights* (Hart Publishing, Oxford 2004); with reference to the Inter-American Court of Human Rights, L Lixinski, 'Treaty Interpretation by the Inter-American Court of Human Rights: Expansionism at the Service of the Unity of International Law' (2010) 21 EJIL 585.

[7] For a discussion of the VCLT articles on interpretation, see Chapter 19; R Gardiner, *Treaty Interpretation* (OUP, Oxford 2008); A Orakhelashvili, *The Interpretation of Acts and Rules in Public International Law* (OUP, Oxford 2008); U Linderfalk, *On the Interpretation of Treaties: The Modern International Law as Expressed in the 1969 Vienna Convention on the Law of Treaties* (Springer, Dordecht 2007).

[8] For Article 31's text, see Chapter 19, 475.

[9] For Article 32's text, see Chapter 19, 475–6.

[10] See Gardiner (n 7) 29–33.

[11] For a classical defence of this position see A McNair, *The Law of Treaties* (Clarendon Press, Oxford 1961) 364–83. Cf I Sinclair, *Vienna Convention on the Law of Treaties* (2nd edn MUP, Manchester 1984) 114–19.

with McNair, suggested a 'sliding scale' approach to what interpretation entails.[12] Interpretation is only required when the wording of the treaty is not clear. In that sense, the more literally unclear a provision becomes, the more necessary it is to refer to context. If context does not bring clarity, object and purpose should be employed as a last resort.

Since 1969, however, there has been wider support for a holistic approach to Article 31. This approach emphasizes the importance of an interpreter's judgment as to how the wording, context, and object and purpose interact with each other.[13] The original source for this perspective lies with ILC Commentaries on the draft VCLT describing treaty interpretation as a 'single combined operation' where wording, context, and object and purpose are 'thrown into a crucible',[14] which subsequently led this approach to be called the 'crucible approach'.[15]

The European Court of Human Rights (ECtHR) was an early subscriber to the crucible approach. It interpreted Article 31 in the same way and applied it in the famous *Golder* case even before the VCLT came into force:

In the way in which it is presented in the 'general rule' in Article 31 of the Vienna Convention, the process of interpretation of a treaty is a unity, a single combined operation; this rule, closely integrated, places on the same footing the various elements enumerated in the four paragraphs of the Article.[16]

What the ILC and the ECtHR have in common is their understanding of what Article 31 instructs the interpreter to do. Instead of conceiving Article 31 as a mechanistic formula, they regard it as guiding the interpreter's judgment as to what measure of wording, context, and object and purpose are relevant.[17] In the practice of treaty interpretation, however, it may be difficult to distinguish whether an interpreter is carrying out a mechanistic interpretation or exercising interpretive judgment. The difference between these approaches is often one of description of the method of the interpreter rather than the outcome of interpretation. It is possible to conceive the McNair argument about a lexical priority to 'wording of the text' at face value as not too far removed from that of the 'crucible' interpretation. Indeed, it is reasonable to suggest that if the wording of a treaty is very clear and is widely agreed by all interpreters then one does not need to carry out a detailed analysis of the context and the treaty's object and purpose. This does not, however, mean that the treaty text is not in need of interpretation or that interpre-

---

[12] McNair (n 11) 365.

[13] See Gardiner (n 7) 9–10; Van Damme (n 5) 619–20.

[14] [1966] YBILC, vol II, 219–20 [8]; cf also ILC Study Group, 'Fragmentation of International Law: Difficulties Arising from the Diversification and Expansion of International Law' (13 April 2006) UN Doc A/CN.4/L.682 [428].

[15] Gardiner (n 7) 9–10.

[16] *Golder v United Kingdom* (App no 4451/70) (1975) 1 EHRR 524 [30].

[17] DM McRae, 'Approaches to Interpretation of Treaties: the European Court of Human Rights and the WTO Appellate Body' in S Breitenmoser and others (eds), *Human Rights, Democracy and the Rule of Law: Liber Amicorum Luzuis Wildhaber* (Nomos Verlagsgesellschaft, Baden-Baden 2007) 1407.

tation is an activity separate from understanding the wording of a text.[18] It simply means that the meaning that emerges from the text 'fits' with the context and the object and purpose of the treaty so well that the interpreters do not find themselves in strong disagreement about that meaning.

Consider the example of Article 1 of Protocol No 6 to the European Convention for the Protection of Human Rights and Fundamental Freedoms (ECHR). This article concerns the abolition of the death penalty, stating: 'The death penalty shall be abolished. No-one shall be condemned to such penalty or executed.'[19] There is nothing in this text that is ambiguous. The first sentence clearly prohibits a practice. The second sentence is clear with respect to whom the article covers and how an interpreter should deal with whether death penalty moratoriums satisfy the conditions of the first part of the article. In this respect, there is a strong and tight overlap between the object and purpose of the article and its wording—the absolute prohibition of the death penalty in theory and in practice.[20]

Such strong overlap between wording and object and purpose, however, is not often the case in human rights treaty provisions—hence the controversy about the relevant regime of interpretation. This is primarily because the provisions of human rights treaties often do not lend themselves easily to tight wording. They state rights in abstract ways without stating in detail what they require for their application. One obvious explanation for this is the treaty negotiation process and the difficulties of getting agreements on certain words or concepts.[21] Commentators in other fields of international law would concur, however, that this is not necessarily a problem *sui generis* with respect to human rights treaties, but generally permeates all international law treaty-drafting processes.[22]

There is, however, a deeper explanation for the frequent lack of clear fit between the ordinary wording of human rights treaties, their context, and their object and purpose, which makes human rights treaties a demanding case for interpretation. This explanation is based on the very nature of the conceptual structure of these treaty provisions. As many commentators have noted, human rights treaties do not create reciprocal obligations between States parties, but instead create obligations

---

[18] See on this point and the distinction between neutral and semantic concepts, R Dworkin, *Justice in Robes* (Harvard University Press, London 2006).

[19] Protocol No 6 to the Convention for the Protection of Human Rights and Fundamental Freedoms Concerning the Abolition of the Death Penalty (28 April 1983) Eur TS No 114 reprinted in [1983] 22 ILM 539, Art 1.

[20] Cf Higgins (n 6) 6–7 (raising the point with respect to prohibitive provisions of the ICCPR).

[21] For an historical account, see B Simpson, *Human Rights and the End of the Empire: Britain and the Genesis of the European Convention* (OUP, Oxford 2004); for a contemporary account, see A Dhir, 'Human Rights Treaty Drafting through the Lens of Mental Disability: The Proposed International Convention on Promotion and Protection of the Rights and Dignity of Persons with Disabilities' (2005) 41 Stanford J Intl L 181.

[22] For debates on similar ambiguity in international trade law, cf eg P Linsday, 'The Ambiguity of GATT Article XXI: Subtle Success or Rampant Failure?' (2003) 52 Duke L J 1277; and in international criminal law, cf G Fletcher and JD Ohlin, 'Reclaiming Fundamental Principles of Criminal Law in the Darfur Case' (2005) 3 J Intl Crim Justice 539–61.

Treaty Interpretation

for States in relation to their treatment of individuals under their jurisdiction.[23] More importantly, this observation about the nature of human rights treaties is a descriptive statement, rather than a statement of *lex ferenda*.

Human rights law provisions in UN and regional human rights treaties regulate the conduct of States towards individuals by way of assigning rights to individuals and correlative duties to States. This is *the* common feature of all human rights treaty structures.[24] Each treaty text lists the rights that individuals are entitled to claim from State authorities.[25] These rights are formulated in general wording. They do not often include information about in what contexts they apply, what types of relationships they cover, where they apply, and what kinds of circumstances, if any, would allow their legitimate restriction. Consider Article 7 of the International Covenant on Civil and Political Rights (ICCPR):

No one shall be subjected to torture or to cruel, inhuman or degrading treatment or punishment. In particular, no one shall be subjected without his free consent to medical or scientific experimentation.[26]

The obligations of States with respect to these rights are characteristically not listed in the treaty texts themselves, but rather stated in a single, all-encompassing provision that assigns States duties to respect and ensure treaty rights.[27] Article 2 (1)–(2) of the ICCPR provide an example of this effect:

(1) Each State Party to the present Covenant undertakes to respect and to ensure to all individuals within its territory and subject to its jurisdiction the rights recognized in the present Covenant, without distinction of any kind, such as race, colour, sex, language, religion, political or other opinion, national or social origin, property, birth or other status.

(2) Where not already provided for by existing legislative or other measures, each State Party to the present Covenant undertakes to take the necessary steps, in accordance with its constitutional processes and with the provisions of the present Covenant, to adopt such laws or other measures as may be necessary to give effect to the rights recognized in the present Covenant.[28]

---

[23] M Craven, 'Legal Differentiation and the Concept of the Human Rights Treaty in International Law' (2000) 11 EJIL 489, 513–17.

[24] Human rights treaty structures differ, in this respect from other categories of normative treaties, notably those for international humanitarian law, international criminal law, and international environmental law.

[25] The only exception to this rule is the assignment of duties to individuals in the African (Banjul) Charter on Human and People's Rights (adopted 27 June 1981, entered into force 21 October 1986) 1520 UNTS 217, ch 2.

[26] ICCPR (adopted 16 December 1966, entered into force 23 March 1976) 999 UNTS 171, Art 7.

[27] See European Convention for the Protection of Human Rights and Fundamental Freedoms (opened for signature 4 November 1950, entered into force 3 September 1953) 213 UNTS 222, Art 1 ('ECHR'); American Convention on Human Rights (opened for signature 22 November 1969, entered into force 18 July 1978) 1144 UNTS 123, Art 1(1)–(2); International Covenant on Economic, Social and Cultural Rights (adopted 19 December 1966, entered into force 3 January 1976) 993 UNTS 3, Art 1 ('ICESCR'); Banjul Charter (n 25) Art 1.

[28] ICCPR (n 26) Art 2(1)–(2).

It is not a mere coincidence that neither the exact scope of States' rights nor their duties are specified in detail in human rights treaties. This lack of precision is a function of the non-mechanical context in which human rights claims arise. Human rights treaties apply to a much larger universe of situations than many other international treaties. By their very nature, human rights provisions need to be interpreted in the light of changing political, social, and economic justifications of State policies. Human rights treaty law interpreters have to decide which interests of specific individuals are so important that they need to be safeguarded from policies that seem to respect or make better-off the majority of individuals under a particular jurisdiction. The key trigger for the interpretative task to start is a claim on behalf of an individual that her situation is within the scope of a human rights treaty, ie that she has a claim grounded in human rights law against the State. Does the lack of access to disabled facilities in a police detention centre constitute degrading treatment with respect to a disabled detainee even if there is no such intention to mistreat on the part of the authorities?[29] Does handing out leaflets in a privatized shopping mall that has been historically a public space come under the scope of freedom of assembly?[30] What responsibility does a State have with respect to actions of non-State military forces acting in its territory?[31] None of these questions can be resolved solely by analysing (respectively) the text of the right to be free from torture, inhuman, or degrading treatment; the right to freedom of assembly; or the right to life provisions in various human rights treaties.

With respect to State duties, as the term 'legislative and other measures' in ICCPR Article 2(2) points out, there is an inherent flexibility as to how States parties can respect and ensure compliance with a human right provision.[32] The application of human rights treaties require that such measures are given the requisite 'effect'. This can only be done by assessing whether the conduct of the State authorities are corresponding to an appropriate conception of their duties under human rights treaties.

It should be clear by now that the core activity of international human rights treaty application involves subsuming particulars under generals in the domain of the relationship between the State and the individual. Descriptively, this means that situations when only the wording (or wording together with the treaty context) paves the way for the meaning of the text are limited by nature; the structure of human rights treaties themselves demands an onerous interpretive framework to operate. This primarily means that any interpreting agent has to specify what types of duties States have towards individuals in an infinite number of situations and why such duties must trump other duties the States have under particular condi-

---

[29] *Price v United Kingdom* (App no 33394/96) ECHR 10 July 2001 [30].

[30] Cf *Appleby and others v United Kingdom* (App no 44306/98) ECHR 6 May 2003 [48]–[49].

[31] *Case of the Rochela Massacre v Colombia* Inter-American Court of Human Rights Series C No 163 (11 May 2007) [66]–[68].

[32] Indeed, the new generation human rights treaties specify a wide range of general obligations that flow from human rights treaties. Cf Art 4 of the UN Convention on the Rights of Persons with Disabilities (adopted 13 December 2006, entered into force 3 May 2008) 2515 UNTS 3 ('Disabilities Convention').

tions. Human rights listed in treaties range among civil, political, economic, social, and cultural rights. There are also cross-cutting human rights treaties that focus on all types of rights with respect to vulnerable or special groups, such as women, children, the disabled, the next of kin of the disappeared, or torture victims.[33] Each of these treaties requires a complex analysis of the duties of States with respect to different kinds of rights and with respect to different kinds of vulnerable groups. Such duties range from duties to respect, protect, and fulfil human rights to duties to promote human rights.[34] Even prohibitive and absolute provisions of human rights treaties, most notably the prohibition on torture, show that duty specification in concrete instances of an alleged violation requires a more burdensome interpretive process.[35]

Does this conceptual structure of human rights treaties mean that human rights treaty interpretation is all about 'object and purpose'? Does the lack of clarity of the scope of rights and the lack of duty specification mean that the wording, the context, and the history of texts are disregarded altogether at the expense of a teleological interpretation? If we took this view, most interpreters of human rights treaties would be natural rights lawyers or moral philosophers in disguise for whom Article 31 of the VCLT is merely a cloak for pursuing a purposeful type of interpretation.

This argument, however, does not survive close scrutiny. An important part of the response to this argument requires going back to the hierarchical distinction McNair drew between wording, context, and object and purpose. The crucible interpretation approach requires that the three components of interpretation fit

---

[33] International Convention on the Elimination of All Forms of Racial Discrimination (opened for signature 7 March 1966, entered into force 4 January 1969) 660 UNTS 195; Convention on the Elimination of All Forms of Discrimination Against Women (adopted 18 December 1979, entered into force 3 September 1981) 1249 UNTS 13 ('CEDAW'); Convention against Torture and other Cruel, Inhuman or Degrading Treatment or Punishment (adopted 10 December 1984, entered into force 26 June 1987) 1465 UNTS 85 ('CAT'); Convention on the Rights of the Child (adopted 20 November 1989, entered into force 2 September 1990) 1577 UNTS 3; International Convention on the Protection of the Rights of All Migrant Workers and Members of their Families (adopted 18 December 1990, entered into force 1 July 2003) 2220 UNTS 3; Disabilities Convention (n 32); International Convention for the Protection of All Persons from Enforced Disappearance (adopted 20 December 2006, entered into force 23 December 2010) UN Doc A/61/488 reprinted in (2007) 14 IHRR 582.

[34] The duty specification with respect to individual human rights treaties follows different trajectories. For example, the ECHR and the American Convention on Human Rights, employ a negative obligation and positive obligation framework, specifying a range of duties on an article-by-article and case-by-case basis. See Mowbray (n 6) 7–220. The ICESCR follows a tri-partite conceptual framework, with duties to respect, protect, and fulfil. See Committee on Economic, Social and Cultural Rights (CESCR), 'General Comment 12: The right to adequate food (art 11)' UN Doc E/C.12/1999/5. CEDAW has a four-layer duty framework, with duties to respect, protect, fulfil, and actively promote. See Committee on the Elimination of All Forms of Discrimination against Women, 'General Comment 28' (16 December 2010) CEDAW/C/GC/28. Cf IE Koch, 'Dichotomies, Trichotomies or Waves of Duties?' (2005) 5 Human Rts L Rev 81–103.

[35] For interpretive difficulties on torture with respect to a single human rights treaty, see *Ireland v United Kingdom* (1976) 19 Ybk 512 [163] (EComHR) (on the minimum level of severity); *Soering v United Kingdom* (App no 14038/88) (1989) 11 EHRR 439 [88]–[91] (on deportation and real risk of torture); *Cakici v Turkey* (App no 23657/94) ECHR 8 July 1999 [98]–[99] (on the treatment of the next of kin of the disappeared).

together. It does not, however, tell us what measure of use of these methods constitutes a perfect fit. As the earlier prohibition of the death penalty example shows, it cannot automatically be assumed that wording is never enough to interpret a human rights treaty. In the case of most human rights treaty provisions, however, the vague wording of rights, and the blanket provisions of duties, logically necessitates visiting the object and purpose of the treaty and its fit with the wording and context. This is not, as I have been careful to emphasize, because the subject matter is 'human rights' as the *droit de l'hommiste* charge would have it, or because human rights treaty interpreters are natural rights lawyers. On the contrary, the argument is functional and descriptive. The claim that insists that human rights treaties have an exceptional regime of interpretation favours a very particular—not a widely shared—interpretation of Article 31 of the VCLT; it favours a hierarchical ordering of wording, context, and object and purpose. But the crucible approach, which has received widespread support, demands that the wording, context, and the object and purpose fit. In sum, human rights treaty interpretation, regardless of the theoretical orientation of the interpreter, is complex and demanding. Human rights treaty interpreters disagree about the best interpretation of human rights treaties.[36] Despite such criticism of actual practice, however, there does not seem to be evidence to suggest that the crucible approach cannot accommodate the interpretive problems of human rights treaty provisions.

II. The Reservations to Human Rights Treaties Debate: Evidence of an Exceptional Interpretive Regime?

The debate concerning reservations to human rights treaties is complex and long-standing. It has attracted a considerable amount of debate amongst public international lawyers and human rights lawyers, especially after the delivery of General Comment 24 of the Human Rights Committee (HRC),[37] reactions to these comments by France, the United Kingdom, and the United States in 1994[38] and the ILC's subsequent work on reservations to treaties.[39] This chapter cannot do

---

[36] Cf generally F Ni Aolain, 'The Emergence Of Diversity: Differences in Human Rights Jurisprudence' (1995) 19 Fordham Intl L J 101.

[37] HRC, 'General Comment No 24: General comment on issues relating to reservations made upon ratification or accession to the Covenant or the Optional Protocols thereto, or in relation to declarations under article 41 of the Covenant' (4 November 1994) CCPR/C/21/Rev.1/Add.6.

[38] 'Observation by France on GC No 24 on Reservations to the ICCPR' (8 September 1995) CCPR A/51/40, 104–6; 'Observation by the United States of America on General Comment No 24' (28 March 1995) CCPR A/50/40/Annex VI 126–29; 'Observations by the United Kingdom on GC No 24' (21 July 1995) CCPR A/50/40/Annex VI 130–34.

[39] The ILC's decades-long work culminated in August 2011 with adoption of the *Guide to Practice on Reservations to Treaties* <http://untreaty.un.org/ilc/texts/instruments/english/draft%20articles/1_8_2011.pdf> forthcoming [2011] YBILC, vol II(2) ('Guide to Practice'); see also A Pellet, 'Second report on reservations to treaties' [1996] YBILC, vol II(1), 37; A Pellet, 'Third report on reservations to treaties' [1998] YBILC, vol II(1), 221; A Pellet, 'Fifth report on reservations to treaties' [2000] YBILC, vol II(1), 139; A Pellet, 'Seventh report on reservations to treaties' [2002] YBILC, vol II, 3; A Pellet, 'Eighth report on reservations to treaties' (2003) UN Doc A/CN.4/535.

justice to the whole literature that has developed surrounding this matter.[40] Rather, I focus on this debate only to the extent it indirectly asks whether human rights treaty bodies' and regional courts' interpretations of the VCLT's articles on reservations (Articles 19 and 20) are consistent with Article 31's interpretative guidance or whether, instead, they reflect the adoption of an exceptional regime of interpretation.[41]

The debate surrounding reservations to human rights treaties centres on the important problem of the legal consequences of reservations to duly entered into human rights law treaties by individual States parties.[42] Article 19 of the VCLT provides that States can enter reservations to treaties upon signature or ratification, provided that reservations are expressly envisaged in the treaty or if the treaty is silent with regard to reservations. This is on the condition that the reservations are compatible with the treaty's object and purpose.[43] The interpretive difficulty lies with deciding whether under Article 19 of the VCLT a reservation that is incompatible with the object and the purpose of a treaty is a reservation at all and who should decide on this matter and to what effect.[44]

There are two possible approaches to this issue. On one account, the reservations regime is primarily interactional. It is up to States parties themselves to decide whether a reservation entered by one party is contrary to the treaty's object and purpose. If one State party makes this determination with respect to another party's reservation, there are two possible legal effects, either (a) that treaty is not in force between those two States at all, or (b) the treaty is in force between the two parties, but without the reservation having any legal effect. If the State objects to a reservation on grounds other than it being against the object and the purpose of the treaty, the treaty would be in force between those two States minus the provision with the reservation, even if a third State party had objected to the same reservation on the grounds that it is against the treaty's object and the purpose and, therefore, not a valid reservation. Based on bilateral objections to reservations, this approach leads to a fragmentation of the legal effects of a treaty.

---

[40] Cf generally C Redgwell, 'Reservations to Treaties and Human Rights Committee General Comment 24' (1997) 46 ICLQ 390; B Simma, 'Reservations to Human Rights Treaties: Some Recent Developments' in G Hafner and others (eds), *Liber Amicorum Professor Seidl-Hohenweldern* (Kluwer Law International, The Hague 1998) 659–80; R Baratta, 'Should Invalid Reservations to Human Rights Treaties be Disregarded?' (2000) 11 EJIL 413; J Klabbers, 'Accepting the Unacceptable? A Nordic Approach to Reservations to Multilateral Treaties' (2000) 69 Nordic J Intl L 179.

[41] Similarly, one could analyse interpretative issues surrounding withdrawals from human rights treaties. For a discussion of North Korea's attempted ICCPR denunciation, see Chapter 25, Part I.A, 639 *et seq*.

[42] VCLT Art 2(1)(d) defines reservations as statements that purport 'to exclude or to modify the legal effect of certain provisions of the treaty' with respect to the reserving State. For more on reservations, see Chapter 11.

[43] VCLT Art 19.

[44] The meaning of VCLT Arts 20, 21, and 22 (concerning the entry of objections to reservations, the legal effects of such objections, and the withdrawal of objections) all depend on this prior question. For a detailed discussion, see F Hampson, 'Expanded working paper on the question of reservations to human rights treaties, prepared in accordance with [UNHRC] Sub-Commission decision 2001/17' (8 August 2003) UN Doc E/CN.4/Sub.2/2003/WP.2.

On the alternative, second account, Article 19 of the VCLT is interpreted so that whether a reservation is contrary to the treaty's object and the purpose becomes a question lexically prior to whether States can object to a State party's statement. Under this approach, an interactional regime applies only if the reservation is compatible with the treaty's object and purpose. This latter account was favoured by the ICJ in its advisory opinion on *Reservations to the Genocide Convention*:

A State which has made and maintained a reservation which has been objected to by one or more of the parties to the Convention but not by others, can be regarded as being a party to the Convention *if the reservation is compatible with the object and purpose of the Convention.*[45]

It should become clear by this point that the problem of whether an exceptional regime governs reservations to human rights treaties is not really all that exceptional. Rather than an interpretative question specific to human rights, the issue is the interpretation of Article 19 of the VCLT generally. Indeed, either interpretation discussed above has consequences not only for reservations to human rights treaties, but for all treaties, particularly those that do not regulate bilateral relations, but demand objective application of provisions to all member States in an equal manner.

The reason that the interpretive dispute with respect to Article 19 is amplified in the case of human rights treaties is primarily because of (i) the number of vague and unclear reservations human rights treaties attract; (ii) the lack of an adequate practice amongst States in objecting to such reservations; and (iii) the presence of treaty-monitoring bodies or courts. In carrying out their monitoring or adjudicatory mandates these institutions have had to tackle the problem of statements in the form of reservations, or otherwise, and decide whether they have to take such statements into account when monitoring compliance or adjudicating. When doing so, these bodies and courts are faced with a familiar problem in general international law, namely, the legal significance of lack of State practice. It is not clear whether a reservation is widely accepted amongst States by looking at the sheer number of objections. It is also not clear whether a monitoring body severing or accepting a reservation is accepted to have the authority to do so. This situation is simply *not* governed by the VCLT. There are no provisions in the VCLT that regulate the relationship between international courts or treaty monitoring bodies, on the one hand, and the reserving States and those that object or do not object to such reservations, on the other. This is why the response of such bodies to the problem, when faced with a concrete reservation, has primarily developed through the practice of these institutions and subsequent acquiescence or reactions from States.

The ECtHR has led the way in arguing that it has the power to determine whether a statement, however phrased, is a valid reservation or not. According to the ECtHR, given that the reserving States agree that the Court is competent in adjudicating the cases before it, those States cannot have the benefit of that

---

[45] *Reservations to the Convention on the Prevention and Punishment of the Crime of Genocide* (Advisory Opinion) [1951] ICJ Rep 15, 23 [10] (emphasis added).

statement in the course of the proceedings if the ECtHR deems the reservation invalid.[46] The Court also rejected the interactional account altogether in carrying out its own task and held that: 'The silence of the depositary and the Contracting States does not deprive the Convention institutions of the power to make their own assessment.'[47]

This interpretation is in line with the ICJ's interpretation in the *Reservations* case of the admissibility of reservations.[48] Some commentators (most notably the ILC's Special Rapporteur on Reservations to Treaties, Alain Pellet) have proposed, however, to read the ECtHR case law with respect to severing invalid reservations as regional customary law, rather than a generally applicable interpretation of Article 19 of the VCLT. This means, therefore, that the approach of severing inadmissible reservations would not be available to UN human rights bodies and other third party adjudicators/interpreters outside of Europe.[49] It is not clear, however, whether Pellet's views should prevail. It is true that ECHR States parties appear to have acquiesced in the ECtHR's interpretation severing reservations incompatible with a treaty's object and purpose. It is also important, however, to note that the structure of the ECtHR argument does not rely exclusively on the *sui generis* nature of the European human rights treaty system, and could be read as a more general interpretation of Article 19 of the VCLT.[50] The ILC's 2011 *Guide to Practice on Reservations to Treaties* suggests a middle ground—a presumption of severability subject to an interpretation of the State's intent in determining the legal effects of an invalid reservation—but it remains to be seen if States and other international actors will adopt this approach.[51]

When the HRC issued its General Comment 24 and defended the lexical priority of the object and purpose test to the interactional account, it drew strong criticism from the United States, France, and the United Kingdom. These States primarily argued that the decision of whether a reservation is incompatible with the object and the purpose of a treaty rests with States and not with the treaty monitoring body and thus the Human Rights Committee did not have legally binding authority to severe reservations.[52] The thrust of their objections emphasized the centrality of State consent to be bound by treaties and the legal status of human rights treaty monitoring bodies in international law. Unlike human rights courts, whose judgments are legally binding, the general comments, concluding observations, and views of treaty monitoring bodies are not legally binding. As far as the applicability of the VCLT's interpretative regime to treaty bodies' interpretation of Article 19 of the VCLT is concerned, therefore, this dispute is more accurately conceived as one over how to interpret the extent of authority granted to treaty-monitoring bodies. There is not, in this sense, exceptional interpretive regimes governing reservations to human rights treaties, since Article 31 of the

---

[46] *Belilos v Switzerland* (App no 10328/83) ECHR 29 April 1988 [50]–[55].
[47] Ibid [47]   [48] See generally *Reservations* case (n 45).
[49] [1997] YBILC, vol II(2), 49 [83]–[85].
[50] Hampson (n 44) [35].   [51] Guide to Practice (n 39) Guideline 4.5.3.
[52] See n 38 for references to the French, US, and UK Comments.

VCLT does not favour the interpretations of a group of States, nor does it regulate interpretation focusing on the authenticity of the interpreters.

This discussion shows, therefore, that as a matter of *lex lata* the exceptionalist versus specialist divide is part of a larger debate about the meaning of Articles 19 and 31 of the VCLT. When human rights treaty law is placed in the VCLT context, the interpretation of human rights treaty provisions or reservations to human rights treaties do not necessarily turn on an exceptionalist vision of human rights, but a more general debate about the provisions of the VCLT itself.

III. Specialized Interpretive Principles in the Field of Human Rights Treaty Law

The preceding section has shown that human rights treaties do not require exceptional rules of interpretation that are hermeneutically sealed off from the VCLT regime. On the contrary, interpretation of human rights treaties is a case of applying Article 31 of the VCLT to a particular domain of international law. Human rights courts often echo the fact that human rights treaties and the VCLT are not competing frameworks. Consider this ECtHR statement:

The Court recalls that the Convention must be interpreted in the light of the rules set out in the Vienna Convention 1969 (*Golder v. the United Kingdom* judgment of 21 February 1975, Series A no. 18, § 29) .... The Court must also take into account any relevant rules of international law when examining questions concerning its jurisdiction and, consequently, determine State responsibility in conformity with the governing principles of international law, although it must remain mindful of the Convention's special character as a human rights treaty (the above-cited *Loizidou judgment* (merits), at §§ 43 and 52). The Convention should be interpreted as far as possible in harmony with other principles of international law of which it forms part.[53]

The focus in this section is on the specialized principles of interpretation in the human rights field as a case of fully applying Article 31. The aim here is not to go through the jurisprudence of all human rights treaties. Neither is it to document the inconsistencies of interpretations within the same or across different institutions—something which has attracted much commentary.[54] Rather, the aim is to show that the application of Article 31 has led to the adoption and elaboration of an effectiveness approach to human rights treaty interpretation. In other words, human rights interpreters across a diversity of treaty contexts have come to view the interaction between wording, context, and object and purpose as requiring 'effective, real, and concrete' protection of human rights provisions.

---

[53] *Bankovic and others v Belgium and 16 other NATO States* (App no 52207/99) ECHR 12 December 2001 [55]–[57].

[54] MB Dembour, *Who Believes in Human Rights? Reflections on the European Convention* (CUP, Cambridge 2006); K Mechlem, 'Treaty Bodies and the Interpretation of Human Rights' (2009) 42 Vanderbilt J Transnatl L 905.

A. The effectiveness approach and human rights treaties

Even though all human rights treaties have their own distinct context and wording, there is nevertheless significant convergence around the notion that the core interpretive task for any interpreter is to make human rights treaty provisions 'effective, real, and practical' for individuals as right-holders under international law.[55] This is sometimes called the principle of effectiveness (*ut res magis valeat quam pereat*).[56] Effectiveness is an overarching approach to human rights treaty interpretation. It animates a range of other more fine-grained, specific interpretive principles developed in the context of each human rights treaty. Examples include the interpretive principles of 'autonomous concepts', 'living instrument', and 'practicality' in the ECtHR context;[57] the 'responsiveness to African circumstances' in the case of the African Commission on Human and People's Rights;[58] the consideration of the 'real situation' in the case of the Inter-American Court of Human Rights;[59] and the 'dynamic instrument doctrine' put forward by the Committee against All Forms of Discrimination against Women.[60] These principles all derive from the interpretive consensus that interpretations that are devoid of actual effect for human rights protections do not cohere with good faith interpretations of the wording and context of human rights treaties in the light of their object and purpose.[61]

As Gardiner explains the principle of effectiveness has two aspects.[62] The first aspect directs the interpreter to give meaning to each and every treaty provision so that each term has effect rather than no effect.[63] This aspect comes from the good faith requirement of Article 31. The second aspect involves taking a teleological approach to interpretation and this is associated with the demands of the treaty's object and purpose. In human rights treaty interpretation we find that interpreters have developed both aspects of effectiveness, often in tandem with each other.

---

[55] The ECtHR explains its mission as making '[the European Convention on Human Rights] safeguards practical and effective'. *Loizidou v Turkey* (Preliminary Objections) (1995) 20 EHRR 99, 102.

[56] D Rausching, *The Vienna Convention on the Law of Treaties, Travaux Préparatoires* (Metzner, Frankfurt 1978) 251. For a discussion of this principle's operation in the international organizations' context, see Chapter 20, Part I.B.1, 512 *et seq*.

[57] *Tyrer v United Kingdom* (App nos 5856/72) (1978) 2 EHRR 1, 15–16 [31]; *Chassagnou and others v France* (App nos 25088/94, 28331/95, 28443/95) (1999) 29 EHRR 615 [100]; *Selmouni v France* (App no 25803/94) (1999) 29 EHRR 32 [101].

[58] *The Social-Economic Rights Action Centre and the Centre for Economic and Social Rights/Nigeria* Decision on Communication No 155/96 (2001) African Commn on Human and Peoples' Rights [68].

[59] *Right to Information on Consular Assistance in the Framework of the Guarantees of the Due Process Law* (Advisory Opinion) Inter-American Court of Human Rights Series A No 16 (1 October 1999) [121]; *Juridical Condition and Rights of Undocumented Migrants* (Advisory Opinion) Inter-American Court of Human Rights Series A No 18 (17 September 2003) [121].

[60] CEDAW, 'General Recommendation No 25: Temporary Social Measures' UN Doc HRI/Gen/1/Rev.7 270 [3] ('The Convention is a living instrument').

[61] See *Tyrer* (n 57) 15–16 [31]; *Case of the Mapiripan Massacre v Colombia* Inter-American Court of Human Rights Series C No 134 (15 September 2005) [104]–[108].

[62] Gardiner (n 7) 159–61; Chapter 19, Part III.B, 495 *et seq*.

[63] See *The Corfu Channel Case (United Kingdom v Albania)* (Merits) [1949] ICJ Rep 4 [29].

The first aspect of effectiveness in the human rights treaty context means that the interpretation of provisions should have real effect in terms of the concrete and actual lives of individuals who are the recognized right-holders of human rights treaty law. That is, human rights interpretations must have 'practical effect'. The ECtHR case of *Airey* is a helpful demonstration of this aspect.[64] The case involved whether the right of access to court involved a duty to provide legal aid. The Irish government argued that there was no duty to provide legal aid because the applicant can exercise her right by appearing in person. The ECtHR rejected this argument on the grounds that the human rights treaties require effective rights, not merely formal rights. In a well-known quote, the Court summed up the good faith aspect of effectiveness: 'The Convention is intended to guarantee rights that are not theoretical or illusory, but rights that are practical and effective.'[65] According to this first version, effectiveness instructs the interpreters to attribute 'sincerity' to the original intensions of the drafters (ie the context) in realizing human rights of individuals. The distinction between formalistic protection versus effective protection offers an animating reason to choose between conflicting understandings of the wording of the text. Good faith effectiveness also requires the interpreter to take into account the ability of existing frameworks to protect individual rights over time.

The second version of effectiveness offers a deeper account of what really makes a human rights provision effective. It is teleological in the sense that it goes beyond an analysis of whether an existing protection is formal or effective as a matter of fact and asks the question of under what kinds of circumstances human rights treaty provisions can be trumped by other concerns[66] or legitimately infringed. This version of effectiveness hinges on the question of whether treaty texts in principle should be interpreted in favour of the particular individual right and expanding correlating duties or in favour of the public interest that would restrict or not recognize a right or its correlating duty.[67] A common trend amongst human rights interpreting bodies has been to adopt an understanding that favours the first option and thereby to assert that the protection of human rights has priority to sovereign rights.[68] The 'living instrument' doctrine of the ECtHR, which disregards the original intent of the drafters in favour of assessing rights in present conditions, develops this aspect of effectiveness.[69] The HRC's view on the interpretation of the

---

[64] *Airey v Ireland* (App no 6289/73) (1981) 3 EHRR 305.

[65] Ibid [24].

[66] See eg R Dworkin, *Justice for Hedgehogs* (Harvard University Press, Cambridge 2011) 227–331 (articulating rights as trumps).

[67] This latter approach resonates with the notion of 'restrictive interpretation', which presumes that the drafters intended to leave States freedom of action (or inaction) in cases of ambiguity. Cf eg L Crema, 'Disappearance and New Sightings of Restrictive Interpretation(s)' (2010) 21 EJIL 681.

[68] This general principle is not without problems as priority does not mean absolute priority. Cf B Çalı, 'Balancing Human Rights: Methodological Problems with Weights, Scales and Proportions' (2007) 29 HRQ 251; MK Addo and N Grief, 'Does Article 3 of the European Convention on Human Rights Enshrine Absolute Rights?' (1998) 9 EJIL 510.

[69] See eg *Loizidou v Turkey* (App no 15318/89) 23 EHHR 513 [71] (holding that the living instrument doctrine not only applies to the Convention's substantive provisions, but also to those that govern the operation of the Convention machinery).

right to life is a good example of problematizing original intent in favour of teleological effectiveness:

noting that . . . The expression 'inherent right to life' cannot be properly understood in a restrictive manner, and [that] the protection of this right requires that States adopt positive measures.[70]

This general preference for expansive interpretations of rights and duties and restrictive interpretations of sovereignty, however, also comes with problems. Central questions in this regard are whether teleological effectiveness equals unwarranted expansionism and whether international human rights treaty interpreters that are beyond the reach of domestic democratic accountability impose their subjective views on States under this so-called principle of 'effective interpretation'.[71] There is no clear indication, however, that this is the automatic outcome of effectiveness in human rights treaty interpretation. The function of the teleological aspect of effectiveness in the case of human rights treaties is better understood as shifting the burden of proof from the individual to the State in justifying the infringement of, or lack of measures for protecting, rights.[72]

The effectiveness principle articulated by the Inter-American Court of Human Rights comes closest to the full-blown teleological interpretation that sceptics have in mind. This Court holds that interpretation in favour of the individual (which it calls the principle of *pro-homine*) must be followed even if this comes at the expense of the wording or context.[73] The (former) European Commission on Human Rights, and subsequently the ECtHR, was more cautious in defining the parameters of effectiveness. The Commission, for example, held that effectiveness requires seeking:

the interpretation that is most appropriate in order to realise the aim and achieve the objective of the treaty, not that which would restrict to the greatest possible degree the obligations undertaken by the parties.[74]

Here the notion of 'greatest possible degree' indicates that effectiveness is not about burdening the State with a large range of impractical or unrealistic obligations and that the interpretation that may seem the most beneficial to the individual may not be chosen due to other principles at work. Most notably, the doctrine of margin of appreciation, which calls for deference to interpretations of domestic institutions based on concerns for the appropriate forum to resolve conflicts between rights and

---

[70] HRC, 'General Comment No 6, The Right to Life' (1982) UN Doc HRI/Gen/1/Rev.7 128 [4]–[5].

[71] For an account offering a general scepticism towards effectiveness as a subjective imposition, see M Waibel, 'Demystifying the Art of Interpretation' (2011) 22 EJIL 571, 582.

[72] This may occur, eg, in cases of declarations of states of emergency to derogate from protection of rights temporally pursuant to ICCPR Art 4. Cf HRC, 'General Comment 29, States of Emergency (article 4)' (2001) UN Doc CCPR/C/21/Rev.1/Add.11. Or, in cases interpreting the ICESCR's 'progressive realization' clauses. Cf CESCR's 'General Comment 12' (n 34).

[73] *19 Tradesmen v Colombia* Inter-American Court of Human Rights Series C No 109 (5 July 2004) [173].

[74] *Wemhoff v Germany* (App no 2122/64) (1968) 1 EHRR 55, 75.

public interest, is held to work against *pro-homine* interpretations.[75] In other words, effectiveness in the eyes of the European Commission and the ECtHR cuts both ways. Human rights treaty obligations cannot be interpreted in expansive ways without regard to whether or not it is reasonable, realistic, or legitimate for States to have these correlating obligations. Effectiveness is neither about 'inflation of rights' nor about 'inflation of duties'.

In light of the above, could the overarching effectiveness approach be regarded in itself as being a radical departure from Article 31 of the VCLT? Here, it is important to distinguish the different conceptions of effectiveness employed by treaty interpreting bodies. Various courts and treaty monitoring bodies can be criticized on the grounds that in their application of effectiveness they do not pay adequate attention to treaty wording and context or that too radical departure from the wording of human rights treaty provisions makes interpretation unpredictable. Even in such cases, however, the reactions of the States to those interpretations should be taken into account. Evidence of compliance with the interpretations of such bodies, for example, may suggest that the parties accept the special meaning given to the text.[76]

But the rejection of effectiveness as animating how provisions should be interpreted itself does not stand up to close scrutiny. First, there is the question of 'if not effectiveness, then what'? Given the vague wording that is not just an accidental feature but a necessity in the human rights treaty domain, it is clear that a reading that simply emphasizes the wording of the provisions does not in itself offer serious mileage. Second, the adoption of a restrictive interpretation approach not only sits uncomfortably with the object and purpose of human rights treaties, but also with their context. The effectiveness principle is not exclusively about giving effect to the object and purpose of the treaty. It is also about interpreting the context as one of 'sincerity' on the part of contracting States in their commitment to the effective realization of human rights and constraining their own sovereignty to achieve this. Effectiveness as an overarching approach both in its practical and teleological versions, therefore, is better conceived as a holistic attempt to apply the VCLT in this domain of international law.

B. Effectiveness and the role of general international law in the interpretation of human rights treaties

If effectiveness animates the measure of text, context, and object and purpose in human rights treaty interpretation, it remains to ask how does effectiveness interact

---

[75] The ECtHR is the only treaty body that explicitly applies the margin of appreciation as a general principle to counterbalance effectiveness in some instances. See E Benvenisti, 'Margin Of Appreciation, Consensus, and Universal Standards' (1999) 31 NYU J Intl L & Poly 843, 844. For a confined use of the margin of appreciation in cases of nationality rights, see *Proposed Amendments to the Naturalization Provisions of the Constitution of Costa Rica* (Advisory Opinion) Inter-American Court of Human Rights Series A No 4 (19 January 1984) [62].

[76] In this respect, human rights courts are in a better position than human rights treaty monitoring bodies in giving special meaning to the texts of human rights treaties. The legally binding nature of their decisions gives additional effect to their interpretations.

with the additional requirement in Article 31(3) of the VCLT, requiring parties to take into account 'any relevant rules of international law applicable in the relations between the parties'? There is strong evidence that human rights treaty interpreters do this, locating their work as part of, and not in isolation from, general international law and other related treaties and instruments.[77] This is in line with a more general duty to attempt to reach coherence amongst different bodies of international law, even though this may not be possible in each concrete instance.[78]

Human rights interpreters interact with Article 31(3) in two directions.[79] First, Article 31(3) may lead to the accumulation of interpretation. Second, Article 31(3) may lead to conflicts in interpretation. In the case of accumulation, other international law obligations or treaties regulating similar subject matters serve as a means of reaching a coherent or overlapping interpretation of human rights treaty provisions by cumulatively confirming a particular interpretation. The comparative method employed by the Inter-American Court of Human Rights and the ECtHR explicitly point in this direction.[80] Both courts in their judgments cite other international treaty law obligations, ranging from UN human rights treaties[81] to statutes of international criminal courts.[82] This practice of paying attention to the general and regional human rights treaty context enables interpreters to solidify and harmonize the meanings of human rights treaty provisions.[83]

Second, interpreters interact with other human rights treaties and the general international legal context as a matter of actual or potential conflict. Effectiveness and coherence may pull in opposite directions in these cases. Conflict implies that the 'taking into account' language of Article 31(3) ultimately takes the form of resolving conflicts between a particular human rights treaty and relevant international law (including other human rights treaties). Three further specialized rules of interpretation have emerged in human rights treaty interpretive practice in this respect that warrant attention.

For starters, there is the self-contained autonomous meaning rule, which addresses the question of whether certain words raised in various legal contexts must

---

[77] Cf *Golder* (n 16) [29]; *Al-Adsani v United Kingdom* (2001) 34 EHRR 273 [55]; *Right to Information on Consular Assistance* (n 59) [113].

[78] Cf *Andrajeva v Latvia* (App no 55707/00) ECHR 18 February 2009 [75].

[79] For an elaboration of these two modes of interaction, see J Pauwelyn, *Conflict of Norms in Public International Law: How WTO Law Relates to Other Rules of International Law* (CUP, Cambridge 2003) 161–212.

[80] With respect to freedom of expression provisions, see eg 'The Last Temptation of Christ' Case (Olmedo-Bustos et al) v Chile Inter-American Court of Human Rights Series C No 73 (5 February 2001) [69] (citing *Sunday Times v United Kingdom* (App no 6538/74) (1979) 2 EHRR 245 [59]–[65]).

[81] *Soering* (n 35) [88] (citing CAT); *Opuz v Turkey* (App no 33401/02) ECHR 9 June 2009 [72]–[77] (citing CEDAW).

[82] *Case of Bámaca-Velasques v Guatemala* Inter-American Court of Human Rights Series C No 70 (25 November 2000) 17 (citing the Rome Statute of the International Criminal Court).

[83] A good example of this is the interpretation of the exhaustion of domestic remedy clauses across treaty contexts. All regional courts have confirmed that only those remedies that are 'effective' need to be exhausted. *Velasquez Rodriguez v Honduras* Inter-American Court of Human Rights Series C No 4 (29 July 1988) [63]–[64]; *Akdivar v Turkey* (App no 21893/93) ECHR 30 August 1996 [66]–[69].

always have the same meaning.[84] If the answer to this is negative, then human rights treaty interpreters have an argument for declaring some international law as not 'relevant' to the interpretation of a particular treaty. The interpretive difference in defining the concept of 'jurisdiction' clauses in human rights treaties and general international law is a good illustration of this. In general international law, jurisdiction points to the authority of the State to regulate its subjects *in principle*.[85] In contrast, in human rights treaty law, jurisdiction has been interpreted to mean 'effective control' over persons by the authorities of any State.[86] That is, even though a State may not have jurisdiction over a person in the general international law sense, it may nevertheless have jurisdiction over that person in the human rights treaty law sense if it can be proven that the State has 'effective' control over the exercise of a particular right of an individual.[87] This development in itself, however, does not modify the concept of jurisdiction in public international law. By introducing a different or 'specialized' conception of jurisdiction via an effectiveness approach, this sets out a particular pathway of interaction with Article 31(3).

Next, there is the priority of a particular human rights treaty provision over other rules of international law. This may have the consequence of declaring that another body of international law is not relevant to the human rights treaty interpretation context. The priority of human rights treaties or their individual provisions have been argued on two grounds. The first ground involves establishing that a human rights treaty provision is *jus cogens* and subsequently arguing that it takes priority because of its *jus cogens* qualification.[88] The second ground is to argue that human rights treaty obligations are more prominent than other treaty obligations because of the comparative prominence of the treaty's subject matter or the particular nature of the obligations attached to specific rights in the treaties. The 2006 case

---

[84] A similar interpretive principle exists in the context of the relationship between domestic law and human rights treaty law called the 'autonomous concepts doctrine'. This doctrine holds that treaty words have a self-contained, independent meaning if the word overlaps with the wording of domestic law. *Konig v Germany* (App no 6232/73) ECHR 28 June 1978 [88]–[89].

[85] V Lowe, 'Jurisdiction' in MD Evans (ed), *International Law* (2nd edn OUP, Oxford 2006) 335.

[86] Committee against Torture, 'Conclusions and Recommendations of the Committee Against Torture regarding United States of America' (25 July 2006) CAT/C/USA/CO/2 [14]–[15]; HRC, 'Concluding Observations of the Human Rights Committee regarding United States of America' (15 September 2006) CCPR/C/USA/CO/3 [10]. The Security Council, the UN General Assembly as well as treaty interpreting bodies and regional courts endorse this view. See UNSC Res 1265 (17 September 1999) UN Doc S/Res/1265 [4]; UNGA, 'Respect for human rights in armed conflicts' UNGA Res 3319 (XXIX) (14 December 1974); HRC, 'General Comment 31, The Nature of the Legal Obligation Imposed on States Parties to the Covenant' (29 March 2004) UN Doc A/59/40 [10]; *Legality of the Threat or Use of Nuclear Weapons* (Advisory Opinion) [1996] ICJ Rep 226 [10]–[18] ('*Nuclear Weapons*'); *Case Concerning Armed Activities on the Territory of the Congo (DRC v Uganda)* [2005] ICJ Rep 168, 185; *Sergio Euben Lopez Burgos v Uruguay*, Communication No R.12/52 (1981) UN Doc Supp No 40 A/36/40 [12]; *Loizidou* (n 55) [62].

[87] M Milanovic, 'From Compromise to Principle: Clarifying the Concept of State Jurisdiction in Human Rights Treaties' (2008) 8 Human Rts L Rev 411, 416. Some States challenge this specialized interpretation of jurisdiction. Cf eg Fourth Periodic Report of the United States of America to the UN Committee on Human Rights concerning the International Covenant on Civil and Political Rights (30 December 2011) at <http://www.state.gov/j/drl/rls/179781.htm> [504]–[505].

[88] Case T-315/01 *Kadi v Council and Commission* [2005] ECR II-3649 [226]; Case T-306/01 *Yusuf & Al Barakaat* [2005] ECR II-3533 [277]; HRC, General Comment 24 (n 37) [10].

of *Sawhoyamaxa Indigenous Community v Paraguay* of the Inter-American Court of Human Rights, which concerned a conflict between a Paraguayan bilateral investment treaty and the American Convention on Human Rights, is an example of the prominent subject matter argument.[89] The Court argued that the normative-multilateral nature of human rights treaties gives them priority over bilateral non-human rights law treaties even if those treaties post-date the human rights treaty in question, and thereby rule out the use of the later-in-time (*lex posterior*) maxim. The rationale for giving the human rights treaty priority was because a reciprocal bilateral obligation that a State agrees to undertake cannot override a non-reciprocal obligation that the State already has.[90] The decision of the Grand Chamber of the European Court of Justice in the cases of *Kadi and Al Barakaat* invokes the non-derogable nature of the right to fair trial for the EU as the central reason for its priority over UN law.[91] This suggests that interpreters may rank provisions of individual treaties, rather than the treaties themselves, as more prominent obligations.

There are important differences between arguments for *jus cogens* priority and priority based on the prominence of human rights treaties or individual provisions. Whilst the former is an absolute formulation, the latter is a relative ordering where the prominence of human rights treaties has to be pitted against the prominence of other treaty obligations.[92]

Finally, there is the rule of 'accommodation' of relevant international law in the interpretation of human rights treaties. Unlike the first two rules, this rule takes account of the relevant international law in interpreting human rights treaties when the relationship is characterized as one of conflict. The rule of accommodation is most relevant when there is a clash between human rights treaties and other treaties that are also non-reciprocal and have a prominent normative character. Two possible scenarios of accommodation may occur. In the first scenario, relevant international law fully displaces human rights treaty law because it is shown that a normatively prior duty exists in relevant international law and fulfilling the human rights law duties would require a State to be in violation of those duties (in which case the priority rule operates in the opposite direction). The most illustrative instance of this scenario is the interaction between international human rights law in conflict with UN Charter law (in particular chapter 7 of the UN Charter).[93] In a second scenario, some provisions of human rights treaties are interpreted in light of the relevant international law where that law is shown to be *lex specialis*. Conflicts between human rights treaty provisions with respect to the right to life and

---

[89] Inter-American Court of Human Rights Series C No 146 (29 March 2006).
[90] Ibid [140]–[141].
[91] Joined Cases C-402/05 P and C-415/05 P *Kadi and Al Barakaat International Foundation v Council and Commission* [Grand Chamber, 2008] ECR I-06531 [316].
[92] B Simma, 'Harmonising Investment Protection and International Human Rights: First Steps towards a Methodology' in C Binder and others (eds), *International Investment Law for the 21st Century, Essays in Honour of Christoph Schreuer* (OUP, Oxford 2009) 678.
[93] *Nuclear Weapons* (n 86) Dispositif [2c].

international humanitarian law (*jus in bello*) provisions on military necessity are examples of this.[94]

This discussion shows that taking into account relevant international law in the interpretive exercise is a complex task. It first requires filtering what constitutes relevant international law. If a body of law is declared relevant, it must be decided whether that international law modifies or confirms the interpretation of a human rights treaty carried out prior to taking into account such law. The practice shows that other international law can be (i) excluded, (ii) deemed to displace human rights treaty interpretation altogether, or (iii) included as *lex specialis*. Whilst the effectiveness principle remains intact in the first scenario, it is weighed against other interpretive principles in the latter two.

IV. The Interpretive Forum: Interpretation of Human Rights Treaties by Specialized or General International Bodies or Domestic Courts

It may be argued that effectiveness and coherency interact differently when the interpretive fora are different. That is, the way in which Article 31 operates is relative to the legal context. There is some merit to this view, but caution is also advised to not take the relativity of interpretive frameworks too far. Rather, the difference that the forum brings to interpretative strategies is better conceived as one of emphasis rather than one of kind.

Non-specialized international courts and institutions find themselves in a position to take into account human rights treaty law under different circumstances than specialized institutions. As discussed above, specialized human rights interpreters are motivated by identifying the most effective protection for the individual right holder in the light of the constraints of the wording, context, and taking into account any relevant international law. Generalists, however, would be motivated by identifying the full range of relevant international law and would exclusively focus on human rights treaty law only if the priority rule applies. For specialists in other fields, on the other hand, human rights treaty law may only be a candidate for relevant international law in interpreting their core domain, be it trade, environment, or international criminal law. Whilst there is a forceful case for specialist human rights interpreters to defer to the effective interpretation of human rights treaties, this would not necessarily be the case for non-specialised interpreters. There is emerging evidence, especially from the ICJ, however, that the effectiveness principle has permeated interpretation of human rights treaty law by non-specialists.[95] In the contentious case of the *DRC v Uganda*, for example, the

---

[94] N Prud'homme, 'Lex specialis: Oversimplifying a more Complex and Multifaceted Relationship' (2007) 40 Israel L Rev 355, 395.

[95] See for example, *Nuclear Weapons* (n 86) [25] accepting that the ICCPR continues to apply in time of war except in cases of lawful derogations. See also *Legal Consequences of the Construction of a Wall in the Occupied Palestinian Territory* (Advisory Opinion) [2004] ICJ Rep 106–13.

ICJ largely analysed the situation in Uganda through the lens of human rights treaty law in areas that were occupied by the Ugandan forces as well as in areas where there was no occupation, but civilians were nevertheless affected by the actions of Ugandan armed forces.[96] This analysis was possible because human rights law did not conflict with any prior duties that Uganda had under international law.

Finally, there is the question of whether interpretive principles developed by specialized bodies can have the same currency when received by domestic courts. Domestic courts are similar to specialized human rights treaty interpreters in the sense that their interpretive functions take place in the context of individual rights claims in most cases.[97] Unlike specialist or generalist international interpreters, however, domestic courts often pit the effectiveness principle against the principles of integrity, coherency, and stability of domestic law in the light of the domestic legal doctrine concerning the authority of international human rights case law in the domestic context. Whilst the transnationalist models of interpretation give primacy to the case law, nationalist models of interpretation are more sceptical of the direct authority of interpretive principles of international courts.[98] The case for the 'nationalist' model's self-contained interpretations of human rights treaties by domestic courts in light of the *domestic system's* object and purposes does not survive scrutiny under the VCLT. Any interpreter is actually under a duty to consider the *treaty's* object and the purpose. Furthermore, domestic interpretations of an international human rights treaty that significantly diverge from the interpretations of its final interpreter (such as a regional human rights court) are likely to raise questions about whether domestic courts enjoy the authority to offer autonomous interpretations of multilateral human rights treaties. Ultimately, however, whether the principles developed by regional courts and specialized bodies have direct effect and are legally binding on the domestic interpretation process depends on the status of such interpretations in domestic law.[99] It is nevertheless safe to argue that the effectiveness principle may at the very least have persuasive value in domestic courts.

Conclusion

This chapter surveyed the existing rules for human rights treaty interpretation. It has shown that human rights treaties do not have an exceptional regime of treaty interpretation. There are specific approaches to interpreting human rights treaties to the extent required by the interpretive task before the interpreter. In this respect, it is only natural that there are some special rules in each domain of international law. Importantly, special does not mean rules that are out of touch with general

---

[96] *Armed Activities on the Territory of the Congo* (n 86) 185.
[97] There are exceptions; eg Constitutional Courts with no right to individual petition.
[98] See Chapter 15, Part III, 379 *et seq.*   [99] Ibid.

international law. Special simply means the approaches mentioned herein are a necessity for the everyday business of interpretation.

This chapter has further shown that special rules of interpretation called for by human rights treaties have been crystallized under the overarching umbrella of effectiveness. Effectiveness is a general direction for making sense of the wording, context, and the object and purpose of human rights treaties. It is demanded by the circumstances of the human rights treaties themselves, which regulate the rights of individuals to which States have correlating duties to give effect. In other words, effectiveness is not a preferred principle by some. Rather, it flows from the relationship of the treaty's wording, context, and the object and purpose. This overarching principle has given rise to many more specific principles in the context of each treaty and its interpreting body, including mediating principles that show the limits of effectiveness. An important consequence of the employment of effectiveness has been to disregard original intent and formal protection of rights in favour of dynamic interpretation and practical protection of rights.

The chapter has attempted to avoid discussing interpretive conflicts that exist between different institutions over different rights provisions, as well as jurisdictional clauses. Instead, as a matter of a general argument, the aim has been to show that specialization is an inevitable consequence and that there are good reasons for why this has taken the effectiveness route in the case of human rights treaties. The last section turned its attention to the interaction of human rights treaties with general international law and other relevant instruments and treaties. This showed that effectiveness, non-reciprocity, and normative hierarchy are three key concepts that animate human rights treaties' interaction with other parts of international law.

What this overall discussion shows is that Article 31 of the VCLT is a flexible regime. The principle that it covers—that of crucible interpretation—is too abstract not to be applicable to human rights treaties. What is at stake in human rights treaty interpretation, as well as in other fields of international law, is precisely to work out how to give full effect to Article 31 in every-day applications. As this chapter has explained, this task cannot but be controversial.

Recommended Reading

M Craven, 'Legal Differentiation and the Concept of the Human Rights Treaty in International Law' (2000) 11 EJIL 489

JS Davidson, *The Inter-American Human Rights System* (Aldershot, Dartmouth 1996)

M Fitzmaurice, 'Dynamic (evolutive) interpretation of treaties' (2008) 21 Hague Ybk Intl L 101

M Fitzmaurice, 'Dynamic (evolutive) interpretation of treaties' (2009) 22 Hague Ybk Intl L 3

M Forowics, *The Reception of International Law in the European Court of Human Rights* (OUP, Oxford 2010)

R Higgins, 'Human Rights: Some Questions of Integrity' (1989) 52 Modern L Rev 1

M Kamminga and M Shenin (eds), *The Impact of Human Rights Law on General International Law* (OUP, Oxford 2009)

L Lijnzaad, *Reservations to UN Human Rights Treaties: Ratify and Ruin?* (Martinus Nijhoff, Dordrecht 1995)

L Lixinski, 'Treaty Interpretation by the Inter-American Court of Human Rights: Expansionism at the Service of the Unity of International Law' (2010) 21 EJIL 585

JG Merrills, *The Development of International Law by the European Court of Human Rights* (2nd edn MUP, Manchester 1993)

M Milanovic, 'From Compromise to Principle: Clarifying the Concept of State Jurisdiction in Human Rights Treaties' (2008) 8 Human Rts L Rev 411

A Mowbray, *The Development of Positive Obligations Under the European Convention on Human Rights by the European Court of Human Rights* (Hart Publishing, Oxford 2004)

A Orakhelashvili, 'Restrictive Interpretation of the Human Rights Treaties in the Recent Jurisprudence of the European Court of Human Rights' (2005) 14 EJIL 529

C Redgwell, 'Reservations to Treaties and Human Rights Committee General Comment No 24' (1997) 46 ICLQ 390

B Simma, 'International Human Rights and General International Law: A Comparative Analysis' (1993) *Collected Courses of the Academy of European Law*, vol IV(2), 163

J Tobin, 'Seeking to Persuade: A Constructive Approach to Human Rights Treaty Interpretation' (2010) 23 Harvard Human Rts J 1

C Trindade, 'Coexistence and Coordination of Mechanisms of Protection of Human Rights' (1987) 202 RcD 9

DF Vagts, 'Treaty Interpretation and the New Ways of Law Reading' (1993) 4 EJIL 499

SECTION V

AVOIDING OR EXITING TREATY COMMITMENTS

22

The Validity and Invalidity of Treaties

Jan Klabbers

Introduction

It may well be the case, as a seasoned international law practitioner once suggested, that the validity or invalidity of treaties is a topic of no practical significance whatsoever.[1] Few treaties have ever been declared invalid and, indeed, it is quite rare for States even to argue that a treaty they are parties to should be declared invalid.[2] Moreover, it is by no means clear who should declare a treaty invalid and whether, for instance, this could be done by a court in one of the States that are parties to the treaty. In short, validity is a topic shrouded in mystery and practically not terribly relevant. And yet, the 1969 Vienna Convention on the Law of Treaties (VCLT) would have had a gaping hole in its middle if it had not paid any attention to the validity or invalidity of treaties: no legal system can do without rules on the validity of legal instruments, be it legislation, contracts, or treaties.

This chapter aims systematically to discuss the rules on validity of treaties as laid down in the VCLT, while paying attention (if and when appropriate) to the corresponding position under the 1986 Vienna Convention[3] as well as the presence (or lack) of relevant State practice (Part III). Before doing so, it will address a few peculiarities about the function of validity that underlies the Vienna Convention(s) (Part II), and it will start with some general reflections on validity (Part I), inspired by the curious circumstance that each and every lawyer will have some intuitive understanding of what validity refers to, yet scholarly exposés on validity are few and far between.

---

[1] See A Aust, *Modern Treaty Law and Practice* (CUP, Cambridge 2000) 252 ('It has to be said . . . that the subject is not of the slightest importance in the day-to-day work of a foreign ministry'). In the second edition, the statement has been toned down a little. See A Aust, *Modern Treaty Law and Practice* (2nd edn CUP, Cambridge 2007) 312.

[2] While I would hesitate to make the absolute claim that no tribunal has ever found a treaty to be invalid, the fact is that I have been unable to find examples of such findings.

[3] Vienna Convention on the Law of Treaties between States and International Organizations or between International Organizations (adopted 21 March 1986, not yet in force) [1986] 25 ILM 543 ('1986 VCLT').

I. The Concept of Validity

Legal systems typically need rules to establish whether the norms prevailing in them are valid or invalid, and they need these for at least two reasons. A first reason is to enable the legal system to distinguish between law and non-law. After all, it cannot be the case that every utterance of normative import or intent will be seen as law: a formal criterion of legal validity serves to distinguish the legal from the moral, the social, or the courteous, and serves to distinguish the accepted from the merely desirable. Such a criterion may focus on the identity of the aspiring law-giver, or may focus on the law-making process itself. Thus, most international lawyers would probably maintain that the Pope cannot make law for the global society: he lacks the power to do so these days, even though a few centuries ago this was less clear. Whatever the Pope says may be authoritative, but it will not be regarded as international law. That is not to say that the Pope cannot make law at all, but merely that he cannot make valid international law. Likewise, treaties consented to by States tend to be regarded as law (or at least as sources of obligations[4]), even though other instruments accepted by States and their representatives—think of resolutions adopted at ministerial conferences or within international bodies—may not qualify as law.

A second reason why legal systems insist on rules on validity is to protect basic values of the system. Few domestic legal systems will recognize a contract to kill as a valid legal contract, simply because few domestic legal systems think murder is a great idea. Less obviously, many legal systems will insist that the signing of wills be witnessed by several people so as to establish that those wills are the result of an underlying intention rather than the result of coercion, and likewise insist on marriages being witnessed and performed by duly authorized individuals. Here then, the value to be protected is the reality of the consent of the author. And as the examples already suggest, both reasons for having validity rules—to distinguish law from non-law and to protect basic values—tend to shade into each other. Thus, formal thresholds ('a valid decision requires a 2/3 majority') typically exist to protect a minority, because protecting minorities against the tyranny of the majority can be seen as a value in its own right. Discussing validity then is by no means an exercise in fatuousness or eccentricity, much less even legalism; instead, validity 'deals with the practical problem of determining what rules are to be used in legal reasoning, a choice on which the freedom or the well-being of individuals or communities depends'.[5]

The statement that a rule or an instrument is valid, then, typically suggests that it is applicable within a certain community, and must be accepted as such by the members of that community. It does not necessarily follow that such a rule or

---

[4] On the distinction, see GG Fitzmaurice, 'Some Problems Regarding the Formal Sources of International Law' in FM van Asbeck et al (eds), *Symbolae Verzijl* (Martinus Nijhoff, The Hague 1958) 153–76.

[5] See G Sartor, 'Legal Validity as Doxastic Obligation' (2000) 19 Law and Philosophy 585, 611.

instrument is also binding. While, arguably, it used to be the case that there was a high correspondence between 'legally valid' and 'legally binding' rules and instruments (so much so that in Kelsen's days, the two concepts could still be treated as synonymous[6]), it is now quite plausible to suggest that documents devoid of legally binding force should nonetheless be tested for validity. Surely, a General Assembly resolution endorsing genocide should be held invalid regardless of its non-legal nature because it undermines a fundamental community value, in much the same way as a General Assembly resolution 'adopted' by only five member States will not be considered valid: it will be deemed to lack the required support.[7]

It bears repetition to say that validity is not the same as 'bindingness'; rather, it is to say that the binding nature of an instrument follows—or may follow—from its validity.[8] Consequently, the binding nature of an instrument can be affected by considerations of validity or invalidity, but also by other concerns. Thus, it may happen that a treaty never enters into force: it never becomes binding law, but not because of a defect relating to its validity. Or a treaty may be terminated, in which case it stops being valid and binding law but, again, its bindingness does not end because of a transgression of any of the grounds of validity.[9]

Following Kelsen, norms or instruments are valid along a number of different dimensions. Writing three quarters of a century ago, Kelsen distinguished two such dimensions, holding that a valid norm is always valid in relation to time and space: 'That a norm is valid will always mean that it is valid in some space or another and for some time or another...'[10] Later, in the specific context of international law, Kelsen added that the sphere of validity of an international legal norm also encompasses the personal and material spheres: whose behavior does the norm regulate, and which behavior does it regulate?[11] Importantly though, for Kelsen the first two spheres (time and place) pertained to the rule or instrument as such, whereas the personal and material spheres pertained to the human behaviour that the rule or instrument applied to: hence, the latter two have different objects, so to speak. In other words, following this model, the Genocide Convention is valid law for many States (place) since its entry into force in 1951 (time), telling States and other actors (persons) not to engage in genocide (material).

---

[6] In his *Principles of International Law*, Kelsen clearly thinks of validity and bindingness as one and the same when observing that the validity starts when the treaty enters into force and may be affected by, eg, dissolution of the treaty by mutual consent. See H Kelsen, *Principles of International Law* (Rinehard, New York 1952) 355–6. MacCormick is not entirely convinced that this was actually Kelsen's position; referring to Kelsen's *Pure Theory of Law*, he speaks of this being Kelsen's opinion 'or perhaps of his translators'. See N MacCormick, *Institutions of Law: An Essay in Legal Theory* (OUP, Oxford 2007) 160–1.

[7] See similarly IF Dekker, 'Making Sense of Accountability in International Institutional Law' (2005) 36 Netherlands Ybk Intl L 83–118.

[8] See MacCormick (n 6) 162–3.

[9] See similarly M Kohen, 'Article 42—Convention de 1969' in O Corten and P Klein (eds), *Les Conventions de Vienne sur le Droit des Traités: Commentaire Article par Article* (Bruylant, Brussels 2006) 1593, 1598–600.

[10] See H Kelsen, *Introduction to the Problems of Legal Theory* (Litschewski Paulson and Paulson (trs), Clarendon Press, Oxford 1992) (first published 1934) 12.

[11] See Kelsen, *Principles* (n 6) 93.

Much confusion concerning the idea of validity has stemmed from the circumstance that different approaches to law entertain different criteria of validity: positivists typically rely on procedural processes to determine validity, while naturalists emphasize axiological validity, and realists tend to think that a rule is valid only if it is actually respected. Still, as Giovanni Sartor has pointed out, for everyday purposes these distinctions need not detain any analysis. For everyday purposes, it suffices to proclaim that validity is doxastic in nature: what matters is that valid norms need to be accepted by their audiences, not why they must be so accepted.[12] That is not to say such grounds are irrelevant: they will, for example, come back in discussing whether instruments need be considered invalid in their entirety, or whether they are only partly invalid. The positivist position often boils down to stating that no severance is possible: adoption via the wrong procedure affects the entire instrument, not just a part of it. On the other hand, the naturalist and the realist may well be able to live with severance. Chances are, that a treaty contains many provisions which are just or which are respected, and only a single provision that is considered unjust, or that is ignored in practice.

The international legal order, unwritten and especially unsystematic as it mostly is, has rules on validity just like any legal order, but few of these are explicitly formulated for the purpose of establishing validity. International law is mostly concerned with facilitating agreement, and thus not 'big' on formalities, and this circumstance, as we will see, will affect the rules on validity considerably. Although seemingly international law is stricter when it comes to the identity of possible law-makers (not everyone is entitled to participate), even here the law seems to facilitate and follow political necessity.[13] The tension, in other words, is between formalism (with which validity rules are usually associated) and the pragmatics of political agreement. This is, to some extent, a false tension, but that does not render it less relevant, if only because it is often repeated. One of the reasons why this is a false dichotomy is that with respect to treaties, as discussed below, the main validity requirement resides in State consent: without consent, there will be no valid treaty. This is not to say that consent is necessarily the only validity criterion (it is not, as *jus cogens* considerations may also play a role), nor is it automatically to suggest that all instruments consented to are therefore treaties (although an argument can be made that consent creates a rebuttable presumption that a treaty has actually been concluded). What it does suggest though, is that the formalism often associated with validity criteria and the pragmatics of political agreement, when it comes to international law, tend to go hand in hand: if States reach political agreement, the most relevant validity requirement (for all practical purposes, that is) has been met.[14]

---

[12] See Sartor (n 5).

[13] It is, for example, rarely argued that liberation movements cannot conclude valid agreements because they are not among the generally accepted subjects of international law just yet. See in more detail J Klabbers, '(I Can't Get No) Recognition: Subjects Doctrine and the Emergence of Non-state Actors' in J Petman and J Klabbers (eds), *Nordic Cosmopolitanism: Essays in International Law for Martti Koskenniemi* (Martinus Nijhoff, Leiden 2003) 351–69.

[14] I explore this in greater detail in Chapter 3 of J Klabbers, A Peters, and G Ulfstein, *The Constitutionalization of International Law* (OUP, Oxford 2009).

International law's validity rules are not, however, limited to the role of consent in treaty-making. Notwithstanding the informality of the international legal order, with some deduction one can identify other rules of validity; for example the rules on decision-making within international organizations (IOs). It is clear that the UN General Assembly needs to be able to command a majority for most of its binding decisions on topics such as the UN budget; a decision endorsed by a mere minority will not be accepted as valid. Likewise, a binding decision by the Security Council will only be deemed valid if it commands a three-fifths majority and as long as this majority includes the concurring votes of the permanent members. While admittedly the meaning of 'concurring vote' has undergone some change since the Charter was concluded,[15] the basic principle still stands: a decision which is not supported by the concurring votes of the permanent members will not be considered valid.[16]

International courts and tribunals have not been overly verbose on validity in international law, perhaps because there is room for the argument that validity can practically only be enforceable in a highly institutionalized legal order comprising compulsory jurisdiction. Although it is, one would think, only open to courts or similar institutions to declare legal instruments to be invalid (a statement to that effect by, say, the President of the United States, or the Queen of the United Kingdom, will always run the risk of being considered self-serving), the international legal order is not quite sufficiently organized. Indeed, typically, decisions on validity (at least practically, if not necessarily conceptually) presuppose compulsory jurisdiction: where two States agree that a treaty concluded between them is invalid, such invalidity is difficult to disentangle from, eg, termination by common accord.[17] Moreover, it can be postulated that the efficacy of a system of rules on validity benefits from being embedded in a hierarchical and harmonized legal order: an instrument cannot be considered invalid in one corner of the legal system, yet be considered valid in a different location within that same legal system.[18] Here Kelsen's four dimensions of validity may prove illuminating: a treaty between Germany and France is valid law for those two States, but inapplicable (rather than invalid) elsewhere, and it would be inappropriate to proclaim it valid for Germany but invalid for France.

---

[15] See *Legal Consequences for States of the Continued Presence of South Africa in Namibia (South West Africa) Notwithstanding Security Council Resolution 297 (1970)* (Advisory Opinion) [1971] ICJ Rep 16 [22].

[16] Much the same applies to the rules on admission or expulsion of member States. See *Competence of the General Assembly for the Admission of a State to the United Nations* (Advisory Opinion) [1950] ICJ Rep 4 ('*UN Admissions* case').

[17] See already B Simma, 'Termination or Suspension of Treaties: Two Recent Austrian Cases' (1978) 21 German Ybk Intl L 74–96.

[18] The rationale is that a number of important procedural issues remain open unless there is some organized legal order within which validity issues are embedded, with one pressing example being the question whether a court should only look into validity if it is raised by one of the parties to a dispute, or whether it should do so *ex officio*. In *Oscar Chinn*, for example, the Permanent Court of International Justice (PCIJ) chose to stay close to the parties' arguments. See *The Oscar Chinn Case (UK v Belgium)* [1934] PCIJ Rep Series A/B No 63.

It is precisely this problem which has caused such an uproar in the wake of the decision of the Court of Justice of the EU in *Kadi*. The Court's decision to invalidate (in part) the EU Regulation implementing Security Council sanctions strongly suggests that there is a problem with the underlying Security Council resolution: if invalid in the EU, can these sanctions still plausibly be considered valid elsewhere? On the other hand, *Kadi* raises the question whether a domestic or regional legal order can substitute its own validity criteria (*in casu*: EU Regulations should conform to EU human rights standards, even when importing verbatim Security Council resolutions) for those of the more centralized legal order?[19]

Perhaps because of the above-mentioned conceptual and political issues, the International Court of Justice (ICJ) itself has not been very outspoken. On some occasions it has addressed the validity of decisions of IOs, but without being able or willing to produce a general theory on validity or invalidity. In *IMCO Maritime Safety Committee*, the ICJ held that a decision had been adopted in violation of IMCO's constituent document.[20] In *WHA*,[21] it found that the World Health Assembly lacked the power to ask the same ICJ for an advisory opinion (although it seemed to found its decision predominantly on the basis, not of the World Health Organization (WHO) Constitution, but on the place of the WHO within the UN family—a position that is not explicitly written down anywhere[22]). By contrast, in *Certain Expenses* it accepted that UN organs are presumed to act *intra vires* and are themselves to be the first arbiters of the legality of their own action.[23] And in *Namibia*, the ICJ had no problem accepting that the procedure for making valid decisions by the Security Council had changed through practice.[24] The one thing connecting these four decisions would be the proposition that the Court is reluctant to subject the activities of the leading political institutions of global governance to strict legal scrutiny (something also confirmed by its reluctance to engage with an argument that the Security Council had unwittingly contributed to the Bosnian genocide[25]), but that it is a bit quicker to do so when the activities of politically less important institutions (IMCO, WHO) are at stake. Yet even this highly abstract conclusion is possibly not airtight: in *Admissions II*, the ICJ accepted that the two main political organs—the General Assembly and the Security Council—are engaged in some kind of institutional balance.[26] This, in turn, would suggest that

---

[19] See Case C-402/05 P, *Kadi v Council and Commission* [2008] ECR I-6351.

[20] See *Constitution of the Maritime Safety Committee of the Inter-Governmental Maritime Consultative Organization* (Advisory Opinion) [1960] ICJ Rep 150, 171.

[21] See *Legality of the Use by a State of Nuclear Weapons in Armed Conflict* (Advisory Opinion) [1996] ICJ Rep 66.

[22] See J Klabbers, 'Global Governance at the ICJ: Re-reading the WHA Opinion' (2009) 13 Max Planck Ybk UN L 1–28.

[23] See *Certain Expenses of the United Nations (Article 17, Paragraph 2, of the Charter)* (Advisory Opinion) [1962] ICJ Rep 151, 168.

[24] See *South West Africa* case (n 15) [22].

[25] See *Case Concerning Application of the Convention on the Prevention and Punishment of the Crime of Genocide (Bosnia-Herzegovina v Yugoslavia (Serbia and Montenegro))* (Order) [1993] ICJ Rep 325.

[26] See generally *UN Admissions* case (n 16).

even their freedom is hemmed in—at least in situations where they threaten to step on each other's toes.

Be that as it may, the ICJ has offered no consistent or coherent view on the validity of international institutional law, let alone international law more generally. And the ICJ is not alone: none of the other relevant international law actors have pronounced, let alone agreed, on the issue. As such, a general theory on (in)validity in international law remains to be formulated.

II. Validity and Treaties

The only explicit validity rules circulating in the international legal order are the rules on validity and invalidity of treaties, as laid down in Articles 46 through 53 of the VCLT. In essence, most of these (Articles 46 through 52) deal with defects in the consent of a State to be bound, underlining the point made above that consent is practically speaking the most relevant general validity requirement when it comes to treaties.[27] Such defects can have three broad sources: they can be based on improper procedure or authorization; they can be the result of something misleading; or they can be the result of coercion. In all cases, the underlying rationale is that the consent to be bound has been affected: but for the affecting circumstance, the State concerned would not (or would most likely not) have expressed its consent to be bound.[28] The one remaining article deals with the substance of a treaty: a treaty concluded in violation of a *jus cogens* norms is void. The emphasis on defects in State consent makes theoretical sense. Treaties are typically conceptualized as the result of a *consensus ad idem*; if so, a premium is placed on the reality of this *consensus*, and if the *consensus ad idem* is affected by fraud, coercion, or misrepresentation, it follows that there is not really a *consensus ad idem* and thus, in a meaningful way, no treaty. The required underlying political agreement[29] would be absent.

In light of earlier work on validity, it is useful to note that the VCLT's drafters no longer regarded treaty conflicts as sources of invalidity. Amongst pre-Vienna Convention legal thought, the connection of treaty conflict to invalidity had been par for the course. In one of the few monographs on the topic, Vitta devoted quite a bit of attention to conflicts with other treaties and with existing norms of

[27] There are implicit rules hidden in the definition of treaties in the 1969 and 1986 VCLT, to the effect that, for purposes of those conventions, treaties can only be concluded by States or IOs. This is without prejudice though to the possibility of other actors concluding agreements which, under customary international law, could qualify as treaties.

[28] The International Law Commission (ILC), in the commentary accompanying its final draft articles, made this point explicitly when discussing fraud. Fraud would potentially nullify a treaty, if it would have induced a State 'to give a consent to a treaty which it would not otherwise have given'. See [1966] YBILC, vol II, 177, 245.

[29] Note that the term 'political agreement' here is not used as an alternative to 'legal agreement', but rather as the first step towards the latter: States reach agreement in the body politic which, if it passes the validity test, automatically becomes a legal agreement. For further detail, see J Klabbers, *The Concept of Treaty in International Law* (Kluwer Law International, The Hague 1996).

customary international law as potential sources of invalidity,[30] as did McNair in his *magnum opus*.[31] Indeed, the International Law Commission's (ILC's) second Special Rapporteur on the law of treaties, Hersch Lauterpacht, started his discussion of treaty conflict with a draft article to the effect that treaties which would conflict with other treaties would be invalid, only to realize quickly that such a rule would be too rigid to be of much use: subsequent paragraphs of the same draft article allowed for some broadly worded exceptions.[32]

Still, decent policy arguments could be invoked for viewing treaty conflict as an issue of validity.[33] Two arguments in particular come to mind. First, there is the argument that allowing for treaty conflicts would amount to stimulating the breach of existing treaties: nullity here would be conceptualized as the sanction for such a breach. Second, this would apply with special force if the earlier treaty has a legislative or even constitutional character, as judges Van Eysinga and Schücking found in the 1934 *Oscar Chinn* case.[34] To their mind, a bilateral Anglo–Belgian agreement on trade and transport in the Congo ran foul of an earlier multilateral treaty establishing the general legal framework for the treatment of Africa by its European colonizers, and thus should have been held invalid.[35]

The ILC's first Special Rapporteur on the law of treaties, JL Brierly, never got around to discussing validity and quickly resigned, having confessed to being less than fully interested in codification generally.[36] His three successors (Lauterpacht, Fitzmaurice, and Waldock), however, all devoted considerable attention to issues of validity, and it is fair to say that at least in quantitative terms, the topic of validity ranks among the more central ones of the VCLT.[37] The Convention not only contains eight articles detailing grounds of invalidity, but also four articles devoted (in part) to setting up the role of invalidity provisions,[38] and another four devoted (again, in part) to elements of procedure.[39] In addition, the VCLT has three articles spelling out the consequences of invalidity.[40] Hence, almost a quarter of the VCLT's eighty-five articles have to do, in one way or another, with the invalidity of treaties. This contrasts sharply to other branches of the law of treaties, which (regardless of their pivotal importance and intellectual complexities) have been

---

[30] See E Vitta, *La validité des traités internationaux* (Brill, Leiden 1940) 172–215.

[31] See A McNair, *The Law of Treaties* (Clarendon Press, Oxford 1961) 213–36.

[32] For brief discussion, see J Klabbers, 'Beyond the Vienna Convention: Conflicting Treaty Provisions' in E Cannizzaro (ed), *The Law of Treaties beyond the Vienna Convention* (OUP, Oxford 2011) 192–205.

[33] For a more general discussion, see Chapter 18 ('Treaty Conflicts and Normative Fragmentation').

[34] See *Oscar Chinn* (n 18) (dissenting opinions of Judges van Eysinga and Schüking).

[35] It is possibly a useful reminder of the contextuality of most things that many might nowadays agree that the earlier agreement—the General Act of the Berlin Conference—itself would be invalid due to its conflict with a *jus cogens* norm.

[36] See JL Brierly, 'The Codification of International Law' (1948) 47 Michigan L Rev 2–10.

[37] For brief and convenient discussions on an article-by-article basis, see ME Villiger, *Commentary on the 1969 Vienna Convention on the Law of Treaties* (Martinus Nijhoff, Leiden 2009).

[38] VCLT Arts 42–5.

[39] VCLT Arts 65–8.

[40] For ease of reference, I include Art 64 (on the later emergence of a new *jus cogens* norm). The other two are VCLT Arts 69 and 71.

dealt with in far fewer provisions. For example, the regime on reservations, arguably the central topic of the VCLT, is addressed in five articles (six, if the definition of Article 2, paragraph 1(d) is included).

One of the hallmarks of the VCLT's approach, and a clear indication that the intention was to create something of a 'self-contained regime', ie a regime that tolerates no interference from elsewhere,[41] is the circumstance that Article 42(1) stipulates that the validity of a treaty 'may be impeached only through the application of the present Convention'. In other words: the list of grounds of invalidity is meant to be exhaustive, no reasons for invalidating a treaty can be put forward which cannot be found in the Vienna Convention. Still, the ILC did not pay too much attention to this in its commentary, mostly justifying the closed nature of its listing of grounds of invalidity by reference to the need for 'stability of treaties'. Validity was supposed to be the normal state of affairs, 'which may be set aside only on the grounds and under the conditions provided for' according to the draft of what would become Article 42.[42]

Yet, closing off the Convention's validity regime is awkward, for a variety of reasons. First, it may be difficult to squeeze some past examples into the VCLT framework. For instance, it is sometimes claimed that the infamous Munich agreement, by which Hitler's Germany gained control over Czechoslovakia, should be declared invalid, but on which exact ground remains an open question. Reuter, in his classic textbook, treats 'Munich' as an example of fraud,[43] but this, somehow, is less than fully convincing. Hitler's intentions, one might surmise, were perfectly clear: those intentions were nasty, no doubt, but not necessarily fraudulent.

Second, and related, there is the jurisprudential staple that rules are by their very nature both over-inclusive and under-inclusive.[44] In particular, the latter is relevant here, as it suggests that occasions may arise where something happens that would warrant the treaty to be invalidated, yet that would be impossible to fit plausibly into the VCLT categories.[45] One example may be bribery of a negotiator that is not attributable to a State, yet without which the treaty would not have been concluded. As a matter of legal systematics, so the Commission must have thought, such a case has no place in the law of treaties, dealing as it does with relations between States. Yet surely, as a practical matter, bribery by the private sector may be the more obvious concern. Following the letter of the Vienna Convention and its

---

[41] See eg M Koskenniemi, *Fragmentation of International Law: Difficulties Arising from the Diversification and Expansion of International Law. Report of the Study Group of the International Law Commission* (Erik Castrén Institute, Helsinki 2007) [124].

[42] See [1966] YBILC, vol II, 236.

[43] See P Reuter, *Introduction au droit des traités*, Cahier (ed) (3rd edn Presses Universitaires de France, Geneva 1995) 156–7 and accompanying endnote.

[44] The best treatment, quite possibly, is F Schauer, *Playing by the Rules: A Philosophical Examination of Rule-based Decision-making in Law and in Life* (Clarendon Press, Oxford 1991).

[45] The ILC, it seems, was well aware of the issue, given the care with which it made clear that obsolescence and desuetude would be instances of termination by common agreement, and thus covered by the parallel idea relating to treaty termination.

legislative history,[46] it would be very difficult to invalidate a treaty on grounds of private sector bribery of a State representative.[47]

Third, it was probably a bit naïve at any rate to suppose that political practice could be closed off by means of a rigid, if reluctant, *Grundnorm*, as I have called it elsewhere (with a wink and a nod to Kelsen).[48] Post-Vienna Convention practice suggests that authors and even courts do not hesitate to bring within the VCLT's reach all sorts of activities that the VCLT itself excluded from its scope. In particular, arguments have been made to the effect that the classic maxim *rebus sic stantibus* (which, to be sure, is not a ground of invalidity but justifies unilateral treaty termination or suspension) covers occurrences such as a succession of States[49] and even the outbreak of armed conflict.[50] But, the VCLT explicitly excludes these from its own scope and thus, logically, also from the scope of the *rebus sic stantibus* maxim.[51] Even the circumstance that an entire convention has been devoted to State succession in respect of treaties (or that, later, the effect of armed conflict on treaties has come to be regarded as a topic fit for separate study and perhaps codification by the ILC) has not deterred such arguments.[52] In this light, it was not too difficult to predict that, all good intentions on the part of the ILC notwithstanding, the closing off of the invalidity and termination regimes would not meet with great success.

Those intentions of an exhaustive list were furthermore dealt something of a blow when the same ILC saw fit, in the same Vienna Convention, to include a rule that goes a long way towards establishing the opposite of what Article 42 aims to achieve. Whereas Article 42 aims to turn the law of treaties into a self-contained regime, Article 31(3)(c), containing the so-called principle of systemic integration,[53] aims to do the opposite.[54] It opens the door for all possible arguments in interpreting treaties. This too was, no doubt, defensible in its own right, if only to underline that international law is something of a unitary legal order, but the

---

[46] The ILC explicitly explained that in order to nullify a treaty, 'the corrupt acts must be shown to be directly or indirectly imputable to the other negotiating State'. See [1966] YBILC, vol II, 245.

[47] Incidentally, 'buying' votes or trading votes at law-making conferences may come close, but at least the latter is often seen as fairly innocent. See eg O Eldar, 'Vote-trading in International Institutions' (2008) 19 EJIL 3–41.

[48] See J Klabbers, 'Reluctant *Grundnormen*: Articles 31(3)(c) and 42 of the Vienna Convention on the Law of Treaties and the Fragmentation of International Law' in M Craven, M Fitzmaurice, and M Vogiatzi (eds), *Time, History and International Law* (Martinus Nijhoff, Leiden 2007) 141–61.

[49] See eg S Oeter, 'State Succession and the Struggle over Equity' (1995) 38 German Ybk Intl L 73–102.

[50] See Case C-162/96 *Racke v Hauptzollamt Mainz* [1998] ECR I-3655.

[51] VCLT Art 73 provides: 'The provisions of the present Convention shall not prejudge any question that may arise in regard to a treaty from a succession of States or from the international responsibility of a State or from the outbreak of hostilities between States.'

[52] This refers to the 1978 Vienna Convention on Succession of States in Respect of Treaties (concluded 23 August 1978, entered into force 6 November 1996) 1946 UNTS 3, and to the ILC's ongoing study of the effect of armed conflict on treaties, carried out by Ian Brownlie and, since 2009, Lucius Caflisch.

[53] See generally C MacLachlan, 'The Principle of Systemic Integration and Article 31(3)(c) of the Vienna Convention' (2005) 54 ICLQ 279–32; M Koskenniemi (n 41).

[54] VCLT Art 31(3)(c) holds that in the interpretation of treaties, due account shall be taken of 'any relevant rules of international law applicable in the relations between the parties'.

combination of the two was always likely to be problematic.[55] As things stand, it is unlikely that Article 42 either reflected customary international law in 1969 or has since crystallized into customary international law, if only because, as a provision, it is geared to the internal workings of the VCLT itself, and can have no meaningful existence outside the scope of the Convention. That does not mean, however, that no additional grounds of invalidity can be found, and as noted, a case has been made for conflicting treaties to result in invalidity. While this is no longer done (partly, no doubt, because inapplicability of conflicting provisions is so much less dramatic than invalidity, and thus politically far more opportune), it cannot be excluded that other grounds of invalidity may arise or, alternatively, that considerations which are now seen to lead to termination, such as the fundamental change of circumstances, may come to be treated as grounds of invalidity.

III. The Grounds of Invalidity

As noted, the Vienna Convention's provisions on validity largely focus on defects in the consent of treaties. This is most readily explained by the circumstance that the VCLT focuses on treaties as instruments, rather than as obligations.[56] Treaties, in other words, are conceptualized not in terms of their substance, but as agreements (or, more likely perhaps, disagreements[57]) reached by States and reduced to writing: form takes precedence over substance. This orientation automatically turns the prism towards the formal characteristics of treaties, ranging from means of expressing consent to be bound to means for limiting consent, and including defects in the consent. There are, in the Convention, only two exceptions to this: one is the reference to *jus cogens* as a validity criterion, the other is formed by the repeated references to the 'object and purpose' of treaties.[58] That is not to say that international law is 'big' on formalities after all, but it is to say that considerations of form help the system to channel substance and, what is more, this emphasis on form in the VCLT is required in particular so as not to interfere with substance. Simply put, international law is (barring *jus cogens* considerations) simply not interested in what States agree, but only in that they reach agreement.

A. Constitutional concerns

The first two grounds of invalidity as mentioned in the VCLT and the 1986 VCLT relate to the propriety of a State's consent in light of its own constitutional order.

---

[55] See further Klabbers, Reluctant *Grundnormen* (n 48).

[56] See generally S Rosenne, 'Bilateralism and Community Interest in the Codified Law of Treaties', in W Friedmann, L Henkin, and O Lissitzyn (eds), *Transnational Law in a Changing Society: Essays in Honor of Philip C. Jessup* (Columbia University Press, New York 1972) 202–27.

[57] In Philip Allott's lovely phrase, treaties are a 'disagreement reduced to writing'. See P Allott, 'The Concept of International Law' (1999) 10 EJIL 31, 43.

[58] On the latter, see J Klabbers, 'Some Problems regarding the Object and Purpose of Treaties' (1997) 8 Finnish Ybk Intl L 138–60.

Article 46 does so explicitly under reference to a State's treaty-making rules,[59] while Article 47, in less spectacular fashion, deals with a representative's authority to express consent to be bound.[60] The ILC, in its commentary, made abundantly clear that in both cases the provisions represented an *ultimum remedium*. Given the expectation that governments should know what they are doing and that they have all sorts of possibilities to intervene between signing a treaty and its eventual entry into force,[61] Articles 46 and 47 should not be invoked too lightly.[62] This is reflected in their wording which, in both cases, is cast in negative form: the grounds should not be invoked, unless there is a very good reason to do so.

Article 46, as noted, addresses a violation of domestic treaty-making provisions, providing that a State may not invoke a violation thereof unless the violation concerned a rule of fundamental importance and was manifest. The initial ILC draft had clearly been considered inadequate, as it never defined what 'manifest' meant, and made no distinction between fundamental and less fundamental domestic provisions. Consequently, both elements were added at the Vienna Conference, partly on the basis of an amendment proposed by the United Kingdom.[63]

The requirement that the domestic rule at issue must be a rule of fundamental importance is sometimes taken to mean that only violations of constitutional provisions can qualify under Article 46,[64] but this, surely, is untenable. For one thing, it would be difficult to pinpoint with any precision which rules in the United Kingdom, in the absence of a single written constitutional document, qualify as 'constitutional'. More importantly though, it would amount to ordering States what to put in their constitutions: there are States where the constitutions remain

---

[59] VCLT Art 46 provides, in relevant part, that a State 'may not invoke the fact that its consent to be bound by a treaty has been expressed in violation of its internal law regarding competence to conclude treaties as invalidating its consent unless that violation was manifest and concerned a rule of its internal law of fundamental importance'.

[60] VCLT Art 47 provides: 'If the authority of a representative to express the consent of a State to be bound by a particular treaty has been made subject to a specific restriction, his omission to observe that restriction may not be invoked as invalidating the consent expressed by him unless the restriction was notified to the other negotiating States prior to his expressing such consent.'

[61] Even in respect of treaties in simplified form, a government has 'the necessary means of controlling the acts of its representative and of giving effect to any constitutional requirements'. See [1966] YBILC, vol II, 242.

[62] Additionally, the ICJ hinted that acquiescence may play a role here as well: in a boundary dispute between Cameroon and Nigeria, it noted that Nigeria only invoked invalidity a few years after the agreement had been concluded, and had even failed to do so when the treaty was amended. See *Land and Maritime Boundary between Cameroon and Nigeria (Cameroon v Nigeria; Equatorial Guinea Intervening)* [2002] ICJ Rep [267].

[63] The definition of 'manifest' was proposed by the United Kingdom; the limitation to rules of fundamental importance seems to have been added by the Drafting Committee, in the spirit of an adopted but differently worded amendment proposed by Peru and Ukraine. See UN Conference on the Law of Treaties, Official Records: Documents of the Conference (1969) UN Doc A/CONF/39/11/Add.2, 165–6.

[64] See SE Nahlik, 'The Grounds of Validity and Termination of Treaties' (1971) 65 AJIL 736–56.

silent on the precise treaty-making procedure to be followed and where, instead, the matter is organized in generic legislation.[65]

Still, it is clear that elements of domestic procedure laid down in some inter-ministerial circular or internal memorandum will not qualify. The least one can do is expect governments, if they want their treaty-making provisions to be taken seriously, to take them seriously enough themselves to be given some recognizable and cognizable legal form. This also follows from the requirement that a violation must be 'manifest': this is defined by Article 46(2) of the VCLT as 'objectively evident to any State conducting itself in the matter in accordance with normal practice and in good faith'. It will normally be next to impossible for a treaty partner to know the contents of a circular or aide-memoire in force in the other State. Indeed, it is no coincidence that the one time the ICJ addressed Article 46, the claim faltered precisely on this ground. Cameroon, so the Court stipulated, could not have known the details of Nigeria's treaty-making provisions when Nigeria invoked Article 46 to get a boundary agreement declared invalid. The Court drily suggested that limitations on a Head of State's treaty-making capacity could not be relied upon 'unless at least properly publicized', and even more drily remarked that 'there is no general legal obligation for States to keep themselves informed of legislative and constitutional developments in other States which are or may become important for the international relations of these States'.[66]

It is perhaps no surprise that the arena for making 'Article 46 arguments' is the domestic political arena rather than its international counterpart. It turns out that the Article is sometimes invoked as a domestic politico-legal argument by domestic forces opposed to a particular treaty. Thus, the Article 46 argument was made by members of the US Senate in objection to the conclusion of the Panama Treaty in 1977.[67] Still, such appeals are bound to remain unsuccessful and, in the curious way of some law, self-defeating: a veritable Catch-22. The very invocation of Article 46 domestically would seem to suggest that there is some uncertainty as to the treaty-making procedure to be used; and if that is the case, then a violation can hardly ever qualify as 'manifest'.

The 1986 VCLT, although not in force, adds that the validity of IO treaties can possibly be affected by the rules of the organization but, again, in very limited circumstances. The Court of Justice of the EU (CJEU) seems to have relied to some

---

[65] An example is the Netherlands, where treaty-making is governed by a State Act. For a general overview in Dutch, see EW Vierdag, *Het Nederlandse Verdragenrecht* (Tjeenk Willink, Zwolle 1995); for a brief discussion in English, see J Klabbers, 'The New Dutch Law on the Approval of Treaties' (1995) 44 ICLQ 629–43.

[66] See *Land and Maritime Boundary between Cameroon and Nigeria* (n 62) [265], [266] respectively. In a similar vein, the arbitral panel in *Guinea-Bissau v Senegal* reached the conclusion that a 1960 boundary agreement concluded between colonizers France and Portugal had been validly concluded because France was entitled, in good faith, to expect that the treaty was valid despite not being submitted to Portugal's Parliament. Note though that the tribunal explicitly did not base itself on VCLT Art 46 which, in 1960, did not yet exist as such. See *Case Concerning the Arbitral Award of 31 July 1989 (Guinea-Bissau v Senegal)* 83 ILR 1 [54], [59].

[67] See generally T Meron, 'Article 46 of the Vienna Convention on the Law of Treaties (*Ultra Vires* Treaties)' (1979) 50 BYBIL 175–99.

extent on this provision when suggesting in the case *France v Commission* that an agreement concluded by the European Commission (instead of the EU—or, at the time the European Community—as such) would nonetheless be seen as binding upon the EU. In doing so, the Court rejected the Commission's claim that it had merely concluded an administrative agreement, and seemed to suggest that even if internally ultra vires, the agreement would still produce legal effects under international law.[68] Admittedly, the Court did not specifically refer to Article 46 or its counterpart in customary international law, but it seems likely that its opinion was informed by Article 46, as something of a background consideration. Indeed, the Court must have realized that an appeal to internal EU rules as grounds for invalidity would not be likely to impress the Commission's treaty partner too much.[69]

Whether Article 46 qualifies as customary international law would seem debatable. There is little practice, after all, and while the rule is sometimes invoked, it is rarely honoured. But this perhaps points to a more general theoretical problem: the rules making up the law of treaties are not quite comparable to 'regular' rules of behaviour. Whereas it makes sense to discuss, say, diplomatic relations in terms of customary law, the law of treaties is largely residual in nature, and facilitates the creation and maintenance of legal relations between States. It does not, however, consist of clear injunctions or prohibitions. Hence, it may not be all that useful to discuss the law of treaties in terms of customary international law to begin with. That said, a provision such as Article 46 makes eminent sense, but does so perhaps more as a logical necessity than as the crystallization of many instances of State practice.[70]

More generally, in light of the wide variety of possible ways to express consent, which may include opting-in or opting-out procedures, it becomes even more difficult than before to get a sense of each other's treaty-making provisions and whether these have actually been respected. Much the same applies to domestic procedures, where phenomena such as tacit approval by parliaments may be difficult to distinguish, from the outside, from situations where parliaments are not consulted or their prerogatives circumvented. All this conspires to make successful invocation of Article 46 less, rather than more, likely.

B. Error, fraud, corruption

Article 48 addresses the issue of errors in the formation of treaties, and specifically excludes linguistic errors from its scope: these can be rectified in accordance with

---

[68] See Case C-327/91 *France v Commission* [1994] ECR I-3641. Bothe reaches a similar conclusion: see M Bothe, 'Article 46—Convention de 1986', in *Les Conventions de Vienne* (n 9) 1719, 1721.

[69] As a technical matter, the EU is neither bound by the 1969 nor the 1986 VCLT. Still, the CJEU (as well as the General Court, previously known as the Court of First Instance) has on various occasions applied the law of treaties, typically by invoking the customary status of the rule concerned. See generally J Klabbers, 'Re-Inventing the Law of Treaties: The Contribution of the EC Courts' (1999) 30 Netherlands Ybk Intl L 45–74.

[70] What I have in mind here is an argument comparable to Fitzmaurice's claim that *pacta sunt servanda* is best seen as a kind of natural rule, natural in the sense that it would be difficult to imagine a legal order without such a rule. See Fitzmaurice (n 4).

Article 79.[71] If linguistic errors do not, as such, affect a treaty's validity, then the most common errors will be geographical representations. However, as these typically illustrate graphically what is also expressed in words and in terms of geographical coordinates, maps too are unlikely to be declared invalid. That leaves, for all practical purposes, a fairly empty category: the error may only be invoked if it 'relates to a fact or situation which was assumed' to exist at the time of conclusion, and if it formed 'an essential basis' of a State's consent to be bound. Indeed, Article 48 was largely drawn from the ICJ's reasoning in the *Temple* case, which declined to find that an error in a map invalidated a border treaty, since errors to which a State has itself contributed cannot be invoked by that same State, if the State knew of the error, or if it was 'put . . . on notice of a possible error'.[72]

In this light, it is perhaps no coincidence that one of the few examples ever mentioned is a hypothetical, launched by the US representative to the 1968 Vienna Conference, Richard Kearney. Kearney, worried about an earlier draft which suggested that the error could only be invoked if it was literally part of the treaty, provided the example of a treaty for the sharing of hydroelectric power. Such a treaty, he opined, might be based on a mistaken calculation of the capacity of turbines, and thus give rise to all sorts of mistaken figures.[73] By the same token, one might consider an agreement on fisheries, based on assumptions regarding the whereabouts of the fish stock, to be invalidated on ground of error should those assumptions prove wrong.

Kearney's main concern with respect to his turbine example was that the underlying calculation would not necessarily itself be part of the treaty, and that thus a requirement that the error be 'in the treaty' might be too strict. The US tabled a formal amendment to delete the words 'in a treaty', but withdrew it upon the explanation of Special Rapporteur Sir Humphrey Waldock that the reference was meant so as not to broaden the scope by allowing States to refer to all possible sorts of facts so as to invalidate a treaty. Creating a nexus to the treaty itself was considered necessary and, apparently, this reply persuaded the US representative.[74]

Generally, errors are not lightly to be presumed. A political miscalculation by a statesman can hardly qualify. Accordingly, the claim that Norway's Foreign Minister Ihlén did not realize the consequences of what he was doing when he promised not to contest Denmark's sovereignty over Eastern Greenland was rightly dismissed by the Permanent Court of International Justice (PCIJ).[75] After all, allowing such a claim to serve as a ground of invalidity would open Pandora's Box: it is part of the

---

[71] VCLT Art 48 provides in relevant part that a State may invoke an error in a treaty to invalidate consent 'if the error relates to a fact or situation which was assumed by that State to exist at the time when the treaty was concluded and formed an essential basis of its consent to be bound by the treaty'.

[72] See *Case concerning the Temple at Preah Vihear (Cambodia v Thailand)* (Merits) [1962] ICJ Rep 6 [26].

[73] See UN Conference on the Law of Treaties, Summary Records of the First Session (26 March–24 May 1968) UN Doc A/CONF/39/11, 249 ('Vienna Conference, First Session').

[74] See ibid 254.

[75] See *Legal Status of Eastern Greenland* [1933] PCIJ Rep Series A/B No 53.

art of statesmanship that one can (or should) make a reasonable assessment of the consequences of political action.

Sometimes errors may be the result of deliberate misrepresentations, or fraud. Fraud is dealt with in Article 49 and, again, the practical utility would seem limited.[76] As noted, Hitler's conduct at Munich is sometimes treated as fraudulent, but this has neither resulted in the formal invalidity of the Munich agreement nor has it been established that his conduct was, in fact, fraudulent. More generally, it would seem that there are no recorded instances of fraud,[77] although it cannot be excluded that this owes something to possible embarrassment on the part of States having been defrauded. The ILC, in the commentary to its 1966 draft articles, defined fraud as including 'any false statement, misrepresentation or other deceitful proceedings by which a State is induced to give a consent to a treaty which it would not otherwise have given'.[78] This then helps distinguish fraud from error: fraud is by definition deceitful, whereas errors may also be the result of an honest mistake.

If fraud needs to be distinguished from error, it also needs to be distinguished from corruption of a State's representative, which is addressed in Article 50.[79] Tellingly perhaps, both (draft) articles were discussed together during the 1968 Vienna Conference, and several possible examples were listed which could fall within either category—or both. Courtesies, small gifts, and honorary decorations would not be unusual in diplomatic practice, but would hardly amount to fraud or corruption, so the *communis opinio* held. As a result, the entire discussion of fraud and corruption got mired into discussion of either what the two terms mean in various domestic legal systems, or whether the consequence of their presence should be relative or absolute invalidity of the treaty concerned. And as if that discussion was not unstructured enough, the representative of the Holy See (French law professor René-Jean Dupuy) felt the need to introduce the desirability of *jus cogens* at this juncture, blissfully oblivious as to whether or not this was the relevant moment for discussing *jus cogens*.[80] In all, the preparatory works on both Articles 49 and 50 therewith ooze a rarefied atmosphere, akin to people desperately trying to remember why, on the hottest day during an extremely warm summer, they brought their winter coats with them. Moreover, there is the risk, elegantly formulated by the UK representative, Sir Ian Sinclair, that where practice is very rare, trying to regulate it may be counterproductive. As Sir Ian put it, aiming to include fraud as a ground for invalidity 'might encourage States to invoke grounds of fraud more frequently'.[81]

---

[76] VCLT Art 49 reads: 'If a State has been induced to conclude a treaty by the fraudulent conduct of another negotiating State, the State may invoke the fraud as invalidating its consent to be bound by the treaty.'

[77] See Aust, 2nd edn (n 1) 316.

[78] See [1966] YBILC, vol II, 245.

[79] VCLT Art 50 holds: 'If the expression of a State's consent to be bound by a treaty has been procured through the corruption of its representative directly or indirectly by another negotiating State, the State may invoke such corruption as invalidating its consent to be bound by the treaty.'

[80] See Vienna Conference, First Session (n 73) 258–9.

[81] Ibid 261.

As with Article 46, it is difficult to maintain that the provisions on error, fraud, and corruption have crystallized into customary international law. Useful as such provisions no doubt are, practice would simply seem to be too scarce to meaningfully speak of customary international law. Again, the better view may be that such provisions need a place in any legal order for the simple reason that one cannot do business on the basis of error, fraud, or corruption. Doing business, whether between individuals or States, needs to be based, to some extent at least, on mutual trust, so it makes sense to have rules protecting this minimum amount of trust.

C. Coercion

Politically, the more relevant concerns relate to coercion of States and their representatives, and these are dealt with in two separate articles (Articles 52 and 51, respectively). In both cases, the result will be absolute nullity. Originally, the big political issue was the discussion of how exactly to define coercion: would it cover only military coercion, or also pressure by other means, such as economic or political pressure? In this light, Article 51 is the relatively simpler of the two, dealing with coercion against a State's representatives.[82] What the Commission had in mind, it seems, was physical violence: it referred to 'third-degree methods of pressure' being employed against Czechoslovakia's President and Foreign Minister by Nazi-Germany, aspiring to create a German protectorate over Moravia and Bohemia.[83] In addition to physical violence though, the ILC also memorably remarked that a threat to ruin a diplomat's career 'by exposing a private indiscretion' could qualify as coercion.[84]

Note that Article 51 is drafted in a peculiar manner. Taken literally, the text suggests that what is invalidated in case of coercion of a representative is the act by which the State expresses consent to be bound, rather than the treaty itself. Taken literally, this may have serious consequences, as the treaty—in case of bilateral treaties—then remains unfinished (ie not concluded). The legal effects of a treaty not being concluded differ from those of an invalidated treaty, especially if the defect has been identified only after the treaty already entered into force.

Perhaps surprisingly, during the Vienna Conference the US tabled an amendment allowing for relative nullity. As Herbert Briggs, a member of the US delegation (as well as the US member of the ILC) argued, it might be the case that the State whose consent is procured by the coercion of its representative nonetheless finds that, on balance, the agreement is worth keeping. If so, absolute nullity appears to be too strong a sanction.[85] While some western States endorsed the US proposal, the US amendment and similar ones tabled by Australia and France were eventually rejected, and one can only speculate that their western origins did

---

[82] VCLT Art 51 states: 'The expression of a State's consent to be bound by a treaty which has been procured by the coercion of its representative through acts or threats directed against him shall be without any legal effect.'

[83] See [1966] YBILC, vol II, 246.

[84] Ibid.   [85] See Vienna Conference, First Session (n 73) 267.

them no favours: in all likelihood, rich nations are the ones expected to be most likely to engage in subtle forms of coercion.

Again, there is (fortunately perhaps) a dearth of actual cases, and it would for that reason be difficult to maintain that the coercion of representatives is part of customary international law. Again though, it cannot completely be excluded that the lack of cases owes something to the understandable reticence of those who have been coerced to make the coercion public, in particular when it concerns 'private indiscretions' being exposed.

Rather more explosive was the situation concerning coercion of the State itself, which eventually found provision in Article 52 of the VCLT.[86] The underlying idea is simple enough: States should not impose their wills on other States, and every treaty resulting from an attempt to do so suffers from a lack in the required *consensus ad idem*. Still, to give effect to such a position is not at all easy: Grotius already struggled with it. Curiously, when discussing promises, Grotius claimed that while a coerced promise is binding, the coercing agent should release the promisor of his obligation.[87] This would have the dual advantage of keeping the sanctity of promises intact, while securing the justice of preventing damage. More generally, he pointed out that fear has no place in the formation of contracts,[88] and that the conclusion of unequal treaties was not a particularly good idea.[89] Here too, problems of delimitation came up. Thus, Grotius noted that treaties between victors and vanquished may qualify as unequal treaties, but that such treaties could also be concluded 'between more powerful and less powerful peoples that have not even engaged in war with each other'.[90]

Indeed, it turned out that these two examples of unequal treaties (victory treaties, and treaties between States with huge power differences) would create systemic puzzles for international lawyers. The first is the phenomenon of the peace treaty which, almost by definition, is the result of coercion, and thus raises the issue of demarcating the just from the unjust use of coercion. The easy answer is to refer to the prohibition of the use of force contained in the UN Charter, and Article 52 of the VCLT duly takes this step: coercion is defined as the use of force 'in violation of the principles of international law embodied in the Charter of the United Nations'. While this may be easy to apply in some cases (think of the Iraqi invasion of Kuwait in 1990), difficulties may nonetheless occur. It might be difficult to identify which of the parties used force in violation of the Charter's principles, and which party used force in legitimate self-defense. Perhaps then the smarter cause is to forego the temptation of imposing an all too victorious peace treaty upon the vanquished— something Woodrow Wilson repeatedly advocated during the First World War when publicly announcing to be striving for a 'peace without victory'.[91] Even so, his attempt to secure a peace without victory after the First World War bore no

---

[86] VCLT Art 52 reads: 'A treaty is void if its conclusion has been procured by the threat or use of force in violation of the principles of international law embodied in the Charter of the United Nations.'

[87] See H Grotius, *On the Law of War and Peace* (Kelsey (trs), Clarendon Press, Oxford 1925) 334.

[88] See ibid 348.   [89] See ibid 396.   [90] Ibid 397.

[91] See the fine biography by JM Cooper, Jr, *Woodrow Wilson: A Biography* (Knopf, New York 2009).

fruit. The Versailles Treaty, negotiated without Germany's participation between the victorious powers, is often seen as the textbook example of a treaty procured by means of coercion.[92]

During the 1968 Vienna Conference, a number of mainly non-aligned nations tabled an amendment that the notion of coercion should not only address military force, but also the more subtle emanations of political and economic pressure. This came as no surprise: a similar discussion had taken place within the ILC, as the Commission's final report recalled.[93] The amendment would eventually not be taken on board and would not even be voted on. While many States had expressed their support, others found that the inclusion of economic and political pressure would fatally undermine the stability of treaty relations, and it was even pointed out that economic and political pressure can take many forms: the industrial State without natural resources can just as easily be bullied into accepting a treaty by a State richer in natural resources as the other way around.[94] In order to prevent a stalemate, the Dutch representative, Willem Riphagen, proposed to append a declaration condemning the use of political and economic pressure in the conclusion of treaties while keeping Article 52 limited to coercion as embodied in the UN Charter. This was accepted; the earlier amendment was dropped without a vote, and the Final Act of the Vienna Conference included a declaration condemning coercion also by non-forceful means.[95]

While Article 52 gave rise to lots of discussion both before and during the Vienna Conference, its practical impact seems to have remained fairly limited, at least if discussion in the literature is a reliable yardstick: relatively few scholarly works have been devoted to coercion in the law of treaties, and those which touch upon the topic tend to focus either on the use of force in general,[96] or concentrate on the category of unequal treaties and tend to do so from a largely historical perspective.[97] Likewise, there is little recorded State practice. Aust mentions the possible example of a military agreement concluded between the Federal Republic of Yugoslavia (FRY) and NATO, with the FRY complaining about duress, only to dismiss it.[98] Perhaps this follows logically from the problem of delimitation between justifiable and unjustifiable pressure, and the intricate problem of proving coercion in the conclusion of treaties. As the Court of Arbitration deciding the *Dubai-Sharjah Border Arbitration* sensibly remarked, pressure of some sort or another is endemic in international negotiations, yet '[m]ere influences and

---

[92] For further discussion, see also J Klabbers, 'Clinching the Concept of Sovereignty: *Wimbledon Redux*' (1998) 3 ARIEL L 345–67.

[93] See [1966] YBILC, vol II, 246.

[94] The point was made by Eduardo Jiménez de Aréchaga, the representative of Uruguay. See Vienna Conference, First Session (n 73) 277.

[95] See ibid 328–9.

[96] The same is observed by HG de Jong, 'Coercion in the Conclusion of Treaties' (1984) 15 Netherlands Ybk Intl L 209–47.

[97] A fine example is M Craven, 'What Happened to Unequal Treaties? The Continuities of Informal Empire' (2005) 74 Nordic J Intl L 335–82.

[98] See Aust, 2nd edn (n 1) 318.

pressures cannot be equated with the concept of coercion as it is known in international law'.[99]

D. *Jus cogens*

By contrast, much ink has been spilt on the concept of *jus cogens*—the idea that there are certain peremptory norms of international law that States cannot derogate from via treaty.[100] The idea of *jus cogens* gained momentum when the Nazi-regime in Germany prompted Alfred Verdross to write a brief note on forbidden treaties in international law.[101] Still, the notion is problematic within the VCLT system. Since the Vienna Convention conceptualizes treaties as instruments rather than obligations, it follows that considerations relating to the substance of treaties (as opposed to their formal characteristics) have a hard time being integrated. Yet *jus cogens* focuses precisely on considerations of substance: it aims to limit the contractual freedom of States by stipulating that States are not allowed to conclude treaties to engage in certain activities. This is intuitively attractive: inasmuch as domestic legal orders are unwilling to accept and recognize certain contracts (eg a contract to kill), so too is international law unwilling to allow States to conclude treaties providing for genocide, slavery, aggression, or racial segregation. What renders this problematic are two factors. First, there is no agreement as to which norms belong to the corpus of *jus cogens*; second, there is a lack of clarity as to how norms come to be recognized as such.

The first of these did not bother the ILC too much: it felt confident that the 'full content of this rule' could be elaborated in State practice and in the case law of international tribunals. This had the advantage, from the drafters' point of view, of not closing off the discussion: it allowed for the inclusion of new rules over time, and ensured that the drafters did not have to make difficult, perhaps impossible, choices. Put differently: it is unlikely that any list of *jus cogens* norms would have been accepted by the Vienna Conference, and even if such a list would have made the grade, it would probably have deterred quite a few States from ratifying the Vienna Convention. Hence, playing down the relevance of such a list was useful for purposes of completing the Convention, but has resulted in a veritable explosion of suggestions since 1969.

That would not be much of a problem, arguably, if it would have been possible to find a workable method for the identification of *jus cogens* norms. Article 53 does prescribe such a method: a rule of *jus cogens* is defined as a norm 'from which no derogation is permitted' and which is 'accepted and recognized by the international

---

[99] See *Dubai-Sharjah Border Arbitration* (1981) 91 ILR 543, 571.

[100] Some of the more useful works include L Hannikainen, *Peremptory Norms (Jus Cogens) in International Law* (Finnish Lawyers' Publishing Company, Helsinki 1988); G Gaja, 'Jus Cogens Beyond the Vienna Convention' (1981/III) 172 RcD 271–316, and, more recently, A Paulus, '*Jus Cogens* in a Time of Hegemony and Fragmentation—An Attempt at a Re-appraisal' (2005) 74 Nordic J Intl L 297–334. A broader critique of some of the thinking underlying the *jus cogens* idea and similar trends is P Weil, 'Towards Relative Normativity in International Law?' (1983) 77 AJIL 413–42.

[101] See A Verdross, 'Forbidden Treaties in International Law' (1937) 31 AJIL 571–7.

community of States as a whole' as such a non-derogable norm.[102] There is some agreement that it relates to norms of high moral fibre (the prohibitions of genocide, torture, apartheid, slavery, and aggression are often mentioned), but even this does not close the ranks. Much trouble is caused by the absence of an international legislature to decide on what counts as a *jus cogens* prohibition. Article 53 tries to compensate for this by suggesting that it is 'the international community of States as a whole' which decides, but given that no such community exists in institutionalized form, authors have had a free hand in suggesting norms for inclusion, and have not hesitated to utilize this freedom.

The ICJ has been rather quiet on this front: it took until 2006 before the Court was willing to classify the genocide prohibition as a *jus cogens* norm, while simultaneously noting that violation of such a norm as such would not grant the Court jurisdiction.[103] In earlier decisions and opinions, the Court had sometimes hinted at *jus cogens*, but never actively used the term.[104] For example, in its opinion on the legality of nuclear weapons, the ICJ held that two norms of humanitarian law are amongst the 'intransgressible principles' of international law, but stopped short of referring to them as *jus cogens*—intentionally, we may presume.[105] By the same token, on another occasion, the Court classified self-determination as an '*erga omnes* principle', but did not refer to it as a *jus cogens* rule.[106]

Other international tribunals have sometimes found *jus cogens* norms to exist, most emphatically perhaps the International Criminal Tribunal for the former Yugoslavia (ICTY) in *Furundžija* with its conclusion that the prohibition on torture so qualifies.[107] Then again, in one sense at least *Furundžija* was a relatively easy case: there was no need to pit the *jus cogens* prohibition of torture against any other rules of international law to establish its peremptory status. Where such a need has arisen, courts have been a bit less emphatic. Thus, the European Court of Human Rights has held that while the torture-prohibition forms part of the *jus cogens* corpus, this does not set aside the immunity of States from civil suit, although it may affect their immunity from criminal proceedings.[108] More generally, it will surely be the case that the mere label of *jus cogens* does not bring political

---

[102] VCLT Art 53 reads: 'A treaty is void if, at the time of its conclusion, it conflicts with a peremptory norm of general international law. For the purposes of the present Convention, a peremptory norm of general international law is a norm accepted and recognized by the international community of States as a whole as a norm from which no derogation is permitted and which can be modified only by a subsequent norm of general international law having the same character.' It follows, that agreement between a group of like-minded States on the non-derogability of a certain norm does not automatically turn that norm into a norm of *jus cogens*.

[103] See *Case Concerning Armed Activities on the Territory of the Congo* (*Democratic Republic of the Congo v Rwanda*) (New Application: 2002) [2006] ICJ Rep 6 [64].

[104] In *Military and Paramilitary Activities in and against Nicaragua* (*Nicaragua v USA*) [1986] ICJ Rep 14 [190], the ICJ used the term but did so while citing the ILC and the parties to the dispute; it is doubtful whether this can be regarded as an unqualified endorsement.

[105] See *Legality of the Threat or Use of Nuclear Weapons* (Advisory Opinion) [1996] ICJ Rep 226 [79].

[106] See *East Timor* (*Portugal v Australia*) [1995] ICJ Rep 90 [29].

[107] See *Prosecutor v Furundžija* (Case IT-95-17/1) (1998) 121 ILR 213.

[108] See *Al-Adsani v United Kingdom* (Decision of 21 November 2001) App No 35763/97 [61].

debate to a halt. It is one thing to agree that genocide or torture are *jus cogens*, but quite another to agree on what constitutes genocide or torture.

Domestic courts have been somewhat less hesitant than the ICJ in identifying the existence of a *jus cogens*, but have been reluctant to actually apply *jus cogens*. They have sometimes held, for example, that perpetrators could benefit from sovereign immunity. Thus, in *Siderman de Blake*,[109] a US court held that torture qualified as a *jus cogens* norm, but that the government of Argentina was immune from suit. In *Princz*,[110] another US court reached a similar conclusion with respect to the genocide perpetrated by Nazi-Germany before and during the Second World War. These positions, however, seem conceptually awkward: if a norm is one from which no derogation is permitted, then surely sovereign immunity should not function as a shield.

Upholding immunity even for *jus cogens* violations can be—and has been—rationalized by making a rigid distinction between substantive law and procedural rules: on such a construction, the fact that the States concerned could not be sued does not detract from their possible guilt and from the fundamental nature of the rules breached. Yet somehow this seems too clever by half.[111] Perhaps a more plausible explanation may be that for many domestic courts, particularly those whose legal systems do not automatically incorporate international law, upholding an international *jus cogens* norm over considerations of sovereign immunity would typically imply an unwanted result: the prevalence of international law over domestic law, as immunity law is typically regulated in domestic legislation.[112] On the other hand, if *jus cogens* is regarded as domestic law, a different result may follow. Indeed, the decision of Italy's Court of Cassation in *Ferrini* goes some way towards this: the Court held that Germany could not invoke immunity in respect of allegations of forced labour during the Second World War, and specifically invoked the domestication of 'fundamental human rights': these 'automatically become an integral part of Italian law'.[113] On such a reading, any conflict between international law and domestic law dissipates, and *jus cogens* can come to be applied as a matter of domestic law.

---

[109] See *Siderman de Blake v Republic of Argentina*, 965 F.2d 699 (9th Cir).

[110] See *Hugo Princz v Federal Republic of Germany*, 26 F.3d 1166 (DC cir 1994). Moreover, the court found that engaging in an act prohibited by *jus cogens* does not constitute an implied waiver to immunity.

[111] Such a construction is hinted at by Zimmermann, noting that *jus cogens* rules and rules on immunity are best seen 'as involving two different sets of rules which do not interact with each other'. See A Zimmermann, 'Sovereign Immunity and Violations of International *Jus Cogens*—Some Critical Remarks' (1995) 16 Michigan J Intl L 433, 438. In a similar vein, see J Finke, 'Sovereign Immunity: Rule, Comity or Something Else?' (2010) 21 EJIL 853, 869.

[112] Surely, the European Court of Human Rights too would be sensitive to such a concern; it is keen not to be seen as replacing the domestic law of its member States.

[113] See *Ferrini v Federal Republic of Germany* (Court of Cassation Italy, Judgment of 11 March 2004) 128 ILR 658, 666. Note, however, that the ICJ recently rejected this approach and held that the decision of Italy's Court of Cassation was not in conformity with international law, upholding a strict separation between substance and process. See *Jurisdictional Immunities of the State (Germany v Italy; Greece Intervening)*, Judgment of 3 February 2012.

The reluctance of the ICJ, and the conceptual awkwardness of other courts, may well find its source in the general reluctance of States to accept the ultimate price to pay for acceptance of the *jus cogens* category. In the end, it would seem that the *jus cogens* notion is only workable within a hierarchical system of law (unlike the still predominantly horizontal international legal order), and with an acceptance of the possibility of legislation by majority.[114] Surely, the position, sometimes heard in the 1970s and 1980s, that the apartheid prohibition was accepted as a norm of *jus cogens*, but that this could not affect South Africa because of its non-acceptance thereof, bordered on the bizarre.[115] The one State that engages in an unwanted practice cannot escape from universal condemnation by acting as a persistent objector, at least not without diluting the very idea of *jus cogens*. *Jus cogens* should either be imperative enough to bind all, or it is not *jus cogens*.

As the above suggests, *jus cogens* has started to live a life outside the limited context of the conclusion of treaties. One may even stipulate that empirically, it seems to have been a reasonable success within the law of treaties. After all, few treaties are concluded in order to facilitate genocide, slavery, or apartheid. While the relevance of facts is never self-evident, this may be taken as a sign that States do not conclude such treaties because they think such treaties will be invalid— although it may also mean that they refrain from concluding such treaties because they think them distasteful, impractical, or not in their best interest. That said, the recent popularity of treaties which facilitate torture through so-called extraordinary rendition casts some doubt on whether the torture prohibition still qualifies as a *jus cogens* norm: if too many States engage in torture, then either all those activities are invalid or, more likely perhaps, the conclusion must be reached that the norm is no longer recognized as one from which no derogation is permitted.

The more common usage of *jus cogens* would seem to be as a yardstick for the legality of official behaviour more generally. The scenarios in cases such as *Al-Adsani*, *Ferrini*, *Princz*, and *Siderman de Blake* did not involve treaty-making by the UK, Nazi-Germany, or Argentina, but concerned the way in which those States treated individuals. By the same token, *Furundžija* and the ICJ's *Armed Activities* case did not involve the validity of treaties. The ICJ has once been called upon (without answering the call) to assess the legality of a Security Council resolution in light of a proposed *jus cogens* norm: this arose when Bosnia complained that an arms embargo imposed on both Bosnia and Serbia during the Yugoslav conflict affected Bosnia's capacity for self-defense, and therewith contributed to ethnic cleansing or even genocide.[116] In short: the idea of *jus cogens* is no longer limited to being a

---

[114] In particular, France was troubled by the very category of *jus cogens*: troubled enough not to sign the Vienna Convention. See generally O Deleau, 'Les positions francaises à la Conférence de Vienne sur le droit des traités' (1969) 15 Annuaire Français de Droit International 7–23.

[115] Cassese came very close to such a position when allowing for application of the persistent objector doctrine to the creation of *jus cogens* norms. See A Cassese, *International Law in a Divided World* (Clarendon Press, Oxford 1986) 178.

[116] See *Case Concerning Application of the Convention on the Prevention and Punishment of the Crime of Genocide (Bosnia-Herzegovina v Yugoslavia (Serbia and Montenegro))* (Order) [1993] ICJ Rep 325.

validity test for treaties (if it ever was), but has come to assume the role of a general—and genuine—*ordre public* notion.

Conclusions

At the end of the day, the notion of validity (or invalidity) seems to have little practical effect in the law of treaties, and, if *jus cogens* be excepted, has not given rise to much theoretical reflection either. There is widespread agreement that some rules on validity are useful and required, and there is widespread agreement that the consent defects identified by Articles 46–52 are amongst the rules that should be present, and that the *jus cogens* idea is, well, a really good idea as such. The precise details, however, remain to be filled in.

It is therefore, naturally, no coincidence that also the procedure invented in the Vienna Convention to address issues of validity and invalidity (Articles 65–8 of the VCLT), has remained a dead letter. Such a procedure was considered necessary, quite obviously so, as soon as provisions on invalidity were introduced: it would not be a good idea to have States proclaim the invalidity of treaties left, right, and centre. Still, in the absence of instances of State practice, the procedures too have remained under-utilized.

And perhaps this relative neglect of validity is as it should be. A legal order in which the contractual activities of its main members are often invalidated would be a highly problematic legal order. Likewise, a legal order where invalidity is the norm, rather than a rare exception, has quite a problem. And even then, it is one thing to invalidate treaties, but quite another to scrutinize the acts of public authorities within any given legal order; it is surely no coincidence that the *jus cogens* notion has come to be seen as a test of the validity of the exercise of public authority rather than of treaties alone. Still, in the absence—or very limited existence—of global public authorities and the necessary presumption of validity of treaties, it stands to reason that the notion of invalidity does not do much work in the international legal order.

Recommended Reading

A Aust, *Modern Treaty Law and Practice* (2nd edn CUP, Cambridge 2007) 312–23

O Corten and P Klein (eds), *Les Conventions de Vienne sur le Droit des Traités: Commentaire Article par Article* (Bruylant, Brussels 2006)

M Craven, 'What Happened to Unequal Treaties? The Continuities of Informal Empire' (2005) 74 Nordic J Intl L 335–82

HG de Jong, 'Coercion in the Conclusion of Treaties' (1984) 15 Netherlands Ybk Intl L 209–47

GG Fitzmaurice, 'Some Problems Regarding the Formal Sources of International Law', in FM van Asbeck et al (eds), *Symbolae Verzijl* (Martinus Nijhoff, Leiden 1958) 153–76

D Greig, *Invalidity and the Law of Treaties* (BIICL, London 2006)

P Guggenheim, 'La validité et la nullité des actes juridiques internationaux' (1949/I) 74 RcD 191–268

L Hannikainen, *Peremptory Norms (Jus Cogens) in International Law* (Finnish Lawyers' Publishing Company, Helsinki 1988)

H Kelsen, *Introduction to the Problems of Legal Theory* (Litschewski Paulson and Paulson trs) (Clarendon Press, Oxford 1992, first published in 1934)

J Klabbers, 'Law-making and Constitutionalism', in J Klabbers, A Peters, and G Ulfstein, *The Constitutionalization of International Law* (Oxford University Press, Oxford 2009) 81–125

J Klabbers, 'Reluctant *Grundnormen*: Articles 31(3)(c) and 42 of the Vienna Convention on the Law of Treaties and the Fragmentation of International Law' in M Craven, M Fitzmaurice, and M Vogiatzi (eds), *Time, History and International Law* (Martinus Nijhoff, Leiden 2007) 141–61

A McNair, *The Law of Treaties* (Clarendon Press, Oxford 1961)

T Meron, 'Article 46 of the Vienna Convention on the Law of Treaties (*Ultra Vires* Treaties)' (1979) 50 BYBIL 175–99

SE Nahlik, 'The Grounds of Validity and Termination of Treaties' (1971) 65 AJIL 736–56

P Reuter, *Introduction au droit des traits* (Cahier (ed), 3rd edn Presses Universitaires de France, Geneva 1995)

G Sartor, 'Legal Validity as Doxastic Obligation' (2000) 19 Law and Philosophy 585–625

A Verdross, 'Forbidden Treaties in International Law' (1937) 31 AJIL 571–7

ME Villiger, *Commentary on the 1969 Vienna Convention on the Law of Treaties* (Martinus Nijhoff, Leiden 2009)

E Vitta, *La validité des traités internationaux* (Brill, Leiden 1940)

23

Reacting against Treaty Breaches

Bruno Simma and Christian J Tams

Introduction

States regularly proclaim the sanctity of treaty obligations and few principles are as firmly established as *pacta sunt servanda*.[1] Yet, treaty breaches are by no means exceptional: adapting one of international law's most celebrated statements, one might even say that 'almost all nations, almost all the time, consider their rights under a given treaty to be violated'.[2] By way of a snapshot, at the time of writing, six of nine active contentious cases pending before the International Court of Justice (ICJ) involve claims, by one State, that a certain treaty has been violated.[3] And this ignores the many treaty breaches that do not reach the spotlight, but are addressed quietly (eg by means of a phone call between representatives of the States concerned) or are not addressed at all. Against this background, a recent textbook is surely right to state that 'most disputes between states, and especially those which are referred to international adjudication, involve, mainly or partly, the interpretation or application of a treaty'.[4]

The frequency of real or alleged treaty breaches is neither a source for major concern, nor should it come as a great surprise. With treaty commitments covering ever greater areas of international relations, it is only natural that some of them should occasionally be breached. Nobody is perfect, and States certainly are not. More importantly, not all treaty breaches are intentional, or show disrespect for international law as a system, let alone its ground rule of *pacta sunt servanda*. Often, breaches result from mere oversights or lack of information: to give just one example, before States like Paraguay, Germany, and Mexico were beginning to

---

[1] In the introductory lines of its commentary on draft Art 23 (which eventually became Art 26 of the 1969 Vienna Convention on the Law of Treaties (VCLT)), the International Law Commission (ILC) observed: 'Pacta sunt servanda—the rule that treaties are binding on the parties and must be performed in good faith—is the fundamental principle of the law of treaties' [1966] YBILC, vol II, 211.

[2] Cf L Henkin, *How Nations Behave* (2nd edn Columbia University Press, New York 1979) 47 ('almost all nations observe almost all principles of international law and almost all of their obligations almost all the time').

[3] For a list of ICJ cases see <http://www.icj-cij.org/docket/index.php?p1=3&p2=1>. The figures given exclude proceedings that remain on the Court's docket after a judgment on the merits has been rendered, as well as requests for interpretations of earlier judgments.

[4] A Aust, *Modern Treaty Law and Practice* (2nd edn CUP, Cambridge 2007) 352.

raise the matter, few people were likely to be aware of the requirements imposed by the Vienna Convention on Consular Relations (VCCR) with respect to consular notification.[5] Or, treaty disputes may be due to different, plausible interpretations of a given treaty commitment—eg with respect to the scope of an obligation to prevent the commission of acts of genocide, as was the case in the recent proceedings between Bosnia and Serbia before the ICJ.[6] Finally, at times, conflicting obligations may even require States to disregard obligations arising under one treaty to comply with the demands of another—in which case, conflict resolution techniques such as the *lex specialis* principle, or *jus cogens,* may clarify questions of precedence.[7] And, of course, not every treaty breach is in itself dramatic; the spectre of what is covered by the term 'treaty breach' is huge. It comprises acts of aggression amounting to a large-scale violation of Article 2(4)[8] of the UN Charter just as it does one State's imposition of an 11 per cent *ad valorem* import tax on foreign goods where a treaty bound the tariff to 10.9 per cent.

Against this background, it seems natural that real or alleged treaty breaches are by no means an exceptional feature of international law in its 'age of treaties'. The real question is whether international law provides means and methods to respond to them. This chapter addresses that question. We do so in four steps. First, we provide an overview of the international regime governing reactions against treaty breaches. In the next two sections, we analyse the two most relevant generally available means of response under the law of treaties and the law of State responsibility respectively. Our final section offers some concluding observations. In addressing questions of treaty breaches and responses, we will focus on rules of international law regulating inter-State behaviour. Notwithstanding this restriction, it seems clear that treaty breaches can be committed by and against different (non-State) subjects of international law, notably by and against international organizations. While these raise some special problems (eg relating to determining whether the organization itself or its members bear responsibility[9]), they are in principle subject to the rules developed to govern inter-State relations.[10]

---

[5] Cf Vienna Convention on Consular Relations (adopted 24 April 1963, entered into force 19 March 1967) 596 UNTS 261, Art 36 (VCCR). For details on the 'litigation saga' see eg B Simma and C Hoppe, 'From *LaGrand* and *Avena* to *Medellin*—A Rocky Road Toward Implementation' (2005) 14 Tulane J Intl Comp L 7.

[6] *Case Concerning the Application of the Convention on the Prevention and Punishment of the Crime of Genocide (Bosnia and Herzegovina v Serbia and Montenegro)* (Judgment) [2007] ICJ Rep 43.

[7] For many details on these—and other—conflicts see the ILC Study Group, 'Fragmentation of International Law: Difficulties Arising from the Diversification and Expansion of International Law' (13 April 2006) UN Doc A/CN.4/L.682.

[8] See eg UNGA Res 3314 (XXIX) (14 December 1974), fifth preambular paragraph, describing aggression as 'the most serious and dangerous form of the illegal use of force'.

[9] For brief comment on this see B Simma and C Tams, 'Article 60 (1986)' in O Corten and P Klein (eds), *The Vienna Convention on the Law of Treaties: A Commentary* (OUP, Oxford 2011) vol II, [3]–[4].

[10] Leaving aside the inclusion of references to 'international organizations', Art 60 of the 1986 Vienna Convention on the Law of Treaties between States and International Organizations or between International Organizations (adopted 21 March 1986, not yet in force) [1986] 25 ILM 543 follows the wording of Art 60 of the 1969 VCLT (addressed below, in Part II). By the same token, Arts 51–7 of the 2011 Draft Articles on the Responsibility of International Organizations adapt Arts 49–54 of the Articles on the Responsibility of States for Internationally Wrongful Acts (addressed below, in Part III) with only minor modifications. See also Chapter 3, Part III, 84 *et seq.*

I. Specific and General Rules Governing Reactions Against Treaty Breaches: An Overview

A. Responses 'in [their] infinite variety'[11]

Just as treaty breaches are manifold, so are the possible reactions against them. The point may be illustrated by reverting to the examples of treaty breaches just mentioned and to consider possible responses. State A's aggression in scenario 1 could prompt State B—the victim of the armed attack—to resort to self-defence under Article 51 of the UN Charter. State C might want to refer to Article 51 to justify its military support for State B ('collective self-defence'), while State D might decide to freeze assets to exercise pressure on State A. Other States are likely to protest against the violation of international law, while the Security Council could address the matter by imposing sanctions or encouraging enforcement action in defence of State B's territorial integrity.

In scenario 2, the limited violation of tariff bindings by State X is most likely to be addressed bilaterally, through diplomatic channels, perhaps with the assistance of other States, if State Y (whose exports are affected) does not decide to ignore the matter altogether so as not to jeopardize its friendly relations with State X. In a variation to scenario 2 (which one might refer to as scenario 2*bis*), violations of tariff bindings that are of a more relevant character might prompt State Y to respond in kind by disregarding its own tariff bindings. If the matter is governed by World Trade Organization (WTO) law, State Y might institute panel proceedings under the WTO Dispute Settlement Understanding. Alongside these more formal responses, States X and Y, but presumably also other States with some interest in the matter, might seek a friendly settlement, which might involve consultations, expressions of concern, incentives, or protests against State X's disregard of international trade rules.

B. Treaty-specific rules and general legal concepts

From this briefest of illustrations, it becomes clear that the range of possible reactions against treaty breaches is vast. A State's reaction against a treaty breach depends on a variety of factors, including *inter alia* (i) the character or gravity of the breach; (ii) the relations between the States involved in the dispute; (iii) the competence of international institutions to address the matter; and (iv) more particularly, the availability of an independent forum for dispute resolution. More importantly, the scenarios illustrate that a State's response to a treaty breach may be governed by two different categories of rules.[12] The first category comprises what might be termed 'treaty-specific' reactions: a treaty can itself regulate reactions

---

[11] Cf R Baxter, 'International Law "In Her Infinite Variety"' (1980) 29 ICLQ 549.
[12] The following distinction draws on C Tams, 'Enforcement' in G Ulfstein and others (eds), *Making Treaties Work* (CUP, Cambridge 2007) 395–6.

against breaches of its provisions. In scenario 1 above, State B's reliance on self-defence would be 'treaty-specific', as Article 51 of the UN Charter permits a specific form of self-help against a particular breach of the same treaty (namely a qualified use of force against a breach amounting to an 'armed attack'). By the same token, State C could avail itself of the treaty-specific possibility of aiding the victim of an armed attack by means of collective self-defence, just as the Security Council could make use of its treaty-specific enforcement competence under (and subject to the requirements of) Chapter VII of the UN Charter. In scenario *2bis,* State Y's decision to institute WTO dispute settlement proceedings would also be 'treaty-specific', as WTO law envisages Panel and Appellate Body proceedings as suitable modes for resolving disputes about violations of the covered agreements.

However, not all treaties address reactions against breaches, and even those that do need not be exhaustive in their regulation. Irrespective of any treaty-specific provision, reactions against treaty breaches can be based on general legal concepts, which comprise the second category of rules governing responses to treaty breach. In the scenarios mentioned above, State D's decision to freeze State A's assets (unless authorized by the Security Council) cannot be based on a specific treaty provision and therefore must be justified differently. Similarly, if State Y decides to respond to State X's violation of tariff bindings by levying excessive import duties, it is unlikely that there will be a treaty-specific rule justifying such a tit-for-tat response. More generally, few treaties lay down express rules governing protests against treaty breaches. The legality of these responses depends then, not on the express terms of the treaty whose breach prompted them, but on general rules external to the treaty.

The distinction between treaty-specific and general rules governing reactions against treaty breaches is of considerable importance. While the treaty itself is the obvious *locus* for addressing questions of breaches and responses, treaty-specific rules are of limited relevance for a study on general aspects of treaty law. They are no doubt common and, taken together, constitute an important element of the international regime governing responses against treaty breaches. But precisely because of their heterogeneity, they escape easy classifications. There are but few limits to the creativity of treaty parties in designing regimes of reactions against treaty breaches, and few models that have not been tried out. In fact, the two simplified scenarios already mentioned reveal the spectre of approaches, ranging from bilateral consultations to legal or quasi-legal proceedings, but also encompassing the (potentially massive) use of military force in self-defence. To provide an overview over treaty-specific rules 'in [their] infinite variety'[13] would be impossible; what is more, it would be of limited utility as treaty-specific rules are by definition of no general relevance outside the specific treaty's field of application. For this reason, the subsequent discussion focuses on responses available under general concepts.

---

[13] Baxter (n 11) 549.

C. Intrinsically lawful responses versus responses presupposing title to respond

Excluding reactions based on treaty-specific provisions considerably narrows the scope of inquiry. It may be further restricted on the basis of functional criteria. Notably, a second distinction can be drawn between responses that depend on a title, or justification; and responses that are permissible as a matter of course. This latter category would comprise protests, or forms of pressure that are unfriendly, but intrinsically lawful (often described as retorsions[14]). International law does not regulate these responses in any detail—and it opts against regulation deliberately, as the responses do not reach the threshold of (prima facie) illegality. Like treaty-based responses, intrinsically lawful reactions can be hugely relevant: very often, pro-tests—especially by a large group of States—may be an extremely effective way of resolving a dispute about treaty breaches. On the other hand, they may sometimes exacerbate tensions and deepen existing frictions.

By contrast, responses that cross the threshold of (prima facie) illegality require regulation. Of course, international law must permit effective responses against treaty breaches, but it cannot give carte blanche to responding States. Not surpris-ingly, it seeks to strike a balance between the two competing considerations. This balancing exercise has been influenced by changing views of treaty stability and effectiveness within the international community, and is reflected in the general legal regimes permitting coercive responses against treaty breaches.

D. Treaty law responses versus countermeasures

International law enshrines two main categories of coercive responses against treaty breaches: (i) the suspension or termination of treaties under the law of treaties, and (ii) the non-performance of obligations justified as a countermeasure under the law of State responsibility.[15] The first of these is of obvious relevance: given that treaty breaches affect treaty obligations, one would expect the general law of treaties to address the matter—eg by laying down a general provision on potential responses. This general provision is Article 60 of the 1969 Vienna Convention on the Law of Treaties (VCLT), which puts forward a very nuanced and highly influential regime governing responses to treaty breaches. As discussed in the next section, it

---

[14] ILC, 'Articles on the Responsibility of States for Internationally Wrongful Acts, with Commen-taries' [2001] YBILC, vol II, 128 [3] (ASR). For more on retorsion, see eg OY Elagab, *The Legality of Non-Forcible Countermeasures in International Law* (OUP, Oxford 1987) 4, 29–30; KJ Partsch, 'Retorsion' in R Bernhardt (ed), *Encyclopaedia of Public International Law* (Amsterdam, Elsevier 2000) vol IV, 232.

[15] For a more detailed assessment see B Simma, 'Reflections on Article 60 of the Vienna Conven-tion on the Law of Treaties and Its Background in General International Law' (1970) 20 ÖZÖR 19–23, 52–5. See also J Crawford, 'Third Report on State Responsibility' UN Doc A/CN.4/507/Add.2, [324]–[325]; R Provost, 'Reciprocity in Human Rights and Humanitarian Law' (1994) 65 BYBIL 398–400.

draws fine distinctions based on the impact of the breach, and on the character of the treaty affected, while also clarifying which obligations are 'sacrosanct' and cannot be suspended or terminated even in cases of breach.

The general law of treaties does not exhaustively regulate responses to treaty breaches. It might have done so; however, the VCLT as the key text setting out the law of treaties addresses treaty breaches only in passing.[16] As a consequence, there remains room for responses based, not on the general law of treaties, but on the law of State responsibility, which is detailed in the 2001 Draft Articles on State Responsibility (ASR). In State responsibility 'jargon', a treaty breach amounts to an internationally wrongful act, and entails the ensuing duties of cessation (where applicable) and reparation.[17] More importantly, the general rules of responsibility also contain provisions governing the invocation of responsibility and inducing the wrongdoer to return to legality by way of countermeasures.[18] Countermeasures can in fact be taken against all forms of wrongful acts, but it is clear that they are *also* available against treaty breaches. They permit 'the non-performance for the time being of international obligations of the State taking the measures towards the responsible State'[19] (having violated a treaty). And they are subject to a number of conditions and exclusionary clauses.

On the face of it, countermeasures and treaty law responses may seem similar. Subject to certain conditions, both are available against a treaty breach. Both concepts allow for reactions that take the form of suspension of treaty benefits. And, of course, States invoking the two concepts must establish an entitlement to do so—they must be affected by the previous breach against which their response is directed. Yet, notwithstanding these commonalities, international law draws a fine, conceptual distinction between countermeasures, on the one hand, and treaty law responses on the other.[20] It does so, moreover, for good reasons. Despite their similarities, the two types of responses serve different purposes. Countermeasures aim to compel the defaulting State to cease its violation of international law and/or

---

[16] See S Rosenne, *Breach of Treaty* (Grotius, Cambridge 1985) 3–8. Rosenne rightly notes that the VCLT approach deliberately distinguishes the 'law of treaties' from the 'law of obligations' imposed by treaties. Ibid 4. This distinction, he observed, 'made it necessary to find another basis for the systematic classification and treatment of the law of international obligations as such . . . This was found in a thorough reconstruction of the nature, scope and treatment of the law of State responsibility'. Ibid. The ICJ has emphasized this as well. *Gabčikovo-Nagymaros Project (Hungary v Slovakia)* (Judgment) [1997] ICJ Rep 7 [47] (the VCLT 'confines itself to defining—in a limitative manner—the conditions in which a treaty may lawfully be denounced or suspended; while the effects of a denunciation or suspension seen as not meeting those conditions are, on the contrary, expressly excluded from the scope of the Convention by operation of Article 73. It is moreover well established that, when a State has committed an internationally wrongful act, its international responsibility is likely to be involved whatever the nature of the obligation it has failed to respect'); VCLT Art 73 (VCLT is 'without prejudice' to questions arising from a treaty on 'the international responsibility of a State').

[17] ASR (n 14) Arts 2, 30, and 31.

[18] Ibid Arts 22, 49–54.

[19] Ibid Art 49(1).

[20] For further details on this point see B Simma and C Tams, 'Article 60 (1969)' in O Corten and P Klein (eds), *The Vienna Convention on the Law of Treaties: A Commentary* (OUP, Oxford 2011) vol II, [4], [69]–[73].

restore the situation that would have existed had there been no such violation.[21] In contrast, treaty law responses aim to remedy a situation in which the balance of rights and obligations within a treaty relationship has been upset due to a prior breach by the defaulting State.[22] At least in theory, treaty law responses must be restricted to synallagmatic pairs of obligations. In contrast, a party resorting to countermeasures may choose—subject to a number of specific exceptions— which obligation it intends to violate. In addition, both forms of reaction may be distinguished by their effect on the norm in question. A countermeasure constitutes the (justified) violation of a binding norm; it has no effect on the continued existence of the norm as such. In contrast, reactions under Article 60 of the VCLT involve the temporary or permanent extinction of a norm; ie they— at least temporarily—remove the underlying legal bond between the disputing parties.[23] This difference is reflected in the different legal regimes governing countermeasures and treaty law responses.

II. The Law of Treaties: Article 60 of the VCLT

The regime set out in Article 60 constitutes an ambitious attempt to categorize the system of treaty-based responses against violations of international agreements. Within the framework of the general law of treaties, it aims at balancing two competing considerations, namely the need for effective responses against treaty breaches and the overarching interest in preserving treaty commitments. This balancing exercise has resulted in a very complex and perhaps overambitious regime. It is characterized by four features: (a) the decision to make treaty-based responses dependent on a qualified ('material') breach; (b) an attempt to restrict the scope of the right; (c) the development of a complex categorization of treaties with a view to identifying States entitled to respond against breaches; and (d) the submission of the right to suspend or terminate treaties to cumbersome procedural preconditions.

A. The requirement of a material breach

Pursuant to the opening phrases of Article 60(1) and (2) of the VCLT, suspension and termination of treaties can only be sought in response to breaches of a *material* character.[24] With a view to ensuring the stability of treaty relations, drafters thus

---

[21] See ASR (n 14) Art 49(1) (countermeasures are taken 'in order to induce that State to comply with its obligations'); for commentary, see also ibid 129–30 [7].

[22] F Capotorti, '*L'extinction et la suspension des traités*' (1971-III) 134 RdC 548–9; Simma (n 15) 20–1.

[23] Cf Crawford (n 15) [324]–[325] (referencing the *Gabčikovo-Nagymaros Case* (n 16) 39 [48]). See also Provost (n 15) 398–9.

[24] Cf [1966] YBILC, vol II, 255 [7]. The term 'material breach' was adopted in 1963 upon the proposal of the ILC's Special Rapporteur, Sir Humphrey Waldock; it substituted the term 'fundamental breach' suggested by the previous Special Rapporteur, Sir Gerald Fitzmaurice. See H Waldock, 'Second Report on the Law of Treaties' [1963] YBILC, vol II, 75 [11] ('Waldock, Second Report');

chose not to codify any remedies against immaterial breaches,[25] an approach followed for both termination and mere suspension of treaties.[26] Article 60(3) 'defines' a material breach by distinguishing two cases. The first of these is an obvious one: pursuant to Article 60(3)(a), the repudiation of a treaty (ie any attempt by a State to relieve itself from its obligations[27]) will generally[28] constitute a material breach. While practice applying paragraph 3(a) is sparse,[29] the *Namibia* case provides an illustration. There, the ICJ held that by disregarding obligations deriving from the 1922 agreement, South Africa had 'disavowed' the mandate,[30] which the majority considered to amount to a repudiation.[31]

The more relevant aspect of the material breach 'definition' is given in Article 60 (3)(b), which qualifies as material any 'violation of a provision essential to the accomplishment of the object or purpose of the treaty'. In so doing, it adopts an understanding of 'material breach' that may at first seem counterintuitive. Contrary to what might be expected, there is no reference to the breach's *intensity* or *gravity*; instead, the provision's focus is on the character of the treaty obligation. This notably means that Article 60 does not permit responses against grave breaches of treaty provisions that are not essential.[32] Conversely, but more controversially, the textual analysis clarifies that trivial breaches of essential provisions can constitute material breaches under Article 60(3)(b). Whether this is indeed a desirable

GG Fitzmaurice, 'Second Report on the Law of Treaties' [1957] YBILC, vol II, 31 (draft Art 19(2)) ('Fitzmaurice, Second Report').

[25] This raises the question whether reactions against immaterial breaches are permitted under general international law; see Part III, 595 *et seq*.

[26] In contrast, Fitzmaurice had drawn a distinction between suspension and termination. In his view, at least partial suspension would have been justified in response to breaches of a lesser character, cf Fitzmaurice, Second Report (n 24) 30 (draft Art 18); GG Fitzmaurice, 'Fourth Report on the Law of Treaties' [1957] YBILC, vol II, 50 (draft Art 37) ('Fitzmaurice, Fourth Report').

[27] See UN Conference on the Law of Treaties, Summary Records of Second Session, (9 April to 22 May 1969) UN Doc A/CONF.39/11/Add.1, 115 [73] ('Vienna Conference, Second Session'); P Reuter, *Introduction au droit des traités* (PUF, Paris 1995) 182 (note to paragraph 301). During the Vienna Conference, various delegations submitted alternative proposals substituting the term 'repudiation', see M Gomaa, *Suspension or Termination of Treaties on Grounds of Breach* (Martinus Nijhoff, Leiden 1996) 26 n4.

[28] This does not comprise repudiations 'sanctioned by the present Convention', ie cases in which a State is entitled not to perform a treaty pursuant to VCLT Arts 46–64.

[29] See Gomaa (n 27) 151. The provision was unsuccessfully raised in some cases before municipal courts, see eg Australian Federal Court, *Hempel and Another v Attorney-General* (Judgment) (1987) 87 ILR 159, 163.

[30] *Legal Consequences for States of the Continued Presence of South Africa in Namibia (South-West Africa)* (Advisory Opinion) [1971] ICJ Rep 16, 47 [95].

[31] Ibid; see also ibid 218 (Separate Opinion of Judge de Castro). It must be noted however that the Court did not clearly distinguish between cases of 'repudiation' (Art 60(3)(a)) and 'violations of essential provisions' (Art 60(3)(b)). In an Annex to his dissenting opinion, Sir Gerald Fitzmaurice criticized the majority's approach: in his view, South Africa had denied the obligation's existence, which was not the same as to repudiate it. Ibid Annex [6].

[32] The drafting history is very clear on this point: At the Vienna Conference, delegates rejected a Finnish proposal pursuant to which grave breaches of treaties should generally give rise to a right to suspend performance or terminate the treaty, irrespective of the essential (or otherwise) character of the provision affected. UN Conference on the Law of Treaties, Official Records: Documents of the Conference (1968–1969) UN Doc A/CONF.39/14/Add.2, 181 [522] ('Vienna Conference, Official Records').

approach may be open to debate,[33] especially since earlier draft provisions had required a *substantial violation*.[34] The clear wording of Article 60(3)(b), however, admits of little doubt in this respect.[35]

Neither the text of the provision nor the International Law Commission's (ILC's) commentary clarify what is meant by an 'essential provision'. It is clear from the wording that the determination has to be made in light of, and with reference to, the treaty's object and purpose.[36] The term 'essential' suggests that the provision in question must have been at the heart of a treaty.[37] However, from the *travaux,* it appears that the ILC did not intend this to be overly restrictive; hence it considered that provisions of an ancillary character could be essential.[38] This statement (which may surprise at first sight) has to be seen in the context of debates about dispute settlement clauses. These clauses are typically not a treaty's one and only central aspect, and yet, the drafters were keen to clarify that their violation could amount to a 'material breach'.[39]

Given the absence of clear normative guidance, it is no surprise that courts and tribunals charged with applying Article 60 have not come up with comprehensive definitions. Some judgments in fact merely restate the necessity of distinguishing between 'normal' and 'material' treaty violations.[40] Statements made in proceedings before Austrian courts would seem to confirm that provisions may acquire an 'essential' status over time if the normative framework of the treaty changes.[41] Finally, from the ICJ's approach in the *Nicaragua* case, it may be inferred that

---

[33] DW Greig, 'Reciprocity, Proportionality, and the Law of Treaties' (1994) 34 VJIL 342–3; P Malanczuk, *Akehurst's Modern Introduction to International Law* (7th edn Routledge, London 1997) 143.

[34] See Waldock, Second Report (n 24) draft Art 20 (providing that '[a] material breach of a treaty results from . . . a breach so substantial as to be tantamount to setting aside any provisions . . . the failure to perform which is not compatible with the effective fulfilment of the object and purpose of the treaty'); [1966] YBILC, vol II, 255 [6]; F Kirgis, 'Some Lingering Questions About Article 60 of the Vienna Convention on the Law of Treaties' (1989) 22 Cornell Int L J 554.

[35] See Gomaa (n 27) 33.

[36] As the ILC made clear in its commentary, this primarily requires an analysis of the reasons that led to the conclusion of the treaty. [1966] YBILC, vol II, 255 [9]. By way of illustration, cf *Military and Paramilitary Activities in and against Nicaragua (Nicaragua v United States of America)* (Judgment) [1986] ICJ Rep 14, 137 [273].

[37] Gomaa (n 27) 31.

[38] [1966] YBILC, vol II, 255 [9]; see also Waldock, Second Report (n 24) 75 [11]. In order to broaden the scope of the provision, the ILC replaced Fitzmaurice's term 'fundamental breach' by the notion of a 'material breach'. For Fitzmaurice's use of terminology, cf Fitzmaurice, Second Report (n 24) 31 (draft Art 19(2)).

[39] See Waldock, Second Report (n 24) 75 [11]; for a different interpretation of Art 60(3)(b) see the statement of the Uruguayan delegate Jiménez de Arechaga. UN Conference on the Law of Treaties, Summary Records of the First Session (26 March–24 May 1968) UN Doc A/CONF.39/11, 356 [39] ('Vienna Conference, First Session'). Apart from the example of dispute settlement clauses, no other examples of such 'essential ancillary' character are given.

[40] See eg *Malachtou v Armefti and Armefti* (Judgment of the Cyprus Supreme Court of 20 January 1987) 88 ILR 199, 210.

[41] See the position taken by the Austrian Government in a Swiss–Austrian dispute relating to the right to acquire real property under a Treaty of Establishment of 1875, noted by P Fischer and G Hafner, 'Austrian Practice in International Law' (1976) 26 ÖZÖR 301, 345–6. The case is discussed in B Simma, 'Termination and Suspension of Treaties. Two Recent Austrian Cases' (1978) 21 German Ybk Intl L 74.

flagrant violations of generally formulated treaty obligations are likely to be seen as 'material breaches' in the sense of Article 60(3)(b). There, the Court considered the mining of Nicaraguan ports and direct attacks on ports and oil installations to be material breaches of the bilateral Friendship, Commerce and Navigation (FCN) Treaty, while US import restrictions on Nicaraguan sugar and its efforts to prevent international organizations from granting loans to Nicaragua were held not to be 'material'.[42] Of course, none of these attempts to explain the concept of 'material breach' is in itself fully satisfactory. Generally, international practice and jurisprudence still seem to grapple with applying the curious 'definition' in Article 60(3) to specific instances.

B. The scope of the right

Article 60 not only elaborates upon conditions restricting the suspension/termination of a treaty; it also regulates the scope of that right. It does so, however, in a rather rudimentary, and not always compelling, way. To some extent, the regulation had to remain fragmentary, as material breaches, depending on the circumstances, may produce very different effects. Some undermine the treaty as a whole, others affect only some of its aspects—and responding States will tailor their responses accordingly. Even so, Article 60 presents a curious mix of strict limitations and non-regulation. Three features stand out.

First, contrary to what might be suggested by its title—'Termination or suspension of the operation of a treaty...'—Article 60 deliberately limits the right of termination. Both Article 60(1) (dealing with material breach and bilateral treaties) and 60(2)(a) (dealing with collective responses to material breach) do deal with suspension and termination, but States' individual responses under Article 60(2)(b) and 2(c) (dealing with multilateral treaty breach in the absence of unanimity) are restricted to the *suspension* of an agreement. The exclusion of termination in the latter two provisions reflects the drafters' opinion that in the case of multilateral treaties, the interest of third parties in the stability of treaty relations had to be taken into account.[43]

Second, compared to responsibility-based responses (addressed below), Article 60 severely limits the discretion of States in choosing how to respond to material breaches. Article 60(1) and (2) make it clear that the responding party may only suspend or terminate the *same* treaty breached by the defaulting State. Article 60 does not justify the suspension or termination of *other* treaties. This reflects the purpose of treaty-based responses, which are designed to re-establish the balance of rights between treaty parties, and as a matter of principle, seems uncontroversial. One might query, however, whether the principle should have been qualified.

---

[42] *Nicaragua* case (n 36) 138 [275]–[276].
[43] See [1966] YBILC, vol II, 255 [7]. For multilateral treaties that are bilateral in application (the subject of Art 60(2)(a)), this approach seems misleading; any response to their violation, whether termination or suspension, would only affect the two parties to the dispute. The complete exclusion of termination thus seems unwarranted here. Simma (n 15) 67–8; Gomaa (n 27) 104.

Notably, the ILC discussed whether (exceptionally) responding States could suspend or terminate *another* treaty, if it was closely linked to the one materially breached.[44] This indeed would have been preferable, especially for formally distinct treaties that could only be agreed by way of a 'package deal'.[45] The ILC's decision not to include any provision on interrelated treaties however answered this question in the negative.[46]

Third, and in contrast, within the framework of the same treaty, responding parties enjoy a wide measure of discretion to choose which parts they wish to suspend, terminate, or leave intact. In particular, they may decide whether to suspend or terminate a treaty *in whole or in part*.[47] As Article 44(2) makes clear, this freedom is not affected by the VCLT rules on separability, which, in view of the drafters, would have imposed too big a restraint.[48] Perhaps more surprisingly, Article 60 does not require responses to be proportionate. This was deliberate in so far as the drafters decided against including a requirement of 'qualitative proportionality',[49] that is, a duty of responding parties to limit their reactions to the very obligations that had been materially breached, or that were connected to them in some way.[50] It is another question whether responding States have to observe the limits of quantitative proportionality, ie restrict themselves to responses of similar intensity.[51] The question may arise in particular where a State seeks to respond against trivial violations of essential provisions.[52] In this case, Article 60 does not seem to limit the intensity of reactions—once there has been a material breach, the

---

[44] [1963] YBILC, vol I, 121 [79] (De Luna); cf also A Verdross and B Simma, *Universelles Völkerrecht* (3rd edn Duncker & Humblot, Berlin 1984) 520 n42. E Schwelb, 'Termination or Suspension of the Operation of a Treaty as a Consequence of its Breach' (1967) 7 IJIL 316–17; A McNair, *Law of Treaties* (Clarendon, Oxford 1961) 571; Simma (n 15) 22; M Virally, 'Le principe de la réciprocité en droit international contemporain' (1967-III) 122 RdC 1, 44–5.

[45] By way of example, one might think of the German–Polish negotiations of October 1975, which led to the conclusion of two distinct, but interrelated treaties; the first obliging Germany to grant Poland a credit, the other obliging Poland to modify its hitherto restrictive rules on the freedom of movement. For references see Verdross and Simma (n 44) 520 n42.

[46] Cf G Arangio-Ruiz, 'Third Report on State Responsibility' [1991] YBILC, vol II, 23 [72].

[47] This applies to all responses under Art 60, even though the wording of Art 60(2)(a) remains misleading. For details see the debates at the Vienna Conference, First Session (n 39) 167 [30], 168 [32].

[48] As pointed out by Waldock (Expert Consultant), the rules laid down in Art 44 (then draft Art 41) could in some situations have even prevented responding parties from suspending the very provision that had been violated by the defaulting party, cf Vienna Conference, First Session (n 39) 237 [40]. See further Waldock's explanation for draft Art 26 of the 1963 draft. Waldock, Second Report (n 24) 90 [1]. The Vienna debates (which, at least initially, were controversial) are reproduced in Vienna Conference, First Session (n 39) 229–34.

[49] Cf Simma (n 15) 21–2, 78; Arangio-Ruiz (n 46) 24 [77].

[50] Notably, during the Vienna conference, delegates rejected a US amendment that would have limited reactions to responses in kind: see Vienna Conference, Official Records (n 32) 181 [522]; Vienna Conference, First Session (n 39) 389.

[51] On quantitative proportionality see ASR (n 14) Art 51, pursuant to which '[c]ountermeasures must be commensurate with the injury suffered, taking into account the gravity of the internationally wrongful act and the rights in question', a topic discussed at nn 106–13 and accompanying text.

[52] See Part II.A, 582–3, for comment on the curious way Art 60 seeks to define 'material breach'. Where a trivial breach of an essential provision qualifies as a material breach, it could not be said that proportionality was 'pre-built into the mechanism' of Art 60. Cf Gomaa (n 27) 120.

responding State is free to suspend (or indeed terminate) the treaty in whole or in part. The better view would presumably be to 'read' proportionality into the text of the provision. There is considerable evidence that it constitutes an overriding principle *generally* governing reactions against breaches of international law.[53] However, the matter is far from settled, and the text itself does not support this more restrictive approach.[54]

Finally, the right to suspend or terminate a treaty is restricted by the exclusionary clause of Article 60(5) of the VCLT, which declares certain treaty provisions to be sacrosanct.[55] Under this provision, States may not suspend or terminate 'provisions relating to the protection of the human person contained in treaties of a humanitarian character, in particular to provisions prohibiting any form of reprisals against persons'. The purpose of the clause is to protect the beneficiaries of humanitarian treaties from losing their rights in the course of inter-State disputes.[56] The drafting history suggests that despite the curious wording, this exclusion is intended to cover provisions of international humanitarian law and international human rights law.[57] The ICJ, in *Namibia*, seemed to consider Article 60(5) to reflect general international law.[58] However, upon reflection, its relevance—at least within human rights law proper—is more limited than is usually assumed. This is so because very often, material breaches of human rights treaties do not affect any other treaty party in a particular way. Hence, often no other State has standing to suspend or terminate human rights treaties. Article 60(5), of course, clarifies this and thus removes legal uncertainty; however, even without its inclusion, human rights provisions would have effectively been protected against suspension and termination.[59]

Interestingly, Article 60(5) is the only exclusionary clause expressly restricting the right to suspend or terminate treaties. While seeking to declare human rights provisions sacrosanct, the drafters did not include a more comprehensive exclusion. Since the adoption of the provision, it has occasionally been discussed whether States should be precluded from suspending or terminating treaty provisions that

---

[53] In the words of Willem Riphagen, 'a "rule of [quantitative] proportionality" would seem to govern in principle all . . . legal consequences [of an internationally wrongful act]'. ILC, 'Preliminary Report on State Responsibility' [1980] YBILC, vol II, 112 [27]; see also Verdross and Simma (n 44) 520 [816].

[54] Contrast, for example, the parties' different approaches in the *ICAO Council* case: in the view of India, reactions under Art 60 did not have to be proportionate. *Appeal Relating to the Jurisdiction of the ICAO Council (India v Pakistan)* [1972] ICJ Pleadings 422 [52] (Reply by India). Predictably, Pakistan took the opposite approach. Ibid 384 [38] (Counter-Memorial of Pakistan).

[55] Article 60(5), however, does not affect States' right to denounce treaties of a humanitarian character. On the drafting history of the provision, see E Schwelb, 'The Law of Treaties and Human Rights' (1973–1975) 16 Archiv des Völkerrechts 1, 14–26.

[56] For the drafting process see Vienna Conference, First Session (n 39) 354 [12]; Vienna Conference, Second Session (n 27) 112 [20]; Vienna Conference, Official Records (n 32) 269 (quoting UN Doc A/CONF.39/L31).

[57] See Vienna Conference, First Session (n 39) 354 [12] (Mr Bindschedler) and further G Barile, 'The Protection of Human Rights in Article 60, Paragraph 5 of the Vienna Convention on the Law of Treaties' in *International Law at the Time of its Codification. Essays in Honour of Roberto Ago* (Giuffre, Milan 1987) vol II, 3–14.

[58] *Namibia* case (n 30) 47 [95].

[59] The point is explored in Simma and Tams (n 20) [45].

enshrine provisions of a peremptory nature.[60] Such an approach would indeed seem implicit in the rationale underlying *jus cogens* norms, as norms 'from which no derogation is permitted'.[61] However, Article 60 fails to take up the matter, and given the paucity of practice, it is no surprise that uncertainties remain.

C. Standing to suspend or terminate treaties

As the suspension or termination of a treaty affects its international obligations, a State invoking Article 60 must be legally entitled to do so. In this respect, two aspects need to be distinguished. Of course, any response finds its ultimate justification in the prior breach by the other State party. However, that in itself is not enough: in addition, the responding State must have been affected by that prior breach. It must have 'standing' to react. Standing is addressed in Article 60(1) and (2), which distinguish between bilateral and multilateral treaties and collective and individual responses. The result is a very complex regime of 'standing to respond against treaty breaches'. This regime is not beyond criticism, but it has had a lasting influence on our understanding of the character of multilateral obligations more generally and in a modified way reappears in the relevant provisions addressing standing to invoke State responsibility.

That the regime of standing is so complex is due to the rise of multilateral treaty obligations. Within the framework of a multilateral treaty, it may be extremely difficult to assess which of the parties should be entitled to respond against another party's material breach. Of course, some treaties say so expressly (eg by recognizing a right of each State party to respond against breaches[62]) and within regimes providing for regular recourse to third-party dispute resolution, courts, or tribunals have explored requirements of *locus standi*.[63] But in the absence of such treaty-specific approaches, the general rules governing standing to raise breaches of multilateral obligations are by no means easy to assess.

At the outset, it is worth noting that bilateral treaties present few problems. Where one State violates a bilateral treaty in a material way, the other party obviously has standing to respond to that breach. Subject to the exclusions

---

[60] See eg ibid [49]–[51].

[61] VCLT Art 53.

[62] See eg European Convention on Human Rights (adopted 4 November 1950, entered into force 3 September 1953) ETS 5, Art 33 (ECHR); American Convention on Human Rights (adopted 22 November 1969, entered into force 18 July 1978) 1144 UNTS 123, Art 45; African Charter on Human and Peoples' Rights (adopted 27 June 1981, entered into force 21 October 1986) [1982] 21 ILM 58, Art 47; Constitution of the International Labour Organization (adopted 9 October 1946, entered into force 20 April 1948) 15 UNTS 35, Art 26; Treaty on the Functioning of the European Union (TFEU), Art 259 (formerly Art 227 of the Treaty establishing the European Community).

[63] See eg the jurisprudence of WTO Panels and the Appellate Body on questions of standing to bring WTO complaints: WTO, *European Communities—Regime for the Importation, Sale and Distribution of Bananas* ('*Bananas III*')—*Report of the Panel* (22 May 1997) WT/DS27/R [7.46]–[7.51], and *Bananas III—Appellate Body Report* (9 September 1997) WT/DS27/AB/R [131]–[136], respectively. For comment see J Waincymer, *WTO Litigation: Procedural Aspects of Formal Dispute Settlement* (Cameron, London 2002) 154–7.

mentioned in Article 60(5) of the VCLT, all bilateral treaties can therefore be suspended or terminated in response to material breaches.

With respect to multilateral treaties, matters are more complex.[64] During the *travaux,* and ever since, the key question has been whether the position of States parties to multilateral treaties should be assimilated to that of States under bilateral treaties, ie within a clearly defined reciprocal legal relationship. On this, the ILC's debates reveal considerable uncertainty.[65] Drafters on the one hand acknowledged that all parties had an interest in the treaty's observance. On the other hand, they accepted that not all multilateral treaties could be treated alike and that material violations would not always affect all parties in the same way. The ILC initially favoured the first of these approaches and stressed the solidarity of all parties within a multilateral treaty framework: according to draft Article 42(2)(a), adopted in 1963, 'any other party' could respond to breaches of multilateral treaties by way of suspension.[66] This was refreshingly simple, but critically received by governments[67] and in the literature[68]—especially since the 'solidarity view' neglected that a material breach might affect different parties very differently, and because it seemed to place insufficient emphasis on the stability of treaty relations.[69] Taking up these concerns, the eventual standing regime moved away from the 'solidarity approach'. In so doing, the drafters managed to ensure (more) treaty stability, but had to embrace complexity. The regime eventually put forward in Article 60(2) is best understood in terms of one restrictive rule and two more liberal exceptions.

1. The restrictive rule

The *restrictive rule* is found in Article 60(2)(b), pursuant to which 'specially affected' States are entitled to suspend (but not terminate) treaties. The attribute 'specially affected' is not defined, but it clearly was introduced to indicate the move away from the solidarity approach. In order to be specially affected, a party to a treaty must have been individually injured by the material breach in question; the general interest in seeing the terms of the treaty observed (which is shared by 'any

---

[64] It is worth noting that notwithstanding the heterogeneity of multilateral treaties (which under the VCLT scheme cover narrow tripartite agreements just as much as universal law-making agreements), the drafters of the VCLT put forward one rule for all of them.

[65] For further details, see Simma and Tams (n 20) [26]–[40].

[66] [1963] YBILC, vol II, 204. This was based on Waldock's draft (Waldock, Second Report (n 24) 72 (Art 20(4)(a))), which however went further in accepting a right of 'any other party' to suspend or terminate the treaty in relation to the defaulting State. Within the ILC, Waldock's attempt to broaden the circle of parties entitled to respond to material breaches of multilateral treaties was endorsed inter alia by Rosenne (who later changed his view on the matter), Castren, and Briggs. See [1966] YBILC, vol I(1), 60 [26], 61 [40], [47]. The opposite view was taken by Verdross, [1963] YBILC, vol I, 294 [62]; and, in 1966, by Cadieux, de Luna, and Rosenne, [1966] YBILC, vol I(1), 62 [60], 63 [70], and 128 [7].

[67] See eg [1966] YBILC, vol II, Annex, 381 §17 (the Netherlands); and cf Simma (n 15) 69–70.

[68] See eg Schwelb (n 44) 321–6; Rolin, 'Statement' (1967) 52 Annuaire de l'Institut de Droit International, vol II, 359–61.

[69] One recurring point of concern was that draft Art 42(2)(a) would have permitted non-compliance with standard-setting conventions protecting collective interests: cf Schwelb (n 44) 321–6; Rolin (n 68) 359–61.

party to the treaty') will thus not be sufficient.[70] In practice, such 'special effects' are accepted in mainly two scenarios.

First, one State may have a particular interest in seeing a multilateral obligation performed. This is notably the case for multilateral obligations that—despite binding a plurality of States—are performed in a strictly bilateral context. Like bilateral treaties, these obligations are based on synallagmatic relations, giving rise to reciprocal rights and duties between pairs of States. Duties under multilateral diplomatic or consular agreements provide a classic example: while the treaties in question are multilateral, obligations arising under them are to be performed between pairs of receiving and sending States. The same would seem to apply to obligations arising under multilateral treaties on judicial assistance, the exchange of trade benefits, or conventions in the field of humanitarian law. In all these cases, the 'litmus test' is whether the multilateral treaty's application takes place between pairs of States and in what has been described as a 'quasi-bilateral' setting. If this is the case, a material breach of the multilateral treaty will 'specially affect' the other State party to the quasi-bilateral setting: the sending or receiving State; the State having requested judicial assistance; the State party to an armed conflict; or the State profiting directly from an exchange of benefits.

Second, even where the obligation is to be performed outside quasi-bilateral settings, the effect of the material breach may still 'specially affect' one State.[71] It may occur, for example, where a State violates treaty-based rights of foreign nationals (which would specially affect the State of nationality); where one State's material breach of an environmental obligation produces particularly grave effects on the territory of another State (such as the coastal State suffering from an oil spill); or, arguably, where one State party has a special responsibility to guarantee a treaty status (such as a special right to protect nationals of another State belonging to a distinct ethnic group).[72] Of course, these examples merely illustrate the general approach, and there is no hard and fast rule comprehensively defining instances of special effects based on special consequences. Thus, Article 60(2)(b), on the one hand, sets out a flexible requirement of 'special effects', but on the other hand, in requiring some form of special effect in the first place, requires States seeking to respond against a treaty breach to establish some form of individual injury.

2. Two liberal exceptions

There are two limited settings where this rather restrictive approach limiting standing to respond against material breaches is given up. The first of these exceptions is found in Article 60(2)(a), which addresses collective responses. As is

---

[70] See DN Hutchinson, 'Solidarity and Breaches of Multilateral Treaties' (1988) 59 BYBIL 188–9; Schwelb (n 44) 324.

[71] Cf Provost (n 15) 401; Schwelb (n 44) 324.

[72] Schwelb (n 44) 324. See for example Annex IV and Art 10(2) of the 1946 Peace Treaty with Italy, providing for a right of protection of the Austrian Government with respect to German-speaking inhabitants of South Tyrol; and the decision by the European Commission on Human Rights in *Austria v Italy* (App 788/60) (1961) 4 Yearbook 116, 142 (EComHR).

clear from the text, when acting collectively, all other parties enjoy wide freedom to react against material breaches of multilateral treaties. They can suspend the treaty in whole or in part or terminate it either in the relations between themselves and the defaulting State, or as between all the parties. In other words, they may choose between finally or temporarily expelling the violator from the treaty, or bringing the whole treaty relationship to an end. In order to do so, however, they have to act unanimously. This may be a realistic option in treaties with a limited number of parties, but it is increasingly difficult in universal multilateral treaty regimes with wide membership. It does not come as a surprise, then, that Article 60(2)(a) has been of limited practical relevance. In its 1971 advisory opinion on *Namibia*, the ICJ seemed to interpret the termination of the mandate for South West Africa as an exercise of the Article 60(2)(a) right.[73] Perhaps the suspension of Egypt's membership in the Organisation of the Islamic Conference (OIC), in 1979, could be seen as another instance on point (provided one is willing to accept that Egypt's entering into peace agreements with Israel could amount to a material breach of the OIC Charter).[74] Yet these are isolated—and dubious—incidents.

The second exception is found in Article 60(2)(c). It is equally of rather limited practical relevance, but conceptually important. It recognizes that, for a small circle of obligations, each party to a treaty can respond to material breaches individually, irrespective of any special injury, thus accepting the premise of the 'solidarity approach'. It does so however only with respect to a very narrowly formulated category of obligations, namely so-called 'integral' obligations.[75] These are described, in rather complicated terms, as obligations 'a material breach of [which] by one party radically changes the position of every party with respect to the further performance of its obligations'. The provision refers back to a category of treaties, initially described by Sir Gerald Fitzmaurice,[76] that operate on the basis of 'global reciprocity'.[77] The objective of such treaties can only be achieved through the interdependent performance of obligations by all parties.[78] Examples discussed by

---

[73] Cf *Namibia* case (n 30) 47 [94]. This interpretation would be problematic because the UNGA's resolution was not unanimous, but adopted by 114 votes to 2 with 3 abstentions. As evident from the wording of the provision, Art 60(2)(a), however, requires unanimity.

[74] See OIC Charter, 914 UNTS 103 and OIC Resolution 18/10-P of 12 May 1979. The case is discussed in KD Magliveras, *The Exclusion from Participation in International Organisations* (Brill, Leiden 1999) 237–8.

[75] For brief comments see M Fitzmaurice and O Elias, *Contemporary Issues in the Law of Treaties* (Eleven Intl Pub, Utrecht 2005) 158–64; LA Sicilianos, 'The Classification of Obligations and the Multilateral Dimension of the Relations of International Responsibility' (2002) 13 EJIL 1127.

[76] Fitzmaurice, Second Report (n 24) 31, 54 [126] (draft Art 19(1)(ii)(b) and (iii) and commentary); GG Fitzmaurice, 'Third Report on the Law of Treaties' [1958] YBILC, vol II, 27–8, 41 [78] and 44 [91]–[93] (draft Art 18(2), 19(a) and commentary), Fitzmaurice, Fourth Report (n 26) 45–6, 66 [82], 70 [102].

[77] Sicilianos (n 75) 1135.

[78] Crawford (n 15) [91]; J Crawford, 'The Standing of States: A Critique of Article 40 of the ILC's Draft Articles on State Responsibility', in D Fairgrieve (ed), *Judicial Review in International Perspective: Liber Amicorum in Honour of Lord Slynn of Hadley* (Kluwer Law International, The Hague 2000) 29–32 ('Crawford, The Standing of States'); C Feist, *Kündigung, Rücktritt und Suspendierung von multilateralen Verträgen* (Duncker & Humblot, Berlin 2001) 49–52; Gomaa (n 27) 34–5; Simma (n 15) 76; Sicilianos (n 75) 348.

the drafters include disarmament treaties or treaties prohibiting the use of particular weapons; to these, treaties prohibiting the acquisition of territory by force may be added.[79] In order to be meaningful, the VCLT drafters assumed, these treaties would have to be performed by every party vis-à-vis every other party. Conversely, one party's non-compliance would affect all other parties to the treaty. Hence, all other parties are entitled to respond to material breaches. What is more, because of the obligations' interdependent (or 'integral') structure, responses cannot be restricted to relations between the defaulting and responding party because the responding party's suspension would necessarily be a violation of its obligation vis-à-vis all other (non-defaulting) parties. Article 60(2)(c) spells out the implications of this 'global reciprocity' concept; and exceptionally allows for responses by each and every treaty party.

As is clear from the preceding paragraphs, to lay down a general regime governing standing to respond against breaches has been a considerable challenge. The ILC's debate on what became Article 60 is relevant precisely because it marked one of the first occasions at which the UN's main codification body discussed questions of standing in depth, and in full awareness of the rise of multilateralism. Not surprisingly, then, Article 60's approach has 'spilled over' into subsequent attempts to formulate rules of standing, notably in the context of the ILC's State responsibility project. That said, as much as it was a 'first', the ILC's Article 60 debates were also a 'last' in some respects. They reflect the international community's approach to standing at a time when the key concepts giving expression to collective interests were only beginning to be considered. While a 'solidarity approach' was considered, the drafters did not discuss public interest concepts such as obligations *erga omnes* (to be defined, one year after the VCLT's adoption, as obligations in whose observance 'all States can be held to have a legal interest'[80]), and they decided not to reflect the new category of *jus cogens* within a regime governing standing against treaty breaches. On that basis, they generally favoured a restrictive regime of standing that remained premised on specially sustained injury, resisting the temptation to turn Article 60 into an instrument of public interest enforcement.

D. Procedural conditions governing the exercise of the right of response

A mere two years after the VCLT's opening for signature, the ICJ held that Article 60 might 'in many respects be considered as a codification of existing international law on the subject'.[81] In line with this statement, the preceding discussion has treated Article 60 and treaty-based responses under customary international law together. With respect to the procedural conditions governing the exercise of the right, matters are different. The VCLT subjects individual responses to a

---

[79] See eg Fitzmaurice, Second Report (n 24) 54 [126] and n73.
[80] *Barcelona Traction, Light and Power Company, Limited (Belgium v Spain)* (Judgment) [1970] ICJ Rep 3 [33].
[81] *Namibia* case (n 30) 47 [94]–[95].

cumbersome regime that, to date, has not been applied; and customary international rules on treaty-based responses do not contain equivalent restrictions.

Article 60(1), 2(b), and 2(c) (ie those provisions addressing individual responses) expressly provide that the responding State is entitled to *invoke* the prior breach *as a ground* for suspension or termination.[82] This formula clarifies that the Article 60 invocation does not itself affect the treaty relationship, but that the legal effects of suspension or termination are only entailed according to the procedural rules of Articles 65–68 of the VCLT.[83] A responding State's intention to suspend or terminate a treaty in whole or in part therefore only takes effect once the procedure of Articles 65–68 has been followed.[84] And this is by no means a mere formality. Rather, these provisions envisage the notification of any claims; the lapse of a three-month period during which other parties can protest; dispute resolution by a method chosen by the responding and protesting parties; and, failing their agreement on a mode of dispute resolution, a process of mandatory conciliation pursuant to VCLT Annex 1.[85]

Predictably, the 'procedural straightjacket' set out in Articles 65 to 68 has not proved particularly popular. States and other actors of international law have drawn a distinction between Article 60's substantive aspects—which, by and large, they have applied as customary international law—and its procedural implementation mechanism. In practice, this has meant that States affected by a material breach have suspended or terminated treaties without instituting the VCLT's dispute settlement procedures. In line with that understanding, the ICJ, in *Armed Activities (DRC v Rwanda)* expressly noted that Article 66 (providing for compulsory conciliation) was not 'declaratory of customary international law'.[86] In the *Racke case,* which concerned the parallel problem whether responses based on the *clausula rebus sic stantibus* would require prior attempts at dispute settlement, the European Court of Justice adopted the same line of reasoning, holding that 'the specific procedural requirements there [ie in Article 65 of the VCLT] laid down do not form part of customary international law'.[87] While some decisions have taken a more favourable position,[88] the more convincing view is that Articles 65–68 do not

---

[82] In the ILC's draft articles, this formula was used only for [1] and [2(b)]; the ILC's version of [2(c)] had entitled parties 'to suspend the operation of the treaty'. The inconsistency between [2(b)] and [2(c)] was removed following a proposal by the UK. Vienna Conference, Official Records (n 32) 269 (quoting UN Doc A/CONF.39/L.29); for the relevant debates see Vienna Conference, First Session (n 39) 478, 484; Vienna Conference, Second Session (n 27) 115.

[83] Gomaa (n 27) 98.

[84] Kirgis maintains that Arts 65 to 68 do not apply to partial suspension of treaties, as neither Art 65 nor Art 42(2) referred to it. See Kirgis (n 34) 558. The argument is however not convincing, as the Art 60 formula 'to invoke as a ground' is to be understood as a comprehensive reference to the procedure envisaged in Arts 65–68.

[85] For details, including on the dramatic debates surrounding the adoption of Arts 65 *et seq*, see I Sinclair, *The Vienna Convention on the Law of Treaties* (2nd edn MUP, Manchester 1984) 226–33.

[86] [2006] ICJ Rep 6 [125].

[87] *Racke GmbH and Co v Hauptzollamt Mainz*, Case C-162/96 [1998] ECR I-3655 [52]–[59].

[88] See especially the *Gabčíkovo-Nagymaros* case, where the ICJ's judgment noted that '[b]oth Parties agree[d] that Articles 65 to 67 of the Vienna Convention on the Law of Treaties, if not codifying customary law, at least generally reflect customary international law and contain[ed] certain procedural

reflect general international law. This in turn provides some justification for the approach of States just described: because of its temporal restrictions[89] and still rather modest ratifications record,[90] the VCLT more often than not, is not applicable *as treaty law*, but merely in so far as it reflects custom. As Articles 65 to 68 do not reflect custom, States enjoy considerable leeway in seeking to avoid the cumbersome implementation procedure governing the exercise of the right to suspend or terminate a treaty.[91]

E. Interim conclusions

The preceding considerations suggest that Article 60 has shaped our thinking about responses against treaty breaches, but that it is not immune from criticism. Drafters were keen to ensure that States would not lightly suspend (let alone terminate) treaties—hence the requirement that the right to suspend/terminate presupposes a prior *material* breach, the cumbersome conditions governing its exercise, the restriction of responses to *the treaty affected by the prior breach*, and the rather cautious approach to standing. If one accepts the drafters' approach, one might wonder whether the notion of 'material breach' ought not to have been defined differently, or why the scope of the right is not limited by a proportionality test.

Yet, more fundamentally, it seems that the drafters may have lost sight of the necessary balance between the need to ensure the stability of treaties, while also permitting effective responses against breaches. Article 60 is really designed to address major ruptures in treaty relations, but leaves the smaller, 'everyday' problems unaddressed. In hindsight, the regime devised in Article 60 may well have been an over-ambitious attempt to 'civilize' inter-State relations. Article 60 certainly achieves its aim—that is, to preserve the stability of treaties. But by subjecting treaty suspension and termination to rather stringent conditions, the drafters inadvertently restricted Article 60's 'appeal' to States seeking to respond against another State's treaty breaches. Not surprisingly, treaties adopted after the VCLT have increasingly formulated treaty-specific rules on responses against breaches. And perhaps more importantly, with respect to general concepts, the VCLT's narrow approach has meant that responding States intending to suspend treaty obligations have relied, not on the general law of treaties, but on the law of State

---

principles which are based on an obligation to act in good faith'. *Gabčikovo-Nagymaros* case (n 16) [109].

[89] Cf VCLT Arts 4 and 84(2) (providing for non-retroactivity).

[90] Forty-two years after its adoption, the Convention has been ratified, or acceded to, by 111 States (cf <http://treaties.un.org/pages/ViewDetailsIII.aspx?&src=UNTSONLINE&mtdsg_no=XXIII~1&chapter=23&Temp=mtdsg3&lang=en>). Prominent 'non-ratifying' States include France, the US, India, and Indonesia.

[91] For further comment on this point see ME Villiger, *Commentary on the 1969 Vienna Convention on the Law of Treaties* (Martinus Nijhoff, Leiden 2009) 813–14; Verdross and Simma (n 44) [840]; J Verhoeven, '*Jus cogens* and Reservations or "Counter-Reservations" to the Jurisdiction of the International Court of Justice' in K Wellens (ed), *International Law: Theory and Practice; Essays in Honour of Eric Suy* (Martinus Nijhoff, Leiden 1998) 199–200.

responsibility instead. Inadvertently, then, Article 60's limited 'appeal' may have paved the way for a 'renaissance' of the concept of countermeasures.

III. The Law of State Responsibility: Countermeasures

The second general concept permitting otherwise illegal responses against treaty breaches is that of countermeasures. The concept of countermeasures is situated within the law of State responsibility and has been shaped by that doctrine rather than by the general law of treaties. As noted above,[92] conceptually, countermeasures follow a different rationale than Article 60 treaty-based responses: their aim is not to re-establish a balance of rights among treaty partners, but to induce or compel the State responsible for a treaty breach back into compliance. Compared to treaty-based responses, countermeasures are a broader concept, and their regulation under international law is more flexible. In order to bring out these features, this section clarifies the legal regime of countermeasures by comparing it to Article 60 treaty-based responses. This comparative approach will enable us to highlight four main aspects of the countermeasures regime: (i) the possibility of resorting to countermeasures against *any* treaty breach; (ii) the wide discretion of States in calibrating their response; limited largely by the requirement of proportionality; (iii) the different approach to the problem of standing; and (iv) the decision not to submit countermeasures to far-reaching procedural preconditions.

A. The requirement of a prior breach

The first element is that in order to be justified, a countermeasure 'must be taken in response to a previous international wrongful act of another State and must be directed against that State'.[93] This is at times formulated as a limitation, indicating that it is not sufficient for the responding State to *consider* international law to have been breached.[94] And indeed, in prescribing that there must be an *actual* breach, the international legal regime of countermeasures embraces an objective standard. Of course, this is fully in line with the overall legal regime governing responses to wrongfulness, and should not be read to require an objective assessment of the situation *by a third party*. A responding State remains free to determine whether there has been a breach, but does so at its own risk.[95]

---

[92] See nn 20–3 and accompanying text.

[93] *Gabčíkovo-Nagymaros* case (n 16) 55 [83].

[94] ASR (n 14) [3] (commentary to ASR Art 49). Clarification of this point is often felt to be necessary, since the *Air Services* arbitral award misleadingly stated that 'each State establishes for itself its legal situation vis-à-vis other States'. *Case Concerning the Air Services Agreement of 27 March 1946* [1978] 54 ILR 304 [81].

[95] The matter is, of course, different if applicable rules make resort to countermeasures dependent upon some form of authorization, such as within the WTO regime. Cf WTO Dispute Settlement Understanding [1994] 33 ILM 1226, Annex 2, Art 22; WTO, *United States–Sections 301–10 of the Trade Act of 1974—Panel Report* (22 December 1999) WT/DS152/R [7.35]–[7.46]. On procedural preconditions restricting the resort to countermeasures see nn 135–9 and accompanying text.

From a comparative perspective, what stands out in this element is not the decision to require the actual commission of a breach, but the fact that, unlike in the law of treaties, *any* actual breach can be met by way of a countermeasure. There are two aspects to this. First, the formulation very clearly brings out the breadth of the concept of countermeasures, which is available against all 'previous international wrongful act[s] of another State', including (but not limited to) treaty breaches.[96] Second, and more pertinently, unlike Article 60, there is no threshold requirement. Countermeasures can be taken against all treaty breaches, irrespective of their material character. This means that, even within the field of treaty breaches, countermeasures have a wider scope of application than treaty-based measures. Conversely, the decision to leave out any threshold requirement reinforces the need for limits on the scope of responses, notably through the concept of proportionality.

B. The scope of the right to respond

The breadth of the concept of countermeasures is reflected in the rules governing the scope of the right to resort to them. These rules are clearly influenced by the purpose of countermeasures as an instrument of law enforcement. Beyond that, moreover, countermeasures are characterized by their flexibility. Unlike treaty-based responses, States enjoy an extremely wide margin of discretion in choosing how to respond to treaty breaches via countermeasures. This wide discretion in turn is limited by the overarching requirement that countermeasures must be proportionate, as well as by a range of exclusionary clauses protecting particularly important obligations. Against this background, the legal rules governing the scope of countermeasures can be presented in four steps.

1. *Countermeasures focus on inducing compliance*

As an enforcement concept, countermeasures must be taken for a specific purpose. They must 'induce the wrongdoing State to comply with its obligations under international law'.[97] This limited function implies that countermeasures are not designed to alter the underlying legal relationship between the responding and targeted State. Rather, they merely justify non-compliance with international law for an interim period and a specific purpose.[98] It follows that countermeasures— notwithstanding the negative connotations of the traditional term 'reprisals'—are

---

[96] This is in line with the international law approach to questions of responsibility generally, which does not draw distinctions between breaches of treaty and breaches of general international law: cf ASR (n 14) Art 12 ('There is a breach of an international obligation by a State when an act of that State is not in conformity with what is required of it by that obligation, regardless of its origin or character').

[97] *Gabčikovo-Nagymaros* case (n 16) [85]. This is taken up in ASR (n 14) Art 49(1).

[98] Cf ibid Art 49(2) ('Countermeasures are limited to the non-performance for the time being of international obligations of the State taking the measures towards the responsible State').

not an instrument of private vengeance and must not be used as a form of punishment.[99]

While firmly established conceptually (and indispensable as a matter of legal policy), these guidelines are rather difficult to translate into strict rules in practice. The prohibition against punishment mainly goes to the State's motivation in adopting countermeasures. This, however, is difficult to police, especially since—like punishment—countermeasures are by definition coercive. As for the interim character of countermeasures, the general rule is that countermeasures be temporary and reversible. But Article 49(3) of the ASR deliberately opts against any absolute approach, instead stating that '[c]ountermeasures shall, *as far as possible*, be taken in such a way as to permit the resumption of performance of the obligations in question' (emphasis added).[100] Even with this caveat, it is clear that countermeasures only justify non-compliance as long as this is required to induce compliance.[101]

2. Countermeasures are not limited to the treaty breached

It is with respect to the choice of obligations that can be violated that countermeasures are most clearly different from treaty-based responses. Unlike Article 60 of the VCLT, the law of countermeasures does not prescribe which obligations can be disregarded in order to induce the targeted State back into compliance. Subject to a number of exclusionary rules (addressed below), this is a matter for the responding State to decide. There are two aspects to this. First, given the general character of the concept, it is clear that countermeasures cannot be restricted to the non-performance of obligations *under the same treaty.* Second, and less obviously, international law has refrained from formulating special rules for responses that affect obligations connected to the ones initially breached.[102] A responding State may no doubt choose to take such so-called 'reciprocal countermeasures',[103] but the legal regime of countermeasures does not require it to do so, nor indeed does it subject reciprocal countermeasures to a special legal regime.[104] As a consequence, the circle of obligations that can be disregarded by way of countermeasures is much wider than those affected by treaty-based responses. A responding State can respond against treaty breaches notably by violating its obligations towards the targeted State under *other treaties,* or indeed under *general international law.* For example, a breach of a bilateral treaty on economic cooperation may be met with economic sanctions violating WTO law. Or, violations of diplomatic immunity

---

[99] ASR (n 14) 130 [1] (commentary on Art 49).

[100] For details see ibid 131 [9]; *Gabčikovo-Nagymaros* case (n 16) [87].

[101] This is expressly spelled out in ASR (n 14) Arts 52(3)(a), 53.

[102] For a discussion of whether such 'reciprocal countermeasures' are subject to an autonomous regime see Crawford (n 15) [327]–[329]. For an attempt to formulate autonomous rules cf W Riphagen, 'Sixth Report on State Responsibility' [1985] YBILC, vol II(1), 10 (draft Art 8 of Part Two, drawing on PCIJ's judgment in *Diversion of Water from the Meuse* [1937] PCIJ Rep Series A/B No 70, 4, 50, 77).

[103] See eg the *Air Services* arbitration (n 94) 304.

[104] See eg ASR (n 14) 128–9 [4]–[5].

may prompt the freezing of assets. The law of countermeasures does not presuppose any nexus, or requirement of qualitative proportionality,[105] between the initial violation and the response thereto. This flexibility, in turn, reinforces the need for some limitations on the response, which are found in exclusionary clauses and the overarching requirement of proportionality.

3. Proportionality: countermeasures must be commensurate with the injury suffered

Proportionality—in its 'quantitative' variant[106]—is the key substantive criterion limiting the exercise of the right to take countermeasures. It is a common limitation on responses against wrongfulness and a crucial element in the quest to 'tame' countermeasures specifically. Its application to the law of countermeasures raises few conceptual problems: what is required is a comparison between the effects of the initial breach and the responding State's reaction. In the words of the ICJ (endorsed by the ILC), 'the effects of a countermeasure must be commensurate with the injury suffered'.[107] This indeed is a necessary limitation, one instrumental to ensuring that countermeasures do not become measures of punishment and which helps keep its results acceptable. As the ILC's work clarifies, the proportionality comparison is primarily between the levels of injury (ie quantitative), but also the importance of the interest protected by the rule infringed and the seriousness of the breach.[108]

While relatively unproblematic conceptually, the *application* of proportionality poses two problems. First, because States have discretion in choosing which obligations they intend to disregard to induce the targeted State back into compliance, any proportionality analysis may involve a comparison between 'disparate integers'[109] or 'apples and oranges'.[110] This is not a specific problem of countermeasures. Still the problem can be easily seen in this context by considering, for example, the possibility of responding to a prior violation of an FCN treaty by adopting a travel ban. The two acts are so different that it is not easy to assess their equivalence. Second, the absence of a regular scrutiny procedure further complicates matters. As shown below, as a matter of principle, countermeasures are not

---

[105] Cf the terminology used at nn 49–51 and accompanying text.

[106] Ibid.

[107] ASR (n 14) Art 51. This goes back to the ICJ's judgment in the *Gabčikovo-Nagymaros* case (n 16) [85]–[87]. For earlier attempts to formulate versions of a proportionality requirement cf *Air Services* arbitration (n 94) [83] ('It is generally agreed that all counter-measures must, in the first instance, have some degree of equivalence with the alleged breach'); *Naulilaa Award* (1930) 2 RIAA 1011, 1028 ('[E]ven if one were to admit that the law of nations does not require that the reprisal should be approximately in keeping with the offence, one should certainly consider as excessive and therefore unlawful reprisals out of all proportion to the act motivating them').

[108] ASR (n 14) 135 [6] (commentary to Art 51).

[109] T Franck, 'On Proportionality of Countermeasures in International Law' (2008) 102 AJIL 715, 729.

[110] M Schmitt, 'Fault Lines in the Law of Attack' in S Breau and A Jachec-Neale (eds), *Testing the Boundaries of International Law* (BIICL, London 2006) 293.

subject to any form of prior authorization or independent assessment; like other private responses, they are to be taken by the responding State on the basis of its own (auto-)assessment of the situation.[111]

Both problems, taken together, limit the effectiveness of a proportionality principle in taming countermeasures, but do not render it pointless. Quite to the contrary, in the absence of regular independent assessments, it is the unorganized international legal community that evaluates responses, through statements, protests or approval, whether tacit or express. In its evaluation, the community is guided by occasional pronouncements by international courts and tribunals, which—notwithstanding the absence of *regular* judicial scrutiny—have assessed the proportionality of countermeasures in cases such as *Naulilaa, Air Services*, and *Gabcikovo*.[112] Based on these pronouncements, international practice, and clarification exercises like the ILC's work on State responsibility, the notion of proportionality—it is submitted—can be applied meaningfully. Indeed, it acts as the most important restraint on countermeasures.[113]

4. Countermeasures must not affect obligations under rules of jus cogens *and dispute settlement procedures*

Finally, beyond the overarching requirement of proportionality, international law shields a number of particularly important obligations from the application of countermeasures. Within the ILC's text, these exclusions are spelled out in Article 50 of the ASR. They follow the same logic as the exclusionary clause of Article 60(5) of the VCLT, but (having been adopted in 2001) are more up-to-date with contemporary international law.[114] In essence, two categories of obligations cannot be disregarded by way of countermeasure. First, countermeasures do not justify the non-performance of obligations imposed by rules of *jus cogens.* This takes account of the fact that modern international law accepts *jus cogens* effects beyond the VCLT[115] and that fundamental substantive interests protected by the concept cannot be opted out of unilaterally.[116] It follows that obligations flowing from recognized peremptory rules—notably the duty not to use force in violation of the UN Charter, or obligations under peremptory rules of human rights law or international humanitarian law—must not be the subject of countermeasures.

---

[111] See nn 135–9 and accompanying text.

[112] See *Naulilaa Award* (n 107) 1101; *Air Services* arbitration (n 94) 304; *Gabčikovo-Nagymaros* case (n 16) 7, respectively.

[113] Cf Franck (n 109) 764.

[114] Contrast the authors' more sceptical analysis of Art 60(5) at nn 54–61 and accompanying text.

[115] Within the ILC's text on State responsibility, see notably ASR (n 14) Arts 26, 40–1. For an early and balanced study of these and other instances see G Gaja, 'Jus Cogens Beyond the Vienna Convention' (1981) 172 RdC 273. For an ambitious attempt to 'peremptorise' broad areas of international law, see A Orekhelashvili, *Peremptory Norms in International Law* (OUP, Oxford 2006).

[116] In the words of the ILC, '[e]vidently, a peremptory norm, not subject to derogation as between two States even by treaty, cannot be derogated from by unilateral action in the form of countermeasures'. ASR (n 14) 132 [9] (Commentary to Art 50).

Second, good reasons suggest that countermeasures may not affect obligations that were agreed precisely to peacefully resolve disputes between the responding State and the targeted State. This implies that, as the ICJ put it in the *ICAO Council* case when speaking about treaty suspension, 'a merely unilateral suspension [cannot] per se render jurisdictional clauses inoperative, since one of their purposes might be, precisely, to enable the validity of the suspension to be tested'.[117] It follows that where States are bound by dispute settlement provisions covering the dispute in question, the responding State is not relieved from fulfilling these obligations when resorting to countermeasures.[118] According to the ILC, the same rationale applies to minimum obligations designed to ensure the inviolability of diplomatic and consular immunities. Following this argument—which draws some support from the ICJ's *Tehran Hostages* judgment[119]—countermeasures ought not to affect the existence of basic channels of communication since they may be a conduit for the resolution of the dispute.[120]

C. Standing to take countermeasures

Given the broad character of the concept, the identification of States entitled to resort to countermeasures assumes particular importance. Not surprisingly, there is much debate about 'standing to take countermeasures'. The ILC's work on State responsibility—which addresses the matter within the framework of the rules governing the implementation of responsibility—has helped clarify some of the issues, but leaves open one crucial question. The regime set out in Articles 42 and 49 of the ILC's text to a large extent follows the VCLT rules on standing to suspend or terminate treaties, while Article 54 points to an unresolved question ignored by Article 60 of the VCLT.

Articles 42 and 49 of the ASR deal with standing on the basis of the *acquis* of agreed rules devised in Article 60 of the VCLT.[121] In essence, these provision recognize the right of States to resort to countermeasures if the obligation breached was owed to them bilaterally or if the breach of a multilateral obligation 'specially affected' them (because of the quasi-bilateral structure of performance or because the wrongful act had produced specific, individualized consequences).[122] What is more, the standing regime set out in the ASR follows Article 60 even into the

---

[117] *Appeal Relating to the Jurisdiction of the ICAO Council (India v Pakistan)* [1972] ICJ Rep 46, 53.

[118] ASR (n 14) Art 50(2)(a).

[119] *United States Diplomatic and Consular Staff in Tehran* [1980] ICJ Rep 3 [83]–[86] (misleadingly describing diplomatic law as a 'self-contained regime', which 'on the one hand, lays down the receiving State's obligations regarding the facilities, privileges and immunities to be accorded to diplomatic missions and, on the other, foresees their possible abuse by members of the mission and specifies the means at the disposal of the receiving State to counter any such abuse'). For a critical analysis cf B Simma, 'Self-contained regimes' (1985) Netherlands Ybk Intl L 111.

[120] ASR (n 14) 133–4 [14]–[15] (commentary to Art 50).

[121] See Part II.C, 588 *et seq*. During the course of its second reading on State responsibility, the ILC deliberately opted to follow the VCLT Art 60 approach: cf ASR (n 14) 117 [4]; J Crawford, The Standing of States (n 78) 23.

[122] Cf ASR (n 14) Art 42(a) and 42(b)(i).

muddy terrain of integral obligations.[123] Taking up the rationale of 'global reciprocity'[124] informing Article 60(2)(c) of the VCLT, Article 42(b)(ii) of the ASR accepts that where an interdependent/integral obligation has been breached '[t]he other States parties . . . must all be considered as individually entitled to react to a breach', including by means of countermeasures.[125]

In another respect, however, debates about standing to take countermeasures have moved beyond the Vienna Convention *acquis*. There is much debate about a new version of the 'solidarity approach'[126] to questions of standing—namely the question whether States could resort to countermeasures in order to defend collective interests protected by treaties dealing with humanitarian matters or other public policy concerns.[127] These renewed discussions are part of a more general debate about the right of individual States to act as guardians of collective interests.[128] Given the crucial role of multilateral treaties as 'workhorses of community interest',[129] this general debate directly implicates the legal regime(s) governing responses to treaty breaches. The international community has yet to reach agreement on this matter, but developments since the mid-1960s (when the VCLT rules were drafted) point in favour of allowing 'solidarity measures'.

In its 1970 judgment in the *Barcelona Traction* case, the ICJ accepted that all States can be held to have a legal interest in seeing certain fundamental rules complied with (which it termed obligations *erga omnes*).[130] Since 1970, States have accepted the rationale behind this *erga omnes* dictum and, on a number of occasions, have taken countermeasures in response to grave and systematic breaches of collective interest provisions.[131] In its work on State responsibility, the ILC considered these instances to be too sporadic to amount to a settled practice, and was cautious not to endorse expressly a right of individual States, irrespective of any individual injury, to take 'solidarity measures'.[132] However, it did embrace the idea of collective interest enforcement in Article 48 of its text and accepted that a practice was emerging.[133] Other bodies, such as the *Institut de droit international* have (rightly) gone beyond the ILC's approach and recognized that where a State is responsible for a 'widely acknowledged grave breach of a treaty protecting obligations *erga omnes*, 'all the States to which the obligation is owed: . . . are entitled to

---

[123] Ibid 119 [13]–[14] (commentary to Art 42).

[124] Sicilianos (n 75) 1135.

[125] ASR (n 14) 119 [14] (commentary to Art 42). For critical comment see Tams (n 12).

[126] Cf n 69 and accompanying text.

[127] For details see M Akehurst, 'Reprisals by Third States' (1970) 44 BYBIL 1; J Charney, 'Third State Remedies in International Law' (1989) 10 Michigan J Intl L 57; C Tams, *Enforcing Obligations Erga Omnes in International Law* (CUP, Cambridge 2005) 198 *et seq.*

[128] On which see C Tams, 'Individual States as Guardians of Community Interests' in U Fastenrath and others (eds), *From Bilateralism to Community Interest. Essays in Honour of Judge Bruno Simma* (OUP, Oxford 2011) 379.

[129] B Simma, 'From Bilateralism to Community Interest' (1994) 250 RdC 217, 322.

[130] *Barcelona Traction* (n 80) 32–3 [33]–[34].

[131] For details see Tams (n 127) 198–249.

[132] See ASR (n 14) 140 [3] (commentary to Art 54, noting 'Practice on this subject is limited and rather embryonic').

[133] Ibid (listing some of the more prominent examples).

take non-forcible counter-measures under conditions analogous to those applying to a State specially affected by the breach'.[134] Indeed, this last position seems to reflect the current state of the law and marks the acceptance of a modest version of the solidarity approach within the law of countermeasures.

D. Procedural conditions governing the exercise of the right to countermeasures

The question remains whether States seeking to resort to countermeasures need to comply with procedural requirements. Just as with treaty-based measures, this is a matter of some controversy.[135] From a policy perspective, the imposition of procedural conditions has seemed to many to be the best way of taming the archaic countermeasures concept. During the first reading of the ILC's work on State responsibility, the ILC's Special Rapporteur Arangio Ruiz submitted far-reaching proposals in this respect. He proposed to require the prior exhaustion 'of all the amicable settlement procedures available under general international law, the United Nations Charter or any other dispute settlement instrument to which [a State seeking redress] is a party' and a system for 'post-countermeasures' dispute settlement.[136] These proposals certainly marked one of the high-points of attempts to 'civilize' the private enforcement of international law, but they proved overly ambitious. Stressing the legitimacy of countermeasures (which were a fact of life and served to uphold the rule of law), States and commentators argued for a leaner regime, which would balance the interests of responding and targeted States in a more nuanced way.[137] Debates eventually resulted in ASR Article 52, which requires responding States to give 'advance warning' to the targeted State and provide it with an opportunity to respond to the claims underlying the dispute.[138]

Beyond this minimum requirement, Article 52 deliberately refrains from making resort to countermeasures dependent on the prior exhaustion of further dispute settlement procedures (nor does it establish mechanisms for 'post-countermeasures' dispute settlement). It does, however, recognize the primacy of third party dispute resolution in two settings. First, it affirms that comprehensive dispute settlement systems can exclude the availability of coercive self-help altogether. Second, it excludes resorting to countermeasures in situations in which the underlying dispute

---

[134] Institut de droit international, 'Resolution on "Obligations and Rights Erga Omnes in International Law"' in [2006] 71 Annuaire de l'Institut de droit international 289.

[135] See notably the symposium on 'Counter-measures and Dispute Settlement' in (1994) EJIL, vol 5 (contributions by G Arangio-Ruiz, V Vereshchetin, M Bennouna, J Crawford, C Tomuschat, D Bowett, B Simma, and L Condorelli).

[136] See notably G Arangio-Ruiz, 'Fourth Report on State Responsibility' [1992] YBILC, vol II(1), 1; G Arangio-Ruiz, 'Fifth Report on State Responsibility' [1993] YBILC, vol II(1), 1 (proposals for draft Art 12 and a 'dispute settlement annex').

[137] See eg B Simma, 'Counter-measures and Dispute Settlement: A Plea for a Different Balance' (1995) 5 EJIL 102 (on which the subsequent observations draw).

[138] See ASR (n 14) Art 52(1) ('[b]efore taking countermeasures, an injured State shall: (a) call upon the responsible State, in accordance with Article 43, to fulfil its obligations under Part Two; (b) notify the responsible State of any decision to take countermeasures and offer to negotiate with that State').

is pending before a court or tribunal, with the caveat that where the dispute settlement process breaks down, the right to take countermeasures revives. These safeguards are complemented by the provision—mentioned above, as part of the exclusionary clauses[139]—that countermeasures must not affect dispute settlement obligations agreed between the disputing parties. Taken together, it would seem that the more modest system devised by the ILC indeed preserves existing institutionalized dispute settlement without 'choking' countermeasures.

Conclusion

The legal regime governing countermeasures differs markedly from the treaty law rules permitting the suspension or termination of treaties in response to breaches. Mindful not to lay down overly restrictive rules that States would merely circumvent, the international community's 'agents' of legal development—the ILC, States in their comments on the ILC's work, and international courts and tribunals—have devised a regime that is considerably more flexible than that of Article 60, and which permits the suspension of treaty obligations under less stringent conditions. The difference can be explained by reference to differences between the enforcement concept of countermeasures, on the one hand, and the defensive concept of treaty law responses on the other. But presumably, they are *also* a reflection of a more sceptical approach towards over-ambitious attempts to civilize inter-State relations. As the more flexible general concept permitting coercive responses against treaty breaches, countermeasures thus still retain their role as an important feature of the international regime governing response against treaty breaches.

If nevertheless, even resort to the more flexible concept of countermeasures today is rather rare, then this reflects the increasing prominence of treaty-specific regimes providing for 'tailor-made' rules on responses against treaty breaches. Modern treaty regimes in fields such as international environmental law, arms control, or human rights law have reached a degree of sophistication that general legal concepts (like countermeasures or treaty law responses) simply cannot match. If we may be permitted to adapt a well-known statement by a well-known international lawyer, coercive responses to treaty breaches—whether justified as countermeasures or under Article 60 of the VCLT—today seem to be 'vehicle[s] that hardly ever leav[e] the garage'.[140] Yet, like rarely used vehicles, they do remain around, ready to be taken out for the occasional trip, when the circumstances so require. Thus, they should not be discarded lightly.

---

[139] See nn 114–20 and accompanying text.

[140] Cf I Brownlie, 'Comment' in J Weiler and A Cassese (eds), *Change and Stability in International Law-Making* (Walter de Gruyter, Berlin 1988) 108, 110. The original statement referred to *jus cogens*. Developments since 1988 show that even vehicles that at one point hardly left the garage may become rather over-used subsequently.

Recommended Reading

DW Bowett, 'Treaties and State Responsibility' in D Bardonnet and others (eds), *Le droit international au service de la paix, de la justice et du développement. Mélanges Michel Virally* (Pédone, Paris 1991) 137

F Capotorti, 'L'extinction et la suspension des traités' (1971-III) 134 RdC 417

OY Elagab, *The Legality of Non-Forcible Countermeasures in International Law* (OUP, Oxford 1987)

C Feist, *Kündigung, Rücktritt und Suspendierung von multilateralen Verträgen* (Duncker & Humblot, Berlin 2001)

M Gomaa, *Suspension or Termination of Treaties for Grounds of Breach* (Martinus Nijhoff, Leiden 1996)

DW Greig, 'Reciprocity, Proportionality, and the Law of Treaties' (1994) 34 VJIL 295

DN Hutchinson, 'Solidarity and Breaches of Multilateral Treaties' (1988) 59 BYBIL 151

FL Kirgis, 'Some Lingering Questions About Article 60 of the Vienna Convention on the Law of Treaties' (1989) 22 Cornell Intl L J 549

R Mazzeschi Pisillo, 'Termination and Suspension of Treaties on Grounds of Breach' in B Simma and M Spinedi (eds), *United Nations Codification of State Responsibility* (Oceana, New York 1987) 57

S Rosenne, *Breach of Treaty* (Grotius, Cambridge 1985)

E Schwelb, 'Termination or Suspension of a Treaty as a Consequence of its Breach' (1967) 7 IJIL 309

LA Sicilianos, 'The Relationship Between Reprisals and Denunciation or Suspension of a Treaty' (1993) 4 EJIL 341

B Simma, 'From Bilateralism to Community Interest' (1994) 250 RdC 217

B Simma, 'Reflections on Article 60 of the Vienna Convention on the Law of Treaties and Its Background in General International Law' (1970) 20 ÖZÖR 5

B Simma and C Tams, 'Article 60 (1969)' in O Corten and P Klein (eds), *The Vienna Conventions on the Law of Treaties: A Commentary* (OUP, Oxford 2011) vol II, 1352

BP Sinha, *Unilateral Denunciation of Treaty Because of Prior Violations of Obligations by Other Party* (Martinus Nijhoff, Leiden 1966)

CJ Tams, *Enforcing Obligations* Erga Omnes *in International Law* (CUP, Cambridge (revised paperback) 2010)

24

Exceptional Circumstances and Treaty Commitments

Malgosia Fitzmaurice

Introduction

Much of the existing law of treaties promotes the stability and security of treaty relations. The fundamental principle *pacta sunt servanda* reflects this idea by requiring that parties must perform their obligations in good faith for all valid treaties in force.[1] But the law of treaties does not favour stability and security exclusively. Escape valves do exist, permitting parties to terminate or suspend their obligations for various reasons. In some cases, the law of treaties does so to promote consent, such as where termination or suspension occurs in conformity with the parties' own agreement, whether in the treaty itself or some later instrument.[2] In a different set of cases—those involving material breach—the behaviour of other parties provides an alternative basis for a State to abrogate the treaty or suspend its own performance.[3]

This chapter deals with a third condition—the existence of 'exceptional circumstances'—that States can invoke to avoid (or remove) their treaty obligations. The following doctrines that may serve this purpose are analysed: (i) supervening impossibility of performance; (ii) fundamental change of circumstances; and (iii) necessity.[4] The first two grounds are codified in Articles 61 and 62 of the 1969 Vienna Convention on the Law of Treaties (VCLT). Necessity belongs to the

---

[1] VCLT Art 26 ('Every treaty in force is binding upon the parties to it and must be performed by them in good faith').

[2] See Chapter 25, Part II, 641 *et seq.*

[3] See Chapter 23, Part II, 582 *et seq* .

[4] Although not the focus of this chapter, the VCLT also permits treaty termination or suspension if: (i) all the parties to a treaty conclude a later treaty that they intended to govern or the provisions of the later treaty are so incompatible with the earlier treaty that the two cannot apply at the same time; or (ii) if the treaty conflicts with a new pre-emptory norm of general international law. VCLT Arts 59 and 64. In addition, the VCLT makes clear that certain external developments do not give cause for termination or suspension. Thus, a reduction in the number of parties below that necessary for entry into force does not offer a basis for termination unless the treaty otherwise provides. Ibid Art 55. Similarly, the severance of diplomatic or consular relations does not affect treaty relations unless the existence of such relations is indispensable for the treaty's application. Ibid Art 63.

realm of State responsibility (namely, Article 25 of the International Law Commission's Articles on State Responsibility (ASR)). As with the broader relationship between the law of treaties and the law of State responsibility, the doctrine of necessity's relationship with the law of treaties remains unclear and, despite certain case law, it is one of the most taxing areas of international law.[5]

I. Supervening Impossibility of Performance

The doctrine of supervening impossibility of performance is an uncontroverted basis for States to terminate or suspend their treaty obligations.[6] Article 61 of the VCLT expresses the fundamental elements of the rule:

1. A party may invoke the impossibility of performing a treaty as a ground for terminating or withdrawing from it if the impossibility results from the permanent disappearance or destruction of an object indispensable for the execution of the treaty. If the impossibility is temporary, it may be invoked only as a ground for suspending the operation of the treaty.

2. Impossibility of performance may not be invoked by a party as a ground for terminating, withdrawing from or suspending the operation of a treaty if the impossibility is the result of a breach by that party either of an obligation under the treaty or of any other international obligation owed to any other party to the treaty.

Unlike other bases for terminating or suspending a treaty, however, the doctrine of impossibility has gone largely un-theorized. Moreover, practically speaking, it has proven extraordinarily difficult for States to invoke.

As a threshold matter, the doctrine on supervening impossibility of performance needs to be distinguished from the exception of non-performance. The exception of non-performance purports to relieve a party from the obligation to perform where the other party has failed to perform the same or a related obligation.[7] The legal basis for this exception, however, has not received sufficient analysis. It was not included in the VCLT nor—despite extensive discussion—the codification of the 2001 ASR. Some viewed the exception of non-performance as 'a circumstance precluding wrongfulness' or a kind of countermeasure for another State's wrongful act or omission. Others, however, now view it as a rule of treaty interpretation, rather than a secondary rule suitable for the ASR.[8]

---

[5] See eg J Crawford and S Olleson, 'The Exception of Non-performance: Links between the Law of Treaties and the Law of State Responsibility' (2000) 21 Australian Ybk Intl L 55.

[6] See eg *Gabčíkovo-Nagymaros Project (Hungary v Slovakia)* (Judgment) [1997] ICJ Rep 7; ME Villiger, *Commentary on the 1969 Vienna Convention on the Law of Treaties* (Martinus Nijhoff, Leiden 2009) 761; see also Crawford and Olleson (n 5) 62.

[7] Crawford and Olleson (n 5) 56.

[8] The ASR is an attempt to codify 'secondary rules', that is the conditions under which international legal responsibility arises and the legal consequences that flow therefrom, as distinct from codifying the 'primary rules', which are the actual conventional and customary obligations of international law. J Crawford, 'Third Report on State Responsibility', UN Doc A/CN.4/507/Add.1-4 (2000); Draft Articles on the Responsibility of States for Internationally Wrongful Acts with Commentaries [2001] YBILC, vol II(2) (UN Doc A/56/10, as corrected) ('ASR').

Today, there remain many unresolved questions concerning the exception of non-performance, such as its relationship with *force majeure* (a circumstance precluding wrongfulness) and, generally, the principle of *pacta sunt servanda*. As a result, it is easy to see this exception's potential confusion with the doctrine of impossibility, particularly where one party's wrongful behaviour makes it impossible for the other party to perform its obligations. But, there are at least two differences between these concepts. First, the exception of non-performance need not be limited to cases where a party cannot possibly perform; its wider meaning encompasses cases where a party may not perform because it is *unfair* to require performance because the other party has not performed its own (reciprocal) obligations. Moreover, the functions of the two doctrines are distinct. The exception of non-performance conditions a State's legal responsibility for its acts or omissions; the doctrine of impossibility provides a basis for terminating or suspending the treaty itself. Termination or suspension of a treaty may, of course, have consequences for a party's obligation to perform, but that is not their focus, which lies instead with whether there are treaty obligations at all. Thus, more careful analysis is required of the relationship between the institutions of termination and suspension of treaties and exceptions to performance obligations, whether as part of the law of treaties or the law of State responsibility.[9]

A. Views of the International Law Commission

Within the broad issue of termination or suspension of treaties, supervening impossibility of performance has been analysed less than other doctrines such as fundamental change of circumstances. However, it was extensively discussed during the codification process of the VCLT by the International Law Commission (ILC). And even, prior to this, Fitzmaurice had already made some pertinent observations on what circumstances would make performance impossible.[10] Fitzmaurice's examples referred to the extinction of the physical object to which the treaty relates, such as: the disappearance of an island owing to subsidence in the seabed; the drying up of the bed of a river permanently; the destruction of a railway by an earthquake; the destruction of a plant, installation, canal, lighthouse, etc. He also noted that under certain circumstances the legal character of this exception may generate difficulties in interpretation. The question may arise to what extent granting rights in respect of an object involves a guarantee to maintain the object itself, or to refrain from all action liable to interfere with it. As an example, Fitzmaurice posed the question whether granting fishery rights in a river implies an obligation not to divert the water or impair the fisheries. According to him, answering such questions must depend on the interpretation of the treaty. Fitzmaurice also noted that certain authors wanted to divide the impossibility doctrine into physical and juridical impossibilities. However, he believed that allowing juridical impossibility would present inherent difficulties because a State

---

[9] Crawford and Olleson (n 5) 73.
[10] GG Fitzmaurice, 'Second Report on the Law of Treaties' [1957] YBILC, vol II, 50 [97].

would always be able to obtain release from its treaty obligations by entering into other incompatible obligations.[11]

Fitzmaurice was more open, in contrast, to recognizing supervening impossibility of performance for treaty regulations due to the disappearance of the treaty field of action. Examples would include: treaties regulating certain matters regarding a system of capitulatory rights (after the disappearance of the system) and treaties concerning certain matters arising from a customs union after the disappearance of such a union. Fitzmaurice believed termination or suspension of such obligations could be based either on the doctrine of supervening impossibility of performance or fundamental change of circumstances, revealing the inherent difficulties in achieving clean-cut differences between various doctrines aimed at releasing a State from its treaty obligations. Indeed, Fitzmaurice explained that in these types of cases, it is not so much that performance has become impossible, but:

rather that performance would, even if possible, be absurd, inappropriate and meaningless, and that it is really no longer a question of performance, because there is no longer any sphere or field of action to which the treaty relates, or in which performance can take place.[12]

Sir Humphrey Waldock made similar observations in his own reports on the law of treaties.[13] His comments on draft Article 21 (supervening impossibility of performance) took the view that the doctrine of supervening impossibility needed to be understood very strictly to separate cases falling under its remit and those falling under the doctrine of *rebus sic stantibus* (fundamental change of circumstances). Waldock, however, did not offer any precise guidance on the boundaries separating these two doctrines. He also disagreed with Fitzmaurice on whether the disappearance of one of the parties fell under the law of treaties or larger questions of State succession.[14]

The ensuing ILC discussion addressed how widely to define impossibility, how to distinguish it from fundamental change of circumstances, and how to differentiate it from the law of State responsibility. Mr De Luna thought the doctrine should include practical or relative impossibility, together with its incontrovertible application to factual impossibility of performance of an absolute character, which involves the disappearance or destruction of an object of a treaty. However, such a broadening of the scope of the applicability of this doctrine would, as observed by Fitzmaurice, undermine the principle *pacta sunt servanda*. De Luna also admitted that relative impossibility of performance could prove troublesome regarding a clear-cut distinction from the doctrine of fundamental change of circumstances, which according to him was applicable where the treaty lost all its meaning. For De Luna, the difference between these two doctrines was primarily based on the premise that, according to the doctrine of supervening impossibility,

---

[11] Ibid 50–1 [97]–[99].   [12] Ibid 51 [101].
[13] H Waldock, 'Second Report on the Law of Treaties' [1963] YBILC, vol II, 79.
[14] Ibid 78.

performance without being totally impossible has been rendered extremely difficult due to supervening circumstances.[15]

In addition to discussing what conditions could generate supervening impossibility of performance, the ILC discussion also evidenced unresolved difficulties in separating the law of treaties and the law of State responsibility. Tunkin viewed the reasons for a State's non-fulfilment of its obligations and its resulting responsibilities as separate issues belonging to the topic of State responsibility. He maintained that for State responsibility to arise from non-performance of a treaty there must be a valid treaty in operation; however, the ILC draft Article (43(1) and (2)) provided for the treaty's suspension or termination due to the supervening impossibility of performance. Therefore, Tunkin believed that in those circumstances there would be no treaty in operation.[16]

The ILC's attempt to make a significant distinction between the law of treaties and the law of State responsibility regarding supervening impossibility of performance was ultimately inconclusive. Mr De Arechaga distinguished two substantively different types of responsibility to clarify the issue: the first type derives from the treaty (analogous to liability *ex contractu* in private law) and the second type arises in certain cases outside the treaty.[17] The dilemma of separating these two areas (the law of treaties and the law of State responsibility), was also reflected in the views of the Special Rapporteur, Waldock. He argued that certain cases should be treated as cases of *force majeure*, particularly where a substantial doubt existed as to the permanence of the impossibility since that situation 'might simply be treated as a case where *force majeure* could be pleaded as a defence exonerating a party from liability for non-performance'.[18] In general, the Commission viewed impossibility under the topic of *force majeure* as belonging to the realm of State responsibility rather than the law of treaties.

Mr Ago also questioned whether the physical impossibility of carrying out a treaty necessarily always means that the legal obligation created by the treaty ceases to exist. He contrasted two distinct situations. The first arises when impossibility supervenes without any fault on the invoking State's part such that it might not only be factually impossible to carry out the treaty, but the State could decide that it is no longer legally bound to implement that treaty. The second arises when the State *is* responsible, in whole or in part, for creating the conditions of impossibility of performance, such that the State might find it impossible to execute the treaty, but could not declare itself free from having to implement that treaty. This later limit on impossibility ended up being reflected in paragraph 2 of Article 61. During

---

[15] ILC, 'Summary record of the 697th meeting' (1966) UN Doc A/CN.4/SR.697, [4]–[12].

[16] Ibid [3].

[17] Ibid [22]. De Arechaga did not specify *what* cases outside the treaty would entail responsibility, noting:

> If the Commission wished to cover both types of responsibility, it could say that there was always a responsibility for certain forms of conduct, independently of the obligations under the treaty. In consequence of the recent developments of public international law, and more particularly of the law of treaties, the duty to make reparation and the duty to be vigilant were becoming generalized.

[18] Ibid [23].

the VCLT Diplomatic Conference, additional proposals were made to broaden Article 61's scope, such as instances of impossibility to make certain payments due to financial difficulties. The participating States chose not to do this, but recognized that such a situation may be treated as a circumstance precluding wrongfulness.[19]

B. The relevant case law

Supervening impossibility of performance was pleaded in two early cases before the Permanent Court of International Justice (PCIJ), but the Court rejected the claims in both instances.[20] In 1991, the *Libyan Arab Foreign Investment Company v Burundi Arbitration* case faced the question of impossibility raised under a plea of *force majeure*.[21] The Arbitral Tribunal declined, however, to accept this plea, because 'the alleged impossibility [was] not the result of an irresistible force or an unforeseen external event beyond the control of Burundi. In fact, the impossibility was a result of a unilateral decision of a State'.[22]

Undoubtedly, the most relevant case applying the doctrine of supervening impossibility of performance was the *Gabčikovo-Nagymaros* case.[23] The case originated from a dispute regarding the implementation of the 1977 Treaty Concerning the Construction and Operation of the Gabčikovo-Nagymaros System of Locks between Czechoslovakia and Hungary. The 1977 Treaty provided for construction of two series of locks at Gabčikovo (situated in Czechoslovak territory) and Nagymaros (situated in Hungarian territory) to establish 'a single and indivisible operational system of works'.[24] In its Judgment, the International Court of Justice (ICJ) emphasized the project's integrated character, 'with the two contracting parties on an equal footing in respect of the financing, construction and operation of the works'.[25] The Court also noted that the 1977 Treaty provided for a flexible framework and that the Parties in practice acknowledged it.[26] In terms of its functions, one purpose of the Treaty was to provide energy, but it also sought improvement of the navigability of the Danube, flood control, regulation of ice discharge, and the protection of the natural environment.[27]

In 1989, Hungary unilaterally suspended and subsequently sought to terminate the Treaty with the Slovak Republic (which became a Party after the so-called 'Velvet Revolution' that created separate Czech and Slovak Republics). The Slovak

---

[19] UN Conference on the Law of Treaties, Summary Records of First Session (26 March-24 May 1968) UN Doc A/Conf.39/11, 361–89 ('Vienna Conference, First Session').
[20] *Case Concerning the Payment of Various Serbian Loans Issued in France (France v. Yugoslavia)* PCIJ Rep Series A No 20 (July 12) [83]; *Case Concerning the Payment in Gold of Brazilian Federal Loans Contracted in France (France v Brazil)* PCIJ Rep Series A No 21 (July 12) [83].
[21] (1991) 96 ILR 279, 318.
[22] Ibid [53].
[23] *Gabčikovo-Nagymaros* case (n 6).
[24] Treaty Concerning the Construction and Operation of the Gabcikovo-Nagymaros System of Locks (Czechoslovakia-Hungary) (16 September 1977) 1109 UNTS 235, Art 1(1).
[25] *Gabčikovo-Nagymaros* case (n 6) [20].
[26] Ibid [138].   [27] Ibid [135].

Republic started to put into operation a unilateral alternative locks system, the so-called 'Variant C' solution and submitted the dispute to the ICJ.

As Johann Lammers observed, this case created a host of issues relating to the law of treaties and the law of State responsibility.[28] The first group of issues related to Hungary's various grounds for justifying termination of the 1977 Treaty (eg supervening impossibility of performance, fundamental change of circumstances, material breach, reciprocal non-compliance), while the second group of issues related to questions of State responsibility and its relationship to the law of treaties (eg whether a state of necessity served as a circumstance precluding the wrongfulness of any Hungarian act).

In terms of supervening impossibility of performance, Hungary specifically sought to rely on VCLT Article 61. Hungary argued that the essential object of the 1977 Treaty—namely the joint economic investment undertaken by two Parties, which was compatible with environmental protection—had permanently disappeared and that 'the Treaty had thus become impossible to perform'.[29] The Court, however, decided that Hungary's interpretation of impossibility was not in conformity with either the terms of its formulation in Article 61 or the intentions of the Diplomatic Conference that adopted the VCLT.[30] The Court decided not to engage in the discussion (originally suggested by Fitzmaurice) as to whether the term 'object' in Article 61 can encompass disappearance of a legal regime. It found 'even if that were the case, it would have to conclude that in this instance that regime had not definitively ceased to exist'.[31] The Court pointed out (as it did repeatedly throughout the Judgment) that the 1977 Treaty included provisions enabling the Parties to make necessary adjustments between economic and environmental issues. Moreover, the Court observed that the impossibility of joint exploitation was in fact caused by Hungary's failure to carry out most of the work for which it was responsible under the Treaty. The Court relied on Article 61(2) of the VLCT to prohibit Hungary from invoking impossibility of performance when it results from a party's own breach of an obligation stemming from a treaty.

C. State practice

Just because international tribunals have rarely relied on supervening impossibility of performance to terminate or suspend a treaty, does not mean that State practice does not rely on the doctrine. Although harder to document and still relatively rare, States have invoked supervening impossibility in situations not subject to judicial settlement. For example, impossibility might arise for defence treaties among militaries when one State (such as Costa Rica or Panama) abolishes its military (although other States might challenge that claim in accordance with Article 61(2) because the State's acts create the conditions leading to impossibility of perfor-

---

[28] J Lammers, 'The Gabčikovo-Nagymaros Case Seen in Particular From the Perspective of the Law of International Watercourses and the Protection of the Environment' (1998) 11 LJIL 287, 289–90.

[29] *Gabčikovo-Nagymaros* case (n 6) [103].

[30] Ibid [102].   [31] Ibid [103].

mance). Aust notes a further example in British attempts to invoke supervening impossibility to justify housing Argentina POW's on its ships in violation of the fourth Geneva Convention where its tents had been destroyed.[32]

Finally, it is also worth recalling that even if there is an undoubted supervening impossibility of performance, the doctrine does not terminate or suspend treaties automatically. To invoke the doctrine, a State must notify the other party per specific procedures for termination or suspension laid out in the VCLT.[33]

D. Conclusions on the supervening impossibility of performance

There are a host of other questions about the impossibility doctrine that remain open, including the difference between factual and legal impossibility and the role of fault. Thus, although the final text of Article 61 codifies the fundamental issues concerning supervening impossibility of performance, outstanding issues remain subject to interpretation by States and international courts and tribunals. It must be observed that, somewhat surprisingly, the majority of scholars do not perceive this doctrine to be in any way controversial or giving rise to unresolved issues. For example, Nahlik in his seminal essay noted that '[t]here can hardly be any objection to the inclusion of "supervening impossibility of performance" among the causes of the termination of treaties', this doctrine originates from an ancient concept of civil law, and it has always been considered to be a principle admitted by the general law of nations.[34] However, the formulation of Article 61 and the approach of the Court in the *Gabčikovo-Nagymaros* case clearly indicate that States can only invoke supervening impossibility as a ground for exiting treaty commitments in exceptional circumstances more often identified in theory than in practice. Even then, the applicability of this doctrine is problematic due to the unresolved issues about its relationship to the law of State responsibility and what exactly qualifies as the 'permanent disappearance or destruction of an object indispensible for the execution of the treaty', which may lead to misunderstanding and confusion in practice.

II. Fundamental Change of Circumstances

The notion that a State may terminate or suspend its treaty obligations if circumstances have changed fundamentally since the treaty entered into force (*rebus sic stantibus*) has received extensive attention from scholars, courts, and States. Today, it is considered part of customary international law and codified in Article 62 of the VCLT. Nevertheless, although recognizing the doctrine's existence, international tribunals have rarely applied it. At the same time, its negative formulation in

---

[32] A Aust, *Modern Treaty Law & Practice* (2nd edn CUP, Cambridge 2007) 296–7.
[33] VCLT Arts 65–8.
[34] SE Nahlik, 'The Grounds of Invalidity and Termination of Treaties' (1971) 65 AJIL 736, 747.

Article 62 means that, in practice, it remains difficult for States to assert as a basis for terminating or suspending treaties.

A. Views of the International Law Commission

The doctrine of *clasula rebus sic stantibus* is a well-established principle in contract law, dating back to the early commentaries of Thomas of Aquin.[35] Gentili transferred the idea to international law, asserting that a treaty did not have to be observed if the conditions of affairs changed, providing that the change was unforeseeable.[36] Vattel voiced a similar view; where the promise of an engagement was given dependent on certain circumstances, a change in those circumstances would result in exemption from the engagement, provided that those circumstances were essential for the promise that otherwise would not have been made.[37] Grotius, however, had a more restrictive view, denying that continuation of present conditions is a tacit condition of promises.[38] In practice, the *rebus sic stantibus* doctrine gained importance especially as States increasingly invoked it in their attempts to escape treaty obligations during the nineteenth century and in the inter-war period.[39]

An analysis of this doctrine constituted a substantive part of the work by Rapporteurs Fitzmaurice and Waldock.[40] Their analysis and the ensuing discussion within the ILC and during the Diplomatic Conference contributed to what became initially draft Article 59 and finally Article 62 of the VCLT. In broad brushstrokes, both Rapporteurs and the ILC were aware of the dangers of such a provision to the stability of treaties. The majority of the Commission viewed this *rebus sic stantibus* principle as operating in tension with that of *pacta sunt servanda*.[41]

---

[35] I Sinclair, *The Vienna Convention on the Law of Treaties* (2nd edn MUP, Manchester 1984) 192–3 (citing Aquin's *Summa Theologiae* II/2, qu.110).

[36] *De Jure Belli Liberi Tres*, 1598. See Sinclair (n 35) 192.

[37] E de Vattel, *The Law of Nations or the Principles of Natural Law Applied to Conduct and to the Affairs of Nations and of Sovereigns* (CG Fenwick (trs), Carnegie Institute, Washington 1916) (1758) vol III, chap XVII, 211 [296]. See Sinclair (n 35) 192.

[38] H Grotius, *De jure belli ac pacis libri tres* (reprinted Clarendon Press, Oxford 1925) (1646) vol II, chap XXV.2, 424.

[39] In particular, Russia invoked this doctrine to justify its assertion in 1870 that the provisions of the 1956 Treaty on neutralization of the Black Sea were no longer binding upon it. Later, this doctrine was abused as a result of its indiscriminate invocation by States in the period preceding the First World War to escape from inconvenient treaty obligations. See Sinclair (n 35) 193.

[40] On this doctrine see: A Vamvoukos, *Termination of Treaties in International Law: The Doctrines of Rebus Sic Stantibus and Desuetude* (Clarendon Press, Oxford 1985); Sinclair (n 35); OJ Lissitzyn, 'Treaties and Changed Circumstances *(rebus sic stantibus)*' (1967) 61 AJIL 895; G Haraszti, 'Treaties and the Fundamental Change of Circumstances' (1975) 146 RcD 1; R Mullerson, 'The ABM Treaty: Changed Circumstances, Extraordinary Events, Supreme Interests and International Law' (2001) 59 ICLQ 509.

[41] However, there were also different views. For example, Mr Stuyt of the Netherlands suggested that:

> [o]nce a treaty came into existence, it had to be executed in good faith; otherwise it remained a dead letter. But whether or not the treaty remained binding, despite a fundamental change of circumstances, was an entirely different matter. It was a practical problem and could not be solved merely by referring to the logical principle of good faith.

Vienna Conference, First Session (n 19) 367 [18].

Fitzmaurice noted that the doctrine of *rebus sic stantibus* had a long tradition in law in general and should, in some way, be included in the text of the VCLT.[42] He advanced three theories that could establish the juridical basis for this doctrine.[43] The first theory rested on the implied intention of the parties: the presumption that the parties to a treaty expected the continued existence of the circumstances that formed the fundamental basis of their agreement. They had an implicit intention by which the treaty would come to an end in the event of an essential change of those circumstances. The second theory was based on the premise that international law contains an objective rule allowing the parties to a treaty to require its termination due to an essential change of circumstances. The third theory was a combination of the first two, implying a condition into every treaty for termination or suspension if there is an essential change of circumstances, but basing this implication on an objective rule of law, regardless of the intention of the parties. Both Fitzmaurice and Waldock supported the second of these theories. As Waldock phrased it, 'the *rebus sic stantibus* doctrine is an objective rule of law rather than a presumption as to the original intention of the parties to make the treaty subject to an implied condition'.[44]

The discussion within the ILC stressed the exceptional character of this doctrine. It had been suggested by some members that a provision on fundamental change of circumstances should have procedural safeguards, requiring, for example, the exhaustion of negotiations or even a jurisdictional clause to protect parties to a treaty against threats to its stability.[45] These suggestions were not included in the VCLT, but they evidence the ILC's great caution in drafting this provision.

The ILC and the Diplomatic Conference strove to introduce in draft Article 59 a proper balance between stability and change. To this end, it was decided that this fundamental change of circumstances doctrine does not bestow an automatic right to repudiate the treaty but only a right to request that other parties to the treaty release the State from its obligations.[46] The prevailing, albeit, reluctant view was also that this doctrine was a principle of general international law and that in contemporary practice its application was not confined, as some had argued, only to so-called perpetual treaties.[47] The restrictive character of this doctrine was maintained by the Commission's negative phrasing of the article and the exclusion from it of any treaty establishing a boundary, as a defence against this doctrine becoming a source of tensions if applied in that context.[48] The ILC also relied on the principle

---

[42] Fitzmaurice, Second Report (n 10) [141]–[163] (Art 21 of the Draft Code on the Law of Treaties and commentary).

[43] Ibid [146]–[148].

[44] Waldock, Second Report (n 13) 83.

[45] ILC, 'Summary record of the 835th meeting' UN Doc A/CN.4/SR.835 [3].

[46] Vienna Conference, First Session (n 19) 369–70 [35]–[40].

[47] ILC, 'Report of the International Law Commission on the Work of the Second Part of the Eighteenth Session 4 May–19 July 1966, Official Records of the General Assembly, Twenty-first Session, Supplement No. 9' UN Doc A/6309/Rev.1, 257–8; Lissitzyn (n 40) 912–22.

[48] *Case Concerning the Frontier Dispute (Burkina Faso v Mali)* (Judgment) [1986] ICJ Rep 554 [17] (viewing this exclusion to cover 'both delimitation treaties and those ceding or attributing territory').

of international law that a party cannot take advantage of its own wrong-doing.[49] As a result, the fundamental change of circumstances doctrine may not be invoked if the changes are brought about by a treaty breach by the party invoking the doctrine or by that party's breach of an international obligation owed to the other parties to the treaty.

In its final form, Article 62 of the VCLT contains the following conditions for a treaty's termination or suspension based on a fundamental change of circumstances: (i) change with regard to circumstances existing at the time of the treaty's conclusion (unforeseen by the treaty parties) in principle must not be invoked as a ground for the treaty's termination, unless (ii) the existence of those circumstances constituted an essential basis for the parties' consent to be bound by a treaty, and (iii) the effect of the change radically transforms the extent of obligations still to be performed under the treaty. The ILC, however, provided no guidance as to the meaning of the terms 'radically' or 'extent'.[50]

B. Relevant case law and other instances of this doctrine's application

Unlike supervening impossibility of performance, the change of circumstances doctrine has been invoked in a number of cases. However, courts are very cautious; while admitting the doctrine's existence as matter of principle, the majority of cases have not found sufficient grounds for its actual application.[51]

1. *The* Free Zones *case*[52]

Although the PCIJ did not rule on *rebus sic stantibus* in its Judgment,[53] this case is noteworthy for the Parties' pronouncements on the conditions for applying this doctrine, pronouncements that the ILC considered while drafting Article 62. Both the French and Swiss Governments invoked *rebus sic stantibus* as a basis for terminating a treaty. France argued, however, that this principle did not permit the unilateral denunciation of a treaty that was allegedly out of date.[54] The Swiss Government pleaded that there were differing views regarding the *rebus sic stantibus*

---

[49] *Case Concerning the Factory at Chorzów (Germany v Poland)* (Jurisdiction) [1927] PCIJ Rep Series A No 9 141–2 [87].

[50] See F Kirgis, 'Proposed Missiles and the ABM Treaty' (2001) ASIL Insights <http://www.asil.org/insigh70.cfm>.

[51] R Jennings and A Watts (eds), *Oppenheim's International Law Vol 1: Peace* (9th edn OUP, Oxford 1992) 1307.

[52] *Case of the Free Zones of Upper Savoy and the District of Gex (France v Switzerland)* [1932] PCIJ Rep Series A/B No 46.

[53] The PCIJ said that:

[a]s the French argument fails on the facts, it becomes unnecessary for the Court to consider any of the questions of principle which arise in connection with the theory of the lapse of treaties by reason of change of circumstances, such as the extent to which the theory can be regarded as constituting a rule of international law, the occasions on which and the method by which effect can be given to the theory if recognised, and the question whether it would apply to treaties establishing rights.

Ibid 186.

[54] Ibid 578–9 and 405–15.

doctrine, and disputed the existence in international law of a right that could be enforced through the decision of a competent tribunal regarding treaty termination due to changed circumstances. Switzerland further argued that: (i) the circumstances that allegedly changed were those upon which the treaty Parties had entered, provided those conditions continued; (ii) in any event, the doctrine does not apply to treaties creating territorial rights; and (iii) France allowed too long a period to lapse after the alleged changes of circumstances had manifested themselves before making its plea.[55]

2. *The* Fisheries Jurisdiction *cases*[56]

These are important cases as the ICJ dealt with the subject matter of the fundamental change of circumstances doctrine soon after the VCLT's signing. The ICJ relied on VCLT Article 62's formulation of this doctrine, indicating that it 'may in many respects be considered as a codification of existing customary law on the subject'.[57] Regarding the doctrine's application, the Court had to analyse a 1961 Agreement between Iceland and the United Kingdom that allegedly came to an end as result of (i) changes in fishing techniques and (ii) the international law on fisheries. The Court applied the conditions for invoking this principle very strictly regarding both alleged grounds of its applicability. The Court stated as follows:

in order that a change of circumstances may give rise to a ground for invoking the termination of a treaty it is also necessary that it should have resulted in a radical transformation of the extent of the obligations still to be performed. The change must have increased the burden of the obligations to be executed to the extent of rendering the performance something essentially different from that originally undertaken.[58]

In rejecting the fundamental change of circumstances claim, the Court emphasized the importance of the non-foreseeability criterion embodied in Article 62(1) of the VCLT, which disavows the doctrine's application if the change of circumstances was foreseen by the Parties at the time of the Agreement's conclusion. The Court also attached great importance to the VCLT's procedural requirement that a third party determine if the particular situation merited the operation of the doctrine of fundamental change of circumstances, since that process helps preserve the stability of treaties.[59] Such a procedural requirement was already included in the compromisory clause referring the case to the ICJ. Briggs, in particular, noted the Court's cautious attitude in applying this doctrine and its punctilious emphasis on the fulfilment of all relevant conditions (including the procedural ones).[60]

---

[55] Ibid 463–76.

[56] *Fisheries Jurisdiction Case (United Kingdom v Iceland)* (Jurisdiction) [1973] ICJ Rep 4 ('*UK Fisheries Jurisdiction* Case'); *Fisheries Jurisdiction Case (Federal Republic of Germany v Iceland)* [1973] ICJ Rep 49.

[57] *UK Fisheries Jurisdiction Case* (n 56) [36].

[58] Ibid [43].

[59] Sinclair (n 35) 195.

[60] HW Briggs, 'Unilateral Denunciation of Treaties: The Vienna Convention and the International Court of Justice' (1974) 68 AJIL 51, 68.

3. The Gabčikovo-Nagymaros case[61]

In addition to claiming supervening impossibility of performance, Hungary also identified several substantive elements that allegedly had fundamentally changed at the time it notified the Czechoslovak Government about the 1977 Treaty's termination. These elements included: (i) the notion of 'socialist integration' for which the 1977 Treaty was initially a vehicle, had since ceased to exist; (ii) the 'single and indivisible operational system', which was substituted by a unilateral scheme; (iii) the fact that the basis of the planned joint investment had been frustrated by the emergence of both States as market economies; (iv) the change in Czechoslovakia's attitude, which turned the framework treaty into an immutable form; and finally (v) the transformation of a Treaty consistent with 'environmental protection' into 'a prescription for environmental disaster'.[62] Slovakia argued that the changes identified by Hungary had not altered the nature of the obligations under the Treaty from those initially undertaken, so Hungary was not entitled to terminate the Treaty.[63]

The Court reiterated that Article 62 of the VCLT reflected customary international law, albeit again with the qualification 'in many respects'.[64] The Court found that the political situation was relevant to the 1977 Treaty's conclusion. However, the treaty's object and purpose, namely a joint investment programme for the production of energy, the control of floods and the improvement of navigation on the Danube, were not so closely linked to political conditions that changes in those conditions would radically alter the extent of the obligations still to be performed.[65] Thus, the collapse of the communist regime and the aim of strengthening communist economic cooperation were not viewed by the Court as sufficiently fundamental as to constitute valid grounds for the termination of the 1977 Treaty. The Court expressed the view that even though the project's profitability had diminished by 1992, it had not done so to the extent as to 'radically' transform the Parties' obligations. Likewise, the new developments in environmental knowledge were not completely unforeseen; Articles 15, 19, and 20 of the 1977 Treaty allowed the Parties, according to the Court, to consider such changes and accommodate them when implementing provisions of the 1977 Treaty. The Court summed up its analysis as follows:

The changed circumstances advanced by Hungary are, in the Court's view, not of such a nature, either individually or collectively, that their effect would radically transform the extent of the obligations still to be performed in order to accomplish the Project. A fundamental change of circumstances must have been unforeseen; the existence of the circumstances at the time of the Treaty's conclusion must have constituted an essential basis of the consent of the parties to be bound by the Treaty. The negative and conditional wording of Article 62 of the Vienna Convention on the Law of Treaties is a clear indication

---

[61] For the statement of facts see text accompanying nn 23–7.
[62] *Gabčikovo-Nagymaros* case (n 6) [95].   [63] Ibid.
[64] Ibid [42].   [65] Ibid [104].

moreover that the stability of treaty relations requires that the plea of fundamental change of circumstances be applied only in exceptional cases.[66]

From this case (and the *Fisheries Jurisdiction* cases), it appears that the ICJ will treat the plea of fundamental change of circumstances in the most restrictive manner, according absolute priority to the stability of treaties, a principle which appears to trump the invocation of the doctrine of fundamental changes. The present author has doubts if at any time this doctrine will gain more currency in the Court's practice. Until the present, it has remained only a theoretical possibility for treaty termination or suspension.

4. Racke v Hauptzollamt Mainz[67]

Uniquely, in this European Court of Justice (ECJ) case, the plea of fundamental change of circumstances succeeded. The case arose from the suspension by the Council of Ministers of the European Communities (EC) of a Cooperation Agreement between the EC and Yugoslavia in 1991 following the outbreak of hostilities in the region. An importer of Yugoslav wines who became liable for higher import duties as a result of the suspension litigated the case before the German courts. The ECJ gave a preliminary ruling concerning the validity of the suspension in which it listed two conditions for successfully claiming fundamental change of circumstances. First, the Court identified the essential basis for the Parties' consent, finding it necessary that there was 'a situation of peace in Yugoslavia, indispensable for neighbourly relations, and the existence of institutions capable of ensuring implementation of the cooperation envisaged by the Agreement throughout the territory of Yugoslavia'. The ECJ found that these conditions were no longer the case on the facts. Second, the ECJ emphasized that the fundamental change of circumstances must radically transform the extent of obligations undertaken by the Parties. In this respect, the ECJ ruled that it was sufficient that no purpose was served by continuing to grant preferences with a view to stimulating trade where Yugoslavia was breaking up, since 'the customary international law rules in question [do] not require an impossibility to perform obligations'. Accordingly, the plea of fundamental change of circumstances was upheld, provided that no 'manifest error of assessment' existed in the Council's appreciation of the situation and its invocation of the plea.[68]

It may be noted that the ECJ was not as strict as the ICJ in applying the doctrine of fundamental change of circumstances.[69] Commentators have observed that this case's special features, such as the fact of persistent war in a neighbouring country

---

[66] Ibid.

[67] Case C-162/96 [1998] ECR-1-3655. See also J Klabbers, 'Re-inventing the Law of Treaties: The Contribution of the EC Courts' (1999) 30 Netherlands Ybk Intl L 45, 57–9; O Elias, 'General International Law and the European Court of Justice: From Hypothesis to Reality?' (2000) 31 Netherlands Ybk Intl L 3, 17–22.

[68] *Racke* (n 67) [53]–[57].

[69] Klabbers (n 67) 59.

(in spite of a ceasefire agreement, the Resolution of the Security Council determined that the war constituted a threat to international peace and security), influenced the decision of the ECJ and the Council.[70] It was also observed that the ECJ adopted perhaps a more lenient stand due to the fact that an individual (as opposed to an EC organ) pleaded the fundamental change of circumstances, raising the issue of whether an individual can even rely on customary international law to challenge the validity of EC law.[71] More importantly, the ECJ's observations on the doctrine of fundamental change of circumstances were not at the core of its Judgment, which was a matter of judicial review of the Council of Ministers' decision. The importance of the ECJ's statements on applying the doctrine of fundamental change of circumstances may thus be limited to this particular case, which is how the ECJ viewed its own role.[72]

Even though Article 73 of the 1969 VCLT specifically excludes the outbreak of hostilities from its scope, *Racke* also illustrates how questions may still arise as to whether such a situation qualifies as a fundamental change of circumstances.[73] Doctrinal views on this subject are inconclusive and the practice is not uniform.[74] Some authors view the effect of armed conflict on treaties as similar or even coterminous with a fundamental change of circumstances, accepting that a treaty can be suspended or terminated on this basis.[75] But there are few examples of State

---

[70] Ibid; Elias (n 67) 21–2.

[71] As Klabbers noted:

> This focus on the individual's position, tuning the Court's mind to the needs and interests of individuals, may have caused the Court to misconstrue the case as one in which the trader invoked the *rebus sic stantibus* doctrine ... [I]t transpires that the opening up of international actors may well have consequences for the application of the law of treaties. One may wonder whether the Court would have come up with such a relaxed version of *rebus sic stantibus* had the case been brought by one of the Community institutions ... and it seems questionable that the Council would have argued it with fervour had Yugoslavia complained against the suspension.

Klabbers (n 67) [59].

[72] The ECJ opined that:

> [B]ecause of the complexity of the rules in question and the imprecision of some of the concepts to which they refer, judicial review must necessarily, and in particular in the context of a preliminary reference for an assessment of validity, be limited to the question whether, by adopting the suspending regulation, the Council made manifest errors of assessment concerning the conditions for applying those rules

Racke (n 67) [52]. See also Aust (n 32) 299.

[73] For recent discussion of armed conflicts and treaties generally, see ILC Secretariat, 'The Effect of Armed Conflict on Treaties: an Examination of Practice and Doctrine' (2005) UN Doc A/CN.4/550, 68–71 [120]–[126] ('ILC Memorandum').

[74] I Brownlie, 'First Report on Effects of Armed Conflict on Treaties' (2005) UN Doc A/CN/4/522, 7 [12]. Government comments to the ILC confirmed a lack of agreement on the scope of the problem. ILC, 'Effects of armed conflicts on treaties, Comments and information received from Governments' (2005) UN Doc A/CN.4/622.

[75] ILC Memorandum (n 73) 68–9 [121] (citing B Conforti and A Labella, 'Invalidity and Termination of Treaties: Role of National Courts' (1990) 1 EJIL 44; *Restatement (Third) of the Foreign Relations Law of the United States* (1987) §336(e); SH McIntyre, *Legal Effects of World War II on Treaties of the United Nations* (Martinus Nijhoff, The Hague, 1958) 25; I Brownlie, *Principles of Public International Law* (6th edn OUP, Oxford 2003) 592). The Italian Court of Cassation reached a similar result, holding that armed conflict 'cannot bring about the extinction of treaties, but may contribute to

reliance on this theory.[76] US President Franklin D Roosevelt invoked *rebus sic stantibus* to suspend American obligations under the International Load Line Convention of 1930, but his move engendered much criticism.[77] Briggs characterized it as against the treaty's provisions, while Rank suggested Roosevelt had not fulfilled the necessary conditions for invoking that doctrine (although Rank accepted that, under the right conditions, a State might terminate or suspend a treaty because of a situation of armed conflict).[78]

5. Fundamental change of circumstances and State practice: the ABM Treaty

The Load Line Convention example reveals that, although courts have only occasionally applied the fundamental change of circumstances doctrine, States can still invoke it outside the judicial context. The Netherlands, for example, apparently relied on *rebus sic stantibus* in 1982 to suspend a development assistance agreement with Surinam when the government the Netherlands had agreed to assist was overthrown in a *coup d'etat* with a rash of accompanying human rights violations.[79]

States may also address the potential for fundamental changes in circumstances in advance in the treaty itself. Since fundamental change of circumstances is not regarded as *jus cogens*, parties can confirm, modify, or even waive its application in their treaties.[80] Thus, in the bilateral 1972 Anti-Ballistic Missile Treaty (ABM Treaty) between the United States and the Soviet Union, the Parties included a termination clause that contained a variation on the fundamental change of circumstances rule. Article XV(2) allowed each Party 'in exercising its national sovereignty' to withdraw from the Treaty 'if it decides that extraordinary events related to the subject matter of this Treaty have jeopardised its national interests'. In 2001, US President George W Bush announced US withdrawal from the treaty, noting that the circumstances affecting US national security had changed fundamentally and the United States faced different types of threats than those it faced during the Cold War. According to President Bush, the ABM Treaty imposed on

---

a supervening impossibility and perhaps to a change in the circumstances (*rebus sic stantibus*)'. *Lanificio Branditex v Società Azais e Vidal* (1975) Italian Ybk Intl L 232–3.

[76] In 1939, the French Foreign Ministry argued that war was a changed circumstance to terminate its acceptance of compulsory jurisdiction of the PCIJ. A Kiss, '*L'extinction des traités dans la praqtique française*' (1959) 5 AFDI 784, 795.

[77] Opinion of Acting Attorney General Francis Biddle on Suspension of the International Load Line Convention, 40 Op Att Gen (1949) 69; R Rank, *Modern War and the Validity of Treaties: A Comparative Study*, Vol I (1952) 38; R Rank, *Modern War and the Validity of Treaties: A Comparative Study* (1952) vol II, 337–8 ('Rank 2'); HW Briggs, 'The Attorney General Invokes Rebus Sic Stantibus'(1942) 36 AJIL 89.

[78] Briggs (n 77) 96; Rank 2 (n 77) 338–9, 340–1; ILC Memorandum (n 73) 69–71 [123]–[124], [126].

[79] Villiger (n 6) 772.

[80] Ibid 771. Examples of such clauses can be found in Section VI of this Volume.

the United States such conditions as to generally impair its homeland security.[81] Some commentators argued that the existence of Article XV(2) precluded US reliance on the doctrine of fundamental change of circumstances to terminate that treaty.[82] Others, including the author, believe that the US termination may be viewed both as an issue of the proper interpretation of Article XV(2) as well as an independent claim for fundamental change of circumstances.[83]

It may be argued that some, but not all, conditions imposed by the VCLT for invoking a fundamental change of circumstances were met in this instance. The VCLT requirement of change relative to the circumstances existing at the time of conclusion of the treaty (a temporal issue) was satisfied. In other words, the United States had a valid argument that circumstances which led to this treaty no longer existed. But the requirement that this be a 'fundamental' change is more difficult to assess, as there is no definition of this term and what can be described as 'fundamental' will depend on the circumstances in question. In this case, the end of the Cold War and the emergence of new threats from so-called 'rogue' States would be the main 'fundamental' change of circumstance. In the *Gabčikovo-Nagymaros* case, the Court confirmed that a change of political circumstances was 'certainly relevant'.[84] The political circumstances surrounding the conclusion of the ABM Treaty appear to be even more compelling than those in *Gabčikovo-Nagymaros*, therefore giving credibility to the US argument and satisfying that requirement of Article 62 of the VCLT. On the other hand, a host of other considerations in the ABM analysis sets it apart from *Gabčikovo-Nagymaros*.[85] The latter analysis was done by the ICJ (a third party adjudicator) in a formal and legal setting, whereas the ABM Treaty termination issues were discussed at political and diplomatic levels. The facts of the case and the Parties' arguments might have differed if they had occurred before a third party in a judicial setting. Likewise, the Russian view that the US *rebus sic stantibus* argument was not compelling would have been perhaps assessed differently in a more formal process.

Next there is the requirement that the change must not be foreseen by the Parties. In this instance, the question is whether the United States and the Soviet Union did foresee that the Cold War might end one day or that threats might arise from an actor not a Party to the Treaty. On this point, Article XIII of the ABM Treaty provides that:

1. To promote the objectives and implementation of this Treaty, the Parties shall establish promptly a Standing Consultative Commission within the framework of which they will: . . .

(d) consider possible changes in the strategic situation which have bearing on provisions of this Treaty;

---

[81] GW Bush, 'President Discusses National Missile Defence' (Remarks, 13 December 2001) <http://2001-2009.state.gov/t/ac/rls/rm/2001/6847.htm.>

[82] Vamvoukos (n 40) 200–6.

[83] See in-depth M Fitzmaurice and O Elias, 'The Doctrine of Fundamental Change of Circumstances' in M Fitzmaurice and O Elias (eds), *Contemporary Issues in the Law of Treaties* (Eleven International Publishing, Utrecht 2005) 185–98.

[84] *Gabčikovo-Nagymaros* case (n 6) [104].

[85] Fitzmaurice and Elias (n 83) 188.

The Standing Consultative Commission was established in 1972 by a Memorandum of Understanding and was used regularly by both Parties for various purposes,[86] including five-year periodic reviews of the Treaty required by its Article XIV(2).

These Articles provided room for the ABM Treaty to accommodate change of the kind that arose and allegedly gave rise to the issue of fundamental change of circumstances here; namely, changes in the strategic situation. That strategic situation was clearly at the heart of the conclusion of the ABM Treaty; but, Articles XIII and XIV(2) render the argument that any such changes were not foreseen in the Treaty lacking in credibility. The provisions in question gave an opportunity for the Parties to both modify (Article XIII/XIV(2)) and terminate (Article XIV) the Treaty.

The last requirement to be fulfilled is that the effect of the change must radically transform the 'extent' of the remaining obligations to be fulfilled under the treaty. For the ABM Treaty, the issue is whether the perceived threats to the United States in 1972 and 2001 changed radically, as they were no longer coming from the Soviet Union but from 'rogue' States. This is a matter of extensive disagreement, with varying views that: the threat posed by 'rogue' States is not real; that actual threats can be dealt with by technologies; and that diplomacy aimed at dealing with the missile proliferation problem was preferred, rather than abrogating the ABM Treaty. The argument can be made, however, that the new type of threats, coming not from the Soviet Union but from the 'rogue' States, has transformed radically the US commitment to control its nuclear weapons, due to the fundamental change of circumstances (unforeseen by the Parties at the time of the Agreement's conclusion). Therefore, it can be argued that the original obligation has changed radically, and the United States faces a new type of a threat.

In such a sensitive case concerning national security, moreover, these arguments are only speculative, since not all the arguments are known. This case is thus different from an invocation of the doctrine of fundamental change of circumstances in a judicial context, where all the facts have to be argued and presented to other Parties and a third party adjudicator.

6. Procedural requirements for the application of the doctrine of fundamental change of circumstances

Article 65(1) to (3) of the VCLT lays out a certain procedural requirement for applying the doctrine of fundamental change of circumstances. Its legal character, however, remains unclear. In particular, two issues can be identified: (i) whether this requirement is a norm of customary international law and (ii) whether it is an indispensable element of the doctrine as formulated in Article 62 of the VCLT.

---

[86] 'Treaty between the United States of America and the Union of Soviet Socialist Republics on the Limitation of Anti-Ballistic Missile Systems' (signed 26 May 1972, entered into force 3 October 1972) 944 UNTS 13, Arts XIII–XIV('ABM Treaty').

In the *Fisheries Jurisdiction* case, the ICJ attached great importance to the 'procedural complement to the doctrine of changed circumstances'.[87] It did not expressly say, however, that customary law required claims under the doctrine be submitted to a third party. Briggs, however, considered the Court's finding to be 'an essential part of the doctrine'.[88] In contrast, in the *Racke* case, the ECJ stated that Article 65 was not binding on the Council (which had not complied with its procedural requirements) on the basis that it was not a part of customary international law and the EC was not a party to the VCLT. As regards the ABM Treaty, it may be said that the VCLT was not binding on Russia (the Soviet Union acceded to the VCLT in 1986)[89] and the United States is not a party. At any rate, since the United States followed the ABM Treaty's own termination procedure, it can hardly be said that that this case depended solely on the operation of the doctrine of fundamental change of circumstances as a ground for the treaty's termination.

Article 65 remains important, however, particularly as its existence indicates a shift from subjective auto-interpretation to the possibility of a more objective legal ruling on 'fundamental change of circumstances' claims.[90] Under the auto-interpretative subjective doctrine, the State wishing to withdraw from a treaty is the sole arbiter of whether a fundamental change of circumstances has occurred. The announcement of this would be sufficient, and most importantly, other parties would have no part in the termination of the treaty. Such a situation clearly does not contribute to maintaining the stability of treaty relations between States. At the other end of the spectrum, international law could require third-party adjudication in all cases where fundamental change of circumstances is invoked. The VCLT took a middle way, including elements of decision-making by the other parties to the treaty, and in extreme cases, requiring the involvement of a third-party adjudicator. If a party to a treaty notifies other parties of its wish to withdraw or terminate the treaty, there are two possible scenarios: (i) either no party raises any objection; or (ii) one or more other parties objects, and they must seek a solution through the means indicated in Article 33 of the UN Charter.

There is a consensus in the literature that a plea of fundamental change of circumstances entitles a party with the legal right to demand either that: (i) the parties or a competent international tribunal should declare the termination or suspension of the treaty, or (ii) the parties should negotiate for its revision in good faith with a view to resolving the dispute.[91] It has been suggested that where the rights to negotiate or submit to third-party adjudication are invoked, the other party (or parties) to the treaty are under a corresponding obligation to comply *and* if that corresponding obligation is not fulfilled, the State invoking the plea is entitled

---

[87] *UK Fisheries Jurisdiction* case (n 56) [45].

[88] Briggs (n 60) 68.

[89] According to Art 4 of the VCLT, it does not apply to treaties such as the ABM Treaty that entered into force before the VCLT.

[90] See B Cheng, 'The Future of State Practice in a Divided World' in R St J MacDonald and J Johnston (eds), *The Structure of International Law: Essays in Legal Philosophy and Theory* (Martinus Nijhoff, Dordrecht 1983) 513.

[91] Vamvoukos (n 40) 206–14.

to terminate or suspend the treaty's operation.[92] However, neither the VCLT nor any other agreement includes a conventional obligation to submit the case to the ICJ or another third party. It would appear that negotiations in good faith are the only requirement. The question then left is the legal position if those negotiations do not produce a solution, either in the form of an agreement that a treaty should be terminated, or an agreement to modify it (both of which are consensual solutions, rather than a separately and distinctly identifiable consequence of the legal doctrine of fundamental change of circumstances).

C. Conclusion on the fundamental change of circumstances doctrine

Many theoretical and practical aspects of the requirements of the doctrine of fundamental change of circumstances remain not yet fully explored. The lack of extensive State practice makes further analysis mainly speculative. Nevertheless, the legal construct of Article 62 of the VCLT has shifted the doctrine's focus from a unilateral, subjective process into an objective procedure where other treaty parties may participate in assessing pleas of fundamental change of circumstances.

The relevant ICJ case law leads to the conclusion that, although the Court in principle affirms the existence of this doctrine, in practice, difficulties arise even when it is invoked. The Court has jointly evaluated all elements of this doctrine and applied them to the cases at hand very restrictively. The doctrine's application in the ECJ's *Racke* case was less restrictive but, as explained above, many extra-legal considerations may have contributed to that outcome. It may thus be said that the doctrine of fundamental change of circumstances is an exception in international law, used very sparingly by States and treated with great circumspection by the ICJ.

As to the procedural requirements for applying this doctrine, this topic remains largely unexplored both from the theoretical and practical points of view. It would be purely speculative to predict whether its status will change or remain the same.

III. The State of Necessity and Treaty Obligations

A. General introduction

The state of necessity is not part of the law of treaties but belongs to the law of State responsibility and forms one of the circumstances precluding wrongfulness, codified in Article 25 of the 2001 ASR (formerly draft Article 33).[93] Like a fundamental change of circumstances, the doctrine of necessity takes a negative formulation; it may not be invoked unless the act done out of necessity is the 'only way for the

---

[92] Ibid.

[93] See eg M Agius 'The Invocation of Necessity in International Law' [2009] Netherlands Intl L Rev 95 ('Agius, NILR'); M Agius, LLM dissertation [2006] 'The Invocation of Necessity in International Law' <http://www.uppsalajuristernasalumnistiftelse.se/wp-content/uploads/2012/02/Maria-Agius-The-Invocation-of-Necessity-in-International-Law.pdf> ('Agius, LLM dissertation') and also volume 41 of the Netherlands Yearbook of International Law devoted to the state of necessity.

State to safeguard an essential interest against grave and imminent peril; and does not seriously impair an essential interest of the State or States towards which the obligation exists, or of the international community as a whole'.[94] Similarly, it cannot be invoked if the international obligation in question excludes invoking necessity or the State contributed to the situation of necessity.[95] A state of necessity frequently constitutes a separate ground for States attempting to terminate (or suspend) their treaty obligations, as evidenced by the *Gabčikovo-Nagymaros* case. In doing so, it exemplifies the troublesome relationship between the law of treaties and the law of State responsibility, which are at times almost impossible to distinguish.

B. The relevant case law

The most instructive illustration of cross-fertilization between the law of treaties and the law of State responsibility (specifically, the plea of necessity) is the aforementioned *Gabčikovo-Nagymaros* case.[96] It is a classical case not only regarding its treatment of necessity in international environmental law, but also in its general approach to international law. There, the ICJ analysed not only the general aspects of this plea, but also the relationship between a state of necessity (and generally the law of State responsibility) and the law of treaties.

Hungary justified its termination of the 1977 Treaty by suggesting that act safeguarded its essential interests, specifically the health and vital interests of the population, particularly in the Szigetköz region. Hungary further argued that the ecological dangers posed by the 1977 Treaty were: (i) of an 'exceptional' character and threatened a 'major interest' of the State; (ii) 'imminent'; and (iii) impossible to avert by means other than termination. The exceptional character of the interests involved severe pollution, a threat to the quality of drinking water, agriculture, and the essential interest of Hungary in maintaining its natural environment.[97] Hungary also emphasized the imminent nature of the peril, particularly after Czechoslovakia put into operation 'Variant C'. Finally, Hungary stressed the unavoidable character of its decision to terminate the project:

The termination of the 1977 Treaty was the last possible legal reaction to Czechoslovakia's illegitimate and persistent refusal of meaningful negotiations, which was only underscored by Czechoslovakia's perseverance with Variant C in spite of Hungary's urgent invitations to discontinue work as highly damaging and incompatible with the 1977 Treaty.[98]

Hungary stressed that it did not contribute to the occurrence of the state of necessity.[99]

The Slovak Republic presented a vigorous reply to Hungarian assertions of a state of necessity. Further, it argued that an 'ecological state of necessity' did not exist either at the time of suspending the works, or at the time of Hungary's

---

[94] ASR (n 8) Art 26.   [95] Ibid Art 25.
[96] For the statement of facts see text accompanying nn 23–7.
[97] J Crawford, *The International Law Commission's Articles on State Responsibility* (CUP, Cambridge 2002) 287–8.
[98] Ibid 291.   [99] Ibid.

termination notice. Slovakia even expressed some doubts as to whether there could be an 'ecological state of necessity', since such a plea would seriously undermine the stability of the law of treaties.[100] In any case, the Slovak Republic suggested that when the Treaty was concluded, the best possible evidence of the project's expected environmental impact was offered. It also claimed that Hungary did not believe that a state of necessity existed when it unlawfully suspended, abandoned, and terminated its performance under the 1977 Treaty. The Slovak Memorial argued: '[t]o invoke a State of ecological necessity, a State must believe it exists. And it must have held that deep and genuine belief at the moment it decided to act contrary to its international obligations'.[101] The Slovak Republic asserted that Hungary's actions were dictated by financial difficulties and its own perceptions of its energy needs rather than a state of necessity.[102] Finally, it argued that in invoking the state of necessity, Hungary ignored the provisions of the 1977 Treaty, which had its own dispute settlement procedure based on objective data and its own built-in mechanism for constant monitoring of environmental conditions. The Slovak position was that:

[f]ull use of such mechanisms therefore precluded the unobserved development of any situation which could be characterised as a state of necessity and any negative developments could be resolved within the 1977 Treaty framework.[103]

Thus, the Slovak Republic introduced two elements to necessity not found in draft Article 33 or the final Article 25. First, Slovakia adopted 'a subjective approach', ie requiring the true belief of a State (Hungary) that the necessity exists. Second, it suggested that the dispute settlement procedure contained in the Treaty could preclude the emergence of a situation of necessity.[104] In doing so, the Republic of Slovakia revealed the complexities of this institution and the lack of any agreement by States as to what constitutes a plea of necessity.

The Court itself analysed the state of necessity against the background of Article 33 of the ILC 1980 draft Articles, ascertaining that it is a circumstance precluding wrongfulness recognized by international customary law.[105] The Court confirmed that the state of necessity was not confined to the traditional grounds for its invocation, such as a grave danger to the existence of the State itself.[106] The Court, following the ILC's findings, also acknowledged that safeguarding the

---

[100] ICJ, P Tomka, 'Verbatim Record of Oral Arguments in the *Case concerning Gabčikovo-Nagymaros Project*' (15 April 1997, The Hague) UN Doc CR.97/15, 60.

[101] Slovak Republic, 'Memorial Submitted to the ICJ for the *Case Concerning the Gabčikovo-Nagymaros Project*' (2 May 1994) vol I, 324.

[102] Ibid 325.

[103] Ibid 332.

[104] Slovakia could also have argued that Art 25(2)(a) precludes the possibility of relying on the plea of the state of necessity as 'the international obligation in question excluded the possibility of invoking necessity', which may (albeit implicitly) indicate that the relevant existing treaty obligation precludes reliance on the plea of necessity.

[105] *Gabčikovo-Nagymaros* case (n 6) [51].

[106] Ibid [53].

ecological balance could be considered an 'essential interest' of all States.[107] However, the Court confirmed the exceptional character of necessity as a circumstance precluding wrongfulness and the stringent conditions attached to its invocation.[108]

For its part, the Court questioned the existence in 1989 of the threat of 'a grave and imminent peril' and whether Hungary's suspension and termination of the 1977 Treaty and the abandonment of the works were the only method of safeguarding its essential interest against this peril. Regarding the erection of the Gabčikovo-Nagymaros barrage system, the Court stated that '[t]he Court considers, however, that, serious though these uncertainties might have been they could not, alone, establish the objective existence of a "peril" in the sense of a component element of a state of necessity'.[109] The Court further explained that 'peril' in the context of a state of necessity 'certainly evokes the idea of "risk"; that is precisely what distinguishes "peril" from material damage'.[110] A state of necessity can only exist with a 'peril', 'duly established' at 'the relevant point of time'. Further, the Court added 'the mere apprehension of a possible "peril" could not suffice' to establish the state of necessity.[111] This follows from the requirement that a 'peril' must at the same time be 'grave' and 'imminent'. The Court analysed the notion of 'imminence' as synonymous with 'immediacy' or 'proximity'. According to the ILC, an 'extremely grave and imminent peril' must be a threat to a State's interest at the actual time. The Court added, however, that in its view a 'peril' appearing over a long period of time might be considered 'imminent' 'as soon as it is established at the relevant point of time; that the realization of that peril, however far off it might be, is not thereby any less certain and inevitable'.[112]

Against this background, the Court analysed the Gabčikovo-Nagymaros system of locks and barrages. As to the Nagymaros portion of the project, the Court viewed the dangers alleged by Hungary as of an uncertain character and therefore saw no 'grave and imminent' peril at the time of the suspension and abandonment of the works by Hungary. The ICJ observed, moreover, that the peril invoked by Hungary had already been present before 1989 and could not entirely be ascribed to work on the Nagymaros dam. The Court stressed that even if the system's erection would have created serious risks, Hungary had at its disposal other means besides the project's suspension and abandonment. The use of such, more costly techniques, according to the Court, was 'not determinative of the state of necessity'.[113] The Court invoked similar reasoning to deny Hungary's plea of necessity in relation to the quality of certain ground and surface water and the effects on fauna and flora.[114]

As with fundamental change of circumstances, a separate, vital issue for determining the existence of the state of necessity is: who can authoritatively make such a

---

[107] See eg R Boed, 'State of Necessity as a Justification for Internationally Wrongful Act' (2000) 3 Yale Human Rights and Development L J 12.

[108] *Gabčikovo-Nagymaros* (n 6) [51]; P Okowa, 'Defences in the Jurisprudence of International Tribunals' in GS Goodwin-Gill and S Talmon (eds), *The Reality of International Law: Essays in Honour of Ian Brownlie* (OUP, Oxford 1999) 392.

[109] *Gabčikovo-Nagymaros* case (n 6) [54].

[110] Ibid.   [111] Ibid.   [112] Ibid.   [113] Ibid [55].   [114] Ibid [56].

factual assessment, the State claiming necessity or a third party? It may be inferred from the judgment in the *Gabčikovo-Nagymaros* case that:

> the current position is that the assessment must indeed be determined by a State, but that such an assessment may be scrutinized by affected parties, the international community as a whole and, as seen from case law, international legal bodies to which the case may be rendered. The very idea behind regime building efforts in the field of state responsibility builds upon the desire not to give much latitude to States, as regards the circumstances under which they may deviate from their international undertakings.[115]

Finally, the Court stated that even if it had been established that there was a state of necessity in 1989 linked to the performance of the 1977 Treaty, Hungary would not have been permitted to rely upon that state of necessity as it had helped, by act or omission, to bring it about.[116]

All told, the ICJ decision confirmed several legal characteristics of the state of necessity. First, the Court incontrovertibly reiterated that ecological concerns can give rise to the invocation of the plea of necessity. It clarified the question of who decides on the factual existence of necessity and it came up with a two-tiered test; the first tier comprises a subjective test, ie the State itself decides on the existence of a state of necessity. However, it cannot be the sole judge thereof; therefore, a second, objective tier is introduced and is applied by other States (the community of States) or judicial bodies. The Court also analysed the notion of 'imminence' as synonymous with 'immediacy' or 'proximity.' According to the ILC, an 'extremely grave and imminent peril' must be a certain and inevitable threat to the State's interest at the actual time.[117]

Other issues about necessity were not fully resolved. In the view of the present author, the Court did not deal in a persuasive manner with fundamental differences between the law of treaties and the law of State responsibility. Additionally, some of the Court's legal analysis of the elements of necessity (such as the above-mentioned notion of 'imminence') was very complicated and it is difficult to envisage how such a definition will be reflected in State practice. It may also be noted that although it cited, on several occasions, its reliance on customary international law regarding necessity and draft Article 33, it introduced elements that were not essential parts of those constructs, including 'a subjective approach', that is, the true belief of a State that the necessity exists.

IV. Distinguishing Supervening Impossibility of Performance, Fundamental Change of Circumstances and the Law of State Responsibility (Including the Plea of Necessity)

As mentioned above, the relationship between (i) the law of treaty doctrines on supervening impossibility of performance and fundamental change of circumstances and (ii) the law of State responsibility doctrines of *force majeure* (Article 23

---

[115] Agius, LLM dissertation (n 93) 16.   [116] *Gabčikovo-Nagymaros* (n 6) [57].
[117] Ibid [54].

of the ASR) and the plea of necessity (Article 25 of the ASR), remain, in the view of the present author, unresolved. Certain commentators have promoted the view that there is a fast and clear distinction between the realm of the law of treaties and that of State responsibility by relying on the two systems' different objectives. As crafted in Articles 61 and 62, impossibility and fundamental change of circumstances regulate the future of any treaty relationship between the Parties. In contrast, the law of State responsibility does not terminate or suspend the treaty; rather, it provides a State with a defence to preclude the wrongfulness of a past failure to perform that treaty.[118] The idea of a clear distinction is further supported by the possibility of a temporary suspension of treaty relations as a part of the law of treaties.[119]

There is, however, a more elaborate explanation regarding the relationship between Article 61 and *force majeure* (Article 23). It is based on the premise that *force majeure* embraces supervening impossibility of performance but is a wider concept, meaning that *force majeure* operates even when there is no impossibility of performance.[120] Verhoeven argued that a supervening impossibility 'necessarily constitutes *force majeure*, at least when it does not result from a breach by the State invoking it of its obligations'.[121] He operates from the premise that:

it seems reasonable to consider that the impossibility of performance that justifies the termination of the treaty under Article 61 of the Vienna Convention is fulfilled when *force majeure* under Article 23 is definitive, even if it is true that this leads to a particularly flexible interpretation of the notion of 'object indispensible for the execution of the treaty'.[122]

Verhoeven's views are confusing, however, as the invocation of circumstances precluding wrongfulness (such as *force majeure* or the state of necessity) only follows from the commission of an internationally wrongful act. It cannot be invoked in other circumstances, which do not involve wrongfulness, but prima facie resemble factually the circumstances that allow the invocation of some of the circumstances precluding wrongfulness (eg supervening impossibility, which can arise without wrongful acts by any State).[123]

---

[118] R Lefeber, 'The *Gabčikovo-Nagymaros* Project and the Law of State Responsibility' (1998) 11 LJIL 612.

[119] [1966] YBILC, vol II, 256.

[120] J Verhoeven, 'The Law of State Responsibility and the Law of Treaties' in J Crawford, A Pellet, and S Olleson (eds), *The Law of International Responsibility* (OUP, Oxford 2010) 108.

[121] Ibid.   [122] Ibid.

[123] As Sørensen explained regarding the state of necessity:

There are particular rules of international law making allowance for varying degrees of necessity, but these cases have a meaning and a scope entirely outside the traditional doctrine of state of necessity. Thus, for instance, vessels in distress are allowed to seek refuge in a foreign port, even if it is closed . . . ; in the case of famine in a country, a foreign ship proceeding to another port may be detained and its cargo expropriated . . . In these cases—in which adequate compensation must be paid—it is not the doctrine of the state of necessity which provides the foundation of the particular rules, but humanitarian considerations, which do not apply to the State as a body politic but are designed to protect essential rights of human beings in a situation of distress.

M Sørensen (ed), *Manual of Public International Law* (Macmillan, London 1968) 54.

Verhoeven's views are inconsistent, moreover, with the Court's adoption in *Gabčikovo-Nagymaros* of a strict division between the law of treaties and the law of State responsibility. The Court said as follows:

A determination of whether a convention is or is not in force, and whether it has or has not been properly suspended or denounced, is to be made pursuant to the law of treaties. On the other hand, an evaluation of the extent to which the suspension or denunciation of a convention, seen as incompatible with the law of treaties, involves the responsibility of the State which proceeded to it, is to be made under the law of State responsibility.[124]

The Court gave no guidance on how to assess the extent to which State responsibility is involved. The general gist of the Court's statement, however, is that the non-performance of a treaty under Article 61 should be assessed on the basis of the law of treaties not the law of State responsibility.

These differences of opinion demonstrate the problematic (and still unclarified) relationship between the law of treaties and the law of State responsibility. The borders between the two areas of law are often blurred. Attempts to distinguish them are not fully convincing and leave the possibility for confusion. The *Rainbow Warrior* Arbitration provides a useful example.[125] In 1985 the 'Rainbow Warrior' was sunk in New Zealand waters by two secret service French agents. The dispute was initially resolved via a 1986 Agreement which prescribed that these agents were to be transferred to the remote island of Hao for the period of three years, with any earlier release requiring the mutual consent of both governments. However, later in 1986, before this period expired, France removed them from Hao and transferred them to France on the basis of ill health and pregnancy without the agreement of New Zealand. In the ensuing arbitration (required under the terms of the 1986 Agreement), France invoked *force majeure* and distress (circumstances precluding wrongfulness) as justifying its non-compliance with the Agreement's terms.[126] New Zealand strenuously objected to such an explanation, relying exclusively on the law of treaties. It argued that in cases of a breach of a treaty, the only excuses available under the law of treaties were acceptable grounds to suspend, terminate, or invalidate treaties. Thus, France could only invoke supervening impossibility of performance under Article 61 to terminate its 1986 treaty commitments; but here the conditions for its invocation were not met. The Tribunal, however, accepted the French position and reasoned that the breach of a treaty can be justified on the grounds of a general law of State responsibility (even where there was no ground to terminate the treaty according to the law of treaties). As Susan Marks argued, this 'puts into question the continued operation of the provisions of the Vienna Convention relating to the termination, suspension and invalidity of treaties'.[127] She explained further that:

---

[124] *Gabčikovo-Nagymaros* case (n 6) [47].
[125] *New Zealand v France* (Arbitration Tribunal) (1990) 82 ILR 499.
[126] S Marks, 'Treaties, State Responsibility and Remedies' (1990) 49 CLJ 387, 388.
[127] Ibid.

[i]f a state wishing to avoid its obligations under a treaty can justify breaching the treaty by reference to the full range of excuses known to the law of state responsibility, why should it pay any heed to the stricter grounds and procedures applicable under the law of treaties?[128]

States cannot freely choose the rules applicable in cases of breach of an international obligation. Non-compliance with treaty provisions should result in the application of the VCLT's relevant rules. Indeed, the different spheres of the law of treaties and the law of State responsibility were emphasized by the ILC during its codification of the rules of State responsibility several times, particularly in discussing counter-measures and material breach of a treaty. However, several scholars favour the approach adopted by the Arbitral Tribunal in the *Rainbow Warrior* case and argue that:

[t]he circumstances precluding wrongfulness cannot logically be precluded by the existence of provisions concerning termination, suspension or impossibility of performance, as circumstances precluding wrongfulness cancelled not the operation of the treaty, but only liability for what was unquestionably illegal conduct. The regimes are to be considered as complements to one another: a state whose act of termination or suspension is incompatible with the law of treaties may still escape responsibility if it can rely on the general excuses under the law of state responsibility.[129]

Such an argument, although logical and neat, cannot be fully supported by theory, the practice of States or the relevant jurisprudence, especially the *Gabčikovo-Nagymaros* case.

Fundamental change of circumstances gives rise to similar confusion and mis-conceptions regarding the state of necessity. The predominant view is that the invocation of a state of necessity does not terminate treaty relations but only justifies non-compliance; rules of State responsibility such as necessity could be treated as emergency rules that do not affect treaty relations between States and are temporary in character.[130] But such a distinction does not conform to State practice or the case law (eg the *Gabčikovo-Nagymaros* case); necessity is often pleaded as a ground for the termination of treaties, which are primary rules. Even if we adhere to the view that under the law of treaties, the treaty remains operative, rules of State responsibility like necessity excuse the wrongfulness of a State's non-performance of its treaty commitments and prevent the liability of a State. In doing so, they defeat to a certain extent the stability of treaties and the fundamental principle of *pacta sunt servanda*.[131]

Crawford explained that circumstances precluding wrongfulness:

operate more as a shield than a sword. While they may protect the State against an otherwise well-founded accusation of wrongful conduct, they do not strike down the obligation, and the underlying source of the obligation, the primary rule, is not affected by them *as such*.[132]

---

[128] Ibid.   [129] Agius, NILR (n 93) 113.
[130] Ibid 113–14.   [131] *Gabčikovo-Nagymaros* case (n 6) [46]–[47].
[132] J Crawford, 'Second Report on State Responsibility (2nd Addendum, 30 April 1999)' UN Doc A/CN.4/498/Add.2 [224].

As the Special Rapporteur reminds us, this issue was already raised by Fitzmaurice in 1959, during the ILC's work on the codification of the law of treaties.[133] The difficulties regarding the clear-cut distinction between these two regimes may be due to the fact that although each set of norms to some degree regulates the same fields and the same situations:

the law of State responsibility is separate from the law treaties ... Nevertheless, international practice has confirmed that whenever State responsibility is incurred, the State has a right to invoke the circumstances precluding wrongfulness, as well as defenses under the law of treaties.[134]

General Conclusions

Supervening impossibility of performance and fundamental change of circumstances constitute classical means of suspending and terminating treaty obligations. The relevant provisions of the VCLT adopt a very restrictive approach to the invocation of any grounds that would undermine the stability of treaties, especially fundamental change of circumstances. Such a restrictive approach is further strengthened by the existence of procedural rules to accompany any invocation of exceptional circumstances.

The relevant case law, particularly that of the ICJ, upholds such strict application of exceptional circumstances. The ECJ was less exacting in one instance, but as suggested in the literature, that may have been caused by several circumstances peculiar to that case. The case of the ABM Treaty, moreover, indicates that where international adjudication is absent, the application of fundamental change of circumstances may not strictly follow the requirements of VCLT Article 62 but instead rely to a great degree on extra-legal factors.

Finally, it must be noted that these exceptional circumstances are frequently confused with the rules on State responsibility, such as those concerning the state of necessity as a circumstance States may invoke to preclude liability for conduct that would otherwise be wrongful. In the case law, it is quite noticeable that States are unsure which set of rules to apply in cases of attempts to exit a treaty. Various explanations presented in the relevant literature are unconvincing as how to differentiate among the potentially applicable doctrines. Similarly, State practice indicates that there is a lack of certainty as to how and when to apply particular

---

[133] J Crawford, 'Second Report on State Responsibility (3rd Addendum, 1 April 1999)' UN Doc A/CN.4/498/Add.3, 27–33; [1999] YBILC, vol II(2), 82–4; Fitzmaurice also stated as follows:

some of the grounds justifying non-performance of a particular treaty obligation are identical with some of those causing or justifying the *termination* of a treaty. Yet ... the two subjects are quite distinct, if only because in the case of termination ... the treaty ends altogether, while in the other [situation] ... it does not in general do so, and (if a paradox is permissible) the non-performance is not only justified, but 'looks towards' a resumption of performance so soon as the factors causing and justifying the non-performance are no longer present.

[1959] YBILC, vol II, 41.

[134] Agius, LLM dissertation (n 93) 43.

provisions. At present, moreover, as noted in the *Gabčikovo-Nagymaros* case, it appears that rules of State responsibility precluding wrongfulness such as necessity may undermine the stability of treaties and the universality of *pacta sunt servanda*.

Finally, as observed above, recourse to the State responsibility regime may be more lenient than the law of treaties in nullifying the relevant rules of the law of treaties regarding treaty termination or suspension.

Recommended Reading

M Agius, 'The Invocation of Necessity in International Law' (2009) 56 Netherlands Intl L Rev 95

J Crawford and S Olleson, 'The Exception of Non-Performance: Links between the Law of Treaties and the Law of State Responsibility' (2000) 21 Australian Ybk Intl L 55

M Fitzmaurice, 'The Gabcikovo-Nagymaros Case: the Law of Treaties' (1998) 11 LJIL 321

M Fitzmaurice and O Elias, 'The Doctrine of Fundamental Change of Circumstances' in M Fitzmaurice and O Elias (eds), *Contemporary Issues in the Law of Treaties* (Eleven International Publishing, Utrecht 2005) 185

G Haraszti, 'Treaties and the Fundamental Change of Circumstances' (1975) 146 RcD 1

OJ Lissitzyn, 'Treaties and Changed Circumstances' (1967) 61 AJIL 895

R Mullerson, 'The ABM Treaty: Changed Circumstances, Extraordinary Events, Supreme Interests and International Law' (2000) 59 ICLQ 509

SE Nahlik, 'The Grounds of Invalidity and Termination of Treaties' (1971) 65 AJIL 747

M Shaker, 'Fundamental Change of Circumstances or the International Law Commission and the Doctrine of "*rebus sic stantibus*"' (1967) Rev Egypt Dr Intl 109

I Sinclair, *The Vienna Convention on the Law of Treaties* (2nd edn MUP, Manchester 1984)

DF Vagts, '*Rebus* Revisited: Changed Circumstances in Treaty Law' (2005) 43 Colum J Transnat'l L 459

A Vamvoukos, *Termination of Treaties in International Law: The Doctrine of Rebus Sic Stantibus and Desuetude* (Clarendon Press, Oxford 1985)

ME Villiger, *Commentary on the 1969 Vienna Convention on the Law of Treaties* (Martinus Nijhoff, Leiden 2009)

25

Terminating Treaties

Laurence R Helfer

Introduction

An old adage says that no one likes to talk about divorce before a wedding. Yet that is, in effect, precisely what States do when they negotiate new treaties. Buried in the back of most international agreements are provisions that describe procedures for the treaty parties to end their relationship. In addition, no fewer than thirteen articles of the 1969 Vienna Convention on the Law of Treaties (VCLT) contain termination, denunciation, or withdrawal rules that apply when States do not negotiate treaty-specific rules on these topics.[1] These 'exit' provisions share a distinctive attribute: they authorize one treaty member acting unilaterally or all treaty parties acting collectively to end their obligations under an international agreement.[2] The act of exiting pursuant to these provisions is thus distinguishable from a termination or withdrawal in response to breach by another treaty party.[3]

---

[1] VCLT Arts 42–5, 54–6, 65–8, 70–1. The VCLT applies only to treaties between States. Agreements involving international organizations are governed by the Vienna Convention on the Law of Treaties between States and International Organizations or between International Organizations (adopted 21 March 1986, not yet in force) [1986] 25 ILM 543 ('1986 VLCT'). The first seventy-two articles of the 1986 VCLT—which is widely regarded as reflecting customary international law—address the same subjects as Arts 1 through 72 of the original VCLT. Anthony Aust, *Modern Treaty Law and Practice* (2nd edn CUP, Cambridge 2007) 7–8 and n7. Inasmuch as the 1986 VCLT's provisions relating to termination, denunciation, or withdrawal are materially indistinguishable from those of the VCLT, this chapter focuses only on the VCLT.

[2] LR Helfer, 'Exiting Treaties' (2005) 91 Virginia L R 1579, 1582 (explaining that 'exit clauses create a lawful, public mechanism for a state to terminate its treaty obligations or withdraw from membership in an intergovernmental organization').

[3] Eg MM Gomaa, *Suspension or Termination of Treaties on Grounds of Breach* (Martinus Nijhoff, The Hague 1996) 167–8; S Rosenne, *Breach of Treaty* (Grotius, Cambridge 1985) 117–25; AE David, *The Strategy of Treaty Termination: Lawful Breaches and Retaliations* (Yale University Press, New Haven 1975) 159–202. For a discussion of treaty breach, see Chapter 23. It is also important to distinguish denunciation, withdrawal, and termination of a treaty pursuant to its terms from the termination or suspension of a treaty due to supervening impossibility or fundamental change of circumstances. For further discussion of those topics, see Chapter 24, Parts I and II, 606 *et seq*. For a review of the literature on the design and use of treaty suspension and derogation clauses, see LR Helfer, 'Flexibility in International Agreements' in J Dunoff and M Pollack (eds), *International Law and International Relations: Taking Stock: Insights from Interdisciplinary Scholarship* (CUP, Cambridge 2012).

The structure and operation of treaty exit provisions were long overlooked by most legal scholars and political scientists.[4] Over the last decade, that silence has ended as commentators in both fields have devoted fresh attention to the design and use of international agreements in general and treaty flexibility mechanisms in particular. This chapter reviews the findings of this research as it applies to treaty exit rules and discusses its practical, theoretical, and normative implications.

Part I provides an overview of the international law rules governing exit from multilateral and bilateral treaties, including key provisions of the VCLT. Part II highlights the wide variations in the design and invocation of treaty termination, denunciation, and withdrawal clauses using illustrations from a range of subject areas. Part III sets forth a theory of treaty exit. It argues that termination, denunciation, and withdrawal clauses are tools for managing risk—a pervasive feature of international affairs.[5] A concluding section briefly identifies avenues for future research on treaty exit that may aid scholars and practitioners alike.

I. The International Law of Treaty Termination, Withdrawal, and Denunciation

It is helpful to begin with a definition of key terms. *Denunciation* and *withdrawal* are used interchangeably to refer to a unilateral act by which a nation that is currently a party to a treaty ends its membership in that treaty.[6] In the case of multilateral agreements, denunciation or withdrawal generally does not affect the treaty's continuation in force for the remaining parties.[7] For bilateral agreements, in contrast, denunciation or withdrawal by either party results in the *termination* of

---

[4] Eg A McNair, *The Law of Treaties* (Clarendon Press, Oxford 1961) 510 (stating that treaty clauses permitting unilateral denunciation 'occur[] so frequently that [they] hardly require[] illustration' or discussion).

[5] RB Bilder, *Managing the Risks of International Agreement* (University of Wisconsin Press, Madison 1981), is an early and influential analysis of treaty flexibility mechanisms as risk management tools.

[6] UN Office of Legal Affairs, *Final Clauses of Multilateral Treaties Handbook* (UN Sales No E04V3 2003) 109 ('Final Clauses Handbook') ('The words denunciation and withdrawal express the same legal concept'). Anthony Aust asserts that 'although the term denunciation is sometimes used in relation to a multilateral treaty, the better term is *withdrawal*, since if a party leaves a multilateral treaty that will not normally result in its termination'. A Aust, *Handbook of International Law* (CUP, Cambridge 2010) 93. Although there is much to recommend this view, in fact multilateral agreements use both terms interchangeably.

[7] There are a number of exceptions. If a multilateral agreement, such as the Comprehensive Nuclear-Test-Ban Treaty (adopted 10 September 1996, not yet in force) [1996] 35 ILM 1439, Art XIV(1), requires a particular State to join the agreement as a condition of its entry into force and that State subsequently withdraws from the treaty, 'it can be assumed that . . . the treaty would be terminated'. ME Villiger, *Commentary on the 1969 Vienna Convention on the Law of Treaties* (Martinus Nijhoff, Leiden 2009) 694. Termination also occurs when a multilateral treaty specifies that it shall no longer be in force if denunciations reduce the parties to below a specified number. Eg Convention on the Political Rights of Women (adopted 20 December 1952, entered into force 7 July 1954) 193 UNTS 135, Art 8(2) (providing that the convention 'shall cease to be in force as from the date when the denunciation which reduces the number of Parties to less than six becomes effective'). However, the default rule in VCLT Art 55 allows the treaty to continue in force unless it specifies a minimum number of required parties.

the treaty for both parties. The termination of a multilateral agreement occurs when the treaty ceases to exist for all States parties.[8]

It is also useful to situate denunciation, withdrawal, and termination within a broader group of mechanisms and doctrines concerning treaty dissolution. For example, Article 59 of the VCLT describes situations in which a treaty 'shall be considered as terminated if all the parties to it conclude a later treaty relating to the same subject matter'.[9] Another temporal incompatibility provision appears in Article 64 of the VCLT, which provides that a treaty terminates if it conflicts with a newly emerged peremptory norm.[10] In addition, Article 61 of the VCLT authorizes a party to 'invoke the impossibility of performing a treaty as a ground for terminating or withdrawing from it if the impossibility results from the permanent disappearance or destruction of an object indispensable for the execution of the treaty'.[11] The VCLT's exit provisions, together with those set forth in the agreement itself, are intended to be exhaustive.[12] In practice, however, a treaty may end in other ways, such as upon the performance of all of its obligations, by implication, or by falling into desuetude.[13]

The foundational principle of State consent governs the design and operation of all treaty exit clauses. At the negotiation stage, State representatives have free reign to choose the substantive and procedural rules that will govern the future cessation of their relationship. Once those rules have been adopted as part of the final text, however, a State that ratifies or accedes to the treaty also accepts any conditions or restrictions on termination, withdrawal, or denunciation that the treaty contains.[14] Unilateral exit attempts that do not comply with these conditions or restrictions are ineffective. A State that ceases performance after such an attempt remains a party to the treaty, albeit one that may be in breach of its obligations.[15] However, the treaty parties may waive these conditions or restrictions and permit unilateral withdrawal, or terminate the treaty, 'at any time by consent of all the parties after consultation with the other contracting States'.[16]

In sum, States are the undisputed masters of treaty exit rules. As illustrated in Part II, they have utilized that power to negotiate a diverse array of termination,

---

[8] Villiger (n 7) 685.

[9] VCLT Art 59 (identifying those situations as occurring when '(a) it appears from the later treaty or is otherwise established that the parties intended that the matter should be governed by that treaty; or (b) the provisions of the later treaty are so far incompatible with those of the earlier one that the two treaties are not capable of being applied at the same time').

[10] Ibid Art 64. For additional discussion, see N Kontou, *The Termination and Revision of Treaties in the Light of New Customary International Law* (Clarendon Press, Oxford 1994).

[11] VCLT Art 61. For a discussion of impossibility, see Chapter 24, Part I, 606 *et seq*.

[12] VCLT Art 42(2) ('The termination of a treaty, its denunciation or the withdrawal of a party, may take place only as a result of the application of the provisions of the treaty or of the present Convention').

[13] Aust (n 1) 305–7.

[14] VCLT Art 54(a) ('The termination of a treaty or the withdrawal of a party may take place . . . in conformity with the provisions of the treaty'); Villiger (n 7) 685 (characterizing Art 54(a) as 'independent of the will of the parties in a particular situation'). Reservations to withdrawal, denunciation, or termination clauses are extremely rare.

[15] Helfer (n 2) 1589 n23.

[16] VCLT Art 54(b).

denunciation, and withdrawal clauses and to invoke those clauses in a wide variety of circumstances. But what if a treaty omits such clauses entirely? In such a situation, the VCLT provides default rules to govern the end of the parties' relationship.

A. Treaties with no provision for termination, denunciation, or withdrawal

The most important—and the most controversial—of these exit default rules is Article 56(1) of the VCLT, which provides that a treaty that contains no provisions for termination, denunciation, or withdrawal 'is not subject to denunciation or withdrawal unless: (a) it is established that the parties intended to admit the possibility of denunciation or withdrawal; or (b) a right of denunciation or withdrawal may be implied by the nature of the treaty'.[17] Article 56(2), in turn, requires twelve months' notice before a withdrawal or denunciation effectuated pursuant to either of these clauses takes effect.[18]

Article 56 reflected an uneasy compromise among the members of the International Law Commission (ILC) as to whether States may exit from treaties that do not contain an express denunciation or withdrawal clause. In his 1957 report to the ILC, Sir Gerald Fitzmaurice wrote that such treaties should be assumed to be of 'indefinite duration, and only terminable . . . by mutual agreement on the part of all the parties'.[19] Fitzmaurice also acknowledged, however, the possibility of several exceptions:

This assumption, however, may be negatived in any case *(a)* by necessary inference to be derived from the terms of the treaty generally, indicating its expiry in certain events, or an intention to permit unilateral termination or withdrawal; *(b)* should the treaty belong to a class in respect of which, *ex naturae*, a faculty of unilateral termination or withdrawal must be deemed to exist for the parties if the contrary is not indicated—such as treaties of alliance, or treaties of a commercial character.[20]

Sir Humphrey Waldock revisited the issue in a subsequent report to the ILC. The report included a detailed draft article on 'treaties containing no provisions regarding their duration and termination'.[21] Waldock disagreed with Fitzmaurice that there was a presumption against exit from treaties that lack

---

[17] Ibid Art 56(1). Another default rule is the presumption that exit rights 'may be exercised only with respect to the whole treaty'. Villiger (n 7) 564; VCLT Art 44(1) ('A right of a party, provided for in a treaty or arising under article 56, to denounce, withdraw from or suspend the operation of the treaty may be exercised only with respect to the whole treaty unless the treaty otherwise provides or the parties otherwise agree').

[18] VCLT Art 56(2). Whether these VCLT rules constitute customary international law is an open question, but at least one scholar insists they have such status. See eg Villiger (n 7) 689 (discussing customary law basis of VCLT Art 54(b)); ibid 705 (noting it was 'doubtful' if Art 56 reflected customary international law at the time of the VCLT's adoption, but contending that it has since 'generated a new rule of customary law').

[19] GG Fitzmaurice, 'Second Report on the Law of Treaties' [1957] YBILC, vol II, 16, 22.

[20] Ibid.

[21] H Waldock, 'Second Report on the Law of Treaties' [1963] YBILC, vol II, 36 (draft Art 17).

a withdrawal or denunciation clause, and he reviewed State practice to identify the types of agreements for which exit was or was not permitted. The former category included:

(i) a commercial or trading treaty, other than one establishing an international regime for a particular area, river or waterway; (ii) a treaty of alliance or of military co-operation . . . ; (iii) a treaty for technical co-operation in economic, social, cultural, scientific, communications or any other such matters . . . ; (iv) a treaty of arbitration, conciliation or judicial settlement [and] 'a treaty which is the constituent instrument of an international organization'.[22]

In contrast, Waldock asserted that a treaty 'shall continue in force indefinitely' if it:

(a) is one establishing a boundary between two States, or effecting a cession of territory or a grant of rights in or over territory; (b) is one establishing a special international regime for a particular area, territory, river, waterway, or airspace; (c) is a treaty of peace, a treaty of disarmament, or for the maintenance of peace; (d) is one effecting a final settlement of an international dispute; (e) is a general multilateral treaty providing for the codification or progressive development of general international law.[23]

Treaties not referenced in either list would be subject to a presumption against withdrawal 'unless it clearly appears from the nature of the treaty or the circumstances of its conclusion that it was intended to have only a temporary application'.[24] Waldock's proposed typology divided the ILC and the VCLT's drafters.[25] The result was the compromise reflected in Article 56(1), quoted above, which refers to the treaty's (frequently undefined) nature and the parties' (often ambiguous) intent.

In the years following the ILC reports, scholars have continued to debate the types of treaties whose nature implies a right to withdraw as well as the evidence needed to demonstrate that the parties recognized the possibility of unilateral exit even if they failed to memorialize such an option in the treaty.[26] State practice has also been divided on these two issues. Several States have purported to quit multilateral conventions, including those establishing international organizations, notwithstanding the absence of an express exit clause.[27] Others have withdrawn without providing the one-year notice that Article 56(2) requires.[28] Some of these actions

---

[22] Ibid draft Art 17(3)(a) and (b).   [23] Ibid draft Art 17(4).
[24] Ibid draft Art 17(5).
[25] Eg T Christakis, 'Article 56' in O Corten and P Klein (eds), *The Vienna Convention on the Law of Treaties: A Commentary* (OUP, Oxford 2011) vol II, 1257–66; M Fitzmaurice and O Elias, *Contemporary Issues in the Law of Treaties* (Eleven International Publishing, Utrecht 2005) 357.
[26] Eg K Widdows, 'The Unilateral Denunciation of Treaties Containing No Denunciation Clause' (1982) 53 BYBIL 83 (summarizing these debates).
[27] Prominent examples of denunciations of multilateral organizations included the withdrawal of Indonesia from the UN in 1965; of Czechoslovakia, Hungary, and Poland from UNESCO in the 1950s; and of the Soviet Union and eight Eastern European States from WHO in the same period. N Feinberg, 'Unilateral Withdrawal from an International Organization' (1963) 39 BYBIL 189, 204–11; E Schwelb, 'Withdrawal from the United Nations: The Indonesian Intermezzo' (1967) 61 AJIL 661, 666–71; Widdows (n 26) 99–102. For an overview of State practice prior to the Second World War, see Christakis (n 25) 1262–3.
[28] For example, the US purported to withdraw from the Optional Protocol to the Vienna Convention on Consular Relations with immediate effect. J Quigley, 'The United States' Withdrawal

triggered objections from other treaty parties.[29] In the case of international organizations, the withdrawing States soon rejoined the organizations, acquiesced in the characterization of their conduct as a temporary cessation of participation, and paid a portion of the dues assessed against them during their absence.[30]

A recent and high profile dispute involving Article 56 of the VCLT concerns North Korea's attempt to denounce the International Covenant on Civil and Political Rights (ICCPR) in 1997. In response to the State's action, the UN Human Rights Committee (HRC) issued a General Comment concluding that the ICCPR was not capable of denunciation or withdrawal.[31] Tracking Article 56's two-part inquiry, the Committee first explained that the absence of an exit clause was not an oversight, inasmuch as the ICCPR's First Optional Protocol and other contemporaneously negotiated human rights conventions expressly provided for withdrawal.[32] It then reasoned that the rights protected by the ICCPR 'belong to the people living in the territory of the State party' and cannot be divested by changes in government or State succession.[33] As a result, the treaty 'does not have a temporary character typical of treaties where a right of denunciation is deemed to be admitted, notwithstanding the absence of a specific provision to that effect'.[34]

---

from International Court of Justice Jurisdiction in Consular Cases: Reasons and Consequences' (2009) 19 Duke J Comp & Intl L 263, 265–6, 292–3 ('United States, in its communication to the U.N. Secretary-General gave no time period, apparently purporting to make its withdrawal effective immediately').

[29] A notable example occurred in 1971 when Senegal notified the UN Secretary-General of denunciations of the Convention on the Territorial Sea and the Contiguous Zone (adopted 29 April 1958, entered into force 10 September 1964) 516 UNTS 205, and the Convention on Fishing and Conservation of the Living Resources of the High Seas (adopted 29 April 1958, entered into force 20 March 1966) 559 UNTS 285. Senegal justified its actions by asserting that the treaties '"profited the wealthier, the better equipped, and not the under-developed, the poorer" who could only attest, powerless, to the over-exploitation of biological resources situated in high seas areas adjacent to their territorial waters'. D Bardonnet, 'La denunciation par le gouvernement sénégalais de la Convention sur la mer territoriale et la zone continiguë et de la Convention sur la pêche et la conservation des sources biologiques de la haute mer' (1972) 18 Annuaire Française de Droit International 123, 133 (quoting declaration of Senegalese President). In response, the United Kingdom objected on the ground that the conventions were 'not susceptible to unilateral denunciation' and that it 'therefore cannot accept the validity or effectiveness of the purported denunciation by the Government of Senegal'. UN Treaty Collection, Law of the Sea, Convention on the Territorial Sea and the Contiguous Zone, *Multilateral Treaties Deposited with the Secretary General* (MTDSG) <http://treaties.un.org/Pages/ViewDetails.aspx?src=TREATY&mtdsg_no=XXI-1&chapter=21&lang=en, Chapter XXI>.

[30] Eg M Akehurst, 'Withdrawal from International Organisations' (1979) 32 Current Legal Prob 143, 146–49.

[31] UNHRC, 'General Comment 26' (1997) UN Doc CCPR/C/21/Rev1/Add8/Rev1 [5].

[32] Ibid [2].   [33] Ibid [4].

[34] Ibid [3]; E Evatt, 'Democratic People's Republic of Korea and the ICCPR: Denunciation as an Exercise of the Right of Self-defence?'(1998) 5 Australia J Human Rts 215, 219–20. In part in reliance on the Committee's analysis, most commentators have concluded that human rights treaties that lack an express exit clause—including the International Covenant on Economic, Social and Cultural Rights (adopted 16 December 1966, entered into force 3 January 1976) 993 UNTS 3; Convention on the Elimination of All Forms of Discrimination Against Women (adopted 18 December 1979, entered into force 3 September 1981) 1249 UNTS 13; International Convention for the Protection of All Persons from Enforced Disappearance (adopted 20 December 2006, entered into force 23 December 2010) [2007] 4 IHRR 582, and the Second Optional Protocol to the ICCPR Aiming at the Abolition of the Death Penalty (adopted 15 December 1989, entered into force 11 July 1991) 1642 UNTS

The UN Secretary-General also rejected North Korea's purported denunciation, although he relied on a different legal theory. In the Secretary-General's view, unilateral exit from the ICCPR was precluded by Article 54 of the VCLT, which he interpreted as permitting North Korea to withdraw only with the consent of all of the other treaty parties.[35] The UN Treaty Section referred to this interpretation in a notification sent to these States in response to North Korea's action, and '[a]t least one State, Denmark, sent a Notification to the Secretary-General agreeing with his understanding of Article 54 and stating that it did not consent to [North Korea's] withdrawal'.[36] North Korea 'appears to have accepted' that unilateral withdrawal from the ICCPR is not legally permissible.[37] In 2000, the country 'submitted its long overdue second periodic report' to the HRC and 'participated in the examination of that report' in the following year.[38]

B. The legal effects of exit

In addition to providing default exit rules for treaties that lack express exit provisions, the VCLT sets forth important principles concerning the legal consequences of exit. Article 70 provides that 'the termination of a treaty under its provisions or in accordance with the present Convention ... releases the parties from any obligation further to perform the treaty'.[39] Termination does not, however, 'affect any right, obligation or legal situation of the parties created through the execution of the treaty prior to' the date that the termination takes effect.[40] Nor does it 'impair the duty of any State to fulfil any obligation embodied in the treaty to which it would be subject under international law independently of the treaty'[41]—an implicit reference to customary international law. These limitations are equally applicable to a State that unilaterally withdraws from or denounces a multilateral treaty.[42]

414—are not susceptible to unilateral denunciation or withdrawal. Eg Helfer (n 2) 1642 n172; Villiger (n 7) 703; Y Tyagi, 'The Denunciation of Human Rights Treaties' (2008) 79 BYBIL 86, 126–33.

[35] Article 54 provides that '[t]he termination of a treaty or the withdrawal of a party may take place: (a) in conformity with the provisions of the treaty; or (b) at any time by consent of all the parties after consultation with the other contracting States'. VCLT Art 54.

[36] E Bates, 'Avoiding Legal Obligations Created by Human Rights Treaties' (2008) 57 ICLQ 751, 755; H Klingenberg, 'Elements of Nordic Practice 1998: Denmark' (1999) 68 Nordic J Intl L 163, 164 (indicating that '[o]ther states communicated similar responses').

[37] Aust (n 1) 291.

[38] Bates (n 36) 755–6.

[39] VCLT Art 70(1)(a).

[40] Ibid Art 70(1)(b).

[41] Ibid Art 43.

[42] Ibid Arts 43, 70(2). A few multilateral human rights and humanitarian law conventions reiterate that an exiting State's obligations continue until the date that a denunciation or withdrawal takes effect. Eg American Convention on Human Rights (adopted 22 November 1969, entered into force 18 July 1978) 1144 UNTS 123, Art 78(2). The drafters of other multilateral agreements, accepting Art 70's invitation to contract around the VCLT default rules, expressly indicate which obligations survive a State's unilateral exit. Eg UN Convention on the Law of the Sea (10 December 1982, entered into force 16 November 1994) 1833 UNTS 397, Art 317(2) (providing that a denunciation does not affect the 'financial and contractual obligations' accrued while a State was a party).

These rules function as a deterrent to exit. As explained below, the overwhelming majority of denunciation and withdrawal clauses require prior notice to other treaty parties. Notice is also required when a State asserts a basis for terminating or withdrawing from a treaty pursuant to the VCLT.[43] During the notice period, the legal obligations of all States parties—including the nation that seeks to withdraw from or terminate the agreement—continue unabated. States also remain responsible for any breaches that occur prior to or during the notice period, a responsibility that survives the State's withdrawal or the treaty's end.[44] Taken together, these provisions restrict States from using exit to avoid accountability for past violations of international law. They also discourage precipitous and opportunistic withdrawals in which a State seeks to exit and then immediately violate a rule that it previously accepted as binding.[45]

II. The Design and Invocation of Termination, Withdrawal, and Denunciation Clauses

In contrast to issues relating to when an international agreement implicitly precludes exit, scholars have devoted less attention to express denunciation, withdrawal, and termination clauses. This Part reviews the findings of several recent studies that reveal a wide variation in the design of these clauses and in the situations in which States invoke the clauses to end their treaty-based relationships. This variation suggests that treaty exit provisions are not mere boilerplate provisions but rather a tool for States to manage the risks of international cooperation.

Treaty provisions that authorize unilateral denunciation and withdrawal are pervasive. They are found in a wide array of multilateral and bilateral agreements governing key transborder regulatory issues, including human rights, arms control, trade, investment, and environmental protection. A 2010 study based on a random sample of 142 international agreements published in the United Nations Treaty Series (UNTS) found that 60 per cent of treaties surveyed contain an exit clause. However, the incidence of these clauses 'varies by issue area, with human rights

---

[43] VCLT Art 65(1) ('A party which, under the provisions of the present Convention, invokes . . . a ground for . . . terminating [a treaty], withdrawing from it or suspending its operation, must notify the other parties of its claim'); see also ibid Art 67 (requiring that notices of withdrawal, denunciation, or termination be in writing and be made by officials with actual treaty-making powers or those possessing full powers); ibid Art 68 (providing that notice of withdrawal, denunciation or termination may be revoked at any time before taking effect).

[44] Eg *Roodal v Trinidad and Tobago*, Case 12.342, Inter-Am Comm'n HR 89, OEA/ser L/V/II114, doc 5 rev (2001) <http://cidh.org/annualrep/2001eng/TT12342.htm> (concluding that '[n]otwithstanding Trinidad and Tobago's denunciation of the Convention [on 26 May 1999], the Commission will retain jurisdiction over complaints of violations of the Convention by Trinidad and Tobago in respect of acts taken by that State prior to' the date the denunciation became effective as well as over 'acts taken by the State prior to [that date] even if the effects of those acts continue or are not manifested until after that date').

[45] LR Helfer, 'Exiting Custom: Analogies to Treaty Withdrawals' (2010) 21 Duke J Comp & Intl L 65, 78–9.

agreements almost always incorporating them but more than half of the security agreements in the sample failing to do so'.[46]

More intriguingly, denunciation clauses impose different types and degrees of restrictions on a State's ability to withdraw from a treaty and from the obligations it imposes. Handbooks and model treaty rules published by the UN and other international organizations (IOs) on the 'final clauses' of treaties demonstrate wide variation in express exit provisions.[47] A review of these drafting guides reveals that denunciation and withdrawal clauses cluster around five ideal types:

(1) treaties that may be denounced at any time;

(2) treaties that preclude denunciation for a fixed number of years, calculated either from the date the agreement enters into force or from the date of ratification by the State;

(3) treaties that permit denunciation only at fixed time intervals;

(4) treaties that may be denounced only on a particular occasion, identified either by time period or upon the occurrence of a particular event; and

(5) treaties whose denunciation occurs automatically upon the State's ratification of a subsequent agreement.[48]

Examples of each type of clause can be found in Section VI(21) of this volume.

Divergences also exist as to the procedures for providing notice of a denunciation, including the period of time that must elapse before a denunciation takes effect, to whom notice must be given, and whether the denouncing State's obligations continue after the withdrawal takes effect. For some categories of treaties, such as humanitarian law conventions, the effective date of withdrawal is contingent upon external events, such as the cessation of an existing armed conflict.[49] Others, most notably bilateral investment agreements (BITs), 'contain a continuing effects

---

[46] B Koremenos and A Nau, 'Exit, No Exit' (2010) 21 Duke J Comp & Intl L 81, 106. The study's findings may be influenced by the fact that a large majority of treaties in the random sample are bilateral. Ibid 112–19. An earlier survey found that just nearly 90 per cent of bilateral and multilateral treaties registered with the UN between 1967 and 1971 contained denunciation or withdrawal clauses. Widdows (n 26) 95.

[47] In 1951, 1957, and 2003, the UN Office of Legal Affairs published a Handbook of Final Clauses. The Handbook is a reference tool of examples from existing treaties intended to assist State representatives who draft international agreements. Eg Final Clauses Handbook (n 6). See also Committee of Ministers, Council of Europe, Model Final Clauses for Conventions and Agreements Concluded within the Council of Europe (February 1980) <http://conventions.coe.int/Treaty/EN/Treaties/Html/ClausesFinales.htm>; H Blix and JH Emerson (eds), *The Treaty Maker's Handbook* (Oceana Publications, New York 1973) ('Treaty Maker's Handbook') (collecting examples of final clauses).

[48] Helfer (n 2) 1597 (reviewing handbooks of final clauses).

[49] Common Art 63 of the four Geneva Conventions of 1949 provides that a denunciation takes effect one year after notification. However, a notice of denunciation 'made at a time when the denouncing Power is involved in a conflict shall not take effect until peace has been concluded, and until after operations connected with the release and repatriation of the persons protected by the present Convention have been terminated'. Eg Geneva Convention for the Amelioration of the Condition of the Wounded and Sick in Armed Forces in the Field (opened for signature 12 August 1949, entered into force 21 October 1950) 75 UNTS 31, Art 63.

clause that provides that investments made, acquired, or approved prior to the date of the termination of the treaty will be protected by the treaty's provisions for a further period of ten, fifteen, or twenty years'.[50]

The most common unilateral exit clauses require advance notice (most often of twelve or six months)[51] of a decision to withdraw, sometimes with the additional condition that the treaty have been in force for a specified number of years.[52] The large majority of exit provisions do not, however, require a State to justify its decision to withdraw. To the contrary, notices of denunciation and withdrawal are generally short, stylized letters of two or three paragraphs that inform the treaty depository that a State is quitting a particular agreement on a specified future date.[53] A few treaties—most notably arms control agreements—require States to explain a decision to withdraw,[54] although they generally allow the denouncing nation to decide whether the factual predicate for withdrawal has been satisfied.[55] In addition, States often provide explanations when denouncing international labour conventions, although the treaties do not require them to do so.[56]

Treaty termination clauses are also highly diverse. Negotiators can implicitly address the issue of termination by specifying a treaty's duration. Common examples include agreements that have a fixed term of years, often with a presumption of renewal or an expectation of renegotiation.[57] At the other end of the

[50] JW Salacuse, 'The Emerging Global Regime for Investment' (2010) 51 HILJ 427, 471–2.

[51] The date that a notice of denunciation, withdrawal, or termination takes effect is calculated differently depending on whether the treaty lists the notice period in days or months. For further discussion, see Chapter 7, Part IV, 204.

[52] Eg Koremenos and Nau (n 46) 106–7; G Haraszti, *Some Fundamental Problems of the Law of Treaties* (Akadémiai Kiadó, Budapest 1973) 264.

[53] Treaty Maker's Handbook (n 47) 114–16.

[54] Eg Convention on the Prohibition of the Use, Stockpiling, Production and Transfer of Anti-Personnel Mines and on their Destruction (adopted 18 September 1997, entered into force 1 March 1999) 2056 UNTS 211, Art 20 ('Land Mines Convention') (requiring a State to provide 'a full explanation of the reasons motivating [its] withdrawal'). For additional analysis, see A Chayes, 'An Inquiry into the Workings of Arms Control Agreements' (1972) 85 Harvard L Rev 905, 957–8.

[55] Eg Treaty on the Limitation of Anti-Ballistic Missile Systems (US-USSR) (adopted 26 May 1972, entered into force 3 October 1972) 944 UNTS 13, Art XV (recognizing a right to withdraw if either party 'decides that extraordinary events related to the subject matter of this Treaty have jeopardized its supreme interests' and requiring notice 'of the extraordinary events the notifying Party regards as having jeopardized its supreme interests'). The events surrounding North Korea's exit from the Nuclear Non-Proliferation Treaty, which contains a similarly worded withdrawal clause, engendered extensive analysis of the 'extraordinary events' standard and its self-judging character. Eg M Asada, 'Arms Control Law in Crisis? A Study of the North Korean Nuclear Issue' (2004) 9 J Conflict & Sec L 331; AF Perez, 'Survival of Rights Under the Nuclear Non-Proliferation Treaty: Withdrawal and the Continuing Right of International Atomic Energy Agency Safeguards' (1994) 34 VJIL 749.

[56] K Widdows, 'The Denunciation of International Labour Conventions' (1984) 33 ICLQ 1052, 1055.

[57] Eg JR Crook, 'United States, Russia Sign New Strategic Arms Reduction Treaty; Senate Begins Hearings' (2010) 104 AJIL 514, 515 (explaining that the duration of the New START Treaty between the Russian Federation and the United States 'will be ten years, unless superseded by a subsequent agreement' and that the parties 'may agree to extend the Treaty for a period of no more than five years'); B Koremenos, 'Can Cooperation Survive Changes in Bargaining Power? The Case of Coffee' (2002) 31 J Legal Studies 259, 274–6 ('Koremenos, Coffee Agreements') (analysing International

spectrum are multilateral conventions that are intended to continue in force indefinitely.[58] For treaties that include express termination clauses, common provisions include: termination upon the occurrence of a particular event; the entry into force of a later treaty; prior written notice (with cessation of the agreement to take effect after a specified period of time); and the decision of a body established pursuant to the treaty.[59] A treaty that does not contain an express termination clause is considered to continue indefinitely, although it may be terminated at any time by consent of all the parties.[60] Examples of clauses governing treaty termination and duration are included in Section VI(23) of this volume.

As with unilateral withdrawal provisions, the incidence and type of termination clauses vary by issue area and by type of agreement. Multilateral human rights and environmental protection treaties, for example, often do not include express termination provisions.[61] In contrast, many bilateral agreements contain two modes of termination: (i) an initial term after which the treaty ends unless the parties have expressly or tacitly extended it, and (ii) termination upon notice. These 'flexible provisions enable the parties to keep their options open'.[62] A 2005 study based on a random sample of 146 treaties in the UNTS found that two-thirds have a finite duration, but that the percentage of finite treaties varied across subject areas, ranging from a high of nearly 80 per cent of economic agreements to a low of 44 per cent of human rights agreements.[63]

In contrast to the design of denunciation, withdrawal, and termination clauses, far less attention has been devoted to how often or in which circumstances States actually invoke these provisions.[64] The conventional wisdom holds that unilateral exit is an extremely rare event, a supposition based on anecdotal evidence of a few high-profile denunciations and withdrawals. A 2005 study provided a more comprehensive empirical analysis using data collected from the treaty offices of several IOs. The study identified 1,546 instances of denunciation and withdrawal from 5,416 multilateral agreements registered with the UN between 1945 to 2004.[65] It also found that, although older treaties are denounced more frequently than

---

Coffee Agreements, which had durations of five to seven years with the expectation of renegotiation); B Koremenos, 'Loosening the Ties that Bind: A Learning Model of Agreement Flexibility' (2001) 55 Intl Org 289, 305 ('Koremenos, Loosening the Ties') (analysing the Nuclear Non-Proliferation Treaty, which 'entered into force in 1970 for a period of twenty-five years' and whose parties 'reconvened [in 1995] and decided to extend the treaty indefinitely').

[58] Land Mines Convention (n 54) Art 20(1) ('This Convention shall be of unlimited duration').

[59] Eg Aust (n 1) 278–88; Final Clauses Handbook (n 6) 114–17.

[60] VCLT Art 54(b).

[61] Final Clauses Handbook (n 6) 117.

[62] Aust (n 1) 284.

[63] B Koremenos, 'Contracting around International Uncertainty' (2005) 99 American Political Science Rev 549, 557.

[64] This omission is especially striking with regard to treaty terminations. For two notable exceptions, see Koremenos, Coffee Agreements (n 57) (analysing International Coffee Agreements); Koremenos, Loosening the Ties (n 57) (analysing the Nuclear Non-Proliferation Treaty).

[65] Helfer (n 2) 1601–7. Of the 5,416 multilateral agreements in the study, 191, or 3.5 per cent, have been denounced at least once. This small percentage suggests that a few multilateral treaties have turned out badly and resulted in withdrawals by multiple States.

recently adopted ones, the rate of exit 'has held relatively constant or declined only slightly over the last fifty years, even after controlling for the large increase in ratifications and the emergence of new nations in the 1960s and 1970s'.[66] Based on these findings, the study concluded that 'denunciations and withdrawals are a regularized component of modern treaty practice—acts that are infrequent but hardly the isolated or aberrant events that the conventional wisdom suggests'.[67]

Data from the 2005 study, supplemented with more recent examples, reveal that denunciations and withdrawals can be grouped into four broad categories. These categories are not mutually exclusive. There may be more than one explanation for a State's decision to exit in a particular instance, and multiple States that exit the same treaty may have different reasons for doing so. Nevertheless, the four categories provide a basic framework for reviewing the empirical landscape of treaty denunciations and withdrawals.

The most high profile and often the most controversial of these involve States that quit a treaty to challenge disfavoured international legal rules or rebuke international institutions. In the late 1990s, for example, three Caribbean States denounced human rights treaties and withdrew from the jurisdiction of international human rights bodies in response to treaty interpretations that resulted in the *de facto* abolition of the death penalty in those countries.[68] More recently, several Latin American States denounced investment agreements and their associated dispute settlement mechanisms, charging that the international investment regime 'is not transparent, . . . does not account for the disparity in economic situation of regime members', is staffed by arbitrators who 'have an investor bias [and whose] decisions infringe on the legitimate exercise of sovereignty by host countries'.[69] These and other examples[70] illustrate how States use unilateral exit to disengage from or radically reconfigure existing forms of international cooperation.[71]

---

[66] Ibid 1604–05.   [67] Ibid 1602.

[68] LR Helfer, 'Overlegalizing Human Rights: International Relations Theory and the Commonwealth Caribbean Backlash Against Human Rights Regimes' (2002) 102 Columbia L Rev 1832 (analysing denunciations of the American Convention on Human Rights and the First Optional Protocol to the ICCPR by Guyana, Jamaica, and Trinidad and Tobago).

[69] Salacuse (n 50) 469. Bolivia (in 2007) and Ecuador (in 2010) withdrew from the Washington Convention establishing the International Centre for the Settlement of Investment Disputes (ICSID) (18 March 1965, entered into force 14 October 1966) 575 UNTS 159. During the same period, Ecuador denounced nine BITs and Venezuela terminated its BIT with the Netherlands. The States have also announced their intention to renegotiate other BITs to which they are parties. Ibid 469–70.

[70] A related phenomenon is exit that is associated with the creation of a new treaty regime. In 1992, for example, Iceland denounced the International Convention for the Regulation of Whaling (2 December 1946, entered into force 10 November 1948) 161 UNTS 72, and, together with other pro-whaling States, established the North Atlantic Marine Mammal Commission. DD Caron, 'The International Whaling Commission and the North Atlantic Marine Mammal Commission: The Institutional Risks of Coercion in Consensual Structures' (1995) 89 AJIL 154, 155. Iceland rejoined the Convention in 2002.

[71] In the Caribbean example, the States that denounced human rights treaties established a new Caribbean Court of Justice to, *inter alia*, review appeals in death penalty cases. Helfer (n 68) 1882–4. Several of the Latin American nations that withdrew from international investment treaties are advocating for a 'Bolivarian alternative to free trade'. A Tzanakopoulos, 'Denunciation of the ICSID Convention under the General International Law of Treaties' in R Hofmann and CM Tams (eds),

Second, withdrawing from an agreement (or threatening to withdraw) can increase a denouncing nation's negotiating leverage with other States parties and its influence in IOs. The United States' denunciation in the 1970s and 1980s of the agreements establishing the International Labour Organization (ILO) and the United Nations Educational, Social and Cultural Organization (UNESCO) follow this pattern. In each instance, the United States used exit and threats of exit—and the loss of organizational support and funding these entailed—to pressure the organizations' members to change their behaviour, after which it rejoined the treaties. The Soviet Union and its allies pursued a similar approach in the 1950s, temporarily withdrawing from but later rejoining the World Health Organization (WHO), UNESCO, and the ILO. In the mid-1990s, the United States and the European Communities used an exit strategy to close the Uruguay Round of trade talks that created the World Trade Organization (WTO). They withdrew from the old General Agreement on Tariffs and Trade—a treaty that gave special benefits to developing States—and then ratified the new WTO Agreement as a 'single undertaking', forcing developing States to accept a broad package of obligations favourable to US and European interests.[72] These examples reveal how States use exit and threats of exit to increase their voice within treaty-based negotiating forums and to reshape treaty commitments to more accurately reflect their interests.[73]

A third circumstance concerns what might be termed 'forced exit', which occurs when one State or group of States requires another nation to withdraw from a treaty as a condition of joining or retaining membership in an IO. The most striking example of forced exit occurred in the mid-2000s, when the European Union (EU) demanded that States seeking EU membership denounce BITs with the United States that had been in force since the early 1990s. The EU 'announced that the treaties, which broadly prohibited, among other things, discrimination against foreign investment, violated European (protectionist) laws that had governed the region's economic policies for nearly fifty years'.[74] Commentators have noted the possibilities of similar forced exits from bilateral trade and investment agreements between the United States and the members of Mercosur, South America's largest regional trading block.[75] These examples starkly illustrate that exit sits at the intersection of law and power in international relations.[76]

International Investment Law and General International Law: From Clinical Isolation to Systemic Integration (Nomos Verlagsgesellschaft Mbh & Co, Baden Baden 2011) 75–93.

[72] For additional discussion of these examples and supporting authorities, see Helfer (n 2) 1584.

[73] The foundational framework for analysing the relationship between exit and voice in the domestic context is AO Hirschman, *Exit, Voice and Loyalty: Responses to Decline in Firms, Organizations, and States* (Harvard University Press, Cambridge 1970).

[74] C Brummer, 'The Ties that Bind? Regionalism, Commercial Treaties and the Future of Global Economic Integration' (2007) 60 Vanderbilt L Rev 1349, 1372. The EU later modified this position somewhat, declaring that all incompatible BIT provisions would have to be removed from the treaties by amendment. The States seeking accession to the EU complied with this demand. Ibid 1379.

[75] Ibid 1389.

[76] For a recent discussion of the distributional implications of exit costs for powerful and weaker States, see T Meyer, 'Power, Exit Costs, and Renegotiation in International Law' (2010) 51 HILJ 379.

A fourth and very different type of exit occurs when the denunciation of one treaty is linked to joining a later-negotiated agreement that relates to the same subject matter. In the ILO and the International Maritime Organization, for example, the ratification of certain revising conventions or protocols triggers the automatic or compulsory denunciation of earlier agreements. Similarly, a few Council of Europe treaties that supersede earlier agreements on the same topic require ratifying States to denounce the earlier agreements as a condition of membership. Such paired treaty actions update a State's international obligations without diminishing its overall level of commitment. Unlike the three circumstances discussed above, denunciations and withdrawals of this type are also fundamentally cooperative in nature. They often occur in groups or waves, a pattern which suggests an attempt to shift to a new equilibrium point that benefits all or most States parties.[77]

III. Exit Clauses as Risk Management Tools

The wide variation in the design and use of termination, denunciation, and withdrawal clauses suggests that States pay close attention to the conditions and contours of exit, both when they negotiate international agreements and when they evaluate the costs and benefits of continuing to comply with those agreements over time. To many commentators anxious to demonstrate that States obey international law, the pervasiveness of these exit options is not something to be advertised, let alone celebrated.[78] For risk-averse governments, however, exit clauses are a rational response to a world plagued by uncertainty, one in which States negotiate commitments with imperfect information about the future and the preferences of other treaty parties.

To see why this is so, consider the perspective of government officials negotiating a treaty. In an ideal world, the negotiators would hammer out an agreement that maximizes joint gains and induces all affected States to join the treaty and invest the material resources and political capital needed to comply with its terms. In practice, however, numerous types of uncertainty limit the ability of negotiators to achieve such a salutary result. These include uncertainty about the preferences of other States, uncertainty about their behaviour, and uncertainty about future events such as 'unanticipated circumstances or shocks', or 'new demands from domestic coalitions or clusters of States wanting to change important rules or procedures'.[79]

---

[77] For additional discussion of these examples and supporting authorities, see Helfer (n 2) 1609–10, 1645–6. Note that even if a later treaty does not expressly provide for the denunciation of an earlier convention, the same result may be achieved by VCLT Art 59, which creates a default rule that allows for the termination of an earlier treaty by implication if all the parties to that agreement conclude a later treaty relating to the same subject matter.

[78] Eg CW Jenks, *A New World of Law? A Study of the Creative Imagination in International Law* (Longmans, Green & Co, London 1969) 180 (deploring treaty withdrawals as 'a mask for anarchy, a practice which weakens the whole structure of treaty-created international obligations').

[79] B Koremenos and others, 'The Rational Design of International Institutions' (2001) 55 Intl Org 761, 773.

Negotiators must also contend with the fact that treaties are voluntary instruments; even for States that actively participate in the drafting process, ratification is never guaranteed. The consensual nature of international agreements means that States will join a treaty only if the anticipated benefits of doing so outweigh the expected costs.

In terms of their benefits, denunciation, withdrawal, and termination clauses reduce the uncertainties that are pervasive in international affairs. They do so by providing what is, in effect, an insurance policy—a low cost option for States to end treaty-based cooperation if an agreement turns out badly. All other things being equal, exit clauses encourage ratification by a larger number of States than would join the treaty in the absence of such a clause.[80] Such clauses also enable the negotiation of deeper or broader commitments than would otherwise be attainable.[81] And they encourage treaty parties to address openly the consequences of changed circumstances rather than remaining as parties but committing surreptitious violations.[82] Taken together, these factors counsel negotiators to include broad and permissive exit provisions in treaties.

Although the *ex ante* benefits of exit are considerable, treaties that permit easy denunciation may also create impediments to future cooperation. One concern is that a State will invoke a denunciation or withdrawal clause (or credibly threaten to do so) whenever economic, political, or other pressures make compliance costly or inconvenient. Seen from this vantage point, an exit provision enables a State to quit a treaty and, after the withdrawal takes effect, engage in conduct that would have been a violation had it remained a member of the agreement. But the risks of exit extend beyond such opportunistic behaviour. States that prefer to cooperate but fear that their treaty partners may withdraw from the agreement also have less incentive to invest in treaty compliance. These deterrents to cooperation favour making treaties more durable and binding by eliminating or restricting exit opportunities—a position directly contrary to the *ex ante* perspective that favours broad exit rights.

These competing perspectives on the benefits and costs of exit suggest that a key challenge that negotiators face is not to close exit options but rather to set optimal conditions on exit *ex ante* so as to deter opportunistic invocations of exit *ex post*. Exit clauses that are too capacious will encourage self-serving denunciations and lead to a breakdown in cooperation. Exit provisions that are too onerous will reduce such behaviour, but may prevent the parties from reaching agreement in the

---

[80] As Harold Tobin observed nearly eighty years ago, a State's ability to quit a treaty after it enters into force 'facilitates the securing of the consent of doubtful states to conventions aiming at universality, by removing the fear that changed conditions will make continued adherence inconvenient or even dangerous'. H Tobin, *The Termination of Multipartite Treaties* (Columbia University Press, New York 1933) 202.

[81] Helfer (n 2) 1599; cf Tobin (n 80) 179–80 (explaining that where 'conditions are particularly liable to change', a denunciation or termination clause 'may materially assist those who are attempting to secure acceptance of a draft').

[82] Helfer (n 2) 1590 ('A state that . . . follows the specified procedures [of an exit clause] and explains the basis for its actions projects a real (if somewhat backhanded) respect for international rules, particularly where it is possible to profess adherence in theory but fail to comply in fact').

first instance or trigger widespread violations if the costs of compliance rise unexpectedly. These alternative vantage points help to explain the diversity of exit clauses and the different uses of those clauses reviewed in Part II above. Such variation reflects the efforts of negotiators to calibrate the costs of exit in light of the often divergent preferences of States and the myriad transborder cooperation problems they seek to resolve.

Conclusion

This chapter has analysed the different mechanisms that States invoke to end their treaty-based relationships, including express termination, denunciation, and withdrawal clauses and the default rules provided by the VCLT. The chapter has argued that these 'exit' provisions help States to mitigate the uncertainties that are endemic to international affairs.

In closing, it is important to stress that treaty exit clauses do not exist in a vacuum. Rather, they operate in tandem with other flexibility devices—such as reservations, amendment rules, escape clauses, and renegotiation provisions—that treaty-makers use to manage risk. The relationship among these flexibility tools has long been a concern of government officials and commentators interested in improving the treaty-making process.[83] It would be useful to link these studies to recent scholarship analysing the form and substance of international agreements.[84] Such research might consider how States select from among a diverse array of flexibility mechanisms, and how they actually exercise the mechanisms available to them. The findings of these studies could also aid negotiators in designing treaties that more effectively address the diverse array of legal issues that are subject to international regulation.

Recommended Reading

M Akehurst, 'Withdrawal from International Organisations' (1979) 32 Current Legal Problems 143

RB Bilder, *Managing the Risks of International Agreement* (University of Wisconsin Press, Madison 1981)

E Evatt, 'Democratic People's Republic of Korea and the ICCPR: Denunciation as an Exercise of the Right of Self-defence?' (1998) 5 Australia J Human Rts 215

N Feinberg, 'Unilateral Withdrawal from an International Organization' (1963) 39 BYBIL 189

---

[83] See generally Bilder (n 5); Treaty Maker's Handbook (n 47).

[84] Eg AT Guzman, 'The Design of International Agreements' (2005) 16 EJIL 579; O Hathaway, 'Between Power and Principle: An Integrated Theory of International Law' (2005) 72 U Chicago L Rev 469; LR Helfer, 'Nonconsensual International Lawmaking' 2008 U Illinois L Rev 71; K Raustiala, 'Form and Substance in International Agreements' (2005) 99 AJIL 581.

LR Helfer, 'Exiting Custom: Analogies to Treaty Withdrawals' (2010) 21 Duke J Comp & Intl L 65

LR Helfer, 'Exiting Treaties' (2005) 91 Virginia L R 157

LR Helfer, 'Flexibility in International Agreements' in J Dunoff and M Pollack (eds), *International Law and International Relations: Insights from Interdisciplinary Scholarship* (CUP, Cambridge 2012)

LR Helfer, 'Overlegalizing Human Rights: International Relations Theory and the Commonwealth Caribbean Backlash Against Human Rights Regimes' (2002) 102 Columbia L Rev 1832

MF Imber, *The USA, ILO, UNESCO and IAEA: Politicization and Withdrawal in the Specialized Agencies* (Palgrave Macmillan, New York 1989)

N Kontou, *The Termination and Revision of Treaties in the Light of New Customary International Law* (Clarendon Press, Oxford 1994)

B Koremenos and A Nau, 'Exit, No Exit' (2010) 21 Duke J Comp & Intl L 81

T Meyer, 'Power, Exit Costs, and Renegotiation in International Law' (2010) 51 HILJ 379

B Ress, 'Ex Ante Safeguards Against Ex Post Opportunism in International Treaties: Theory and Practice of International Public Law' (1994) 150 J Institutional and Theoretical Economics 279

E Schwelb, 'Withdrawal from the United Nations: The Indonesian Intermezzo' (1967) 61 AJIL 661

H Tobin, *The Termination of Multipartite Treaties* (Columbia University Press, New York 1933)

Y Tyagi, 'The Denunciation of Human Rights Treaties' (2008) 79 BYBIL 86

K Widdows, 'The Unilateral Denunciation of Treaties Containing No Denunciation Clause' (1982) 53 BYBIL 83

SECTION VI

TREATY CLAUSES

Introduction

The preceding chapters cover the key treaty issues of today, explaining, in narrative form, how the relevant treaty theories, rules, and practices operate. But understanding may emerge from *examples* as much as *explanations*. Thus, the current Section offers a sampling of clauses from existing treaties to supplement the explanations that precede it.[1]

Judge Richard Baxter once famously described the 'infinite variety' by which States could make normative commitments.[2] His description could just as easily be limited to treaty-making itself. The UN has now registered more than 64,000 treaties, and, by all accounts, there are many more treaties that go unregistered. The form of these agreements varies widely. Treaties may employ an array of titles and include any number of instruments. The parties vary by number (from bilateral relations to multilateral treaties to those with universal aspirations) and identity (including States, International Organizations (IOs), and other qualified subjects of international law). Treaty-making may occur on virtually any subject matter of concern to treaty-makers, and they have an equally wide spectrum of regulatory tools for embodying such commitments.[3] In short, treaties have a nearly infinite variety of their own.

Thus, what follows is no more (and no less) than a *sampling* of recent treaty clauses. To capture the full diversity of approaches treaty-makers have employed—if even possible—would exceed the bounds of this volume. Nor should the inclusion of certain clauses be read as empirical evidence in any social science sense. Certainly, in some cases, a clause is sampled because it appears to be the predominant approach (eg the 'all States' formula for universal multilateral treaties), just as the inclusion of a range of clauses (eg for a treaty's relationship with other treaties) may offer a sense of a treaty-maker's options. But the inclusion of any particular clause is not intended as descriptive 'proof' of how States or other actors behave; it is not designed to link the use of that clause to a particular treaty subject or function. Whatever utility such a project might have, it is not the present one.[4]

What the current set of sample clauses *does* offer is a different lens for understanding the earlier explanations of treaty law and practice. It is one thing to read how treaty-makers construct their commitments and quite another to see the precise wording by which they do so. In some cases, clauses will illustrate how parties have applied the VCLT such as its various procedures for States to consent

---

[1] This sampling is limited to treaty texts. Models and examples of other treaty-related instruments (eg full powers, Final Acts, instruments of ratification) are available elsewhere. See eg A Aust, *Modern Treaty Law and Practice* (2nd edn CUP, Cambridge 2007); DB Hollis and others (eds), *National Treaty Law and Practice* (Martinus Nijhoff, Leiden 2005). The UN also provides examples in its *Treaty Handbook*. UN Office of Legal Affairs, *Treaty Handbook* (2006) <http://treaties.un.org>.

[2] RR Baxter, 'International Law in "Her Infinite Variety"' (1980) 29 ICLQ 549.

[3] For a survey of the various functions treaty regulations perform see Chapter 1 (Part II.C).

[4] For that sort of project, see B Koremenos and T Betz, 'The Design of Dispute Settlement Procedures in International Agreements' in JL Dunoff and MA Pollack (eds), *International Law and International Relations: Synthesizing Insights from Interdisciplinary Scholarship* (CUP, Cambridge 2012).

to be bound. Where the VCLT 'rules'—and by extension customary international law—empower treaty-makers to make decisions (such as who may participate or the permissibility of reservations), the sampled clauses indicate the choices made. And where international law provides a 'default' rule, clauses can reveal not just how States implement it, but also the variations they have adopted. In certain instances, such as treaty amendments, the extent of the departure from the default rule is particularly striking.

Thus, sampling treaty clauses provides a richer appreciation for the relationship between the law of treaties and the actual practice of those who make them. The diversity of these clauses may also have more practical utility—as an aid to those who work with treaties. Blix and Emerson's *Treaty Maker's Handbook* has remained relevant for four decades precisely because it gave those negotiating treaties precedents that they could adopt or adjust to new circumstances.[5] As a result, in several cases a clause is included here, not because it is in any way representative of treaty practice, but precisely because it reflects a creative or innovative example that others might wish to consider using in the future.

Of course, not every good example or innovative idea can fit within a sample set. And experienced readers will no doubt marvel at one or more omitted examples that they would have considered essential for inclusion. In such instances, there are other sources on which readers may rely, most notably the UN's 2003 Handbook on *Final Clauses of Multilateral Treaties*.[6] In the end, however, any deficiencies in the clauses assembled may be a function of the sampling approach as much as the sample set itself. The fact that the *Guide to Treaties* cannot mark every approach to treaty-making should not diminish its utility with respect to the examples it does provide. Current treaty practice is, moreover, both broad and deep. Whatever value sampling examples may have, the law of treaties still leaves treaty-makers essentially as masters of their agreements. In that role, they must recognize that cooperation and coordination can (and sometimes should) adopt new forms or approaches than those that came before.

The clauses that follow are organized around the life-cycle of a treaty, rather than the order in which they may be drafted or appear. The treaty-drafting process is so idiosyncratic as to defy easy summary given variations in participants, timeframes, subject matters, locations, and political will. Similarly, although most (but not all) common types of treaty clauses appear at the end of the text as so-called 'final clauses', they do not necessarily arise in any particular order. Moreover, it must be emphasized that not all the topics addressed here will find their way into any particular treaty. The inclusion of specific clauses is largely a function of the treaty-makers' specific preferences (and sometimes their attention to detail). Most of those preferences will centre on *substantive* provisions addressing a specific subject area or regulatory form that are less interesting to treaty law and practice generally. The current sample set does not, therefore, survey variations *within* specific subject areas

---

[5] H Blix and J Emerson, *The Treaty Maker's Handbook* (Oceana, Dobbs Ferry 1973).
[6] The UN Handbook is available online at <http://treaties.un.org/doc/source/publications/FC/English.pdf>.

(eg clauses to protect human rights or the environment) nor does it examine non-obligatory forms of regulation (eg how a treaty may constitute an IO). Such important issues are better dealt with in the relevant literature for each specific subject.

The treaty topics sampled focus on issues likely to arise in many and, in some cases, all treaties. This *Guide* includes twenty-three types of clauses, which can be divided into six groups. For starters, there are clauses that address whether an instrument is a treaty, what its object or purpose is and who can participate in its formation or operation. Second, there are clauses dealing with the procedures for consenting to be bound by the treaty, including those for reservations, declarations, and notifications. A third set of clauses focuses on constituting the treaty, establishing its scope, the procedures and conditions for entry into force, and any subsequent dissemination conditions. Fourth, an array of clauses deals with treaty application, whether in terms of timing, territory, disputes, or a treaty's relationship to other treaties or factual circumstances. A fifth group of clauses examines how treaties may be amended. Finally, the survey concludes with clauses that examine different ways treaty obligations end, whether temporarily via suspension, or permanently through a party's withdrawal or denunciation or the treaty's own termination.

Each sampled clause is preceded by a *very* brief description of its nature and purpose, including, where relevant, references to earlier chapters. Excerpts are in English and are authentic texts unless otherwise indicated. Space constraints require limiting excerpts to the relevant wording. Thus, where a particular clause is of interest, readers are advised to proceed to examine the treaty from which it is taken, including its text, context, and object and purpose (and perhaps even subsidiary materials) to illuminate why the particular wording was chosen. To facilitate such research, each excerpt is accompanied by a heading (where relevant) and a citation that identifies: (a) the relevant section, article, or paragraph from which it is taken; (b) the treaty title; (c) for bilateral and plurilateral treaties, the parties; (d) the year it was adopted, signed, or opened for signature; and (e) the relevant volume of the *United Nations Treaty Series* (UNTS), *International Legal Materials* (ILM) or some other location where it may be found. In the current Information Age, treaty texts (particularly multilateral ones) are available online and may regularly be found by inserting the title into an internet search engine. Such searches may actually be the easiest way to access the treaties sampled here.

Initial Decisions on Treaty-Making

1. Distinguishing Political Commitments from Treaties

As Chapter 1 explains, the dominant view is that States, IOs, and other qualified subjects make treaties when they manifest their intent to conclude an agreement governed by international law, whether in writing or some other recorded form.[7] But, as Chapter 2 details, treaties are not the only form of agreement international actors may conclude; they may opt instead to conclude a political commitment, where they intend their agreement to have exclusively political or moral (and not legal) force.[8] Discerning what the participants intended—namely, a treaty or a political commitment—is not always easy. Many treaty texts make no mention that the parties intend to conclude one or that the agreement be governed by international law. In such cases, any manifestation of treaty intent rests on the terms used, the surrounding circumstances, or even a baseline presumption that inter-State agreements are treaties absent evidence to the contrary.

Agreement participants have, however, developed a variety of ways to manifest a contrary intent. Sometimes that intent is evidenced by the forum where the agreement is adopted (such as the G8 or OSCE) or the surrounding circumstances (eg the Copenhagen Accord).[9] In other cases, however, participants may use a clause to signal their intentions. Some clauses declaim any intention that the commitment be legally binding; others affirmatively characterize the commitment as a political one. Clauses indicating that the agreement will not be registered (which the UN Charter requires for *all* treaties) are an alternative vehicle for indicating a political commitment. The ability of these clauses to definitively deny an agreement treaty status remains unresolved. Nevertheless, to the extent participants wish to make clear their non-treaty intentions at the outset, these types of clauses may offer the best available means for doing so.

---

[7] Chapter 1 (Part II.A.4).

[8] As noted in Chapter 1, a third form of inter-State agreement is also possible, where agreements have legal force, but are governed by domestic, as opposed to international, law. Ibid (Part II.B.3).

[9] See Copenhagen Accord (18 December 2009) in UNFCCC, 'Report of the Conference on its Fifteenth Session' UN Doc FCC/CP/2009/11/Add.1.

A. Explicitly not legally binding

- Memorandum of Principles and Procedures between the Republic of Moldova and the State of North Carolina (USA) Concerning their Desire to Strengthen their Good Relations (2010) <http://www.secretary.state.nc.us/partnership/pdf/NC-Moldova%20Agreement%201-20-10.pdf>:

  A. This Memorandum does not create any obligations that constitute a legally binding agreement under international law . . .

- Memorandum of Understanding for the Conservation and Management of Shared Polar Bear Populations (US Department of Interior-Environment Canada) (2008) <http://graphics8.nytimes.com/packages/pdf/national/20080515polar_memo.pdf>:

  This Memorandum of Understanding is not legally binding and creates no legally binding obligations on the Participants.

- Title, *Non-Legally Binding* Authoritative Statement of Principles for a Global Consensus on the Management, Conservation and Sustainable Development of all Types of Forests (1992) 31 ILM 882 (emphasis added).

B. Explicitly politically binding

- Title, *Political Declaration*, International Carbon Action Partnership (2007) <http://www.icapcarbonaction.com/index.php?option=com_content&view=article&id=12&Itemid=4> (emphasis added).

- First Paragraph, Founding Act on Mutual Relations, Cooperation and Security (NATO) (1997) 36 ILM 1006:

  The North Atlantic Treaty Organization and its member States, on the one hand, and the Russian Federation, on the other hand, hereinafter referred to as NATO and Russia, based on an enduring political commitment undertaken at the highest political level, will build together a lasting and inclusive peace in the Euro-Atlantic area on the principles of democracy and cooperative security.

- Paragraph 101, CSCE Document of the Stockholm Conference on Confidence- and Security-Building Measures and Disarmament in Europe (1986) 26 ILM 190:

  The measures adopted in this document are politically binding and will come into force on 1 January 1987.

C. Not eligible for registration with the UN

- Part X(39), CSCE Code of Conduct on Politico-Military Aspects of Security (1994) DOC.FSC/1/95:

The provisions adopted in this Code of Conduct are politically binding. Accordingly, this Code is not eligible for registration under Article 102 of the Charter of the United Nations. This Code will come into effect on 1 January 1995.

• Title IV, European Energy Charter (1991) <http://www.encharter.org/fileadmin/user_upload/document/EN.pdf#page=211>:

The signatories request the Government of The Netherlands, President-in-office of the Council of the European Communities, to transmit to the Secretary-General of the United Nations the text of the European Energy Charter which is not eligible for registration under Article 102 of the Charter of the United Nations.

• Testimonium, Final Act of the Conference on Security and Co-operation in Europe (The Helsinki Final Act) (1975) 14 ILM 1293:

The Government of the Republic of Finland is requested to transmit to the Secretary-General of the United Nations the text of this Final Act, which is not eligible for registration under Article 102 of the Charter of the United Nations, with a view to its circulation to all the members of the Organization as an official document of the United Nations.

2. Object and Purpose

A treaty's 'object and purpose' is an amorphous, but important, concept throughout the law of treaties. As Chapter 8 discusses, parties who sign a treaty subject to ratification are obliged not to defeat a treaty's object and purpose. Reservations are only permissible where they are compatible with the treaty's object and purpose, a mandate examined in Chapter 12. As explained in both Chapters 19 and 21, a treaty's object and purpose is a significant component of the 'crucible' approach to treaty interpretation and plays an important role in reconciling different language texts as well. A multilateral treaty's object and purpose restricts the scope of any treaty modification or suspension by only some of its parties.[10] As Chapter 16 notes, moreover, a treaty's object and purpose may limit when succession is possible.[11] Finally, as examined in Chapter 23, the concept of 'material breach' involves violations of treaty provisions 'essential to the accomplishment of the object or purpose of the treaty'.[12]

There is no fixed procedure for determining what a treaty's object and purpose is (let alone whether it has the same meaning in each context it applies). The concept is so flexible as to risk indeterminacy on occasion.[13] Indeed, as an interpretative

---

[10] See eg VCLT Arts 41(1)(b), 58(1)(b).

[11] See Chapter 16 (Part II.D. 423 *et seq*).

[12] VCLT Art 60(3)(b); see also Chapter 23 (Part II.A, 582 *et seq*). The 1986 VCLT contains similar references to object and purpose. See Vienna Convention on the Law of Treaties between States and International Organizations or between International Organizations (1986, not yet in force) 25 ILM 543.

[13] See generally J Klabbers, 'Some Problems Regarding the Object and Purpose of Treaties' (1997) Finnish Ybk Intl L 138.

matter, Article 31 of the VCLT presents a tautology where it would determine a treaty's object and purpose in 'light of its object and purpose'.[14]

On occasion, parties use treaty text to list one or more of its objects/objectives (the desired end result), its purpose(s) (its *raison d'être*), or both.[15] The relevant language may be found in the preamble or a specific treaty clause. In certain cases, a treaty may purport to identify some overarching object or purpose not just for itself but for related agreements, such as Protocols to a Framework Convention. Caution is warranted, however, in treating any description of a treaty's object or purpose as determinative. In most cases, the instrument as a whole must be considered. Nonetheless, these clauses are of value in such inquiries and warrant careful attention.

A. Clauses listing a treaty's objective(s)

• Article 1, Stockholm Convention on Persistent Organic Pollutants (2001) 2256 UNTS 119:

Mindful of the precautionary approach as set forth in Principle 15 of the Rio Declaration on Environment and Development, the objective of this Convention is to protect human health and the environment from persistent organic pollutants.

• Article 102, North American Free Trade Agreement (NAFTA) (1992) 32 ILM 612:

1. The objectives of this Agreement, as elaborated more specifically through its principles and rules, including national treatment, most-favored-nation treatment and transparency, are to:

   a) eliminate barriers to trade in, and facilitate the cross-border movement of, goods and services between the territories of the Parties;
   b) promote conditions of fair competition in the free trade area;
   c) increase substantially investment opportunities in the territories of the Parties;
   d) provide adequate and effective protection and enforcement of intellectual property rights in each Party's territory;
   e) create effective procedures for the implementation and application of this Agreement, for its joint administration and for the resolution of disputes; and
   f) establish a framework for further trilateral, regional and multilateral cooperation to expand and enhance the benefits of this Agreement.

2. The Parties shall interpret and apply the provisions of this Agreement in the light of its objectives set out in paragraph 1 and in accordance with applicable rules of international law.

---

[14] WA Schabas, 'Reservations to Human Rights Treaties: Time for Innovation and Reform' (1994) 18 Canadian Ybk Intl L 39, 48.

[15] Such decoupling of a treaty's objectives and purposes is, however, inconsistent with the prevailing view that a treaty's object and purpose is a 'comprehensive blanket term'. Klabbers (n 13) 148.

- Article 2(1), UN Framework Convention on Climate Change (1992) 1771 UNTS 107:

  The ultimate objective of this Convention and any related legal instruments that the Conference of the Parties may adopt is to achieve, in accordance with the relevant provisions of the Convention, stabilization of greenhouse gas concentrations in the atmosphere at a level that would prevent dangerous anthropogenic interference with the climate system. Such a level should be achieved within a time frame sufficient to allow ecosystems to adapt naturally to climate change, to ensure that food production is not threatened and to enable economic development to proceed in a sustainable manner.

- Article 3, Convention for the Conservation of Southern Bluefin Tuna (1993) 1819 UNTS 359:

  The objective of this Convention is to ensure, through appropriate management, the conservation and optimum utilisation of southern bluefin tuna.

- Article 1, Convention on the Civil Aspects of International Child Abduction (1980) 1343 UNTS 89:

  The objects of the present Convention are:
  (a) to secure the prompt return of children wrongfully removed to or retained in any Contracting State; and
  (b) to ensure that rights of custody and of access under the law of one Contracting State are effectively respected in the other Contracting States.

B. Clauses listing a treaty's purpose(s)

- Article 1, UN Convention on the Rights of Persons with Disabilities (2006) 2515 UNTS 3:

  The purpose of the present Convention is to promote, protect and ensure the full and equal enjoyment of all human rights and fundamental freedoms by all persons with disabilities, and to promote respect for their inherent dignity...

- Preamble, Agreement Concerning the Encouragement and Reciprocal Protection of Investments (China-Jamaica) (1994) <http://www.unctad.org/sections/dite/iia/docs/bits/china_jamaica.pdf>:

  The Government of the People's Republic of China and the Government of Jamaica... Desiring to encourage, protect, and create favorable conditions for investment by investors of one Contracting Party in the territory of the other Contracting Party; Desiring to strengthen economic co-operation between both States on the basis of the principles of mutual respect, sovereign equality, and mutual benefit;
  Have agreed as follows:...

C. Clauses indicative of a treaty's object and purpose

- Article 1, Agreement Concerning Cooperation To Suppress The Proliferation Of Weapons Of Mass Destruction, Their Delivery Systems, And Related Materials By Sea (Malta-US) (2007) <http://www.state.gov/t/isn/trty/81883.htm>:

1. The object and purpose of this Agreement is to promote cooperation between the Parties to enable them to prevent the transportation by sea of items of proliferation concern.

- Chapter 1, Articles 1–2, Agreement Establishing the Latin American Energy Organization (1973) 1000 UNTS 117:

Article 1

To establish a regional body which shall be called the "Latin American Energy Organization" (hereinafter referred to as the Organization or OLADE), with headquarters in the city of Quito, Ecuador.

Article 2

The Organization is an instrument for cooperation, coordination, and consultation, with its own juridical identity, whose fundamental purpose is the integration, protection, conservation, rational utilization, marketing, and defense of the energy resources of the Region.

3. Participation Conditions for States

In the bilateral context, State participation in a treaty is largely subsumed into the question of whether the two States wish to make a treaty and at what level (government-to-government, agency-to-agency, etc) to do so.[16] In the multilateral context, however, negotiating States may set conditions for participation. They may opt to pursue a 'closed' treaty, limiting participation only to those involved in the original negotiations and those they invite in by some agreed procedure. Or, they may open the treaty up to some number of other States based on certain qualifying conditions such as geography or participation in an activity. Most protocols limit participation to parties to the original treaty, but this is not legally required.

For treaties that aspire to universal membership, the so-called 'Vienna formula' became popular during the Cold War because it allowed for participation beyond UN General Assembly (UNGA) member States. Since 1973, the UNGA has had an understanding that the UN Secretary-General, as depositary, will follow UNGA practice (or seek its opinion) on questions of which entities constitute States.[17] As a result, the so-called 'all States' formula now predominates for such multilateral treaties. For further discussion of treaty participation issues, see Chapter 7.

A. Closed treaties

- Preamble, Article XXVII–VIII, Amazon Cooperation Treaty (1978) 1202 UNTS 51:

---

[16] See Chapter 1 (Part II.A.2, 21 *et seq*).
[17] See [1973] UNJY 79.

The Republics of Bolivia, Brazil, Colombia, Ecuador, Guyana, Peru, Suriname and Venezuela...

RESOLVE to sign the following Treaty...

ARTICLE XXVII. This Treaty shall remain in force for an unlimited period of time, and shall not be open to adherence.

ARTICLE XXVIII. This Treaty shall be ratified by all the Contracting Parties and the instruments of ratification shall be deposited with the Government of the Federative Republic of Brazil...

B. Participation by invitation

- Article 16.1, Framework Agreement on a Multilateral Nuclear Environment Programme in the Russian Federation (2003) [2003] OJ L155/37:

  This Agreement shall be open for accession by any State, intergovernmental organization or regional economic integration organization being subject to public international law upon invitation by the MNEPR Committee.

- Article 37, International Sugar Agreement (1992) 1703 UNTS 203:

  This Agreement shall be open for signature at the United Nations Headquarters from 1 May until 31 December 1992 by any Government invited to the United Nations Sugar Conference, 1992.

1. *Requiring a consensus of the parties*

- Articles 34–35(1)–(2), Convention on the Protection of the Marine Environment of the Baltic Sea (1992) 2099 UNTS 195:

  Article 34
  This Convention shall be open for signature in Helsinki from 9 April 1992 until 9 October 1992 by States and by the European Economic Community participating in the Diplomatic Conference on the Protection of the Marine Environment of the Baltic Sea Area held in Helsinki on 9 April 1992.

  Article 35
  1. This Convention shall be subject to ratification or approval.
  2. This Convention shall, after its entry into force, be open for accession by any other State or regional economic integration organization interested in fulfilling the aims and purposes of this Convention, provided that this State or organization is invited by all the Contracting Parties...

2. *Requiring a majority vote of the parties*

- Articles 29(1)–(2), Constitutive Act of the African Union (2000) 2158 UNTS 3:

  1. Any African State may, at any time after the entry into force of this Act, notify the Chairman of the Commission of its intention to accede to this Act and to be admitted as a member of the Union.

2. The Chairman of the Commission shall, upon receipt of such notification, transmit copies thereof to all Member States. Admission shall be decided by a simple majority of the Member States. The decision of each Member State shall be transmitted to the Chairman of the Commission who shall, upon receipt of the required number of votes, communicate the decision to the State concerned.

3. Requiring a majority of parties not to object

• Articles 13–14, Agreement Establishing the International Organisation of Vine and Wine (2001) [2004] ATS 3:

Article 13
This Agreement shall be open for signature by all Member States of the International Vine and Wine Office until 31 July 2001. This Agreement shall be subject to acceptance, approval, ratification or accession.

Article 14
Any state not referred to in Article 13 of this Agreement may apply to become a member. Applications for membership shall be made directly to the O.I.V, with a copy to the Government of the French Republic, which shall notify signatories of, or Parties to the Agreement of such applications. The O.I.V shall provide information to its members concerning applications for membership and any observations made. Members have six months in which to inform the O.I.V of their opinion. The application shall be accepted if at the expiration of six months from the date of notification a majority of members has not opposed it. The depository shall notify the State of the outcome of its application. If the application is successful, the State concerned shall have twelve months within which to deposit its instrument of accession with the depository. States referred to in Article 13 that have not signed this Agreement within the given time limit may accede at any time.

C. Conditional participation

1. Open to States who engage in particular activity

• Article 35(2), Convention on the Conservation and Management of Highly Migratory Fish Stocks in the Western and Central Pacific Ocean (2000) 40 ILM 277:

After the entry into force of this Convention, the Contracting Parties may, by consensus, invite other States and regional economic integration organizations, whose nationals and fishing vessels wish to conduct fishing for highly migratory fish stocks in the Convention Area to accede to this Convention.

• Paragraph 21, Constitution of the Association of Natural Rubber Producing Countries (1968) 1045 UNTS 173:

The Constitution of the Association shall come into force definitely on such date as when at least four Governments of countries producing natural rubber have deposited instruments of [approval], acceptance or accession. Thereafter the Government of any country producing natural rubber which ratifies the Constitution of the Association and has deposited its instrument of approval, acceptance or accession shall become a Member of the Association.

2. *Participation limited to members of a specific organization*

- Article 17(1), WIPO Copyright Treaty (1996) 2186 UNTS 121:

Any Member State of WIPO may become Party to this Treaty.

3. *Participation limited to States from within a specific region*

- Articles 18, 20, Inter-American Convention to Prevent and Punish Torture (1985) OAS Treaty Series No 67:

Article 18
This Convention is open to signature by the member states of the Organization of American States.

Article 20
This Convention is open to accession by any other American state ...

- Article 10(1), European Agreement Concerning the International Carriage of Dangerous Goods by Inland Waterways (2000) UN Doc ECE/TRANS/ADN/ CONF/2000/CRP.10:

Member States of the Economic Commission for Europe whose territory contains inland waterways, other than those forming a coastal route, which form part of the network of inland waterways of international importance as defined in the European Agreement on Main Inland Waterways of International Importance (AGN) may become Contracting Parties to this Agreement ...

4. *Open to parties to an existing treaty*

- Article IX(1), COE Protocol amending the Convention on Mutual Administrative Assistance in Tax Matters (2010) CETS No 208:

This Protocol shall be open for signature by the Signatories to the Convention. It is subject to ratification, acceptance or approval. A signatory may not ratify, accept or approve this Protocol unless it has previously or simultaneously ratified, accepted or approved the Convention ...

5. *Participation based on acceptance of a political commitment*

- Article 38, Energy Charter Treaty (1994) 2080 UNTS 95:

This Treaty shall be open for signature at Lisbon from 17 December 1994 to 16 June 1995 by the states and Regional Economic Integration Organizations which have signed the [European Energy] Charter.

6. *Multiple bases for participation*

- Section XI, Article XI.1, Convention on the Recognition of Qualifications Concerning Higher Education in the European Region (1997) 2136 UNTS 3:

   This Convention shall be open for signature by:
   a. the member States of the Council of Europe;
   b. the member States of the UNESCO Europe Region;
   c. any other signatory, contracting State or party to the European Convention of the Council of Europe and/or the UNESCO Convention on the Recognition of Studies, Diplomas and Degrees concerning Higher Education in the States belonging to the Europe Region, which have been invited to the Diplomatic Conference entrusted with the adoption of this Convention.

D. Open treaties

1. *'All States' formula*

- Articles 46–48, Convention on the Rights of the Child (1989) 1577 UNTS 3:

   Article 46
   The present Convention shall be open for signature by all States.

   Article 47
   The present Convention is subject to ratification...

   Article 48
   The present Convention shall remain open for accession by any State...

2. *The 'Vienna formula'*

- Article 20, UN Framework Convention on Climate Change (1992) 1771 UNTS 107:

   This Convention shall be open for signature by States Members of the United Nations or of any of its specialized agencies or that are Parties to the Statute of the International Court of Justice...

3. *Protocol open to participation by 'any State'*

- Article 9(2), Optional Protocol to the Convention on the Rights of the Child on the Involvement of Children in Armed Conflict (2000) 2173 UNTS 222:

   2. The present Protocol is subject to ratification and is open to accession by any State...

4. Participation Conditions for Non-State Actors

Besides States, a number of non-State actors make treaties. Their ability to do so depends on: (a) the non-State actor having competence over the treaty's subject matter and the authority to make a treaty on that subject; and (b) the willingness of the other party or parties to enter into treaty relations with it. As Chapter 3 explores, the treaty-making capacity of IOs is now well-established and has generated its own Vienna Convention. Today, most IO treaty-making is bilateral (such as cooperation, relationship, or headquarters agreements) where any question of IO participation is settled through the conclusion of the treaty itself.[18] In contrast, in the multilateral context, many treaties involve matters where either the IO lacks the competence to perform or States are unwilling to allow the IO to become a party.[19] Thus, many multilateral treaties limit participation to States only. In some cases, however, a clause may specifically authorize IO participation, with or without conditions.

Unlike IOs generally, one IO—the EU—does have extensive experience making both bilateral *and* multilateral treaties. Treaties allow (and condition) this participation in different ways. Many contain a so-called 'REIO clause', allowing 'regional economic integration organizations' that have competence over the treaty's subject matter and an attendant treaty-making capacity to become parties. Some REIO clauses envision the REIO participating in lieu of its member States. Others contemplate shared competences among the REIO and its member States (a 'mixed agreement'). Mixed agreements regularly include detailed provisions on the treaty's legal effects given the division of competences between the organization and its member States. For some time, the European Community (EC) was the primary (if not the only) example of a REIO. The Treaty of Lisbon has since supplanted the EC with the EU, whose competence is not limited to economic matters. Thus, recent multilateral treaties have restyled their participation clauses to refer to a 'Regional Integration Organization' (RIO). Neither RIO nor REIO clauses are exclusive to the EU; nothing precludes an IO from invoking one if it actually possesses sufficient competence and treaty-making capacity to do so.[20] At the same time, several recent treaties have moved away from the RIO/REIO clause model, opting to simply authorize EU participation specifically. Chapter 4 covers EU treaty law and practice in much more detail.

Beyond IOs and the EU, 'other subjects of international law' may make treaties, albeit in more exceptional circumstances. The same conditions of competence, capacity, and willingness to enter into a treaty apply. But, as Chapter 5 details, the actors involved are more diverse and include integral territorial units, external territories, insurgent groups, Special Administrative Regions (SARs), Associated States, and *sui generis* entities like Taiwan. As with IOs, most treaties involving

---

[18] See eg Agreement on Cooperation (Europol-Russian Federation) (2003) <http://www.mid.ru/bdomp/ns-dos.nsf/162979df2beb9880432569e70041fd1e/0604c28d811b8da243256de1003d3e10!OpenDocument>. For an example of an IO-IO agreement, see the Agreement between the International Criminal Court and the EU on cooperation and assistance (2005) <http://register.consilium.eu.int/pdf/en/05/st14/st14298.en05.pdf>.

[19] Some of these treaties may, however, accord IOs a non-party role (eg as observers) to treaty meetings. The extent of such participation is usually detailed in the relevant rules of procedure rather than in the treaty itself.

[20] The Organization of African Unity's participation in the Agreement establishing the Common Fund for Commodities (1980) is one of the few non-European examples of this occurring. See Final Clauses Handbook (n 6) 23.

'other subjects' are bilateral without any specific clause(s) on participation.[21] Occasionally, however, States may conclude treaties that contemplate treaty-making by non-State actors. More rarely, a multilateral treaty may employ various categories of entities (eg territories, fishing entities, customs unions) via which certain non-State actors may participate.

A. Participation limited to States

- Article 24(1), (3), International Convention for the Suppression of Acts of Nuclear Terrorism (2005) 2445 UNTS 89:

  1. This Convention shall be open for signature by all States from 14 September 2005 until 31 December 2006 at United Nations Headquarters in New York...
  3. This Convention shall be open to accession by any State. The instruments of accession shall be deposited with the Secretary-General of the United Nations.

B. Participation by IOs

1. *Generally*

- Articles IV–VI, Agreement on the Establishment of the International Vaccine Institute (1996) 1979 UNTS 199:

  ARTICLE IV SIGNATURE

  This Agreement shall be open for signature by all states and intergovernmental organizations at Headquarters of the United Nations, New York...

  ARTICLE V CONSENT TO BE BOUND

  This Agreement shall be subject to ratification, acceptance or approval by the signatory states and intergovernmental organizations referred to in Article IV.

  ARTICLE VI ACCESSION

  After the expiration of the period specified in Article IV, the present Agreement shall remain open for accession by any state or intergovernmental organization, contingent upon approval by the Board of Trustees of the Institute by simple majority.

2. *By invitation*

- Article 8, Agreement Establishing the International Organisation of Vine and Wine (2001) [2004] ATS 3:

---

[21] See eg Agreement on the Promotion and Reciprocal Protection of Investment (Costa Rica-The Republic of China) (1999) <http://www.unctad.org/sections/dite/iia/docs/bits/Costa_rica_taiwan. pdf> (Costa Rica-Taiwan BIT); Basic Agreement on the Region of Eastern Slavonia, Baranja, And Western Sirmium (The Erdut Agreement) (1995) UN Doc A/50/757 (peace agreement between Croatia and a sub-State unit involving local Serb authorities); Agreement on the Protection of the River Scheldt (France-Netherlands-Walloon Region-Flemish Region-Brussels-Capital Region) (1994) 34 ILM 851.

An international intergovernmental organisation may participate in or be a member of the O.I.V. and may help to fund the O.I.V. under conditions determined, on a case by case basis, by the General Assembly on a proposal from the Executive Committee.

3. *With specific competences*

- Article 26(1)(ii), Singapore Treaty on the Law of Trademarks (2006) <http://www.wipo.int/treaties/en/ip/singapore/singapore_treaty.html>:

  [Eligibility] The following entities may sign and, subject to paragraphs (2) and (3) and Article 28(1) and (3), become party to this Treaty...
  (ii) any intergovernmental organization which maintains an Office in which marks may be registered with effect in the territory in which the constituting treaty of the intergovernmental organization applies, in all its Member States or in those of its Member States which are designated for such purpose in the relevant application, provided that all the Member States of the intergovernmental organization are members of the Organization...

C. EU participation

1. *As a qualified 'intergovernmental organisation'*

- Article 17, WIPO Copyright Treaty (1996) 2186 UNTS 121:

  ... The Assembly may decide to admit any intergovernmental organisation to become Party to this Treaty which declares that it is competent in respect of, and has its own legislation binding on all its Member States on, matters covered by this Treaty and that it has been duly authorised, in accordance with its internal procedures, to become Party to this Treaty.

  The European Community, having made the Declaration referred to in the preceding paragraph in the Diplomatic Conference that has adopted this Treaty, may become Party to this Treaty.

- Annex IX, Articles 1–4, UN Convention on the Law of the Sea (1982) 1833 UNTS 3:

  #### Article 1 – Use of terms
  For the purposes of article 305 and of this Annex, 'international organization' means an intergovernmental organization constituted by States to which its member States have transferred competence over matters governed by this Convention, including the competence to enter into treaties in respect of those matters.

  #### Article 2 – Signature
  An international organization may sign this Convention if a majority of its member States are signatories of this Convention. At the time of signature an international organization shall make a declaration specifying the matters governed by this Convention in respect of which competence has been transferred to that organization by its member States which are signatories, and the nature and extent of that competence.

Article 3 – Formal confirmation and accession

1. An international organization may deposit its instrument of formal confirmation or of accession if a majority of its member States deposit or have deposited their instruments of ratification or accession.
2. The instruments deposited by the international organization shall contain the undertakings and declarations required by articles 4 and 5 of this Annex.[22]

2. As a REIO

• Articles 2(a)–(b), 23–26, Stockholm Convention on Persistent Organic Pollutants (2001) 2256 UNTS 119:

ARTICLE 2 – Definitions

(a) 'Party' means a State or regional economic integration organization that has consented to be bound by this Convention and for which the Convention is in force;
(b) 'Regional economic integration organization' means an organization constituted by sovereign States of a given region to which its member States have transferred competence in respect of matters governed by this Convention and which has been duly authorized, in accordance with its internal procedures, to sign, ratify, accept, approve or accede to this Convention . . .

ARTICLE 23 – Right to vote

1. Each Party to this Convention shall have one vote, except as provided for in paragraph 2.
2. A regional economic integration organization, on matters within its competence, shall exercise its right to vote with a number of votes equal to the number of its member States that are Parties to this Convention. Such an organization shall not exercise its right to vote if any of its member States exercises its right to vote, and vice versa.

ARTICLE 24 – Signature

This Convention shall be open for signature at Stockholm by all States and regional economic integration organizations on 23 May 2001, and at the United Nations Headquarters in New York from 24 May 2001 to 22 May 2002.

ARTICLE 25 – Ratification, Acceptance, Approval or Accession

1. This Convention shall be subject to ratification, acceptance or approval by States and by regional economic integration organizations. It shall be open for accession by States and by regional economic integration organizations from the day after the date on which the Convention is closed for signature. Instruments of ratification, acceptance, approval or accession shall be deposited with the depositary.
2. Any regional economic integration organization that becomes a Party to this Convention without any of its member States being a Party shall be bound by all the obligations under the Convention. In the case of such organizations, one or more of whose member States is a Party to this Convention, the organization and its member States shall decide on their respective responsibilities for the performance of their

---

[22] Additional Annex IX provisions cover the extent of IO participation, rights and obligations, declarations of competence, responsibility and liability, and dispute settlement. The EU which joined UNCLOS in 1998 as the European Community is the only IO to have done so.

obligations under the Convention. In such cases, the organization and the member States shall not be entitled to exercise rights under the Convention concurrently.

3. In its instrument of ratification, acceptance, approval or accession, a regional economic integration organization shall declare the extent of its competence in respect of the matters governed by this Convention. Any such organization shall also inform the depositary, who shall in turn inform the Parties, of any relevant modification in the extent of its competence...

ARTICLE 26 – Entry into force

1. This Convention shall enter into force on the ninetieth day after the date of deposit of the fiftieth instrument of ratification, acceptance, approval or accession.

2. For each State or regional economic integration organization that ratifies, accepts or approves this Convention or accedes thereto after the deposit of the fiftieth instrument of ratification, acceptance, approval or accession, the Convention shall enter into force on the ninetieth day after the date of deposit by such State or regional economic integration organization of its instrument of ratification, acceptance, approval or accession.

3. For the purpose of paragraphs 1 and 2, any instrument deposited by a regional economic integration organization shall not be counted as additional to those deposited by member States of that organization.

3. As a REIO provided one member State also participates

- Article 67(3), UN Convention Against Corruption (2003) 2349 UNTS 41:

  3. This Convention is subject to ratification, acceptance or approval. Instruments of ratification, acceptance or approval shall be deposited with the Secretary-General of the United Nations. A regional economic integration organization may deposit its instrument of ratification, acceptance or approval if at least one of its member States has done likewise. In that instrument of ratification, acceptance or approval, such organization shall declare the extent of its competence with respect to the matters governed by this Convention. Such organization shall also inform the depositary of any relevant modification in the extent of its competence.

4. As a REIO in lieu of member States

- Article XXVII 1(c), 2, Convention for the Strengthening of the Inter-American Tropical Tuna Commission (2003) <http://www.iattc.org/PDFFiles2/Antigua_Convention_Jun_2003.pdf>:

  1. This Convention shall be open for signature at Washington from November 14, 2003, until December 31, 2004, by...
     (c) States and regional economic integration organizations which are not Parties to the 1949 Convention and whose vessels have fished for fish stocks covered by this Convention at any time during the four years preceding the adoption of this Convention and that participated in the negotiation of this Convention; and
  2. In relation to the regional economic integration organizations referred to in paragraph 1 of this Article, no member State of such organizations may sign this Convention unless it represents a territory which lies outside the territorial scope of the treaty establishing the organization and provided that such member State's participation be limited to representing only the interests of that territory.

5. As a RIO

- Articles 42–44, Convention on the Rights of Persons with Disabilities (2006) 2515 UNTS 3:

Article 42 – Signature

The present Convention shall be open for signature by all States and by regional integration organizations at United Nations Headquarters in New York as of 30 March 2007.

Article 43 – Consent to be bound

The present Convention shall be subject to ratification by signatory States and to formal confirmation by signatory regional integration organizations. It shall be open for accession by any State or regional integration organization which has not signed the Convention.

Article 44 – Regional integration organizations

1. 'Regional integration organization' shall mean an organization constituted by sovereign States of a given region, to which its member States have transferred competence in respect of matters governed by this Convention. Such organizations shall declare, in their instruments of formal confirmation or accession, the extent of their competence with respect to matters governed by this Convention. Subsequently, they shall inform the depositary of any substantial modification in the extent of their competence.
2. References to 'States Parties' in the present Convention shall apply to such organizations within the limits of their competence.
3. For the purposes of article 45, paragraph 1 [on entry into force], and article 47, paragraphs 2 and 3 [on Amendments], any instrument deposited by a regional integration organization shall not be counted.
4. Regional integration organizations, in matters within their competence, may exercise their right to vote in the Conference of States Parties, with a number of votes equal to the number of their member States that are Parties to this Convention. Such an organization shall not exercise its right to vote if any of its member States exercises its right, and vice versa.

6. As the EU specifically

- Article 75, COE Convention on preventing and combating violence against women and domestic violence (2011) CETS No 210:

1. This Convention shall be open for signature by the member States of the Council of Europe, the non-member States which have participated in its elaboration and the European Union.
2. This Convention is subject to ratification, acceptance or approval. Instruments of ratification, acceptance or approval shall be deposited with the Secretary General of the Council of Europe.
3. This Convention shall enter into force on the first day of the month following the expiration of a period of three months after the date on which 10 signatories, including at least eight member States of the Council of Europe, have expressed their consent to be bound by the Convention in accordance with the provisions of paragraph 2.

4. In respect of any State referred to in paragraph 1 or the European Union, which subsequently expresses its consent to be bound by it, the Convention shall enter into force on the first day of the month following the expiration of a period of three months after the date of the deposit of its instrument of ratification, acceptance or approval.

- Article 59(2), Protocol No 14 to the European Convention for the Protection of Human Rights and Fundamental Freedom (2004) CETS No 194:

The European Union may accede to this Convention.

D. Participation by 'other subjects of international law'

1. By associated States and certain other territories

- Article 305(c)–(e), UN Convention on the Law of the Sea (1982) 1833 UNTS 3:[23]

This Convention shall be open for signature by . . .

(c) all self-governing associated States which have chosen that status in an act of self-determination supervised and approved by the United Nations in accordance with General Assembly resolution 1514 (XV) and which have competence over the matters governed by this Convention, including the competence to enter into treaties in respect of those matters;

(d) all self-governing associated States which, in accordance with their respective instruments of association, have competence over the matters governed by this Convention, including the competence to enter into treaties in respect of those matters;

(e) all territories which enjoy full internal self-government, recognized as such by the United Nations, but have not attained full independence in accordance with General Assembly resolution 1514 (XV) and which have competence over the matters governed by this Convention, including the competence to enter into treaties in respect of those matters;

2. By a 'fishing entity'

- Article XXVIII(1), Convention for the Strengthening of the Inter-American Tropical Tuna Commission (2003) <http://www.iattc.org/PDFFiles2/Antigua_Convention_Jun_2003.pdf>:[24]

1. Any fishing entity whose vessels have fished for fish stocks covered by this Convention at any time during the four years preceding the adoption of this Convention may express its firm commitment to abide by the terms of this Convention and comply with any conservation and management measures adopted pursuant thereto, by:

---

[23] Two self-governing Associated States—the Cook Islands and Niue—joined UNCLOS pursuant to Art 305.

[24] On 17 August 2010, Chinese Taipei filed a written communication of commitment pursuant to Art XXVIII. See <http://www.iattc.org/IATTCdocumentationENG.htm>.

(a) signing, during the period referred to in Article XXVII(1) of this Convention, an instrument drafted to this effect in accordance with a resolution to be adopted by the Commission under the 1949 Convention; and/or

(b) during or after the above-mentioned period, providing a written communication to the Depositary in accordance with a resolution to be adopted by the Commission under the 1949 Convention...

3. By a 'separate customs territory'

• Article XII(1)–(2), Marrakesh Agreement Establishing the World Trade Organization (1994) 1867 UNTS 3:[25]

1. Any State or separate customs territory possessing full autonomy in the conduct of its external commercial relations and of the other matters provided for in this Agreement and the Multilateral Trade Agreements may accede to this Agreement, on terms to be agreed between it and the WTO. Such accession shall apply to this Agreement and the Multilateral Trade Agreements annexed thereto.

2. Decisions on accession shall be taken by the Ministerial Conference. The Ministerial Conference shall approve the agreement on the terms of accession by a two-thirds majority of the Members of the WTO.

4. Participation authorized by separate treaty

• Article XX, Agreement with respect to Social Security (US-Canada) (1981) 35 UST 3403:

The Competent Authority of the United States and the authorities of the provinces of Canada may conclude understandings concerning any social security legislation within the provincial jurisdiction insofar as those understandings are not inconsistent with the provisions of this Agreement.[26]

5. Participation authorized by the responsible State

• Preamble, Agreement for the Exchange of Information for the Purpose of the Prevention of Fiscal Evasion and the Allocation of Rights of Taxation With Respect to Income of Individuals (Japan-Bermuda) (2010) <http://www.oecd.org/dataoecd/21/2/44538948.pdf>:

The Government of Japan and the Government of Bermuda, the Government of Bermuda having been duly authorised by the Government of the United Kingdom of Great Britain and Northern Ireland, Desiring to conclude an Agreement for the exchange of information for the purpose of the prevention of fiscal evasion and the allocation of rights of taxation with respect to income of individuals, Have agreed as follows...

---

[25] Chinese Taipei acceded to the WTO Agreement under Art XII on 1 January 2002. Hong Kong and Macau are original WTO members by virtue of earlier accession to the 1947 GATT pursuant to a similar clause (Art XXXIII).

[26] The Understanding and Administrative Arrangement (US-Quebec) (1983) TIAS 10,863 was concluded pursuant to this clause.

5. NGO Involvement

Non-governmental organizations (NGOs) do not have the capacity to conclude treaties in their own name. Nevertheless, NGOs have played an increasing role in the formation, implementation, and enforcement of certain multilateral treaties. Chapter 6 discusses these roles and assesses the NGO's significance to international law and international relations. In terms of formation, NGOs frequently push for treaty negotiations and informally lobby States on their substance. IO procedural rules may give NGOs a more formal role as observers with a right to speak (but not vote).[27] Such participation is only occasionally reflected in the treaty text itself. Treaties will more often provide for NGO participation *after* the agreement is in force; the ILO even (uniquely) goes so far as to incorporate them among member representatives. Other clauses provide for parties to cooperate with NGOs or use the information or services they provide. In a few cases, an NGO may be given standing to complain about potential treaty violations.

A. NGO participation in treaty meetings

1. As representatives of members

* Article 3(1), (5), ILO Constitution, as amended (1972) <http://www.ilo.org/ilolex/english/constq.htm>:

    1. The meetings of the General Conference of representatives of the Members shall be held from time to time as occasion may require, and at least once in every year. It shall be composed of four representatives of each of the Members, of whom two shall be Government delegates and the two others shall be delegates representing respectively the employers and the workpeople of each of the Members.
    5. The Members undertake to nominate non-Government delegates and advisers chosen in agreement with the industrial organizations, if such organizations exist, which are most representative of employers or workpeople, as the case may be, in their respective countries.

2. As observers

* Article 11(1), (4), Convention on the Prohibition of the Use, Stockpiling, Production and Transfer of Anti-Personnel Mines and on their Destruction (1997) 2056 UNTS 211:

    1. The States Parties shall meet regularly in order to consider any matter with regard to the application or implementation of this Convention . . .
    4. States not parties to this Convention, as well as the United Nations, other relevant international organizations or institutions, regional organizations, the International

---

[27] See eg Rule 31(1)–(4), Rules of Procedure, Conference of the Parties, WHO Framework Convention on Tobacco Control (2006) <http://www.who.int/fctc/cop/rules_procedure/en/index.html> (rules on NGOs as observers).

Committee of the Red Cross and relevant non-governmental organizations may be invited to attend these meetings as observers in accordance with the agreed Rules of Procedure.

- Article 23(5), Convention on Biological Diversity (1992) 1760 UNTS 79:

  ...Any other body or agency, whether governmental or nongovernmental, qualified in fields relating to conservation and sustainable use of biological diversity, which has informed the Secretariat of its wish to be represented as an observer at a meeting of the Conference of the Parties, may be admitted unless at least one third of the Parties present object. The admission and participation of observers shall be subject to the rules of procedure adopted by the Conference of the Parties.

B. NGO participation in implementing treaty obligations

- Article 23(5)(g), WHO Framework Convention on Tobacco Control (2003) 2302 UNTS 166:

  5. The Conference of the Parties shall keep under regular review the implementation of the Convention and take the decisions necessary to promote its effective implementation and may adopt protocols, annexes and amendments to the Convention, in accordance with Articles 28, 29 and 33. Towards this end, it shall...

     (g) request, where appropriate, the services and cooperation of, and information provided by, competent and relevant organizations and bodies of the United Nations system and other international and regional intergovernmental organizations and nongovernmental organizations and bodies as a means of strengthening the implementation of the Convention...

- Article 15(2), 44(4), Rome Statute of the International Criminal Court (1998) 2187 UNTS 3:

  Article 15. Prosecutor
  2. The Prosecutor shall analyse the seriousness of the information received. For this purpose, he or she may seek additional information from States, organs of the United Nations, intergovernmental or non-governmental organizations, or other reliable sources that he or she deems appropriate, and may receive written or oral testimony at the seat of the Court.

  Article 44. Staff
  4. The Court may, in exceptional circumstances, employ the expertise of gratis personnel offered by States Parties, intergovernmental organizations or non-governmental organizations to assist with the work of any of the organs of the Court. The Prosecutor may accept any such offer on behalf of the Office of the Prosecutor. Such gratis personnel shall be employed in accordance with guidelines to be established by the Assembly of States Parties.

- Article 5(2), Marrakesh Agreement Establishing the World Trade Organization (1994) 1867 UNTS 3:

  The General Council may make appropriate arrangements for consultation and cooperation with non-governmental organizations concerned with matters related to those of the WTO.

- Article XII(1), Convention on International Trade in Endangered Species of Wild Fauna and Flora (CITES) (1973) 993 UNTS 243:

  ... To the extent and in the manner [the Secretariat] considers appropriate, he may be assisted by suitable inter-governmental or non-governmental international or national agencies and bodies technically qualified in protection, conservation and management of wild fauna and flora.

C. NGO rights and standing

- Article 34, European Convention for the Protection of Human Rights and Fundamental Freedoms, as amended (2010) CETS No 194:

  The Court may receive applications from any person, non-governmental organisation or group of individuals claiming to be the victim of a violation by one of the High Contracting Parties of the rights set forth in the Convention or the Protocols thereto. The High Contracting Parties undertake not to hinder in any way the effective exercise of this right.

- Article 14(1), North American Agreement on Environmental Cooperation (Canada-Mexico-US) (1993) 32 ILM 1480:

  The Secretariat may consider a submission from any non-governmental organization or person asserting that a Party is failing to effectively enforce its environmental law, if the Secretariat finds that the submission:

  (a) is in writing in a language designated by that Party in a notification to the Secretariat;
  (b) clearly identifies the person or organization making the submission;
  (c) provides sufficient information to allow the Secretariat to review the submission, including any documentary evidence on which the submission may be based;
  (d) appears to be aimed at promoting enforcement rather than at harassing industry;
  (e) indicates that the matter has been communicated in writing to the relevant authorities of the Party and indicates the Party's response, if any; and
  (f) is filed by a person or organization residing or established in the territory of a Party.

Conditions on Joining a Treaty

6. Consent to be Bound

To become a party to a treaty, States, IOs, and other qualified subjects of international law must first express their consent to be bound by it. Generally, they do so through a concrete act that manifests a willingness to accept the international legal commitment embodied in the agreement. The VCLT identifies five vehicles for expressing consent: (i) definitive signature; (ii) an exchange of instruments constituting a treaty; (iii) ratification; (iv) acceptance or approval; and (v) accession. To that list, the 1986 VCLT adds (vi) an 'act of formal confirmation' for IO consent.[28] Each of these methods is explained and explored in detail in Chapter 7.

Most treaties will contain one or more clauses designating which method(s) of consent are acceptable. Bilateral treaties may contain clauses providing for consent via an exchange of notes, letters, or instruments of ratification. Or, they may contain clauses where the exchange brings the treaty into force, in which case the exchange also impliedly (and simultaneously) constitutes consent. In these cases, consent occurs by the act of the exchange itself, such that if the exchange is not simultaneous, it is effective on the date the later instrument is received. As for definitive signature, it may be contemplated expressly or be inferred whenever a treaty provides that signature brings the agreement into force.

Multilateral treaties may contain a clause providing for just one method of consent, but more often list an array of ways by which States or others may consent to be bound. Where ratification is a listed option—whether alone, or alongside options for acceptance or approval[29]—the treaty will usually include an additional clause on (simple) signature.[30] Signature clauses indicate who may sign the treaty, and now regularly include details on where signature may occur, at what point the treaty will be 'open for signature' and for how long. Accession clauses may be included where a treaty was not open for signature or to permit consent by States that did not (or could not) sign the treaty. Clauses on IO consent by formal confirmation are less frequent, and IOs like the EU frequently express their consent by signature followed by acceptance or approval

---

[28] 1986 VCLT Art 11(2).

[29] As Chapter 7 explains, acceptance or approval are generally interchangeable terms that follow the same rules (and have the same legal effects) as ratification unless the treaty otherwise provides. Acceptance or approval clauses are often paired with ratification clauses to accommodate those States who prefer to avoid using ratification for domestic reasons. See Chapter 7 (Part III.D, 199 *et seq*).

[30] For further discussion of simple signature and its legal effects, see Chapter 8.

instead. In cases of ratification, acceptance, approval, accession, or formal confirmation, consent to be bound will generally be effective from the date the relevant instrument is deposited or exchanged.

A State only becomes a 'party' to a treaty when it has consented to be bound by the treaty *and* that treaty is in force. When a State consents to a treaty that is not yet in force, it is referred to as a 'contracting State'. The label 'signatory' applies to States during the period following their simple signature but prior to the expression of consent by ratification, acceptance or approval. Finally, it must be emphasized, as both VCLTs acknowledge, that consent may also occur 'by any other means if so agreed'.[31] This leaves room for an array of additional (and often creative) methods for expressing consent to bound, just a few of which are included below.[32]

A. Consent by definitive signature

1. *Expressly*

- Article 36(1)–(2)(a), International Tropical Timber Agreement (2006) [2007] OJ L262/8:

  1. This Agreement shall be open for signature, at United Nations Headquarters from 3 April 2006 until one month after the date of its entry into force, by Governments invited to the United Nations Conference for the Negotiation of a Successor Agreement to the International Tropical Timber Agreement, 1994.
  2. Any Government referred to in paragraph 1 of this article may:
     (a) At the time of signing this Agreement, declare that by such signature it expresses its consent to be bound by this Agreement (definitive signature)...

- Article 9, Agreement concerning the Establishing of Global Technical Regulations for Wheeled Vehicles, Equipment and Parts which can be fitted and/or be used on Wheeled Vehicles (1998) 2119 UNTS 129:

  9.1 Countries and regional economic integration organizations specified in Article 2 may become Contracting Parties to this Agreement by...
  9.1.1. signature without reservation as to ratification, acceptance or approval;

2. *By implication*

- Paragraph 4, Understanding regarding the Implementation of the 1963 Basic Agreement for the Peace Corps Program (Colombia-US Peace Corps) (2010) TIAS 10–511:

  This Understanding shall enter into force and be binding under international law upon signature.

---

[31] VCLT Art 11; 1986 VCLT Art 11.
[32] For examples of clauses dealing with consent to treaty amendments, see headings 19–20 of this Section.

- Article 15, Agreement on Audio-visual Relations (Canada-Germany) (2004) Canadian No E104998:

This Agreement shall enter into force on the date of its signature.

B. Consent by exchange of instruments

1. By exchange of notes

- Article 20(1), Agreement for the Exchange of Information for the Purpose of the Prevention of Fiscal Evasion and the Allocation of Rights of Taxation With Respect to Income of Individuals (Japan-Bermuda) (2010) <http://www.oecd.org/dataoecd/21/2/44538948.pdf>:

This Agreement shall be approved in accordance with the legal procedures of each of the Contracting Parties and shall enter into force on the thirtieth day after the date of exchange of diplomatic notes indicating such approval.

2. By exchange of notifications

- Article XI, Agreement for Cooperation in the Field of Fusion Energy Research (European Atomic Energy Community-India) (2009) [2010] OJ L242/26:

This Agreement shall enter into force on the date on which the Parties have notified each other in writing that their respective internal procedures necessary for its entry into force have been completed, and shall remain in force for five (5) years.

- Article 13, Agreement on the Promotion and Reciprocal Protection of Investments (Greece-South Africa) (1998) <http://www.unctad.org/sections/dite/iia/docs/bits/greece_southafrica.pdf>:

This Agreement shall enter into force thirty days after the date on which the Contracting Parties have exchanged written notifications informing each other that the procedures required by their respective laws to this end have been completed.

3. By exchange of notes (or letters) constituting the treaty[33]

- Exchange of Notes Amending Chapter 4 of Annex IV of the Treaty concerning Pacific Salmon (Canada-US) (2010) <http://www.state.gov/documents/organization/179954.pdf>:

DEPARTMENT OF STATE
WASHINGTON
December 21, 2010

Excellency:

---

[33] Diplomatic Notes are usually reserved for communications among Embassies and Foreign Ministries; letters are commonly used in communications involving another State agency.

I have the honor to acknowledge receipt of your diplomatic note No. UNEN0075 dated December 21, 2010, which reads as follows:

'I have the honour to refer to the recent recommendations of the Pacific Salmon Commission relating to Chapter 4 of Annex IV of the Treaty between the Government of Canada and the Government of the United States of America Concerning Pacific Salmon, signed at Ottawa on 28 January 1985, as amended ("the Treaty"). That chapter is scheduled to expire by its own terms on 31 December 2010. I therefore have the honour to propose an agreement between our two Governments, pursuant to Article XIII of the Treaty, to amend Annex IV as follows:

Annex IV, Chapter 4, Paragraph 1 be amended to read "The provisions of this Chapter shall apply for the period 2005 through 2012."

If the proposal set forth in this Note is acceptable to your Government, I have the honour to propose that this Note, which shall be equally authentic in the English and French languages, and your affirmative reply shall constitute an Agreement between our Governments, which shall enter into force on the date of your reply, and shall continue in force for a period of two years from January 1, 2011.

Please accept, Madam Secretary, the assurances of my highest consideration.'

I am pleased to inform you that the Government of the United States of America accepts the proposal set forth in your diplomatic note. The Government of the United States of America further agrees that your diplomatic note, together with this reply, shall constitute an Agreement between the United States of America and Canada, which shall enter into force on the date of this note, and shall continue in force for a period of two years from January 1, 2011.

Accept, Excellency, the renewed assurances of my highest consideration.

For the Secretary of State: [signature]

4. By exchange of instruments of ratification

• Article 23(1), Agreement on Social Security (Australia-Italy) (1993) [2000] ATS 29:

This Agreement shall be ratified by both Parties in accordance with their respective procedures and shall enter into force on the first day of the month following that in which there has been an exchange of instruments of ratification.

C. Consent by ratification

1. By ratification exclusively

• Article 6(1), Treaty of Lisbon Amending the Treaty on European Union and the Treaty Establishing the European Community (2007) [2007] OJ C306/1:

This Treaty shall be ratified by the High Contracting Parties in accordance with their respective constitutional requirements. The instruments of ratification shall be deposited with the Government of the Italian Republic.

• Article 29(1), Convention for the Avoidance of Double Taxation and the Prevention of Fiscal Evasion with respect to Taxes on Income and on Capital (Canada-Gabon) (2002) Canadian Treaty Series 2008/5:

This Convention shall be ratified and the instruments of ratification shall be exchanged as soon as possible.

2. By ratification where the treaty is open for signature indefinitely

- Article 25(1), (3), Convention on the Elimination of All Forms of Discrimination against Women (1979) 1249 UNTS 13:

  1. The present Convention shall be open for signature by all States. . . .
  3. The present Convention is subject to ratification. Instruments of ratification shall be deposited with the Secretary-General of the United Nations.

3. By ratification requiring signature prior to treaty's entry into force

- Articles 15–16, Convention on the Prohibition of the Use, Stockpiling, Production, and Transfer of Anti-Personnel Mines and on their Destruction (1997) 2056 UNTS 211:

  Article 15
  This Convention, done at Oslo, Norway, on 18 September 1997, shall be open for signature at Ottawa, Canada, by all States from 3 December 1997 until 4 December 1997, and at the United Nations Headquarters in New York from 5 December 1997 until its entry into force.

  Article 16
  This Convention is subject to ratification, acceptance or approval of the Signatories . . .

4. By ratification requiring treaty signature within a defined period

- Articles 24–25(1), Rotterdam Convention on the Prior Informed Consent Procedure for Certain Hazardous Chemicals and Pesticides in International Trade (1998) 2244 UNTS 337:

  Article 24 Signature
  This Convention shall be open for signature at Rotterdam by all States and regional economic integration organizations on the 11th day of September 1998, and at United Nations Headquarters in New York from 12 September 1998 to 10 September 1999.

  Article 25 Ratification, acceptance, approval or accession
  1. This Convention shall be subject to ratification, acceptance or approval by States and by regional economic integration organizations . . .

D. By acceptance or approval

1. By acceptance only

- Article XIII(1)–(2), Agreement for the Establishment of the Regional Commission for Fisheries (1999) <http://www.fao.org/Legal/treaties/028t-e.htm>:

  1. In accordance with Article I.2, this Agreement shall be open to acceptance by Members and Associate Members of the Organization as well as by non-member

States of the Organization that are coastal States or Associate Members whose territories are situated wholly or partly within the Area defined in Article IV.

2. Acceptance of this Agreement by any Member or Associate Member of the Organization that is a coastal State or Associate member whose territories are situated wholly or partly within the Area defined in Article IV, shall be effected by the deposit of an instrument of acceptance with the Director-General of the Organization, the depositary of this Agreement, and shall take effect on receipt of such instrument by the Director-General . . .

2. *By acceptance or approval*

• Articles 38–39, Energy Charter Treaty (1994) 2080 UNTS 95:

ARTICLE 38 SIGNATURE

This Treaty shall be open for signature at Lisbon from 17 December 1994 to 16 June 1995 by the states and Regional Economic Integration Organizations which have signed the Charter.

ARTICLE 39 RATIFICATION, ACCEPTANCE OR APPROVAL

This Treaty shall be subject to ratification, acceptance or approval by signatories. Instruments of ratification, acceptance or approval shall be deposited with the Depository.

E. By accession

1. *Accession at any time*

• Article 25(1)–(3), International Convention for the Suppression of the Financing of Terrorism (1999) 2178 UNTS 197:

1. This Convention shall be open for signature by all States from 10 January 2000 to 31 December 2001 at United Nations Headquarters in New York.

2. This Convention is subject to ratification, acceptance or approval . . .

3. This Convention shall be open to accession by any State. The instruments of accession shall be deposited with the Secretary-General of the United Nations.

2. *Accession once treaty no longer open to signature*

• Article 25(1), Stockholm Convention on Persistent Organic Pollutants (2001) 2256 UNTS 119:

This Convention shall be subject to ratification, acceptance or approval by States and by regional economic integration organizations. It shall be open for accession by States and by regional economic integration organizations from the day after the date on which the Convention is closed for signature . . .

3. *Accession once treaty is in force*

• Article XIII, Comprehensive Nuclear-Test-Ban Treaty (1996, not yet in force) <http://www.ctbto.org/the-treaty>:

Any State which does not sign this Treaty before its entry into force may accede to it at any time thereafter.

4. *By accession to make a bilateral agreement into a multilateral one*

- Article 23.1, Free Trade Agreement (Australia-US) (2004) [2005] ATS 1:

  1. Any country or group of countries may accede to this Agreement subject to such terms and conditions as may be agreed between such country or countries and the Parties and following approval in accordance with the applicable legal procedures of each country.

  2. This Agreement shall not apply as between any Party and any acceding country or group of countries if, at the time of the accession, either Party does not consent to such application.

5. *By accession only*

- Article 43(1), Revised General Act for the Pacific Settlement of International Disputes (1949) 71 UNTS 101:

  The present General Act shall be open to accession by the members of the United Nations, by the non-member States which shall have become parties to the Statute of the International Court of Justice or to which the General Assembly of the United Nations shall have communicated a copy for this purpose.

F. By formal confirmation

- Article 43, Convention on the Rights of Persons with Disabilities (2006) 2515 UNTS 3:

  The present Convention shall be subject to ratification by signatory States and to formal confirmation by signatory regional integration organizations . . .

G. Consent by a combinations of methods

1. *By ratification or accession*

- Articles 25(1)–(2), 26, Convention Against Torture and Other Cruel, Inhuman or Degrading Treatment or Punishment (1984) 1465 UNTS 85:

  Article 25
  1. This Convention is open for signature by all States.
  2. This Convention is subject to ratification. Instruments of ratification shall be deposited with the Secretary-General of the United Nations.
  Article 26
  This Convention is open to accession by all States. Accession shall be effected by the deposit of an instrument of accession with the Secretary-General of the United Nations.

2. *By ratification, acceptance, approval, or accession*

- Article 16(1)–(3), Convention on the Prohibition of the Use, Stockpiling, Production and Transfer of Anti-Personnel Mines and on their Destruction (1997) 2056 UNTS 211:

  1. This Convention is subject to ratification, acceptance or approval of the Signatories.
  2. It shall be open for accession by any State which has not signed the Convention.
  3. The instruments of ratifications, acceptance, approval or accession shall be deposited with the Depositary.

3. *By signature, ratification, acceptance, approval, or accession*

- Article 12(1)–(2), International Convention on Arrest of Ships (1999) UN Doc A/CONF.188.6:

  1. This Convention shall be open for signature by any State at the Headquarters of the United Nations, New York, from 1 September 1999 to 31 August 2000 and shall thereafter remain open for accession.
  2. States may express their consent to be bound by this Convention by:
     (a) signature without reservation as to ratification, acceptance or approval; or
     (b) signature subject to ratification, acceptance or approval, followed by ratification, acceptance or approval; or
     (c) accession.

H. Consent by 'any other means so agreed'

1. *Initialling pursuant to separate agreement*

- Articles I–II, Agreement on Initialing the General Framework Agreement for Peace in Bosnia and Herzegovina (Dayton Agreement) (1995) <http://www.ohr.int/dpa/default.asp?content_id=380>:[34]

  Article I. The negotiation of the General Framework Agreement for Peace in Bosnia and Herzegovina and its Annexes has been completed. The Parties, and the Entities that they represent, commit themselves to signature of these Agreements in Paris in their present form, in accordance with Article III, thus establishing their entry into force and the date from which the Agreements shall have operative effect.

  Article II. The initialing of each signature block of the General Framework Agreement for Peace in Bosnia and Herzegovina and its Annexes today hereby expresses the consent of the Parties, and the Entities that they represent, to be bound by such Agreements.

---

[34] The text of the referenced Dayton Agreement is available at [1996] 35 ILM 75.

2. *By adoption of a Resolution of Approval*

- Text on the Establishment of a Preparatory Commission for the Comprehensive Test-Ban Organization (1996) [1999] UKTS 46:

  The States Signatories of the Comprehensive Nuclear Test-Ban Treaty, adopted by the General Assembly at New York on 10 September 1996,
    Having decided to take all necessary measures to ensure the rapid and effective establishment of the future Comprehensive Nuclear Test-Ban Treaty Organization, Having decided to this end to establish a Preparatory Commission,

    1. Approve the Text on the Establishment of a Preparatory Commission for the Comprehensive Nuclear Test-Ban Treaty Organization, as annexed to the present resolution;
    2. Request the Secretary-General of the United Nations, in accordance with General Assembly resolution 50/245, of 10 September 1996, on the Comprehensive Nuclear Test-Ban Treaty, to provide the services required to initiate the work of the Preparatory Commission for the Comprehensive Nuclear Test-Ban Treaty Organization, including the Meeting of States Signatories and the First Session of the Preparatory Commission.

3. *Consent subject to additional conditions*

- Article XII(1), Marrakesh Agreement establishing the World Trade Organization (1994) 1867 UNTS 3:

  Any State or separate customs territory possessing full autonomy in the conduct of its external commercial relations and of the other matters provided for in this Agreement and the Multilateral Trade Agreements may accede to this Agreement, on terms to be agreed between it and the WTO. Such accession shall apply to this Agreement and the Multilateral Agreements annexed thereto.

- Article 41, International Sugar Agreement (1992) 1703 UNTS 203:

  This Agreement shall be open to accession by the Governments of all states upon conditions established by the Council. Upon accession, the State concerned shall be deemed to be listed in the annex to this Agreement, together with its votes as laid down in the conditions of accession. Accession shall be effected by the deposit of an instrument of accession with the depositary. Instruments of accession shall state that the Government accepts all the conditions established by the Council.

- Article 4(3)–(5), Convention on Prohibitions or Restrictions of the Use of Certain Conventional Weapons which May be Deemed to be Excessively Injurious or to Have Indiscriminate Effects (1980) 1342 UNTS 137:

  3. Expressions of consent to be bound by any of the Protocols annexed to this Convention shall be optional for each State, provided that at the time of the deposit of its instrument of ratification, acceptance or approval of this Convention or accession thereto, that State shall notify the Depositary of its consent to be bound by any two or more of these Protocols.

4. At any time after the deposit of its instrument of ratification, acceptance or approval of this Convention or accession thereto, a State may notify the Depositary of its consent to be bound by any annexed Protocol by which it is not already bound.

5. Any Protocol by which a High Contracting Party is bound shall for that Party form an integral part of this Convention.

7. Reservations

Reservations are unilateral statements by a State (or an IO such as the EU) in signing or consenting to be bound by a multilateral treaty that purport 'to exclude or to modify the legal effect of certain provisions of the treaty in their application' to that State or IO.[35] A reservation is generally permitted except where: (a) the treaty explicitly prohibits reservations; (b) the treaty permits *some* reservations but not the one made; or (c) the reservation is otherwise 'incompatible with the object and purpose of the treaty'.[36]

Chapter 11 deals with the extraordinarily complicated law and practice currently surrounding reservations. There are a host of outstanding issues—What statements constitute a reservation? When and how is a reservation incompatible with a treaty's object and purpose? What legal effects flow from a reservation? And just who has authority to decide the answers to these questions? The ILC has recently revisited the topic, and time will tell what effect its involvement will have.[37]

In the current environment, treaty clauses offer a way to mitigate some (but certainly not all) of the issues reservations raise. Whether because of a failure to agree, political objections, or general inattention, a treaty may not contain any provision on reservations. But, as the VCLT envisions, negotiators can use clauses to regulate whether and how reservations may be made. A treaty can, of course, expressly prohibit *all* reservations. Or, it might authorize all reservations not incompatible with the treaty's object and purpose. In between these poles, treaty clauses can specify provisions, parts, subjects, or factual circumstances in relation to which reservations will (or will not) be permitted.

As a general rule, 'unless the treaty otherwise provides, a reservation may be withdrawn at any time'[38] by the State or IO that made it; the consent of other parties is not required. In practice, treaties tend not to alter this default rule, but rather reiterate it. In contrast, the issue of modifying existing reservations tends not to be addressed by treaties at all.

---

[35] VCLT Art 2(d); 1986 VCLT Art 2(d). Reservations formulated in signing a treaty subject to ratification, acceptance, approval, or act of formal confirmation require confirmation at the time the State or IO consents to be bound. VCLT Art 23(2); 1986 VCLT Art 23(2).

[36] VCLT Art 19; 1986 VCLT Art 19. Reservations may also be prohibited implicitly. For example, even though ILO treaties do not expressly prohibit reservations, it is generally accepted that the nature of the ILO regime precludes them.

[37] See eg ILC, 'Guide to Practice on Reservations to Treaties' (forthcoming in [2011] YBILC, vol II (2)) <http://untreaty.un.org/ilc/texts/instruments/english/draft%20articles/1_8_2011.pdf>.

[38] VCLT Art 22(1).

A. Clauses prohibiting treaty reservations entirely

- Article 25, Convention on Contact concerning Children (2003) CETS No 192:

  No reservation may be made in respect of any provision of this Convention.

- Article 30, Optional Protocol to the Convention against Torture and other Cruel, Inhuman or Degrading Treatment or Punishment (2002) 2375 UNTS 237:

  No reservations shall be made to the present Protocol.

- Article 120, Rome Statute of the International Criminal Court (1998) 2187 UNTS 3:

  No reservations may be made to this Statute.

- Article XVI(5), Marrakesh Agreement establishing the World Trade Organization (1994) 1867 UNTS 3:

  No reservations may be made in respect of any provision of this Agreement. Reservations in respect of any of the provisions of the Multilateral Trade Agreements may only be made to the extent provided for in those Agreements. Reservations in respect of a provision of a Plurilateral Trade Agreement shall be governed by the provisions of that Agreement.

B. Reservations expressly permitted

1. *Generally*

- Article 14(1), Tampere Convention on the Provision of Telecommunication Resources for Disaster Mitigation and Relief Operations (1998) 2296 UNTS 5:

  When definitively signing, ratifying or acceding to this Convention or any amendment hereto, a State Party may make reservations.

2. *Except those incompatible with the treaty's object and purpose*

- Article 51(2), Convention on the Rights of the Child (1989) 1577 UNTS 3:

  A reservation incompatible with the object and purpose of the present Convention shall not be permitted.

3. *Only where authorized by the treaty*

- Article 98, United Nations Convention on Contracts for the International Sale of Goods (1980) 1489 UNTS 3:

  No reservations are permitted except those expressly authorized in this Convention.

4. For all provisions except certain articles

- Article 42(1), Convention Relating to the Status of Refugees (1951) 189 UNTS 137:

  At the time of signature, ratification or accession, any State may make reservations to articles of the Convention other than to articles 1, 3, 4, 16 (1), 33, 36–46 inclusive.

5. For certain provisions or parts of the treaty only

- Article 42, Convention on Cybercrime (2001) 2296 UNTS 167:

  By a written notification addressed to the Secretary General of the Council of Europe, any State may, at the time of signature or when depositing its instrument of ratification, acceptance, approval or accession, declare that it avails itself of the reservation(s) provided for in Article 4, paragraph 2, Article 6, paragraph 3, Article 9, paragraph 4, Article 10, paragraph 3, Article 11, paragraph 3, Article 14, paragraph 3, Article 22, paragraph 2, Article 29, paragraph 4, and Article 41, paragraph 1. No other reservation may be made.

- Article 24(2), International Convention for the Suppression of the Financing of Terrorism (1999) 2178 UNTS 197:

  Each State may at the time of signature, ratification, acceptance or approval of this Convention or accession thereto declare that it does not consider itself bound by paragraph 1 [on binding dispute resolution by arbitration or the ICJ]. The other States Parties shall not be bound by paragraph 1 with respect to any State Party which has made such a reservation.

- Article 21(1)–(4), Trademark Law Treaty (1994) 2037 UNTS 35:

  (1) [Special Kinds of Marks] Any State or intergovernmental organization may declare through a reservation that, notwithstanding Article 2(1)(a) and (2)(a), any of the provisions of Articles 3(1) and (2), 5, 7, 11 and 13 shall not apply to associated marks, defensive marks or derivative marks. Such reservation shall specify those of the aforementioned provisions to which the reservation relates.

  (2) [Modalities] Any reservation under paragraph (1) shall be made in a declaration accompanying the instrument of ratification of, or accession to, this Treaty of the State or intergovernmental organization making the reservation.

  (3) [Withdrawal] Any reservation under paragraph (1) may be withdrawn at any time.

  (4) [Prohibition of Other Reservations] No reservation to this Treaty other than the reservation allowed under paragraph (1) shall be permitted.

- Article XXIII(1)–(2), Convention on International Trade in Endangered Species of Wild Fauna and Flora (CITES) (1973) 993 UNTS 243:

  1. The provisions of the present Convention shall not be subject to general reservations. Specific reservations may be entered in accordance with the provisions of this Article and Articles XV and XVI.
  2. Any State may, on depositing its instrument of ratification, acceptance, approval or accession, enter a specific reservation with regard to:

(a) any species included in Appendix I, II or III; or

(b) any parts or derivatives specified in relation to a species included in Appendix III.

6. For parts other than the main treaty text

- Article XXII, Convention on the Prohibition of the Development, Production, Stockpiling and use of Chemical Weapons and on their Destruction (1992) 1974 UNTS 45:

The Articles of this Convention shall not be subject to reservations. The Annexes of this Convention shall not be subject to reservations incompatible with its object and purpose.

7. With respect to excluding certain subjects

- Article 10(1), International Convention on Arrest of Ships (1999) UN Doc A/Conf.188/6:

1. Any State may, at the time of signature, ratification, acceptance, approval, or accession, or at any time thereafter, reserve the right to exclude the application of this Convention to any or all of the following:
(a) ships which are not seagoing;
(b) ships not flying the flag of a State Party;
(c) claims under article 1, paragraph 1 (s).

8. Dependent on the existence of certain factual conditions

- Article 2(1)–(3), Second Optional Protocol to the International Covenant on Civil and Political Rights Aiming at the Abolition of the Death Penalty (1989) 1642 UNTS 414:

1. No reservation is admissible to the present Protocol, except for a reservation made at the time of ratification or accession that provides for the application of the death penalty in time of war pursuant to a conviction for a most serious crime of a military nature committed during wartime.

2. The State Party making such a reservation shall at the time of ratification or accession communicate to the Secretary-General of the United Nations the relevant provisions of its national legislation applicable during wartime.

3. The State Party having made such a reservation shall notify the Secretary-General of the United Nations of any beginning or ending of a state of war applicable to its territory.

- Article 32(4), Convention on Psychotropic Substances (1971) 1019 UNTS 175:

A State on whose territory there are plants growing wild which contain psychotropic substances from among those in Schedule I and which are traditionally used by certain small, clearly determined groups in magical or religious rites, may, at the time of signature, ratification or accession, make reservations concerning these plants, in respect of the provisions of article 7, except for the provisions relating to international trade.

9. So long as it relates to one or more specific provisions

- Article 13, Inter-American Convention on Personality and Capacity of Juridical Persons in Private International Law (1984) 1752 UNTS 237:

  Each State may, at the time of signature, ratification or accession, make reservations to this Convention, provided that each reservation concerns one or more specific provisions.

C. Admissibility of reservations

1. Admissible on unanimous acceptance or in the absence of objections

- Article XII, Agreement to Promote Compliance with International Conservation and Management Measures by Fishing Vessels on the High Seas (1993) 2221 UNTS 91:

  Acceptance of this Agreement may be made subject to reservations which shall become effective only upon unanimous acceptance by all Parties to this Agreement. The Director-General shall notify forthwith all Parties of any reservation. Parties not having replied within three months from the date of the notification shall be deemed to have accepted the reservation. Failing such acceptance, the State or regional economic integration organization making the reservation shall not become a Party to this Agreement.

2. Incompatible or inhibitive if two-thirds of the parties object

- Article 20(1)–(2), International Convention on the Elimination of All Forms of Racial Discrimination (1966) 660 UNTS 195:

  1. The Secretary-General of the United Nations shall receive and circulate to all States which are or may become Parties to this Convention reservations made by States at the time of ratification or accession. Any State which objects to the reservation shall, within a period of ninety days from the date of the said communication, notify the Secretary-General that it does not accept it.

  2. A reservation incompatible with the object and purpose of this Convention shall not be permitted, nor shall a reservation the effect of which would inhibit the operation of any of the bodies established by this Convention be allowed. A reservation shall be considered incompatible or inhibitive if at least two thirds of the States Parties to this Convention object to it.

3. Permitted absent objection by one-third of parties

- Article 32(3), Convention on Psychotropic Substances (1971) 1019 UNTS 175:

  A State which desires to become a Party but wishes to be authorized to make reservations other than those made in accordance with paragraphs 2 and 4 may inform the Secretary-General of such intention. Unless by the end of twelve months after the date of the Secretary-General's communication of the reservation concerned, this reservation has been objected to by one third of the States that have signed without reservation of ratification, ratified or acceded to this Convention before the end of that period, it shall be deemed to be permitted, it being understood however that States which have objected to the reservation need not assume towards the reserving State any legal obligation under this Convention which is affected by the reservation.

D. Withdrawing reservations

1. Withdrawal at any time

- Article 46(2), Convention on the Rights of Persons with Disabilities (2006) 2515 UNTS 3:

Reservations may be withdrawn at any time.

2. Effective on notice

- Article 28(3), Convention on the Elimination of All Forms of Discrimination Against Women (1979) 1249 UNTC 13:

Reservations may be withdrawn at any time by notification to this effect addressed to the Secretary-General of the United Nations, who shall then inform all States thereof. Such notification shall take effect on the date on which it is received.

3. Partial withdrawal permitted

- Article 15, Convention on Customs Treatment of Pool Containers Used in International Transport (1994) 2000 UNTS 289:

... Any Contracting Party which has entered reservations may withdraw them, in whole or in part, at any time, by notification to the depositary specifying the date on which such withdrawal takes effect.

8. Declarations and Notifications

Reservations are not the only statements that may accompany treaty signature or consent. The most important alternatives are: (i) interpretative declarations; (ii) optional declarations; (iii) mandatory declarations; and (iv) notifications.[39] As Chapter 11 explains, States frequently issue 'interpretative declarations'. Unlike reservations, interpretative declarations do not purport to modify or exclude the treaty's provisions; rather, they clarify how the State understands the treaty's scope or meaning.[40] Thus, whatever interpretative significance they have, such declarations do not alter the treaty commitments assumed. In contrast, optional declarations do

---

[39] There is also a fifth option, where States make 'political' statements in signing, ratifying, or acceding that are not intended to have legal effects with respect to the treaty itself. See Chapter 11 (Part I, n12 and accompanying text).

[40] The ILC has suggested, however, that 'conditional interpretative declarations' (those that condition consent on the specific interpretation proposed) should be treated like reservations. See Guide to Practice (n 37) Guideline 1.4.

allow States or IOs to assume additional or different commitments on joining the treaty than those they would have absent a declaration. Mandatory declarations are also legally binding on their authors. These are issued on joining the treaty (or soon thereafter) in response to requirements for information on how the declaration's author will perform the treaty, whether by giving content to a particular provision, delimiting competences, or choosing to opt in (or out) of some specific obligation or procedure. Notifications may perform similar functions, or may simply pass along relevant information concerning the treaty and its implementation.

Treaties only occasionally contain provisions for interpretative declarations. In contrast, optional and mandatory declarations are almost always responsive to particular treaty clauses. Those clauses are often quite specific in terms of the declaration's required timing, scope, or format. The same holds true for clauses involving notifications. Moreover, unlike reservations clauses, provisions on declarations and notifications may be found throughout the treaty text, not just in its final clauses.

A. Provision for interpretative declarations

- Articles 42–43, Agreement for the Implementation of the Provisions of the United Nations Convention on the Law of Sea of 10 December 1982 Relating to the Conservation and Management of Straddling Fish Stocks and Highly Migratory Fish Stocks (1995) 2167 UNTS 3:

Article 42
No reservations or exceptions may be made to this agreement.

Article 43
Article 42 does not preclude a State or entity, when signing, ratifying or acceding to this Agreement, from making declarations or statements, however phrased or named, with a view, <u>inter alia</u>, to the harmonization of its laws and regulations with the provisions of this Agreement, provided that such declarations or statements do not purport to exclude or to modify the legal effect of the provisions of this Agreement in their application to that State or entity.

B. Provisions for optional declarations

1. *That modify the commitment otherwise assumed*

- Article 10(2), International Convention on Arrest of Ships (1999) UN Doc A/CONF.188.6:

A State may, when it is also a State Party to a specified treaty on navigation on inland waterways, declare when signing, ratifying, accepting, approving or acceding to this Convention, that rules on jurisdiction, recognition and execution of court decisions provided for in such treaties shall prevail over the rules contained in article 7 of this Convention.

- Article 124, Rome Statute of the International Criminal Court (1998) 2187 UNTS 3:

Notwithstanding article 12, paragraphs 1 and 2, a State, on becoming a party to this Statute, may declare that, for a period of seven years after the entry into force of this Statute for the State concerned, it does not accept the jurisdiction of the Court with respect to the category of crimes referred to in article 8 when a crime is alleged to have been committed by its nationals or on its territory. A declaration under this article may be withdrawn at any time. The provisions of this article shall be reviewed at the Review Conference convened in accordance with article 123, paragraph 1.

2. That add to the commitment otherwise assumed

- Article 20(3), Basel Convention on the Control of Transboundary Movements of Hazardous Wastes and their Disposal (1989) 1673 UNTS 57:

When ratifying, accepting, approving, formally confirming or acceding to this Convention, or at any time thereafter, a State or political and/or economic integration organization may declare that it recognizes as compulsory ipso facto and without special agreement, in relation to any Party accepting the same obligation:
(a) submission of the dispute to the International Court of Justice; and/or
(b) arbitration in accordance with the procedures set out in Annex VI.
Such declaration shall be notified in writing to the Secretariat which shall communicate it to the Parties.

- Article 22(1), (8), Convention against Torture and Other Cruel, Inhuman or Degrading Treatment or Punishment (1984) 1465 UNTS 85:

1. A State Party to this Convention may at any time declare under this article that it recognizes the competence of the Committee to receive and consider communications from or on behalf of individuals subject to its jurisdiction who claim to be victims of a violation by a State Party of the provisions of the Convention. No communication shall be received by the Committee if it concerns a State Party which has not made such a declaration ...
8. The provisions of this article shall come into force when five States Parties to this Convention have made declarations under paragraph 1 of this article. Such declarations shall be deposited by the States Parties with the Secretary-General of the United Nations, who shall transmit copies thereof to the other States Parties. A declaration may be withdrawn at any time by notification to the Secretary-General. Such a withdrawal shall not prejudice the consideration of any matter which is the subject of a communication already transmitted under this article; no further communication by or on behalf of an individual shall be received under this article after the notification of withdrawal of the declaration has been received by the Secretary-General, unless the State Party has made a new declaration.

C. Provisions for mandatory declarations

1. That clarify or elaborate on the content of the obligations assumed

- Article 3(2), Optional Protocol to the Convention on the Rights of the Child on the Involvement of Children in Armed Conflict (2000) 2173 UNTS 222:

Each State Party shall deposit a binding declaration upon ratification of or accession to this Protocol that sets forth the minimum age at which it will permit voluntary recruitment into its national armed forces and a description of the safeguards that it has adopted to ensure that such recruitment is not forced or coerced.

- Article III(1)(a)(i), (ii), (v), Convention on the Prohibition of the Development, Production, Stockpiling and Use of Chemical Weapons and on their Destruction (1992) 1974 UNTS 45:

Each State Party shall submit to the Organization, not later than 30 days after this Convention enters into force for it, the following declarations, in which it shall:

(a) With respect to chemical weapons:
  (i) Declare whether it owns or possesses any chemical weapons, or whether there are any chemical weapons located in any place under its jurisdiction or control;
  (ii) Specify the precise location, aggregate quantity and detailed inventory of chemical weapons it owns or possesses, or that are located in any place under its jurisdiction or control...
  (v) Provide its general plan for destruction of chemical weapons that it owns or possesses, or that are located in any place under its jurisdiction or control...

2. That declare the extent of competence

- Article 25(3), Stockholm Convention on Persistent Organic Pollutants (2001) 2256 UNTS 119:

In its instrument of ratification, acceptance, approval or accession, a regional economic integration organization shall declare the extent of its competence in respect of the matters governed by this Convention. Any such organization shall also inform the depositary, who shall in turn inform the Parties, of any relevant modification in the extent of its competence.

- Article 47(2)(a), Agreement for the Implementation of the Provisions of the United Nations Convention on the Law of Sea of 10 December 1982 Relating to the Conservation and Management of Straddling Fish Stocks and Highly Migratory Fish Stocks (1995) 2167 UNTS 3:

In cases where an international organization referred to in Annex IX, article 1, of the Convention has competence over all the matters governed by this Agreement, the following provisions shall apply to participation by such international organization in this Agreement:

(a) at the time of signature or accession, such international organization shall make a declaration stating:
  (i) that it has competence over all the matters governed by this Agreement;
  (ii) that, for this reason, its member States shall not become States Parties, except in respect of their territories for which the international organization has no responsibility; and
  (iii) that it accepts the rights and obligations of States under this Agreement;

3. That require a selection among alternatives

- Article 1(B)(1), Convention Relating to the Status of Refugees (1951) 189 UNTS 137:

For the purposes of this Convention, the words 'events occurring before 1 January 1951' in article 1, section A, shall be understood to mean either

(a) 'events occurring in Europe before 1 January 1951'; or
(b) 'events occurring in Europe or elsewhere before 1 January 1951' and each Contracting State shall make a declaration at the time of signature, ratification or accession, specifying which of these meanings it applies for the purpose of its obligations under this Convention.

D. Conditions on the formation and withdrawal of declarations

- Article 97, UN Convention on Contracts for the International Sale of Goods (1980) 1489 UNTS 3:

    1. Declarations made under this Convention at the time of signature are subject to confirmation upon ratification, acceptance or approval.
    2. Declarations and confirmations of declarations are to be in writing and be formally notified to the depositary.
    3. A declaration takes effect simultaneously with the entry into force of this Convention in respect of the State concerned. However, a declaration of which the depositary receives formal notification after such entry into force takes effect on the first day of the month following the expiration of six months after the date of its receipt by the depositary. Reciprocal unilateral declarations under article 94 take effect on the first day of the month following the expiration of six months after the receipt of the latest declaration by the depositary.
    4. Any State which makes a declaration under this Convention may withdraw it at any time by a formal notification in writing addressed to the depositary. Such withdrawal is to take effect on the first day of the month following the expiration of six months after the date of the receipt of the notification by the depositary.
    5. A withdrawal of a declaration made under article 94 renders inoperative, as from the date on which the withdrawal takes effect, any reciprocal declaration made by another State under that article.

E. Notifications

- Article 7(3), International Convention for the Suppression of the Financing of Terrorism (1999) 2178 UNTS 197:

    Upon ratifying, accepting, approving or acceding to this Convention, each State Party shall notify the Secretary-General of the United Nations of the jurisdiction it has established in accordance with paragraph 2. Should any change take place, the State Party concerned shall immediately notify the Secretary-General.

- Article 45(4), Convention on Road Traffic (1968) 1042 UNTS 17:

    On signing this Convention or on depositing its instrument of ratification or accession, each State shall notify the Secretary-General of the distinguishing sign it has selected for display in international traffic on vehicles registered by it, in accordance with Annex 3 to this Convention. By a further notification addressed to the Secretary-General, any State may change a distinguishing sign it has previously selected.

Constituting the Treaty and its Dissemination

9. Languages

Most treaties as part of their final clauses or testimonium will address the language(s) in which the treaty is 'Done...in' or concluded. Treaties may be negotiated and concluded in a single language, which may or may not be the native language of the negotiating parties. More often, however, the treaty text will be finalized or 'authenticated' in multiple languages (and sometimes irrespective of what language(s) the negotiations themselves employ).[41] In such cases, it is important to recall that there is only a single 'treaty', consisting of all the different languages in which it is finalized.[42]

Article 33(1) of the VCLT makes clear that 'when a treaty has been authenticated in two or more languages, the text is equally authoritative in each language, unless the treaty provides or the parties agree that, in case of divergence, a particular text shall prevail'. Where a treaty is authenticated in multiple languages, it may simply confirm the general rule. In the UN context, for example, treaties are generally equally authentic in the UN's six official languages—Arabic, Chinese, English, French, Russian, and Spanish. In other cases, a clause or testimonium may provide that one or more of a treaty's authenticated texts should prevail in cases of divergence.

It is also possible that a treaty will be translated into languages other than the authenticated ones. Article 33(2) of the VCLT indicates that in such circumstances, another 'version' may be considered 'an authentic text only if the treaty so provides or if the parties so agree'. Thus, a treaty may contain a clause contemplating future authentication in additional languages. Or, additional authenticated languages may be added by separate agreement.

---

[41] Although many multilateral negotiating conferences conduct formal negotiations in multiple 'working' or 'official' languages, informal negotiations often occur in a single language, which today is mostly English but still occasionally French. Thus, a treaty is regularly drawn up in a single language, and translated into other texts. A process known as, of all things, the *toilette finale*, is then employed prior to authentication to ensure that all language texts are consistent.

[42] The issues of authentication and multiple language texts are discussed in Chapter 7 (Part II.C–D, 188 *et seq*) while Chapter 19 (Part II.C, 490 *et seq*) discusses how different languages impact treaty interpretation.

A. Original authentic texts

1. A single authentic text

- Testimonium, Agreement concerning Air Services (UK-Trinidad and Tobago) (2010) [2011] UKTS 7:

  In witness whereof the undersigned, being duly authorised by their respective Governments have signed this Agreement.
  Done in duplicate at Port of Spain this sixteenth day of March 2010 in the English language.

- Testimonium, Central European Free Trade Agreement (Czech Republic-Hungary-Poland-Slovakia) (1992) 34 ILM 8:

  Done at Krakow this 21st day of December 1992 in a single authentic copy in the English language which shall be deposited with the Government of Poland.

2. Two or more equally authentic texts

- Article 33, UN Convention on Jurisdictional Immunities of States and Their Property (2004) UN Doc A/59/508:

  The Arabic, Chinese, English, French, Russian and Spanish texts of the present Convention are equally authentic.

- Testimonium, Convention on the Recognition of Qualifications Concerning Higher Education in the European Region (1997) 2136 UNTS 3:

  Done at Lisbon on 11 April 1997, in the English, French, Russian and Spanish languages, the four texts being equally authoritative.[43]

- Testimonium, Agreement on the Settlement of Certain Outstanding Claims (US-Albania) (1995) 34 ILM 597:

  Done at Tirana, in duplicate in the English and Albanian languages, both languages being equally authentic, this 10th day of March, 1995.

3. Two or more equally authentic texts, with a prevailing language in the case of divergence

- Testimonium, Agreement on the reciprocal promotion and protection of investments (Qatar-Italy) (2003) 2296 UNTS 239:

  Done at Rome on 22-03-00 in two originals, in the Arabic, Italian and English languages, all texts being equally authentic.
  In case of any divergence, the English text shall prevail.

---

[43] For a discussion of what 'authoritative' means see Chapter 19 (Part II.C, 490 *et seq*).

• Testimonium, Optional Protocol on the Compulsory Settlement of Disputes Relating to the Constitution of the International Telecommunication Union, to the Convention of the International Telecommunication Union and to the Administrative Regulations (1992) 1825 UNTS 3:

IN WITNESS WHEREOF, the respective Plenipotentiaries have signed this Protocol in each of the Arabic, Chinese, English, French, Russian and Spanish languages, in a single copy within which, in case of discrepancy, the French text shall prevail . . .

B. Authentication of other language versions

1. *Pursuant to the original treaty*

• Testimonium, Agreement on Mutual Legal Assistance in Criminal Matters (EU-Japan) (2009) [2010] OJ L39/20:

DONE in duplicate, in the English and Japanese languages, both texts being equally authentic, and signed at Brussels on the thirtieth day of November 2009, and at Tokyo on the [fifteenth] day of December 2009. This Agreement shall also be drawn up in the Bulgarian, Czech, Danish, Dutch, Estonian, Finnish, French, German, Greek, Hungarian, Italian, Latvian, Lithuanian, Maltese, Polish, Portuguese, Romanian, Slovak, Slovenian, Spanish and Swedish languages, and the Contracting Parties shall authenticate those language versions by an exchange of diplomatic notes.

• Testimonium, International Tropical Timber Agreement (1983) 1393 UNTS 671:

DONE at Geneva on the eighteenth day of November, one thousand nine hundred and eighty-three, the texts of this Agreement in the Arabic, English, French, Russian and Spanish languages being equally authentic. The authentic Chinese text of this Agreement shall be established by the depositary and submitted for adoption to all signatories and States and intergovernmental organizations which have acceded to this Agreement.

2. *By subsequent agreement*

• Articles I–II, Protocol 1 on the Authentic Trilingual Text of the Convention on International Civil Aviation (Chicago, 1944) (1968) 740 UNTS 21:

Article I
The text of the Convention in the French and Spanish languages annexed to this Protocol, together with the text of the Convention in the English language, constitutes the text equally authentic in the three languages as specifically referred to in the last paragraph of the Convention.

Article II
If a State party to this Protocol has ratified or in the future ratifies any amendment made to the Convention in accordance with Article 94(a) thereof, then the text of such amendment in the English, French and Spanish languages shall be deemed to refer to the text, equally authentic in the three languages, which results from this Protocol.

10. Annexes

Annexes are important instruments attached to a treaty's text. Together with that text (and the preamble) annexes form part of the treaty's 'context' for interpretative purposes under Article 31 of the VCLT. Annexes thus must be differentiated from other instruments (eg declarations, final acts, agreed minutes) accompanying a treaty's conclusion. Although they usually do not contain the treaty's core commitments, Annexes perform important functions, including (but not limited to) dividing parties into groups, listing individual party commitments, designating materials subject to regulation, providing technical standards, or offering understandings of the treaty's main provisions. Annexes may have other titles, including schedule, appendix, or protocol (although a protocol may also be a separate treaty so care should be taken in using that term).

Where annexes are present, a clause will frequently clarify that they are an 'integral' part of the treaty, although sometimes their status is left to inference. In other cases, a clause may qualify more precisely the annexes' relationship to the rest of the treaty, by limiting it to interpretative purposes or making its application voluntary.[44] Finally, some treaties are concluded without annexes but contain a provision for their future adoption.

A. Annexes as integral parts of the treaty

- Article XIV(1), Treaty on Measures for the Further Reduction and Limitation of Strategic Offensive Arms (US-Russian Federation) (New START Agreement) (2010) 50 ILM 340:

  This Treaty, including its Protocol, which is an integral part thereof, shall be subject to ratification in accordance with the constitutional procedures of each Party...

- Article 17, Intergovernmental Agreement on the Asian Highway Network (2003) 2323 UNTS 37:

  Annexes I, II and III to the Agreement shall form an integral part of this Agreement.

- Article XX(1), (3), WTO General Agreement on Trade in Services (1994) 33 ILM 1167:

  1. Each Member shall set out in a schedule the specific commitments it undertakes under Part III of this Agreement...
  3. Schedules of specific commitments shall be annexed to this Agreement and shall form an integral part thereof.

---

[44] For a discussion of annex amendments and related clauses, see heading 20 of this section.

B. Differently titled attachments

- Article 15, Fisheries Partnership Agreement (EU-Solomon Islands) (2010) [2010] OJ L190/3:

  The Protocol and the Annex shall form an integral part of this Agreement.

C. Qualifications on annex's relationship to the treaty

- Article 20, Convention on International Customs Transit Procedures for the Carriage of Goods by Rail Under Cover of SMGS Consignment Notes (2006, not yet in force) <http://treaties.un.org/doc/source/RecentTexts/XI_-C_6_english.pdf>:

  The Explanatory Notes set out in Annex 2 to this Convention describe certain recommended practices and interpret certain provisions of this Convention. They constitute an integral part of the Convention. They do not modify the provisions of this Convention, but merely make their contents, meaning and scope more precise.

- Technical Annex, Protocol on Explosive Remnants of War to the Convention on Prohibitions or Restrictions on the Use of Certain Conventional Weapons which may be deemed to be Excessively Injurious or to have Indiscriminate Effects (Protocol V) (2003) 2399 UNTS 100:

  This Technical Annex contains suggested best practice for achieving the objectives contained in Articles 4, 5 and 9 of this Protocol. This Technical Annex will be implemented by High Contracting Parties on a voluntary basis.

D. Provision for future annexes

- Article 29, WHO Framework Convention on Tobacco Control (2003) 2302 UNTS 166:

  1. Annexes to this Convention and amendments thereto shall be proposed, adopted and shall enter into force in accordance with the procedure set forth in Article 28.
  2. Annexes to the Convention shall form an integral part thereof and, unless otherwise expressly provided, a reference to the Convention constitutes at the same time a reference to any annexes thereto.
  3. Annexes shall be restricted to lists, forms and any other descriptive material relating to procedural, scientific, technical or administrative matters.

11. Entry into Force

A treaty becomes legally binding when it enters into force. It does so, however, only for those who have consented to it. Absent provisions giving rise to third party rights or obligations of the sort discussed in Chapter 13, treaties are binding on

States, IOs, or other qualified subjects of international law only if and when they individually consent to be bound.[45] Where a treaty is open to additional participants, they may consent after the treaty has initially entered into force, in which case the treaty will enter into force for them individually on the date of that consent or some specified date thereafter.

Chapter 7 reviews the relevant law and practice relating to entry into force. Like other areas of treaty law, the primary rule defers to treaty-makers; Article 24 of the VCLT provides that a treaty enters into force 'in such manner and upon such date as it may provide or as the negotiating States may agree'.[46] The manner of that agreement varies depending on whether a treaty is bilateral or multilateral.

Bilateral treaties regularly provide for entry into force on the occurrence of a specific act (eg signature) or date (eg a certain number of days after an exchange of instruments). A multilateral treaty's entry into force will require the consent of at least two States (or other qualified actors) and its final clauses may require larger numbers of States or the consent of specific ones. The treaty may also provide for entry into force on a specific date or the satisfaction of certain conditions that can range widely in terms of their complexity. Responsibility for determining whether (and when exactly) the conditions necessary for entry into force are fulfilled usually lies with any designated depositary and, in the absence of one, the parties themselves.

It is important, moreover, to distinguish a treaty's entry into force from its legal effects. Certain treaty provisions (such as an entry into force clause) must necessarily have legal effect before a treaty enters into force. And after it enters into force, a treaty may apply its provisions retroactively or leave their effectiveness to some later date.

A. Bilateral agreements: entry into force

1. On signature

- Article 11, Agreement on British Armed Forces' Training in Canada (Canada-UK) (2006) Canada Treaty Series 2006/17:

  This Agreement shall enter into force upon signature...

- Article 7, Agreement on intensifying and broadening the Agreement of 28 May 1997 on customs co-operation and mutual assistance in customs matters to include co-operation on Container Security and related matters (EC-US) (2004) [2004] OJ L304/34:

---

[45] Where a treaty provision codifies (or comes to codify) customary international law, it may bind non-parties, but it does so by virtue of the provision's status as custom, not by virtue of *pacta sunt servanda*.

[46] Where a treaty is silent on its entry into force—which is very rare today—it is presumed to enter into force on signature or whenever the negotiating States have otherwise indicated their consent to be bound.

This Agreement shall enter into force upon signature by the Parties which shall have the effect of expressing their consent to be bound. If the Agreement is not signed the same day on behalf of both Parties, the Agreement shall enter into force on the day on which the second signature is affixed.

2. On exchange of instruments of ratification

- Article XIV, Treaty on Measures for the Further Reduction and Limitation of Strategic Offensive Arms (US-Russian Federation) (New START Agreement) (2010) 50 ILM 340:

  This Treaty, including its Protocol, which is an integral part thereof, shall be subject to ratification in accordance with the constitutional procedures of each Party. This Treaty shall enter into force on the date of the exchange of instruments of ratification.

3. On a date following exchange of notifications concerning the completion of procedures necessary for entry into force

- Article 22, Agreement on Mutual Administrative Assistance in Customs Matters (The Netherlands-Philippines) (2011) 2011 Trb 67:

  This Agreement shall enter into force on the first day of the second month after the Contracting Parties have notified each other in writing through diplomatic channels that the constitutional or internal requirements for the entry into force of this Agreement have been complied with.

- Article 11, Agreement for the Promotion and Protection of Investments (Hong Kong Special Administrative Region-Thailand) (2005) <http://www.unctad. org/sections/dite/iia/docs/bits/thailand_hongkong.PDF>:

  This Agreement shall enter into force thirty days after the date on which the Contracting Parties have notified each other in writing that their respective requirements for the entry into force of this Agreement have been complied with.

4. On satisfaction of multiple conditions

- Article 6, Agreement on Trade in Bananas (EU-US) (2010) [2010] OJ L141/6:

  The United States and the EU shall notify each other in writing of the completion of the internal procedures necessary for the entry into force of this Agreement. This Agreement shall enter into force on the later of: (a) the date of the last notification referred to in the previous sentence; and (b) the date of entry into force of the [General Agreement on Trade in Bananas] ...

B. Multilateral treaties: entry into force

1. On a set date with exchange of notifications

- Article 2203, North American Free Trade Agreement (1992) 32 ILM 612:

  This Agreement shall enter into force on January 1, 1994, on an exchange of written notifications certifying the completion of necessary legal procedures.

2. On a date following deposit of ratification instruments by all negotiating parties

- Article 6, Treaty of Lisbon Amending the Treaty on European Union and the Treaty Establishing the European Community (2007) [2007] OJ C306/1:

  1. This Treaty shall be ratified by the High Contracting Parties in accordance with their respective constitutional requirements...

  2. This Treaty shall enter into force on 1 January 2009, provided that all the instruments of ratification have been deposited, or, failing that, on the first day of the month following the deposit of the instrument of ratification by the last signatory State to take this step.

3. On a date following deposit of a specific number of instruments [47]

- Article 126(1), Rome Statute of the International Criminal Court (1998) 2187 UNTS 3:

  This Statute shall enter into force on the first day of the month after the 60th day following the date of the deposit of the 60th instrument of ratification, acceptance, approval or accession with the Secretary-General of the United Nations.

- Article 58, Geneva Convention for the Amelioration of the Condition of the Wounded and Sick in Armed Forces in the Field (1949) 75 UNTS 31:

  The present Convention shall come into force six months after not less than two instruments of ratification have been deposited.

4. On a date following deposit of a specific number of instruments, including those of certain States or percentages of States

- Article 42(1), International Coffee Agreement (2007) [2008] OJ L186/13:

  This Agreement shall enter into force definitively when signatory Governments holding at least two-thirds of the votes of the exporting Members and signatory Governments holding at least two-thirds of the votes of the importing Members, calculated as at 28 September 2007, without reference to possible suspension under the terms of Article 21, have deposited instruments of ratification, acceptance or approval. Alternatively, it shall enter into force definitively at any time if it is provisionally in force in accordance with the provisions of paragraph 2 of this Article and these percentage requirements are satisfied by the deposit of instruments of ratification, acceptance or approval.

---

[47] In cases where a regional economic integration organization (REIO) or regional integration organization (RIO) joins a treaty in addition to its member States, the treaty will normally not count their instruments of acceptance or approval for purposes of determining when it enters into force. Samples of such clauses are included under this heading at B.6, but are not otherwise repeated here.

- Article 28.1, International Treaty on Plant Genetic Resources for Food and Agriculture (2001) 2400 UNTS 303:

  Subject to the provisions of Article 29.2, this Treaty shall enter into force on the ninetieth day after the deposit of the fortieth instrument of ratification, acceptance, approval or accession, provided that at least twenty instruments of ratification, acceptance, approval or accession have been deposited by Members of FAO.

- Article 25(3)(a)–(b), International Space Station Agreement (1998) TIAS 12927:

  (a) This Agreement shall enter into force on the date on which the last instrument of ratification, acceptance, or approval of Japan, Russia and the United States has been deposited. The Depositary shall notify all signatory States of this Agreement's entry into force.

  (b) This Agreement shall not enter into force for a European Partner State before it enters into force for the European Partner. It shall enter into force for the European Partner after the Depositary receives instruments of ratification, acceptance, approval, or accession from at least four European signatory or acceding States, and, in addition, a formal notification by the Chairman of the ESA Council.

5. On a date following deposit of a specific number of instruments, including an IO's

- Article 69(4), Convention on Jurisdiction and the Recognition and Enforcement of Judgments in Civil and Commercial Matters (2007) [2007] OJ L339/3:

  The Convention shall enter into force on the first day of the sixth month following the date on which the European Community and a Member of the European Free Trade Association deposit their instruments of ratification.

6. On a date following deposit of a specific number of instruments not including those of an IO

- Article 38(1), United Nations Convention Against Transnational Organized Crime (2000) 2225 UNTS 209:

  This Convention shall enter into force on the ninetieth day after the date of deposit of the fortieth instrument of ratification, acceptance, approval or accession. For the purpose of this paragraph, any instrument deposited by a regional economic integration organization shall not be counted as additional to those deposited by member States of such organization.

7. Following deposit of a specific number of instruments and entry into force of the underlying treaty

- Article 22(1), Protocol Against the Smuggling of Migrants by Land, Sea and Air, Supplementing the United Nations Convention Against Transnational Organized Crime (2000) 2241 UNTS 507:

This Protocol shall enter into force on the ninetieth day after the date of deposit of the fortieth instrument of ratification, acceptance, approval or accession, except that it shall not enter into force before the entry into force of the Convention.

8. *On a set date or later date following satisfaction of conditions*

• Article 16(1), Montreal Protocol on Substances that Deplete the Ozone Layer (1987) 1522 UNTS 3:

This Protocol shall enter into force on 1 January 1989, provided that at least eleven instruments of ratification, acceptance, approval of the Protocol or accession thereto have been deposited by States or regional economic integration organizations representing at least two thirds of 1986 estimated global consumption of the controlled substances, and the provisions of paragraph 1 of Article 17 of the Convention have been fulfilled. In the event that these conditions have not been fulfilled by this date, the Protocol shall enter into force on the ninetieth day following the date on which the conditions have been fulfilled.

9. *By mutual agreement of certain parties*

• Article 42(4), International Coffee Agreement (2007) [2008] OJ L186/13:

If this Agreement has not entered into force definitively or provisionally by 25 September 2009 under the provisions of paragraph 1 or 2 of this Article, those signatory Governments which have deposited instruments of ratification, acceptance or approval, in accordance with their laws and regulations, may, by mutual consent, decide that it shall enter into force definitively among themselves.

C. Joining a treaty after conditions for its entry into force are satisfied

• Article 45(1)–(2), Convention on the Rights of Persons with Disabilities (2006) 2515 UNTS 3:

1. The present Convention shall enter into force on the thirtieth day after the deposit of the twentieth instrument of ratification or accession.

2. For each State or regional integration organization ratifying, formally confirming or acceding to the Convention after the deposit of the twentieth such instrument, the Convention shall enter into force on the thirtieth day after the deposit of its own such instrument.

• Article 22(2), Protocol Against the Smuggling of Migrants by Land, Sea and Air, Supplementing the United Nations Convention Against Transnational Organized Crime (2000) 2241 UNTS 507:

For each State or regional economic integration organization ratifying, accepting, approving or acceding to this Protocol after the deposit of the fortieth instrument of such action, this Protocol shall enter into force on the thirtieth day after the date of deposit by such State or organization of the relevant instrument or on the date this Protocol enters into force pursuant to paragraph 1 of this article, whichever is later.

- Article 126(2), Rome Statute of the International Criminal Court (1998) 2187 UNTS 3:

  For each State ratifying, accepting, approving or acceding to this Statute after the deposit of the 60th instrument of ratification, acceptance, approval or accession, the Statute shall enter into force on the first day of the month after the 60th day following the deposit by such State of its instrument of ratification, acceptance, approval or accession.

D. Entry into force differentiated from effect

1. Retroactive effect

- Exchange of Notes constituting an Agreement to further amend and extend the Agreement concerning Space Vehicle Tracking and Communications Facilities of 29 May 1980, as amended (Australia-US) (2000) [2000] ATS 32:

  . . . The Agreement shall enter into force with retroactive effect from 26 February 2000, when the Government of Australia advises, via the diplomatic channel, that it has completed the domestic processes necessary to give effect to this Agreement.

- Exchange of Letters Amending the Memorandum on the Canada-ASEAN Regional Training Program (ASEAN-Canada) (1996) <http://www.asean.org/4729.htm>:

  I have the honour to confirm that Your Excellency's letter and this reply shall constitute an agreement on the amendments to the Memorandum of Understanding (MOU) for the Project 'The Canada-ASEAN Regional Training Program (RTP)', by which Vietnam is included in the project, with the revised MOU entering into force on the date of this reply [25 July 1996] with retroactive effect to 31 March 1996.

2. Delayed effect following entry into force

- Article 29(2), Convention for the Avoidance of Double Taxation and the Prevention of Fiscal Evasion with Respect to Taxes on Income and Capital (Canada-Gabon) (2002) Canada Treaty Series 2008/5:

  The Convention shall enter into force upon the exchange of instruments of ratification and its provisions shall have effect:

  (a) in respect of taxes withheld at the source on amounts paid or credited to non-residents, on or after the first day of January in the calendar year immediately following that in which the exchange of instruments of ratification takes place; and
  (b) in respect of other taxes, for taxation years beginning on or after the first day of January in the calendar year immediately following that in which the exchange of instruments of ratification takes place.

12. The Depositary

The depositary plays a critical role as the treaty's custodian. Of course, not every treaty will have a depositary (bilateral treaties generally do not), but many large multilateral treaties require one given the complications of treaty-related acts and communications among dozens of actors over long periods of time. The depositary may be the State hosting the negotiations, but more often will be an IO or the IO's chief administrative officer. Chapter 10 discusses when and how the most prominent depositary—the Secretary-General of the United Nations—performs depositary functions.[48]

It is now standard practice for a treaty to designate its own depositary either in a stand-alone clause or more indirectly.[49] Rarely, more than one depositary may be designated for political or symbolic reasons, but that practice is generally discouraged because of how it complicates depositary functions. As for those functions, some depositary duties—such as facilitating signature or receipt of instruments of ratification—necessarily commence on the treaty text's adoption. That text does not, however, need to detail all depositary functions since the VCLT is now widely recognized as having already done so. Nonetheless, treaties will often direct performance in ways that allow the depositary to perform its duties.

A. Designating the depositary directly

1. A State

- Article 58(2), Convention on the International Recovery of Child Support and Other Forms of Family Maintenance (2007) 47 ILM 257:

  [The Convention] shall be ratified, accepted or approved and the instruments of ratification, acceptance or approval shall be deposited with the Ministry of Foreign Affairs of the Kingdom of the Netherlands, depositary of the Convention.

2. An IO

- Article 53(5), Montreal Convention for the Unification of Certain Rules for International Carriage by Air (1999) 2242 UNTS 309:

  Instruments of ratification, acceptance, approval or accession shall be deposited with the International Civil Aviation Organization, which is hereby designated the Depositary.

3. An IO's Chief Administrative Officer

- Article 41, Convention on the Rights of Persons with Disabilities (2006) 2515 UNTS 3:

  The Secretary-General of the United Nations shall be the depositary of the present Convention.

---

[48] Chapter 10 also assesses the UN Secretary-General's central role in registering and publishing treaties in accordance with Art 102 of the UN Charter.

[49] The designation does not, however, have to be included in the treaty; as VCLT Art 76 recognizes, negotiating parties may designate a depositary 'in some other manner' such as by adoption of a separate decision.

4. A joint depositary

- Article XI.9(1), Convention on the Recognition of Qualifications concerning Higher Education in the European Region (1997) 2136 UNTS 3:

  The Secretary General of the Council of Europe and the Director-General of the United Nations Educational, Scientific and Cultural Organization shall be the depositories of this Convention.

B. Designating the depositary indirectly

- Article 128, Rome Statute of the International Criminal Court (1998) 2187 UNTS 3:

  The original of this Statute, of which the Arabic, Chinese, English, French, Russian and Spanish texts are equally authentic, shall be deposited with the Secretary-General of the United Nations, who shall send certified copies thereof to all States.

C. Provisions specifying depositary functions

- Articles 38(2)–(3)–40, International Convention for the Protection of All Persons from Enforced Disappearance (2007) 14 IHHR 582:

  ### Article 38
  2. ... Instruments of ratification shall be deposited with the Secretary-General of the United Nations.
  3. ... Accession shall be effected by the deposit of an instrument of accession with the Secretary-General.

  ### Article 39
  1. This Convention shall enter into force on the thirtieth day after the date of deposit with the Secretary-General of the United Nations of the twentieth instrument of ratification or accession.
  2. For each State ratifying or acceding to this Convention after the deposit of the twentieth instrument of ratification or accession, this Convention shall enter into force on the thirtieth day after the date of the deposit of that State's instrument of ratification or accession.

  ### Article 40
  The Secretary-General of the United Nations shall notify all States Members of the United Nations and all States which have signed or acceded to this Convention of the following:

    (a) Signatures, ratifications and accessions under article 38;
    (b) The date of entry into force of this Convention under article 39.

- Article 22(2), Convention on Customs Treatment of Pool Containers used in International Transport (1994) 2000 UNTS 289:

  The functions of the Secretary-General of the United Nations as depositary shall be as set out in Part VII of the Vienna Convention on the Law of Treaties, concluded at Vienna on 23 May 1969.

Applying the Treaty

13. Provisional Application

Provisional application is the agreement of some or all negotiating participants to apply one or more of a treaty's substantive provisions in advance of the treaty's initial entry into force (or pending its individual entry into force for those agreeing to provisional application).[50] That agreement may come in the text of the treaty to be provisionally applied or in some 'other manner so agreed', such as a protocol, exchange of notes, or IO resolution.[51] When or how provisional application begins may vary, just as its scope may be unqualified or subject to a signatory's constitution, laws, or regulations. Chapter 9 surveys the complex history of provisional application, its legal effects, and the recent attention the concept has received in international arbitral circles.

In practice, provisional application clauses may limit its duration (i) to a specific timeframe, which may or may not be extended, or (ii) until such time as the treaty enters into force. Article 25(2) of the VCLT provides that a party may terminate provisional application on notice '[u]nless the treaty otherwise provides or the negotiating States have otherwise agreed'. Thus, any right to withdraw or terminate provisional application may be conditioned on the expiration of an agreed notice period. Finally, it is important not to confuse provisional application clauses with those for provisional entry into force, which are still employed in certain contexts (eg multilateral commodity agreements) to avoid gaps in coverage among successive short-term treaties.[52]

A. The timing of provisional application

1. On signature

- Article 18(7), Framework Agreement on a Multilateral Nuclear Environmental Programme in the Russian Federation (2003) 2265 UNTS 5:

  This agreement shall be applied on a provisional basis from the date of its signature.

---

[50] Certain non-substantive treaty provisions may have legal effect from the treaty's adoption. See VCLT Art 24(4). For a detailed discussion of entry into force, see Chapter 7 (Part IV, 201 *et seq*).

[51] See VCLT Art 25(1); 1986 VCLT Art 25(1).

[52] A recent example of a provisional entry into force clause is included in Chapter 9 (Part II.D, 233).

- Paragraph 8(b), Geneva Agreement on Trade in Bananas (2010) [2010] OJ L141/3:

  Notwithstanding subparagraph (a), the signatories agree to provisionally apply paragraphs 3, 6 and 7 from the day of signature of this Agreement.

2. On signature, absent a declaration to the contrary

- Article 45(1)–(2), Energy Charter Treaty (1994) 2080 UNTS 95:

  (1) Each signatory agrees to apply this Treaty provisionally pending its entry into force for such signatory in accordance with Article 44, to the extent that such provisional application is not inconsistent with its constitution, laws or regulations.

  (2) (a) Notwithstanding paragraph (1) any signatory may, when signing, deliver to the Depository a declaration that it is not able to accept provisional application. The obligation contained in paragraph (1) shall not apply to a signatory making such a declaration. Any such signatory may at any time withdraw that declaration by written notification to the Depository.

  (b) Neither a signatory which makes a declaration in accordance with subparagraph (a) nor Investors of that signatory may claim the benefits of provisional application under paragraph (1).

  (c) Notwithstanding subparagraph (a), any signatory making a declaration referred to in subparagraph (a) shall apply Party VII provisionally pending the entry into force of the Treaty for such signatory in accordance with Article 44, to the extent that such provisional application is not inconsistent with its laws or regulations.[53]

3. By declaration or notification

- Article 38, International Tropical Timber Agreement (2006) [2007] OJ L262/8:

  A signatory Government which intends to ratify, accept or approve this Agreement, or a Government for which the Council has established conditions for accession but which has not yet been able to deposit its instrument may, at any time, notify the depositary that it will apply this Agreement provisionally in accordance with its laws and regulations, either when it enters into force in accordance with Article 39 or, if it is already in force, at a specified date.

- Article 15, Convention on Assistance in the Case of a Nuclear Accident or Radiological Emergency (1986) 1457 UNTS 133:

  A State may, upon signature or at any later date before this Convention enters into force for it, declare that it will apply this Convention provisionally.

4. From a specified date

- Article 25(1), Air Transport Agreement (US/EU Open Skies Agreement) (2007) 46 ILM 470:

---

[53] The entirety of Art 45 is reproduced in Chapter 9 (Part III.B, 242).

Pending entry into force pursuant to Article 26:
The Parties agree to apply this Agreement from 30 March 2008 . . .

- Article 7(2), Agreement on Certain Aspects of Air Services (EC-Australia) (2008) [2008] OJ L149/65:

  Notwithstanding paragraph 1, the Contracting Parties agree to provisionally apply this Agreement from the first day of the month following the date on which the Contracting Parties have notified each other of the completion of the procedures necessary for this purpose.

5. *After consent to be bound, pending entry into force*

- Article 18, Convention on the Prohibition of the Use, Stockpiling, Production and Transfer of Anti-Personnel Mines and on their Destruction (1997) 2056 UNTS 211:

  Any State may at the time of its ratification, acceptance, approval or accession, declare that it will apply provisionally paragraph 1 of Article 1 of this Convention pending its entry into force.

6. *By other means*

- Article 7(1)–(2), Agreement relating to the Implementation of Part XI of the United Nations Convention on the Law of the Sea of 10 December 1982 (1994) 1836 UNTS 3:

  1. If on 16 November 1994 this Agreement has not entered into force, it shall be applied provisionally pending its entry into force by:

     (a) States which have consented to its adoption in the General Assembly of the United Nations, except any such State which before 16 November 1994 notifies the depositary in writing either that it will not so apply this Agreement or that it will consent to such application only upon subsequent signature or notification in writing;

     (b) States and entities which sign this Agreement, except any such State or entity which notifies the depositary in writing at the time of signature that it will not so apply this Agreement;

     (c) States and entities which consent to its provisional application by so notifying the depositary in writing;

     (d) States which accede to this Agreement.

  2. All such States and entities shall apply this Agreement provisionally in accordance with their national or internal laws and regulations, with effect from 16 November 1994 or the date of signature, notification of consent or accession, if later . . .

B. Provisional application agreements beyond the treaty text

1. *By exchange of notes*

- Agreement on the Arbitration relating to the Reactivation and Modernization of the Iron Rhine (Belgium-Netherlands) (2003) 2332 UNTS 481 (PCA translation from Dutch):

> The Ministry of Foreign Affairs has the honour to confirm that the Government of the Kingdom of the Netherlands can agree with the above-mentioned proposals and that the Note of the Embassy of Belgium and this affirmative Note together constitute an agreement between the Kingdom of the Netherlands and the Kingdom of Belgium which shall be applied provisionally from the day on which this affirmative Note is received . . .

2. *By separate protocol*

- Protocol on the Provisional Application of the Agreement Establishing an International Science and Technology Center (1993) [1994] OJ L64/2:

> The United States of America, Japan, the Russian Federation, and the European Atomic Energy Community and the European Community, acting as one party, hereinafter referred to as the 'Signatory Parties',
>
> Recognizing the importance of the Agreement Establishing an International Science and Technology Center, signed in Moscow on November 27, 1992, hereinafter referred to as the 'Agreement',
>
> HAVE AGREED AS FOLLOWS:
>
> Article I
> 1. The Agreement shall be provisionally applied in accordance with its terms by the Signatory Parties from the date of the last notification of the Signatory Parties of the completion of internal procedures necessary for entry into force of this Protocol.
> 2. The Agreement shall be applied provisionally until its entry into force in accordance with Article XVIII thereof . . .
>
> Article III
> Any of the Parties may withdraw from this Protocol six months from the date on which written notification is provided to the other parties.
>
> Article IV
> 1. Any state desiring to become a Party to the Agreement in accordance with Article XIII thereof, after fulfilling the conditions set forth in that Article, and after completing its internal procedures that will be necessary for accession to the Agreement, shall notify the Signatory Parties of its intention to provisionally apply the Agreement in accordance with this Protocol.
> 2. The provisional application by that State shall begin from the date of notification referred to in Paragraph (1) of this Article . . .

3. *By IO resolution*

- ITU Resolution, 'Provisional application of certain provisions of the Radio Regulations as revised by WRC-07 and abrogation of certain Resolutions and Recommendations' (2007) ITU Resolution 97 (WRC-07):

The World Radiocommunication Conference (Geneva, 2007),
considering
a) that this Conference has adopted a partial revision to the Radio Regulations (RR) in accordance with its terms of reference which will enter into force on 1 January 2009;
b) that some of the provisions, as amended by this conference, need to apply provisionally as of an earlier date; . . .

resolves

1. that, as of 17 November 2007, the following provisions of the RR, as revised or established by this conference, shall provisionally apply [list omitted] . . .

C. Duration and termination of provisional application

1. Duration for a specified period of time

• Article XVIII(2), Treaty on Open Skies (1992) Canada Treaty Series 2002/3:

This provisional application shall be effective for a period of 12 months from the date when this Treaty is opened for signature. In the event that this Treaty does not enter into force before the period of provisional application expires, that period may be extended if all the signatory States so decide. The period of provisional application shall in any event terminate when this Treaty enters into force. However, the States Parties may then decide to extend the period of provisional application in respect of signatory States that have not ratified this Treaty.

2. Termination effective on the treaty's entry into force or a date certain

• Article 7(3), Agreement relating to the Implementation of Part XI of the United Nations Convention on the Law of the Sea of 10 December 1982 (1994) 1836 UNTS 3:

Provisional application shall terminate upon the date of entry into force of this Agreement. In any event, provisional application shall terminate on 16 November 1998 if at that date the requirement in article 6, paragraph 1, of consent to be bound by this Agreement by at least seven of the States (of which at least five must be developed States) referred to in paragraph 1(a) of resolution II has not been fulfilled.

3. Limitations on duration combined with options for termination

• Article 8(4), Agreement Concerning the Participation of the Government of the Kingdom of Norway in the Work of the Agency (IAEA-Norway) (1975) 14 ILM 641:

4. Provisional application of this Agreement shall continue until:
   - this Agreement enters into force, or
   - 60 days after the Agency receives notification that the Government will not consent to be bound by this Agreement, or
   - the time limit for notification of consent by the Government, referred to in paragraph 1 above, expires.

4. Withdrawal effective on notice

• Article 5, Arrangement on Provisional Application of the Agreement on the Establishment of the ITER [International Thermonuclear Experimental Reactor] International Fusion Energy Organization for the Joint Implementation of the ITER Project (2006) [2006] OJ L358/62:

A Party may withdraw from this Arrangement upon 120 days' written notice to the other Parties.

• Article 45(3), Energy Charter Treaty (1994) 2080 UNTS 95:

(a) Any signatory may terminate its provisional application of this Treaty by written notification to the Depository of its intention not to become a Contracting Party to the Treaty. Termination of provisional application for any signatory shall take effect upon the expiration of 60 days from the date on which such signatory's written notification is received by the Depository.

(b) In the event that a signatory terminates provisional application under subparagraph (a), the obligation of the signatory under paragraph (1) to apply Parts III and V with respect to any Investments made in its Area during such provisional application by Investors of other signatories shall nevertheless remain in effect with respect to those Investments for twenty years following the effective date of termination, except as otherwise provided in subparagraph (c).

(c) Subparagraph (b) shall not apply to any signatory listed in Annex PA. A signatory shall be removed from the list in Annex PA effective upon delivery to the Depository of its request therefor.

14. Territorial and Extraterritorial Application

Chapter 12 addressed the territorial application of treaties, including Article 29 of the VCLT's relatively short treatment: 'unless a different intention appears from the treaty or is otherwise established, a treaty is binding upon each party in respect of its entire territory'. Territorial application clauses address the geographic space within which a party is responsible for treaty compliance. These clauses may reinforce the VCLT's integral territorial application principle. Alternatively, they may express a 'different intention', whether by specifying the applicable territory or allowing a State, on notice, to extend (or exclude) the treaty's application to some or all of its non-metropolitan territory. A 'territorial clause' allows a State comprised of two or more territorial units to indicate to which unit(s) a treaty applies, either at the time it joins the treaty or, in some cases, at any time subsequently. Finally, some clauses may extend (directly or indirectly) a treaty's application extraterritorially.

A. Application to all territories

1. *Mandatory application*

- Article IX, Convention on the International Right of Correction (1953) 435 UNTS 191:

    The provisions of the present Convention shall extend to or be applicable equally to a contracting metropolitan State and to all the territories, be they Non-Self-Governing, Trust or Colonial Territories, which are being administered or governed by such metropolitan State.

2. *Mandatory application except where consent of territorial unit required*

- Article 27, Convention on Psychotropic Substances (1971) 1019 UNTS 175:

    The Convention shall apply to all non-metropolitan territories for the international relations of which any Party is responsible except where the previous consent of such a territory is required by the Constitution of the Party or of the territory concerned, or required by custom. In such a case the Party shall endeavor to secure the needed consent of the territory within the shortest period possible, and when the consent is obtained the Party shall notify the Secretary-General. The Convention shall apply to the territory or territories named in such a notification from the date of its receipt by the Secretary-General. In those cases where the previous consent of the non-metropolitan territory is not required, the Party concerned shall, at the time of signature, ratification or accession, declare the non-metropolitan territory or territories to which this Convention applies.

B. Application to specified territories

- Article 355(1)–(5), Consolidated Version of Treaty on the Functioning of the European Union [2010] OJ C83/47:

    1. The provisions of the [EU] Treaties shall apply to Guadeloupe, French Guiana, Martinique, Réunion, Saint-Barthélemy, Saint-Martin, the Azores, Madeira and the Canary Islands in accordance with Article 349.
    2. The special arrangements for association set out in Part Four shall apply to the overseas countries and territories listed in Annex II.

        The Treaties shall not apply to those overseas countries and territories having special relations with the United Kingdom of Great Britain and Northern Ireland which are not included in the aforementioned list.

    3. The provisions of the Treaties shall apply to the European territories for whose external relations a Member State is responsible.
    4. The provisions of the Treaties shall apply to the Åland Islands in accordance with the provisions set out in Protocol 2 to the Act concerning the conditions of accession of the Republic of Austria, the Republic of Finland and the Kingdom of Sweden.

5. Notwithstanding Article 52 of the Treaty on European Union and paragraphs 1 to 4 of this Article:

(a) the Treaties shall not apply to the Faeroe Islands;

(b) the Treaties shall not apply to the United Kingdom Sovereign Base Areas of Akrotiri and Dhekelia in Cyprus except to the extent necessary to ensure the implementation of the arrangements set out in the Protocol on the Sovereign Base Areas of the United Kingdom of Great Britain and Northern Ireland in Cyprus annexed to the Act concerning the conditions of accession of the [certain listed States] to the European Union and in accordance with the terms of that Protocol;

(c) the Treaties shall apply to the Channel Islands and the Isle of Man only to the extent necessary to ensure the implementation of the arrangements for those islands set out in the Treaty concerning the accession of new Member States to the European Economic Community and to the European Atomic Energy Community signed on 22 January 1972.

• Article 1, Agreement for the Exchange of Information Relating to Taxes (US-UK) (2001) <http://www.oecd.org/dataoecd/20/17/35514531.pdf?contentId =35514532>:

... The territorial scope of this agreement, in respect of the United Kingdom, is the territory of the Cayman Islands.

• Article 1, Protocol 1 to the South Pacific Nuclear Free Zone Treaty (1986) 1971 UNTS 470:

Each Party undertakes to apply, in respect of the territories for which it is internationally responsible situated within the South Pacific Nuclear Free Zone, the prohibitions contained in Articles 3, 5 and 6 ... and the safeguards specified in Article 8(2)(c) and Annex 2 of the Treaty.

C. Exclusion of non-metropolitan territory

1. Treaty limited to metropolitan territory

• Article 15, Agreement on the Export and Enforcement of Social Security Benefits (The Netherlands-Belize) (2005) 2387 UNTS 319:

In relation to the Kingdom of the Netherlands, this Agreement shall apply only to the territory of the Kingdom in Europe.

• Article 19, Agreement Providing for the Reciprocal Recognition and Enforcement of Maintenance Orders (UK-Ireland) (1974) 990 UNTS 69:

This Agreement shall not apply to the non-metropolitan territories for the international relations of which the United Kingdom is responsible.

2. Exclusion of non-metropolitan territory on notice

• Article 15, Agreement Concerning the Establishing of Global Technical Regulations For Wheeled Vehicles, Equipment and Parts which Can Be Fitted and/ or Be Used on Wheeled Vehicles (1998) 2119 UNTS 129:

15.1 This Agreement shall extend to the territory or territories of a Contracting Party for whose international relations such Contracting Party is responsible, unless the Contracting Party otherwise specifies, prior to entry into force of the agreement for that Contracting Party.

15.2 Any Contracting Party may denounce this Agreement separately for any such territory or territories in accordance with Article 12.

- Article 66, Convention establishing the Multilateral Investment Guarantee Agency (1985) 1508 UNTS 99:

This Convention shall apply to all territories under the jurisdiction of a member including the territories for whose international relations a member is responsible, except those which are excluded by such member by written notice to the depository of this Convention either at the time of ratification, acceptance or approval or subsequently.

D. Extension to non-metropolitan territory

1. On notice

- Article 9, European Agreement relating to Persons Participating in Proceedings of the European Court of Human Rights (1996) 2135 UNTS 181:

1. Any Contracting State may, when depositing its instrument of ratification, acceptance or approval or at any later date, by declaration addressed to the Secretary General of the Council of Europe, extend this Agreement to any territory or territories specified in the declaration and for whose international relations it is responsible or on whose behalf it is authorized to give undertakings.

2. This Agreement shall enter into force for any territory or territories specified in a declaration made pursuant to paragraph 1 on the first day of the month following the expiration of one month after the date of receipt of the declaration by the Secretary General.

3. Any declaration made pursuant to paragraph 1 may, in respect of any territory mentioned in such declaration, be withdrawn according to the procedure laid down for denunciation in Article 10 of this Agreement.

- Article XII, Convention on the Prevention and Punishment of the Crime of Genocide (1948) 78 UNTS 277:

Any Contracting Party may at any time, by notification addressed to the Secretary-General of the United Nations, extend the application of the present Convention to all or any of the territories for the conduct of whose foreign relations that Contracting Party is responsible.

2. On agreement of the parties

- Article 14, Agreement concerning Mutual Assistance in the Investigation, Restraint and Confiscation of the Proceeds of Crime other than Drug Trafficking (UK-Mexico) (1996) 1945 UNTS 317:

This Agreement shall apply:

(a) in relation to the United Kingdom:
    (i) to England and Wales, Scotland and Northern Ireland; and
    (ii) to any territory for the international relations of which the United Kingdom is responsible and to which this Agreement shall have been extended, subject to any modifications agreed, by agreement between the Parties. Such extension may be terminated by either Party by giving six months' written notice to the other through the diplomatic channel; and
(b) in relation to the United Mexican States, to the territory of the United Mexican States.

• Article 16, Agreement on the Promotion and Protection of Investments (1988) (New Zealand-China) 1787 UNTS 185:

This Agreement shall not apply to the Cook Islands, Niue and Tokelau unless the Contracting Parties have exchanged notes agreeing the terms on which this Agreement shall so apply.

E. Territorial clauses

• Article 20(1)–(3), Convention on the Law Applicable to Certain Rights in Respect of Securities Held with an Intermediary (2006) 46 ILM 649:

1. A Multi-unit State may, at the time of signature, ratification, acceptance, approval or accession, make a declaration that this Convention shall extend to all its territorial units or only to one or more of them.
2. Any such declaration shall state expressly the territorial units to which this Convention applies.
3. If a State makes no declaration under paragraph (1), this Convention extends to all territorial units of that State.

• Article 35(1)–(5), United Nations Convention on the Assignment of Receivables in International Trade (2001) 41 ILM 776:

(1) If a State has two or more territorial units in which different systems of law are applicable in relation to the matters dealt with in this Convention, it may at any time declare that this Convention is to extend to all its territorial units or only one or more of them, and may at any time substitute another declaration for its earlier declaration.
(2) Such declarations are to state expressly the territorial units to which this Convention extends.
(3) If, by virtue of a declaration under this article, this Convention does not extend to all territorial units of a State and the assignor or the debtor is located in a territorial unit to which this Convention does not extend, this location is considered not to be in a Contracting State.
(4) If, by virtue of a declaration under this article, this Convention does not extend to all territorial units of a State and the law governing the original contract is the law in force in a territorial unit to which this Convention does not extend, the law governing the original contract is considered not to be the law of a Contracting State.
(5) If a State makes no declaration under paragraph 1 of this article, the Convention is to extend to all territorial units of that State.

F. Extraterritorial applications

1. *Application irrespective of territory*

- Article IV, Convention on the Prohibition of the Development, Production and Stockpiling of Bacteriological (Biological) and Toxin Weapons, and on Their Destruction (1972) 1015 UNTS 163:

  Each State Party to this Convention shall, in accordance with its constitutional process-es, take any necessary measures to prohibit and prevent the development, production, stockpiling, acquisition or retention of the agents, toxins, weapons, equipment and means of delivery specified in Article I of the Convention, within the territory of such State, under its jurisdiction or under its control anywhere.

2. *Application to territory outside of State territory*

- Article 1(4), Agreement on Reciprocal Encouragement and Protection of In-vestments (Spain-China) (1992) 1746 UNTS 167:

  The term 'territory' designates the land territory and territorial waters of each of the Contracting Parties. This Agreement shall also apply to investments made by investors of either Contracting Party in the exclusive economic zone and the continental shelf that extends outside the limits of the territorial waters of the other Contracting Party, over which they have or may have sovereign rights and jurisdiction for the purpose of prospecting, exploration and conservation of natural resources, pursuant to international law.

- Article IV(1), Treaty Relating to Extradition (Thailand-Philippines) (1981) 1394 UNTS 3:

  A reference in this Treaty to the territory of a Party is a reference to all the territory under the jurisdiction of that Party and to vessels and aircraft registered in that Party if any such aircraft is in flight or if any such vessel is on the high seas when the crime is committed.

- Article VI, The Antarctic Treaty (1959) 402 UNTS 71:

  The provisions of the present Treaty shall apply to the area south of 60° South latitude, including all ice shelves, but nothing in the present Treaty shall prejudice or in any way affect the rights, or the exercise of the rights, of any State under international law with regard to the high seas within that area.

3. *Application where State has jurisdiction*

- Article 2(1), Convention on the Rights of the Child (1989) 1577 UNTS 3:

  States Parties shall respect and ensure the rights set forth in the present Convention to each child within their jurisdiction without discrimination of any kind, irrespective of the child's or his or her parent's or legal guardian's race, colour, sex, language, religion, political or other opinion, national, ethnic or social origin, property, disability, birth or other status.

• Article 1(1), American Convention on Human Rights (1969) 1144 UNTS 123:

> The States Parties to this Convention undertake to respect the rights and freedoms recognized herein and to ensure to all persons subject to their jurisdiction the free and full exercise of those rights and freedoms, without any discrimination for reasons of race, color, sex, language, religion, political or other opinion, national or social origin, economic status, birth, or any other social condition.

15. Federal States

Federal States may encounter difficulties in applying treaties on matters constitutionally committed to their sub-federal units. In such cases, a federal State may not be able to join the treaty without some accommodation either by its sub-federal units or other parties to the treaty. As Chapter 12 explains, one solution is to include a 'territorial clause' where the treaty may apply to some of a State's sub-federal territorial units but not others.[54] In addition, some treaties may include a 'federal State clause' that limits the scope of the treaty's obligations to those that the federal State's government has constitutional authority to assume.[55] Unitary States tend to resist such clauses because they lead to unequal treaty rights and obligations. As a result, the traditional federal State clause is not widely used today. Instead, modern treaties may contain clauses that: (a) authorize limited exceptions to a treaty's obligations for federal States; (b) differentiate implementation among federal and non-federal States; (c) limit treaty obligations to the 'national' level; or (d) reject any accommodation for federal States.

Moreover, although not sampled here, it is important to recognize that where a treaty neither prohibits nor permits federalism accommodations, several federal States have made reservations to limit their obligations to those areas of legislative jurisdiction that the federal government has assumed.[56] On occasion, other States have objected to such reservations.[57] Alternatively, a federal State may issue an interpretative declaration to explain how federalism affects its implementation of

---

[54] See heading 14.E for examples of territorial clauses.

[55] See Chapter 12 (Part II.B, 313 *et seq*).

[56] For example, the United States deposited a 'federalism' reservation to criminalization obligations that fell within areas traditionally reserved to its States under the 2000 UN Transnational Organized Crime Convention. See Multilateral Treaties Deposited with the Secretary General ('MTDSG'), Ch XVIII.12 <http://treaties.un.org/Pages/ViewDetails.aspx?src=TREATY&mtdsg_no=XVIII-12&chapter=18&lang=en#EndDec>. It was not clear, however, that the US Constitution prohibited federal implementation of those obligations. See DB Hollis, 'Executive Federalism: Forging New Constraints on the Treaty Power' (2005) 79 So Cal L Rev 1327.

[57] Canada reserved out of obligations falling 'outside of federal legislative jurisdiction' under the 1991 Espoo Convention on Transboundary Environmental Impact Assessment, prompting Spain and Sweden to object that the reservation was too imprecise and incompatible with the treaty's object and purpose. See MTDSG, Ch XXVII.4 <http://treaties.un.org/pages/ViewDetails.aspx?src=TREATY&mtdsg_no=XXVII-4&chapter=27&lang=en>.

the treaty.[58] For further discussion of reservations, objections to reservations, and interpretative declarations, see Chapter 11.

A. Clauses excepting federal States from certain treaty obligations

1. *Federal State clauses*

• Article 35, Convention for the Safeguarding of the Intangible Cultural Heritage (2003) 2368 UNTS 3:

The following provisions shall apply to States Parties which have a federal or non-unitary constitutional system:

(a) with regard to the provisions of this Convention, the implementation of which comes under the legal jurisdiction of the federal or central legislative power, the obligations of the federal or central government shall be the same as for those States Parties which are not federal States;

(b) with regard to the provisions of this Convention, the implementation of which comes under the jurisdiction of individual constituent States, countries, provinces or cantons which are not obliged by the constitutional system of the federation to take legislative measures, the federal government shall inform the competent authorities of such States, countries, provinces or cantons of the said provisions, with its recommendation for their adoption.

• Article XI, Convention on the Recognition and Enforcement of Foreign Arbitral Awards (New York Convention) (1958) 330 UNTS 3:

In the case of a federal or non-unitary State, the following provisions shall apply:

(a) With respect to those articles of this Convention that come within the legislative jurisdiction of the federal authority, the obligations of the federal Government shall to this extent be the same as those of Contracting States which are not federal States;

(b) With respect to those articles of this Convention that come within the legislative jurisdiction of constituent states or provinces which are not, under the constitutional system of the federation, bound to take legislative action, the federal Government shall bring such articles with a favourable recommendation to the notice of the appropriate authorities of constituent states or provinces at the earliest possible moment;

(c) A federal State Party to this Convention shall, at the request of any other Contracting State transmitted through the Secretary-General of the United Nations, supply a statement of the law and practice of the federation and its constituent units in regard to any particular provision of this Convention, showing the extent to which effect has been given to that provision by legislative or other action.

• Article 19(7)(a)–(b)(i)–(iv), Constitution of the International Labour Organization, as amended (1972) <http://www.ilo.org/ilolex/english/constq.htm>:

---

[58] Australia, for example, issued an understanding on how federalism meant its implementation of the International Covenant on Civil and Political Rights would be distributed among the Commonwealth and its constituent states and territories. See MTDSG, ch IV.4 <http://treaties.un.org/pages/ViewDetails.aspx?src=TREATY&mtdsg_no=IV-4&chapter=4&lang=en>.

In the case of a federal State, the following provisions shall apply:

(a) in respect of Conventions and Recommendations which the federal government regards as appropriate under its constitutional system for federal action, the obligations of the federal State shall be the same as those of Members which are not federal States;

(b) in respect of Conventions and Recommendations which the federal government regards as appropriate under its constitutional system, in whole or in part, for action by the constituent states, provinces, or cantons rather than for federal action, the federal government shall:

(i) make, in accordance with its Constitution and the Constitution of the states, provinces or cantons concerned, effective arrangements for the reference of such Conventions and Recommendations not later than eighteen months from the closing of the session of the Conference to the appropriate federal, state, provincial or cantonal authorities for the enactment of legislation or other action;

(ii) arrange, subject to the concurrence of the state, provincial or cantonal Governments concerned, for periodical consultations between the federal and the state, provincial or cantonal authorities with a view to promoting within the federal State co-ordinated action to give effect to the provisions of such Conventions and Recommendations;

(iii) inform the Director-General of the International Labour Office of the measures taken in accordance with this article to bring such Conventions and Recommendations before the appropriate federal, state, provincial or cantonal authorities regarded as appropriate and of the action taken by them;

(iv) in respect of each such Convention which it has not ratified, report to the Director-General of the International Labour Office, at appropriate intervals as requested by the Governing Body, the position of the law and practice of the federation and its constituent States, provinces or cantons in regard to the Convention, showing the extent to which effect has been given, or is proposed to be given, to any of the provisions of the Convention by legislation, administrative action, collective agreement, or otherwise; . . .

2. *Clause that authorizes limited exceptions for federal States*

• Article 41(1)–(3), Convention on Cybercrime (2001) 2296 UNTS 167:

1. A federal State may reserve the right to assume obligations under Chapter II of this Convention consistent with its fundamental principles governing the relationship between its central government and constituent States or other similar territorial entities provided that it is still able to co-operate under Chapter III.

2. When making a reservation under paragraph 1, a federal State may not apply the terms of such reservation to exclude or substantially diminish its obligations to provide for measures set forth in Chapter II. Overall, it shall provide for a broad and effective law enforcement capability with respect to those measures.

3. With regard to the provisions of this Convention, the application of which comes under the jurisdiction of constituent States or other similar territorial entities, that are not obliged by the constitutional system of the federation to take legislative measures, the federal government shall inform the competent authorities of such States of the said provisions with its favourable opinion, encouraging them to take appropriate action to give them effect.

B. Differentiating federal versus non-federal State implementation

1. Explicitly

- Article 6(1)–(2), Convention on Protection of Children and Cooperation in respect of Intercountry Adoption (1993) 1870 UNTS 167:

    1. A Contracting State shall designate a Central Authority to discharge the duties which are imposed by the Convention upon such authorities.

    2. Federal States, States with more than one system of law or States having autonomous territorial units shall be free to appoint more than one Central Authority and to specify the territorial or personal extent of their functions. Where a State has appointed more than one Central Authority, it shall designate the Central Authority to which any communication may be addressed for transmission to the appropriate Central Authority within that State.

2. Implicitly

- Paragraph 27, Explanatory Report, COE Criminal Law Convention on Corruption (1999) CETS No 173:

    ... [I]t should be noted that it was the intention of the drafters of the Convention that Contracting parties assume obligations under this Convention only to the extent consistent with their Constitution and the fundamental principles of their legal system, including, where appropriate, the principles of federalism.

C. Obligations imposed only at the 'national' level

- Article 8(2), WHO Framework Convention on Tobacco Control (2003) 2302 UNTS 166:

    Each Party shall adopt and implement in areas of existing national jurisdiction as determined by national law and actively promote at other jurisdictional levels the adoption and implementation of effective legislative, executive, administrative and/or other measures, providing for protection from exposure to tobacco smoke in indoor workplaces, public transport, indoor public places and, as appropriate, other public places.

D. Clauses that deny any accommodation to federal States

- Article 41, International Convention for the Protection of All Persons from Enforced Disappearance (2007) 14 IHHR 582:

    The provisions of this Convention shall apply to all parts of federal States without any limitations or exceptions.

- Article 9, Second Optional Protocol to the International Covenant on Civil and Political Rights Aiming at the Abolition of the Death Penalty (1989) 1642 UNTS 414:

The provisions of the present Protocol shall extend to all parts of federal States without any limitations or exceptions.

16. Relationships to Other Treaties

The proliferation of treaties across—and within—subject areas raises important questions about what to do when treaties conflict. As Chapter 18 explains, the VCLT default rules provide a complicated, and yet, incomplete response. Those rules do, however, allow parties to draft clauses that may avoid (or mitigate) treaty conflicts in at least four ways.

First, where there is a unity of parties, Article 59 of the VCLT allows a later treaty to terminate or suspend an earlier one on the 'same subject matter' if the later treaty so provides or the parties intention to do so is 'otherwise established'.[59] Thus, a clause may indicate that a treaty supersedes, replaces, or suspends a prior treaty. Second, a clause may indicate that the treaty takes priority over some or all other treaties without purporting to terminate or suspend them. Third, as Article 30(2) of the VCLT directs, where a treaty indicates that it is subject to another 'earlier or later treaty', the other treaty's provisions will prevail in case of incompatibility.

Fourth, Article 41 of the VCLT allows treaty clauses providing for *modifications*—subsequent agreements to modify a multilateral treaty by some, but not all, of its parties.[60] Such modification clauses are not a regular feature of treaty-making, but they do appear occasionally. When they do, authorization often comes with a caveat; any modifications must be consistent with, or improve upon, the original treaty's commitments. Notice requirements may also be imposed, which either reiterate or adjust those found in the VCLT itself.[61]

Finally, it is important to recognize that the various ways of dealing with relationships among treaties are not mutually exclusive. A treaty may use a combination of them to afford a comprehensive picture of its relations to other treaties.

---

[59] Termination or suspension may also occur by implication for other successive treaties on the 'same subject matter'. See VCLT Art 59(1)(b). When a treaty is not terminated or suspended under Art 59, *lex posterior* applies among common parties—'the earlier treaty applies only to the extent its provision are compatible with those of the later treaty'. Ibid Art 30(3). Unfortunately, the VCLT leaves ambiguous what constitutes the 'same subject matter' and has no clear rule for treaty conflicts where party unity is absent. For more discussion of the VCLT default rules, see Chapter 18 (Part III.C, 461 *et seq*).

[60] VCLT Art 41(1)(b) also indicates that modifications are acceptable in the absence of textual authorization where they: (i) are not prohibited by the treaty; (ii) do not negatively impact other parties' rights or their performance obligations; *and* (iii) do not derogate from the original treaty in a way incompatible with 'the effective execution of the object and purpose of the treaty as a whole'. Where either ground for a modification is satisfied, it overrides the VCLT's default rules on applying successive treaties relating to the same subject matter. See ibid Art 30(5).

[61] Unless a treaty otherwise provides, VCLT Art 41(2) requires parties making a modification to notify other parties 'of their intention to conclude the agreement and of the modification to the treaty for which it provides'.

A. Supersession clauses

- Article XIV(4), Treaty on Measures for the Further Reduction and Limitation of Strategic Offensive Arms (US-Russian Federation) (New START Agreement) (2010) 50 ILM 340:

  As of the date of its entry into force, this Treaty shall supersede the Treaty between the United States of America and the Russian Federation on Strategic Offensive Reductions of May 24, 2002, which shall terminate as of that date.

- Article 22(1)–(2), Air Transport Agreement (US/EU Open Skies Agreement) (2007) 46 ILM 470:

  1. During the period of provisional application pursuant to Article 25 of this Agreement, the bilateral agreements listed in section 1 of Annex 1, shall be suspended, except to the extent provided in section 2 of Annex 1.
  2. Upon entry into force pursuant to Article 26 of this Agreement, this Agreement shall supersede the bilateral agreements listed in section 1 of Annex 1, except to the extent provided in section 2 of Annex 1.

- Article XXVI, Food Aid Convention (1999) 2073 UNTS 135:

  This Convention shall replace the Food Aid Convention, 1995, as extended, and shall be one of the constituent instruments of the International Grains Agreement, 1995.

B. Clauses providing for the priority of the present treaty

1. Present treaty prevails over all treaties

- Article 103, Charter of the United Nations (1945) TS No 993:

  In the event of a conflict between the obligations of the Members of the United Nations under the present Charter and their obligations under any other international agreement, their obligation under the present Charter shall prevail.

2. Present treaty prevails over past and future treaties

- Article 21, African Union Convention on Preventing and Combating Corruption (2003) 43 ILM 5:

  Subject to the provisions of Article 4 paragraph 2, this Convention shall in respect to those State Parties to which it applies, supersede the provisions of any treaty or bilateral agreement governing corruption and related offences between any two or more State Parties.

- Article 11(5), International Convention for the Suppression of the Financing of Terrorism (1999) 2178 UNTS 197:

  The provisions of all extradition treaties and arrangements between States Parties with regard to offences set forth in article 2 shall be deemed to be modified as between States Parties to the extent that they are incompatible with this Convention.

3. Present treaty prevails over earlier treaties

- Article 27, Singapore Treaty on Trademarks (2006) <http://www.wipo.int/treaties/en/ip/singapore/singapore_treaty.html>:

  (1) [*Relations Between Contracting Parties to Both This Treaty and the TLT 1994*] This Treaty alone shall be applicable as regards the mutual relations of Contracting Parties to both this Treaty and the TLT 1994.

  (2) [*Relations Between Contracting Parties to This Treaty and Contracting Parties to the TLT 1994 That Are Not Party to This Treaty*] Any Contracting Party to both this Treaty and the TLT 1994 shall continue to apply the TLT 1994 in its relations with Contracting Parties to the TLT 1994 that are not party to this Treaty.

- Article 9, Free Trade Agreement (Ukraine-Tajikistan) (2001) <http://wits.worldbank.org/GPTAD/PDF/archive/Tajikistan-ukraine.pdf>:

  The provisions of the present Agreement shall prevail over the provisions of bilateral agreements concluded earlier between the Parties to the extent when the latter are either not compatible with the first or identical to them, except for the provisions of bilateral and multilateral agreements in the area of transports, which set out the procedure and terms of carriage.

4. Present treaty prevails over IO member's constituent instrument

- Annex IX, Article 4(6), United Nations Convention on the Law of the Sea (1982) 1833 UNTS 3:

  In the event of a conflict between the obligations of an international organization under this Convention and its obligations under the agreement establishing the organization or any acts relating to it, the obligations under this Convention shall prevail.

5. Obligation to eliminate incompatibilities with respect to existing treaties with third-parties

- Article 351, Consolidated Version of Treaty on the Functioning of the European Union [2010] OJ C83/47:

  The rights and obligations arising from agreements concluded before 1 January 1958 or, for acceding States, before the date of their accession, between one or more Member States on the one hand, and one or more third countries on the other, shall not be affected by the provisions of the Treaties.

  To the extent that such agreements are not compatible with the Treaties, the Member State or States concerned shall take all appropriate steps to eliminate the incompatibilities established. Member States shall, where necessary, assist each other to this end and shall, where appropriate, adopt a common attitude.

  In applying the agreements referred to in the first paragraph, Member States shall take into account the fact that the advantages accorded under the Treaties by each Member State form an integral part of the establishment of the Union and are thereby inseparably linked with the creation of common institutions, the conferring of powers upon them and the granting of the same advantages by all the other Member States.

6. *Future treaties must be compatible with the present treaty*

- Article XVIII, Treaty for Amazonian Cooperation (1978) 1202 UNTS 51:

  Nothing contained in this Treaty shall in any way limit the rights of the Contracting Parties to conclude bilateral or multilateral agreements on specific or generic matters, provided that these are not contrary to the achievement of the common aims for cooperation in the Amazonian region stated in this instrument.

- Article 8, North Atlantic Treaty (NATO Treaty) (1949) 34 UNTS 243:

  Each Party declares that none of the international engagements now in force between it and any other of the Parties or any third State is in conflict with the provisions of this Treaty, and undertakes not to enter into any international engagement in conflict with this treaty.

C. Clauses providing for the priority of another treaty

1. *No effect on one or more other agreements*

- Article 2, Agreement on Cooperation in the Field of Internal Security and the Fight against Crime (France-Russian Federation) (2003) 2476 UNTS 145:

  ... This Agreement shall not affect the rights and obligations of the Parties under other international agreements, including those dealing with mutual legal assistance in criminal and extradition matters.

- Article VII, Agreement on Science and Technology Cooperation (UK-Russian Federation) (1996) 1945 UNTS 351:

  The provisions of this Agreement shall not affect the rights and obligations of the Parties arising under their international agreements with third Parties.

- Article 11(3), WTO Agreement on the Application of Sanitary and Phytosanitary Measures (1994) 1867 UNTS 493:

  Nothing in this Agreement shall impair the rights of Members under other international agreements, including the right to resort to the good offices or dispute settlement mechanisms of other international organizations or established under any international agreement.

- Article 12, Convention on Assistance in the Case of a Nuclear Accident or Radiological Emergency (1986) 1457 UNTS 133:

  This Convention shall not affect the reciprocal rights and obligations of States Parties under existing international agreements which relate to the matters covered by this Convention, or under future international agreements concluded in accordance with the object and purpose of this Convention.

2. Existing treaties prevail

- Article 50, Convention on the International Recovery of Child Support and Other Forms of Family Maintenance (2007) 47 ILM 257:

  This Convention does not affect the Hague Convention of 1 March 1954 on civil procedure, the Hague Convention of 15 November 1965 on the Service Abroad of Judicial and Extrajudicial Documents in Civil or Commercial Matters and the Hague Convention of 18 March 1970 on the Taking of Evidence Abroad in Civil or Commercial Matters.

- Article 22(1), Convention on Biological Diversity (1992) 1760 UNTS 79:

  The provisions of this Convention shall not affect the rights and obligations of any Contracting Party deriving from any existing international agreement, except where the exercise of those rights and obligations would cause a serious damage or threat to biological diversity.

- Article 5(1)–(2), Protocol on Environmental Protection to the Antarctic Treaty (1991) 30 ILM 1455:

  1. This Protocol shall supplement the Antarctic Treaty and shall neither modify nor amend that Treaty.
  2. Nothing in this Protocol shall derogate from the rights and obligations of the Parties to this Protocol under the other international instruments in force within the Antarctic Treaty system.

- Article XV, Agreement on Air Quality (Canada-US) (1991) 1852 UNTS 79:

  Nothing in this Agreement shall be deemed to diminish the rights and obligations of the Parties in other international agreements between them, including those contained in the Boundary Waters Treaty and the Great Lakes Water Quality Agreement of 1978, as amended.

3. Future treaties prevail

- Article V, Agreement regarding Cooperation to Facilitate the Provision of Assistance (US-Russian Federation) (1992) 2264 UNTS 11:

  The Parties recognise that further arrangements or agreements may be necessary or desirable with respect to particular United States assistance activities. In case of any inconsistency between this Agreement and any such further written agreement, the provisions of such further written agreements shall prevail.

- Article 90, United Nations Convention on Contracts for the International Sale of Goods (1980) 1489 UNTS 3:

  This Convention does not prevail over any international agreement which has already been or may be entered into and which contains provisions concerning the matters governed by this Convention, provided that the parties have their places of business in States parties, to such agreement.

4. Existing or future treaties giving greater benefits prevail

- Article 40(1), Council of Europe Convention on Action against Trafficking in Human Beings (2005) 45 ILM 12:

  This Convention shall not affect the rights and obligations derived from other international instruments to which Parties to the present Convention are Parties or shall become Parties and which contain provisions on matters governed by this Convention and which ensure greater protection and assistance for victims of trafficking...

- Article 20, Berne Convention for the Protection of Literary and Artistic Works of 9 September 1886, as revised (1967) 828 UNTS 221:

  The Governments of the countries of the Union reserve the right to enter into special agreements among themselves, in so far as such agreements grant to authors more extensive rights than those granted by the Convention, or contain other provisions not contrary to this Convention. The provisions of existing agreements which satisfy these conditions shall remain applicable.

- Article 53, European Convention for the Protection of Human Rights and Fundamental Freedoms, as amended (2010) CETS No 194:

  Nothing in this Convention shall be construed as limiting or derogating from any of the human rights and fundamental freedoms which may be ensured under the laws of any High Contracting Party or under any other agreement to which it is a party.

D. Modifications and supplementary agreements

1. Modifications permitted if compatible with the present treaty

- Article 2(2), WHO Framework Convention on Tobacco Control (2003) 2302 UNTS 166:

  The provisions of the Convention and its protocols shall in no way affect the right of Parties to enter into bilateral or multilateral agreements, including regional or subregional agreements, on issues relevant or additional to the Convention and its protocols, provided that such agreements are compatible with their obligations under the Convention and its protocols. The Parties concerned shall communicate such agreements to the Conference of the Parties through the Secretariat.

- Article 8, Convention on Environmental Impact Assessment in a Transboundary Context (1991) 1989 UNTS 309:

  The Parties may continue existing or enter into new bilateral or multilateral agreements or other arrangements in order to implement their obligations under this Convention. Such agreements or other arrangements may be based on the elements listed in Appendix VI.

- Article 11(1)–(2), Basel Convention on the Control of Transboundary Movements of Hazardous Wastes and their Disposal (1989) 1673 UNTS 57:

1. Notwithstanding the provisions of Article 4 paragraph 5, Parties may enter into bilateral, multilateral, or regional agreements or arrangements regarding trans-boundary movement of hazardous wastes or other wastes with Parties or non-Parties provided that such agreements or arrangements do not derogate from the environmentally sound management of hazardous wastes and other wastes as required by this Convention. These agreements or arrangements shall stipulate provisions which are not less environmentally sound than those provided for by this Convention in particular taking into account the interests of developing countries.

2. Parties shall notify the Secretariat of any bilateral, multilateral or regional agreements or arrangements referred to in paragraph 1 and those which they have entered into prior to the entry into force of this Convention for them, for the purpose of controlling transboundary movements of hazardous wastes and other wastes which take place entirely among the Parties to such agreements. The provisions of this Convention shall not affect transboundary movements which take place pursuant to such agreements provided that such agreements are compatible with the environmentally sound management of hazardous wastes and other wastes as required by this Convention.

- Article 73(2), Vienna Convention on Consular Relations (1963) 596 UNTS 261:

  Nothing in the present Convention shall preclude States from concluding international agreements confirming or supplementing or extending or amplifying the provisions thereof.

2. Modifications permitted without conditions on consistency with the present treaty

- Article 9, Convention on Early Notification of a Nuclear Accident (1986) 1439 UNTS 275:

  In furtherance of their mutual interests, States Parties may consider, where deemed appropriate, the conclusion of bilateral or multilateral arrangements relating to the subject matter of this Convention.

3. Supplementary agreements permitted with IO's member States

- Article 18, Agreement on Extradition (EU-US) (2003) 43 ILM 749:

  This Agreement shall not preclude the conclusion, after its entry into force, of bilateral Agreements between a Member State and the United States of America consistent with this Agreement.

E. Comprehensive treatment of relations with other treaties

- Article 311(1)–(6), United Nations Convention on the Law of the Sea (1982) 1833 UNTS 3:

  1. This Convention shall prevail, as between States Parties, over the Geneva Conventions on the Law of the Sea of 29 April 1958.

2. This Convention shall not alter the rights and obligations of States Parties which arise from other agreements compatible with this Convention and which do not affect the enjoyment by other States Parties of their rights or the performance of their obligations under this Convention.

3. Two or more States Parties may conclude agreements modifying or suspending the operation of provisions of this Convention, applicable solely to the relations between them, provided that such agreements do not relate to a provision derogation from which is incompatible with the effective execution of the object and purpose of this Convention, and provided further that such agreements shall not affect the application of the basic principles embodied herein, and that the provisions of such agreements do not affect the enjoyment by other States parties of their rights or the performance of their obligations under this Convention.

4. States Parties intending to conclude an agreement referred to in paragraph 3 shall notify the other States Parties through the depositary of this Convention of their intention to conclude the agreement and of the modification or suspension for which it provides.

5. This article does not affect international agreements expressly permitted or preserved by other articles of this Convention.

6. States Parties agree that there shall be no amendments to the basic principle relating to the common heritage of mankind set forth in article 136 and that they shall not be party to any agreement in derogation thereof.

17. Derogations

For all the stability of the treaty commitment, its application can be quite flexible. As the foregoing has shown, treaties may fluctuate as to when application begins, where the treaty applies, and how they deal with conflicts. A treaty's application may also turn on whether any of its obligations are subject to derogation.

A *derogation* clause refers to a treaty provision that authorizes a party to exclude the application of some or all of the treaty's other provisions whether due to the occurrence of specific factual circumstance (such as a public emergency) or on the basis of a stated purpose (such as protection of essential security interests).[62] Such exclusions allow parties to accept treaty commitments while managing the risks they impose by preserving party autonomy in specific core areas or exceptional circumstances. Where a treaty contains a derogation provision, the scope of the party's commitment to perform is adjusted to permit otherwise non-compliant behaviour. Thus, derogations modify the original scope of the obligation assumed, in contrast to doctrines like impossibility or necessity, which excuse behaviour in breach of pre-existing obligations.[63]

The law surrounding derogations is complex and underdeveloped. There are conflicting views, for example, on how self-judging the invocation of a derogation

---

[62] International investment law sometimes refers to these as clauses on 'non-precluded measures'.
[63] For more on these concepts see Chapter 24.

may be.[64] Similarly, it may be difficult to differentiate derogations from provisions that simply outline the contours of the obligation itself. That distinction may not matter much, since determining an obligation's original scope and the availability of any exceptions to it are both interpretative exercises that will be governed by the same rules on treaty interpretation. In any case, derogation clauses are now a regular feature of treaty-making, most often visible in the human rights, trade, and investment contexts. Like the diversity of treaty regulations themselves, derogations are diverse in both form and content. The following examples thus illustrate only a few of the more frequent formulations a derogation clause may adopt.

A. Derogations based on factual conditions

- Article 4, International Covenant on Civil and Political Rights (1966) 999 UNTS 171:

  (1) In time of public emergency which threatens the life of the nation and the existence of which is officially proclaimed, the States Parties to the present Covenant may take measures derogating from their obligations under the present Covenant to the extent strictly required by the exigencies of the situation, provided that such measures are not inconsistent with their other obligations under international law and do not involve discrimination solely on the ground of race, colour, sex, language, religion or social origin.

  (2) No derogation from articles 6, 7, 8 (paragraphs 1 and 2), 11, 15, 16 and 18 may be made under this provision.

  (3) Any State Party to the present Covenant availing itself of the right of derogation shall immediately inform the other States Parties to the present Covenant, through the intermediary of the Secretary-General of the United Nations, of the provisions from which it has derogated and of the reasons by which it was actuated. A further communication shall be made, through the same intermediary, on the date on which it terminates such derogation.

B. Derogations based on the purpose(s) of the behaviour

1. *Based on non-precluded measures*

- Article 15, Free Trade Agreement (Israel-Slovakia) (1996) 1995 UNTS 3:

  This Agreement shall not preclude prohibitions or restrictions on imports, exports or goods in transit justified on grounds of public morality, public policy or public security; of the protection of health and life of humans, animals or plants, including environmental measures necessary to protect human, animal or plant life or health; of

---

[64] The current weight of judicial authority, however, appears to deny them this character. See eg *Oil Platforms (Islamic Republic of Iran v United States)* [2003] ICJ Rep 161; *CMS Gas Transmission Company v Argentine Republic* (Award) (2005) ICSID Case No ARB/01/8; *LG&E Energy Corp v Argentine Republic* (Decision on Liability) (2006) ICSID Case No ARB/02/1; *Enron Corporation Ponderosa Asset v Argentine Republic* (Decision on Liability) (2006) ICSID Case No ARB/01/3.

the protection of national treasures possessing artistic, historic or archaeological value; of the protection of intellectual property, or of the rules relating to gold or silver or to the conservation of exhaustible natural resources. Such prohibitions or restrictions shall not, however, constitute means of arbitrary discrimination or a disguised restriction on trade between the Parties.

- Article XX, General Agreement on Tariffs and Trade (1947), as amended (1955) 278 UNTS 200:

Subject to the requirement that such measures are not applied in a manner which would constitute a means of arbitrary or unjustifiable discrimination between countries where the same conditions prevail, or a disguised restriction on international trade, nothing in this Agreement shall be construed to prevent the adoption or enforcement by any contracting party of measures:

(a) necessary to protect public morals;

(b) necessary to protect human, animal or plant life or health;

(c) relating to the importations or exportations of gold or silver;

(d) necessary to secure compliance with laws or regulations which are not inconsistent with the provisions of this Agreement, including those relating to customs enforcement, the enforcement of monopolies operated under paragraph 4 of Article II and Article XVII, the protection of patents, trademarks and copyrights, and the prevention of deceptive practices;

(e) relating to the products of prison labour;

(f) imposed for the protection of national treasures of artistic, historic or archaeological value;

(g) relating to the conservation of exhaustible natural resources if such measures are made effective in conjunction with restrictions on domestic production or consumption;

(h) undertaken in pursuance of obligations under any intergovernmental commodity agreement which conforms to criteria submitted to the contracting parties and not disapproved by them or which is itself so submitted and not so disapproved;

(i) involving restrictions on exports of domestic materials necessary to ensure essential quantities of such materials to a domestic processing industry during periods when the domestic price of such materials is held below the world price as part of a governmental stabilization plan; Provided that such restrictions shall not operate to increase the exports of or the protection afforded to such domestic industry, and shall not depart from the provisions of this Agreement relating to non-discrimination;

(j) essential to the acquisition or distribution of products in general or local short supply; Provided that any such measures shall be consistent with the principle that all contracting parties are entitled to an equitable share of the international supply of such products, and that any such measures, which are inconsistent with the other provisions of the Agreement shall be discontinued as soon as the conditions giving rise to them have ceased to exist. The contracting parties shall review the need for this sub-paragraph not later than 30 June 1960.

2. Regarding acts in furtherance of essential security interests

- Article 15, Agreement on the Promotion and Protection of Investments (Finland-Tanzania) (2001) 2201 UNTS 61:

1. Nothing in this Agreement shall be construed as preventing a Contracting Party from taking any action necessary for the protection of its essential security interests in time of war or armed conflict, or other emergency in international relations.
2. Provided that such measures are not applied in a manner which would constitute a means of arbitrary or unjustifiable discrimination by a Contracting Party, or a disguised investment restriction, nothing in this Agreement shall be construed as preventing the Contracting Parties from taking any measure necessary for the maintenance of public order.
3. The provisions of this Article shall not apply to Article 5, Article 6 or paragraph 1(e) of Article 7 of this Agreement.

• Article 73, Agreement on Trade-Related Aspects of Intellectual Property (TRIPS Agreement), Marrakesh Agreement establishing the World Trade Organization (1994) 1867 UNTS 3:

Nothing in this Agreement shall be construed:

(a) to require a Member to furnish any information the disclosure of which it considers contrary to its essential security interests; or
(b) to prevent a Member from taking any action which it considers necessary for the protection of its essential security interests;
   (i) relating to fissionable materials or the materials from which they are derived;
   (ii) relating to the traffic in arms, ammunition and implements of war and to such traffic in other goods and materials as is carried on directly or indirectly for the purpose of supplying a military establishment;
   (iii) taken in time of war or other emergency in international relations; or
(c) to prevent a Member from taking any action in pursuance of its obligations under the United Nations Charter for the maintenance of international peace and security.

3. Avoiding acts impairing essential interests

• Article 3(1)(a), Treaty on Mutual Legal Assistance in Criminal Matters (UK-US) (1994) 1967 UNTS 101:

(1) The Central Authority of the Requested Party may refuse assistance if:
   (a) the Requested Party is of the opinion that the request, if granted, would impair its sovereignty, security, or other essential interests or would be contrary to important public policy . . .

• Article 13, Agreement on cooperation and mutual assistance in customs matters (Poland-Uzbekistan) (2003) 2369 UNTS 171:

1. If the Customs authority considers that the assistance requested might be prejudicial to the sovereignty, security, public order or other essential interests of its State, or would cause violation of a secret that is protected by the law, it may refuse providing the assistance or may provide it only if certain conditions are met.
2. If assistance is refused the decision and the reasons for the refusal shall be immediately notified in writing to the requesting authority.
3. If one of the Customs authorities requests assistance that it would not be able to give if requested it should draw attention to that fact in the request. Compliance with such a request will be within the discretion of the requested authority.

4. Regarding the environment

- Article XVII(2)–(3), Agreement for the promotion and protection of investments (Latvia-Canada) (1995) 2012 UNTS 13:

  (2) Nothing in this Agreement shall be construed to prevent a Contracting Party from adopting, maintaining or enforcing any measure otherwise consistent with this Agreement that it considers appropriate to ensure that investment activity in its territory is undertaken in a manner sensitive to environmental concerns.

  (3) Provided that such measures are not applied in an arbitrary or unjustifiable manner, or do not constitute a disguised restriction on international trade or investment, nothing in this Agreement shall be construed to prevent a Contracting Party from adopting or maintaining measures, including environmental measures:
      (a) necessary to ensure compliance with laws and regulations that are not inconsistent with the provisions of this Agreement;
      (b) necessary to protect human, animal or plant life or health; or
      (c) relating to the conservation of living or non-living exhaustible natural resources.

5. Based on the availability of resources or application of local law

- Article III(4), Agreement concerning Defense Communications Services (New Zealand-US) (1992) 1937 UNTS 283:

  The parties recognize that the implementation of this Agreement is subject to the laws of NZ and the US and the authorization and appropriation of funds.

- Article XIV(1), Agreement on Air Quality (Canada-US) (1991) 1852 UNTS 79:

  The obligations undertaken under this Agreement shall be subject to the availability of appropriated funds in accordance with the respective constitutional procedures of the Parties.

18. Dispute Settlement

Disputes are an inevitable feature of international relations, and treaty relations are no exception. Frequently, States end up disagreeing over what a treaty requires, privileges, or permits (not to mention how it applies in specific situations). Somewhat surprisingly, international law does not actually require States to settle all such disputes. As the UN Charter articulates, only those 'likely to endanger the maintenance of international peace and security'—require resolution.[65] And many treaties do little to change this situation, including *no* provisions on dispute settlement. Other treaties, however, actually do bind parties to settle disputes. In some cases, a treaty's whole objective is establishing a

---

[65] UN Charter Art 33. The Charter famously insists on the peaceful resolution of these disputes through 'negotiation, enquiry, mediation, conciliation, arbitration, judicial settlement, resort to regional agencies or arrangements, or other peaceful means of their own choice'.

dispute settlement mechanism, such as the ICJ Statute, or more recently, the WTO Dispute Settlement Understanding.[66] In other cases, a treaty combines substantive regulations with procedural requirements on issues of implementation or compliance. In terms of dispute settlement, the options range from simply calling for negotiations to binding judicial proceedings, with a host of options in between.[67]

Thus, when it comes to dispute resolution clauses, the options are manifold. Generally, they tend to take one (or more) of three forms: (i) voluntary procedures involving the parties themselves; (ii) voluntary procedures involving a third party mediator; or (iii) compulsory binding dispute settlement. Binding dispute settlement may come at the election of one or all disputing parties and in recent years has extended to some individual complainants. Treaties often elaborate—in great detail—specific dispute settlement procedures. The results in some cases, such as UNCLOS[68] or NAFTA,[69] are simply too lengthy for sampling purposes. The dispute resolution clauses that follow thus focus on demonstrating the range of choices, without necessarily conveying all the details that accompany each selection.

A. Procedures involving parties themselves

1. Through consultations only

- Article 18, Treaty Concerning Defense Trade Cooperation (US-UK) (2007) Senate Treaty Doc No 110-7:

  Any disputes between the Parties arising out of or in connection with this Treaty shall be resolved through consultations between the Parties and shall not be referred to any court, tribunal, or third party.

2. Through any agreed-upon means

- Article XXV, Convention on the Protection of the Black Sea Against Pollution (1992) 1764 UNTS 3:

  In case of a dispute between Contracting Parties concerning the interpretation and implementation of this Convention, they shall seek a settlement of the dispute through negotiations or any other peaceful means of their own choice.

---

[66] Dispute Settlement Understanding, Marrakesh Agreement Establishing the World Trade Organization (1994) 1867 UNTS 4.

[67] Nor is dispute settlement the only vehicle for ensuring treaty performance. Alternatives include: multilateral environmental agreement 'non-compliance procedures'; human rights treaty body supervision; arms control inspection and verification regimes; and exclusion clauses authorizing termination or suspension of breaching parties' treaty rights. Although not sampled here, these are tools treaty-makers should consider. See generally G Ulfstein and others (eds), *Making Treaties Work—Human Rights, Environment, and Arms Control* (CUP, Cambridge 2007).

[68] See UN Convention on the Law of the Sea (1982) 1833 UNTS 3, Arts 186–191, 264–265, 279–299, Annexes V–VIII.

[69] North American Free Trade Agreement (NAFTA) (1992) 32 ILM 605, chs 11, 19, 20.

B. Procedures involving third parties

1. *Referral to a treaty body*

- Article 50, International Cocoa Agreement (2010) [2011] OJ L259/8:

    1. Any dispute concerning the interpretation or application of this Agreement which is not settled by the parties to the dispute shall, at the request of either party to the dispute, be referred to the Council for decision.
    2. When a dispute has been referred to the Council under paragraph 1 of this article and has been discussed, Members holding not less than one third of the total votes, or any five Members, may require the Council, before giving its decision, to seek the opinion on the issues in dispute of an ad hoc advisory panel to be constituted as described in paragraph 3 of this article.
    3. (a) Unless the Council decides otherwise, the ad hoc advisory panel shall consist of:
        (i) Two persons, one having wide experience in matters of the kind in dispute and the other having legal standing and experience, nominated by the exporting Members;
        (ii) Two persons, one having wide experience in matters of the kind in dispute and the other having legal standing and experience, nominated by the importing Members; and
        (iii) A chairman selected unanimously by the four persons nominated under (i) and (ii) above or, if they fail to agree, by the Chairman of the Council.
        (b) Nationals of Members shall not be ineligible to serve on the ad hoc advisory panel.
        (c) Persons appointed to the ad hoc advisory panel shall act in their personal capacities and without instructions from any Government.
        (d) The costs of the ad hoc advisory panel shall be paid by the Organization.
    4. The opinion of the ad hoc advisory panel and the reasons therefore shall be submitted to the Council, which, after considering all the relevant information, shall decide the dispute.

- Article XVI, Treaty on Conventional Armed Forces in Europe (1990) 2443 UNTS 3:

    1. To promote the objectives and implementation of the provisions of this Treaty, the States Parties hereby establish a Joint Consultative Group.
    2. Within the framework of the Joint Consultative Group, the States Parties shall:
        (A) address questions relating to compliance with or possible circumvention of the provisions of this Treaty;
        (B) seek to resolve ambiguities and differences of interpretation that may become apparent in the way this Treaty is implemented ...
        (I) consider matters of dispute arising out of the implementation of this Treaty.
    3. Each State Party shall have the right to raise before the Joint Consultative Group, and have placed on its agenda, any issue relating to this Treaty.
    4. The Joint Consultative Group shall take decisions or make recommendations by consensus. Consensus shall be understood to mean the absence of any objection by any representative of a State Party to the taking of a decision or the making of a recommendation ...

6. Nothing in this Article shall be deemed to prohibit or restrict any State Party from requesting information from or undertaking consultations with other States Parties on matters relating to this Treaty and its implementation in channels or fora other than the Joint Consultative Group.

C. Binding dispute settlement

1. Through a treaty-specific court

- Articles 32, 55, European Convention for the Protection of Human Rights and Fundamental Freedoms, as amended (2010) CETS No 194:

ARTICLE 32 – Jurisdiction of the Court
1. The jurisdiction of the Court shall extend to all matters concerning the interpretation and application of the Convention and the Protocols thereto which are referred to it as provided in Articles 33, 34, 46 and 47.
2. In the event of dispute as to whether the Court has jurisdiction, the Court shall decide.

ARTICLE 55 – Exclusion of other means of dispute settlement
The High Contracting Parties agree that, except by special agreement, they will not avail themselves of treaties, conventions or declarations in force between them for the purpose of submitting, by way of petition, a dispute arising out of the interpretation or application of this Convention to a means of settlement other than those provided for in this Convention.

2. Through arbitration at the election of one party

- Article 8(2), Agreement on the participation of the Russian Federation in the European Union military operation in the Republic of Chad and in the Central African Republic (EU-Russian Federation) (2008) [2008] OJ L307/16:

Any financial claims or disputes, that have not been resolved in accordance with paragraph 1 of this Article, may be submitted to a mutually agreed conciliator or mediator. Any claims or disputes which have failed to be settled by such conciliation or mediation may be submitted by either Party to an arbitration tribunal . . .

3. Through arbitration by mutual agreement

- Article XVIII, Convention on International Trade in Endangered Species of Wild Fauna and Flora (CITES) (1973) 993 UNTS 243:

1. Any dispute which may arise between two or more Parties with respect to the interpretation or application of the provisions of the present Convention shall be subject to negotiation between the Parties involved in the dispute.
2. If the dispute cannot be resolved in accordance with paragraph 1 of this Article, the Parties may, by mutual consent, submit the dispute to arbitration, in particular that of the Permanent Court of Arbitration at The Hague, and the Parties submitting the dispute shall be bound by the arbitral decision.

4. *Unilateral ICJ Referral*

- Article IX, Convention on the Prevention and Punishment of the Crime of Genocide (1948) 78 UNTS 277:

  Disputes between the Contracting Parties relating to the interpretation, application or fulfilment of the present Convention, including those relating to the responsibility of a State for genocide or for any of the other acts enumerated in article III, shall be submitted to the International Court of Justice at the request of any of the parties to the dispute.

5. *ICJ Referral on mutual agreement of disputing parties*

- Article 24, Treaty for the Prohibition of Nuclear Weapons in Latin America (1967) 634 UNTS 281:

  Unless the Parties concerned agree on another mode of peaceful settlement, any question or dispute concerning the interpretation or application of this Treaty which is not settled shall be referred to the International Court of Justice with the prior consent of the Parties to the controversy.

6. *Referral to arbitration or the ICJ*

- Article 35(2)–(4), UN Transnational Organized Crime Convention (2000) 2225 UNTS 209:

  2. Any dispute between two or more States Parties concerning the interpretation or application of this Convention that cannot be settled through negotiation within a reasonable time shall, at the request of one of those States Parties, be submitted to arbitration. If, six months after the date of the request for arbitration, those States Parties are unable to agree on the organization of the arbitration, any one of those States Parties may refer the dispute to the International Court of Justice by request in accordance with the Statute of the Court.
  3. Each State Party may, at the time of signature, ratification, acceptance or approval of or accession to this Convention, declare that it does not consider itself bound by paragraph 2 of this article. The other States Parties shall not be bound by paragraph 2 of this article with respect to any State Party that has made such a reservation.
  4. Any State Party that has made a reservation in accordance with paragraph 3 of this article may at any time withdraw that reservation by notification to the Secretary-General of the United Nations.

- Article 18, Stockholm Convention on Persistent Organic Pollutants (2001) 2256 UNTS 119:

  1. Parties shall settle any dispute between them concerning the interpretation or application of this Convention through negotiation or other peaceful means of their own choice.
  2. When ratifying, accepting, approving or acceding to the Convention, or at any time thereafter, a Party that is not a regional economic integration organization may declare in a written instrument submitted to the depositary that, with respect to any dispute concerning the interpretation or application of the Convention, it

recognizes one or both of the following means of dispute settlement as compulsory in relation to any Party accepting the same obligation:

(a) Arbitration in accordance with procedures to be adopted by the Conference of the Parties in an annex as soon as practicable;

(b) Submission of the dispute to the International Court of Justice.

3. A Party that is a regional economic integration organization may make a declaration with like effect in relation to arbitration in accordance with the procedure referred to in paragraph 2 (a).

D. Individual right to dispute settlement procedures

- Article 23(1)–(3), Double Taxation Agreement and Protocol (Hong Kong-UK) (2010) <http://www.hmrc.gov.uk/taxtreaties/in-force/hong-kong-uk-dta.pdf>:

  1. Where a person considers that the actions of one or both of the Contracting Parties result or will result for him in taxation not in accordance with the provisions of this Agreement, he may, irrespective of the remedies provided by the domestic laws of those Parties, present his case to the competent authority of the Contracting Party of which he is a resident . . . The case must be presented within three years from the first notification of the action resulting in taxation not in accordance with the provisions of this Agreement.

  2. The competent authority shall endeavour, if the objection appears to it to be justified and if it is not itself able to arrive at a satisfactory solution, to resolve the case by mutual agreement with the competent authority of the other Contracting Party, with a view to the avoidance of taxation which is not in accordance with this Agreement. Any agreement reached shall be implemented notwithstanding any time limits in the domestic laws of the Contracting Parties.

  3. The competent authorities of the Contracting Parties shall endeavour to resolve by mutual agreement any difficulties or doubts arising as to the interpretation or application of this Agreement. They may also consult together for the elimination of double taxation in cases not provided for in this Agreement.

- Article VII(2)-(3), Treaty Concerning the Reciprocal Encouragement and Protection of Investment (US-Argentina) (1991) 31 ILM 124:

  2. In the event of an investment dispute, the parties to the dispute should initially seek a resolution through consultation and negotiation. If the dispute cannot be settled amicably, the national or company concerned may choose to submit the dispute for resolution:
     (a) to the courts or administrative tribunals of the Party that is a party to the dispute; or
     (b) in accordance with any applicable, previously agreed dispute-settlement procedures; or
     (c) in accordance with the terms of paragraph 3.

  3. (a) Provided that the national or company concerned has not submitted the dispute for resolution under paragraph 2 (a) or (b) and that six months have elapsed from the date on which the dispute arose, the national or company concerned may choose to

consent in writing to the submission of the dispute for settlement by binding arbitration:

> (i) to the International Centre for the Settlement of Investment Disputes ("Centre"]) ... provided that the Party is a party to such convention; or
>
> (ii) to the Additional Facility of the Centre, if the Centre is not available; or
>
> (iii) in accordance with the Arbitration Rules of the United Nations Commission on International Trade Law (UNICTRAL); or
>
> (iv) to any other arbitration institution, or in accordance with any other arbitration rules, as may be mutually agreed between the parties to the dispute.

(b) Once the national or company concerned has so consented, either party to the dispute may initiate arbitration in accordance with the choice so specified in the consent. . . .

Amendments

19. Standard Amendment Procedures

A defining feature of the treaty is its stability; treaties are serious commitments meant to last over time. Nevertheless, treaties may require adjustment for various reasons. The primary, although not exclusive,[70] means of doing so is through an amendment. Amendments formally make changes to a treaty's text, whether its main provisions or any annexes.

Today, a treaty usually specifies its own procedures for amendment.[71] This is not, however, universally true, and the VCLT provides a default framework where treaties are silent on the subject.[72] Sometimes, a treaty will contain provisions for a general review of the *whole* treaty. Although these 'revision' clauses were once distinguished from amendment procedures, that is no longer the case. Revision clauses now either set the stage for applying the treaty's amendment procedures, or where the treaty is silent, those of the VCLT.

In terms of amendment procedures themselves, treaties may adopt one of two standard formulations.[73] First, bilateral treaties (and occasionally multilateral ones) operate on the basis of *unanimity*; an amendment requires the agreement and consent of *all* parties to enter into force, and when it does, all parties are equally bound. A second, different formulation is frequently employed in treaty texts anticipating a large number of parties, where an amendment *only binds those parties that consented to it*. The singularity of this result is masked by a complicated set of procedures for: (i) proposing amendments; (ii) the parties' adoption of an amendment; and (iii) its entry into force. Although unanimity is not required for entry

[70] Other alternatives include: (i) a stand-alone treaty (a 'protocol') that supplements the original treaty; (ii) a new treaty that supersedes the earlier one; (iii) decisions of an authorized treaty body; or (iv) (more controversially) treaty interpretation. On superseding treaties, see Chapter 18; treaty bodies, Chapter 17; and interpretation, Chapter 19.

[71] Occasionally, a Framework Convention will specify procedures not only for its own amendment, but also for Protocols concluded under its auspices. See eg Art 9 of the Vienna Convention for the Protection of the Ozone Layer (1985) 1513 UNTS 293. A protocol may, however, delineate its own amendment procedures. See eg Final Clauses Handbook (n 6) 102–4.

[72] VCLT Arts 39–40.

[73] These procedures may be available on the treaty's entry into force or the treaty may require some period of time to elapse before amendments may be proposed. Amendments are not, however, possible until *after* a treaty enters into force. Revising a treaty's terms beforehand generally requires a separate agreement or protocol. See eg Agreement relating to the Implementation of Part XI of the United Nations Convention on the Law of the Sea of 10 December 1982 (1994) 1836 UNTS 3.

into force, approval requirements may otherwise vary at all three stages. Thus, these clauses differ widely in their details even as they structurally end in the same place, stipulating individual consent for any treaty amendment that enters into force.

Both standard formulations leave individual parties in control of decisions as to whether to consent to an amendment.[74] As Chapter 14 explains, this may not always be a good thing; it may delay or obstruct necessary changes to a treaty or create layers of complicated relations among parties to treaties in their original formulation and those that consented to one (or more) amended versions of it. As a result of these difficulties, alternative or 'simplified' amendment procedures have emerged that are sampled in the next section. For now, it is enough to emphasize that these simplified processes are not just substitutes for standard amendment procedures; they may operate in concert with them as well. A robust amendment clause may thus differentiate treaty provisions for which dynamic amendment procedures are appropriate from others provisions to which more standard procedures apply.

A. Procedures for revision or review

- Article 15(1)–(2), International Convention on Arrest of Ships (1999) UN Doc A/CONF.188.6:

   1. A conference of States Parties for the purpose of revising or amending this Convention shall be convened by the Secretary-General of the United Nations at the request of one third of the States Parties.

- Article 123, Rome Statute of the International Criminal Court (1998) 2187 UNTS 3:

   1. Seven years after the entry into force of this Statute the Secretary-General of the United Nations shall convene a Review Conference to consider any amendments to this Statute. Such review may include, but is not limited to, the list of crimes contained in article 5. The Conference shall be open to those participating in the Assembly of States Parties and on the same conditions.
   2. At any time thereafter, at the request of a State Party and for the purposes set out in paragraph 1, the Secretary-General of the United Nations shall, upon approval by a majority of States Parties, convene a Review Conference.
   3. The provisions of article 121, paragraphs 3 to 7 [on amendments], shall apply to the adoption and entry into force of any amendment to the Statute considered at a Review Conference.

B. Amendments binding by unanimity

1. Bilateral treaties

- Articles XIII, XIV(1), Agreement for Co-operation in the Peaceful Uses of Nuclear Energy (Canada-Jordan) (2009) Canada Treaty Series 2009/9:

---

[74] When a State joins an amended treaty, it normally consents to that treaty as amended, although the VCLT acknowledges that it can express a 'different intention'. VCLT Art 40(5).

ARTICLE XIII

This Agreement may be amended at any time with the written consent of the Parties. Any amendment to this Agreement shall enter into force in accordance with the provisions of paragraph 1 of Article XIV.

ARTICLE XIV

1. This Agreement shall enter into force on the date of the last note of an exchange of diplomatic notes in which the Parties notify each other of the completion of their internal procedures necessary for the entry into force of this Agreement.

• Article 9, Agreement on the Framework for Security Cooperation (Australia-Indonesia) (2006) [2008] ATS 3:

This Agreement may be amended in writing by mutual consent by both Parties. Any amendment to this Agreement shall come into force on the date of later notification by either Party of the completion of its ratification procedure for the amendment.

• Article 22(3), Treaty on Extradition (Canada-South Africa) (2001) Canada Treaty Series 2001/20:

This Treaty may be amended by mutual consent.

• Article 17, Memorandum of Agreement on the Establishment of a Joint Center for the Exchange of Data from Early Warning Systems and Notifications of Missile Launches (Russian Federation-US) (2000) <http://www.state.gov/t/isn/4799.htm#treaty>:

Amendments to this Memorandum shall enter into force upon agreement by the Parties in the Joint Commission.

2. Multilateral treaties

• Article 28, Agreement on the Establishment of the ITER International Fusion Energy Organization for the Joint Implementation of the ITER Project (2006) [2006] OJ L358/62:

1. Any Party may propose an amendment to this Agreement.
2. Proposed amendments shall be considered by the Council, for recommendation to the Parties by unanimity.
3. Amendments are subject to ratification, acceptance or approval in accordance with the procedures of each Party and shall enter into force 30 days after the deposit of the instruments of ratification, acceptance or approval by all Parties.

• Article 27, Agreement Concerning Cooperation on the Civil International Space Station (1998) TIAS 12927:

This Agreement, including its Annex, may be amended by written agreement of the Governments of the Partner States for which this Agreement has entered into force. Amendments to this Agreement, except for those made exclusively to the Annex, shall be subject to ratification, acceptance, approval, or accession by those States in accordance with their respective constitutional processes. Amendments made exclusively to the Annex shall require only a written agreement of the Governments of the Partner States for which this Agreement has entered into force.

- Article X(2), Marrakesh Agreement Establishing the World Trade Organization (1994) 1867 UNTS 3:

  Amendments to the provisions of this Article and to the provisions of the following Articles shall take effect only upon acceptance by all Members:
  Article IX of this Agreement;
  Articles I and II of GATT 1994;
  Article II:1 of GATS;
  Article 4 of the Agreement on TRIPS.

- Article 21, Convention for the Conservation of Southern Bluefin Tuna (1993) 1819 UNTS 359:

  1. Any Party may at any time propose an amendment to this Convention.
  2. If one-third of the Parties request a meeting to discuss a proposed amendment the Depositary shall call such a meeting.
  3. An amendment shall enter into force when the Depositary has received instruments of ratification, acceptance or approval thereof from all the Parties.

C. Amendments binding those parties that consent to them[75]

1. Requiring consent from three-fourths of the parties

- Article 21, Rotterdam Convention on the Prior Informed Consent Procedure for Certain Hazardous Chemicals and Pesticides in International Trade (1998) 2244 UNTS 337:

  1. Amendments to this Convention may be proposed by any Party.

  2. Amendments to this Convention shall be adopted at a meeting of the Conference of the Parties. The text of any proposed amendment shall be communicated to the Parties by the Secretariat at least six months before the meeting at which it is proposed for adoption. The Secretariat shall also communicate the proposed amendment to the signatories to this Convention and, for information, to the Depositary.

  3. The Parties shall make every effort to reach agreement on any proposed amendment to this Convention by consensus. If all efforts at consensus have been exhausted, and no agreement reached, the amendment shall as a last resort be adopted by a three-fourths majority vote of the Parties present and voting at the meeting.

  4. The amendment shall be communicated by the Depositary to all Parties for ratification, acceptance or approval.

---

[75] As noted, clauses may differ by how amendment proposals are made, amendments are adopted *and* entry into force occurs. Although these examples are organized around the entry into force threshold, each amendment provision should be read *in toto*. Requirements for proposing or adopting amendments may impact the threshold chosen for entry into force. For example, amendments under the Convention on the Conservation and Management of High Migratory Fish Stocks in the Western and Central Pacific Ocean enter into force following the consent of only a majority of the parties, but that amendment must first be adopted by consensus.

5. Ratification, acceptance or approval of an amendment shall be notified to the Depositary in writing. An amendment adopted in accordance with paragraph 3 shall enter into force for the Parties having accepted it on the ninetieth day after the date of deposit of instruments of ratification, acceptance or approval by at least three fourths of the Parties. Thereafter, the amendment shall enter into force for any other Party on the ninetieth day after the date on which that Party deposits its instrument of ratification, acceptance or approval of the amendment.

2. *Requiring consent from two-thirds of the parties*

- Article 26, International Convention for the Suppression of Acts of Nuclear Terrorism (2005) 2445 UNTS 89:

  1. A State Party may propose an amendment to this Convention. The proposed amendment shall be submitted to the depositary, who circulates it immediately to all States Parties.

  2. If the majority of the States Parties request the depositary to convene a conference to consider the proposed amendments, the depositary shall invite all States Parties to attend such a conference to begin no sooner than three months after the invitations are issued.

  3. The conference shall make every effort to ensure amendments are adopted by consensus. Should this not be possible, amendments shall be adopted by a two-thirds majority of all States Parties. Any amendment adopted at the conference shall be promptly circulated by the depositary to all States Parties.

  4. The amendment adopted pursuant to paragraph 3 of the present article shall enter into force for each State Party that deposits its instrument of ratification, acceptance, accession or approval of the amendment on the thirtieth day after the date on which two thirds of the States Parties have deposited their relevant instrument. Thereafter, the amendment shall enter into force for any State Party on the thirtieth day after the date on which that State deposits its relevant instrument.

3. *Requiring consent from two-thirds of the parties and UNGA approval*

- Article 12, Optional Protocol to the Convention on the Rights of the Child on the Involvement of Children in Armed Conflict (2000) 2173 UNTS 222:

  1. Any State Party may propose an amendment and file it with the Secretary-General of the United Nations. The Secretary General shall thereupon communicate the proposed amendment to States Parties, with a request that they indicate whether they favour a conference of States Parties for the purpose of considering and voting upon the proposals. In the event that, within four months from the date of such communication, at least one third of the States Parties favour such a conference, the Secretary-General shall convene the conference under the auspices of the United Nations. Any amendment adopted by a majority of States Parties present and voting at the conference shall be submitted to the General Assembly for approval.

  2. An amendment adopted in accordance with paragraph 1 of the present article shall enter into force when it has been approved by the General Assembly of the United Nations and accepted by a two-thirds majority of States Parties.

3. When an amendment enters into force, it shall be binding on those States Parties that have accepted it, other States Parties still being bound by the provisions of the present Protocol and any earlier amendments that they have accepted.

4. Requiring consent from two-thirds of the parties that were parties at the time of the adoption of the amendment

- Article 30(4), UN Convention to Combat Desertification in those Countries Experiencing Serious Drought and/or Desertification, particularly in Africa (1994) 1954 UNTS 3:

Instruments of ratification, acceptance, approval or accession in respect of an amendment shall be deposited with the Depositary. An amendment adopted pursuant to paragraph 3 shall enter into force for those Parties having accepted it on the ninetieth day after the date of receipt by the Depositary of an instrument of ratification, acceptance, approval or accession by at least two thirds of the Parties to the Convention which were Parties at the time of the adoption of the amendment.

5. Requiring consent from a majority of the parties

- Article 40, Convention on the Conservation and Management of Highly Migratory Fish Stocks in the Western and Central Pacific Ocean (2000) 2275 UNTS 43:

1. Any member of the Commission may propose amendments to this Convention to be considered by the Commission. Any such proposal shall be made by written communication addressed to the Executive Director at least 60 days before the meeting of the Commission at which it is to be considered. The Executive Director shall promptly circulate such communication to all members of the Commission.

2. Amendments to this Convention shall be considered at the annual meeting of the Commission unless a majority of the members request a special meeting to consider the proposed amendment. A special meeting may be convened on not less than 60 days notice. Amendments to this Convention shall be adopted by consensus. The text of any amendment adopted by the Commission shall be transmitted promptly by the Executive Director to all members of the Commission.

3. Amendments to this Convention shall enter into force for the Contracting Parties ratifying or acceding to them on the thirtieth day following the deposit of instruments of ratification or accession by a majority of Contracting Parties. Thereafter, for each Contracting Party ratifying or acceding to an amendment after the deposit of the required number of such instruments, the amendment shall enter into force on the thirtieth day following the deposit of its instrument of ratification or accession.

6. Requiring consent of the majority of parties who voted for adoption of the amendment

- Article XV, Convention on the Prohibition of the Development, Production, Stockpiling and Use of Chemical Weapons and on their Destruction (1992) 1974 UNTS 45:

1. Any State Party may propose amendments to this Convention...

2. The text of a proposed amendment shall be submitted to the Director-General for circulation to all States Parties and to the Depositary. The proposed amendment shall be considered only by an Amendment Conference. Such an Amendment Conference shall be convened if one third or more of the States Parties notify the Director-General not later than 30 days after its circulation that they support further consideration of the proposal. The Amendment Conference shall be held immediately following a regular session of the Conference unless the requesting States Parties ask for an earlier meeting. In no case shall an Amendment Conference be held less than 60 days after the circulation of the proposed amendment.

3. Amendments shall enter into force for all States Parties 30 days after deposit of the instruments of ratification or acceptance by all the States Parties referred to under subparagraph (b) below:
   (a) When adopted by the Amendment Conference by a positive vote of a majority of all States Parties with no State Party casting a negative vote; and
   (b) Ratified or accepted by all those States Parties casting a positive vote at the Amendment Conference...

7. *On a date set by a Plenipotentiary Conference*

- Article 55(3)–(4), (6), Constitution of the International Telecommunication Union, as amended (2010) <http://www.itu.int/pub/S-CONF-PLEN-2011/en>:

   3. The quorum required at any Plenary Meeting of the Plenipotentiary Conference for consideration of any proposal for amending this Constitution or modification thereto shall consist of more than one half of the delegations accredited to the Plenipotentiary Conference.

   4. To be adopted, any proposed modification to a proposed amendment as well as the proposal as a whole, whether or not modified, shall be approved, at a Plenary Meeting, by at least two-thirds of the delegations accredited to the Plenipotentiary Conference which have the right to vote.

   6. Any amendments to this Constitution adopted by a plenipotentiary conference shall, as a whole and in the form of one single amending instrument, enter into force at a date fixed by the conference between Member States having deposited before that date their instrument of ratification, acceptance or approval of, or accession to, both this Constitution and the amending instrument. Ratification, acceptance or approval of, or accession to, only a part of such an amending instrument shall be excluded.

8. *Without specifying a threshold for entry into force*

- Article 39, UN Transnational Organized Crime Convention (2000) 2225 UNTS 209:

   1. After the expiry of five years from the entry into force of this Convention, a State Party may propose an amendment and file it with the Secretary-General of the United Nations, who shall thereupon communicate the proposed amendment to the States Parties and to the Conference of the Parties to the Convention for the purpose

of considering and deciding on the proposal. The Conference of the Parties shall make every effort to achieve consensus on each amendment. If all efforts at consensus have been exhausted and no agreement has been reached, the amendment shall, as a last resort, require for its adoption a two-thirds majority vote of the States Parties present and voting at the meeting of the Conference of the Parties.

2. Regional economic integration organizations, in matters within their competence, shall exercise their right to vote under this article with a number of votes equal to the number of their member States that are Parties to this Convention. Such organizations shall not exercise their right to vote if their member States exercise theirs and vice versa.

3. An amendment adopted in accordance with paragraph 1 of this article is subject to ratification, acceptance or approval by States Parties.

4. An amendment adopted in accordance with paragraph 1 of this article shall enter into force in respect of a State Party ninety days after the date of the deposit with the Secretary-General of the United Nations of an instrument of ratification, acceptance or approval of such amendment.

5. When an amendment enters into force, it shall be binding on those States Parties which have expressed their consent to be bound by it. Other States Parties shall still be bound by the provisions of this Convention and any earlier amendments that they have ratified, accepted or approved.

20. Simplified Amendment Procedures

The default rule for amending treaties involves the proposal and adoption of amendments that individual parties may then decide to consent to be bound by (or not). But these are *default* rules; they apply 'except in so far as the treaty may otherwise provide'.[76] As Chapter 14 surveys, many modern multilateral treaties have adopted different—or 'simplified'—amendment procedures. Despite the label, these provisions are among the most complex in treaty practice. They reflect the treaty-makers' accommodations of various interests—eg the need for party consent, the consistency of commitments parties assume, and the ability to adapt quickly to changing circumstances—in light of the different functions a treaty may be asked to perform.

First, where a treaty addresses technical, scientific, or administrative matters, amendments regularly assume the *tacit* consent of all parties for purposes of their entry into force, subject to an 'opt-out' for parties that do not wish to be bound by specific amendments (or on occasion the tacit amendment process itself). Such matters are often addressed in an annex (or a treaty body decision). In the bilateral context, a similar procedure even allows one side with technical expertise to amend certain parts of the treaty for both parties.

---

[76] VCLT Art 39. The 1986 VCLT reiterates this rule and adds that IO consent to an amendment 'shall be governed by the rules of that organization'. 1986 VCLT Art 39.

Second, where it is important for policy or logistical reasons that parties operate with the same set of commitments—as in the case of treaty provisions governing IO operations—a clause may provide for amendment by some specified majority, who bring the amendment into force for *all* parties including those that did not consent to be bound. Alternatively, the clause may stipulate that once a certain majority threshold is passed, non-consenting parties may (or must) withdraw from the treaty itself.

A third (more infrequent) type of simplified amendment procedure combines the process of adopting and bringing an amendment into force, empowering a vote of the treaty's plenary body to bind all parties. To the extent this process minimizes opportunities for domestic review of treaty amendments, it is often limited to institutional matters, topics that do not involve 'new' obligations, timing questions, or (like tacit consent) technical subjects.

In many cases, a single treaty will have multiple functions. As a result, a treaty may contain elaborate amendment clauses that provide different sets of procedures for each of the different types of commitments the treaty and its annexes contain.

A. Amendment by tacit consent with an opt-out

1. Where parties may opt-out of individual amendments

- Article 22(2)–(4), Rotterdam Convention on the Prior Informed Consent Procedure for Certain Hazardous Chemicals and Pesticides in International Trade (1998) 2244 UNTS 337:

  2. Annexes shall be restricted to procedural, scientific, technical or administrative matters.

  3. The following procedure shall apply to the proposal, adoption and entry into force of additional annexes to this Convention:

     (a) Additional annexes shall be proposed and adopted according to the procedure laid down in paragraphs 1, 2 and 3 of Article 21;[77]

     (b) Any Party that is unable to accept an additional annex shall so notify the Depositary, in writing, within one year from the date of communication of the adoption of the additional annex by the Depositary. The Depositary shall without delay notify all Parties of any such notification received. A Party may at any time withdraw a previous notification of non-acceptance in respect of an additional annex and the annex shall thereupon enter into force for that Party subject to subparagraph (c) below; and

     (c) On the expiry of one year from the date of the communication by the Depositary of the adoption of an additional annex, the annex shall enter into force for all Parties that have not submitted a notification in accordance with the provisions of subparagraph (b) above.

  4. Except in the case of Annex III, the proposal, adoption and entry into force of amendments to annexes to this Convention shall be subject to the same procedures as for the proposal, adoption and entry into force of additional annexes to the Convention.

---

[77] Article 21 is excerpted in heading 19, sampling 'Standard' Amendment procedures.

2. Where parties may opt-in or out of the tacit consent process on joining the treaty

- Article 16(2)(e)(ii), (f), International Convention on the Control of Harmful Anti-Fouling Systems on Ships (2001) IMO Doc AFS/CONF/26:

    (e) An amendment shall be deemed to have been accepted in the following circumstances . . .

        (ii) An amendment to an Annex shall be deemed to have been accepted at the end of twelve months after the date of adoption or such other date as determined by the Committee. However, if by that date more than one-third of the Parties notify the Secretary-General that they object to the amendment, it shall be deemed not to have been accepted.

    (f) An amendment shall enter into force under the following conditions . . .

        (ii) An amendment to Annex 1 shall enter into force with respect to all Parties six months after the date on which it is deemed to have been accepted, except for any Party that has:

            (1) notified its objection to the amendment in accordance with subparagraph (e) (ii) and that has not withdrawn such objection;

            (2) notified the Secretary-General, prior to the entry into force of such amendment, that the amendment shall enter into force for it only after a subsequent notification of its acceptance; or

            (3) made a declaration at the time it deposits its instrument of ratification, acceptance or approval of, or accession to, this Convention that amendments to Annex 1 shall enter into force for it only after the notification to the Secretary-General of its acceptance with respect to such amendments. . . .

B. Amendment by majority consent

1. By ratification of seven-eighths of the parties (with an option for non-consenting parties to withdraw)

- Article 121(3)–(4), (6), Rome Statute of the International Criminal Court (1998) 2187 UNTS 3:

    3. The adoption of an amendment at a meeting of the Assembly of States Parties or at a Review Conference on which consensus cannot be reached shall require a two-thirds majority of States Parties.

    4. Except as provided in paragraph 5, an amendment shall enter into force for all States Parties one year after instruments of ratification or acceptance have been deposited with the Secretary-General of the United Nations by seven-eighths of them.

    6. If an amendment has been accepted by seven-eighths of States Parties in accordance with paragraph 4, any State Party which has not accepted the amendment may withdraw from this Statute with immediate effect, notwithstanding article 127, paragraph 1, but subject to article 127, paragraph 2, by giving notice no later than one year after the entry into force of such amendment.

2. *By three-fourths of the parties*

- Article 17(3), Convention Establishing the World Intellectual Property Organization (WIPO) (1967) 828 UNTS 3:

  (3) Any amendment shall enter into force one month after written notifications of acceptance, effected in accordance with their respective constitutional processes, have been received by the Director General from three–fourths of the States Members of the Organization, entitled to vote on the proposal for amendment pursuant to paragraph (2), at the time the Conference adopted the amendment. Any amendment thus accepted shall bind all the States which are Members of the Organization at the time the amendment enters into force or which become Members at a subsequent date, provided that any amendment increasing the financial obligations of Member States shall bind only those States which have notified their acceptance of such amendment...

3. *By three-fourths of the parties (with non-consenting parties free to withdraw or remain if IO consents)*

- Article X(3), Marrakesh Agreement Establishing the World Trade Organization (1994) 1867 UNTS 3:

  Amendments to provisions of this Agreement, or of the Multilateral Trade Agreements in Annexes 1A and 1C, other than those listed in paragraphs 2 and 6, of a nature that would alter the rights and obligations of the Members, shall take effect for the Members that have accepted them upon acceptance by two thirds of the Members and thereafter for each other Member upon acceptance by it. The Ministerial Conference may decide by a three-fourths majority of the Members that any amendment made effective under this paragraph is of such a nature that any Member which has not accepted it within a period specified by the Ministerial Conference in each case shall be free to withdraw from the WTO or to remain a Member with the consent of the Ministerial Conference.

4. *By two-thirds of the parties*

- Article X(4), Marrakesh Agreement Establishing the World Trade Organization (1994) 1867 UNTS 3:

  Amendments to provisions of this Agreement or of the Multilateral Trade Agreements in Annexes 1A and 1C, other than those listed in paragraphs 2 and 6, of a nature that would not alter the rights and obligations of the Members, shall take effect for all Members upon acceptance by two thirds of the Members.

5. *By at least two-thirds of the contracting parties (with the possibility that non-consenting parties will cease to be parties to the treaty)*

- Article 94, Convention on International Civil Aviation (1944) 15 UNTS 295:

  (a) Any proposed amendment to this Convention must be approved by a two-thirds vote of the Assembly and shall then come into force in respect of States which have ratified such amendment when ratified by the number of contracting States specified by the Assembly. The number so specified shall not be less than two-thirds of the total number of contracting States.

(b) If in its opinion the amendment is of such a nature as to justify this course, the Assembly in its resolution recommending adoption may provide that any State which has not ratified within a specified period after the amendment has come into force shall thereupon cease to be a member of the Organization and a party to the Convention.

6. *Tacit consent by provisional application*

- Article 54(217D (3 *penter*)), (218(4)), (221A(5*bis*)), Constitution of the International Telecommunication Union (ITU), as amended (2010) <http://www.itu.int/pub/S-CONF-PLEN-2011/en>:

217D(3 *penter*) Any revision of the Administrative Regulations shall apply provisionally, as from the date of entry into force of the revision, in respect of any Member State that has signed the revision and has not notified the Secretary-General of its consent to be bound . . . Such provisional application only takes effect if the Member State in question did not oppose it at the time of signature of the revision.

218(4) Such provisional application shall continue for a Member State until it notifies the Secretary-General of its decision concerning its consent to be bound by any such revision.

221A(5 *bis*) If a Member State fails to notify the Secretary-General of its decision concerning its consent to be bound under No. 218 above within thirty-six months following the date or dates of entry into force of the revision, that Member State shall be deemed to have consented to be bound by that revision.

C. Amendment by adoption

1. *By adoption*

- Article 122, Rome Statute of the International Criminal Court (1998) 2187 UNTS 3:

1. Amendments to provisions of this Statute which are of an exclusively institutional nature, namely, article 35, article 36, paragraphs 8 and 9, article 37, article 38, article 39, paragraphs 1 (first two sentences), 2 and 4, article 42, paragraphs 4 to 9, article 43, paragraphs 2 and 3, and articles 44, 46, 47 and 49, may be proposed at any time, notwithstanding article 121, paragraph 1, by any State Party . . .

2. Amendments under this article on which consensus cannot be reached shall be adopted by the Assembly of States Parties or by a Review Conference, by a two-thirds majority of States Parties. Such amendments shall enter into force for all States Parties six months after their adoption by the Assembly or, as the case may be, by the Conference.

- Article XX(2), Constitution of the Food and Agriculture Organization of the United Nations (with Annexes) (1945) [1991] OJ C/238:

An amendment not involving new obligations for Member Nations or Associate Members shall take effect forthwith, unless the resolution by which it is adopted provides otherwise...

2. *By adoption in the absence of objection from the contracting parties*

• Articles 25(2), (9), 27, Convention on International Customs Transit Procedures for the Carriage of Goods by Rail Under Cover of SMGS Consignment Notes (2006) <http://treaties.un.org/doc/source/RecentTexts/XI_C_6_english.pdf>:

ARTICLE 25

2. The members of the Committee shall be the Contracting Parties...
9. Proposals shall be put to the vote. Each Contracting Party represented at the meeting shall have one vote...Proposed amendments shall be adopted by a two-thirds majority of those present and voting.

ARTICLE 27

1. In accordance with article 25 of this Convention, the Committee may recommend amendments to this Convention.
2. The text of any amendment so recommended shall be communicated by the depositary to all Contracting Parties to this Convention and to the other signatories.
3. Except as provided for under article 28, any recommended amendment communicated in accordance with paragraph 2 of this article shall enter into force with respect to all Contracting Parties 3 months after the expiry of a period of 18 months following the date of communication of the recommended amendment if no objection to the recommended amendment has been notified during that period to the depositary by a Contracting Party.
4. If any objection to the recommended amendment has been notified to the depositary by a Contracting Party before the expiry of the period of 18 months specified in paragraph 3 of this article, the amendment shall be deemed not to have been accepted and shall have no effect.

• Article 16, European Agreement on Important International Combined Transport Lines and Related Installations (1991) 1746 UNTS 3:

1. Annexes III and IV to this Agreement may be amended in accordance with the procedure specified in this article.
2. At the request of a Contracting Party, any amendment proposed by it to annexes III and IV shall be considered by the Working Party on Combined Transport of the United Nations Economic Commission for Europe.
3. If the amendment is adopted by a two-thirds majority of the Contracting Parties present and voting, the amendment shall be communicated by the Secretary-General of the United Nations to all Contracting Parties for acceptance.
4. Any proposed amendment communicated in accordance with paragraph 3 of this article shall be deemed accepted unless, within a period of six months following the date of its communication, one fifth or more of the Contracting Parties have notified the Secretary-General of the United Nations of their objection to the proposed amendment.
5. Any amendment accepted in accordance with paragraph 4 of this article shall be communicated by the Secretary-General to all Contracting Parties and shall enter

into force three months after the date of its communication with respect to all Contracting Parties except those which, prior to the date of its entry into force, have notified the Secretary-General that they did not accept the proposed amendment

6. If one fifth or more of the Contracting Parties have notified an objection to the proposed amendment in accordance with paragraph 4 above, the amendment shall be deemed not to have been accepted and shall have no effect whatsoever.

3. Authority to make 'changes' under different procedures than amendments

- Article XV(4)–(5), Convention on the Prohibition of the Development, Production, Stockpiling and Use of Chemical Weapons and on their Destruction (1992) 1974 UNTS 45:

4. In order to ensure the viability and the effectiveness of this Convention, provisions in the Annexes shall be subject to changes in accordance with paragraph 5, if proposed changes are related only to matters of an administrative or technical nature. All changes to the Annex on Chemicals shall be made in accordance with paragraph 5. Sections A and C of the Confidentiality Annex, Part X of the Verification Annex, and those definitions in Part I of the Verification Annex which relate exclusively to challenge inspections, shall not be subject to changes in accordance with paragraph 5.

5. Proposed changes referred to in paragraph 4 shall be made in accordance with the following procedures:

   (a) The text of the proposed changes shall be transmitted together with the necessary information to the Director-General. Additional information for the evaluation of the proposal may be provided by any State Party and the Director-General. The Director-General shall promptly communicate any such proposals and information to all States Parties, the Executive Council and the Depositary;

   (b) Not later than 60 days after its receipt, the Director-General shall evaluate the proposal to determine all its possible consequences for the provisions of this Convention and its implementation and shall communicate any such information to all States Parties and the Executive Council;

   (c) The Executive Council shall examine the proposal in the light of all information available to it, including whether the proposal fulfils the requirements of paragraph 4. Not later than 90 days after its receipt, the Executive Council shall notify its recommendation, with appropriate explanations, to all States Parties for consideration. States Parties shall acknowledge receipt within 10 days;

   (d) If the Executive Council recommends to all States Parties that the proposal be adopted, it shall be considered approved if no State Party objects to it within 90 days after receipt of the recommendation. If the Executive Council recommends that the proposal be rejected, it shall be considered rejected if no State Party objects to the rejection within 90 days after receipt of the recommendation;

   (e) If a recommendation of the Executive Council does not meet with the acceptance required under subparagraph (d), a decision on the proposal, including whether it fulfils the requirements of paragraph 4, shall be taken as a matter of substance by the Conference at its next session;

   (f) The Director-General shall notify all States Parties and the Depositary of any decision under this paragraph;

   (g) Changes approved under this procedure shall enter into force for all States Parties 180 days after the date of notification by the Director-General of their approval unless another time period is recommended by the Executive Council or decided by the Conference.

4. Procedure for 'adjustments'

- Article 2(9), Montreal Protocol on Substances that Deplete the Ozone Layer (1987) 1522 UNTS 3:

  (a) Based on the assessments made pursuant to Article 6, the Parties may decide whether:
    (i) Adjustments to the ozone depleting potentials specified in Annex A should be made and, if so, what the adjustments should be; and
    (ii) Further adjustments and reductions of production or consumption of the controlled substances from 1986 levels should be undertaken and, if so, what the scope, amount and timing of any such adjustments and reductions should be;
  (b) Proposals for such adjustments shall be communicated to the Parties by the Secretariat at least six months before the meeting of the Parties at which they are proposed for adoption;
  (c) In taking such decisions, the Parties shall make every effort to reach agreement by consensus. If all efforts at consensus have been exhausted, and no agreement reached, such decisions shall, as a last resort, be adopted by a two-thirds majority vote of the Parties present and voting representing at least fifty per cent of the total consumption of the controlled substances of the Parties;
  (d) The decisions, which shall be binding on all Parties, shall forthwith be communicated to the Parties by the Depositary. Unless otherwise provided in the decisions, they shall enter into force on the expiry of six months from the date of the circulation of the communication by the Depositary.

5. Adoption of amendments by one party only

- Article 16, Protocol Additional to the Agreements for the Application of Safeguards (Congo-IAEA) (2011) IAEA INFCIRC/831/Add.1:

  b. The list of activities specified in Annex I, and the list of equipment and material specified in Annex II, may be amended by the [IAEA] Board [of Governors] upon the advice of an open-ended working group of experts established by the Board. Any such amendment shall take effect four months after its adoption by the Board.

D. Combining standard and simplified amendment procedures

- Articles 21–22, Stockholm Convention on Persistent Organic Pollutants (2001) 2256 UNTS 119:

  Article 21 Amendments to the Convention
  1. Amendments to this Convention may be proposed by any Party.
  2. Amendments to this Convention shall be adopted at a meeting of the Conference of the Parties. The text of any proposed amendment shall be communicated to the Parties by the Secretariat at least six months before the meeting at which it is proposed for adoption. The Secretariat shall also communicate proposed amendments to the signatories to this Convention and, for information, to the depositary.

3. The Parties shall make every effort to reach agreement on any proposed amendment to this Convention by consensus. If all efforts at consensus have been exhausted, and no agreement reached, the amendment shall as a last resort be adopted by a three-fourths majority vote of the Parties present and voting.

4. The amendment shall be communicated by the depositary to all Parties for ratification, acceptance or approval.

5. Ratification, acceptance or approval of an amendment shall be notified to the depositary in writing. An amendment adopted in accordance with paragraph 3 shall enter into force for the Parties having accepted it on the nineteenth day after the date of deposit of instruments of ratification, acceptance or approval by at least three-fourths of the Parties. Thereafter, the amendment shall enter into force for any other Party on the nineteenth day after the date on which that Party deposits its instrument of ratification, acceptance or approval of the amendment.

Article 22 Adoption and amendment of annexes

1. Annexes to this Convention shall form an integral part thereof and, unless expressly provided otherwise, a reference to this Convention constitutes at the same time a reference to any annexes thereto.

2. Any additional annexes shall be restricted to procedural, scientific, technical or administrative matters.

3. The following procedure shall apply to the proposal, adoption and entry into force of additional annexes to this Convention:

   (a) Additional annexes shall be proposed and adopted according to the procedure laid down in paragraphs 1, 2 and 3 of Article 21;

   (b) Any Party that is unable to accept an additional annex shall so notify the depositary, in writing, within one year from the date of communication by the depositary of the adoption of the additional annex. The depositary shall without delay notify all Parties of any such notification received. A Party may at any time withdraw a previous notification of non-acceptance in respect of any additional annex, and the annex shall thereupon enter into force for that Party subject to subparagraph (c); and

   (c) On the expiry of one year from the date of the communication by the depositary of the adoption of an additional annex, the annex shall enter into force for all Parties that have not submitted a notification in accordance with the provisions of subparagraph (b).

4. The proposal, adoption and entry into force of amendments to Annex A, B or C shall be subject to the same procedures as for the proposal, adoption and entry into force of additional annexes to this Convention, except that an amendment to Annex A, B or C shall not enter into force with respect to any Party that has made a declaration with respect to amendment to those Annexes in accordance with paragraph 4 of Article 25, in which case any such amendment shall enter into force for such a Party on the nineteenth day after the date of deposit with the depositary of its instrument of ratification, acceptance, approval or accession with respect to such amendment.

5. The following procedure shall apply to the proposal, adoption and entry into force of an amendment to Annex D, E or F:

   (a) Amendments shall be proposed according to the procedure in paragraphs 1 and 2 of Article 21;

   (b) The Parties shall take decisions on an amendment to Annex D, E or F by consensus; and

(c) A decision to amend Annex D, E or F shall forthwith be communicated to the Parties by the depositary. The amendment shall enter into force for all Parties on a date to be specified in the decision.

6. If an additional annex or an amendment to an annex is related to an amendment to this Convention, the additional annex or amendment shall not enter into force until such time as the amendment to the Convention enters into force.

The End of Treaty Relations

21. Withdrawal or Denunciation

The terms 'withdrawal' and 'denunciation' may be used interchangeably to refer to the unilateral act by which a party to a treaty seeks to terminate its party status.[78] Withdrawal or denunciation may be authorized by the treaty's own terms. Where the treaty is silent, the default rule disfavours withdrawal absent a showing that the parties intended to allow it or if such a right may be implied from the nature of the treaty.[79] Where available, withdrawal or denunciation has significant legal effects. In the bilateral context, treaty relations end on the effective date of one side's withdrawal or denunciation. In the multilateral context, the withdrawing party becomes free of its performance obligations *vis-à-vis* other parties, even as it remains on the hook for 'any right, obligation, or legal situation' that arose by virtue of the treaty's execution *before* the effective date of the party's withdrawal.[80] The treaty remains in force, however, for other parties *inter se*.

As Chapter 25 explains, treaty provisions on withdrawal or denunciation allow parties to manage the risks of entering into the treaty commitment in the first place. Today, treaties regularly include provisions on withdrawal or denunciation. The key question in such clauses pertains to *when* a party may withdraw, whether at any time, at some fixed interval(s), or based on certain conditions. Other important variations involve the required notification period and whether there is a need to cite some extraordinary circumstances.[81] In some situations, moreover, a party's actions with respect to one treaty may lead to the constructive withdrawal or denunciation of another one.

---

[78] These acts should be distinguished from cases of 'exclusion', where treaties provide procedures for bringing a breaching party's treaty membership to an end. Eg International Coffee Agreement (2007) [2008] OJ L186/13, Art 46.

[79] VCLT Art 56(1); 1986 VCLT Art 56(1). Where a right to withdraw or denounce can be implied, VCLT Art 56(2) requires twelve months notice to exercise it. Another default rule limits withdrawal or denunciation to the whole treaty unless the particular provision(s) are separable. See VCLT Art 44.

[80] VCLT Art 70(2); 1986 VCLT Art 70(2). Pursuant to VCLT Art 43, withdrawal or denunciation also does nothing to impair the requirements of customary international law, a point occasionally reiterated in withdrawal and denunciation clauses specifically.

[81] The self-judging character of these conditions is a matter of some debate. See Chapter 24 (Part II.B.5, 620 *et seq*).

A. Withdrawal or denunciation at any time

1. *Effective immediately*

- Article XV(1), Articles of Agreement of the International Monetary Fund (1945) 2 UNTS 39:

  Any member may withdraw from the Fund at any time by transmitting a notice in writing to the Fund at its principal office. Withdrawal shall become effective on the date such notice is received.

2. *On notice*

- Article VIII(4), Agreement for Cooperation on a Joint Clean Energy Research and Development Center (US Dept of Energy-Republic of India Planning Commission) (2010) <http://www.state.gov/documents/organization/159460.pdf>:

  This Agreement may be terminated by mutual written agreement, or by either Party in writing at any time upon ninety days' written notice to the other Party . . .

- Article 70(1), UN Convention Against Corruption (2003) 2349 UNTS 41:

  A State Party may denounce this Convention by written notification to the Secretary-General of the United Nations. Such denunciation shall become effective one year after the date of receipt of the notification by the Secretary-General.

3. *On notice, with continuing legal effects*

- Article 18, Agreement on the Security and Exchange of Classified Information (ESA-EU) (2008) [2008] OJ L219/59:

  This Agreement may be denounced by one Party by giving written notice of denunciation to the other Party. Such denunciation shall take effect six months after receipt of notification by the other Party, but shall not affect obligations already contracted under the provisions of this Agreement. In particular, all classified information provided or exchanged pursuant to this Agreement shall continue to be protected in accordance with the provisions set forth herein.

- Article 12(2)–(3), Agreement for the Promotion and Protection of Investments (Panama-South Korea) (2001) <http://www.unctad.org/sections/dite/iia/docs/bits/korea_panama.pdf>:

  (2) This Agreement shall remain in force for a period of ten (10) years and shall remain in force thereafter indefinitely unless either Contracting Party notifies the other Contracting Party, in writing, one (1) year in advance of its intention to terminate this Agreement.

  (3) In respect of investments made prior to the termination of this Agreement, the provisions of Article 1 to 11 of this Agreement shall remain in force for a further period of ten (10) years from the date of termination.

- Article 24(4), Treaty establishing the Organisation of Eastern Caribbean States (1981) 1338 UNTS 97:

  Any Member State which withdraws from the Organisation during the period of its operation has no claim to any part of the proceeds until the liquidation of the assets of the Organisation on the termination of this Treaty at which time it shall be entitled to the value of its assets as at the date of withdrawal.

- Article 78(2), American Convention on Human Rights (1969) 1144 UNTS 123:

  1. The States Parties may denounce this Convention at the expiration of a five-year period from the date of its entry into force and by means of notice given one year in advance...
  2. Such a denunciation shall not have the effect of releasing the State Party concerned from the obligations contained in this Convention with respect to any act that may constitute a violation of those obligations and that has been taken by that state prior to the effective date of denunciation.

B. Conditional right of withdrawal or denunciation

1. At any time after a specific period of time has passed

- Article XXI(1), Agreement for the Establishment of the Indian Ocean Tuna Commission (1993) [1996] ATS 20:

  Any Member of the Commission may withdraw from this Agreement at any time after the expiry of two years from the date upon which the Agreement entered into force with respect to that Member, by giving written notice of such withdrawal to the Director-General...

2. Only at fixed intervals

- Article 22, ILO Convention No 189, Domestic Workers Convention (2011) <http://www.ilo.org/ilolex/english/convdisp1.htm>:

  1. A Member which has ratified this Convention may denounce it after the expiration of ten years from the date on which the Convention first comes into force, by an act communicated to the Director-General of the International Labour Office for registration. Such denunciation shall not take effect until one year after the date on which it is registered.
  2. Each Member which has ratified this Convention and which does not, within the year following the expiration of the period of ten years mentioned in the preceding paragraph, exercise the right of denunciation provided for in this Article, will be bound for another period of ten years and, thereafter, may denounce this Convention within the first year of each new period of ten years under the terms provided for in this Article.

3. On notice after a specific period of time has passed

- Article 17(3), Agreement on the Promotion and Protection of Investments (Egypt-Finland) (2004) 2309 UNTS 261:

  This Agreement shall remain in force for a period of twenty (20) years and shall thereafter remain in force on the same terms until either Contracting party notifies the other in writing of its intention to terminate the Agreement in twelve (12) months.

- Article 35(2)–(4), Berne Convention for the Protection of Literary and Artistic Works, as amended (1971) 1161 UNTS 3:

  (2) Any country may denounce this Act by notification addressed to the Director General. Such denunciation shall constitute also denunciation of all earlier Acts and shall affect only the country making it, the Convention remaining in full force and effect as regards the other countries of the Union.
  (3) Denunciation shall take effect one year after the day on which the Director General has received the notification.
  (4) The right of denunciation provided by this Article shall not be exercised by any country before the expiration of five years from the date upon which it becomes a member of the Union.

4. On notice with an explanation

- Article 20, Treaty Concerning Defense Trade Cooperation (US-UK) (2007) <http://www.state.gov/t/pm/rls/othr/misc/92770.htm>:

  2. The Parties shall have the right to withdraw from this Treaty in accordance with this Article. If a Party decides that extraordinary events related to the subject matter of this Treaty have jeopardized its national interests it shall give notice of its intention to withdraw from this Treaty to the other Party. Such notice of intention to withdraw shall include a statement of the extraordinary events the notifying Party regards as having jeopardized its national interests. The Parties shall commence consultation within 30 days of the provision of the notice of intention to withdraw with the aim of allowing the continuation of this Treaty. If, after such consultation, the notifying Party does not agree to the continuation of this Treaty, the withdrawal of the notifying Party shall take effect upon the expiry of 6 months from the provision of the notice of intention to withdraw.

- Article X(1), Treaty on the Non-Proliferation of Nuclear Weapons (1968) 729 UNTS 161:

  Each Party shall in exercising its national sovereignty have the right to withdraw from the Treaty if it decides that extraordinary events, related to the subject matter of this Treaty, have jeopardized the supreme interests of its country. It shall give notice of such withdrawal to all other Parties to the Treaty and to the United Nations Security Council three months in advance. Such notice shall include a statement of the extraordinary events it regards as having jeopardized its supreme interests.

5. *When another party has given notice of withdrawal or denunciation*

- Article XXXI(1)–(2), Convention on the Conservation of Antarctic Marine Living Resources (1980) 1329 UNTS 47:

  1. Any Contracting Party may withdraw from this Convention on 30 June of any year, by giving written notice not later than 1 January of the same year to the Depositary, which, upon receipt of such a notice, shall communicate it forthwith to the other Contracting Parties.
  2. Any other Contracting Party may, within sixty days of the receipt of a copy of such a notice from the Depositary, give written notice of withdrawal to the Depositary in which case the Convention shall cease to be in force on 30 June of the same year with respect to the Contracting Party giving such notice.

6. *Effective only under certain conditions*

- Article 20(3)–(4), Convention on the Prohibition of the Use, Stockpiling, Production and Transfer of Anti-Personnel Mines and on their Destruction (1997) 2056 UNTS 211:

  3. ... withdrawal shall only take effect six months after the receipt of the instrument of withdrawal by the Depositary. If, however, on the expiry of that six-month period, the withdrawing State Party is engaged in an armed conflict, the withdrawal shall not take effect before the end of the armed conflict.
  4. The withdrawal of a State Party from this Convention shall not in any way affect the duty of states to continue fulfilling the obligations assumed under any relevant rules of international law.

C. Constructive withdrawal

- Article XII(1)(a)–(b), The Antarctic Treaty (1959) 402 UNTS 71:

  (a) The present Treaty may be modified or amended at any time by unanimous agreement of the Contracting Parties whose representatives are entitled to participate in the meetings provided for under Article IX. Any such modification or amendment shall enter into force when the depositary Government has received notice from all such Contracting Parties that they have ratified it.
  (b) Such modification or amendment shall thereafter enter into force as to any other Contracting Party when notice of ratification by it has been received by the depositary Government. Any such Contracting Party from which no notice of ratification is received within a period of two years from the date of entry into force of the modification or amendment in accordance with the provisions of subparagraph 1(a) of this Article shall be deemed to have withdrawn from the present Treaty on the date of the expiration of such period.

- Article 27(3), Kyoto Protocol to the UN Framework Convention on Climate Change (1997) 2303 UNTS 148:

  Any Party that withdraws from the [UN Framework Convention on Climate Change] shall be considered as also having withdrawn from this Protocol.

22. Suspension

Suspension is a pause button for the law of treaties; it puts a treaty's application on hold. It may occur among all the parties, or only some of them, just as it may apply to the treaty as a whole or only some of its provisions. When all parties are involved, suspension works like withdrawal and termination; it can occur pursuant to the treaty's terms or where all parties consent.[82] Where only some parties seek suspension *inter se*, it functions like a treaty modification.[83] Individual parties may seek suspension due to breach, impossibility, or a fundamental change of circumstances.[84] But implying a unilateral right to suspend a treaty where it only provides for withdrawal or denunciation is harder; that view appears inconsistent with the VCLT's own differentiation between the two concepts.[85] Whatever its availability, suspension ceases performance obligations for its duration, leaving other treaty relations intact. Suspension presumes a limited duration, however, one where parties may resume their prior relationship at the expiration of the suspension period or via some later agreement.[86]

Treaties only occasionally include provisions for suspension, primarily in bilateral relations. Where they occur, suspension clauses authorize suspension generally, or limit its application to certain circumstances (eg breach) or conditions.

A. Suspension generally authorized

- Article 25, Voluntary Partnership Agreement on Forest Law Enforcement, Governance and Trade in Timber Products into the Community (EC-Ghana) (2009) [2010] OJ L70/3:

  1. Either Party may suspend the application of this Agreement. The decision on suspension and the reasons for that decision shall be notified to the other Party in writing.
  2. The conditions of this Agreement will cease to apply 30 calendar days after such notice is given.

---

[82] Like withdrawal or denunciation, any contracting States must be consulted if the parties are otherwise prepared to agree to suspension outside the treaty's terms. VCLT Art 57; 1986 VCLT Art 57.

[83] Suspension *inter se* requires a provision authorizing it. Alternatively, it may occur if there is: (i) no provision prohibiting it; (ii) the suspension does not affect the other parties' enjoyment of treaty rights or their performance of its obligations; (iii) it is compatible with the treaty's object and purpose; and (iv) other parties are given appropriate notice. VCLT Art 58; 1986 VCLT Art 58.

[84] On breach, see Chapter 23; on impossibility and fundamental change of circumstances, see Chapter 24.

[85] But Russia has asserted such a right in suspending its performance of the Treaty on Conventional Armed Forces in Europe. See DB Hollis, 'Russia Suspends CFE Treaty Participation' (July 2007) 11 ASIL Insight.

[86] See VCLT Art 72(1). During a treaty's suspension, the VCLT also obligates parties to refrain from acts that would interfere with the resumption of treaty operations, although the content of this obligation—like the one following signature—is ambiguous. Hollis (n 85); VCLT Art 72(2).

- Section 5, Memorandum of Understanding Concerning a Working Holiday Program (Denmark-Canada) (2005) 2374 UNTS 283:

  Either of the Governments may suspend the foregoing provisions in whole or in part temporarily through an exchange of notes.

B. Suspension for non-compliance

- Article 21, Agreement on the Processing and Transfer of Financial Messaging Data from the European Union to the United States for the Purposes of the Terrorist Finance Tracking Program (EU-US) (2010) [2010] OJ L195/5:

  Either Party may suspend the application of this Agreement with immediate effect, in the event of breach of the other Party's obligations under this Agreement, by notification through diplomatic channels.

- Article 13, Exchange of Letters relating to the Provisional Application of the Fisheries Partnership Agreement (EC-Denmark/Greenland) (2006) [2007] OJ L27/17:

  1. Application of this Agreement may be suspended at the initiative of one of the Parties if the undertakings in this Agreement, in the opinion of this Party, has been seriously infringed by the other Party. Such suspension shall require the Party concerned to notify its intention in writing at least six months before the date on which suspension is due to take effect. On receipt of this notification, the Parties shall enter into consultations with a view to resolving their differences amicably.
  2. Payment of the financial contribution referred to in Article 7 and the fishing possibilities referred to in Article 5 shall be reduced proportionately, according to the duration of the suspension.

C. Suspension for specified reasons

- Article 6, Agreement on the use of Two Tracks of the Slovenian State Territory in the area of the 'Dreilendereck' Skiing Region (Austria-Slovenia) (1995) 2404 UNTS 307:

  Each Contracting Party may temporarily suspend the validity of this Agreement for reasons of public order and security as well as on account of contagious diseases or epidemics in neighbouring regions of the other Contracting Party. The other Contracting Party must be informed thereof without delay through diplomatic channels.

- Paragraph 6, Exchange of Notes Constituting an Agreement in regard to the Mutual Abolition of Visas (Ireland-Poland) (1992) 1745 UNTS 77:

  The Government of the Republic of Poland or the Government of Ireland may temporarily suspend the foregoing provisions in whole or in part for reasons of public policy. In any such case the suspension and the lifting of that suspension shall be notified to the other Government through the diplomatic channel and shall have effect immediately upon such notification.

23. Duration and Termination

How long do treaty relations last? As with so many earlier issues, treaty-makers largely control their agreement's final fate. A treaty terminates—meaning that it ceases to exist for all parties—in conformity with its provisions. Where there are no termination provisions (and even if there are) the parties may always agree collectively to terminate their treaty at any time.[87] In terms of legal effects, termination 'releases the parties from any obligation further to perform the treaty' unless it provides otherwise or the parties otherwise agree.[88] That said, as with withdrawal or denunciation, any rights, obligations, or legal situations produced while the treaty *was* in force remain.[89] Chapter 25 details the relevant law and practice surrounding questions of treaty duration and termination.

In practice, most treaties contain provisions on duration or termination. Some expressly cabin the length of the commitment upfront, giving a treaty a set end date. Other clauses anticipate a repeating term, either at the election of the parties or automatically absent a contrary decision. But when a treaty's term expires, so too does the treaty. In contrast, a treaty may have no fixed duration, adopting an indefinite term, which runs unless and until the parties trigger the termination provisions, if any.

Termination provisions, therefore, offer an alternative exit option to parties. Instead of—and often in addition to—a specific duration for a treaty's existence, a treaty can specify the procedures or conditions for ending it. In the bilateral context, provisions for withdrawal or denunciation serve this function, where one party's withdrawal notice effects a termination of the treaty, usually after the passage of some set notice period. In other contexts, termination may follow the occurrence of a specific event or condition. Depending on the nature of the treaty, a termination provision may also include 'transitional' provisions to deal with any remaining treaty rights or obligations. Finally, in some cases, a treaty may have no provision on duration or termination as happens quite frequently in both the human rights and multilateral environmental treaty contexts.

A. Treaty duration

1. A fixed term

- Article VI(3), Agreement on Bilateral Cooperation in Industrial Research and Development (Canada-Israel) (2006) Canada Treaty Series 2006/9:

   This Agreement shall remain in force for a period of five years, unless terminated by either Party.

---

[87] VCLT Art 54; 1986 VCLT Art 54. Where the parties intend to terminate, the VCLT requires them to first consult with any 'contracting States'—those who consented to the treaty but for whom it has yet to enter into force. Ibid Art 54(b).
[88] VCLT Art 70(1)(a); 1986 VCLT Art 70(1)(a).
[89] VCLT Art 70(1)(b); 1986 VCLT Art 70(1)(b).

2. A fixed term extending an earlier agreement

- Exchange of Notes to Extend the Agreement relating to Scientific and Technical Cooperation (South Korea-US) (2009) <http://www.state.gov/documents/organization/130469.pdf>:

  The Embassy of Korea refers to the Department of State's Note dated July 1, 2009, which reads as follows:

  ...

  > On behalf of the Government of the United States of America, the Department of State proposes to extend the 1999 Agreement for an additional period until July 2, 2014.

  ...

  The Embassy further informs the Department of State that the above proposal is acceptable to the Government of the Republic of Korea and confirms, on behalf of the Government of the Republic of Korea, that the Department of State's Note and this Note in reply shall constitute an agreement between our two Governments in this matter, which shall enter into force on July 2, 2009.

3. A fixed term with limited extension options

- Article 44(1)–(3), International Tropical Timber Agreement (2006) [2007] OJ L262/8:

  1. This Agreement shall remain in force for a period of 10 years after its entry into force unless the Council, by special vote in accordance with article 12, decides to extend, renegotiate or terminate it in accordance with the provisions of this article.
  2. The Council may, by special vote in accordance with article 12, decide to extend this Agreement for two periods, an initial period of five years and an additional one of three years.
  3. If, before the expiry of the 10-year period referred to in paragraph 1 of this article, or before the expiry of an extension period referred to in paragraph 2 of this article, as the case may be, the new Agreement to replace this Agreement has been negotiated but has not yet entered into force either definitively or provisionally, the Council may, by special vote in accordance with article 12, extend this Agreement until the provisional or definitive entry into force of the new Agreement.

4. A fixed term that renews automatically unless terminated

- Article 19, Agreement on Development Co-Operation (Australia-Pakistan) (1991) [1991] ATS 35:

  This Agreement shall enter into force on the date of signature, and shall remain in force for an initial period of three years. Thereafter it shall be automatically renewed for subsequent periods of one year, unless either Government gives written notice, at least 6 months before the expiry of a period of validity, of its desire to terminate the Agreement.

5. A fixed term that parties may agree to extend affirmatively

- Article VII(19), Agreement Concerning Cooperating Communications Networks, (Australia-US) (1990) [1990] ATS 5:

This Agreement shall come into force on signature and shall remain in force for a period of five years. The term may be extended only by the specific written concurrence of both Parties.

6. A fixed term subject to extensions and conditions

- Article XXV, Food Aid Convention (1999) 2073 UNTS 135:

  (a) This Convention shall remain in force until and including 30 June 2002, unless extended under paragraph (b) of this Article or terminated earlier under paragraph (f) of this Article, provided that the Grains Trade Convention, 1995, or a new Grains Trade Convention replacing it, remains in force until and including that date.
  (b) The Committee may extend this Convention beyond 30 June 2002 for successive periods not exceeding two years on each occasion, provided that the Grains Trade Convention, 1995, or a new Grains Trade Convention replacing it, remains in force during the period of the extension.

7. Unlimited duration but with a right of withdrawal or denunciation

- Article 8, Agreement on 'Working Holiday' Arrangements (Australia-Belgium) (2002) [2004] ATS 13:

  This Agreement is concluded for an indeterminate period. It can be terminated by either of the Parties with three months written notice to the other Party via diplomatic channels.

- Article XVI, Convention on the Prohibition of the Development, Production, Stockpiling and Use of Chemical Weapons and on their Destruction (1992) 1974 UNTS 45:

  1. This Convention shall be of unlimited duration.
  2. Each State Party shall, in exercising its national sovereignty, have the right to withdraw from this Convention if it decides that extraordinary events, related to the subject-matter of this Convention, have jeopardized the supreme interests of its country. It shall give notice of such withdrawal 90 days in advance to all other States Parties, the Executive Council, the Depositary and the United Nations Security Council. Such notice shall include a statement of the extraordinary events it regards as having jeopardized its supreme interests.

B. Treaty termination[90]

1. On the completion of a specific operation or activity

- Article 19(1), Agreement on the status of the European Union-led Forces in the Central African Republic (2008) (Central African Republic-EU) [2008] OJ L136/46 (trans):

---

[90] For examples of treaty termination in the bilateral context, see heading 21, 'Withdrawal or Denunciation'. For examples of termination by supersession, see heading 16, 'Relationships to Other Agreements'.

This Agreement shall enter into force on the day on which it is signed and shall remain in force until the date of departure of the last EUFOR element and of the last EUFOR personnel, as notified by EUFOR.

• Article 27(2), Headquarters Agreement Between the Government of Australia and the Commission for the Conservation of Southern Bluefin Tuna (1998) [1999] ATS 6:

This Agreement may be terminated by a joint decision of the Government and the Commission. In the event of the Headquarters of the Commission being moved from Australia, this Agreement shall, after a period reasonably required for such transfer and the disposal of the property of the Commission in Australia, cease to be in force. In either event, the date on which the Agreement terminates shall be confirmed by an exchange of notes between the Government and the Commission.

2. Termination on the withdrawal of certain parties

• Article XVII, Convention for a North Pacific Marine Science Organization (1990) <http://www.pices.int/about/convention.aspx>:

1. This Convention shall be terminated upon the withdrawal of three of the signatory states listed in Article XIII.
2. The effective date of termination shall be one year after the deposit with the Depositary of the number of withdrawals required to terminate the Convention in accordance with paragraph 1 above.

3. Termination when the number of parties is reduced below a minimum threshold[91]

• Article 27, Convention on the Contract for the International Carriage of Passengers and Luggage by Road (1973) 1774 UNTS 109:

If, after the entry into force of this Convention, the number of Contracting Parties is reduced, as a result of denunciations, to less than five, the Convention shall cease to be in force from the date on which the last of such denunciations takes effect.

4. Termination by decision of a treaty body

• Article 62(5), International Cocoa Agreement (2010) [2011] OJ L259/8:

The Council may at any time decide to terminate this Agreement. Such termination shall take effect on such date as the Council shall decide, provided that the obligations of Members under Article 25 shall continue until the financial liabilities relating to the operation of this Agreement have been discharged. The Council shall notify the Depositary of any such decision.

---

[91] But see VCLT Art 55 ('Unless the treaty otherwise provides, a multilateral treaty does not terminate by reason only of the fact that the number of the parties falls below the number necessary for its entry into force').

5. *Termination on entry into force of a later treaty*

- Article 44(4), International Tropical Timber Agreement (2006) [2007] OJ L262/8:

If the new Agreement is negotiated and enters into force during any period of extension of this Agreement under paragraph 2 or paragraph 3 of this article, this Agreement, as extended, shall terminate upon the entry into force of the new Agreement.

6. *Post-termination transitional provisions*

- Article 62(6), International Cocoa Agreement (2010) [2011] OJ L259/8:

Notwithstanding the termination of this Agreement by any means whatsoever, the Council shall remain in being for as long as necessary to carry out the liquidation of the Organization, settlement of its accounts and disposal of its assets. The Council shall have during that period the necessary powers for the conclusion of all administrative and financial matters.

- Article 44(6), International Tropical Timber Agreement (2006) [2007] OJ L262/8:

Notwithstanding the termination of this Agreement, the Council shall continue in being for a period not exceeding 18 months to carry out the liquidation of the Organization, including the settlement of accounts, and, subject to relevant decisions to be taken by special vote in accordance with article 12, shall have during that period such powers and functions as may be necessary for these purposes.

Index

Lightning Source UK Ltd.
Milton Keynes UK
UKOW05f2355120314

228018UK00001B/1/P